Experience adventures on the road with us

Bungle Bungle Caravan Park

Congratulations!

You've purchased Australia's most comprehensive Caravan Park guide.

As the authors of Camps Australia Wide, we welcome you to our community of travellers across Australia.

We invite you to receive even more value from your book, with our newsletters. Each fortnight we share our favourite places, new free and budget campgrounds, plus new and featured caravan and tourist parks across our beautiful country.

There's even more news and tips on our Facebook and Instagram pages for you, and we'd love to hear about you and your travels.

Over 20 years of research and knowledge has been transferred into our easy to use guides, in a simple format that makes it easier for you choose where to stay. We have also listened to feedback from our readers, and improved the layout in our latest edition (making sure font sizes stayed the same) so the book was lighter and easier to travel with.

In Caravan Parks 5, we have over 2,240 listings, 876 public dump points, with the very latest Hema maps. You can see facilities of each at a glance - with coloured symbols that tell you everything from where you can bring your pet (do call the park before you arrive), to boat ramps and big rigs!

As the third owner of CAMPS, our first RV trip around Australia with our four children was life changing. We are passionate about giving everyone the opportunity to experience the freedom of life on the road – and we know our guides will help you make memories that are priceless.

When we see our books, they are circled and scrawled on, with tips from other travellers swapped over firesides and camp kitchens. Make sure you use it to plan your travels, not just navigate your way around each state.

We look forward to many more hours on the road, chatting at happy hours, verifying parks and camps so you can experience the best of travel in Australia.

We look forward to hearing from you and hope to see you on the road,

Heatley & Michelle Gilmore

Receive our email ***newsletters*** www.campsaustraliawide.com

Like us on ***Facebook*** www.facebook.com/CampsAustraliaWide/

Follow us on ***Instagram*** @campsaustraliawide

Thanks for purchasing our book. SCAN ME

Discover our App

(ADVERTORIAL)

Common rail diesel fuel systems – prevent expensive water damage

With common rail diesel fuel systems found on late-model vehicles, water in the fuel is causing some large repair bills. When I say large, I mean budget breakers. How about $10,000 to $20,000 bills?

Rust formation can occur within minutes of water being introduced to the system, and rust particles cause rapid wear to the diesel pump and injectors due to their abrasive nature. Water, of course, should not be present in diesel fuel; however, it is difficult for fuel outlets in Australia to ensure that diesel fuel is free of water.

When a tanker delivers a fresh fuel load to the service station, water at the bottom of the tank gets stirred up, mixing with the diesel fuel, allowing what is sometimes many litres of water to be pumped into your fuel tank.

A modern diesel engine consumes only a small portion of the fuel it draws, circulating the rest back into the tank. Fuel-water separator traps (as used by Water Watch) help in removing the water content by separating water from fuel in every cycle. A fuel-water separator has the ability to remove free, dispersed and emulsified water with greater than 95 per cent efficiency.

Research indicates that in high-pressure fuel systems typical of common rail, mechanical filtration is extremely difficult, as not all dispersed and emulsified water can be captured by even the most advanced filters.

Modern common rail systems are typically equipped with a 'water in fuel' warning light to alert operators to the presence of free water, but those warning lights are not activated by untreated emulsified water (commonly found in motor vehicles).

Secondary filters will cause a restriction to fuel flow in common rail diesel vehicles because the filter medium is a physical barrier designed to trap particles. Placing a secondary filter on a vehicle is a duplication of the original equipment manufacturer (OEM) filter already on the vehicle, which provides little protection against water damage.

How do you prevent water passing into the diesel pump and beyond?

Water Watch detects a very small quantity of water before it enters the OEM filter. Water Watch separates and removes both water and particles from the fuel flow, alerting the driver that water is present in the vehicle's fuel by a recurring beep and a warning LED light. It is then easy to pull over, turn the engine off, drain the water, restart the engine and continue driving. Water Watch is not a filter and therefore will not give restriction to fuel flow.

Find out more information at www.waterindiesel.com

Acknowledgements

Camps Australia Wide Pty Ltd

PO Box 204 Rainbow Beach
Queensland Australia 4581
Phone: (07) 5474 2542
Email: info@campsaustraliawide.com
Website: www.campsaustraliawide.com

Fifth edition published November 2018
Reprinted September 2019
ISBN: 9780992573270

Proprietors of Caravan Parks Australia Wide:
Michelle and Heatley Gilmore
Compiled, Designed and Published by:
Michelle and Heatley Gilmore

Research:
Julie Simpson, Jacqueline Wardle, Philip and Cathryn Fennell, Leisa Cooper, Michelle and Heatley Gilmore

Field Research:
Michelle and Heatley Gilmore,
Philip and Cathryn Fennell

Production and Prepress:
Allan and Linda Shearer - Shearer Publishing Systems
Gavin James www.mapuccino.com.au
Leanne Collett www.floweringdesign.com.au

Cover Design:
Leanne Collett www.floweringdesign.com.au

Photography:
Michelle and Heatley Gilmore,
Philip and Cathryn Fennell

Base Maps:
Hema Maps Pty Ltd

Printed by C&C Offset Printing Co Ltd, China

Front Cover: The Streaky Bay Islands Caravan Park, South Australia. Image by Chris, Vee and Tilly's big lap

Back Cover: Simpsons Gap, Tjoritja / West MacDonnell National Park, Northern Territory. Image Michelle Gilmore

Longreach Tourist Park, Queensland by Alan Unkles

Contents

***Top Image** Reflections Caravan Park, Forster NSW by Darlene and Stephen Collins*
***Circle Image** Nullarbor Roadhouse by Zahlis Big Lap*

How to use this Guide

Layout of the Guide

For simplicity this book is divided into different coloured sections for each State or Territory (ACT is included in NSW). These sections are listed in the following sequence in the book >

QUEENSLAND
NEW SOUTH WALES (including ACT)
VICTORIA
TASMANIA
SOUTH AUSTRALIA
WESTERN AUSTRALIA
NORTHERN TERRITORY

EACH STATE SECTION CONTAINS, IN SEQUENCE:

A set of maps of the latest edition of the Hema Road Atlas.

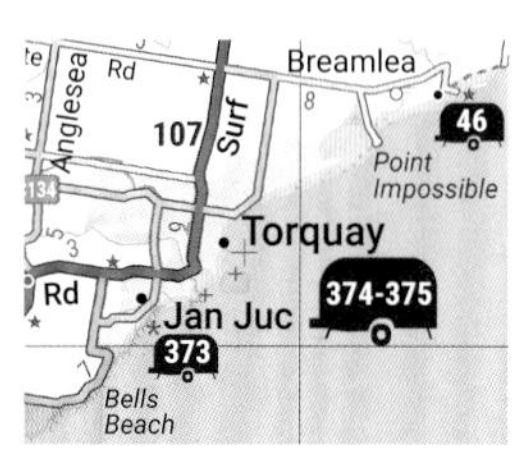

Numbered caravan symbols have been placed on the maps. Although we have endeavoured to place these symbols in as accurate a position as possible, please note this location is an indication only. Where the park is in a town the symbol is placed next to that town name due to scale and space restriction.

A listing of all caravan parks by locality

The listing contains details of all caravan parks of the State by locality. These are alphabetically listed.

Port Sorell

44 Moomba Holiday & Caravan Park
24 Kermode St. 500m E of PO
www.moombacaravanpark.com
03 6428 6140 HEMA 106 C1 41 09 50 S 146 33 00 E

The remaining sections are:

A listing of dump points for each state

An index of towns/localities of caravan parks across Australia

The index lists the localities and the page on which the detailed information can be found.

How to find the listing for a caravan park

USING THE MAPS

From the maps, note the identification numbers of caravan parks in your area of interest, or the town/locality. Then simply go to the site pages for that State to find out those caravan parks. Alternatively visit the index to find out what page the locality's listings are on.

USING LOCALITY INFORMATION

Because caravan parks are listed alphabetically under localities, simply refer to the listing for the relevant State and find the alphabetically-listed locality. If the locality is not found, look for other possible names for that locality or refer to the map.

Abbreviations – Some abbreviations have been used to condense the amount of text used in the listings.

They are:

Rd	Road	**Cnr**	corner
Ave	Avenue	**Jcn**	junction
Hwy	Highway	**NP**	National Park
St	Street	**PO**	Post Office
m	metre	**N**	north
km	kilometre	**S**	south
R	right	**E**	east
L	left	**W**	west

GPS CO-ORDINATES

As a further aid to navigation GPS co-ordinates have been added to each listing. The format used is d° m' s" (degrees, minutes, seconds).

THE SAMPLE BELOW EXPLAINS HOW EACH CARAVAN PARK IS LAID OUT FOR EASY INTERPRETATION.

Most of the symbols are self-explanatory, but some have been designed to fit certain criteria. Please note that an abbreviated version of this legend is provided on the last page of the book.

EXPLANATION OF SYMBOLS

PRICING

The price symbols have three categories to assist you when budgeting your travels. The prices are based on the standard off season rate for a powered site for two adults for one night.

Please note: The majority of parks have pricing system based on seasons. Prices in peak seasons (Christmas, Easter etc) and during school holidays will often differ – expect to pay a premium at these times. Peak seasons vary around the country so please check before you travel.

$27 & under

$28 to $39

$40 & over

Please note that these prices were correct at the time of printing. Prices may change without notice.

ENSUITE CABINS

These cabins will have one or more bedrooms, a combined kitchen/living area with an en-suite shower/toilet.

CABINS

These cabins will have one or more bedrooms, and a combined kitchen/living area. Guests use the communal toilet and showers.

POWERED SITE

These sites may have a concrete pad and/or grassed area, with a power point for your vehicle.

ENSUITE SITE

Powered sites that have individual amenities.

DRIVE THROUGH SITE

Sites that a caravan or motorhome can drive directly into and out of without having to reverse or unhitch. Drive through sites are popular when in transit and just overnight.

TENT SITE

Typically tent sites are on a grassed area (subject to local conditions). They may be among the powered sites or in a separate area close to the communal toilets and showers

BBQ

Some caravan parks provide a free gas or electric barbeque for guests, while others may charge a small fee for the use of the facility. Please clean after use.

BOAT RAMP

This caravan park has boat launch facilities nearby. The ramp may be properly built or may be adapted from local conditions. In most cases they are suitable for small 'tinnies'. Check local conditions for tidal flow and other hazards.

The CAMPS team at Derby W.A.

CAMP KITCHEN

A number of caravan parks provide a camp kitchen which generally consists of a BBQ, with perhaps a hot plate or stove, communal refrigerator and an area for dishwashing. A camp kitchen is generally a covered area with communal seating and dining tables.

SWIMMING POOL

Swimming pools in caravan parks are generally saltwater. They may be shaded and some are heated.

CHILDREN'S PLAYGROUND

At least one playground is provided inside the caravan park.

DISABLED FACILITIES

Generally there is at least one dedicated toilet and shower, in some parks this facility is unisex.

WIRELESS INTERNET

Wireless internet facilities are provided in the caravan park. Fees may apply.

MOTORHOME FRIENDLY

Many caravan parks now provide suitable and often bigger areas to accommodate various sized motorhomes. Each park has its own regulations and size limitation for motorhomes and will often only have a limited number of such sites available.

We advise motorhome travellers to check and book in advance to ensure your choice of park. Note that some parks charge an extra fee for any large motorhome that takes up more than one standard caravan site.

DUMP POINT

This symbol advises that the park or site has a central dump point. These dump points are generally provided for the disposal of cassette toilets. For those vehicles with holding tanks you will need to check with the facility operator to ensure that there is access for the disposal of black or grey water.

CARAVAN PARK AFFILIATION

Listings for caravan parks which have industry affiliations include the appropriate logo.

PETS - Pets are allowed at these parks with 'conditions'.

It is highly recommended that you contact the park prior to deciding to use the park, as some parks limit the animal size and only permit animals in off-peak periods. Management reserve the right to amend the park's policy at no notice (and often do!) so to avoid any disappointment make a phone call.

Many parks now require a fee and/or bond from the pet's owners as part of the conditions of entry to that park. As a general rule pets must always be on a lead, the owners must collect and dispose of any droppings, pets must travel with the owner and not be left unattended in the park. Pets are rarely permitted in cabins, villas or on site vans. Guide dogs may be an exception.

PETS NOT ALLOWED

Pets are not allowed at this site.

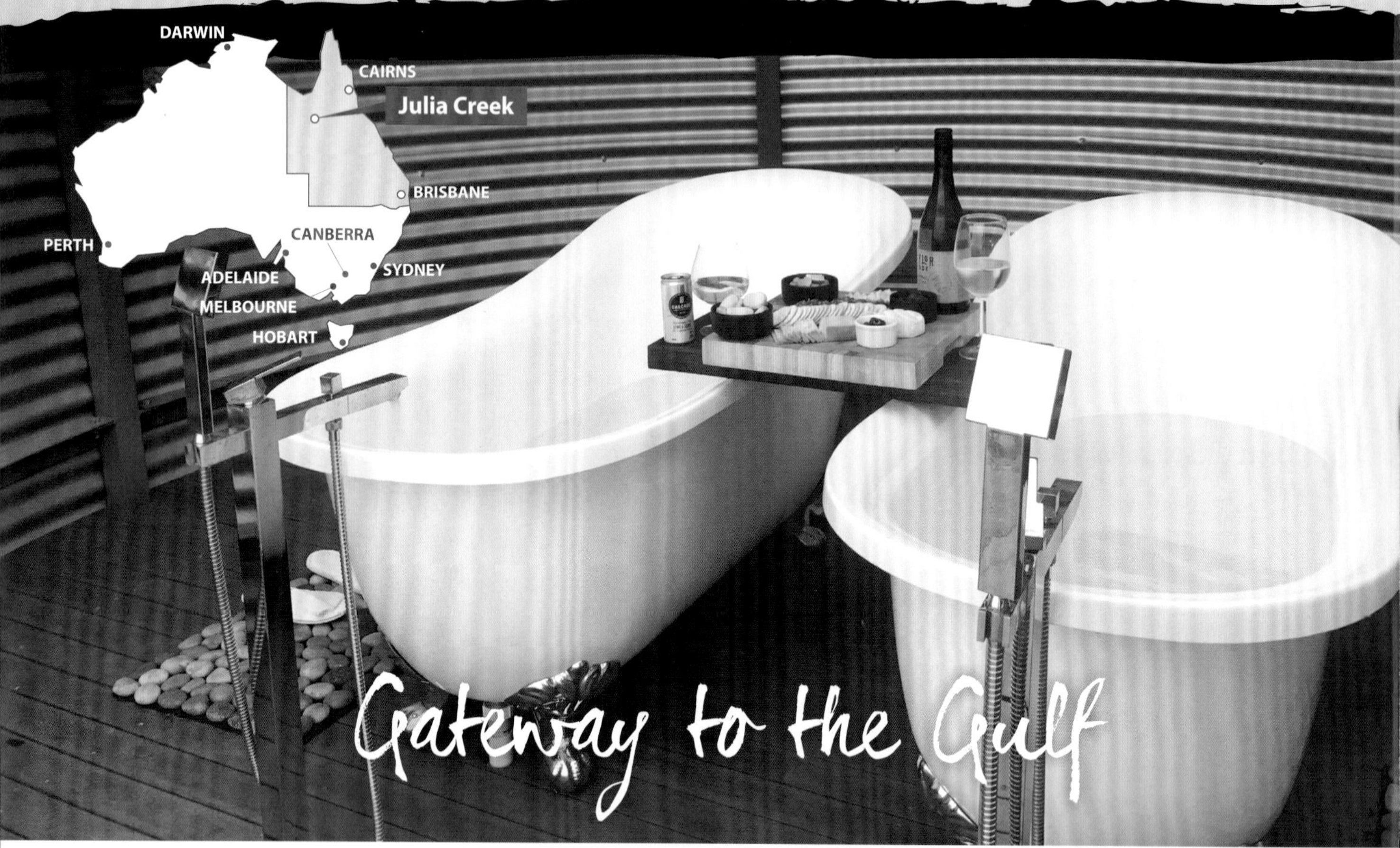

Important: Updating This Book

A free user-friendly searchable update service is provided on our website via the 'Updates' tab. Changes will undoubtedly occur, especially over time after the book's release. So it's important to check regularly for updates. Updates for this edition are provided for two years from the date first published.

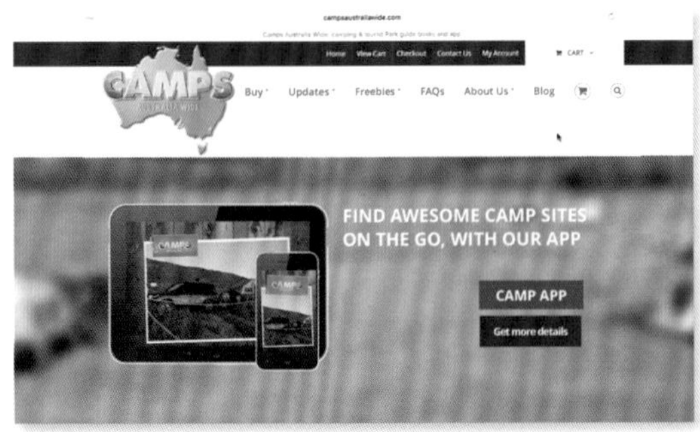

STEP 1

On the Camps Australia Wide website (www.campsaustraliawide.com) select the 'Updates' tab.

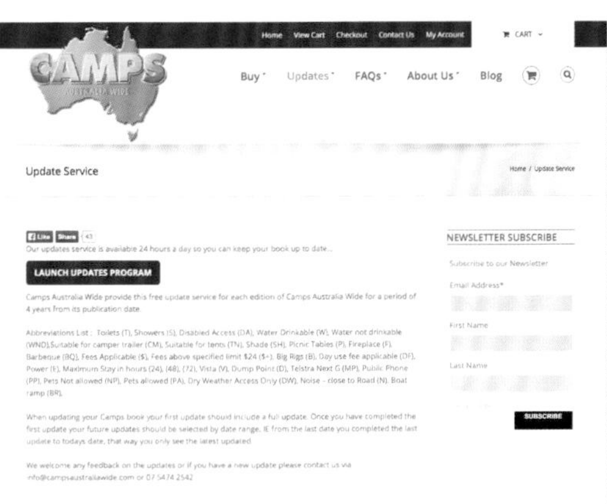

STEP 2

Selecting the 'Updates' tab will direct to the 'Update Service' page which gives you an option to 'Launch Updates Program'. When that is selected, the Updates Program will display in a window floating above the web page.

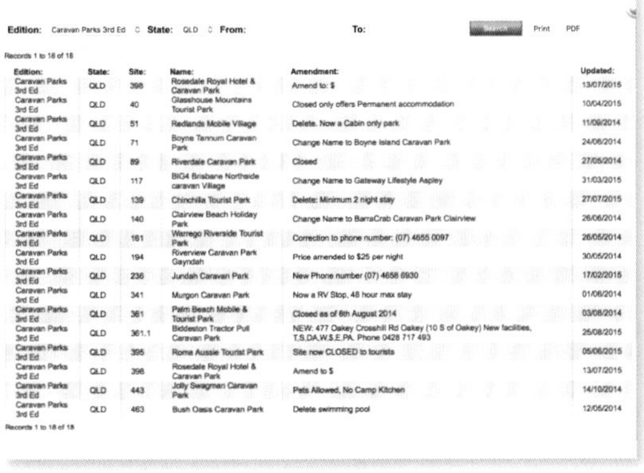

Edition: Caravan Parks 3rd Ed **State:** QLD **From:** **To:** Print PDF

Records 1 to 18 of 18

Edition:	State:	Site:	Name:	Amendment:	Updated:
Caravan Parks 3rd Ed	QLD	398	Rosedale Royal Hotel & Caravan Park	Amend to: $	13/07/2015
Caravan Parks 3rd Ed	QLD	40	Glasshouse Mountains Tourist Park	Closed only offers Permanent accommodation	10/04/2015
Caravan Parks 3rd Ed	QLD	51	Redlands Mobile Village	Delete. Now a Cabin only park	11/09/2014
Caravan Parks 3rd Ed	QLD	71	Boyne Tannum Caravan Park	Change Name to Boyne Island Caravan Park	24/06/2014
Caravan Parks 3rd Ed	QLD	89	Riverdale Caravan Park	Closed	27/05/2014
Caravan Parks 3rd Ed	QLD	117	BIG4 Brisbane Northside caravan Village	Change Name to Gateway Lifestyle Aspley	31/03/2015
Caravan Parks 3rd Ed	QLD	139	Chinchilla Tourist Park	Delete: Minimum 2 night stay	27/07/2015
Caravan Parks 3rd Ed	QLD	140	Clairview Beach Holiday Park	Change Name to BarraCrab Caravan Park Clairview	26/06/2014
Caravan Parks 3rd Ed	QLD	161	Warrego Riverside Tourist Park	Correction to phone number: (07) 4655 0097	26/05/2014
Caravan Parks 3rd Ed	QLD	194	Riverview Caravan Park Gayndah	Price amended to $25 per night	30/05/2014
Caravan Parks 3rd Ed	QLD	236	Jundah Caravan Park	New Phone number (07) 4658 6930	17/02/2015
Caravan Parks 3rd Ed	QLD	341	Murgon Caravan Park	Now a RV Stop, 48 hour max stay	01/06/2014
Caravan Parks 3rd Ed	QLD	361	Palm Beach Mobile & Tourist Park	Closed as of 8th August 2014	03/08/2014
Caravan Parks 3rd Ed	QLD	361.1	Biddeston Tractor Pull Caravan Park	NEW: 477 Oakey Crosshill Rd Oakey (10 S of Oakey) New facilities, T,S,DA,W,$,E,PA. Phone 0428 717 493	25/08/2015
Caravan Parks 3rd Ed	QLD	395	Roma Aussie Tourist Park	Site now CLOSED to tourists	05/06/2015
Caravan Parks 3rd Ed	QLD	398	Rosedale Royal Hotel & Caravan Park	Amend to $	13/07/2015
Caravan Parks 3rd Ed	QLD	443	Jolly Swagman Caravan Park	Pets Allowed, No Camp Kitchen	14/10/2014
Caravan Parks 3rd Ed	QLD	463	Bush Oasis Caravan Park	Delete swimming pool	12/06/2014

Records 1 to 18 of 18

STEP 3

The Updates Program window. Here choices are made as to publication, edition, state, and dates.

For the first update leave the date fields blank. For subsequent updates just enter the date range using the pop-up calendar to show new updates only.

PRINTING If the Print button is obscured, simply use the scroll bar to reveal it.

FEEDBACK

We always welcome feedback and updates on existing caravan parks and also if you find a park we have missed, or a newly opened one please let us know. Please email us on : **talktous@campsaustraliawide.com**

0 200 400 km

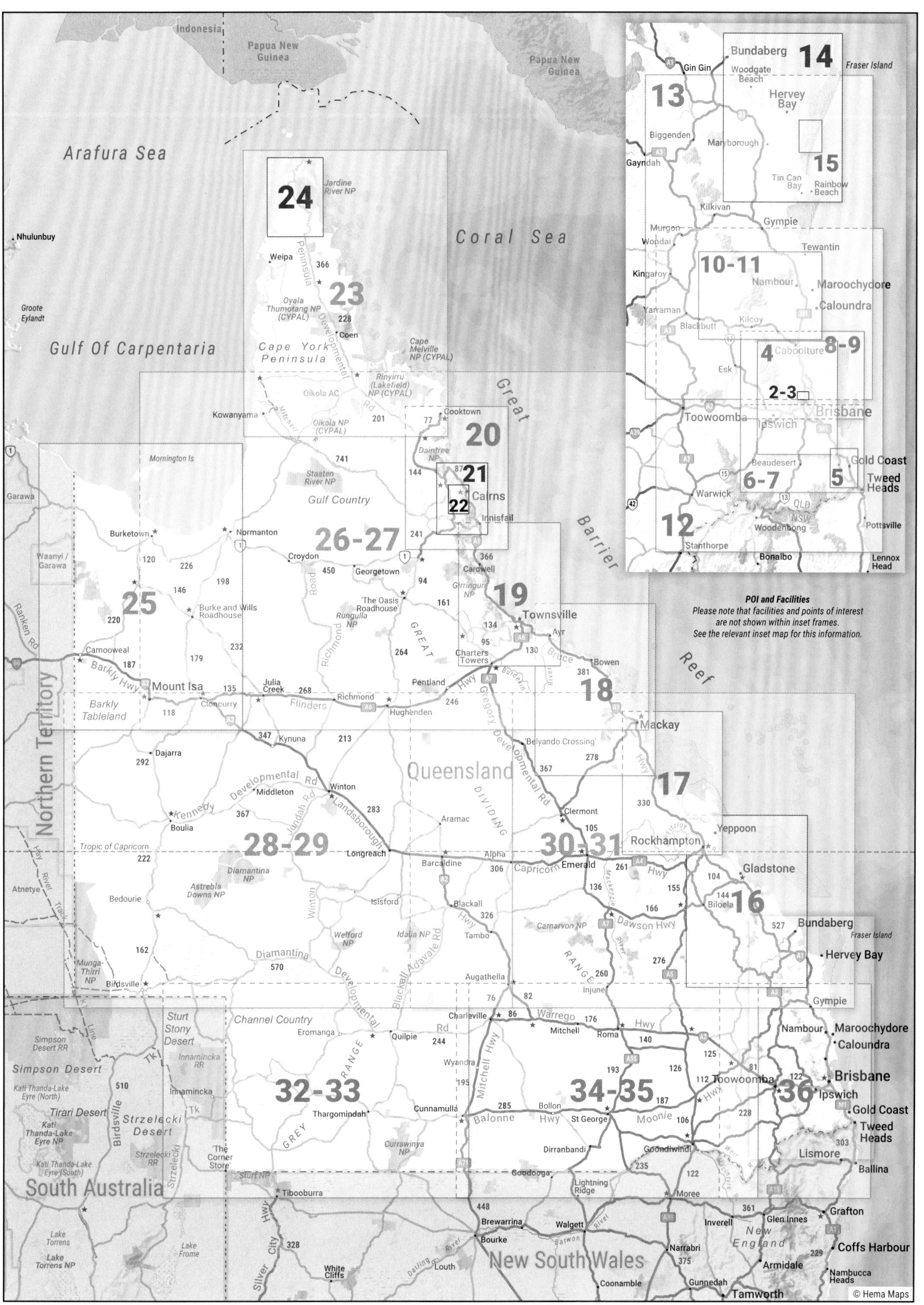
Indonesia
Papua New Guinea
Arafura Sea
Coral Sea
Gulf Of Carpentaria
Great Barrier Reef
Nhulunbuy
Groote Eylandt
Cape York Peninsula
Weipa
Coen
Cooktown
Cairns
Innisfail
Cardwell
Townsville
Ayr
Bowen
Charters Towers
Mackay
Yeppoon
Rockhampton
Gladstone
Bundaberg
Hervey Bay
Gympie
Nambour
Maroochydore
Caloundra
Brisbane
Ipswich
Gold Coast
Tweed Heads
Toowoomba
Lismore
Ballina
Grafton
Coffs Harbour
Armidale
Tamworth
Burketown
Normanton
Croydon
Georgetown
Mount Isa
Cloncurry
Julia Creek
Richmond
Hughenden
Pentland
Camooweal
Dajarra
Kynuna
Winton
Middleton
Boulia
Longreach
Barcaldine
Aramac
Alpha
Emerald
Clermont
Blackall
Tambo
Isisford
Bedourie
Birdsville
Augathella
Charleville
Quilpie
Eromanga
Mitchell
Roma
St George
Cunnamulla
Thargomindah
Dirranbandi
Goondiwindi
Moree
Bourke
Brewarrina
Walgett
Narrabri
Tibooburra
Queensland
Northern Territory
South Australia
New South Wales
Simpson Desert
Strzelecki Desert
Channel Country
Gulf Country
Barkly Tableland
Tropic of Capricorn
POI and Facilities
Please note that facilities and points of interest are not shown within inset frames.
See the relevant inset map for this information.
2-3
4
5
6-7
8-9
10-11
12
13
14
15
16
17
18
19
20
21
22
23
24
25
26-27
28-29
30-31
32-33
34-35
36
© Hema Maps

Inner Brisbane

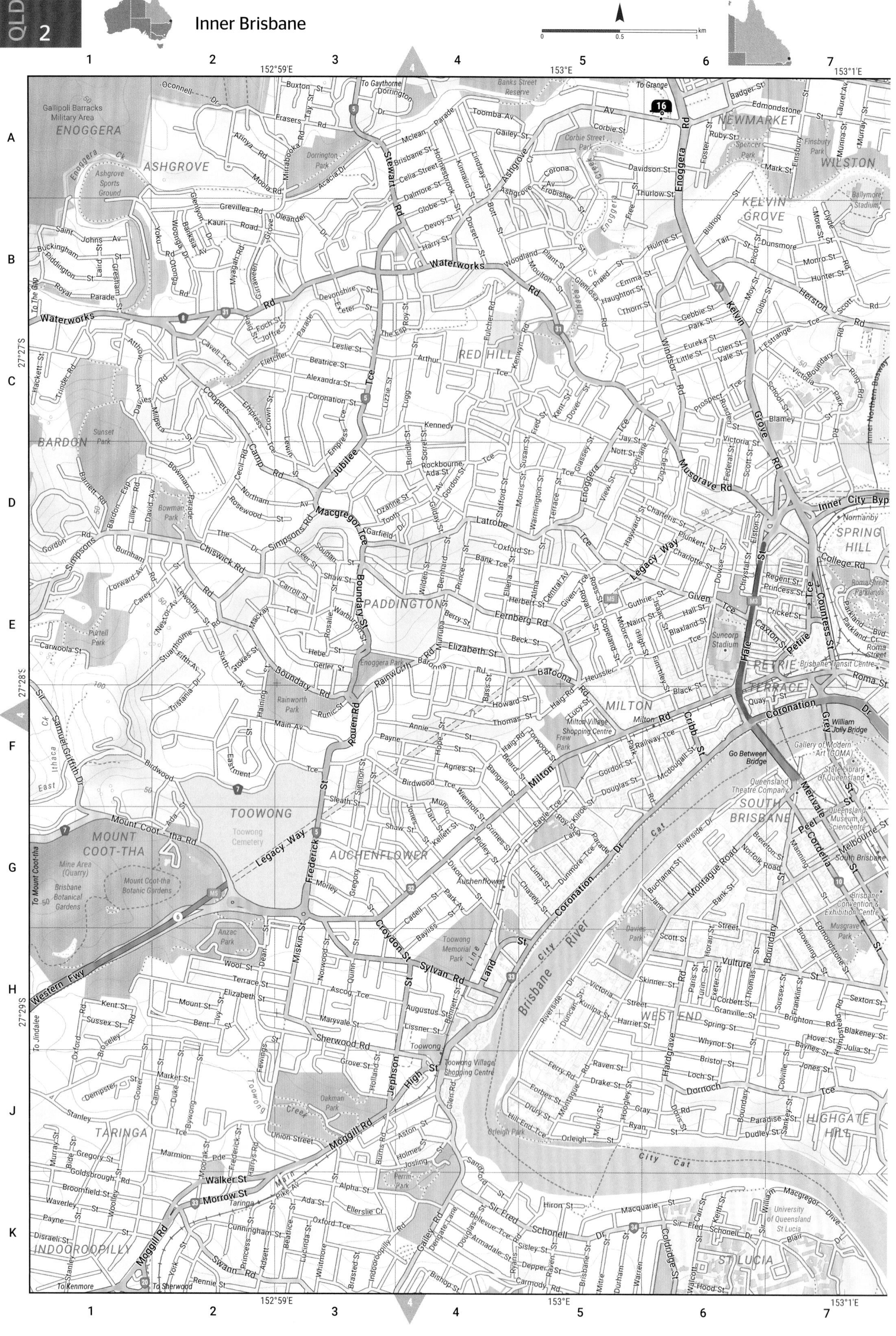

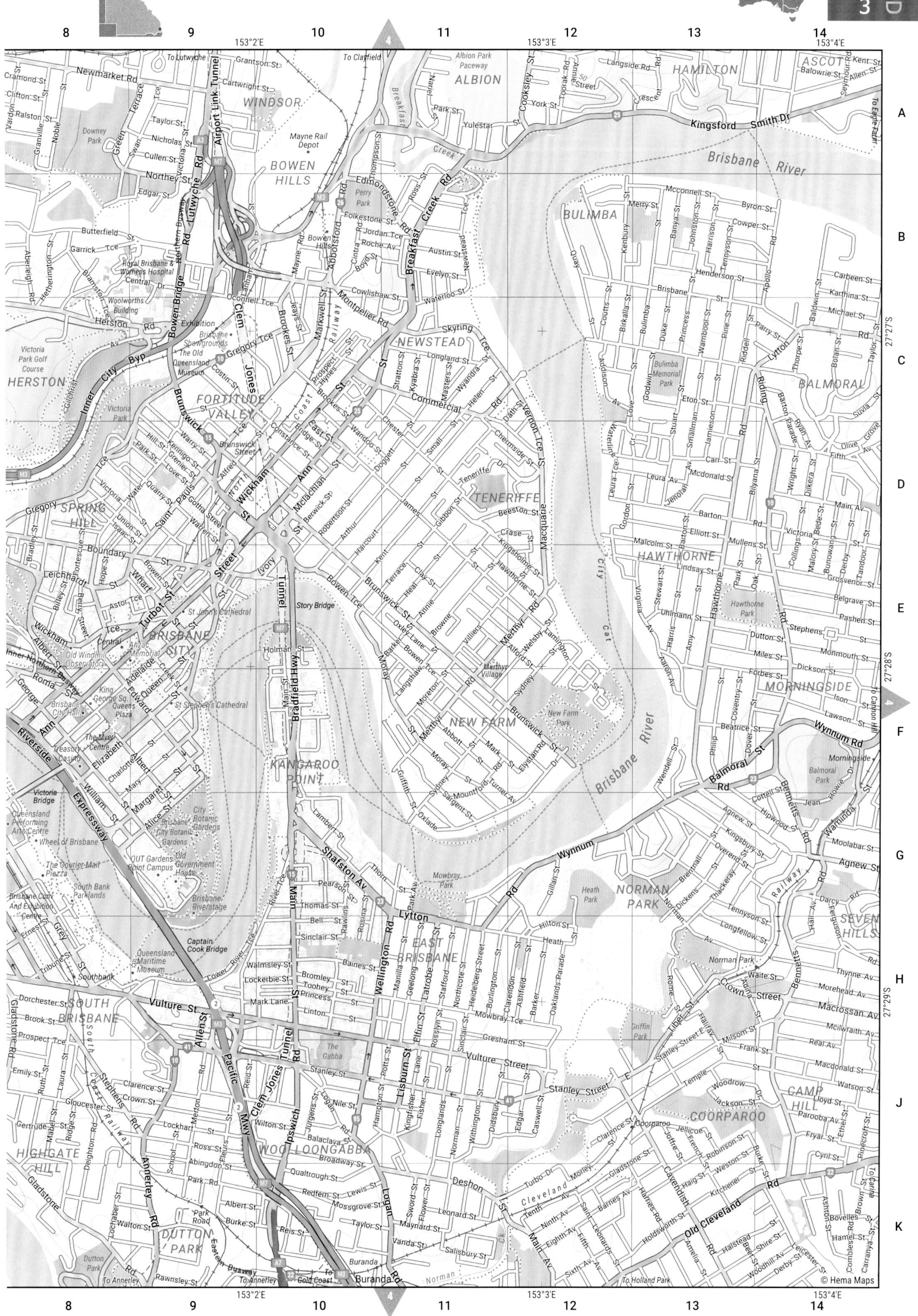
8
9
10
11
12
13
14
153°2'E
153°3'E
153°4'E
A
B
C
D
E
F
G
H
J
K
27°27'S
27°28'S
27°29'S
WINDSOR
ALBION
HAMILTON
ASCOT
BOWEN HILLS
BULIMBA
HERSTON
NEWSTEAD
FORTITUDE VALLEY
BALMORAL
SPRING HILL
TENERIFFE
HAWTHORNE
BRISBANE CITY
MORNINGSIDE
NEW FARM
KANGAROO POINT
NORMAN PARK
SEVEN HILLS
EAST BRISBANE
SOUTH BRISBANE
CAMP HILL
COORPAROO
HIGHGATE HILL
WOOLLOONGABBA
DUTTON PARK
Brisbane River
Kingsford Smith Dr
Inner City Byp
Riverside Expressway
Pacific Mwy
Wynnum Rd
Lytton Rd
Vulture St
Stanley Street
Old Cleveland Rd
Shafston Av
Bradfield Hwy
Story Bridge
Victoria Bridge
Captain Cook Bridge
Mayne Rail Depot
Victoria Park Golf Course
Royal Brisbane & Womens Hospital
The Gabba
New Farm Park
Hawthorne Park
Bulimba Memorial Park
Balmoral Park
Heath Park
Mowbray Park
Downey Park
Perry Park
Dutton Park
Griffin Park
City Botanic Gardens
St Stephen's Cathedral
St John's Cathedral
Old Windmill Observatory
Queensland Performing Arts Centre
Wheel of Brisbane
South Bank Parklands
Queensland Maritime Museum
To Clayfield
To Lutwyche
To Eagle Farm
To Cannon Hill
To Carina
To Holland Park
To Annerley
Gold Coast
© Hema Maps

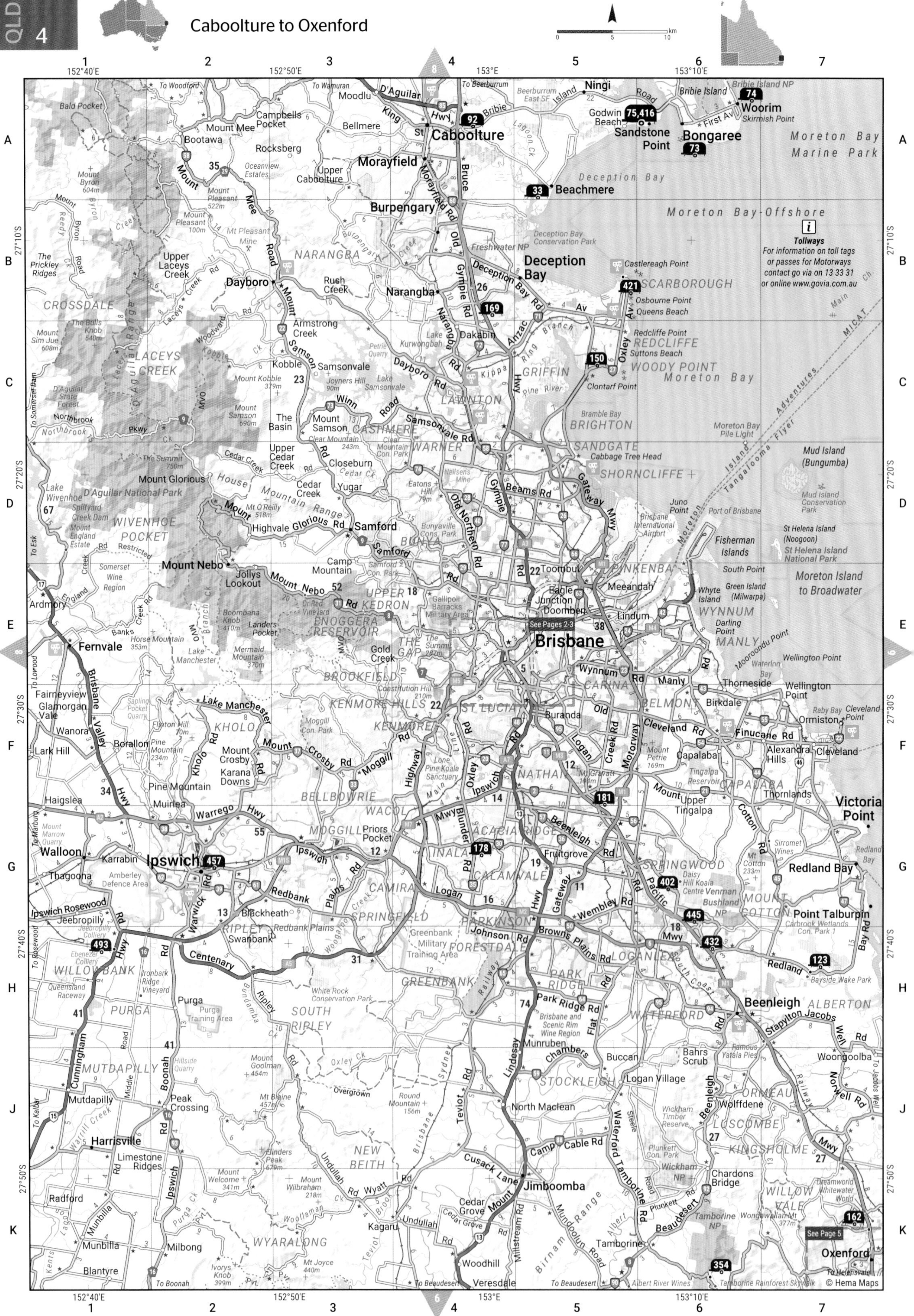
Caboolture
Morayfield
Burpengary
Narangba
Deception Bay
Beachmere
Bribie Island
Woorim
Bongaree
Sandstone Point
Godwin Beach
Ningi
Moreton Bay Marine Park
Moreton Bay-Offshore
Tollways
For information on toll tags or passes for Motorways contact go via on 13 33 31 or online www.govia.com.au
SCARBOROUGH
REDCLIFFE
WOODY POINT
Moreton Bay
Dayboro
Samford
Mount Nebo
Mount Glorious
D'Aguilar National Park
Fernvale
Brisbane
See Pages 2-3
Mud Island (Bungumba)
St Helena Island (Noogoon)
Moreton Island to Broadwater
WYNNUM
MANLY
Cleveland
Victoria Point
Redland Bay
Ipswich
Springwood
Beenleigh
Jimboomba
Tamborine
Oxenford
See Page 5
Walloon
Harrisville
Peak Crossing
Logan Village
© Hema Maps

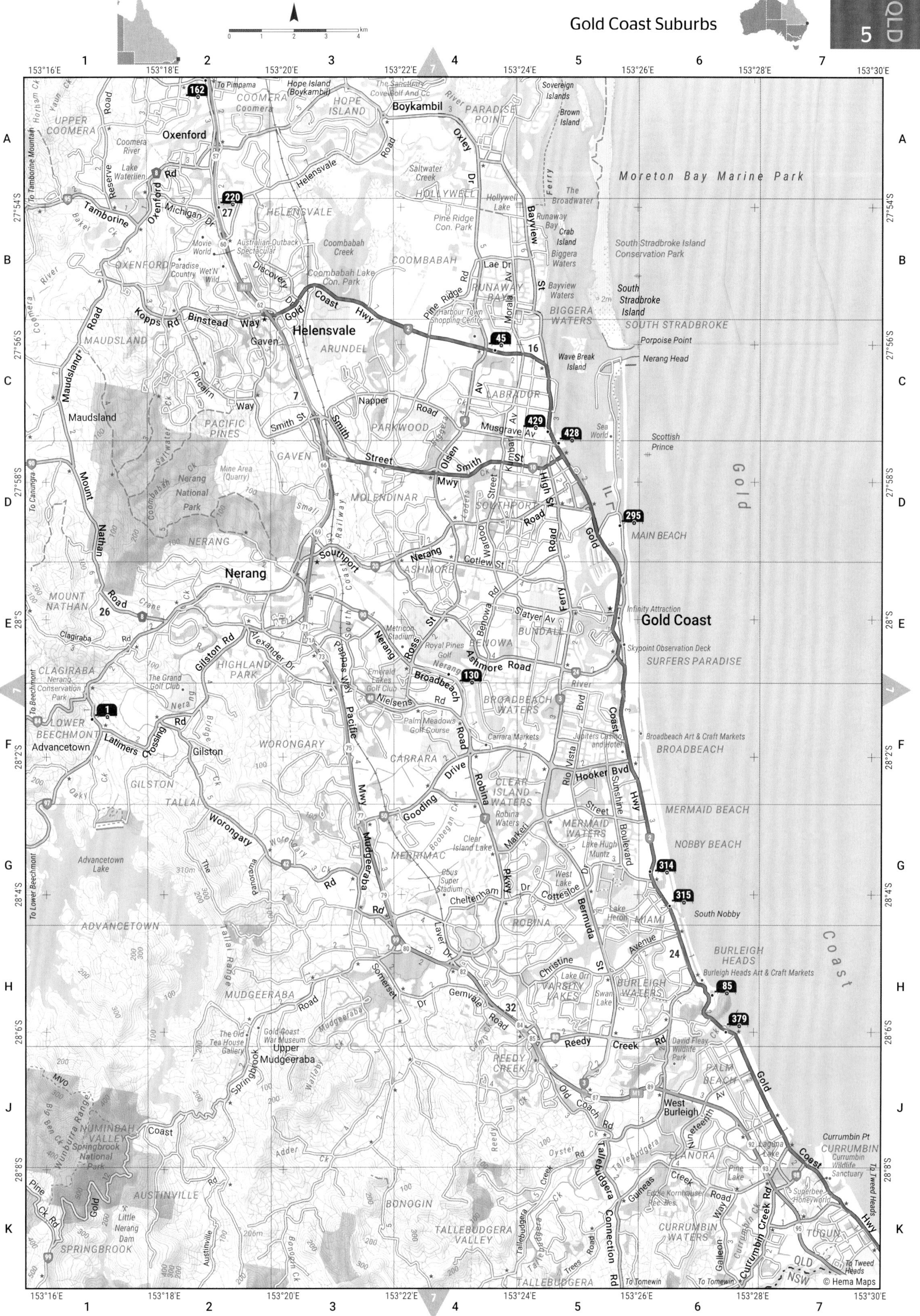
Oxenford
Helensvale
Nerang
Gold Coast
Boykambil
Maudsland
Advancetown
Gilston
Upper Mudgeraba
West Burleigh
Moreton Bay Marine Park
South Stradbroke Island
Main Beach
Surfers Paradise
Broadbeach
Mermaid Beach
Nobby Beach
Burleigh Heads
Currumbin
Tugun
Gold Coast
© Hema Maps

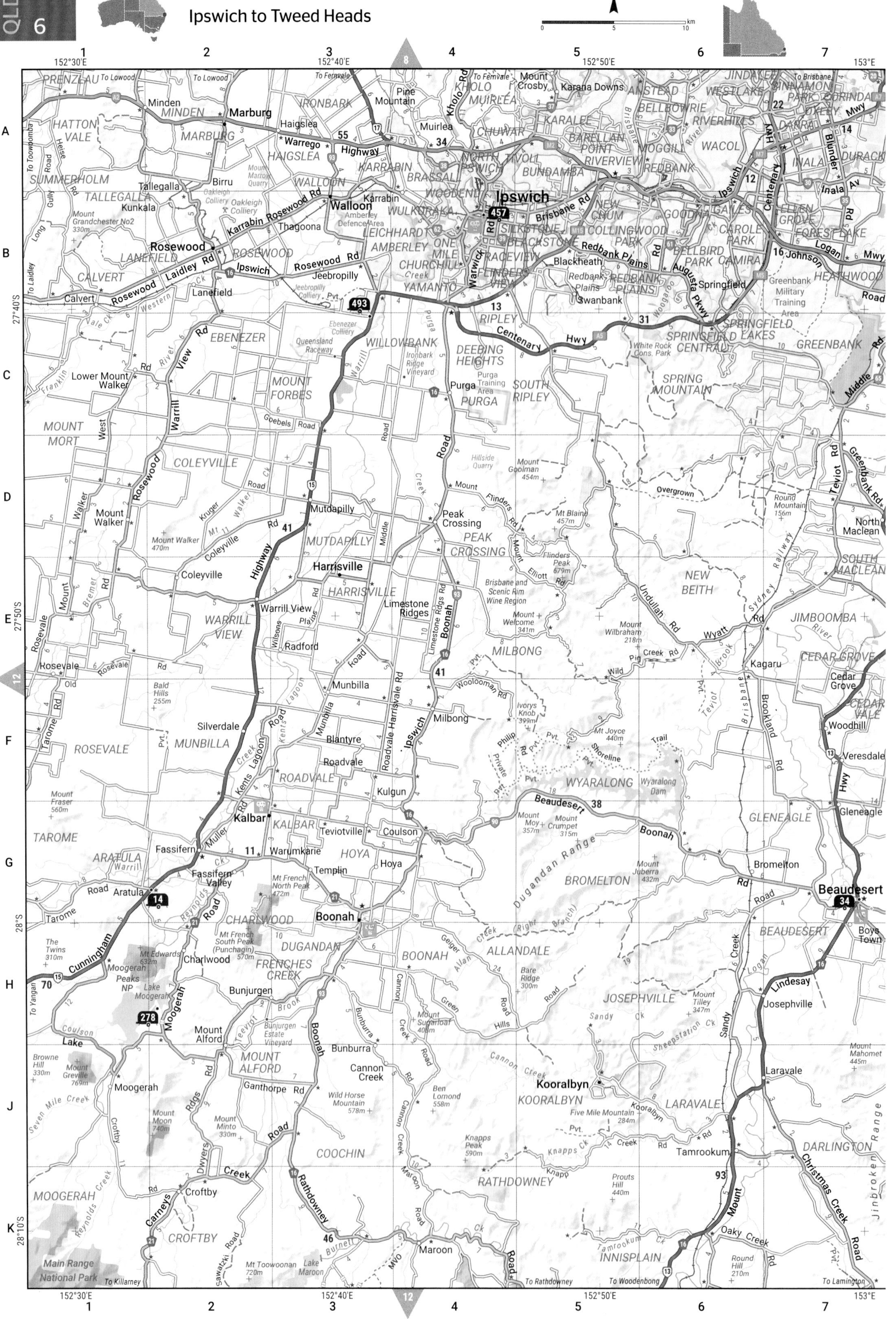
Ipswich
Marburg
Minden
Rosewood
Walloon
Thagoona
Karrabin
Haigslea
Tallegalla
Kunkala
Birru
Calvert
Lanefield
Jeebropilly
Blackheath
Springfield
Swanbank
Purga
Peak Crossing
Mutdapilly
Harrisville
Coleyville
Warrill View
Radford
Limestone Ridges
Munbilla
Silverdale
Blantyre
Roadvale
Kulgun
Kalbar
Teviotville
Coulson
Fassifern
Warumkarie
Hoya
Templin
Fassifern Valley
Aratula
Boonah
Charlwood
Bunjurgen
Mount Alford
Moogerah
Bunburra
Cannon Creek
Ganthorpe
Croftby
Maroon
Kooralbyn
Tamrookum
Laravale
Josephville
Beaudesert
Bromelton
Gleneagle
Veresdale
Woodhill
Cedar Grove
Kagaru
North Maclean
Lower Mount Walker
Mount Walker
Rosevale
Milbong
Pine Mountain
Muirlea
Mount Crosby
Karana Downs
Greenbank Military Training Area
Boys Town
Oaky Creek
Cunningham Highway
Warrego Highway
Centenary Hwy
Ipswich Mwy
Logan Mwy
Mount Lindesay Hwy
Main Range National Park
Moogerah Peaks NP
Lake Moogerah
Wyaralong Dam
Dugandan Range
Jinbroken Range
To Lowood
To Fernvale
To Brisbane
To Toowoomba
To Laidley
To Yangan
To Killarney
To Rathdowney
To Woodenbong
To Lamington
152°30'E
152°40'E
152°50'E
153°E
27°40'S
27°50'S
28°S
28°10'S
0 5 10 km

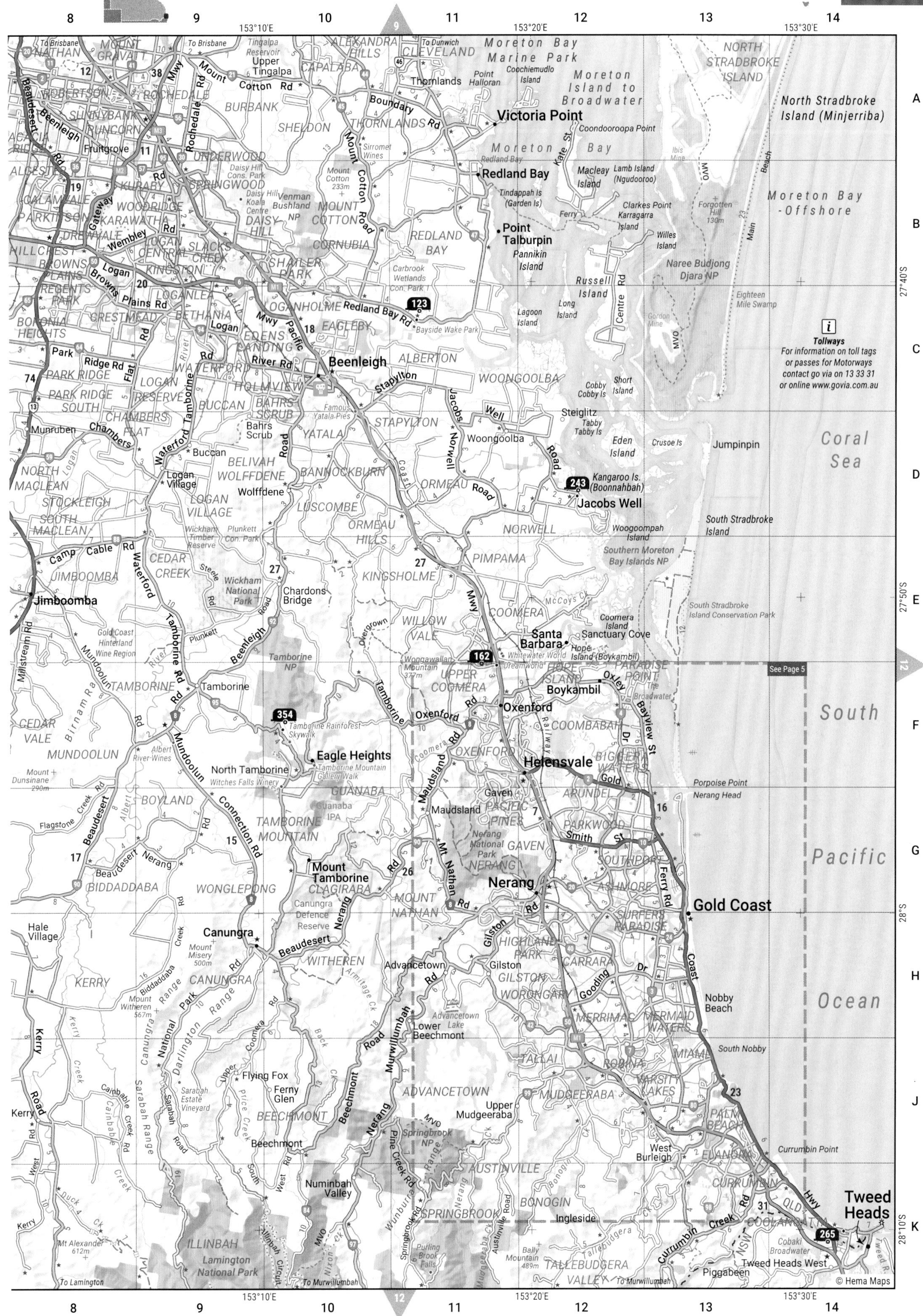
153°10'E
153°20'E
153°30'E
27°40'S
27°50'S
28°S
28°10'S
Moreton Bay Marine Park
Moreton Island to Broadwater
North Stradbroke Island
North Stradbroke Island (Minjerriba)
Moreton Bay
Moreton Bay - Offshore
Victoria Point
Redland Bay
Point Talburpin
Cleveland
Thornlands
Capalaba
Mount Gravatt
Rochedale
Springwood
Daisy Hill
Logan
Beenleigh
Eagleby
Loganholme
Yatala
Stapylton
Woongoolba
Jacobs Well
Kangaroo Is. (Boonnahbah)
Naree Budjong Djara NP
Russell Island
Macleay Island
Lamb Island (Ngudooroo)
Coochiemudlo Island
Jumpinpin
South Stradbroke Island
Southern Moreton Bay Islands NP
South Stradbroke Island Conservation Park
Tollways
For information on toll tags or passes for Motorways contact go via on 13 33 31 or online www.govia.com.au
Coral Sea
South Pacific Ocean
Jimboomba
Logan Village
Wolffdene
Chardons Bridge
Pimpama
Coomera
Santa Barbara
Sanctuary Cove
Hope Island (Boykambil)
Oxenford
Helensvale
Boykambil
Paradise Point
Tamborine
Tamborine NP
Tamborine Rainforest Skywalk
Eagle Heights
North Tamborine
Mount Tamborine
Canungra
Nerang
Gold Coast
Southport
Surfers Paradise
Nobby Beach
Mudgeeraba
Advancetown
Lower Beechmont
Beechmont
Flying Fox
Ferny Glen
Numinbah Valley
Springbrook NP
Lamington National Park
Kerry
Hale Village
Tweed Heads
Tweed Heads West
Piggabeen
Currumbin Point
Ingleside
West Burleigh
Pacific Mwy
Gold Coast Hwy
See Page 5
© Hema Maps

Lake Somerset to Victoria Point

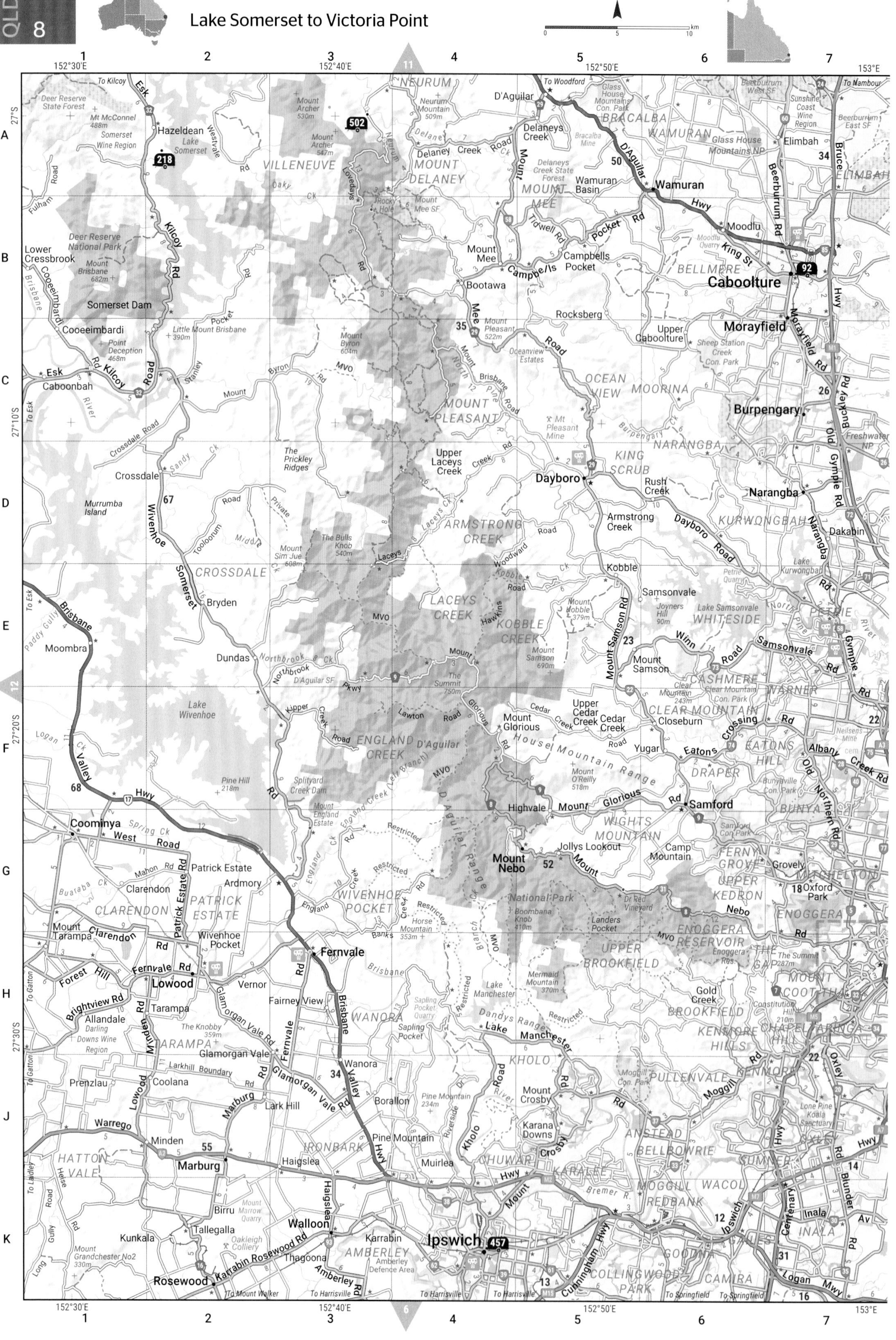

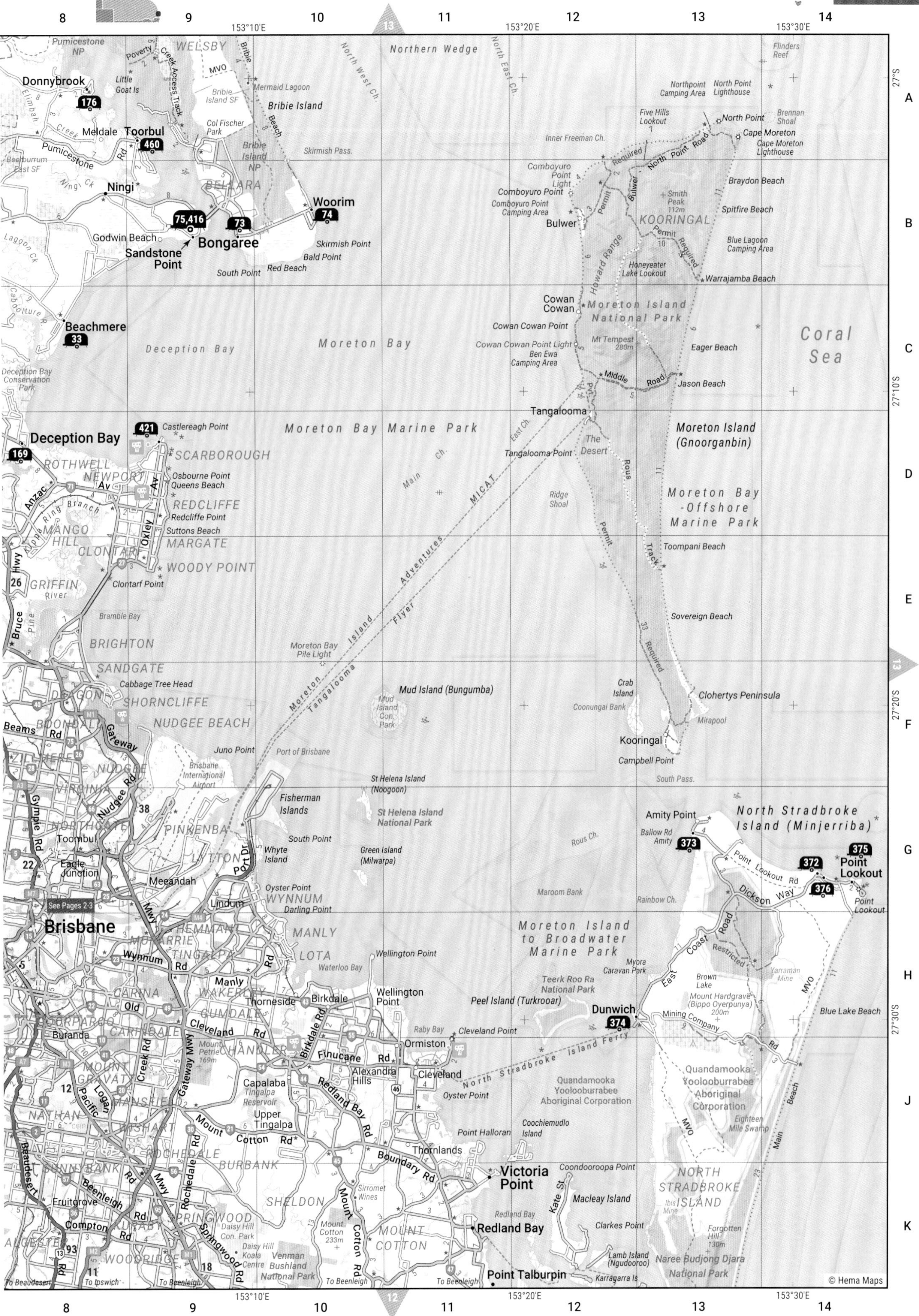
Donnybrook
Toorbul
Meldale
Ningi
Woorim
Bongaree
Sandstone Point
Godwin Beach
Beachmere
Bribie Island
Bribie Island NP
Deception Bay
Moreton Bay
Moreton Bay Marine Park
Northern Wedge
Bulwer
Cowan Cowan
Tangalooma
Kooringal
Moreton Island National Park
Moreton Island (Gnoorganbin)
Moreton Bay -Offshore Marine Park
Coral Sea
North Point
Cape Moreton
Mud Island (Bungumba)
St Helena Island National Park
Amity Point
North Stradbroke Island (Minjerriba)
Point Lookout
Dunwich
Moreton Island to Broadwater Marine Park
Peel Island (Turkrooar)
Brisbane
Scarborough
Redcliffe
Sandgate
Wynnum
Manly
Cleveland
Capalaba
Victoria Point
Redland Bay
Point Talburpin
Macleay Island
North Stradbroke Island
Naree Budjong Djara National Park
Quandamooka Yoolooburrabee Aboriginal Corporation
See Pages 2-3
© Hema Maps

Blackbutt to Noosa Heads

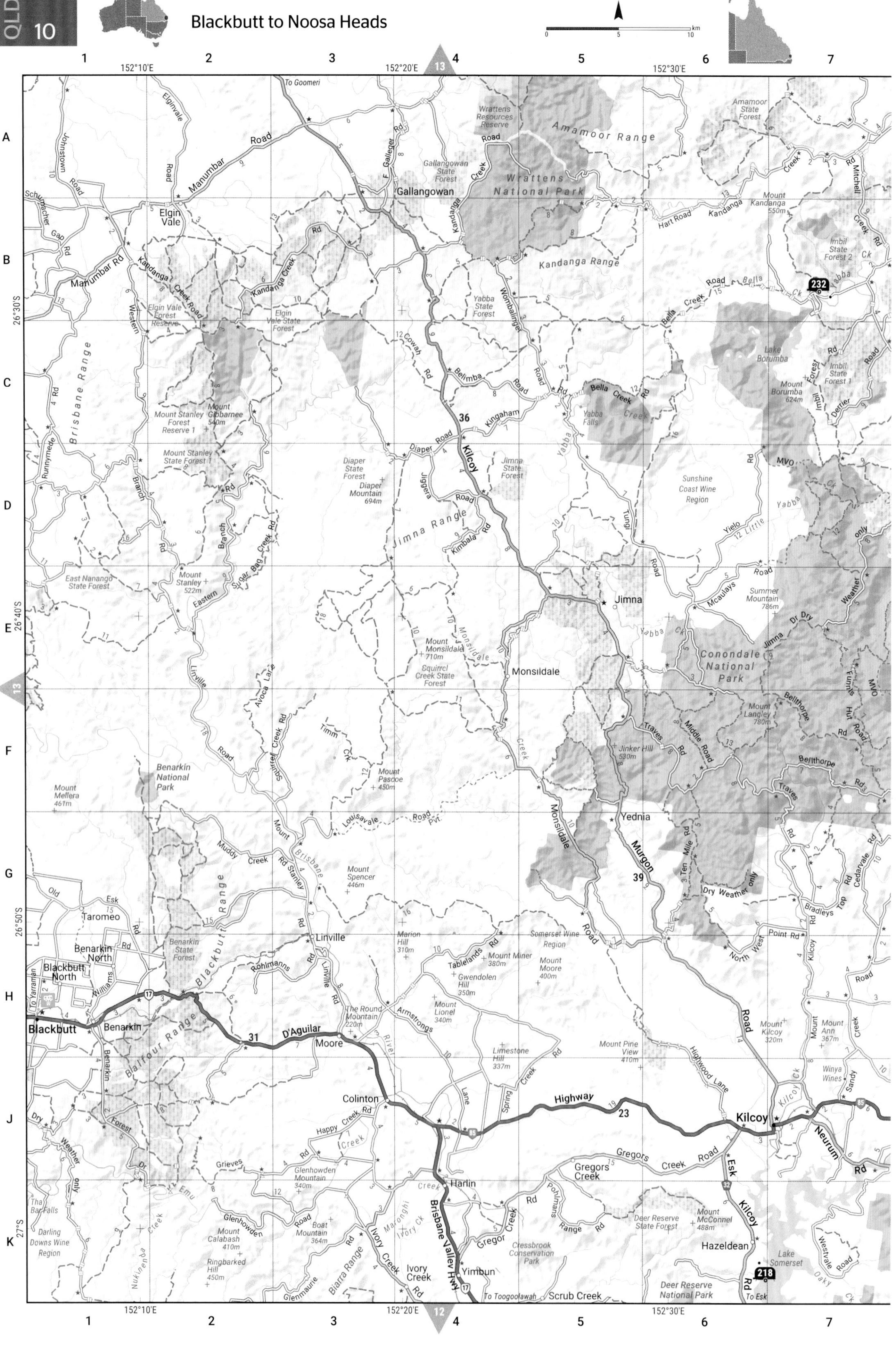

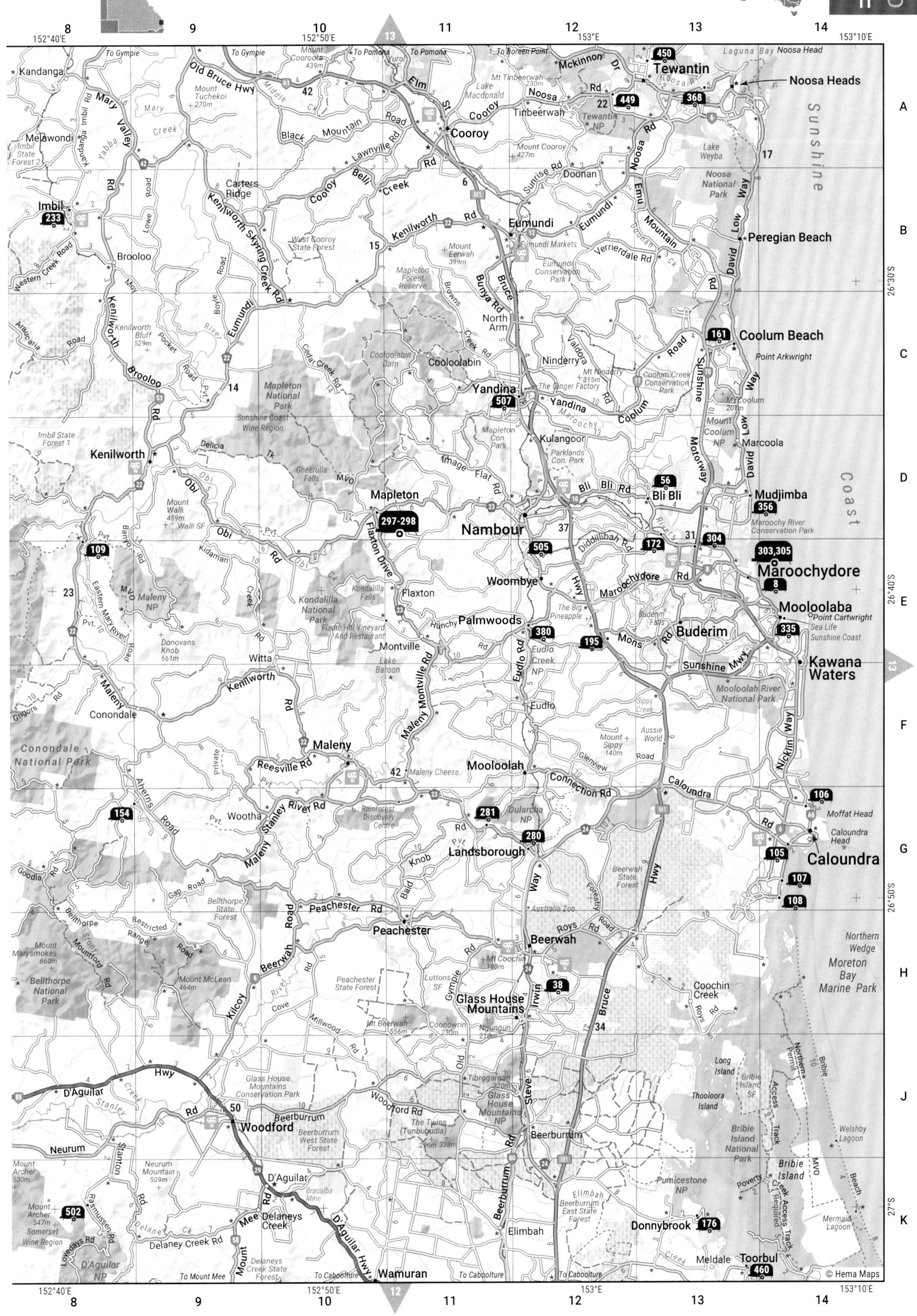

Gympie to Brunswick Heads

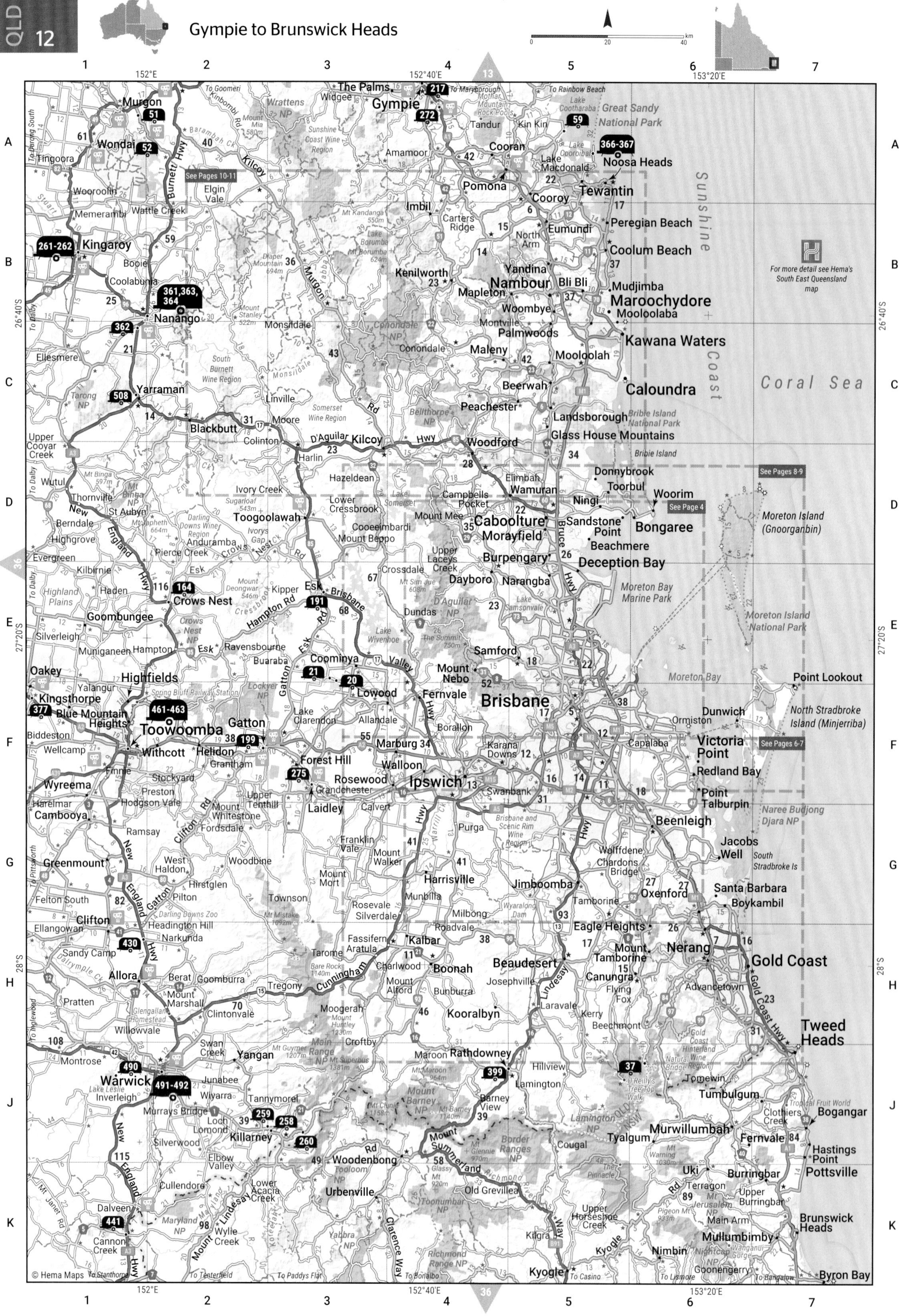

Hervey Bay
For more detail see Hema's Fraser Island map
Great Sandy Marine Park
Great Sandy NP
Corroboree Beach
The Cathedrals
The Declivity
Cathedral Beach
Dipuying
Happy Valley
Be croc wise
Estuarine crocodile sightings have been reported on the west coast of Fraser Island and the Great Sandy Strait.
-Camp at least 50m from the water's edge.
-Never clean fish or discard fish or food scraps near the water's edge, campsites or boat ramps.
-Take care when launching or retrieving your boat.
Eurong
Fraser Island
Dilli Village
North Spit
South Spit
Coral Sea
Rainbow Beach
Tin Can Bay
Cooloola Cove
See Page 14
For more detail see Hema's South East Queensland map
South Pacific Ocean
New Moonta
Weithew
Wallaville
Mount Perry
Gayndah Mt Perry Rd
Cordalba
Booyal
Apple Tree Creek
Childers
Good Night Scrub NP
Woodgate Beach
Burrum Coast NP
Burrum Heads
Toogoom
Dundowran Beach
Hervey Bay
Craignish
Dundowran
Takura
Nikenbah
Booral
Kingfisher Bay
River Heads
Howard
Torbanlea
Duckinwilla
Maryborough West
Maryborough
Biggenden
Mount Lawless
North Aramara
Aramara
Thinoomba
Yerra
Brooweena
Mount Walsh NP
Ban Ban Springs
Glenbar
Tiaro
Tinnanbar
Aranbanga
'Dovedale'
Ban Ban National Park
Burnett Range
Glenbar NP
Marodian
Gootchie
Bauple
Beninbi NP
'Ettiewyn'
Grongah NP
Miva
Kadina
Tansey
Windera
Kilkivan
Cloyna
Nangur NP
Goomeri
Lower Wonga
Gympie
The Palms
Widgee
Gympie South
Hivesville
Mondure
Murgon
Wondai
Tingoora
Wooroolin
Wattle Creek
Gordonbrook
Memerambi
Kingaroy
Boole
Coolabunia
Nanango
Kumbia
Ellesmere
Tarong NP
Yarraman
Blackbutt
Bunya Mtns NP
Upper Cooyar Creek
Maclagan
Wutul
Thornville
Quinalow
Peranga
Kulpi
Rosalie
Brymaroo
Acland
Silverleigh
Devon Park
Oakey
Kingsthorpe
Goombungee
Muniganeen
Yalangur
Highfields
Crows Nest
Hampton
Haden
Kilbirnie
Evergreen
Highgrove
Berndale
St Aubyn
Pierce Creek
Anduramba
Bells Pinch
Toogoolawah
Ivory Creek
Cooeeimbardi
Lower Cressbrook
Mount Beppo
Eskvale
Kipper
Esk
Ravensbourne
Buaraba
Coominya
Allandale
Lowood
Fernvale
Mount Nebo
Samford
Brisbane
Dundas
Lake Wivenhoe
Crossdale
Dayboro
Upper Laceys Creek
Narangba
Burpengary
Morayfield
Caboolture
Bongaree
Woorim
Beachmere
Deception Bay
Moreton Bay
Tangalooma Flyer
Moreton Island National Park
Moreton Island (Gnoorganbin)
Cape Moreton
Eager Beach
Toompani Beach
Clohertys Peninsula
North Stradbroke Island (Minjerriba)
Point Lookout
Mount Mee
Campbells Pocket
Wamuran
Elimbah
Ningi
Toorbul
Donnybrook
Bribie Island National Park
Moreton Bay Marine Park
Woodford
Kilcoy
D'Aguilar Hwy
Harlin
Hazeldean
Moore
Colinton
Linville
Yednia
Monsildale
Somerset Wine Region
Beerwah
Glass House Mountains
Peachester
Landsborough
Maleny
Conondale
Conondale NP
Caloundra
Mooloolah
Kawana Waters
Buderim
Mooloolaba
Maroochydore
Nambour
Palmwoods
Montville
Mapleton
Kenilworth
Yandina
Bli Bli
Mudjimba
Coolum Beach
Peregian Beach
North Arm
Eumundi
Cooroy
Carters Ridge
Imbil
Noosa Heads
Tewantin
Lake Macdonald
Cooran
Pomona
Kin Kin
Tandur
Amamoor
Gallangowan
Elgin Vale
Kingaroy
See Pages 10-11
See Pages 8-9
See Page 4
© Hema Maps

Fraser Island

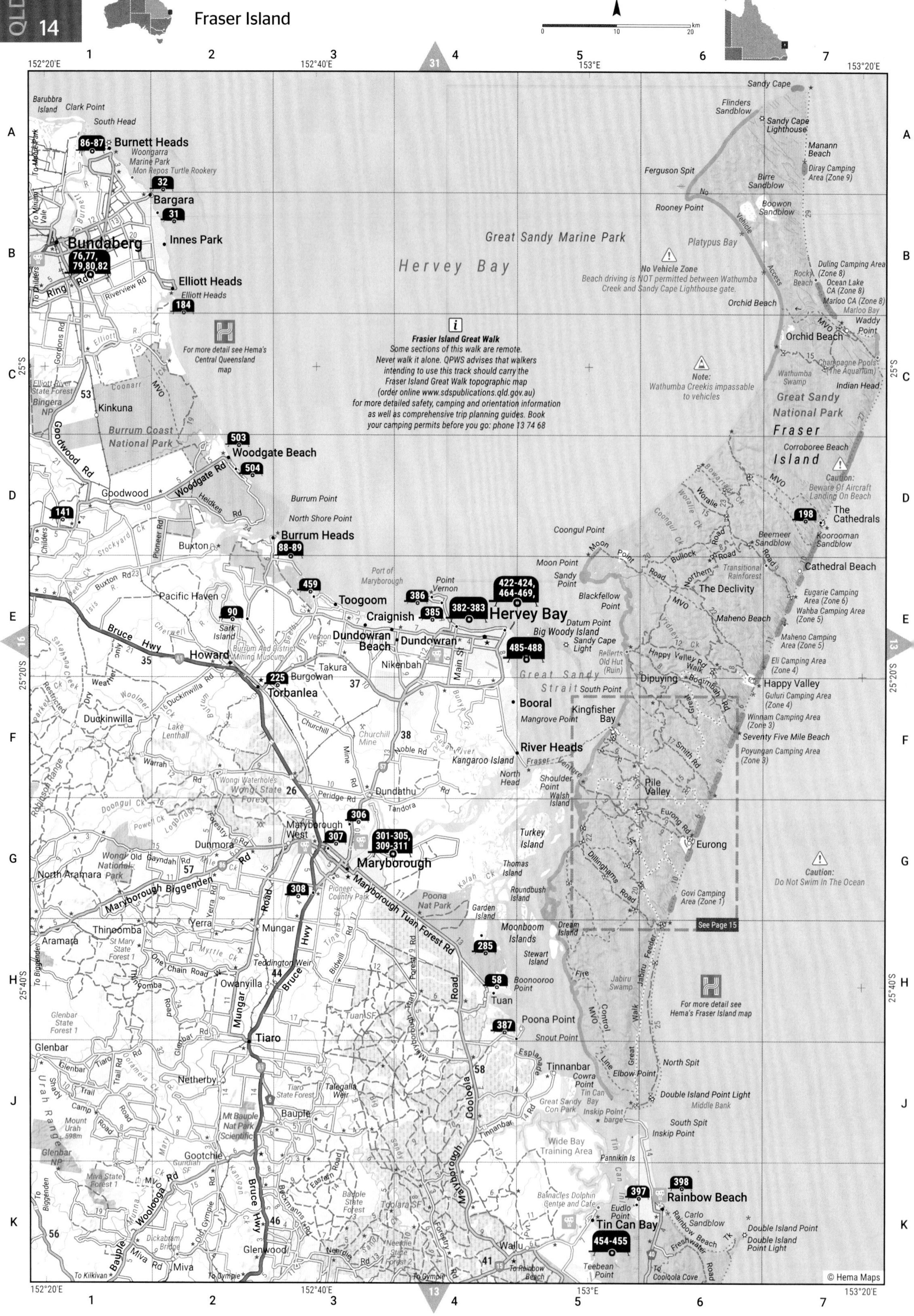

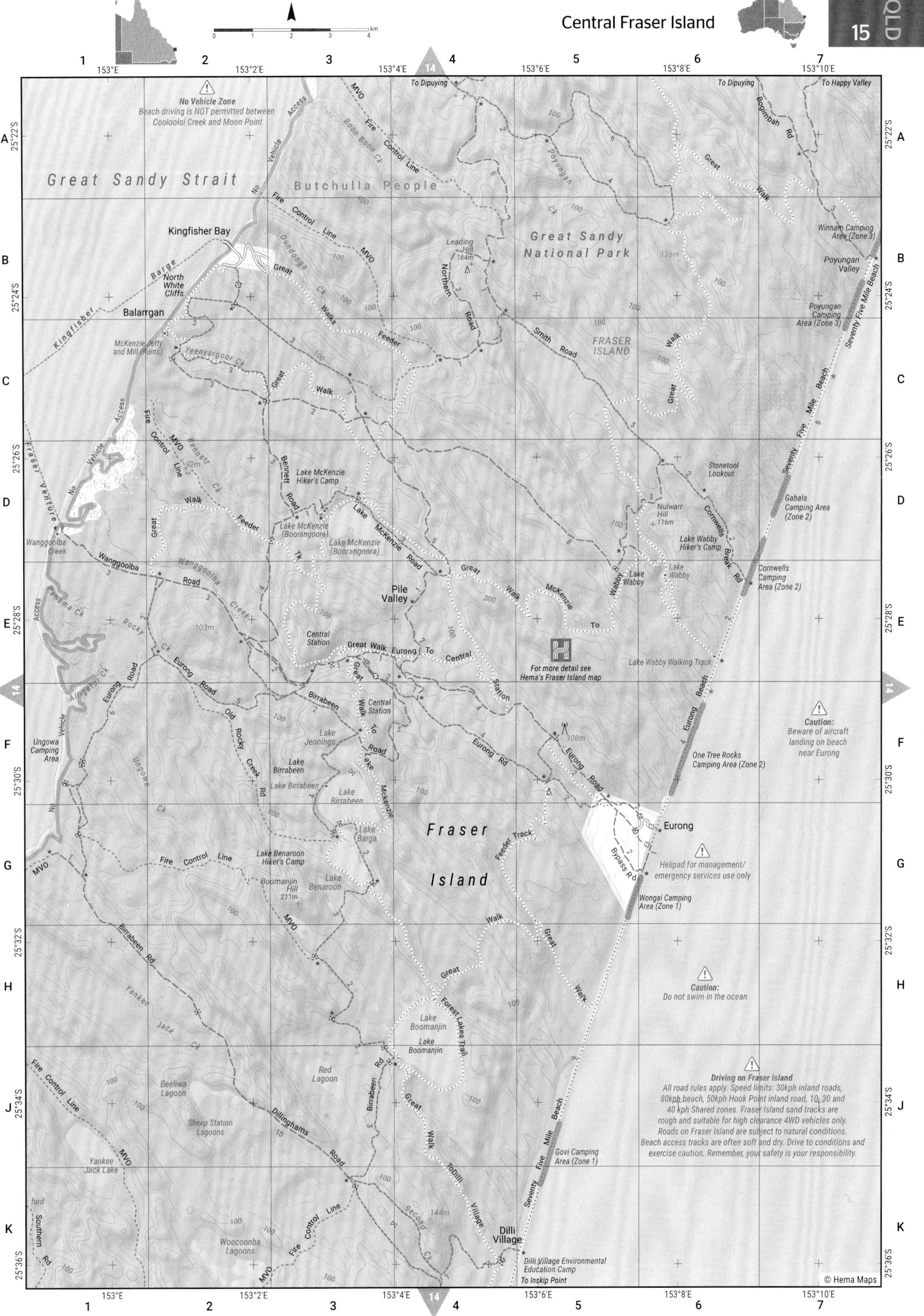
Great Sandy Strait
Kingfisher Bay
Balarrgan
North White Cliffs
Butchulla People
Great Sandy National Park
FRASER ISLAND
No Vehicle Zone
Beach driving is NOT permitted between Cooloolooi Creek and Moon Point
Leading Hill 184m
Lake McKenzie Hiker's Camp
Lake McKenzie (Boorangoora)
Pile Valley
Central Station
Lake Jennings
Lake Birrabeen
Lake Barga
Lake Benaroon Hiker's Camp
Lake Benaroon
Boomanjin Hill 211m
Lake Boomanjin
Red Lagoon
Beeliwa Lagoon
Sheep Station Lagoons
Yankee Jack Lake
Woocoonba Lagoons
Fraser Island
Nulwarr Hill 116m
Stonetool Lookout
Lake Wabby Hiker's Camp
Lake Wabby
Gabala Camping Area (Zone 2)
Cornwells Camping Area (Zone 2)
One Tree Rocks Camping Area (Zone 2)
Eurong
Wongai Camping Area (Zone 1)
Govi Camping Area (Zone 1)
Dilli Village
Dilli Village Environmental Education Camp
To Inskip Point
Winnam Camping Area (Zone 3)
Poyungan Valley
Poyungan Camping Area (Zone 3)
Seventy Five Mile Beach
Ungowa Camping Area
McKenzie Jetty and Mill (Ruins)
Wanggoolba Creek
For more detail see Hema's Fraser Island map
Caution: Beware of aircraft landing on beach near Eurong
Helipad for management/ emergency services use only
Caution: Do not swim in the ocean
Driving on Fraser Island
All road rules apply. Speed limits: 30kph inland roads, 80kph beach, 50kph Hook Point inland road, 10, 30 and 40 kph Shared zones. Fraser Island sand tracks are rough and suitable for high clearance 4WD vehicles only. Roads on Fraser Island are subject to natural conditions. Beach access tracks are often soft and dry. Drive to conditions and exercise caution. Remember, your safety is your responsibility.
To Dipuying
To Happy Valley
© Hema Maps

Rockhampton to Bundaberg

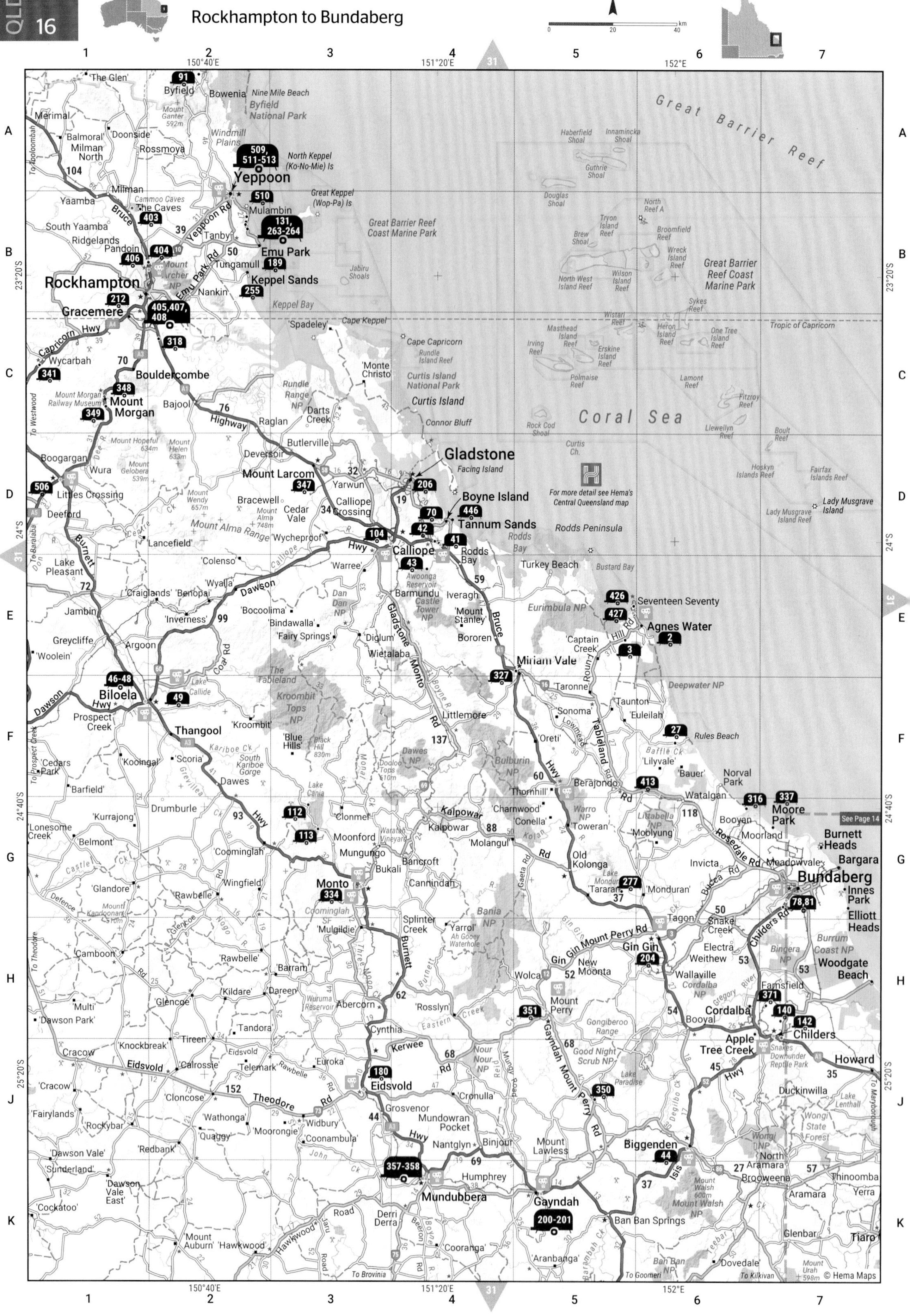

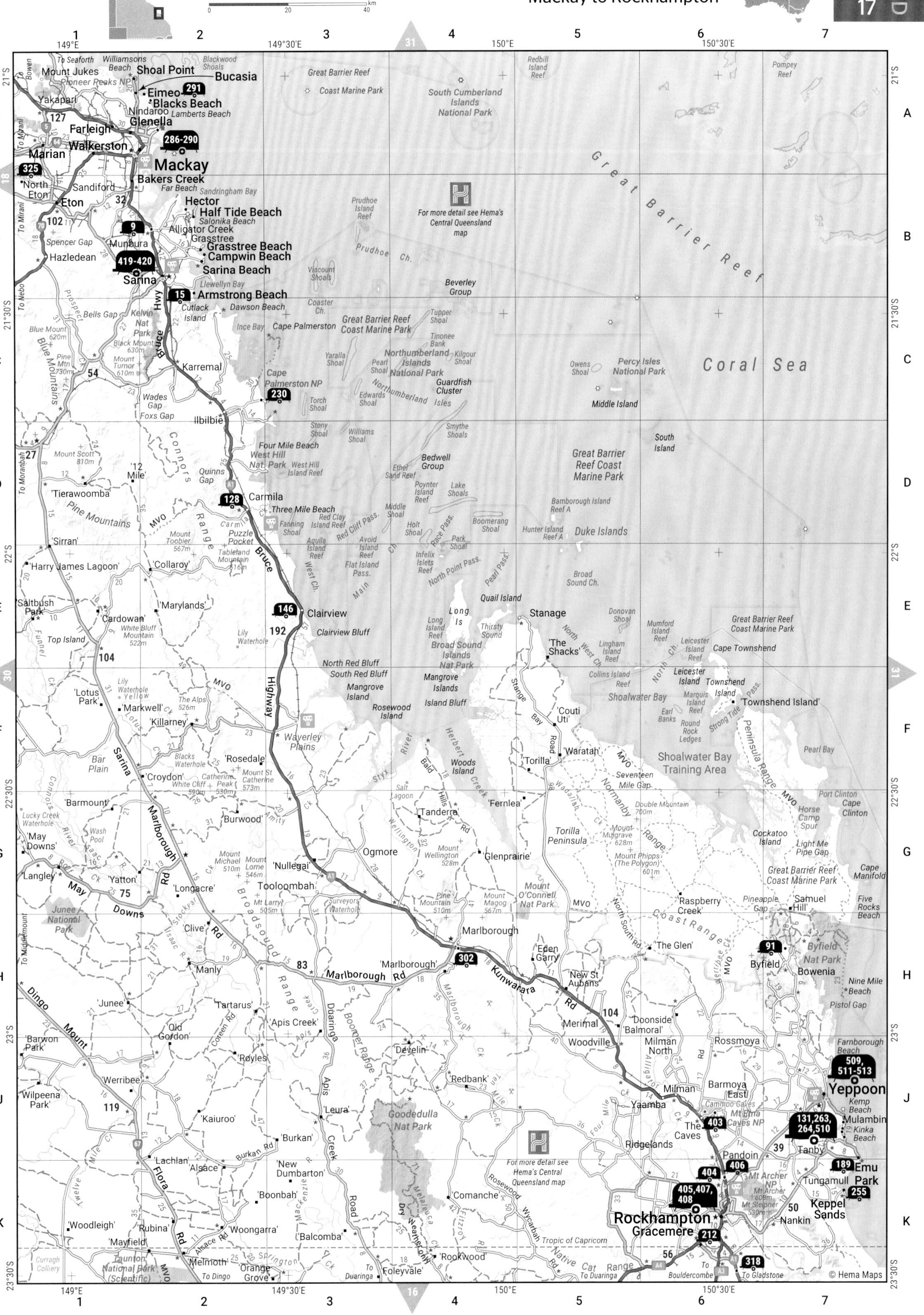
Mackay
Shoal Point
Bucasia
Eimeo
Blacks Beach
Glenella
Farleigh
Walkerston
Marian
Bakers Creek
Hector
Half Tide Beach
Grasstree Beach
Campwin Beach
Sarina Beach
Sarina
Armstrong Beach
Karremal
Ilbilbie
Carmila
Clairview
Great Barrier Reef
Coral Sea
South Cumberland Islands National Park
Percy Isles National Park
Northumberland Islands National Park
Cape Palmerston NP
Great Barrier Reef Coast Marine Park
Broad Sound Islands Nat Park
Shoalwater Bay Training Area
For more detail see Hema's Central Queensland map
Stanage
Ogmore
Tooloombah
Marlborough
Byfield
Bowenia
Yeppoon
Emu Park
Keppel Sands
Rockhampton
Gracemere
Goodedulla Nat Park
Junee National Park
Tropic of Capricorn
© Hema Maps

Ayr to Sarina

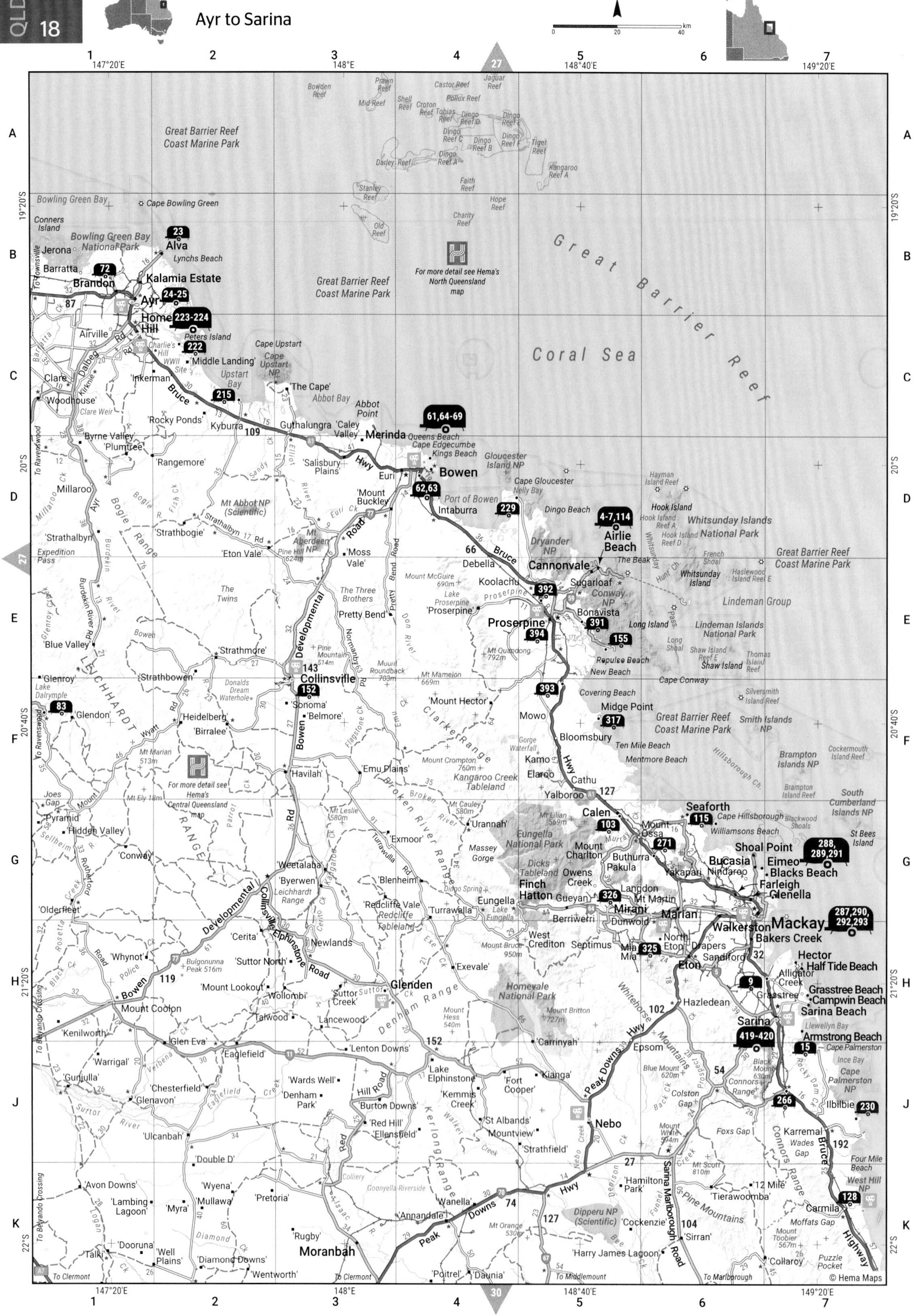

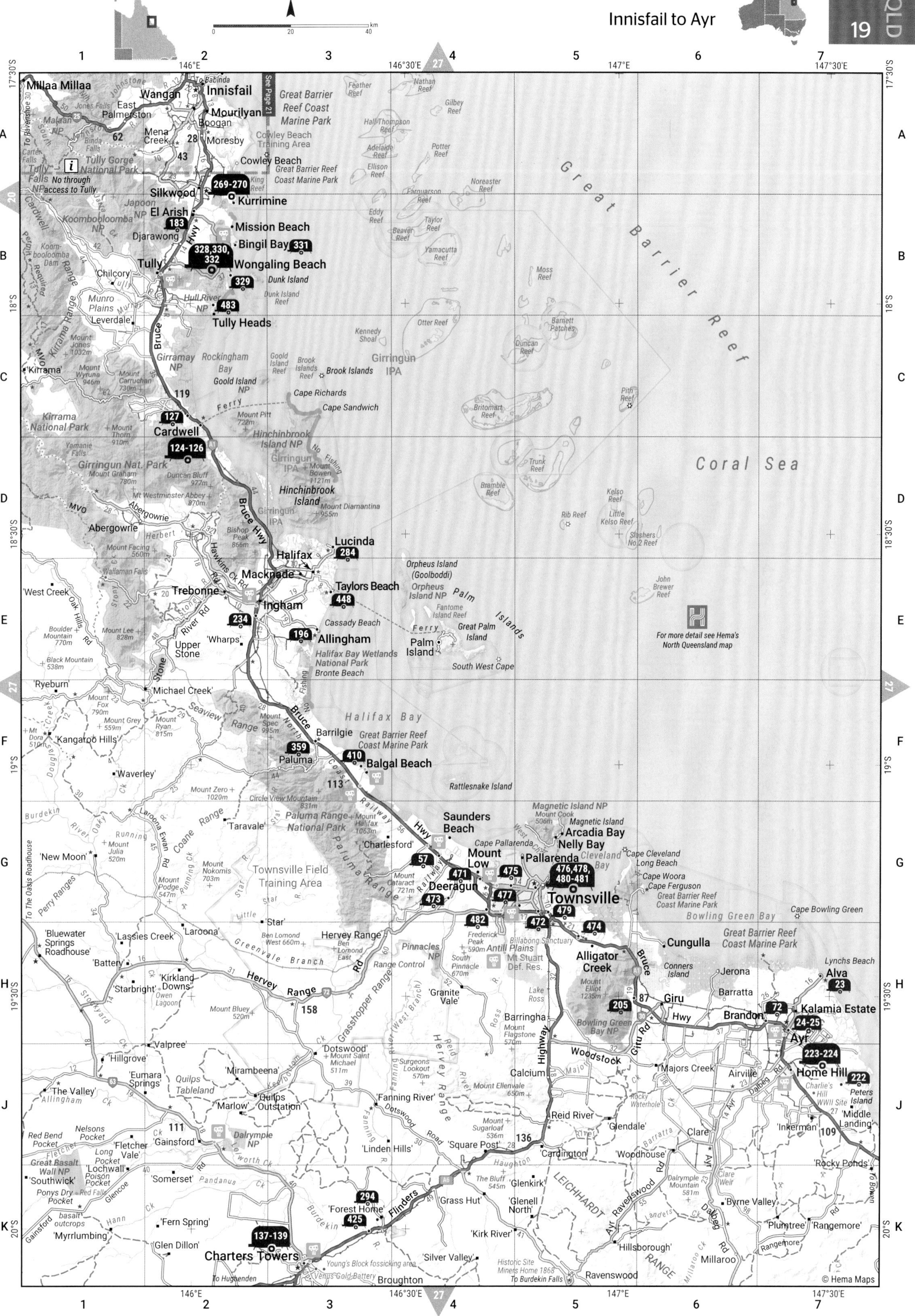
Millaa Millaa
Wangan
Innisfail
Mourilyan
Boogan
Moresby
Cowley Beach
Great Barrier Reef Coast Marine Park
Silkwood
Kurrimine
El Arish
Mission Beach
Bingil Bay
Wongaling Beach
Dunk Island
Tully
Tully Heads
Great Barrier Reef
Girringun IPA
Cardwell
Hinchinbrook Island
Coral Sea
Lucinda
Halifax
Macknade
Taylors Beach
Trebonne
Ingham
Allingham
Palm Island
Halifax Bay
Barrilgie
Paluma
Balgal Beach
Rattlesnake Island
Saunders Beach
Magnetic Island NP
Arcadia Bay
Nelly Bay
Pallarenda
Mount Low
Deeragun
Townsville
Cungulla
Alligator Creek
Giru
Alva
Brandon
Kalamia Estate
Ayr
Home Hill
Charters Towers
Ravenswood
For more detail see Hema's North Queensland map
© Hema Maps

Cooktown to Tully

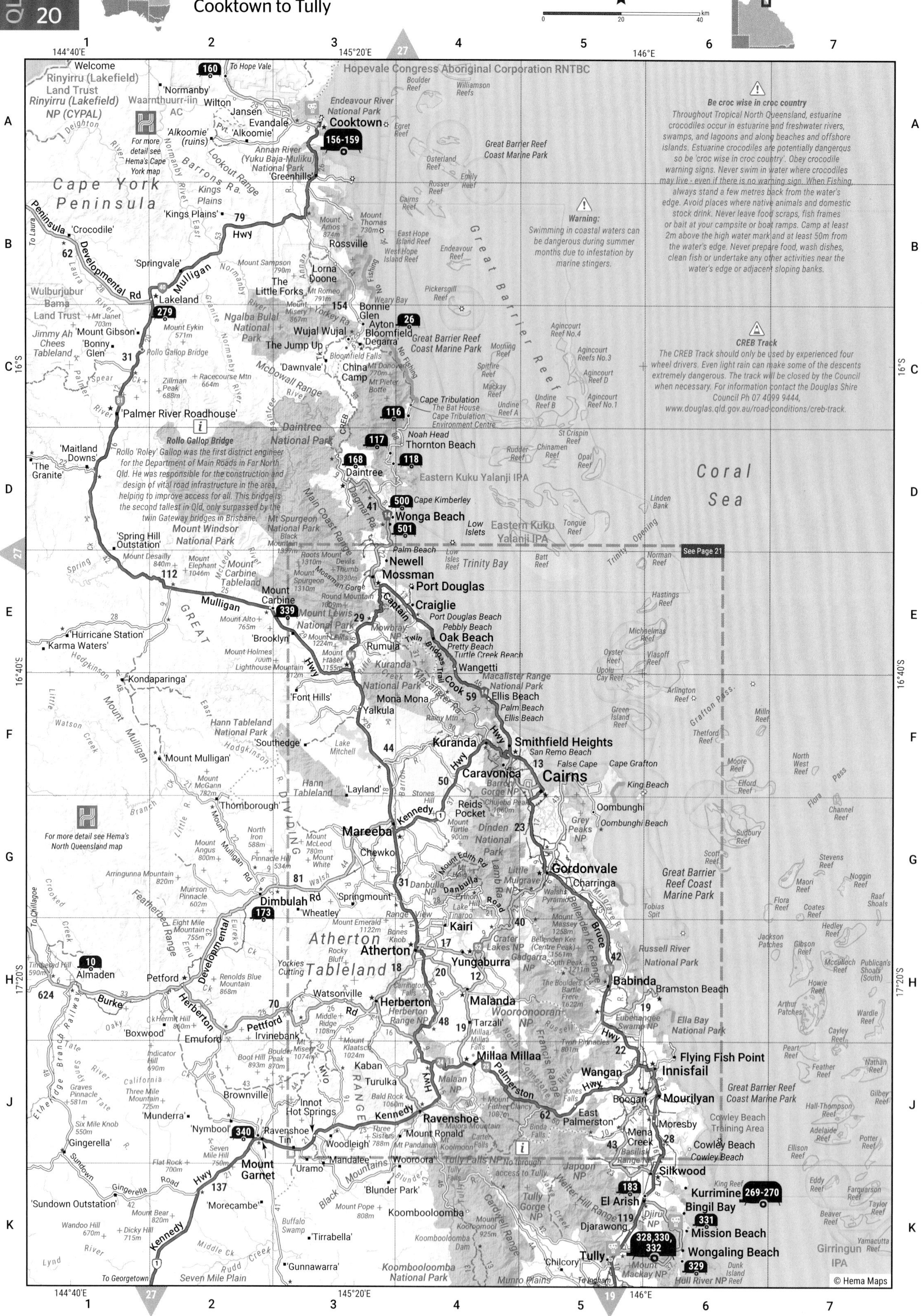

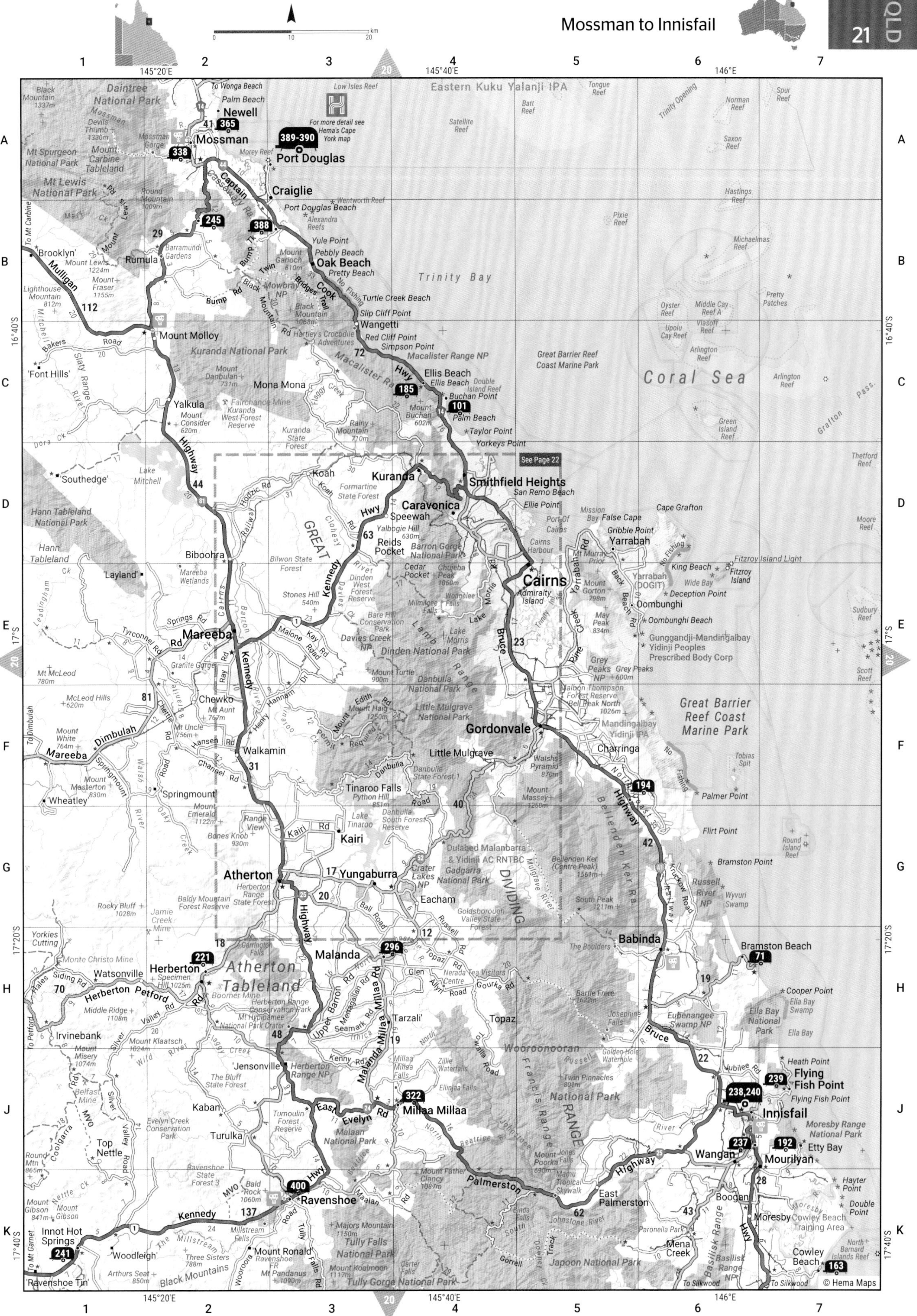
Mossman
Port Douglas
Craiglie
Oak Beach
Trinity Bay
Coral Sea
Great Barrier Reef Coast Marine Park
Kuranda
Smithfield Heights
Caravonica
Cairns
Mareeba
Gordonvale
Atherton
Yungaburra
Malanda
Babinda
Millaa Millaa
Innisfail
Ravenshoe
Herberton
Atherton Tableland
Mourilyan
Flying Fish Point
Etty Bay
Bramston Beach
Wangan
East Palmerston
Innot Hot Springs
Yarrabah
Kuranda National Park
Daintree National Park
Mt Lewis National Park
Wooroonooran National Park
Tully Falls National Park
Tully Gorge National Park
Japoon National Park
See Page 22
For more detail see Hema's Cape York map
© Hema Maps

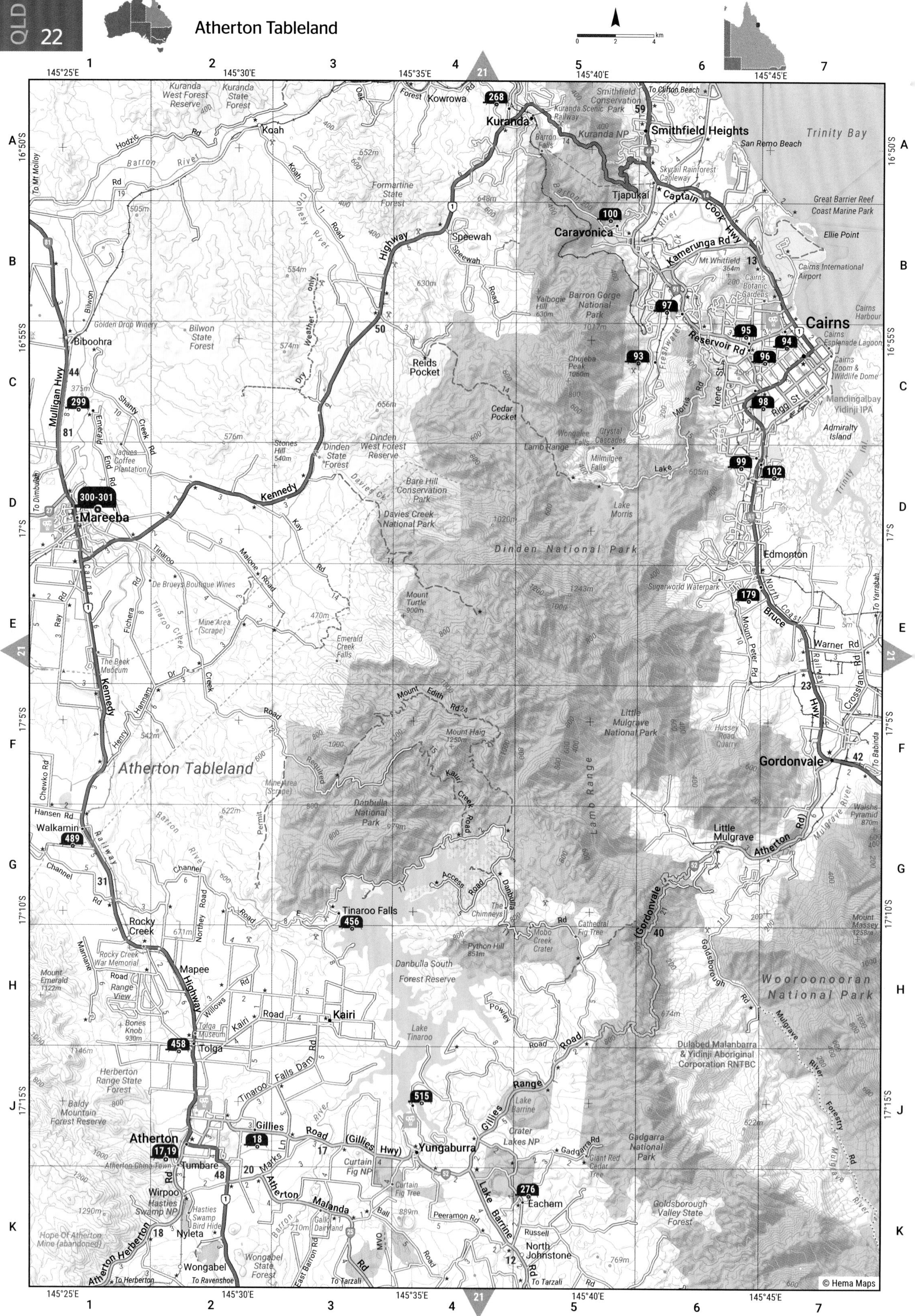
Kuranda
Kowrowa
Smithfield Heights
Trinity Bay
San Remo Beach
Koah
Tjapukai
Caravonica
Speewah
Kamerunga Rd
Captain Cook Hwy
Great Barrier Reef Coast Marine Park
Ellie Point
Cairns International Airport
Barron Gorge National Park
Cairns
Reservoir Rd
Biboohra
Bilwon State Forest
Mulligan Hwy
Reids Pocket
Cedar Pocket
Mareeba
Kennedy
Dinden National Park
Davies Creek National Park
Edmonton
Sugarworld Waterpark
Bruce Hwy
Warner Rd
Atherton Tableland
Little Mulgrave National Park
Gordonvale
Walkamin
Danbulla National Park
Little Mulgrave
Tinaroo Falls
Rocky Creek
Mapee
Wooroonooran National Park
Kairi
Tolga
Lake Tinaroo
Gillies Hwy
Atherton
Yungaburra
Crater Lakes NP
Gadgarra National Park
Tumbare
Eacham
Malanda
Wirpoo
Hasties Swamp NP
Nyleta
North Johnstone
Wongabel
Goldsborough Valley State Forest
To Herberton
To Ravenshoe
To Tarzali
© Hema Maps

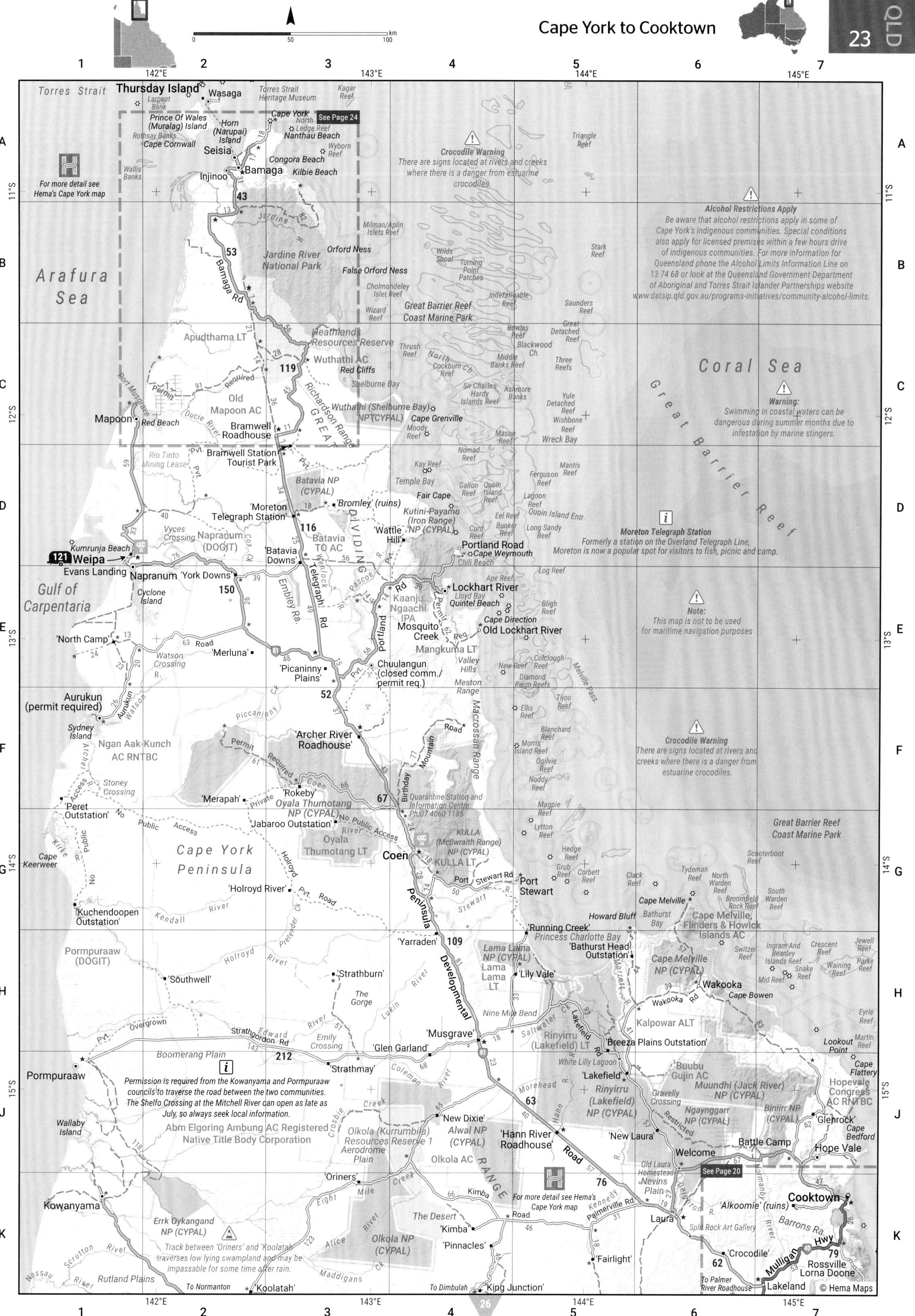
Crocodile Warning
There are signs located at rivers and creeks where there is a danger from estuarine crocodiles.
Alcohol Restrictions Apply
Be aware that alcohol restrictions apply in some of Cape York's indigenous communities. Special conditions also apply for licensed premises within a few hours drive of indigenous communities. For more information for Queensland phone the Alcohol Limits Information Line on 13 74 68 or look at the Queensland Government Department of Aboriginal and Torres Strait Islander Partnerships website www.datsip.qld.gov.au/programs-initiatives/community-alcohol-limits.
For more detail see Hema's Cape York map
Warning:
Swimming in coastal waters can be dangerous during summer months due to infestation by marine stingers.
Moreton Telegraph Station
Formerly a station on the Overland Telegraph Line, Moreton is now a popular spot for visitors to fish, picnic and camp.
Note:
This map is not to be used for maritime navigation purposes
Crocodile Warning
There are signs located at rivers and creeks where there is a danger from estuarine crocodiles.
Permission is required from the Kowanyama and Pormpuraaw councils to traverse the road between the two communities. The Shelfo Crossing at the Mitchell River can open as late as July, so always seek local information.
Track between 'Oriners' and 'Koolatah' traverses low lying swampland and may be impassable for some time after rain.
For more detail see Hema's Cape York map
See Page 24
See Page 20
Coral Sea
Great Barrier Reef
Arafura Sea
Gulf of Carpentaria
Cape York Peninsula
© Hema Maps

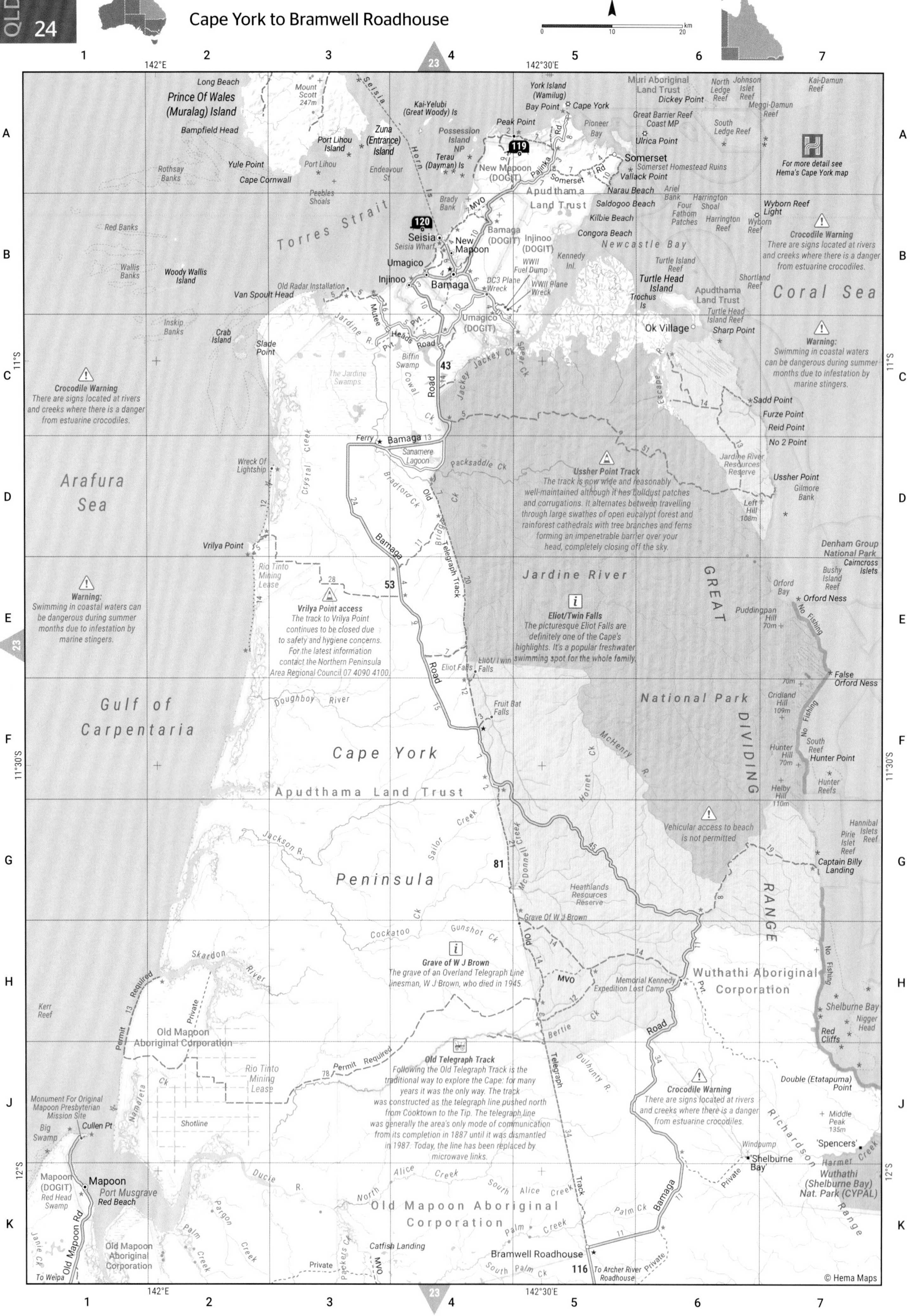
Prince Of Wales (Muralag) Island
Long Beach
Mount Scott 247m
Bampfield Head
Rothsay Banks
Yule Point
Cape Cornwall
Port Lihou Island
Port Lihou
Zuna (Entrance) Island
Kai-Yelubi (Great Woody) Is
Possession Island NP
Terau (Dayman) Is
Endeavour St
Peebles Shoals
Torres Strait
York Island (Wamilug)
Bay Point
Cape York
Peak Point
Pioneer Bay
New Mapoon (DOGIT)
Somerset
Somerset Homestead Ruins
Vallack Point
Muri Aboriginal Land Trust
Dickey Point
Great Barrier Reef Coast MP
Ulrica Point
North Ledge Reef
Johnson Islet Reef
Meggi-Damun Reef
South Ledge Reef
Kai-Damun Reef
For more detail see Hema's Cape York map
Apudthama Land Trust
Narau Beach
Saldogoo Beach
Kilbie Beach
Congora Beach
Newcastle Bay
Ariel Bank
Four Fathom Patches
Harrington Shoal
Harrington Reef
Wyborn Reef Light
Wyborn Reef
Crocodile Warning
There are signs located at rivers and creeks where there is a danger from estuarine crocodiles.
Brady Bank
Seisia
Seisia Wharf
New Mapoon
Bamaga (DOGIT)
Injinoo (DOGIT)
Umagico
Injinoo
Bamaga
WWII Fuel Dump
DC3 Plane Wreck
WWII Plane Wreck
Kennedy Inl.
Turtle Island Reef
Turtle Head Island
Trochus Is
Apudthama Land Trust
Shortland Reef
Coral Sea
Turtle Head Island Reef
Sharp Point
Ok Village
Red Banks
Wallis Banks
Woody Wallis Island
Old Radar Installation
Van Spoult Head
Inskip Banks
Crab Island
Slade Point
Jardine R.
Mutee Heads Rd
Heads Road
Biffin Swamp
Umagico (DOGIT)
Jackey Jackey Ck
The Jardine Swamps
Cowal Ck
Escape R.
Warning:
Swimming in coastal waters can be dangerous during summer months due to infestation by marine stingers.
Sadd Point
Furze Point
Reid Point
No 2 Point
Crocodile Warning
There are signs located at rivers and creeks where there is a danger from estuarine crocodiles.
Ferry
Bamaga
Sanamere Lagoon
Packsaddle Ck
Ussher Point Track
The track is now wide and reasonably well-maintained although it has bulldust patches and corrugations. It alternates between travelling through large swathes of open eucalypt forest and rainforest cathedrals with tree branches and ferns forming an impenetrable barrier over your head, completely closing off the sky.
Jardine River Resources Reserve
Ussher Point
Gilmore Bank
Left Hill 108m
Arafura Sea
Wreck Of Lightship
Crystal Creek
Bradford Ck
Old Bridge Ck
Bamaga
Telegraph Track
Vrilya Point
Denham Group National Park
Cairncross Islets
Bushy Island Reef
Orford Bay
Orford Ness
Rio Tinto Mining Lease
Jardine River
GREAT
Warning:
Swimming in coastal waters can be dangerous during summer months due to infestation by marine stingers.
Vrilya Point access
The track to Vrilya Point continues to be closed due to safety and hygiene concerns. For the latest information contact the Northern Peninsula Area Regional Council 07 4090 4100.
Eliot/Twin Falls
The picturesque Eliot Falls are definitely one of the Cape's highlights. It's a popular freshwater swimming spot for the whole family.
Puddingpan Hill 70m
No Fishing
Eliot Falls
Eliot/Twin Falls
Road
False Orford Ness
Gulf of Carpentaria
Doughboy River
Fruit Bat Falls
National Park
Cridland Hill 109m
DIVIDING
Cape York
McHenry R.
South Reef
Hunter Point
Hunter Hill 70m
Hunter Reefs
Helby Hill 110m
Apudthama Land Trust
Hornet Ck
Vehicular access to beach is not permitted
Jackson R.
Sailor Creek
McDonnell Creek
Hannibal Islets Reef
Pirie Islet Reef
Captain Billy Landing
Peninsula
RANGE
Heathlands Resources Reserve
Grave Of W J Brown
Cockatoo Ck
Gunshot Ck
Grave of W J Brown
The grave of an Overland Telegraph Line linesman, W J Brown, who died in 1945.
Old Telegraph Track
Skardon River
Memorial Kennedy Expedition Lost Camp
MVO
Wuthathi Aboriginal Corporation
Pvt. Road
Kerr Reef
Permit Required
Private
Old Mapoon Aboriginal Corporation
Bertie Ck
Shelburne Bay
Nigger Head
Red Cliffs
Rio Tinto Mining Lease
Permit Required
Old Telegraph Track
Following the Old Telegraph Track is the traditional way to explore the Cape: for many years it was the only way. The track was constructed as the telegraph line pushed north from Cooktown to the Tip. The telegraph line was generally the area's only mode of communication from its completion in 1887 until it was dismantled in 1987. Today, the line has been replaced by microwave links.
Dulhunty R.
Crocodile Warning
There are signs located at rivers and creeks where there is a danger from estuarine crocodiles.
Double (Etatapuma) Point
Monument For Original Mapoon Presbyterian Mission Site
Big Swamp
Cullen Pt
Namaleta Ck
Shotline
Richardson Range
Middle Peak 135m
Windpump
Shelburne Bay
'Spencers'
Harmer Creek
Wuthathi (Shelburne Bay) Nat. Park (CYPAL)
Mapoon (DOGIT)
Mapoon
Red Head Swamp
Port Musgrave
Red Beach
Ducie R.
Alice Creek
North Alice Creek
South Alice Creek
Private
Old Mapoon Aboriginal Corporation
Pargon Creek
Palm Ck
Palm Creek
Bamaga Road
Janie Ck
Old Mapoon Rd
Old Mapoon Aboriginal Corporation
Palm Creek
Catfish Landing
Packers Ck
Private
Bramwell Roadhouse
South Palm Ck
To Archer River Roadhouse
To Weipa
© Hema Maps

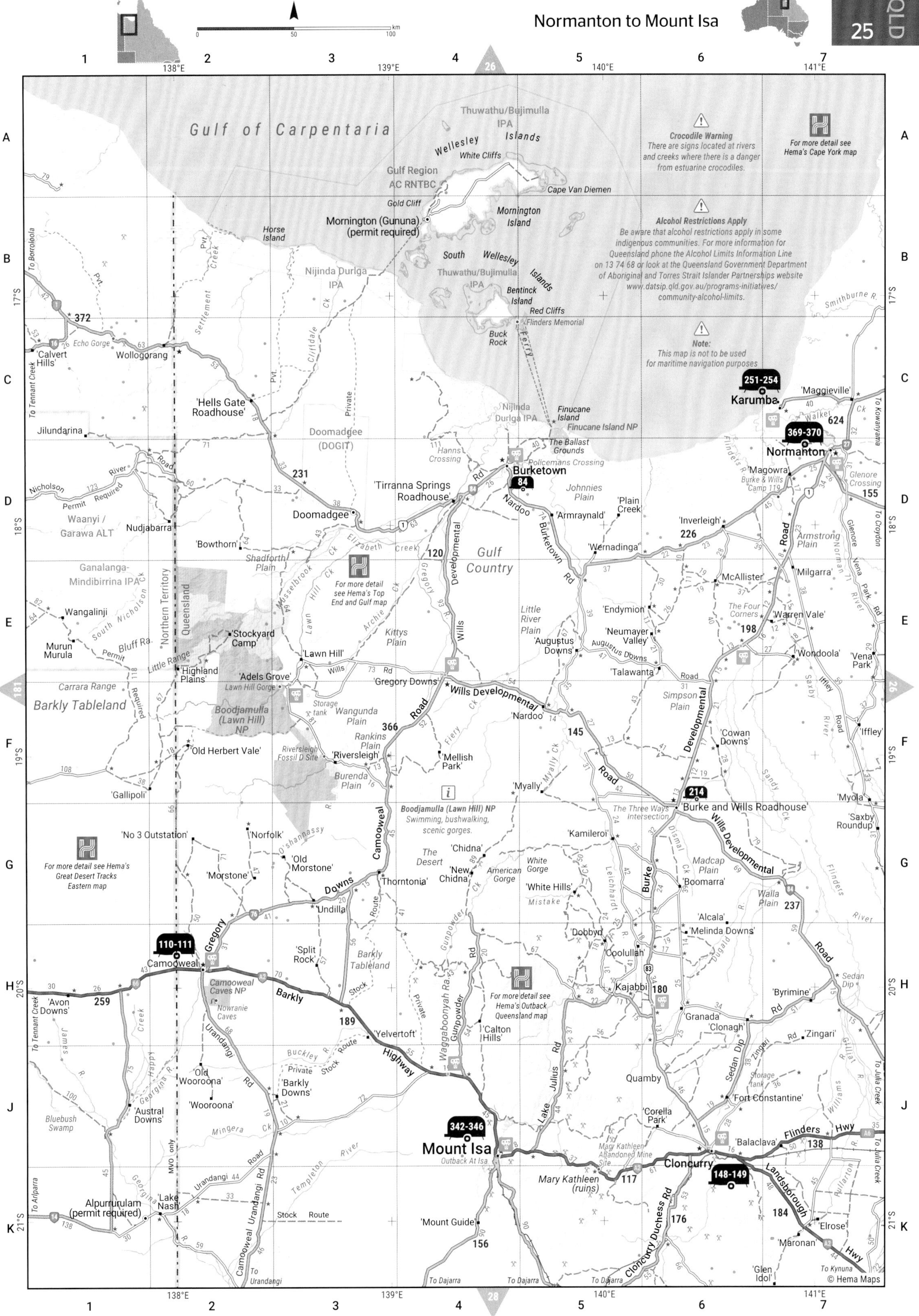
Gulf of Carpentaria
Thuwathu/Bujimulla IPA
Wellesley Islands
White Cliffs
Gulf Region AC RNTBC
Cape Van Diemen
Gold Cliff
Mornington (Gununa) (permit required)
Mornington Island
Horse Island
South Wellesley Islands
Thuwathu/Bujimulla IPA
Nijinda Durlga IPA
Bentinck Island
Red Cliffs
Flinders Memorial
Buck Rock
Ferry
Crocodile Warning
There are signs located at rivers and creeks where there is a danger from estuarine crocodiles.
For more detail see Hema's Cape York map
Alcohol Restrictions Apply
Be aware that alcohol restrictions apply in some indigenous communities. For more information for Queensland phone the Alcohol Limits Information Line on 13 74 68 or look at the Queensland Government Department of Aboriginal and Torres Strait Islander Partnerships website www.datsip.qld.gov.au/programs-initiatives/community-alcohol-limits.
Note:
This map is not to be used for maritime navigation purposes
To Borroloola
372
'Calvert Hills'
Echo Gorge
Wollogorang
To Tennant Creek
'Hells Gate Roadhouse'
Jilundarina
Nicholson River Road
Permit Required
Waanyi / Garawa ALT
Nudjabarra
231
Doomadgee
Doomadgee (DOGIT)
Hanns Crossing
Nijinda Durlga IPA
Finucane Island
Finucane Island NP
The Ballast Grounds
Policemans Crossing
Burketown
84
'Tirranna Springs Roadhouse'
Johnnies Plain
'Plain Creek'
'Armraynald'
Nardoo Burketown Rd
Karumba
251-254
'Maggieville'
624
369-370
Normanton
'Magowra'
Burke & Wills Camp 119
Glenore Crossing
155
To Kowanyama
To Croydon
'Inverleigh'
226
Armstrong Plain
'Bowthorn'
Shadforth Plain
Elizabeth Creek
120
Gulf Country
For more detail see Hema's Top End and Gulf map
'Wernadinga'
'McAllister'
'Milgarra'
Ganalanga-Mindibirrina IPA
Northern Territory
Queensland
Wangalinji
Murun Murula
Bluff Ra.
'Stockyard Camp'
Kittys Plain
'Lawn Hill'
Little River Plain
'Augustus Downs'
'Endymion'
'Neumayer Valley'
The Four Corners
198
'Warren Vale'
'Wondoola'
'Vena Park'
Little Range
'Highland Plains'
'Adels Grove'
Lawn Hill Gorge
Carrara Range
Barkly Tableland
Boodjamulla (Lawn Hill) NP
Storage tank
Wangunda Plain
'Gregory Downs'
Wills Developmental Rd
'Nardoo'
'Talawanta'
Simpson Plain
145
'Iffley'
366
Rankins Plain
Riversleigh Fossil D Site
'Riversleigh'
'Mellish Park'
'Old Herbert Vale'
'Cowan Downs'
'Gallipoli'
Burenda Plain
Boodjamulla (Lawn Hill) NP
Swimming, bushwalking, scenic gorges.
'Myally'
214
The Three Ways Intersection
'Burke and Wills Roadhouse'
'Myola'
'Saxby Roundup'
For more detail see Hema's Great Desert Tracks Eastern map
'No 3 Outstation'
'Norfolk'
'Old Morstone'
'Morstone'
Camooweal Road
The Desert
'Chidna'
'New Chidna'
American Gorge
White Gorge
'White Hills'
Mistake
'Kamileroi'
Madcap Plain
'Boomarra'
Walla Plain
237
Thorntonia
Downs
Undilla
'Split Rock'
Barkly Tableland
'Dobbyn'
Coolullah
'Alcala'
'Melinda Downs'
110-111
Camooweal
Camooweal Caves NP
Nowranie Caves
259
'Avon Downs'
Barkly Highway
189
'Yelvertoft'
For more detail see Hema's Outback Queensland map
'Calton Hills'
Kajabbi
180
'Byrimine'
Granada
'Clonagh'
'Zingari'
Sedan Dip
'Old Wooroona'
'Wooroona'
'Barkly Downs'
Buckley R.
Stock Route
Quamby
'Fort Constantine'
'Austral Downs'
Bluebush Swamp
Mingera Ck
342-346
Mount Isa
Outback At Isa
'Corella Park'
Mary Kathleen Abandoned Mine Site
Mary Kathleen (ruins)
117
Cloncurry
148-149
'Balaclava'
Flinders Hwy
138
To Julia Creek
Landsborough Hwy
184
'Elrose'
'Maronan'
Alpurrurulam (permit required)
'Lake Nash'
Urandangi Road
Templeton River
Stock Route
'Mount Guide'
156
176
Cloncurry Duchess Rd
'Glen Idol'
To Kynuna
To Urandangi
To Dajarra
To Arlparra
© Hema Maps

Mount Isa to Cooktown

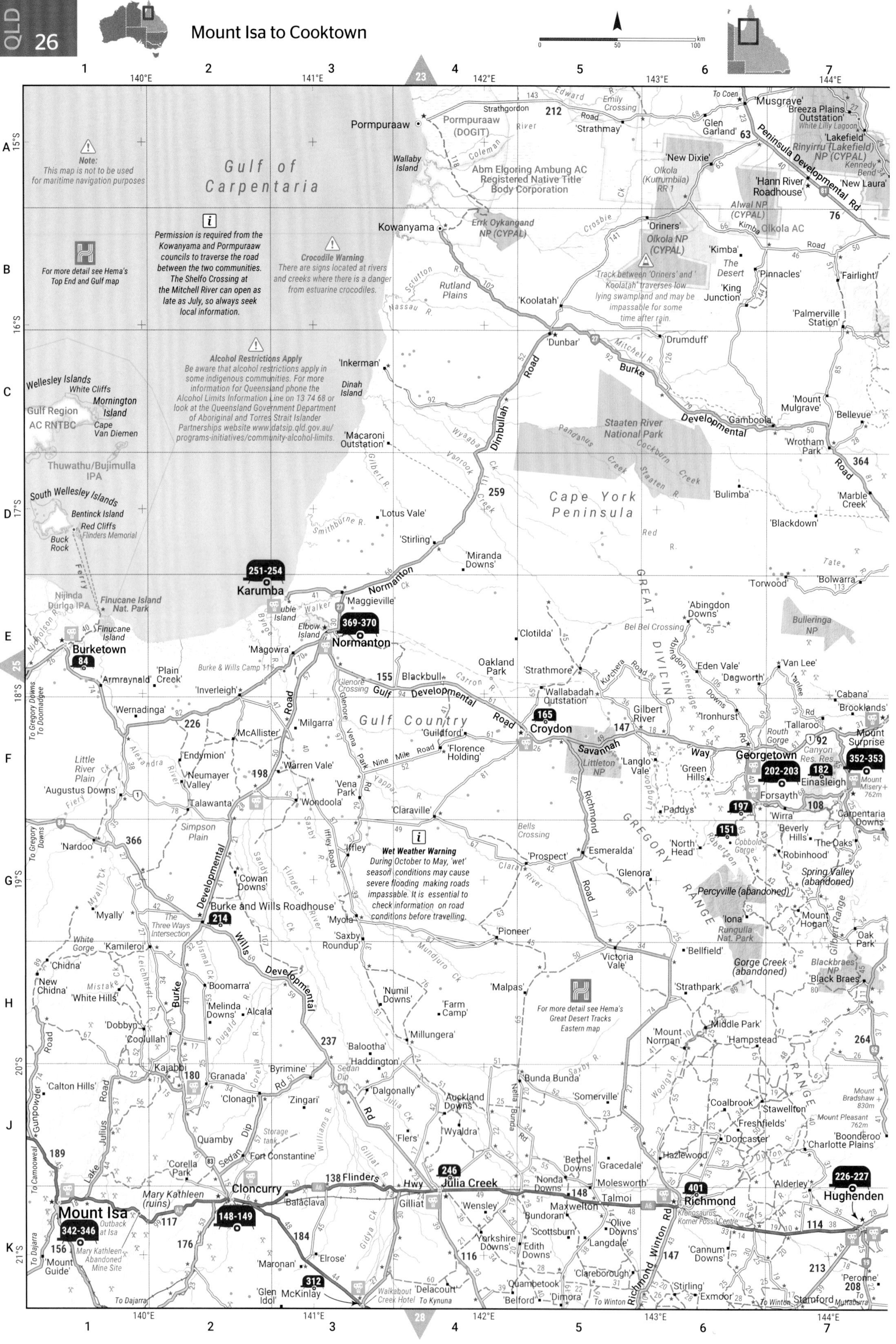

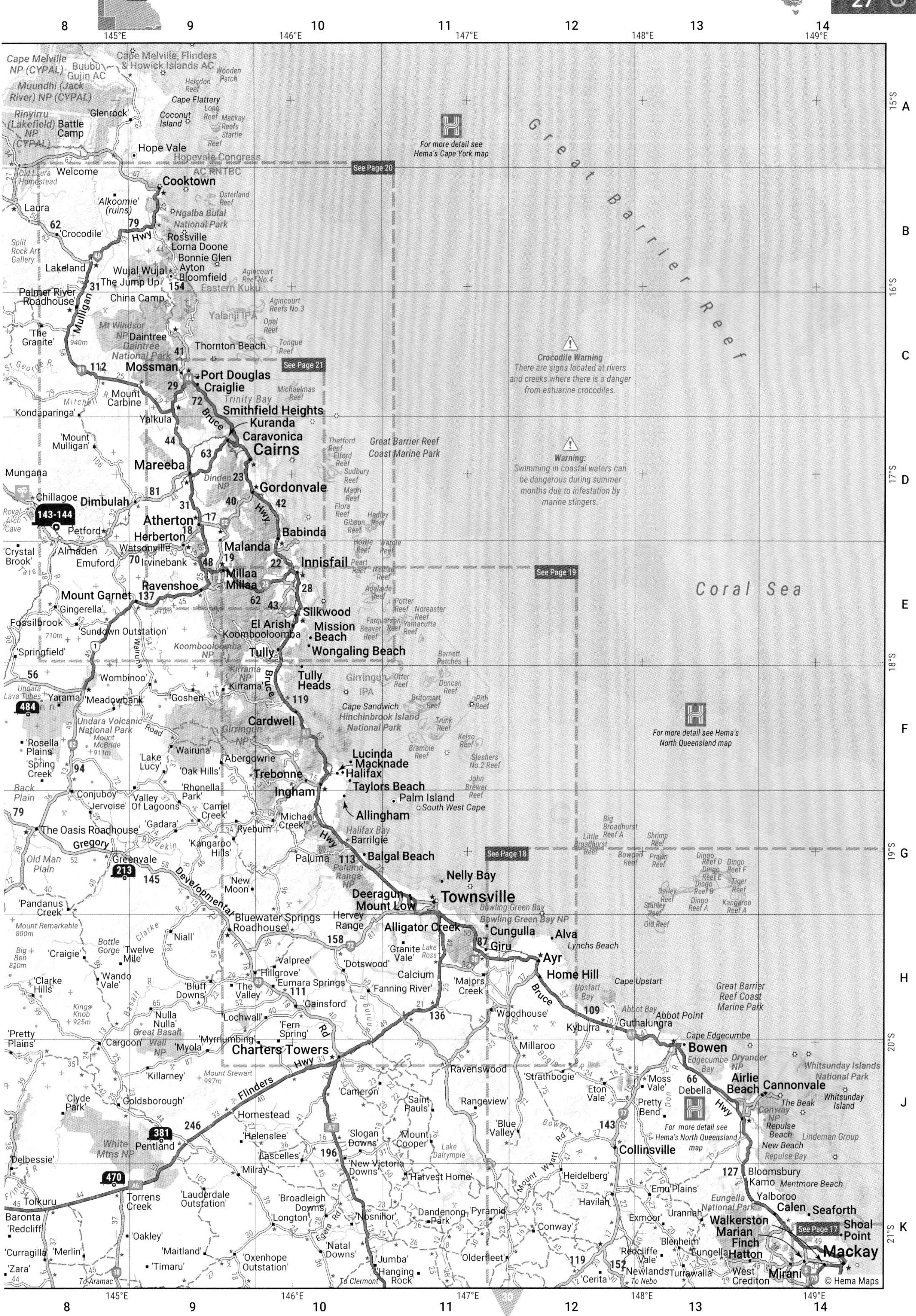

Great Barrier Reef
Coral Sea
For more detail see Hema's Cape York map
See Page 20
See Page 21
See Page 19
See Page 18
See Page 17
Crocodile Warning
There are signs located at rivers and creeks where there is a danger from estuarine crocodiles.
Warning:
Swimming in coastal waters can be dangerous during summer months due to infestation by marine stingers.
For more detail see Hema's North Queensland map
For more detail see Hema's North Queensland map
Great Barrier Reef Coast Marine Park
Cooktown
Cairns
Townsville
Mackay
Bowen
Charters Towers
Mossman
Port Douglas
Mareeba
Atherton
Innisfail
Tully
Cardwell
Ingham
Ayr
Home Hill
Airlie Beach
Cannonvale
Collinsville
Pentland
143-144
484
213
381
470
© Hema Maps

Mount Isa to Augathella

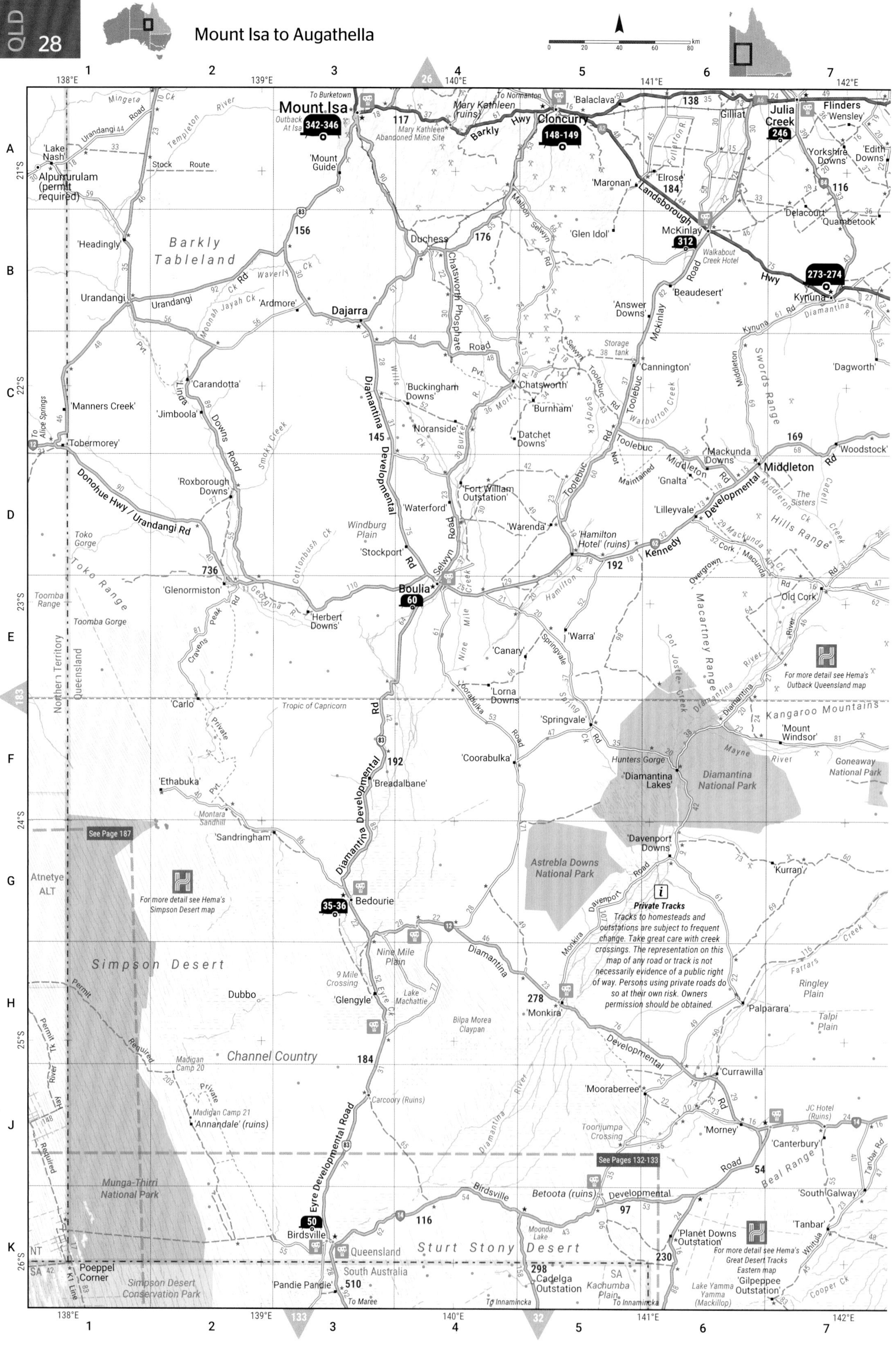

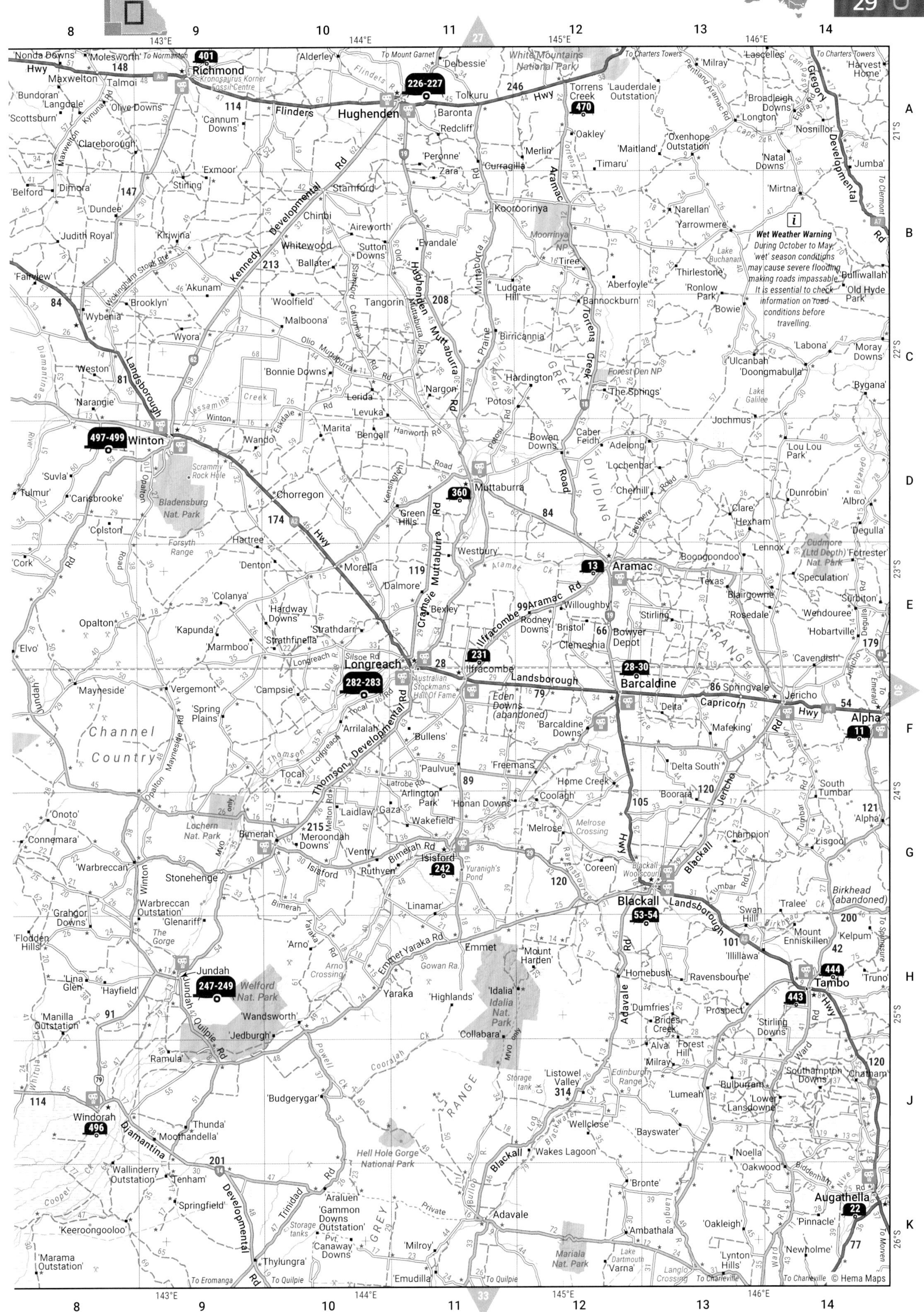
Richmond
Kronosaurus Korner Fossil Centre
Hughenden
Flinders
Hwy
Torrens Creek
White Mountains National Park
Maxwelton
Kennedy Developmental Rd
Hughenden Muttaburra Rd
Muttaburra
Stamford
Chinbi
Whitewood
Tangorin
Kooroorinya
Moorrinya NP
Tiree
Landsborough Hwy
Winton
Scrammy Rock Hole
Bladensburg Nat. Park
Forsyth Range
Chorregon
Morella
Opalton
Longreach
Australian Stockmans Hall Of Fame
Ilfracombe
Eden Downs (abandoned)
Barcaldine
Aramac
Great Dividing Range
Forest Den NP
The Springs
Lake Galilee
Jericho
Alpha
Capricorn Hwy
Gregory Developmental Rd
Wet Weather Warning
During October to May, 'wet' season conditions may cause severe flooding making roads impassable. It is essential to check information on road conditions before travelling.
Cudmore (Ltd Depth) Nat. Park
Channel Country
Thomson Developmental Rd
Lochern Nat. Park
Stonehenge
Isisford
Yuranigh's Pond
Blackall
Blackall Woolscour
Tambo
Augathella
Jundah
Welford Nat. Park
Windorah
Idalia Nat. Park
Emmet
Yaraka
Arno Crossing
Gowan Ra.
Mount Harden
Edinburgh Range
Hell Hole Gorge National Park
Grey Range
Adavale
Mariala Nat. Park
Lake Dartmouth
Langlo Crossing
Birkhead (abandoned)
To Normanton
To Mount Garnet
To Charters Towers
To Clermont
To Emerald
To Springsure
To Morven
To Charleville
To Quilpie
To Eromanga
© Hema Maps

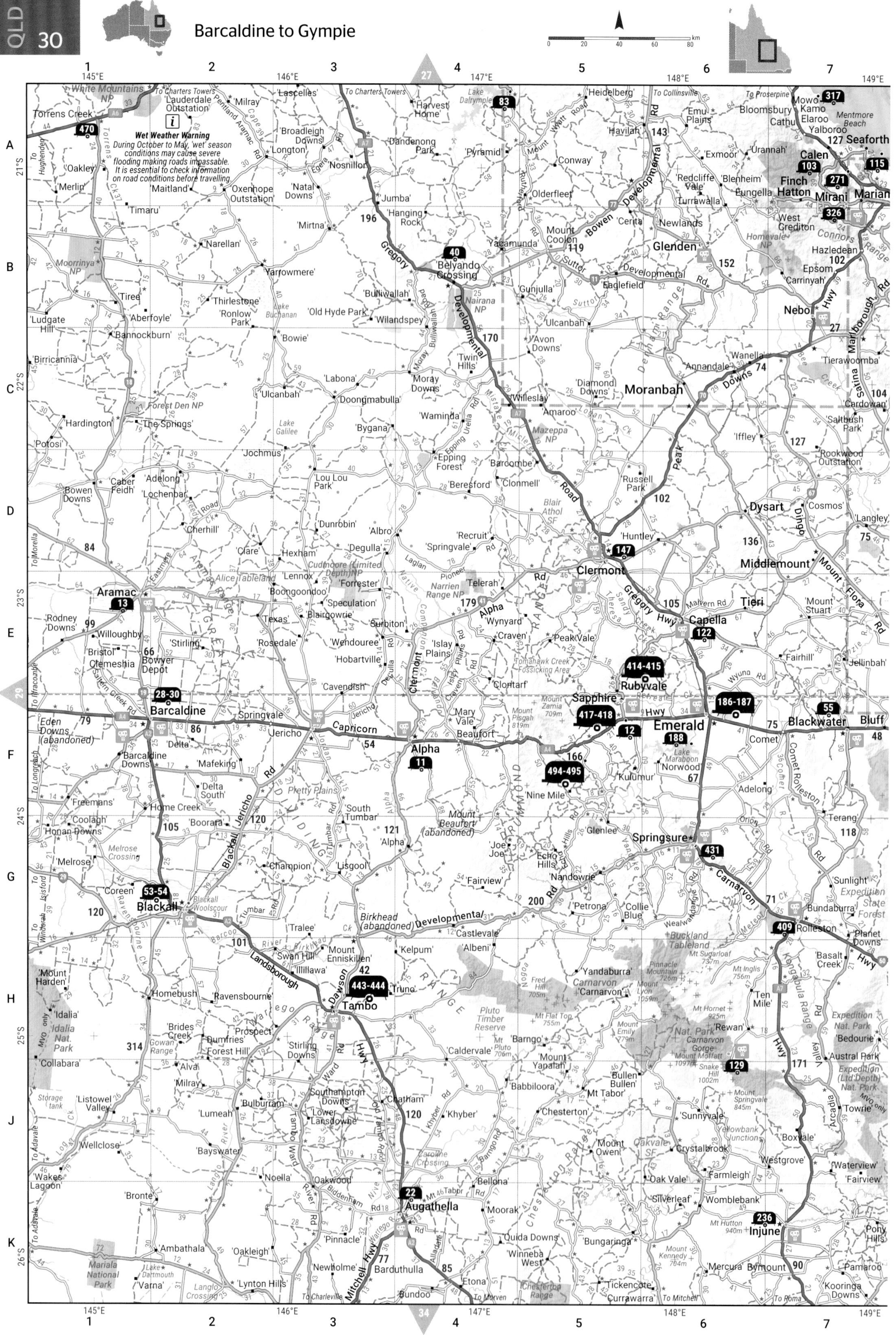
Wet Weather Warning
During October to May, 'wet' season conditions may cause severe flooding making roads impassable. It is essential to check information on road conditions before travelling.
Barcaldine
Aramac
Blackall
Tambo
Augathella
Alpha
Jericho
Clermont
Moranbah
Emerald
Capella
Tieri
Dysart
Middlemount
Blackwater
Springsure
Rolleston
Injune
Sapphire
Rubyvale
Glenden
Nebo
Mirani
Finch Hatton
Seaforth
Bluff
Comet
Capricorn Hwy
Gregory Developmental Road
Landsborough Hwy
Dawson Hwy
Carnarvon Hwy
Peak Downs Hwy
Mitchell Hwy

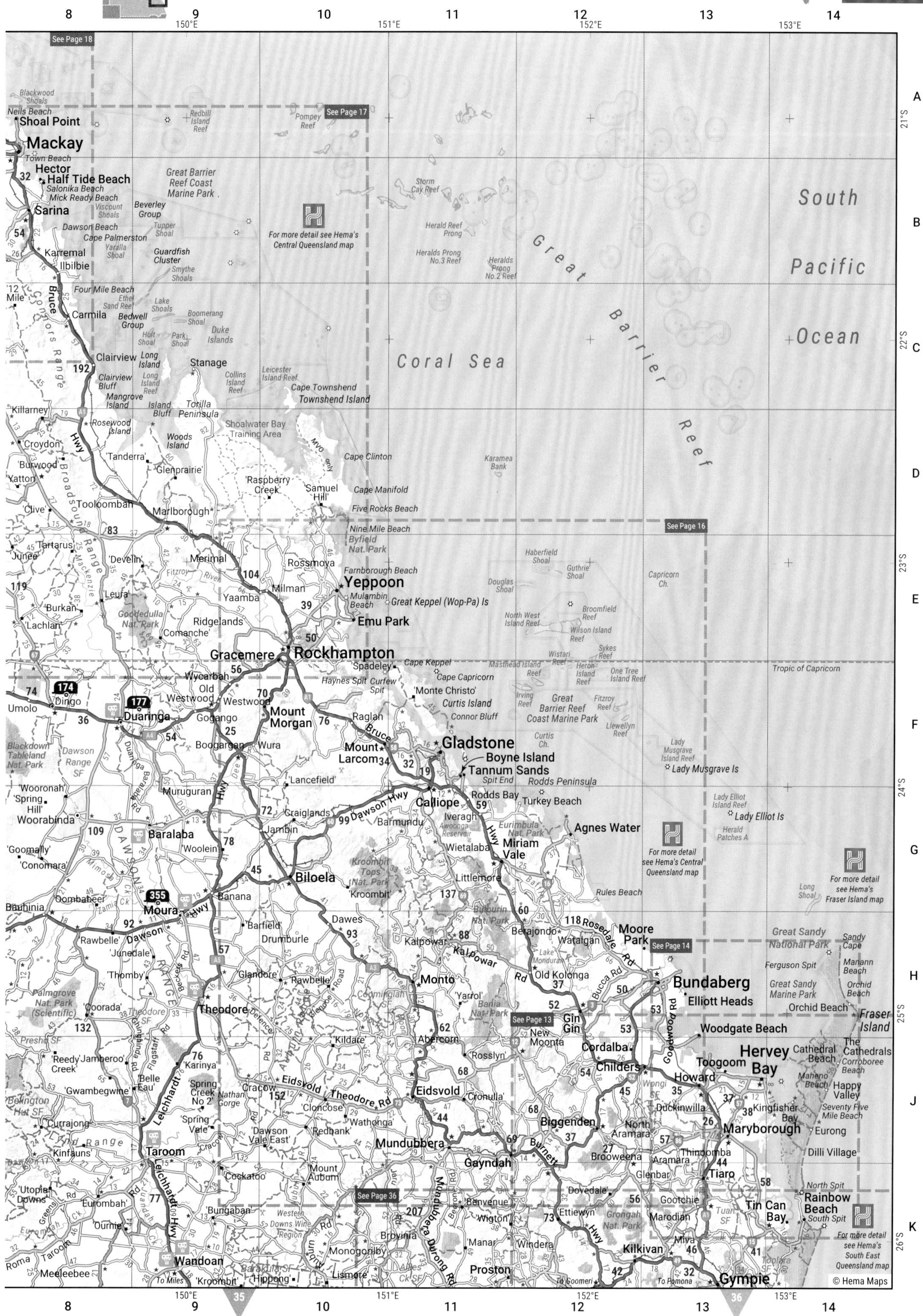

Mackay
Sarina
Carmila
Clairview
Marlborough
Yeppoon
Emu Park
Rockhampton
Gracemere
Mount Morgan
Gladstone
Boyne Island
Tannum Sands
Calliope
Agnes Water
Miriam Vale
Biloela
Moura
Theodore
Taroom
Wandoan
Monto
Eidsvold
Mundubbera
Gayndah
Biggenden
Childers
Bundaberg
Hervey Bay
Maryborough
Tin Can Bay
Rainbow Beach
Gympie
Coral Sea
Great Barrier Reef
South Pacific Ocean
Tropic of Capricorn
For more detail see Hema's Central Queensland map
For more detail see Hema's Fraser Island map
For more detail see Hema's South East Queensland map
© Hema Maps

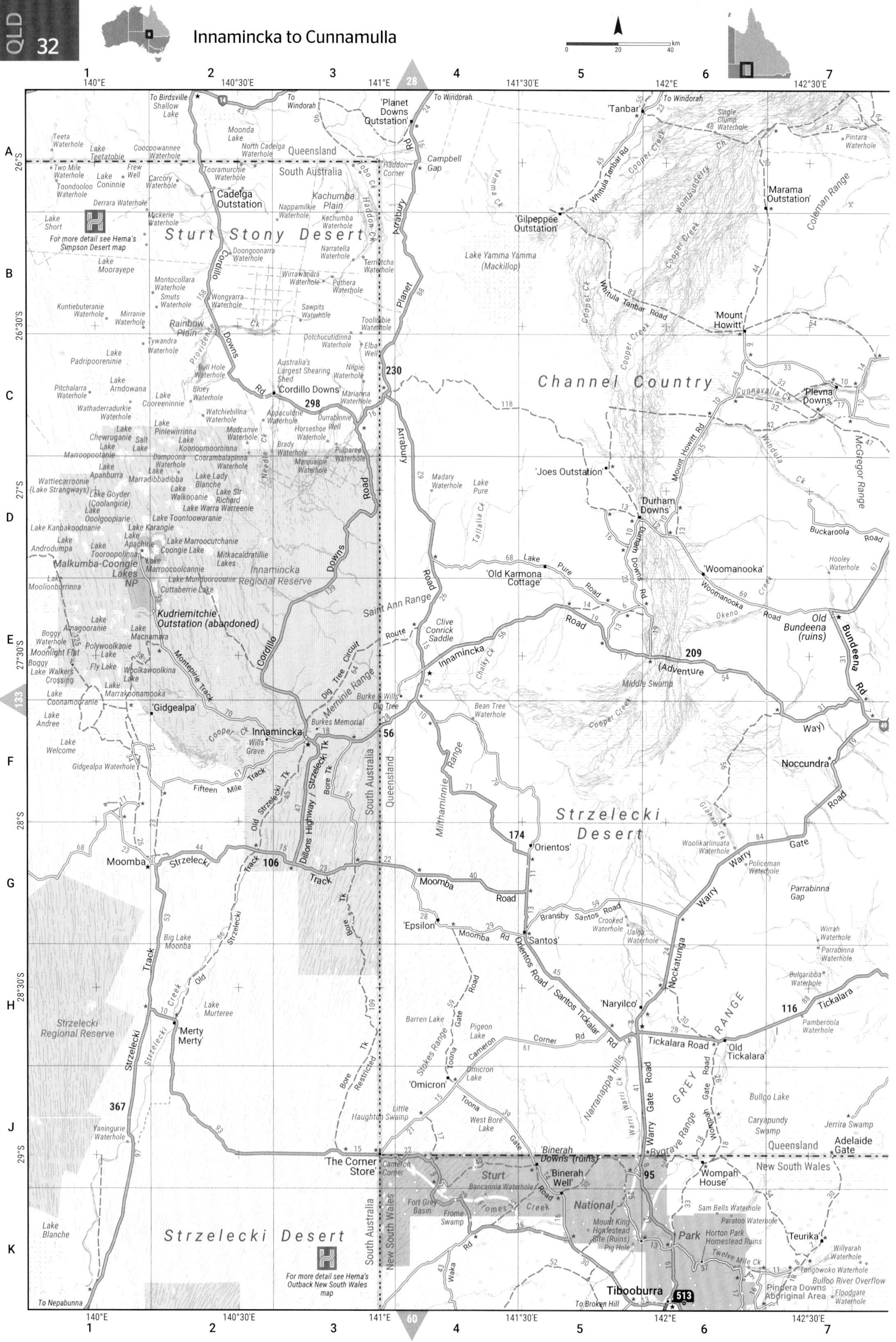
140°E
140°30'E
141°E
141°30'E
142°E
142°30'E
26°S
26°30'S
27°S
27°30'S
28°S
28°30'S
29°S
km
0
20
40
28
133
60
To Birdsville
Shallow Lake
To Windorah
'Planet Downs Outstation'
'Tanbar'
Teeta Waterhole
Lake Teetatobie
Coocoowannee Waterhole
Moonda Lake
North Cadelga Waterhole
Queensland
South Australia
Haddon Corner
Campbell Gap
Single Clump Waterhole
Pintara Waterhole
Two Mile Waterhole
Toondooloo Waterhole
Lake Coninnie
Frew Well
Carcory Waterhole
Tooramurchie Waterhole
Cadelga Outstation
Kachumba Plain
Nappamilkie Waterhole
Kachumba Waterhole
Derrara Waterhole
Mickerie Waterhole
Lake Short
For more detail see Hema's Simpson Desert map
Sturt Stony Desert
Whitula Tanbar Rd
Cooper Creek
Wombunderry Ch
Marama Outstation'
Coleman Range
'Gilpeppee Outstation'
Yamma Ck
Doongoonarra Waterhole
Narratella Waterhole
Territcha Waterhole
Lake Yamma Yamma (Mackillop)
Lake Moorayepe
Montocollara Waterhole
Smuts Waterhole
Wongyarra Waterhole
Wirrawandra Waterhole
Puthera Waterhole
Kuntiebuteranie Waterhole
Mirranie Waterhole
Sawpits Waterhole
Toolimbie Waterhole
Cordillo Downs Rd
Rainbow Plain
Providence Ck
Planet Rd
Arrabury Rd
Whitula Tanbar Road
Cooper Ck
'Mount Howitt'
Tywandra Waterhole
Ootchucutidinna Waterhole
Elba Well
Lake Padripooreninie
Australia's Largest Shearing Shed
Nilpie Waterhole
Bull Hole Waterhole
230
Channel Country
Lake Arndowana
Pitchalarra Waterhole
Bluey Waterhole
'Cordillo Downs'
Marianna Waterhole
Cunnavalla Ck
'Plevna Downs'
Lake Cooreeninnie
298
Wathaderradurkie Waterhole
Watchiebillina Waterhole
Appaculdrie Waterhole
Durrabinnie Well
Lake Piniewirrinna
Lake Chewruganie
Salt Lake
Mudcamie Waterhole
Horseshoe Waterhole
Lake Koonoomoorninna
Mount Howitt Rd
Windula Ck
McGregor Range
Marroopootanie
Dampoona Waterhole
Coorambalapinna Waterhole
Brady Waterhole
Pulparee Waterhole
Marqualpie Waterhole
Needle Ck
Lake Apanburra
Marradibbadibba
Lake Lady Blanche
'Joes Outstation'
Madary Waterhole
Lake Pure
Wattiecarroonie (Lake Strangways)
Lake Goyder (Coolangirie)
Lake Walkooanie
Lake Sir Richard
Lake Warra Warreenie
'Durham Downs'
Lake Ooolgoopiarie
Lake Toontoowaranie
Tallalia Ck
Lake Kanbakoodnanie
Lake Karangie
Lake Apachie
Buckaroola Road
Lake Androdumpa
Lake Marroocutchanie
Coongie Lake
Lake Tooroopolinna
Lake Marroocoolcannie
Mitkacaldratillie Lakes
Malkumba-Coongie Lakes NP
Innamincka Regional Reserve
Durham Downs Rd
'Old Karmona Cottage'
Lake Pure Road
'Woomanooka'
Hooley Waterhole
Lake Moolionburrinna
Lake Mundooroounie
Cuttaberrie Lake
Woomanooka Road
Okeno
Kudriemitchie Outstation (abandoned)
Saint Ann Range
Clive Conrick Saddle
Road
Old Bundeena (ruins)
Bundeena Rd
Lake Amagooranie
Boggy Waterhole
Polywoolkanie Lake
Lake Macnamara
Moonlight Flat
Boggy Lake
Fly Lake
Walkers Crossing
Woolkawoolkina Lake
Montepirie Track
Cordillo Downs Road
Dig Tree Circuit
Route
Innamincka
Chalky Ck
209
(Adventure Way)
Middle Swamp
Lake Coonamoorranie
Lake Marrakoonamooka
Merninie Range
Burke & Wills Dig Tree
Bean Tree Waterhole
'Gidgealpa'
Lake Andree
Burkes Memorial
Cooper Ck
Innamincka
Wills Grave
56
Lake Welcome
Gidgealpa Waterhole
Noccundra
Fifteen Mile Track
Old Strzelecki Tk
Dillons Highway / Strzelecki Tk
Bore Tk
South Australia
Queensland
Milthaminnie Range
Strzelecki Desert
Graham Ck
174
'Orientos'
Woolikarlinuata Waterhole
Noccundra Road
Warry Warry Gate
Policeman Waterhole
Moomba
Strzelecki Track
106
Moomba Road
Parrabinna Gap
'Epsilon'
Moomba Rd
Bransby
Santos Road
Crooked Waterhole
Ualga Waterhole
'Santos'
Wirrah Waterhole
Parrabinna Waterhole
Big Lake Moomba
Strzelecki Track
Old Strzelecki Creek
Nockatunga
Bulgaribba Waterhole
Orientos Road / Santos Tickalar Rd
'Naryilco'
Grey Range
116
Tickalara
Lake Murteree
Strzelecki Regional Reserve
'Merty Merty'
Barren Lake
Pigeon Lake
Stokes Range
Toona Gate Road
Cameron Corner Rd
Tickalara Road
'Old Tickalara'
Pamberoola Waterhole
Omicron Lake
'Omicron'
Bore Restricted Tk
Narranappa Hills
Warri Warri Ck
Warry Gate Road
Wompah Gate Road
Bulloo Lake
367
Little Haughton Swamp
West Bore Lake
Caryapundy Swamp
Jerrira Swamp
Yaningurie Waterhole
Adelaide Gate
Queensland
New South Wales
'The Corner Store'
'Binerah Downs' (ruins)
Bygrave Range
95
'Wompah House'
Cameron Corner
'Binerah Well'
Sturt National Park
Bancannia Waterhole
Fort Grey Basin
Frome Swamp
Fromes Creek
Sam Bells Waterhole
Paratoo Waterhole
Mount King Homestead Site (Ruins)
Pig Hole
Horton Park Homestead Ruins
'Teurika'
Lake Blanche
Strzelecki Desert
For more detail see Hema's Outback New South Wales map
Twelve Mile Ck
Willyarah Waterhole
Tongowoko Waterhole
Bulloo River Overflow
Pindera Downs Aboriginal Area
Floodgate Waterhole
Waka Rd
Tibooburra
513
To Broken Hill
To Nepabunna
A
B
C
D
E
F
G
H
J
K
1
2
3
4
5
6
7

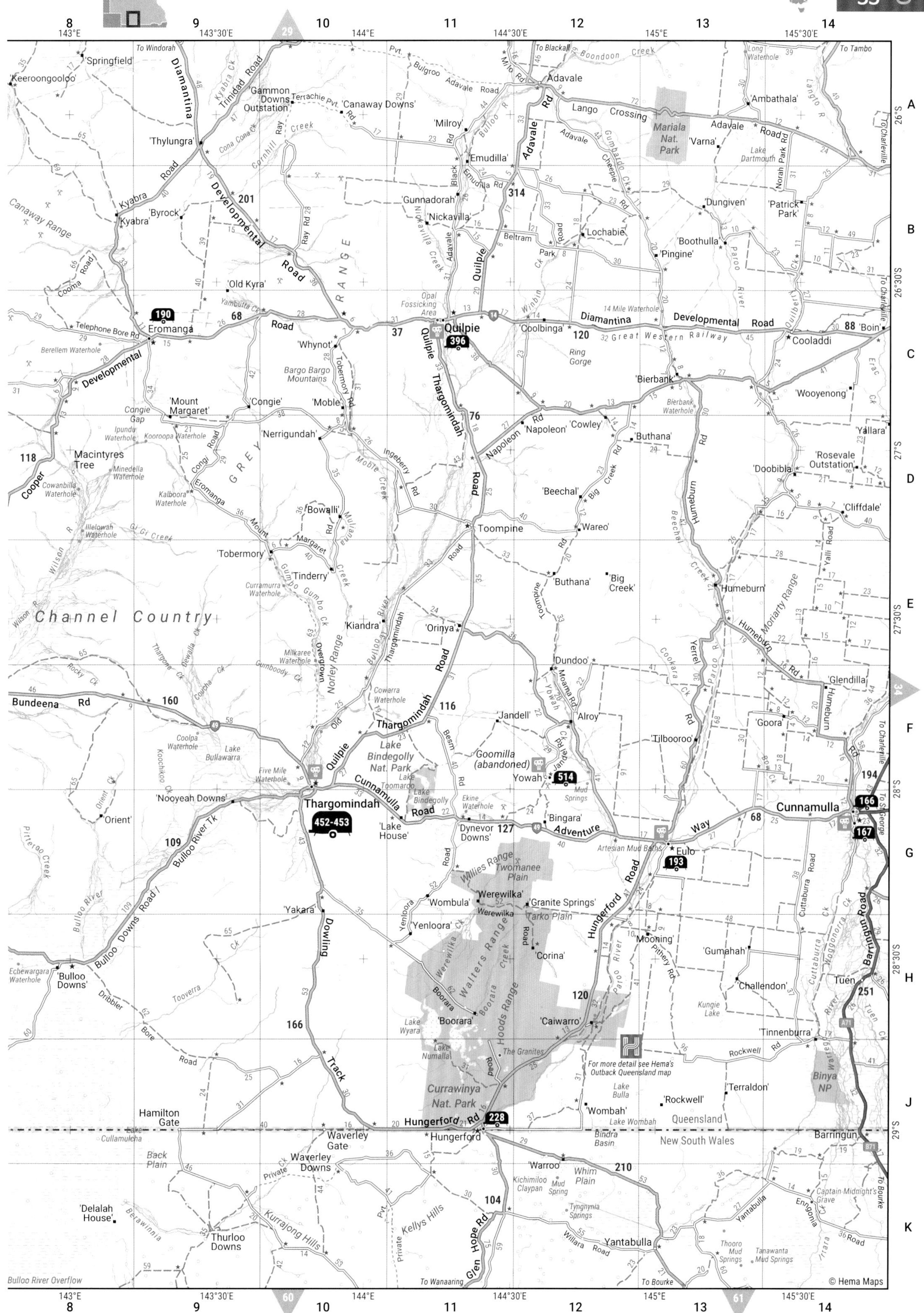

Channel Country
Quilpie
Thargomindah
Cunnamulla
Eromanga
Adavale
Toompine
Eulo
Hungerford
Yowah
Yantabulla
Barringun
Diamantina Developmental Road
Adventure Way
Currawinya Nat. Park
Lake Bindegolly Nat. Park
Mariala Nat. Park
Binya NP
Grey Range
Queensland
New South Wales
For more detail see Hema's Outback Queensland map
© Hema Maps

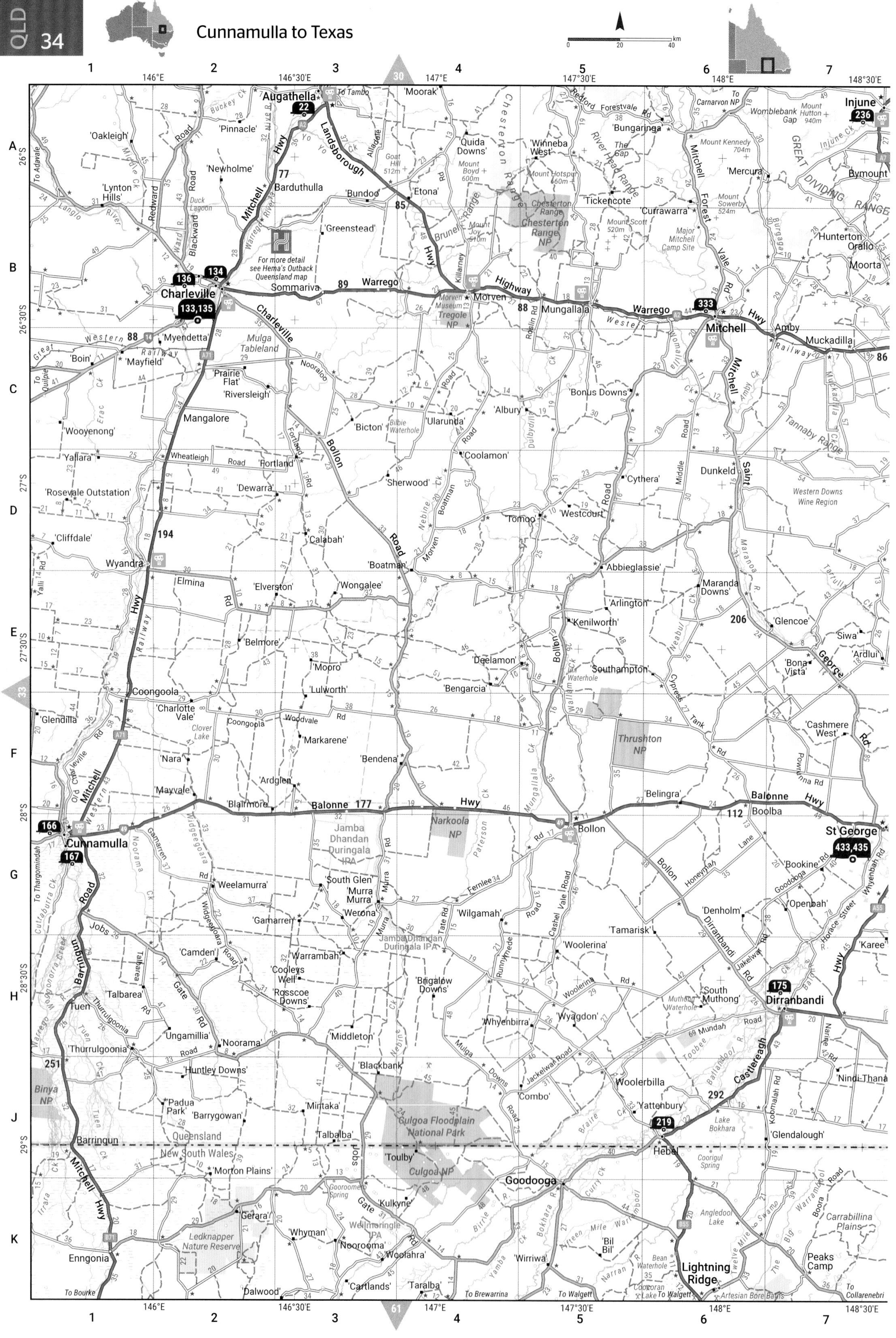

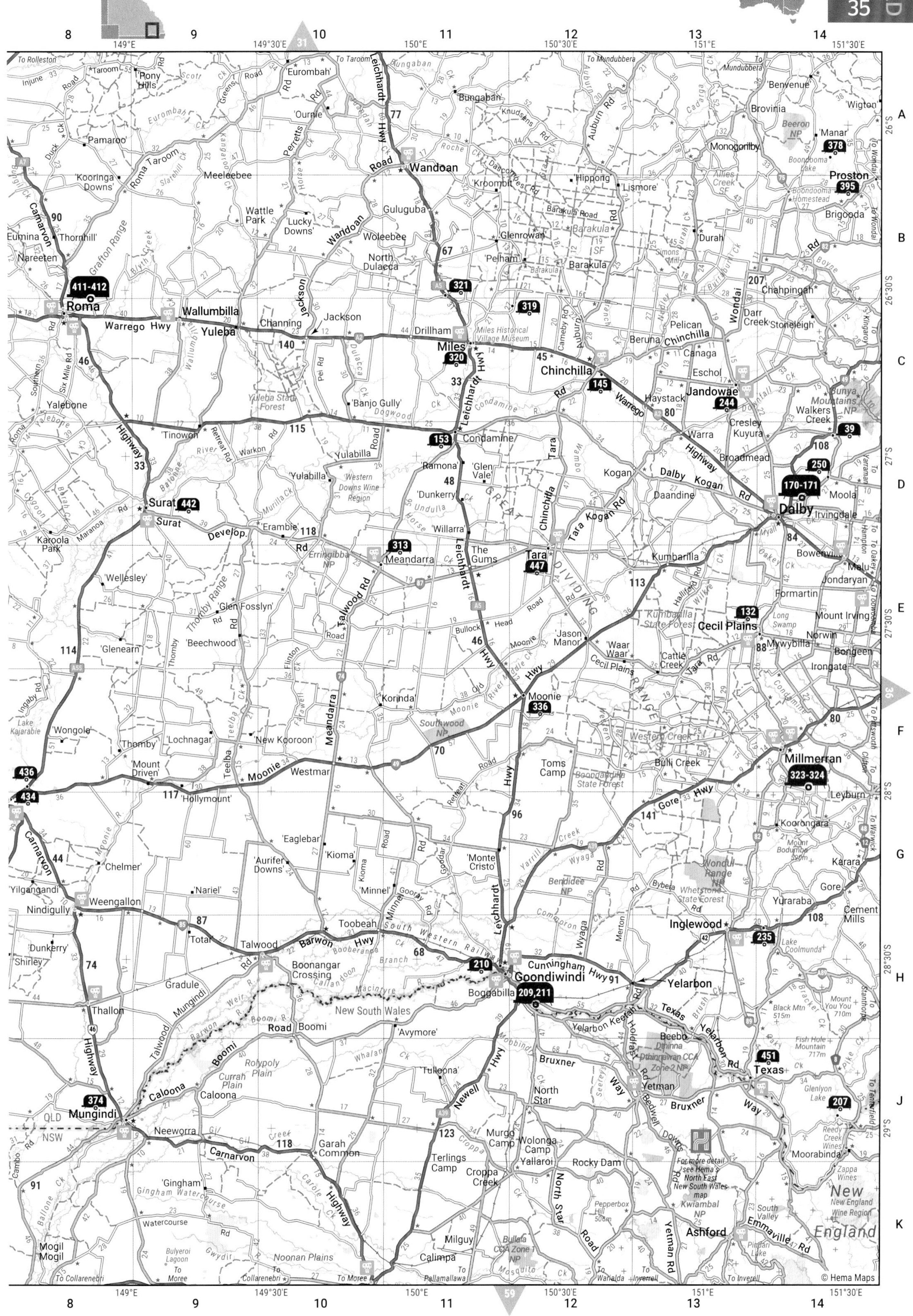
Roma
Wallumbilla
Yuleba
Jackson
Channing
Drillham
Miles
Chinchilla
Wandoan
Guluguba
Woleebee
North Dulacca
Meeleebee
Wattle Park
'Lucky Downs'
'Pamaroo'
'Kooringa Downs'
'Thornhill'
Eumina
Nareeten
'Eurombah'
'Ournie'
'Pony Hills'
'Bungaban'
'Kroombit'
'Hippong'
'Lismore'
Barakula
'Glenrowan'
'Pelham'
'Durah'
Brovinia
'Benvenue'
'Wigton'
'Manar'
Monogorilby
Proston
Brigooda
Chahpingah
Darr Creek
'Stoneleigh'
Pelican
Beruna
Canaga
Eschol
Jandowae
Haystack
Walkers Creek
Cresley
Kuyura
Warra
Broadmead
Kogan
Daandine
Dalby
Moola
Irvingdale
Bowenville
Jondaryan
Formartin
Mount Irving
Norwin
Bongeen
Irongate
Mywybilla
Cecil Plains
Kumbarilla
Yalebone
'Tinowon'
Condamine
'Ramona'
'Glen Vale'
'Dunkerry'
'Willarra'
Yulabilla
'Yulabilla'
'Banjo Gully'
Western Downs Wine Region
Surat
'Karoola Park'
'Erambie'
Meandarra
Erringibba NP
The Gums
Tara
'Wellesley'
'Glen Fosslyn'
'Beechwood'
'Glenearn'
'Jason Manor'
'Waar Waar'
'Cattle Creek'
'Korinda'
Moonie
Southwood NP
Toms Camp
Western Creek
Bulli Creek
Millmerran
Leyburn
'Wongole'
'Thomby'
'Lochnagar'
'New Kooroon'
'Mount Driven'
Westmar
'Hollymount'
'Eaglebar'
'Kioma'
'Aurifer Downs'
'Minnel'
'Monte Cristo'
Bendidee NP
Inglewood
'Kooroongara'
Karara
Gore
Yuraraba
Cement Mills
'Chelmer'
'Yilgangandi'
Weengallon
Nindigully
'Nariel'
'Totar'
Talwood
Toobeah
'Dunkerry'
'Shirley'
Boonangar Crossing
Goondiwindi
Boggabilla
Yelarbon
Texas
Gradule
Thallon
New South Wales
Boomi
'Avymore'
Rolypoly Plain
Currah Plain
Caloona
'Tulloona'
Bruxner
North Star
Yetman
Mungindi
QLD
NSW
Neeworra
Garah
Common
Terlings Camp
Murgo Camp
Wolonga Camp
Yallaroi
Rocky Dam
Croppa Creek
'Gingham'
Watercourse
Milguy
Calimpa
Mogil Mogil
Noonan Plains
Bullala CCA Zone 1 NP
Kwiambal NP
Ashford
Emmaville Rd
South Valley
'Moorabinda'
New England
Glenlyon Lake
Warrego Hwy
Leichhardt Hwy
Carnarvon Hwy
Moonie Hwy
Gore Hwy
Cunningham Hwy
Barwon Hwy
Newell Hwy
Bruxner Way
Dalby Kogan Rd
Tara Kogan Rd
Great Dividing Range
411-412
321
319
320
153
145
244
378
395
207
250
39
170-171
442
313
447
132
336
323-324
436
434
210
209,211
235
451
374
207
For more detail see Hema's North East New South Wales map
© Hema Maps

Rainbow Beach to Ballina

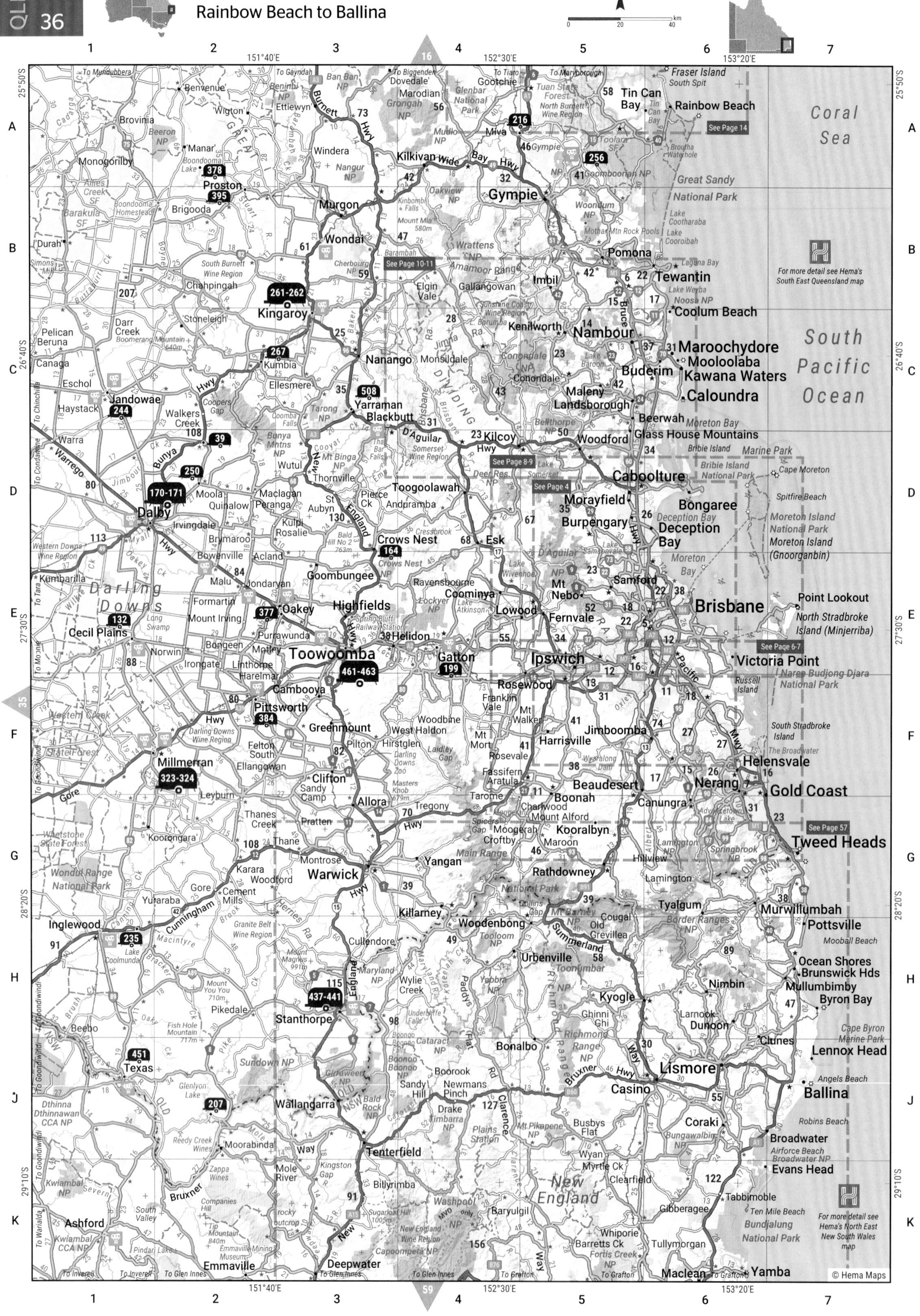

Advancetown

1 Advancetown Caravan Park
376 Nerang-Murwillumbah Rd
07 5533 2147 HEMA 5 F1 28 01 27 S 153 16 47 E

Agnes Water

2 Agnes Water Beach Holidays
Jeffrey Court
www.agneswaterbeach.com.au
07 4974 7279 HEMA 16 E6 24 12 37 S 151 54 27 E

3 The Reef Caravan Park
34 Rocky Crossing Rd
07 4974 7547 HEMA 16 E5 24 14 50 S 151 51 39 E

Airlie Beach

4 BIG4 Adventure Whitsunday Resort
25-29 Shute Harbour Rd
www.adventurewhitsunday.com.au
07 4948 5400 HEMA 18 E5 20 17 13 S 148 40 45 E

5 Discovery Parks Airlie Beach
Cnr Shute Harbour Rd & Ferntree Rd. Jubilee Pocket, 2.5 km from PO
www.discoveryparks.com.au
07 4946 6727 HEMA 18 E5 20 17 02 S 148 44 18 E

6 Flametree Tourist Village
2955 Shute Harbour Rd
www.flametreevillage.com.au
07 4946 9388 HEMA 18 E5 20 16 37 S 148 45 11 E

7 Island Gateway Holiday Park
Cnr Shute Harbour Rd & Jubilee Pocket Rd
www.islandgateway.com.au
07 4946 6228 HEMA 18 E5 20 16 53 S 148 43 44 E

Alexandra Headland

8 Alex Beach Cabins & Tourist Park
21-23 Okinja Rd
www.alexbeach.com.au
07 5443 2356 HEMA 11 E13 26 39 58 S 153 06 11 E

Alligator Creek

9 Moana Caravan Park
92259 Bruce Hwy. Alligator Creek via Mackay
www.moanacaravanpark.com.au
07 4956 4165 HEMA 17 B2 21 19 15 S 149 11 30 E

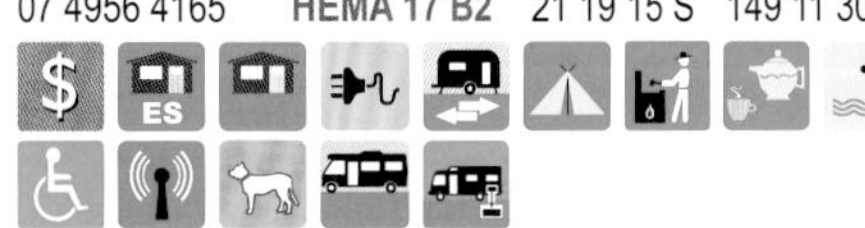

Almaden

10 Tamarind Gardens Caravan Park
Schools Rd
07 4094 8201 HEMA 20 H1 17 20 15 S 144 40 41 E

Alpha

11 Alpha Caravan & Villa Park
Cnr of Capricorn Hwy & Hooper St
www.alpha-caravan-park.com
07 4985 1337 HEMA 29 F14 23 39 12 S 146 38 14 E

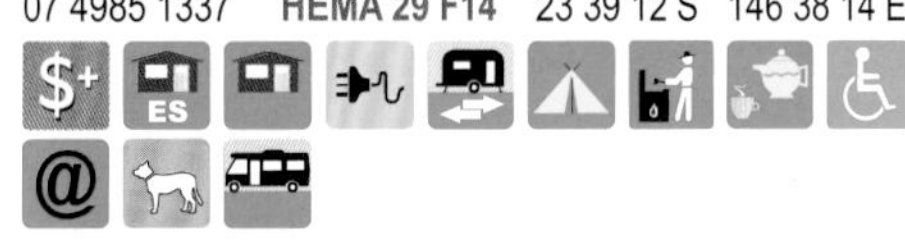

Anakie

12 Anakie Gemfields Caravan Park
7 Richardson St
07 4985 4142 HEMA 30 F5 23 33 08 S 147 44 41 E

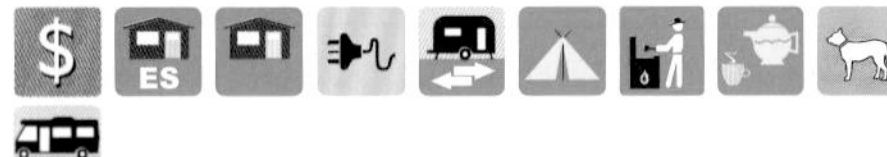

Aramac

13 Aramac Shire Caravan Park & Camping Grounds
Booker St
07 4652 9999 HEMA 29 E12 22 58 02 S 145 14 20 E

Aratula

14 Aratula Village Gap View Motel & Caravan Park
6757 Cunningham Hwy
www.aratulavillage.com.au
07 5463 8161 HEMA 6 G2 27 58 57 S 152 32 52 E

Armstrong Beach

15 Armstrong Beach Caravan Park
66 Melba St
07 4956 2425 HEMA 17 B2 21 27 08 S 149 17 26 E

Ashgrove

16 Newmarket Gardens Caravan Park
199 Ashgrove Ave. 4 km NW of PO
www.newmarketgardens.com.au
07 3356 1458 HEMA 2 A6 27 26 17 S 153 00 21 E

Atherton

17 Atherton Halloran's Leisure Park
152 Robert St
www.halloransleisurepark.com
07 4091 4144 HEMA 22 J2 17 16 11 S 145 29 23 E

18 Atherton Holiday Park
64-72 Mountain View Drive
www.athertonholidaypark.com
07 4091 1099 HEMA 22 J2 17 15 44 S 145 30 28 E

19 BIG4 Atherton Woodlands Tourist Park
141 Herberton Rd
www.woodlandscp.com.au
07 4091 1407 HEMA 22 K2 17 16 55 S 145 28 09 E

Atkinson Dam

20 Atkinson Dam Holiday Park
381 Atkinson Dam Rd
www.atkinsondamholidaypark.com.au
07 5426 4211 HEMA 12 E3 27 25 12 S 152 27 11 E

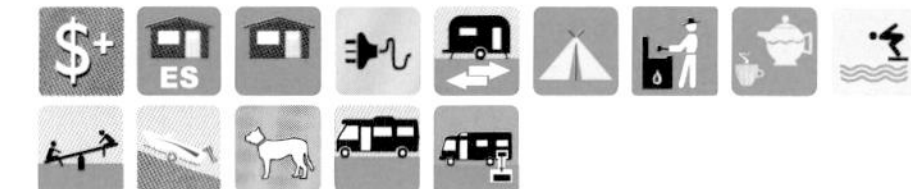

21 Atkinson Dam Waterfront Caravan Park
545 Atkinson Dam Rd
07 5426 4151 HEMA 12 E3 27 24 54 S 152 26 14 E

Augathella

22 Augathella Motel & Caravan Park
Matilda Hwy
www.augathella.com
07 4654 5255 HEMA 34 A3 25 47 36 S 146 35 35 E

Ayr

23 Alva Beach Tourist Park
36 Braby St
www.alvabeachtouristpark1.net.au
07 4783 3383 HEMA 18 B2 19 27 32 S 147 28 51 E

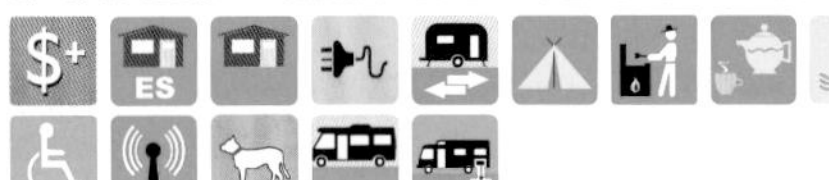

24 BIG4 Ayr Silver Link Caravan Village
34 Norham Rd. 2 km from CBD
www.big4.com.au
07 4783 3933 HEMA 18 B1 19 34 32 S 147 24 54 E

25 Burdekin Cascades Caravan Park
228 Queen St. 500m from CBD
www.burdekincascades.com.au
07 4783 1429 HEMA 18 B1 19 34 48 S 147 24 06 E

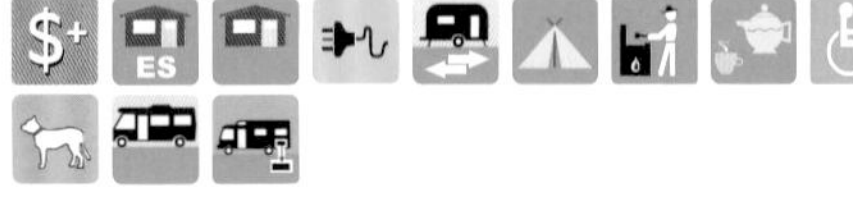

Ayton

26 Bloomfield Beach Camp & Cabins
Bloomfield Rd
www.bloomfieldbeach.com.au
07 4060 8207 HEMA 20 C3 15 54 40 S 145 21 07 E

Baffle Creek

27 Baffle Creek Caravan & Camping Park
1384 Coast Rd
www.bafflecreekcaravanandcampingpark.com
07 4156 6421 HEMA 16 F6 24 30 18 S 152 00 06 E

Barcaldine

28 Barcaldine Tourist & Caravan Park
51- 65 Box St
www.barcaldinetouristandcaravanpark.com.au
07 4651 6066 HEMA 29 F12 23 33 48 S 145 17 00 E

29 Homestead Caravan Park
Landsborough Hwy. 300m W of PO
www.homesteadcvpark.com.au
07 4651 1308 HEMA 29 F12 23 33 18 S 145 17 00 E

30 Roses-N-Things
44 Coolibah St
www.kuiparks.com.au
0427 223 930 HEMA 29 F12 23 33 44 S 145 16 50 E

Bargara

31 Absolute Oceanfront Tourist Park
117 Woongarra Scenic Dr
www.oceanfrontpark.com.au
07 4159 2436 HEMA 14 B2 24 50 03 S 152 28 18 E

32 Bargara Beach Caravan Park
25 Fred Courtice Ave, Nielson Park
www.bargarabeachcaravanpark.com.au
07 4159 2228 HEMA 14 A1 24 48 24 S 152 27 21 E

Beachmere

33 Beachmere Caravan Park
10-26 Biggs Ave
www.moretonbay.qld.gov.au
07 5496 8077 HEMA 4 A5 27 07 54 S 153 03 09 E

Beaudesert

34 Beaudesert Caravan & Tourist Park
Albert St
07 5541 1368 HEMA 6 G7 27 59 31 S 153 00 16 E

Bedourie

35 Bedourie Caravan Park
Herbert St. Please pay at Visitor Centre
07 4746 1040 HEMA 28 G3 24 21 45 S 139 28 12 E

36 Simpson Desert Oasis Caravan Park & Camping Ground
1 Herbert St
www.simpsondesertoasis.com.au
07 4746 1291 HEMA 28 G3 24 21 23 S 139 28 16 E

Beechmont

37 Binna Burra Mountain Lodge & Campsite
Binna Burra Rd, Lamington National Park. Camper Van sites only
07 5533 3622 HEMA 12 J6 28 11 56 S 153 11 14 E

Beerwah

38 Beerwah Caravan Park
205 Burys Rd
07 5494 0365 HEMA 11 H12 26 52 30 S 152 58 43 E

Bell

39 Bell Tourist Park
40 Cedarvale Rd
www.belltouristpark.com.au
07 4663 1265 HEMA 35 D14 26 55 57 S 151 26 49 E

Belyando

40 Belyando Crossing Service Station Caravan Park
Gregory Developmental Rd. No water hook up available
07 4983 5269 HEMA 30 B4 21 31 56 S 146 58 23 E

Benaraby

41 Boyne River Tourist Park
Bruce Hwy
www.boynerivertp.com.au/
07 4975 0769 HEMA 16 D4 24 00 21 S 151 20 12 E

42 Greenacres Motel & Van Park
Bruce Hwy. N end of town
www.greenacresvanpark.com.au
07 4975 0136 HEMA 16 D4 24 00 04 S 151 19 31 E

43 Lake Awoonga Caravan Park
865 Awoonga Dam Rd
www.lakeawoongacaravanpark.com
07 4975 0155 HEMA 16 E4 24 04 15 S 151 18 12 E

Biggenden

44 Mountain View Caravan Park
Walsh St
07 4127 1399 HEMA 13 C2 25 30 49 S 152 02 25 E

Biggera Waters

45 NRMA Treasure Island Holiday Park

117 Brisbane Rd
www.treasureisland.com.au
07 5500 8666 HEMA 5 C4 27 56 05 S 153 23 35 E

Biloela

46 Biloela Caravan Park

98-100 Dawson Hwy
07 4992 1211 HEMA 16 F1 24 24 28 S 150 29 43 E

47 Boomerang Caravan Park

2-10 Dunn St
www.ozzyparks.com.au
07 4992 1815 HEMA 16 F1 24 24 09 S 150 30 35 E

48 Discovery Holiday Parks Biloela

1-31 Valentine Plains Rd
www.discoveryholidayparks.com.au
07 4992 2618 HEMA 16 F2 24 24 26 S 150 31 01 E

49 Lake Callide Retreat

119 Lake Callide Drive
07 4993 9010 HEMA 16 F2 24 22 22 S 150 36 40 E

Birdsville

50 Birdsville Caravan Park

1 Florence St
www.birdsvillecaravanpark.com
07 4656 3214 HEMA 28 K3 25 53 59 S 139 21 15 E

Bjelke Petersen Dam

51 Barambah Bush Caravan Park

332 Borcherts Hill Rd, via Murgon
www.barambahbush.com.au
07 4168 1085 HEMA 12 A1 26 15 23 S 151 58 51 E

Bjelke Petersen Dam (Moffatdale)

52 Yallakool Caravan Park

Haager Dr
www.yallakoolpark.com.au
07 4168 4746 HEMA 12 A1 26 18 17 S 151 59 41 E

Blackall

53 Barcoo Hotel Caravan Park

95 Shamrock St. Entry to sites off Spring Ln
07 4657 4197 HEMA 29 G13 24 25 24 S 145 27 53 E

54 Blackall Caravan Park

53 Garden St
www.blackallcaravanpark.com.au
07 4657 4816 HEMA 29 G13 24 25 38 S 145 28 06 E

Blackwater

55 Discovery Holiday Parks Blackwater

74 Littlefield St
www.discoveryholidayparks.com.au
07 4982 5611 HEMA 30 F7 23 35 06 S 148 52 17 E

Bli Bli

56 Bli Bli Riverside Caravan Village

297 David Low Way. 500m E of Bli Bli Castle
www.riversideblibli.com.au
07 5448 5207 HEMA 11 D13 26 37 20 S 153 02 30 E

Bluewater

57 Bluewater Caravan Park

41420 Bruce Hwy
www.bluewatercaravanpark.com.au
07 4778 6118 HEMA 19 G4 19 11 51 S 146 34 43 E

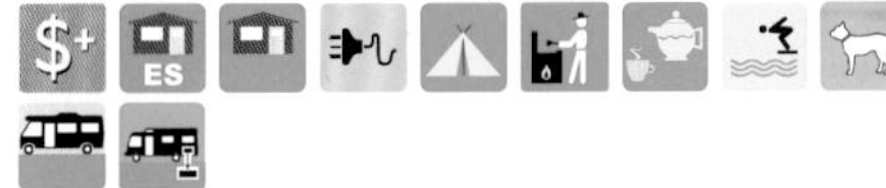

Boonooroo

58 Boonooroo Caravan Park

18 Oak St
07 4129 8211 HEMA 14 H4 25 40 25 S 152 53 07 E

Boreen Point

59 Boreen Point Camp Ground

The Esplanade. Apply online 1 week prior to bring pet
www.noosaholidayparks.com.au
07 5485 3244 HEMA 13 F5 26 17 14 S 152 59 31 E

Boulia

60 Boulia Caravan Park

Diamantina Development Rd
07 4746 3320 HEMA 28 E4 22 54 36 S 139 55 04 E

Bowen

61 BIG4 Bowen Coral Coast Beachfront Holiday Park

Cnr of Horseshoe Bay & The Soldiers Rds
www.big4bowen.com.au
1800 602 469 HEMA 18 D4 19 59 08 S 148 14 40 E

62 Bowen Holiday Park

18540 Bruce Hwy
www.bowenholidaypark.com.au
07 4786 1366 HEMA 18 D4 20 01 49 S 148 12 52 E

63 Bowen Palms Caravan Park

18477 Bruce Hwy
www.bowenpalms.com.au
07 4786 2994 HEMA 18 D4 20 02 05 S 148 13 05 E

64 Harbour Lights Caravan Park

40 Santa Barbara Pde
07 4786 1565 HEMA 18 D4 20 00 54 S 148 15 07 E

65 Horseshoe Bay Resort

1 Horseshoe Bay Rd
www.horseshoebayresortbowen.com.au
07 4786 2564 HEMA 18 D4 19 58 48 S 148 15 35 E

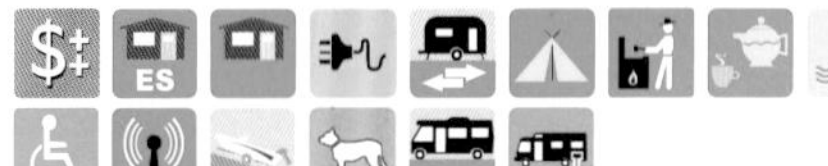

66 Queens Beach Caravan Park

160 Mount Nutt Rd
www.qbtvbowen.com.au
07 4785 1313 HEMA 18 D4 19 58 54 S 148 13 48 E

67 Rose Bay Caravan Park
Banyan Dr
07 4786 2388 HEMA 18 D4 19 59 31 S 148 15 54 E

68 Tropical Beach Caravan Park
Howard St
www.tropicalbeachcaravanparkbowen.com.au
07 4785 1490 HEMA 18 D4 19 59 09 S 148 14 32 E

69 Wangaratta at the Beach Caravan Park
66 Golf Links Rd
07 4785 1152 HEMA 18 D4 19 58 54 S 148 13 59 E

Boyne Island

70 Boyne Island Caravan Park
1 Jacaranda Dr
www.boyneislandcaravanpark.com.au
07 4973 8888 HEMA 16 D4 23 57 43 S 151 20 43 E
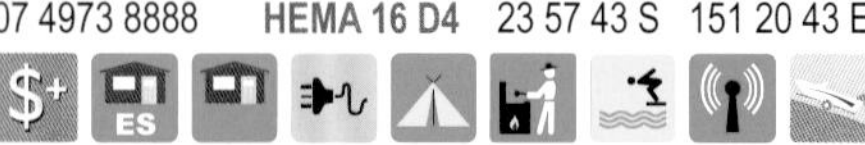

Bramston Beach

71 Bramston Beach Caravan Park & Campground
96 Evans Rd
07 4067 4121 HEMA 21 H6 17 21 08 S 146 01 25 E

Brandon

72 Hotel Brandon Caravan Park
54 Drysdale St
07 4782 5255 HEMA 18 B1 19 33 14 S 147 21 13 E
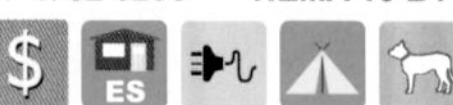

Bribie Island

73 Bongaree Caravan Park
25-47 Welsby Pde
07 3408 1054 HEMA 4 A6 27 04 52 S 153 09 31 E

74 Bribie Island Caravan Park
40 Jacana Ave
www.bribieislandcaravanpark.com.au
07 3408 1134 HEMA 4 A6 27 04 05 S 153 12 06 E

75 Silver Shores Caravan Park
1 Kal-Ma-Kuta Drv
07 5497 5566 HEMA 4 A6 27 04 06 S 153 08 00 E

Bundaberg

76 BIG4 Cane Village Holiday Park
94 Twyford St. 5 km from PO
www.big4.com.au
07 4155 1022 HEMA 14 B1 24 53 26 S 152 18 58 E

77 Bundaberg East Cabin & Tourist Park
83 Princess St. 2 km from PO
www.bundabergtouristpark.com.au
07 4152 8899 HEMA 14 B1 24 51 18 S 152 22 29 E

78 Bundaberg Park Lodge
20 Childers Rd. 3 km S of PO
www.bundypl.com.au
07 4155 1969 HEMA 16 G7 24 54 49 S 152 18 18 E
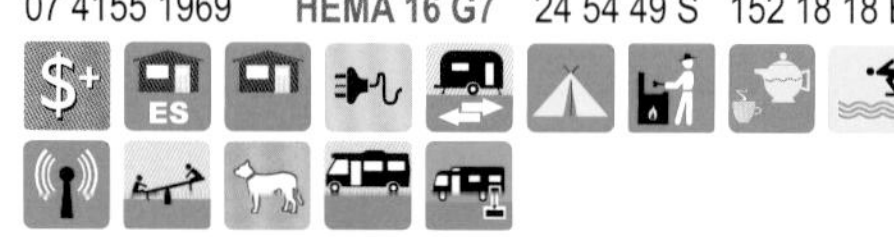

79 Glenlodge Caravan Village
321 Goodwood Rd
www.glenlodge.com.au
07 4153 1515 **HEMA 14 B1** 24 54 22 S 152 21 59 E

80 Midtown Caravan Park
61 Takalvan St. 2.5 km S of PO
www.midtowncaravanpark.com.au
07 4152 2768 **HEMA 14 B1** 24 52 44 S 152 19 42 E

81 Oakwood Caravan Park
15 Old Gin Gin Rd
www.oakwoodvanpark.com.au
07 4159 9332 **HEMA 16 G7** 24 51 07 S 152 17 33 E

Bundaberg North

82 AAOK Riverdale Caravan Park
6 Perry St
www.riverdalecaravanpark.com.au
07 4153 6696 **HEMA 14 B1** 24 51 38 S 152 20 58 E

Burdekin Falls Dam

83 Burdekin Falls Dam Caravan Park
Burdekin Falls Dam Rd
07 4770 3177 **HEMA 18 F1** 20 38 28 S 147 08 47 E

Burketown

84 Burketown Caravan Park
Solman St
www.burketowncaravanpark.net.au
07 4745 5118 **HEMA 25 D4** 17 44 32 S 139 32 47 E

Burleigh Heads

85 Burleigh Beach Tourist Park
Goodwin Tce
www.goldcoasttouristparks.com.au
07 5667 2750 **HEMA 5 H6** 28 05 28 S 153 27 18 E

Burnett Heads

86 Burnett Heads Lighthouse Holiday Park
Paul Mittleheuser St. 500m from PO
www.bundabergholidayparks.com.au
07 4159 4313 **HEMA 14 A1** 24 45 48 S 152 24 29 E

87 Oaks Beach Caravan & Relocatable Homes Village
Cnr Burnett Heads Rd & Rowlands Rd
07 4159 4353 **HEMA 14 A1** 24 46 13 S 152 24 52 E

Burrum Heads

88 Burrum Heads Beachfront Tourist Park
42 Burrum St
www.beachfronttouristparks.com.au
07 4129 5138 **HEMA 14 D2** 25 11 01 S 152 36 44 E

89 Hillcrest Holiday Park
1 Howard St
www.burrumheadshillcrestholidaypark.com
07 4129 5179 **HEMA 14 D2** 25 11 08 S 152 36 32 E

Burrum River

90 Australian Adventure Park
805 Burrum Heads Road
www.australianadventurepark.com
07 4186 7606 HEMA 14 E2 25 16 18 S 152 34 51 E

Byfield

91 Ferns Hideaway Resort & Caravan Park
67 Cahills Rd. GPS at entry
www.fernshideawayresort.com
07 4935 1235 HEMA 16 A2 22 49 29 S 150 39 18 E

Caboolture

92 Caboolture River Caravan Park
26 Burnett Rd. 2.5 km NE of PO
www.caboolturerivercaravanpark.com
07 5495 1041 HEMA 4 A4 27 05 17 S 152 58 27 E

Cairns

93 BIG4 Cairns Crystal Cascades Holiday Park
The Rocks Rd, Redlynch
www.crystalcascades.com.au
07 4039 1036 HEMA 22 C6 16 55 34 S 145 41 47 E

94 Cairns Holiday Park
12-30 Little St, Manunda
www.cairnsholidaypark.com.au
07 4051 1467 HEMA 22 C7 16 54 45 S 145 45 26 E
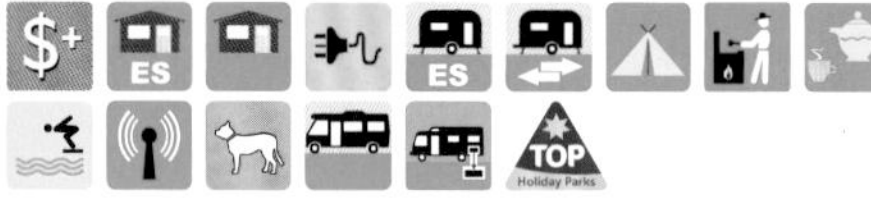

95 Cairns Sunland Leisure Park
49 Little Pease St. 4 km W of PO
www.cairnssunland.com.au
07 4053 6888 HEMA 22 C6 16 55 04 S 145 44 25 E

96 Cairns Villa & Leisure Park
28 Pease St
www.cairnsvilla.com.au
07 4053 7133 HEMA 22 C6 16 55 15 S 145 44 26 E

97 Cool Waters Holiday Park
Cnr Brinsmead Rd & View St. 7 km NW of Cairns PO
www.coolwatersholidaypark.com.au
07 4034 1949 HEMA 22 B6 16 54 18 S 145 42 32 E

98 First City Caravilla
1 Kelly St, Earlville
www.caravilla.com.au
07 4054 1403 HEMA 22 C6 16 56 18 S 145 44 36 E

99 Ingenia Holidays Cairns Coconut
23-51 Anderson Rd
www.ingeniaholidays.com.au
07 4054 6644 HEMA 22 D6 16 58 04 S 145 44 38 E

100 Lake Placid Tourist Park
Lake Placid Rd. 3 km S of Skyrail
www.lakeplacidtouristpark.com
07 4039 2509 HEMA 22 B5 16 52 10 S 145 40 29 E

101 NRMA Palm Cove Holiday Park
149 Williams Esplanade
www.palmcovehp.com.au
07 4055 3824 HEMA 21 C4 16 44 26 S 145 40 16 E

102 White Rock Leisure Park
1 Skull Rd. 6 km S of PO
www.whiterockleisurepark.com.au
07 4036 2523 HEMA 22 D6 16 58 14 S 145 44 46 E

Calen

103 St Helens Gardens Tourist Park
Bruce Highway, 6 Ferris Rd, 1 km S of PO
www.sthelensgardens.com.au
07 4958 8152 HEMA 18 G5 20 54 15 S 148 46 48 E

Calliope

104 Calliope Caravan Park
65 Stowe Rd. 1 km from PO
www.calliopecaravanpark.com
07 4975 7472 HEMA 16 D3 23 59 59 S 151 11 29 E

Caloundra

105 Caloundra Big4
44 Maloja Ave
www.caloundraholidaypark.com.au
07 5491 1564 HEMA 11 G14 26 48 16 S 153 07 28 E

106 Dicky Beach Family Holiday Park
1 Beerburrum St. 800m NW of PO
www.sunshinecoastholidayparks.com.au
07 5491 3342 HEMA 11 G14 26 46 59 S 153 08 14 E

107 Golden Beach Holiday Park
1 Onslow St
www.goldenbeachholidaypark.com.au
07 5492 4811 HEMA 11 G14 26 49 27 S 153 07 13 E

108 Military Jetty Caravan Park
131 The Esplanade (Golden Beach)
07 5492 1288 HEMA 11 G14 26 50 01 S 153 07 07 E

Cambroon

109 Cambroon Caravan & Camping Park
2951 Maleny Kenilworth Rd
www.cambrooncaravanpark.com.au
07 5446 0002 HEMA 11 E8 26 38 23 S 152 41 07 E

Camooweal

110 Camooweal Roadhouse Caravan Park
Barkly Hwy
www.camoowealroadhouse.net.au
07 4748 2155 HEMA 25 H2 19 55 15 S 138 07 08 E

111 Post Office Hotel
Barkly Hwy
07 4748 2124 HEMA 25 H2 19 55 19 S 138 07 11 E

Cania Gorge

112 Cania Gorge Caravan & Tourist Park
54 Park Rd. Approval for pets prior to arrival
www.caniagorge.com.au
07 4167 8188 HEMA 16 G3 24 39 41 S 150 57 48 E

113 Cania Gorge Tourist Retreat
1253 Cania Gorge Rd
www.caniagorgeretreat.com.au
07 4167 8110 HEMA 16 G3 24 43 20 S 150 59 31 E

Cannonvale

114 Seabreeze Tourist Park
234 Shute Harbour Rd
www.seabreezepark.com.au
07 4946 6379 HEMA 18 E5 20 16 30 S 148 42 09 E

Cape Hillsborough

115 Cape Hillsborough Nature Resort
51 Risley Parade
www.capehillsboroughresort.com.au
07 4959 0152 HEMA 18 G6 20 55 28 S 149 02 52 E

Cape Tribulation

116 Cape Tribulation Camping
Lot 11 Cape Tribulation Rd. 37 km N of Daintree Ferry
www.capetribcamping.com.au
07 4098 0077 HEMA 20 C4 16 06 36 S 145 27 25 E

117 Lync - Haven Rainforest Retreat
Lot 44 Cape Tribulation Rd
07 4098 9155 HEMA 20 D3 16 11 29 S 145 24 53 E

118 Rainforest Village
Lot 1 Cape Tribulation Rd. 17 km N of Daintree Ferry
www.rainforestvillage.com.au
07 4098 9015 HEMA 20 D3 16 12 51 S 145 25 19 E

Cape York

119 Cape York Camping
Punsand Bay. Via Bamaga
www.capeyorkcamping.com.au
07 4069 1722 HEMA 24 A5 10 43 19 S 142 27 47 E

120 Seisia Holiday Park
6 Koraba Rd
www.seisiaholidaypark.com
07 4203 0992 HEMA 24 B4 10 50 51 S 142 22 05 E

121 Weipa Caravan Park & Camping Ground
Kerr Point Rd
www.campweipa.com.au
07 4069 7871 HEMA 23 D1 12 38 20 S 141 51 38 E

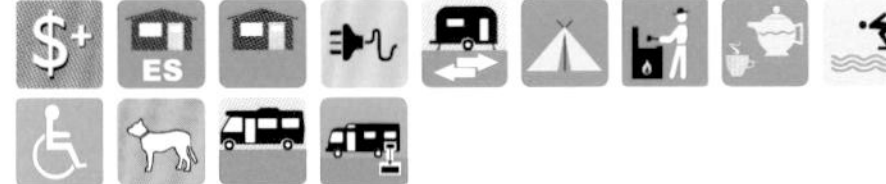

Capella

122 Capella Van Park
13 Langton St. 1 km N of PO
07 4984 9615 HEMA 30 E6 23 04 42 S 148 01 18 E

Carbrook

123 Aquatic Gardens Caravan Park
833-901 Beenleigh-Redland Bay Rd
07 3287 6474 HEMA 7 C11 27 41 12 S 153 15 50 E

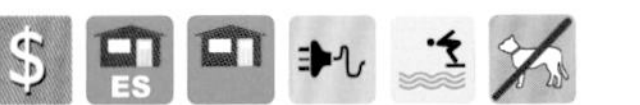

Cardwell

124 Cardwell Beachcomber Motel & Tourist Park
43a Marine Pde. 1.5 km N of PO
www.cardwellbeachcomber.com.au
07 4066 8550 HEMA 19 C2 18 15 20 S 146 01 06 E

125 Cardwell Van Park
107 Roma St. 1 km from PO
www.familyparks.com.au
07 4066 8689 HEMA 19 C2 18 15 54 S 146 01 23 E

126 Kookaburra Holiday Park
175 Bruce Hwy. 800m N of PO
www.kookaburraholidaypark.com.au
07 4066 8648 HEMA 19 C2 18 15 37 S 146 01 18 E

127 Meunga Creek Caravan Park
12 Ellerbeck Rd (Ellerbeck) 5 km N of Cardwell on Bruce Hwy
07 4066 8710 HEMA 19 C2 18 14 27 S 145 59 27 E

Carmila

128 Carmila Caravan Park & Motel
1 Music St
07 4950 2227 HEMA 17 D2 21 54 30 S 149 24 34 E

Carnarvon National Park

129 Takarakka Bush Resort
Carnarvon Gorge Rd
www.takarakka.com.au
07 4984 4535 HEMA 30 H6 25 04 13 S 148 16 17 E

Carrara

130 River Gardens Caravan Park
672 Nerang Broadbeach Rd
07 5594 4211 HEMA 5 E4 28 00 48 S 153 22 48 E

Causeway Lake

131 Causeway Caravan Park
11 Causeway Esplanade
www.causewaycaravanpark.com.au
07 4933 6356 HEMA 16 B2 23 11 54 S 150 47 16 E

Cecil Plains

132 Cecil Plains Rural Retreat Caravan Park
Taylor St. Payment & keys see notice board or call
0428 913 779 HEMA 35 E14 27 31 59 S 151 11 45 E

Charleville

133 Bailey Bar Caravan Park
196 King St. 1.5 km S of PO
www.charlevillebaileybar.com.au
07 4654 1744 HEMA 34 B2 26 23 58 S 146 15 14 E

134 Charleville Bush Caravan Park
Lot 1 Frawley St, 2 km NW of PO on the Diamantina Development Road. No smoking policy, unsuitable for children. No credit card facilities
0428 545 200 HEMA 34 B2 26 23 43 S 146 13 13 E

135 Cobb & Co Caravan Park
1 Ridgeway St
www.caravanparkscharleville.com.au
07 4654 1053 HEMA 34 B2 26 23 44 S 146 15 08 E

136 Evening Star Tourist Park
818 Adavale Road, 9 km NW of Charleville on the Charleville-Adavale Rd
www.eveningstar.com.au
07 4654 2430 HEMA 34 B2 26 21 59 S 146 09 37 E

Charters Towers

137 Aussie Outback Oasis Cabin & Van Village
76 Dr George Ellis Dr. 3 km E of PO
www.big4.com.au
07 4787 8722 HEMA 19 K3 20 03 46 S 146 16 56 E

138 Charters Towers Tourist Park
37 Mt Leyshon Rd
www.charterstowerstouristpark.com.au
07 4787 7944 HEMA 19 K3 20 05 36 S 146 15 40 E

139 Dalrymple Tourist Van Park
24 Dalrymple Rd (Lynd Hwy). 2 km N of PO next to Golf Course
www.dalrymplevanpark.com.au
07 4787 1121 HEMA 19 K3 20 03 26 S 146 15 24 E

Childers

140 Childers Tourist Park & Camp
111 Stockyard Rd. 7 km SE of PO
www.childerstouristparkandcamp.com.au
07 4126 1371 HEMA 13 A3 25 11 50 S 152 17 53 E

141 Iron Ridge Park
1472 Goodwood Rd, Redridge via Childers (15 km)
www.ironridgepark.com.au
07 4126 8410 HEMA 14 D1 25 10 06 S 152 22 29 E

142 Site Closed

Chillagoe

143 Chillagoe Observatory & Eco Lodge
1 Hospital Ave
www.coel.com.au
07 4094 7155 HEMA 27 D8 17 08 55 S 144 31 39 E

144 Chillagoe Tourist Village
40-50 Queen St
www.chillagoeaccommodationvillage.com.au
07 4094 7177 HEMA 27 D8 17 09 20 S 144 31 28 E

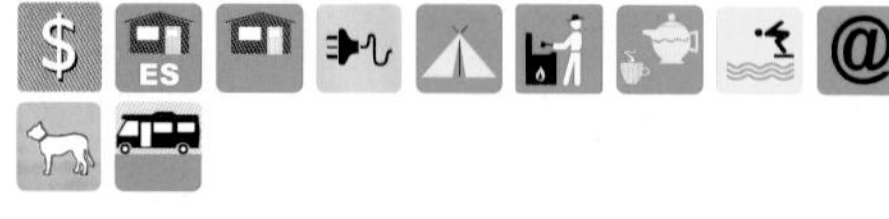

Chinchilla

145 Chinchilla Tourist Park
264 Zeller St. Via Carmichael Rd (Tara Bypass).
www.chinchillatouristpark.com.au
07 4669 1465 HEMA 35 C12 26 45 14 S 150 38 37 E

Clairview Beach

146 BarraCrab Caravan Park
1 Colonial Dr
07 4956 0190 HEMA 17 E3 22 07 16 S 149 32 07 E

Clermont

147 Clermont Caravan Park
1 Haig St
www.clermontcaravanpark.com.au
07 4983 1927 HEMA 30 D5 22 49 39 S 147 38 46 E

Cloncurry

148 Cloncurry Caravan Park Oasis
McIlwraith St. 1.5 km from PO
07 4742 1313 HEMA 25 J6 20 42 24 S 140 31 02 E

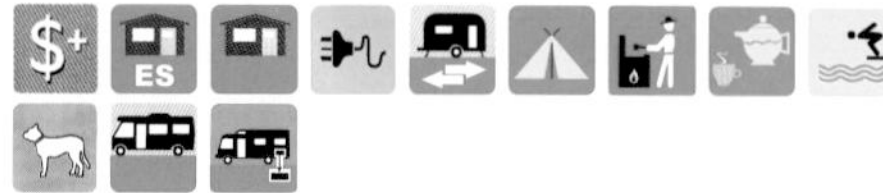

149 Discovery Holiday Parks Cloncurry
2 McIlwraith St
07 4742 2300 HEMA 25 J6 20 42 26 S 140 31 33 E

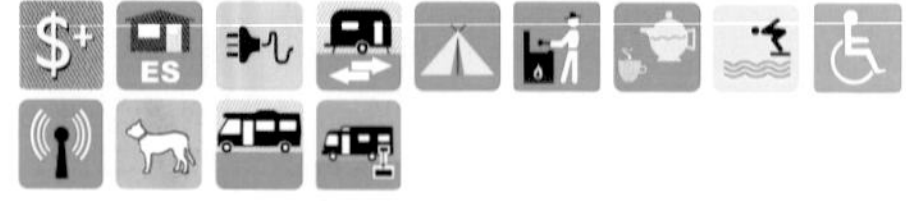

Clontarf

150 Bells Caravan Park
39 Thompson Cres
07 3283 2317 HEMA 4 C5 27 15 20 S 153 05 30 E

Cobbold Gorge

151 Cobbold Gorge Village
Agate Creek Rd
www.cobboldgorge.com.au
07 4062 5470 HEMA 26 G6 18 47 43 S 143 25 24 E

Collinsville

152 Collinsville Caravan Park
4 Doonan St. Limited sites
07 4785 6859 HEMA 18 E3 20 33 03 S 147 50 54 E

Condamine

153 Condamine River Caravan Park
8 Wambo St
www.condaminerivercaravanpark.com.au
07 4627 7179 HEMA 35 D11 26 55 36 S 150 07 59 E

Conondale

154 Crystal Waters Eco Caravan Park
65 Kilcoy Ln. 9 km S of Conondale
www.crystalwaters.org.au
07 5494 4550 HEMA 11 G8 26 46 54 S 152 43 00 E

Conway Beach

155 Conway Beach Tourist Park
10 Daniel St
www.conwaybeach.com.au
07 4947 3147 HEMA 18 E5 20 28 40 S 148 44 17 E

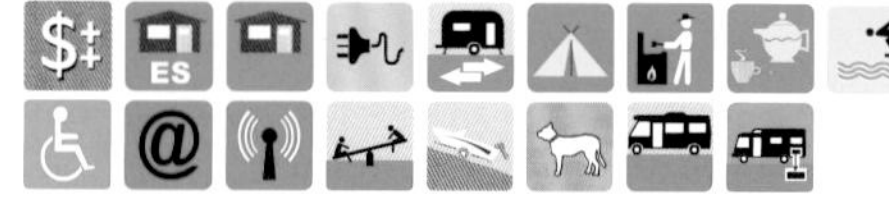

Cooktown

156 Cooktown Caravan Park
14-16 Hope St. 1.5 km S of PO
www.cooktowncaravanpark.com
07 4069 5536 HEMA 20 A3 15 29 00 S 145 14 50 E

157 Cooktown Holiday Park
35-41 Charlotte St
www.cooktownholidaypark.com.au
07 4069 5417 HEMA 20 A3 15 28 34 S 145 14 44 E

158 Cooktown Orchid Travellers Park
Cnr Charlotte St & Walker St. 500m S of PO
07 4069 6400 **HEMA 20 A3** 15 28 10 S 145 14 54 E

159 Cooktown Peninsula Caravan Park
64 Howard St. 1 km S of PO
www.peninsulacaravanpark.com
07 4069 5107 **HEMA 20 A3** 15 28 35 S 145 15 27 E

160 Endeavour Falls Tourist Park
3040 Endeavour Valley Rd
www.endeavourfallstouristpark.com.au
07 4069 5431 **HEMA 20 A2** 15 22 16 S 145 01 44 E

Coolum Beach

161 Coolum Beach Holiday Park
David Low Way. 1 km E of PO
07 5446 1474 **HEMA 11 C13** 26 31 44 S 153 05 28 E

Coomera

162 Secura Lifestyle North Gold Coast
2 Reserve Rd
www.securalifestyle.com.au
07 5573 1665 **HEMA 5 A2** 27 52 09 S 153 18 44 E

Cowley Beach

163 Cowley Beach Caravan Park
Bambarook Rd
www.cowleybeachcaravanpark.com.au
07 4065 4806 **HEMA 21 K7** 17 41 47 S 146 06 41 E

Crows Nest

164 Crows Nest Caravan Park
New England Hwy. 1 km S of PO
www.crowsnestcaravanpark.com.au
07 4698 1269 **HEMA 12 E2** 27 16 23 S 152 03 20 E

Croydon

165 Croydon Caravan Park
Cnr of Brown St & Aldridge St
07 4745 6238 **HEMA 26 F5** 18 12 09 S 142 14 43 E
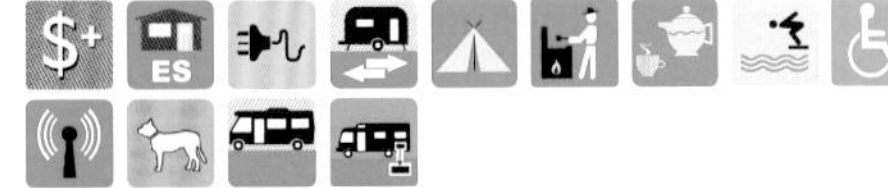

Cunnamulla

166 The Cunnamulla Tourist Park
65 Watson St
www.cunnamullapark.com
07 4655 1421 **HEMA 33 G14** 28 04 30 S 145 41 04 E
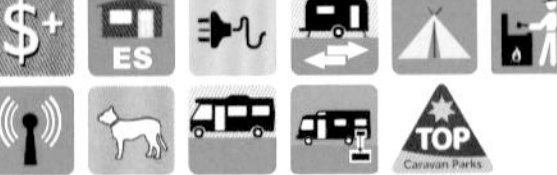

167 Warrego Riverside Tourist Park
322 Weir Rd
07 4655 0097 **HEMA 33 G14** 28 06 07 S 145 41 23 E

Daintree

168 Daintree Riverview Lodges & Van Park
2 Stewart St, Daintree Village
www.daintreeriverview.com
0409 627 434 **HEMA 20 D3** 16 15 01 S 145 19 05 E

Dakabin

169 Watson Park Convention Centre
337 Old Gympie Rd, check in with caretaker
www.sq.adventist.org.au/campgrounds
07 3204 6544 **HEMA 4 B4** 27 13 13 S 152 59 21 E

Dalby

170 Dalby Tourist Park
32 Myall St
www.dalbytouristpark.com.au
07 4662 4793 **HEMA 35 D14** 27 11 08 S 151 16 01 E

171 Pioneer Caravan Park
28 Black St
07 4662 1811 **HEMA 35 D14** 27 10 38 S 151 14 38 E
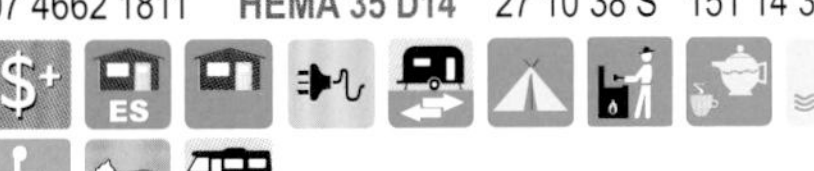

Diddillibah

172 Rivershore Resort
99 David Low Way
www.rivershore.com.au
07 5458 2200 **HEMA 11 D13** 26 38 12 S 153 02 42 E

Dimbulah

173 Dimbulah Caravan Park
Burke Developmental Rd. 1 km W of PO
07 4093 5242 **HEMA 20 G2** 17 09 05 S 145 06 20 E

Dingo

174 Dingo Caravan Park
26 Cairns St
07 4935 9121 **HEMA 31 F8** 23 38 33 S 149 19 48 E

Dirranbandi

175 Dirranbandi Caravan Park
45 Kirby St
07 4625 8707 **HEMA 34 H7** 28 34 53 S 148 13 44 E

Donnybrook

176 Donnybrook Caravan Park
10 Alice St
www.moretonbay.qld.gov.au
07 5498 8219 **HEMA 9 A8** 27 00 03 S 153 04 13 E

Duaringa

177 Duaringa Hotel & Caravan Park
20 Edward St. 1 km from Capricorn Hwy over railway line
07 4935 7202 **HEMA 31 F8** 23 42 46 S 149 40 12 E

Durack

178 Durack Gardens Caravan & Relocatable Homepark
758 Blunder Rd
www.durackgardens.com.au
07 3372 7300 **HEMA 4 G4** 27 35 55 S 152 59 17 E

Edmonton

179 Barrier Reef Tourist Park
69 Bruce Hwy. 12 km S of Cairns
www.barrierreeftouristpark.com.au
07 4055 4544 **HEMA 22 E6** 17 01 27 S 145 44 47 E

Eidsvold

180 Eidsvold Caravan Park

3 Esplanade St. 500m from PO

07 4165 1168 HEMA 16 J3 25 22 06 S 151 07 23 E

Eight Mile Plains

181 Brisbane Holiday Village

10 Holmead Rd

www.brisbaneholidayvillage.com.au

07 3341 6133 HEMA 4 G5 27 34 11 S 153 05 33 E

Einasleigh

182 Copperfield Lodge Camping & Caravan Park

Barootа St. Open Easter to first weekend in Oct. No children

www.copperfieldlodge.com

07 4062 5102 HEMA 26 F7 18 30 35 S 144 05 37 E

El Arish

183 Diggers Creek Motel & Caravan Park

6 Bruce Hwy

www.diggerscreek.com.au

07 4068 5281 HEMA 19 B2 17 47 48 S 146 00 31 E

Elliott Heads

184 Elliott Heads Holiday Park

Lihs St

07 4159 6193 HEMA 14 B2 24 55 17 S 152 29 28 E

Ellis Beach

185 Ellis Beach Oceanfront Bungalows & Leisure Park

Captain Cook Hwy

www.ellisbeach.com

07 4055 3538 HEMA 21 C4 16 43 32 S 145 38 46 E

Emerald

186 Emerald Cabin & Caravan Village

64 Opal St

www.emeraldcabinandcaravanvillage.com.au

07 4982 1300 HEMA 30 F6 23 31 17 S 148 10 01 E

187 Emerald Tourist Park

43 Robert St

www.villagenational.com.au

07 4982 1589 HEMA 30 F6 23 31 51 S 148 09 26 E

188 Lake Maraboon Holiday Village

Fairburn Dam access Rd. 17 km W of Emerald

07 4982 3677 HEMA 30 F6 23 39 30 S 148 04 36 E

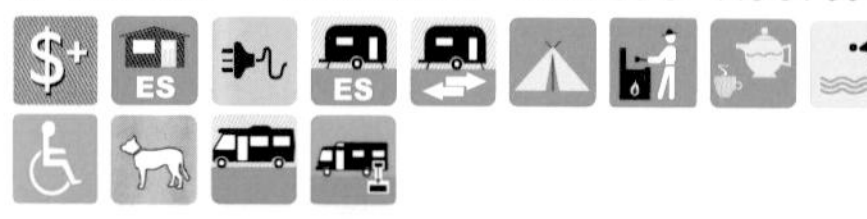

Emu Park

189 Fishermans Beach Holiday Park

67 Pattison St

www.fishermansbeachhp.com.au

07 4847 6002 HEMA 16 B2 23 15 14 S 150 49 27 E

Eromanga

190 Eromanga Motel & Caravan Park

Webber St

07 4656 3276 HEMA 33 C9 26 40 10 S 143 16 20 E

Esk

191 Esk Caravan Park

16 Hassall Street

www.eskcaravanpark.com.au

07 5424 1466 HEMA 12 E3 27 14 20 S 152 25 23 E

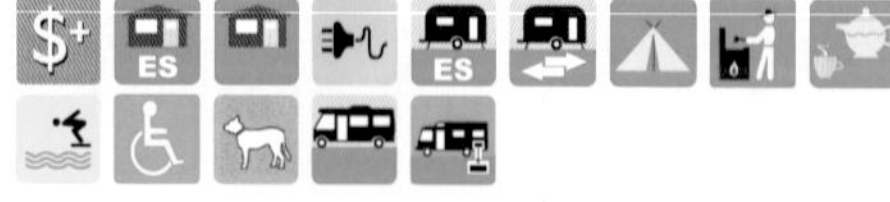

Etty Bay

192 Etty Bay Caravan Park

The Esplanade

07 4063 2314 HEMA 21 J7 17 33 28 S 146 05 23 E

Eulo

193 Eulo Queen Hotel & Caravan Park

Leo St

www.euloqueenhotel.com.au

07 4655 4867 HEMA 33 G13 28 09 37 S 145 02 49 E

Fishery Falls

194 Fishery Falls Holiday Park

69479 Bruce Hwy

www.fisheryfalls.com.au

07 4067 5283 HEMA 21 F5 17 10 55 S 145 53 08 E

Forest Glen

195 Forest Glen Holiday Resort

71 Owen Creek Rd

www.forestglenresort.com.au

07 5476 6646 HEMA 11 E12 26 41 36 S 153 00 40 E

Forrest Beach

196 Forrest Beach Hotel

1 Ash St. Via Ingham

www.forrestbeachhotel.com.au

07 4777 8700 HEMA 19 E3 18 42 55 S 146 17 48 E

Forsayth

197 Forsayth Tourist Park

First St

07 4062 5324 HEMA 26 F6 18 35 16 S 143 36 06 E

Fraser Island

198 Cathedrals on Fraser

Lot 53, Fraser Island Road

www.cathedralsonfraser.com.au

07 4127 9177 HEMA 14 D7 25 09 59 S 153 16 56 E

Gatton

199 Gatton Caravan Park

291 Eastern Dr

www.gattoncaravanpark.com

07 5462 1198 HEMA 12 F3 27 33 19 S 152 17 19 E

Gayndah

200 Riverside Gayndah Caravan Park & Motel

11 Dalgangal Rd
www.riversidegayndah.com
07 4161 1911 **HEMA 16 K5** 25 37 10 S 151 36 33 E

201 Riverview Caravan Park

3 Barrow St. 1 km N of PO
www.caravanparkgayndah.com.au
07 4161 1280 **HEMA 16 K5** 25 37 17 S 151 36 10 E

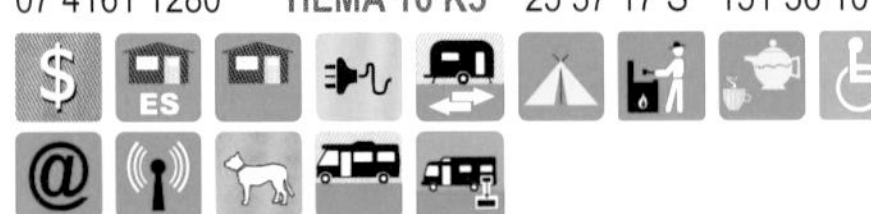

Georgetown

202 Goldfields Caravan Park

2 St. George St
07 4062 1269 **HEMA 26 F6** 18 17 14 S 143 32 58 E

203 Midway Caravan Park

1 North St. 500m N of PO
07 4062 1219 **HEMA 26 F6** 18 17 22 S 143 32 48 E

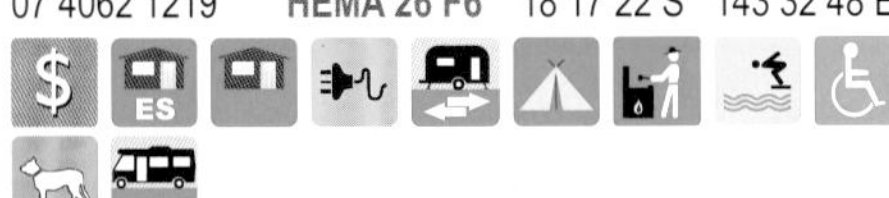

Gin Gin

204 Puma Caravan Park and Roadhouse

2 Mulgrave St
07 4157 2192 **HEMA 16 H6** 24 58 56 S 151 57 02 E

Giru

205 Mountain View Lake Holiday Park

Bruce Hwy. Palm Creek, 7 km W of Giru turnoff
07 4782 9122 **HEMA 19 H5** 19 30 19 S 147 02 17 E

Gladstone

206 Kin Kora Village Tourist & Residential Home Park

Olsen Ave, off Dawson Hwy
07 4978 5461 **HEMA 16 D4** 23 52 33 S 151 14 17 E

Glenlyon Dam

207 Glenlyon Dam Tourist Park

Glenlyon Dam Rd
www.glenlyondamtouristpark.com.au/
02 6737 5266 **HEMA 35 J14** 28 57 56 S 151 28 21 E

Goomeri

208 Goomeri Roadhouse Caravan Park

Moore St (Burnett Hwy)
07 4168 4203 **HEMA 13 E2** 26 11 10 S 152 04 07 E

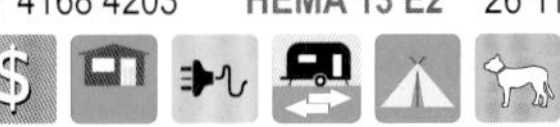

Goondiwindi

209 Goondiwindi Holiday Park

36 Old Cunningham Hwy. 2.5 km NE of PO
www.gundystar.com.au
07 4671 2900 **HEMA 35 H12** 28 31 58 S 150 19 15 E

210 Goondiwindi Tourist Park

20 Hungerford St
www.goondiwinditouristpark.com.au
07 4671 2566 **HEMA 35 H11** 28 31 21 S 150 17 23 E

211 Rivergums Caravan Park

1-5 Delacy St. Limited sites
www.rivergumsgoondiwindi.com.au
07 4671 1383 **HEMA 35 H11** 28 33 02 S 150 18 41 E

Gracemere

212 Gracemere Caravan Park

118 Old Capricorn Hwy
07 4933 1310 **HEMA 16 B1** 23 25 27 S 150 27 44 E

Greenvale

213 Greenvale Caravan Park & Cabins

3 Kylee Crt
07 4788 4155 **HEMA 27 G8** 19 00 04 S 144 59 00 E

Gregory Downs

214 Burke & Wills Roadhouse

Burke Developmental Rd, no water available
07 4742 5909 **HEMA 25 G6** 19 13 37 S 140 20 49 E

Gumlu

215 Molongle Creek Caravan Park

583 Molongle Beach Rd
07 4784 8009 **HEMA 18 C2** 19 50 09 S 147 41 58 E

Gunalda

216 Windsong Cabins & Cafe
Cnr Bruce Hwy & Balkin St
www.windsongcabins.com
07 5484 6262 HEMA 13 D4 25 59 12 S 152 34 01 E

Gympie

217 Gympie Caravan Park
1 Jane St
07 5483 6800 HEMA 13 E4 26 11 09 S 152 39 09 E

Hazeldean

218 Lake Somerset Holiday Park
78 Kirkleagh Road on Esk-Kilcoy Rd
07 5497 1093 HEMA 8 A2 27 01 06 S 152 33 25 E

Hebel

219 Hebel Caravan Park
William St, at General Store
07 4625 0920 HEMA 34 J6 28 58 18 S 147 47 44 E

Helensvale

220 Gold Coast Holiday Park
66-86 Siganto Dr
www.goldcoastholidaypark.com.au
07 5514 4400 HEMA 5 B2 27 54 00 S 153 18 57 E

Herberton

221 Wild River Caravan Park
23 Holdcroft Dr
07 4096 2121 HEMA 21 H2 17 22 03 S 145 23 20 E

Home Hill

222 Groper Creek Caravan Park
Groper Creek. Via Home Hill
www.gropercreek.com.au
07 4782 0186 HEMA 18 C2 19 41 28 S 147 31 52 E

223 Home Hill Caravan Park
Cnr Eighth St & Eleventh Ave
www.homehillcp.com.au
07 4782 2498 HEMA 18 C1 19 39 44 S 147 25 05 E

224 Michelle's Caravan Park
158 Eighth Ave
07 4782 1101 HEMA 18 C1 19 39 35 S 147 24 41 E

Howard

225 Burrum River Caravan Park
141 Old Bruce Hwy
www.burrumrivercaravanpark.com
1800 649 721 HEMA 14 E2 25 19 50 S 152 34 44 E

Hughenden

226 Hughenden Allen Terry Caravan Park
2 Resolution St
www.hughendenvanpark.com.au
07 4741 1190 HEMA 26 K7 20 50 57 S 144 11 46 E

227 Rest Easi Motel & Caravan Park
11 Flinders Hwy
07 4741 1633 HEMA 26 K7 20 50 55 S 144 11 59 E

Hungerford

228 Southern Cross Caravan Park
Hungerford Rd
07 4655 4064 HEMA 33 J11 28 59 51 S 144 24 35 E

Hydeaway Bay

229 Hydeaway Bay Caravan & Camping Park
414 Hydeaway Bay Dr
www.hydeawaybaycaravanpark.com.au
07 4945 7170 HEMA 18 D4 20 05 12 S 148 29 13 E

Ilbilbie

230 Cape Palmerston Holiday Park
989 Greenhill Rd
07 4950 3987 HEMA 17 C2 21 40 45 S 149 26 36 E

Ilfracombe

231 Ilfracombe Caravan Park
Murray St
07 4658 1510 HEMA 29 F11 23 29 24 S 144 30 35 E

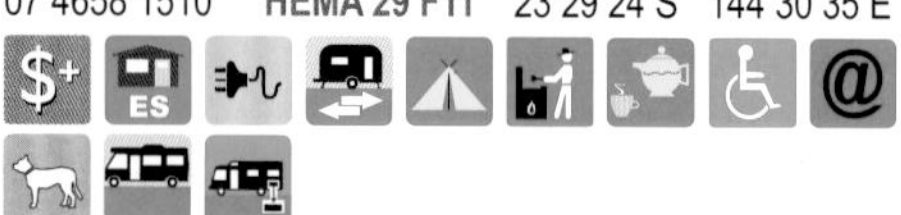

Imbil

232 Borumba Deer Park
1133 Yabba Creek Rd
www.borumbadeerpark.com
07 5484 5196 HEMA 10 B7 26 29 29 S 152 36 03 E

233 Imbil Camping Retreat
1 Imbil Island Road, Imbil, pet security deposit
www.imbilcampingretreat.com.au
0447 135 471 HEMA 11 B8 26 27 32 S 152 40 54 E

Ingham

234 Palm Tree Caravan Park
Bruce Hwy. 3 km S of PO
www.palmtreecaravanpark.com.au
07 4776 2403 HEMA 19 E2 18 40 37 S 146 09 07 E

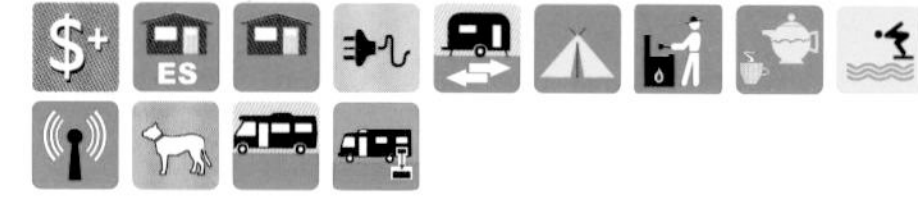

Inglewood

235 Lake Coolmunda Caravan Park
Coolmunda Dam Access Rd, off Cunningham Hwy. 13 km E of Inglewood
www.coolmundacaravan.com.au
07 4652 4171 HEMA 35 H14 28 24 34 S 151 12 45 E

Injune

236 Injune Caravan Park
3rd Ave
07 4626 1881 HEMA 34 A7 25 50 43 S 148 34 01 E

Innisfail

237 August Moon Caravan Park
Bruce Hwy. 4 km S of PO
www.augustmoon.com.au
07 4063 2211 HEMA 21 J6 17 33 28 S 146 02 07 E

238 BIG4 Innisfail Mango Tree Tourist Park
2-6 Couche St. 2 km S of PO
www.mangotreepark.com.au
07 4061 1656 HEMA 21 J6 17 32 40 S 146 01 49 E

239 Flying Fish Point Tourist Park
39 Elizabeth St. Flying Fish Point 7 km NE of Innisfail
www.ffpvanpark.com.au
07 4061 3131 HEMA 21 J7 17 29 59 S 146 04 34 E

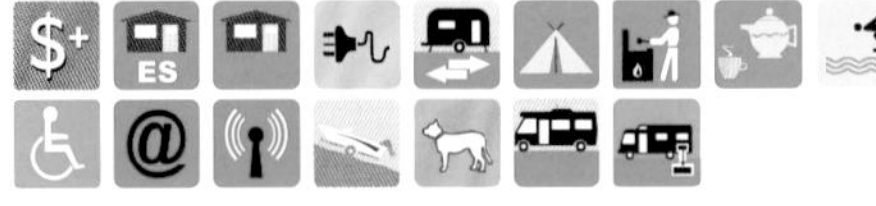

240 River Drive Van Park
7 River Ave
www.riverdrivecaravanpark.com.au
07 4061 2515 HEMA 21 J6 17 32 06 S 146 01 49 E

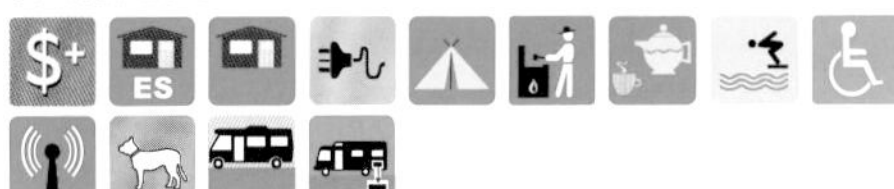

Innot Hot Springs

241 Hot Springs Leisure & Health Park
Kennedy Hwy
07 4097 0136 HEMA 21 K1 17 39 58 S 145 14 19 E

Isisford

242 Golden West Hotel Caravan Park
Cnr St Helena & Mark St
07 4658 8380 HEMA 29 G11 24 15 30 S 144 26 29 E

Jacobs Well

243 Jacobs Well Tourist Park
1161 Pimpama-Jacobs Well Rd
www.goldcoasttouristparks.com.au
07 5667 2760 HEMA 7 D12 27 46 50 S 153 21 54 E

Jandowae

244 AAOK Jandowae Accommodation Park
104 High St 1.5 km S of PO
www.jandowaeaccommodationpark.com.au
07 4668 5071 HEMA 35 C13 26 47 12 S 151 06 46 E

Julatten

245 Tableland Caravan Park
1045 Rex Hwy
07 4094 1145 HEMA 21 B2 16 32 44 S 145 22 59 E

Julia Creek

246 Julia Creek Caravan Park
Old Normanton Rd
www.jccaravanpark.com.au
07 4746 7108 HEMA 26 K4 20 39 09 S 141 44 41 E

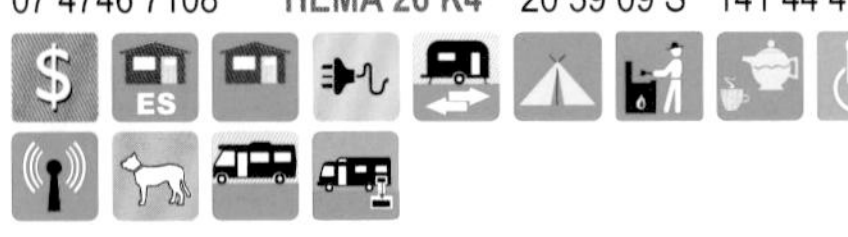

Jundah

247 Site Closed

248 Jundah Caravan Park
2 Dickson St, no bookings, pay general store or Info Centre
07 4658 6930 HEMA 29 H9 24 49 43 S 143 03 33 E

249 Jundah Hotel Caravan Park
12 Dickson St
07 4658 6166 HEMA 29 H9 24 49 45 S 143 03 32 E

Kaimkillenbun

250 Glasbys Caravan Park
82 Mofatt St. 27 km from Bunya Mtns
07 4663 4228 HEMA 35 D14 27 03 39 S 151 26 03 E

Karumba

251 Gulf Country Caravan Park
69 Yappar St
www.gulfcountrycaravanpark.com.au
07 4745 9148 HEMA 25 C7 17 29 21 S 140 50 08 E

252 Karumba Point Service Station Caravan Park
37 Karumba Point Rd
07 4745 9318 HEMA 25 C7 17 27 29 S 140 49 59 E

253 Karumba Point Sunset Caravan Park
53 Palmer St
www.sunsetcp.com.au
07 4745 9277 HEMA 25 C7 17 27 50 S 140 49 46 E

254 Karumba Point Tourist Park
2 Col Kitching Dr
www.karumbapoint.com.au
07 4745 9306 HEMA 25 C7 17 27 19 S 140 50 07 E

Keppel Sands

255 Keppel Sands Caravan Park
38 Taylor St
07 4934 4899 HEMA 16 B2 23 19 28 S 150 47 24 E

Kia Ora

256 Standown Caravan Park
91 Radtke Rd
07 5486 5144 HEMA 13 E5 26 02 08 S 152 47 32 E

Kilkivan

257 Kilkivan Bush Camping Park
Rossmore Rd
www.bushcamping.com.au
07 5484 1340 HEMA 13 E3 26 07 01 S 152 17 25 E

Killarney

258 Killarney Sundown Motel Tourist Park
2-4 Pine St
07 4664 1318 HEMA 12 J3 28 20 29 S 152 17 46 E

259 Killarney View Cabins & Caravan park
Cnr O'Maras Rd & Claydon Rd
www.killarneyviewcaravanpark.com.au
07 4664 1522 HEMA 12 J2 28 19 46 S 152 17 11 E

260 Queen Mary Falls Caravan Park
676 Spring Creek Rd
www.queenmaryfallscaravanpark.com.au
07 4664 7151 HEMA 12 J3 28 20 30 S 152 22 17 E

Kingaroy

261 BIG4 Kingaroy Holiday Park
48 Walter Rd
www.kingaroyholidaypark.com.au
07 4162 1808 HEMA 12 B1 26 33 19 S 151 50 23 E

262 Kingaroy Showgrounds Caravan Park
31 Youngman St
07 4162 5037 HEMA 12 B1 26 32 49 S 151 49 56 E

Kinka Beach

263 Coolwaters Holiday Park
760 Scenic Hwy
www.coolwaters.com.au
07 4939 6102 HEMA 16 B2 23 12 18 S 150 47 11 E

264 Island View Caravan Park
946 Scenic Hwy
www.island-view.com.au
07 4939 6284 HEMA 16 B2 23 12 58 S 150 47 31 E

Kirra

265 Kirra Beach Tourist Park
10 Charlotte St
www.goldcoasttouristparks.com.au
07 5667 2740 HEMA 7 K14 28 10 12 S 153 31 19 E

Koumala

266 Koumala Caravan Park
2-4 Mumby St
07 4950 3657 HEMA 17 C2 21 36 35 S 149 14 49 E

Kumbia

267 Kumbia Caravan Park
Bell St
07 4164 4375 HEMA 13 G1 26 41 23 S 151 39 18 E

Kuranda

268 Kuranda Rainforest Accommodation Park
88 Kuranda Heights Rd. 2 km N of PO
www.kurandarainforestpark.com.au
07 4093 7316 HEMA 22 A4 16 48 57 S 145 37 39 E

Kurrimine Beach

269 King Reef Resort
75 Jacobs Rd. 800m S of PO. Beachfront
www.kingreef.com.au
07 4065 6144 HEMA 19 B2 17 46 51 S 146 06 08 E

270 Kurrimine Beach Holiday Park
9 Coyle St
www.kurrimine.com.au
07 4065 6166 HEMA 19 B2 17 47 00 S 146 05 53 E

Kuttabul

271 Jolimont Caravan Park
Cnr Watts Rd & Bruce Hwy
07 4954 0170 HEMA 18 G6 21 00 25 S 148 52 27 E

Kybong

272 Gold Nugget Roadhouse Caravan Park
690 Bruce Hwy. 6 km S of Gympie, limited sites
0418 871 116 HEMA 12 A4 26 14 17 S 152 41 56 E

Kynuna

273 Blue Heeler Caravan Park
Hulbert St
07 4746 8650 HEMA 28 B7 21 34 43 S 141 55 23 E

274 Kynuna Roadhouse Caravan Park
Landsborough Hwy
07 4746 8683 HEMA 28 B7 21 34 44 S 141 55 13 E

Laidley

275 Laeta Living Laidley
25 Campbell St. 600m NE of PO
07 5465 3506 HEMA 12 F3 27 37 31 S 152 23 52 E

Lake Eacham

276 Lake Eacham Tourist Park
Lakes Dr
www.lakeeachamtouristpark.com
07 4095 3730 HEMA 22 K5 17 17 44 S 145 38 07 E

Lake Monduran

277 Lake Monduran Holiday Park
1 Claude Wharton Dr
www.lakem.com.au
07 4157 3881 HEMA 16 G5 24 52 32 S 151 51 09 E

Lake Moogerah

278 Lake Moogerah Caravan Park
Muller Park Rd
www.moogerah.com
07 5463 0141 HEMA 6 H2 28 02 46 S 152 33 09 E

Lakeland

279 Lakeland Caravan Park
1 Sesame St
07 4060 2033 HEMA 20 B2 15 51 32 S 144 51 17 E
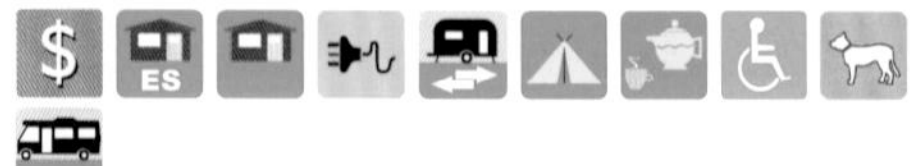

Landsborough

280 Landsborough Pines Caravan Park & Villas
Steve Irwin Way. 300m from railway station
www.landsboroughpines.com.au
07 5494 1207 HEMA 11 G12 26 48 46 S 152 58 00 E

281 Ocean View Tourist Park
2 Old Maleny Rd
www.oceanviewtouristpark.com.au
07 5494 1171 HEMA 11 G11 26 47 37 S 152 56 07 E

Longreach

282 Longreach Caravan Park
180 Ibis St
07 4658 1770 HEMA 29 F11 23 26 45 S 144 14 31 E

283 Longreach Tourist Park
12 Thrush Rd. 1 km E of PO
www.longreachtouristpark.com.au
07 4658 1781 HEMA 29 F11 23 26 34 S 144 15 52 E

Lucinda

284 Wanderers Holiday Village
49 Bruce Pde. 200m from PO
www.wanderers-lucinda.com.au
07 4777 8213 HEMA 19 D3 18 31 40 S 146 20 01 E

Maaroom

285 Maaroom Caravan Park
32 Granville Rd
www.maaroomcaravanpark.com
07 4129 8222 HEMA 14 H4 25 36 44 S 152 52 15 E

Mackay

286 Andergrove Van Park
40-68 Beaconsfield Rd East, Nth Mackay
www.andergrovevanpark.com
07 4942 4922 HEMA 17 A2 21 06 31 S 149 10 31 E

287 Bakers Creek Caravan Park
106 Main St, Bakers Creek, Self contained RV prices available
www.mycowaccommodation.com.au
07 4952 2806 HEMA 17 B1 21 12 47 S 149 08 49 E

288 Big 4 Mackay Marine Tourist Park
265 Harbour Rd
www.mmtp.com.au
07 4955 1496 HEMA 17 A2 21 06 46 S 149 12 26 E

289 Bucasia Beachfront Caravan Resort
2 Bucasia Esp
www.bucasiabeach.com.au
07 4954 6375 HEMA 17 A2 21 02 13 S 149 10 03 E

290 Central Tourist Park
15 Malcomson St
07 4957 6141 HEMA 17 A2 21 07 26 S 149 11 07 E

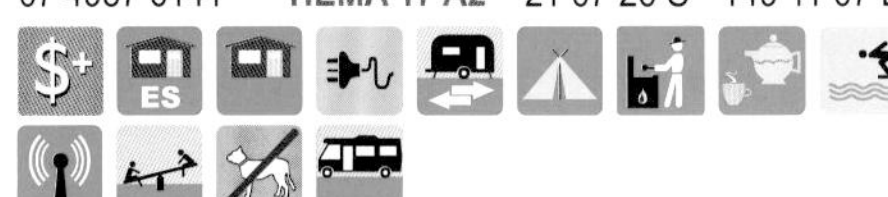

291 Mackay Blacks Beach Holiday Park
16 Bourke St, Blacks Beach
07 4954 9334 HEMA 17 A2 21 03 09 S 149 11 24 E

292 Premier Caravan Park
152 Nebo Rd
www.premiercp.com.au
07 4957 6976 HEMA 17 A2 21 09 16 S 149 09 55 E

293 The Park
284 Farrellys Ln
www.theparkmackay.com.au
07 4952 1211 HEMA 17 A1 21 11 07 S 149 09 07 E

Macrossan

294 Bivouac Junction Outback Holiday Camp
Burdekin Downs Rd
www.bivouacjunctionholidays.com
07 4787 3804 HEMA 19 K3 19 58 58 S 146 26 04 E

Main Beach

295 Main Beach Tourist Park
Main Beach Pde
www.goldcoasttouristparks.com.au
07 5667 2720 HEMA 5 D5 27 58 38 S 153 25 42 E

Malanda

296 Malanda Falls Caravan Park
38 Park Ave
07 4096 5314 HEMA 21 H3 17 21 13 S 145 35 18 E

Mapleton

297 Lilyponds Holiday Park
26 Warruga St. 300m NW of PO
www.lilyponds.com.au
07 5445 7238 HEMA 11 D10 26 37 16 S 152 51 48 E

298 Mapleton Cabins & Caravan Park
85 Obi-Obi Rd. 600m W of PO
www.mapletoncabinscaravans.com.au
07 5445 7135 HEMA 11 D10 26 37 43 S 152 51 35 E

Mareeba

299 Mareeba Country Caravan Park
Emerald End Rd
07 4092 3281 HEMA 22 C1 16 56 54 S 145 25 51 E

300 Riverside Caravan Park
13 Egan St
07 4092 2309 HEMA 22 D1 17 00 04 S 145 25 39 E

301 Tropical Tablelands Caravan Park
3 Kenneally Rd
07 4092 1158 HEMA 22 D1 17 00 45 S 145 25 51 E

Marlborough

302 Marlborough Motel & Van Park
Bruce Hwy
www.marlborough.net.au
07 4935 6112 HEMA 17 H4 22 49 25 S 149 53 34 E

Maroochydore

303 Cotton Tree Holiday Park
2-36 Cotton Tree Pde, Cotton Tree
07 5459 9070 HEMA 11 E13 26 39 14 S 153 06 00 E

304 Maroochy River Park Caravan Park
Cnr Bradman Ave & Diura St
www.maroochyriverpark.com.au
07 5443 3033 HEMA 11 E13 26 38 36 S 153 03 59 E

305 Maroochydore Beach Holiday Park
Melrose Pde. 1 km S of PO
07 5443 1167 HEMA 11 E13 26 39 36 S 153 06 14 E

Maryborough

306 Cheery Nomad RV Park & Farmstay
113 Lawson St, off Fazio Rd
www.cheerynomad.com.au
0414 754 638 HEMA 14 G3 25 29 34 S 152 42 28 E

307 City Caravan Park
125 Alderidge St
07 4121 4467 HEMA 14 G3 25 31 07 S 152 40 52 E

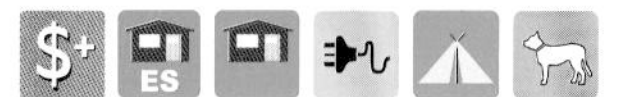

308 Country Stopover Caravan Park
22623 Bruce Hwy
07 4121 2764 HEMA 14 G3 25 33 58 S 152 39 44 E

309 Huntsville Caravan Park
23 Gympie Rd
www.huntsvillecaravanpark.com.au
07 4121 4075 HEMA 14 G3 25 32 45 S 152 41 05 E

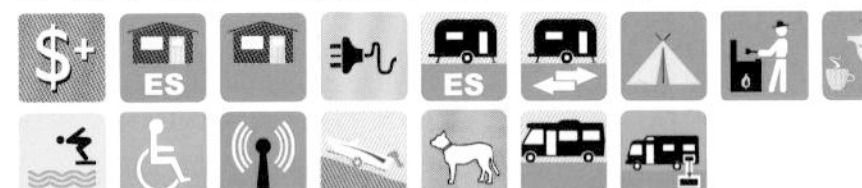

310 Maryborough Caravan Park
209 Gympie Rd
www.ozzyparks.com.au
07 4121 6379 HEMA 14 G3 25 33 23 S 152 40 12 E

311 Wallace Motel & Caravan Park
22 Ferry St. 1 km SW of PO
www.wallacecaravanpark.com.au
07 4121 3970 HEMA 14 G3 25 32 32 S 152 41 20 E

McKinlay

312 Walkabout Creek Hotel & Van Park
Cnr Middleton St & Landsborough Hwy
07 4746 8424 HEMA 26 K3 21 16 19 S 141 17 23 E

Meandarra

313 Meandarra Caravan Park
Gibson St. Fees collected
0400 656 190 HEMA 35 E10 27 19 36 S 149 52 51 E

Miami

314 Nobby Beach Holiday Park
2200 Gold Coast Hwy. 100m S of PO
www.nobbybeachholidayvillage.com.au
07 5572 7533 HEMA 5 G6 28 03 40 S 153 26 13 E

315 Ocean Beach Tourist Park
2 Hythe St. 500m N of PO
www.gctp.com.au/oceanbeach
07 5667 2710 HEMA 5 G6 28 04 10 S 153 26 34 E

Miara

316 Miara Holiday Park
1200 Miara Rd. (Via Yandaran)
07 4156 1171 HEMA 16 G6 24 40 04 S 152 12 05 E

Midge Point

317 Travellers Rest Caravan & Camping Park
29 Jackson St
www.toptouristparks.com.au
07 4947 6120 HEMA 18 F5 20 39 17 S 148 43 06 E

Midgee

318 Kangaroo Country Caravan Park
59741 Bruce Hwy. Limited sites
www.kangaroocountrycaravanpark.com
07 4921 1799 HEMA 16 C2 23 29 34 S 150 32 30 E

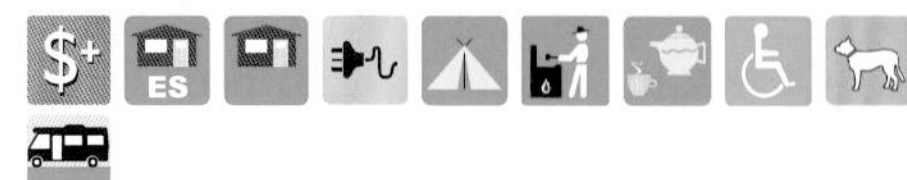

Miles

319 Columboola Country Caravan Park
Ryalls Rd
07 4665 8293 HEMA 35 C12 26 32 46 S 150 19 52 E

320 Miles Crossroads Caravan Park
132 Murilla St
07 4627 2165 HEMA 35 C11 26 39 36 S 150 11 42 E

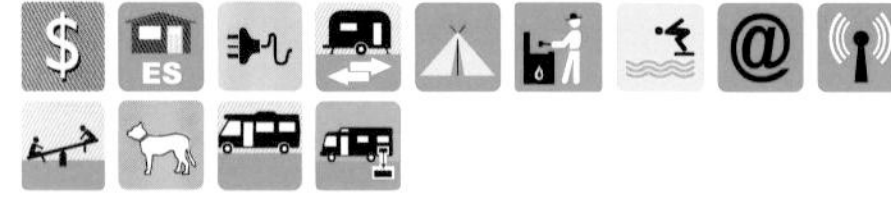

321 Possum Park Caravan & Camping Park
36865 Leichhardt Hwy
www.possumpark.com.au
07 4627 1651 HEMA 35 B11 26 30 49 S 150 06 00 E

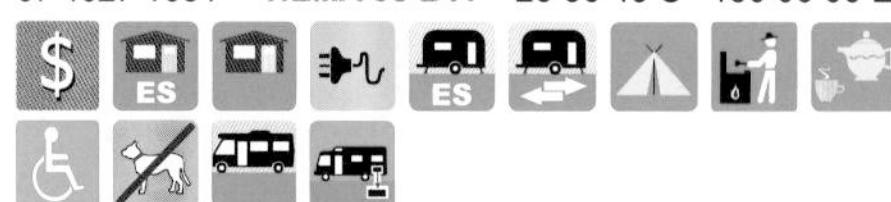

Millaa Millaa

322 Millaa Millaa Tourist Park
86 Millaa Millaa - Malanda Rd
www.millaapark.com
07 4097 2290 HEMA 21 J3 17 31 01 S 145 36 24 E

Millmerran

323 Millmerran Caravan Park
89 Campbell St
07 4695 1572 HEMA 35 F14 27 52 46 S 151 16 08 E

324 Millmerran Village Caravan Park
59-81 Bruce Rd. 700m NW of PO
07 4695 2020 HEMA 35 F14 27 52 20 S 151 15 54 E

Mirani

325 Kinchant Waters Leisure Resort
Lot 10 Kinchant Dam Rd
www.kinchantwaters.com.au
07 4954 1453 HEMA 17 B1 21 13 14 S 148 53 34 E

326 Mirani Caravan Park
Caroline St, next to swimming pool
07 4959 1239 HEMA 18 G6 21 09 42 S 148 51 59 E

Miriam Vale

327 Star Roadhouse Caravan Park
Bruce Hwy, N end of town
07 4974 5249 HEMA 16 E5 24 19 34 S 151 33 12 E

Mission Beach

328 Bali Hai Beach Front Cabin & Camping Village
Cnr Wongaling Beach Rd & Banfield Pde
07 4068 8812 HEMA 19 B2 17 53 45 S 146 05 52 E

329 Beachcomber Coconut Caravan Village
Kennedy Esp
www.beachcombercoconut.com.au
07 4068 8129 HEMA 19 B2 17 56 12 S 146 05 39 E

330 Dunk Island View Caravan Park
21 Webb Rd. Wongaling Beach
www.dunkislandviewcaravanpark.com
07 4068 8248 HEMA 19 B2 17 54 16 S 146 05 47 E

331 Mission Beach Hideaway Holiday Village
58-60 Porters Promenade
www.missionbeachhideaway.com.au
07 4068 7104 HEMA 19 B2 17 51 54 S 146 06 29 E

332 Tropical Hibiscus Caravan Park
2008 Tully Mission Beach Rd, Wongaling Beach
www.thcp.com.au
07 4068 8138 HEMA 19 B2 17 53 47 S 146 05 29 E

Mitchell

333 Major Mitchell Caravan Park
Warrego Hwy
www.majormitchellcaravanpark.com.au
07 4623 6600 HEMA 34 B6 26 29 10 S 147 59 00 E

Monto

334 Monto Caravan Park
16 Flinders St
www.montocaravanpark.com.au
07 4166 1492 HEMA 16 G3 24 51 52 S 151 06 48 E

Mooloolaba

335 Mooloolaba Beach Holiday Park
100 Parkyn Pde
www.sunshinecoastholidayparks.com.au
07 5444 1201 HEMA 11 E14 26 40 57 S 153 07 20 E

Moonie

336 Moonie Crossroads Motel Caravan Park
Cnr Moonie Hwy & Leichhardt Hwy
www.mooniecrossroads.com.au
07 4665 0200 HEMA 35 F12 27 43 03 S 150 22 11 E

Moore Park

337 Moore Park Beach Holiday Park
2 Park Drive
07 4154 8388 HEMA 16 G7 24 42 58 S 152 16 40 E

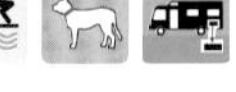

Mossman

338 Mossman Riverside Leisure Park
Cnr Foxton Ave & Park St. 1 km N of PO
www.mossmanriversideleisurepark.com.au
07 4098 2627 HEMA 21 A2 16 27 16 S 145 22 20 E

Mount Carbine

339 Mt Carbine Caravan Park
6806 Mulligan Hwy
www.mtcarbine.com
07 4094 3160 HEMA 20 E2 16 31 42 S 145 08 21 E

Mount Garnet

340 Mount Garnet Travellers Park
2 Nymbool Rd
07 4097 9335 HEMA 20 J2 17 40 08 S 145 06 17 E

Mount Hay

341 Mount Hay Gemstone Tourist Park
3665 Capricorn Hwy
07 4934 7183 HEMA 16 C1 23 33 32 S 150 12 11 E

Mount Isa

342 AAOK Moondarra Caravan Park
2 Lake Moondarra Rd
www.moondarraaccommodation.com.au
07 4743 9780 HEMA 25 J4 20 40 56 S 139 29 51 E

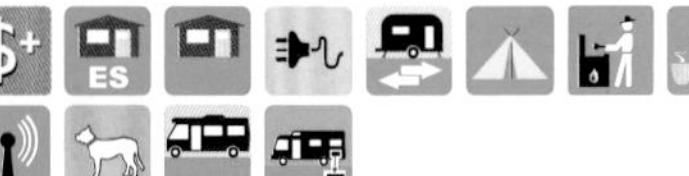

343 Discovery Holiday Parks Argylla
Barkly Hwy (140 Marian St). 2 km E of PO
www.discoveryholidayparks.com.au
07 4743 4733 HEMA 25 J4 20 43 25 S 139 30 59 E

344 Discovery Holiday Parks Mount Isa
185 West St. 1.5 km S of PO
www.discoveryholidayparks.com.au
07 4743 4676 HEMA 25 J4 20 42 30 S 139 29 42 E

345 Mount Isa Caravan Park
112 Marian St. 900m E of Outback@Isa centre
www.mtisacaravanpark.com.au
07 4743 3252 HEMA 25 J4 20 43 28 S 139 30 34 E

346 Sunset Top Tourist Park
14 Sunset Dr. 1.6 km N of PO
07 4743 7668 HEMA 25 J4 20 42 34 S 139 30 00 E

Mount Larcom

347 Mt. Larcom Tourist Park
7 Balfour Street
0413 411 924 HEMA 16 D3 23 48 54 S 150 58 55 E

Mount Morgan

348 Mount Morgan Motel & Van Park
Cnr Burnett Hwy & Showgrounds Rd
07 4938 1952 HEMA 16 C1 23 39 37 S 150 23 13 E

349 Silver Wattle Caravan Park
Burnett Hwy. 1 km S of CBD
www.silverwattlecaravanpark.com.au
07 4938 1550 HEMA 16 C1 23 39 48 S 150 23 28 E

Mount Perry

350 Mingo Crossing Caravan & Recreation Park
2670 Gayndah Mount Perry Rd (28 km S of Mount Perry Town)
www.bundabergregion.org
07 4161 6200 HEMA 13 B1 25 23 38 S 151 46 38 E

351 Mt Perry Caravan Park
54 Heusman St
0427 563 271 HEMA 13 A1 25 10 29 S 151 38 24 E

Mount Surprise

352 Bedrock Village Caravan Park

Garnet St. 500m E of PO
www.bedrockvillage.com.au
07 4062 3193 HEMA 26 F7 18 08 39 S 144 19 13 E

353 Mount Surprise Tourist Park Motel & Roadhouse

23 Garland St
1800 447 982 HEMA 26 F7 18 08 50 S 144 19 06 E

Mount Tamborine

354 Tamborine Mountain Caravan & Camping

Cnr Cedar Creek Rd & Tamborine Mountain Rd
www.tamborine.info
07 5545 0034 HEMA 7 F10 27 54 11 S 153 10 53 E

Moura

355 Moura Accommodation Village & Caravan Park

Okano St. 1 km E of PO
07 4997 1432 HEMA 31 H9 24 33 47 S 149 58 37 E

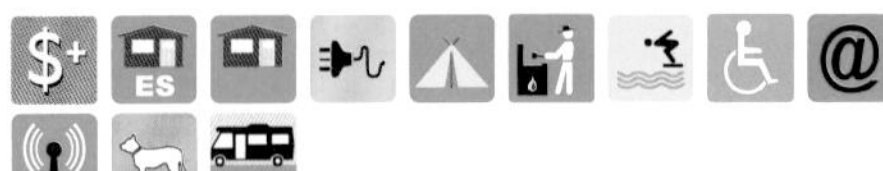

Mudjimba

356 Mudjimba Beach Holiday Park

3-35 Cottonwood St
www.sunshinecoastholidayparks.com.au
07 5448 7157 HEMA 11 D13 26 37 02 S 153 05 57 E

Mundubbera

357 Big Mandarin & Citrus Country Caravan Park

1 Ann St
07 4165 4549 HEMA 16 K4 25 35 00 S 151 18 01 E

358 Mundubbera Three Rivers Tourist Park

37 Strathdee St
07 4165 3000 HEMA 16 K4 25 35 12 S 151 18 04 E

Mutarnee

359 Crystal Creek Caravan Park

Cnr Bruce Highway & Barrilgie Rd
www.crystalcreekcaravanpark.com.au
07 4770 8198 HEMA 19 F3 18 57 02 S 146 17 05 E

Muttaburra

360 Muttaburra Caravan Park

Cnr Mary & Bridge Sts. Caretaker collects fee
07 4658 7191 HEMA 29 D11 22 35 36 S 144 33 07 E

Nanango

361 Homestead Caravan Park & Cabins

17 Arthur St
www.homesteadcaravanpark.com.au
07 4163 1733 HEMA 12 B1 26 40 53 S 151 59 55 E

362 Nanango Caravan & Motorhome Park

13673 D'Aguilar Hwy. 4 km S of PO
www.nanangocaravanandmotorhomepark.lifestylesforyou.com
07 4163 2322 HEMA 12 C1 26 41 46 S 151 58 42 E

363 Nanango RV & Caravan Park

Elk St A/H 0400 631 677
www.nanangorvpark.com.au
07 4163 1677 HEMA 12 B2 26 40 07 S 152 00 03 E

364 Twin Gums Caravan Park

Cnr of Scott St & Arthur St. 1.5 km from PO
07 4163 1376 HEMA 12 B1 26 40 49 S 151 59 54 E

Newell Beach

365 Newell Beach Caravan Park

44 Marine Pde
www.newellbeachcaravanpark.com.au
07 4098 1331 HEMA 21 A2 16 25 31 S 145 24 22 E

Noosa North Shore

366 Noosa North Shore Beach Campground

240 Wilderness Track. Limited powered sites
www.noosaholidayparks.com.au
07 5449 8811 HEMA 13 F6 26 20 00 S 153 03 36 E

367 Noosa North Shore Resort

Beach Rd
www.noosanorthshoreretreat.com.au
07 5447 1225 HEMA 12 A5 26 21 16 S 153 03 07 E

Noosaville

368 Noosa River Holiday Park

4 Russell St
www.noosaholidayparks.com.au
07 5449 7050 HEMA 11 A13 26 23 40 S 153 04 23 E

Normanton

369 Normanton Tourist Park

14 Brown St. 80m from PO
www.normantontouristpark.com.au
07 4745 1121 HEMA 25 D7 17 40 10 S 141 04 42 E

370 The Gulfland Motel & Caravan Park

11 Landsborough St
www.gulflandmotelandcaravanpark.com
07 4745 1290 HEMA 25 D7 17 40 40 S 141 04 08 E

North Isis via Childers

371 Lake Redbrook Holiday Retreat

122 Farnsfield Rd
07 4126 6961 HEMA 13 A3 25 09 33 S 152 15 26 E

North Stradbroke Island

372 Adder Rock Camping Ground

East Coast Rd, Point Lookout
www.straddiecamping.com.au
07 3409 9668 HEMA 9 G14 27 25 22 S 153 30 55 E

373 Amity Point Camping Ground
Claytons Rd
www.straddiecamping.com.au
07 3409 9668 **HEMA 9 G13** 27 24 05 S 153 26 19 E

374 Bradburys Beach Camping Ground
Flinders Ave, Dunwich. No on site manager check in at Dunwich Booking Centre prior
07 3409 9668 **HEMA 9 H12** 27 29 41 S 153 24 07 E

375 Cylinder Beach Camping Ground
East Coast Rd, Point Lookout. No on site manger check in at Dunwich Booking Centre prior
www.straddiecamping.com.au
07 3409 9668 **HEMA 9 G14** 27 25 37 S 153 32 03 E

376 Home Beach Camp Ground
East Coast Rd, Point Lookout
www.straddiecamping.com.au
07 3409 9668 **HEMA 9 G14** 27 25 30 S 153 31 09 E

Oakey

377 Oakridge Motel & Tourist Park
56 Toowoomba Rd (Warrego Hwy)
www.oakridgemoteltouristpark.com.au
07 4691 3330 **HEMA 12 F1** 27 27 25 S 151 43 30 E

Okeden

378 Lake Boondooma Caravan & Recreation Park
40 Bushcamp Road
www.lakeboondooma.com.au
07 4168 9694 **HEMA 35 A14** 26 05 38 S 151 26 27 E

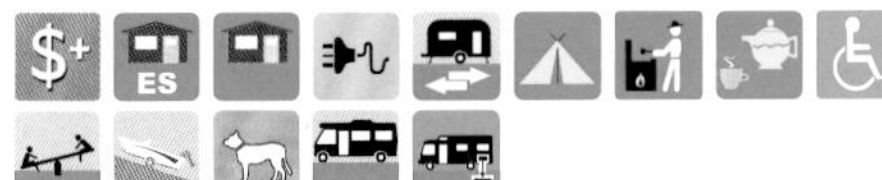

Palm Beach

379 Tallebudgera Creek Tourist Park
1544 Gold Coast Hwy
www.gctp.com.au/tallebudgera
07 5581 7700 **HEMA 5 H6** 28 06 00 S 153 27 32 E

Palmwoods

380 Palmwoods Tropical Village
18 Landershute Rd. 1.8 km SW of PO
www.palmwoodspark.com.au
07 5445 9450 **HEMA 11 E12** 26 41 45 S 152 56 41 E

Pentland

381 Pentland Caravan Park
Flinders Hwy
07 4788 1148 **HEMA 27 J9** 20 31 19 S 145 24 03 E

Pialba

382 Coconut Grove Caravan Park
Cnr Main St & McLiver St
07 4128 2142 **HEMA 14 E4** 25 17 29 S 152 50 17 E

383 Pialba Beachfront Tourist Park
The Esplanade. 400m NW of PO
www.beachfronttouristparks.com.au
07 4128 1399 **HEMA 14 E4** 25 16 44 S 152 50 22 E

Pittsworth

384 Pittsworth Shady Rest Caravan Park
Cnr McIntrye & Yandilla Sts
www.pittsworthshadyrest.com
07 4693 1440 **HEMA 36 F2** 27 43 02 S 151 37 44 E

Point Vernon

385 Point Vernon Holiday Park
26 Corser St. 3.5 km NE PO
www.pvhp.com.au
07 4128 1423 **HEMA 14 E4** 25 15 15 S 152 49 17 E

386 Sunlodge Oceanfront Tourist Park
26 Mant St. 5 km NW of PO
www.beachfronttouristpark.com.au
07 4128 1692 **HEMA 14 E4** 25 14 53 S 152 48 33 E

Poona

387 Poona Palms Caravan Park
Cnr Owen Cox St & Boronia Dr, Poona
www.poonapalms.com.au
07 4129 8167 **HEMA 14 H4** 25 43 20 S 152 54 46 E

Port Douglas

388 BIG4 Port Douglas Glengarry Holiday Park
70 Mowbray River Rd. 8 Km S of PO
www.glengarrypark.com.au
07 4098 5922 **HEMA 21 B3** 16 33 18 S 145 28 24 E

389 Pandanus Caravan Park
107 Davidson St
07 4099 5944 **HEMA 21 A3** 16 29 41 S 145 27 49 E

390 Tropic Breeze Caravan Park
24 Davidson St
07 4099 5299 **HEMA 21 A3** 16 29 16 S 145 27 55 E

Preston

391 Taylorwood Tourist Park
670 Conway Rd
www.taylorwoodresort.com
0417 646 075 **HEMA 18 E5** 20 24 20 S 148 40 15 E

Proserpine

392 Gunna Go Caravan Park
13067 Bruce Hwy. 6 km N of PO
www.gunnagocaravanpark.weebly.com
07 4945 1540 **HEMA 18 E5** 20 21 06 S 148 33 22 E

393 O'Connell River Whitsunday Tourist Park
OConnell River, Bruce Hwy. 22 km S of PO
07 4947 5148 **HEMA 18 F5** 20 33 57 S 148 37 00 E

394 Proserpine Tourist Park
79-83 Anzac Rd. 1.3 Km W of PO
07 4945 0490 **HEMA 18 E5** 20 24 15 S 148 34 18 E

Proston

395 Proston Caravan Park
Boondooma Rd, Next to Showgrounds. Pay at Rural Supplies Store, Murphys Way. AH call for amenities key
07 4168 9000 **HEMA 35 B14** 26 09 39 S 151 35 55 E

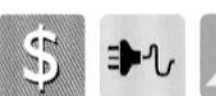

Quilpie

396 Channel Country Tourist Park & Spas
21 Chipu St
www.channelcountrytouristpark.com
07 4656 2087 **HEMA 33 C11** 26 37 01 S 144 15 51 E

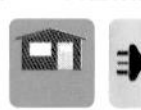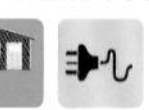

Rainbow Beach

397 Rainbow Beach Holiday Park
308 Carlo Rd, Carlo Point. 2.5 km W of PO
www.caravanparkescapes.com.au
07 5486 3200 **HEMA 14 K5** 25 53 59 S 153 03 36 E

398 Rainbow Beach Holiday Village
13 Rainbow Beach. 50m S of PO
www.rainbowbeachholidayvillage.com
07 5486 3222 **HEMA 14 K6** 25 54 12 S 153 05 35 E

Rathdowney

399 Rathdowney Caravan Park
Running Creek Rd, just E of the PO
0467 684 879 **HEMA 12 J5** 28 12 42 S 152 51 55 E

Ravenshoe

400 Tall Timbers Motel & Caravan Park
Kennedy Hwy
07 4097 6325 **HEMA 21 K3** 17 37 02 S 145 29 06 E

Richmond

401 Lakeview Caravan Park
109 Goldring St
07 4741 3772 **HEMA 26 K6** 20 44 06 S 143 08 46 E

Rochedale

402 Brisbane Gateway Resort
200 School Rd
www.gatewayvillage.com.au
07 3341 6333 **HEMA 4 G5** 27 35 25 S 153 06 34 E

Rockhampton

403 Capricorn Caves Tourist Park
30 Olsens Caves Rd. 23 km N of Rockhampton
07 4934 2883 **HEMA 16 B1** 23 09 57 S 150 29 26 E

404 Country Club for Accommodation
Bruce Hwy. Nth Rockhampton
www.overnightrockhampton.wordpress.com/
07 4936 1022 **HEMA 16 B2** 23 17 59 S 150 30 48 E

405 Discovery Holiday Parks Rockhampton
394 Yamba Rd (Bruce Hwy)
www.discoveryholidayparks.com.au
07 4926 3822 HEMA 16 B2 23 20 43 S 150 31 18 E

406 Parkhurst Motel & Caravan Park
Bruce Hwy. 8 km N of PO
07 4936 1126 HEMA 16 B2 23 17 50 S 150 30 46 E

407 Riverside Tourist Park
2 Reaney St. 800m from PO
www.riversiderockhampton.com.au
07 4922 3779 HEMA 16 B2 23 22 18 S 150 30 52 E

408 Southside Holiday Park
283 Lower Dawson Rd. 4.4 km SW of PO
www.southsidevillage.com.au
07 4927 3013 HEMA 16 B1 23 24 10 S 150 30 15 E

Rolleston

409 Rolleston Caravan Park
Cnr Comet St & Meteor St
07 4984 3145 HEMA 30 G7 24 27 54 S 148 37 21 E

Rollingstone

410 Rollingstone Beach Caravan Resort
14 Hencamp Creek Rd
www.rollingstonebeach.com.au
07 4770 7277 HEMA 19 F3 19 00 12 S 146 23 44 E

Roma

411 Roma Big Rig Tourist Park
4 McDowall St. 1 km from PO
www.bigrig.net.au
07 4622 2538 HEMA 35 C8 26 34 23 S 148 47 54 E

412 Villa Holiday Park
67-75 Northern Rd. 1.5 km N of Roma
www.villaholidaypark.com.au
07 4622 1309 HEMA 35 C8 26 33 38 S 148 47 09 E

Rosedale

413 Rosedale Royal Hotel & Caravan Park
2 Wills Rd
07 4156 5322 HEMA 16 F6 24 37 44 S 151 54 59 E

Rubyvale

414 Gemseekers Caravan Park
10 Vane Tempest Rd. 300m NW of PO
www.gemseekers.com.au
07 4985 4175 HEMA 30 E5 23 25 01 S 147 41 50 E
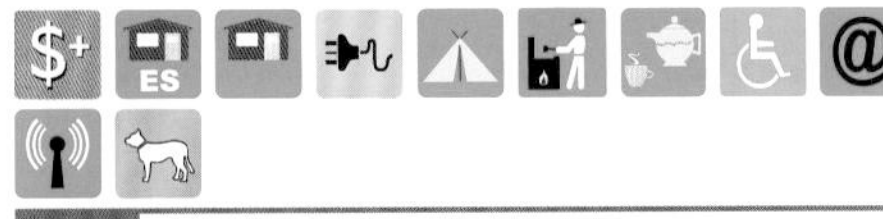

415 Rubyvale Caravan Park
16 Main St
www.rubyvalecaravanpark.com.au
07 4985 4118 HEMA 30 E5 23 25 08 S 147 41 52 E

Sandstone Point

416 Sandstone Point Holiday Resort
1800 Bribie Island Rd
www.sandstonepointholidayresort.com.au
07 3450 0732 HEMA 4 A6 27 04 38 S 153 08 28 E

Sapphire

417 Blue Gem Tourist Park
Main Rd
www.bluegemtouristpark.com.au
07 4985 4162 HEMA 30 F5 23 27 59 S 147 43 22 E
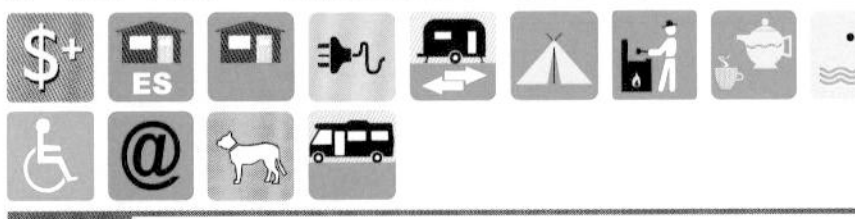

418 Sapphire Caravan Park
57 Sunrise Rd
www.sapphirecaravanpark.com.au
07 4985 4281 HEMA 30 F5 23 27 35 S 147 42 57 E

Sarina

419 Sarina Palms Caravan Village
31 Anzac St
www.sarinapalms.com.au
07 4956 1892 HEMA 17 B2 21 25 17 S 149 12 42 E

420 Tropicana Caravan Park
4 Greetham Street
07 4956 1480 HEMA 17 B2 21 25 36 S 149 12 27 E
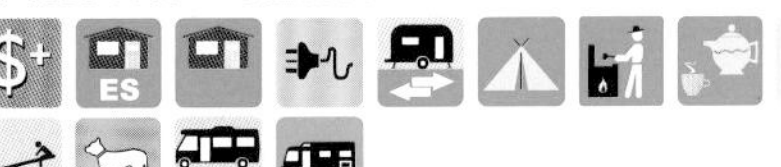

Scarborough

421 Scarborough Holiday Village
Reef Point Esplanade
www.scarboroughholidayvillage.com.au
07 3203 8864 HEMA 4 B5 27 11 34 S 153 06 39 E

Scarness

422 Discovery Boat Harbour Holiday Parks Hervey Bay
295 Boat Harbour Dr
www.discoveryholidayparks.com.au
07 4128 2762 HEMA 14 E4 25 17 24 S 152 51 00 E

423 Fraser Coast Top Tourist Caravan Park
21 Denmans Camp Rd
www.frasercoasttoptouristpark.com.au
07 4124 6237 HEMA 14 E4 25 17 11 S 152 51 39 E

424 Scarness Beachfront Tourist Park
Esplanade. 1.5 km W of PO
www.beachfronttouristparks.com.au
07 4128 1274 HEMA 14 E4 25 17 02 S 152 51 20 E

Sellheim

425 Burdekin Duck Roadhouse
Flinders Hwy
07 4787 3587 HEMA 19 K3 20 00 26 S 146 24 52 E

Seventeen Seventy

426 1770 Camp Grounds
641 Captain Cook Dr
www.1770campingground.com.au
07 4974 9286 HEMA 16 E5 24 09 45 S 151 53 06 E

427 Captain Cook Holiday Village
Captain Cook Dr
www.1770holidayvillage.com.au
07 4974 9219 HEMA 16 E5 24 10 59 S 151 53 08 E

Southport

428 Broadwater Tourist Park

169 Marine Pde
www.gctp.com.au/bwater
07 5667 2730 HEMA 5 D5 27 57 26 S 153 24 39 E

429 Southport Tourist Park

6 Frank St
07 5531 2281 HEMA 5 C5 27 57 16 S 153 24 28 E

Spring Creek

430 Spring Creek Caravan Park

New England Hwy. Via Allora
07 4697 3397 HEMA 12 H1 27 57 00 S 151 59 28 E

Springsure

431 Springsure Roadhouse & Caravan Park

86 William St
www.springsureroadhouseandcaravanpark.com.au
07 4984 1418 HEMA 30 G6 24 07 28 S 148 05 50 E

Springwood

432 Springtime Gardens Holiday Park

13 Old Chatswood Rd
www.springtimegardens.com.au/
07 3208 8184 HEMA 4 G6 27 38 05 S 153 08 16 E

St George

433 Kamarooka Tourist Park

56 Victoria St
07 4625 3120 HEMA 34 G7 28 02 01 S 148 35 12 E

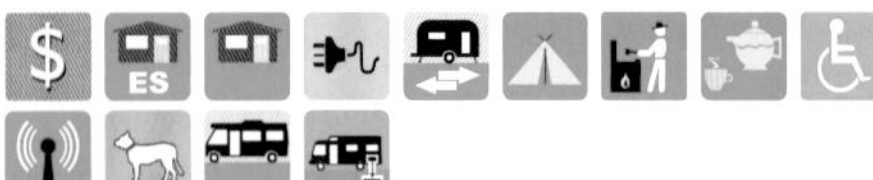

434 Pelican Rest Tourist Park

12022 Carnarvon Hwy
www.pelicanrest.com.au
07 4625 3398 HEMA 35 G8 28 01 37 S 148 35 58 E

435 St George Caravan Park

221 Victoria St
07 4625 5778 HEMA 34 G7 28 02 39 S 148 34 13 E

436 St George Riverfront Tourist Park

12747 Carnarvon Hwy 9 km N of St George
07 4625 5546 HEMA 35 F8 27 59 17 S 148 39 24 E

Stanthorpe

437 Blue Topaz Caravan Park & Camping Ground

26806 New England Hwy. Severnlea. 5 km S of PO
www.bluetopazcaravanpark.com
07 4683 5279 HEMA 36 H3 28 41 50 S 151 54 21 E

438 Country Style Tourist Accommodation Park

27156 New England Hwy. Glen Aplin. 8 km S of PO
www.countrystyleaccommodation.com.au
07 4683 4358 HEMA 36 H3 28 43 24 S 151 53 19 E

439 Sommerville Valley Tourist Park

63 Sommerville Lane. 12 km SE of Stanthorpe
www.sommervillevalley.com.au
07 4681 4200 HEMA 36 H3 28 42 36 S 152 00 13 E

440 Top of the Town Tourist Park

10 High St. 1.5 km N of PO
www.topoftown.com.au
07 4681 4888 HEMA 36 H3 28 38 40 S 151 56 50 E

441 The Happy Apple Resort

11 Munson Lane, Thulimbah
www.happyapple.com.au
07 4685 2880 HEMA 36 H3 28 32 57 S 151 56 50 E

Surat

442 Surat Caravan Park

47 Burrowes St. Pay at New Royal Hotel opposite
07 4626 5218 HEMA 35 D9 27 09 05 S 149 03 59 E

Tambo

443 Tambo Caravan Park

58 Arthur St
07 4654 6463 HEMA 29 H14 24 53 06 S 146 14 52 E

444 Tambo Mill Motel & Van Park

Landsborough Hwy
www.tambomill.com.au
07 4621 7000 HEMA 29 H14 24 53 01 S 146 15 08 E

Tanah Merah

445 Galaxy Caravan Park

3813 Pacific Hwy. Limited sites
07 3209 8434 HEMA 4 H6 27 39 36 S 153 10 04 E

Tannum Sands

446 Discovery Holiday Parks Tannum Sands

20 Millenium Esplanade. 1 km S of PO. Limited pet friendly sites, call ahead
www.discoveryholidayparks.com.au
07 4973 7201 HEMA 16 D4 23 57 18 S 151 22 37 E

Tara

447 Tara Caravan Park

78 Milne St
0455 211 173 HEMA 35 E12 27 16 30 S 150 27 06 E

Taylors Beach

448 Taylors Beach Holiday Park

87-99 John Dory St
www.taylorsbeach.net
07 4777 8560 HEMA 19 E3 18 37 27 S 146 19 33 E

Tewantin

449 Ingenia Holidays BIG4 Noosa

141 Cooroy Noosa Rd
www.ingeniaholidays.com.au/noosa/
07 5447 1712 HEMA 11 A12 26 23 53 S 153 00 55 E

450 Noosa Caravan Park

143 Moorindil St
www.noosacaravanpark.com.au
07 5449 8060 HEMA 11 A13 26 22 47 S 153 02 13 E

Texas

451 Texas Caravan Park
2 Avon St
www.texasvanpark.com.au
07 4653 1194 HEMA 35 J13 28 50 56 S 151 10 08 E

Thargomindah

452 Napunyah Caravan Park
Powell St
07 4621 8000 HEMA 33 F10 27 59 49 S 143 49 31 E

453 Thargomindah Explorers Caravan Park
88 Dowling St. 500m W of PO
07 4655 3307 HEMA 33 F10 27 59 51 S 143 49 11 E
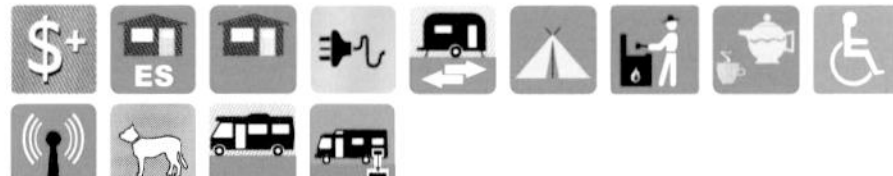

Tin Can Bay

454 Kingfisher Caravan Park
44 The Esplanade. 400m N of PO
www.kingfishercaravanpark.com.au
07 5486 4198 HEMA 14 K5 25 54 33 S 153 00 26 E

455 Tin Can Bay Tourist Park
54-74 Trevally St. 1.5 km S of PO
www.tincanbaytouristpark.com.au
07 5486 4411 HEMA 14 K5 25 55 23 S 153 00 23 E

Tinaroo Falls

456 Lake Tinaroo Holiday Park
Tinaroo Falls Dam Rd
07 4095 8232 HEMA 22 G3 17 10 19 S 145 32 43 E

Tivoli

457 Ipswich Caravan Village
95 Mt Crosby Rd. Limited sites
www.ipswichcaravanvillage.com
07 3281 7951 HEMA 6 B4 27 35 09 S 152 46 32 E

Tolga

458 Tolga Cabins & Van Park
Tate Rd, off Kennedy Hwy
0427 775 802 HEMA 22 J2 17 13 41 S 145 28 44 E

Toogoom

459 Serenity Caravan Park
39 Moreton St
07 4128 0164 HEMA 14 E3 25 14 52 S 152 39 47 E

Toorbul

460 Toorbul Caravan Park
120 The Esplanade
www.moretonbay.qld.gov.au
07 5498 8701 HEMA 9 A9 27 01 53 S 153 05 48 E

Toowoomba

461 BIG4 Toowoomba Garden City Holiday Park
34A Eiser St. 3 km S of PO
www.big4toowoombagchp.com.au
07 4635 1747 HEMA 12 F1 27 35 15 S 151 56 10 E

462 Jolly Swagman Caravan Park
47 Kitchener St. 1 km SE of PO
www.swagmanpark.com
07 4632 8735 HEMA 12 F1 27 34 09 S 151 57 48 E

463 Toowoomba Motor Village
821 Ruthven St. Kearney Springs
www.toowoombamotorvillage.com.au
07 4635 8186 HEMA 12 F1 27 35 17 S 151 56 54 E

Torquay

464 Discovery Parks Fraser Street
20 Fraser St
www.discoveryholidayparks.com.au
07 4124 9999 HEMA 14 E4 25 17 15 S 152 52 20 E

465 Ingenia Holidays Harvey Bay
105 Truro St. 1 km E of PO
www.ingeniaholidays.com.au
07 4125 1103 HEMA 14 E4 25 17 11 S 152 52 49 E

466 Lazy Acres Caravan Park
91 Exeter St. 1.2 km S of PO
www.lazyacres.com.au
07 4125 3815 HEMA 14 E4 25 17 41 S 152 52 11 E

467 Palms Caravan Park
67 Truro St. 600m SE of PO
www.palmsherveybay.com.au
07 4125 1704 HEMA 14 E4 25 17 13 S 152 52 35 E

468 Shelly Beach Caravan Park
61 Ocean St
07 4125 1105 HEMA 14 E4 25 17 06 S 152 52 45 E

469 Torquay Beachfront Caravan Park
The Esplanade. 500m E of PO.
www.beachfronttouristparks.com.au
07 4125 1578 HEMA 14 E4 25 17 02 S 152 52 27 E

Torrens Creek

470 Exchange Hotel Caravan Park
34 Flinders Hwy
07 4795 5990 HEMA 27 K8 20 46 12 S 145 01 09 E

Townsville

471 BIG4 Townsville Woodlands Holiday Park
548 Bruce Hwy. 15 km N of PO
www.big4woodlands.com.au
07 4751 6955 HEMA 19 G4 19 14 23 S 146 39 51 E

472 BIG4 Walkabout Palms Townsville
6 University Rd, Wulguru. 7 km S of PO
www.discoveryholidayparks.com.au
07 4778 2480 HEMA 19 G5 19 19 04 S 146 48 43 E

473 Black River Stadium Caravan Park
772 Black River Rd
www.blackriverstadium.com.au
07 4788 8322 HEMA 19 G4 19 17 19 S 146 36 03 E

474 Bush Oasis Caravan Park
1 Muntalunga Dr, 18 km S of PO
www.bushoasiscaravanpark.com.au
07 4778 8301 HEMA 19 H5 19 22 30 S 146 54 14 E

475 Coconut Glen Van Village
910 Ingham Rd
www.coconutglen.com
07 4774 5101 HEMA 19 G4 19 15 44 S 146 42 50 E
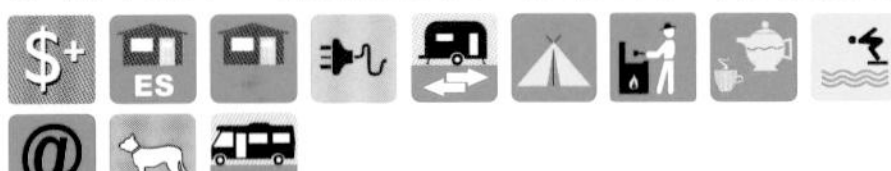

476 Coral Coast Tourist Park
547 Ingham Rd
www.coralcoastpark.com.au
07 4774 5205 HEMA 19 G4 19 15 43 S 146 44 53 E

477 Riverside Convention Centre Seventh Day Adventist
55 Leopold St. CLOSED Friday - Sunday
www.riverscc.com.au
07 4779 6708 HEMA 19 G5 19 18 20 S 146 46 04 E

478 Rowes Bay Caravan Park
46 Heatleys Pde
www.rowesbaycp.com.au
07 4771 3576 HEMA 19 G5 19 14 30 S 146 47 29 E

479 Secura Lifestyle Magnetic Gateway Townsville
88 Minehane St, Cluden
www.securalifestyle.com.au
07 4778 2412 HEMA 19 G5 19 19 11 S 146 50 08 E

480 Secura Lifestyle The Lakes Townsville
196 Woolcock St, Currajong. 2.5 km SW of PO
www.securalifestyle.com.au/parks/lakes/
07 4725 1577 HEMA 19 G5 19 16 17 S 146 47 03 E

481 Town & Country Caravan Park
16 Kings Rd. West End
07 4772 1487 HEMA 19 G5 19 16 09 S 146 47 35 E

482 Townsville Tourist & Lifestyle Village
405 Hervey Range Rd
www.townsvilletouristvillage.com.au
07 4773 2419 HEMA 19 G4 19 19 06 S 146 41 28 E

Tully

483 Googarra Beach Caravan Park
7 Tully Heads Rd. 16 km E of PO
www.googarrabeach.com.au
07 4066 9325 HEMA 19 B2 18 00 06 S 146 03 13 E

Undara

484 Undara Experience
Georgetown - Mount Garnet Rd, Undara Volcanic National Park
www.undara.com.au
07 4097 1900 HEMA 27 F8 18 12 07 S 144 34 21 E

Urangan

485 Harbour View Caravan Park
1 Jetty Rd. 1.8 km SE of PO
www.caravanparkherveybay.net.au
07 4128 9374 HEMA 14 E4 25 17 41 S 152 54 27 E

486 Hervey Bay Caravan Park
85 Margaret St. 1 km NW of PO
www.hervey-bay-park.com.au
07 4128 9553 HEMA 14 E4 25 17 24 S 152 53 20 E

487 Pier Caravan Park
Cnr King & Pier Street
www.caravanparkherveybay.com.au
1300 743 742 HEMA 14 E4 25 17 06 S 152 54 06 E

488 Windmill Caravan Park
17 Elizabeth St. 1 km N of PO
www.windmillpark.com.au
07 4128 9267 HEMA 14 E4 25 16 59 S 152 53 51 E

Walkamin

489 Walkamin Central Van Park
Wattle St
07 4093 3561 HEMA 22 G1 17 07 56 S 145 25 41 E

Warwick

490 Lake Leslie Tourist Park
113 Saddledam Rd. Lake Leslie Dam via Warwick
www.lakeleslietouristpark.com.au
07 4661 9166 HEMA 12 J1 28 13 37 S 151 55 29 E

491 Rose City Caravan Park
Cnr Glengallan Rd & New England Hwy
07 4661 1662 HEMA 12 J2 28 11 36 S 152 02 39 E

492 Warwick Freedom Lifestyle Park
98 Wallace St, New England Hwy. 2 km S of PO
www.warwick.freedomlifestyleparks.com.au
07 4661 2874 HEMA 12 J2 28 13 44 S 152 01 06 E

Willowbank

493 Willowbank Caravan Village
Coopers Rd
07 5464 3166 HEMA 6 B3 27 40 14 S 152 41 20 E

Willows Gemfields

494 Gem Air Village Caravan Park
Village Rd
www.gemairvillage.com
07 4985 5124 HEMA 30 F5 23 44 19 S 147 32 16 E

495 Willows Gemfield Caravan Park
30 Willows Rd
07 4985 5128 HEMA 30 F5 23 44 32 S 147 32 16 E

Windorah

496 Windorah Caravan Park
Albert St, caretaker collects fees
07 4656 3063 HEMA 29 J8 25 25 13 S 142 39 09 E

Winton

497 Matilda Country Tourist Park
43 Chirnside St
www.matildacountrytouristpark.com
07 4657 1607 HEMA 29 D9 22 22 47 S 143 02 32 E

498 Pelican Fuel Stop & Caravan Park
92 Elderslie St
07 4657 1478 HEMA 29 D9 22 23 25 S 143 02 05 E

499 Tattersalls Hotel Van Park
Werna St, next to hotel. Pay fees at hotel
07 4657 1309 HEMA 29 D9 22 23 25 S 143 02 11 E

Wonga Beach

500 Pinnacle Village Holiday Park
40 Vixies Rd
www.pinnaclevillage.com
07 4098 7566 HEMA 20 D3 16 19 50 S 145 25 14 E

501 Wonga Beach Caravan Park
The Esplanade
07 4098 7514 HEMA 20 D3 16 20 48 S 145 24 53 E

Woodford

502 Neurum Creek Bush Retreat
268 Rasmussen Rd
www.ncbr.com.au
07 5496 3692 HEMA 8 A3 26 59 54 S 152 41 12 E

Woodgate

503 Woodgate Beach Hotel Tourist Park
195 Esplanade
07 4126 8988 HEMA 14 D2 25 05 32 S 152 33 14 E

504 Woodgate Beach Tourist Park
88 Esplanade
www.woodgatebeachtouristpark.com
07 4126 8802 HEMA 14 D2 25 06 38 S 152 34 02 E

Woombye

505 Rainforest Holiday Village
557 Nambour Connection Rd. 2.5 km S of PO
www.rainforestholidayvillage.com.au
07 5442 1153 HEMA 11 E12 26 38 43 S 152 57 41 E

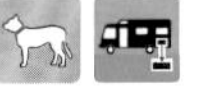

Wowan

506 Wowan Caravan Park
Don St
07 4937 1542 HEMA 16 D1 23 54 42 S 150 11 39 E

Yandina

507 Yandina Caravan Park
1519 Nambour North Connection Rd
www.yandinacaravanpark.com/
07 5446 7332 HEMA 11 C12 26 34 02 S 152 57 18 E

Yarraman

508 Yarraman Caravan Park
12121 D'Aguilar Hwy
www.yarramancp.com.au
07 4163 8185 HEMA 12 C1 26 50 03 S 151 58 29 E

Yeppoon

509 Beachside Caravan Park
Farnborough Rd
07 4939 3738 HEMA 16 B2 23 07 11 S 150 44 57 E

510 BIG4 Capricorn Palms Holiday Village
Wildin Way. Mulambin Beach
www.big4.com.au
07 4933 6144 HEMA 16 B2 23 11 06 S 150 47 23 E

511 Blue Dolphin Caravan Park
74 Whitman St
07 4939 3140 HEMA 16 B2 23 07 59 S 150 44 38 E

512 Maine Caravan Park
70 Queen St, entry via John St
07 4938 3099 HEMA 16 B2 23 07 47 S 150 44 31 E

513 Poinciana Tourist Park
9 Scenic Hwy
www.poincianatouristpark.com
07 4939 1601 HEMA 16 B2 23 08 41 S 150 45 28 E

Yowah Opal Field

514 Artesian Waters Caravan Park
10 Bluff Rd
www.yowahcaravanpark.com
07 4655 4953 HEMA 33 F12 27 58 15 S 144 38 17 E

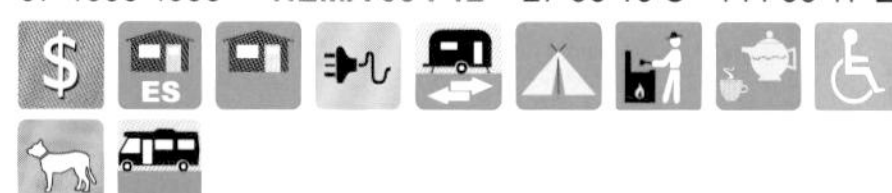

Yungaburra

515 Lakeside Motor Inn & Caravan Park
2 Tinaburra Drive
07 4095 3563 HEMA 22 J4 17 15 05 S 145 35 00 E

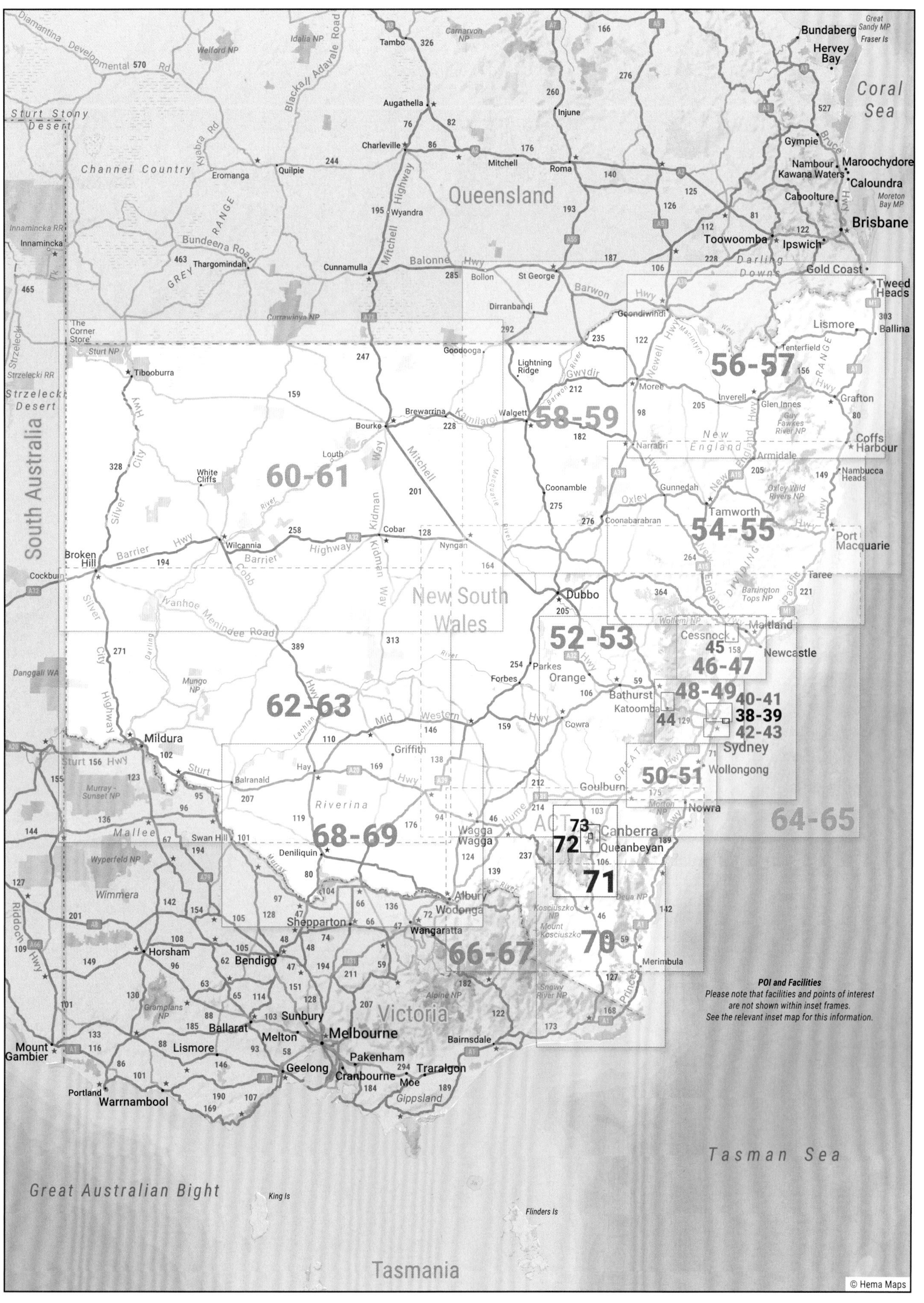
0
200
400
km
Queensland
New South Wales
Victoria
South Australia
ACT
Tasmania
Coral Sea
Tasman Sea
Great Australian Bight
Channel Country
Sturt Stony Desert
Strzelecki Desert
Riverina
Mallee
Wimmera
Gippsland
New England
Darling Downs
Bundaberg
Hervey Bay
Gympie
Maroochydore
Nambour
Kawana Waters
Caloundra
Caboolture
Brisbane
Ipswich
Toowoomba
Gold Coast
Tweed Heads
Lismore
Ballina
Tenterfield
Grafton
Glen Innes
Inverell
Moree
Goondiwindi
Coffs Harbour
Armidale
Nambucca Heads
Tamworth
Gunnedah
Narrabri
Port Macquarie
Taree
Coonabarabran
Coonamble
Walgett
Lightning Ridge
Dubbo
Maitland
Cessnock
Newcastle
Bathurst
Katoomba
Orange
Parkes
Forbes
Cowra
Sydney
Wollongong
Goulburn
Nowra
Canberra
Queanbeyan
Merimbula
Wagga Wagga
Griffith
Hay
Balranald
Deniliquin
Albury
Wodonga
Wangaratta
Shepparton
Mildura
Swan Hill
Horsham
Bendigo
Ballarat
Sunbury
Melton
Melbourne
Geelong
Pakenham
Cranbourne
Moe
Traralgon
Bairnsdale
Lismore
Mount Gambier
Portland
Warrnambool
Broken Hill
Cockburn
Wilcannia
White Cliffs
Tibooburra
The Corner Store
Bourke
Brewarrina
Cobar
Nyngan
Louth
Goodooga
Dirranbandi
St George
Bollon
Cunnamulla
Thargomindah
Innamincka
Eromanga
Quilpie
Charleville
Augathella
Tambo
Mitchell
Roma
Injune
Wyandra
56-57
58-59
60-61
54-55
52-53
45
46-47
48-49
44
40-41
38-39
42-43
50-51
64-65
62-63
68-69
66-67
70
71
72
73
POI and Facilities
Please note that facilities and points of interest are not shown within inset frames.
See the relevant inset map for this information.
© Hema Maps

Inner Sydney

0 0.5 1 km

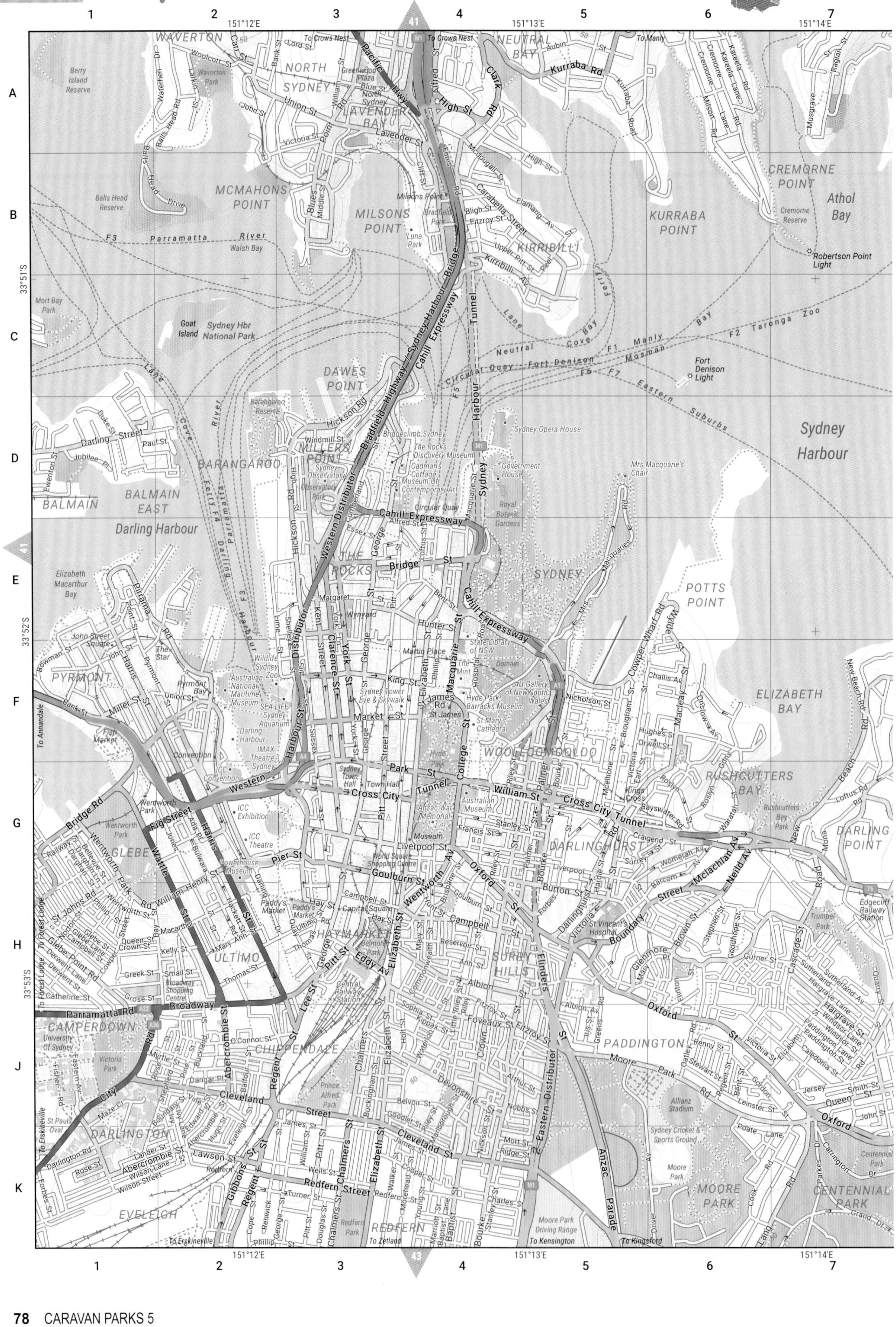

1 2 3 4 5 6 7

151°12'E 151°13'E 151°14'E

A B C D E F G H J K

33°51'S 33°52'S 33°53'S

41
43

WAVERTON
NORTH SYDNEY
LAVENDER BAY
NEUTRAL BAY
MCMAHONS POINT
MILSONS POINT
KIRRIBILLI
KURRABA POINT
CREMORNE POINT
Athol Bay
Robertson Point Light
Berry Island Reserve
Balls Head Reserve
Parramatta River
Walsh Bay
Mort Bay Park
Goat Island
Sydney Hbr National Park
DAWES POINT
Fort Denison Light
Sydney Harbour
Sydney Opera House
Government House
Royal Botanic Gardens
Mrs Macquarie's Chair
BARANGAROO
MILLERS POINT
BALMAIN
BALMAIN EAST
Darling Harbour
THE ROCKS
SYDNEY
POTTS POINT
ELIZABETH BAY
Elizabeth Macarthur Bay
PYRMONT
WOOLLOOMOOLOO
RUSHCUTTERS BAY
DARLING POINT
DARLINGHURST
GLEBE
ULTIMO
HAYMARKET
SURRY HILLS
PADDINGTON
CAMPERDOWN
University of Sydney
CHIPPENDALE
DARLINGTON
EVELEIGH
REDFERN
Allianz Stadium
Sydney Cricket & Sports Ground
MOORE PARK
CENTENNIAL PARK
Edgecliff Railway Station
Central Railway Station
Sydney Harbour Bridge
Cahill Expressway
Western Distributor
Eastern Distributor
Cross City Tunnel
Anzac Parade
Parramatta Rd
Broadway
Cleveland Street
Oxford St
William St
To Crows Nest
To Manly
To Annandale
To Forest Lodge
To Erskineville
To Zetland
To Kensington
To Kingsford

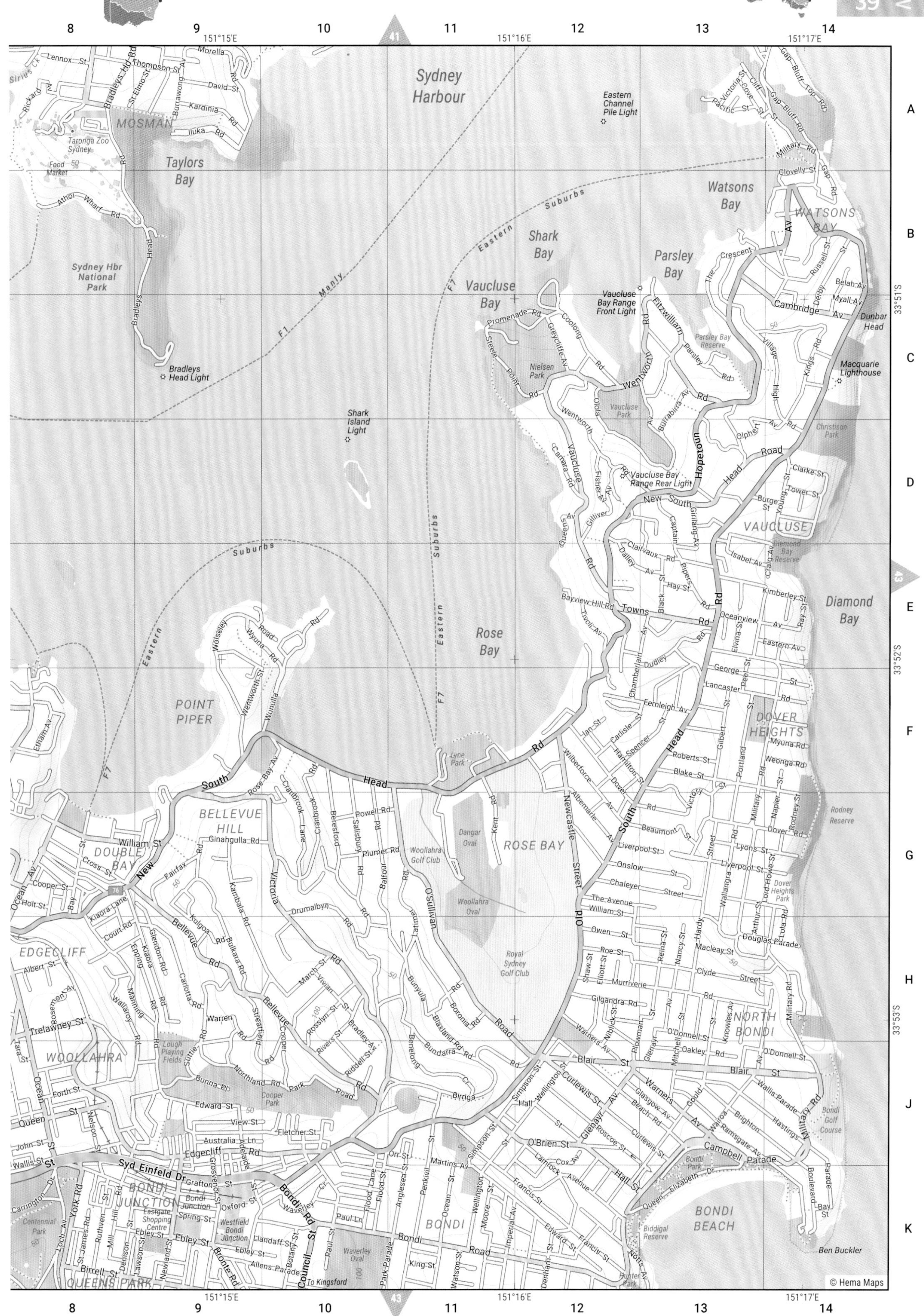
8
9
10
11
12
13
14
151°15'E
151°16'E
151°17'E
41
43
A
B
C
D
E
F
G
H
J
K
33°51'S
33°52'S
33°53'S
Sydney Harbour
Taylors Bay
MOSMAN
Taronga Zoo Sydney
Food Market
Sydney Hbr National Park
Bradleys Head Light
Eastern Channel Pile Light
Watsons Bay
WATSONS BAY
Shark Bay
Parsley Bay
Vaucluse Bay
Vaucluse Bay Range Front Light
Dunbar Head
Macquarie Lighthouse
Nielsen Park
Parsley Bay Reserve
Vaucluse Park
Christison Park
Shark Island Light
Vaucluse Bay Range Rear Light
VAUCLUSE
Diamond Bay Reserve
Diamond Bay
Rose Bay
POINT PIPER
Lyne Park
BELLEVUE HILL
DOUBLE BAY
ROSE BAY
Dangar Oval
Woollahra Golf Club
Woollahra Oval
Royal Sydney Golf Club
DOVER HEIGHTS
Rodney Reserve
Dover Heights Park
NORTH BONDI
EDGECLIFF
WOOLLAHRA
Lough Playing Fields
Cooper Park
Bondi Golf Course
Bondi Park
BONDI BEACH
Bidigal Reserve
Ben Buckler
Hunter Park
BONDI
BONDI JUNCTION
Eastgate Shopping Centre
Westfield Bondi Junction
Centennial Park
Waverley Oval
QUEENS PARK
To Kingsford
Manly
F1
F7
Eastern Suburbs
South Head Rd
New South Head Rd
Old South Head Rd
Syd Einfeld Dr
Bondi Rd
Campbell Parade
Military Rd
Bellevue Rd
Victoria Rd
O'Sullivan Rd
Newcastle Street
Towns Rd
Hopetoun Av
Vaucluse Rd
Wentworth Rd
Blair St
Curlewis St
Warners Av
© Hema Maps

Northern Sydney Suburbs

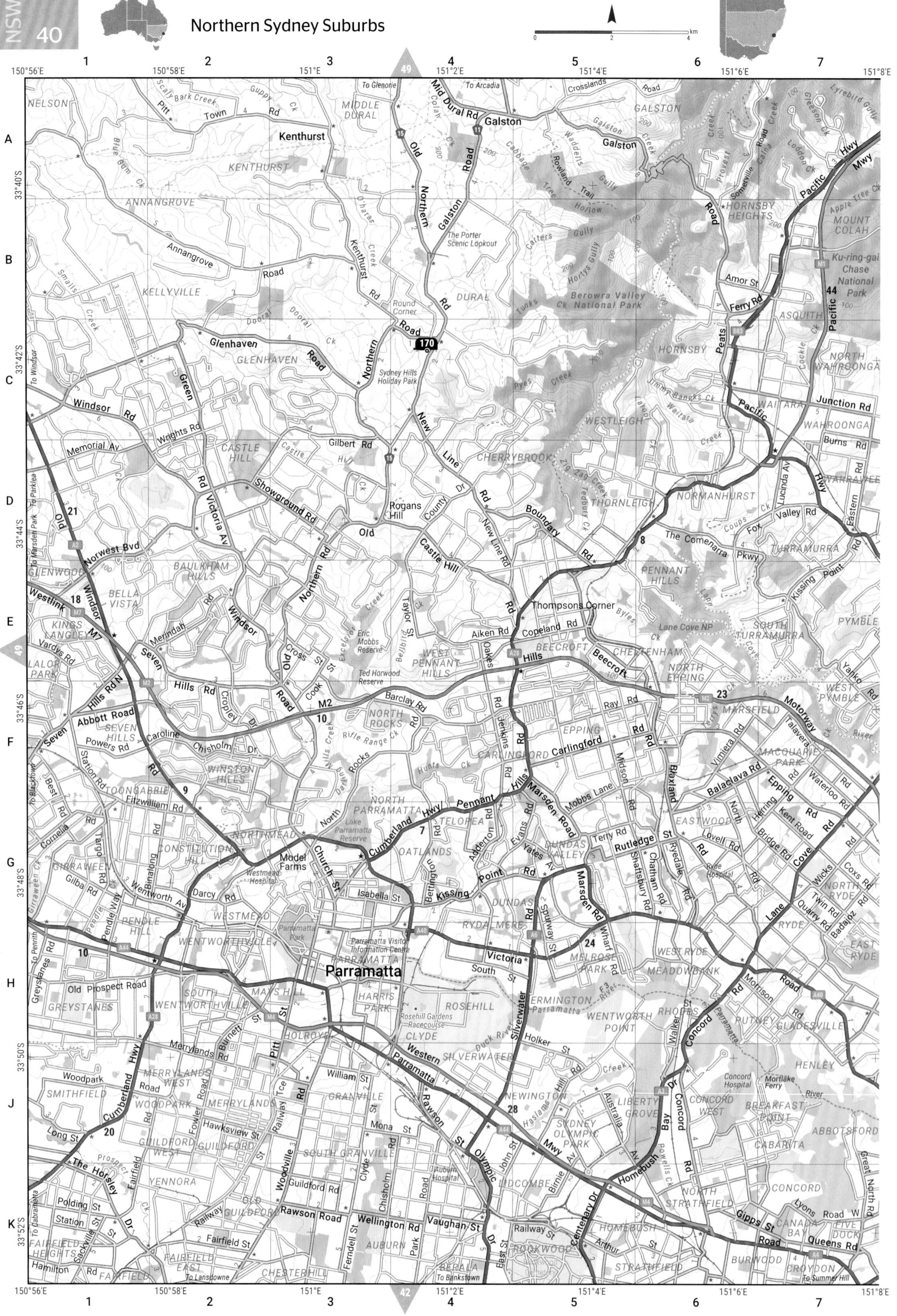

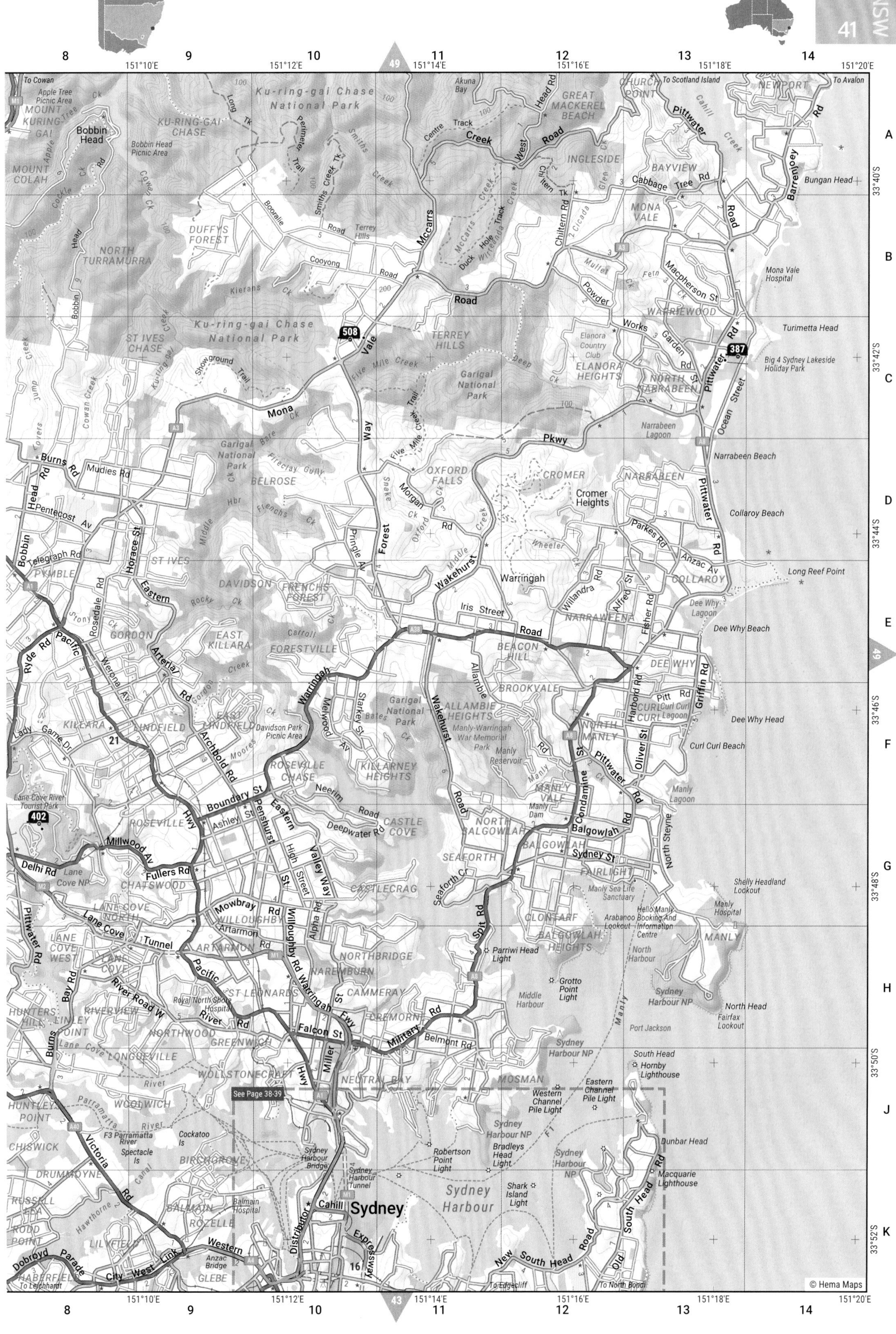

Ku-ring-gai Chase National Park
Garigal National Park
Sydney Harbour
Sydney
MOUNT KURING-GAI
Bobbin Head
MOUNT COLAH
NORTH TURRAMURRA
DUFFYS FOREST
TERREY HILLS
INGLESIDE
MONA VALE
BAYVIEW
NEWPORT
CHURCH POINT
GREAT MACKEREL BEACH
WARRIEWOOD
ELANORA HEIGHTS
NORTH NARRABEEN
NARRABEEN
COLLAROY
CROMER
OXFORD FALLS
BELROSE
ST IVES
ST IVES CHASE
PYMBLE
GORDON
DAVIDSON
FRENCHS FOREST
FORESTVILLE
EAST KILLARA
KILLARA
LINDFIELD
EAST LINDFIELD
BEACON HILL
BROOKVALE
ALLAMBIE HEIGHTS
NARRAWEENA
DEE WHY
CURL CURL
NORTH MANLY
MANLY VALE
KILLARNEY HEIGHTS
ROSEVILLE
ROSEVILLE CHASE
CASTLE COVE
CASTLECRAG
NORTH BALGOWLAH
BALGOWLAH
SEAFORTH
FAIRLIGHT
CLONTARF
BALGOWLAH HEIGHTS
MANLY
CHATSWOOD
WILLOUGHBY
ARTARMON
NORTHBRIDGE
NAREMBURN
CAMMERAY
CREMORNE
ST LEONARDS
LANE COVE
LANE COVE NORTH
LANE COVE WEST
RIVERVIEW
NORTHWOOD
GREENWICH
LONGUEVILLE
WOLLSTONECRAFT
NEUTRAL BAY
MOSMAN
HUNTERS HILL
LINLEY POINT
WOOLWICH
HUNTLEYS POINT
CHISWICK
DRUMMOYNE
BIRCHGROVE
BALMAIN
ROZELLE
RUSSELL LEA
RODD POINT
LILYFIELD
GLEBE
HABERFIELD
To Cowan
To Scotland Island
To Avalon
To Leichhardt
To Edgecliff
To North Bondi
See Page 38-39
Bungan Head
Mona Vale Hospital
Turimetta Head
Big 4 Sydney Lakeside Holiday Park
Narrabeen Lagoon
Narrabeen Beach
Collaroy Beach
Long Reef Point
Dee Why Lagoon
Dee Why Beach
Dee Why Head
Curl Curl Beach
Manly Lagoon
Shelly Headland Lookout
Manly Hospital
North Head
Fairfax Lookout
Port Jackson
South Head
Hornby Lighthouse
Dunbar Head
Macquarie Lighthouse
Sydney Harbour NP
Middle Harbour
Grotto Point Light
Parriwi Head Light
Western Channel Pile Light
Eastern Channel Pile Light
Bradleys Head Light
Robertson Point Light
Shark Island Light
Sydney Harbour Bridge
Sydney Harbour Tunnel
Cockatoo Is
Spectacle Is
F3 Parramatta River
Balmain Hospital
Royal North Shore Hospital
Lane Cove NP
Lane Cove River Tourist Park
Davidson Park Picnic Area
Manly-Warringah War Memorial Park
Manly Reservoir
Manly Dam
Manly Sea Life Sanctuary
Arabanoo Lookout
Hello Manly Booking And Information Centre
Elanora Country Club
Cromer Heights
Warringah
Apple Tree Picnic Area
Bobbin Head Picnic Area
Akuna Bay
Pittwater Rd
Mona Vale Rd
Wakehurst Pkwy
Forest Way
Warringah Rd
Pacific Hwy
Military Rd
Spit Rd
Victoria Rd
Cahill Expressway
Western Distributor
City West Link
Dobroyd Parade
Lane Cove Tunnel
Falcon St
Miller St
Boundary St
Eastern Arterial Rd
Archbold Rd
Burns Rd
Mowbray Rd
Epping Rd
Barrenjoey Rd
Ocean Street
Condamine St
Sydney St
Balgowlah Rd
Harbord Rd
Old South Head Rd
New South Head Road
508
387
402
21
16
151°10'E
151°12'E
151°14'E
151°16'E
151°18'E
151°20'E
33°40'S
33°42'S
33°44'S
33°46'S
33°48'S
33°50'S
33°52'S
49
43
© Hema Maps

Southern Sydney Suburbs

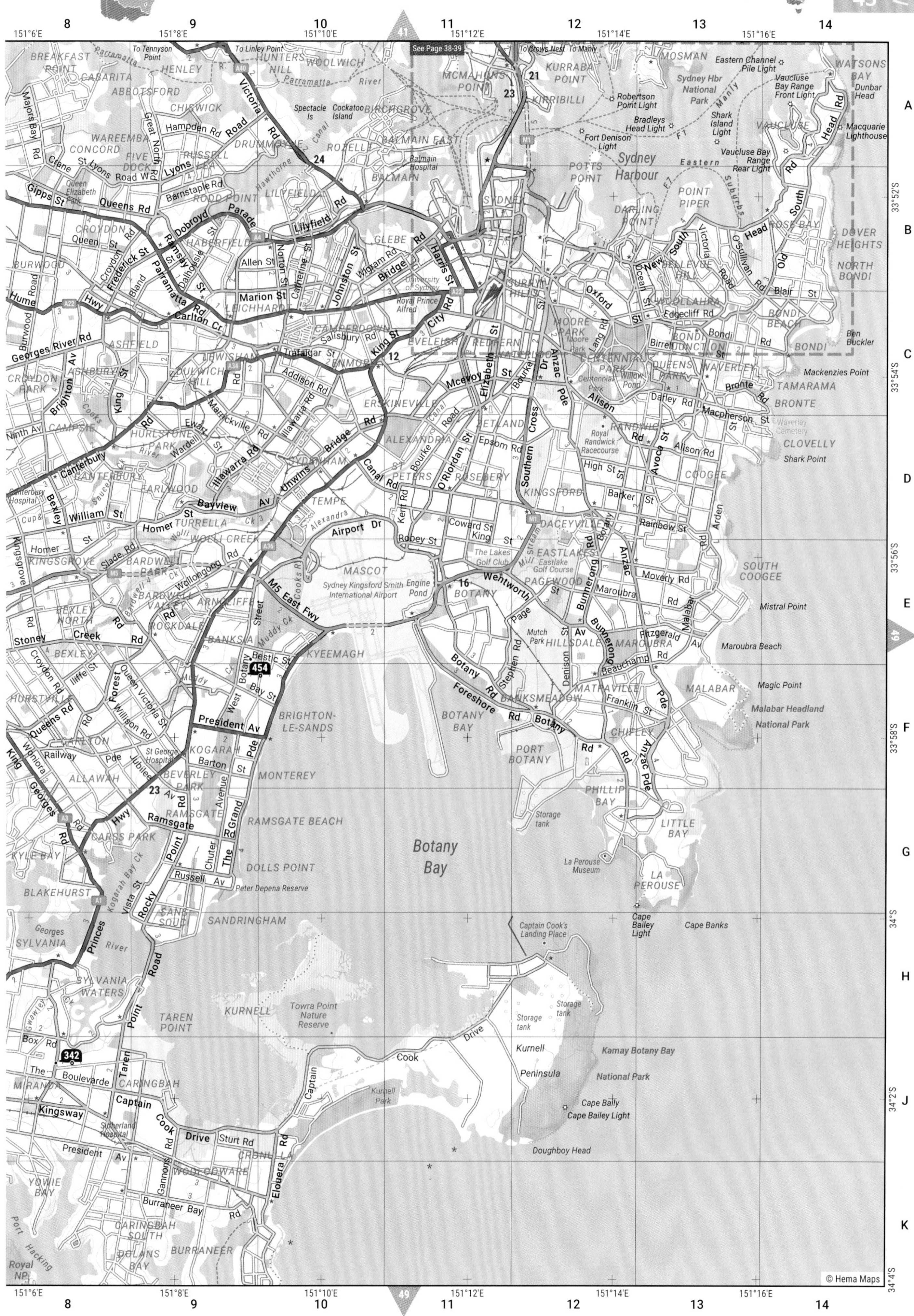
Botany Bay
Sydney Harbour
See Page 38-39
© Hema Maps

Bells Line Of Road to Wentworth Falls

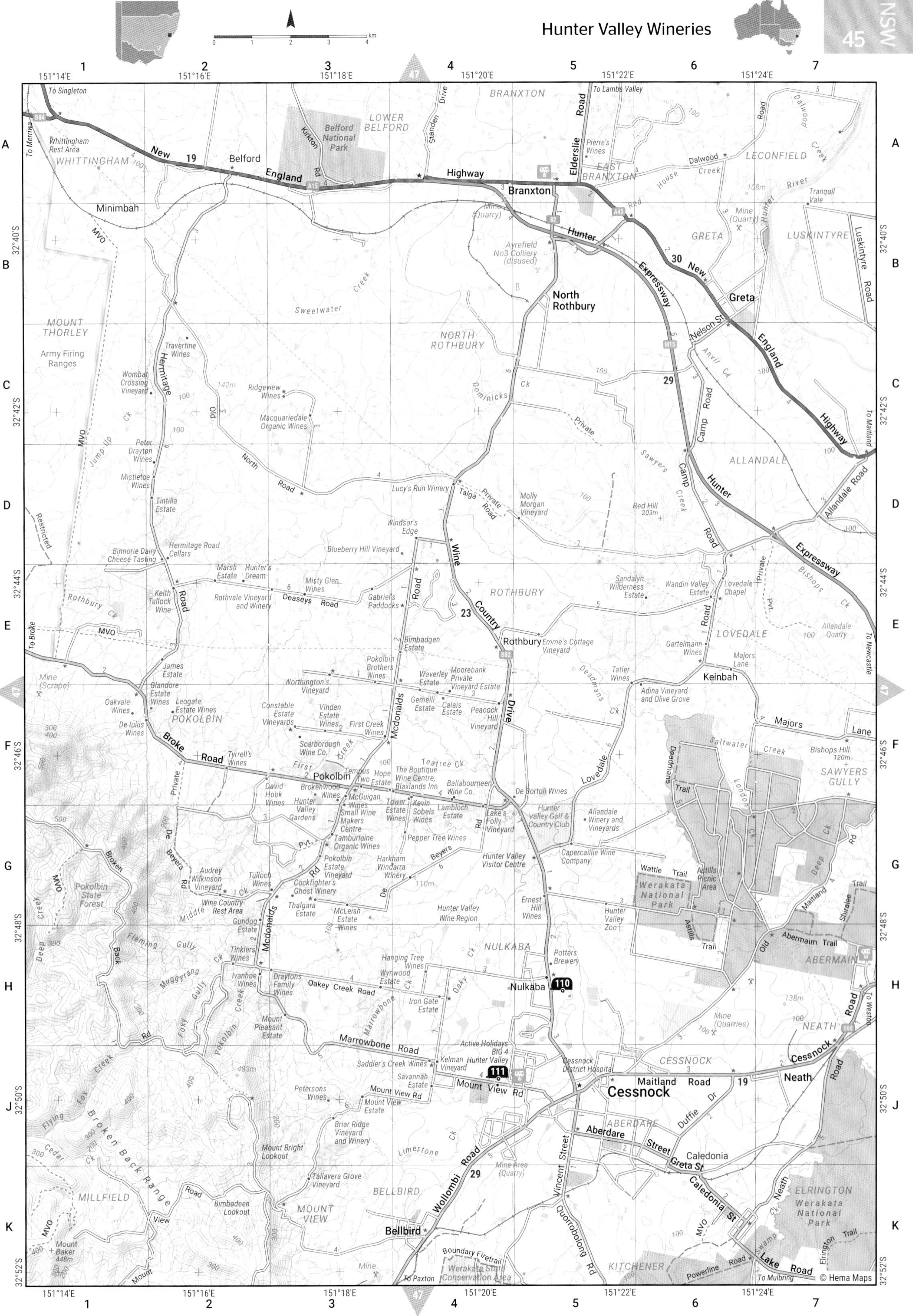
To Singleton
New England Highway
Belford
Belford National Park
LOWER BELFORD
BRANXTON
Branxton
To Lambs Valley
Eldersile Road
Pierre's Wines
EAST BRANXTON
Dalwood
LECONFIELD
Tranquil Vale
LUSKINTYRE
Luskintyre Road
Hunter River
Whittingham Rest Area
WHITTINGHAM
Minimbah
To Merriwa
Mine (Quarry)
Ayrefield No3 Colliery (disused)
Hunter Expressway
North Rothbury
GRETA
Greta
Nelson St
MOUNT THORLEY
Army Firing Ranges
Travertine Wines
Wombat Crossing Vineyard
Hermitage Road
Ridgeview Wines
Macquariedale Organic Wines
NORTH ROTHBURY
Dominicks Ck
Sweetwater Creek
Camp Road
Peter Drayton Wines
Mistletoe Wines
Tintilla Estate
North Road
Lucy's Run Winery
Talga Road
Molly Morgan Vineyard
Red Hill 203m
ALLANDALE
Allandale Road
To Maitland
Restricted
Binnorie Dairy Cheese Tasting
Hermitage Road Cellars
Windsor's Edge
Blueberry Hill Vineyard
Wine Country Drive
Marsh Estate
Hunter's Dream
Rothvale Vineyard and Winery
Deaseys Road
Misty Glen Wines
Gabriel's Paddocks
Keith Tulloch Wine
Rothbury Ck
ROTHBURY
Sandalyn Wilderness Estate
Wandin Valley Estate
Lovedale Chapel
LOVEDALE
Bishops Ck
Allandale Quarry
To Newcastle
To Broke
Bimbadgen Estate
Rothbury
Emma's Cottage Vineyard
Gartelmann Wines
Majors Lane
James Estate
Pokolbin Brothers Wines
Worthington's Vineyard
Waverley Estate
Moorebank Private Vineyard Estate
Tatler Wines
Keinbah
Adina Vineyard and Olive Grove
Mine (Scrape)
Glandore Estate Wines
Oakvale Wines
Leogate Estate Wines
POKOLBIN
De Iuliis Wines
Constable Estate Vineyards
Vinden Estate Wines
Gemelli Estate
Calais Estate
Peacock Hill Vineyard
First Creek Wines
Majors Lane
Saltwater Creek
Bishops Hill 120m
SAWYERS GULLY
Broke Road
Tyrrell's Wines
Scarborough Wine Co.
Pokolbin
Tempus Two
Hope Estate
The Boutique Wine Centre, Blaxlands Inn
Ballabourneen Wine Co.
De Bortoli Wines
Deadmans Trail
London Ck
David Hook Wines
Brokenwood Wines
McGuigan Wines
Hunter Valley Gardens
Small Wine Makers Centre
Tower Estate Wines
Kevin Sobels Wines
Lambloch Estate
Lake's Folly Vineyard
Hunter Valley Golf & Country Club
Allandale Winery and Vineyards
Tamburlaine Organic Wines
Pepper Tree Wines
Capercaillie Wine Company
Pokolbin State Forest
Broken Back
Audrey Wilkinson Vineyard
Tulloch Wines
Pokolbin Estate Vineyard
Harkham Windarra Winery
Hunter Valley Visitor Centre
Wattle Trail
Astills Picnic Area
Werakata National Park
Wine Country Rest Area
Cockfighter's Ghost Winery
Thalgara Estate
McLeish Estate Wines
Ernest Hill Wines
Hunter Valley Zoo
Hunter Valley Wine Region
Astills Trail
Abermain Trail
ABERMAIN
Gundog Estate
Middle Ck
Fleming Gully
Tinklers Wines
NULKABA
Potters Brewery
Hanging Tree Wines
Wynwood Estate
Ivanhoe Wines
Draytons Family Wines
Oakey Creek Road
Nulkaba
110
Iron Gate Estate
Muggyrang Gully
Foxy Gully
Mount Pleasant Estate
Mine (Quarries)
NEATH
To Weston
Marrowbone Road
Active Holidays BIG 4 Hunter Valley
Saddler's Creek Wines
Kelman Vineyard
111
Savannah Estate
Cessnock District Hospital
CESSNOCK
Maitland Road
Cessnock Road
Neath
483m
Petersons Wines
Mount View Rd
Mount View Estate
Cessnock
ABERDARE
Aberdare Street
Duffie Dr
Flying Fox Creek
Broken Back Range
Briar Ridge Vineyard and Winery
Mount Bright Lookout
Limestone Ck
Caledonia
Greta St
Cedar Ck
Wollombi Road
Mine Area (Quarry)
Tallavera Grove Vineyard
Vincent Street
Caledonia St
ELRINGTON
Werakata National Park
MILLFIELD
Road
Bimbadeen Lookout
MOUNT VIEW
BELLBIRD
Neath Road
View
Bellbird
Quorrobolong Rd
Mount Baker 448m
Boundary Firetrail
Werakata State Conservation Area
Mine
To Paxton
KITCHENER
Powerline Road
Lake Road
Elrington Trail
To Mulbring
© Hema Maps

Putty Road to Newcastle

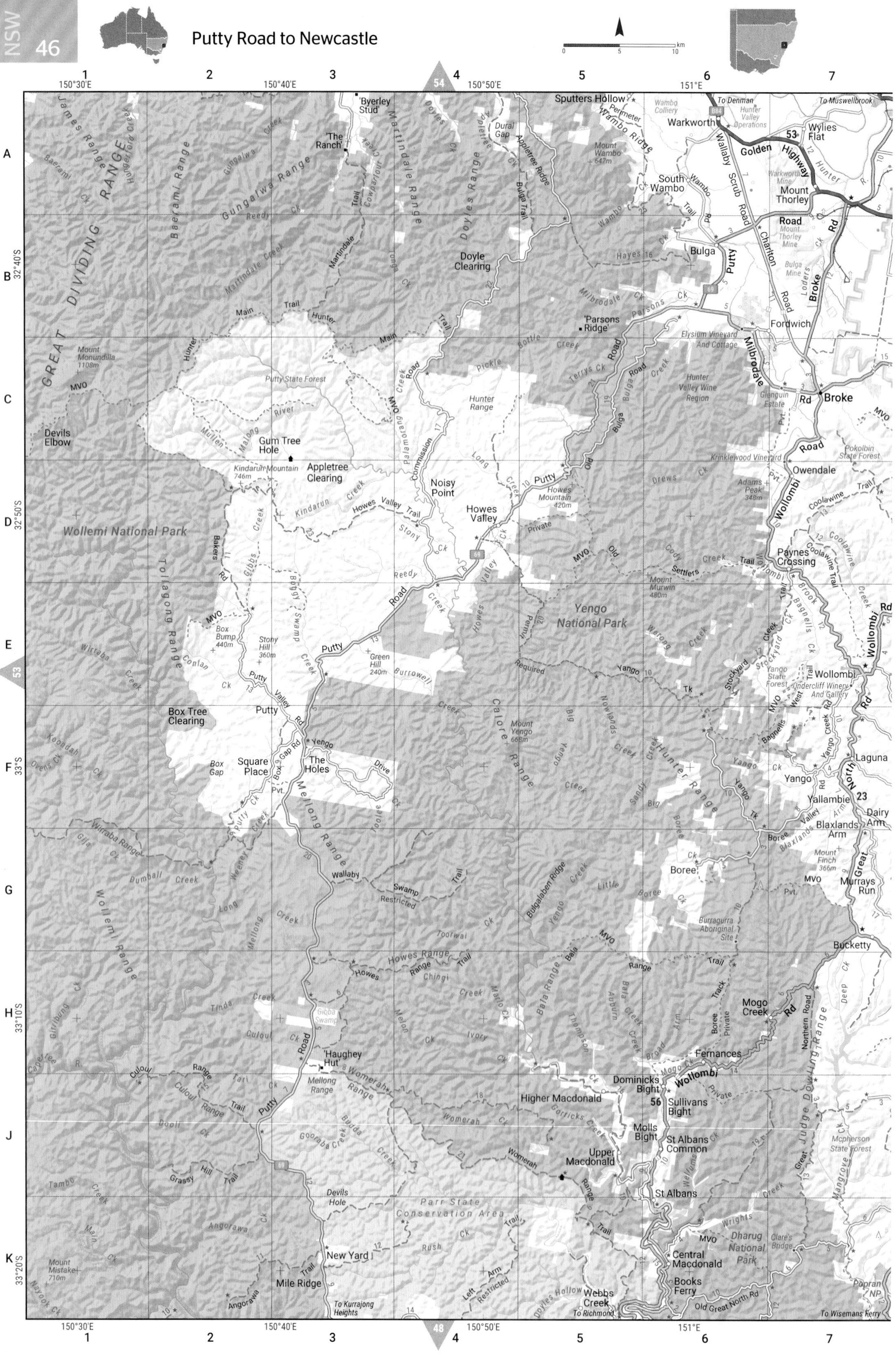

Singleton
Branxton
Greta
Lochinvar
Maitland
Cessnock
Kurri Kurri
Weston
Paterson
Raymond Terrace
Medowie
Newcastle
Toronto
Swansea
Morisset
Budgewoi
Wyong
The Entrance
Tasman Sea
See Page 45
© Hema Maps

Lithgow to Sydney

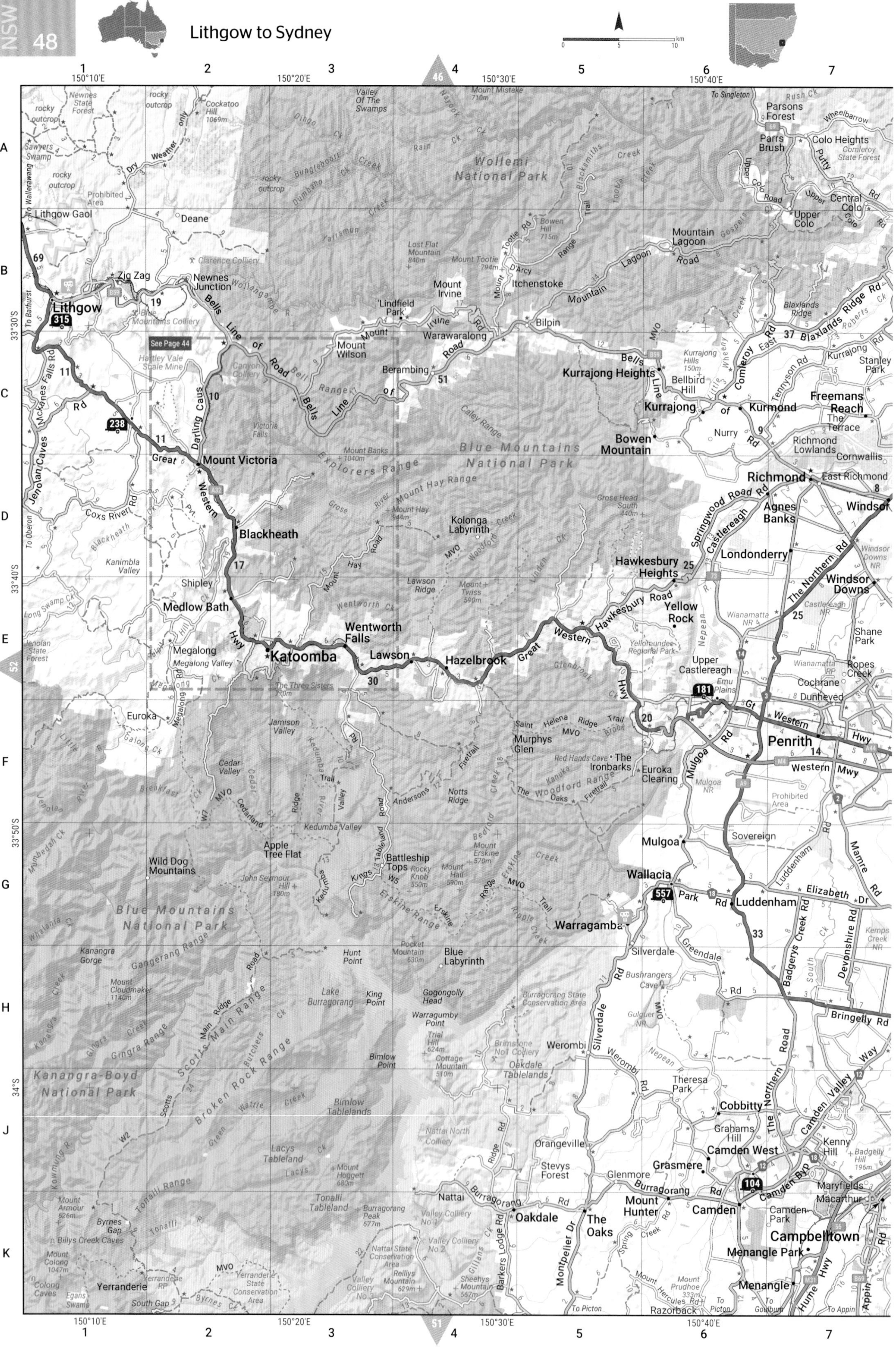

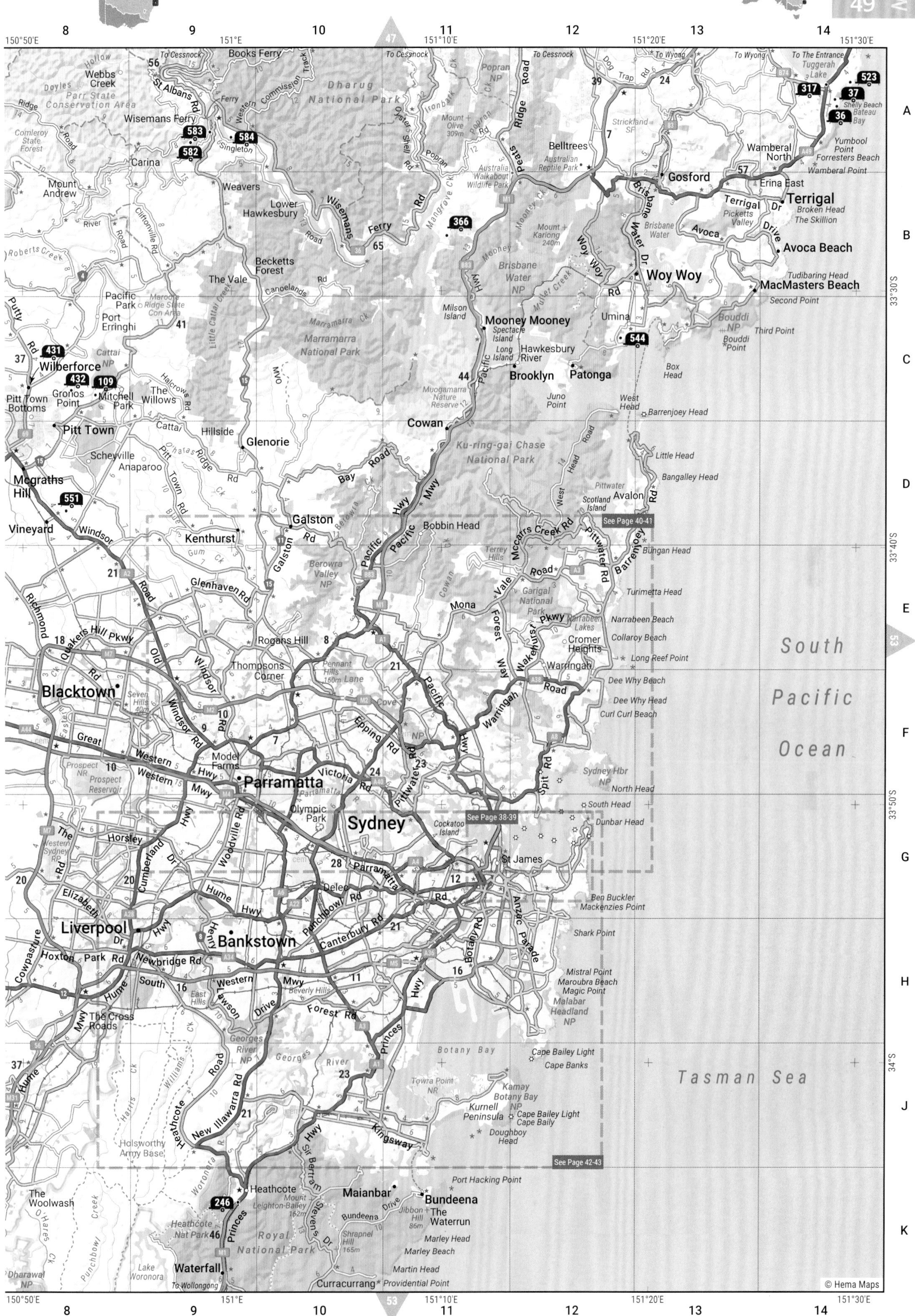

Wisemans Ferry
Books Ferry
Webbs Creek
Parr State Conservation Area
Comleroy State Forest
Carina
Singleton
Weavers
Lower Hawkesbury
Dharug National Park
Mount Olive 309m
Australia Walkabout Wildlife Park
Australian Reptile Park
Belltrees
Gosford
Wamberal North
Erina East
Terrigal
Broken Head
The Skillion
Picketts Valley
Avoca Beach
Tudibaring Head
MacMasters Beach
Second Point
Third Point
Bouddi NP
Bouddi Point
Woy Woy
Umina
Brisbane Water NP
Mount Kariong 240m
Strickland SF
To The Entrance
Tuggerah Lake
Shelly Beach
Bateau Bay
Yumbool Point
Forresters Beach
Wamberal Point
To Cessnock
To Wyong
Popran NP
Mount Andrew
Roberts Creek
Becketts Forest
The Vale
Pacific Park
Maroota Ridge State Con Area
Port Erringhi
Marramarra National Park
Milson Island
Mooney Mooney
Spectacle Island
Long Island
Hawkesbury River
Brooklyn
Patonga
Box Head
Juno Point
West Head
Barrenjoey Head
Muogamarra Nature Reserve
Cowan
Ku-ring-gai Chase National Park
Little Head
Bangalley Head
Pittwater
Scotland Island
Avalon
Bungan Head
Turimetta Head
Narrabeen Beach
Collaroy Beach
Long Reef Point
Dee Why Beach
Dee Why Head
Curl Curl Beach
Wilberforce
Cattai NP
Gronos Point
Mitchell Park
The Willows
Pitt Town Bottoms
Pitt Town
Hillside
Glenorie
Scheyville
Anaparoo
Mcgraths Hill
Vineyard
Galston
Kenthurst
Bobbin Head
Terrey Hills
Berowra Valley NP
Garigal National Park
Mona Vale
Cromer Heights
Warringah
Rogans Hill
Thompsons Corner
Pennant Hills 160m
Blacktown
Seven Hills 40m
Model Farms
Parramatta
Prospect NR
Prospect Reservoir
Olympic Park
Sydney
Cockatoo Island
Sydney Hbr NP
North Head
South Head
Dunbar Head
St James
Horsley
Western Sydney RP
Liverpool
Bankstown
Ben Buckler
Mackenzies Point
Shark Point
Mistral Point
Maroubra Beach
Magic Point
Malabar Headland NP
Hoxton Park
East Hills
Beverly Hills
The Cross Roads
Georges River NP
Botany Bay
Cape Bailey Light
Cape Banks
Towra Point NR
Kamay Botany Bay NP
Kurnell Peninsula
Cape Baily
Doughboy Head
Holsworthy Army Base
Heathcote
Maianbar
Bundeena
Port Hacking Point
Jibbon Hill 86m
The Waterrun
Marley Head
Marley Beach
Martin Head
Providential Point
Curracurrang
Royal National Park
Shrapnel Hill 165m
Mount Leighton-Bailey 162m
Heathcote Nat Park
The Woolwash
Lake Woronora
Dharawal NP
Waterfall
To Wollongong
South Pacific Ocean
Tasman Sea
See Page 40-41
See Page 38-39
See Page 42-43
© Hema Maps

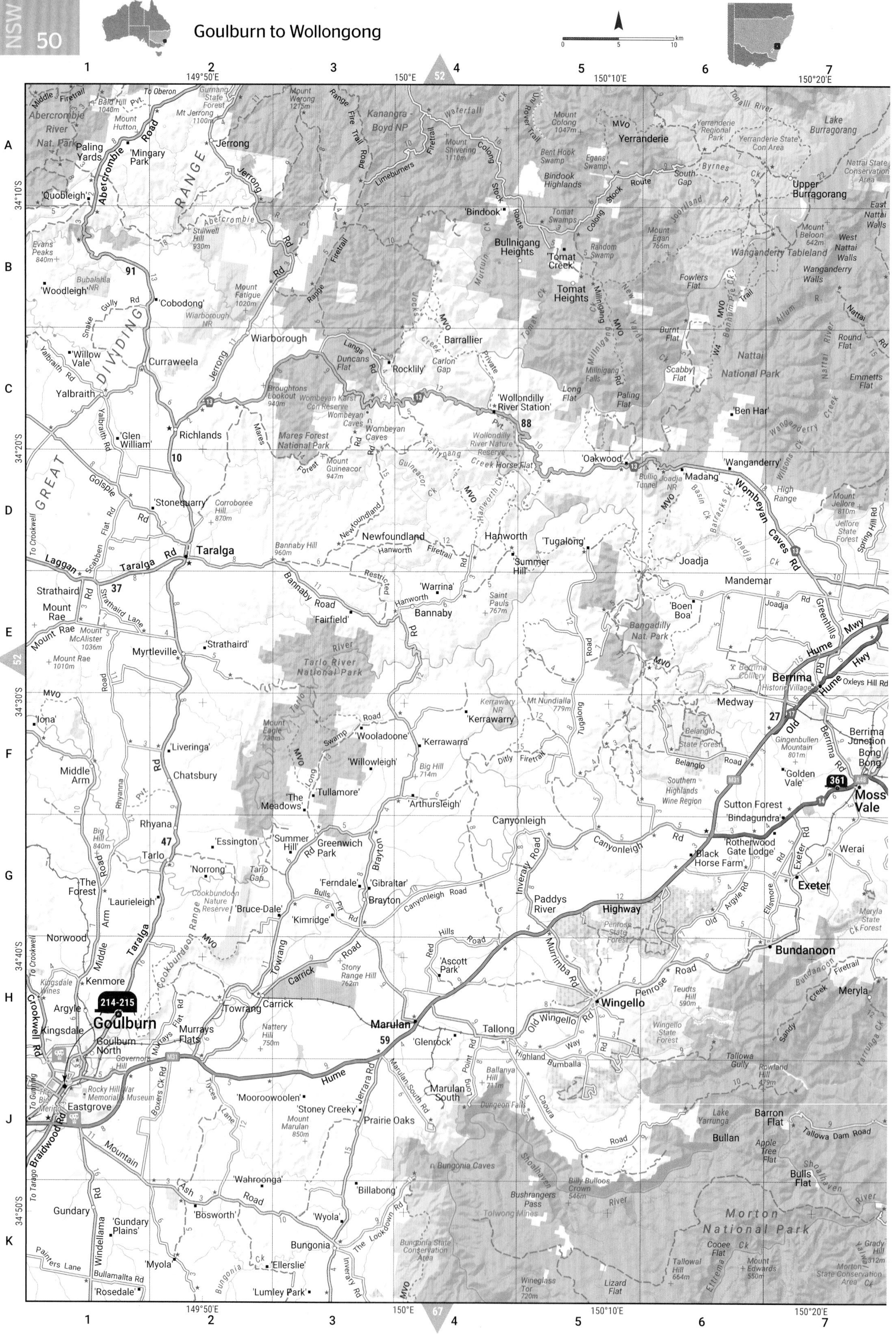

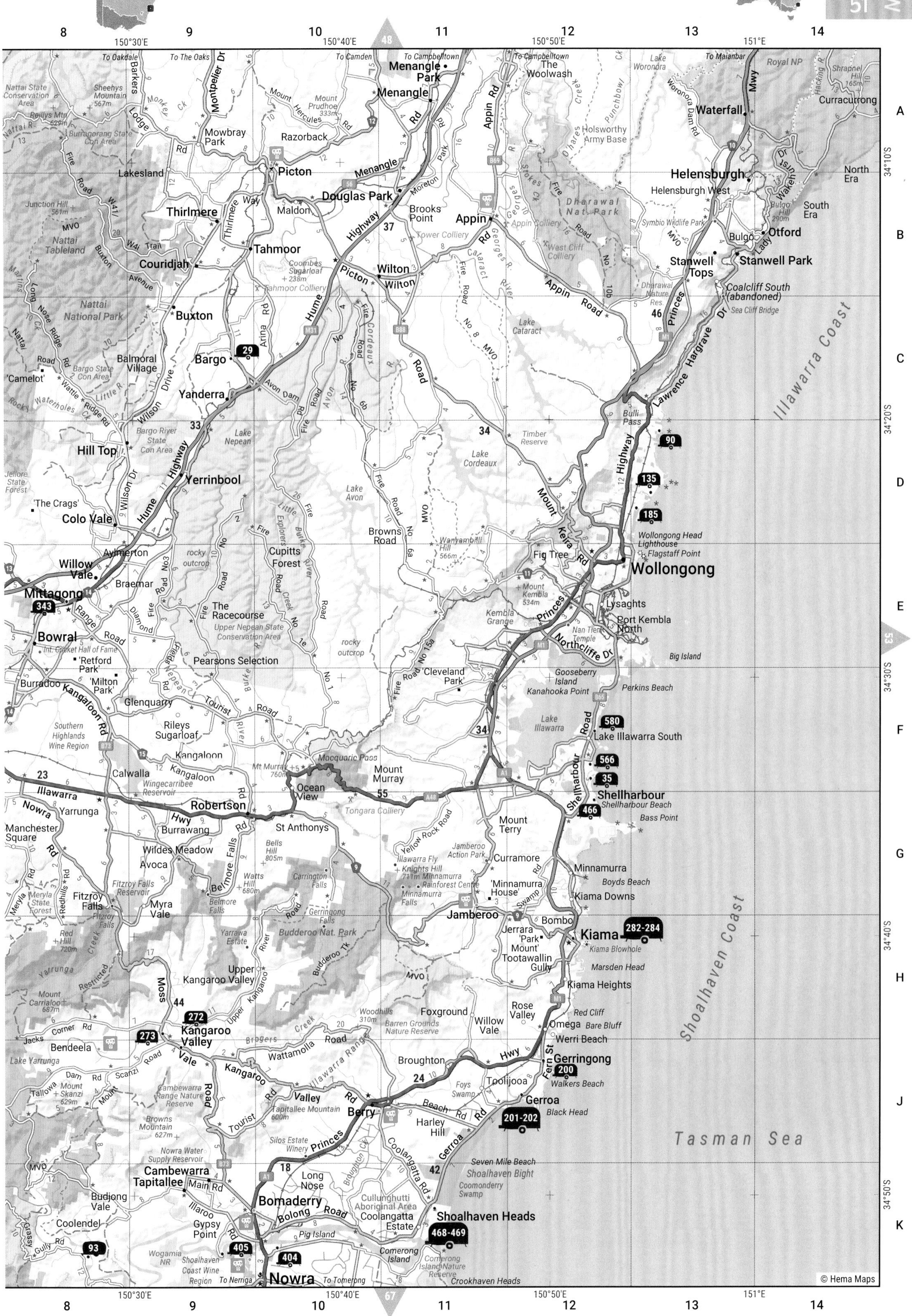
Wollongong
Picton
Kiama
Nowra
Bomaderry
Shellharbour
Helensburgh
Bowral
Mittagong
Robertson
Berry
Gerringong
Appin
Tasman Sea
Illawarra Coast
Shoalhaven Coast
© Hema Maps

Goulburn to Newcastle

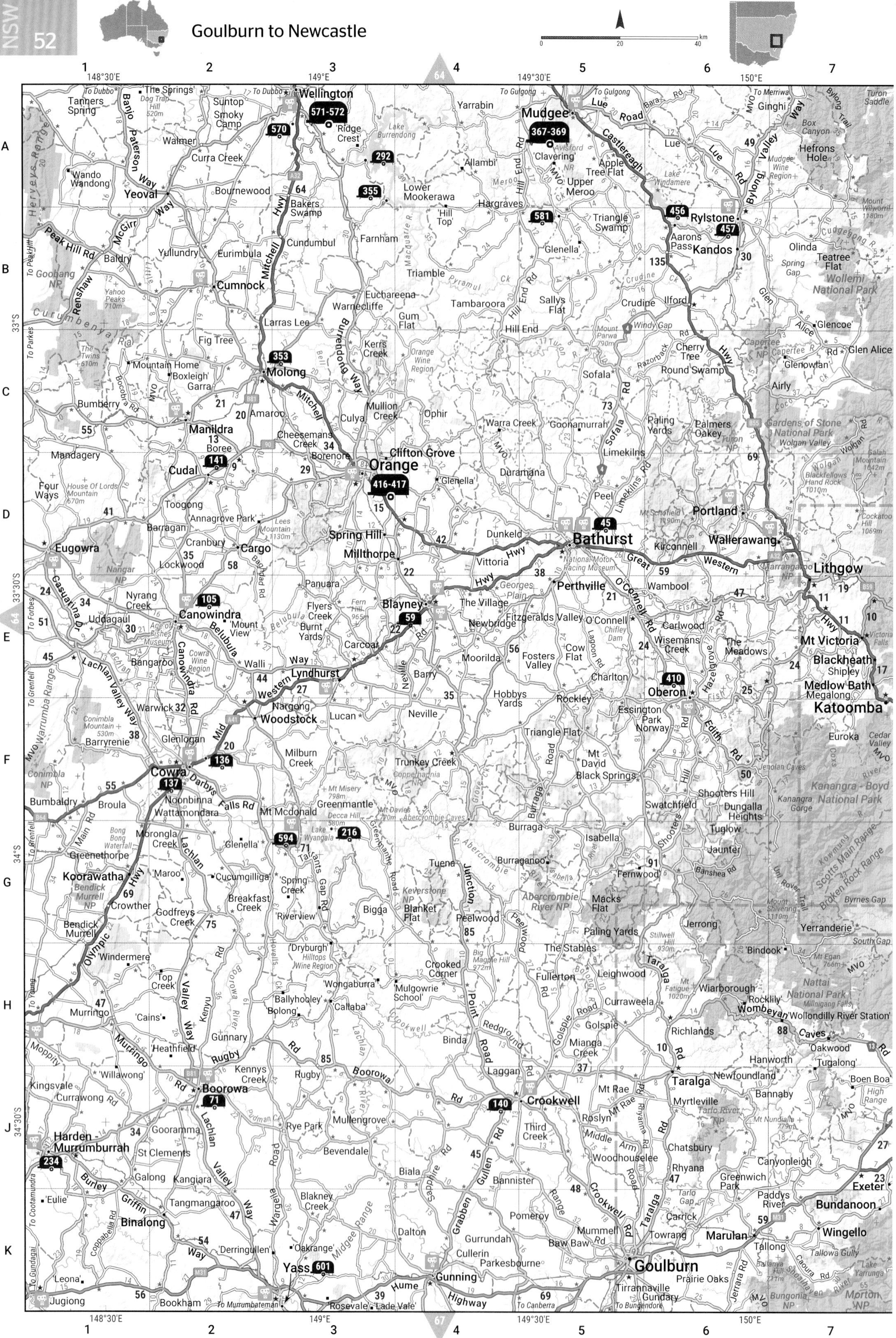

Singleton
Warkworth
Mount Thorley
Branxton
North Rothbury
Greta
Lochinvar
Paterson
Clarence Town
Sinclairs Point
Seaham
Wallalong
Brandy Hill
Windella Downs
Hinton
Maitland
Raymond Terrace
Medowie
Soldiers Pt
Karuah
Tea Gardens
Hawks Nest
Salamander Bay
Nelson Bay
Corlette
Fingal Bay
Boat Harbour
Mullwee
Port Stephens - Great Lakes Marine Park
Stockton Beach
Newcastle
Bar Beach
Bulga
Broke
Rothbury
Gillieston Heights
Pokolbin
Weston
Neath
Heddon Greta
Kurri Kurri
Cessnock
Bellbird
Paynes Crossing
Howes Valley
Sweetmans Creek
Millfield
Paxton
Ellalong
Kitchener
Seahampton
Mulbring
Minmi
Brookstown
Killingworth
Brunkerville
Quorrobolong
Yango
Eglinford
Laguna
Awaba
Toronto
Nine Mile Beach
Wollemi National Park
Yengo Nat. Park
Putty Square Place
Putty State Forest
Gum Tree Hole
'Parsons Ridge'
'Holbrook'
Devils Elbow
Yallambie
Watagan
Avondale
Dora Creek
Yarrawonga Park
Bonnells Bay
Morisset
Mannering Park
Swansea
Silverwater
Mirrabooka
Nords Wharf
Gwandalan
Chain Valley Bay
Budgewoi
Bucketty
Mogo Creek
Fernances
'Haughey Hut'
Higher Macdonald
Upper Macdonald
St Albans
Devils Hole
Parr State Conservation Area
Lakes Beach
Wyong
Palmdale
The Entrance
Shelly Beach
Colo Heights
Weavers
Mountain Lagoon
Gosford
Forresters Beach
The Skillion
Terrigal
Avoca Beach
Picketts Valley
MacMasters Beach
Woy Woy
Mooney Mooney
Patonga
Brooklyn
Becketts Forest
Marramarra NP
Warawaralong
Kurrajong Heights
Kurrajong
Kurmond
Freemans Reach
Wilberforce
Pitt Town
Bowen Mountain
Richmond
Agnes Banks
Windsor
Mcgraths Hill
Vineyard
Londonderry
Hawkesbury Heights
Yellow Rock
Windsor Downs
Cowan
Glenorie
Galston
Kenthurst
Avalon
Ku-ring-gai Chase NP
Lawson
Penrith
Blacktown
Shane Park
Dunheved
Collaroy Beach
Narrabeen Beach
Dee Why Beach
Curl Curl Beach
Sydney
The Ironbarks
Battleship Tops
Mulgoa
Wallacia
Warragamba
Parramatta
Luddenham
Liverpool
Bankstown
Ben Buckler
Maroubra Beach
Cape Banks
Botany Bay
Werombi
Theresa Park
The Cross Roads
Cobbitty
Camden West
Grasmere
The Oaks
Oakdale
Camden
Mt Hunter
Campbelltown
Cape Baily
Kurnell Peninsula
Maianbar
Bundeena
Marley Beach
Menangle Park
Menangle
Helensburgh
Garie Beach
Picton
Douglas Park
Appin
Thirlmere
Tahmoor
Couridjah
Wilton
Buxton
Bargo
Waterfall
Otford
Stanwell Park
Stanwell Tops
'Camelot'
Yanderra
Hill Top
Yerrinbool
Colo Vale
Willow Vale
Mittagong
Bowral
Berrima
Pearsons Selection
Wollongong
Moss Vale
Perkins Beach
Lake Illawarra South
Calwalla
Shellharbour
Yarrunga
Robertson
Curramore
Shellharbour Beach
Fitzroy Falls
Myra Vale
Jamberoo
Kiama
Boyds Beach
Bare Bluff
Red Cliff
Walkers Beach
Gerringong
Gerroa
Seven Mile Beach
Foxground
Kangaroo Valley
Morton Nat. Park
Budjong Vale
Tapitallee
Cambewarra
Berry
Harley Hill
Bomaderry
Shoalhaven Heads
South Pacific Ocean
Tasman Sea
See Page 46-47
See Page 48-49
See Page 50-51
For more detail see Hema's South East New South Wales map
© Hema Maps

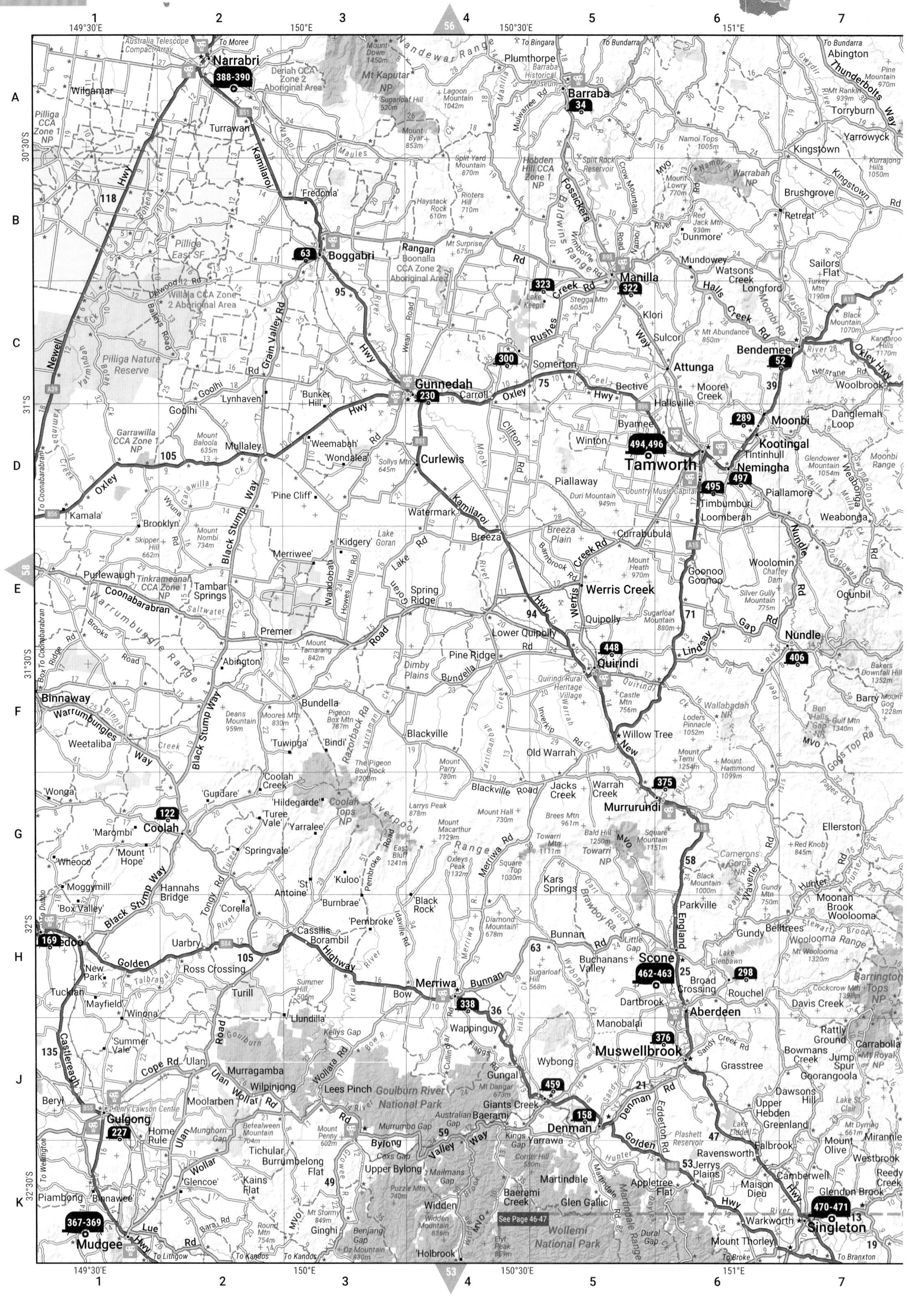

Narrabri to Port Macquarie

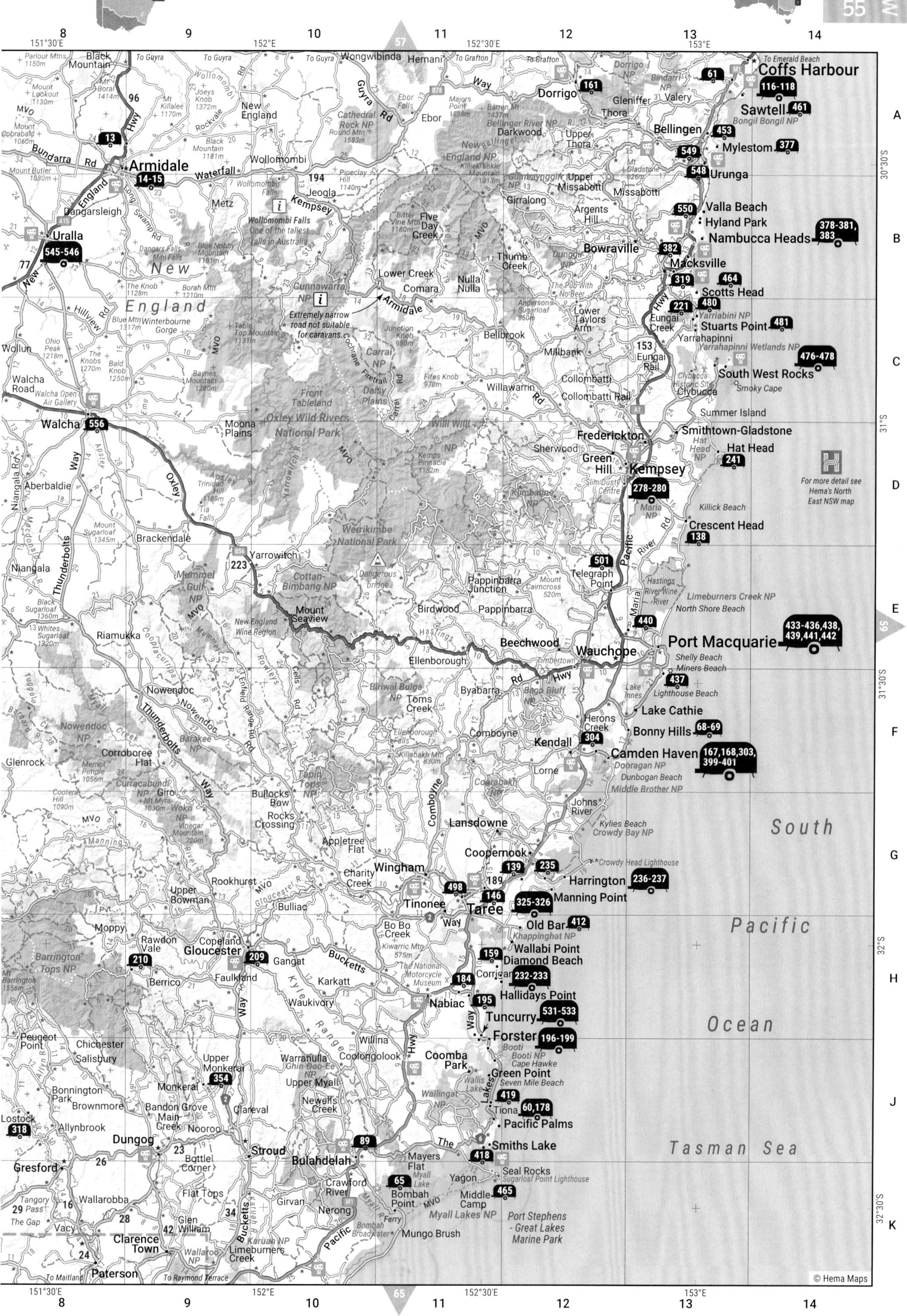
Coffs Harbour
116-118
61
Sawtell
461
Bongil Bongil NP
Dorrigo
161
Dorrigo NP
Bindarri NP
Glenifffer
Valery
Thora
Bellingen
453
Mylestom
377
549
548
Urunga
Darkwood
Upper Thora
New England NP
Bellinger River NP
Gumbaynggirr NP
Upper Missabotti
Missabotti
Girralong
Argents Hill
550
Valla Beach
Hyland Park
Nambucca Heads
378-381, 383
Bowraville
382
Macksville
319
464
Scotts Head
221
480
Stuarts Point
481
Eungai Creek
Yarrahapinni
Yarriabini NP
Yarrahapinni Wetlands NP
153
Eungai Rail
476-478
South West Rocks
Smoky Cape
Clybucca
Collombatti
Collombatti Rail
Summer Island
Smithtown-Gladstone
Frederickton
Hat Head NP
Hat Head
241
Sherwood
Green Hill
Kempsey
278-280
Maria NP
For more detail see Hema's North East NSW map
Killick Beach
Crescent Head
138
501
Telegraph Point
Limeburners Creek NP
North Shore Beach
440
Port Macquarie
433-436,438, 439,441,442
Shelly Beach
Miners Beach
437
Lighthouse Beach
Lake Innes
Lake Cathie
Bonny Hills
68-69
304
Camden Haven
167,168,303, 399-401
Dooragan NP
Dunbogan Beach
Middle Brother NP
Kendall
Herons Creek
Lorne
Johns River
Kylies Beach
Crowdy Bay NP
Wauchope
Beechwood
Pappinbarra
Pappinbarra Junction
Birdwood
Ellenborough
Byabarra
Bago Bluff
Comboyne
Lansdowne
Coopernook
139
235
Crowdy Head Lighthouse
Harrington
236-237
Manning Point
325-326
146
Taree
498
189
Wingham
Tinonee
Old Bar
412
Khappinghat NP
Wallabi Point
159
Diamond Beach
232-233
Hallidays Point
184
Nabiac
195
Tuncurry
531-533
Forster
196-199
Booti Booti NP
Cape Hawke
Green Point
Seven Mile Beach
419
60,178
Tiona
Pacific Palms
Smiths Lake
418
Seal Rocks
Sugarloaf Point Lighthouse
465
Yagon
Middle Camp
Myall Lakes NP
Port Stephens - Great Lakes Marine Park
65
Bombah Point
Mungo Brush
89
Bulahdelah
Crawford River
Nerong
Girvan
Mayers Flat
Coolongolook
Coomba Park
Wallingat NP
Willina
Stroud
209
Gloucester
Gangat
Karkatt
Faulkland
Copeland
Rawdon Vale
210
Barrington Tops NP
Berrico
Moppy
Bo Bo Creek
The National Motorcycle Museum
Kiwarric Mtn 575m
Waukivory
Warranulla
Upper Myall
Newells Creek
Clareval
354
Monkerai
Upper Monkerai
Bandon Grove
Main Creek
Nooroo
Chichester
Salisbury
Peugeot Point
Bonnington Park
Brownmore
Allynbrook
Lostock
318
Dungog
Gresford
Bottle Corner
Flat Tops
Wallarobba
Tangory Pass
The Gap
Vacy
Glen William
Clarence Town
Paterson
Limeburners Creek
Karuah NP
Wallaroo NP
To Maitland
To Raymond Terrace
Armidale
14-15
13
Uralla
545-546
Dangarsleigh
Metz
Wollomombi
Wollomombi Falls One of the tallest falls in Australia
Jeogla
194
New England
Ebor
Hernani
Wongwibinda
Cathedral Rock NP
Five Day Creek
Lower Creek
Comara
Nulla Nulla
Thumb Creek
Bellbrook
Millbank
Lower Taylors Arm
Willawarrin
Cunnawarra NP
Extremely narrow road not suitable for caravans.
Carrai NP
Daisy Plains
Front Tableland
Oxley Wild Rivers National Park
Willi Willi NP
Moona Plains
Walcha
556
Walcha Road
Wollun
Aberbaldie
Brackendale
Yarrowitch
223
Werrikimbe National Park
Cottan-Bimbang NP
Dangerous bridge
Mount Seaview
New England Wine Region
Riamukka
Mummel Gulf NP
Niangala
Nowendoc
Nowendoc NP
Corroboree Flat
Glenrock
Giro
Woko NP
Bullocks Bow
Rocks Crossing
Tapin Tops NP
Biriwal Bulga NP
Toms Creek
Appletree Flat
Charity Creek
Rookhurst
Upper Bowman
Bulliac
South Pacific Ocean
Tasman Sea
© Hema Maps

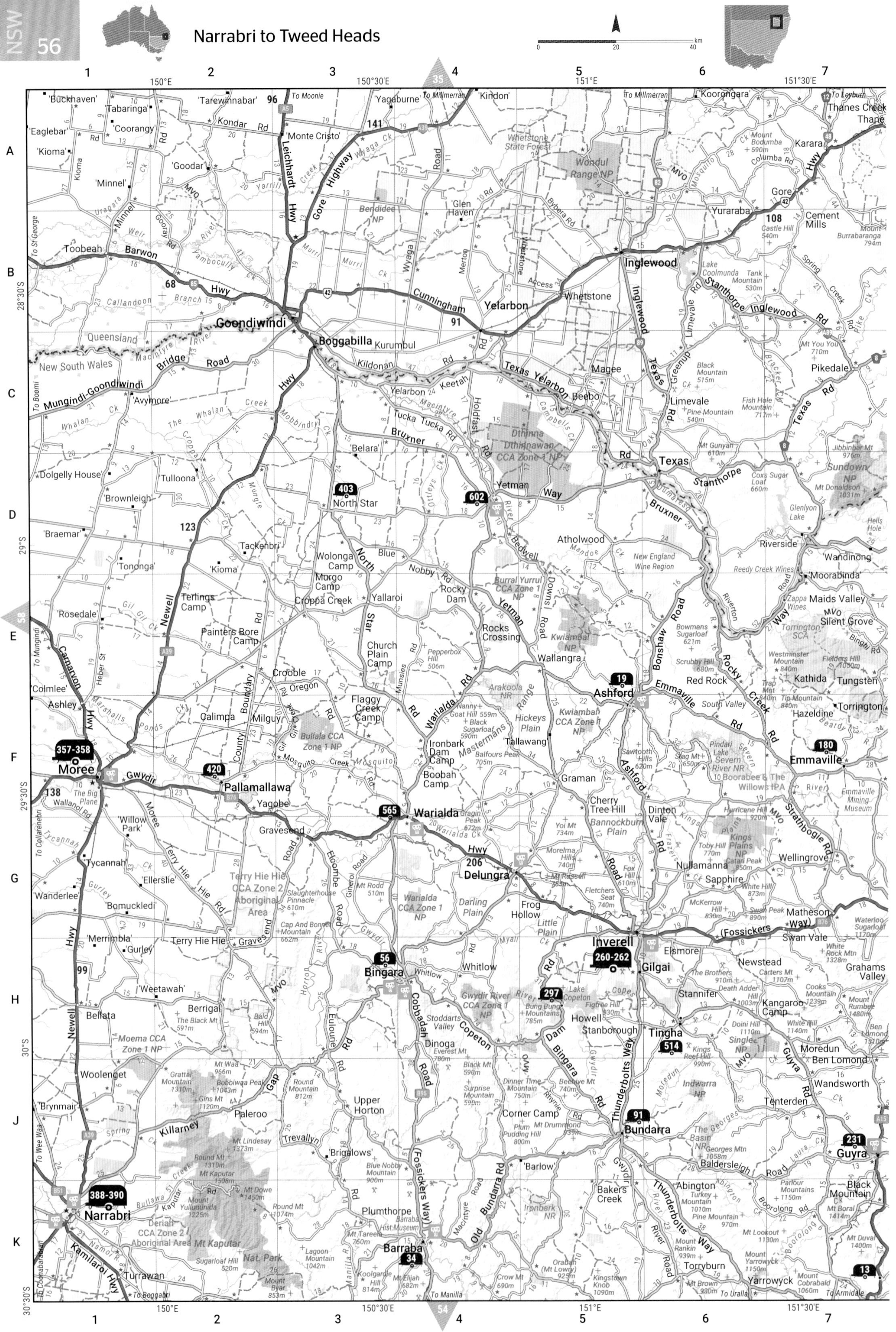
Goondiwindi
Boggabilla
Inglewood
Yelarbon
Texas
Moree
Pallamallawa
Warialda
Delungra
Inverell
Gilgai
Ashford
Emmaville
Bingara
Tingha
Bundarra
Guyra
Narrabri
Barraba
Queensland
New South Wales
Newell Hwy
Gwydir Hwy
Cunningham Hwy
Bruxner Way
Thunderbolts Way
Mt Kaputar Nat. Park
Kamilaroi Hwy
Leichhardt Hwy
Gore Highway
Carnarvon Hwy
Wondul Range NP
Bendidee NP
Kwiambal NP
Sundown NP
Kings Plains NP
Single NP
Indwarra NP
Ironbark NR
North Star
Yetman
Wallangra
Graman
Elsmore
Stannifer
Copeton
Sapphire
Wellingrove
Torrington
Tenterden
Wandsworth
Ben Lomond
Black Mountain
Upper Horton
Plumthorpe
Killarney Gap
Tooheah
Croppa Creek
Terry Hie Hie
Limevale
Pikedale
Thanes Creek
Karara
Gore
Cement Mills
Whetstone
Magee
Beebo
Atholwood
Rocky Dam
Rocks Crossing
Bonshaw
Red Rock
Kathida
Tungsten
Matheson
Swan Vale
Newstead
Kangaroo Camp
Howell
Stanborough
Dinoga
Corner Camp
Bakers Creek
Abington
Torryburn
Yarrowyck
Woolenget
Berrigal
Bellata
Turrawan
Yagobe
Gravesend
Calimpa
Milguy
Crooble
Ashley
Fossickers Way

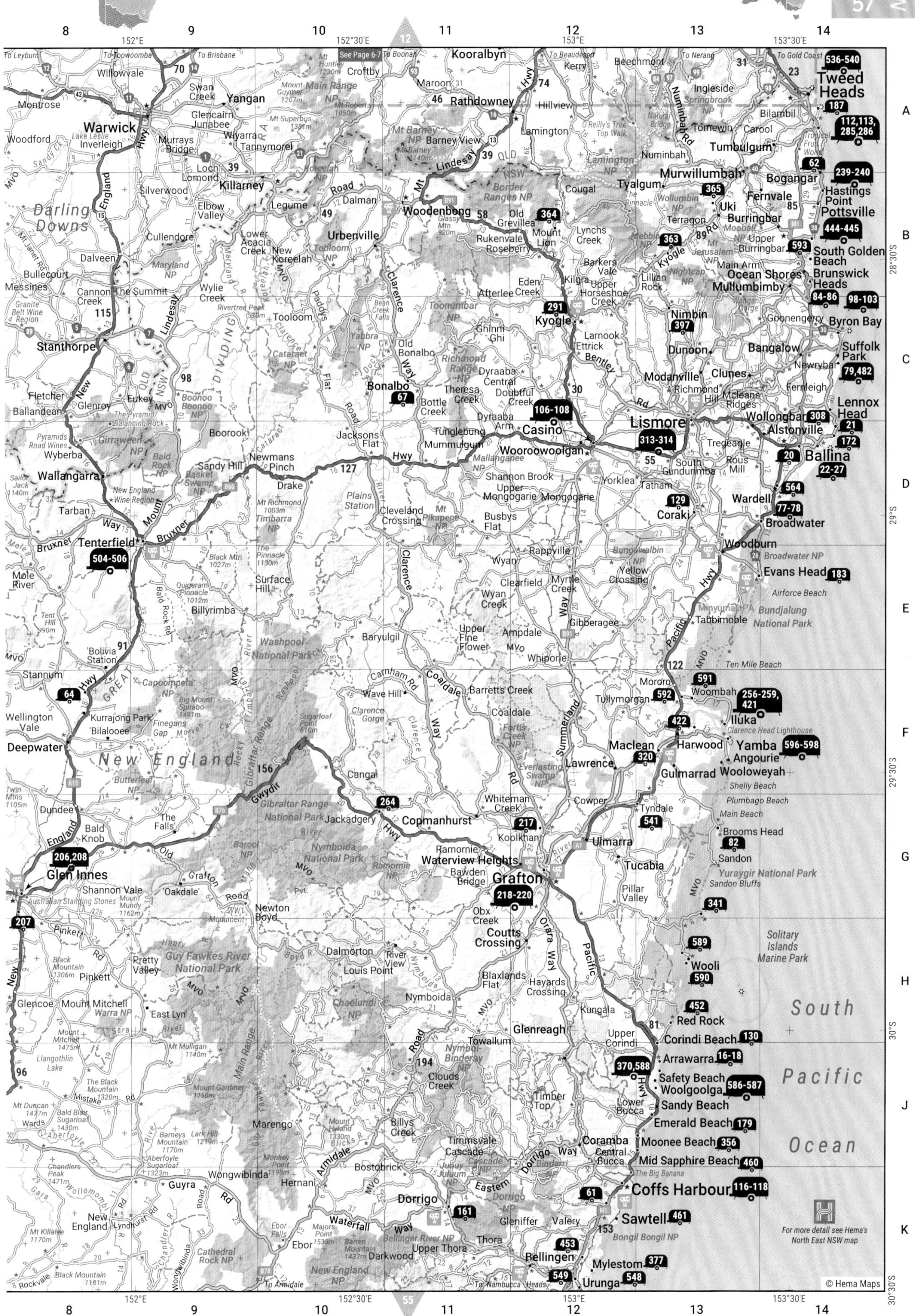
8
9
10
11
12
13
14
152°E
152°30'E
153°E
153°30'E
A
B
C
D
E
F
G
H
J
K
28°30'S
29°S
29°30'S
30°S
30°30'S
To Leyburn
To Toowoomba
To Brisbane
See Page 6-7
To Boonah
To Beaudesert
To Nerang
To Gold Coast
536-540
Tweed Heads
187
112,113, 285,286
Willowvale
Swan Creek
Yangan
Croftby
Kooralbyn
Kerry
Beechmont
Ingleside
Springbrook NP
Bilambil
Montrose
Warwick
Glencairn
Junabee
Maroon
Rathdowney
Hillview
Tomewin
Carool
Tumbulgum
Woodford
Lake Leslie
Inverleigh
Murrays Bridge
Wiyarra
Tannymorel
Mt Barney NP
Barney View
Lamington
Numinbah
Main Range NP
Darling Downs
Loch Lomond
Killarney
Lindesay
Lamington NP
Murwillumbah
62
Silverwood
Elbow Valley
Legume
Dalman
Woodenbong
Border Ranges NP
Cougal
Tyalgum
365
Bogangar
239-240
Hastings Point
Pottsville
Fernvale
Uki
Burringbar
Terragon
Upper Burringbar
444-445
South Golden Beach
593
Cullendore
Lower Acacia Creek
New Koreelah
Urbenville
Old Grevillea
364
Mount Lion
Rukenvale
Roseberry
Lynchs Creek
363
Kyogle
Main Arm
Ocean Shores
Brunswick Heads
Mullumbimby
Dalveen
Maryland NP
Bullecourt
Messines
Cannon Creek
The Summit
Wylie Creek
Eden Creek
Afterlee
Barkers Vale
Kilgra
Upper Horseshoe Creek
Lillian Rock
Nightcap NP
84-86
98-103
Byron Bay
Goonengerry
Granite Belt Wine Region
115
Tooloom
Toonumbar NP
291
Kyogle
Nimbin
397
Stanthorpe
Yabbra NP
Old Bonalbo
Ghinni Ghi
Larnook
Ettrick
Dunoon
Bangalow
Suffolk Park
Newrybar
79,482
Cataract NP
Richmond Range NP
Dyraaba Central
Bentley
Modanville
Clunes
Richmond Hill
McLeans Ridges
Fernleigh
Lennox Head
Fletcher
Ballandean
Glenroy
Eukey
98
Boonoo Boonoo NP
Bonalbo
67
Theresa Creek
Bottle Creek
Doubtful Creek
30
106-108
Casino
Dyraaba Arm
Lismore
Wollongbar
308
Alstonville
21
Tunglebung
Mummulgum
313-314
Tregeagle
172
Ballina
20
22-27
Pyramids Road Wines
Wyberba
Girraween NP
Boorook
Jacksons Flat
Wooroowoolgan
55
South Gundurimba
Rous Mill
Bald Rock NP
Sandy Hill
Newmans Pinch
Hwy
127
Shannon Brook
Tatham
Yorklea
Wallangarra
Basket Swamp NP
Drake
Upper Mongogarie
Mongogarie
564
Sailor Jack
New England Wine Region
Mt Richmond 1003m
Timbarra NP
Plains Station
Cleveland Crossing
Mt Pikapene NP
Busbys Flat
129
Coraki
Wardell
77-78
Broadwater
Tarban
Bruxner
Tenterfield
504-506
Black Mtn 1027m
The Pinnacle 1130m
Wyan
Rappville
Bungawalbin NP
Woodburn
Broadwater NP
Evans Head
183
Mole River
Quigeram Pinnacle 1012m
Surface Hill
Clearfield
Wyan Creek
Myrtle Creek
Yellow Crossing
Airforce Beach
Billyrimba
Gibberagee
Bundjalung National Park
Tabbimoble
Tent Hill 990m
Baryulgil
Upper Fine Flower
Ampdale
'Bolivia Station'
91
Washpool National Park
Whiporie
Ten Mile Beach
122
Stannum
Carnham Rd
Coaldale
Barretts Creek
Mororo
591
Woombah
256-259, 421
64
Capoompeta NP
'Wave Hill'
Tullymorgan
592
Iluka
Wellington Vale
Big Mount Spirabo 1491m
Kurrajong Park
'Bilalooee'
Finegans Gap
Sugarloaf Point 610m
Clarence Gorge
Fortis Creek NP
Coaldale
422
Clarence Head Lighthouse
Deepwater
Gibraltar Range
Maclean
Harwood
Yamba
596-598
Angourie
New England
156
Cangai
Everlasting Swamp NP
Lawrence
320
Gulmarrad
Wooloweyah
Shelly Beach
Twin Mtns 1105m
Butterleaf NP
Gwydir
264
Whiteman Creek
Cowper
Tyndale
Plumbago Beach
Dundee
The Falls
Gibraltar Range National Park
Jackadgery
Copmanhurst
217
541
Main Beach
Bald Knob
Koolkhan
Ulmarra
Brooms Head
82
206,208
Glen Innes
Nymboida National Park
Ramornie
Waterview Heights
Tucabia
Sandon
Yuraygir National Park
Shannon Vale
'Oakdale'
Bawden Bridge
Grafton
218-220
Pillar Valley
Sandon Bluffs
Australian Standing Stones
Mount Mundy 1162m
Newton Boyd
Obx Creek
341
207
Coutts Crossing
Solitary Islands Marine Park
Pinkett
Henry Guy Fawkes River National Park
Dalmorton
River View
589
Black Mountain 1306m
Pretty Valley
Louis Point
Wooli
590
Blaxlands Flat
Hayards Crossing
Glencoe
Mount Mitchell
Warra NP
'East Lyn'
Chaelundi NP
Nymboida
Kungala
452
Red Rock
South
Mount Mitchell 1475m
Mt Mulligan 1140m
Glenreagh
81
Upper Corindi
Corindi Beach
130
Llangothlin Lake
Towallum
Nymboi-Binderay NP
194
Arrawarra
16-18
96
370,588
Safety Beach
Woolgoolga
586-587
Pacific
The Black Mountain 1320m
Mistake
Mount Gardiner 1150m
Clouds Creek
Timber Top
Lower Bucca
Sandy Beach
Mt Duncan 1477m
Wards
Bald Blair
Sugarloaf 1430m
Marengo
Mount Hyland 1330m
Billys Creek
Emerald Beach
179
Aberfoyle
Barneys Mountain 1170m
Lark Hill 1219m
Aberfoyle Sugarloaf 1323m
Timmsvale
Cascade
Coramba
Moonee Beach
356
Ocean
Central Bucca
Mid Sapphire Beach
460
Chandlers Peak 1471m
Wongwibinda
Monkey Point 1198m
Hernani
Bostobrick
The Big Banana
Guyra
Dorrigo
Dorrigo NP
61
Coffs Harbour
116-118
New England
Mt Killiecrankie 1170m
161
Gleniffer
Valery
Sawtell
461
153
Bongil Bongil NP
For more detail see Hema's North East NSW map
Ebor Falls
Ebor
Majors Point 1538m
Waterfall Way
Bellinger River NP
Upper Thora
Thora
Cathedral Rock NP
Barren Mountain 1437m
Darkwood
453
Bellingen
Mylestom
377
New England NP
549
Urunga
548
Rockvale
Black Mountain 1181m
To Armidale
To Nambucca Heads
© Hema Maps
12
55

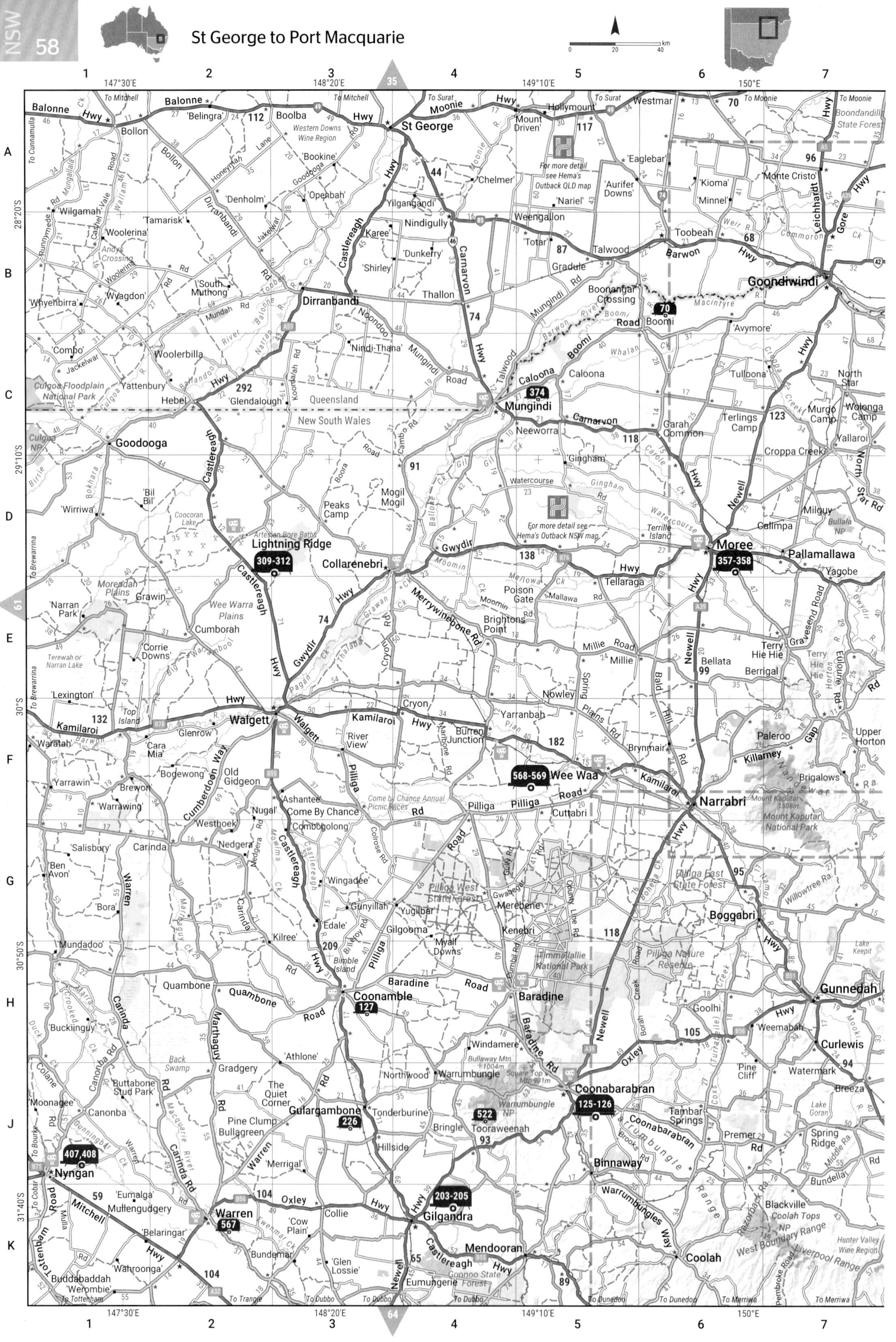

8
9
10
11
12
13
14
150°50'E
151°40'E
152°30'E
153°20'E
36
65
A
B
C
D
E
F
G
H
J
K
28°20'S
29°10'S
30°S
30°50'S
31°40'S
See Page 12
See Page 56-57
See Page 54-55
Bulli Creek
Western Creek State Forest
To Millmerran
Ellangowan
Clifton
Sandy Camp
Allora
To Toowoomba
To Ipswich
Aratula
Fassifern
Beaudesert
Boonah
Helensvale
To Brisbane
Gold Coast
Nerang
Canungra
Tarome
Charlwood
Mt Alford
Kooralbyn
Maroon
Leyburn
Pratten
Thanes Creek
Tregony
Moogerah
Croftby
Yangan
Main Range NP
Rathdowney
Hillview
Lamington
Lamington NP
Tweed Heads
Murwillumbah
'Kooroongara'
Thane
Karara
Whetstone State Forest
Wondul Range National Park
Montrose
Warwick
Woodford
Gore
Yuraraba
Cement Mills
Inglewood
Darling Downs
Killarney
Cougal
Old Grevillea
Tyalgum
Loadstone
Pottsville
Cullendore
Woodenbong
Urbenville
Toonumbar NP
Roseberry
Rukenvale
Eden Creek
Afterlee Creek
Mooball Beach
Ocean Shores
Mullumbimby
Brunswick Heads
Clarkes Beach
Tallow Beach
Cape Byron
Byron Bay
Yelarbon
Cunningham
Wylie Creek
Kyogle
Nimbin
Dunoon
Larnook
Ettrick
Stanthorpe
Pikedale
Beebo
Granite Belt Wine Region
Bonalbo
Richmond Range NP
Lismore
Clunes
Seven Mile Beach
Lennox Head
Ballina
Bruxner
Dthinna Dthinnawan NP
Yetman
Texas
Sundown Nat. Park
Girraween Nat Park
Wallangarra
Sandy Hill
Boorook
Newmans Pinch
Drake
Casino
Robins Beach
Beswicks Beach
Patches Beach
Busbys Flat
Coraki
Rappville
Broadwater
Sandy Beach
Airforce Beach
Evans Head
Tenterfield
Moorabinda
Surface Hill
Wyan
Myrtle Creek
Clearfield
Rocky Dam
Mole River
New England
Billyrimba
Baryulgil
Tabbimoble
Ten Mile Beach
Bundjalung National Park
Gibberagee
Whiporie
Tullymorgan
For more detail see Hema's North East NSW map
Ashford
Emmaville Rd
Emmaville
Deepwater
Washpool NP
Gibraltar Range
Barretts Creek
Yamba
Pippi Beach
Maclean
Shelly Beach
Main Beach
Plumbago Beach
The Red Cliff
Warialda
Dinton Vale
New England Wine Region
Cangai
Lawrence
Copmanhurst
Gibraltar Range NP
Jackadgery
Nymboida National Park
Grafton
Delungra
Fossickers
Sapphire
Swan Vale
Glen Innes
Gwydir
Yuraygir National Park
Tucabia
Sandon Bluffs
Bingara
Inverell
Obx Creek
Coutts Crossing
Blaxlands Flat
Newton Boyd
Pretty Valley
Pinkett
River View
Nymboida
Wooli
Solitary Islands Marine Park
Kangaroo Camp
Guyra
Copeton
Lake Copeton
Tingha
Moredun
Ben Lomond 1510m
Mount Mitchell
'East Lyn'
Hayards Crossing
Kungala
Guy Fawkes River National Park
Chaelundi National Park
The Brothers 1508m
Corindi Beach
Arrawarra
Woolgoolga
Sandy Beach
Emerald Beach
Glenreagh
Clouds Creek
Nymboi-Binderay NP
Corner Camp
Bundarra
Tenterden
Baldersleigh
Marengo
Coffs Harbour
Wongwibinda
Hernani
Dorrigo
Dorrigo NP
Sawtell
Thunderbolts
New England
Barraba
Torryburn
Round Mountain 1583m
Ebor
Majors Point 1538m
Bellingen
North Beach
Urunga
Kingstown
Yarrowyck
Armidale
Waterfall
Brushgrove
'Retreat'
Uralla
Jeogla
New England National Park
Valla Beach
Nambucca Heads
Bowraville
Forster Beach
Macksville
South Pacific Ocean
Manilla
Watsons Creek
Sailors Flat
Longford
Dwyers Range
Cunnawarra NP
Comara
South West Rocks
Smoky Cape
Attunga
Bendemeer
Carrai NP
Green Range
Millbank
Willawarrin
Moonbi
Walcha
Oxley Wild Rivers National Park
Tamworth
Piallaway
Hat Head
Kemps Corner
Willi Willi NP
Kempsey
Killick Beach
Crescent Head
Weabonga
Werrikimbe National Park
Goolawah Beach
Delicate Nobby
North Shore Beach
Yarrowitch
Cottan-Bimbang National Park
Currabubula
Niangala
Pappinbarra Junction
Port Macquarie
Werris Creek
Mummel Gulf National Park
Mount Seaview
Riamukka
Wauchope
Shelly Beach
Miners Beach
Lighthouse Beach
Rainbow Beach
Grants Beach
Tasman Sea
Nundle
Ellenborough
Toms Creek
Nowendoc
Quirindi
Nowendoc National Park
Hunter Valley Wine Region
Comboyne
Hastings River Wine River
Corroboree Flat
Glenrock
Curracabundi National Park
Camden Haven
Dunbogan Beach
Murrurundi
Jacks Creek
Kars Springs
Ellerston
Kangaroo Range
Barrington Tops NP
Bullocks Bow
Appletree Flat
Lansdowne
Kylies Beach
Taree
Harrington
For more detail see Hema's Sydney to Brisbane map
Moppy
To Scone
To Gloucester
To Bulahdelah
To Forster
© Hema Maps

Cameron Corner to Cobar

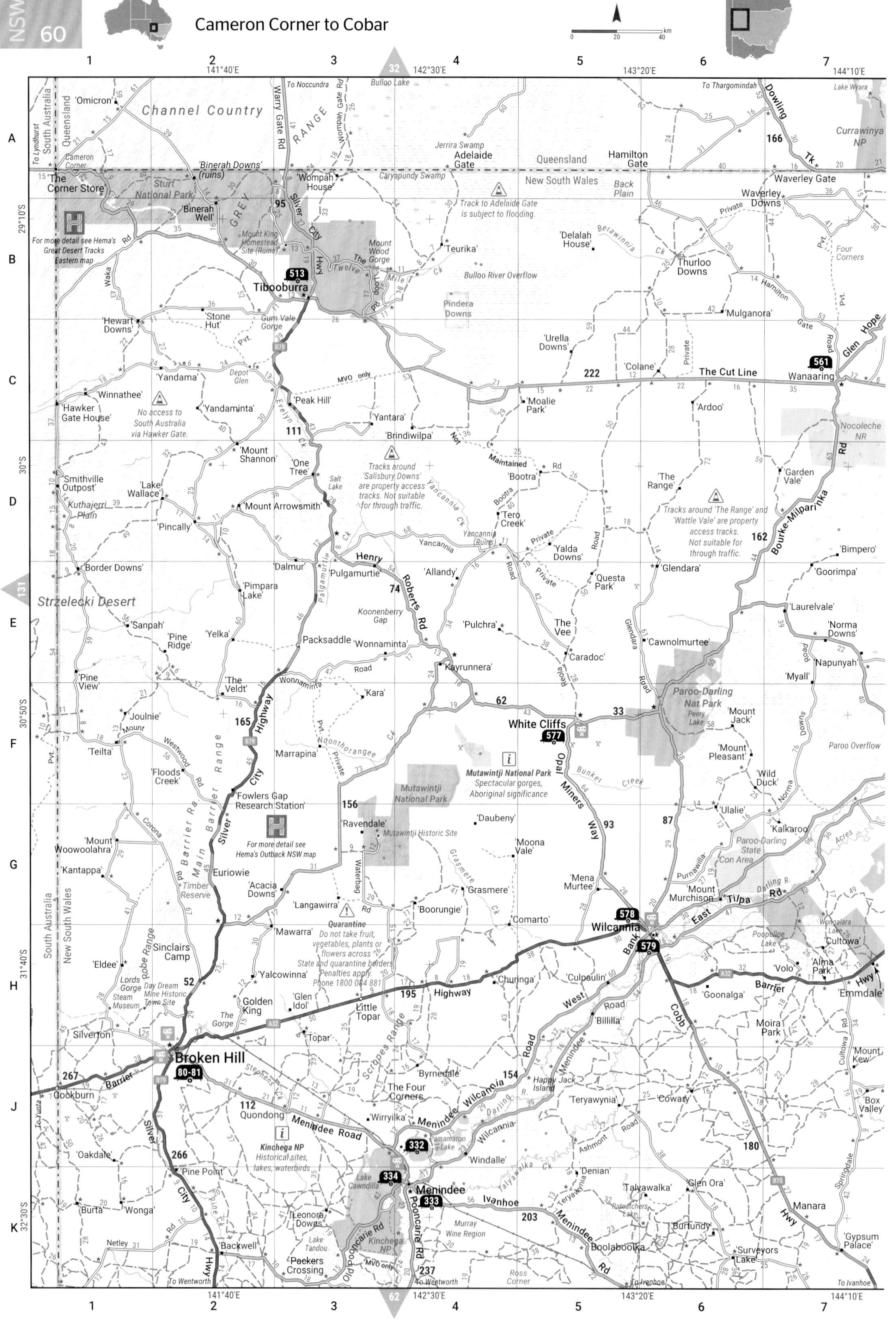

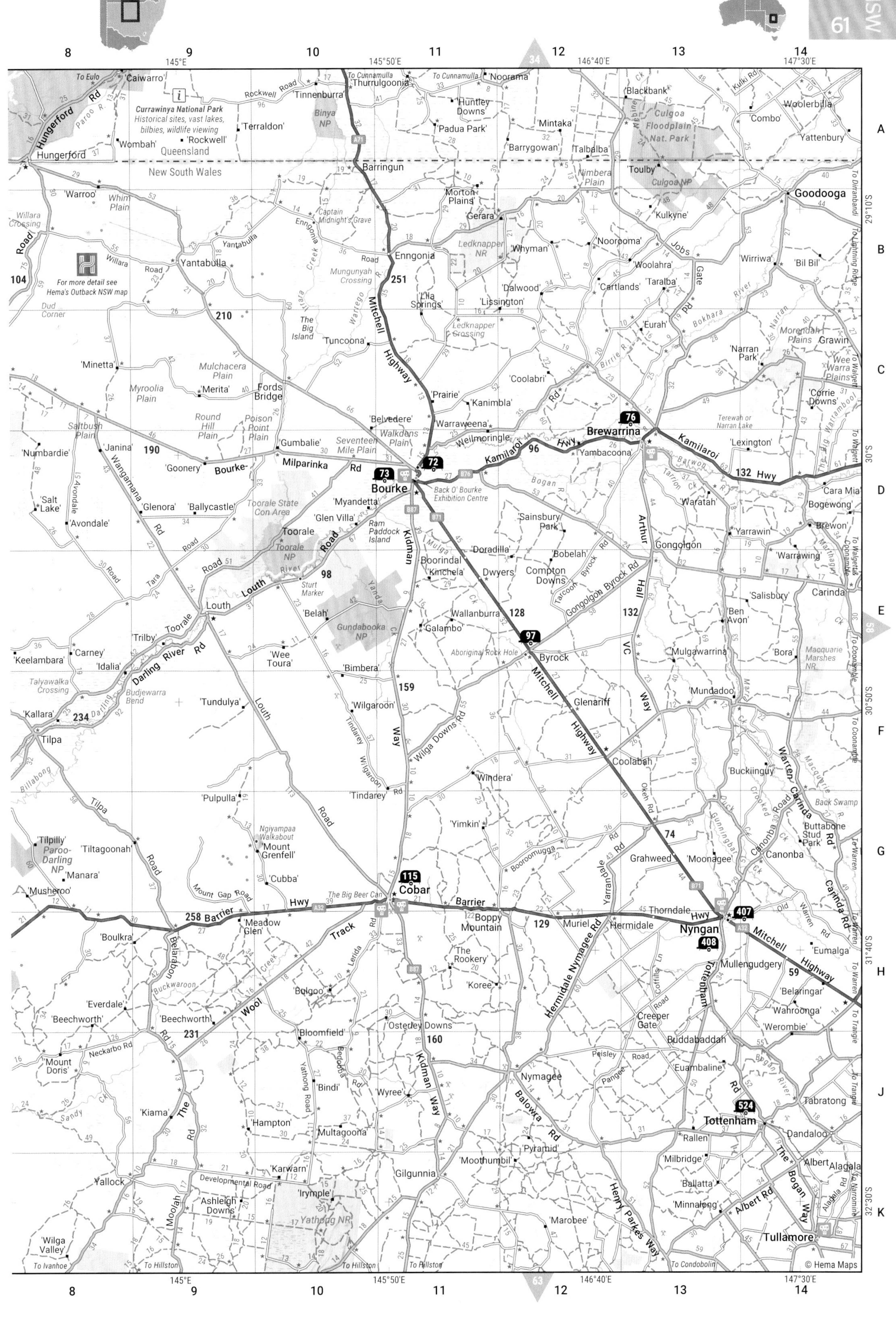

To Eulo
Caiwarro
Currawinya National Park
Historical sites, vast lakes, bilbies, wildlife viewing
Hungerford Rd
Hungerford
Paroo R.
'Wombah'
'Rockwell'
Queensland
New South Wales
'Terraldon'
Rockwell Road
'Tinnenburra'
Binya NP
To Cunnamulla
'Thurrulgoonia'
'Noorama'
'Huntley Downs'
'Padua Park'
'Mintaka'
'Barrygowan'
Talbalba
'Blackbank'
Culgoa Floodplain Nat. Park
Kulki Rd
Woolerbilla
'Combo'
'Yattenbury'
Barringun
'Toulby'
Culgoa NP
Nimbera Plain
Goodooga
'Kulkyne'
'Warroo'
Whim Plain
Willara Crossing
Road
Yantabulla
Willara Road
For more detail see Hema's Outback NSW map
Dud Corner
Captain Midnight's Grave
Enngonia
Creek
Road
Morton Plains
Gerara
Ledknapper NR
'Whyman'
'Nooroama'
'Woolahra'
Jobs Gate Rd
'Wirriwa'
'Bil Bil'
Mungunyah Crossing
Mitchell Highway
'Lila Springs'
'Lissington'
'Dalwood'
'Cartlands'
'Taralba'
Ledknapper Crossing
The Big Island
'Tuncoona'
Warrego
'Eurah'
Bokhara River
Birrie R.
Narran R.
Morendah Plains
Grawin
'Narran Park'
Wee Warra Plains
'Minetta'
Mulchacera Plain
Myroolia Plain
'Merita'
Fords Bridge
'Prairie'
'Coolabri'
'Kanimbla'
'Corrie Downs'
Round Hill Plain
Poison Point Plain
Saltbush Plain
'Belvedere'
Walkdens Plain
'Warraweena'
Weilmoringle
Kamilaroi Hwy
Brewarrina
Kamilaroi Hwy
Terewah or Narran Lake
'Lexington'
'Numbardie'
'Janina'
Wangamana Rd
'Gumbalie'
Seventeen Mile Plain
Milparinka Rd
Bourke-
'Goonery'
'Yambacoona'
Barwon R.
Tarrion Ck
The Big Warrambool
Bourke
Back O' Bourke Exhibition Centre
Bogan R.
'Waratah'
Cara Mia
'Bogewong'
'Salt Lake'
Avondale
'Glenora'
'Ballycastle'
Toorale State Con Area
'Myandetta'
'Glen Villa'
'Avondale'
Toorale
Toorale NP
Ram Paddock Island
Kidman
'Sainsbury Park'
Arthur Hall VC Way
'Yarrawin'
'Brewon'
Gongolgon
'Doradilla'
'Bobelah'
Byrock Rd
Gongolgon Byrock Rd
Marthaguy
'Warrawing'
Boorindal
'Kinchela'
Dwyers
Compton Downs
Tarcoon
Tara Road
Louth Road
Sturt Marker
Yanda Ck
'Salisbury'
Carinda
Louth
'Belah'
Gundabooka NP
Wallanburra
'Galambo'
'Ben Avon'
'Trilby'
Toorale
Darling River Rd
'Carney'
'Keelambara'
'Idalia'
'Wee Toura'
Aboriginal Rock Hole
Byrock
'Mulgawarrina'
'Bora'
Macquarie Marshes NR
Talyawalka Crossing
Budjewarra Bend
'Bimbera'
Mitchell Highway
Glenariff
'Mundadoo'
'Tundulya'
Louth
'Kallara'
Tilpa
'Wilgaroon'
Tindarey
Wilgaroon
Way
Wilga Downs Rd
Coolabah
Warren Carinda Rd
Billabong
'Buckiinguy'
'Windera'
Macquarie R.
Back Swamp
'Tindarey' Rd
'Pulpulla'
Tilpa Road
Road
Oxley Rd
Duck Ck
Crooked Ck
Canonba Road
'Buttabone Stud Park'
'Yimkin'
Ngiyampaa Walkabout
'Mount Grenfell'
'Tilpilly'
Paroo-Darling NP
'Tiltagoonah'
'Manara'
'Cubba'
Booroomugga
Yarrandale Rd
Grahweed
'Moonagee'
Canonba
Gunningbar
'Musheroo'
Mount Gap Road
The Big Beer Can
Cobar
Barrier Hwy
Barrier Hwy
Thorndale
Boppy Mountain
Muriel
Hermidale
Nyngan
Mitchell Highway
Old Warren Rd
Carinda Rd
'Meadow Glen'
Track
Wool
Lerida Rd
'Boulkra'
Belarabon
Creek
'The Rookery'
Hermidale Nymagee Rd
'Eumalga'
Mullengudgery
Tottenham
Coffills Ln
'Koree'
Buckwaroon
'Bulgoo'
'Belaringar'
'Everdale'
'Wahroonga'
'Beechworth'
'Beechworth'
Osterley Downs
Creeper Gate
'Werombie'
'Bloomfield'
Buddabaddah
Kidman Way
'Mount Doris'
Neckarbo Rd
Bedooba
Peisley Road
Pangee
'Euambaline'
Bogan River
Yathong Road
Nymagee
'Bindi'
'Wyree'
Balowra Rd
Tabratong
Sandy Ck
The Rd
'Kiama'
'Hampton'
'Multagoona'
Tottenham
Dandaloo
'Rallen'
'Pyramid'
Henry Parkes Way
The Bogan Way
Developmental Road
'Karwarn'
Gilgunnia
'Moothumbil'
'Milbridge'
Albert
Alagala
Yallock
Moolah
'Irymple'
'Ashleigh Downs'
'Ballatta'
Alagala Rd
Yathong NR
'Marobee'
'Minnalong'
Albert Rd
'Wilga Valley'
Tullamore
To Ivanhoe
To Hillston
To Hillston
To Hillston
To Condobolin
© Hema Maps
To Dirranbandi
To Lightning Ridge
To Walgett
To Coonamble
To Warren
To Trangie
To Narromine
145°E
145°50'E
146°40'E
147°30'E
29°10'S
30°S
30°50'S
31°40'S
32°30'S

Broken Hill to Griffith

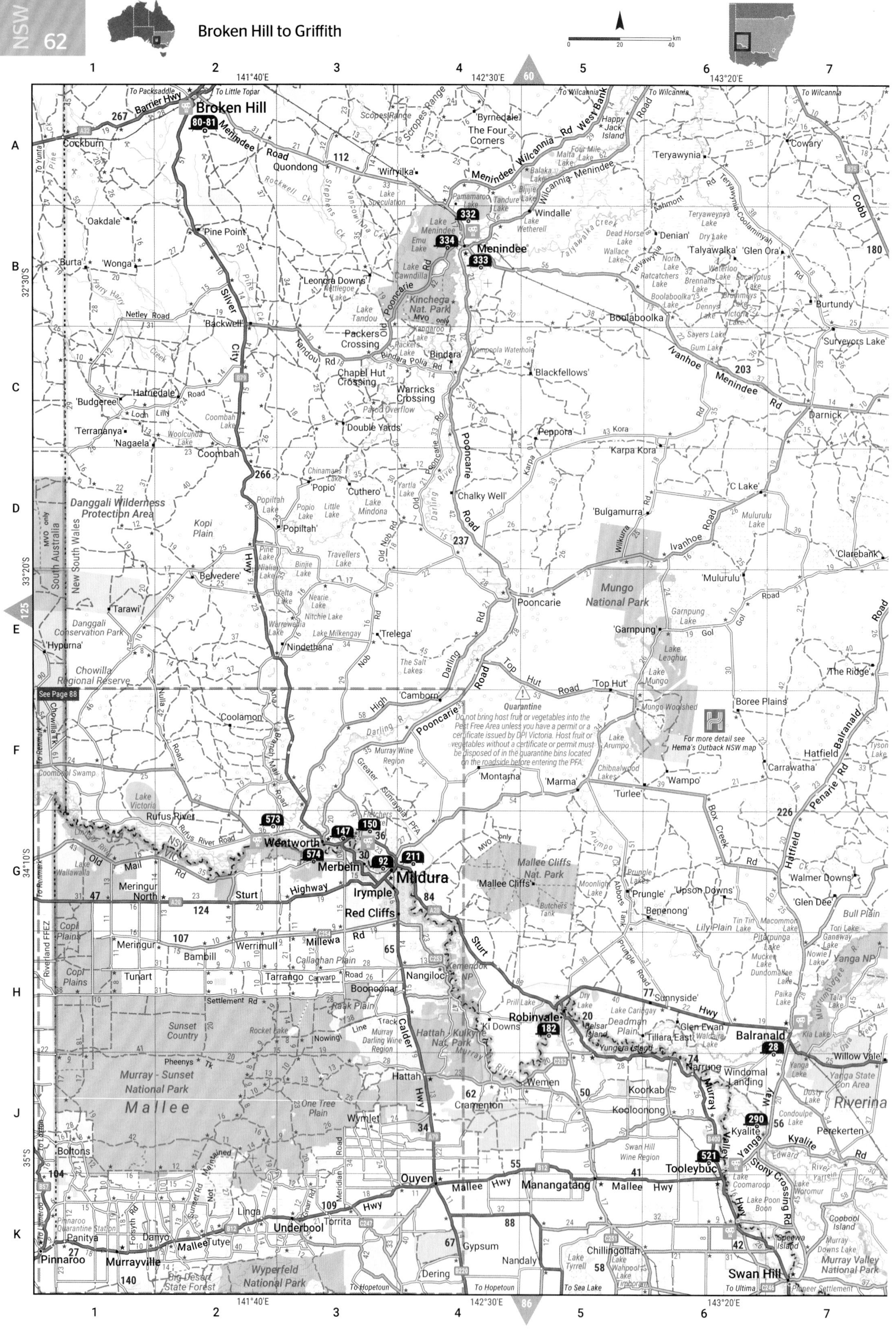

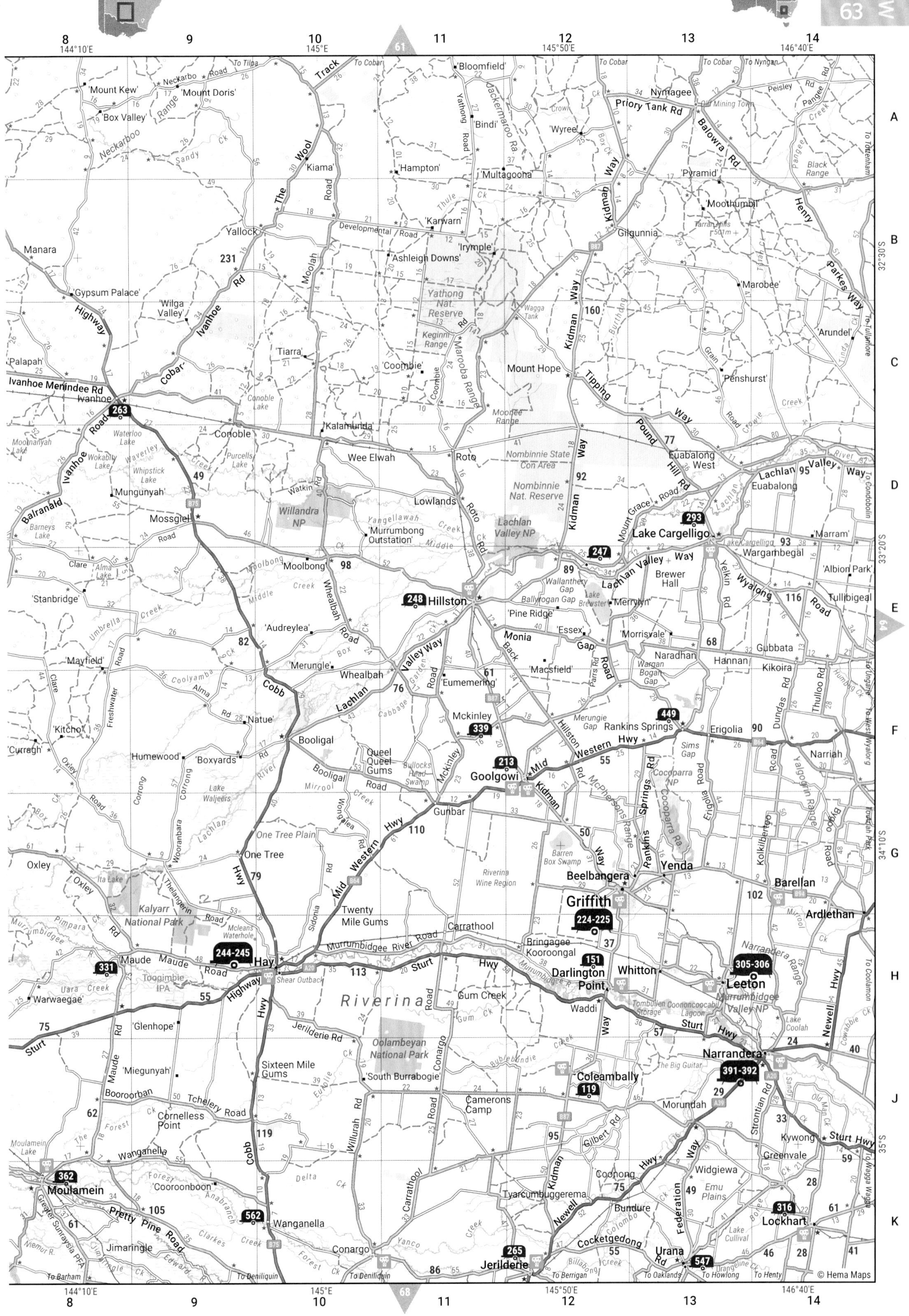

8
9
10
11
12
13
14
144°10'E
145°E
145°50'E
146°40'E
A
B
C
D
E
F
G
H
J
K
32°30'S
33°20'S
34°10'S
35°S
'Mount Kew'
'Mount Doris'
'Box Valley'
Neckarboo Range
'Bloomfield'
'Bindi'
'Wyree'
Nymagee
Priory Tank Rd
Balowra Rd
'Kiama'
'Hampton'
'Multagoona'
'Pyramid'
'Moothumbil'
Black Range
The Wool Track
Kidman Way
Henry Parkes Way
Yallock
'Karwarn'
'Irymple'
Gilgunnia
Manara
'Ashleigh Downs'
'Marobee'
'Gypsum Palace'
Yathong Nat. Reserve
'Wilga Valley'
Keginni Range
160
'Arundel'
Highway
'Tiarra'
'Coombie'
Mount Hope
'Penshurst'
'Palapah'
Ivanhoe Menindee Rd
Ivanhoe
Cobar Rd
Ivanhoe Rd
Tipping Way
Pound Way
Kalamunda
Conoble
Moonee Range
Euabalong West
Wee Elwah
Roto
Nombinnie State Con Area
Nombinnie Nat. Reserve
Lachlan Valley Way
Euabalong
'Mungunyah'
Lowlands
Balranald Road
Willandra NP
Mossgiel
'Murrumbong Outstation'
Lachlan Valley NP
Lake Cargelligo
'Marram'
Wargambegal
'Albion Park'
Moolbong'
'Stanbridge'
Hillston
'Pine Ridge'
'Essex'
Merrylyn'
Brewer Hall
Tullibigeal
'Audreylea'
Monia Back Rd
'Morrisvale'
Gubbata
Naradhan
Hannan
Kikoira
'Mayfield'
'Merungle'
Whealbah
'Eumemering'
'Macsfield'
Wargan Bogan Gap
Mckinley
Rankins Springs
Erigolia
Narriah
'Kitcho'
'Natue'
Booligal
Mid Western Hwy
'Curragh'
'Humewood'
'Boxyards'
Queel Queel Gums
Goolgowi
Cocoparra NP
One Tree Plain
Gunbar
One Tree
Oxley
Kalyarr National Park
Riverina Wine Region
Beelbangera
Yenda
Barellan
Griffith
Ardlethan
Twenty Mile Gums
Carrathool
Bringagee
Kooroongal
Maude
Hay
Darlington Point
Whitton
Leeton
Narrandera Range
Murrumbidgee Valley NP
Toogimbie IPA
Shear Outback
Riverina
Gum Creek
Waddi
'Warwaegae'
Sturt Hwy
'Glenhope'
Jerilderie Rd
Oolambeyan National Park
Narrandera
Newell Hwy
'Miegunyah'
Sixteen Mile Gums
'South Burrabogie'
Coleambally
Boororban
Tchelery Road
Cornelless Point
Camerons Camp
Morundah
Kywong
Greenvale
Wanganella
Moulamein
'Cooroonboon'
Coonong
Tyrcumbuggerema
Widgiewa
Emu Plains
Pretty Pine Road
Bundure
Lockhart
Conargo
Cocketgedong
Jimaringle
Jerilderie
Urana
To Barham
To Deniliquin
To Berrigan
To Oaklands
To Howlong
To Henty
© Hema Maps

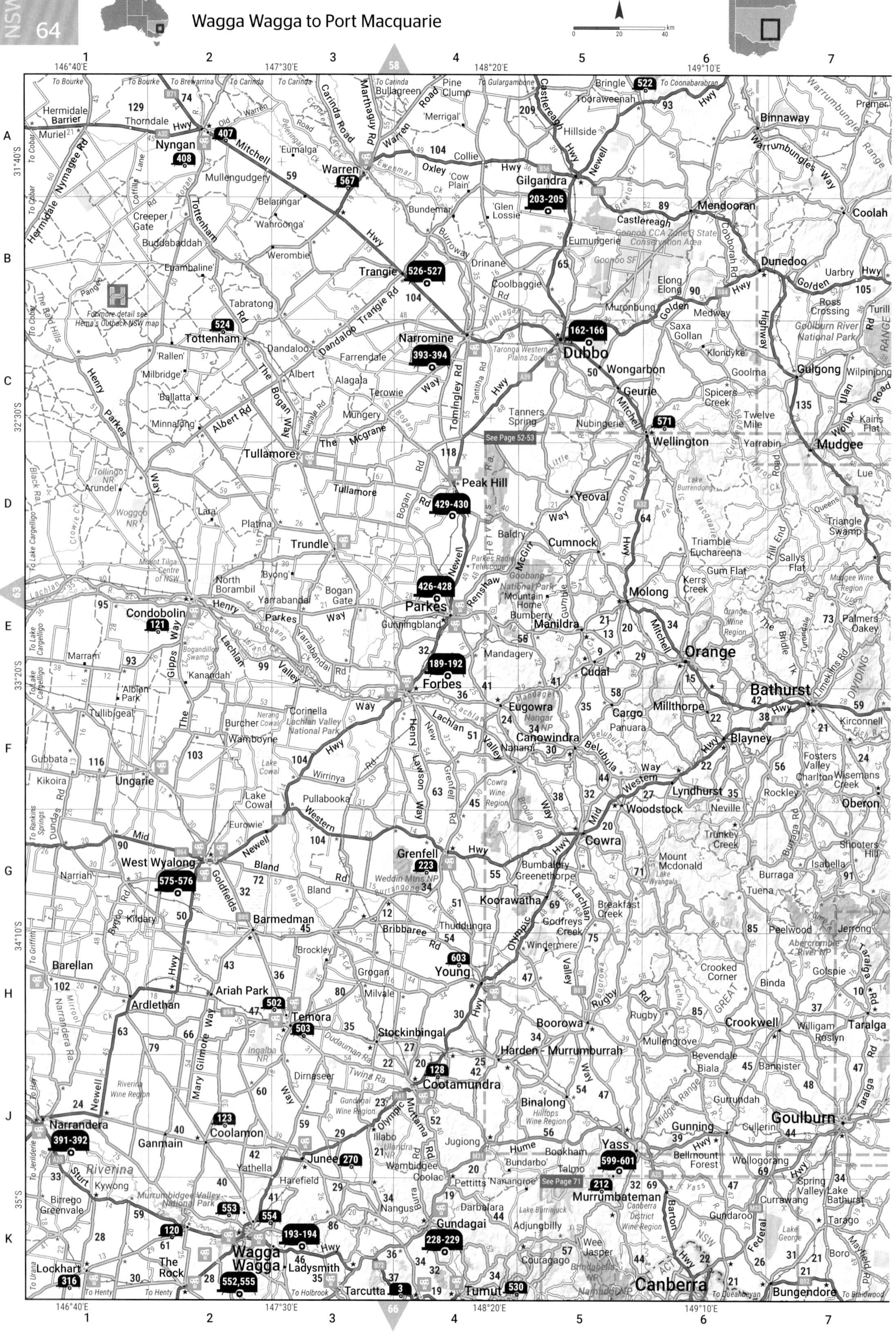
Nyngan
Warren
Gilgandra
Mendooran
Coolah
Binnaway
Dunedoo
Trangie
Narromine
Dubbo
Wongarbon
Geurie
Gulgong
Mudgee
Wellington
Tottenham
Tullamore
Peak Hill
Yeoval
Cumnock
Trundle
Parkes
Condobolin
Molong
Orange
Manildra
Forbes
Eugowra
Cudal
Canowindra
Bathurst
Blayney
Millthorpe
Ungarie
West Wyalong
Grenfell
Cowra
Woodstock
Lyndhurst
Oberon
Barmedman
Young
Koorawatha
Ariah Park
Ardlethan
Temora
Stockinbingal
Boorowa
Harden - Murrumburrah
Cootamundra
Crookwell
Taralga
Binalong
Gunning
Goulburn
Narrandera
Coolamon
Junee
Yass
Murrumbateman
Gundagai
Wagga Wagga
Lockhart
The Rock
Ladysmith
Tarcutta
Tumut
Canberra
Bungendore
For more detail see Hema's Outback NSW map
See Page 52-53
See Page 71

Spring Ridge
Quirindi
Nundle
Nowendoc National Park
Nowendoc
New England
Mount Seaview
Riamukka
Ellenborough
Oxley Hwy
Port Macquarie
Wauchope
North Shore Beach
Miners Beach
Lighthouse Beach
Toms Creek
Comboyne
Rainbow Beach
Grants Beach
Camden Haven
Dunbogan Beach
Kylies Beach
Bundella
Blackville
Coolah Tops National Park
Jacks Creek
Murrurundi
Glenrock
Corroboree Flat
Barrington Tops National Park
Bullocks Flat
Rocks Crossing
Lansdowne
Ellerston
Appletree Flat
Taree
Harrington
Liverpool Range
Towarri NP
Kars Springs
Bunnan
Cassilis
Borambil
Merriwa
Golden
Scone
Rawdon Vale
Gloucester
Belltrees
Peugeot Point
Karkatt
Wallabi Beach
Saltwater Beach
Black Head Beach
For more detail see Hema's Sydney to Brisbane map
Nine Mile Beach
Forster
Tuncurry
Pebbly Beach
Cape Hawke
Seven Mile Beach
Boomerang Beach
Smiths Lake
Davis Creek
Muswellbrook
Bowmans Creek
Upper Monkerai
Monkerai
Warranulla
Upper Myall
Goulburn River National Park
Gooranggoola
Dawsons Hill
Brownmore
Bandon Grove
Newells Creek
Baerami
Denman
Jerrys Plains
Mirannie
Gresford
Dungog
Bulahdelah
Stroud
Mayers Flat
Myall Lakes NP
Submarine Beach
Bombah Point
Mungo Beach
Mungo Brush
Upper Bylong
Martindale
Glen Gallic
Appletree Flat
Singleton
Clarence Town
Nerong
Paterson
Branxton
Pacific
Port Stephens - Great Lakes Marine Park
Jimmys Beach
See Page 54-55
Wollemi National Park
Hefrons Hole
Devils Elbow
Gum Tree Hole
Maitland
Raymond Terrace
Nelson Bay
Medowie
Salamander Bay
Stockton Beach
Broke
Cessnock
Kurri Kurri
Kandos
Howes Valley
Newcastle
Glen Alice
Round Swamp
Glenowlan
Airly
Yango
Laguna
Watagan
Yallambie
Bucketty
Toronto
Nine Mile Beach
Mannering Park
Chain Valley Bay
Birdie Beach
South Pacific Ocean
Gardens of Stone Nat. Park
'Haughey Hut'
Higher Macdonald
Upper Macdonald
Mogo Creek
Fernances
St Albans
Wyong
Tuggerah Lake
Tuggerah Beach
Portland
Colo Heights
Bilpin
Weavers
Forresters Beach
Lithgow
Warawaralong
Gosford
The Skillion
MacMasters Beach
Mooney Mooney
Brooklyn
Patonga
The Meadows
Richmond
Mount Hay Range
Galston
Cowan
Ku-ring-gai Chase National Park
Katoomba
Collaroy Beach
Narrabeen Beach
Curl Curl Beach
Dee Why Beach
Penrith
Blacktown
Blue Mountains National Park
Jenolan Caves Rd
Wallacia
Warragamba
Sydney
Liverpool
Ben Buckler
Maroubra Beach
Kanangra-Boyd National Park
Cape Banks
Kurnell Peninsula
Cape Baily
Tasman Sea
Oakdale
Yerranderie
The Oaks
Campbelltown
Bundeena
Marley Beach
Royal NP
Picton
Thirlmere
Douglas Park
Helensburgh
Buxton
Tahmoor
Bargo
Wombeyan Caves Rd
Newfoundland
Hanworth
Bannaby
Wollongong
Mittagong
Bowral
Greenwich Park
Perkins Beach
Lake Illawarra
Shellharbour Beach
Moss Vale
Robertson
Boyds Beach
Kiama
Bare Bluff
Red Cliff
Walkers Beach
Wingello
Marulan
Kangaroo Valley
Morton National Park
Seven Mile Beach
Shoalhaven Bight
Bomaderry
Nowra
See Page 52-53
See Page 50-51
Culburra Beach
Culburra
Warrain Beach
Jervis Bay
Callala Bay
Old Erowal Bay
Braidwood Rd
Nerriga
Basin View
St Georges Basin
Cape St George
For more detail see Hema's Melbourne to Sydney map
Corang
Shoalhaven Coast Wine Region
Conjola NP
Sussex Inlet
Budawang National Park
To Ulladulla
222
144
148
252-255
483-488
458
294-296
51
142-143
© Hema Maps

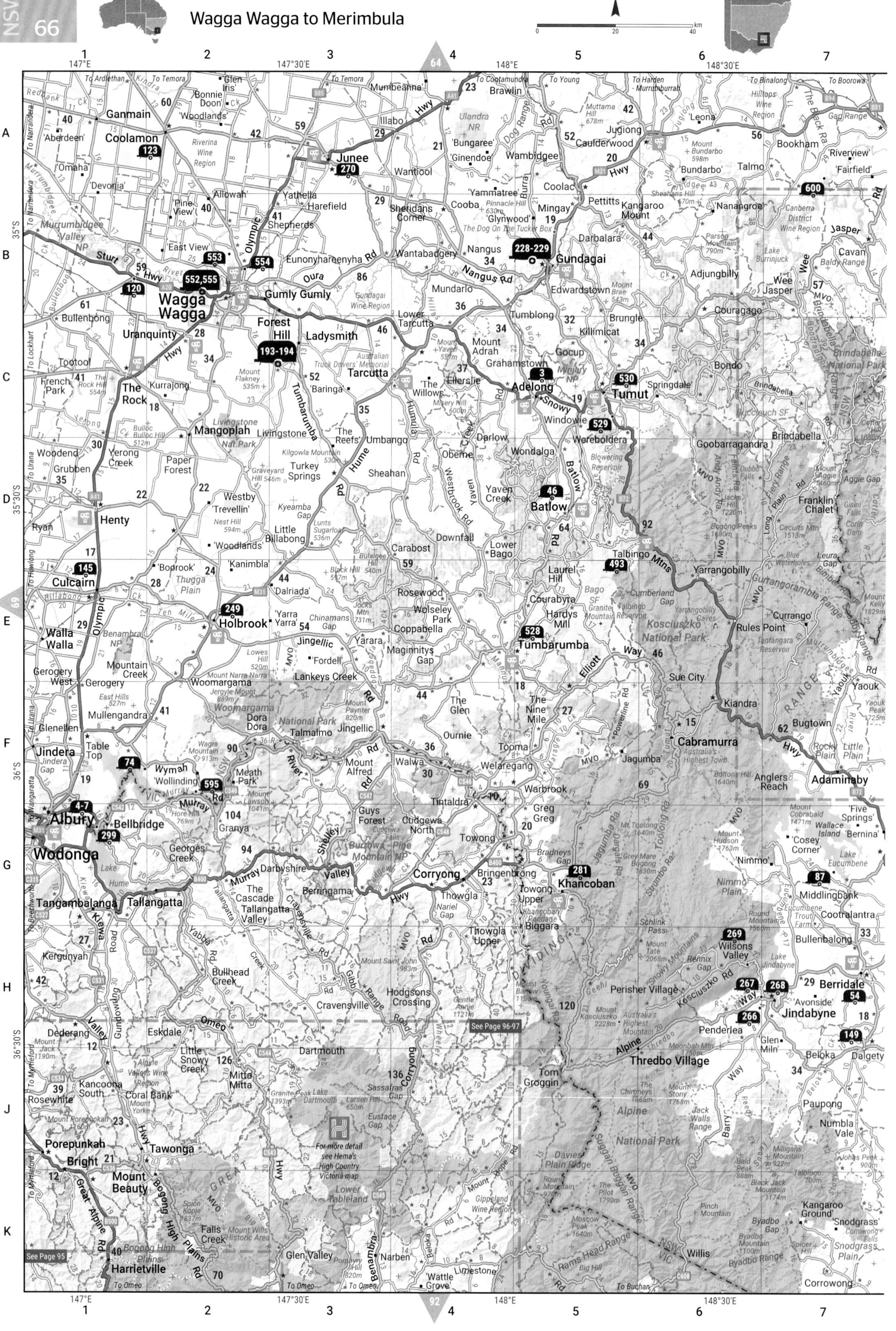
Ganmain
Coolamon
Junee
Wagga Wagga
Gumly Gumly
Forest Hill
Ladysmith
Uranquinty
The Rock
Mangoplah
Tarcutta
Gundagai
Tumut
Adelong
Batlow
Henty
Culcairn
Holbrook
Walla Walla
Tumbarumba
Jindera
Albury
Wodonga
Bellbridge
Corryong
Khancoban
Cabramurra
Adaminaby
Jindabyne
Berridale
Thredbo Village
Tallangatta
Bright
Mount Beauty
Harrietville
Tawonga
Porepunkah
Kosciuszko National Park
Alpine National Park
See Page 96-97
See Page 95
For more detail see Hema's High Country Victoria map

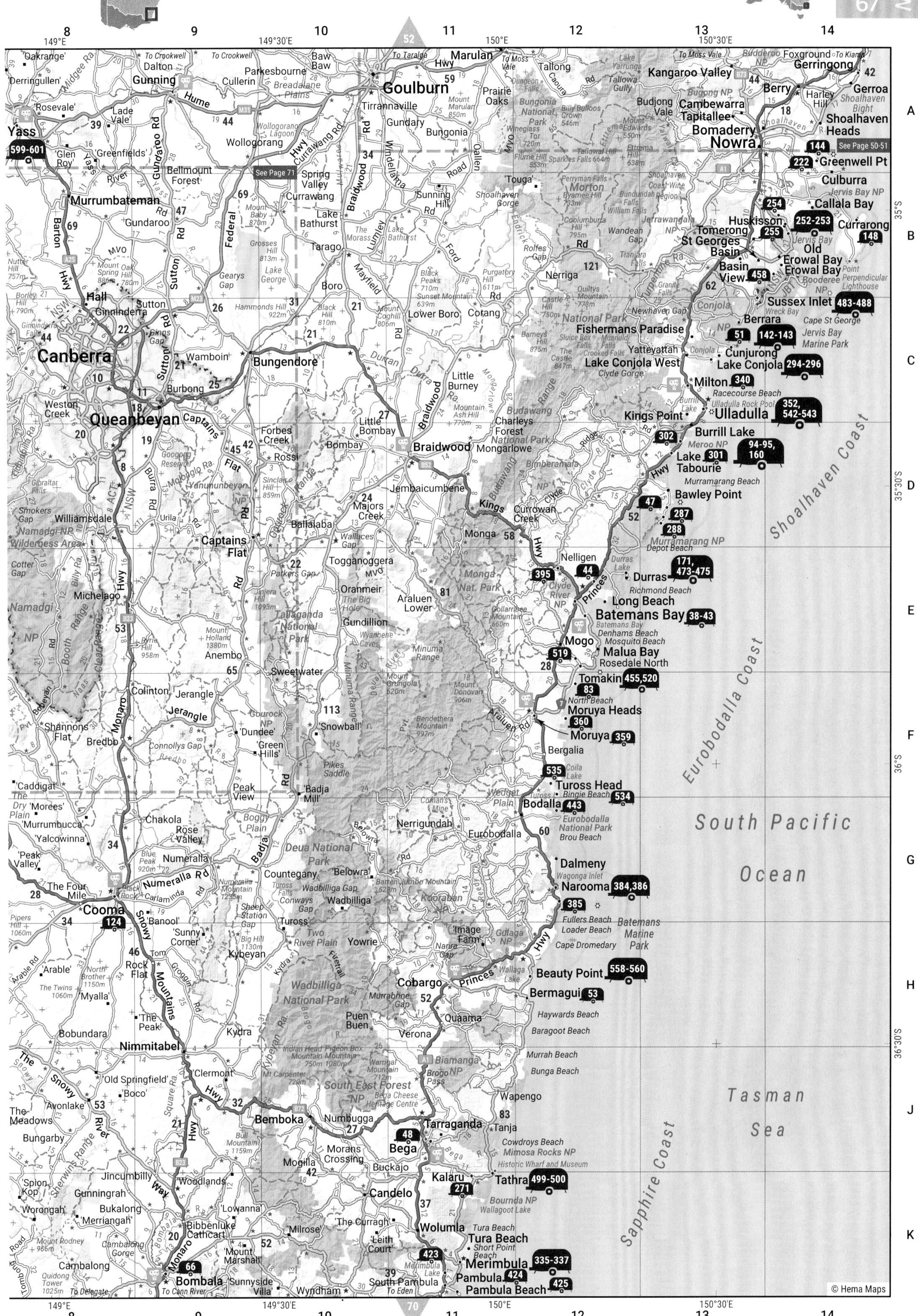

Yass
Gunning
Dalton
Goulburn
Marulan
Tallong
Kangaroo Valley
Foxground
Gerringong
Berry
Gerroa
Shoalhaven Heads
Bomaderry
Nowra
Cambewarra
Tapitallee
Greenwell Pt
Culburra
Callala Bay
Huskisson
Currarong
Tomerong
St Georges Basin
Basin View
Erowal Bay
Old Erowal Bay
Sussex Inlet
Berrara
Cunjurong
Lake Conjola
Fishermans Paradise
Lake Conjola West
Yatteyattah
Milton
Ulladulla
Kings Point
Burrill Lake
Lake Tabourie
Bawley Point
Murramarang NP
Durras
Long Beach
Batemans Bay
Nelligen
Mogo
Malua Bay
Rosedale North
Tomakin
Moruya Heads
Moruya
Bergalia
Tuross Head
Bodalla
Eurobodalla
Dalmeny
Narooma
Beauty Point
Bermagui
Cobargo
Quaama
Tarraganda
Tanja
Bega
Kalaru
Tathra
Candelo
Wolumla
Tura Beach
Merimbula
Pambula
Pambula Beach
South Pambula
Wyndham
Bombala
Cooma
Nimmitabel
Bemboka
Murrumbateman
Hall
Canberra
Queanbeyan
Bungendore
Braidwood
Tarago
Captains Flat
Michelago
Bredbo
Numeralla
Shoalhaven Coast
Eurobodalla Coast
Sapphire Coast
South Pacific Ocean
Tasman Sea
See Page 71
See Page 50-51
© Hema Maps

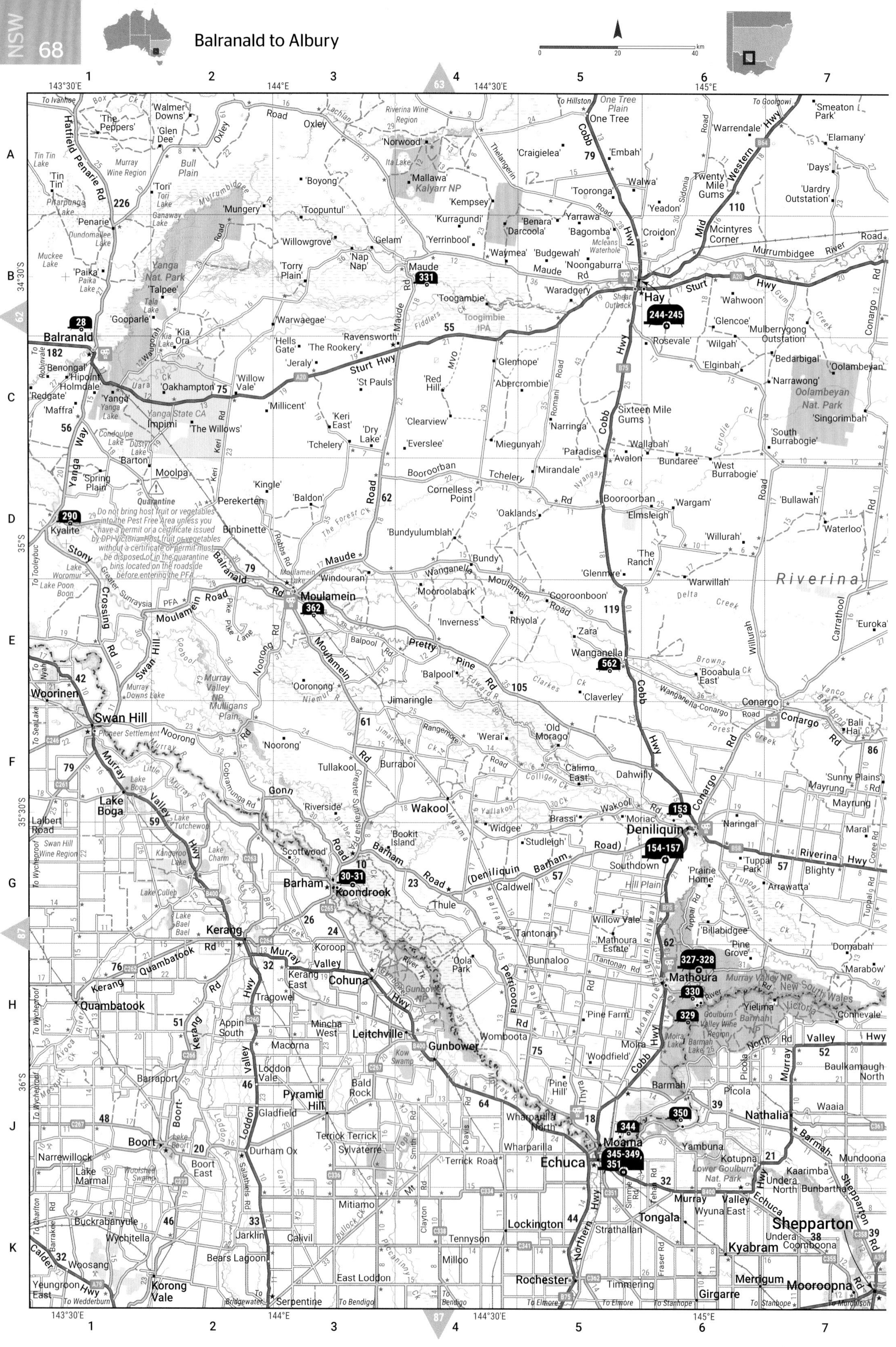

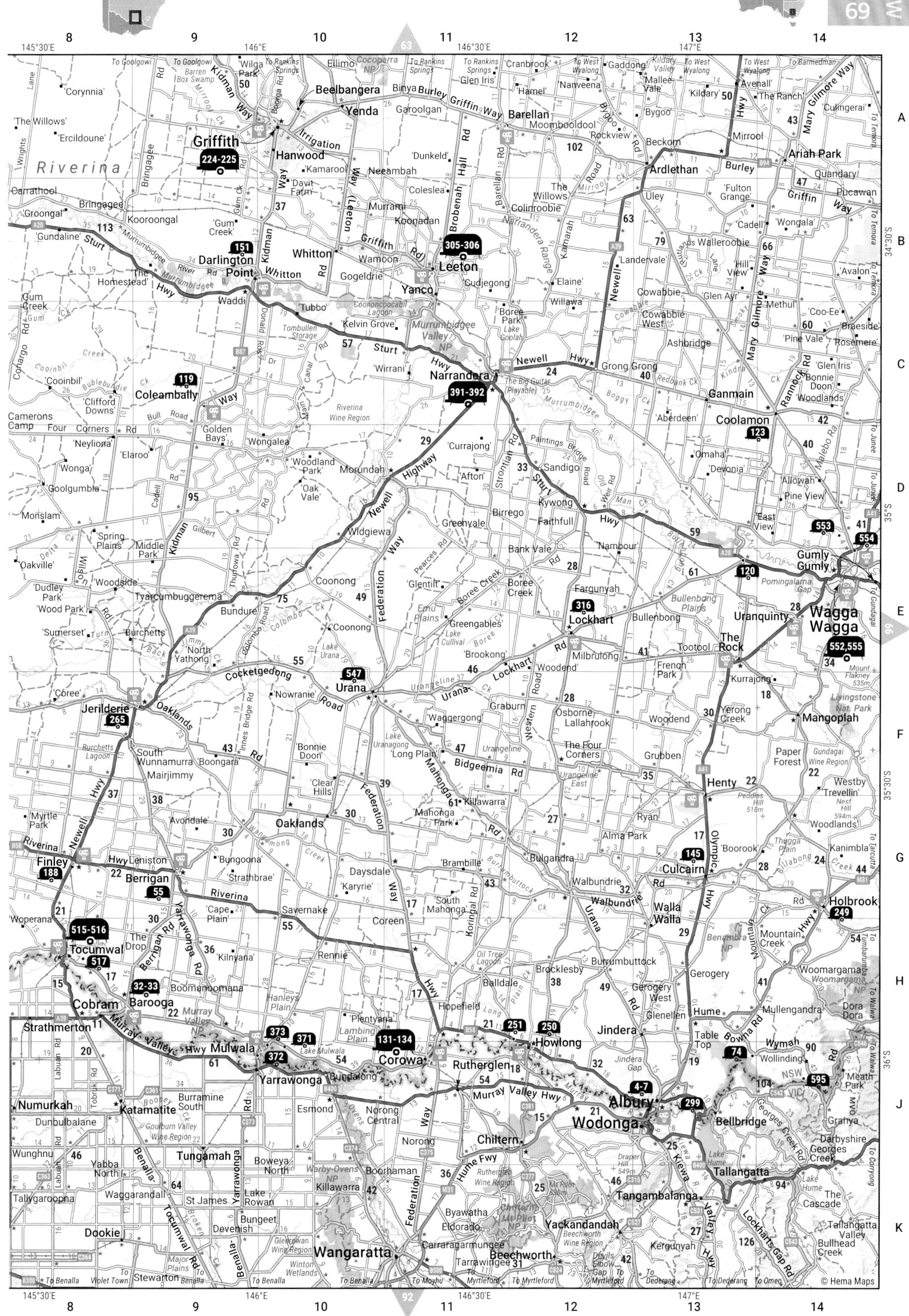
Griffith
Leeton
Narrandera
Darlington Point
Coleambally
Jerilderie
Urana
Lockhart
Coolamon
Wagga Wagga
The Rock
Finley
Berrigan
Tocumwal
Cobram
Barooga
Mulwala
Yarrawonga
Corowa
Howlong
Albury
Wodonga
Holbrook
Culcairn
Henty
Rutherglen
Chiltern
Wangaratta
Beechworth
Yackandandah
Tallangatta
Riverina
© Hema Maps

Orbost to Batemans Bay

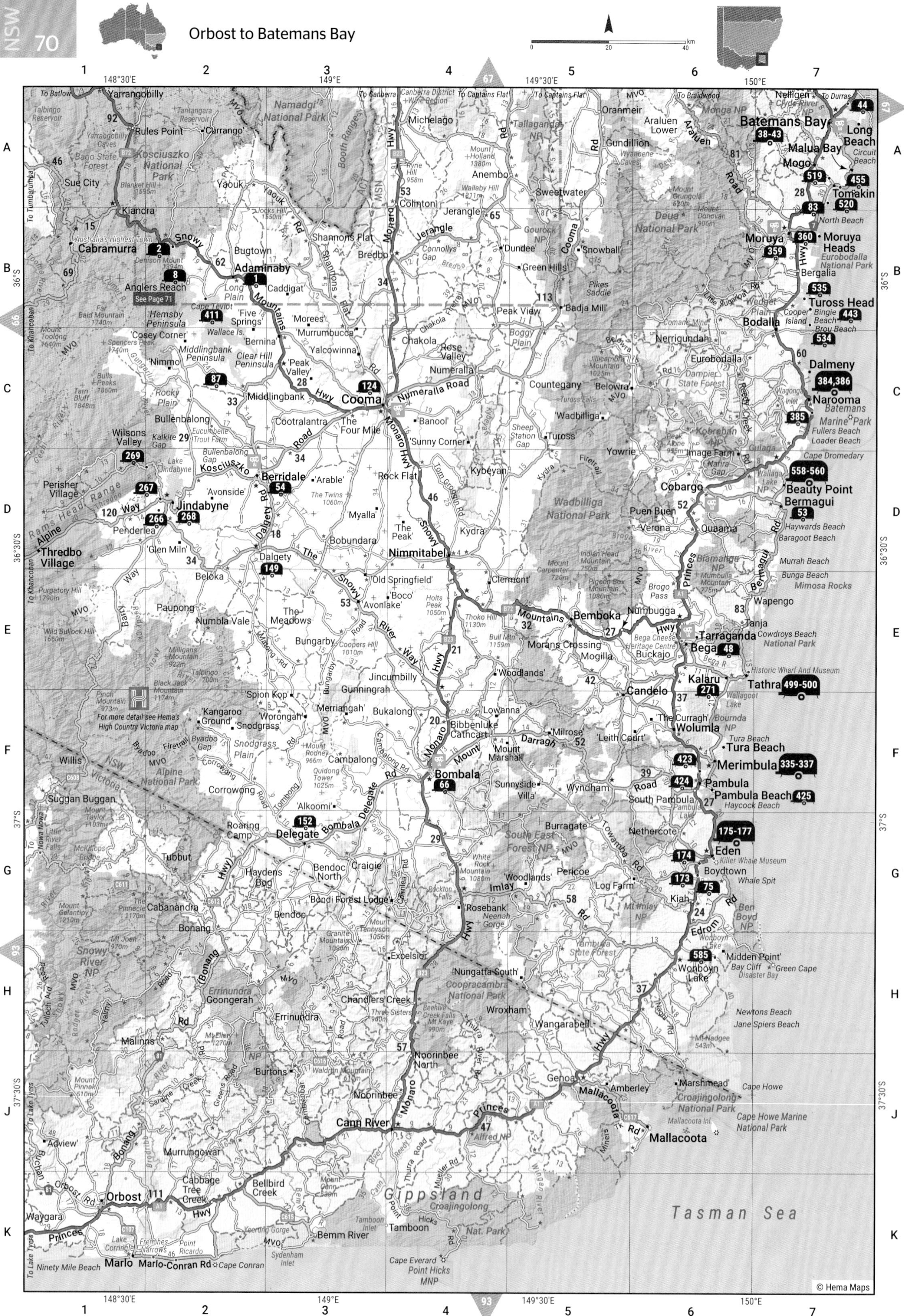

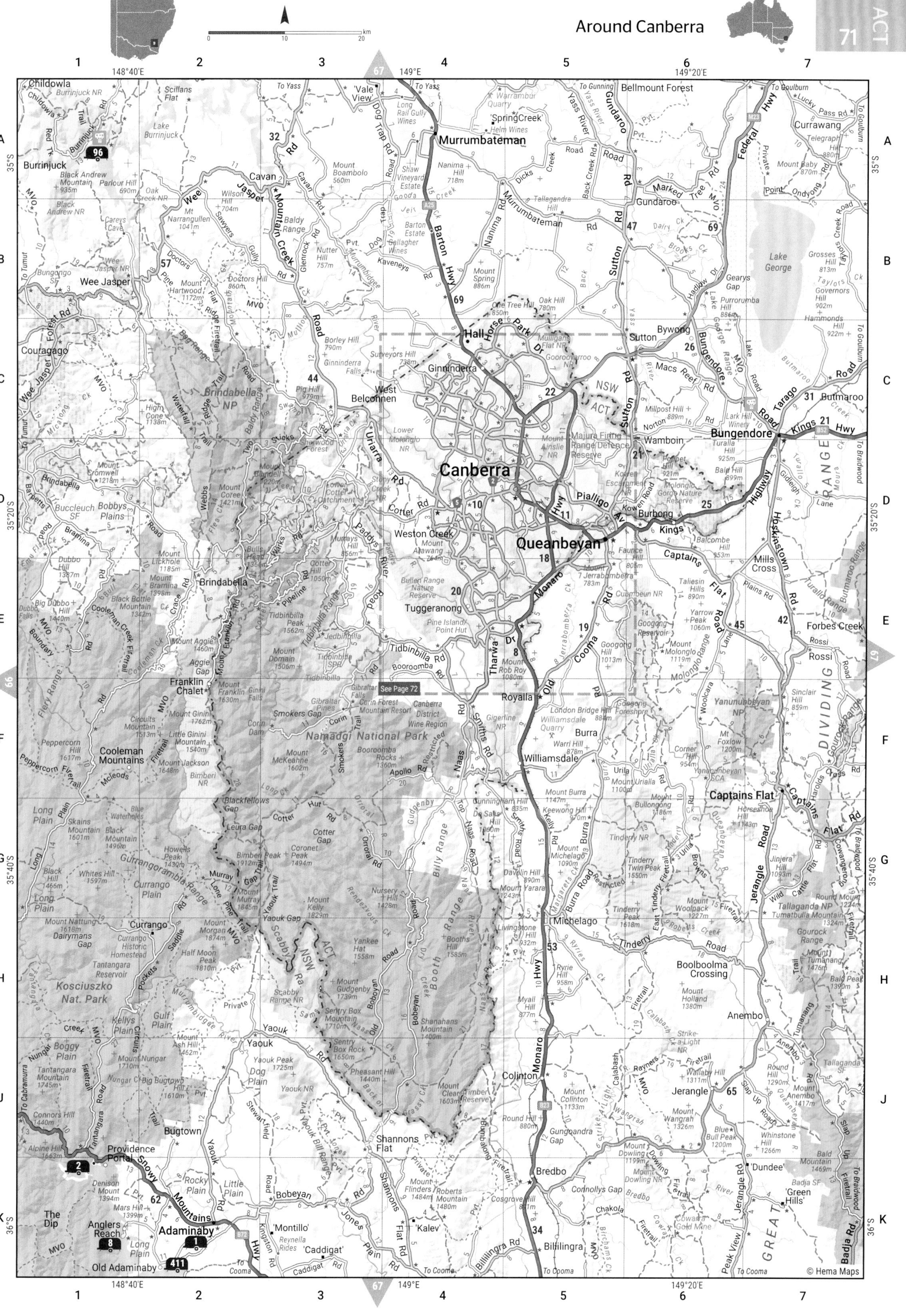
Canberra
Queanbeyan
Murrumbateman
Hall
Bungendore
Captains Flat
Michelago
Bredbo
Adaminaby
Wee Jasper
Brindabella
Tuggeranong
Weston Creek
Belconnen
Namadgi National Park
Kosciuszko Nat. Park
Brindabella NP
Lake George
Tinderry NR
Williamsdale
Royalla
Tharwa
Sutton
Gundaroo
Wamboin
Burbong
Yaouk
Bugtown
Jerangle
Anembo
See Page 72
© Hema Maps

Canberra Throughroads

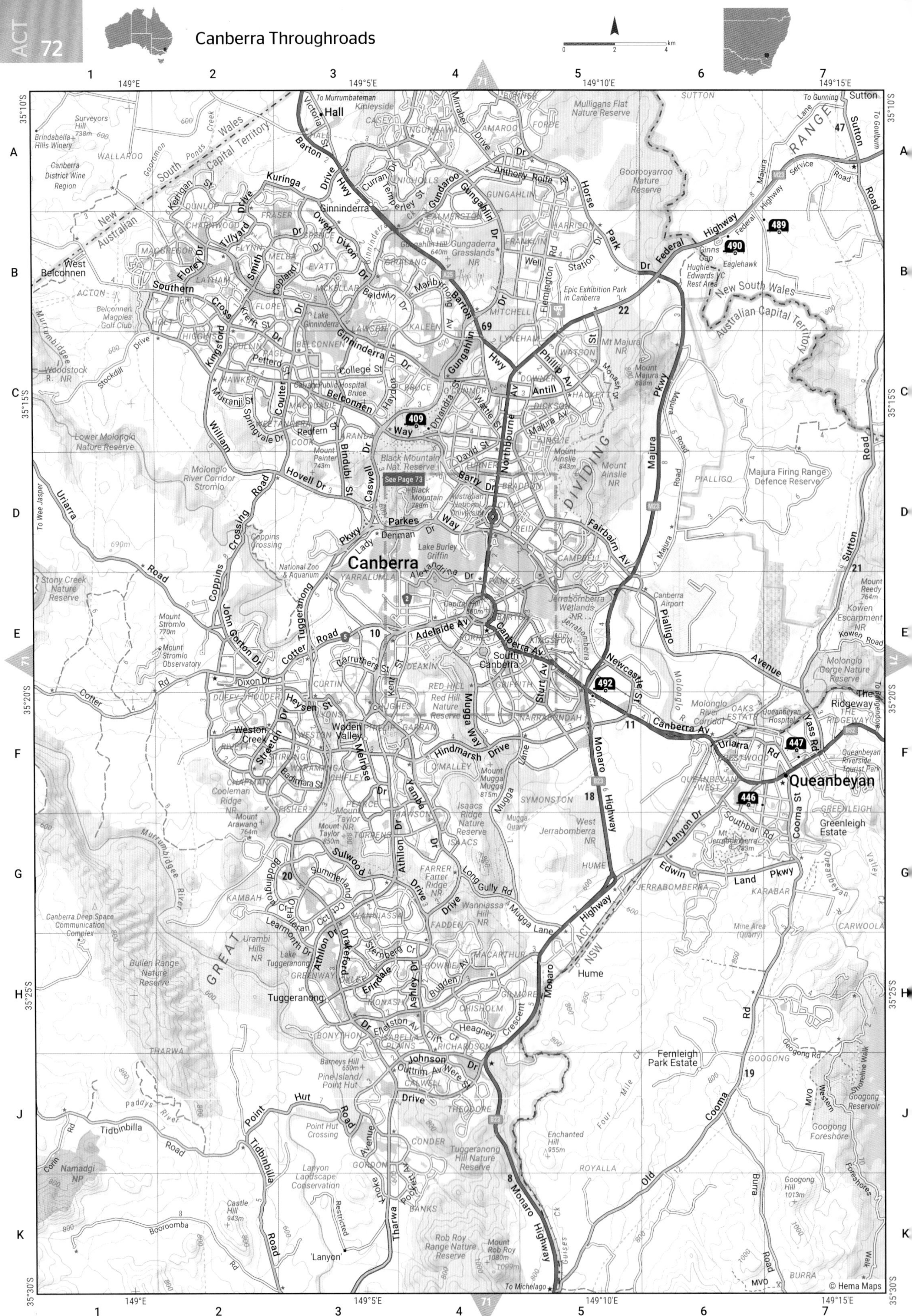

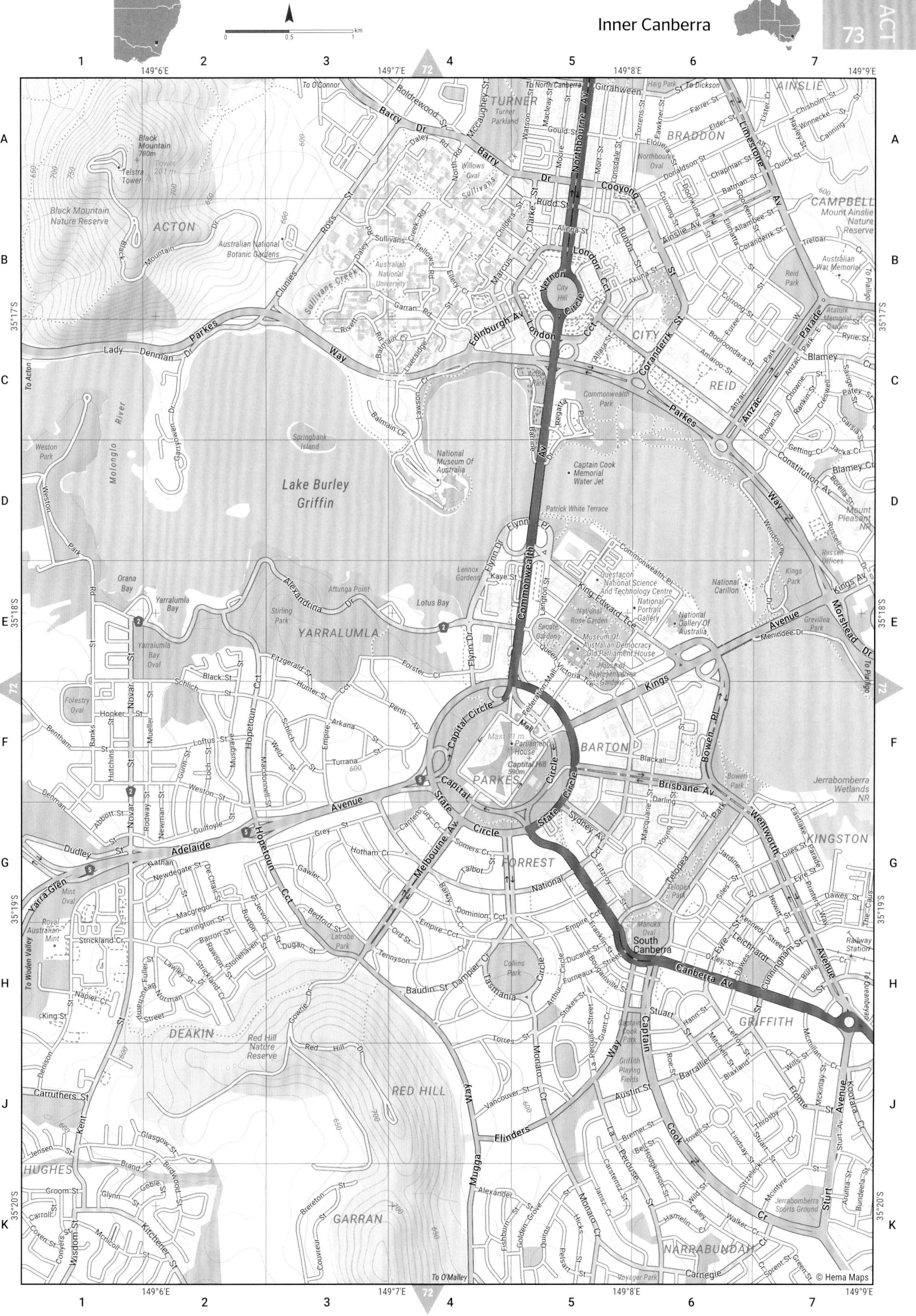
To O'Connor
To North Canberra
To Dickson
TURNER
Turner Parkland
BRADDON
AINSLIE
CAMPBELL
Mount Ainslie Nature Reserve
Australian War Memorial
Black Mountain 780m
Telstra Tower
Black Mountain Nature Reserve
ACTON
Australian National Botanic Gardens
Australian National University
City Hill
CITY
REID
Commonwealth Park
Lake Burley Griffin
Springbank Island
National Museum Of Australia
Captain Cook Memorial Water Jet
Patrick White Terrace
Weston Park
Molonglo River
Orana Bay
Yarralumla Bay
Attunga Point
Lotus Bay
Stirling Park
YARRALUMLA
Lennox Gardens
Questacon National Science And Technology Centre
National Portrait Gallery
National Gallery Of Australia
National Rose Garden
Museum Of Australian Democracy Old Parliament House
National Carillon
Kings Park
Grevillea Park
Russell Offices
Parliament House
Capital Hill 590m
PARKES
BARTON
Bowen Park
Jerrabomberra Wetlands NR
KINGSTON
FORREST
Collins Park
Latrobe Park
Manuka Oval
South Canberra
Telopea Park
Railway Station
GRIFFITH
DEAKIN
Red Hill Nature Reserve
RED HILL
GARRAN
HUGHES
NARRABUNDAH
Jerrabomberra Sports Ground
Royal Australian Mint
Mint Oval
Forestry Oval
To Woden Valley
To Acton
To Pialligo
To Queanbeyan
To O'Malley
Lady Denman Dr
Parkes Way
Commonwealth Av
Northbourne Av
Kings Avenue
Adelaide Avenue
Yarra Glen
Capital Circle
State Circle
Canberra Av
Mugga Way
Constitution Av
Anzac Parade
Limestone Av
Wentworth Avenue
Captain Cook Cr
Hopetoun Cct
Melbourne Av
© Hema Maps

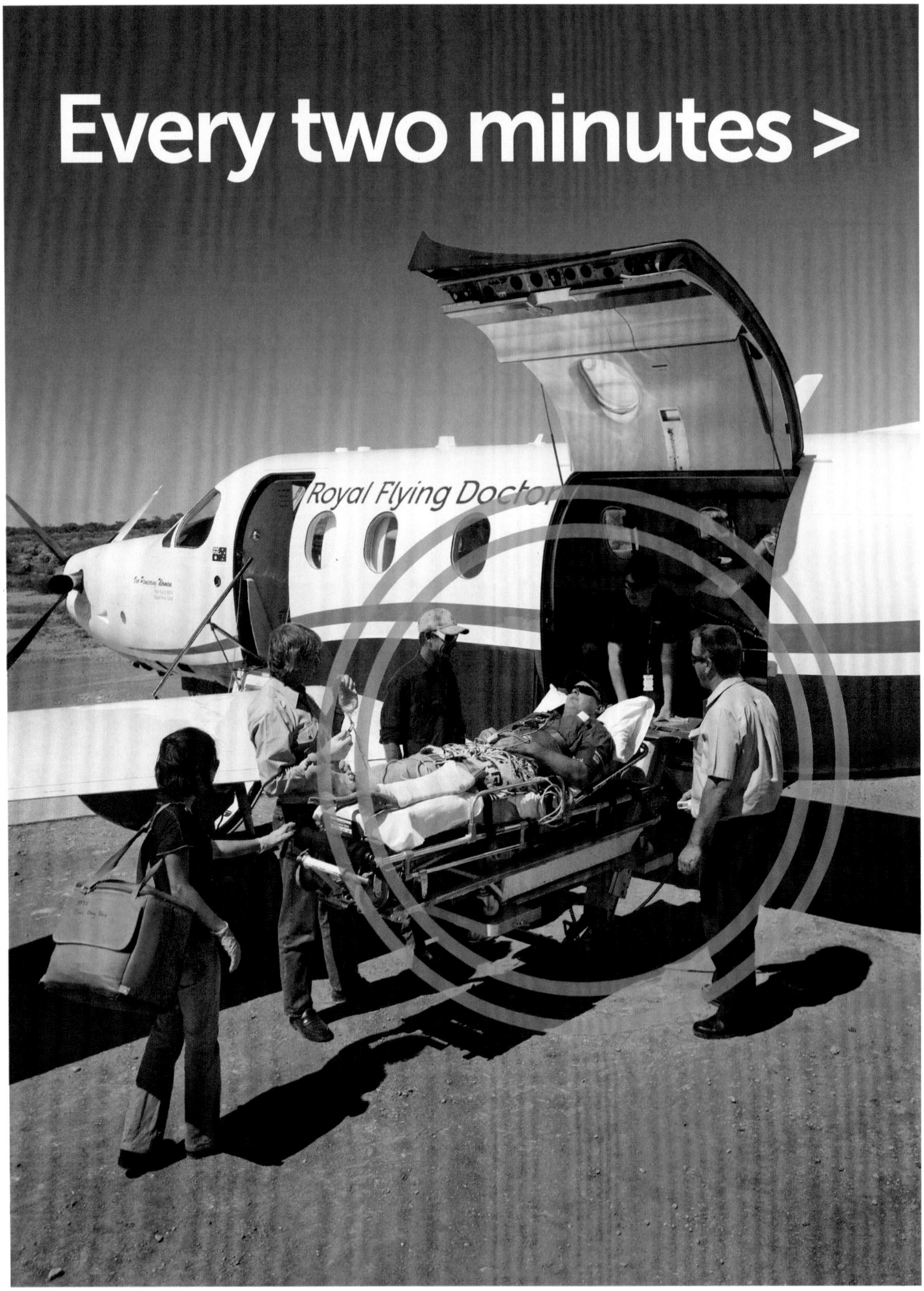

Adaminaby

1 Alpine Tourist Park
2 Lette St, cnr Snowy Mountains Hwy
www.alpinetouristpark.com.au
02 6454 2438 HEMA 71 K2 35 59 48 S 148 46 11 E
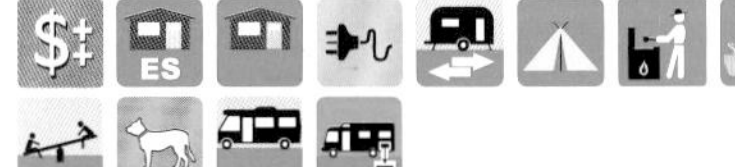

2 Providence Holiday Park
46 Providence Rd, Providence Portal. Camper trailers & tents only
www.providenceholidaypark.com.au
02 6454 2357 HEMA 71 K1 35 56 31 S 148 37 35 E

Adelong

3 Golden Gully Caravan Park
Victoria Hill Rd, behind RSL. Register at Services Club, Tumut St
02 6946 2163 HEMA 66 C5 35 18 25 S 148 03 55 E

Albury

4 Albury All Seasons
481 Wagga Rd. 6 km N of Albury PO
www.alburyallseasons.com.au
02 6025 1619 HEMA 66 F1 36 02 31 S 146 57 08 E

5 Albury Central Park
286 North St. 2 km N of PO
02 60218420 HEMA 66 G1 36 04 03 S 146 56 09 E

6 Big 4 Albury Tourist Park
372 Wagga Rd, Lavington
www.alburytouristpark.com.au/
02 6040 2999 HEMA 66 F1 36 02 54 S 146 56 21 E

7 Ingenia Holidays Albury
508 Wagga Rd, Cnr of Catherine Cres
www.ingeniaholidays.com.au/albury/
02 6040 6275 HEMA 66 F1 36 02 26 S 146 57 31 E
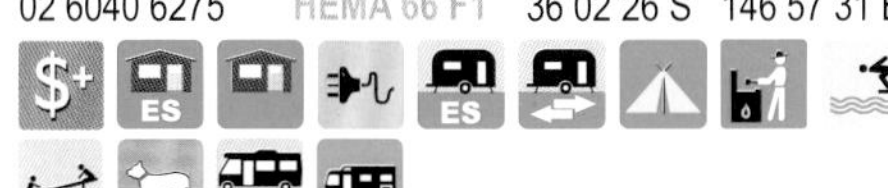

Anglers Reach

8 Anglers Reach Caravan Park
Peninsula Rd.14 km W of Adaminaby PO
www.anglersreach.com
02 6454 2223 HEMA 71 K1 35 59 53 S 148 39 47 E

Anna Bay

9 Bays Holiday Park
23 Port Stephens Dr. 3 km N of PO
www.baysholidaypark.com
02 4982 1438 HEMA 53 A14 32 45 25 S 152 04 03 E

10 Emerald Tiki Village
4296 Nelson Bay Rd
www.tikivillageparkretreat.com.au
02 4982 1422 HEMA 53 A14 32 46 11 S 152 04 05 E

11 Gateway Lifestyle Birubi Beach Holiday Park
37 James Patterson St
www.glhp.com.au/parks/birubi-beach/
02 4982 1263 HEMA 53 B14 32 46 52 S 152 04 50 E
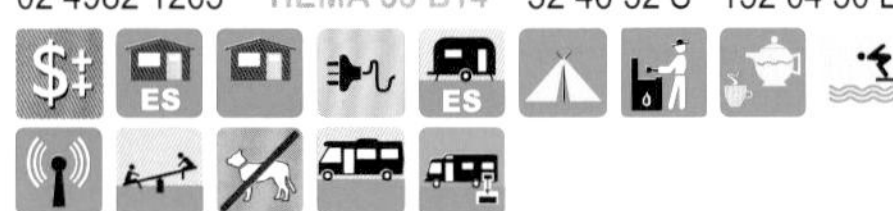

12 Island Leisure Village
Fenningham's Island Rd
www.theisland.com.au
02 4982 1207 HEMA 53 A13 32 45 01 S 152 02 01 E

Armidale

13 Armidale Acres Motor Inn & Van Park
New England Hwy. 6 km N of PO
www.armidaleacres.com.au
02 6771 1281 HEMA 55 A8 30 27 39 S 151 40 53 E

14 Armidale Tourist Park
39 Waterfall Way
www.armidaletouristpark.com.au
02 6772 6470 HEMA 55 A9 30 31 12 S 151 41 03 E

15 BIG4 Armidale Highlander Van Village
76 Glen Innes Rd. 2 km N of PO
www.highlandervanvillage.com
02 6772 4768 HEMA 55 A8 30 29 36 S 151 40 09 E

Arrawarra

16 Arrawarra Beach Holiday Park
46 Arrawarra Beach Rd
www.arrawarrabeachholidaypark.com
02 6649 2753 HEMA 57 J13 30 03 35 S 153 11 47 E

17 Gateway Lifestyle Lorikeet
210 Eggins Close
www.glhp.com.au/parks/lorikeet/
02 6649 2717 HEMA 57 J13 30 02 36 S 153 11 25 E

18 NRMA Darlington Beach Holiday Park
104-134 Eggins Dr
www.darlingtonbeach.com.au
02 6640 7444 HEMA 57 J13 30 02 50 S 153 11 14 E

Ashford

19 Ashford Caravan Park
Bukkulla St, behind the swimming pool
02 6725 4014 HEMA 56 F5 29 19 24 S 151 05 52 E

Ballina

20 Ballina Waterfront Village & Tourist Park
586 River St. 3.5 km S of PO
02 6686 2984 HEMA 57 D14 28 51 54 S 153 31 26 E

21 BIG4 Ballina Headlands Holiday Park
35 Skennars Head Rd
www.ballinaheadlands.com.au
02 6687 7450 HEMA 57 D14 28 49 26 S 153 36 01 E

22 Hibiscus Gardens Caravan Park
491 River St (old Pacific Hwy). 3 km W of PO
02 6686 2394 HEMA 57 D14 28 51 49 S 153 32 03 E

23 Reflections Holiday Parks Ballina
1 River St
www.reflectionsholidayparks.com.au
02 6686 2220 HEMA 57 D14 28 52 22 S 153 33 59 E

24 Discovery Holiday Parks
Ballina
25 Fenwick Dr
www.discoveryholidayparks.com.au
02 6686 3953 HEMA 57 D14 28 52 09 S 153 35 06 E

25 Reflections Holiday Parks
Shaws Bay
1 Brighton St
www.reflectionsholidayparks.com.au
02 6686 2326 HEMA 57 D14 28 52 02 S 153 34 47 E

26 Ballina Beach Village
440 South Ballina Beach Rd
www.ballinabeachvillage.com.au/
02 6686 3347 HEMA 57 D14 28 53 07 S 153 34 10 E

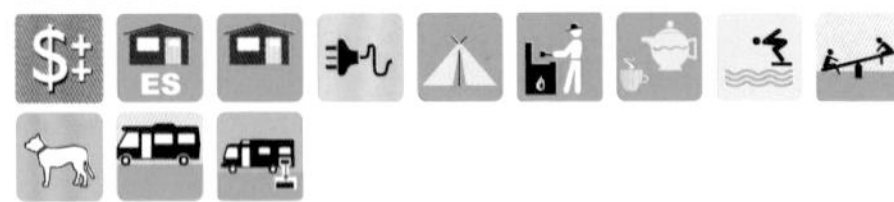

Ballina South

27 Site Closed

Balranald

28 Balranald Caravan park
60 Court St. 800m E of PO
www.balranaldcaravanpark.com.au
03 5020 1321 HEMA 62 H7 34 38 36 S 143 33 56 E

Bargo

29 Avon Caravan Village
79 Avon Dam Rd
www.avoncaravanvillage.com.au
02 4684 1026 HEMA 51 C9 34 18 02 S 150 35 21 E

Barham

30 Barham Caravan & Tourist Park
1 Noorong St. Adjacent to RSL Club
www.barhamcaravan.com.au
03 5453 2553 HEMA 68 G3 35 37 55 S 144 07 40 E

31 Barham Lakes Caravan Park
138 East Barham Rd. 1 km E of PO
www.barham-lakes-caravan-park.com.au
03 5453 2009 HEMA 68 G3 35 38 23 S 144 08 19 E

Barooga

32 Brolgaroo Caravan Park
13 Banker St
03 5873 4331 HEMA 69 H8 35 54 28 S 145 41 20 E

33 Cobram Barooga Golf Resort
Golf Course Rd. 1.2 km W of PO
www.golfresort.com.au
03 5873 4523 HEMA 69 H8 35 54 15 S 145 41 02 E

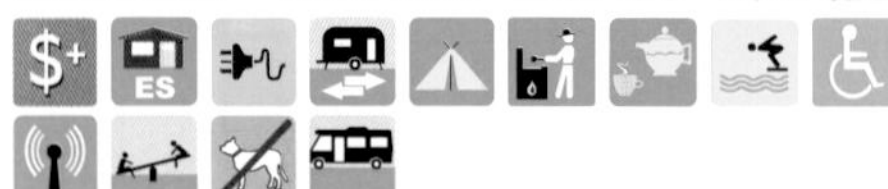

Barraba

34 Barraba Caravan Park
Bridge St. N end of town
www.barrabacaravanpark.com.au
02 6782 1818 HEMA 54 A5 30 22 23 S 150 36 36 E

Barrack Point

35 Surfrider Caravan Park
50 Junction Rd
www.surfridercaravanpark.com.au
02 4295 1941 HEMA 51 F12 34 33 55 S 150 52 00 E

Bateau Bay

36 Blue Lagoon Beach Resort
10 Bateau Bay Rd
www.bluelagoonbeachresort.com.au
02 4332 1447 HEMA 49 A14 33 22 44 S 151 29 05 E

37 Shelly Beach Holiday Park
2 Bateau Bay Rd
www.shellybeachholidaypark.com.au/
02 4332 1107 HEMA 49 A14 33 22 28 S 151 29 00 E

Batehaven

38 Clyde View Holiday Park
107 Beach Rd
www.clydeview.com.au
02 4472 4224 HEMA 67 E12 35 43 56 S 150 12 00 E

Batemans Bay

39 Batemans Bay Beach Resort
51 Beach Rd
www.beachresort.com.au
02 4472 4541 HEMA 67 E12 35 43 38 S 150 11 45 E

40 BIG4 Batemans Bay at Easts Riverside Holiday Park
Wharf Rd. N end of bridge
www.eastsbatemansbay.com.au
02 4472 4048 HEMA 67 E12 35 42 11 S 150 10 55 E

41 Caseys Beach Holiday Park
414 Beach Rd
www.caseysbeach.com.au
02 4472 4226 HEMA 67 E12 35 44 19 S 150 12 35 E

42 Pleasurelea Tourist Resort & Caravan Park
438 Beach Rd
www.pleasurelea.com.au
02 4472 4258 HEMA 67 E12 35 44 32 S 150 12 40 E

43 Shady Willows Holiday Park
Cnr Old Princes Hwy & South St. 1 km S of PO
www.shadywillows.com.au
02 4472 4972 HEMA 67 E12 35 42 59 S 150 10 38 E

44 Batemans Bay North Tourist Park
11195 Princes Hwy. 6 km N of Batemans Bay
02 4478 6060 HEMA 67 E12 35 40 13 S 150 13 10 E

Bathurst

45 BIG4 Bathurst Panorama Holiday Park
250 Sydney Rd
www.bathurstholidaypark.com.au
02 6331 8286 HEMA 52 D5 33 25 11 S 149 37 33 E

Batlow

46 Batlow Caravan Park
Kurrajong Ave
02 6949 1444 HEMA 66 D5 35 31 02 S 148 08 47 E

Bawley Point

47 Racecourse Beach Tourist Park

381 Murramarang Rd. 10 km E of Termeil PO
www.racecoursebeach.com.au
02 4457 1078 HEMA 67 D13 35 32 13 S 150 23 15 E

Bega

48 Bega Caravan Park

256 Princes Hwy. 2 km S of PO
www.begacaravanpark.com.au
02 6492 2303 HEMA 67 J11 36 41 18 S 149 50 20 E

Belmont

49 Belmont Bayview Park

1 Gerald St
www.belbay.com
02 4945 3653 HEMA 47 F12 33 01 50 S 151 39 18 E

Belmont South

50 Belmont Pines Lakeside Holiday Park

24 Paley Cres
www.lakemacholidayparks.com.au
02 4945 4750 HEMA 47 G12 33 03 00 S 151 39 05 E

Bendalong

51 Bendalong Point Holiday Park

Red Point Rd
www.holidayhaven.com.au
02 4444 8860 HEMA 67 C13 35 14 44 S 150 32 08 E

Bendemeer

52 Bendemeer Tourist Park

19 Havannah St
www.bendemeertouristpark.com.au
02 6769 6604 HEMA 54 C7 30 52 50 S 151 09 29 E

Bermagui

53 Reflections Holiday Parks Bermagui

1 Lamont St
www.reflectionsholidayparks.com.au
02 6493 4382 HEMA 67 H12 36 25 31 S 150 04 47 E

Berridale

54 Southern Cross Motor Inn & Tourist Park

1 Middlingbank Rd
02 6456 3289 HEMA 66 H7 36 21 29 S 148 49 50 E

Berrigan

55 Berrigan Caravan Park

104-120 Jerilderie St. 1 km S of PO
www.berrigancaravanpark.com.au
0400 563 979 HEMA 69 G9 35 39 37 S 145 48 49 E

Bingara

56 Bingara Riverside Caravan Park

Copeton Dam Rd
0427 241 300 HEMA 56 H4 29 51 49 S 150 34 38 E

Blackheath

57 Blue Mountains Tourist Park - Blackheath Glen

67-69 Prince Edward St. 500m S of PO
www.bmtp.com.au
02 4787 8101 HEMA 44 F3 33 38 05 S 150 17 29 E

Blacksmiths

58 Blacksmiths Beachside Holiday Park

30 Gommera St. 1.5 km N of Swansea Bridge
www.lakemacholidayparks.com.au
02 4971 2858 HEMA 47 G12 33 04 49 S 151 39 13 E

Blayney

59 Blayney Tourist Park

18 Quamby Place
www.blayneytouristpark.com.au
02 6368 4455 HEMA 52 E4 33 32 15 S 149 14 36 E

Blueys Beach

60 Site Closed

Boambee

61 Koala Villas & Caravan Park

539 Pacific Hwy
www.koalavillas.com.au
02 6653 1109 HEMA 55 A13 30 19 48 S 153 04 55 E

Bogangar

62 Site Closed

Boggabri

63 Boggabri Caravan Park

Laidlaw St
0427 101 142 HEMA 54 B3 30 42 30 S 150 02 45 E

Bolivia

64 Kookaburra Camping & Caravan Park

Cnr New England Hwy & Castlecrag Rd
0429 462 473 HEMA 57 F8 29 20 37 S 151 53 04 E

Bombah Point

65 NRMA Myall Shores Holiday Park

Myall Lakes National Park. Bombah Point Rd, via Buladelah
www.nrmaparksandresorts.com.au
02 4997 4457 HEMA 55 K11 32 30 25 S 152 18 11 E

Bombala

66 Bombala Caravan Park

5 Monaro Hwy
0488 257 928 HEMA 67 K9 36 54 30 S 149 14 20 E

Bonalbo

67 Bonalbo Caravan & Camping Park

Clarence Way
02 6665 1426 HEMA 57 C11 28 44 19 S 152 37 43 E

Bonny Hills

68 Ingenia Holidays BIG4
Bonny Hills
24 Beach St. 500m N of Surf Club
www.ingeniaholidays.com.au
02 6585 5655 HEMA 55 F13 31 35 12 S 152 50 15 E

69 Reflections Holiday Parks
Bonny Hills
Ocean Dr
www.reflectionsholidayparks.com.au
02 6585 5276 HEMA 55 F13 31 35 28 S 152 50 24 E

Boomi

70 Boomi Caravan Park & Artesian Spa
39 Bishop St
02 6753 5336 HEMA 58 B6 28 43 30 S 149 34 43 E

Boorowa

71 Boorowa Caravan Park
Brial St. 1 km N of PO
02 6385 3658 HEMA 52 J2 34 26 04 S 148 43 10 E

Bourke

72 Kidmans Camp
Mitchell Hwy. 7 km N of Bourke
www.kidmanscamp.com.au
02 6872 1612 HEMA 61 D11 30 02 41 S 145 57 26 E

73 Mitchell Caravan Park
Kamilaroi Hwy, Cnr Mitchell St & Becker Sts. 1 km E of Tourist Centre
www.mitchellcaravanpark.com.au
02 6872 2791 HEMA 61 D11 30 05 25 S 145 56 59 E

Bowna

74 Great Aussie Holiday Park
14 Hore Rd
www.greataussieholidaypark.com.au
02 6020 3236 HEMA 66 F1 35 59 42 S 147 08 56 E

Boydtown

75 Boydtown Beach Holiday Park
1 Boydtown Park Rd
www.boydtownbeachholidaypark.com.au
0405 447 361 HEMA 70 G6 37 06 07 S 149 52 34 E

Brewarrina

76 Brewarrina Caravan & Camping Park
27-31 Church St
0491 456 735 HEMA 61 D13 29 58 00 S 146 51 40 E

Broadwater

77 Broadwater Stopover Tourist Park
1 - 5 Pacific Hwy
02 6682 8254 HEMA 57 D14 29 01 12 S 153 25 26 E

78 Sunrise Caravan Park
74 - 92 Pacific Hwy. 1 km N of PO
www.sunrisecaravanpark.com
02 6682 8388 HEMA 57 D14 29 00 54 S 153 25 49 E

Broken Head

79 Broken Head Holiday Park
Beach Rd
www.brokenheadholidaypark.com.au
02 6685 3245 HEMA 57 C14 28 42 16 S 153 36 50 E

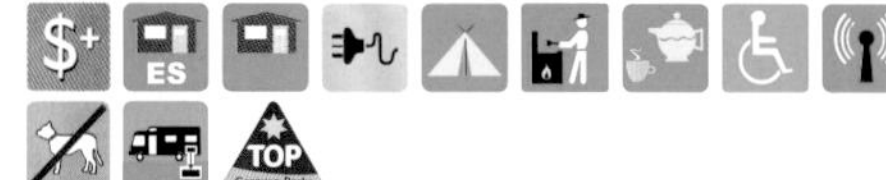

Broken Hill

80 Broken Hill Tourist Park
142 Rakow St. 3.3 km W of PO
www.brokenhilltouristpark.com.au
08 8087 3841 HEMA 60 J2 31 57 41 S 141 26 18 E

81 Lake View Caravan Park
1 Mann St
www.lakeviewcaravanpark.com.au
08 8088 2250 HEMA 60 J2 31 56 38 S 141 29 12 E

Brooms Head

82 Brooms Head Caravan Park
Ocean Rd
www.clarencecoastholidayparks.com.au
02 6646 7144 HEMA 57 G13 29 36 33 S 153 20 16 E

Broulee

83 Ingenia Big4 Broulee
6 Lyttle St
www.ingeniaholidays.com.au/broulee/
02 4471 6247 HEMA 67 F12 35 51 24 S 150 10 28 E

Brunswick Heads

84 Reflections Holiday Parks
Massey Greene
Tweed St. 1 km N of PO
www.reflectionsholidayparks.com.au
02 6685 1329 HEMA 57 B14 28 32 11 S 153 32 54 E

85 Reflections Holiday Parks
Terrace Reserve
Fingal St. 50m E of PO
www.reflectionsholidayparks.com.au
02 6685 1233 HEMA 57 B14 28 32 27 S 153 33 08 E

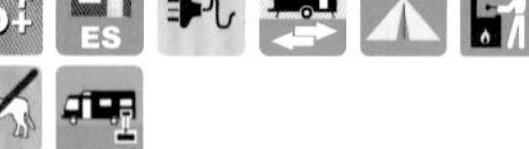

86 Reflections Holiday Parks
Ferry Reserve
Riverside Crescent. 2 km N of PO
www.reflectionsholidayparks.com.au
02 6685 1872 HEMA 57 B14 28 31 59 S 153 32 15 E

Buckenderra

87 Buckenderra Holiday Village
490 Buckenderra Rd (via Cooma)
www.buckenderra.com.au
02 6453 7242 HEMA 66 G7 36 10 55 S 148 45 52 E

Budgewoi

88 Budgewoi Holiday Park
2A Weemala St
www.discoveryholidayparks.com.au
02 4390 9019 HEMA 47 J11 33 14 06 S 151 33 59 E

Bulahdelah

89 Bulahdelah Cabin & Van Park

3 Bulahdelah Way (old Pacific Hwy)
www.bulahdelahcaravanpark.com.au
02 4997 4565 HEMA 55 J10 32 24 02 S 152 12 54 E

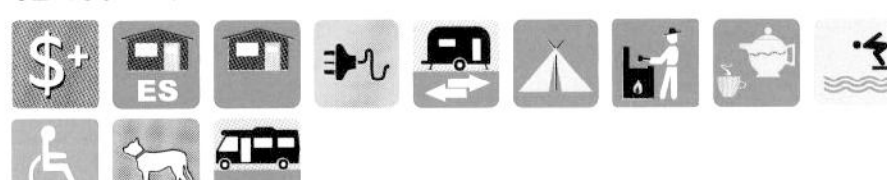

Bulli

90 Bulli Beach Tourist Park

1 Farrell Rd
www.wollongongtouristparks.com.au
02 4285 5677 HEMA 51 D13 34 20 25 S 150 55 22 E

Bundarra

91 Bundarra Caravan Park

Court St. Behind Hotel, payment at Hotel
02 67786300 HEMA 56 J5 30 10 14 S 151 04 35 E

Buronga

92 Buronga Riverside Tourist Park

71a Caravan Park Road
www.burongacaravanpark.com.au
03 5023 3040 HEMA 62 G4 34 10 54 S 142 10 09 E

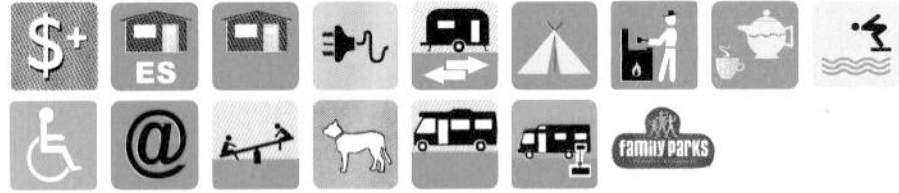

Burrier

93 Gradys Riverside Retreat

674 Burrier Rd. Reservations essential
www.gradys.com.au
02 4421 3282 HEMA 51 K8 34 52 23 S 150 27 44 E

Burrill Lake

94 BIG4 Bungalow Park on Burrill Lake

123 Princess Hwy
www.bungalow-park.com.au
02 4455 1621 HEMA 67 D13 35 23 19 S 150 26 29 E

95 Burrill Lake Tourist park

8 Princess Ave South. 4 km S of PO
www.holidayhaven.com.au
02 4444 8840 HEMA 67 D13 35 23 15 S 150 26 57 E

Burrinjuck

96 Reflections Holiday Parks Burrinjuck Waters

2373 Burrinjuck Rd
www.reflectionsholidayparks.com.au
02 6227 8114 HEMA 71 A1 34 58 46 S 148 37 11 E

Byrock

97 Mulga Creek Hotel Caravan Park

Mitchell Hwy
02 6874 7311 HEMA 61 E12 30 39 47 S 146 24 10 E

Byron Bay

98 Belongil Fields Caravan Park

394 Ewingsdale Rd
www.belongilfields.com.au
02 6680 8999 HEMA 57 C14 28 38 19 S 153 35 29 E

99 Byron Holiday Park

5-37 Brokenhead Rd. 3 km S of PO
www.byronholidaypark.com.au/
02 6685 6751 HEMA 57 C14 28 40 26 S 153 36 42 E

100 Discovery Holiday Parks Byron Bay

399 Ewingsdale Rd
www.discoveryholidayparks.com.au
02 6685 7378 HEMA 57 C14 28 38 10 S 153 35 36 E

101 First Sun Holiday park

Lawson St. 200m N of PO
www.firstsunholidaypark.com.au
02 6685 6544 HEMA 57 C14 28 38 29 S 153 36 42 E

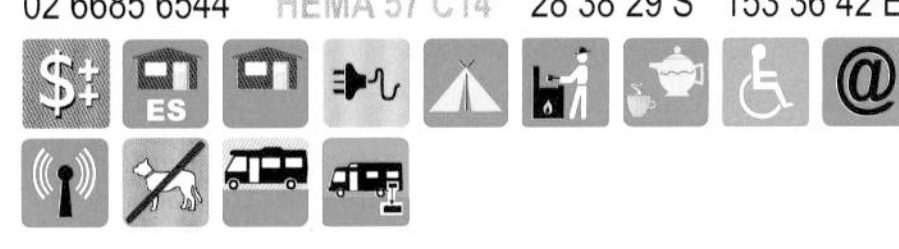

102 Glen Villa Resort

80-86 Butler St. 400m W of PO
www.glenvillaresort.com.au
02 6685 7382 HEMA 57 C14 28 38 50 S 153 36 37 E

103 Reflections Holiday Parks Clarkes Beach

1 Lighthouse Rd
www.reflectionsholidayparks.com.au
02 6685 6496 HEMA 57 C14 28 38 33 S 153 37 23 E

Camden

104 Poplar Tourist Park

21 Macarthur Rd. 800m E of PO
www.poplartouristparkcamden.com.au
02 4658 0485 HEMA 48 J6 34 03 20 S 150 42 25 E

Canowindra

105 Canowindra Caravan Park

Tilga St. Next to swimming pool. 300m S of PO
0428 233 769 HEMA 52 E2 33 34 08 S 148 39 50 E

Casino

106 Browns Caravan Park

60 Hare St. 2 km S of PO
0490 298 534 HEMA 57 D12 28 52 14 S 153 02 18 E

107 Discovery Holiday Parks Casino

115 Johnston St. 2 km E of PO
www.discoveryholidayparks.com.au
02 6662 1572 HEMA 57 D12 28 51 40 S 153 03 44 E

108 Gateway Lifestyle Casino

69 Light St. S side of town, RVs with pets in separate section
www.casinoholidaypark.com.au/
02 6662 1069 HEMA 57 D12 28 52 27 S 153 02 58 E

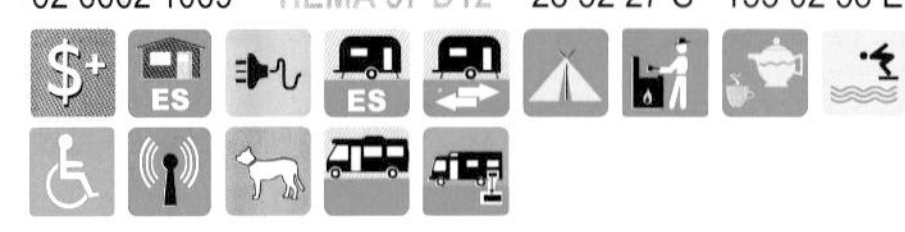

Cattai

109 Riverside Ski Park

307 Cattai Rd. 10 km E of Windsor PO, on Hawkesbury R
02 4572 8764 HEMA 49 C8 33 34 01 S 150 53 27 E

Cessnock

110 Active Holidays Cessnock Wine Country

Cnr Wine Country Dr & O'Connors Rd, Nulkaba
www.winecountrycaravanpark.com.au
02 4990 5819 HEMA 45 H5 32 48 35 S 151 20 57 E

111 Ingenia Holidays BIG4 Hunter Valley

137 Mount View Rd
www.ingeniaholidays.com.au
02 4990 2573 HEMA 45 J4 32 49 50 S 151 20 15 E

Chinderah

112 Chinderah Village Tourist Caravan Park

94 - 104 Chinderah Bay Dr. 5 km S of PO
www.chinderahvillage.com
02 6674 1536 HEMA 57 A14 28 14 06 S 153 33 20 E

113 Tweed River Hacienda Holiday Park

37 Chinderah Bay Dr
www.haciendacv.com.au
02 6674 1245 HEMA 57 A14 28 13 58 S 153 33 21 E

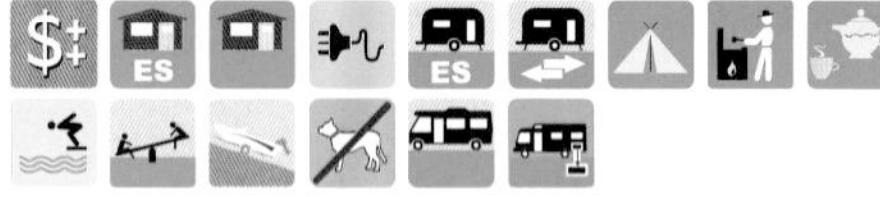

Clarence Town

114 Williams River Holiday Park

Durham St
02 4996 4231 HEMA 47 A14 32 34 56 S 151 46 55 E

Cobar

115 Cobar Caravan Park

101 Marshall St. 1 km W of PO
www.cobarcaravanpark.com.au
02 6836 2425 HEMA 61 G11 31 29 48 S 145 49 32 E

Coffs Harbour

116 Clog Barn Caravan Park

215 Pacific Hwy
www.clogbarn.com.au
02 6652 4633 HEMA 55 A14 30 17 08 S 153 07 32 E

117 Park Beach Holiday Park

1 Ocean Pde
www.coffscoastholidayparks.com.au
02 6648 4888 HEMA 55 A14 30 17 33 S 153 08 15 E

118 Reflections Holiday Parks Coffs Harbour

123 Pacific Hwy. 900m N of PO
www.reflectionsholidayparks.com.au
02 6652 1694 HEMA 55 A13 30 17 33 S 153 07 04 E

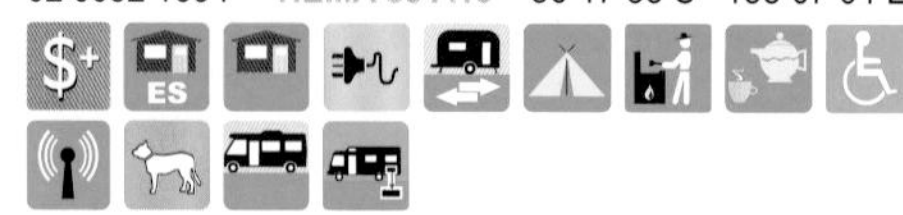

Coleambally

119 Coleambally Caravan Park

Kingfisher Ave
www.coleamballycaravanpark.com.au
02 6954 4100 HEMA 63 J12 34 47 56 S 145 52 48 E

Collingullie

120 Crossroads Hotel

1 Sturt Hwy. Next to Hotel
02 6920 0166 HEMA 66 B1 35 05 16 S 147 07 30 E

Condobolin

121 River View Caravan Park

Diggers Ave. S end of town
02 6895 2611 HEMA 64 E2 33 05 40 S 147 08 50 E

Coolah

122 Coolah Caravan Park

38 Cunningham St. 300m E of PO
www.coolahcp.com.au
02 6377 1338 HEMA 54 G2 31 49 34 S 149 43 26 E

Coolamon

123 Coolamon Caravan Park

70 Bruce St. 600m NE of PO
0417 610 946 HEMA 66 A2 34 48 48 S 147 12 09 E

Cooma

124 Cooma Snowy Mountains Tourist Park

286 (Sharp St) Snowy Mountains Hwy. 1.6 km W of Visitors Info Centre
www.coomatouristpark.com.au
02 6452 1828 HEMA 67 G8 36 14 22 S 149 06 40 E

Coonabarabran

125 Getaway Tourist Park

Newell Hwy. 2 km S of PO
02 6842 1773 HEMA 58 J5 31 17 26 S 149 17 19 E

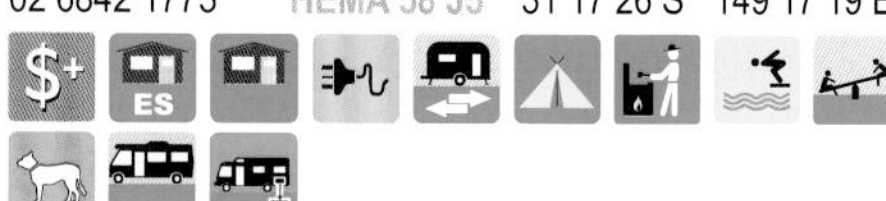

126 John Oxley Caravan Park

Cnr Newell Hwy & Chappel Ave. 1 km N of PO
www.johnoxleycvn.net
02 6842 1635 HEMA 58 J5 31 16 03 S 149 16 36 E

Coonamble

127 Coonamble Riverside Caravan Park

138 Castlereagh St. 1 km S of PO
02 6822 1926 HEMA 58 H3 30 57 48 S 148 23 21 E

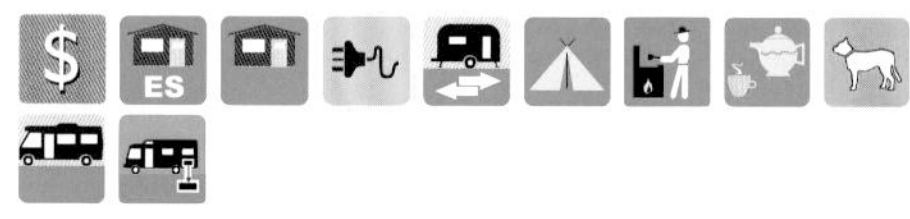

Cootamundra

128 Cootamundra Caravan Park

55 Mackay St. 500m W of PO
www.cootamundracaravanpark.com.au
02 6942 1080 HEMA 64 J4 34 38 21 S 148 01 16 E

Coraki

129 Coraki Riverside Caravan Park and Camping Grounds

81 Richmond Tce
www.kuiparks.com.au
02 6683 1740 HEMA 57 D13 28 59 16 S 153 17 18 E

Corindi Beach

130 Reflections Holiday Parks Corindi Beach

93 Pacific St
www.reflectionsholidayparks.com.au
02 6649 2803 HEMA 57 J13 30 01 43 S 153 12 06 E

Corowa

131 Ball Park Caravan Park

Bridge Rd. 600m S of PO
www.ballparkcp.com.au
02 6033 1426 HEMA 69 J11 36 00 14 S 146 23 43 E

132 Bindaree Motel & Caravan Park
454 Honour Ave. 2 km E of PO
www.bindareeonthemurray.com
02 6033 2500 HEMA 69 J11 35 58 44 S 146 24 21 E

133 Corowa Caravan Park
84 Federation Ave. 1.5 km SW of PO
www.corowacaravanpark.com.au
02 6033 1944 HEMA 69 J11 36 00 25 S 146 22 47 E

134 Rivergum Holiday Retreat
386 Honour Ave
www.rivergumholidayretreat.com.au
02 6033 1990 HEMA 69 J11 35 58 59 S 146 24 09 E

Corrimal

135 Corrimal Beach Tourist Park
1 Lake Parade
02 4285 5688 HEMA 51 D13 34 22 50 S 150 54 56 E

Cowra

136 Cowra Holiday Park
10256 Mid Western Hwy. 4 km E of PO
www.cowraholidaypark.com.au
02 6342 2666 HEMA 52 F2 33 49 10 S 148 44 03 E

137 Cowra Van Park
2a Lachlan St, off Kendall St. 1 km W of PO
www.cowravanpark.com.au
02 6342 1627 HEMA 52 F2 33 50 05 S 148 41 08 E

Crescent Head

138 Crescent Head Holiday Park
Pacific St
www.macleayvalleycoastholidayparks.com.au
02 6566 0261 HEMA 55 D13 31 11 16 S 152 58 44 E

Croki

139 Croki Riverside Caravan Park
23 Reid St
www.croki.com.au
02 6556 3274 HEMA 55 G12 31 52 35 S 152 35 30 E

Crookwell

140 Crookwell Caravan Park
Laggan Rd. Register at Visitor Centre or Council
0408 250 652 HEMA 52 J5 34 27 17 S 149 28 03 E

Cudal

141 Cudal Caravan Park
Main St. 400m E of PO
02 6390 7100 HEMA 52 D2 33 17 03 S 148 44 39 E

Cudmirrah

142 Lakeside Cabins & Holiday Village
36 Goonawarra Dr
www.lakesidecabins.com.au
02 4441 2516 HEMA 67 C13 35 11 43 S 150 33 24 E

143 Swan Lake Tourist Village
4 Goonawarra Dr
www.swanlaketouristvillage.com.au
02 4406 2060 HEMA 67 C13 35 11 42 S 150 33 35 E

Culburra Beach

144 Culburra Beach Holiday Park
2A Prince Edward Ave. 20 km E of Nowra
www.holidayhaven.com.au
02 4429 5405 HEMA 65 J9 34 54 25 S 150 45 47 E

Culcairn

145 Culcairn Caravan Park
11 South St
02 6029 8248 HEMA 66 E1 35 40 13 S 147 02 11 E

Cundletown

146 Dawson River Caravan Park
1 Manning River Dr
02 6553 9237 HEMA 55 G11 31 53 36 S 152 30 22 E

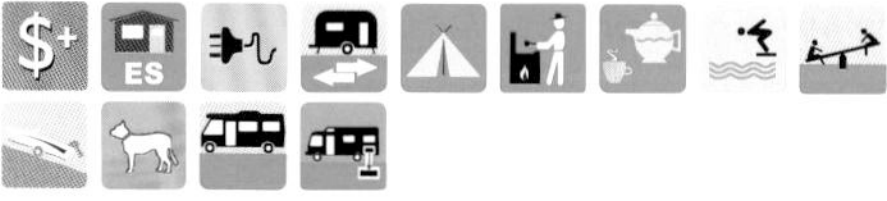

Curlwaa

147 Curlwaa Caravan Park
3 Williamsville Rd (off Silver City Hwy)
www.curlwaacaravanpark.com.au
03 5027 6210 HEMA 62 G3 34 06 45 S 141 59 21 E

Currarong

148 Currarong Beachside Tourist Park
8 Cambewarra Rd
www.holidayhaven.com.au
02 4429 5415 HEMA 67 B14 35 01 00 S 150 49 07 E

Dalgety

149 Snowy River Holiday Park
1 Hamilton St
www.snowyriverholidaypark.com.au
02 6456 5000 HEMA 66 H7 36 30 11 S 148 49 59 E

Dareton

150 Coomealla Club Motel & Caravan Park
Silver City Hwy. 400m NW of PO. Limited sites
www.coomeallaclub.com.au
03 5027 4737 HEMA 62 G3 34 05 38 S 142 02 15 E

Darlington Point

151 Darlington Point Riverside Caravan & Tourist Park
Kidman Way. 200m E of PO
www.darlingtonpointcaravanpark.com
02 6968 4237 HEMA 63 H12 34 34 05 S 146 00 15 E

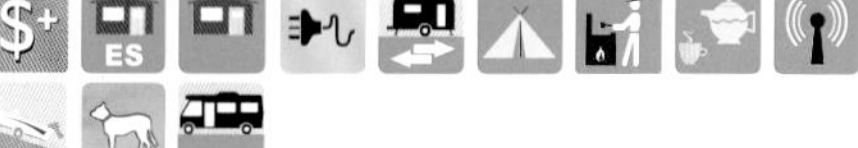

Delegate

152 Delegate Caravan Park
Bill Jeffrey's Memorial Park
02 64584047 HEMA 70 G3 37 02 24 S 148 56 48 E

Deniliquin

153 BIG4 Deniliquin Holiday Park

Lot 100, Ochtertyre St
www.big4.com.au
03 5881 1131 HEMA 68 F6 35 30 47 S 144 55 42 E

154 Deni Car O Tel & Caravan Park

46 Crispe Street
03 5881 1732 HEMA 68 G6 35 32 08 S 144 58 07 E

155 Deniliquin Riverside Caravan park

20-24 Davidson St. 1 km N of PO
www.deniliquinriversidecaravanpark.com.au
03 5881 1284 HEMA 68 G6 35 31 40 S 144 58 08 E

156 McLean Beach Holiday Park

1 Butler St. 1.5 km W of PO
www.mcleanbeachcaravanpark.com.au
03 5881 2448 HEMA 68 G6 35 31 11 S 144 57 36 E

157 Pioneer Tourist Park

167 Hay Rd. (Cobb Hwy) 4 km N of PO
www.pioneertouristpark.com.au
03 5881 5066 HEMA 68 F6 35 30 37 S 144 58 15 E

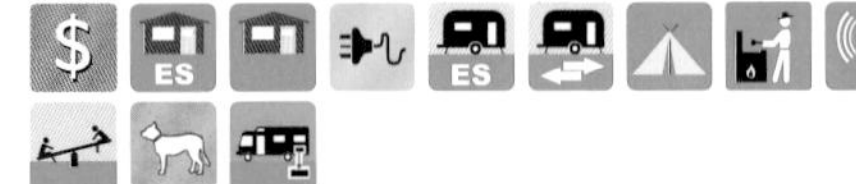

Denman

158 Denman Van Village

6 - 8 Macauley St. 700m S of PO
www.denmanvanvillage.com.au
02 6547 2590 HEMA 54 J5 32 23 40 S 150 41 02 E

Diamond Beach

159 Diamond Beach Holiday Park

Jubilee Parade
www.diamondbeachpark.com.au
02 6559 2910 HEMA 55 H11 32 02 29 S 152 32 26 E

Dolphin Point

160 Dolphins Point Tourist Park

51 Dolphin Point Rd
www.dolphinspoint.com.au
02 4455 1606 HEMA 67 D13 35 23 36 S 150 26 37 E

Dorrigo

161 Dorrigo Mountain Resort

3991 Waterfall Way. 1.5 km E of PO
www.dorrigomountainresort.com.au
02 6657 2564 HEMA 55 A12 30 21 02 S 152 42 57 E

Dubbo

162 Discovery Holiday Parks Dubbo

154 Whylandra St
www.discoveryholidayparks.com.au
02 6884 8633 HEMA 64 C5 32 15 28 S 148 35 11 E

163 Dubbo City Holiday Park

Whylandra St
www.dubbocityholidaypark.com.au
02 6801 4530 HEMA 64 C5 32 14 47 S 148 35 42 E

164 Dubbo Midstate Caravan Park

21 Bourke St. 1 km N of PO
www.dubbomidstate.com.au
02 6882 1155 HEMA 64 C5 32 14 09 S 148 36 36 E

165 Poplars Caravan Park

Cnr Lower Bultje & Bligh Sts
02 6882 4067 HEMA 64 C5 32 15 03 S 148 35 54 E

166 Westview Caravan Park

Westview St. 3.5 km W of PO
www.westviewcaravanpark.com.au
0488 028 992 HEMA 64 C5 32 13 53 S 148 34 33 E

Dunbogan

167 Diamond Waters Caravan Park

152 Diamond Head Rd
www.diamondwaterscaravanpark.com.au
02 6559 9334 HEMA 55 F12 31 40 12 S 152 48 13 E

168 Dunbogan Caravan Park

16A Bell St
www.dunbogancaravanpark.com.au
02 6559 9375 HEMA 55 F12 31 38 49 S 152 48 54 E

Dunedoo

169 Dunedoo Caravan Park

209 Bolaro St, 600m W of PO
02 6375 1455 HEMA 54 H1 32 00 56 S 149 23 22 E

Dural

170 Ingenia Holidays Sydney Hills

269 New Line Rd. 2 km S of PO
www.ingeniaholidays.com.au/sydney-hills
02 9651 2555 HEMA 40 C4 33 41 57 S 151 01 40 E

Durras North

171 Durras Lake North Holiday Park

57 Durras Rd
www.durrasnorthpark.com.au
02 4478 6072 HEMA 67 E12 35 38 09 S 150 18 09 E

East Ballina

172 Flat Rock Tent Park

38 Flat Rock Rd (off Coast Rd). No caravans permitted
www.flatrockcamping.com.au
02 6686 4848 HEMA 57 D14 28 50 37 S 153 36 10 E

Eden

173 Discovery Holiday Parks Eden

731 Princes Hwy. 7 km S of PO
www.discoveryholidayparks.com.au
02 6496 1572 HEMA 70 G6 37 05 58 S 149 52 14 E

174 Eden Beachfront Holiday Park

441 Princes Hwy. 5 km S of Eden on Legges Beach
www.edenbeachfrontholidaypark.com.au
02 6496 1651 HEMA 70 G6 37 04 39 S 149 52 28 E

175 Eden Gateway Holiday Park
99 Princes Hwy
www.edengateway.com.au
02 6496 1798 HEMA 70 G6 37 03 15 S 149 54 09 E

176 Garden of Eden Caravan Park
Cnr Princes Hwy & Barclay St. 2 km N of PO
www.edengarden.biz
02 6496 1172 HEMA 70 G6 37 03 20 S 149 54 16 E

177 Reflections Holiday Parks Eden
Aslings Beach Rd. 2 km E of PO
www.reflectionsholidayparks.com.au
02 6496 1139 HEMA 70 G6 37 03 04 S 149 54 53 E

Elizabeth Beach

178 Pacific Palms Caravan Park
1 Mariana Ave
www.pacificpalmscaravanpark.com.au
02 6554 0209 HEMA 55 J11 32 19 54 S 152 32 02 E

Emerald Beach

179 Discovery Holiday Parks Emerald Beach
73 Fishermans Dr
www.discoveryholidayparks.com.au
02 6656 1521 HEMA 57 J13 30 10 09 S 153 11 13 E

Emmaville

180 Emmaville Caravan Park
Park Rd
0429 347 249 HEMA 55 F7 29 26 51 S 151 36 08 E

Emu Plains

181 Ingenia Holidays Nepean River
91-95 Mackellar St
www.ingeniaholidays.com.au
02 4735 4425 HEMA 48 E6 33 44 37 S 150 40 38 E

Euston

182 Euston Riverfront Caravan Park
27 Murray Tce
03 5026 1543 HEMA 62 H5 34 34 40 S 142 44 42 E

Evans Head

183 Reflections Holiday Parks Evans Head
Park St. 1 km S of PO
www.reflectionsholidayparks.com.au
02 6682 4212 HEMA 57 E14 29 06 55 S 153 25 55 E

Failford

184 Riverside Holiday Park
5 Mill Rd
02 6554 3144 HEMA 55 H11 32 05 33 S 152 26 50 E

Fairy Meadow

185 Wollongong Surf Leisure Resort
201 Pioneer Rd, Fairy Meadow. 5 km N of Wollongong CBD
www.wslr.com.au
02 4283 6999 HEMA 51 D13 34 23 25 S 150 54 15 E

Fingal Bay

186 Fingal Bay Holiday Park
52 Marine Dr
www.beachsideholidays.com.au
02 4981 1473 HEMA 53 A14 32 44 48 S 152 10 09 E

Fingal Head

187 Fingal Holiday Park
Prince St
www.tchp.com.au
07 5524 2208 HEMA 57 A14 28 11 48 S 153 33 58 E

Finley

188 Finley Lakeside Caravan Park
Newell Hwy. 2 km N of PO
www.finleycaravanpark.com.au
03 5883 1170 HEMA 69 G8 35 38 03 S 145 34 49 E

Forbes

189 Apex Riverside Tourist Park
88 Reymond St. 3 km SE of PO
www.apexriversidepark.com.au
02 6851 1929 HEMA 64 F4 33 24 07 S 148 01 05 E

190 BIG4 Forbes Holiday Park
141-145 Flint St
02 6852 1055 HEMA 64 F4 33 24 05 S 148 00 55 E

191 Forbes Caravan and Cabin Park
33/37 Sam St. Off Newell Hwy.1 km N of PO
02 6852 1957 HEMA 64 F4 33 22 33 S 148 00 47 E

192 Forbes River Meadows Caravan Park
Cnr Newell Hwy & River Rd. 1.5 km S of PO
www.forbescaravanpark.com.au
02 6852 2694 HEMA 64 F4 33 23 49 S 147 59 36 E

Forest Hill

193 Airport Tourist Park
36 Allonby Ave
www.airporttouristpark.com.au
02 6922 7271 HEMA 66 B3 35 08 54 S 147 27 57 E

194 Forest Hill Caravan Park
Sturt Hwy
www.foresthillcaravanpark.com.au
02 6922 7219 HEMA 66 B3 35 09 10 S 147 28 48 E

Forster

195 Discovery Holiday Parks Forster
99 Aquatic Rd, Darawank
www.discoveryholidayparks.com.au
02 6554 3123 HEMA 55 H11 32 05 56 S 152 28 15 E

196 Lanis Holiday Island
33 The Lakes Way
www.lanis.com.au
02 6554 6273 HEMA 55 J11 32 11 52 S 152 30 48 E

NEW SOUTH WALES

197 Reflections Holiday Parks Forster Beach
Reserve Road. 200m W of PO
www.reflectionsholidayparks.com.au
02 6554 6269 HEMA 55 H11 32 10 42 S 152 30 33 E

198 Secura Lifestyle Lakeside Forster
13 Tea Tree Rd
www.securalifestyle.com.au
02 6555 5511 HEMA 55 J11 32 13 21 S 152 31 48 E

199 Smugglers Cove Holiday Village
45 The Lakes Way
www.smugglerscove.com.au
02 6554 6666 HEMA 55 J11 32 11 56 S 152 30 50 E

Gerringong

200 Werri Beach Holiday Park
Cnr Pacific Ave & Bridges Rd
www.kiamacoast.com.au
02 4234 1285 HEMA 51 J12 34 44 27 S 150 49 51 E

Gerroa

201 Discovery Holiday Parks Gerroa
107 Crooked River Rd
www.discoveryholidayparks.com.au
02 4234 1233 HEMA 51 J12 34 46 08 S 150 48 31 E

202 Seven Mile Beach Holiday Park
200 Crooked River Rd
www.kiamacoast.com.au
02 4234 1340 HEMA 51 J12 34 46 21 S 150 48 24 E

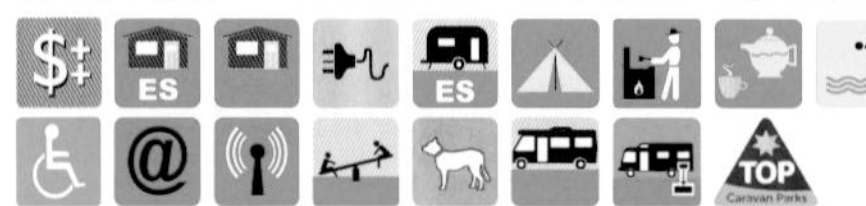

Gilgandra

203 Barneys Caravan Park
173 Miller St. 2 km N of PO
www.barneysandakropolis.com.au
02 6847 2636 HEMA 58 K4 31 42 01 S 148 40 04 E

204 Gilgandra Caravan Park
53 Newell Hwy. 300m N of bridge
www.gilgandracaravanpark.com.au
02 6847 2423 HEMA 58 K4 31 42 55 S 148 40 17 E

205 Rest-A-While Cabin & Van Park
108 Miller St
02 6847 2254 HEMA 58 K4 31 42 25 S 148 40 16 E

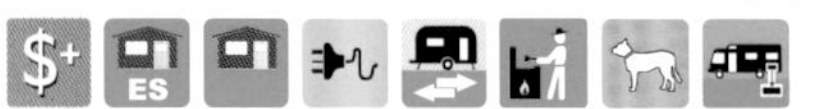

Glen Innes

206 Fossicker Caravan Park
94-96 Church St. 750m S of PO
www.fossickercaravanpark.com.au
02 6732 4246 HEMA 57 G8 29 44 39 S 151 44 12 E

207 Glen Rest Tourist Park
9807 New England Hwy
www.gleninnes.com/glenrestpark/
02 6732 2413 HEMA 57 G8 29 46 15 S 151 43 53 E

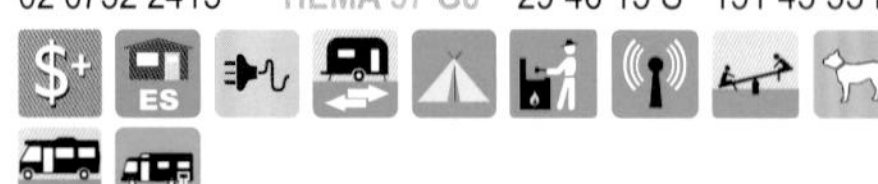

208 Poplar Caravan Park
15 Church St. 1 km S of PO
www.poplarcaravanpark.com.au
02 6732 1514 HEMA 57 G8 29 45 05 S 151 44 09 E

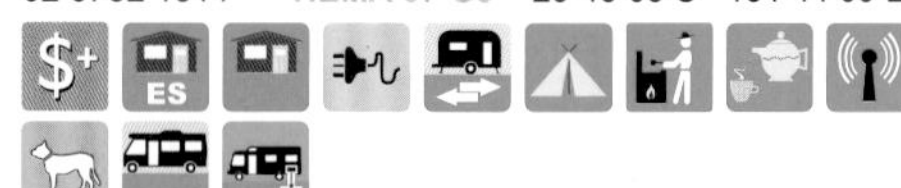

Gloucester

209 Gloucester Holiday Park
1 Denison St. 700m W of PO
www.gloucesterholidaypark.com
02 6558 1720 HEMA 55 H9 32 00 23 S 151 57 12 E

210 Gloucester Tops Riverside Caravan Park
2916 Gloucester Tops Rd
02 6558 3155 HEMA 55 H9 32 03 00 S 151 41 39 E

Gol Gol

211 Rivergardens Holiday Park
Cnr Sturt Hwy & Punt Rd
www.rivergardensholidaypark.com.au
03 5024 8541 HEMA 62 G4 34 10 46 S 142 12 35 E

Good Hope

212 Good Hope Tourist Resort
1087 Good Hope Rd
www.goodhoperesort.com.au
02 6227 1234 HEMA 64 K5 34 55 16 S 148 48 23 E

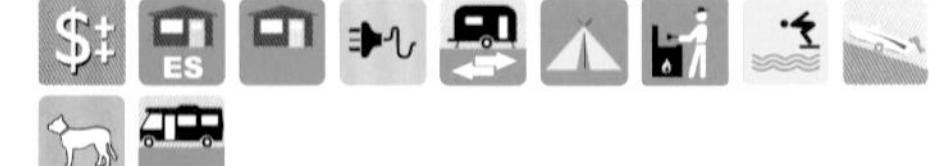

Goolgowi

213 Goolgowi Caravan Park
Napier St. 1 km NE of PO. Pay fees & key collection at Royal Mail Hotel
02 6965 1900 HEMA 63 F12 33 58 47 S 145 42 22 E

Goulburn

214 Goulburn South Caravan Park
149 Hume St. 3 km S of PO
www.goulburnsouthcp.com.au
02 4821 3233 HEMA 50 J1 34 46 13 S 149 41 40 E

215 Governors Hill Carapark
77 Sydney Rd. 3.7 km N of PO
www.big4.com.au
02 4821 7373 HEMA 50 J1 34 44 50 S 149 45 06 E

Grabine

216 Reflections Holiday Parks Grabine Lakeside
2453 Grabine Road
www.reflectionsholidayparks.com.au
02 4835 2345 HEMA 52 G3 33 57 03 S 149 01 44 E

Grafton

217 Big River Holiday Park & Ski Lodge
166 Ski Lodge Rd, Seelands
www.bigriverholidaypark.com.au
02 6644 9324 HEMA 57 G12 29 36 32 S 152 55 30 E

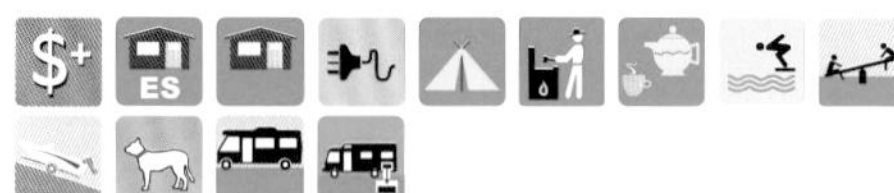

218 Gateway Lifestyle Grafton
598 Summerland Way. 4 km N of PO
www.glhp.com.au/parks/grafton/
02 6642 4225 HEMA 57 G12 29 39 57 S 152 56 15 E

Grafton South

219 Glenwood Tourist Park & Motel
71 Heber St
www.glenwoodtouristpark.com.au
02 6642 3466 HEMA 57 G12 29 42 51 S 152 56 42 E

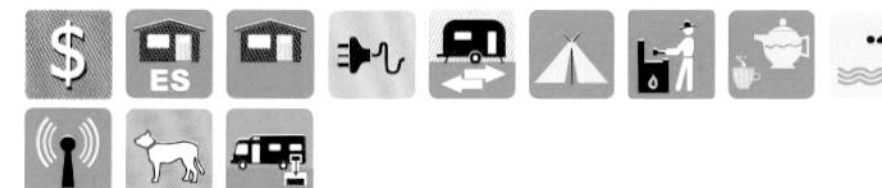

220 Sunset Caravan Park
302 Gwydir Hwy
02 6642 3824 HEMA 57 G12 29 41 43 S 152 54 51 E

Grassy Head

221 Grassy Head Holiday Park
7 Reserve Rd
www.macleayvalleycoastholidayparks.com.au
02 6569 0742 HEMA 55 C13 30 47 35 S 152 59 47 E

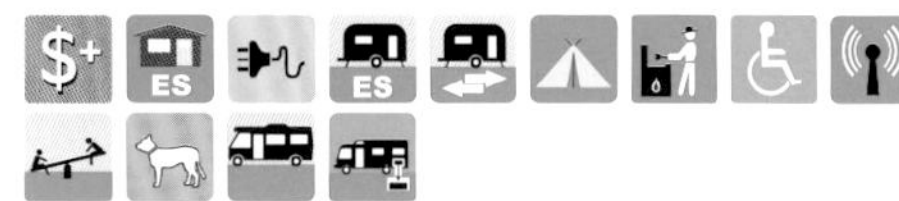

Greenwell Point

222 Coral Tree Lodge Tourist Park
142 Greens Rd
www.coraltreelodge.com.au
02 4447 1358 HEMA 65 J9 34 55 02 S 150 43 56 E

Grenfell

223 Grenfell Caravan Park
Mid Western Hwy. 2 km W of PO
www.grenfellcaravanpark.com.au
02 6343 1194 HEMA 64 G4 33 53 30 S 148 09 06 E

Griffith

224 Griffith Caravan Village
Mackay Ave. 3 km E of PO
www.griffithcaravanvillage.com.au
02 6962 3785 HEMA 63 G13 34 17 47 S 146 04 37 E

225 Griffith Tourist Caravan Park
919 Willandra Ave
www.griffithtouristcaravanpark.com.au
02 6964 2144 HEMA 63 G12 34 17 50 S 146 02 43 E

Gulargambone

226 Gulargambone Caravan Park
17 Skulthorpe St
www.gulargambonecaravanpark.com
02 6825 1666 HEMA 58 J3 31 19 51 S 148 28 12 E

Gulgong

227 Henry Lawson Caravan Park
8 Goolma Rd. 1.5 km W of PO
www.henrylawsoncaravanpark.com.au
02 6374 1294 HEMA 54 J1 32 21 56 S 149 31 30 E

Gundagai

228 Gundagai Cabins & Tourist Park
1 Nangus Rd. 400m S of Visitor Information Centre
www.gundagaitouristpark.com.au
02 6944 4440 HEMA 66 B5 35 03 51 S 148 05 55 E

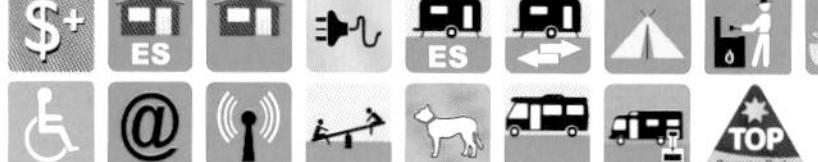

229 Gundagai River Caravan Park
Middleton Dr
www.gundagairivercaravanpark.com.au
02 6944 1702 HEMA 66 B5 35 04 22 S 148 06 22 E

Gunnedah

230 Gunnedah Tourist Caravan Park
51 Henry St. 500m E of PO
www.gunnedahcaravanpark.com.au
02 6742 1372 HEMA 54 C4 30 58 40 S 150 15 39 E

Guyra

231 Guyra Summit Caravan Park
245 Falconer St (New England Hwy)
02 6779 1241 HEMA 56 J7 30 14 04 S 151 40 17 E

Hallidays Point

232 Gateway Lifestyle Beachfront Hallidays Point
21 Redhead Rd
www.glhp.com.au/parks/beachfront/
02 6559 2630 HEMA 55 H11 32 03 36 S 152 32 35 E

233 Big4 Happy Hallidays
517 Blackhead Rd
www.securalifestyle.com.au/parks/happy/
02 6559 2967 HEMA 55 H11 32 03 58 S 152 31 55 E

Harden

234 Harden Caravan Park
Albury St
02 6386 0180 HEMA 52 J1 34 33 21 S 148 22 19 E

Harrington

235 Colonial Holiday Park & Leisure Village

716 Harrington Rd
www.colonialleisure.com
02 6556 3312 HEMA 55 G12 31 52 29 S 152 38 46 E

236 Discovery Holiday Parks Harrington

50 Crowdy St
www.discoveryholidayparks.com.au
02 6556 1228 HEMA 55 G12 31 52 09 S 152 41 42 E

237 Oxley Anchorage Caravan Park

71 Beach St. 800m W of PO
02 6556 1250 HEMA 55 G12 31 52 17 S 152 40 57 E

Hartley

238 Venice Caravan Park

1134 Browns Gap Rd
www.venicecaravanpark.com.au
02 6355 2106 HEMA 48 C1 33 33 38 S 150 12 03 E

Hastings Point

239 North Star Holiday Resort & Caravan Park

1 Tweed Coast Rd
www.northstar.com.au
02 6676 1234 HEMA 57 B14 28 21 20 S 153 34 22 E

240 Hastings Point Holiday Park

Tweed Coast Rd
www.tchp.com.au
02 6676 1049 HEMA 57 B14 28 21 39 S 153 34 29 E

Hat Head

241 Hat Head Holiday Park

Straight St
www.macleayvalleycoastholidayparks.com.au
02 6567 7501 HEMA 55 D13 31 03 21 S 153 03 12 E

Hawks Nest

242 Reflections Holiday Parks Hawks Nest

Booner St
www.reflectionsholidayparks.com.au
02 4997 0239 HEMA 53 A14 32 40 23 S 152 11 00 E

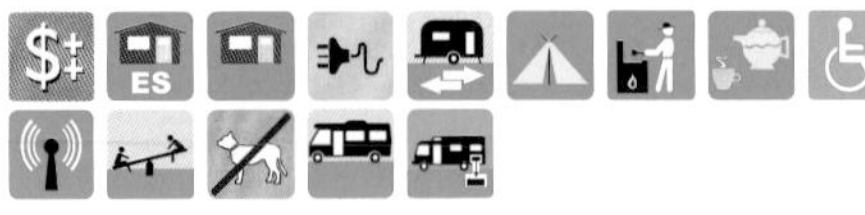

243 Reflections Holiday Parks Jimmys Beach

Coorilla St
www.reflectionsholidayparks.com.au
02 4997 0466 HEMA 53 A14 32 40 41 S 152 10 42 E

Hay

244 Hay Caravan Park

Sturt Hwy
www.haycaravanpark.com.au
02 6993 1415 HEMA 63 H10 34 31 09 S 144 51 26 E

245 Hay Plains Holiday Park

4 Nailor St. 1 km SE of PO
www.big4.com.au
02 6993 1875 HEMA 63 H10 34 31 08 S 144 50 37 E

Heathcote

246 Heathcote Tourist Park

Princes Hwy
02 9520 8816 HEMA 49 K9 34 05 26 S 151 00 16 E

Hillston

247 Billabourie Riverside Tourist Park

Mount Grace Rd. Turn E 38 km N Hillston onto Mount Grace Rd. 10 km to entrance
0427 674 131 HEMA 63 E12 33 22 32 S 145 55 38 E

248 Hillston Caravan Park

101 High St
02 6967 2575 HEMA 63 E11 33 28 49 S 145 32 04 E

Holbrook

249 Holbrook Motor Village

Cnr Bardwell St & Hume Hwy. 800m S of PO
02 6036 3100 HEMA 66 E2 35 43 46 S 147 18 30 E

Howlong

250 Howlong Caravan Park

55 Hume St
www.howlongcaravanpark.com.au
02 6026 5304 HEMA 69 J12 35 59 03 S 146 37 45 E

251 Kismet Riverside Lodge

5189 Riverina Hwy
www.kismetriverside.com
02 6026 5748 HEMA 69 H12 35 57 52 S 146 35 26 E

Huskisson

252 Huskisson Beach Holiday Park

17 Beach St
www.huskissonbeachtouristresort.com.au
1300 733 027 HEMA 67 B14 35 02 44 S 150 40 31 E

253 Huskisson White Sands Holiday Park

2 Beach St
www.holidayhaven.com.au
02 4406 2045 HEMA 67 B14 35 02 36 S 150 40 33 E

254 Jervis Bay Cabins & Hidden Creek Caravan Park

55 Goodland Rd. 4 km W of PO
www.jervisbaycabins.com.au
02 4441 5809 HEMA 67 B14 35 00 25 S 150 38 45 E

255 Jervis Bay Caravan Park

785 Woollamia Rd
www.jervisbaycaravanpark.com.au
02 4441 5046 HEMA 67 B14 35 01 22 S 150 39 39 E

Iluka

256 Anchorage Holiday Park
Marandowie Dr. 2 km N of PO
www.anchorageholidaypark.com.au
02 6646 6210 HEMA 57 F13 29 23 23 S 153 20 55 E

257 Browns Rocks Caravan Park
391 Goodwood Island Rd, Goodwood Island
www.brownsrocks.com.au
02 6646 4324 HEMA 57 F13 29 22 37 S 153 17 42 E

258 Clarence Head Caravan Park
113 Charles St. 200m E of PO
www.ilukacaravanpark.com.au
02 6646 6163 HEMA 57 F13 29 24 43 S 153 21 22 E

259 Iluka Riverside Tourist Park
4 Charles St. 400m N of PO
www.ilukariverside.com.au
02 6646 6060 HEMA 57 F13 29 24 17 S 153 20 51 E

Inverell

260 Fossickers Rest Caravan Park
Lot 3 Lake Inverell Dr. 3 km E of PO
www.fossickersrest.com.au
02 6722 2261 HEMA 56 H6 29 47 10 S 151 08 15 E

261 Inverell Caravan Park
21 Glen Innes Rd. 600m E of PO
www.inverellcaravanpark.com.au
02 6722 3036 HEMA 56 G5 29 46 47 S 151 07 06 E

262 Sapphire City Caravan Park
93-103 Moore St. 2 km E of PO
02 6722 1830 HEMA 56 G6 29 46 32 S 151 07 52 E

Ivanhoe

263 Ivanhoe Caravan Park
30 Columbus St
02 6995 1187 HEMA 63 C8 32 54 03 S 144 18 05 E

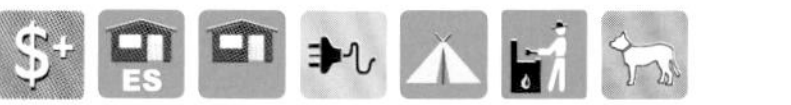

Jackadgery

264 Mann River Caravan Park
4467 Gwydir Hwy
www.mannriver.com.au
02 6647 4662 HEMA 57 G10 29 34 36 S 152 33 03 E

Jerilderie

265 Jerilderie Motel & Caravan Park
121 Newell Hwy
03 5886 1366 HEMA 63 K12 35 21 28 S 145 44 13 E

Jindabyne

266 Adventist Alpine Village
122 Tinworth Dr
www.alpinevillage.com.au
02 6456 2738 HEMA 66 H6 36 25 51 S 148 35 33 E

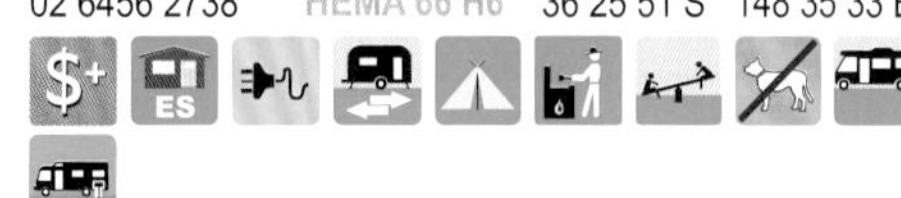

267 Discovery Holiday Parks Jindabyne
6532 Kosciuszko Rd. 2 km S of PO
www.discoveryholidayparks.com.au
02 6456 2099 HEMA 66 H7 36 24 36 S 148 35 47 E

268 Jindabyne Holiday Park
Kosciuszko Rd
www.nrmaparksandresorts.com.au
02 6456 2249 HEMA 66 H7 36 24 49 S 148 37 10 E

269 Kosciuszko Tourist Park
Kosciusko Rd. 14 km NW of PO
www.kosipark.com.au
02 6456 2224 HEMA 66 H6 36 21 04 S 148 33 49 E

Junee

270 Junee Tourist Park
Cnr Broadway & Park Lane. 1.5 km NW of PO
www.juneetouristpark.com.au
02 6924 1316 HEMA 66 A3 34 51 34 S 147 34 34 E

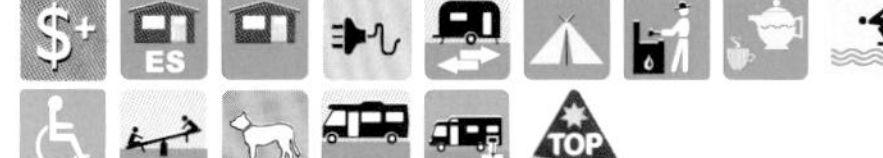

Kalaru

271 Secura Lifestyle Countryside Kalaru
3 Old Wallagoot Rd
www.securalifestyle.com.au
02 6494 1015 HEMA 67 K11 36 44 10 S 149 56 12 E

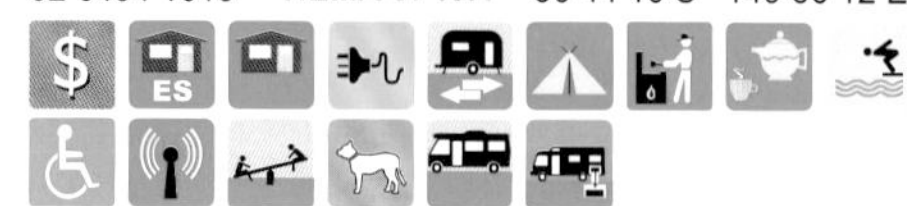

Kangaroo Valley

272 Kangaroo Valley Glenmack Park
215 Moss Vale Rd. 700m E of PO
www.glenmack.com.au
02 4465 1372 HEMA 51 J9 34 44 16 S 150 32 19 E

273 Kangaroo Valley Tourist Park
5 Moss Vale Rd
www.holidayhaven.com.au
02 4406 1900 HEMA 51 H9 34 43 45 S 150 31 19 E

Karuah

274 Australian Motor Homes Caravan Park
4406 Pacific Hwy, 12 Mile Creek N of Karuah
www.caravanparkportstephens.com.au
02 4987 0171 HEMA 47 B14 32 39 09 S 151 52 09 E

275 BIG4 Karuah Jetty Holiday Park
88 Holdom Rd. 1 km NE of PO
www.big4karuahjetty.com.au
02 4997 5520 HEMA 53 A13 32 39 38 S 151 57 49 E

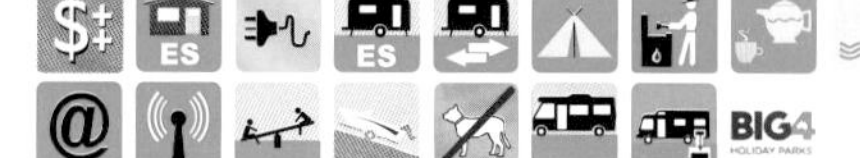

276 Karuah Caravan Park
419 Tarean Rd
0411576030 HEMA 53 A13 32 39 14 S 151 57 49 E

Katoomba

277 Blue Mountains Tourist Park - Katoomba Falls
101 Katoomba Falls Rd. 2 km S of PO
www.bmtp.com.au
02 4782 1835 HEMA 44 K4 33 43 33 S 150 18 12 E

Kempsey

278 Kempsey Tourist Village

325 Macleay Valley Way (Old Pacific Hwy). 3 km S of PO
www.kempseytouristvillage.com.au
02 6562 7666 HEMA 55 D12 31 06 08 S 152 49 53 E

279 Sundowner Caravan Park

161 Macleay Valley Way (Old Pacific Hwy)
02 6562 1361 HEMA 55 D13 31 04 15 S 152 50 42 E

280 Tall Timbers Caravan Park

425 Pacific Hwy. 4 km S of PO
www.allswell.com.au
02 6562 4544 HEMA 55 D12 31 06 39 S 152 49 50 E

Khancoban

281 Khancoban Lakeside Caravan Park

1362 Alpine Way
02 6076 9488 HEMA 66 G5 36 13 11 S 148 07 17 E

Kiama

282 BIG4 Easts Beach Holiday Park

Ocean St
www.eastsbeach.com.au
02 4232 2124 HEMA 51 H12 34 41 21 S 150 51 03 E

283 Kendalls on the Beach Holiday Park

33 Bonaira St
www.kiamacoast.com.au
02 4232 1790 HEMA 51 H12 34 40 57 S 150 51 12 E

284 Surf Beach Holiday Park

20 Bourroul St. 1 km S of PO
www.kiamacoast.com.au
02 4232 1791 HEMA 51 H12 34 40 43 S 150 51 14 E

Kingscliff

285 Ingenia Holidays Kingscliff

46 Wommin Bay Rd
www.ingeniaholidays.com.au/kingscliff/
02 6674 2505 HEMA 57 A14 28 14 12 S 153 33 35 E

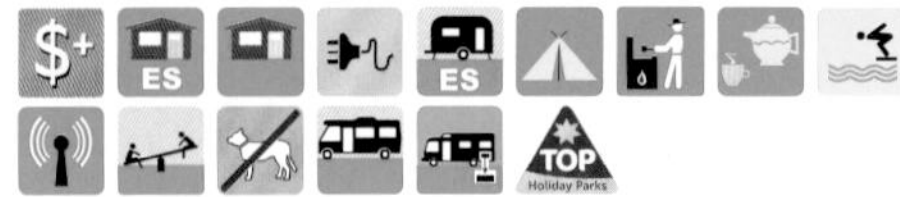

286 Kingscliff North Holiday Park

Marine Pde
www.tchp.com.au/kingscliff-north/
02 6674 1071 HEMA 57 A14 28 14 22 S 153 34 02 E

Kioloa

287 Kioloa Beach Holiday Park

635 Murramarang Rd
www.kioloabeach.com
02 4457 1072 HEMA 67 D13 35 33 20 S 150 22 48 E

288 Merry Beach Caravan Resort

46 Merry Beach Rd
www.merrybeach.com.au
02 4457 1065 HEMA 67 D13 35 33 55 S 150 22 24 E

Kootingal

289 Kootingal Kourt Caravan Park

3 Churchill Dr. 2 km N of PO
02 6760 3103 HEMA 54 D6 31 02 23 S 151 03 31 E

Kyalite

290 Kyalite Pub & Caravan Park

Moulamein Rd
03 5038 2221 HEMA 62 J7 34 56 58 S 143 28 59 E

Kyogle

291 Kyogle Gardens Caravan Park

Summerland Way. 300m N of PO
02 6632 1204 HEMA 57 C12 28 36 57 S 153 00 04 E

Lake Burrendong

292 Reflections Holiday Parks Lake Burrendong

Fashions Mount Rd
www.reflectionsholidayparks.com.au
02 6846 7435 HEMA 52 A3 32 41 24 S 149 06 29 E

Lake Cargelligo

293 Lake View Caravan Park

Cnr of Naradhan St & Wonboyn St. 1.5 km SE of PO
02 6898 1077 HEMA 63 D13 33 18 08 S 146 22 39 E

Lake Conjola

294 Ingenia Holidays Lake Conjola

1 Norman St
www.ingeniaholidays.com.au
02 4456 1407 HEMA 67 C13 35 16 04 S 150 28 42 E

295 Lake Conjola Entrance Tourist Park

1A Lake Conjola Entrance Road
www.holidayhaven.com.au
02 4444 8830 HEMA 67 C13 35 16 07 S 150 29 43 E

296 Lake Conjola Waterfront Holiday Park

2 Aney St
www.lakeconjolaholidaypark.com.au
02 4456 1165 HEMA 67 C13 35 16 06 S 150 29 20 E

Lake Copeton

297 Reflections Holiday Parks Copeton Waters

3533 Copeton Dam Rd
www.reflectionsholidayparks.com.au
02 6723 6269 HEMA 56 H5 29 55 12 S 150 56 18 E

Lake Glenbawn

298 Reflections Holiday Parks Lake Glenbawn
Glenbawn Rd
www.reflectionsholidayparks.com.au
02 6543 7193 HEMA 54 H6 32 06 28 S 150 59 25 E

Lake Hume

299 Lake Hume Tourist Park
37 Murray St
www.lakehumetouristpark.com.au
02 6049 8100 HEMA 66 G1 36 06 09 S 147 02 12 E

Lake Keepit

300 Reflections Holiday Parks Lake Keepit
234 Lake Keepit Rd. Pets in Eastern bush camping area only
www.reflectionsholidayparks.com.au
02 6769 7605 HEMA 54 C4 30 53 45 S 150 30 21 E

Lake Tabourie

301 Lake Tabourie Tourist Park
F595A Princes Hwy
www.holidayhaven.com.au
02 4406 3101 HEMA 67 D13 35 26 25 S 150 24 24 E

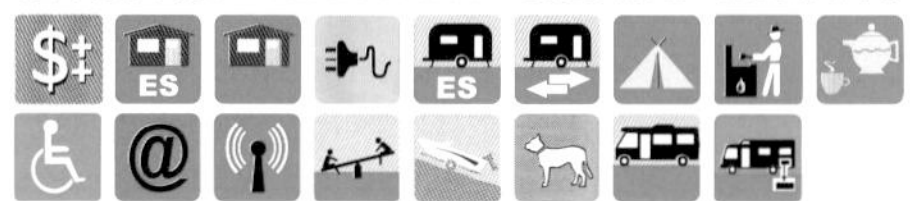

302 Wairo Beach Tourist park
425 Princes Hwy
www.allswell.com.au
02 4457 3035 HEMA 67 D13 35 25 02 S 150 25 11 E

Laurieton

303 Laurieton Gardens Caravan Resort
478 Ocean Dr
www.lgcr.com.au
02 6559 9256 HEMA 55 F12 31 38 38 S 152 47 57 E

304 Laurieton Lakefront Caravan Park & Lifestyle Village
229 Ocean Dr. 3 km W of PO
www.laurietonlakefront.com.au/
02 6559 9086 HEMA 55 F12 31 37 53 S 152 45 57 E

Leeton

305 Leeton Caravan Park
2 Yanco Ave. 2 km SE of PO
02 6953 3323 HEMA 63 H13 34 34 00 S 146 24 40 E

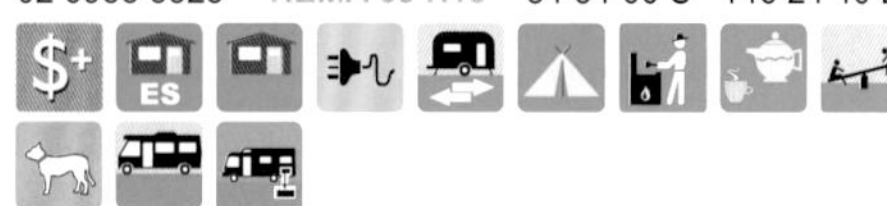

306 Oasis Caravan Park
90 Corbie Hill Rd. 2 km S of PO
02 6953 3882 HEMA 63 H13 34 33 52 S 146 25 22 E

Lemon Tree Passage

307 BIG4 Koala Shores Port Stephens Holiday Park
2 Oyster Farm Rd
www.koalashores.com.au/
1800 463 029 HEMA 53 A13 32 44 19 S 152 01 08 E

Lennox Head

308 Reflections Holiday Parks Lennox Head
Cnr Ross St & Pacific Pde
www.reflectionsholidayparks.com.au
02 6687 7249 HEMA 57 C14 28 47 10 S 153 35 33 E

Lightning Ridge

309 Crocodile Caravan Park
5 Morilla St. 500m W of PO
www.crocodilecaravanpark.com.au
02 6829 0437 HEMA 58 D3 29 25 45 S 147 58 30 E

310 Lightning Ridge Outback Resort & Caravan Park
Cnr of Onyx St & Morilla St
www.lightningridgeoutbackresort.com.au
02 6829 0304 HEMA 58 D3 29 25 44 S 147 58 24 E

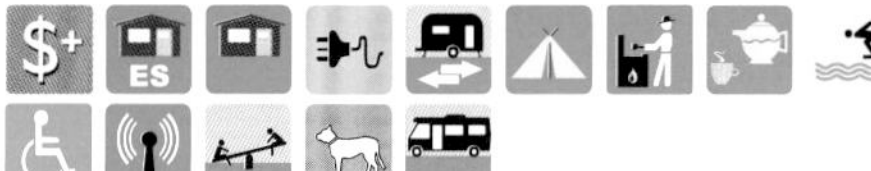

311 Lightning Ridge Tourist Park
44 Harlequin St. 200m SE of PO
02 6829 0532 HEMA 58 D3 29 25 42 S 147 58 54 E

312 Opal Caravan Park
142 Pandora St
www.opalcaravanpark.com.au
02 6829 4884 HEMA 58 D3 29 25 28 S 147 59 43 E

Lismore

313 Lismore Centra Caravan Park
60 Dawson St
02 6621 6581 HEMA 57 D13 28 48 27 S 153 16 56 E

314 Road Runner Caravan Park
61 Caniaba Rd. 3 km S of PO
02 6621 6705 HEMA 57 D13 28 50 26 S 153 15 20 E

Lithgow

315 Lithgow Tourist & Van Park
58 Cooerwull Rd. 1 km W of Visitor Centre
www.lithgowcaravanpark.com.au
02 6351 4350 HEMA 48 B1 33 28 22 S 150 07 48 E

Lockhart

316 Lockhart Caravan Park
162 Green St. 300m W of PO
0458 205 303 HEMA 63 K14 35 13 13 S 146 42 46 E

Long Jetty

317 Lakeview Tourist Park
491 The Entrance Rd
www.lakeviewtouristpark.com.au
02 4332 1515 HEMA 47 K11 33 21 53 S 151 28 35 E

Lostock

318 Lostock Dam Caravan Park
1823 Paterson River Rd
02 4931 7118 HEMA 55 J8 32 19 34 S 151 27 13 E

Macksville

319 Nambucca River Tourist Park
143 Nursery Rd
www.riverpark.com.au
02 6568 1850 HEMA 55 B13 30 42 26 S 152 56 37 E

Maclean

320 Maclean Riverside Caravan Park
109 River St. 1 km N of PO. Limited sites
www.macleanriversidecaravanpark.com.au
02 6645 2987 HEMA 57 F13 29 26 56 S 153 12 06 E

Maitland

321 Coachstop Caravan Park
Cnr Les Darcy Dr & Anzac St
www.coachstop.net.au
02 4933 2950 HEMA 47 C11 32 44 31 S 151 33 53 E

Manilla

322 Manilla Rivergums Caravan Park
86 Strafford St. 2 km E of PO
02 6785 1166 HEMA 54 B5 30 44 40 S 150 43 52 E

323 Manilla Ski Gardens Caravan Park
1 Rushes Creek Rd
02 6785 1686 HEMA 54 C5 30 47 58 S 150 33 56 E

Mannering Park

324 Ingenia Holidays Lake Macquarie
28 Monterey Ave. 300m NE of PO
www.ingeniaholidays.com.au
02 4359 1033 HEMA 47 H11 33 09 03 S 151 32 23 E

Manning Point

325 Gateway Lifestyle East's Ocean Shores
32 Manning St
www.glhp.com.au/parks/manning-point/
02 6553 2624 HEMA 55 G12 31 53 44 S 152 39 46 E

326 Weeroona Holiday Park
21 Main Rd
www.weeroona.com
02 6553 2635 HEMA 55 G12 31 53 44 S 152 39 32 E

Mathoura

327 Gulpa Retreat Tourist Park
32 Picnic Point Rd
www.gulparetreat.com.au
0427 580 904 HEMA 68 H6 35 49 09 S 144 54 38 E

328 Liston Caravan Park
2 Morris St. Pay at Info Centre 23 Moama St
03 5884 3730 HEMA 68 H6 35 48 35 S 144 54 18 E

329 Murraybank Caravan Park
80 Tarragon Rd
www.murraybankcaravanpark.com.au
03 5884 3518 HEMA 68 H6 35 51 21 S 144 59 05 E

330 Picnic Point Caravan Park
Picnic Point Rd
www.picnicpointcaravanpark.com.au
03 5884 3375 HEMA 68 H6 35 51 05 S 144 59 36 E

Maude

331 Maude Hotel & Caravan Park
Yang Yang St, part of Post Office Hotel
02 6993 6112 HEMA 63 H8 34 28 25 S 144 18 07 E

Menindee

332 Copi Hollow Caravan Park
Copi Hollow, 15 km W of Menidee
www.bhsbc.com.au
08 8091 4880 HEMA 60 K4 32 16 08 S 142 23 15 E

333 Menindee Bridge Caravan Park
Pooncarie Rd
08 8091 4282 HEMA 60 K4 32 23 59 S 142 24 48 E

334 Menindee Lakes Caravan Park
Menindee Lakes Shore Dr
08 8091 4315 HEMA 60 K4 32 21 15 S 142 24 12 E

Merimbula

335 BIG4 Merimbula Tween Waters Holiday Park
Dunns Lane
www.tweenwaters.com.au
02 8123 0960 HEMA 70 F6 36 53 50 S 149 54 44 E

336 NRMA Merimbula Beach Holiday Park
2 Short Point Rd. 1.5 km NE of PO
www.merimbulabeachholidaypark.com.au
02 6499 8999 HEMA 70 F6 36 53 15 S 149 55 45 E

337 Sapphire Valley Caravan Park
29 Sapphire Coast Dr
www.sapphirevalleycaravanpark.com.au
02 6495 1746 HEMA 70 F6 36 53 04 S 149 54 18 E

Merriwa

338 Merriwa Caravan Park
152 Bettington St. 600m W of PO
0418 668 402 HEMA 54 H4 32 08 19 S 150 21 01 E

Merriwagga

339 The Old School Camping & Caravan Park
50 Marne St. Manager on site after 4.30pm
02 6965 4484 HEMA 63 F11 33 48 52 S 145 37 38 E

Milton

340 Milton Valley Holiday Park
12 Slaughterhouse Rd, 1 km S of PO
www.miltonvalleyholidaypark.com.au
02 4455 2028 HEMA 67 C13 35 19 47 S 150 26 51 E

Minnie Water

341 Minnie Water Holiday Park
1 Sandon Rd
www.minniewaterholidaypark.com.au
02 6649 7693 HEMA 57 G13 29 46 20 S 153 17 30 E

Miranda

342 Sydney Tourist Park

Cnr Wingello Rd & Bowral Ave
www.sydneytouristpark.com.au
02 9522 7143 HEMA 43 J8 34 01 37 S 151 06 22 E

Mittagong

343 Mittagong Caravan Park

1 Old Hume Hwy
www.mittagongcaravanpark.com.au
02 4871 1574 HEMA 51 E8 34 26 51 S 150 27 26 E

Moama

344 Coco Bend Caravan & Camping Grounds

256 Old Barmah Rd. AH 0400 012 723
03 5482 1652 HEMA 68 J5 36 05 59 S 144 48 16 E

345 Discovery Holiday Parks Maidens Inn

Cnr Chanter & Deniliquin Sts
www.discoveryholidayparks.com.au
03 5480 9253 HEMA 68 J5 36 07 05 S 144 46 32 E

346 Discovery Holiday Parks Moama West

Merool Rd
www.discoveryholidayparks.com.au
03 5482 5500 HEMA 68 J5 36 06 19 S 144 43 53 E

347 Merool on the Murray

131 Merool Rd
www.merool.com.au
03 5480 9111 HEMA 68 J5 36 06 43 S 144 43 45 E

348 Moama Riverside Holiday & Tourist Park

Cnr Cobb Highway & Shaw Street
www.moamariverside.com.au
03 5482 3241 HEMA 68 J5 36 07 01 S 144 45 20 E

349 Moama Waters

96 Old Barmah (Bama) Rd
www.moamawaters.com.au
03 5480 7717 HEMA 68 J5 36 06 38 S 144 47 34 E

350 Morning Glory River Resort

Gilmour Rd, via Barmah Rd
www.morninggloryriverresort.com.au
03 5869 3357 HEMA 68 J6 36 04 50 S 144 57 02 E

351 Murray River Holiday Park

2 Blair St
www.murrayriverholidaypark.com.au
03 5480 9899 HEMA 68 J5 36 06 53 S 144 45 16 E

Mollymook

352 Mollymook Tourist Park

34 Ilett St
www.mollymooktouristpark.com.au
02 4455 1939 HEMA 67 C13 35 20 27 S 150 27 52 E

Molong

353 Molong Caravan Park

Cnr of Watson St & Hill St
02 6366 8328 HEMA 52 C2 33 05 28 S 148 52 16 E

Monkerai

354 Riverwood Downs of Barrington Tops

311 Upper Monkerai Rd
www.riverwooddowns.com.au
02 4994 7112 HEMA 55 J9 32 16 09 S 151 51 35 E

Mookerawa Dam

355 Reflections Holiday Parks Mookerawa Waters

Mookerawa Rd
www.reflectionsholidayparks.com.au
02 6846 8426 HEMA 52 A3 32 45 58 S 149 09 27 E

Moonee Beach

356 Reflections Holiday Parks Moonee Beach

Moonee Beach Rd
www.reflectionsholidayparks.com.au
02 6653 6552 HEMA 57 J13 30 12 36 S 153 09 20 E

Moree

357 Gwydir Carapark & Thermal Pools

Newell Hwy & Amaroo Dr
www.gwydircarapark.com.au
02 6752 2723 HEMA 56 F1 29 29 09 S 149 51 03 E

358 Mehi River Van Park

28 Oak St. 1 km E of PO
02 6752 7188 HEMA 56 F1 29 28 16 S 149 51 03 E

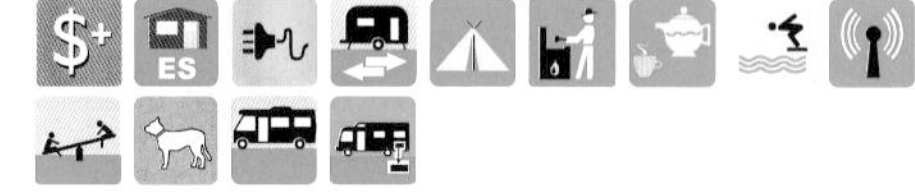

Moruya

359 Riverbreeze Tourist Park

9 Princes Hwy
www.allswell.com.au
02 4474 2370 HEMA 67 F12 35 54 15 S 150 04 54 E

Moruya Heads

360 BIG4 Moruya Heads Easts Dolphin Beach Holiday Park

10 Pedro Point Road (South Head Road)
www.eastsmoruya.com.au
02 4474 2748 HEMA 67 F12 35 55 06 S 150 09 17 E

Moss Vale

361 Moss Vale Village Park

43-53 Willow Dr
www.mossvalevillagecaravanpark.com.au
02 4868 1099 HEMA 50 F7 34 33 12 S 150 21 36 E

Moulamein

362 Moulamein Lakeside Caravan Park

41 Brougham St
www.moulameinlakesidecaravanpark.com
03 5887 5206 HEMA 63 K8 35 05 07 S 144 02 06 E

Mount Burrell

363 Mount Burrell Caravan Park

3220 Kyogle Rd
02 6679 7170 HEMA 57 B13 28 29 12 S 153 13 14 E

Mount Lion

364 Rainforest Gateway Caravan Park

494-540 Grady's Creek Rd. Seasonal opening
02 6636 6114 HEMA 57 B12 28 26 13 S 152 57 34 E

Mount Warning

365 Mt Warning Rainforest Park

153 Mt Warning Rd. 9 km SW of Murwillumbah
www.mtwarningrainforestpark.com
02 6679 5120 HEMA 57 B13 28 23 16 S 153 19 30 E

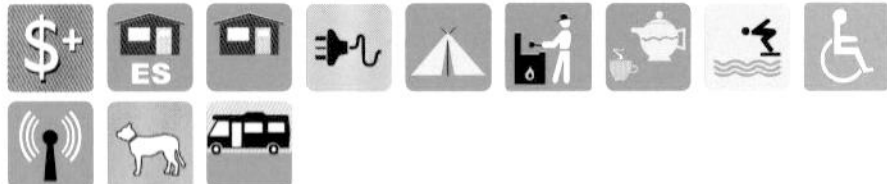

Mount White

366 Greenmans on the Hawkesbury

233 Morgans Rd. Dirt road, some steep access
www.greenmans.com.au
02 4377 1173 HEMA 49 B11 33 27 48 S 151 10 16 E

Mudgee

367 Ingenia Holidays Mudgee

71 Lions Dr
www.ingeniaholidays.com.au
02 6372 1090 HEMA 52 A5 32 36 50 S 149 35 57 E

368 Ingenia Holidays Mudgee Valley

Bell St
www.ingeniaholidays.com.au
02 6372 1236 HEMA 52 A5 32 35 04 S 149 34 13 E

369 Mudgee Riverside Caravan & Tourist Park

22 Short St
www.mudgeeriverside.com.au
02 6372 2531 HEMA 52 A5 32 35 20 S 149 35 02 E

Mullaway

370 Mullaway Beach Holiday & Van Park

2 The Boulevarde. Limited sites
02 6654 1172 HEMA 57 J13 30 04 45 S 153 12 00 E

Mulwala

371 DC on the Lake

3327 Spring Drive
03 5744 1393 HEMA 69 J10 35 58 43 S 146 03 49 E

372 Ski Club Holiday Park

186 Melbourne St. 1 km S of PO
03 5744 1050 HEMA 69 J9 35 59 44 S 146 00 05 E

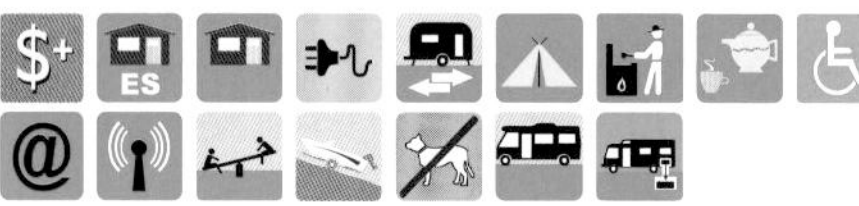

373 Yarrawonga Mulwala Lakeside Holiday Park

102 Corowa Rd. 2 km NE of PO
www.lakesideholidaypark.com.au
03 5743 2888 HEMA 69 J10 35 58 32 S 146 01 26 E

Mungindi

374 Mungindi Caravan Park

Cnr St George & Yarouah Sts
0428 565 128 HEMA 58 C4 28 58 39 S 148 59 52 E

Murrurundi

375 Murrurundi Caravan Park

11 Bernard St. 1 km N of PO
www.murrurundicaravanpark.com.au
02 6546 6288 HEMA 54 G6 31 45 30 S 150 49 21 E

Muswellbrook

376 Riverside Cabin & Van Park

10 Mill St. Limited sites call ahead
www.riversidecabinandvanpark.com.au/
02 6541 2535 HEMA 54 J6 32 16 03 S 150 53 08 E

Mylestom

377 Reflections Hoilday Parks Mylestom

Beach Pde
www.reflectionsholidayparks.com.au
02 6655 4250 HEMA 55 A13 30 27 44 S 153 02 45 E

Nambucca Heads

378 BIG4 Nambucca Beach Holiday Park

26 Swimming Creek Rd. 2 km NE of PO
www.big4nambuccabeachholidaypark.com.au
02 6568 6120 HEMA 55 B13 30 37 49 S 153 00 42 E

379 Foreshore Caravan Park

25 Riverside Dr. 1 km S of PO
www.foreshorecaravanpark.com.au
02 6568 6014 HEMA 55 B13 30 39 01 S 152 59 50 E

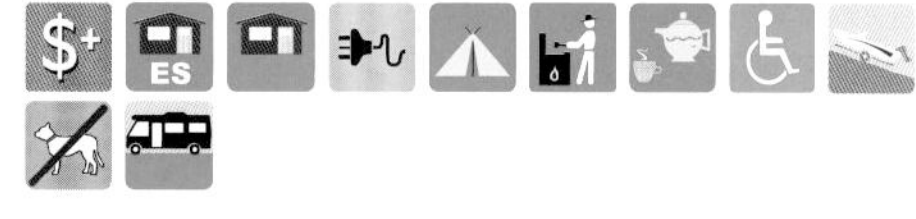

380 Ingenia Holidays White Albatross

52 Wellington Dr
www.ingeniaholidays.com.au
02 6568 6468 HEMA 55 B13 30 38 48 S 153 00 41 E

381 Nambucca Heads Village & Tourist Park

2207 Giinagay Way
02 6568 6647 HEMA 55 B13 30 39 12 S 152 59 20 E

382 Pelican Park

1790 Giinagay Way, 3 km S of Nambucca Heads
www.pelicanpark.com.au
02 6568 6505 HEMA 55 B13 30 40 43 S 152 58 34 E

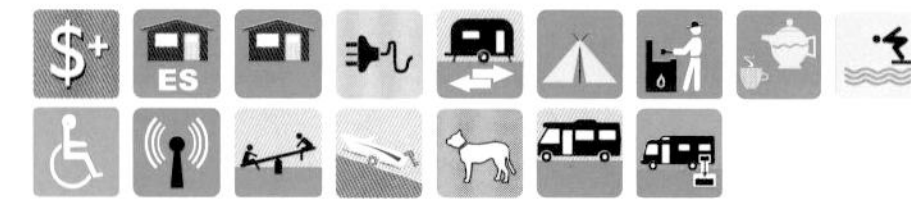

383 Reflections Holiday Parks Nambucca Heads

50 Liston St
www.reflectionsbookings.com.au
02 6568 6547 HEMA 55 B13 30 38 16 S 153 00 51 E

Narooma

384 BIG4 Narooma Easts Holiday Park
41 Princes Hwy
www.eastsnarooma.com.au
02 4476 2046 HEMA 67 G12 36 12 53 S 150 07 31 E

385 Island View Beach Resort
Princes Hwy
www.islandview.com.au
02 4476 2600 HEMA 67 G12 36 14 45 S 150 08 18 E

386 Surf Beach Holiday Park
5 Ballingalla St
www.surfbeachholidaypark.com.au
02 4476 2275 HEMA 67 G12 36 13 23 S 150 08 15 E

Narrabeen

387 NRMA Sydney Lakeside Holiday Park
Lake Park Rd. Off Pittwater Rd
www.sydneylakeside.com.au
02 9913 7845 HEMA 41 C13 33 42 02 S 151 18 09 E

Narrabri

388 Highway Tourist Village & Caravan Park
86-92 Cooma Rd (Newell Hwy). 2 km S of PO
www.narrabricaravanpark.com.au
02 6792 1438 HEMA 54 A2 30 20 03 S 149 46 16 E

389 Narrabri Big Sky Caravan Park
11-35 Tibbereena St. 750m S of PO
www.narrabribigsky.com.au
02 6792 1294 HEMA 54 A2 30 19 50 S 149 47 05 E

390 Narrabri Motel & Caravan Park
52 Cooma Rd (Newell Hwy). 2 km S of PO
www.narrabrimotel.com.au
02 6792 2593 HEMA 54 A2 30 20 16 S 149 46 05 E

Narrandera

391 Lake Talbot Tourist Park
1 Gordon St. 2 km SE of PO
www.laketalbot.com.au
02 6959 1302 HEMA 69 C11 34 45 14 S 146 33 57 E

392 Narrandera Caravan Park
16322 Newell Hwy
www.narranderacaravanpark.com.au
02 6959 2955 HEMA 69 C11 34 45 44 S 146 32 24 E

Narromine

393 Narromine Rockwall Tourist Park
69 Mitchell Highway
0437 656 594 HEMA 64 C4 32 14 13 S 148 14 57 E

394 Narromine Tourist Park & Motel
Mitchell Hwy. 1 km NW of PO
www.narrominetouristpark.com.au
02 6889 2129 HEMA 64 C4 32 13 24 S 148 13 48 E

Nelligen

395 BIG4 Nelligen Holiday Park
Kings Hwy
www.nelligenpark.com.au
02 4478 1076 HEMA 67 E12 35 38 43 S 150 08 05 E

Nelson Bay

396 Halifax Holiday Park
5 Beach Rd. 2 km E of PO
www.beachsideholidays.com.au
02 4981 1522 HEMA 53 A14 32 42 43 S 152 09 36 E

Nimbin

397 Nimbin Caravan Park
29 Sibley St
02 6689 1402 HEMA 57 C13 28 35 39 S 153 13 31 E

Norah Head

398 Norah Head Holiday Park
Victoria St
www.discoveryholidayparks.com.au
02 4396 3935 HEMA 47 J11 33 17 00 S 151 33 58 E

North Haven

399 Brigadoon Holiday Park
Eames Ave
www.brigadoonholidaypark.com.au
02 6559 9172 HEMA 55 F12 31 38 24 S 152 48 27 E

400 Gateway Lifestyle Jacaranda
85 The Parade. 1 km E of PO
www.glhp.com.au/parks/north_haven/
02 6559 9470 HEMA 55 F12 31 38 11 S 152 49 41 E

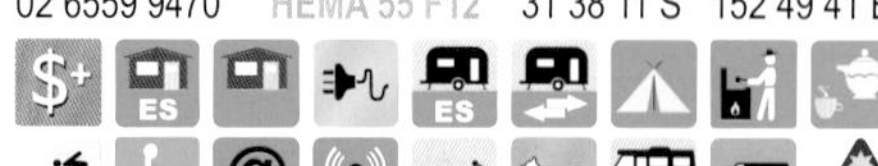

401 Reflections Holiday Parks North Haven
109 The Parade
www.reflectionsholidayparks.com.au
02 6559 9193 HEMA 55 F12 31 38 05 S 152 49 51 E

North Ryde

402 Lane Cove River Tourist Park
Plassey Rd
www.nationalparks.nsw.gov.au
02 9888 9133 HEMA 41 G8 33 47 21 S 151 08 35 E

North Star

403 North Star Caravan Park
1 Wilby St
0458530265 HEMA 56 D3 28 55 55 S 150 23 39 E

Nowra

404 Shoalhaven Caravan Village
17 Terara Rd
www.shoalhavencaravanvillage.com.au
02 4423 0770 HEMA 51 K10 34 52 04 S 150 36 52 E

Nowra North

405 Shoalhaven Ski Park

70 Rockhill Rd
02 4423 2488 HEMA 51 K9 34 52 18 S 150 34 12 E

Nundle

406 Fossickers Tourist Park

103 Jenkins St
www.fossickersatnundle.com.au
02 6769 3355 HEMA 54 E7 31 27 28 S 151 07 41 E

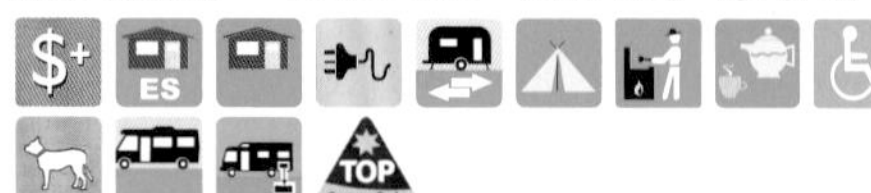

Nyngan

407 Nyngan Leisure & Van Park

12 Old Warren Rd. 3 km E of PO
02 6832 2366 HEMA 58 J1 31 34 00 S 147 12 29 E

408 Nyngan Riverside Tourist Park

Cnr Barrier Hwy & Mitchell Hwy. 2 km N of PO
www.nynganriverside.com.au
02 6832 1729 HEMA 58 J1 31 33 28 S 147 10 48 E

O'Connor

409 Alivio Tourist Park

Kunzea St
www.aliviogroup.com.au
02 6247 5466 HEMA 72 C4 35 15 26 S 149 06 22 E

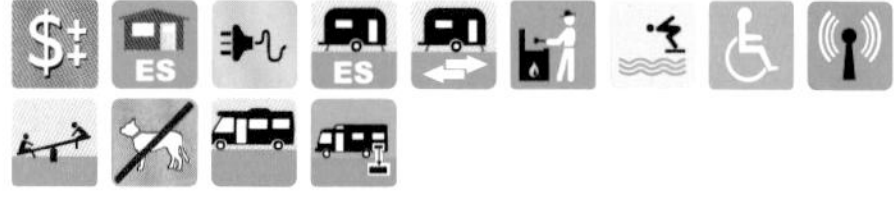

Oberon

410 Jenolan Caravan Park

7 Cunynghame St
www.jenolancaravanpark.com.au
02 6336 0344 HEMA 52 E6 33 42 06 S 149 51 28 E

Old Adaminaby

411 Rainbow Pines Tourist Park

16 Lucas Road
www.rainbowpines.com.au
02 6454 2317 HEMA 71 K2 36 02 22 S 148 42 19 E

Old Bar

412 Lanis On The Beach

Old Bar Rd
www.lanisonthebeach.com.au
02 6553 7274 HEMA 55 H12 31 58 09 S 152 35 31 E

One Mile Beach

413 Ingenia Holidays One Mile Beach

426 Gan Gan Rd
www.ingeniaholidays.com.au
02 4982 1112 HEMA 53 A14 32 46 37 S 152 06 47 E

414 Middle Rock Holiday Resort

554 Gan Gan Rd
www.middlerock.com.au
02 4982 1162 HEMA 53 A14 32 45 56 S 152 06 50 E

415 Site Closed

Orange

416 Canobolas Caravan Park

166-172 Bathurst Rd
www.canobolascaravanpark.com.au/
02 6362 7279 HEMA 52 D3 33 17 47 S 149 07 01 E

417 Colour City Caravan Park

203 Margaret St
02 6393 8980 HEMA 52 D3 33 16 19 S 149 06 33 E

Pacific Palms

418 Sandbar & Bushlands Holiday Parks

3434 The Lakes Way
02 6554 4095 HEMA 55 J11 32 23 00 S 152 31 04 E

419 Sundowner Tiona Tourist Park

4451 The Lakes Way
www.tiona.sundownerholidays.com
02 6554 0291 HEMA 55 J11 32 18 17 S 152 31 12 E

Pallamallawa

420 The Golden Grain Hotel Motel & Caravan Park

59-63 Bingara St
02 6754 9236 HEMA 56 F2 29 28 28 S 150 08 07 E

Palmers Island

421 BIG4 Saltwater @ Yamba Holiday Park

286 O`Keefe`s Ln
www.big4saltwater.com.au
02 6646 0255 HEMA 57 F13 29 23 42 S 153 18 40 E

422 Fishing Haven Caravan Park

35 River Rd
www.fishinghaven.com.au
02 6646 0163 HEMA 57 F13 29 24 47 S 153 16 57 E

Pambula

423 Merimbula Lake Holiday Park

3211 Princes Hwy
www.merimbulalakeholidaypark.com.au
02 6495 6070 HEMA 70 F6 36 54 29 S 149 52 29 E

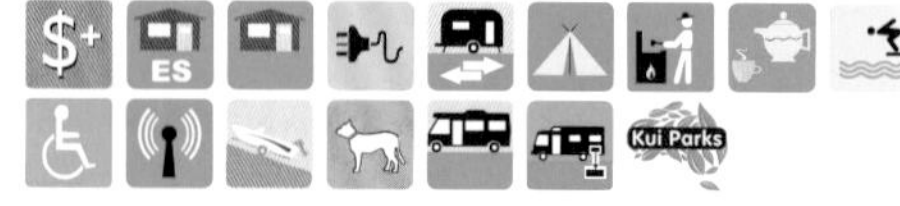

424 Reflections Holiday Parks Pambula

Cnr Toallo St
www.reflectionsholidayparks.com.au
02 6495 6708 HEMA 70 F6 36 55 48 S 149 52 50 E

Pambula Beach

425 Discovery Holiday Parks Pambula Beach

1 Pambula Beach Rd
www.discoveryholidayparks.com.au
02 6495 6363 HEMA 70 F6 36 56 24 S 149 54 23 E

Parkes

426 Parkes Highway Caravan Park

17 Forbes Rd

02 6862 1108 HEMA 64 E4 33 08 42 S 148 10 15 E

427 Parkes Overnighter Caravan Park

48 Bushmans St

02 6862 1707 HEMA 64 E4 33 08 02 S 148 09 57 E

428 Spicer Caravan Park

Victoria St

02 6862 6162 HEMA 64 E4 33 07 53 S 148 10 48 E

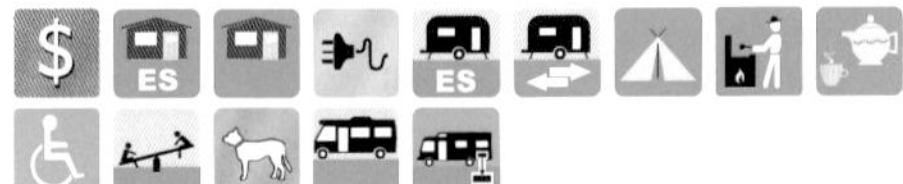

Peak Hill

429 Double D Caravan Park

42 Bogan St

02 6869 1797 HEMA 64 D4 32 43 46 S 148 11 10 E

430 Peak Hill Caravan Park

2 Ween St

www.peakhillcaravanpark.com.au

02 6869 1422 HEMA 64 D4 32 43 17 S 148 11 27 E

Pitt Town

431 Hawkesbury Riverside Tourist Park

505 Pitt Town Bottoms Rd

www.hawkesburycaravanpark.com.au

02 4572 3733 HEMA 49 C8 33 34 19 S 150 50 41 E

432 Percy's Place Caravan Park

190 Hall St

www.percysplacecaravanpark.com.au

02 4580 9919 HEMA 49 C8 33 33 50 S 150 52 18 E

Port Macquarie

433 Edgewater Holiday Park

221 Hastings River Dr

www.edgewaterholidaypark.com.au

02 6583 2799 HEMA 55 E13 31 25 28 S 152 52 30 E

434 Flynns Beach Caravan Park

22 Ocean St

www.flynnsbeachcaravanpark.com.au

02 6583 5754 HEMA 55 E13 31 26 44 S 152 55 32 E

435 Jordans Boating Centre & Caravan Park

McInherney Close

02 6583 1005 HEMA 55 E13 31 25 10 S 152 53 20 E

436 Leisure Tourist Park & Holiday Units

202 Hastings River Dr

www.leisuretouristpark.com.au

02 6584 4555 HEMA 55 E13 31 25 29 S 152 52 30 E

437 Lighthouse Beach Holiday Village

140 Matthew Flinders Dr

www.lighthousebeachholidayvillage.com.au

02 6582 0581 HEMA 55 F13 31 28 55 S 152 55 17 E

438 Marina Holiday Park

52 Settlement Point Rd

www.marinaholidaypark.com

02 6583 2353 HEMA 55 E13 31 24 52 S 152 53 42 E

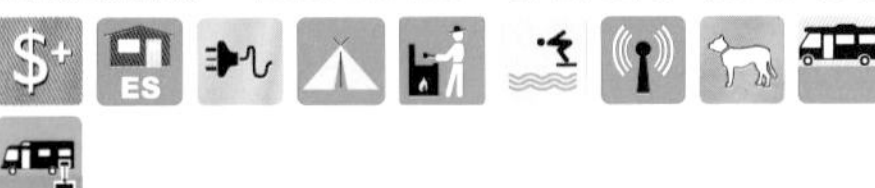

439 Melaleuca Caravan Park

128 Hastings River Dr

www.melaleucacaravanpark.com.au

02 6583 4498 HEMA 55 E13 31 25 39 S 152 52 47 E

440 Riverlodge Tourist Village

340 Blackmans Point Rd

www.riverlodgetouristvillage.com

02 6585 0264 HEMA 55 E13 31 23 55 S 152 50 16 E

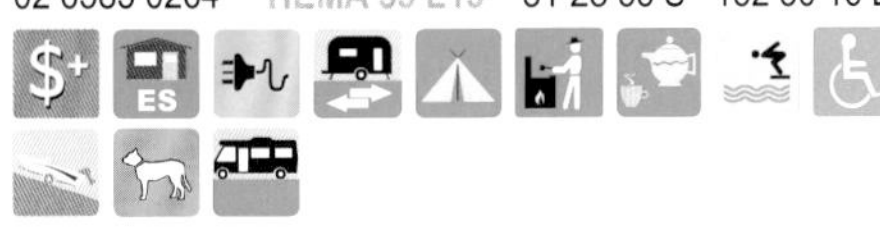

441 Riverside Resort @ Port

259 Hastings River Dr. 3 km N of PO

www.riversideresortatport.com.au/

02 6584 9155 HEMA 55 E13 31 25 20 S 152 52 17 E

442 NRMA Port Macquarie Breakwall Holiday Park

1 Munster St

www.portmacquariebreakwall.com.au/

02 6583 2755 HEMA 55 E13 31 25 41 S 152 54 43 E

Potato Point

443 Beachcomber Holiday Park

Blackfellows Point Rd via Bodalla. Limited solar power

www.beachcomberholidaypark.com.au

02 4473 5312 HEMA 67 G12 36 04 59 S 150 07 57 E

Pottsville

444 Pottsville North Holiday Park

27 Tweed Coast Rd

www.tchp.com.au

02 6676 1221 HEMA 57 B14 28 23 01 S 153 34 01 E

445 Pottsville South Holiday Park

Tweed Coast Rd

www.tchp.com.au

02 6676 1050 HEMA 57 B14 28 23 20 S 153 33 57 E

Queanbeyan

446 Crestview Tourist Park

81 Donald Rd

www.canberracaravanpark.com.au

02 6297 2443 HEMA 72 F6 35 21 48 S 149 13 26 E

447 Queanbeyan Riverside Tourist Park

41 Morisset St

www.qbnriversidetouristpark.com.au

02 6297 4749 HEMA 72 F7 35 20 59 S 149 14 12 E

Quirindi

448 Quirindi Caravan Park

15 Rose St

02 6746 2407 HEMA 54 F5 31 30 37 S 150 41 01 E

Rankins Springs

449 Rankins Springs Caravan Park
Mid Western Hwy
02 6965 1900 HEMA 63 F13 33 50 29 S 146 15 44 E

Raymond Terrace

450 Bellhaven Caravan Park
206 Adelaide St
www.bellhaven.com.au
02 4987 2423 HEMA 47 C13 32 46 50 S 151 44 13 E

451 Pacific Gardens Van Village
2233 Pacific Hwy
02 4987 2224 HEMA 47 C13 32 47 31 S 151 43 25 E

Red Rock

452 Reflections Holiday Parks Red Rock
1 Lawson St
www.reflectionsholidayparks.com.au
02 6649 2730 HEMA 57 H13 29 58 59 S 153 13 45 E

Repton

453 Bellinger River Tourist Park
96 Mylestom Dr
www.bellingerriver.com.au
02 6655 4755 HEMA 55 A13 30 26 20 S 153 01 14 E
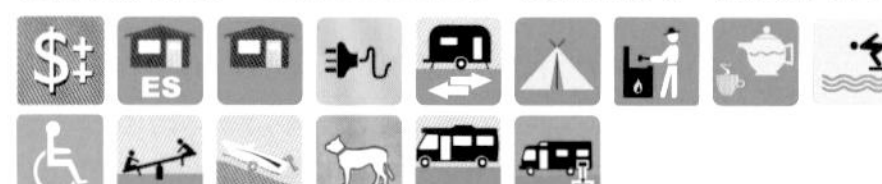

Rockdale

454 Sheralee Caravan Park
88 Bryant St
www.sheraleetouristcaravanpark.com.au
02 9567 7161 HEMA 43 E9 33 57 08 S 151 09 02 E

Rosedale

455 Barlings Beach Tourist Park
1939 George Bass Dr
www.barlingsbeach.com
02 4471 7313 HEMA 67 E12 35 49 35 S 150 12 10 E

Rylstone

456 Cudgegong Waters Caravan Park
1858 Cudgegong Rd. 35 km S of Mudgee
02 6358 8462 HEMA 52 B6 32 48 44 S 149 49 24 E

457 Rylstone Caravan Park
6 Carwell St
0448 251 440 HEMA 52 B6 32 48 02 S 149 58 04 E

Sanctuary Point

458 Palm Beach Caravan Park
103-105 Ethel St. No caravans
www.palmbeachcaravanpark.com.au
02 4443 0356 HEMA 67 B14 35 06 50 S 150 38 01 E

Sandy Hollow

459 Sandy Hollow Tourist Park
1618 Merriwa Rd
www.sandyhollow.com.au
02 6547 4575 HEMA 54 J5 32 20 03 S 150 33 57 E

Sapphire Beach

460 Sapphire Beach Holiday Park
48 Split Solitary Rd
www.sapphirebeachholidaypark.com.au
02 6653 6212 HEMA 57 J13 30 13 43 S 153 09 07 E

Sawtell

461 Sawtell Beach Caravan Park
5 Lyons Rd
www.coffscoastholidayparks.com.au
02 6653 4485 HEMA 55 A13 30 22 22 S 153 05 59 E

Scone

462 Highway Caravan Park
248 New England Hwy. Limited sites
02 6545 1078 HEMA 54 H6 32 03 24 S 150 52 11 E

463 Scone Caravan Park
50 Kelly St. 1 km N of PO
www.sconecaravanpark.com.au
02 6545 2024 HEMA 54 H6 32 02 33 S 150 51 56 E

Scotts Head

464 Reflections Holiday Park Scotts Head
12 Adin St
www.reflectionsholidayparks.com.au
02 6569 8122 HEMA 55 B13 30 44 44 S 152 59 45 E

Seal Rocks

465 Reflections Holiday Parks Seal Rocks
Kinka Road
www.reflectionsholidayparks.com.au
02 4997 6164 HEMA 55 K11 32 25 57 S 152 31 25 E

Shellharbour

466 Shellharbour Beachside Tourist Park
1 John St
www.shellharbourbeachsidetouristpark.com.au
02 4295 1123 HEMA 51 G12 34 34 52 S 150 52 21 E

Shoal Bay

467 Shoal Bay Holiday Park
Shoal Bay Rd
www.beachsideholidays.com.au
02 4981 1427 HEMA 53 A14 32 43 11 S 152 10 15 E

Shoalhaven Heads

468 Mountain View Resort
14 Shoalhaven Heads Rd
www.mtview.com.au
02 4448 7281 HEMA 51 K11 34 50 51 S 150 43 53 E

469 Shoalhaven Heads Tourist Park
49 McIntosh St (End Shoalhaven Hds Rd) 100m E of PO
www.holidayhaven.com.au
02 4429 5409 HEMA 51 K11 34 51 08 S 150 44 46 E

Singleton

470 Country Acres Caravan Park
Maison Dieu Rd. 2 km N of PO
www.countryacres.com.au
02 6572 2328 HEMA 47 A8 32 33 12 S 151 08 55 E

471 Singleton Caracourt Caravan Park
Cnr New England Hwy & Bridgman Rd
02 6572 2886 HEMA 47 A8 32 33 25 S 151 10 02 E

Soldiers Point

472 Ingenia Holidays Soldiers Point
122 Soldiers Point Rd
www.ingeniaholidays.com.au
02 4982 7300 HEMA 53 A14 32 42 39 S 152 04 14 E

South Durras

473 BIG4 South Durras Holiday Park
9 Beagle Bay Rd
www.southdurrasholidaypark.com.au
02 4478 6028 HEMA 67 E12 35 39 19 S 150 17 36 E

474 Lakesea Caravan Park
Durras Lake Rd
www.lakesea.com.au
02 4478 6122 HEMA 67 E12 35 38 41 S 150 17 55 E

475 NRMA Murramarang Beachfront Holiday Park
Banyandah St
www.murramarangresort.com.au
02 4478 6355 HEMA 67 E12 35 40 05 S 150 18 00 E

South West Rocks

476 BIG4 Sunshine South West Rocks
161 Phillip Dr
www.big4southwestrocks.com.au
+61 26566 6142 HEMA 55 C13 30 53 27 S 153 03 50 E

477 Horseshoe Bay Holiday Park
1 Livingstone St
www.macleayvalleycoastholidayparks.com.au
02 6566 6370 HEMA 55 C13 30 53 02 S 153 02 22 E

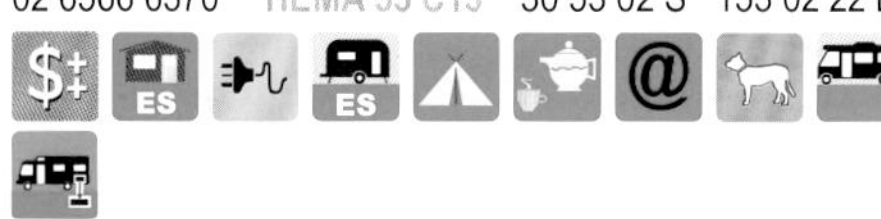

478 Ingenia South West Rocks
Gordon Young Dr
www.ingeniaholidays.com.au
02 6566 6264 HEMA 55 C13 30 53 22 S 153 02 01 E

Stockton

479 Stockton Beach Tourist Park
3 Pitt St
www.stocktonbeach.com
02 4928 1393 HEMA 47 E14 32 54 46 S 151 47 17 E

Stuarts Point

480 Stuarts Point Convention Centre
250 Grassy Head Rd
www.stuartspointconventioncentre.com.au
02 6569 0576 HEMA 55 C13 30 47 57 S 152 59 15 E

481 Stuarts Point Holiday Park
Marine Parade
www.macleayvalleycoastholidayparks.com.au
02 6569 0616 HEMA 55 C13 30 49 14 S 152 59 39 E

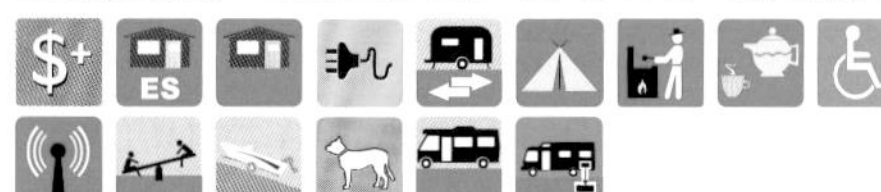

Suffolk Park

482 Suffolk Beachfront Holiday Park
Alcorn St
www.suffolkbeachfront.com.au
02 6685 3353 HEMA 57 C14 28 41 25 S 153 36 46 E

Sussex Inlet

483 Alamein Caravan Park
Alamein Rd
02 4441 2031 HEMA 67 C13 35 10 24 S 150 35 21 E

484 Badgee Caravan Park
148 River Rd
www.badgeepark.com.au
02 4441 2146 HEMA 67 B13 35 09 14 S 150 35 42 E

485 Riverside Caravan Park
96 Sussex Rd
www.riversidetouristpark.com.au
02 4441 2163 HEMA 67 C13 35 10 05 S 150 35 40 E

486 Riviera Caravan Park
158 River Rd
www.rivieracaravanpark.com.au
02 4441 2112 HEMA 67 B13 35 09 15 S 150 35 43 E

487 Seacrest Caravan Park
30 Sussex Rd
www.seacrestcaravanpark.com.au
02 4441 2333 HEMA 67 C13 35 10 08 S 150 35 37 E

488 Sussex Palms Holiday Park
40 Sussex Rd
02 4441 2395 HEMA 67 C13 35 10 04 S 150 35 39 E

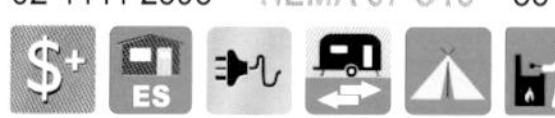

Sutton

489 Capital Country Holiday Park
47 Bidges Rd
02 6230 3433 HEMA 72 B7 35 11 54 S 149 13 29 E

490 Eaglehawk Holiday Park
1246 Federal Hwy
www.eaglehawkpark.com.au
02 6241 6411 HEMA 72 B6 35 12 11 S 149 12 43 E

Swansea

491 Swansea Gardens Lakeside Holiday Parks
15 Wallarah St
www.lakemacholidayparks.com.au
02 4971 2869 HEMA 47 G12 33 04 28 S 151 38 10 E

Symonston

492 Southside Village
Cnr Canberra Ave & Monaro Hwy. 5 km S of PO
www.csmp.net.au
02 6280 6176 HEMA 72 F5 35 19 57 S 149 09 51 E

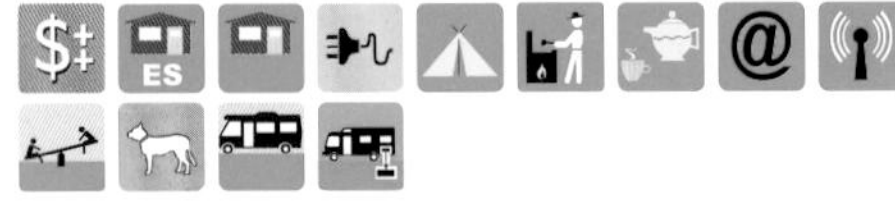

Talbingo

493 Talbingo Tourist Caravan Park
24 Whitty St
www.talbingocaravanpark.com.au
02 6949 5239 HEMA 66 D5 35 35 02 S 148 17 40 E

Tamworth

494 Austin Tourist Park
581 Armidale Rd
www.austintouristpark.com.au
02 6766 2380 HEMA 54 D6 31 06 51 S 150 57 37 E

495 City Lights Caravan Park
612-628 Goonoo Goonoo Rd
www.citylightscaravanpark.com.au
02 6765 7664 HEMA 54 D6 31 08 39 S 150 55 24 E

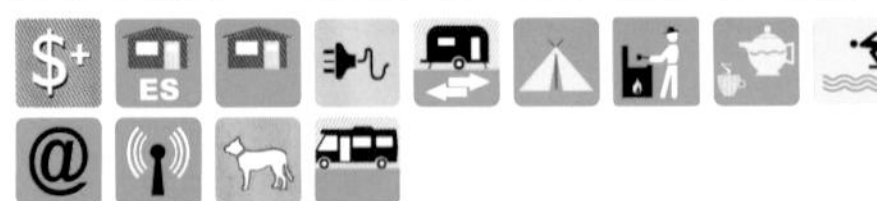

496 Paradise Tourist Park
575 Peel St
www.paradisetouristpark.com.au
02 6766 3120 HEMA 54 D6 31 05 59 S 150 56 15 E

497 Tamworth North Holiday Park
New England Hwy, Nemingha
02 6760 9356 HEMA 54 D6 31 07 24 S 150 59 02 E

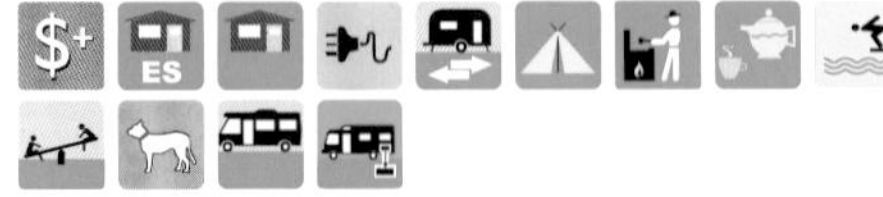

Taree South

498 Twilight Caravan Park
146 Manning River Rd. 3 km S of PO
www.twilightcaravanpark.com.au
02 6552 2857 HEMA 55 G11 31 56 15 S 152 28 03 E

Tathra

499 BIG4 Tathra Beach Holiday Park
41 Andy Poole Dr. 1 km N of PO
www.big4tathrabeach.com.au
02 6494 1350 HEMA 67 J11 36 43 28 S 149 58 43 E

500 Tathra Beachside
2 Andy Poole Dr. 2 km N of PO
www.tathrabeachside.com.au
02 6494 1302 HEMA 67 J11 36 43 28 S 149 58 44 E

Telegraph Point

501 Stoney Park
16 Hacks Ferry Rd
www.stoneypark.com.au
02 6585 0080 HEMA 55 E12 31 19 39 S 152 47 53 E

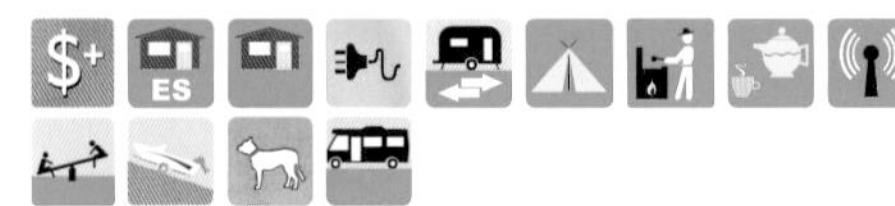

Temora

502 Temora Airfield Tourist Park
Tenefts St
0418 780 251 HEMA 64 H3 34 25 01 S 147 31 01 E

503 Temora Caravan Park
19 Junee Rd
0418 780 251 HEMA 64 H3 34 27 22 S 147 32 05 E

Tenterfield

504 7 Knights Caravan Park
94 Rouse St (New England Hwy)
02 6736 2005 HEMA 57 E8 29 03 44 S 152 01 02 E

505 Craigs Caravan Park
102 Rouse St (enter from Clive St)
www.craigscaravanpark.weebly.com
02 6736 1585 HEMA 57 E8 29 03 40 S 152 00 59 E

506 Tenterfield Lodge & Caravan Park
2 Manners St
www.tenterfieldlodgecaravanpark.com.au
02 6736 1477 HEMA 57 E8 29 03 12 S 152 00 24 E

Teralba

507 Teralba Lakeside Caravan Park
21 Anzac Pde
02 4958 5370 HEMA 47 F12 32 57 53 S 151 36 23 E

Terrey Hills

508 Terrey Hills Caravan Park
319 Mona Vale Road
02 9450 1781 HEMA 41 C10 33 41 47 S 151 13 05 E

The Entrance

509 Blue Bay Camping & Tourist Park
Cnr Bay Rd & Narrawa Ave
www.bluebaytouristpark.com.au
02 4332 1991 HEMA 47 K11 33 21 13 S 151 30 01 E

510 El Lago Waters Tourist Park
11 The Entrance Rd
www.ellago.com.au
02 4332 3955 HEMA 47 K11 33 20 17 S 151 29 46 E

511 Two Shores Holiday Village
200 Wilfred Barrett Dr
www.twoshoresholidayvillage.com.au
02 4332 2999 HEMA 47 K11 33 19 36 S 151 30 37 E

The Entrance North

512 Dunleith Caravan Park
2 Hutton Rd
www.dunleithtouristpark.com.au
02 4332 2172 HEMA 47 K11 33 20 17 S 151 30 13 E

Tibooburra

513 The Granites Motel Caravan Park
Cnr of King St & Brown St
www.tibooburramotel.com.au
08 8091 3305 HEMA 60 B3 29 26 02 S 142 00 33 E

Tingha

514 Tingha Gems Caravan & Camping
91 Swimming Pool Rd
www.tinghagems.com
02 6723 3234 HEMA 56 H6 29 56 45 S 151 12 58 E

Tocumwal

515 BIG4 Tocumwal Tourist Park
1 Bruton St
www.tocumwaltouristpark.com.au
03 5874 2768 HEMA 69 H8 35 48 34 S 145 33 58 E

516 Boomerang Way Tourist Park
65 Murray St
www.boomerangwaytouristpark.com.au
03 5874 2313 HEMA 69 H8 35 48 27 S 145 33 57 E

517 Sport Aviation Holiday Park
87 Babingtons Rd
www.sportaviation.com.au
03 5874 2734 HEMA 69 H8 35 49 04 S 145 35 58 E

Tomago

518 Tomago Village Caravan Park
819 Tomago Rd
www.tomagovillage.com.au
02 4964 8066 HEMA 47 D13 32 49 09 S 151 41 53 E

Tomakin

519 River Haven Tourist Park
476 Tomakin Rd
02 4471 7235 HEMA 67 E12 35 48 35 S 150 10 36 E

520 Tomago River Tourist Park
55 Sunpatch Pde
www.allswell.com.au
02 4471 7235 HEMA 67 E12 35 49 25 S 150 11 12 E

Tooleybuc

521 Tooleybuc Caravan Park
63 Murray St
03 5030 5025 HEMA 62 J6 35 01 46 S 143 20 12 E

Tooraweenah

522 Tooraweenah Caravan Park
Cnr Bridge & Aimee Sts
www.tooraweenahcaravanpark.com
02 6848 1133 HEMA 58 J4 31 26 20 S 148 54 39 E

Toowoon Bay

523 Toowoon Bay Holiday Park
Koongara St
www.discoveryholidayparks.com.au
02 4332 2834 HEMA 47 K11 33 21 47 S 151 29 44 E

Tottenham

524 The State Centre Caravan Park
Tullamore Road. AH 0428 924 126
02 6892 4126 HEMA 61 J14 32 14 44 S 147 21 50 E

Toukley

525 Canton Beach Tourist Park
1 Oleander St
www.discoveryholidayparks.com.au
02 4396 3252 HEMA 47 J11 33 16 29 S 151 32 50 E

Trangie

526 Tandara Caravan Park
55 John St. 500m S of PO
www.tandaracaravanpark.com.au
02 6888 7330 HEMA 64 B4 32 02 11 S 147 58 46 E

527 Trangie Caravan Park
38 Goan St
www.trangiecaravanpark.com.au
02 6888 7511 HEMA 64 B4 32 02 00 S 147 58 36 E

Tumbarumba

528 Tumbarumba Creek Caravan Park
Lauder St
www.tumbarumbacreek.com.au
02 6948 3330 HEMA 66 E4 35 46 24 S 148 00 31 E

Tumut

529 Blowering Holiday Park
511 Snowy Mountians Hwy. 5 km S of PO
02 6947 1383 HEMA 66 C5 35 20 31 S 148 14 44 E

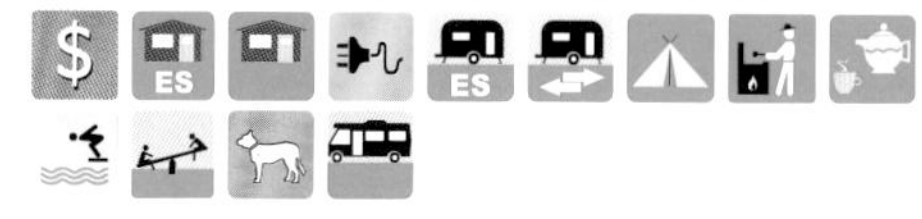

530 Riverglade Caravan Park
Snowy Mountians Hwy
www.riverglade.com.au
02 6947 2528 HEMA 66 C5 35 17 44 S 148 13 17 E

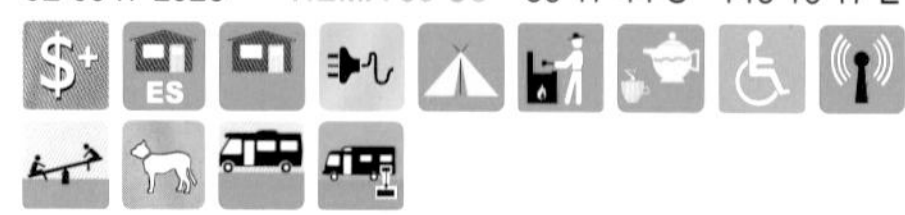

Tuncurry

531 Great Lakes Caravan & Holiday Park
1 Baird St
www.greatlakes.com.au
02 6554 6827 HEMA 55 J11 32 11 00 S 152 29 36 E

532 Reflections Holiday Parks Tuncurry Beach
32 Beach St
www.reflectionsholidayparks.com.au
02 6554 6440 HEMA 55 H11 32 10 18 S 152 30 14 E

533 Twin Dolphins Holiday Park
134 South St
www.twindolphins.com.au
02 6554 7015 HEMA 55 H11 32 10 24 S 152 29 02 E

Tuross Head

534 Tuross Beach Holiday Park
83 Nelson Pde
www.turossbeachholidaypark.com.au
02 4473 8236 HEMA 67 G12 36 03 52 S 150 08 02 E

535 Tuross Lakeside Tourist Park
211 Hector McWilliam Dr
www.turosslakeside.com.au
02 4473 8181 HEMA 67 F12 36 02 03 S 150 07 11 E

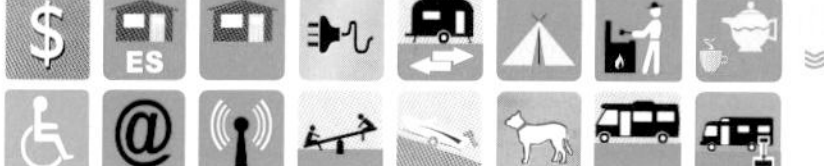

Tweed Heads

536 Pyramid Holiday Park
145 Kennedy Dr
www.pyramidpark.com.au
02 5536 3666 HEMA 57 A14 28 11 13 S 153 31 15 E

Tweed Heads South

537 BIG4 Tweed Billabong Holiday Park
30 Holden St
www.tweedbillabong.com.au
07 5524 2444 HEMA 57 A14 28 11 41 S 153 31 49 E

538 Boyds Bay Holiday Park
3 Dry Dock Rd
www.tchp.com.au
07 5524 3306 HEMA 57 A14 28 11 16 S 153 32 20 E

539 Colonial Tweed Holiday & Home Park
158 Dry Dock Rd
www.colonialtweed.com.au
07 5524 2999 HEMA 57 A14 28 11 37 S 153 31 21 E

540 River Retreat Caravan Park
8 Philp Pde
www.riverretreatpark.com.au
07 5524 2700 HEMA 57 A14 28 11 37 S 153 31 14 E

Tyndale

541 Tyndale Tourist Park & Roadhouse
2848 Pacific Hwy
www.tyndaleroadhouse.com.au
02 6647 6226 HEMA 57 G13 29 33 41 S 153 08 58 E

Ulladulla

542 Kings Point Retreat
300 Kings Point Dr
www.kingspointretreat.com.au
02 4454 4261 HEMA 67 C13 35 22 22 S 150 27 44 E

543 Ulladulla Headland Tourist Park
14 Did-Dell St
www.holidayhaven.com.au
02 4429 8982 HEMA 67 C13 35 21 39 S 150 28 45 E

Umina Beach

544 NRMA Ocean Beach Resort Park
Sydney Ave
www.oceanbeachholidaypark.com.au
02 4379 9444 HEMA 49 C12 33 31 48 S 151 18 39 E

Uralla

545 Country Road Caravan Park
New England Hwy. 1.5 km S of PO
www.countryroadcp.com.au
02 6778 4563 HEMA 55 B8 30 38 56 S 151 29 31 E

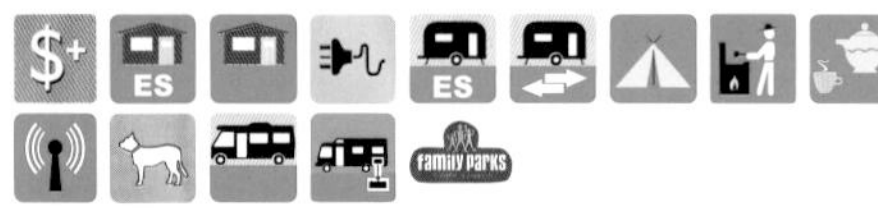

546 Queen Street Uralla Caravan Park
17 Queen St
02 6778 6420 HEMA 55 B8 30 38 17 S 151 30 05 E

Urana

547 Urana Caravan Park & Aquatic Centre
Corowa Rd
02 6920 8192 HEMA 63 K13 35 20 18 S 146 16 23 E

Urunga

548 Reflections Holiday Parks Urunga Head
Hungry Head Rd
www.reflectionsholidayparks.com.au
02 6655 6355 HEMA 55 A13 30 29 48 S 153 01 20 E

549 Urunga Waters Tourist Park
8531 Pacific Hwy
02 6655 6242 HEMA 55 A13 30 28 51 S 153 00 16 E

Valla Beach

550 Valla Beach Tourist Park
1 Regatta Dr, off Ocean View Dr
www.vallabeachtouristpark.com.au
02 6569 5555 HEMA 55 B13 30 36 18 S 153 00 17 E

Vineyard

551 Ingenia Holidays Avina
217 Commercial Rd
www.ingeniaholidays.com.au/avina/
02 9627 1847 HEMA 49 D8 33 38 32 S 150 52 03 E

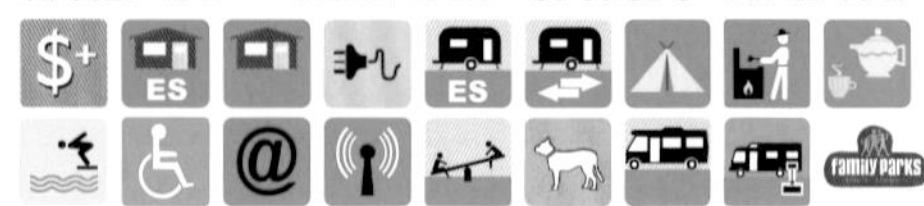

Wagga Wagga

552 BIG4 Wagga Wagga Holiday Park
93 Hammond Ave
www.big4.com.au
02 6921 4287 HEMA 66 B2 35 07 17 S 147 23 19 E

553 Carinya Caravan Park
449 Pine Gully Rd
www.carinyacaravanpark.com.au
02 6933 1256 HEMA 66 B2 35 02 30 S 147 21 00 E

554 Horseshoe Motor Village
23 Horseshoe Rd
www.hmvwagga.com.au
02 6921 6033 HEMA 66 B2 35 04 10 S 147 23 10 E

555 Wagga Beach Caravan Park
2 Johnston St
www.wwbcp.com.au
02 6931 0603 HEMA 66 B2 35 06 21 S 147 22 27 E

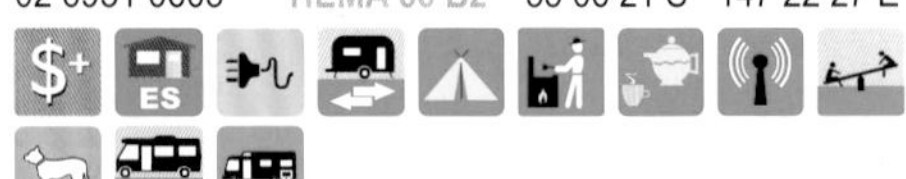

Walcha

556 Walcha Caravan Park
Cnr Middle St & North St
www.walchacaravanpark.com.au
02 6777 2501 HEMA 55 C8 30 58 47 S 151 35 56 E

Wallacia

557 Wallacia Caravan Park

Cnr Silverdale Rd & Alwyn Ave

02 4773 8077 HEMA 48 G6 33 51 49 S 150 38 23 E

Wallaga Lake

558 Ingenia Holidays Ocean Lake

891 Wallaga Lake Rd

www.ingeniaholidays.com.au

02 6493 4055 HEMA 67 H12 36 22 25 S 150 04 18 E

559 Regatta Point Holiday Park

Regatta Point Rd

www.regattapointpark.com.au

02 6493 4253 HEMA 67 H12 36 22 20 S 150 04 11 E

560 Wallaga Lake Holiday Park

186 - 188 Wallaga Lake Rd

www.wallagalakeholidaypark.com.au

02 6493 4655 HEMA 67 H12 36 22 59 S 150 04 13 E

Wanaaring

561 Wanaaring Store & Caravan Park

1 Hebden St

02 6874 7720 HEMA 60 C7 29 42 09 S 144 08 57 E

Wanganella

562 Wanganella Creek Camp Park

32 Murray St

www.wanganellacreekcamppark.com

03 5882 3509 HEMA 63 K10 35 12 57 S 144 48 59 E

Wangi Wangi

563 Wangi Point Lakeside Holiday Park

Watkins Rd

www.lakemacholidayparks.com.au

02 4975 1889 HEMA 47 G12 33 04 21 S 151 36 32 E

Wardell

564 Sandalwood Van & Leisure Park

978 Pimlico Rd

www.sandalwood-van-park.com

02 6683 4221 HEMA 57 D14 28 56 29 S 153 28 21 E

Warialda

565 Warialda Caravan Park

Cnr Holden St & Gwydir Hwy

0427 291 008 HEMA 56 G4 29 32 32 S 150 34 11 E

Warilla

566 Lake Windemere Caravan Park

120 Osborne Pde

02 4296 2610 HEMA 51 F12 34 33 22 S 150 51 59 E

Warren

567 Macquarie Caravan Park

2 Hospital Rd

www.macquarievanpark.com

02 6847 4706 HEMA 58 K2 31 41 43 S 147 50 23 E

Wee Waa

568 Mainway Caravan Park

210 Rose St

02 6795 4268 HEMA 58 F5 30 13 16 S 149 27 12 E

569 Waioma Caravan Park

15 Short St

02 6795 4413 HEMA 58 F5 30 13 46 S 149 26 28 E

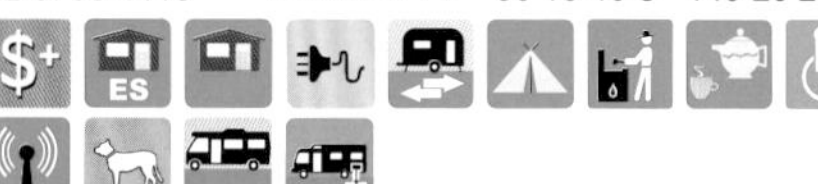

Wellington

570 Wellington Caves Caravan Park & Holiday Complex

101 Caves Rd. 6 km S of PO

www.familyparks.com.au

02 6845 2970 HEMA 52 A3 32 37 14 S 148 56 15 E

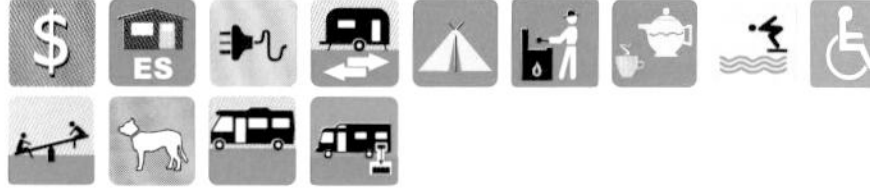

571 Wellington Riverside Park

1 Federal St

www.wellingtonriversidepark.com.au/

02 6845 1370 HEMA 64 C6 32 32 32 S 148 56 37 E

572 Wellington Valley Caravan Park

48 Curtis St

02 6845 2006 HEMA 52 A3 32 33 55 S 148 56 39 E

Wentworth

573 Fort Courage Caravan Park

1703 Old Renmark Rd

03 5027 3097 HEMA 62 G2 34 05 03 S 141 43 53 E

574 Willow Bend Caravan Park

Darling St

www.willowbendcaravanpark.com

03 5027 3213 HEMA 62 G3 34 06 36 S 141 55 12 E

West Wyalong

575 Ace Caravan Park

Cnr Newell & Mid Western Hwys

www.acecaravanpark.com.au

02 6972 3061 HEMA 64 G2 33 55 23 S 147 11 55 E

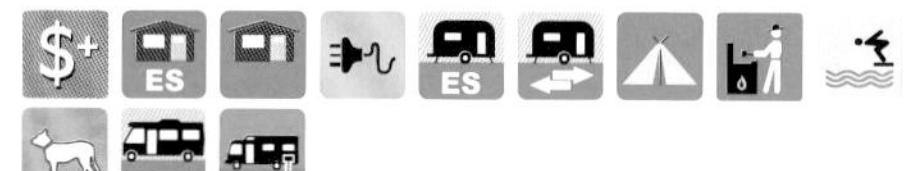

576 West Wyalong Caravan Park

60 Main St

www.westwyalongcaravanpark.com.au

02 6972 3133 HEMA 64 G2 33 55 25 S 147 12 35 E

White Cliffs

577 Opal Pioneer Caravan & Camping Tourist Park

Johnstone St

08 8091 6688 HEMA 60 F5 30 50 58 S 143 05 23 E

Wilcannia

578 Victory Park Caravan Park

Barrier Hwy. Pay at Council Chambers 0900-1500 M-F or contact caretaker, see notice board

08 8091 5803 HEMA 60 H6 31 33 36 S 143 22 52 E

579 Warrawong on the Darling

Barrier Hwy

www.warrawongonthedarling.com.au

0437 010 105 HEMA 60 H6 31 34 03 S 143 23 39 E

Windang

580 Windang Beach Tourist Park
1 Fern St
windangtp@wollongong.nsw.gov.au
02 4297 3166 HEMA 51 F12 34 32 05 S 150 52 12 E

Windeyer

581 Bushlands Tourist Park
1879 Windeyer Rd
www.bushlandstouristpark.com.au
02 6373 8252 HEMA 52 B5 32 47 44 S 149 33 25 E

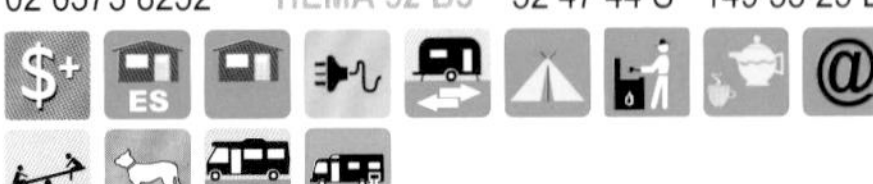

Wisemans Ferry

582 Del Rio Riverside Resort
Chaseling Rd, Webbs Creek
www.delrioresort.com.au
02 4566 4330 HEMA 49 A9 33 24 09 S 150 58 02 E

583 NSW Ski Gardens
2916 River Rd
02 4566 4212 HEMA 49 A9 33 23 45 S 150 58 57 E

584 Rosevale Holiday Park
7123 Wisemans Ferry Rd (BYO drinking water)
02 4566 4207 HEMA 49 A9 33 23 57 S 150 59 58 E

Wonboyn

585 Wonboyn Cabins & Caravan Park
Wonboyn Rd
www.wonboyncabins.com.au
02 6496 9131 HEMA 70 H6 37 15 02 S 149 54 48 E

Woolgoolga

586 Sunset Caravan Park
64 Newman St
www.sunsetcaravanpark.com.au
02 6654 1499 HEMA 57 J13 30 06 32 S 153 11 45 E

587 Woolgoolga Beach Caravan Park
55 Beach St
www.coffscoastholidayparks.com.au
02 6654 1373 HEMA 57 J13 30 06 35 S 153 12 07 E

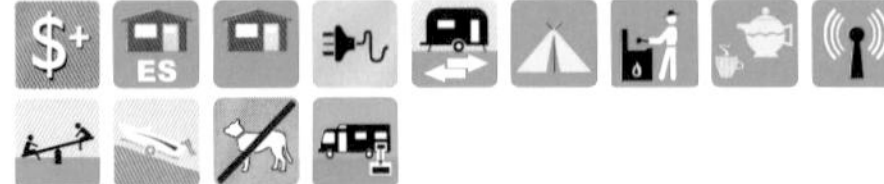

588 Woolgoolga Lakeside Caravan Park
Lot 276 Lake Rd
www.coffscoastholidayparks.com.au
02 6648 4715 HEMA 57 J13 30 06 05 S 153 11 51 E

Wooli

589 BIG4 Solitary Islands Resort
383 North St
www.solitaryislandsresort.com.au
02 6649 7519 HEMA 57 H13 29 51 03 S 153 15 19 E

590 Wooli Camping & Caravan Park
25 Riverside Dr
www.clarenceholidayparks.com.au
02 6649 7671 HEMA 57 H13 29 52 15 S 153 15 52 E

Woombah

591 Bimbimbi Riverside Caravan Park
286 Iluka Rd
02 6646 4272 HEMA 57 F13 29 21 22 S 153 16 37 E

592 Woombah Woods Caravan Park
54 Iluka Rd
www.woombahwoods.com
02 6646 4544 HEMA 57 F13 29 21 12 S 153 15 13 E

Wooyung Beach

593 Wooyung Beach Holiday Park
515 Wooyung Rd
www.wooyungbeach.com.au
02 6677 1300 HEMA 57 B14 28 27 25 S 153 33 09 E

Wyangala Dam

594 Relections Holiday Park Wyangala Waters
2891 Reg Hailstone Way
www.reflectionsholidayparks.com.au
02 6345 0877 HEMA 52 G3 33 57 46 S 148 57 17 E

Wymah

595 Wymah Hideaway
189 Wymah Ferry Rd
www.wymahhideaway.com
02 6020 2035 HEMA 66 F2 36 02 11 S 147 16 10 E

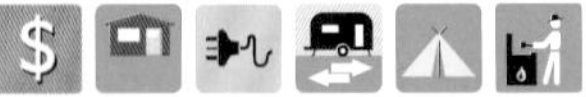

Yamba

596 Blue Dolphin Holiday Resort

31 Yamba Rd. W of PO
www.bluedolphin.com.au
02 6646 2194 HEMA 57 F13 29 26 01 S 153 20 29 E

597 Calypso Holiday Park Yamba

14 Harbour St
www.calypsoyamba.com.au
02 6646 8847 HEMA 57 F13 29 26 05 S 153 21 34 E

598 Gateway Lifestyle Yamba Waters

36 Golding St
www.glhp.com.au/parks/yamba-waters/
02 6646 2930 HEMA 57 F13 29 26 22 S 153 20 29 E

Yass

599 Hume Park Tourist Resort

Good Hope Rd
www.humepark.com.au
02 6227 1235 HEMA 67 A8 34 55 24 S 148 49 09 E

600 Lake Burrinjuck Leisure Resort

590 Woolgarlo Rd, off Burrinjuck Rd
02 6227 7271 HEMA 67 A8 34 53 51 S 148 44 12 E

601 Yass Caravan Park

Cnr Laidlaw & Grampian Sts
02 6226 1173 HEMA 67 A8 34 50 02 S 148 54 30 E

Yetman

602 Yetman Caravan Park

MacIntyre St
07 4675 3231 HEMA 56 D4 28 54 06 S 150 46 42 E

Young

603 Young Caravan Park

17 Edward St
www.youngcaravanpark.com.au
02 6382 2190 HEMA 64 H4 34 18 35 S 148 18 07 E

Key Map

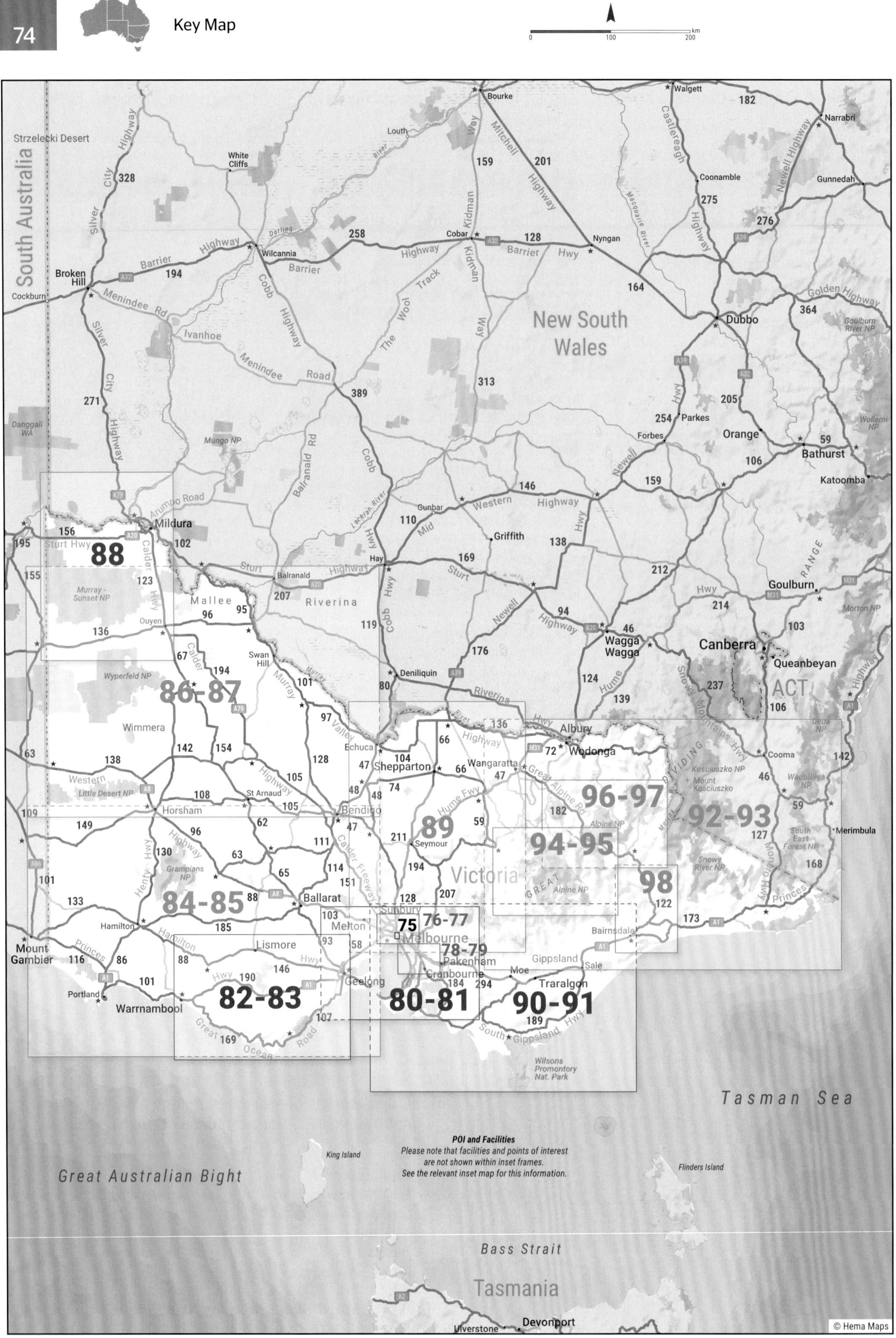

0 100 200 km

88
86-87
84-85
82-83
80-81
75
76-77
78-79
89
90-91
94-95
96-97
92-93
98

South Australia
New South Wales
Victoria
ACT
Tasmania
Great Australian Bight
Bass Strait
Tasman Sea

POI and Facilities
Please note that facilities and points of interest are not shown within inset frames. See the relevant inset map for this information.

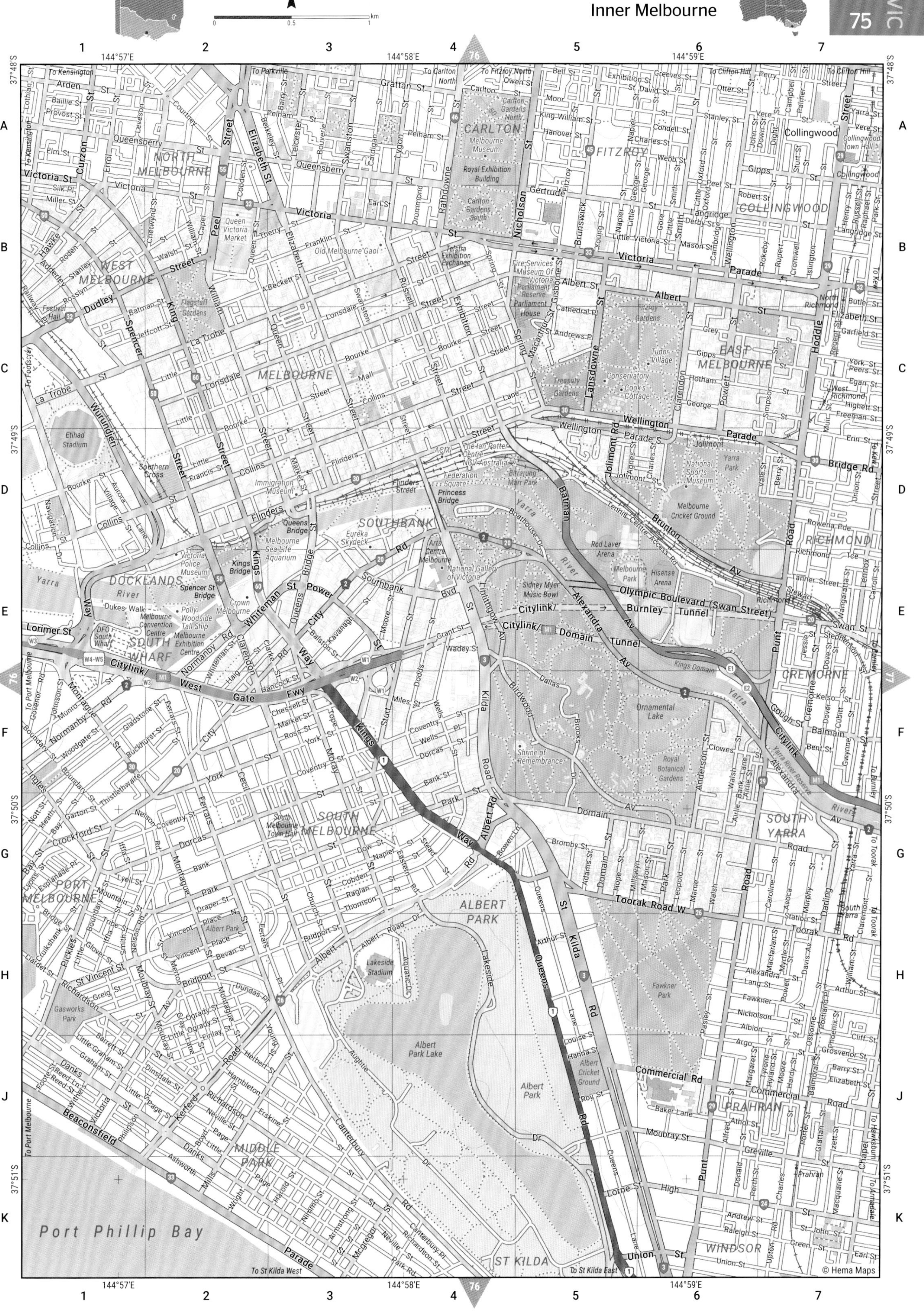
Port Phillip Bay
MELBOURNE
CARLTON
FITZROY
COLLINGWOOD
NORTH MELBOURNE
WEST MELBOURNE
EAST MELBOURNE
RICHMOND
CREMORNE
SOUTHBANK
DOCKLANDS
SOUTH WHARF
SOUTH MELBOURNE
PORT MELBOURNE
ALBERT PARK
MIDDLE PARK
SOUTH YARRA
PRAHRAN
WINDSOR
ST KILDA
© Hema Maps

144°45'E
144°50'E
144°55'E
37°40'S
37°45'S
37°50'S
Bulla
BULLA
DIGGERS REST
To Sunbury
Bulla Rd Sunbury Rd
Woodlands Homestead
Woodlands Historic Park
Gellibrand Hill 202m
Perimeter Rd
Loemans
Organ Pipes NP
Calder Park Raceway
HILLSIDE
CALDER PARK
Sunbury Wine Region
Melbourne International Airport
KEILOR NORTH
Mcnabs
Melton Hwy
KEILOR LODGE
Taylors Lake
SYDENHAM
TAYLORS LAKES
KEILOR DOWNS
TAYLORS HILL
DELAHEY
Taylors Rd
KINGS PARK
BURNSIDE HEIGHTS
Keilor
KEALBA
CAROLINE SPRINGS
ALBANVALE
Main Road W
Main Road E
BURNSIDE
St Albans
ST ALBANS
Cairnlea
CAIRNLEA
Furlong Rd
Western Hwy
Calder Fwy
Tullamarine Fwy
Western Ring Rd
TULLAMARINE
Sharps Rd
KEILOR PARK
KEILOR EAST
Maribyrnong Valley Parklands
SUNSHINE NORTH
Greenvale
GREENVALE
MEADOW HEIGHTS
Somerton Rd
SOMERTON
Cooper St
COOLAROO
CAMPBELLFIELD
Upfield
ATTWOOD
Broadmeadows Valley Park
Dallas
Broadmeadows
DALLAS
WESTMEADOWS
BROADMEADOWS
Camp Rd
JACANA
Jacana
GLADSTONE PARK
Ring Rd
GLENROY
Hilton
Gowrie
FAWKNER
HADFIELD
GOWANBRAE
STRATHMORE HEIGHTS
OAK PARK
Fawkner
Merlynston
PASCOE VALE
ESSENDON FIELDS
Gaffney
Batman St
Othea
Bell St
COBURG NORTH
Murray Rd
NIDDRIE
ESSENDON NORTH
STRATHMORE
Woodland St
PASCOE VALE SOUTH
COBURG
Glenbervie
Rosehill Rd
ESSENDON
Buckley
ESSENDON WEST
Moreland Rd
Moreland
Albion
BRUNSWICK WEST
Anstey
ABERFELDIE
MOONEE PONDS
Victoria St
Dean St
Blyth St
BRUNSWICK
MARIBYRNONG
AVONDALE HEIGHTS
Raleigh Rd
Maribyrnong Rd
Brunswick Rd
Dawson St
Jewell
PARKVILLE
PRINCES HILL
CARLTON NORTH
Western ALBION
Ballarat Rd
Suffolk Road
DEER PARK
Deer Park
RAVENHALL
ARDEER
Tilburn Rd
MAIDSTONE
Mitchell St
ASCOT VALE
Ascot Vale
TRAVANCORE
BRAYBROOK
Devonshire Rd
SUNSHINE WEST
Forrest St
SUNSHINE
Sunshine Golf Course
Flemington Racecourse
FLEMINGTON
Racecourse Rd
Elliott Av
Royal Park
Princes St
South Rd
WEST FOOTSCRAY
Wright St
Sunshine Rd
Barkly St
FOOTSCRAY
KENSINGTON
NORTH MELBOURNE
DERRIMUT
Derrimut Grassland Nature Con. Res.
Andersons Swamp
TOTTENHAM
SEDDON
Dynon
Footscray Rd
CARLTON
Victoria St
Somerville Road
KINGSVILLE
Boundary Road
BROOKLYN
YARRAVILLE
WEST MELBOURNE
Melbourne
TRUGANINA
Geelong Rd
Francis St
DOCKLANDS
Lorimer St
Derrimut
Dohertys Road
Dohertys Rd
Gate
West
SOUTH KINGSVILLE
Yarra River
Kings Domain
LAVERTON NORTH
SPOTSWOOD
Williamstown Rd
SOUTH MELBOURNE
Blackshaws Rd
NEWPORT
ALTONA NORTH
PORT MELBOURNE
Albert Park Lake
Leakes Rd
Princes Freeway
Mason St
Port Melbourne Rear Light
Storage tank
Kororoit Creek Rd
Lawrie Emmins Reserve
Old Geelong Rd
WILLIAMSTOWN NORTH
ALTONA
Hobsons Bay
Beaconsfield Parade
Sayers Rd
WILLIAMS LANDING
Werribee Line
Cherry Lake
Altona Coastal Park
WILLIAMSTOWN
Williamstown Workshop, Piers & Stony Creek Backwash
LAVERTON
Prohibited Area
Civic Pde
SEAHOLME
Williamstown Lighthouse (Inactive)
Laverton
J I Stewart Reserve
Central Av
Queen St
Esplanade
Seaholme
To Geelong
Tasmania Ferry
CityLink and EastLink Tollways
For information on passes and e-TAGs visit www.citylink.com.au or www.eastlink.com.au
Altona Bay
Gellibrand Pile Light (Destroyed)
SEABROOK
ALTONA MEADOWS
Spirit of Tasmania
For more information on the ferry from Devonport to Melbourne, Phone 1800 634 906 or visit www.spiritoftasmania.com.au
Point Ormond
Dunnings Rd
POINT COOK
Point Cook Rd
Sanctuary Lakes Golf Club
Point Cook Coastal Park
Port Phillip Bay
Marine Pde

8 9 10 11 12 13 14
145°E
145°5'E
145°10'E
81
A
B
C
D
E
F
G
H
J
K
37°40'S
37°45'S
37°50'S
EPPING
LALOR
THOMASTOWN
RESERVOIR
PRESTON
THORNBURY
NORTHCOTE
FAIRFIELD
FITZROY NORTH
CLIFTON HILL
ABBOTSFORD
CREMORNE
SOUTH YARRA
PRAHRAN
WINDSOR
ST KILDA EAST
BALACLAVA
RIPPONLEA
ELWOOD
ELSTERNWICK
CAULFIELD NORTH
CAULFIELD EAST
CAULFIELD SOUTH
GLEN HUNTLY
CARNEGIE
HUGHESDALE
MURRUMBEENA
MALVERN EAST
CHADSTONE
OAKLEIGH
ASHBURTON
ASHWOOD
MOUNT WAVERLEY
GLEN IRIS
MALVERN
ARMADALE
TOORAK
KOOYONG
HAWTHORN
HAWTHORN EAST
BURNLEY
RICHMOND
KEW
KEW EAST
BALWYN
BALWYN NORTH
DEEPDENE
CANTERBURY
CAMBERWELL
SURREY HILLS
MONT ALBERT
MONT ALBERT NORTH
BOX HILL
BOX HILL NORTH
BOX HILL SOUTH
BURWOOD
BURWOOD EAST
BLACKBURN
BLACKBURN NORTH
BLACKBURN SOUTH
FOREST HILL
NUNAWADING
MITCHAM
VERMONT
VERMONT SOUTH
WANTIRNA SOUTH
GLEN WAVERLEY
WHEELERS HILL
DONCASTER
DONCASTER EAST
DONVALE
PARK ORCHARDS
TEMPLESTOWE
TEMPLESTOWE LOWER
BULLEEN
WARRANDYTE
NORTH WARRANDYTE
ELTHAM
ELTHAM NORTH
RESEARCH
KANGAROO GROUND
WATTLE GLEN
DIAMOND CREEK
HURSTBRIDGE
YARRAMBAT
PLENTY
MILL PARK
SOUTH MORANG
ST HELENA
GREENSBOROUGH
BRIAR HILL
MONTMORENCY
WATSONIA
WATSONIA NORTH
YALLAMBIE
BUNDOORA
MACLEOD
KINGSBURY
ROSANNA
VIEWBANK
HEIDELBERG
HEIDELBERG WEST
HEIDELBERG HEIGHTS
BELLFIELD
LOWER PLENTY
EAGLEMONT
IVANHOE
IVANHOE EAST
ALPHINGTON
Metropolitan Ring Rd
Hume Freeway
Cooper St
McDonalds Rd
Plenty Rd
Diamond Creek Rd
Settlement Road
Grimshaw St
Greensborough Hwy
Lower Plenty Rd
Rosanna Rd
Templestowe Rd
Manningham Rd
Thompsons Rd
Doncaster Rd
Eastern Freeway
Heidelberg Rd
Burke Rd
Bulleen Rd
Whitehorse Rd
Canterbury Rd
Burwood Hwy
Toorak Rd
Dandenong Rd
Princess Hwy
Monash Freeway
Waverley Rd
Highbury Rd
High Street Rd
Warrigal Road
Middleborough Rd
Springvale Rd
Blackburn Rd
Eastlink
Warrandyte Rd
Kangaroo Ground-Wattle Glen Rd
Heidelberg-Kinglake Rd
Main Hurstbridge Rd
Yarra Valley Parklands
Plenty Gorge Parklands
Dandenong Valley Parklands
See Page 75
76
103
78
© Hema Maps

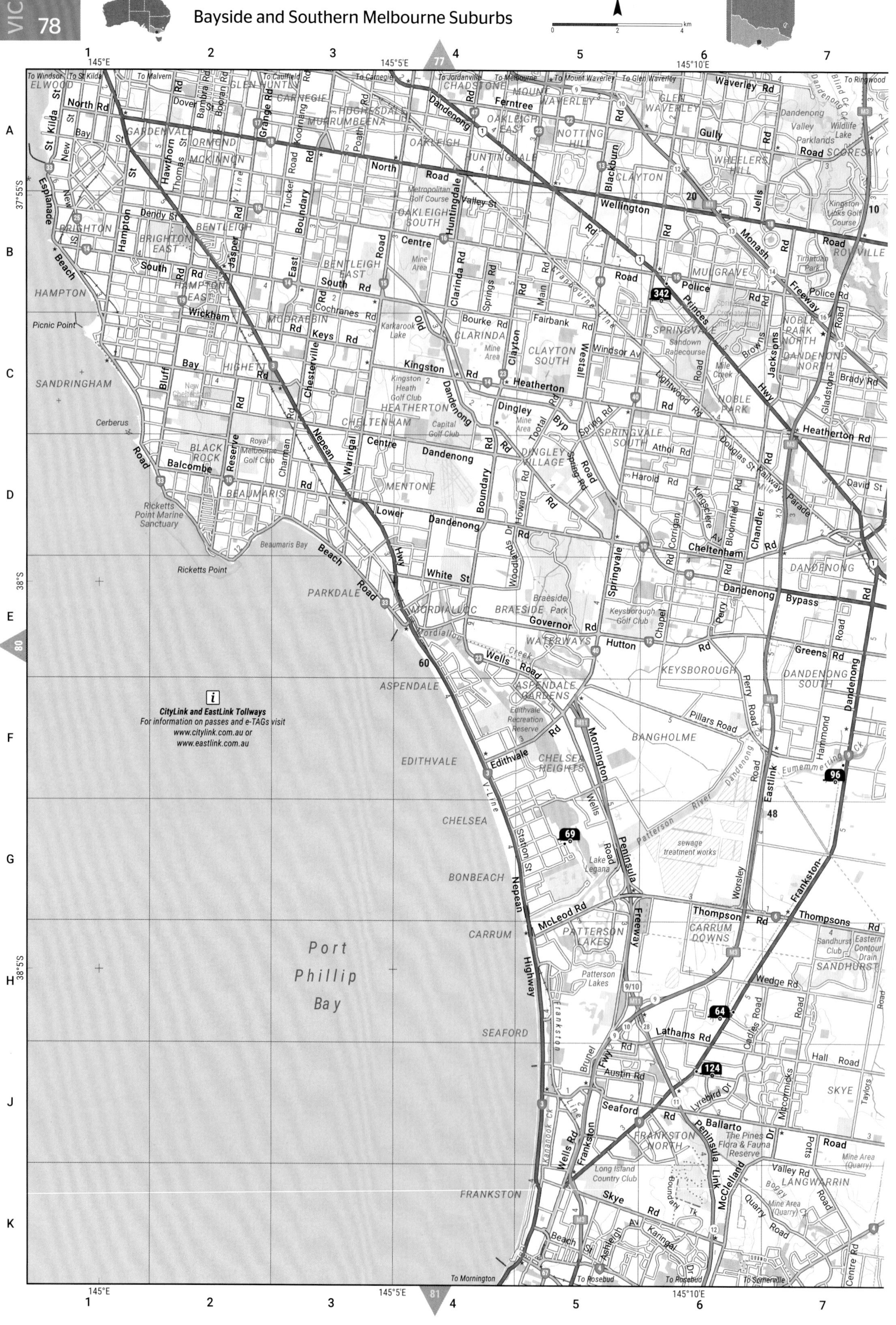
CityLink and EastLink Tollways
For information on passes and e-TAGs visit
www.citylink.com.au or
www.eastlink.com.au
Port Phillip Bay
ELWOOD
BRIGHTON
HAMPTON
SANDRINGHAM
BLACK ROCK
BEAUMARIS
BENTLEIGH
BENTLEIGH EAST
MOORABBIN
HIGHETT
CHELTENHAM
MENTONE
PARKDALE
MORDIALLOC
ASPENDALE
EDITHVALE
CHELSEA
BONBEACH
CARRUM
SEAFORD
FRANKSTON
FRANKSTON NORTH
CLAYTON
CLAYTON SOUTH
CLARINDA
HEATHERTON
DINGLEY VILLAGE
BRAESIDE
WATERWAYS
ASPENDALE GARDENS
CHELSEA HEIGHTS
PATTERSON LAKES
CARRUM DOWNS
BANGHOLME
KEYSBOROUGH
SPRINGVALE
SPRINGVALE SOUTH
NOBLE PARK
NOBLE PARK NORTH
MULGRAVE
DANDENONG
DANDENONG NORTH
DANDENONG SOUTH
SANDHURST
SKYE
LANGWARRIN
ROWVILLE
SCORESBY
WHEELERS HILL
GLEN WAVERLEY
MOUNT WAVERLEY
CHADSTONE
OAKLEIGH
OAKLEIGH EAST
OAKLEIGH SOUTH
NOTTING HILL
HUNTINGDALE
CARNEGIE
MURRUMBEENA
HUGHESDALE
GLEN HUNTLY
ORMOND
MCKINNON
GARDENVALE
Ricketts Point
Ricketts Point Marine Sanctuary
Beaumaris Bay
Picnic Point
To Mornington
To Rosebud
To Somerville
To Ringwood
To Windsor
To St Kilda
To Malvern
To Caulfield
To Carnegie
To Jordanville
To Melbourne
To Mount Waverley
To Glen Waverley

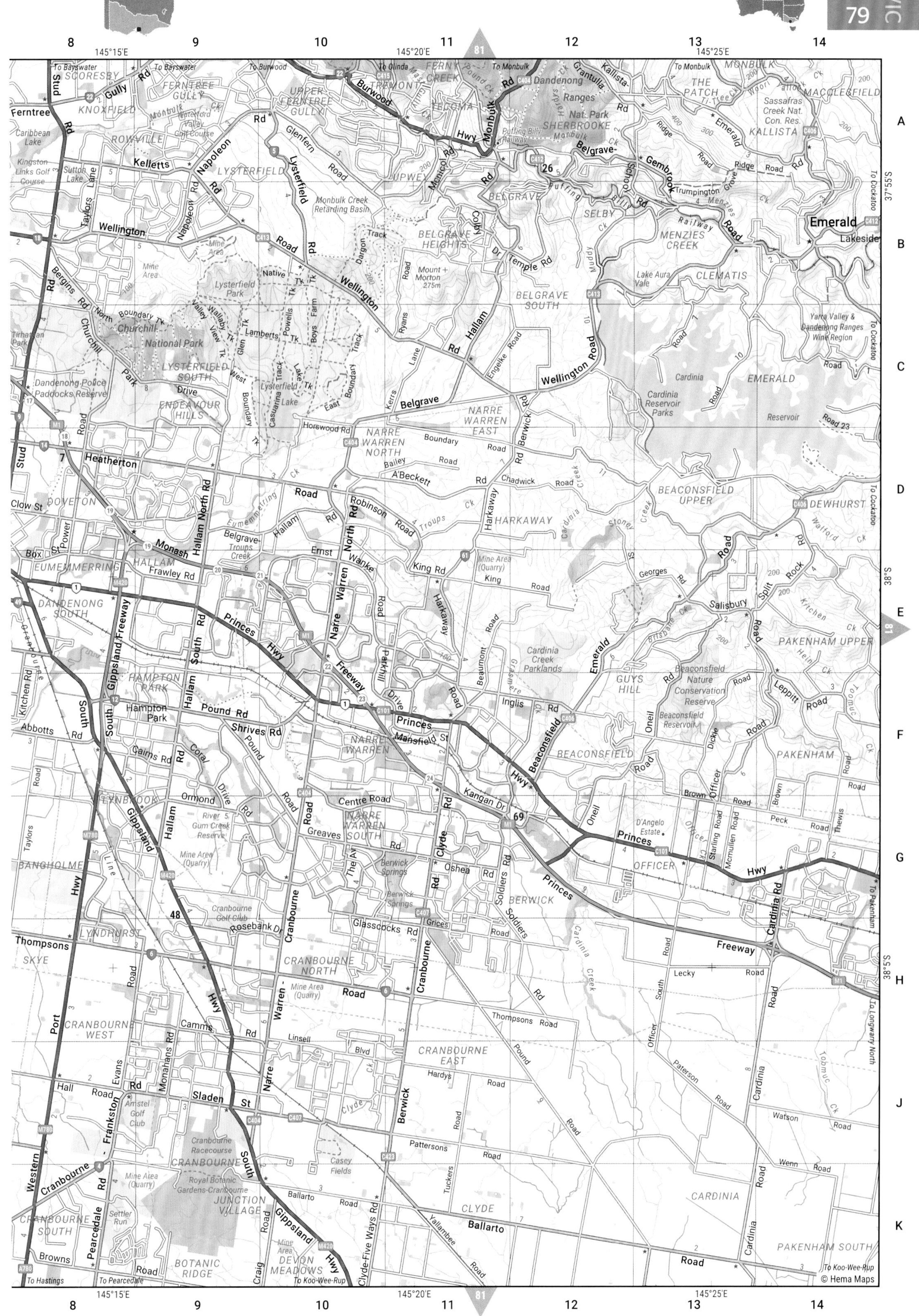
8
9
10
11
12
13
14
145°15'E
145°20'E
145°25'E
37°55'S
38°S
38°5'S
A
B
C
D
E
F
G
H
J
K
81
To Bayswater
To Burwood
To Olinda
To Monbulk
SCORESBY
Ferntree
Gully Rd
KNOXFIELD
FERNTREE GULLY
UPPER FERNTREE GULLY
TREMONT
FERNY CREEK
TECOMA
Dandenong Ranges Nat. Park
SHERBROOKE
Kallista
THE PATCH
MONBULK
MACCLESFIELD
Sassafras Creek Nat. Con. Res.
KALLISTA
ROWVILLE
Caribbean Lake
Kingston Links Golf Course
Sutton Lake
Kelletts
Napoleon Rd
LYSTERFIELD
Burwood Hwy
Monbulk Rd
UPWEY
Belgrave-Gembrook Rd
26
BELGRAVE
SELBY
MENZIES CREEK
Emerald
Lakeside
Wellington Road
Monbulk Creek Retarding Basin
BELGRAVE HEIGHTS
Mount Morton 275m
Lysterfield Park
Churchill National Park
LYSTERFIELD SOUTH
Lake Aura Vale
CLEMATIS
BELGRAVE SOUTH
Yarra Valley & Dandenong Ranges Wine Region
To Cockatoo
Tirhatuan Park
Dandenong Police Paddocks Reserve
ENDEAVOUR HILLS
Lysterfield Lake
Belgrave Hallam Rd
NARRE WARREN EAST
NARRE WARREN NORTH
Cardinia Reservoir Parks
EMERALD
Heatherton
Stud Rd
DOVETON
Clow St
Robinson Road
HARKAWAY
BEACONSFIELD UPPER
DEWHURST
EUMEMMERRING
HALLAM
Monash
Frawley Rd
Belgrave Troups Creek
Hallam North Rd
King Rd
Mine Area (Quarry)
DANDENONG SOUTH
Princes Hwy
Narre Warren North Rd
Cardinia Creek Parklands
PAKENHAM UPPER
HAMPTON PARK
Hampton Park
Hallam South Rd
Pound Rd
Gippsland Freeway
Beaconsfield Nature Conservation Reserve
Beaconsfield Reservoir
GUYS HILL
Abbotts Rd
Shrives Rd
NARRE WARREN
Mansfield St
BEACONSFIELD
PAKENHAM
LYNBROOK
Ormond
Centre Road
Kangan Dr
69
D'Angelo Estate
River Gum Creek Reserve
NARRE WARREN SOUTH
Greaves
Berwick Springs
Clyde Rd
OFFICER
BANGHOLME
Princes Freeway
BERWICK
48
Cranbourne Golf Club
Glasscocks Rd
Grices Road
Thompsons
SKYE
LYNDHURST
CRANBOURNE NORTH
Cranbourne Road
Lecky Road
Cardinia Rd
To Pakenham
CRANBOURNE WEST
Camms Rd
Linsell Blvd
Thompsons Road
CRANBOURNE EAST
Hardys Road
To Longwarry North
Hall Road
Evans Rd
Sladen St
Amstel Golf Club
Cranbourne Racecourse
CRANBOURNE
Casey Fields
Pattersons Road
Western Port Hwy
Cranbourne-Frankston Rd
Royal Botanic Gardens-Cranbourne
JUNCTION VILLAGE
Ballarto Road
CLYDE
CARDINIA
CRANBOURNE SOUTH
Settler Run
Browns Road
BOTANIC RIDGE
DEVON MEADOWS
South Gippsland Hwy
PAKENHAM SOUTH
To Hastings
To Pearcedale
To Koo-Wee-Rup
© Hema Maps

Melbourne and Surrounds

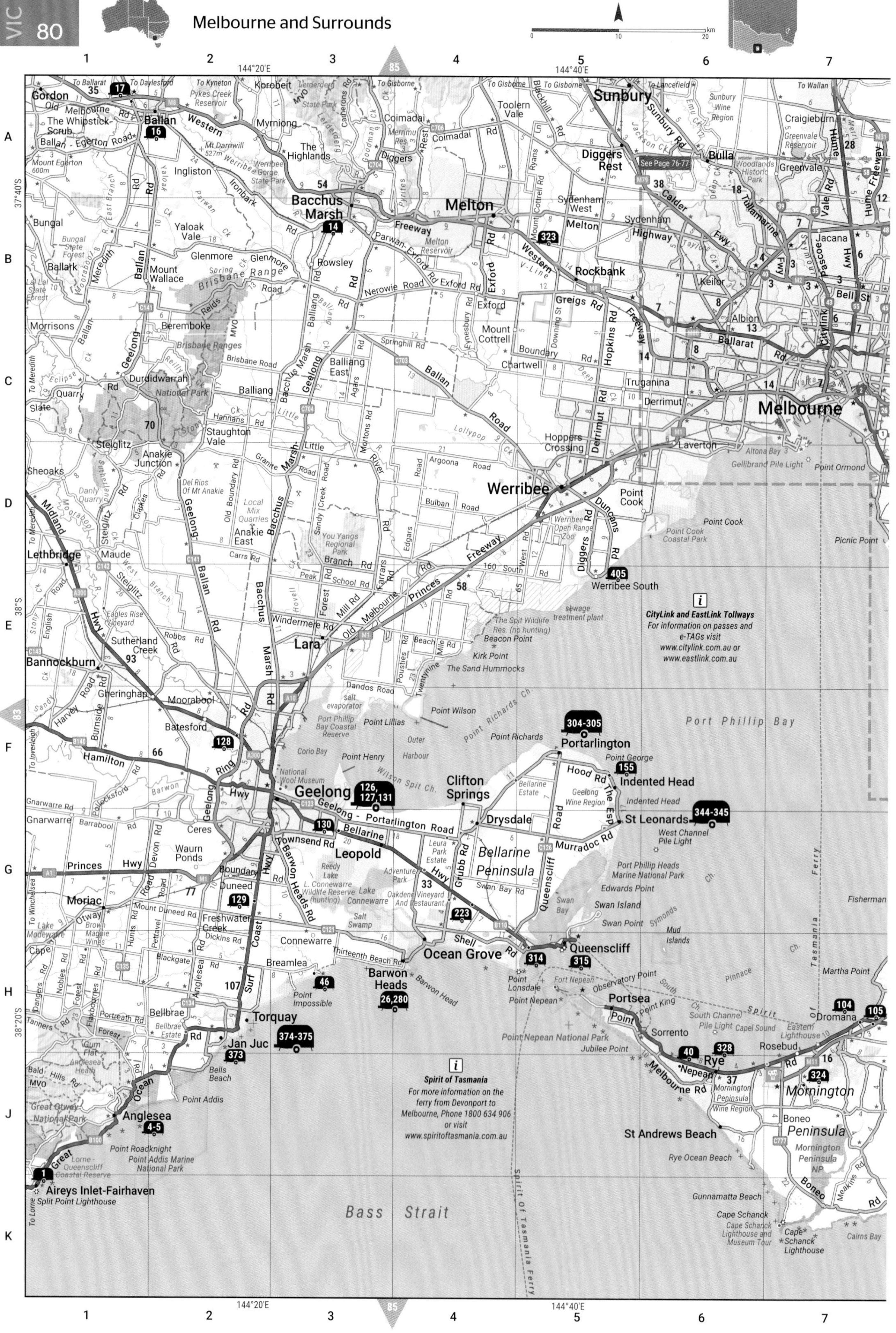

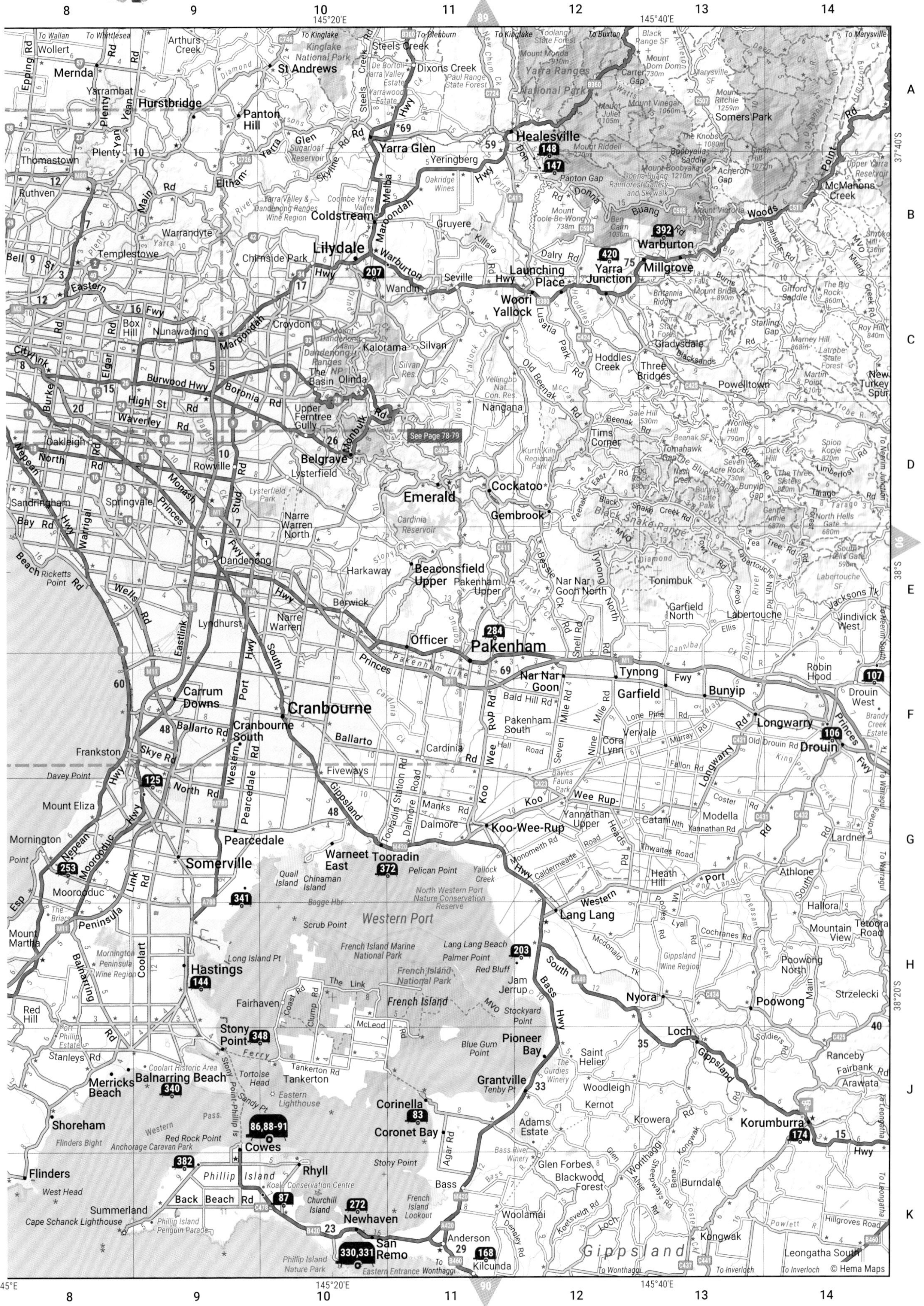
Healesville
Lilydale
Pakenham
Cranbourne
Emerald
Warburton
Drouin
Hastings
Cowes
Western Port
French Island
Phillip Island
Somerville
Frankston
Korumburra
San Remo
Newhaven
Flinders
Gippsland
See Page 78-79
© Hema Maps

Great Ocean Road - Warrnambool to Geelong

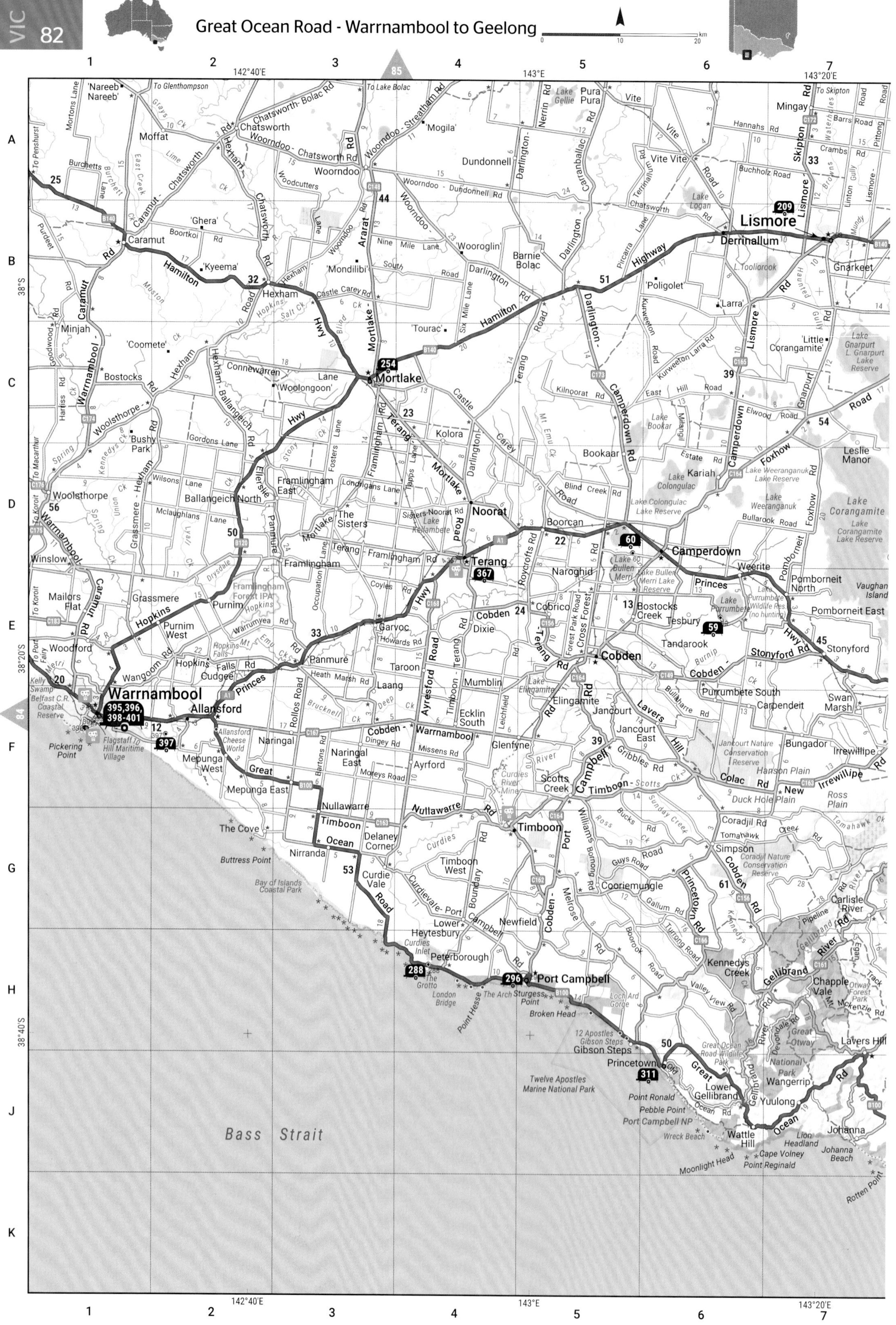

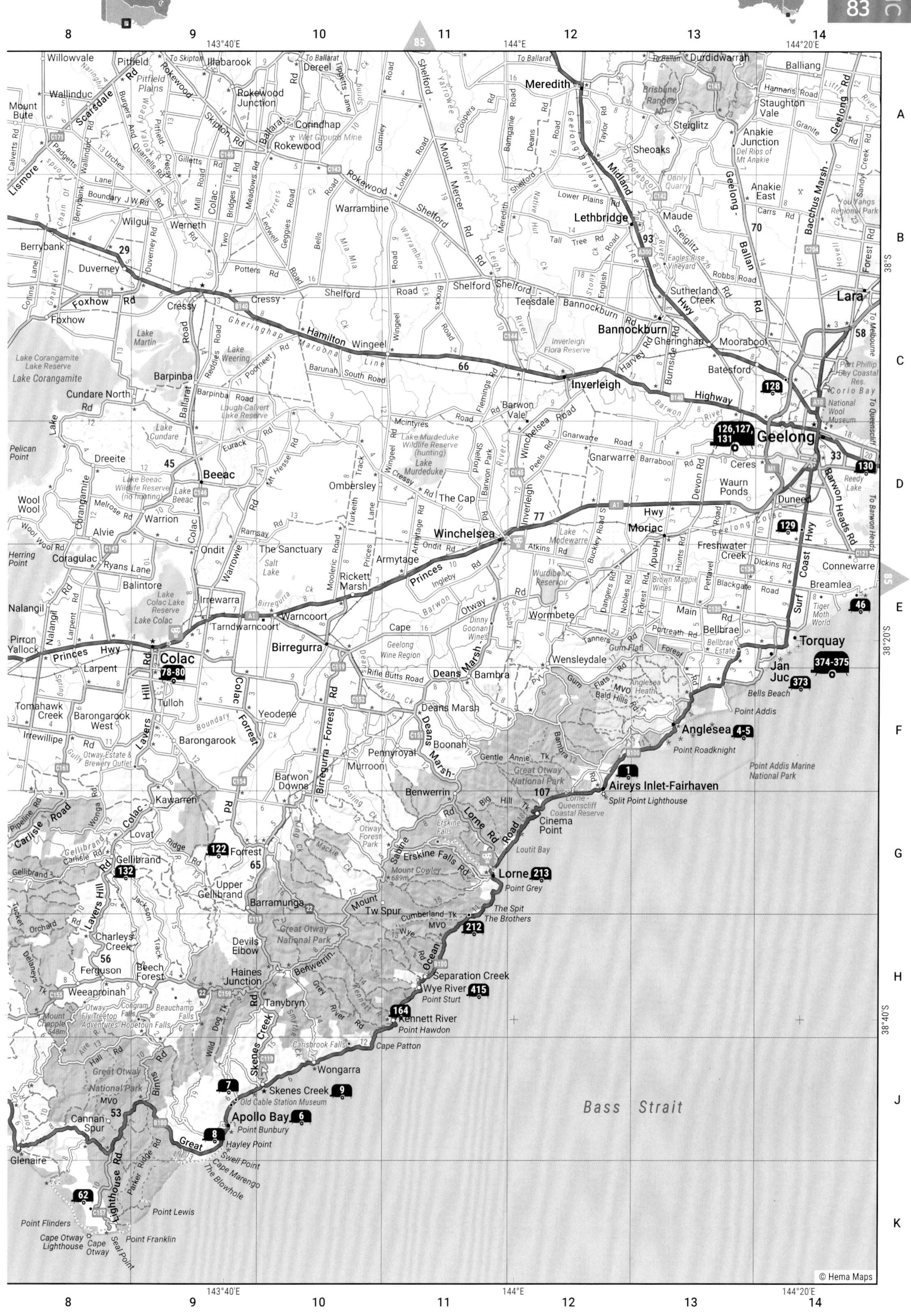
Geelong
Colac
Winchelsea
Lorne
Apollo Bay
Torquay
Anglesea
Aireys Inlet-Fairhaven
Bass Strait
Great Otway National Park
Lake Corangamite
© Hema Maps

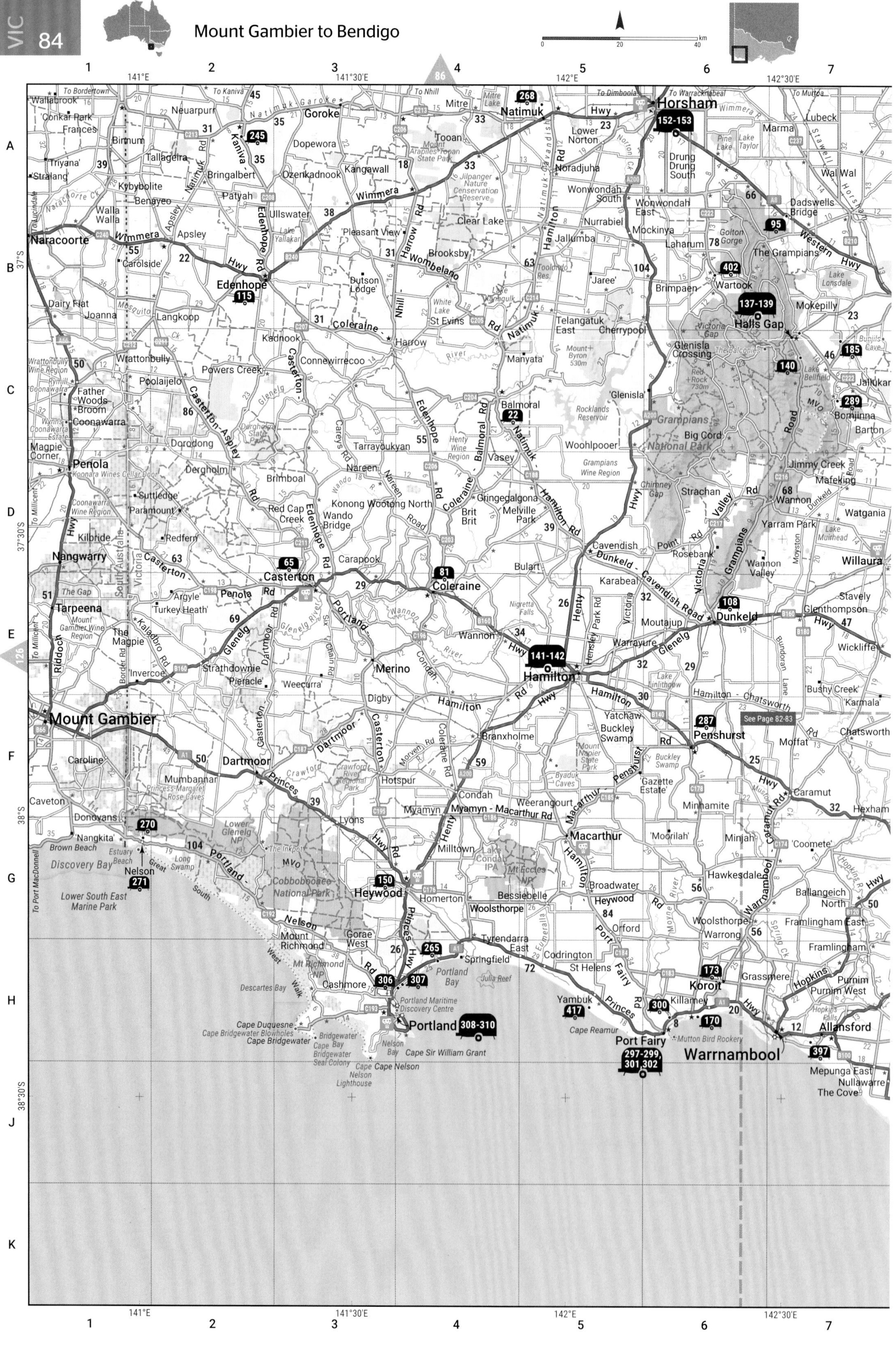

0 20 40 km
141°E
141°30'E
142°E
142°30'E
37°S
37°30'S
38°S
38°30'S
Horsham
Natimuk
Goroke
Mitre
Tooan
Lower Norton
Drung Drung South
Lubeck
Marma
Wal Wal
Dadswells Bridge
Naracoorte
Edenhope
Apsley
Harrow
Brooksby
Wonwondah East
Mockinya
Laharum
Wartook
The Grampians
Halls Gap
Brimpaen
Mokepilly
Glenisla Crossing
Balmoral
Penola
Coleraine
Casterton
Dunkeld
Hamilton
Penshurst
Merino
Digby
Mount Gambier
Dartmoor
Heywood
Portland
Macarthur
Koroit
Port Fairy
Warrnambool
Allansford
Nelson
Caroline
Donovans
Discovery Bay
Lower South East Marine Park
Cape Bridgewater
Cape Nelson
Cape Sir William Grant
Portland Bay
Yambuk
Killarney
Caramut
Hexham
Mepunga East
Nullawarre
The Cove
Willaura
Glenthompson
Moyston
Wickliffe
Grampians National Park
Cobboboonee National Park
Lower Glenelg NP
Mt Eccles NP
See Page 82-83

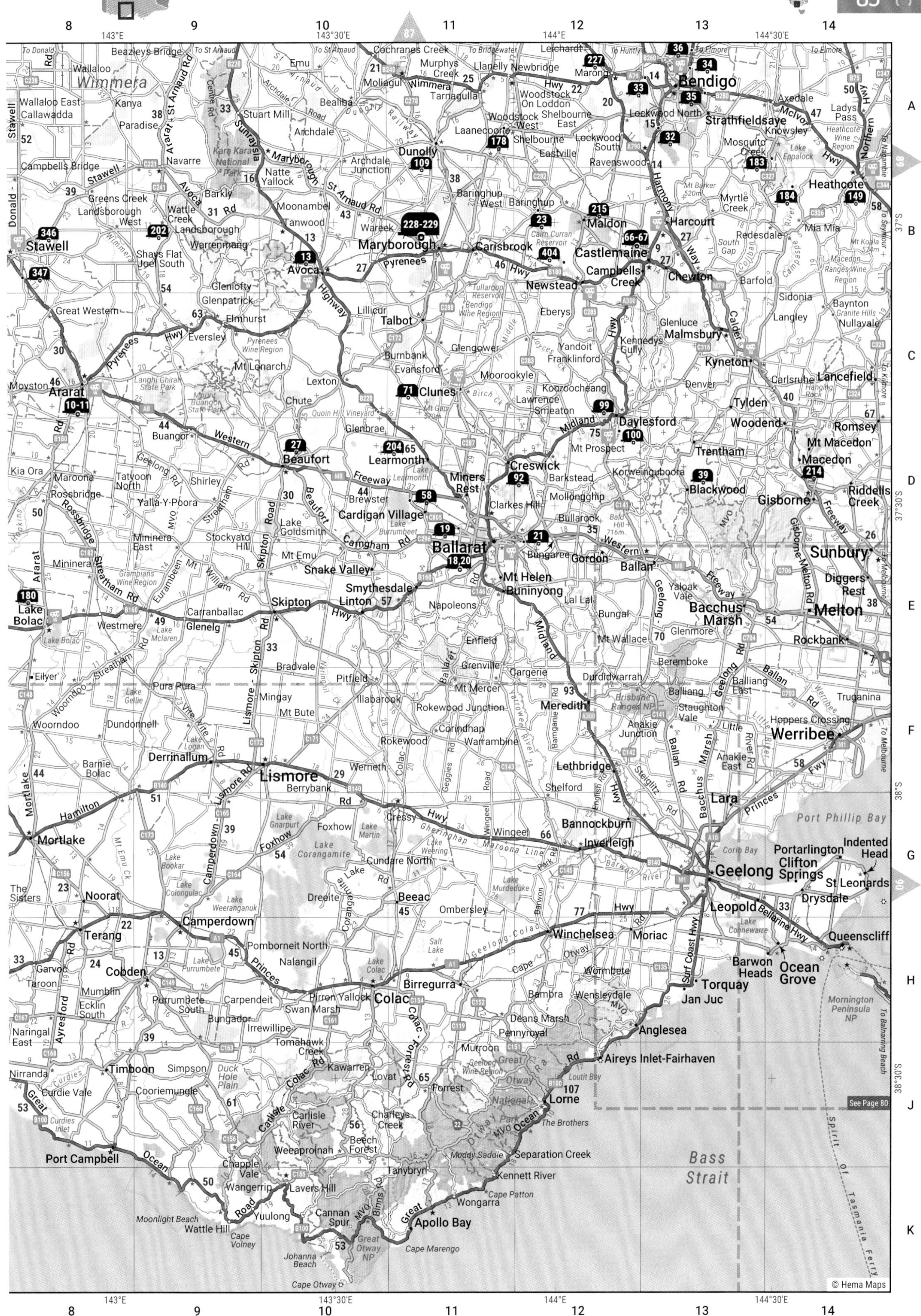
Wimmera
Stawell
Ararat
Lake Bolac
Mortlake
Terang
Noorat
Camperdown
Cobden
Timboon
Port Campbell
Derrinallum
Lismore
Skipton
Beaufort
Avoca
Maryborough
Dunolly
Carisbrook
Talbot
Clunes
Creswick
Learmonth
Ballarat
Mt Helen
Buninyong
Smythesdale
Linton
Snake Valley
Cardigan Village
Daylesford
Castlemaine
Maldon
Newstead
Campbells Creek
Chewton
Harcourt
Bendigo
Strathfieldsaye
Heathcote
Kyneton
Malmsbury
Woodend
Lancefield
Romsey
Macedon
Mt Macedon
Gisborne
Riddells Creek
Sunbury
Diggers Rest
Melton
Bacchus Marsh
Ballan
Gordon
Blackwood
Trentham
Meredith
Lethbridge
Bannockburn
Inverleigh
Geelong
Lara
Werribee
Leopold
Drysdale
Portarlington
Clifton Springs
St Leonards
Indented Head
Queenscliff
Ocean Grove
Barwon Heads
Torquay
Jan Juc
Anglesea
Aireys Inlet-Fairhaven
Lorne
Separation Creek
Kennett River
Wongarra
Apollo Bay
Cape Otway
Winchelsea
Moriac
Colac
Birregurra
Beeac
Cressy
Forrest
Lake Corangamite
Port Phillip Bay
Bass Strait
Spirit of Tasmania Ferry
See Page 80
© Hema Maps

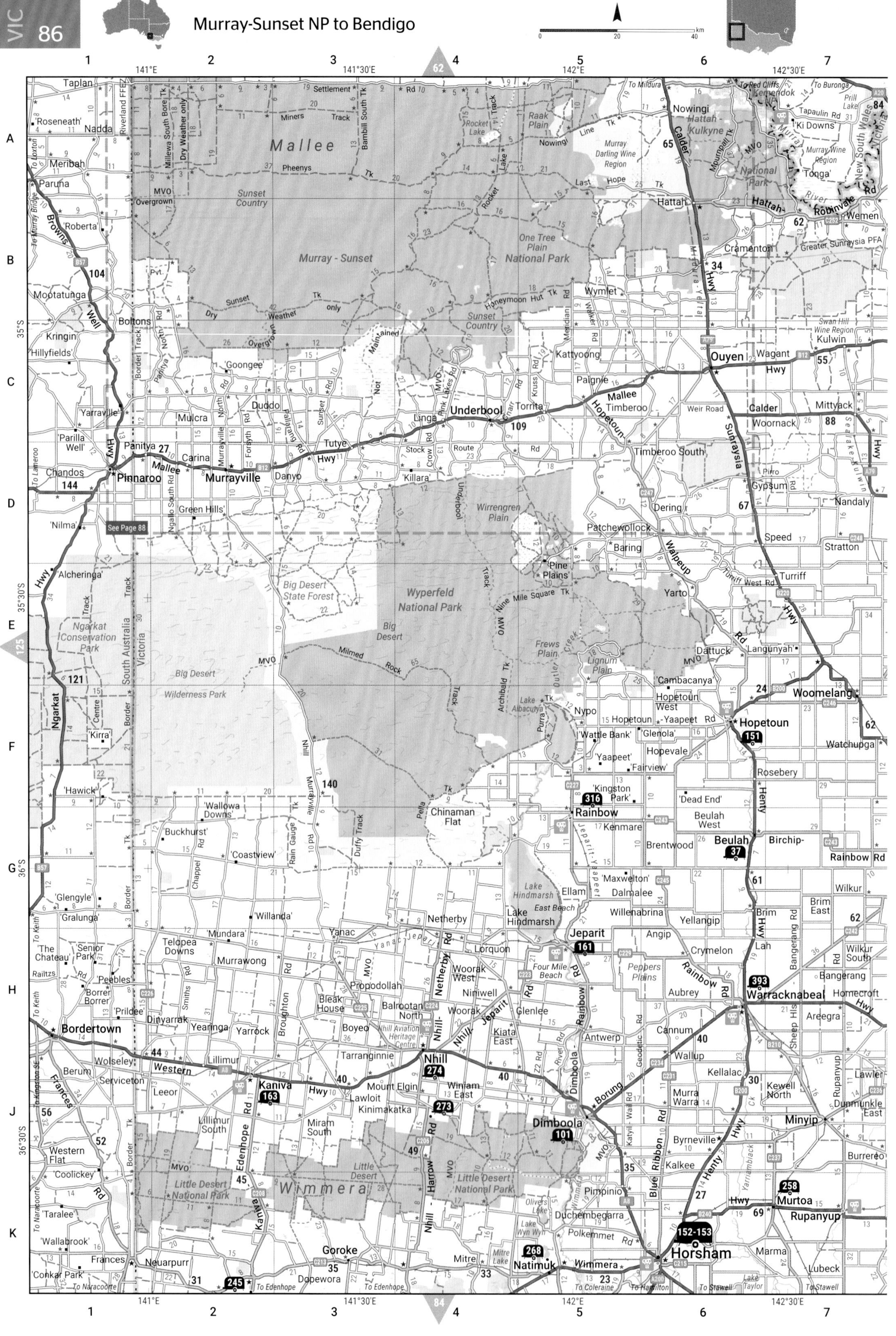
Mallee
Murray - Sunset
Sunset Country
One Tree Plain National Park
Ouyen
Underbool
Pinnaroo
Murrayville
Wyperfeld National Park
Big Desert Wilderness Park
Big Desert State Forest
Ngarkat Conservation Park
Hopetoun
Rainbow
Beulah
Lake Hindmarsh
Jeparit
Warracknabeal
Bordertown
Kaniva
Nhill
Dimboola
Little Desert National Park
Wimmera
Horsham
Natimuk
Goroke
Murtoa
Rupanyup
Minyip
See Page 88

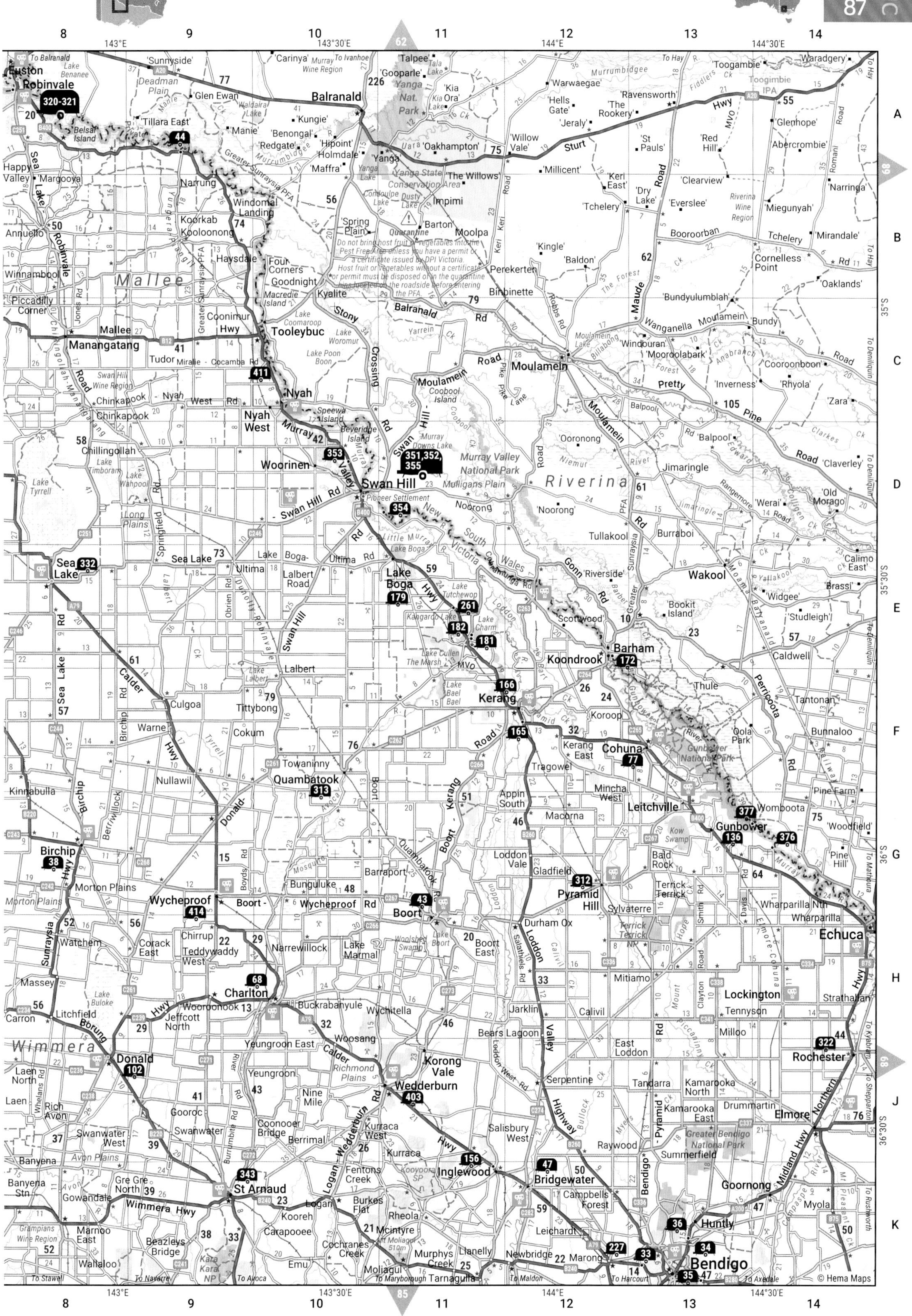
Euston
Robinvale
Balranald
Manangatang
Tooleybuc
Nyah
Nyah West
Woorinen
Swan Hill
Moulamein
Riverina
Mulligans Plain
Murray Valley National Park
Sea Lake
Ultima
Lalbert
Lake Boga
Kerang
Koondrook
Barham
Wakool
Cohuna
Leitchville
Gunbower
Quambatook
Birchip
Wycheproof
Boort
Pyramid Hill
Echuca
Charlton
Donald
Wedderburn
Korong Vale
Inglewood
Bridgewater
St Arnaud
Bendigo
Huntly
Elmore
Rochester
Lockington
Goornong
Mallee
Wimmera
Calder Hwy
Sunraysia Hwy
Murray Valley Hwy
Sturt Hwy
Loddon Valley Highway
Midland Hwy
Northern Hwy
Wimmera Hwy
Borung Hwy
Donald-Swan Hill Rd
Kerang-Koondrook Rd
Gunbower National Park
Greater Bendigo National Park
Mulligans Plain
© Hema Maps

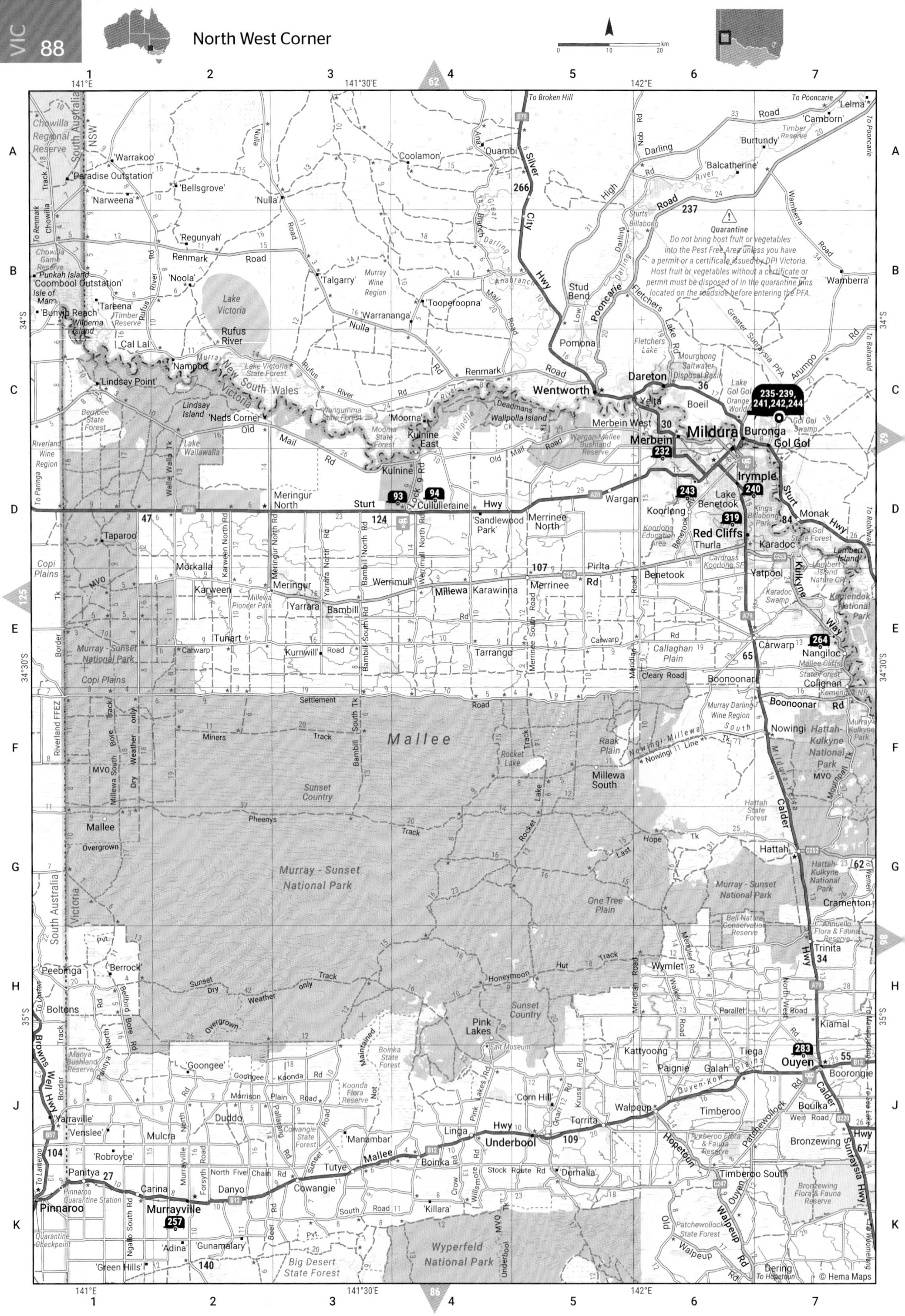
Mildura
Wentworth
Merbein
Irymple
Red Cliffs
Ouyen
Murrayville
Pinnaroo
Underbool
Mallee
Murray - Sunset National Park
Hattah-Kulkyne National Park
Wyperfeld National Park
Quarantine
Do not bring host fruit or vegetables into the Pest Free Area unless you have a permit or a certificate issued by DPI Victoria. Host fruit or vegetables without a certificate or permit must be disposed of in the quarantine bins located on the roadside before entering the PFA.
© Hema Maps

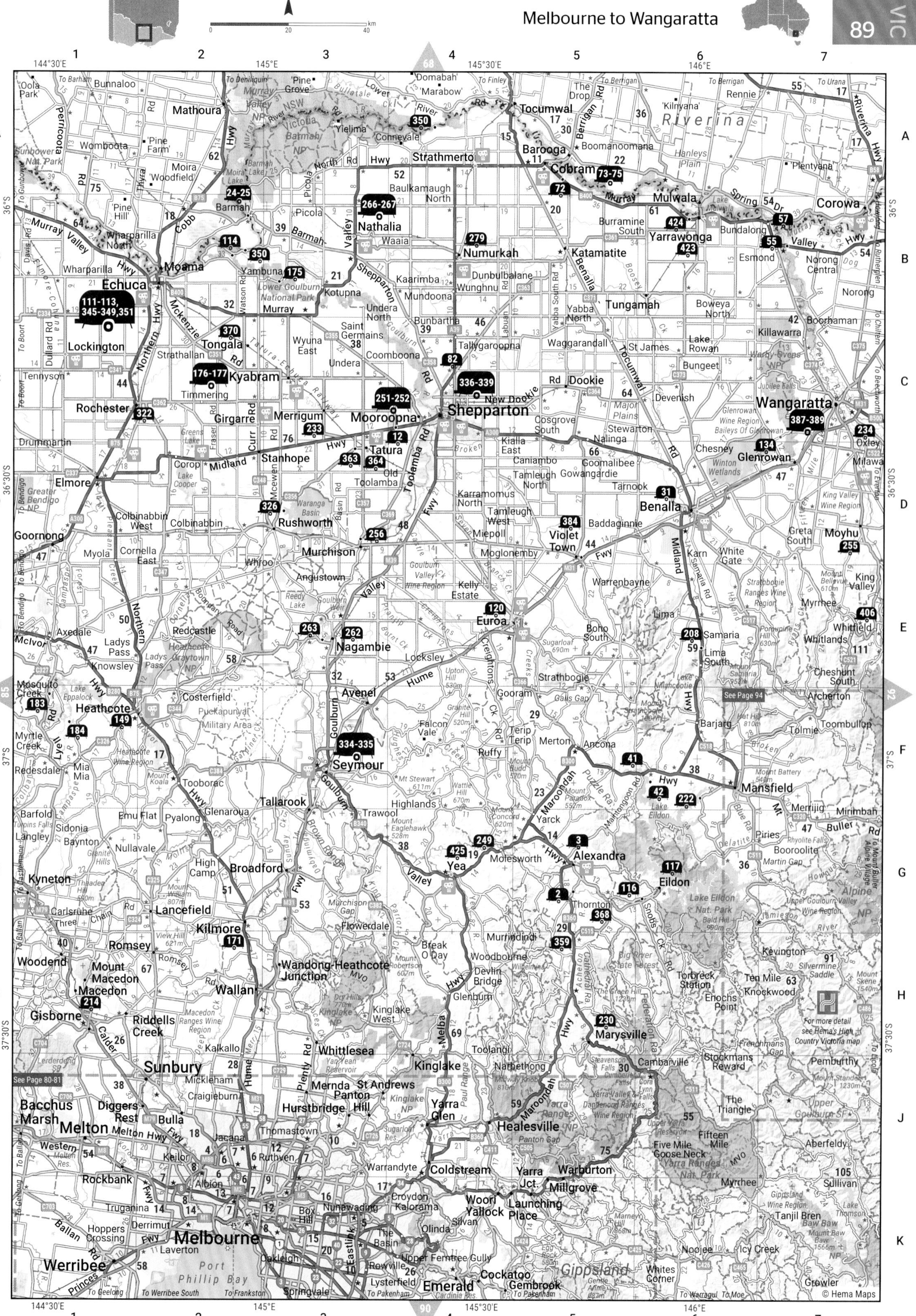
Echuca
Shepparton
Wangaratta
Benalla
Seymour
Melbourne
Mansfield
Kyabram
Mooroopna
Nagambie
Euroa
Yea
Alexandra
Healesville
Kilmore
Sunbury
Melton
Werribee
Cobram
Corowa
Yarrawonga
See Page 94
See Page 80-81
© Hema Maps

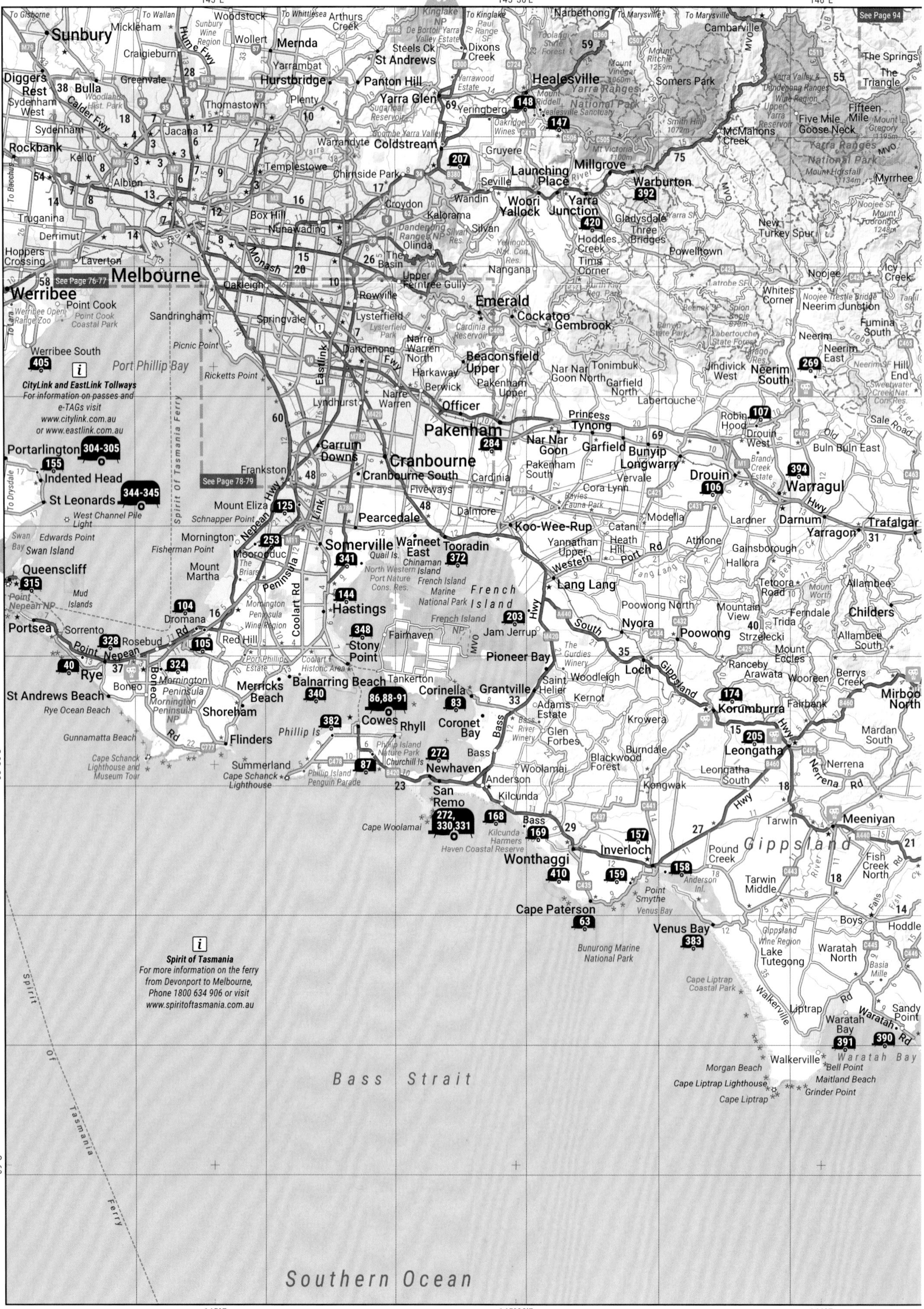
See Page 94
See Page 76-77
See Page 78-79
Sunbury
Mickleham
Woodstock
Arthurs Creek
Kinglake NP
Narbethong
Cambarville
Craigieburn
Wollert
Mernda
Steels Ck
Dixons Creek
St Andrews
Healesville
Yarra Ranges National Park
Somers Park
The Springs
The Triangle
Diggers Rest
Bulla
Greenvale
Yarrambat
Hurstbridge
Panton Hill
Yarra Glen
Yeringberg
Sydenham West
Sydenham
Thomastown
Plenty
Jacana
Warrandyte
Coldstream
McMahons Creek
Five Mile
Fifteen Mile
Goose Neck
Rockbank
Keilor
Templestowe
Chirnside Park
Gruyere
Launching Place
Millgrove
Warburton
Myrrhee
Albion
Seville
Woori Yallock
Yarra Junction
Truganina
Box Hill
Croydon
Wandin
Kalorama
Nunawading
Silvan
Gladysdale
Three Bridges
New Turkey Spur
Derrimut
Olinda
Hoddles Creek
Powelltown
Hoppers Crossing
Laverton
Melbourne
The Basin
Tims Corner
Nangana
Upper Ferntree Gully
Noojee
Icy Creek
Werribee
Oakleigh
Rowville
Emerald
Whites Corner
Neerim Junction
Point Cook
Sandringham
Springvale
Lysterfield
Cockatoo
Gembrook
Fumina South
Werribee South
Picnic Point
Dandenong
Narre Warren North
Neerim
Neerim East
Port Phillip Bay
Ricketts Point
Harkaway
Beaconsfield Upper
Nar Nar Goon North
Tonimbuk
Jindivick West
Neerim South
Hill End
CityLink and EastLink Tollways
For information on passes and e-TAGs visit
www.citylink.com.au
or www.eastlink.com.au
Berwick
Pakenham Upper
Garfield North
Lyndhurst
Narre Warren
Officer
Labertouche
Princess
Tynong
Robin Hood
Drouin West
Sale Road
Portarlington
Pakenham
Nar Nar Goon
Garfield
Bunyip
Buln Buln East
Carrum Downs
Cranbourne
Longwarry
Drouin
Warragul
Indented Head
Frankston
Cranbourne South
Pakenham South
Vervale
St Leonards
Fiveways
Cora Lynn
Mount Eliza
Dalmore
Modella
Pearcedale
Koo-Wee-Rup
Catani
Lardner
Darnum
Trafalgar
Yarragon
West Channel Pile Light
Schnapper Point
Swan Island
Edwards Point
Mornington
Fisherman Point
Somerville
Warneet
Tooradin
Yannathan
Heath Hill
Athlone
Gainsborough
Hallora
Queenscliff
Moorooduc
East
Quail Is.
Chinaman Island
Upper
Lang Lang
Mount Martha
Tetoora Road
Allambee
Mud Islands
French Island
Point Nepean NP
Hastings
Dromana
French Island Marine National Park
Poowong North
Mountain View
Trida
Ferndale
Childers
Portsea
Sorrento
Rosebud
Red Hill
Jam Jerrup
Nyora
Poowong
Strzelecki
Allambee South
Fairhaven
Stony Point
Mount Eccles
Rye
Boneo
Pioneer Bay
Loch
Ranceby
Arawata
Wooreen
Berrys Creek
St Andrews Beach
Rye Ocean Beach
Merricks Beach
Balnarring Beach
Tankerton
Corinella
Grantville
Saint Helier
Woodleigh
Kernot
Korumburra
Fairbank
Mirboo North
Shoreham
Cowes
Rhyll
Coronet Bay
Adams Estate
Krowera
Gunnamatta Beach
Flinders
Phillip Is
Glen Forbes
Leongatha
Mardan South
Cape Schanck Lighthouse and Museum Tour
Summerland
Churchill Is
Bass
Blackwood Forest
Burndale
Nerrena
Cape Schanck Lighthouse
Phillip Island Penguin Parade
Newhaven
Anderson
Woolamai
Kongwak
Leongatha South
San Remo
Kilcunda
Tarwin
Meeniyan
Cape Woolamai
Kilcunda Harmers Haven Coastal Reserve
Wonthaggi
Inverloch
Pound Creek
Gippsland
Fish Creek North
Point Smythe
Anderson Inl.
Tarwin Middle
Cape Paterson
Venus Bay
Boys
Hoddle
Bunurong Marine National Park
Lake Tutegong
Waratah North
Spirit of Tasmania
For more information on the ferry from Devonport to Melbourne, Phone 1800 634 906 or visit www.spiritoftasmania.com.au
Cape Liptrap Coastal Park
Walkerville
Liptrap
Waratah Bay
Sandy Point
Bell Point
Maitland Beach
Grinder Point
Morgan Beach
Cape Liptrap Lighthouse
Cape Liptrap
Bass Strait
Spirit of Tasmania Ferry
Southern Ocean
145°E
145°30'E
146°E
38°S
38°30'S
39°S

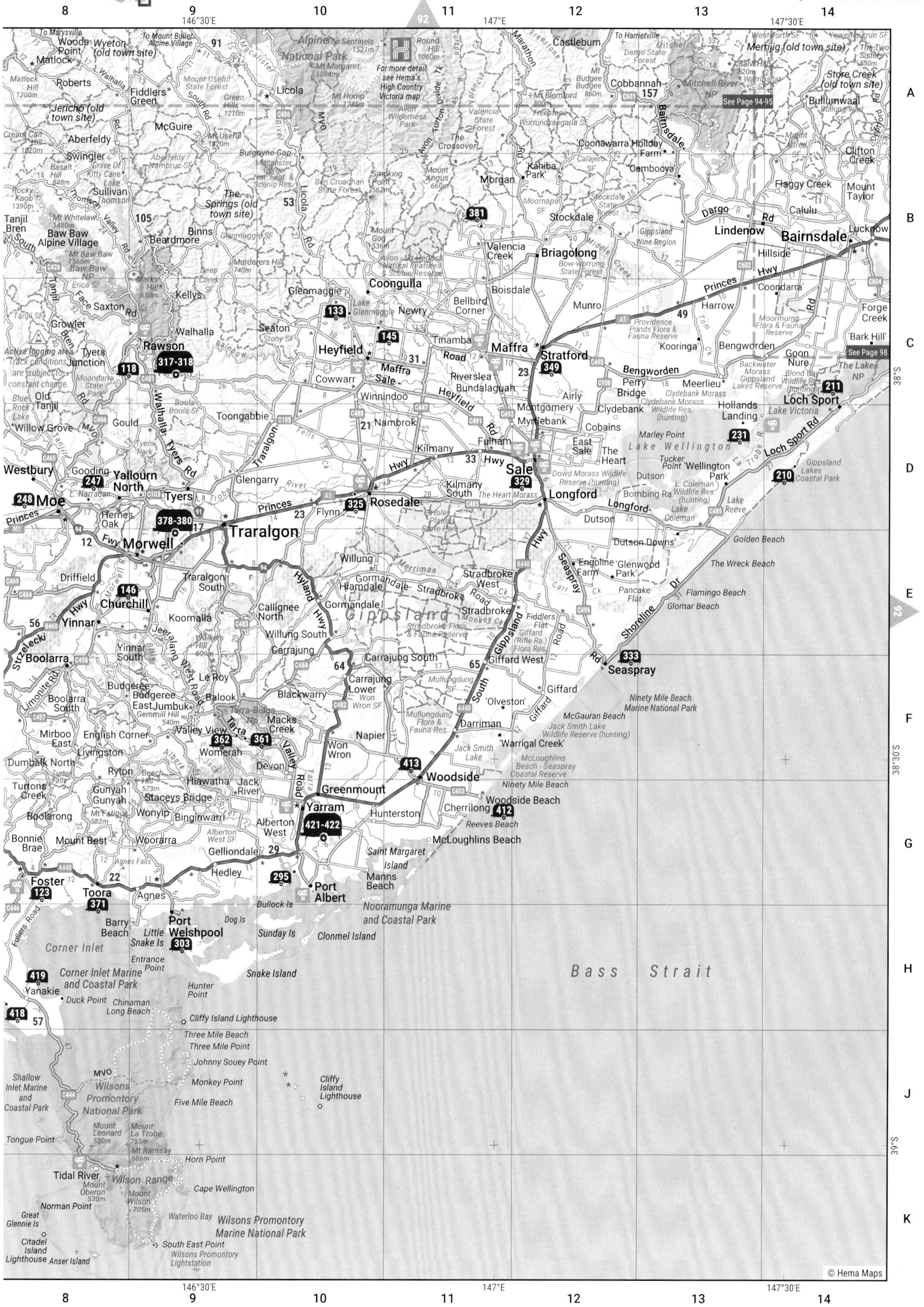

8
9
10
11
12
13
14
146°30'E
147°E
147°30'E
A
B
C
D
E
F
G
H
J
K
38°S
38°30'S
39°S
92
See Page 94-95
See Page 98
For more detail see Hema's High Country Victoria map
Woods Point
Wyeton (old town site)
Matlock
Licola
Castleburn
Cobbannah
Merrijig (old town site)
Store Creek (old town site)
Bullumwaal
Roberts
Fiddlers Green
Jericho (old town site)
McGuire
Aberfeldy
Swingler
Sullivan
Coonawarra Holiday Farm
Camboorya
Clifton Creek
Kahiba Park
Morgan
Flaggy Creek
Mount Taylor
Tanjil Bren
Baw Baw Alpine Village
Beardmore
Binns
The Springs (old town site)
Stockdale
Lindenow
Bairnsdale
Lucknow
Calulu
Hillside
Valencia Creek
Briagolong
Coongulla
Glenmaggie
Boisdale
Bellbird Corner
Newry
Munro
Harrow
Coondarra
Forge Creek
Bark Hill
Kellys
Saxton
Growler
Walhalla
Seaton
Heyfield
Tinamba
Maffra
Stratford
Providence Ponds Flora & Fauna Reserve
Kooringa
Bengworden
Goon Nure
Rawson
Tyers Junction
Cowwarr
Riverslea
Bundalaguah
Airly
Perry Bridge
Meerlieu
Old Tanjil
Winnindoo
Montgomery
Clydebank
Hollands Landing
Loch Sport
The Lakes NP
Lake Victoria
Gould
Toongabbie
Nambrok
Myrtlebank
Cobains
Willow Grove
Kilmany
East Sale
The Heart
Lake Wellington
Marley Point
Tucker Point
Wellington Park
Westbury
Gooding
Yallourn North
Glengarry
Rosedale
Kilmany South
Sale
Dutson
Longford
Moe
Tyers
Hernes Oak
Traralgon
Flynn
Dutson
Bombing Ra
Lake Coleman
Lake Reeve
Morwell
Dutson Downs
Golden Beach
Driffield
Willung
Traralgon South
Gormandale
Hiamdale
Stradbroke West
Engoline Farm
Glenwood Park
The Wreck Beach
Pancake Flat
Flamingo Beach
Glomar Beach
Churchill
Koornalla
Callignee North
Stradbroke
Gippsland
Fiddlers Flat
Yinnar
Willung South
Yinnar South
Carrajung
Boolarra
Carrajung South
Giffard West
Seaspray
Le Roy
Carrajung Lower
Giffard
Ninety Mile Beach Marine National Park
Budgeree
Balook
Blackwarry
Boolarra South
Budgeree East
Jumbuk
Macks Creek
Olveston
McGauran Beach
Darriman
Mirboo East
English Corner
Valley View
Napier
Warrigal Creek
Livingston
Womerah
Won Wron
Jack Smith Lake
Dumbalk North
Devon
Woodside
Ryton
Hiawatha
Jack River
Greenmount
Ninety Mile Beach
Turtons Creek
Gunyah Gunyah
Staceys Bridge
Yarram
Woodside Beach
Boolarong
Wonyip
Binginwarri
Hunterston
Cherrilong
Reeves Beach
Alberton West
Bonnie Brae
Mount Best
Woorarra
McLoughlins Beach
Gelliondale
Saint Margaret Island
Hedley
Manns Beach
Foster
Toora
Agnes
Port Albert
Nooramunga Marine and Coastal Park
Barry Beach
Port Welshpool
Little Snake Is
Dog Is
Sunday Is
Clonmel Island
Corner Inlet
Corner Inlet Marine and Coastal Park
Entrance Point
Snake Island
Bass Strait
Yanakie
Hunter Point
Duck Point
Chinaman Long Beach
Cliffy Island Lighthouse
Three Mile Beach
Three Mile Point
Johnny Souey Point
Shallow Inlet Marine and Coastal Park
Wilsons Promontory National Park
Monkey Point
Cliffy Island Lighthouse
Five Mile Beach
Tongue Point
Horn Point
Tidal River
Wilson Range
Cape Wellington
Norman Point
Great Glennie Is
Waterloo Bay
Wilsons Promontory Marine National Park
South East Point
Wilsons Promontory Lightstation
Citadel Island Lighthouse
Anser Island
© Hema Maps

Wangaratta to Mallacoota

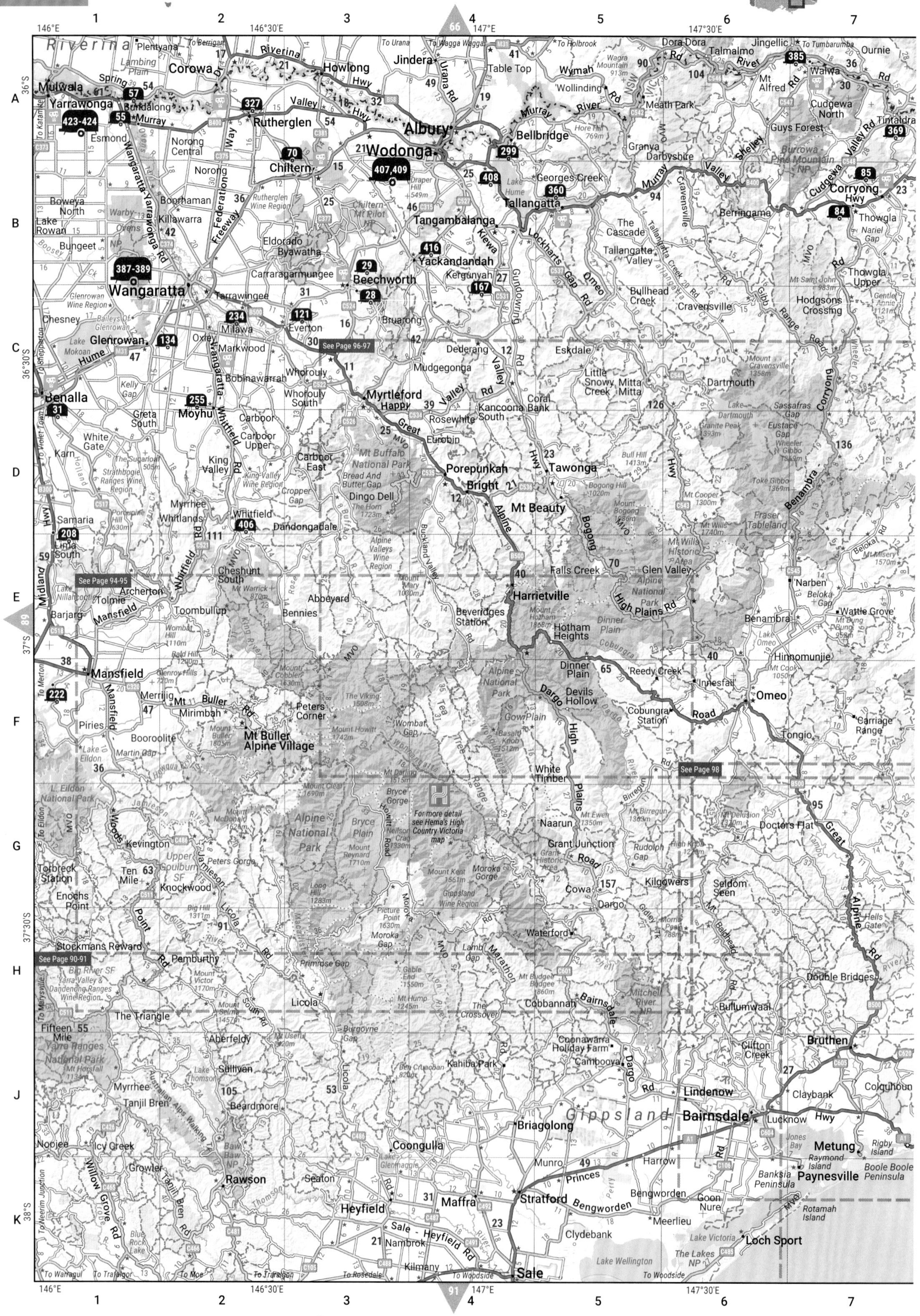

See Page 96-97
See Page 94-95
See Page 98
See Page 90-91
66
89
91

For more detail see Hema's High Country Victoria map

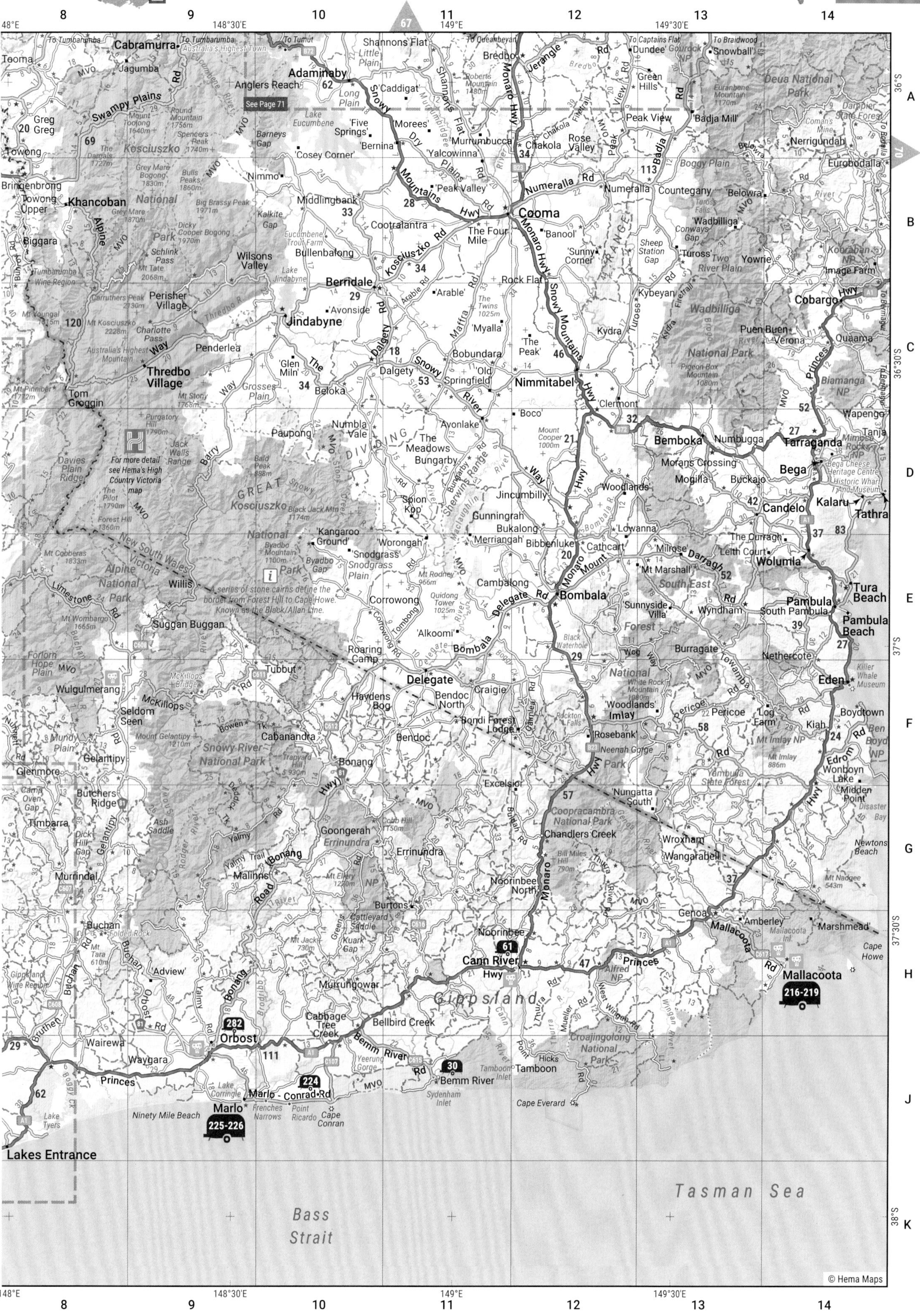

Mansfield to Dargo

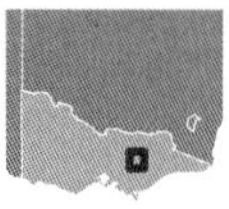

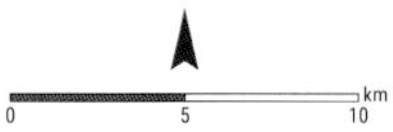

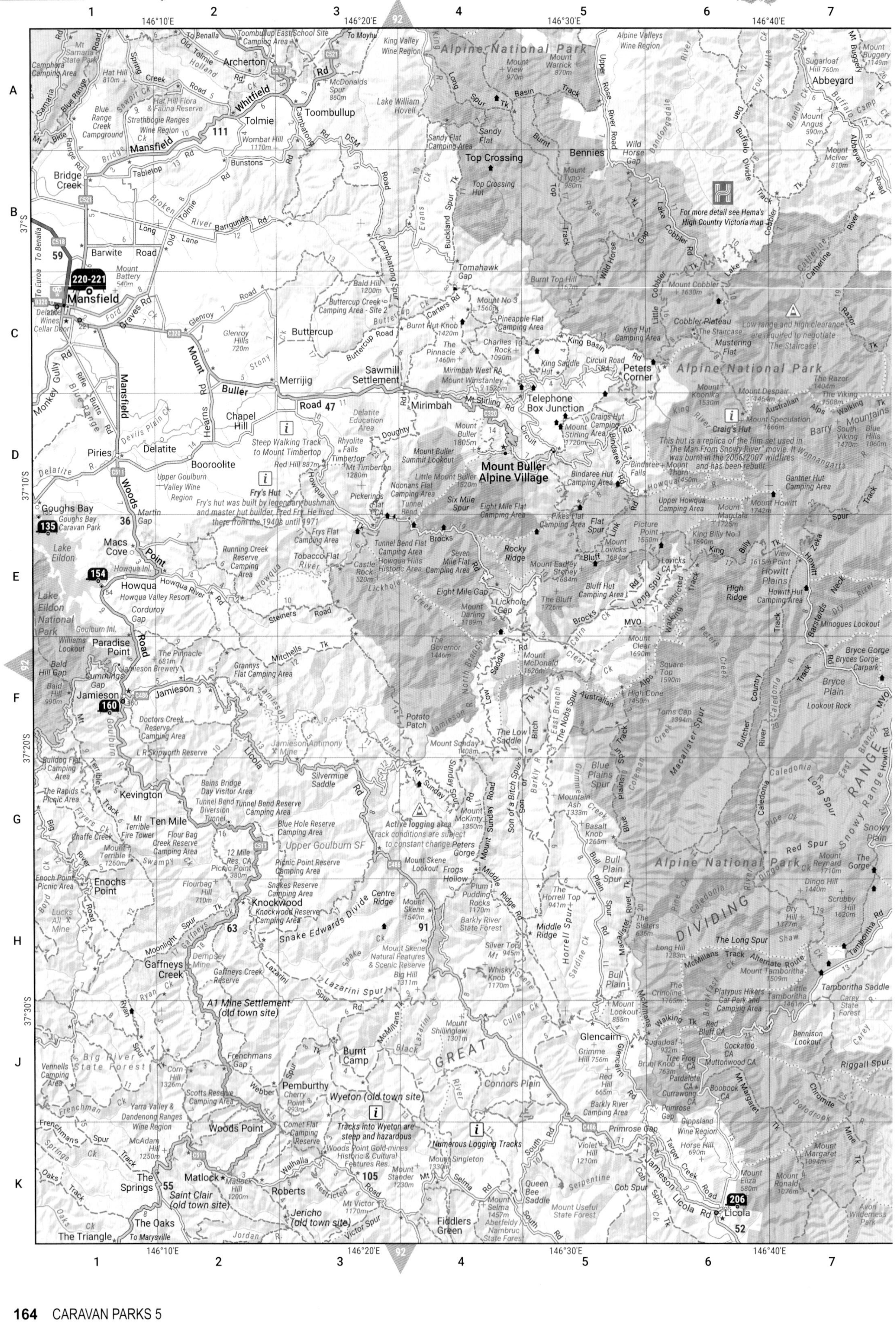

For more detail see Hema's High Country Victoria map

Low range and high clearance are required to negotiate 'The Staircase'.

Craig's Hut
This hut is a replica of the film set used in "The Man From Snowy River" movie. It was burnt in the 2006/2007 wildfires and has been rebuilt.

Steep Walking Track to Mount Timbertop

Fry's Hut
Fry's hut was built by legendary bushman and master hut builder, Fred Fry. He lived there from the 1940s until 1971

Active logging area
Track conditions are subject to constant change

Tracks into Wyeton are steep and hazardous

Numerous Logging Tracks

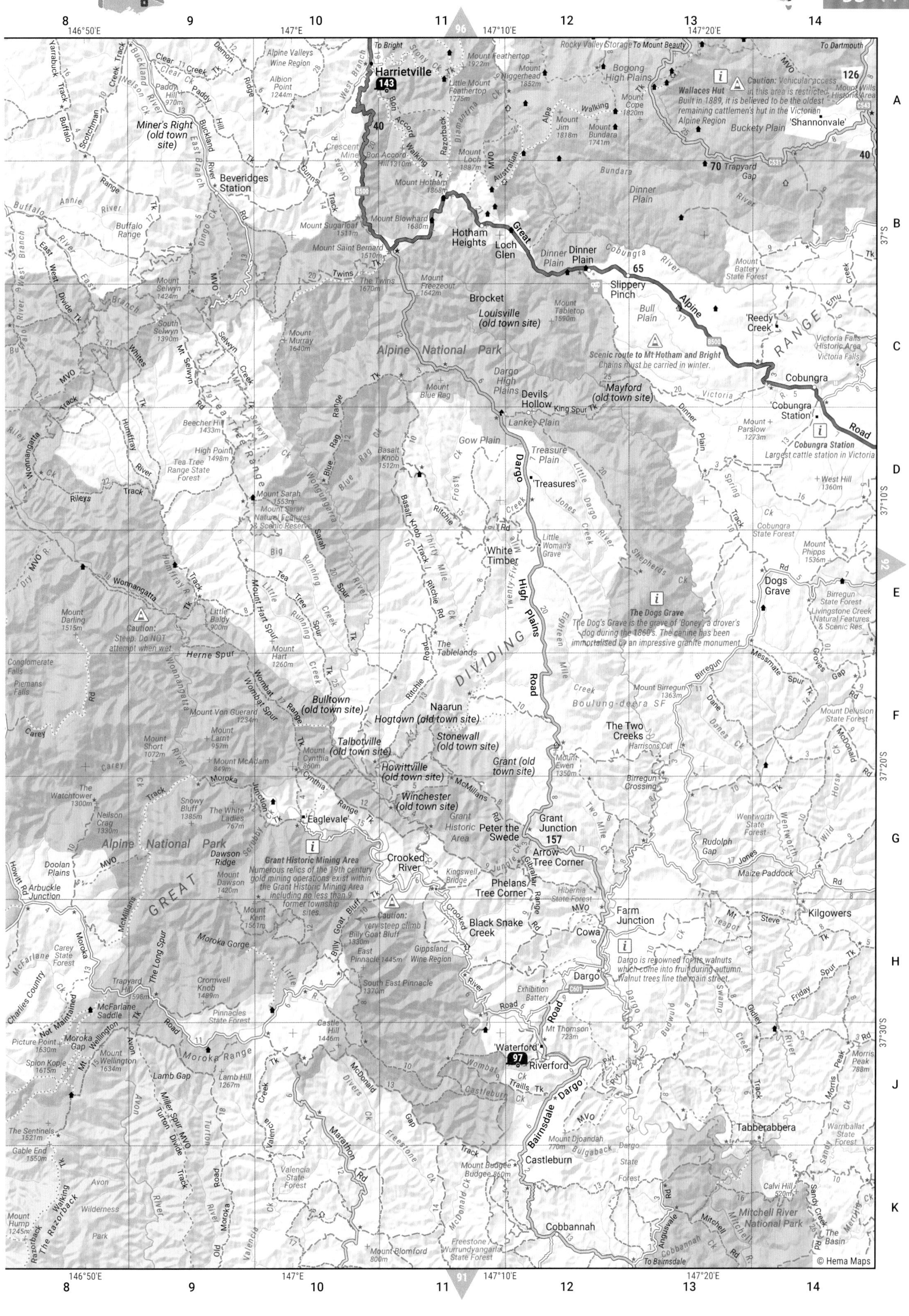
8
9
10
11
12
13
14
146°50'E
147°E
147°10'E
147°20'E
96
91
92
A
B
C
D
E
F
G
H
J
K
37°S
37°10'S
37°20'S
37°30'S
To Bright
Harrietville
143
40
Mount Feathertop 1922m
Little Mount Feathertop 1775m
Mount Niggerhead 1852m
Rocky Valley Storage
To Mount Beauty
Bogong High Plains
Mount Cope 1820m
Mount Jim 1818m
Mount Bundara 1741m
Wallaces Hut
Built in 1889, it is believed to be the oldest remaining cattlemen's hut in the Victorian Alpine Region
Caution: Vehicular access in this area is restricted
To Dartmouth
126
Mount Wills Historic Area
C543
'Shannonvale'
Buckety Plain
40
C531
70
Trapyard Gap
Bundara
Dinner Plain
River
Alpine Valleys Wine Region
Albion Point 1244m
Crescent Mine
Bon Accord Hill 1310m
Bon Accord Walking Tk
Razorback
Diamantina
Mount Loch 1887m
Australian Alps Walking Tk
MVO
Mount Hotham 1868m
Mount Blowhard 1680m
Mount Sugarloaf 1511m
Mount Saint Bernard 1510m
Twins
The Twins 1670m
Mount Freezeout 1642m
B500
Hotham Heights
Loch Glen
Great Alpine Road
Dinner Plain
Dinner Plain
65
Slippery Pinch
Cobungra River
Bull Plain
Mount Tabletop 1590m
Brocket
Louisville (old town site)
Alpine National Park
Mount Murray 1640m
Mount Battery State Forest
'Reedy Creek'
RANGE
Victoria Falls Historic Area
Victoria Falls
Scenic route to Mt Hotham and Bright
Chains must be carried in winter.
Cobungra
'Cobungra Station'
Cobungra Station
Largest cattle station in Victoria
Mount Parslow 1273m
Dargo High Plains
Devils Hollow
King Spur Tk
Mayford (old town site)
Lankey Plain
Mount Blue Rag
Gow Plain
Treasure Plain
'Treasures'
Basalt Knob 1512m
West Hill 1360m
Cobungra State Forest
Mount Phipps 1536m
Miner's Right (old town site)
Beveridges Station
Buffalo Range
Clear Creek Tk
Paddy Hill 970m
Buckland River
Mount Selwyn 1424m
South Selwyn 1390m
Mt Selwyn Rd
Beecher Hill 1433m
High Point 1498m
Tea Tree Range State Forest
Mount Sarah 1553m
Mount Sarah Natural Features & Scenic Reserve
Rileys
Wonnangatta
Dry River
Humffray River Track
Blue Rag Range
Wongungarra
Sarah Spur
White Timber
Little Woman's Grave
Dargo High Plains Road
Dogs Grave
Birregun State Forest
Livingstone Creek Natural Features & Scenic Res.
The Dogs Grave
The Dog's Grave is the grave of 'Boney', a drover's dog during the 1860's. The canine has been immortalised by an impressive granite monument.
Mount Darling 1515m
Caution: Steep. Do NOT attempt when wet.
Little Baldy 900m
Mount Hart Spur
Mount Hart 1260m
Herne Spur
The Tablelands
DIVIDING
Conglomerate Falls
Piemans Falls
Mount Von Guerard 1234m
Wombat Spur
Wombat Range
Bulltown (old town site)
Hogtown (old town site)
Naarun
Stonewall (old town site)
Talbotville (old town site)
Howittville (old town site)
Winchester (old town site)
Grant (old town site)
Mount Ewen 1350m
Mount Birregun 1363m
Boulung-deera SF
The Two Creeks
Harrisons Cut
Birregun Crossing
Mount Delusion State Forest
Mount Larrit 957m
Mount Short 1072m
Mount McAdam 849m
Mount Cynthia 860m
Carey
The Watchtower 1300m
Neilson Crag 1330m
Snowy Bluff 1385m
The White Ladies 767m
'Eaglevale'
Grant Historic Area
Peter the Swede
Grant Junction
157
Arrow Tree Corner
Wentworth State Forest
Rudolph Gap
Maize Paddock
Alpine National Park
Dawson Ridge
Mount Dawson 1420m
Grant Historic Mining Area
Numerous relics of the 19th century gold mining operations exist within the Grant Historic Mining Area including no less than 9 former township sites.
Crooked River
Kingswell Bridge
Phelans Tree Corner
Hibernia State Forest
Doolan Plains
Arbuckle Junction
GREAT
Mount Kent 1561m
Caution: very steep climb
Billy Goat Bluff 1330m
Black Snake Creek
Farm Junction
Cowa
Kilgowers
Mt Teapot
Carey State Forest
Moroka Gorge
East Pinnacle 1445m
Gippsland Wine Region
Dargo is renowned for its walnuts which come into fruit during autumn. Walnut trees line the main street.
Dargo
C601
Trapyard Hill 1598m
The Long Spur
Cromwell Knob 1489m
Pinnacles State Forest
South East Pinnacle 1370m
Exhibition Battery
McFarlane Saddle
Not Maintained
Charles Country
Picture Point 1630m
Moroka Gap
Mt Wellington
Mount Wellington 1634m
Moroka Range
Castle Hill 1446m
Mt Thomson 723m
'Waterford'
97
Riverford
Morris Peak 788m
Spion Kopje 1615m
Lamb Gap
Lamb Hill 1267m
Miller Spur MVO
Turton Divide Track
Marathon Rd
Freestone
Wombat
Castleburn
Traills Tk
Bairnsdale Dargo Road
Tabberabbera
Warriballat State Forest
The Sentinels 1521m
Gable End 1550m
Valencia State Forest
Mount Djoandah 770m
Bulgaback
State Forest
Mount Budgee Budgee 860m
Castleburn
Avon Wilderness Park
The Razorback
Mount Hump 1245m
Calvi Hill 520m
Mitchell River National Park
The Basin
Cobbannah
Freestone Wurrundyangarla State Forest
Mount Blomford 800m
To Bairnsdale
© Hema Maps

Myrtleford to Omeo

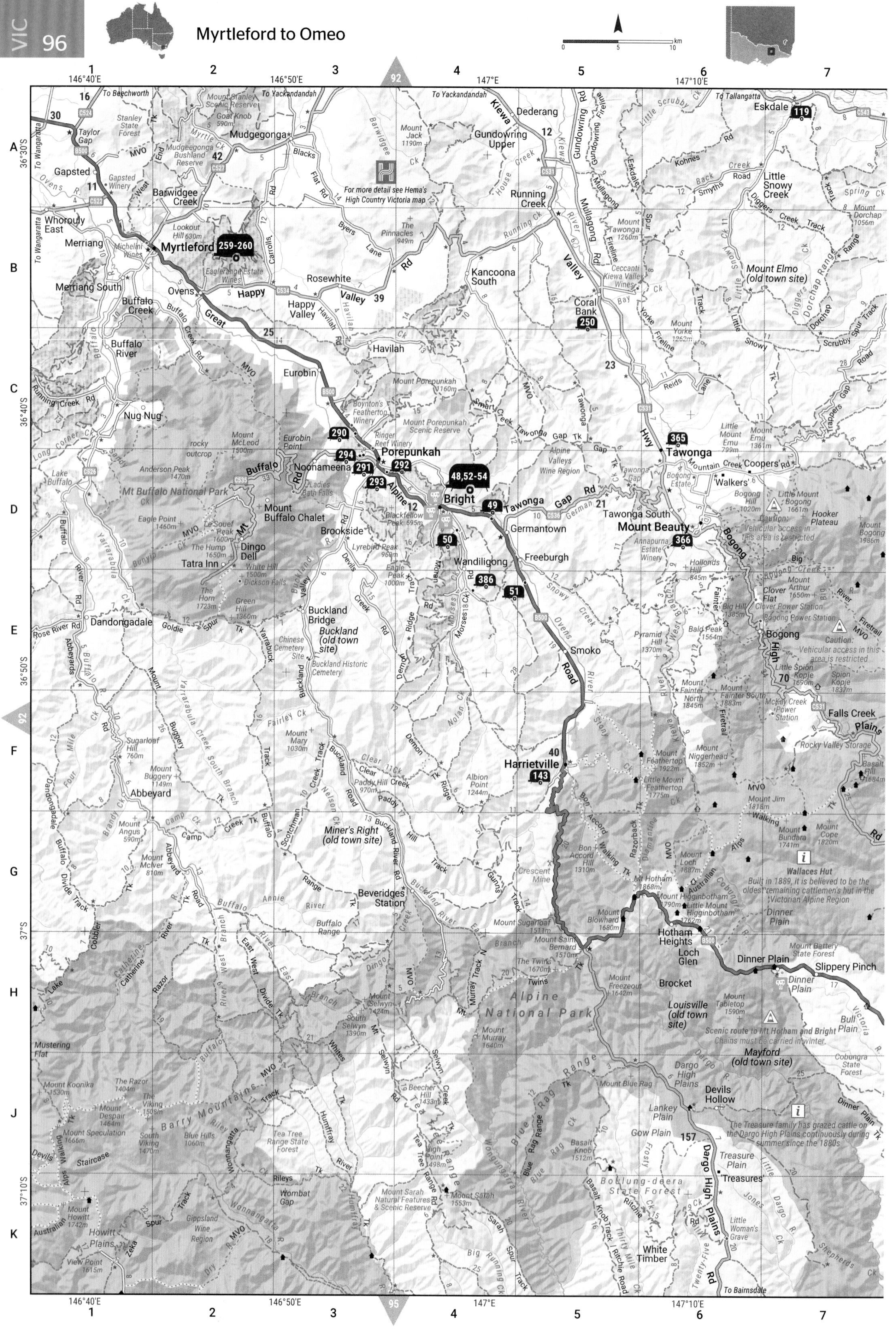

For more detail see Hema's High Country Victoria map

Caution: Vehicular access in this area is restricted

Wallaces Hut
Built in 1889, it is believed to be the oldest remaining cattlemen's hut in the Victorian Alpine Region

The Treasure family has grazed cattle on the Dargo High Plains continuously during summer since the 1880s

Scenic route to Mt Hotham and Bright
Chains must be carried in winter.

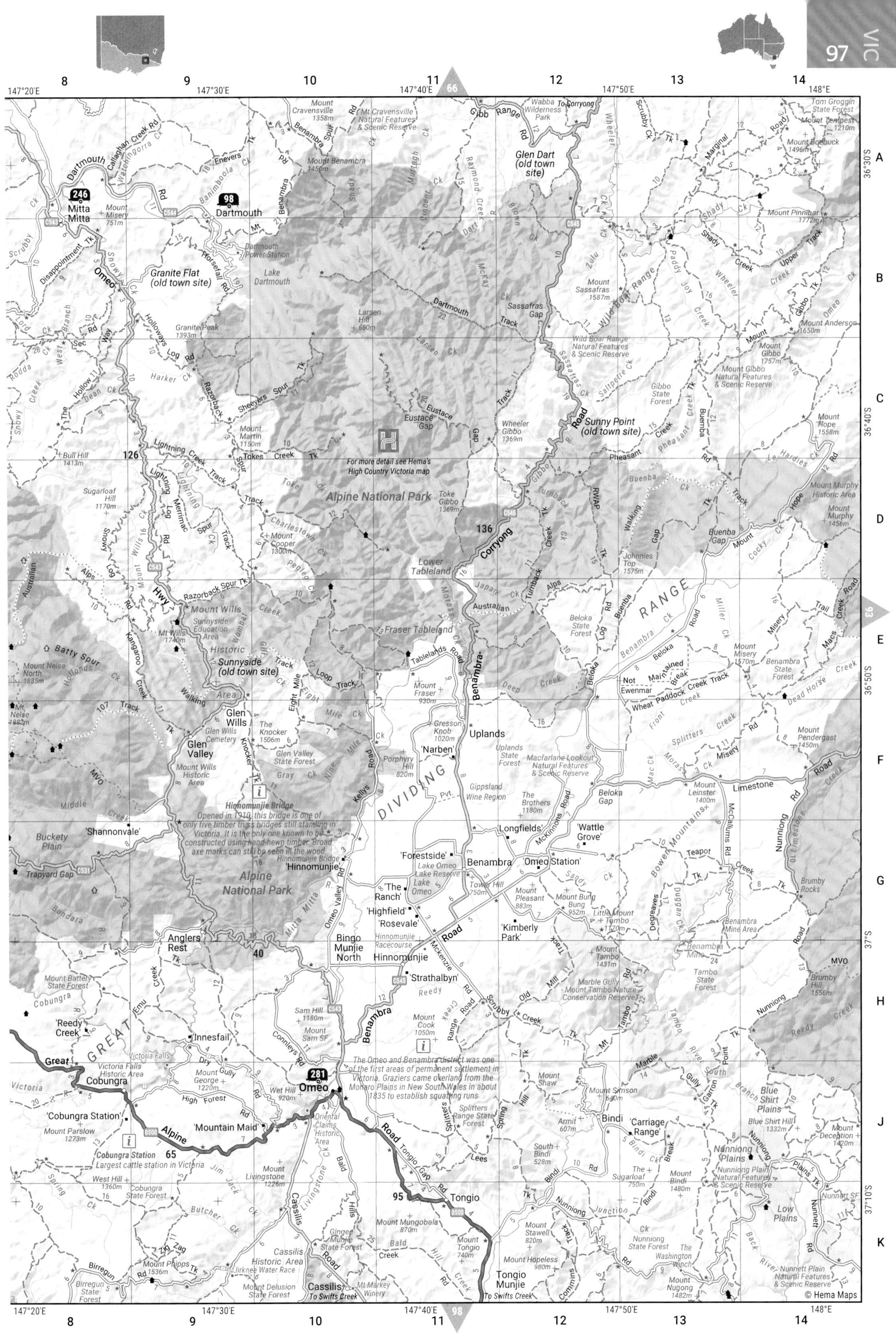

66

For more detail see Hema's High Country Victoria map

Alpine National Park

Hinnomunjie Bridge
Opened in 1910, this bridge is one of only five timber truss bridges still standing in Victoria. It is the only one known to be constructed using hand-hewn timber. Broad axe marks can still be seen in the wood.

The Omeo and Benambra district was one of the first areas of permanent settlement in Victoria. Graziers came overland from the Monaro Plains in New South Wales in about 1835 to establish squatting runs.

Cobungra Station
Largest cattle station in Victoria

Mitta Mitta · Dartmouth · Glen Wills · Glen Valley · Anglers Rest · Benambra · Uplands · Omeo · Cobungra · Cassilis · Tongio · Tongio Munjie · Bindi · Hinnomunjie · Bingo Munjie North

To Corryong · To Swifts Creek

98

© Hema Maps

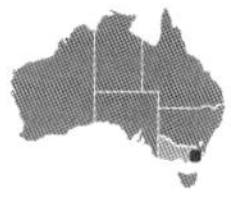

Swifts Creek to Lakes Entrance

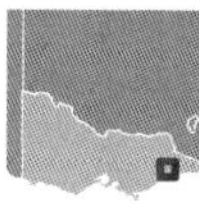

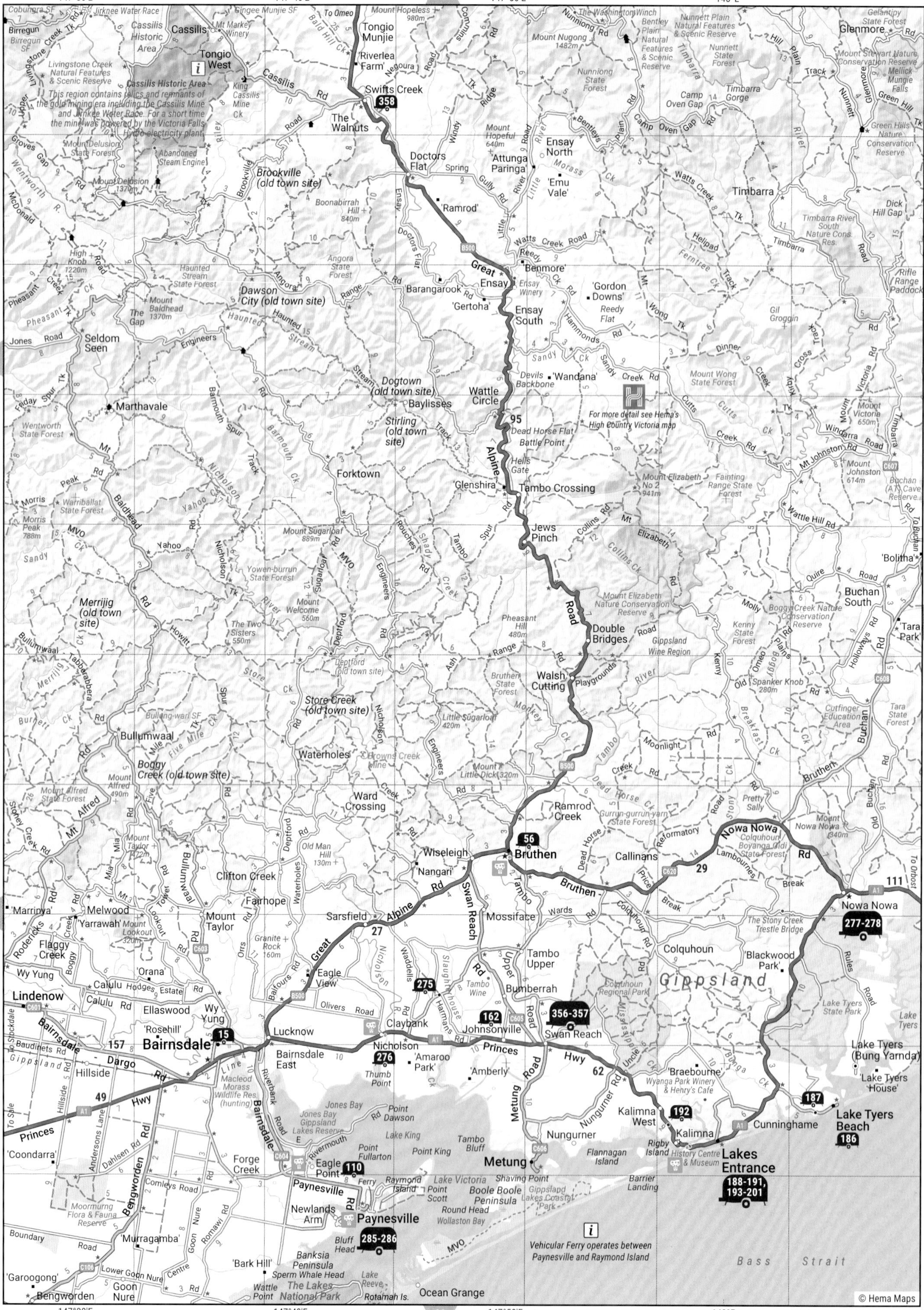
0 5 10 km
1 2 3 4 5 6 7
A B C D E F G H J K
147°30'E 147°40'E 147°50'E 148°E
37°20'S 37°30'S 37°40'S 37°50'S
97 95 93 91 92
Cobungra SF
Jirknee Water Race
Birregun
Birregun SF
Livingstone Creek Tk
Cassilis
Cassilis Historic Area
Mt Markey Winery
Tongio West
Gingee Munjie SF
To Omeo
Tongio Munjie
'Riverlea Farm'
Mount Hopeless 980m
Livingstone Creek Natural Features & Scenic Reserve
Cassilis Historic Area
This region contains relics and remnants of the gold mining era including the Cassilis Mine and Jirnkee Water Race. For a short time the mine was powered by the Victoria Falls Hydro-electricity plant.
King Cassilis Mine Ck
Cassilis Rd
Swifts Creek
358
The Walnuts
Mount Delusion State Forest
Abandoned Steam Engine
Groves Gap
Mount Delusion 1370m
Brookville (old town site)
Doctors Flat
Spring Gully Rd
Boonabirrah Hill 840m
'Ramrod'
Mount Hopeful 640m
'Attunga Paringa'
Ensay North
'Emu Vale'
Little River
The Washington Winch
Nunniong Rd
Mount Nugong 1482m
Bentley Plain Natural Features & Scenic Reserve
Nunnett Plain Natural Features & Scenic Reserve
Nunnett State Forest
Nunniong State Forest
Camp Oven Gap
Timbarra Gorge
Camp Oven Gap Rd
Glenmore
Gelantipy State Forest
Mount Stewart Nature Conservation Reserve
Mellick Munjie Falls
Green Hill Tk
Green Hills Nature Conservation Reserve
Nunnett Rd
Watts Creek Tk
Timbarra
Dick Hill Gap
Timbarra River South Nature Cons. Res.
Helipad Track
Ferntree Ck
Rifle Range Paddock
High Knob 1220m
Haunted Stream State Forest
Angora State Forest
Angora Range
Dawson City (old town site)
'Barangarook'
Great Alpine Road
Ensay
Ensay Winery
'Benmore'
'Gertoha'
Ensay South
'Gordon Downs'
Reedy Flat
Watts Creek Road
Mt Wong Tk
Gil Groggin
Pheasant Creek
Mount Baldhead 1370m
The Gap
Haunted Stream
Jones Road
Seldom Seen
Engineers
Hammonds Rd
Sandy Ck
Dinner Ck
Kings Cross Track
Devils Backbone
'Wandana'
Sandy Creek Rd
Mount Wong State Forest
Dogtown (old town site)
Baylisses
Wattle Circle
Marthavale
Barmouth Spur
Friday Spur Tk
For more detail see Hema's High Country Victoria map
Cutts Creek Rd
Mount Victoria 650m
Windarra Road
Mt Johnston Rd
Mount Johnston 614m
Buchan (A) Caves Reserve
Wentworth State Forest
Stirling (old town site)
95
Dead Horse Flat
Battle Point
Hells Gate
Forktown
'Glenshira'
Tambo Crossing
Mount Elizabeth No 2 941m
Fainting Range State Forest
Morriss Peak 788m
Warriballat State Forest
Mt Baldhead Rd
Yahoo Ck
Nicholson Tk
Mount Sugarloaf 889m
Jews Pinch
Collins Rd
Mt Elizabeth Rd
Wattle Hill Rd
To Buchan
'Bolitha'
Yahoo
Yowen-burrun State Forest
Mount Welcome 560m
Roucheys Rd
Shady Creek
Engineers Rd
Collins Ck
Quire Road
Buchan South
Merrijig (old town site)
The Two Sisters 550m
Pheasant Hill 480m
Mount Elizabeth Nature Conservation Reserve
Molly Boggy Creek Nature Conservation Reserve
Kenny State Forest
Tara Park
Double Bridges
Gippsland Wine Region
Bullumwaal
Tabbarabera
Deptford (old town site)
Range Rd
Walsh Cutting
Playgrounds
Bruthen State Forest
Spanker Knob 280m
Old Omeo Rd
Holloways Rd
Tara State Forest
Store Creek (old town site)
Little Sugarloaf 420m
Cutfinger Education Area
Buchan Rd
Bullung-warl SF
Bullumwaal
Five Mile Ck
Waterholes
Crowns Creek Mine
Mount Little Dick 320m
B500
Moonlight
Boggy Creek (old town site)
Mount Alfred 490m
Mount Alfred State Forest
Ward Crossing
Ramrod Creek
Gurrun-gurrun-yarn State Forest
Dead Horse Ck
Pretty Sally
Reformatory Rd
Nowa Nowa Rd
Mount Nowa Nowa 340m
Colquhoun Boyanga Gidi State Forest
Mt Alfred Rd
Mount Taylor 472m
Old Man Hill 130m
Wiseleigh
'Nangari'
56
Bruthen
Callinans
29
Lambournes
Break
111
To Orbost
Nowa Nowa
277-278
'Marrinya'
Melwood
'Yarrawah'
Mount Lookout 320m
Clifton Creek
Fairhope
Mount Taylor
Sarsfield
Great Alpine Rd
27
Mossiface
Swan Reach Rd
Bruthen - Colquhoun Rd
Wards Rd
C620
The Stony Creek Trestle Bridge
Flaggy Creek
Roderick's
Granite Rock 160m
Tambo Upper
Colquhoun
'Blackwood Park'
Rules Road
Wy Yung
Calulu Hodges Estate Rd
'Orana'
Eagle View
275
Tambo Wine
Bumberrah
Gippsland
Colquhoun Regional Park
Lindenow
C601
Calulu Rd
Ellaswood
Wy Yung
Olivers Road
Claybank
162
Johnsonville
356-357
Swan Reach
Lake Tyers State Park
Lake Tyers
'Rosehill'
Bairnsdale
15
157
Lucknow
Nicholson
276
'Amaroo Park'
Princes Hwy
62
A1
Lake Tyers (Bung Yarnda)
'Lake Tyers House'
To Stockdale
Baudinets Rd
Bairnsdale - Dargo Rd
Hillside
Bairnsdale East
Macleod Morass Wildlife Res. (hunting)
Thumb Point
'Amberly'
Metung Road
'Braebourne'
Wyanga Park Winery & Henry's Cafe
Bunga Ck
Uncle Rd
49
Princes Hwy
To Sale
Andersons Lane
Bengworden Rd
Jones Bay
Jones Bay Gippsland Lakes Reserve
Point Dawson
Lake King
Tambo Bluff
Kalimna West
192
Kalimna
187
Lake Tyers Beach
186
Cunninghame
'Coondarra'
Dahlsen Rd
Forge Creek
Riverbank Road
Rivermouth
Point Fullarton
Point King
Nungurner
Nungurner Rd
Metung
C606
Flannagan Island
Rigby Island
History Centre & Museum
Lakes Entrance
Eagle Point
110
Comleys Road
Paynesville Rd
Ferry
Raymond Island
Lake Victoria
Point Scott
Shaving Point
Boole Boole Peninsula
Gippsland Lakes Coastal Park
Barrier Landing
188-191, 193-201
Moormurng Flora & Fauna Reserve
Newlands Arm
Paynesville
Round Head
Wollaston Bay
Boundary Road
'Murragamba'
Goon Nure Rd
Romawi Rd
Bluff Head
285-286
MVO
Vehicular Ferry operates between Paynesville and Raymond Island
Bass Strait
'Garoogong'
C106
Lower Goon Nure Centre Rd
'Bark Hill'
Banksia Peninsula
Sperm Whale Head
Lake Reeve
Bengworden
Goon Nure
Wattle Point
The Lakes National Park
Rotamah Is.
Ocean Grange
© Hema Maps

Aireys Inlet

1 Aireys Inlet Holiday Park
19-25 Great Ocean Rd. 100m NE of PO
www.aicp.com.au
03 5289 6230 HEMA 80 K1 38 27 27 S 144 06 24 E

Alexandra

2 Breakaway Twin Rivers Caravan Park
91 Breakaway Rd, Acheron. 10 km S of PO
www.thebreakaway.com.au
03 5772 1735 HEMA 89 G5 37 14 23 S 145 42 38 E

3 Park Life Alexandra
5016 Maroondah Hwy. 1 km W of PO
www.parklifealexandra.com
03 5772 1222 HEMA 89 G5 37 11 39 S 145 41 55 E

Anglesea

4 Anglesea Family Caravan Park
35 Cameron Rd. 800m S of PO
www.angleseafamilycaravanpark.com.au
03 5295 1990 HEMA 80 J1 38 24 28 S 144 11 37 E

5 BIG4 Anglesea Holiday Park
45 Murray St. 800m SW of PO
www.big4anglesea.com.au
03 5263 1640 HEMA 80 J1 38 24 34 S 144 10 52 E

Apollo Bay

6 Apollo Bay Holiday Park
27 Cawood St. 700m N of PO
www.apollobayholidaypark.com.au
03 5237 7111 HEMA 83 J9 38 45 01 S 143 40 00 E

7 BIG4 Apollo Bay Pisces Holiday Park
311 Great Ocean Rd. 1.4 km NE of PO
www.piscespark.com.au
03 5237 6749 HEMA 83 J9 38 44 29 S 143 40 31 E

8 Marengo Holiday Park
Marengo Cres, off Great Ocean Rd. 2.5 km S of PO
www.marengopark.com.au
03 5237 6162 HEMA 83 J9 38 46 40 S 143 39 52 E

9 Skenes Creek Caravan Park
2 Great Ocean Rd. 6 km from Apollo Bay, Skenes Creek
www.skenescreek.com
03 5237 6132 HEMA 83 J10 38 43 28 S 143 42 42 E

Ararat

10 Acacia Caravan Park
6 Acacia Ave. 1 km N of PO
www.acaciatouristpark.com
03 5352 2994 HEMA 85 C8 37 16 36 S 142 55 31 E

11 Pyrenees Caravan Park
6003 Pyrenees Hwy (Avoca Rd). 2 km NE of PO
03 5352 1309 HEMA 85 C8 37 16 12 S 142 57 00 E

Ardmona

12 Ardmona Caravan Park
6535 Midland Mwy
0428 729 638 HEMA 89 D4 36 24 10 S 145 17 55 E

Avoca

13 Avoca Caravan Park
2 Liebig St. 1.2 km W of PO
03 5465 3073 HEMA 85 B10 37 05 36 S 143 28 07 E

Bacchus Marsh

14 Bacchus Marsh Caravan Park
26 Main St. 800m W of Main St roundabout
www.bacchusmarshcp.com.au
03 5367 2775 HEMA 80 B3 37 40 17 S 144 25 32 E

Bairnsdale

15 NRMA Bairnsdale Riverside Holiday Park
2 Main St (Princes Hwy). 600m E of PO
www.nrmaparksandresorts.com.au
03 5152 4654 HEMA 98 J2 37 49 31 S 147 38 15 E

Ballan

16 Ballan Caravan Park
45 Jopling St
www.ballancaravanpark.com
03 5368 2755 HEMA 80 A2 37 35 55 S 144 14 08 E

17 Phoenix Park
5623 Geelong Ballan Rd, aprox 600m on the L as you exit the Hwy into Ballan
www.phoenixparkballan.com.au
0431 073 031 HEMA 80 A1 37 35 31 S 144 12 14 E

Ballarat

18 BIG4 Ballarat Goldfields Holiday Park
108 Clayton St
www.ballaratgoldfields.com.au
03 5332 7888 HEMA 85 E11 37 34 19 S 143 52 18 E

19 BIG4 Ballarat Windmill Holiday Park
56 Remembrance Dr. 3 km W of Victory Arch
www.ballaratwindmill.com.au
03 5334 1686 HEMA 85 D11 37 32 21 S 143 46 54 E

20 Eureka Stockade Caravan Park
104 Stawell Street South
www.eurekaholidaypark.com.au
03 5331 2281 HEMA 85 D11 37 33 49 S 143 53 09 E

21 Shady Acres Caravan Park
9435 Western Hwy. 5 km E of PO
www.ballaratcaravanpark.com
03 5334 7233 HEMA 85 D12 37 33 47 S 143 55 46 E

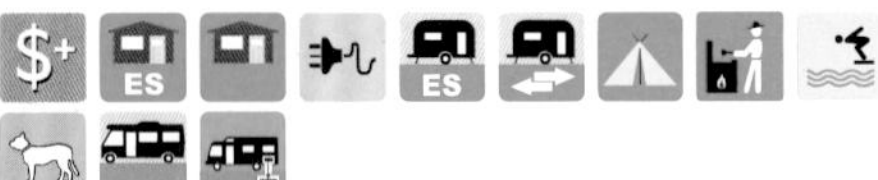

Balmoral

22 Balmoral Caravan Park
5 Glendinning St. 100m N of PO
03 5570 1400 HEMA 84 C4 37 14 49 S 141 50 26 E

Baringhup

23 Loddon House Holiday Park
Maryborough Rd. Adjacent to Loddon River
03 5475 2502 HEMA 85 B12 36 58 42 S 143 57 47 E

Barmah

24 Barmah Bridge Caravan Park
Murray St. Adjacent to Bridge
www.barmahbridgecaravanpark.com.au
03 5869 3225 HEMA 89 B2 36 01 03 S 144 57 24 E

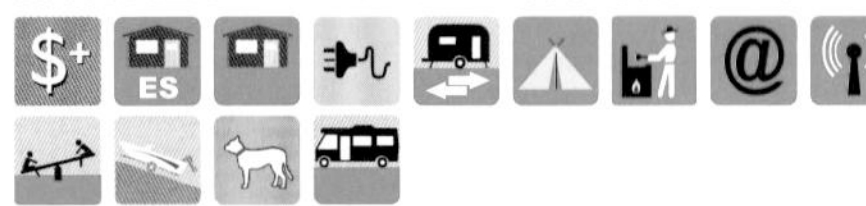

25 Murray Perch Caravan Park
7 Murray St
03 5869 3226 HEMA 89 B2 36 01 06 S 144 57 48 E

Barwon Heads

26 Barwon Heads Caravan Park
Ewing Blyth Dr
www.barwonheadscaravanpark.com.au
03 5254 1115 HEMA 80 H4 38 17 00 S 144 29 37 E

Beaufort

27 Beaufort Lake Caravan Park
39 Park Rd (Skipton Rd)
www.beaufortlakecaravanpark.com.au
03 5349 2196 HEMA 85 D10 37 26 20 S 143 22 49 E

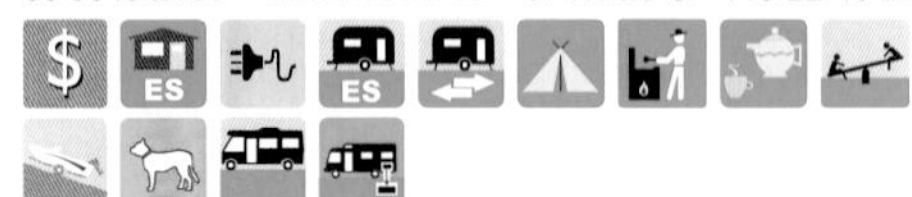

Beechworth

28 Beechworth Holiday Park
151 Stanley Rd. 2.3 km SE of PO
www.beechworthholidaypark.com.au
03 5728 1597 HEMA 92 C3 36 22 07 S 146 42 25 E

29 Lake Sambell Caravan Park
Peach Dr. 1.5 km from PO
www.caravanparkbeechworth.com.au
03 5728 1421 HEMA 92 C3 36 21 28 S 146 42 00 E

Bemm River

30 Bemm River Caravan Park
2-18 Sydenham Inlet Rd
www.bemmrivercaravanpark.com.au
03 5158 4216 HEMA 93 J11 37 45 31 S 148 57 56 E

Benalla

31 Gateway Lifestyle Benalla
115 Sydney Rd. 2.7 km NE of PO
www.glhp.com.au/parks/benalla
03 5762 3434 HEMA 89 D6 36 32 35 S 146 00 30 E

Bendigo

32 A-Line Holiday Village
5615 Calder Hwy, Big Hill. 9.6 km S of fountain
www.alineholidayparkbendigo.com.au
03 5447 9568 HEMA 85 A13 36 49 57 S 144 14 22 E

33 Avondel Caravan Park
723 Calder Hwy, Maiden Gully. 7 km NW of fountain
www.avondelcaravanpark.com.au
03 5449 6265 HEMA 85 A13 36 44 35 S 144 12 31 E

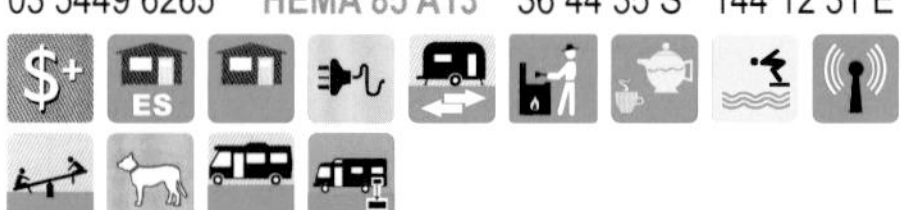

34 BIG4 Bendigo Ascot Holiday Park
15 Heinz St
www.big4bendigo.com.au
03 5448 4421 HEMA 85 A13 36 43 37 S 144 18 49 E

35 BIG4 Bendigo Park Lane Holiday Park
761 McIvor Hwy, Junortoun
www.parklaneholidayparks.com.au
03 5449 3335 HEMA 85 A13 36 46 13 S 144 20 48 E

36 Gold Nugget Tourist Park
293-297 Midland Hwy
www.goldnugget.com.au
03 5448 4747 HEMA 85 A13 36 41 39 S 144 19 02 E

Beulah

37 Beulah Caravan Park
Higgbotham St. In sportsground. Pay & keys at cafe
03 5390 2200 HEMA 86 G6 35 56 28 S 142 25 01 E

Birchip

38 Birchip Motel & Caravan Park
Sunraysia Hwy. Opposite high school
03 5492 2566 HEMA 87 G8 35 58 59 S 142 54 37 E

Blackwood

39 Blackwood Mineral Springs Caravan Park
41 Golden Point Rd. 1 km E of PO
03 5368 6539 HEMA 85 D13 37 28 17 S 144 18 47 E

Blairgowrie

40 Blairgowrie Caravan Park
William Rd
www.mpcp.com.au/caravan-parks
03 59888394 HEMA 80 J6 38 21 57 S 144 46 54 E

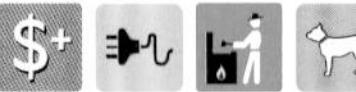

Bonnie Doon

41 Bonnie Doon Caravan Park

Arnot St
www.bonniedooncaravanpark.com.au
03 5778 7254 HEMA 89 F5 37 01 24 S 145 51 17 E

42 Bonnie Doon's Lakeside Leisure Resort

240 Hutchinsons Rd
www.bonniedoonlakeside.com.au
03 5778 7252 HEMA 89 F6 37 02 30 S 145 53 24 E

Boort

43 Boort Lakes Caravan Park

Durham Ox Rd. 300m E of PO. Beside lake
www.boortlakesholidaypark.com.au
03 5455 2064 HEMA 87 H11 36 07 01 S 143 43 48 E

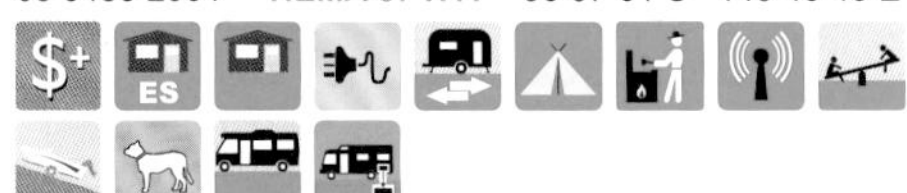

Boundary Bend

44 Boundary Bend General Store & Caravan Park

27 Murray Valley Hwy. 300m W of PO
03 5026 8201 HEMA 87 A9 34 42 55 S 143 08 51 E

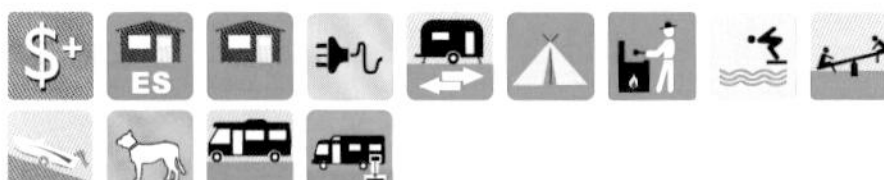

Braybrook

45 Discovery Holiday Parks Melbourne

129 Ashley St. 150m S of Western Hwy
www.discoveryholidayparks.com.au
03 9318 6866 HEMA 76 F4 37 46 59 S 144 51 53 E

Breamlea

46 Breamlea Caravan Park

3 Horwood Dr
03 5264 1352 HEMA 80 H3 38 17 35 S 144 23 52 E

Bridgewater

47 Bridgewater Public Caravan Park

1 Park St. 500m SW of PO
www.bridgewaterpubliccaravanpark.com.au
03 5437 3086 HEMA 87 K12 36 36 19 S 143 56 17 E

Bright

48 BIG4 Bright

1-11 Mountbatten Ave. 500m E of PO
www.big4bright.com.au
03 5755 1064 HEMA 96 D4 36 43 31 S 146 57 54 E

49 Bright Accommodation Park

438 Great Alpine Rd
www.brightaccommodationpark.com.au
03 5750 1001 HEMA 96 D4 36 44 03 S 147 00 14 E

50 Bright Backpackers Outdoor Inn

106 Coronation Ave
www.brightbackpackers.com.au
0418 528 631 HEMA 96 D4 36 44 30 S 146 58 32 E

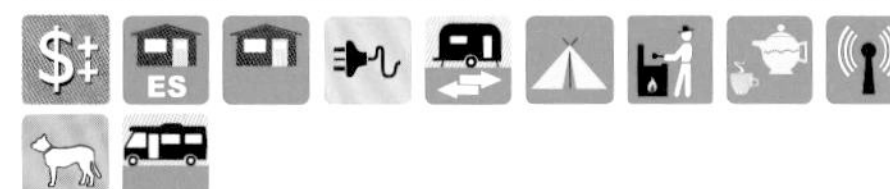

51 Bright Freeburgh Caravan Park

1099 Great Alpine Rd, Freeburgh. 9.7 km SE of Bright PO
www.caravanparkbright.com.au
03 5750 1306 HEMA 96 E5 36 46 30 S 147 01 53 E

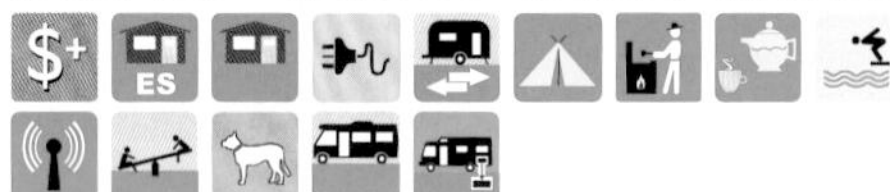

52 Bright Pine Valley Tourist Park

7-15 Churchill Ave
www.brightpinevalley.com.au
03 5755 1010 HEMA 96 D4 36 43 50 S 146 58 15 E

53 Bright Riverside Holiday Park

4 Toorak Ave. 400m N of PO
www.holidayparkbright.com.au
03 5755 1118 HEMA 96 D4 36 43 28 S 146 57 29 E

54 NRMA Bright Holiday Park

Cherry Lane
www.brightholidaypark.com.au
03 5755 1141 HEMA 96 D4 36 43 39 S 146 57 53 E

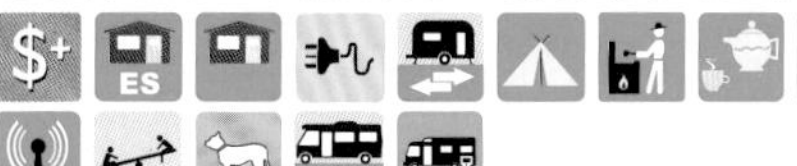

Brimin

55 Bundalong Caravan Park

44 Old Murray Valley Hwy
03 5726 8268 HEMA 92 A1 36 04 10 S 146 12 18 E

Bruthen

56 Bruthen Caravan Park

Tambo Upper Rd. 600m E of PO
03 5157 5753 HEMA 98 G4 37 42 43 S 147 50 08 E

Bundalong

57 Bundalong Holiday Resort

7419A Murray Valley Hwy
www.bundalongholidayresort.com.au
03 5726 8600 HEMA 92 A1 36 01 55 S 146 09 32 E

Burrumbeet

58 Lake Burrumbeet Caravan Park

1185 Remembrance Dr
www.lakeburrumbeetcaravanpark.com
03 5344 0583 HEMA 85 D11 37 29 25 S 143 40 17 E

Camperdown

59 Lake Purrumbete Holiday Park

County Boundary Rd
www.lakepurrumbeteholidaypark.com.au
03 5594 5377 HEMA 82 E6 38 17 34 S 143 13 08 E

60 Lakes & Craters Holiday Park

220 Park Rd
www.lakesandcratersholidaypark.com.au
03 5593 1253 HEMA 82 D5 38 14 08 S 143 07 00 E

Cann River

61 Cann River Rainforest Caravan Park

7536 Princes Hwy. Pay at the Cann River Hotel
03 5158 6369 HEMA 93 H12 37 33 59 S 149 08 46 E

Cape Otway

62 Bimbi Park - Camping Under Koalas
90 Manna Gum Dr
www.bimbipark.com.au
03 5237 9246 HEMA 83 K8 38 49 57 S 143 30 51 E

Cape Paterson

63 Cape Paterson Caravan Park
Cape Paterson Rd
www.cpcp.com.au
03 5674 4507 HEMA 90 G5 38 40 25 S 145 36 57 E

Carrum Downs

64 Carrum Downs Holiday Park
1165 Frankston-Dandenong Rd
www.cpoaus.com.au
03 9782 1292 HEMA 78 H6 38 05 32 S 145 10 44 E

Casterton

65 Island Park Caravan Park
Murray St. Adjacent to swimming pool
0457 414 187 HEMA 84 E3 37 34 58 S 141 24 19 E

Castlemaine

66 BIG4 Castlemaine Gardens Holiday Park
1 Doran Ave (off Walker St). 1.5 km N of PO
www.cgcp.com.au
03 5472 1125 HEMA 85 B13 37 03 13 S 144 12 50 E

67 Castlemaine Central Cabin & Van Park
101 Barker St
www.cabinscastlemaine.com
03 5472 2160 HEMA 85 B13 37 04 07 S 144 12 58 E

Charlton

68 Travellers Rest Caravan Park
45 High St
www.travellersrest.com.au
0448 276 631 HEMA 87 H10 36 16 02 S 143 21 05 E

Chelsea

69 Chelsea Holiday Park
100 Broadway
www.cpoaus.com.au
03 9772 2485 HEMA 78 G5 38 03 22 S 145 07 54 E

Chiltern

70 Lake Anderson Caravan Park
Alliance St. 500m E of PO
www.lakeandersoncaravanpark.com.au
03 5726 1298 HEMA 92 B3 36 09 07 S 146 36 45 E

Clunes

71 Clunes Caravan Park
Purcell St
www.clunescaravanpark.com.au
03 5345 3278 HEMA 85 C11 37 17 35 S 143 47 15 E

Cobram

72 Cobram East Caravan Park
3186 Murray Valley Hwy
03 5872 1207 HEMA 89 A5 35 57 00 S 145 40 52 E

73 Cobram Oasis Tourist Park
Ritchie Rd
www.oasishomes.com.au
03 5871 2010 HEMA 89 A5 35 54 45 S 145 37 56 E

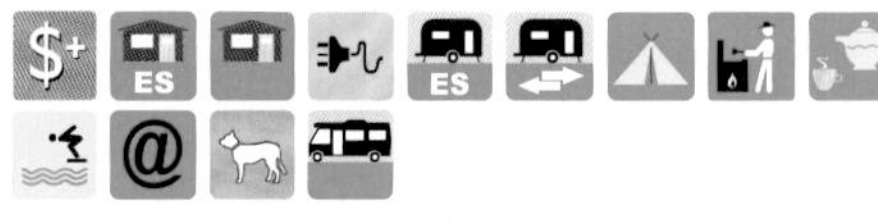

74 Cobram Willows Caravan Park
3 Ritchie Rd, Cnr Murray Valley Hwy. 1.5 km W of PO
www.cobramwillows.com.au
03 5872 1074 HEMA 89 A5 35 55 29 S 145 37 53 E

75 RACV Cobram Resort
Campbell Rd. 2 km E of PO
www.racv.com.au
03 5872 2467 HEMA 89 A5 35 55 51 S 145 39 37 E

Coburg

76 Melbourne BIG4 Holiday Park
265 Elizabeth St. 2 km E off Hume Hwy
www.melbournebig4.com.au
03 9353 8222 HEMA 77 D8 37 43 21 S 144 59 05 E

Cohuna

77 Cohuna Waterfront Holiday Park
58 Island Rd. 1 km N of PO on Gunbower Island
www.cwhp.com.au
03 5456 2562 HEMA 87 F13 35 48 19 S 144 13 33 E

Colac

78 Central Caravan Park
Bruce St, at Showground. 1.2 km E of PO
www.colaccaravanpark.com.au
03 5231 3586 HEMA 83 E9 38 20 09 S 143 36 12 E

79 Colac Otway Caravan & Cabin Park
490 Princes Hwy
www.colacotwaycaravan.com.au
03 5231 5337 HEMA 83 E8 38 20 04 S 143 32 08 E

80 Lake Colac Caravan Park
51 Fryans St
www.lakecolaccaravanpark.com.au
03 5231 5971 HEMA 83 E9 38 19 54 S 143 35 37 E

Coleraine

81 Coleraine Caravan Park
4 Winter St
03 5575 2268 HEMA 84 E4 37 35 50 S 141 41 29 E

Congupna

82 Four Corners Motel & Caravan Park
Goulburn Valley Hwy
03 5829 9404 HEMA 89 C4 36 18 13 S 145 25 55 E

Corinella

83 Corinella Foreshore Caravan Park

3 Peters St
www.corinellaforeshore.com.au
0417 781 141 HEMA 81 J11 38 24 31 S 145 25 20 E

Corryong

84 Colac Colac Caravan Park

1994 Murray Valley Hwy. 7 km S of PO
www.colaccolaccaravanpark.com.au/
02 6076 1520 HEMA 92 B7 36 12 48 S 147 50 10 E

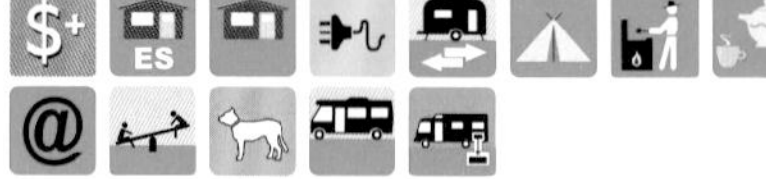

85 Mt Mittamatite Caravan Park

1516 Murray Valley Hwy
02 6076 1152 HEMA 92 B7 36 12 09 S 147 52 59 E

Cowes

86 Amaroo Caravan Park

97 Church St
www.amaroopark.com
03 5952 2548 HEMA 81 J9 38 27 10 S 145 14 11 E

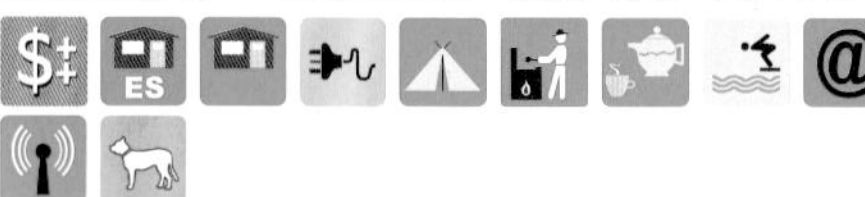

87 Amaze N Things Holiday Park

1805A Phillip Island Rd. 4 km SE of PO
www.amtholidaypark.com.au
03 5952 2020 HEMA 81 K10 38 29 15 S 145 15 44 E

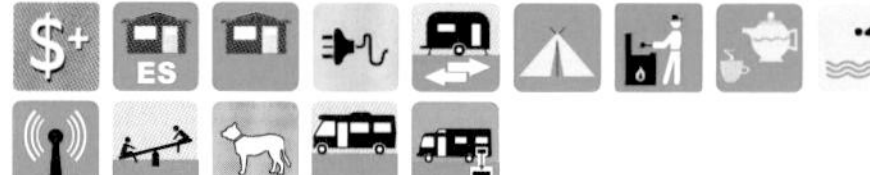

88 Anchor Belle Holiday Park

272 Church St
www.anchorbelle.com.au
03 5952 2258 HEMA 81 J9 38 27 07 S 145 13 00 E

89 Beach Park Tourist Caravan Park

2 McKenzie Rd. 800m W of PO
www.beachpark.com.au
03 5952 2113 HEMA 81 J9 38 27 04 S 145 13 47 E

90 Cowes Foreshore Tourist Park

164 Church St
www.cowesforeshoretouristpark.com.au/
03 5952 2211 HEMA 81 J9 38 27 06 S 145 13 40 E

91 Seaview Holiday Park

411-421 Settlement Rd
www.seaviewholidaypark.com.au
03 5952 2033 HEMA 81 K9 38 27 22 S 145 13 07 E

Creswick

92 Creswick Calembeen Lake Caravan Park

12 Cushing Ave. 900m NW of PO
www.creswickcaravanpark.com.au
03 5345 2411 HEMA 85 D11 37 25 08 S 143 53 32 E

Cullulleraine

93 Bushmans Rest Caravan Park

70 Sturt Hwy
www.bushmansrest.com.au
03 5028 2252 HEMA 88 D4 34 16 23 S 141 35 13 E

94 Lake Cullulleraine Holiday Park

5302 Sturt Hwy
www.lakecullulleraineholidaypark.com.au
03 5028 2226 HEMA 88 D4 34 16 40 S 141 36 00 E

Dadswells Bridge

95 Grampians Edge Caravan Park

20 Krause Road Western Hwy
www.grampiansedgecaravanpark.com.au
03 5359 5241 HEMA 84 B7 36 55 00 S 142 30 29 E

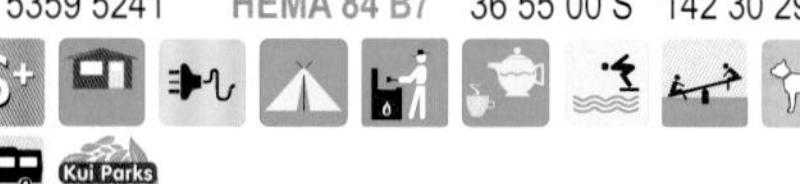

Dandenong

96 BIG4 Dandenong Tourist Park

370 Frankston Rd, Dandenong South. 6 km S of PO
www.big4dtp.com.au
03 9706 5492 HEMA 78 F7 38 02 20 S 145 12 34 E

Dargo

97 Wonnangatta Caravan Park

7611 Dargo Rd. Closed winter, book in advance
03 5140 1265 HEMA 95 J12 37 30 28 S 147 12 03 E

Dartmouth

98 Dartmouth Alpine Caravan Park

14 Dartmouth Rd
02 6072 4218 HEMA 97 B9 36 32 04 S 147 29 58 E

Daylesford

99 Daylesford Holiday Park

Cnr Ballan Rd & Burrall St. 1.7 km S of PO
www.daylesfordholidaypark.com.au
03 5348 3821 HEMA 85 D12 37 21 31 S 144 08 23 E

100 Jubilee Lake Caravan Park

151 Lake Rd
www.jubileelake.com.au
03 5348 2186 HEMA 85 D12 37 22 05 S 144 08 53 E

Dimboola

101 Dimboola Riverside Caravan Park

2 Wimmera St
www.RiversideHolidayParkDimboola.com.au
03 5389 1416 HEMA 86 J5 36 27 24 S 142 01 30 E

Donald

102 Donald Caravan Park

2 Corack Rd. 1 km N of PO
0497 770 064 HEMA 87 J8 36 21 52 S 142 59 16 E

Doncaster

103 Crystal Brook Tourist Park

182 Heidelberg-Warrandyte Rd, Doncaster East
www.cbtp.com.au
03 9844 3637 HEMA 77 E13 37 45 03 S 145 10 35 E

Dromana

104 Kangerong Holiday Park
105 Point Nepean Rd
www.kangerong.com.au
03 5987 2080 HEMA 80 H7 38 19 48 S 144 58 15 E

105 Peninsula Holiday Park
10 Ponderosa Pl. 2 km NW of PO
www.peninsulaholidaypark.com.au
03 5987 2095 HEMA 80 H7 38 19 53 S 144 59 03 E

Drouin

106 El Paso Caravan Park
262 Princes Hwy. 2.3 km W of PO
03 5625 1710 HEMA 81 F14 38 07 14 S 145 50 35 E

107 Glen Cromie Caravan Park
850 Main Neerim Rd
www.glencromie.com.au
03 5626 8212 HEMA 81 F14 38 04 28 S 145 53 37 E

Dunkeld

108 Dunkeld Caravan Park
Cnr of Templeton St & Glenelg Hwy
www.dunkeldcaravanpark.com
03 5577 2578 HEMA 84 E6 37 38 59 S 142 20 44 E

Dunolly

109 Dunolly Caravan Park
46 Desmond St
www.dunollycaravanpark.com.au
03 5468 1262 HEMA 85 A11 36 51 48 S 143 43 49 E

Eagle Point

110 Eagle Point Caravan Park
40 School Rd
03 5156 1183 HEMA 98 J3 37 53 32 S 147 40 53 E

Echuca

111 Discovery Holiday Parks Echuca
75 River Ave
www.discoveryholidayparks.com.au
03 5482 1533 HEMA 89 B2 36 07 30 S 144 47 28 E

112 NRMA Echuca Holiday Park
52 Crofton St. 1 km NW of PO
www.echucacaravanpark.com.au
03 5482 2157 HEMA 89 B2 36 06 58 S 144 44 37 E

113 Rich River Holiday & Lifestyle Village
40 Crescent St. 2 km E of water tower
www.richrivertouristpark.com.au
03 5480 0999 HEMA 89 B2 36 07 37 S 144 46 17 E

114 River Bend Caravan Park
1134 Stewarts Bridge Rd
www.riverbendcaravanpark.com.au
03 5482 6650 HEMA 89 B2 36 05 24 S 144 55 14 E

Edenhope

115 Edenhope Lakeside Tourist Park
Lake St. 100m N of PO
www.edenhopelakeside.com.au
03 5585 1659 HEMA 84 B2 37 02 06 S 141 17 40 E

Eildon

116 Bluegums Riverside Holiday Park
746 Back Eildon Rd. 5 km W of PO
www.bluegumsriverside.com.au/
03 5774 2567 HEMA 89 G6 37 15 08 S 145 52 20 E

117 Eildon Pondage Holiday Park
10 Eildon Rd. 1 km E of PO
www.eildonpondage.com
03 5774 2105 HEMA 89 G6 37 13 44 S 145 55 09 E

Erica

118 Erica Caravan Park
14 Station St
03 5165 3315 HEMA 91 C8 37 58 45 S 146 22 24 E

Eskdale

119 Eskdale Caravan Park
Omeo Hwy
0438 645 846 HEMA 96 A7 36 27 57 S 147 14 53 E

Euroa

120 Euroa Caravan & Cabin Park
73-103 Kirkland Ave. 1 km E of PO
www.euroacaravanpark.com.au
03 5795 2160 HEMA 89 E5 36 45 15 S 145 34 39 E

Everton

121 Everton Caravan & Tourist Park
2121 Great Alpine Rd
www.evertoncaravanpark.com.au
03 5727 0365 HEMA 92 C3 36 25 57 S 146 32 31 E

Forrest

122 The Wonky Stables Holiday Park
1 Station St
www.wonkystables.com.au
03 5236 6275 HEMA 83 G10 38 30 58 S 143 43 02 E

Foster

123 Prom Central Caravan Park
38 Nelson St. 500m E of PO
www.promcentralcaravanpark.com.au
03 5682 2440 HEMA 91 G8 38 39 18 S 146 12 20 E

Frankston

124 Frankston Holiday Park
1325 Frankston Dangenong Rd
www.cpoaus.com.au
03 9786 8355 HEMA 78 J6 38 06 18 S 145 10 07 E

Frankston South

125 BIG4 Mornington Peninsula Holiday Park
2 Robinsons Rd
www.big4mphp.com.au
03 5971 2333 HEMA 81 G9 38 10 27 S 145 08 28 E

Geelong

126 Barwon River Tourist Park
153 Barrabool Rd, Belmont
www.barwoncaravanpark.com.au
03 5243 3842 HEMA 80 G2 38 10 00 S 144 21 00 E

127 Discovery Holiday Parks Geelong
59 Barrabool Rd, Belmont
www.discoveryholidayparks.com.au
03 5243 6225 HEMA 80 G2 38 09 59 S 144 20 15 E

128 Eldorado Tourist Park
360 Ballarat Rd, Batesford
www.eldoradotp.com.au
03 5276 1386 HEMA 80 F2 38 06 10 S 144 18 54 E

129 Geelong Surfcoast Highway Holiday Park
621 Surfcoast Hwy, Mount Duneed
www.geelongsurfcoast.com.au
03 5264 1243 HEMA 80 G2 38 14 07 S 144 20 03 E

130 Moolap Caravan Park
365 Bellarine Hwy, Moolap
03 5250 1381 HEMA 80 G3 38 10 45 S 144 25 27 E

131 Riverglen Holiday Park
75 Barrabool Rd, Belmont
www.riverglenhp.com.au
03 5243 5505 HEMA 80 G2 38 10 01 S 144 20 20 E

Gellibrand River

132 Otways Tourist Park
25 Main Rd
www.otwaystouristpark.com
03 5235 8357 HEMA 83 G8 38 31 27 S 143 32 25 E

Glenmaggie

133 Lake Glenmaggie Caravan Park
Heyfield-Licola Rd
0409 854 106 HEMA 91 C10 37 55 10 S 146 45 19 E

Glenrowan

134 Glenrowan Caravan & Tourist Park
2 Old Hume Hwy
www.glenrowanpark.com.au
03 5766 2288 HEMA 89 D7 36 27 06 S 146 14 13 E

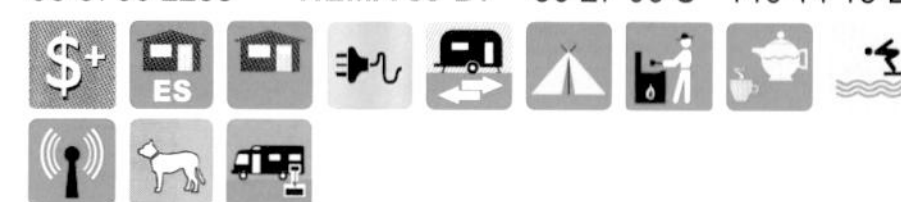

Goughs Bay

135 Goughs Bay Caravan Park
35 Bayside Blvd. 900m S of PO
www.goughsbaycaravanpark.com.au
03 5777 3572 HEMA 94 E1 37 11 12 S 146 04 00 E

Gunbower

136 Gunbower Caravan Park
74-80 Main Rd (Murray Valley Hwy). N end of town 400m from PO
www.gunbowercaravanpark.com.au
03 5487 1412 HEMA 87 G13 35 57 20 S 144 21 47 E

Halls Gap

137 Grampians Parkgate Resort
2372 Grampians Rd. 1.3 km NE of PO
www.parkgateresort.com.au
03 5356 4215 HEMA 84 C7 37 07 44 S 142 32 23 E

138 Halls Gap Caravan & Tourist Park
Cnr School & Grampians Rd
www.hallsgapcaravanpark.com.au
03 5356 4251 HEMA 84 C7 37 08 28 S 142 31 07 E

139 Halls Gap Caravan Park
2223 Grampians Road
www.hallsgapgardenscaravanpark.com.au
03 5356 4244 HEMA 84 C7 37 07 43 S 142 32 21 E

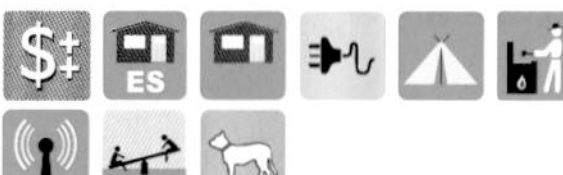

140 Halls Gap Lakeside Tourist Park
23-27 Tymna Dr
www.hallsgaplakeside.com
03 5356 4281 HEMA 84 C7 37 10 22 S 142 32 30 E

Hamilton

141 Hamilton Caravan Park

Cnr Shakespeare & Dickens Sts. 1.7 km NW of PO
www.hamiltoncaravanpark.com.au
03 5572 4235 HEMA 84 E5 37 43 58 S 142 01 11 E

142 Lake Hamilton Motor Village & Caravan Park

8 Ballarat Rd
www.lakehamilton.com.au
03 5572 3855 HEMA 84 E5 37 44 33 S 142 02 02 E

Harrietville

143 Harrietville Cabins & Caravan Park

Camping Park Rd
www.harrietvillecaravanpark.com.au
03 5759 2523 HEMA 95 A10 36 53 37 S 147 03 37 E

Hastings

144 Marina View Van Village

38 Salmon St
www.marinaviewvillage.com.au
03 5979 2322 HEMA 81 H9 38 19 02 S 145 11 38 E

Hayfield

145 Blores Hill Caravan Park

474 Weir Rd
03 5148 2495 HEMA 91 C10 37 56 17 S 146 48 15 E

Hazelwood

146 Hazelwood Pondage Caravan Park

160 Yinnar Rd
03 5163 1566 HEMA 91 E8 38 17 45 S 146 21 28 E

Healesville

147 BIG4 Yarra Valley Holiday Park

419 Don Rd. 5 km SE of PO
www.parklaneholidayparks.com.au
03 5962 4328 HEMA 81 B12 37 40 57 S 145 32 46 E

148 Gateway Lifestyle Healesville

322 Don Rd. 3.9 km SE of PO
www.glhp.com.au/parks/healesville/
03 5962 4398 HEMA 81 B12 37 40 31 S 145 32 26 E

Heathcote

149 Queen's Meadow Caravan Park

3 Barrack St. 500m S of PO
03 5433 2304 HEMA 85 B14 36 55 25 S 144 42 47 E

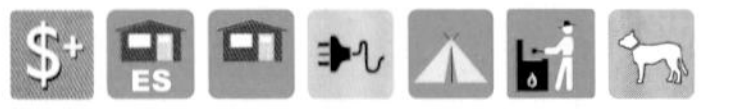

Heywood

150 Pinewood Caravan Park

2 Bell St. 1 km N of PO
www.pinewoodcaravanpark.com.au/
03 5527 1370 HEMA 84 G4 38 07 24 S 141 38 03 E

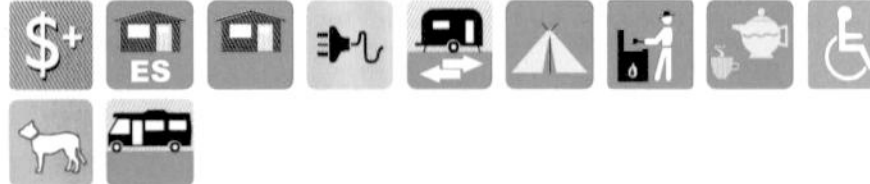

Hopetoun

151 Hopetoun Caravan Park

Austin St
0417 237 587 HEMA 86 F6 35 43 33 S 142 22 02 E

Horsham

152 Horsham Riverside Caravan Park

190 Firebrace St. 1.1 km S of PO
www.horshamriverside.com.au
03 5382 3476 HEMA 84 A6 36 43 23 S 142 11 58 E

153 Wimmera Lakes Caravan Resort

9161 Western Hwy. 3.9 km SE of PO
www.wimmeralakes.com
03 5382 4481 HEMA 84 A6 36 44 39 S 142 13 02 E

Howqua

154 Howqua Valley Holiday Park

2740 Mansfield Woods Point Rd. 27 km S of Mansfield
www.howquavalleyresort.com.au
03 5777 3588 HEMA 94 E1 37 13 50 S 146 07 05 E

Indented Head

155 Bellarine Bayside Holiday Parks

The Esplanade (Anderson Reserve)
www.bellarinebayside.com.au
03 5254 4000 HEMA 80 F5 38 07 59 S 144 42 28 E

Inglewood

156 Inglewood Motel & Caravan Park

4580 Calder Hwy
www.inglewoodmotelcaravanpark.com.au
03 5438 3232 HEMA 87 K11 36 33 56 S 143 51 41 E

Inverloch

157 BIG4 Inverloch Holiday Park

2 Cuttriss St
www.inverlochholidaypark.com.au
03 5674 1447 HEMA 90 G6 38 38 02 S 145 44 26 E

158 Inverloch Foreshore Camping

The Esplanade. 1 km E of PO
www.inverlochforeshorecamping.com.au
03 5674 1236 HEMA 90 G6 38 38 04 S 145 44 38 E

159 RACV Inverloch Resort

70 Cape Paterson-Inverloch Road. 5 km SW of PO
www.racv.com.au
03 5674 0000 HEMA 90 G5 38 38 54 S 145 41 14 E

Jamieson

160 Jamieson Caravan Park

6 Grey St. 200m S of PO
www.jamiesoncaravanpark.com.au
03 5777 0567 HEMA 94 F1 37 18 14 S 146 08 08 E

Jeparit

161 Jeparit Caravan Park

Peterson Ave. 500m SW of PO. See noticeboard for caretaker's details
0408 107 851 HEMA 86 H5 36 08 41 S 141 59 03 E

Johnsonville

162 Lealow Caravan Park
62 Punt Rd. Adjacent to Tambo River Ramp
www.lealow.com.au
03 5156 4237 HEMA 98 J4 37 49 32 S 147 49 45 E

Kaniva

163 Kaniva Caravan Park
Baker St. 400m S of PO
www.kaniva.info/caravan-park
0458 687 054 HEMA 86 J2 36 22 54 S 141 14 25 E

Kennett River

164 Kennett River Holiday Park
1-13 Great Ocean Rd
www.kennettriver.com
03 5289 0272 HEMA 83 H11 38 40 04 S 143 51 40 E

Kerang

165 Ibis Caravan Park
9399 Murray Valley Hwy. 3 km S of PO
www.ibiscaravanpark.com.au
03 5452 2232 HEMA 87 F12 35 45 37 S 143 55 44 E

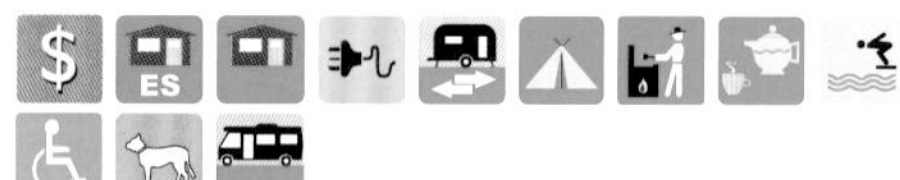

166 Kerang Caravan & Tourist Park
21 Museum Dr. 1 km W of PO
www.kerangcaravanandtouristpark.com.au
03 5452 1161 HEMA 87 F12 35 44 13 S 143 54 49 E

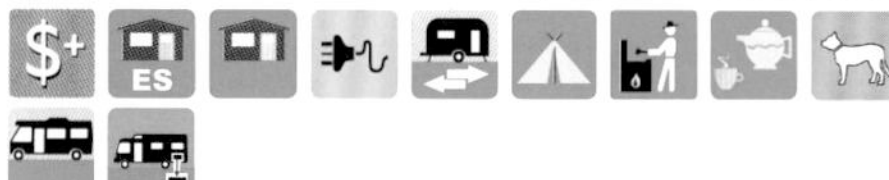

Kergunyah

167 Kergunyah Caravan Park & Store
10 Kergunyah Rd
02 6027 5205 HEMA 92 B4 36 19 40 S 147 01 46 E

Kilcunda

168 Kilcunda Oceanview Holiday Retreat
3560 Bass Hwy
www.kilcundaoceanview.com.au
03 5678 7260 HEMA 81 K11 38 33 06 S 145 28 40 E

169 Powlett River Caravan Park
Mouth of Powlett Rd
03 5678 7520 HEMA 90 G4 38 34 39 S 145 30 49 E

Killarney

170 Killarney Beach Camping Reserve
Mahoneys Rd
www.portfairycaravanparks.com
0428 314 823 HEMA 84 H6 38 21 19 S 142 18 28 E

Kilmore

171 Kilmore Caravan Park
108-110 Northern Hwy
www.kilmorecaravanpark.com.au
03 5782 1508 HEMA 89 G2 37 17 06 S 144 56 59 E

Koondrook

172 Koondrook Caravan Park
Keene St
www.koondrookcaravanpark.com.au
03 5453 2103 HEMA 87 E12 35 38 35 S 144 07 57 E

Koroit

173 Koroit-Tower Hill Caravan Park
High St. 500m SE of PO
www.portfairycaravanparks.com
0436027709 HEMA 84 H6 38 17 48 S 142 22 09 E

Korumburra

174 Korumburra Tourist Park
56 Bourke St
www.korumburratouristpark.com.au
03 5655 2326 HEMA 81 J14 38 25 36 S 145 49 48 E

Kotupna

175 Wakiti Creek Resort
500 Yambuna Bridge Rd
www.wakiticreekresort.com.au
03 5867 3237 HEMA 89 B3 36 08 14 S 145 01 44 E

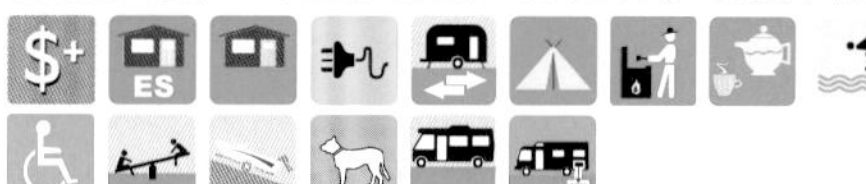

Kyabram

176 Kyabram Caravan & Tourist Park
12 Anderson St. 1.2 km E of PO
www.kyabramcaravanpark.com.au
03 5852 2153 HEMA 89 C2 36 18 55 S 145 03 27 E

177 Western Gums Tourist Park
1220 McEwen Rd
www.westerngums.com.au
03 5852 3310 HEMA 89 C2 36 18 33 S 145 01 53 E

Laanecoorie

178 Laanecoorie Lakeside Park
58 Brownbills Rd
03 5435 7303 HEMA 85 A11 36 49 56 S 143 53 12 E

Lake Boga

179 Lake Boga Caravan Park
153 Murray Valley Hwy
www.lakeboga.com.au
03 5037 2386 HEMA 87 E11 35 27 49 S 143 38 10 E

Lake Bolac

180 Lake Bolac Caravan Park
115 Frontage Rd
www.lakebolac.holiday
03 5350 2329 HEMA 85 E8 37 43 14 S 142 50 26 E

Lake Charm

181 Lake Charm Foreshore Caravan Park
36 Park Rd
www.lakecharmforeshorecaravanpark.com
03 5457 9212 HEMA 87 E11 35 36 31 S 143 48 40 E

182 Pelican Waters Tourist Park
Cnr Benjeroop & Boat Ramp Rd
www.pelicanwaterslakecharm.com.au
03 5457 9318 HEMA 87 E11 35 36 06 S 143 48 44 E

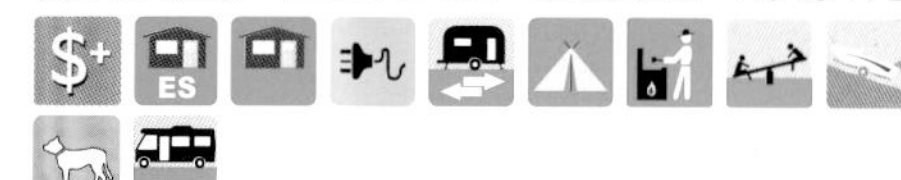

Lake Eppalock

183 Lake Eppalock Holiday Park
1 Gunmins Lane
www.lakeeppalockholidaypark.com.au
03 5439 2538 HEMA 85 A14 36 53 10 S 144 29 59 E

184 Metcalfe Pool Holiday Park
898 North Redesdale Rd
www.metcalfepoolholidaypark.com.au
03 5425 3137 HEMA 85 B14 36 56 10 S 144 32 47 E

Lake Fyans

185 Lake Fyans Holiday Park
650 Mokepilly Rd
www.lakefyansholidaypark.com.au
03 5356 6230 HEMA 84 C7 37 08 35 S 142 38 07 E

Lake Tyers Beach

186 Lake Tyers Camp & Caravan Park
558 Lake Tyers Beach Rd
www.laketyerscaravanpark.com.au
03 5156 5530 HEMA 98 J7 37 51 30 S 148 04 59 E

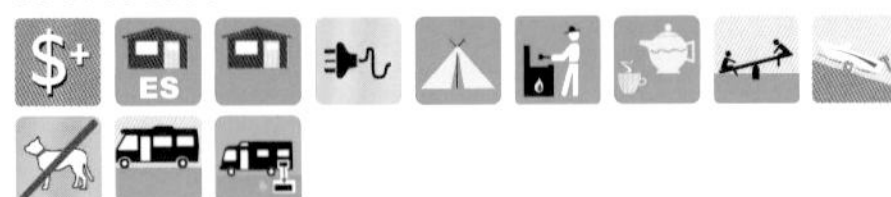

187 Lakes Beachfront Holiday Retreat
430 Lake Tyers Beach Rd
www.lakesbeachfront.com.au
03 5156 5582 HEMA 98 J7 37 51 43 S 148 04 10 E

Lakes Entrance

188 Echo Beach Tourist Park
31-33 Roadknight St. 400m E of footbridge
www.echobeachpark.com
03 5155 2238 HEMA 98 J6 37 52 33 S 147 59 53 E

189 Golden Terrace Holiday Park
651 Esplanade. 1.8 km E of PO
www.goldenterrace.com.au
03 5155 1237 HEMA 98 J6 37 52 38 S 148 00 02 E

190 Idleours Caravan Park
649 Esplanade. 1.7 km E of PO
www.idleours.com.au
03 5155 1788 HEMA 98 J6 37 52 38 S 148 00 00 E

191 Koonwarra Family Holiday Park
683-687 Esplanade. 800m E of footbridge
www.koonwarrapark.com.au
03 5155 1222 HEMA 98 J6 37 52 36 S 148 00 15 E

192 Lakes Caravilla Camping & Caravan Park
3192 Princes Hwy
03 5155 1821 HEMA 98 J6 37 52 10 S 147 57 26 E

193 Lakes Entrance Tourist Park
127 Princes Hwy
www.lakesentrancetouristpark.com
03 5155 1159 HEMA 98 J6 37 51 56 S 148 01 10 E

194 Lakes Haven Caravan Park
3 Jemmeson St
www.lakeshaven.com.au
03 5155 2254 HEMA 98 J6 37 52 32 S 147 59 51 E

195 Lakes Riviera Country Caravan Park
29 Palmers Rd
0418 505 917 HEMA 98 J6 37 52 23 S 148 00 25 E

196 North Arm Tourist Park
76 Marine Pde
www.northarmpark.com
03 5155 2490 HEMA 98 J6 37 52 50 S 147 58 39 E

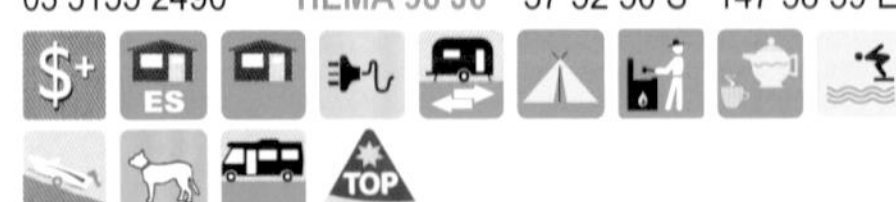

197 NRMA Eastern Beach Holiday Park
42 Eastern Beach Rd
www.easternbeach.com.au
03 5155 1581 HEMA 98 J6 37 52 26 S 148 00 47 E

198 Prime Tourist Park
60 Myer St
www.primetouristpark.com.au
03 5155 1735 HEMA 98 J6 37 52 32 S 147 59 41 E

199 Silver Sands Tourist Park
33 Myer St
www.ssands.com.au
03 5155 2343 HEMA 98 J6 37 52 38 S 147 59 38 E

200 Waters Edge Holiday Park
623 Esplanade
www.watersedgepark.com
03 5155 1914 HEMA 98 J6 37 52 41 S 147 59 49 E

201 Woodbine Tourist Park
33 Church St. 800m E of PO
03 5155 1718 HEMA 98 J6 37 52 44 S 147 59 21 E

Landsborough

202 Landsborough Caravan Park
Burke St, behind Community Resource Centre. Call Info Centre. AH 0408 503 149
03 5356 1000 HEMA 85 B9 37 00 30 S 143 08 11 E

Lang Lang

203 Lang Lang Foreshore Caravan Park
1 Jetty Lane
www.langlangforeshore.com.au
03 5997 5220 HEMA 81 H12 38 18 25 S 145 31 16 E

Learmonth

204 Lake Learmonth Caravan Park
Laidlaw St, Alexander Park
0429 402 149 HEMA 85 D11 37 25 22 S 143 42 39 E

Leongatha

205 Leongatha Caravan Park
14 Turner St. 800m N of PO
03 5662 2753 HEMA 90 F6 38 28 18 S 145 56 52 E

Licola

206 Licola Caravan Park
14 Jamieson Rd
www.licolacaravanpark.com.au
03 5148 8786 HEMA 94 K6 37 37 40 S 146 37 24 E

Lilydale

207 Lilydale Pine Hill Caravan Park
105 Warburton Hwy
www.lilydalepinehill.com.au
03 9735 4577 HEMA 81 B11 37 45 32 S 145 23 31 E

Lima South

208 Midland Holiday Park
3028 Midland Hwy
www.midlandholidaypark.com.au
03 5768 2416 HEMA 89 E6 36 48 01 S 146 00 31 E

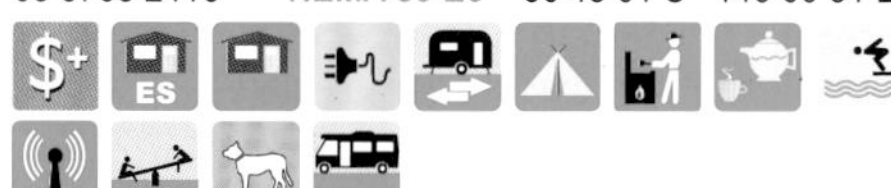

Lismore

209 Browns Water Hole Caravan Park
High St. Contact caretaker for key
0417 071 523 HEMA 82 B7 37 57 16 S 143 20 48 E

Loch Sport

210 90 Mile Beach Holiday Retreat
Track 10 via Longford Loch Sport Rd
www.90milebeachholidayretreat.com
03 5146 0320 HEMA 91 D14 38 07 07 S 147 30 55 E

211 Loch Sport Caravan Park
Charles St
www.lochsportpark.com
03 5146 0264 HEMA 91 D14 38 03 19 S 147 33 57 E

Lorne

212 Cumberland River Holiday Park
2680 Great Ocean Rd. 7 km S of PO
www.cumberlandriver.com.au
03 5289 1790 HEMA 83 H11 38 34 29 S 143 56 56 E

213 Lorne Foreshore Caravan Park
2 Great Ocean Rd
www.lornecaravanpark.com.au
03 5289 1382 HEMA 83 G11 38 32 06 S 143 58 25 E

Macedon

214 Macedon Caravan Park
Cnr Blackforest Dr & McBean Ave. 1.6 km S of PO
www.macedoncaravanpark.com
03 5426 1528 HEMA 85 D14 37 25 53 S 144 33 33 E

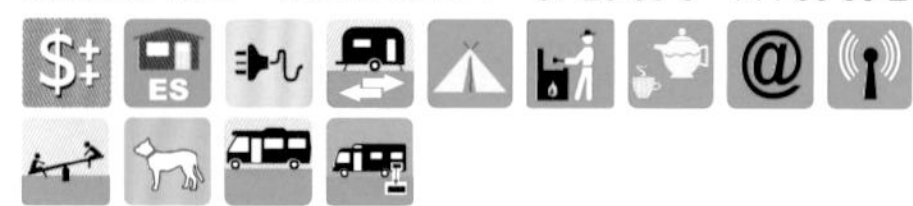

Maldon

215 Maldon Caravan & Camping Park
Hospital St. 600m N of PO
www.maldoncaravanpark.com.au
03 5475 2344 HEMA 85 B12 36 59 41 S 144 03 46 E

Mallacoota

216 A' Wangralea Mallacoota
78 Betka Rd. S of PO
www.mallacootacabins.com
03 5158 0222 HEMA 93 H14 37 33 38 S 149 45 18 E

217 Beachcomber Caravan Park & Log Cabins
85 Betka Rd. 200m S of PO
www.mallacoota.info
03 5158 0233 HEMA 93 H14 37 33 34 S 149 45 18 E

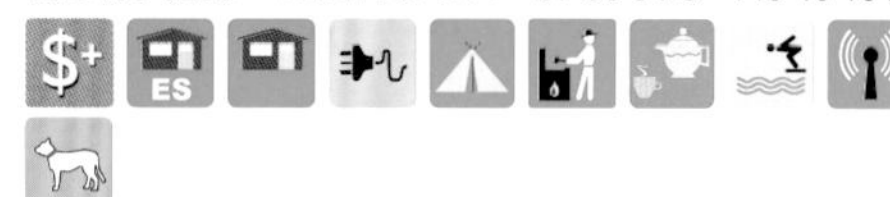

218 Mallacoota Foreshore Holiday Park
Allan Drive
03 5158 0300 HEMA 93 H14 37 33 26 S 149 45 32 E

219 Mallacoota's Shady Gully Caravan Park
Lot 5 Genoa Rd. 1.1 km W of PO
www.mallacootacaravanpark.com
03 5158 0362 HEMA 93 H14 37 33 15 S 149 44 33 E

Mansfield

220 High Country Holiday Park
1 Ultimo St. W of PO
www.highcountryholidaypark.com.au
03 5775 2705 HEMA 94 C1 37 03 11 S 146 04 58 E

221 Mansfield Holiday Park
Mt Buller Rd
www.mansfieldholidaypark.com.au
03 5775 1383 HEMA 94 C1 37 03 41 S 146 06 05 E

222 Mansfield Lakeside Ski Village
540 Howes Creek Rd. 7 km SW of PO
www.mansfieldlakeside.com
03 5775 2735 HEMA 89 F6 37 04 14 S 146 00 25 E

Marcus Hill

223 BIG4 Bellarine Holiday Park
1801 Bellarine Hwy
www.big4bellarine.com.au
03 5251 5744 HEMA 80 G4 38 14 14 S 144 33 54 E

Marlo

224 Jungle Beach Caravan Park & Resort
55 Burbang Rd
03 5154 8219 HEMA 93 J9 37 47 16 S 148 41 58 E

225 Marlo Caravan Park & Motel
10 Argyle Pde
03 5154 8226 HEMA 93 J9 37 47 45 S 148 31 52 E

226 Marlo Ocean Views Caravan & Camping Park
21 Marine Pde
www.marlocamping.com.au
03 5154 8268 HEMA 93 J9 37 47 46 S 148 32 19 E

Marong

227 BIG4 Bendigo Marong Holiday Park
1449 Calder Hwy
www.big4.com.au
03 5435 2329 HEMA 85 A12 36 43 58 S 144 07 46 E

Maryborough

228 Golden Country Motel & Caravan Park
134 Park Rd. 1.6 km N of PO
www.goldencountry.com.au
03 5461 1101 HEMA 85 B11 37 01 55 S 143 44 46 E

229 Maryborough Caravan Park
7 Holyrood Street
www.maryboroughcaravanpark.com.au
03 5460 4848 HEMA 85 B11 37 02 23 S 143 44 39 E

Marysville

230 Marysville Caravan & Holiday Park
1130 Buxton Rd
www.marysvillecaravanpark.com.au
03 5963 3247 HEMA 89 H5 37 30 28 S 145 44 53 E

Meerlieu

231 Roseneath Caravan Park
422 Woodpile Rd, via Hollands Landing Rd. Lakeside
www.roseneathcaravanpark.com.au
03 5157 8298 HEMA 91 D13 38 03 43 S 147 25 37 E

Merbein

232 Merbein Caravan Park
3-4 Box St. 1 km NW of PO
03 5025 2198 HEMA 88 C6 34 09 58 S 142 03 03 E

Merrigum

233 Merrigum Caravan Park
84 Waverley Ave
03 5855 2727 HEMA 89 C3 36 22 26 S 145 07 52 E

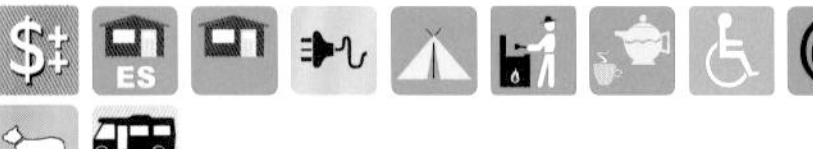

Milawa

234 Milawa Caravan Park
1585 Snow Rd
03 5727 3203 HEMA 89 D7 36 26 57 S 146 25 50 E

Mildura

235 All Seasons Holiday Park
818 Calder Hwy. 400m from PO
www.allseasonsholidaypark.com.au
03 5023 3375 HEMA 88 D6 34 12 45 S 142 08 33 E

236 Apex RiverBeach Holiday Park
435 Cureton Ave. 4.4 km W of PO
www.apexriverbeach.com.au
03 5023 6879 HEMA 88 C6 34 09 09 S 142 09 52 E

237 Site Closed

238 BIG4 Mildura Getaway Holiday Park
472-486 Deakin Ave
www.milduragetaway.com.au
03 5023 0486 HEMA 88 D6 34 12 28 S 142 08 08 E

239 Calder Tourist Park
775-783 Fifteenth St (Calder Hwy)
www.caldercp.com.au
03 5023 1310 HEMA 88 D6 34 12 41 S 142 08 32 E

240 Coachman Tourist Park
2163 Calder Hwy, Irymple. 1 km S of PO
www.coachmanpark.com.au
03 5024 5316 HEMA 88 D6 34 14 15 S 142 10 26 E

241 Golden River Holiday Park
199-205 Flora Ave
www.goldenriverholidaypark.com.au
03 5021 2299 HEMA 88 C6 34 10 30 S 142 07 28 E

242 Sun City Caravan Park
Cnr Cureton Ave & Benetook Ave
www.jonteh1.wixsite.com/suncitycaravanpark
03 5023 2325 HEMA 88 D6 34 11 39 S 142 11 04 E

243 Sun Siesta Caravan Park
Cnr Sturt Hwy & Walnut Ave. 7.5 km SW of PO
03 5023 1185 HEMA 88 D6 34 13 59 S 142 05 45 E

244 The Palms Caravan Park
7 Cureton Ave. 3 km E of PO
www.thepalmscaravanpark.com.au
03 5023 1774 HEMA 88 D6 34 11 53 S 142 11 14 E

Minimay

245 Lake Charlegrark Caravan Park & Cottages
4532 Kaniva-Edenhope Rd
03 5386 6281 HEMA 84 A2 36 46 32 S 141 14 26 E

Mitta Mitta

246 Mitta Mitta Caravan Park
Mitta North Rd. 800m N of general store
02 6072 3568 HEMA 97 A8 36 32 02 S 147 22 26 E

Moe

247 Lake Narracan Caravan & Camping Park
South Shore Rd, Lake Narracan
03 5127 8724 HEMA 91 D8 38 09 46 S 146 18 45 E

248 Moe Gardens Caravan Park
1 Mitchells Rd
www.moegardenscaravanpark.com.au
03 5127 3072 HEMA 91 D8 38 10 39 S 146 15 02 E

Molesworth

249 Molesworth Caravan & Camping Park
Recreation Reserve Rd
www.molesworthreserve.com.au
03 5797 6278 HEMA 89 G4 37 09 49 S 145 32 23 E

Mongans Bridge

250 Mongans Bridge Caravan Park
42 Bay Creek Lane
03 5754 5226 HEMA 96 B5 36 35 05 S 147 05 37 E

Mooroopna

251 Acacia Gardens Caravan Park

6705 Midland Hwy. 3 km W of PO
www.acaciagardenscaravanpark.com.au
03 5825 2793 HEMA 89 C4 36 23 59 S 145 19 10 E

252 Finborough Village

220 McLeenan Rd
www.finbourgh.com
0438 776 492 HEMA 89 C4 36 23 46 S 145 20 41 E

Mornington

253 Mornington Gardens Holiday Village

98 Bungower Rd. 1 km E of Nepean Hwy
www.morningtoncaravanpark.com.au
03 5975 7373 HEMA 81 G8 38 13 26 S 145 04 05 E

Mortlake

254 Mortlake Caravan Park

31 Montgomery Way. 1 km E of PO
0409 428 870 HEMA 82 C3 38 05 01 S 142 48 32 E

Moyhu

255 Moyhu Caravan Park

14 Byrne St
www.moyhucaravanpark.talkspot.com
03 5727 9217 HEMA 89 D7 36 34 37 S 146 22 43 E

Murchison

256 Murchison Caravan Park

101 River Rd, AH 0497 149 058
03 5826 2546 HEMA 89 D3 36 36 17 S 145 13 02 E

Murrayville

257 Murrayville Caravan Park

42 Reed St. 200m S of PO. Honesty box on site.
0457241186 HEMA 88 K2 35 15 57 S 141 10 54 E

Murtoa

258 Murtoa Caravan Park

47 Lake St
0448 511 879 HEMA 86 K7 36 37 18 S 142 27 58 E

Myrtleford

259 Arderns Caravan Park

Willow Grove. 1 km E of PO
03 5752 1394 HEMA 96 B2 36 34 08 S 146 43 45 E

260 Myrtleford Caravan Park

8 Lewis Ave
www.myrtlefordholidaypark.com.au
03 5752 1598 HEMA 96 B2 36 33 50 S 146 43 32 E

Mystic Park

261 Kangaroo Lake Caravan Park

2625 Murray Valley Hwy
www.kangaroo-lake-caravan-park.business.site
03 5457 9333 HEMA 87 E11 35 33 07 S 143 46 13 E

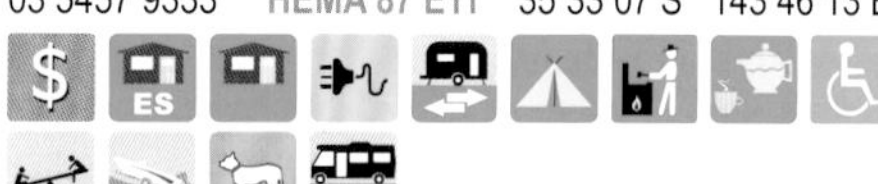

Nagambie

262 Nagambie Caravan Park

143 High St. 1.5 km S of PO
www.nagambiecaravanpark.com.au
03 5794 2681 HEMA 89 E3 36 47 56 S 145 09 01 E

263 Nagambie Lakes Leisure Park

69 Loddings Lane
www.nagambielakespark.com.au
03 5794 2373 HEMA 89 E3 36 47 15 S 145 07 47 E

Nangiloc

264 Nangiloc Caravan Park

Nangiloc Rd. Cnr Brownport Rd
03 5029 1407 HEMA 88 E7 34 27 20 S 142 20 32 E

Narrawong

265 Narrawong Holiday Park

Caravan Park Rd, off Princes Hwy
www.narrawongcaravanpark.com.au
03 5529 5282 HEMA 84 H4 38 15 26 S 141 42 10 E

Nathalia

266 Nathalia Holiday Park

Cnr Blake St & Murray Valley Hwy
www.nathaliamotel.com.au
03 5866 2615 HEMA 89 B3 36 03 42 S 145 12 14 E

267 Riverbank Caravan Park

1-5 Park St
www.riverbankcaravanpark.com.au
03 5866 2821 HEMA 89 B3 36 03 15 S 145 12 35 E

Natimuk

268 Natimuk Lake Caravan Park

597 Lake Rd
0407 800 753 HEMA 84 A5 36 42 56 S 141 56 30 E

Neerim South

269 Neerim South Caravan Park

410 Neerim East Rd
03 5628 1248 HEMA 90 C7 38 00 46 S 145 59 25 E

Nelson

270 Kywong Caravan Park

92 North Nelson Rd
www.kywongcaravanpark.com.au
08 8738 4174 HEMA 84 G1 38 02 20 S 141 00 31 E

271 River Vu Park

31 Kellett St
www.rivervupark.com.au
08 8738 4123 HEMA 84 G1 38 02 57 S 141 00 27 E

Newhaven

272 BIG4 Phillip Island Caravan Park

24 Beach Cres
www.phillipislandcpk.com.au
03 5956 7227 HEMA 81 K10 38 31 00 S 145 21 27 E

Nhill

273 Little Desert Nature Lodge

Via Nhill-Harrow Rd, 16 km S of Nhill
www.littledesertlodge.com.au
03 5391 5232 HEMA 86 J4 36 27 16 S 141 40 05 E

274 Nhill Caravan Park

93 Victoria St (Western Hwy)
www.nhillcaravanpark.com.au
03 5391 1683 HEMA 86 J4 36 20 20 S 141 38 42 E

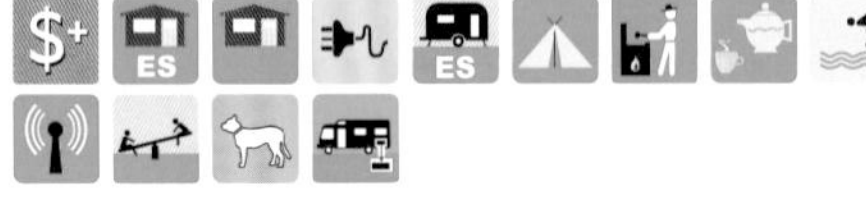

Nicholson

275 Lakes Bushland Caravan Park

363 Stephenson Rd
www.lakesbushland.com.au
03 5156 8422 HEMA 98 H4 37 47 36 S 147 46 55 E

276 Nicholson River Holiday Park

915 Princes Hwy
www.nicholsonriver.com.au
03 5156 8348 HEMA 98 H3 37 48 59 S 147 44 15 E

Nowa Nowa

277 Mingling Waters Bush Retreat

Princes Hwy
www.minglingwaters.com
03 5155 7247 HEMA 98 G7 37 44 03 S 148 05 22 E

278 Nowa Nowa Caravan & Camp Park

Bridge St
www.nowanowacaravanpark.com.au
03 5155 7218 HEMA 98 G7 37 43 48 S 148 05 32 E

Numurkah

279 Numurkah Caravan Park

158 Melville St
www.numurkahcaravanpark.com
03 5862 1526 HEMA 89 B4 36 05 40 S 145 26 30 E

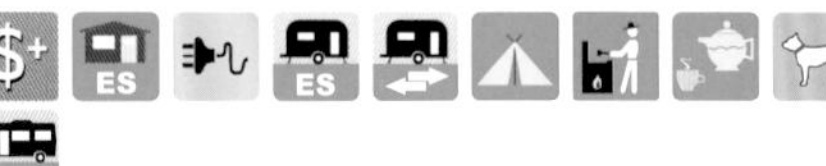

Ocean Grove

280 Riverview Family Caravan Park

Barwon Heads - Ocean Grove Rd
www.riverviewfamilycaravanpark.com.au
03 5256 1600 HEMA 80 H4 38 17 01 S 144 29 37 E

Omeo

281 Omeo Caravan Park

111 Old Omeo Hwy
www.omeocaravanpark.com.au
03 5159 1351 HEMA 97 J10 37 05 26 S 147 35 48 E

Orbost

282 Orbost Caravan Park

2-6 Lochiel St
www.orbostcaravanpark.com.au
03 5154 1097 HEMA 93 J9 37 42 38 S 148 27 14 E

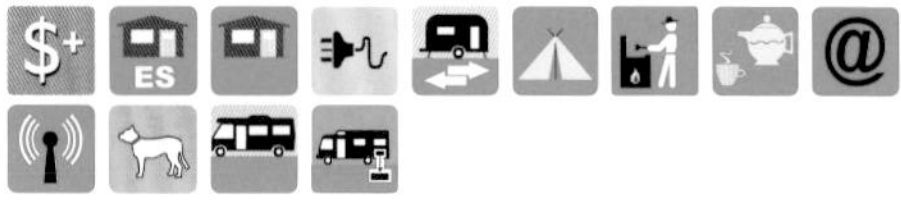

Ouyen

283 Ouyen Caravan Park

10 Calder Hwy
03 5092 1426 HEMA 88 J7 35 04 26 S 142 19 08 E

Pakenham

284 Pakenham Caravan Park

Cnr Princes Hwy & Racecourse Rd
www.pakenhamcaravanparks.com.au
03 5941 2004 HEMA 81 F11 38 04 21 S 145 29 37 E

Paynesville

285 Allawah Caravan Park

79 Slip Rd
www.allawahpark.com.au
03 5156 7777 HEMA 98 K3 37 54 41 S 147 43 35 E

286 Resthaven Caravan Park

414 Gilsenan St
www.resthavenpaynesville.com
03 5156 6342 HEMA 98 K3 37 55 05 S 147 42 51 E

Penshurst

287 Penshurst Caravan Park
Cox St
03 5576 5220 HEMA 84 F6 37 52 26 S 142 17 26 E

Peterborough

288 Great Ocean Road Tourist Park
Cnr Great Ocean Rd & Irvine St
www.gortp.com.au
03 5598 5477 HEMA 82 H4 38 36 15 S 142 52 48 E

Pomonal

289 Grampians Paradise Camping & Caravan Parkland
443 Long Gully Rd
www.grampiansparadise.com.au
03 5356 6309 HEMA 84 C7 37 15 04 S 142 37 42 E

Porepunkah

290 BIG4 Porepunkah Holiday Park
6674 Great Alpine Rd
www.big4.com.au
03 5756 2216 HEMA 96 C3 36 40 47 S 146 53 27 E

291 Mt Buffalo Caravan Park
Harrison Lane off Mt Buffalo Rd
www.mtbuffalocaravanpark.com.au
03 5756 2235 HEMA 96 D3 36 41 37 S 146 53 51 E

292 Porepunkah Bridge Holiday Park
36 Mt Buffalo Rd
www.porepunkahbridge.com.au
03 5756 2380 HEMA 96 D3 36 41 47 S 146 54 23 E

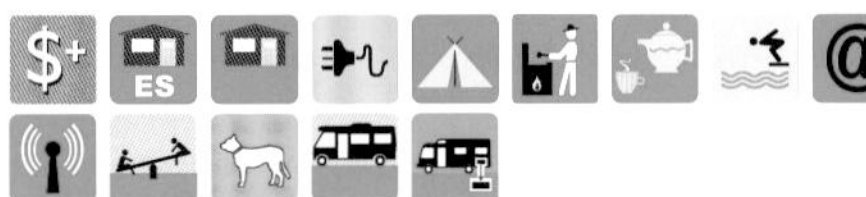

293 Porepunkah Pines Holiday Park
7065 Great Alpine Rd
www.porepunkahholidaypark.com.au
03 5756 2282 HEMA 96 D3 36 42 16 S 146 55 01 E

294 Riverview Caravan Park
Mt Buffalo Rd. 1.8 km SW of PO
www.riverviewcaravanpark.com.au
03 5756 2290 HEMA 96 D3 36 41 38 S 146 53 40 E

Port Albert

295 Port Albert Seabank Caravan Park
95 Old Port Rd, on McMillan Bay
03 5183 2315 HEMA 91 G10 38 38 49 S 146 39 43 E

Port Campbell

296 NRMA Port Campbell Holiday Park
30 Morris St
www.pchp.com.au
03 5598 6492 HEMA 82 H5 38 37 05 S 142 59 44 E

Port Fairy

297 BIG4 Port Fairy Holiday Park
115 Princes Hwy. 1.8 km N of PO
www.big4portfairy.com.au
03 5568 1145 HEMA 84 H6 38 22 30 S 142 13 52 E

298 Catalina Caravan Park
531 Princes Hwy
www.catalinacaravanpark.com.au
0423 302 461 HEMA 84 H6 38 23 06 S 142 13 14 E

299 Gardens by East Beach Caravan Park
111 Griffith St. 700m NE of PO
www.portfairycaravanparks.com
03 5568 1060 HEMA 84 H6 38 22 44 S 142 14 32 E

300 Gum Tree Caravan Park
8 Amble Lane
www.gumtreecaravanpark.com.au
03 5568 1462 HEMA 84 H6 38 21 23 S 142 14 31 E

301 Port Fairy Holiday Park
139 Princes Hwy. 2 km N of PO
www.portfairyholidaypark.com.au
03 5568 1816 HEMA 84 H6 38 22 21 S 142 13 54 E

302 Southcombe by the Sea Caravan Park
James St. 200m S of PO. Open 1st Dec - 30th April
www.portfairycaravanparks.com
03 5568 2677 HEMA 84 H6 38 23 20 S 142 14 04 E

Port Welshpool

303 Long Jetty Foreshore Caravan Park
6 Port Welshpool Rd
www.longjettycaravanpark.com.au
03 5688 1233 HEMA 91 H9 38 41 53 S 146 27 09 E

Portarlington

304 Bellarine Bayside Holiday Parks
Boat Rd (off Sproat St)
www.bellarinebayside.com.au
03 5259 2764 HEMA 80 F5 38 06 46 S 144 38 46 E

305 Dylene Caravan Park
5 Mercer St. 2 km from PO
www.dylenecaravanpark.com.au
03 5259 2873 HEMA 80 F5 38 06 54 S 144 40 13 E

Portland

306 Dutton Way Caravan Park
215 Dutton Way
03 5523 1904 HEMA 84 H4 38 18 20 S 141 36 34 E

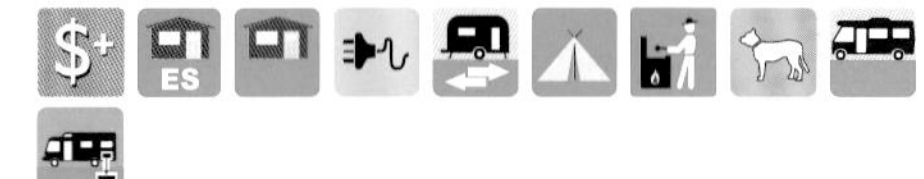

307 Henty Bay Beachfront Holiday Park
342 Dutton Way
www.hentybay.com.au
03 5523 3716 HEMA 84 H4 38 17 57 S 141 37 12 E

308 NRMA Portland Bay Holiday Park
184 Bentinck St. 1 km NE of PO
www.portlandbayhp.com.au
03 5523 1487 HEMA 84 H4 38 20 15 S 141 36 25 E

309 Portland Holiday Village
37 Percy St. 400m S of PO
www.holidayvillage.com.au
03 5521 7567 HEMA 84 H3 38 20 58 S 141 36 12 E

310 Portland Tourist Park
74 Garden St. 1.6 km N of PO
www.holidayvillage.com.au
03 5523 5673 HEMA 84 H3 38 19 55 S 141 36 01 E

Princetown

311 Apostles Camping Park & Cabins
36 Post Office Road
www.apostlescampingpark.com.au
03 5598 8119 HEMA 82 J6 38 41 37 S 143 09 20 E

Pyramid Hill

312 Pyramid Hill Caravan Park
Victoria St. 1 km E of PO
0438 557 012 HEMA 87 G12 36 03 19 S 144 07 30 E

Quambatook

313 Quambatook Caravan Park
Boort Rd
0428 857 122 HEMA 87 F10 35 51 10 S 143 31 31 E

Queenscliff

314 BIG4 Beacon Resort
78 Bellarine Hwy
www.beaconresort.com.au
03 5258 1133 HEMA 80 H5 38 16 17 S 144 37 27 E

315 Queenscliff Tourist Park
134 Hesse St
www.touristparks.queenscliffe.vic.gov.au
03 5258 1765 HEMA 80 H5 38 16 22 S 144 39 28 E

Rainbow

316 Rainbow Caravan Park
2 Railway St. 1 km SW of PO. AH 0429 069 244
03 5395 1062 HEMA 86 G5 35 54 17 S 141 59 35 E

Rawson

317 Mountain Rivers Tourist Park
Caravan Park 11 Depot Rd
www.mountainrivers.com.au
03 5165 3231 HEMA 91 C9 37 57 10 S 146 23 55 E

318 Rawson Caravan Park
Depot Rd
www.rawsoncaravanpark.com.au
03 5165 3439 HEMA 91 C9 37 57 19 S 146 24 19 E

Red Cliffs

319 Red Cliffs Caravan Park
8760 Calder Hwy
www.redcliffscaravanpark.com.au
03 5024 2261 HEMA 88 D6 34 17 51 S 142 11 11 E

Robinvale

320 Robinvale Riverside Caravan Park
Riverside Dr. 1 km N of PO
www.robinvaleaccommodation.com.au
03 5026 4646 HEMA 87 A8 34 34 43 S 142 46 10 E

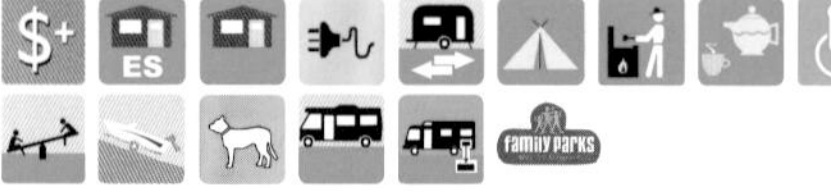

321 Weir Caravan Park
94 Pethard Rd
03 5026 3415 HEMA 87 A8 34 36 00 S 142 45 43 E

Rochester

322 Rochester Caravan & Camping Park
1 Church St
03 5484 1622 HEMA 89 C1 36 21 36 S 144 42 16 E

Rockbank

323 Sundowner Rockbank Caravan Park
2057 Western Hwy
03 9747 1340 HEMA 80 B5 37 43 46 S 144 39 37 E

Rosebud

324 Amberlee Four Star Family Holidays
306 Jetty Rd
www.amberlee.com.au
03 5982 2122 HEMA 80 J7 38 22 50 S 144 54 43 E

Rosedale

325 Rosedale Caravan Park
10 Princes Hwy
03 5199 2202 HEMA 91 D10 38 09 20 S 146 45 51 E

Rushworth

326 Lake Waranga Caravan Park & Holiday Camp
98 Waranga Basin Rd. 4km off Rushworth-Tatura Rd
www.lakewaranga.com
03 5856 1243 HEMA 89 D3 36 33 15 S 145 02 24 E

Rutherglen

327 Rutherglen Caravan & Tourist Park
72 Murray St. 700m SW of PO
www.rutherglencaravanandtouristpark.com.au
02 6032 8577 HEMA 92 A2 36 03 17 S 146 27 27 E

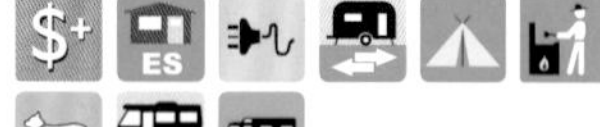

Rye

328 Whitecliffs to Camerons Bight Foreshore Camping
Point Nepean Rd. Open 1st Sep to 30th April. 3 Areas Tyrone, Stringers & Camerons
www.whitecliffs.com.au
03 5985 3288 HEMA 80 J6 38 22 07 S 144 48 48 E

Sale

329 Sale Motor Village
Princes Hwy. 1 km W of PO
www.salemotorvillage.com.au
03 5144 1366 HEMA 91 D12 38 06 45 S 147 03 24 E

San Remo

330 Foreshore Caravan Park
20 Davis Point Rd
03 5678 5251 HEMA 81 K10 38 31 32 S 145 22 07 E

331 San Remo Holiday Park

Mary Grove. 200m W of PO
03 5678 5220 HEMA 81 K10 38 31 21 S 145 22 03 E

Sea Lake

332 Sea Lake Recreation Reserve Caravan Park

71-91 Calder Hwy (community run)
0427 701 261 HEMA 87 E8 35 30 11 S 142 50 57 E

Seaspray

333 Seaspray Caravan Park

1 Futcher St
www.seaspraycaravanpark.com.au
03 5146 4364 HEMA 91 F12 38 22 38 S 147 11 23 E

Seymour

334 Big4 Seymour Holiday Park

30 Trevan St
www.big4seymourholidaypark.com.au
03 5792 1530 HEMA 89 F3 37 01 47 S 145 07 53 E

335 Highlands Caravan Park

33 Emily St (Old Hume Hwy). 500m SW of Police Station
www.highlandscaravanpark.com.au
03 5792 2124 HEMA 89 F3 37 01 16 S 145 07 33 E

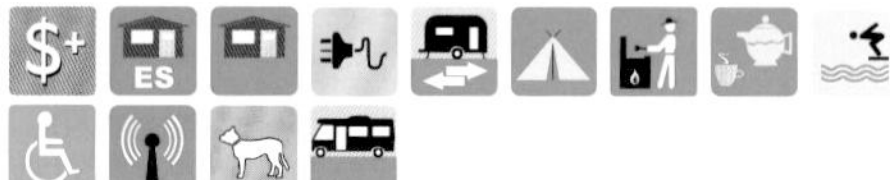

Shepparton

336 BIG4 Shepparton Park Lane Holiday Park

7835 Goulburn Valley Hwy
www.parklaneholidayparks.com.au
03 5823 1576 HEMA 89 C4 36 25 28 S 145 23 22 E

337 Secura Lifestyle Shepparton East

Cnr Midland Hwy & Orrvale Rd. 4 km E of Shepparton PO
www.securalifestyle.com.au
03 5829 2396 HEMA 89 C4 36 23 35 S 145 26 50 E

338 Strayleaves Caravan Park

1 Mitchell St
www.strayleavescaravanpark.com.au
03 5821 1232 HEMA 89 C4 36 22 43 S 145 25 13 E

339 Victoria Lake Holiday Park

536 Wyndham St. 1 km S of PO
www.viclakeholidaypark.com.au
03 5821 5431 HEMA 89 C4 36 23 30 S 145 23 46 E

Somers

340 Somers Cabin Park

93 Camp Hill Rd. 50m N of PO
www.shv.com.au
03 5983 5538 HEMA 81 J9 38 23 34 S 145 09 51 E

Somerville

341 Western Port Harbour Caravan Park

6 Lumeah Rd
03 5977 3344 HEMA 81 G9 38 14 52 S 145 14 40 E

Springvale

342 Sundowner Caravan & Cabin Park

870 Princes Hwy
www.sundownercp.com
03 9546 9587 HEMA 78 B6 37 56 07 S 145 09 34 E

St Arnaud

343 St Arnaud Caravan Park

5 Runge Rd
www.starnaudcaravanpark.com
03 5495 1447 HEMA 87 K9 36 36 43 S 143 15 32 E

St Leonards

344 Bellarine Bayside Holiday Park

Bluff Rd
www.bellarinebayside.com.au
03 5254 4000 HEMA 80 G5 38 10 39 S 144 42 58 E

345 St Leonards Caravan Park

99 Leviens Rd
03 5257 1490 HEMA 80 G5 38 10 44 S 144 42 50 E

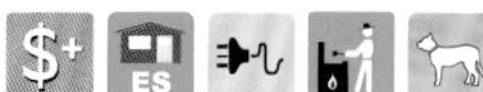

Stawell

346 Stawell Grampians Gate Caravan Park

2 Burgh St
www.stawellgrampiansgatecaravanpark.com.au
03 5358 2376 HEMA 85 B8 37 03 59 S 142 45 49 E

347 Stawell Park Caravan Park

2 Monaghan Rd, Black Range
www.stawellcaravanpark.com.au
03 5358 2709 HEMA 85 B8 37 05 48 S 142 47 34 E

Stony Point

348 Stony Point Caravan Park

1 Stony Point Rd
www.cribpointstonypointforeshore.com.au
03 5983 9242 HEMA 81 J9 38 22 28 S 145 13 16 E

Stratford

349 Stratford On the River Tourist Park

16 McMillan St. 400m S of PO
www.stratfordontheriver.com.au
03 5145 6588 HEMA 91 C12 37 58 11 S 147 04 40 E

Strathmerton

350 Murray River Hideaway Holiday Park

260 Wasers Rd. 17 km NW of PO
www.murrayriverhideaway.com.au
03 5868 2259 HEMA 89 A4 35 51 20 S 145 23 09 E

Swan Hill

351 BIG4 Riverside Swan Hill

1 Monash Dr. 600m SE of PO
www.big4.com.au
03 5032 1494 HEMA 87 D10 35 20 31 S 143 33 49 E

352 BIG4 Swan Hill

186 Murray Valley Hwy. 1.5 km N of PO
www.big4swanhill.com.au
03 5032 4372 HEMA 87 D10 35 19 25 S 143 33 07 E

353 Hilltop Resort
659 Murray Valley Hwy. 5 km NW of PO
www.hilltopresort.com.au
03 5033 1515 HEMA 87 D10 35 17 05 S 143 31 50 E

354 Pental Island Holiday Park
519 Pental Island Rd
www.pentalislandholidaypark.com.au
03 5032 2071 HEMA 87 D10 35 22 38 S 143 36 43 E

355 Swan Hill Holiday Park
5587 Murray Valley Hwy. 3 km S of PO
www.swanhillholidaypark.com.au
03 5032 4112 HEMA 87 D10 35 21 55 S 143 33 42 E

Swan Reach

356 Swan Reach Holiday Park
2143 Princes Hwy. 600m E of Bridge
www.cpoaus.com.au
03 5156 4366 HEMA 98 H5 37 49 20 S 147 52 13 E

357 Tambo River Tourist Park
2040 Princes Hwy
www.tamborivertouristpark.com
03 5156 4314 HEMA 98 H5 37 49 21 S 147 51 31 E

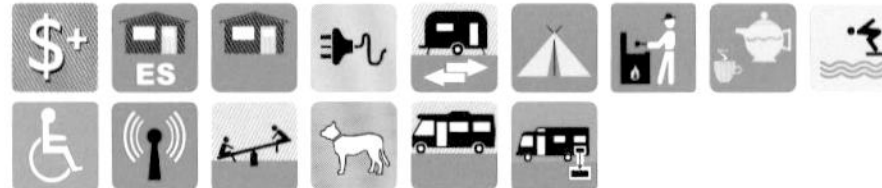

Swifts Creek

358 Swifts Creek Caravan & Tourist Park
McMillan Ave
03 5159 4205 HEMA 98 A3 37 15 47 S 147 43 24 E

Taggerty

359 BIG4 Taggerty Holiday Park
3380 Maroondah Hwy. 400m N of PO
www.big4taggerty.com.au
03 5774 7263 HEMA 89 H5 37 19 06 S 145 42 41 E

Tallangatta

360 Lakelands Caravan Park
Queen Elizabeth Dr
02 6071 2661 HEMA 92 B5 36 12 45 S 147 10 22 E

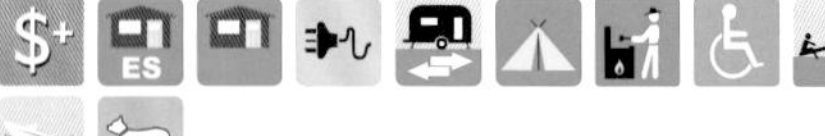

Tarra Valley

361 Best Friend Holiday Retreat
1720 Tarra Valley Rd. Caravan & Camping section closed May-Sep
www.bestfriend.net.au
03 5186 1216 HEMA 91 F9 38 28 28 S 146 34 42 E

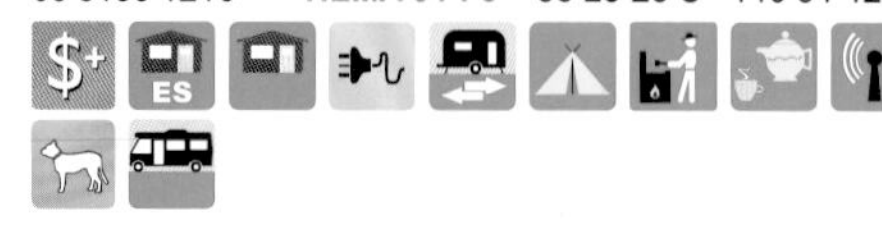

362 Tarra Valley Caravan Park
'Fernholme', 1906 Tarra Valley Rd
www.tarra-valley.com
03 5186 1283 HEMA 91 F9 38 28 14 S 146 33 49 E

Tatura

363 Country Gardens Caravan Park
Cnr Rushworth & Winter Rd
03 5824 2652 HEMA 89 D3 36 26 29 S 145 12 16 E

364 Tatura Caravan Park
23 Hastie St
03 5824 2155 HEMA 89 D3 36 26 45 S 145 13 59 E

Tawonga

365 Tawonga Caravan Park
117 Mountain Creek Rd
www.tawongacaravanpark.com.au
03 5754 4428 HEMA 96 D6 36 41 46 S 147 09 28 E

Tawonga South

366 Mount Beauty Holiday Centre
222-226 Kiewa Valley Hwy
www.holidaycentre.com.au
03 5754 4396 HEMA 96 D6 36 44 08 S 147 09 34 E

Terang

367 Terang Community Caravan Park
Warrnambool Rd off Princes Hwy
03 5592 1687 HEMA 82 D4 38 14 31 S 142 54 34 E

Thornton

368 Thornton Caravan Park
1288 Goulburn Valley Hwy
03 5773 2305 HEMA 89 G5 37 15 16 S 145 47 55 E

Tintaldra

369 Clear Water by the Upper Murray Caravan Park
17 Tintaldra Back Rd
www.clearwatercaravan.com.au
0400232872 HEMA 92 A7 36 02 47 S 147 55 44 E

Tongala

370 Tongala Caravan Park
23 Finlay Rd
www.tongalacaravanpark.com.au
03 5859 0725 HEMA 89 C2 36 15 17 S 144 57 37 E

Toora

371 Toora Tourist Park
South Gippsland Hwy
03 5686 2257 HEMA 91 G8 38 39 42 S 146 19 35 E

Tooradin

372 Tooradin Caravan & Tourist Park
13-17 Tooradin Station Rd
03 5998 3335 HEMA 81 G10 38 12 37 S 145 22 46 E

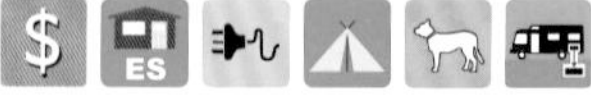

Torquay

373 Jan Juc Park
93 Sunset Strip. 4 km W of PO
www.janjucpark.com.au
03 5261 2932 HEMA 80 H2 38 20 59 S 144 17 28 E

374 Torquay Foreshore Caravan Park
35 Bell St. Community managed. No cats
www.torquaycaravanpark.com.au
03 5261 2496 HEMA 80 H2 38 20 17 S 144 19 09 E

375 Torquay Holiday Park
55 Surfcoast Hwy
www.torquayholidayresort.com.au
03 5261 2493 HEMA 80 H2 38 19 45 S 144 18 59 E

Torrumbarry

376 All the Rivers Run Caravan Park
459 Headworks Rd
www.alltheriversrun.com.au
03 5487 7321 HEMA 87 G13 35 59 17 S 144 30 39 E

377 Torrumbarry Weir Holiday Park
835 Weir Rd
www.twhp.com.au
03 5487 7277 HEMA 87 G13 35 56 41 S 144 27 50 E

Traralgon

378 BIG4 Traralgon Park Lane Holiday Park
5353 Princes Hwy
www.parklaneholidayparks.com.au
03 5174 6749 HEMA 91 E9 38 12 56 S 146 28 41 E

379 Lifestyle Villages Traralgon
35 Airfield Rd
www.villageleisurepark.com.au
03 5174 2384 HEMA 91 E9 38 12 53 S 146 28 32 E

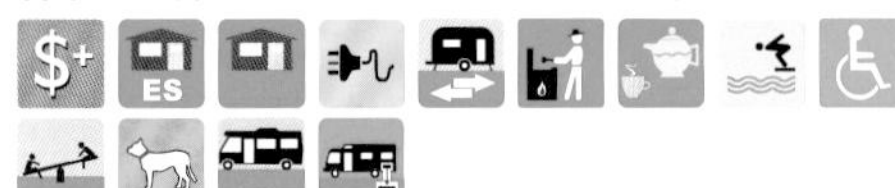

380 Tandara Caravan Park
Cnr Princes Hwy & Village Ave
www.tandaracaravanpark.com
03 5133 6206 HEMA 91 E9 38 13 13 S 146 28 14 E

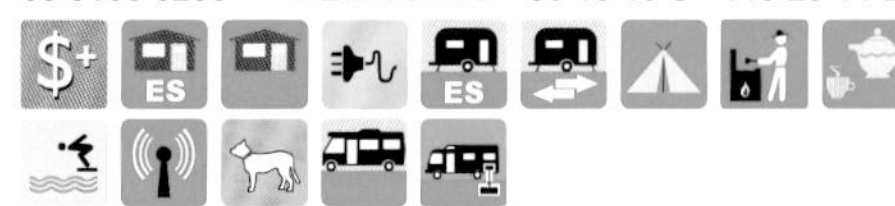

Valencia Creek

381 Valencia Creek Caravan Park
Smyths Rd
03 5145 4210 HEMA 91 B11 37 48 19 S 146 58 40 E

Ventnor

382 Anchorage Caravan Park
Ventnor Rd
03 5956 8218 HEMA 81 K9 38 27 50 S 145 11 46 E

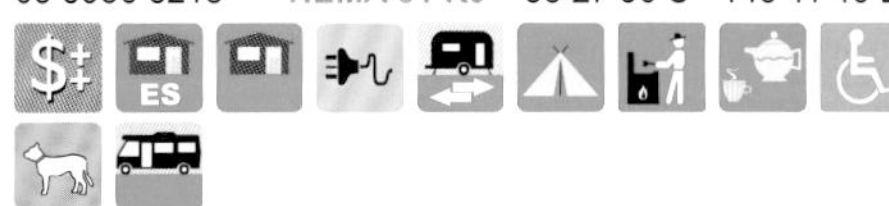

Venus Bay

383 Venus Bay Caravan Park
113A Jupiter Blvd
www.venusbaycaravanpark.com.au
03 5663 7728 HEMA 90 H6 38 42 06 S 145 49 08 E

Violet Town

384 Honeysuckle Caravan Village
154 High St
03 5798 1223 HEMA 89 D5 36 38 14 S 145 43 36 E

Walwa

385 Walwa Riverside Caravan Park
110 River Rd. 1 km N of PO
www.walwariversidecaravanpark.com
02 6037 1388 HEMA 92 A7 35 57 16 S 147 44 14 E

Wandiligong

386 Wandiligong Caravan Park
85 Williams Rd
03 5750 1162 HEMA 96 E4 36 46 49 S 146 59 20 E

Wangaratta

387 BIG4 Wangaratta North Cedars Holiday Park
Old Hume Hwy, North Wangaratta
www.northcedars.com.au
03 5721 5230 HEMA 92 B2 36 19 49 S 146 20 47 E

388 Painters Island Caravan Park
2 Pinkerton Cres
www.paintersislandcaravanpark.com.au
03 5721 3380 HEMA 92 B2 36 20 59 S 146 19 44 E

389 Wangaratta Caravan & Tourist Park
79 Parfitt Rd
www.wangarattacaravanpark.com.au
03 5721 3368 HEMA 92 B2 36 20 44 S 146 20 12 E

Waratah Bay

390 Sandy Point Caravan Park
Beach Pde, Sandy Point
03 5684 1312 HEMA 90 H7 38 49 46 S 146 07 23 E

391 Waratah Bay Caravan Park
Freycinet St
www.waratahbaycaravanpark.com.au
03 5684 1339 HEMA 90 H7 38 48 40 S 146 02 14 E

Warburton

392 Warburton Holiday Park
30 Woods Point Rd
www.warburtonholidaypark.com.au
03 5966 2277 HEMA 81 B13 37 45 11 S 145 42 19 E

Warracknabeal

393 Warracknabeal Caravan Park
2 Lyle St (Dimboola Rd)
0400 915 125 HEMA 86 H6 36 15 11 S 142 23 15 E

Warragul

394 Warragul Gardens Holiday Park
44 Burke St
www.warragulcaravanpark.com.au
03 5623 2707 HEMA 90 D6 38 09 51 S 145 55 31 E

Warrnambool

395 Discovery Holiday Parks Warrnambool
25 Pertobe Rd. 1.8 km S of PO
www.discoveryholidayparks.com.au
03 5561 1514 HEMA 82 F1 38 23 41 S 142 28 27 E

VICTORIA

396 Figtree Holiday Village
33 Lava St
www.figtreepark.com
03 5561 1233 HEMA 82 F1 38 23 04 S 142 29 26 E

397 Hopkins River Caravan Park
125 Jubilee Park Rd, Allansford
www.hopkinsriver.com.au
03 5565 1327 HEMA 82 F2 38 23 59 S 142 34 08 E

398 Shipwreck Bay Holiday Park
Pertobe Rd. Open Dec - Feb only
www.surfsidepark.com.au
03 5559 4720 HEMA 82 F1 38 23 42 S 142 28 33 E

399 Surfside Holiday Park
120 Pertobe Rd
03 5559 4700 HEMA 82 F1 38 23 31 S 142 29 02 E

400 Warrnambool Holiday Park & Motel
Cnr Raglan Pde & Simpson St
www.whpark.com.au
03 5562 5031 HEMA 82 F1 38 23 09 S 142 30 39 E

401 Warrnambool Holiday Village
81 Henna St
www.holidayvillage.com.au
03 5562 3376 HEMA 82 F1 38 22 41 S 142 28 43 E

Wartook Valley

402 Happy Wanderer Holiday Resort & Caravan Park
2493 Northern Grampians Rd
www.happywandererresort.com.au
0404 696 629 HEMA 84 B6 37 01 27 S 142 20 37 E

Wedderburn

403 Wedderburn Pioneer Caravan Park
63 Hospital St
www.pioneercaravanpark.com.au
03 5494 3301 HEMA 87 J11 36 24 47 S 143 36 59 E

Welshmans Reef

404 Welshmans Reef Caravan Park
230 Fishermans Rd
03 5476 2378 HEMA 85 B12 37 04 15 S 144 01 16 E

Werribee

405 Werribee South Caravan Park
39 Beach Rd
www.werribeesouthcaravanpark.com
03 9742 1755 HEMA 80 E5 37 58 22 S 144 41 22 E

Whitfield

406 Valley View Caravan Park
6 Valley View Dr
03 5729 8350 HEMA 89 E7 36 45 46 S 146 24 50 E

Wodonga

407 BIG4 Borderland Wodonga
65 McKoy St, West Wodonga
www.securalifestyle.com.au
02 6024 3906 HEMA 92 B3 36 06 36 S 146 51 24 E

408 Discovery Holiday Parks Lake Hume
Tallangatta Rd (Murray Valley Hwy). 12km from Wodonga
www.discoveryholidayparks.com.au
02 6020 6130 HEMA 92 B3 36 08 31 S 147 00 46 E

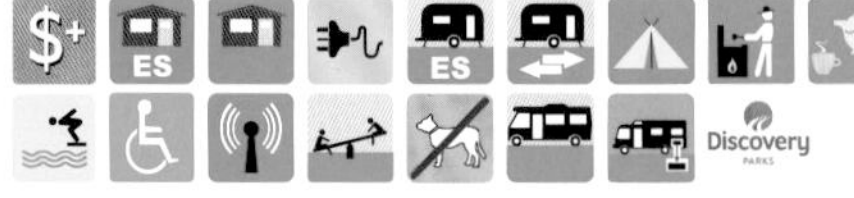

409 Wodonga Caravan & Cabin Park
186 Melbourne Rd
www.wccp.com.au
02 6024 2598 HEMA 92 B3 36 06 46 S 146 51 59 E

Wonthaggi

410 Coalfields Caravan & Residential Park
Cnr Graham St & South Dudley Rd
www.coalfieldscaravanpark.com
03 5672 1798 HEMA 90 G5 38 36 24 S 145 34 51 E

Wood Wood

411 Wood Wood Caravan Park
3559 Murray Valley Hwy
www.woodwoodcaravanpark.com.au
03 5030 5444 HEMA 87 C10 35 06 17 S 143 20 44 E

Woodside

412 Woodside Beach Caravan Park
Woodside Beach Rd. 10 km E of PO
www.woodsidebeachcaravanpark.com.au
03 5187 1214 HEMA 91 G11 38 32 58 S 146 58 39 E

413 Woodside Central Caravan Park
27 Victoria St
03 5187 1446 HEMA 91 F11 38 31 29 S 146 52 34 E

Wycheproof

414 Wycheproof Caravan Park
Calder Hwy, 500m N of PO
03 5493 7278 HEMA 87 G9 36 04 10 S 143 13 33 E

Wye River

415 BIG4 Wye River Holiday Park
Great Ocean Rd
www.big4wyeriver.com.au
03 5289 0241 HEMA 83 H11 38 38 08 S 143 53 18 E

Yackandandah

416 Yackandandah Holiday Park
Myrtleford-Yackandandah Rd
www.yhp.com.au
02 6027 1380 HEMA 92 B4 36 18 54 S 146 50 25 E

Yambuk

417 Yambuk Caravan Park
Yambuk Lake Reserve off Princes Hwy
www.portfairycaravanparks.com/node/21
0419 006 201 HEMA 84 H5 38 20 22 S 142 03 16 E

Yanakie

418 Shallow Inlet Caravan Park
350 Lester Rd. 8 km NW of PO
03 5687 1385 HEMA 91 H8 38 49 08 S 146 10 19 E

419 Yanakie Caravan Park
390 Foley Rd
www.yanakiecaravanpark.com.au
03 5687 1295 HEMA 91 H8 38 48 41 S 146 16 03 E

Yarra Valley

420 Doon Reserve Caravan Park
200 Doon Rd, Yarra Junction
www.doonreserve.com.au
03 5967 1674 HEMA 81 C12 37 46 16 S 145 36 32 E

Yarram

421 Windmill Caravan Park
Commercial Rd (Sth Gippsland Hwy)
03 5182 5570 HEMA 91 G10 38 34 25 S 146 40 24 E

422 Yarram Holiday Park
375 Commercial Rd (Sth Gippsland Hwy)
www.yarramholidaypark.com.au
03 5182 5063 HEMA 91 G10 38 34 09 S 146 40 31 E

Yarrawonga

423 Yarrawonga Holiday Park
Piper St. 500m W of PO
www.yarrawongaholidaypark.com.au
03 5744 3420 HEMA 89 B6 36 00 41 S 145 59 50 E

424 Yarrawonga Westside Carvan Park
254 Murray Valley Hwy
www.yarrawongawestside.com.au
03 5744 3314 HEMA 89 B6 36 01 19 S 145 58 38 E

Yea

425 Yea Riverside Caravan Park
1 Court St
www.yeariverside.com.au
03 5797 2972 HEMA 89 G4 37 12 45 S 145 25 57 E

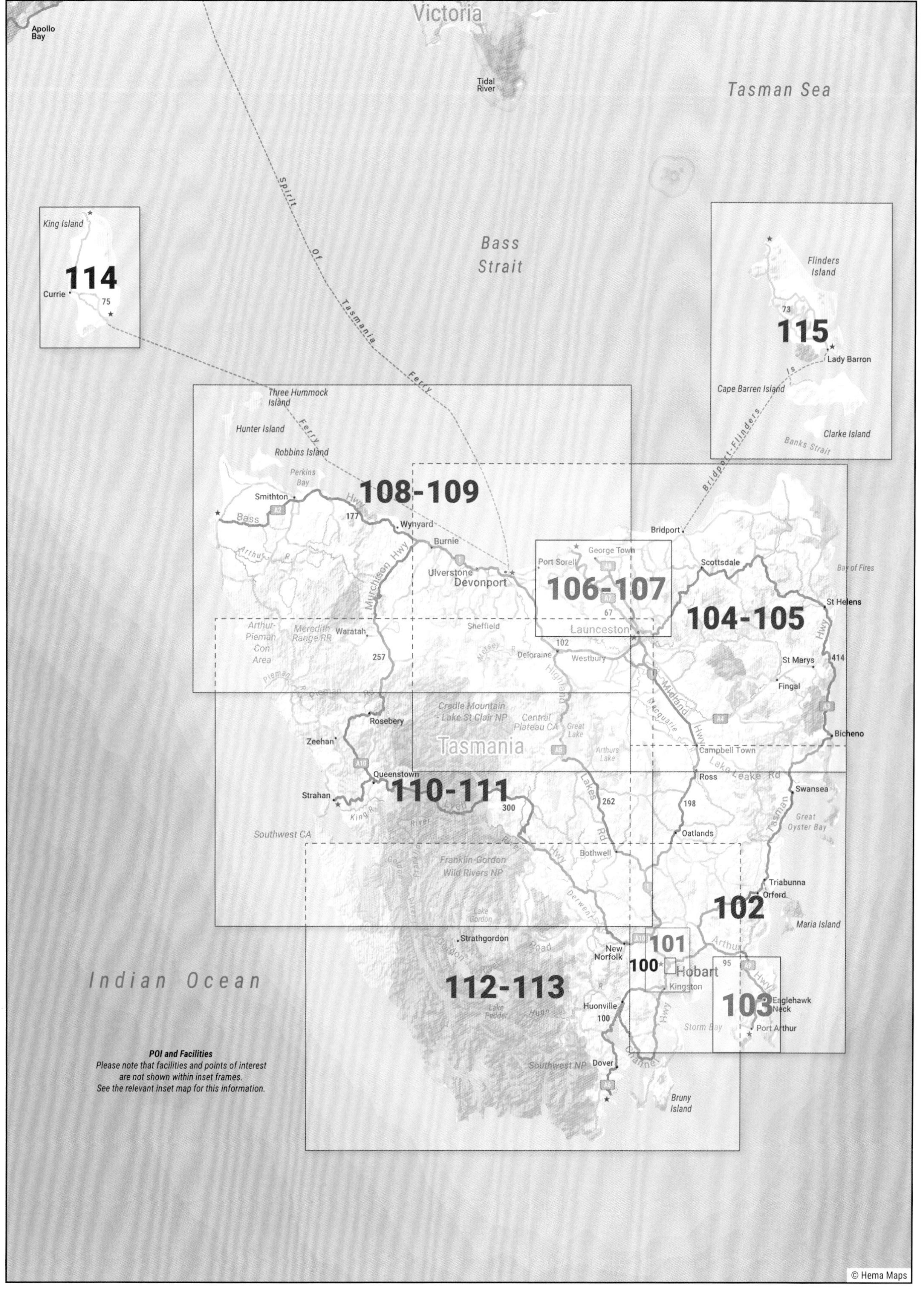
0
50
100
km
Apollo Bay
Victoria
Tidal River
Tasman Sea
Bass Strait
Spirit of Tasmania Ferry
King Island
114
Currie
75
Flinders Island
73
115
Lady Barron
Cape Barren Island
Clarke Island
Banks Strait
Bridport-Flinders Is
Three Hummock Island
Hunter Island
Robbins Island
Perkins Bay
Smithton
108-109
177
Wynyard
Burnie
Ulverstone
Devonport
Port Sorell
George Town
106-107
Launceston
Bridport
Scottsdale
Bay of Fires
St Helens
104-105
St Marys
Fingal
Bicheno
Campbell Town
Arthur-Pieman Con Area
Meredith Range RR
Waratah
257
Sheffield
Deloraine
Westbury
Rosebery
Zeehan
Cradle Mountain - Lake St Clair NP
Central Plateau CA
Great Lake
Tasmania
Arthurs Lake
Queenstown
Strahan
110-111
300
262
Ross
198
Swansea
Great Oyster Bay
Oatlands
Southwest CA
Bothwell
Franklin-Gordon Wild Rivers NP
Triabunna
Orford
102
Maria Island
Lake Gordon
Strathgordon
New Norfolk
101
100
Hobart
Kingston
95
Indian Ocean
112-113
Huonville
Lake Pedder
103
Eaglehawk Neck
Port Arthur
Storm Bay
Southwest NP
Dover
Bruny Island
POI and Facilities
Please note that facilities and points of interest are not shown within inset frames.
See the relevant inset map for this information.
© Hema Maps

Inner Hobart

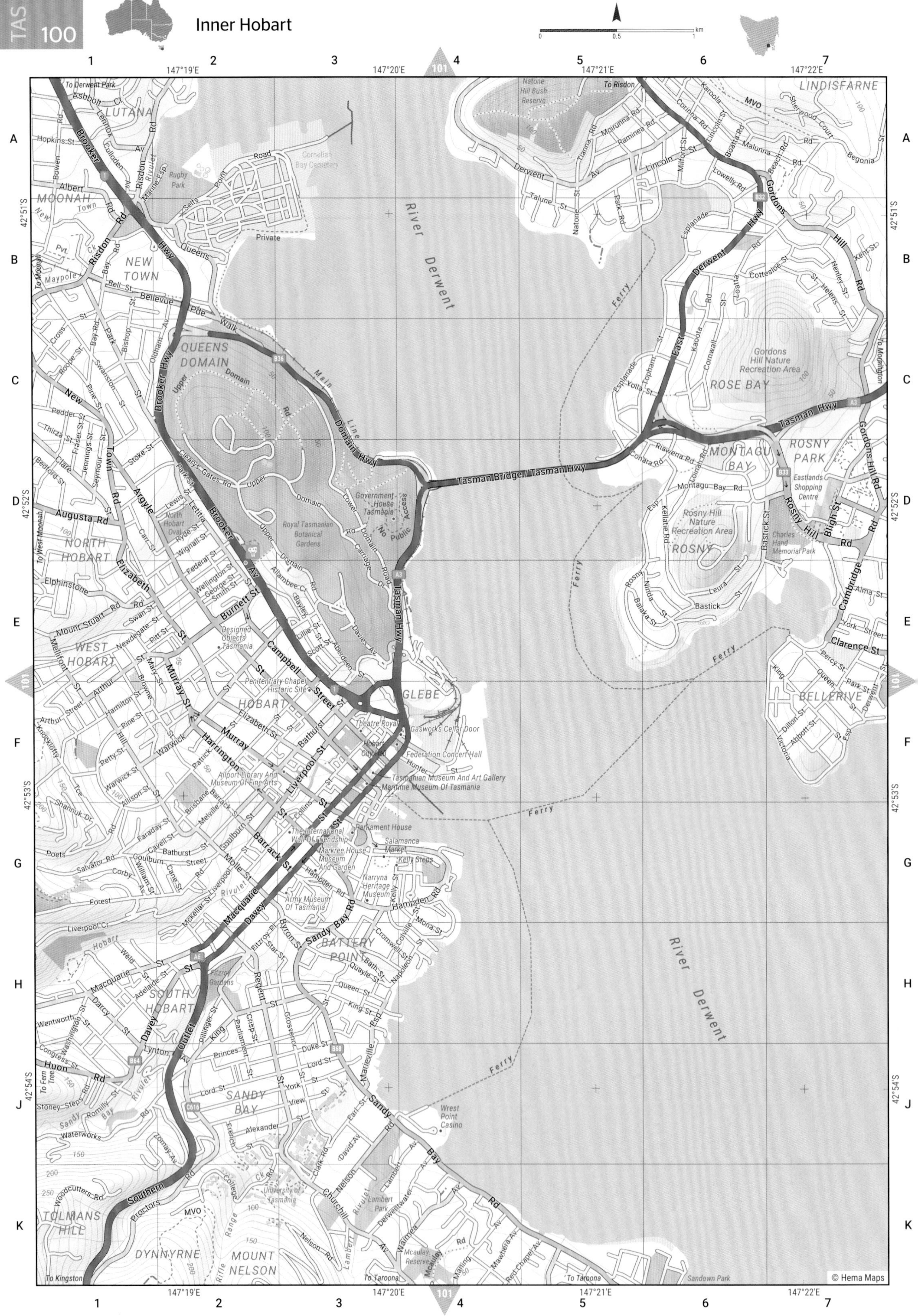

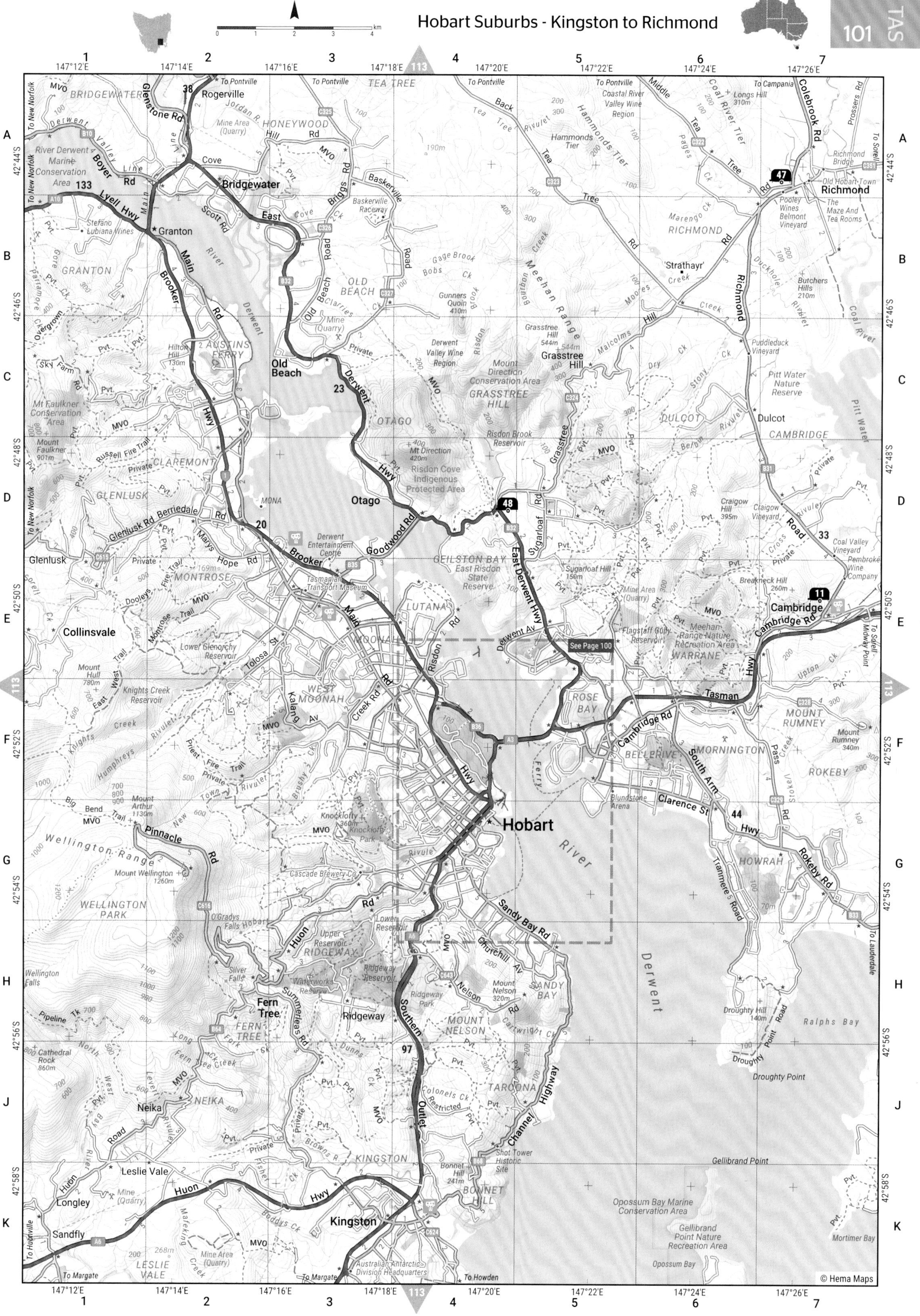
Bridgewater
Granton
Old Beach
Otago
Richmond
Cambridge
Collinsvale
Glenlusk
Hobart
Fern Tree
Ridgeway
Neika
Leslie Vale
Longley
Sandfly
Kingston
Mount Wellington 1260m
Wellington Park
Meehan Range
Grasstree Hill
Derwent River
Tasman Hwy
Brooker Hwy
East Derwent Hwy
Southern Outlet
Channel Highway
Huon Hwy
Lyell Hwy
Sandy Bay Rd
Opossum Bay Marine Conservation Area
Droughty Point
See Page 100
© Hema Maps

Ross to Port Arthur

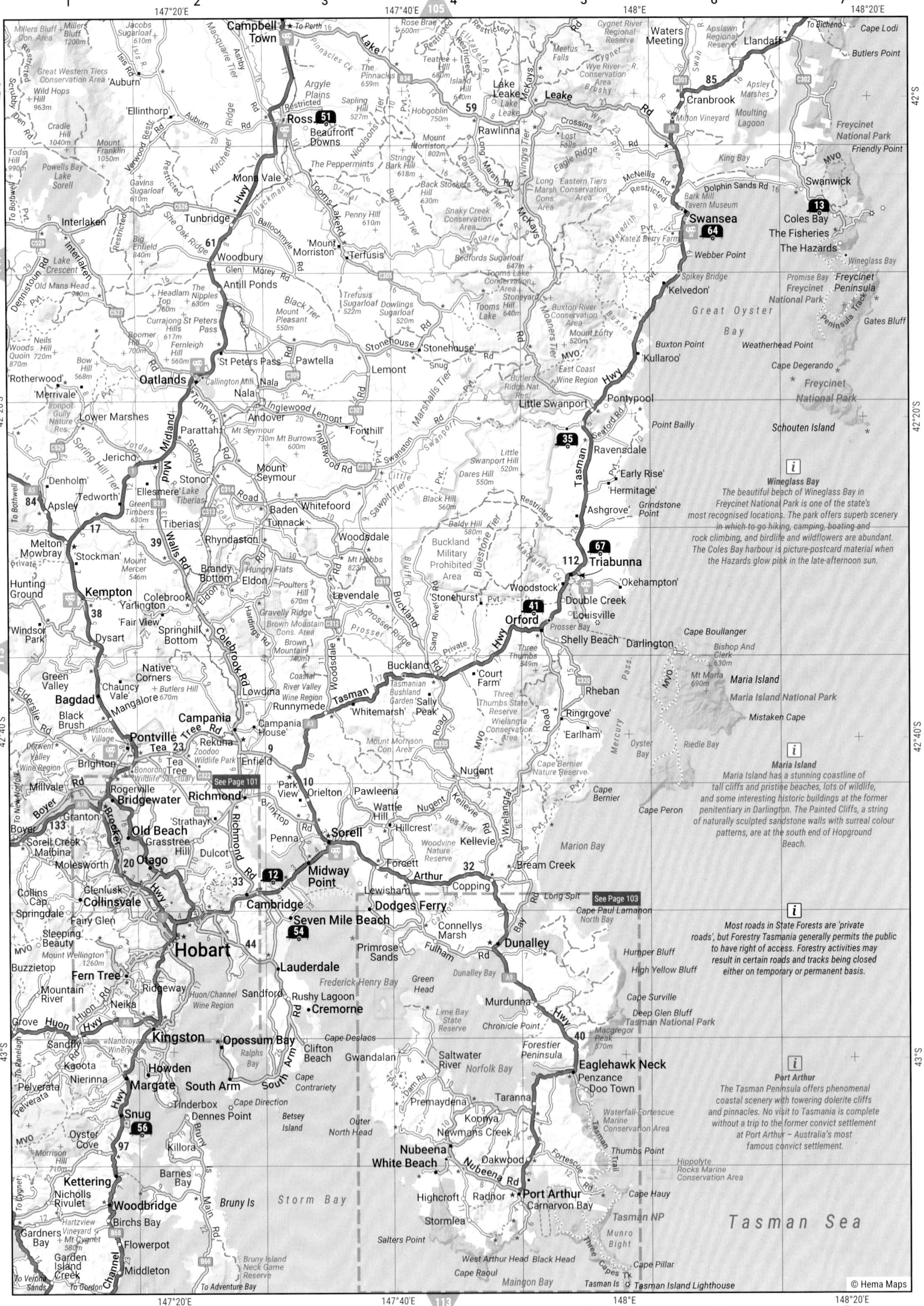

Wineglass Bay
The beautiful beach of Wineglass Bay in Freycinet National Park is one of the state's most recognised locations. The park offers superb scenery in which to go hiking, camping, boating and rock climbing, and birdlife and wildflowers are abundant. The Coles Bay harbour is picture-postcard material when the Hazards glow pink in the late-afternoon sun.

Maria Island
Maria Island has a stunning coastline of tall cliffs and pristine beaches, lots of wildlife, and some interesting historic buildings at the former penitentiary in Darlington. The Painted Cliffs, a string of naturally sculpted sandstone walls with surreal colour patterns, are at the south end of Hopground Beach.

Most roads in State Forests are 'private roads', but Forestry Tasmania generally permits the public to have right of access. Forestry activities may result in certain roads and tracks being closed either on temporary or permanent basis.

Port Arthur
The Tasman Peninsula offers phenomenal coastal scenery with towering dolerite cliffs and pinnacles. No visit to Tasmania is complete without a trip to the former convict settlement at Port Arthur – Australia's most famous convict settlement.

See Page 101

See Page 103

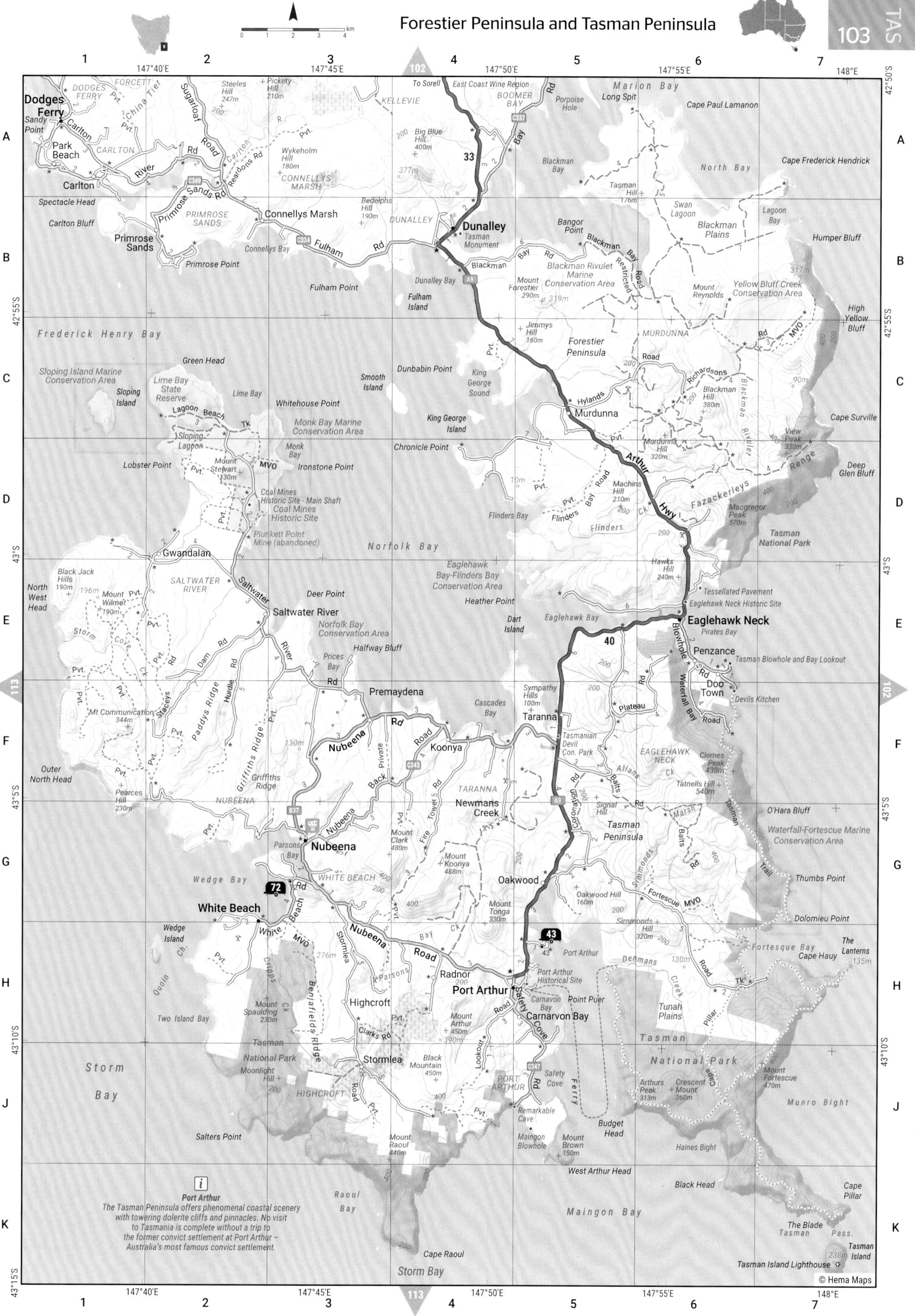
Dodges Ferry
Sandy Point
Park Beach
Carlton
Carlton River
Spectacle Head
Carlton Bluff
Primrose Sands
Primrose Point
Connellys Marsh
Connellys Bay
Fulham Rd
Fulham Point
Fulham Island
Dunalley
Tasman Monument
Dunalley Bay
Marion Bay
Long Spit
Cape Paul Lamanon
Cape Frederick Hendrick
North Bay
Blackman Bay
Bangor Point
Swan Lagoon
Blackman Plains
Lagoon Bay
Humper Bluff
Blackman Rivulet Marine Conservation Area
Yellow Bluff Creek Conservation Area
High Yellow Bluff
Frederick Henry Bay
Green Head
Sloping Island Marine Conservation Area
Sloping Island
Lime Bay State Reserve
Lime Bay
Smooth Island
Dunbabin Point
King George Sound
Forestier Peninsula
Murdunna
Whitehouse Point
Monk Bay Marine Conservation Area
King George Island
Chronicle Point
Cape Surville
Lobster Point
Ironstone Point
Coal Mines Historic Site - Main Shaft
Coal Mines Historic Site
Plunkett Point Mine (abandoned)
Arthur Hwy
Flinders Bay
Deep Glen Bluff
Tasman National Park
Norfolk Bay
Gwandalan
Eaglehawk Bay-Flinders Bay Conservation Area
Heather Point
Tessellated Pavement
Eaglehawk Neck Historic Site
Eaglehawk Neck
Pirates Bay
North West Head
Black Jack Hills
Saltwater River
Deer Point
Norfolk Bay Conservation Area
Halfway Bluff
Dart Island
Eaglehawk Bay
Penzance
Tasman Blowhole and Bay Lookout
Doo Town
Devils Kitchen
Premaydena
Sympathy Hills
Taranna
Cascades Bay
Tasmanian Devil Con. Park
Koonya
Nubeena Rd
Outer North Head
Clemes Peak
Newmans Creek
Tasman Peninsula
O'Hara Bluff
Waterfall-Fortescue Marine Conservation Area
Nubeena
Parsons Bay
Wedge Bay
White Beach
Oakwood
Thumbs Point
Wedge Island
Mount Tonga
Dolomieu Point
Port Arthur
Port Arthur Historical Site
Fortesque Bay
Cape Hauy
The Lanterns
Radnor
Highcroft
Carnarvon Bay
Point Puer
Two Island Bay
Tunah Plains
Stormlea
Safety Cove
Storm Bay
Remarkable Cave
Budget Head
Salters Point
Maingon Blowhole
Mount Brown
Haines Bight
Munro Bight
West Arthur Head
Black Head
Cape Pillar
Raoul Bay
Maingon Bay
The Blade
Tasman Pass.
Tasman Island
Tasman Island Lighthouse
Cape Raoul
Port Arthur
The Tasman Peninsula offers phenomenal coastal scenery with towering dolerite cliffs and pinnacles. No visit to Tasmania is complete without a trip to the former convict settlement at Port Arthur – Australia's most famous convict settlement.
© Hema Maps

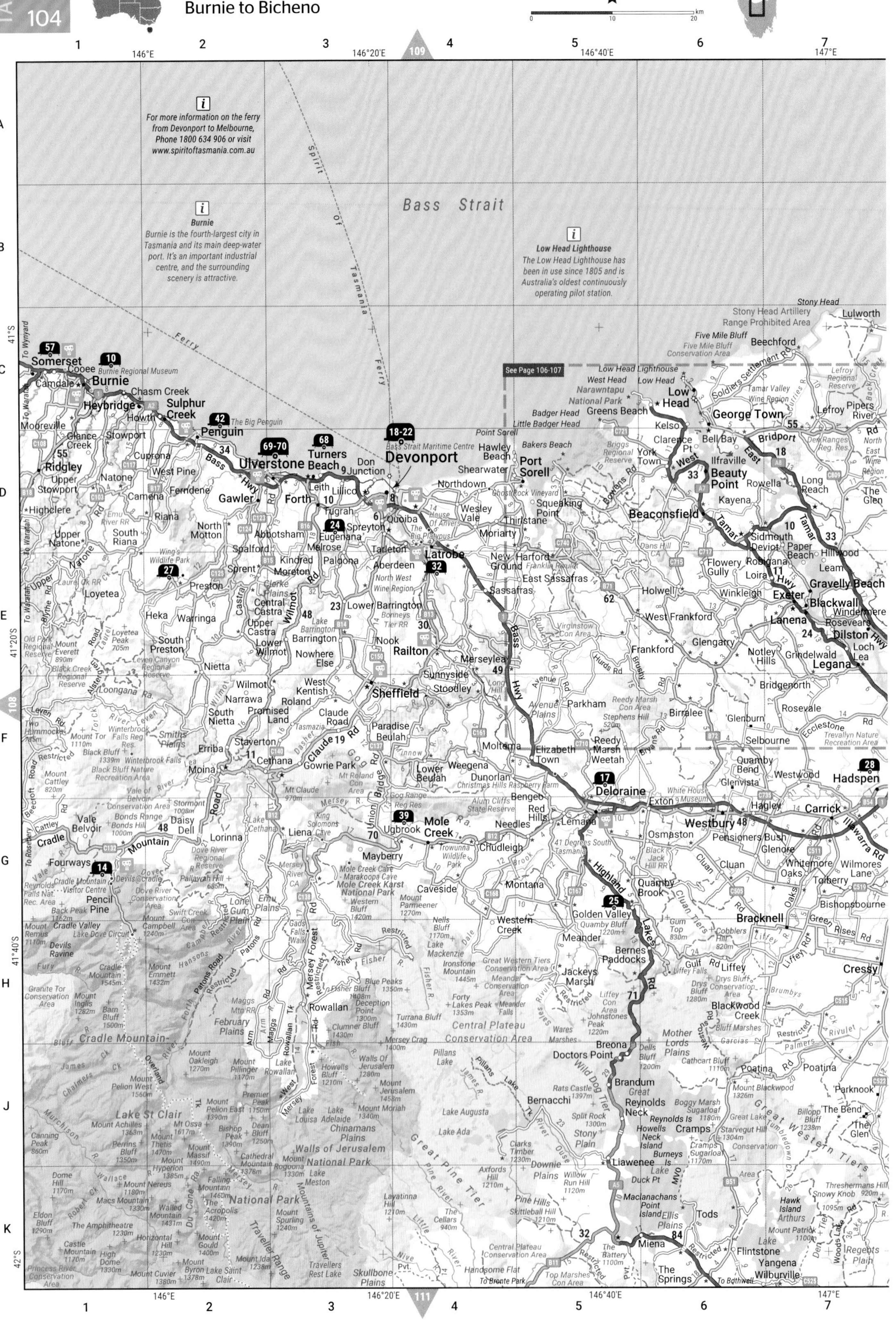
For more information on the ferry from Devonport to Melbourne, Phone 1800 634 906 or visit www.spiritoftasmania.com.au
Burnie
Burnie is the fourth-largest city in Tasmania and its main deep-water port. It's an important industrial centre, and the surrounding scenery is attractive.
Bass Strait
Low Head Lighthouse
The Low Head Lighthouse has been in use since 1805 and is Australia's oldest continuously operating pilot station.
See Page 106-107
Spirit of Tasmania Ferry
Somerset
Burnie
Heybridge
Sulphur Creek
Penguin
Ulverstone
Turners Beach
Devonport
Latrobe
Port Sorell
Low Head
George Town
Beauty Point
Beaconsfield
Exeter
Legana
Sheffield
Railton
Deloraine
Westbury
Carrick
Hadspen
Mole Creek
Cressy
Bass Hwy
Cradle Mountain-Lake St Clair National Park
Walls of Jerusalem National Park
Central Plateau Conservation Area
Great Western Tiers
Great Pine Tier
Lake Augusta
Miena
Liawenee
Bracknell
Poatina
Stony Head
Lulworth
To Bothwell
To Bronte Park

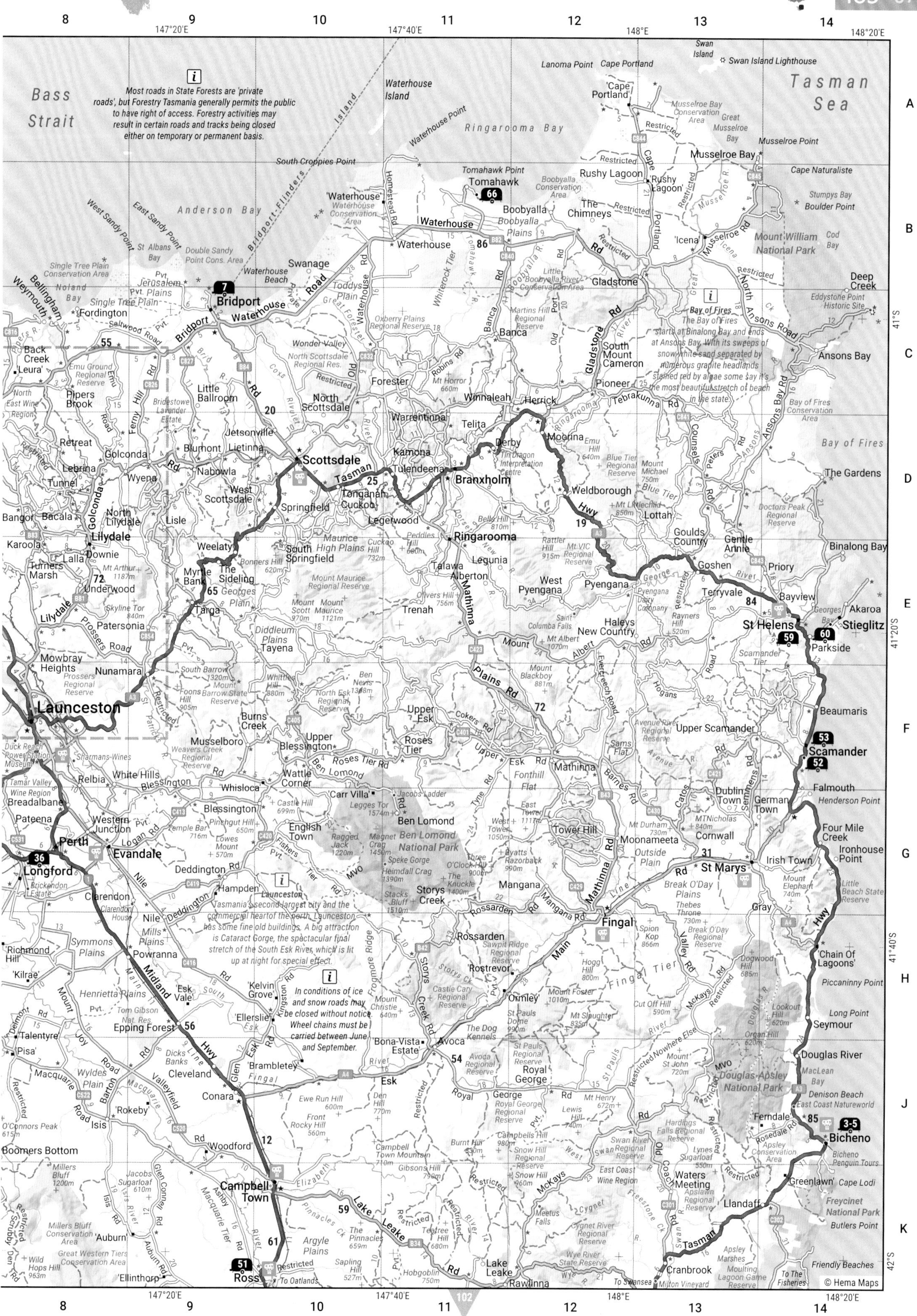
Bass Strait
Tasman Sea
Most roads in State Forests are 'private roads', but Forestry Tasmania generally permits the public to have right of access. Forestry activities may result in certain roads and tracks being closed either on temporary or permanent basis.
Bay of Fires
The Bay of Fires starts at Binalong Bay and ends at Ansons Bay. With its sweeps of snow-white sand separated by numerous granite headlands stained red by algae some say it's the most beautiful stretch of beach in the state.
Launceston
Tasmania's second largest city and the commercial heart of the north, Launceston has some fine old buildings. A big attraction is Cataract Gorge, the spectacular final stretch of the South Esk River, which is lit up at night for special effect.
In conditions of ice and snow roads may be closed without notice. Wheel chains must be carried between June and September.
Waterhouse Island
Ringarooma Bay
Anderson Bay
Swan Island
Swan Island Lighthouse
Lanoma Point
Cape Portland
Musselroe Bay
Mount William National Park
Tomahawk
Bridport
Scottsdale
Branxholm
Derby
Weldborough
Ringarooma
Gladstone
St Helens
Stieglitz
Binalong Bay
Scamander
Beaumaris
Falmouth
St Marys
Fingal
Ben Lomond National Park
Lilydale
Perth
Longford
Evandale
Campbell Town
Ross
Avoca
Douglas-Apsley National Park
Bicheno
Freycinet National Park
Cranbrook
Lake Leake
Tasman Hwy
Midland Hwy
Esk Main Rd
Lake Leake Rd
Mathinna Plains Rd
147°20'E
147°40'E
148°E
148°20'E
41°S
41°20'S
41°40'S
42°S
© Hema Maps

Port Sorell to Launceston

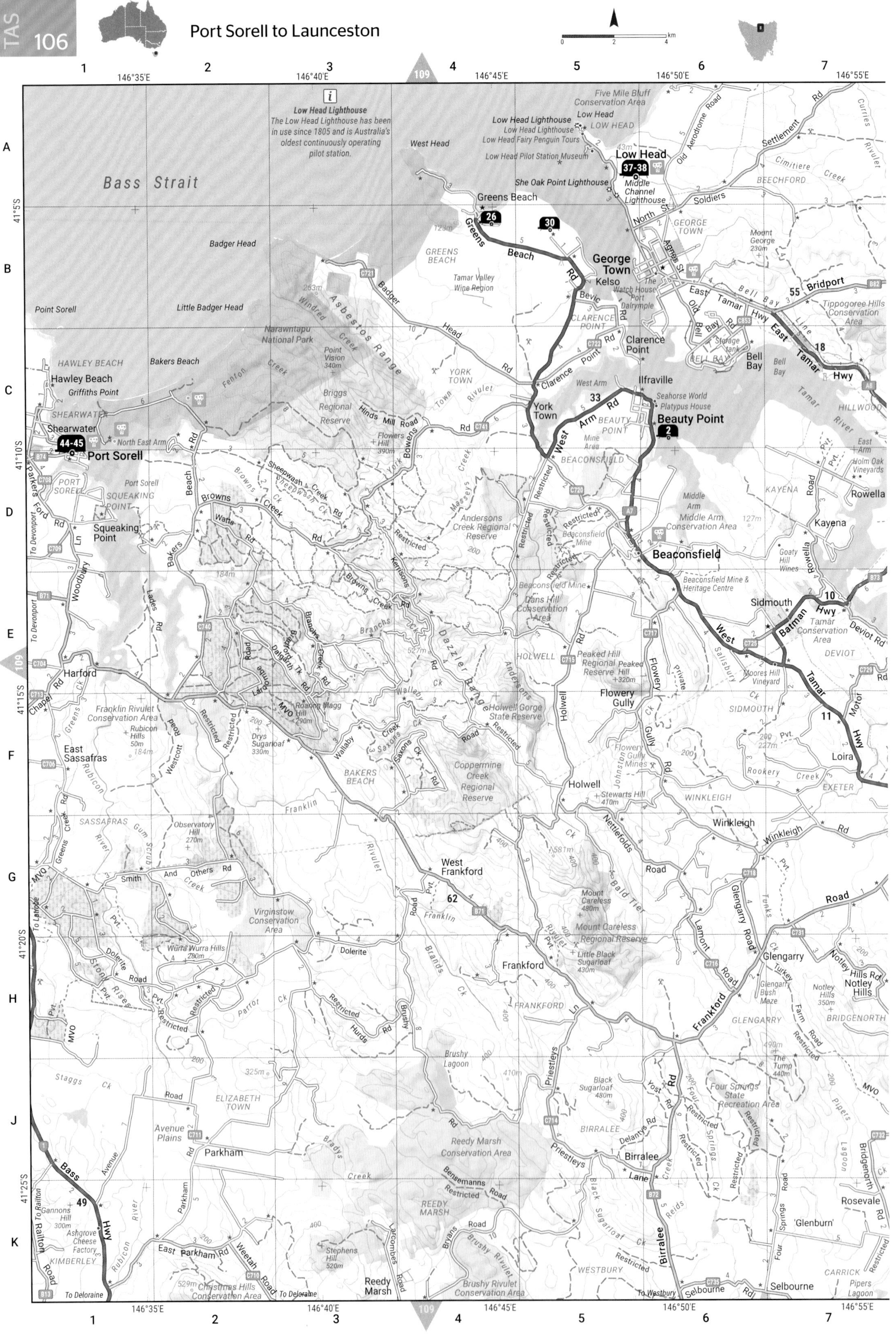

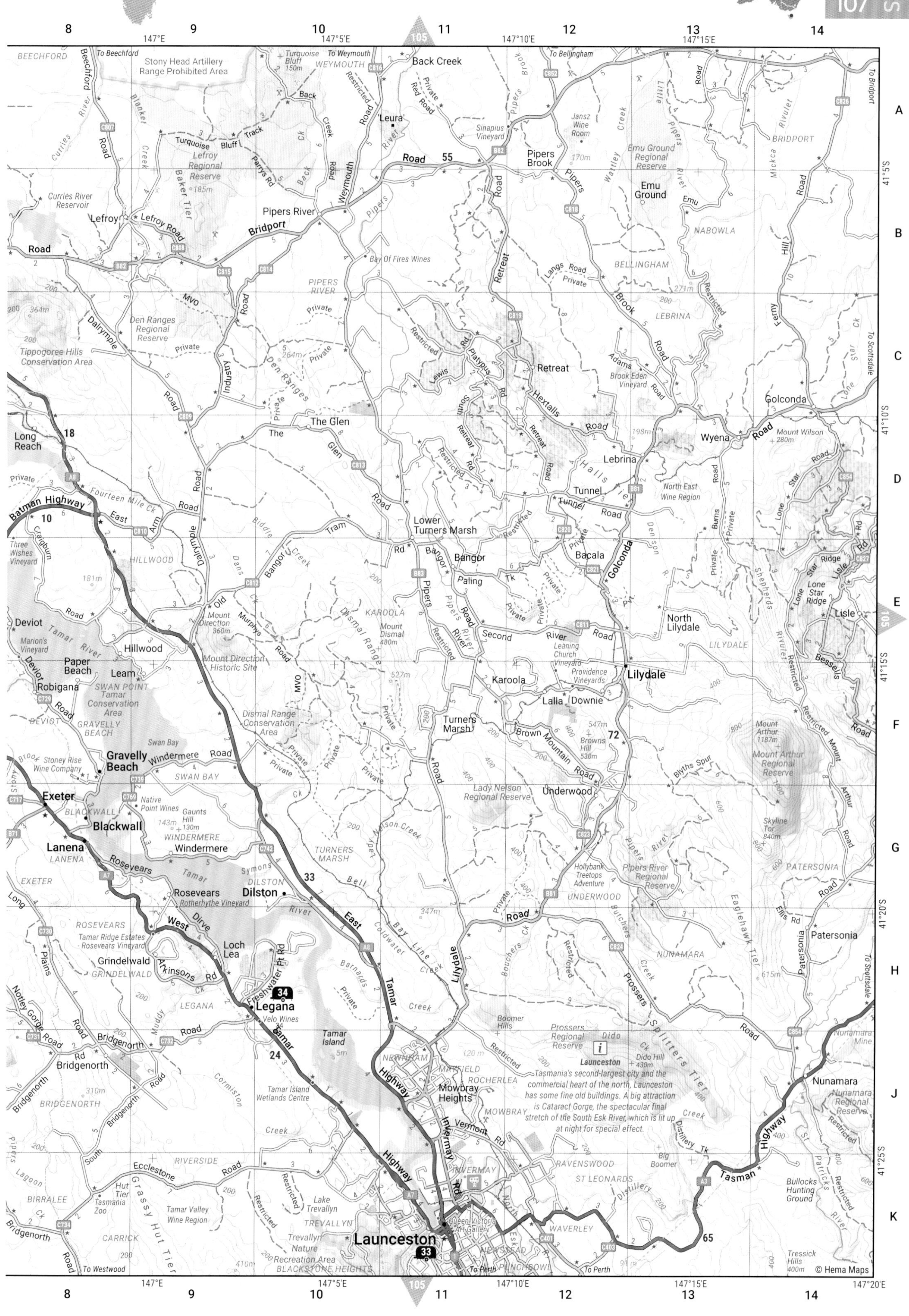

Stony Head Artillery Range Prohibited Area
To Beechford
To Weymouth
To Bellingham
To Bridport
Turquoise Bluff 150m
WEYMOUTH
Back Creek
Leura
Jansz Wine Room
Sinapius Vineyard
Pipers Brook
Emu Ground Regional Reserve
Emu Ground
BRIDPORT
Turquoise Bluff Track
Lefroy Regional Reserve
Curries River Reservoir
Lefroy
Pipers River
Bridport Road
NABOWLA
BELLINGHAM
Bay Of Fires Wines
PIPERS RIVER
Den Ranges Regional Reserve
Tippogoree Hills Conservation Area
LEBRINA
To Scottsdale
Retreat
Brook Eden Vineyard
Golconda
Long Reach
The Glen
Wyena
Mount Wilson 280m
Lebrina
North East Wine Region
Batman Highway
Tunnel
Three Wishes Vineyard
HILLWOOD
Lower Turners Marsh
Bangor
Bacala
Ridge
Lone Star Ridge
Lisle
KAROOLA
Mount Dismal 480m
Deviot
Marion's Vineyard
Mount Direction 360m
Mount Direction Historic Site
North Lilydale
LILYDALE
Hillwood
Paper Beach
Leam
Robigana
SWAN POINT
Tamar Conservation Area
Leaning Church Vineyard
Providence Vineyards
Lilydale
Karoola
Lalla
Downie
DEVIOT
GRAVELLY BEACH
Dismal Range Conservation Area
Turners Marsh
Browns Hill 530m
Mount Arthur 1187m
Mount Arthur Regional Reserve
Swan Bay
Stoney Rise Wine Company
Gravelly Beach
SWAN BAY
Lady Nelson Regional Reserve
Underwood
Exeter
BLACKWALL
Native Point Wines
Gaunts Hill 130m
Blackwall
Skyline Tor 840m
Lanena
LANENA
WINDERMERE
Windermere
TURNERS MARSH
EXETER
DILSTON
Hollybank Treetops Adventure
Pipers River Regional Reserve
PATERSONIA
Rosevears
Rotherhythe Vineyard
Dilston
UNDERWOOD
ROSEVEARS
Tamar Ridge Estates - Rosevears Vineyard
Loch Lea
Paterson
NUNAMARA
Grindelwald
GRINDELWALD
LEGANA
Legana
Velo Wines
Boomer Hills
Prossers Regional Reserve
Nunamara Mine
Bridgenorth
Tamar Island
NEWNHAM
MAYFIELD
ROCHERLEA
Launceston
Dido Hill 430m
Tasmania's second-largest city and the commercial heart of the north, Launceston has some fine old buildings. A big attraction is Cataract Gorge, the spectacular final stretch of the South Esk River, which is lit up at night for special effect.
Nunamara
Nunamara Regional Reserve
Tamar Island Wetlands Centre
Mowbray Heights
MOWBRAY
BRIDGENORTH
RIVERSIDE
Big Boomer
RAVENSWOOD
INVERMAY
ST LEONARDS
Bullocks Hunting Ground
Hut Tier Tasmania Zoo
Tamar Valley Wine Region
Lake Trevallyn
TREVALLYN
BIRRALEE
CARRICK
WAVERLEY
Trevallyn Nature Recreation Area
BLACKSTONE HEIGHTS
Launceston
Queen Victoria Art Gallery
NEWSTEAD
PUNCHBOWL
Tressick Hills 400m
To Westwood
To Perth
© Hema Maps

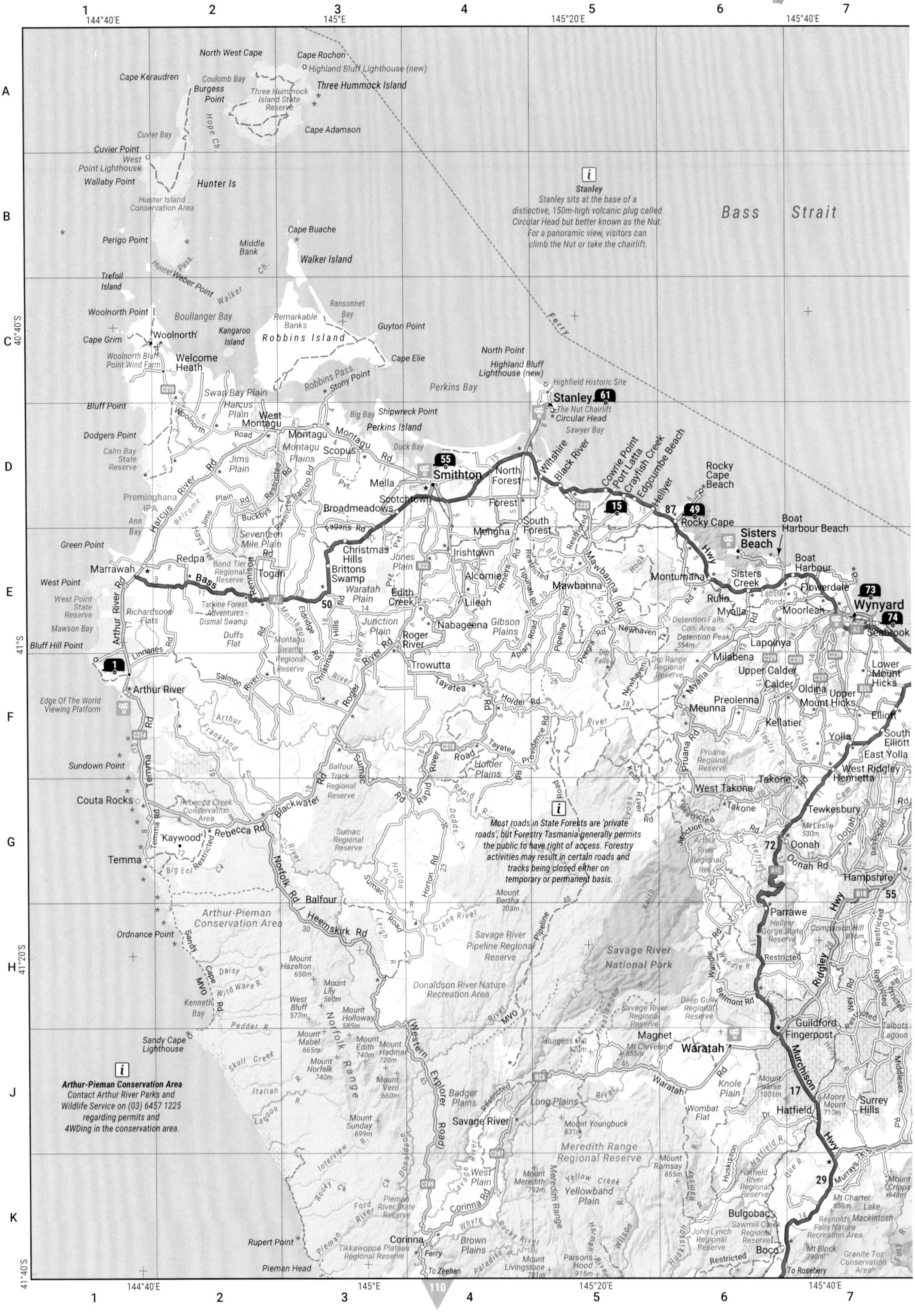

Three Hummock Island to Cressy

Stanley
Stanley sits at the base of a distinctive, 150m-high volcanic plug called Circular Head but better known as the Nut. For a panoramic view, visitors can climb the Nut or take the chairlift.

Most roads in State Forests are 'private roads', but Forestry Tasmania generally permits the public to have right of access. Forestry activities may result in certain roads and tracks being closed either on temporary or permanent basis.

Arthur-Pieman Conservation Area
Contact Arthur River Parks and Wildlife Service on (03) 6457 1225 regarding permits and 4WDing in the conservation area.

110

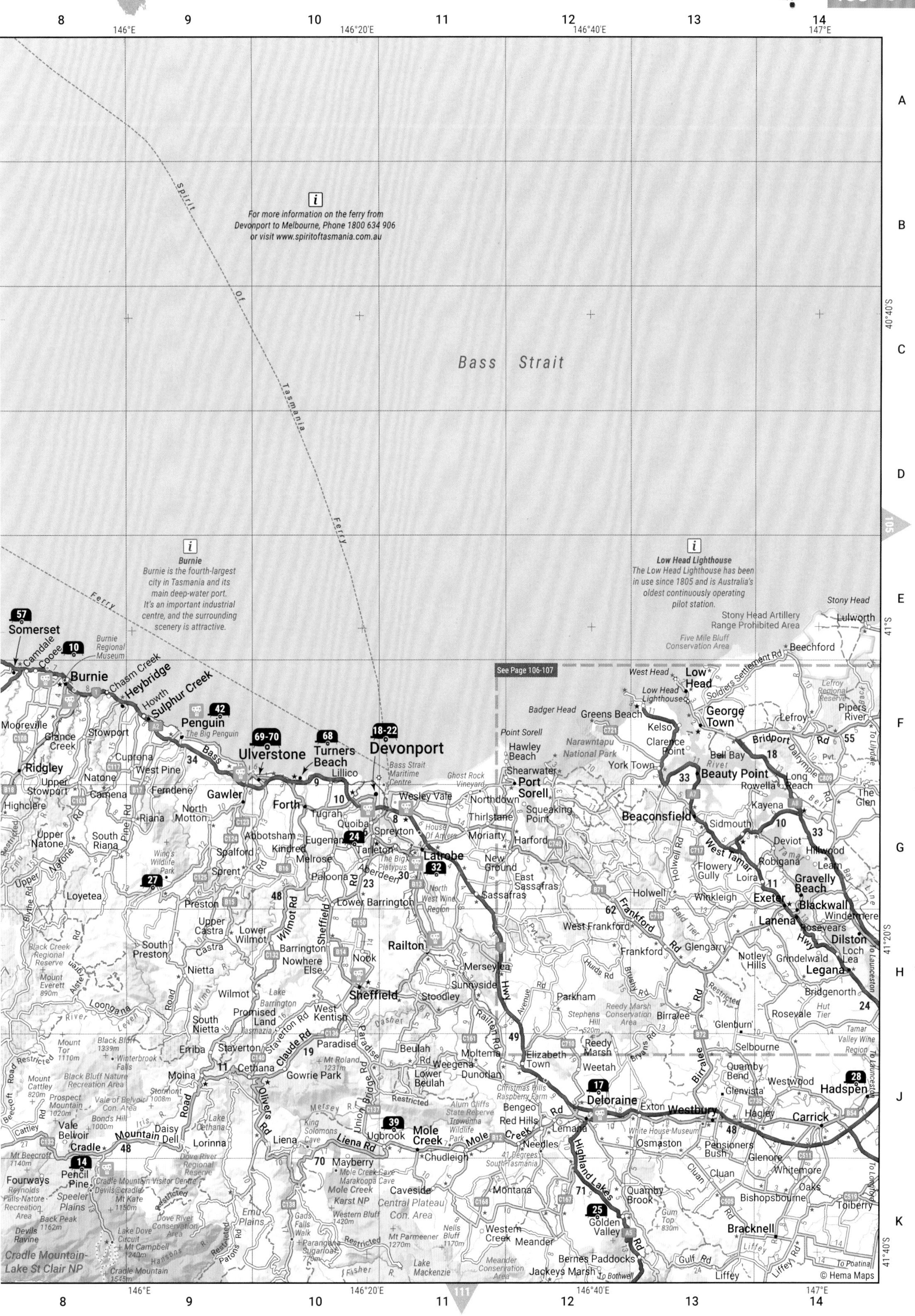
For more information on the ferry from Devonport to Melbourne, Phone 1800 634 906 or visit www.spiritoftasmania.com.au
Bass Strait
Spirit of Tasmania Ferry
Burnie
Burnie is the fourth-largest city in Tasmania and its main deep-water port. It's an important industrial centre, and the surrounding scenery is attractive.
Low Head Lighthouse
The Low Head Lighthouse has been in use since 1805 and is Australia's oldest continuously operating pilot station.
See Page 106-107
Somerset
Burnie
Devonport
Ulverstone
Penguin
Latrobe
Deloraine
Westbury
Sheffield
Railton
Port Sorell
Beaconsfield
George Town
Low Head
Exeter
Legana
Hadspen
Carrick
Cradle Mountain-Lake St Clair NP
© Hema Maps

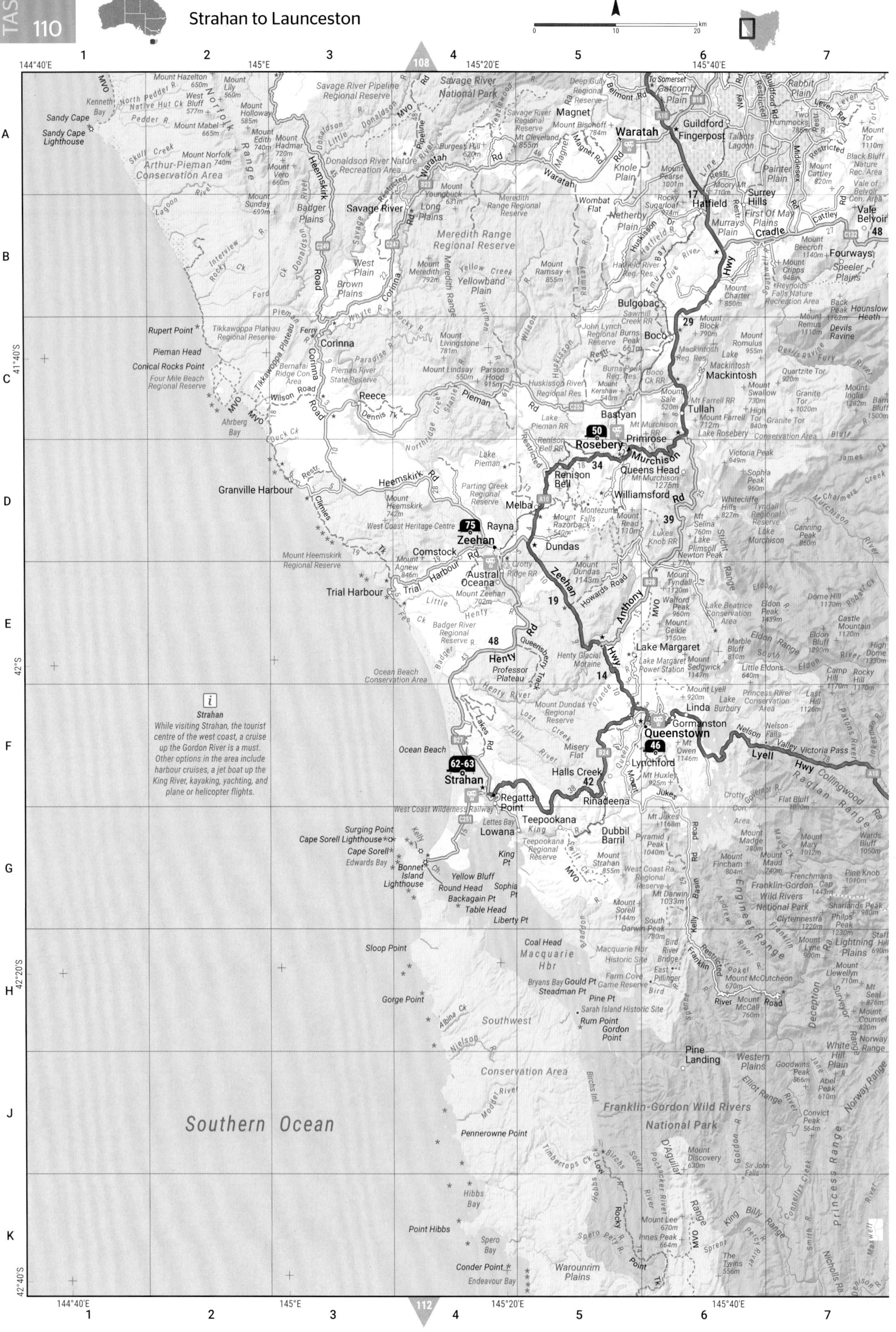
108
112
144°40'E
145°E
145°20'E
145°40'E
41°40'S
42°S
42°20'S
42°40'S
Strahan
While visiting Strahan, the tourist centre of the west coast, a cruise up the Gordon River is a must. Other options in the area include harbour cruises, a jet boat up the King River, kayaking, yachting, and plane or helicopter flights.
Southern Ocean
Sandy Cape
Sandy Cape Lighthouse
Mount Hazelton 650m
Mount Lily 560m
West Bluff 577m
Mount Holloway 585m
Mount Mabel 665m
Mount Edith 740m
Mount Hadmar 720m
Mount Norfolk 740m
Norfolk Range
Arthur-Pieman Conservation Area
Mount Vero 660m
Mount Sunday 699m
Savage River Pipeline Regional Reserve
Savage River National Park
Donaldson River Nature Recreation Area
Savage River
Badger Plains
Long Plains
Mount Youngbuck 631m
Burgess Hill 620m
Meredith Range Regional Reserve
West Plain
Brown Plains
Mount Meredith 792m
Yellowband Plain
Mount Ramsay 855m
Magnet
Mount Bischoff 784m
Waratah
Mt Cleveland 855m
Savage River Regional Reserve
Knole Plain
Wombat Flat
Netherby Plain
Rocky Sugarloaf 974m
Mount Pearse 1001m
Hatfield River Reg. Res.
Deep Gully Regional Reserve
Guildford
Fingerpost
Talbots Lagoon
Hatfield
Moory Mt 710m
Surrey Hills
First Of May Plains
Murrays Plain
Cradle
Rabbit Plain
Two Hummocks 788m
Mount Tor 1110m
Black Bluff Nature Rec. Area
Painter Plain
Mount Cattley 820m
Vale of Belvoir Con. Area
Vale Belvoir
Mount Beecroft 1140m
Fourways
Speeler Plains
Mount Cripps 948m
Reynolds Falls Nature Recreation Area
Mount Charter 850m
Back Peak 1162m
Hounslow Heath
Mount Remus 1110m
Devils Ravine
Mount Romulus 955m
Bulgobac
Boco
Mount Block 790m
John Lynch Regional Reserve
Burns Peak 661m
Mackintosh Reg. Res.
Mackintosh Lake
Mackintosh
Quartzite Tor 920m
Mount Swallow 730m
Granite Tor 1020m
Mount Inglis 1282m
Tullah
Mt Farrell RR
Mount Farrell 712m
High Tor 840m
Granite Tor Conservation Area
Lake Rosebery
Mount Sale 520m
Mount Kershaw 540m
Burns Peak Reg. Res.
Boco Ck RR
Huskisson River Regional Res
Rupert Point
Tikkawoppa Plateau Regional Reserve
Pieman Head
Conical Rocks Point
Four Mile Beach Regional Reserve
Corinna
Ferry
Bernafai Ridge Con Area
Pieman River State Reserve
Reece
Mount Livingstone 781m
Mount Lindsay 550m
Parsons Hood 915m
Lake Pieman RR
Ahrberg Bay
Bastyan
Rosebery
Primrose
Mt Murchison RR
Renison Bell RR
Renison Bell
Queens Head
Mt Murchison 1275m
Williamsford
Victoria Peak 949m
Sophia Peak 960m
Whitecliffe Hills 827m
Tyndall Regional Reserve
Lake Murchison
Canning Peak 860m
Granville Harbour
Lake Pieman
Parting Creek Regional Reserve
Mount Heemskirk 742m
Melba
Montezuma Falls
Mount Razorback 540m
Mount Read 1110m
Lukes Knob RR
Mt Selina 760m
Lake Plimsoll
Newton Peak 770m
West Coast Heritage Centre
Zeehan
Rayna
Dundas
Comstock
Mount Agnew 846m
Austral
Oceana
Crotty Ridge RR
Mount Dundas 1143m
Mount Tyndall 1120m
Mount Heemskirk Regional Reserve
Trial Harbour
Mount Zeehan 702m
Walford Peak 960m
Mount Geikie 1150m
Lake Beatrice Conservation Area
Eldon Peak 1439m
Dome Hill 1170m
Castle Mountain 1120m
Badger River Regional Reserve
Henty
Professor Plateau
Henty Glacial Moraine
Lake Margaret
Lake Margaret Power Station
Mount Sedgwick 1147m
Marble Bluff 810m
Eldon Bluff 1290m
Little Eldons 640m
High Dome 1330m
Camp Hill 1170m
Rocky Hill 1170m
Ocean Beach Conservation Area
Mount Lyell 920m
Lake Burbury
Princess River Conservation Area
Last Hill 1126m
Mount Dundas Regional Reserve
Linda
Gormanston
Queenstown
Nelson Falls
Victoria Pass
Ocean Beach
Misery Flat
Mt Owen 1146m
Lynchford
Halls Creek
Mt Huxley 925m
Strahan
Regatta Point
Rinadeena
Jukes
Flat Bluff 1030m
West Coast Wilderness Railway
Teepookana
Lettes Bay
Lowana
Dubbil Barril
Teepookana Regional Reserve
Mt Jukes 1168m
Pyramid Peak 1040m
Mount Madge 780m
Mount Mary 1012m
Wards Bluff 1050m
Surging Point
Cape Sorell Lighthouse
Cape Sorell
Edwards Bay
Bonnet Island Lighthouse
King Pt
Mount Strahan 855m
West Coast Ra. Regional Reserve
Mount Fincham 804m
Mount Maud 740m
Frenchmans Cap 1443m
Pine Knob 1010m
Yellow Bluff
Round Head
Sophia Pt
Backagain Pt
Table Head
Liberty Pt
Mt Darwin 1033m
Mount Sorell 1144m
Franklin-Gordon Wild Rivers National Park
Sharlands Peak 980m
Clytemnestra 1220m
Philps Peak 1230m
South Darwin Peak 780m
Coal Head
Macquarie Hbr
Macquarie Hbr Historic Site
Bird River Bridge
Engineer Range
Sloop Point
East Pillinger
Farm Cove Game Reserve
Mount Lyne 900m
Lightning Plains
Mount Llewellyn 710m
Bryans Bay
Gould Pt
Steadman Pt
Pine Pt
Mount McCutcheon 670m
Mount McCall 760m
Mt Seal 876m
Gorge Point
Sarah Island Historic Site
Rum Point
Gordon Point
Southwest
Mount Counsel 820m
White Hill Plain
Norway Range
Pine Landing
Western Plains
Goodwins Peak 566m
Abel Peak 610m
Conservation Area
Franklin-Gordon Wild Rivers
National Park
Convict Peak 564m
Pennerowne Point
Mount Discovery 630m
Sir John Falls
Princess Range
Hibbs Bay
Point Hibbs
Mount Lee 670m
Innes Peak 664m
Spero Bay
The Twins 556m
Conder Point
Endeavour Bay
Waraunrim Plains
Lyell Hwy
Murchison Hwy
Zeehan Hwy
Anthony Rd
Heemskirk Rd
Pieman Rd
Corinna Road
Heemskirk Road
Trial Harbour Rd
Queensberry Track
Lakes Rd
Howards Road
Kelly Basin Rd
Mount Road
Raglan Range
Collingwood Range
Deception Range
Elliot Range
D'Aguilar Range
Norway Range
Nelson Valley
Cradle Hwy
Waratah Rd
Magnet Rd
Savage River Rd
Sticht Range
Eldon Range
Meredith Range
Henty River
Little Henty R
King River
Macquarie Harbour

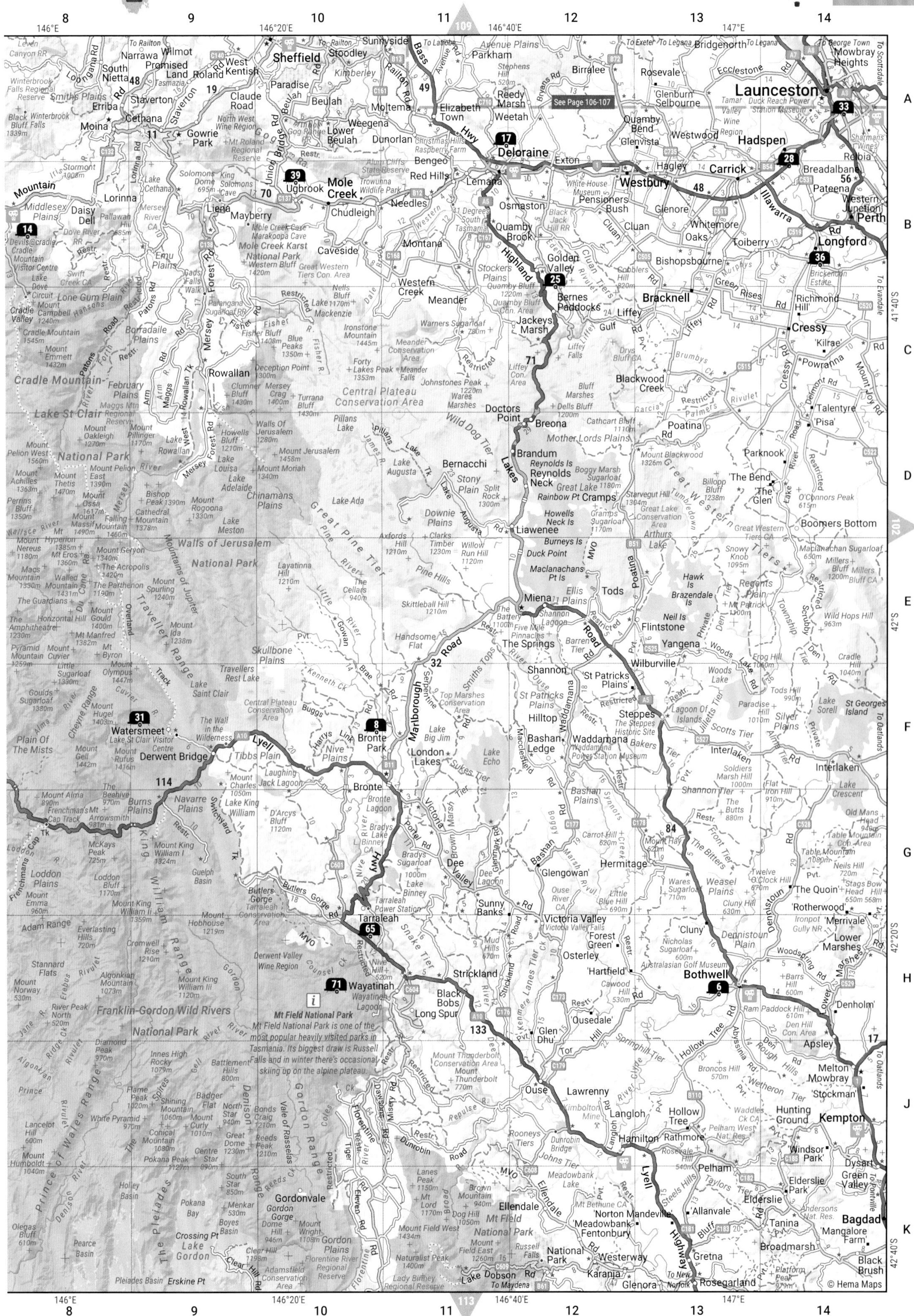
Launceston
Sheffield
Deloraine
Westbury
Hadspen
Carrick
Longford
Perth
Cressy
Bracknell
Mole Creek
Miena
Bothwell
Hamilton
Ouse
Bronte Park
Tarraleah
Wayatinah
Derwent Bridge
Kempton
Bagdad
Central Plateau Conservation Area
Walls of Jerusalem National Park
Cradle Mountain-Lake St Clair National Park
Franklin-Gordon Wild Rivers National Park
Mt Field National Park
Mt Field National Park is one of the most popular heavily visited parks in Tasmania. Its biggest draw is Russell Falls and in winter there's occasional skiing up on the alpine plateau.
See Page 106-107
© Hema Maps

Southern Tasmania

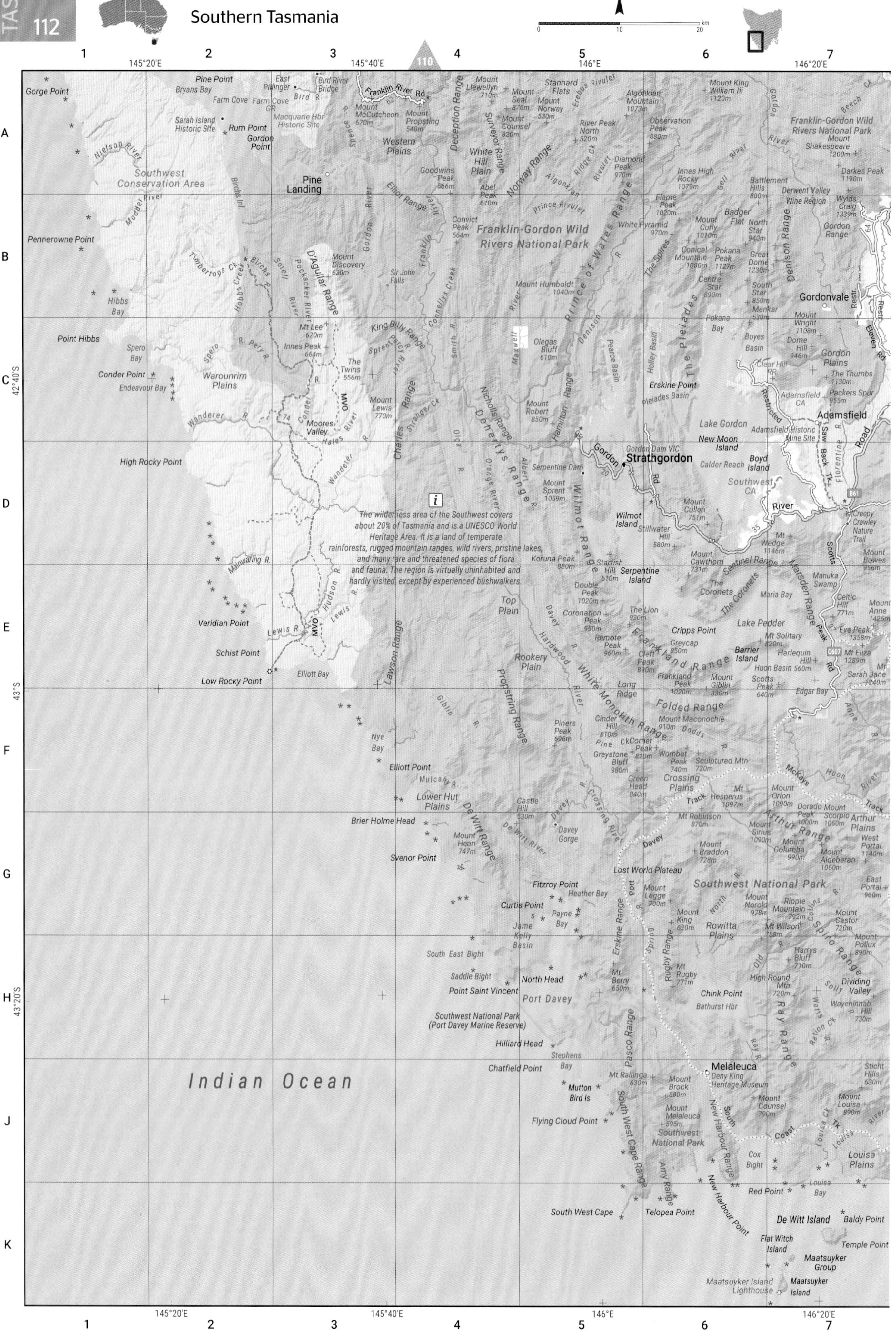

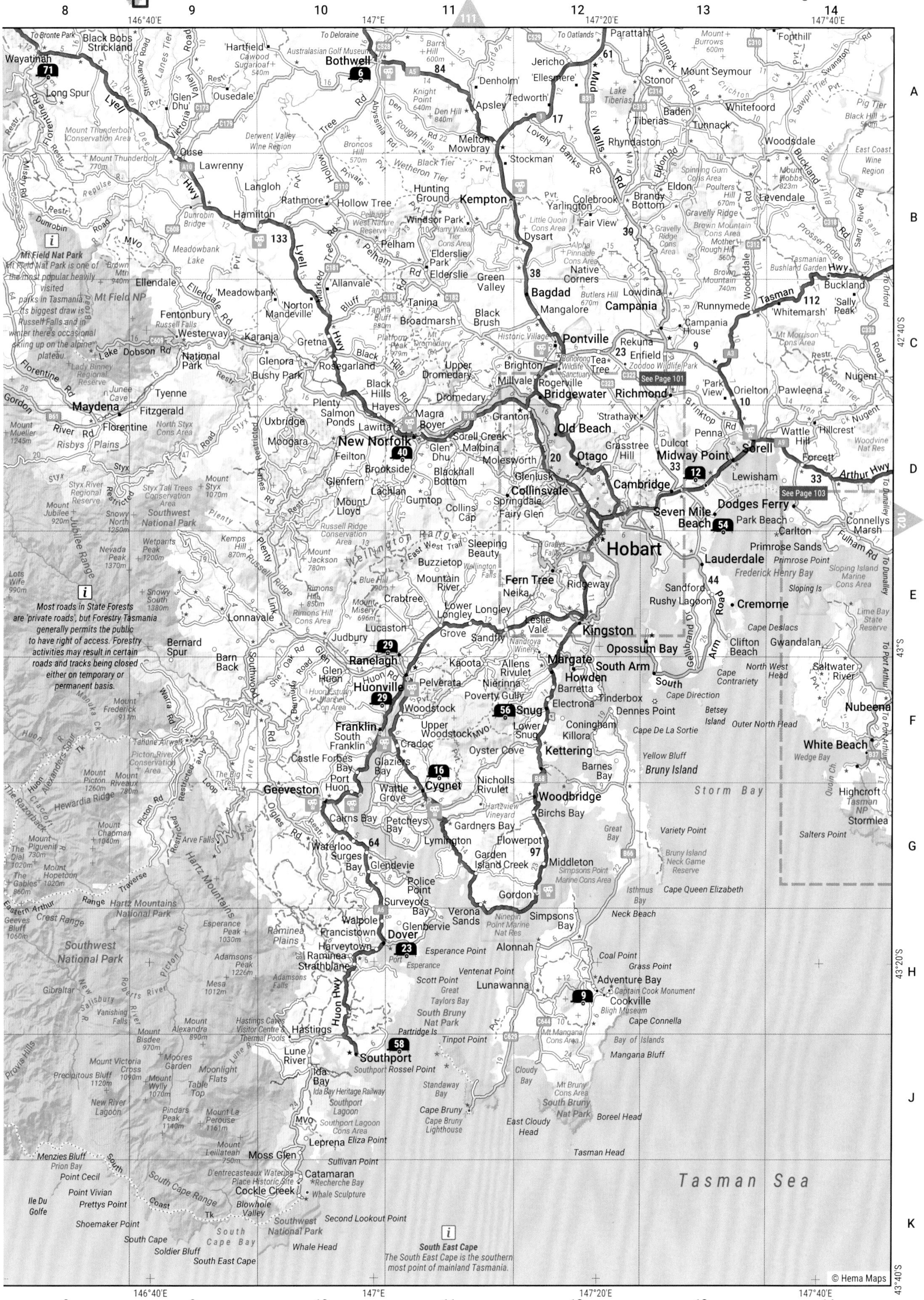
8
9
10
11
12
13
14
146°40'E
147°E
147°20'E
147°40'E
A
B
C
D
E
F
G
H
J
K
42°40'S
43°S
43°20'S
43°40'S
111
102
To Bronte Park
To Deloraine
To Oatlands
Wayatinah
71
Black Bobs
Strickland
Long Spur
Lyell
Ouse
Lawrenny
Hamilton
133
Bothwell
6
84
Jericho
61
Parattah
Stonor
Mount Seymour
Baden
Whitefoord
Tiberias
Tunnack
Rhyndaston
Woodsdale
Apsley
Melton Mowbray
17
Kempton
Colebrook
Eldon
Levendale
Langloh
Hollow Tree
Pelham
Elderslie
Dysart
38
Bagdad
Mangalore
Campania
Lowdina
Runnymede
Buckland
112
Mt Field Nat Park
Mt Field Nat Park is one of the most popular heavily visited parks in Tasmania. Its biggest draw is Russell Falls and in winter there's occasional skiing up on the alpine plateau.
Mt Field NP
Ellendale
Fentonbury
Westerway
National Park
Karanja
Gretna
Glenora
Bushy Park
Rosegarland
Maydena
Fitzgerald
Tyenne
Florentine
Pontville
Brighton
Bridgewater
Richmond
Tea Tree
Rogerville
Enfield
23
9
Orielton
Pawleena
Nugent
10
Plenty
Uxbridge
Moogara
New Norfolk
40
Magra
Boyer
Lawitta
Hayes
Feilton
Glenfern
Lachlan
Mount Lloyd
Molesworth
Granton
Old Beach
20
Otago
Midway Point
12
Sorell
Forcett
Lewisham
33
Cambridge
Collinsvale
Glenlusk
Seven Mile Beach
54
Dodges Ferry
Park Beach
Carlton
Connellys Marsh
Hobart
Lauderdale
44
Primrose Sands
Sandford
Rushy Lagoon
Cremorne
Frederick Henry Bay
Fern Tree
Neika
Ridgeway
Kingston
Opossum Bay
Mountain River
Crabtree
Lucaston
Judbury
29
Ranelagh
Huonville
Glen Huon
Grove
Longley
Sandfly
Leslie Vale
Margate
South Arm
Howden
Barretta
Allens Rivulet
Kaoota
Pelverata
Nierinna
Poverty Gully
Electrona
Tinderbox
Dennes Point
56
Snug
Woodstock
Franklin
South Franklin
Cradoc
Upper Woodstock
Lower Snug
Oyster Cove
Coningham
Kettering
Barnes Bay
Nubeena
White Beach
Most roads in State Forests are 'private roads', but Forestry Tasmania generally permits the public to have right of access. Forestry activities may result in certain roads and tracks being closed either on temporary or permanent basis.
Lonnavale
Bernard Spur
Barn Back
Castle Forbes Bay
Port Huon
Geeveston
Glaziers Bay
16
Cygnet
Wattle Grove
Nicholls Rivulet
Woodbridge
Cairns Bay
Petcheys Bay
Lymington
Gardners Bay
Birchs Bay
Flowerpot
97
Middleton
Garden Island Creek
Gordon
64
Waterloo
Surges Bay
Glendevie
Police Point
Surveyors Bay
Verona Sands
Simpsons Bay
Storm Bay
Bruny Island
Highcroft
Stormlea
Walpole
Francistown
Dover
23
Glenbervie
Harveytown
Strathblane
Esperance Point
Alonnah
Lunawanna
Adventure Bay
Cookville
9
Hartz Mountains National Park
Southwest National Park
Huon Hwy
Hastings
Lune River
Southport
58
Ida Bay
Leprena
Moss Glen
Catamaran
Cockle Creek
Cape Bruny
South Bruny Nat Park
Tasman Sea
South Cape Bay
South East Cape
South East Cape
The South East Cape is the southern most point of mainland Tasmania.
See Page 101
See Page 103
© Hema Maps

King Island

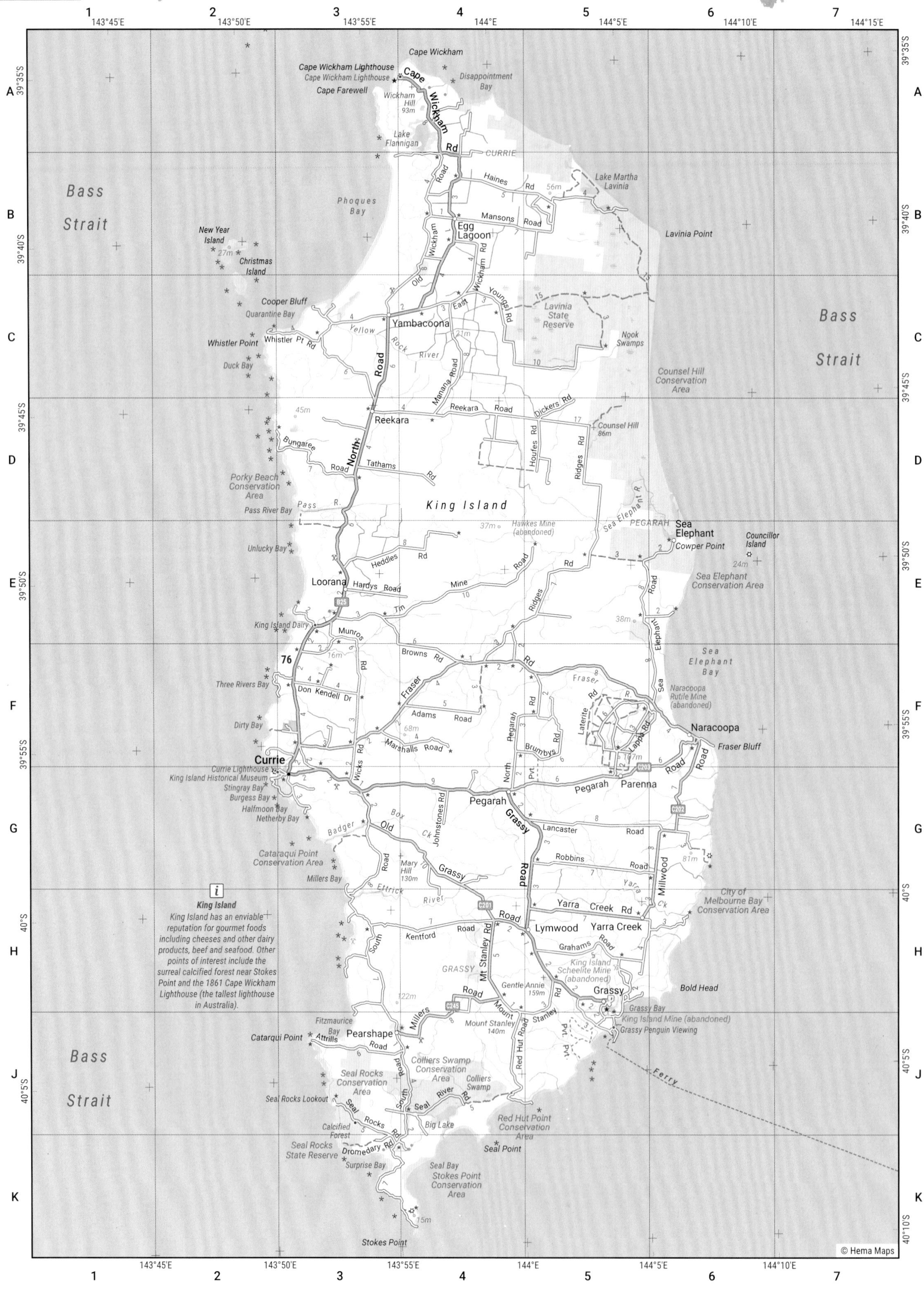

1 2 3 4 5 6 7

143°45'E 143°50'E 143°55'E 144°E 144°5'E 144°10'E 144°15'E

39°35'S 39°40'S 39°45'S 39°50'S 39°55'S 40°S 40°5'S 40°10'S

A B C D E F G H J K

Bass Strait

Cape Wickham
Cape Wickham Lighthouse
Cape Wickham Lighthouse
Cape Farewell
Disappointment Bay
Wickham Hill 93m
Lake Flannigan
Cape Wickham Rd
CURRIE
Haines Rd
Lake Martha Lavinia
56m
Phoques Bay
Mansons Road
Egg Lagoon
Lavinia Point
New Year Island
27m
Christmas Island
Old Wickham Rd
Wickham Rd
Youngs Rd
Lavinia State Reserve
Cooper Bluff
Quarantine Bay
East Rd
Yambacoona
Whistler Point
Whistler Pt Rd
Yellow Rock River
21m
Nook Swamps
Duck Bay
Manana Road
Counsel Hill Conservation Area
Reekara Road
Dickers Rd
Reekara
45m
Counsel Hill 86m
Bungaree Road
North Road
Tathams Rd
Houfes Rd
Ridges Rd
Porky Beach Conservation Area
Pass River Bay
Pass R.
King Island
37m
Hawkes Mine (abandoned)
Sea Elephant R
PEGARAH
Sea Elephant
Cowper Point
Councillor Island
24m
Unlucky Bay
Heddles Rd
Mine Road
Loorana
Hardys Road
Sea Elephant Conservation Area
B25
Tin Mine Rd
Ridges Rd
King Island Dairy
38m
Munros Rd
16m
Browns Rd
76
Sea Elephant Bay
Three Rivers Bay
Don Kendell Dr
Fraser Rd
Fraser R.
Laterite Rd
Naracoopa Rutile Mine (abandoned)
Adams Road
Pegarah Rd
Dirty Bay
68m
Lappa Rd
Naracoopa
Fraser Bluff
Marshalls Road
Brumbys Rd
107m
Currie
Currie Lighthouse
King Island Historical Museum
Stingray Bay
Burgess Bay
Halfmoon Bay
Netherby Bay
Wicks Rd
North Pegarah Pvt
C203
Pegarah Road
Parenna
Johnstones Rd
Pegarah
C202
Badger Box Ck
Old Grassy Road
Grassy Road
Lancaster Road
Cataraqui Point Conservation Area
Millers Bay
Mary Hill 130m
Robbins Road
Millwood Rd
81m
Yarra Ck
Ettrick River
C201
Yarra Creek Rd
City of Melbourne Bay Conservation Area
Kentford Road
Mt Stanley Rd
Lymwood
Yarra Creek
Grahams Road
South Road
GRASSY
King Island Scheelite Mine (abandoned)
Gentle Annie 159m
Grassy
Bold Head
122m
C243
Millers Road
Mount Stanley 140m
Stanley Rd
Grassy Bay
King Island Mine (abandoned)
Grassy Penguin Viewing
Fitzmaurice Bay
Cataraqui Point
Attrills
Pearshape Road
Red Hut Road
Pvt.
Colliers Swamp Conservation Area
Colliers Swamp
Ferry
Seal Rocks Conservation Area
Seal Rocks Lookout
South Road
Seal River Rd
Big Lake
Red Hut Point Conservation Area
Calcified Forest
Seal Rocks Rd
Seal Rocks State Reserve
Dromedary Rd
Seal Point
Surprise Bay
Seal Bay
Stokes Point Conservation Area
15m
Stokes Point

King Island

King Island has an enviable reputation for gourmet foods including cheeses and other dairy products, beef and seafood. Other points of interest include the surreal calcified forest near Stokes Point and the 1861 Cape Wickham Lighthouse (the tallest lighthouse in Australia).

0 5 10 km

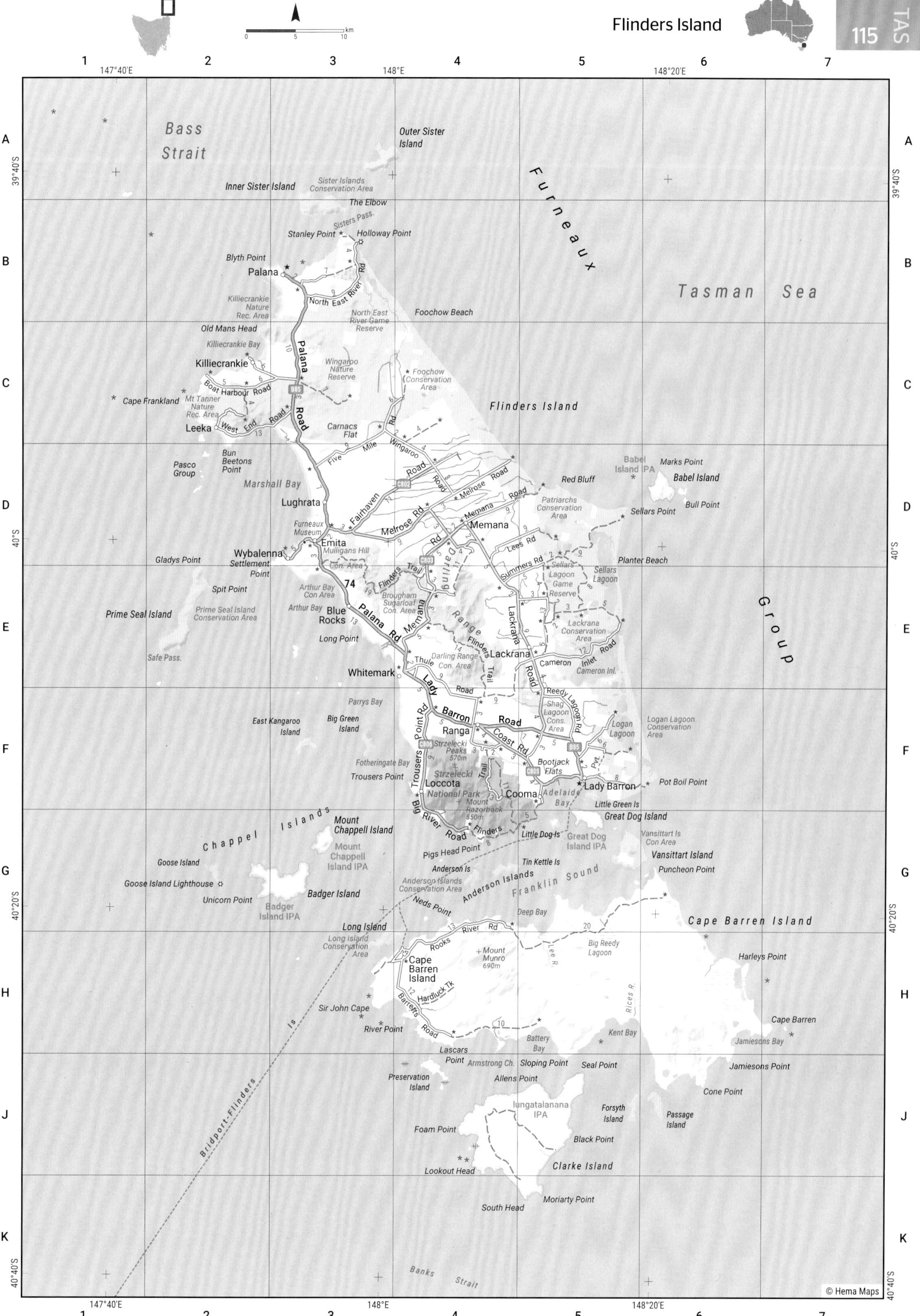
Bass Strait
Furneaux Group
Tasman Sea
Outer Sister Island
Inner Sister Island
Sister Islands Conservation Area
The Elbow
Sisters Pass.
Stanley Point
Holloway Point
Blyth Point
Palana
North East River Rd
North East River Game Reserve
Killiecrankie Nature Rec. Area
Foochow Beach
Old Mans Head
Killiecrankie Bay
Killiecrankie
Palana Road
Wingaroo Nature Reserve
Foochow Conservation Area
Boat Harbour Road
Cape Frankland
Mt Tanner Nature Rec. Area
Flinders Island
Leeka
West End Road
Carnacs Flat
Five Mile Road
Wingaroo Road
Bun Beetons Point
Pasco Group
Marshall Bay
Babel Island IPA
Marks Point
Babel Island
Red Bluff
Fairhaven Road
Melrose Road
Memana Road
Patriarchs Conservation Area
Bull Point
Sellars Point
Lughrata
Furneaux Museum
Emita
Mulligans Hill
Memana
Lees Rd
Wybalenna Settlement Point
Gladys Point
Con. Area
Flinders Trail
Darling Rd
Summers Rd
Sellars Lagoon Game Reserve
Sellars Lagoon
Planter Beach
Spit Point
Arthur Bay Con Area
Arthur Bay
Brougham Sugarloaf Con. Area
Darling Range
Lackrana Road
Lackrana Conservation Area
Prime Seal Island
Prime Seal Island Conservation Area
Blue Rocks
Palana Rd
Memana Rd
Long Point
Flinders Trail
Lackrana
Safe Pass.
Darling Range Con. Area
Thule Road
Cameron Inlet Road
Cameron Inl.
Whitemark
Lady Barron Road
Reedy Lagoon Rd
Parrys Bay
Shag Lagoon Cons. Area
Logan Lagoon Conservation Area
East Kangaroo Island
Big Green Island
Trousers Point Rd
Ranga
Coast Rd
Logan Lagoon
Strzelecki Peaks 570m
Fotheringate Bay
Bootjack Flats
Trousers Point
Strzelecki National Park
Loccota
Cooma
Lady Barron
Pot Boil Point
Mount Razorback 550m
Adelaide Bay
Little Green Is
Great Dog Island
Chappel Islands
Mount Chappell Island
Big River Road
Flinders Trail
Little Dog Is
Great Dog Island IPA
Vansittart Is Con Area
Vansittart Island
Mount Chappell Island IPA
Pigs Head Point
Goose Island
Anderson Is
Tin Kettle Is
Puncheon Point
Goose Island Lighthouse
Anderson Islands Conservation Area
Anderson Islands
Franklin Sound
Badger Island
Unicorn Point
Badger Island IPA
Neds Point
Deep Bay
Long Island
Rooks River Rd
Cape Barren Island
Long Island Conservation Area
Mount Munro 690m
Big Reedy Lagoon
Lee R.
Harleys Point
Cape Barren Island
Hardluck Tk
Rices R.
Sir John Cape
Barrets Road
River Point
Cape Barren
Battery Bay
Kent Bay
Jamiesons Bay
Bridport-Flinders Is
Lascars Point
Armstrong Ch.
Sloping Point
Seal Point
Jamiesons Point
Preservation Island
Allens Point
Cone Point
lungatalanana IPA
Forsyth Island
Passage Island
Foam Point
Black Point
Clarke Island
Lookout Head
Moriarty Point
South Head
Banks Strait
147°40'E
148°E
148°20'E
39°40'S
40°S
40°20'S
40°40'S
© Hema Maps

Arthur River

1 Arthur River Cabin Park
1239 Arthur River Rd
03 6457 1212 HEMA 108 F1 41 02 04 S 144 40 23 E

Beauty Point

2 Beauty Point Tourist Park
36 West Arm Rd. 1 km N of PO
www.beautypointtouristpark.com.au
03 6383 4536 HEMA 106 C5 41 08 40 S 146 48 31 E

Bicheno

3 Bicheno Caravan Park
52 Burgess St. 200m SW of PO
www.bichenocaravanpark.com.au
03 6375 1280 HEMA 105 J14 41 52 39 S 148 18 10 E

4 Bicheno East Coast Holiday Park
4 Champ St. 300m W of PO
www.bichenoholidaypark.com.au
03 6375 1999 HEMA 105 J14 41 52 31 S 148 18 05 E

5 Seaview Holiday Park
29 Banksia St
www.seaviewbicheno.com.au
03 6375 1247 HEMA 105 J14 41 52 28 S 148 17 42 E

Bothwell

6 Bothwell Caravan Park
Market Place. Behind Information Centre
03 6259 5503 HEMA 111 H13 42 22 58 S 147 00 29 E

Bridport

7 Bridport Seaside Caravan Park
83 Bentley St
www.bridportcaravanpark.com.au/
03 6356 1227 HEMA 105 C9 40 59 39 S 147 23 24 E

Bronte Park

8 Bronte Park Village
378 Marlborough Highway
www.bronteparkhighlandcottages.com.au
0409 826 524 HEMA 111 F11 42 08 09 S 146 29 29 E

Bruny Island

9 Captain Cook Holiday Park
786 Adventure Bay Rd, Adventure Bay
www.captaincookpark.com
03 6293 1128 HEMA 113 H12 43 21 54 S 147 20 00 E

Burnie

10 Burnie Ocean View Motel & Holiday Caravan Park
253 Bass Hwy, Cooee. 3 km W of PO
www.burniebeachaccommodation.com.au
03 6431 1925 HEMA 104 C1 41 02 25 S 145 51 50 E

Cambridge

11 Barilla Holiday Park
75 Richmond Rd
www.barilla.com.au
03 6248 5453 HEMA 101 E7 42 49 56 S 147 26 39 E

12 Hobart Airport Tourist Park
2 Flight St
www.hobartairporttouristpark.com.au
1800441184 HEMA 102 G3 42 49 49 S 147 29 35 E

Coles Bay

13 BIG4 Iluka on Freycinet Holiday Park
Esplanade
www.ilukaholidaycentre.com.au
1800 786 512 HEMA 102 B7 42 07 20 S 148 17 05 E

Cradle Mountain

14 Discovery Holiday Parks Cradle Mountain
3832 Cradle Mountain Rd
www.discoveryholidayparks.com.au
03 6492 1395 HEMA 104 G1 41 34 48 S 145 56 16 E

Crayfish Creek

15 Crayfish Creek Van & Cabin Park
20049 Bass Hwy. 8 km NW of Rocky Cape PO
www.crayfishcreekecoaccommodation.com.au
03 6443 4228 HEMA 108 D5 40 51 29 S 145 23 56 E

Cygnet

16 Cygnet Caravan Park
Mary St
0418 532 160 HEMA 113 G11 43 09 22 S 147 04 29 E

Deloraine

17 Deloraine Apex Caravan Park
51 West Pde. 500m S of PO
03 6362 2345 HEMA 104 G5 41 31 39 S 146 39 10 E

Devonport

18 Abel Tasman Caravan Park
6 Wright St, East Devonport
www.abeltasmancaravanpark.com.au
03 6427 8794 HEMA 104 D4 41 10 26 S 146 22 14 E

19 Bay View Holiday Village
2 - 12 North Caroline St, East Devonport. 1 km N of PO
03 6427 0499 HEMA 104 D4 41 10 13 S 146 22 53 E

20 Devonport Holiday Village
20 - 24 North Caroline St, East Devonport. 1 km NE of PO
03 6427 8886 HEMA 104 D4 41 10 25 S 146 22 50 E

21 Discovery Holiday Parks Devonport
13-19 Tarleton St
www.discoveryholidayparks.com.au
03 6427 8418 HEMA 104 D4 41 10 18 S 146 22 29 E

22 Mersey Bluff Caravan Park
41 Bluff Rd
www.merseybluffcaravanpark.com.au/
03 6424 8655 HEMA 104 D3 41 09 44 S 146 21 17 E

Dover

23 Dover Beachside Tourist Park

27 Kent Beach Rd. 1 km SE of PO
www.dovertouristpark.com.au
03 6298 1301 HEMA 113 H11 43 18 55 S 147 01 28 E

Eugenana

24 Lakeside Tourist Caravan Park

76 Lakeside Rd
03 6427 2343 HEMA 104 D3 41 13 38 S 146 18 32 E

Golden Valley

25 Quamby Corner

Golden Valley Rd
www.quambycorner.com
03 6369 5156 HEMA 104 G5 41 37 35 S 146 42 38 E

Greens Beach

26 Greens Beach Caravan & Holiday Park

1774 Greens Beach Rd
www.greensbeachcaravanpark.com.au
03 6383 9222 HEMA 106 B4 41 05 08 S 146 44 49 E

Gunns Plains

27 Wings Wildlife Park

137 Winduss Rd
www.wingswildlife.com.au
03 6429 1151 HEMA 104 E2 41 15 49 S 146 02 43 E

Hadspen

28 Discovery Holiday Parks Hadspen

Cnr Main St & Meander Valley Hwy
www.discoveryholidayparks.com.au
03 6393 6391 HEMA 104 F7 41 30 12 S 147 04 10 E

Huonville

29 Huon Valley Caravan Park

177 Wilmot Rd
www.huonvalleycaravanpark.com.au
0438 304 383 HEMA 113 F11 43 01 01 S 147 02 26 E

Kelso

30 BIG4 Kelso Sands Holiday & Native Wildlife Park

86 Paranaple Rd
www.big4.com.au
03 6383 9130 HEMA 106 B5 41 05 42 S 146 46 41 E

Lake St Clair

31 Lake St Clair Lodge

Lake St Clair National Park. N of Derwent Bridge
www.lakestclairlodge.com.au
03 6289 1137 HEMA 111 F9 42 06 57 S 146 10 32 E

Latrobe

32 Latrobe Mersey River Caravan Park

1 River Rd, cnr Bells Pde
www.latrobemerseycaravan.com.au
03 6426 1944 HEMA 104 D4 41 13 58 S 146 24 09 E

Launceston

33 BIG4 Launceston Holiday Park

94 Glen Dhu St, South Launceston. 2 km S of PO
www.big4launceston.com.au
03 6344 2600 HEMA 105 F8 41 27 25 S 147 08 31 E

34 Launceston Holiday Park Legana

711 West Tamar Hwy, Legana
www.launcestonholidaypark.com.au
03 6330 1714 HEMA 107 J10 41 22 26 S 147 03 09 E

Little Swanport

35 Gumleaves Bush Holidays

Swanston Rd
www.gumleaves.com.au
03 6244 8147 HEMA 102 D5 42 21 01 S 147 54 24 E

Longford

36 Longford Riverside Caravan Park

2A Archer St. 300m NE of PO
www.longfordriversidecaravanpark.com
03 6391 1470 HEMA 105 G8 41 35 26 S 147 07 30 E

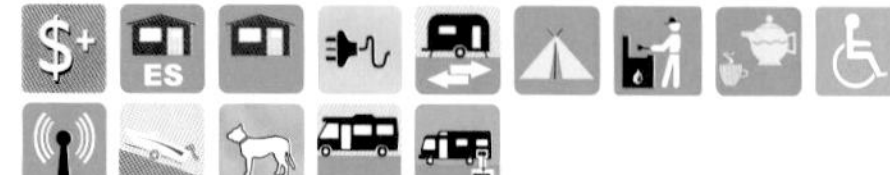

Low Head

37 East Beach Tourist Park

40 Gunn Pde, self contained prices available
03 6382 1000 HEMA 106 A5 41 03 52 S 146 48 19 E

38 Low Head Tourist Park

136 Low Head Rd
www.lowheadtouristpark.com.au
03 6382 1573 HEMA 106 B5 41 05 02 S 146 48 42 E

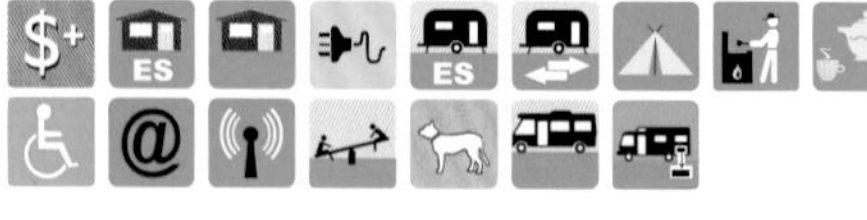

Mole Creek

39 Mole Creek Caravan Park

2 Union Bridge Rd
www.molecreek.net.au
03 6363 1150 HEMA 104 G4 41 33 04 S 146 21 37 E

New Norfolk

40 New Norfolk Caravan Park

1 The Esplanade. 1.5 km N of PO
www.newnorfolkcp.com/
03 6261 1268 HEMA 113 D11 42 46 33 S 147 03 58 E

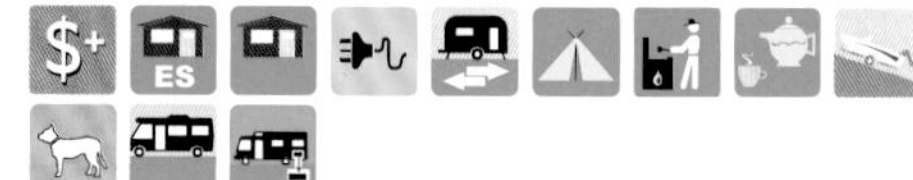

Orford

41 Orford Beachside Holiday Park

77 Tasman Hwy
www.orfordholidaypark.com.au
03 6257 1110 HEMA 102 E5 42 32 59 S 147 52 56 E

Penguin

42 Penguin Caravan Park

6 Johnsons Beach Rd. 1 km W of PO
www.penguincaravanpark.com.au
03 6437 2785 HEMA 104 D2 41 06 24 S 146 04 00 E

Port Arthur

43 BIG4 Port Arthur Holiday Park

Garden Point. 1 km N of PO
www.nrmaparksandresorts.com.au
03 6250 2340 HEMA 103 H5 43 07 57 S 147 51 29 E

Port Sorell

44 Moomba Holiday & Caravan Park

24 Kermode St. 500m E of PO
www.moombacaravanpark.com
03 6428 6140 HEMA 106 C1 41 09 50 S 146 33 00 E

45 Port Sorell Caravan Park

42 Meredith St
www.portsorellcaravanpark.com.au
03 6428 7267 HEMA 106 C1 41 09 53 S 146 33 18 E

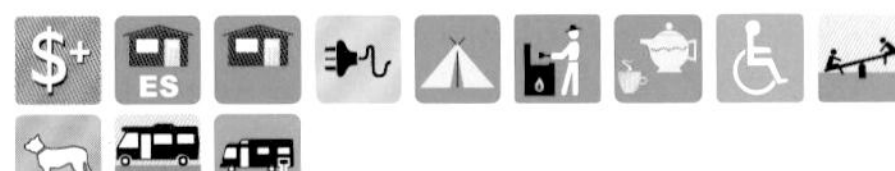

Queenstown

46 Queenstown Cabin & Tourist Park

17 Grafton St
www.queenstowncabinandtouristpark.com.au
03 6471 1332 HEMA 110 F5 42 05 19 S 145 32 42 E

Richmond

47 Richmond Caravan & Cabin Park

48 Middle Tea Tree Rd
www.richmondcaravanpark.com.au
03 6260 2192 HEMA 101 A7 42 44 16 S 147 25 32 E

Risdon Cove

48 Discovery Holiday Parks Hobart

673 East Derwent Hwy. No tents or soft floor camper trailers
www.discoveryholidayparks.com.au
03 6243 9879 HEMA 101 D4 42 48 48 S 147 20 13 E

Rocky Cape

49 Rocky Cape Tavern & Caravan Park

19375 Bass Hwy. Behind tavern
03 6443 4110 HEMA 108 D6 40 53 07 S 145 27 56 E

Rosebery

50 Rosebery Cabin & Tourist Park

1 Park Rd
www.westcoastcabins.com.au
03 6473 1366 HEMA 110 D5 41 46 36 S 145 32 07 E

Ross

51 Ross Caravan Park

Esplanade, via High St
www.rosscaravanpark.com.au
03 6330 1463 HEMA 102 A3 42 01 50 S 147 29 26 E

Scamander

52 Scamander Sanctuary Caravan Park

Winifred Dr
www.scamandersanctuary.com.au/
03 6372 5311 HEMA 105 F14 41 28 02 S 148 15 41 E

53 Scamander Tourist Park

70 - 88 Scamander Ave. 1 km N of PO
www.scamandertouristpark.com.au
03 6372 5121 HEMA 105 F14 41 27 05 S 148 15 54 E

Seven Mile Beach

54 Seven Mile Beach Cabin & Caravan Park

12 Aqua Place
www.hobartcaravanpark.com.au
03 6248 6469 HEMA 102 H3 42 51 15 S 147 30 30 E

Smithton

55 River Breeze Caravan & Cabin Park

69 - 77 Montagu Rd
www.kuiparks.com.au
03 6452 1181 HEMA 108 D4 40 50 26 S 145 06 33 E

Snug

56 Snug Beach Cabin & Caravan Park

35 Beach Rd. 1 km SE of PO
www.snugpark.com.au
03 6267 9138 HEMA 102 J1 43 03 49 S 147 15 40 E

Somerset

57 Somerset Beachside Cabin & Caravan Park

115 Bass Hwy. 1.7 km W of Cam River bridge
www.somersetbeachside.com.au
03 6435 2322 HEMA 104 C1 41 02 04 S 145 49 17 E

Southport

58 Southport Hotel & Caravan Park

8777 Huon Hwy
www.southportcaravanpark.com.au
03 6298 3144 HEMA 113 J10 43 25 29 S 146 58 22 E

St Helens

59 BIG4 St Helens Holiday Park

2 Penelope St. 1.5 km S of PO
www.big4.com.au
03 6376 1290 HEMA 105 E14 41 19 59 S 148 15 12 E

60 Hillcrest Tourist Park

10 Chimney Heights Rd. 7 km S of PO
www.hillcresttouristpark.com.au
03 6376 3298 HEMA 105 E14 41 19 31 S 148 17 47 E

Stanley

61 Stanley Cabin & Tourist Park

23a Wharf Rd. 200m SE of PO
www.stanleycabinpark.com.au
03 6458 1266 HEMA 108 D5 40 45 46 S 145 17 44 E

Strahan

62 Strahan Beach Tourist Park

1 Beach St
www.strahantouristpark.com.au
03 6471 7468 HEMA 110 F4 42 09 10 S 145 19 05 E

63 Strahan Holiday Retreat

8 Innes St West
www.strahanholidaypark.com.au
03 6471 7442 HEMA 110 F4 42 09 09 S 145 19 13 E

Swansea

64 Swansea Holiday Park

2 Bridge St. 1 km SE of PO
www.swansea-holiday.com.au
03 6257 8148 HEMA 102 B6 42 07 43 S 148 04 42 E

Tarraleah

65 Tarraleah Highland Caravan Park

The Edge
www.tarraleah.com
03 6289 0111 HEMA 111 G10 42 18 03 S 146 27 00 E

Tomahawk

66 Tomahawk Tourist Park

1 Main Rd
03 6355 2268 HEMA 105 B11 40 52 32 S 147 46 20 E

Triabunna

67 Triabunna Cabin & Caravan Park

4 Vicary St. 100m S of PO
www.mariagateway.com
03 6257 3575 HEMA 102 E5 42 30 30 S 147 54 40 E

Turners Beach

68 O.C. Ling Memorial Caravan Park

45 The Esplanade
0499 949 584 HEMA 104 D3 41 09 29 S 146 14 35 E

Ulverstone

69 Apex Caravan Park

104 Queen St. 1 km NW of PO
www.apexulverstonecaravanpark.com.au
03 6425 2935 HEMA 104 D2 41 08 42 S 146 09 39 E

70 BIG4 Ulverstone Holiday Park

57 Water St. 1 km NE of PO
www.big4ulverstone.com.au
03 6425 2624 HEMA 104 D3 41 09 15 S 146 10 54 E

Wayatinah

71 Wayatinah Lakeside Caravan Park

Florentine Rd
www.wayatinah.net
03 6289 3317 HEMA 111 H11 42 23 09 S 146 30 19 E

White Beach

72 White Beach Tourist Park

128 White Beach Rd
www.whitebeachtouristpark.com.au
03 6250 2142 HEMA 103 G3 43 06 40 S 147 44 11 E

Wynyard

73 Beach Retreat Tourist Park

30B Old Bass Hwy. 1 km E of PO
www.beachretreattouristpark.com.au/
03 6442 1998 HEMA 108 E7 40 59 22 S 145 44 27 E

74 Leisure Ville Holiday Centre

145 Old Bass Hwy. 3 km E of PO
www.leisureville.com.au
03 6442 2291 HEMA 108 E7 40 59 53 S 145 45 54 E

Zeehan

75 Site Closed

Key Map

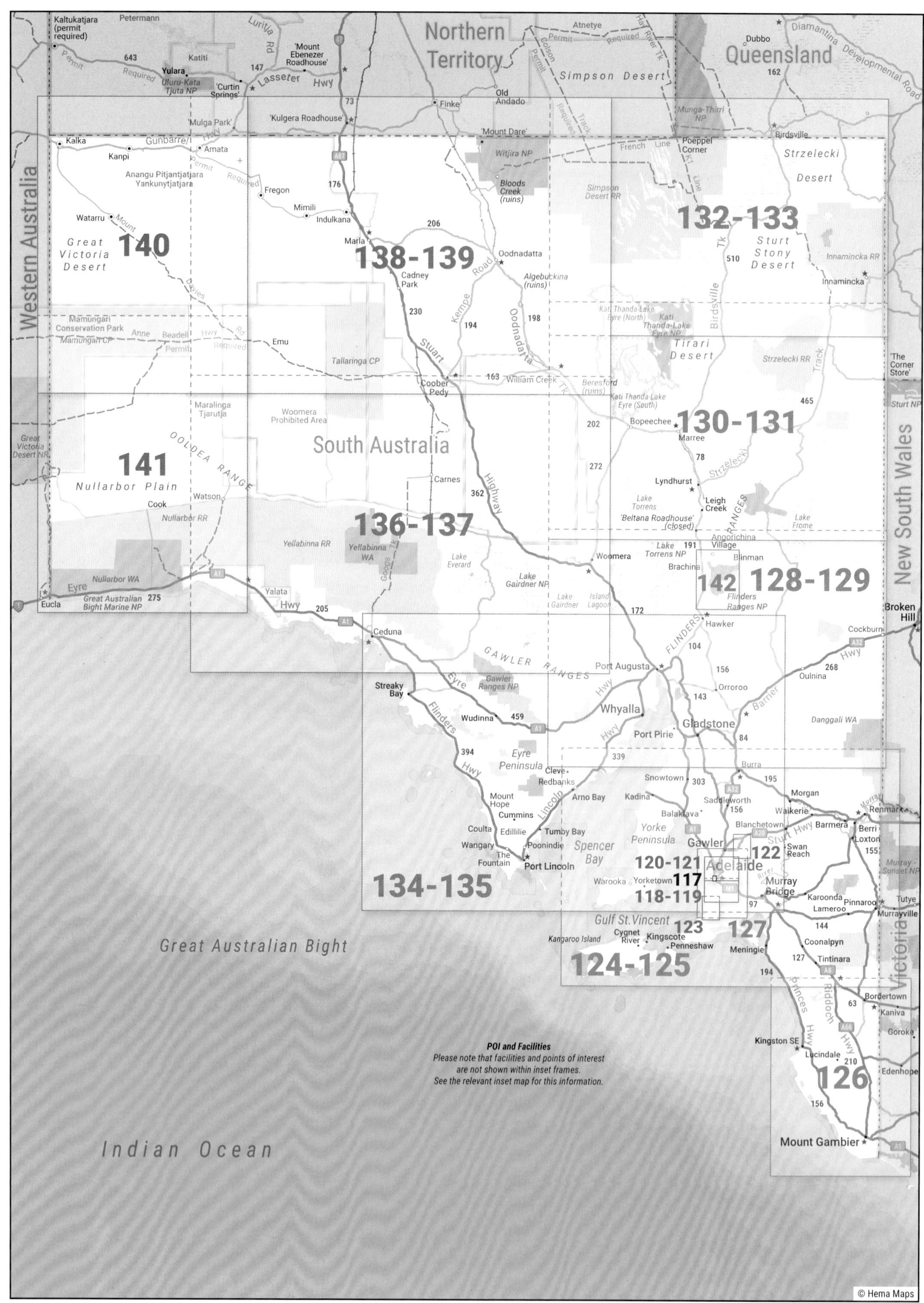

Northern Territory
Queensland
South Australia
New South Wales
Western Australia
Victoria
140
141
138-139
136-137
132-133
130-131
128-129
142
134-135
120-121
122
117
118-119
123
127
124-125
126
Great Australian Bight
Indian Ocean
Adelaide
Port Augusta
Port Lincoln
Ceduna
Coober Pedy
Mount Gambier
Whyalla
Broken Hill
POI and Facilities
Please note that facilities and points of interest are not shown within inset frames.
See the relevant inset map for this information.
© Hema Maps

0
0.5
1
km
138°35'E
138°36'E
138°37'E
34°54'S
34°55'S
34°56'S
34°57'S
120
118
BROMPTON
OVINGHAM
BOWDEN
PROSPECT
FITZROY
MEDINDIE
WALKERVILLE
JOSLIN
GILBERTON
ST PETERS
HACKNEY
COLLEGE PARK
STEPNEY
NORWOOD
KENT TOWN
ROSE PARK
NORTH ADELAIDE
MILE END
MILE END SOUTH
ADELAIDE
EASTWOOD
WAYVILLE
PARKSIDE
UNLEY
FORESTVILLE
GOODWOOD
FULLARTON
City Ring Route
Robe Terrace
Park Tce
Fitzroy Terrace
Main North Rd
O'Connell St
Jeffcott St
Barton Terrace West
Barton Terrace East
Melbourne St
Northcote Tce
Hackney Rd
North Tce
Botanic Rd
War Memorial Drive
Frome Rd
King William Rd
King William St
Montefiore Rd
Port Road
James Congdon Dr
Glover Av
North Terrace
Hindley St
Rundle Mall
Grenfell St
Pirie St
Waymouth St
Flinders St
Franklin St
Wakefield Street
Grote Street
Sir Donald Bradman Drive
West Tce
East Tce
Angas St
Gouger St
Wright St
Carrington St
Halifax St
Sturt St
Gilles St
Gilbert St
South Terrace
Pulteney Street
Hutt Street
Hutt Road
Unley Road
Peacock Rd
Glen Osmond Rd
Glen Osmond Road
Greenhill Road
Greenhill Rd
Fullarton Rd
Anzac Highway
Goodwood Rd
Richmond Rd
Magill Rd
Payneham Rd
The Parade
Bartels Rd
Wakefield Rd
Victoria Square
Central Market
Adelaide Aquatic Centre
North Adelaide Golf Links-North
North Adelaide Golf Links-South
City of Adelaide Golf Links
Carclew House
Women's and Children's Hospital
St Peter's Cathedral
Light's Vision
Adelaide Oval
Karrawirra Parri
Adelaide Zoo
Botanic Park
Adelaide Botanic Garden
National Wine Centre of Australia
University of Adelaide
Art Gallery of South Australia
South Australian Museum
State Library of South Australia
Migration Museum
National War Memorial
Adelaide Festival Centre
Adelaide Convention Centre
Adelaide Casino
SkyCity
Parliament House
Royal Adelaide Hospital
Adelaide Gaol Museum
Adelaide Gondola
Bonython Park
Santos Stadium
Kingston Gardens
Adelaide Parklands Terminal
West Terrace Cemetery
Edwards Park
Veale Gardens
Walyo Yerta Park
Minno Wirra
Adelaide Himeji Garden
Adelaide Reserve
Adelaide Parklands Circuit
Rymill Park
East Terrace Glower
Tandanya National Aboriginal Cultural Institute
Adelaide Town Hall
Adelaide Arcade
Ayers House
Adelaide University Sports Grounds
Nantu Wama
Bickle Reserve
Adelaide Showground
Haigh's Chocolates
Unley Shopping Centre
Unley Oval
Glenelg Tramway
To Devon Park
To Medindie Gardens
To Collinswood
To West Hindmarsh
To Hilton
To Kurralta Park
To Millswood
To Unley Park
To Glenunga
To Toorak Gardens
To Evandale
66
© Hema Maps

Southern Adelaide Suburbs to Mount Barker

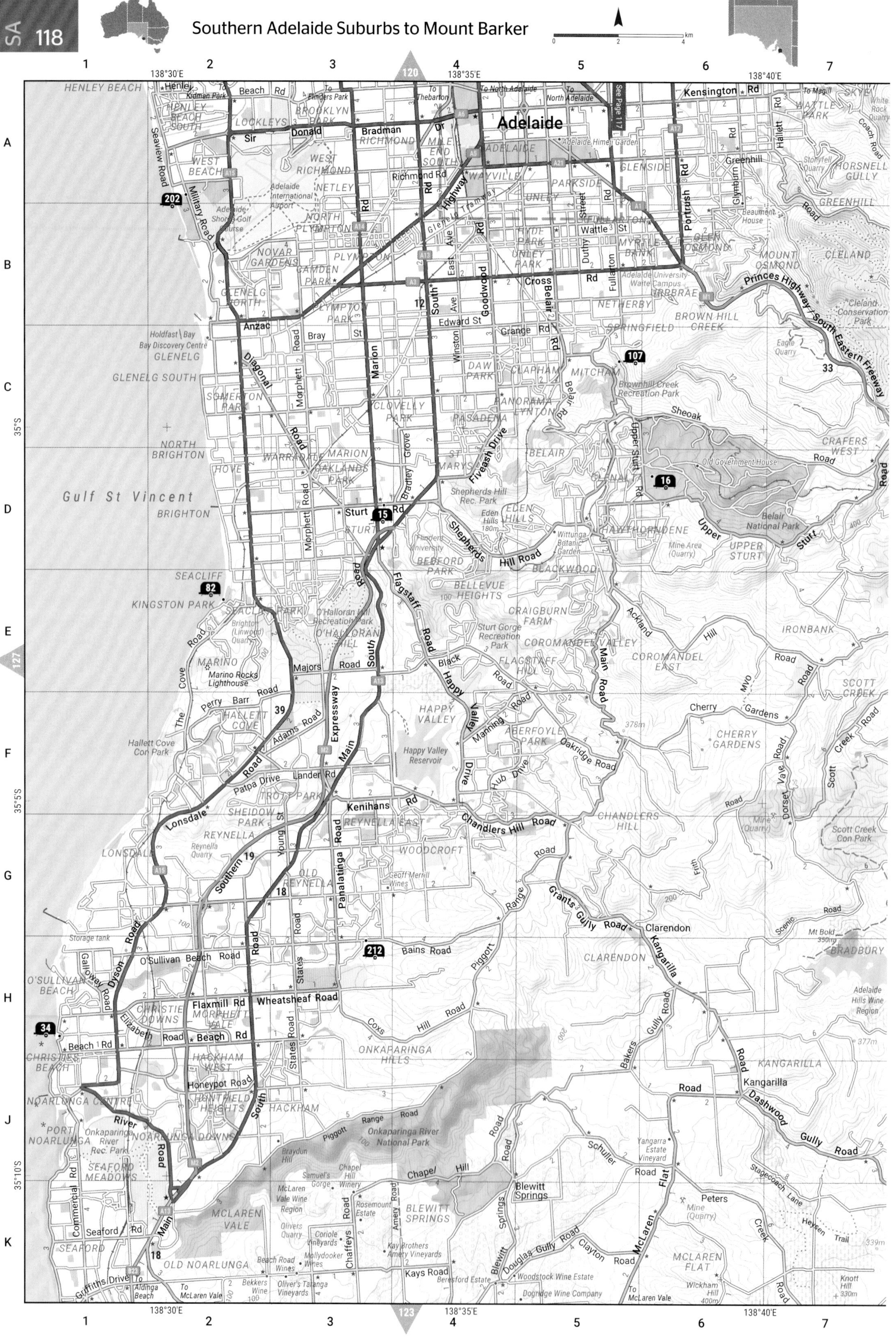

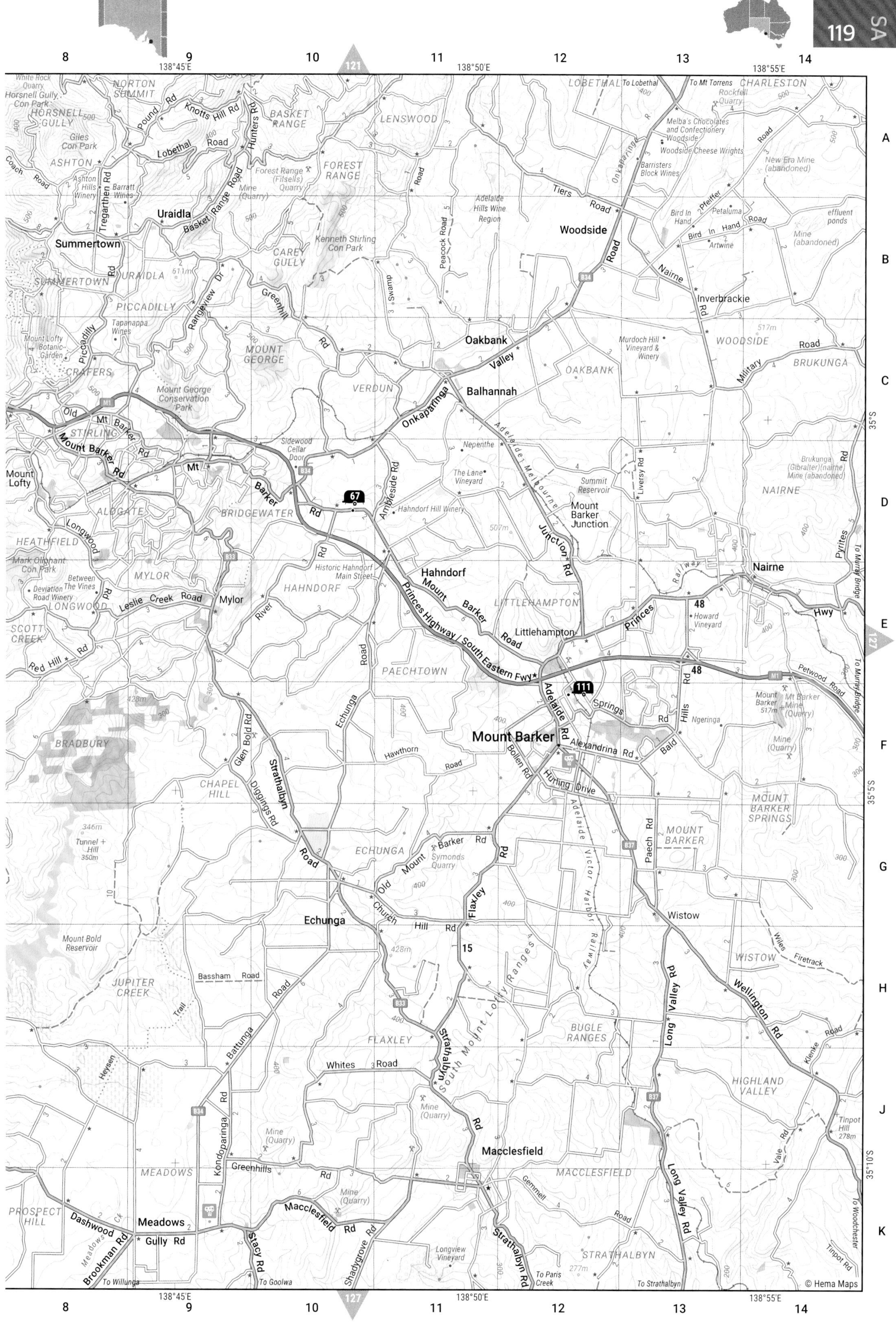

8
9
10
11
12
13
14
121
127
A
B
C
D
E
F
G
H
J
K
138°45'E
138°50'E
138°55'E
35°S
35°5'S
35°10'S
White Rock Quarry
Horsnell Gully Con Park
NORTON SUMMIT
HORSNELL GULLY
Pound Rd
Knotts Hill Rd
Hunters Rd
BASKET RANGE
LENSWOOD
LOBETHAL
To Lobethal
To Mt Torrens
CHARLESTON
Rockfell Quarry
Melba's Chocolates and Confectionery Woodside
Woodside Cheese Wrights
Barristers Block Wines
New Era Mine (abandoned)
Giles Con Park
Lobethal Road
ASHTON
Coach Road
Forest Range (Filsells) Quarry
FOREST RANGE
Ashton Hills Winery
Barratt Wines
Tregarthen Rd
Basket Range Road
Mine (Quarry)
Uraidla
Adelaide Hills Wine Region
Tiers Road
Onkaparinga
Bird In Hand
Pfeiffer
Petaluma
Bird In Hand Road
Artwine
effluent ponds
Mine (abandoned)
Summertown
Kenneth Stirling Con Park
CAREY GULLY
Peacock Road
Woodside
Road
URAIDLA
SUMMERTOWN
Rangeview Dr
Greenhill
Swamp
Nairne
Inverbrackie
Rd
PICCADILLY
Tapanappa Wines
Mount Lofty Botanic Garden
Piccadilly
MOUNT GEORGE
Oakbank
Valley
Murdoch Hill Vineyard & Winery
WOODSIDE
Military
Road
BRUKUNGA
CRAFERS
Mount George Conservation Park
VERDUN
Balhannah
OAKBANK
Onkaparinga
Old Mt Barker Rd
STIRLING
Mount Barker Rd
Sidewood Cellar Door
Nepenthe
Adelaide Melbourne
Liversy Rd
Brukunga (Gibralter) (nairne) Mine (abandoned)
Mount Lofty
Mt Barker Rd
The Lane Vineyard
Summit Reservoir
NAIRNE
ALDGATE
BRIDGEWATER
Ambleside Rd
Hahndorf Hill Winery
Mount Barker Junction
Longwood
HEATHFIELD
507m
Junction Rd
Pyrites
Mark Oliphant Con Park
Historic Hahndorf Main Street
Hahndorf
Railway
Nairne
To Murray Bridge
Between The Vines
Deviation Road Winery
MYLOR
HAHNDORF
Mount Barker Road
LITTLEHAMPTON
Princes
Howard Vineyard
Hwy
LONGWOOD
Leslie Creek Road
Mylor
River
Princes Highway / South Eastern Fwy
Littlehampton
SCOTT CREEK
Red Hill Rd
PAECHTOWN
Petwood Road
Mount Barker 517m
Mt Barker Mine (Quarry)
Adelaide Rd
Springs
Hills Rd
Ngeringa
BRADBURY
Glen Bold Rd
Echunga
Hawthorn Road
Mount Barker
Alexandrina Rd
Bald
Mine (Quarry)
CHAPEL HILL
Diggings Rd
Strathalbyn
Bollen Rd
Hurling Drive
MOUNT BARKER SPRINGS
346m
Tunnel Hill 350m
Road
ECHUNGA
Mount Barker Rd
Symonds Quarry
Adelaide Victor Harbor Railway
Paech Rd
MOUNT BARKER
Old
Flaxley
Church Hill Rd
Echunga
Wistow
Wiles Firetrack
Mount Bold Reservoir
428m
South Mount Lofty Ranges
WISTOW
Bassham Road
Road
JUPITER CREEK
Trail
Long Valley Rd
Wellington Rd
FLAXLEY
BUGLE RANGES
Klenke Road
Heysen
Battunga
Whites Road
Strathalbyn Rd
HIGHLAND VALLEY
Kondoparinga Rd
Mine (Quarry)
Tinpot Hill 278m
Macclesfield
Vale Rd
MEADOWS
Greenhills Rd
MACCLESFIELD
Long Valley Rd
Gemmell Road
PROSPECT HILL
Dashwood
Meadows Ck
Meadows
Gully Rd
Macclesfield Rd
Shadygrove Rd
Brookman Rd
Stacy Rd
Longview Vineyard
STRATHALBYN
277m
To Woodchester
Tinpot Rd
To Willunga
To Goolwa
To Paris Creek
To Strathalbyn
© Hema Maps

Northern Adelaide Suburbs

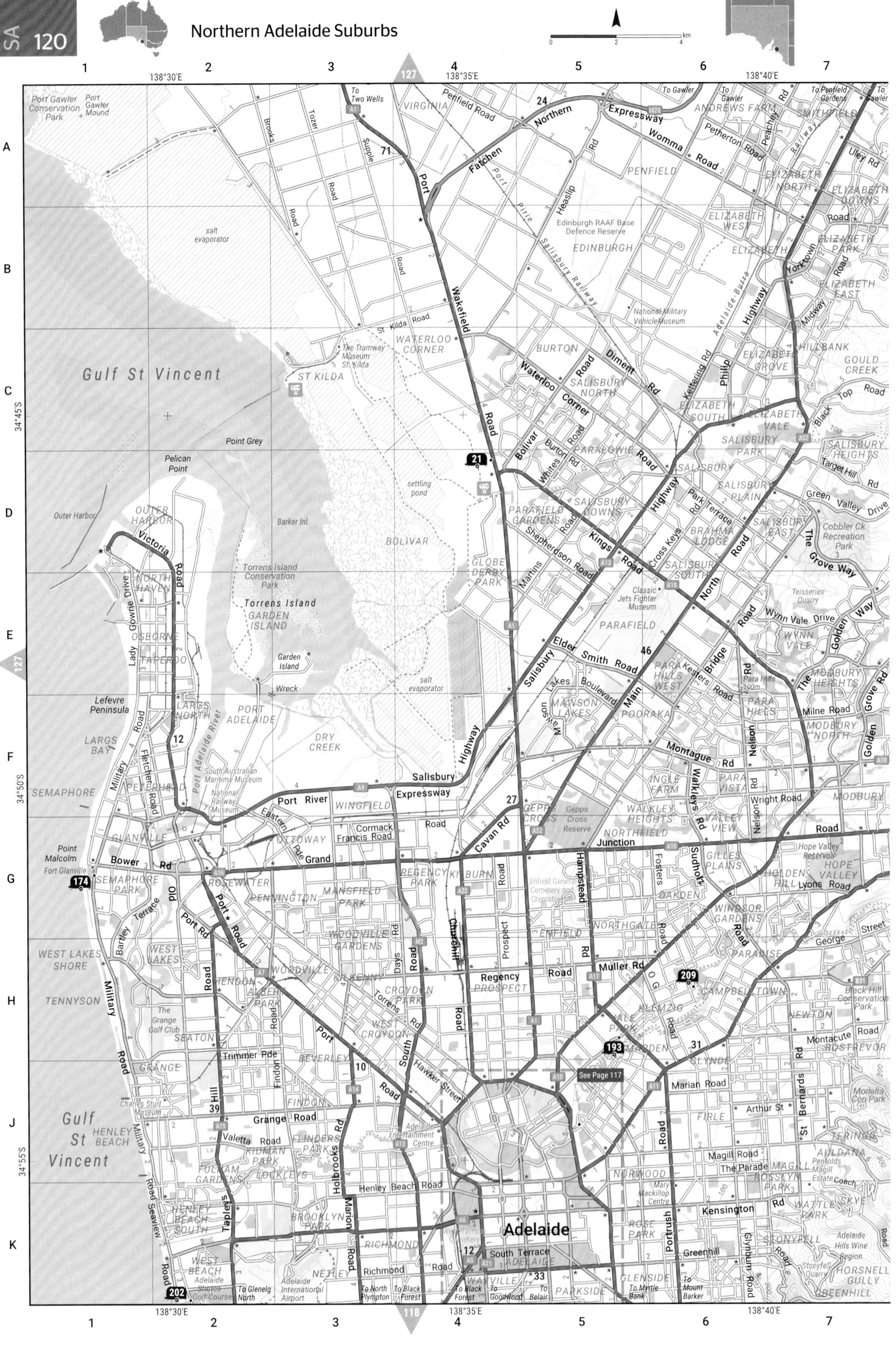

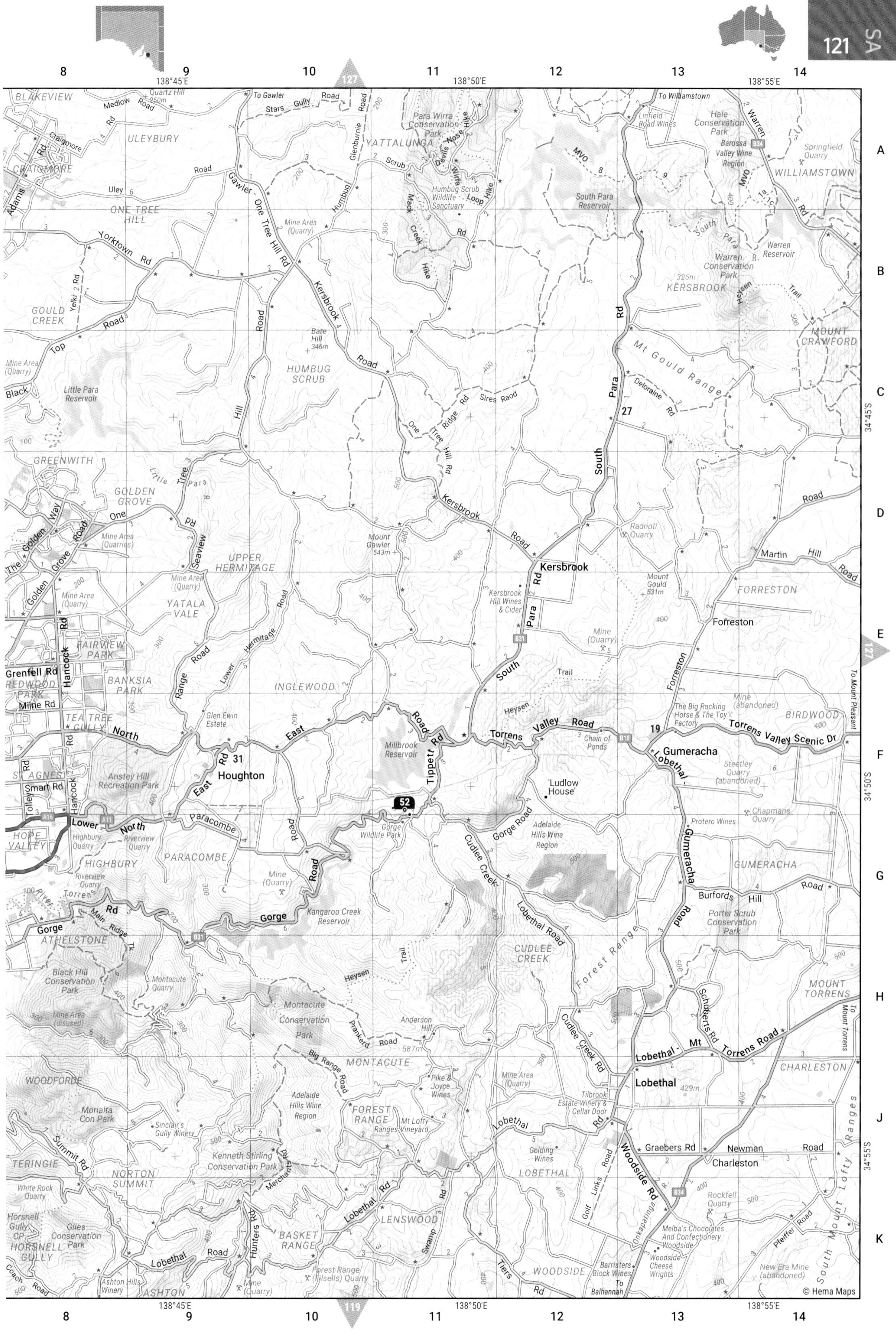

8 9 10 11 12 13 14
138°45'E 138°50'E 138°55'E
127

BLAKEVIEW
Medlow Road
Quartz Hill 250m
To Gawler
Stars Gully Road
Glenburnie Road
Para Wirra Conservation Park
Devils Nose Hike
To Williamstown
Linfield Road Wines
Hale Conservation Park
Warren Road
Barossa Valley Wine Region
Springfield Quarry
WILLIAMSTOWN
ULEYBURY
Craigmore Rd
CRAIGMORE
Adams Rd
Road
Uley
Gawler One Tree Hill Rd
YATTALUNGA
Scrub
Humbug
Mack Creek Hike
Wirra Loop Hike
Humbug Scrub Wildlife Sanctuary
MVO
South Para Reservoir
ONE TREE HILL
Mine Area (Quarry)
Yorktown Rd
Kersbrook Road
Warren Conservation Park
Warren Reservoir
South Para R.
326m
KERSBROOK
Heysen Trail
Yelki Rd
GOULD CREEK
Top Road
Black
Road
Bate Hill 346m
HUMBUG SCRUB
Mt Gould Range
Deloraine Rd
MOUNT CRAWFORD
Mine Area (Quarry)
Little Para Reservoir
One Tree Hill Rd
Ridge Rd
Sires Raod
South Para Rd
27
34°45'S
GREENWITH
Little Para R.
GOLDEN GROVE
One Tree Rd
The Golden Way
Golden Grove Road
Mine Area (Quarries)
Seaview Rd
Kersbrook Road
Radnoti Quarry
Road
Mount Gawler 543m
Martin Hill Road
UPPER HERMITAGE
Kersbrook
Mine Area (Quarry)
Mount Gould 531m
FORRESTON
YATALA VALE
Hermitage Road
Kersbrook Hill Wines & Cider
Forreston
FAIRVIEW PARK
Hancock Rd
Lower Hermitage
Range Road
Mine (Quarry)
B31
Trail
127
To Mount Pleasant
Grenfell Rd
REDWOOD PARK
BANKSIA PARK
INGLEWOOD
South Para Rd
Forreston Rd
Milne Rd
Heysen
Mine (abandoned)
The Big Rocking Horse & The Toy Factory
BIRDWOOD
TEA TREE GULLY
North East Road
Glen Ewin Estate
Tippett Rd
Torrens Valley Road
Chain of Ponds
B10
19
Torrens Valley Scenic Dr
Millbrook Reservoir
Gumeracha
East Rd 31
Houghton
ST AGNES
Smart Rd
Tolley Rd
Hancock Rd
Anstey Hill Recreation Park
Lobethal
Steetley Quarry (abandoned)
'Ludlow House'
34°50'S
52
Chapmans Quarry
A10 A11
Lower North
HOPE VALLEY
Paracombe Road
Gorge Wildlife Park
Gorge Road
Protero Wines
Highbury Quarry
Riverview Quarry
PARACOMBE
Road
Adelaide Hills Wine Region
Cudlee Creek
Gumeracha Road
HIGHBURY
GUMERACHA
Riverview Quarry
Mine (Quarry)
Road
Burfords Hill Road
River Torrens
Gorge Rd
Main Ridge Tk
Gorge
Kangaroo Creek Reservoir
Lobethal Road
Porter Scrub Conservation Park
ATHELSTONE
B31
Forest Range
CUDLEE CREEK
Black Hill Conservation Park
Montacute Quarry
Heysen Trail
Trail
MOUNT TORRENS
Mine Area (disused)
Montacute Conservation Park
Anderson Hill
Schuberts Rd
To Mount Torrens
Prankerd Road
Cudlee Creek Rd
587m
Lobethal - Mt Torrens Road
Big Range Road
MONTACUTE
CHARLESTON
WOODFORDE
Pike & Joyce Wines
Mine Area (Quarry)
Lobethal
429m
Adelaide Hills Wine Region
Tilbrook Estate Winery & Cellar Door
Morialta Con Park
FOREST RANGE
Mt Lofty Ranges Vineyard
Lobethal Rd
Mount Lofty Ranges
Sinclair's Gully Winery
Summit Rd
Kenneth Stirling Conservation Park
Golding Wines
Woodside Rd
Graebers Rd
Newman Road
Charleston
34°55'S
TERINGIE
Merchants Rd
Links Road
LOBETHAL
NORTON SUMMIT
White Rock Quarry
Lobethal Rd
B34
Rockfell Quarry
Onkaparinga R.
Golf
Horsnell Gully CP
Giles Conservation Park
HORSNELL GULLY
Hunters Rd
Swamp Rd
LENSWOOD
Melba's Chocolates And Confectionery Woodside
Pfeffer Road
BASKET RANGE
Woodside Cheese Wrights
South Mount Lofty
Coach Road
Lobethal Road
Forest Range (Filsells) Quarry
Tiers Rd
Barristers Block Wines
New Era Mine (abandoned)
Ashton Hills Winery
ASHTON
Mine (Quarry)
WOODSIDE
To Balhannah
© Hema Maps
138°45'E 138°50'E 138°55'E
119
8 9 10 11 12 13 14

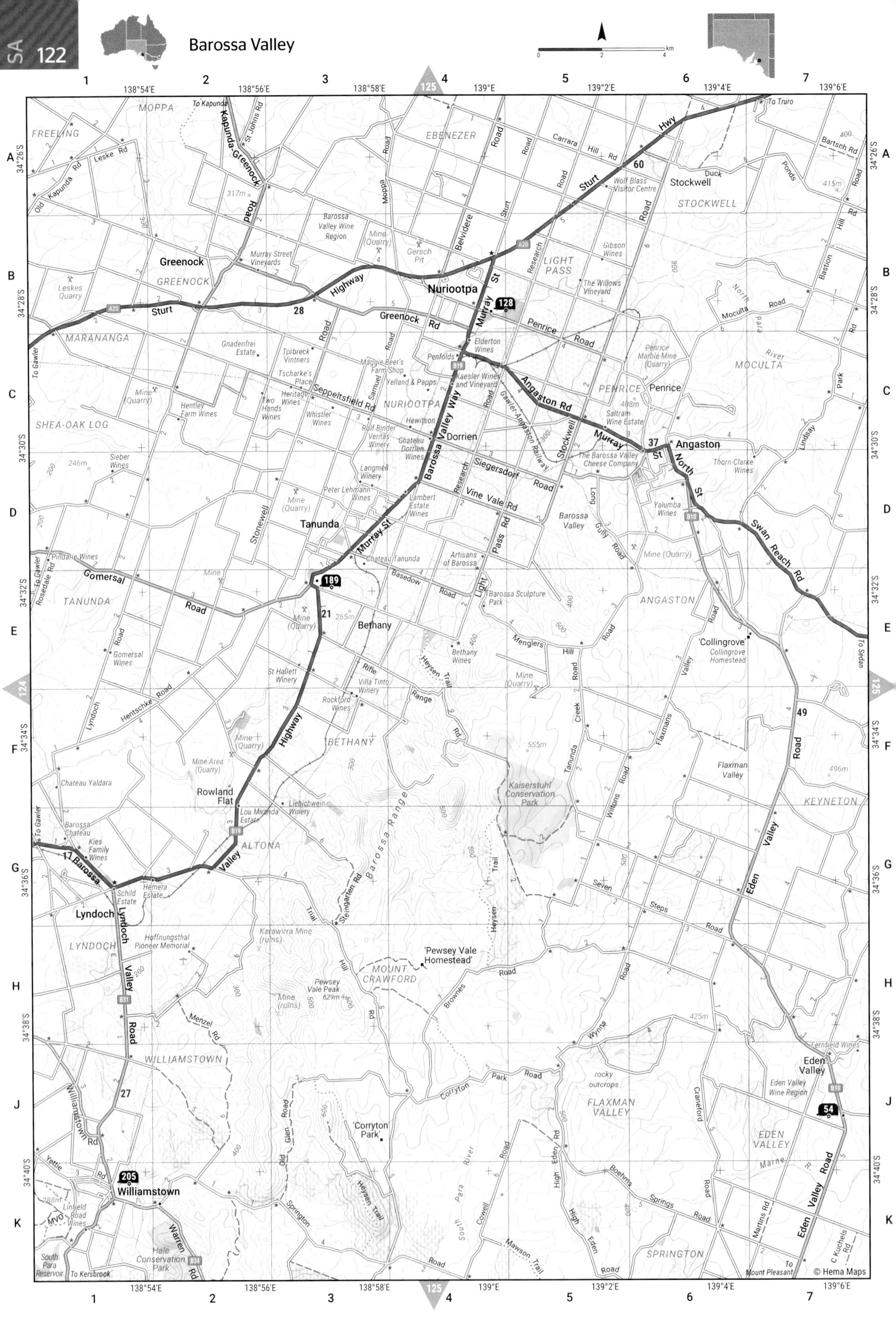
Barossa Valley
Nuriootpa
Tanunda
Angaston
Greenock
Stockwell
Penrice
Dorrien
Bethany
Rowland Flat
Lyndoch
Williamstown
Eden Valley
Sturt Highway
Barossa Valley Way
Angaston Rd
Gomersal Road
Murray St
Swan Reach Rd
Eden Valley Road
Lyndoch Valley Road
Kapunda-Greenock Road
Seppeltsfield Rd
Greenock Rd
Penrice Road
Siegersdorf Road
Vine Vale Rd
Menglers Hill Road
Seven Steps Road
Corryton Park Road
Boehms Springs Road
Barossa Range
Kaiserstuhl Conservation Park
Hale Conservation Park
Heysen Trail
Mawson Trail
MOPPA
FREELING
EBENEZER
STOCKWELL
LIGHT PASS
GREENOCK
MARANANGA
MOCULTA
SHEA-OAK LOG
NURIOOTPA
PENRICE
TANUNDA
ANGASTON
BETHANY
KEYNETON
ALTONA
LYNDOCH
MOUNT CRAWFORD
WILLIAMSTOWN
FLAXMAN VALLEY
EDEN VALLEY
SPRINGTON
To Kapunda
To Truro
To Gawler
To Sedan
To Kersbrook
To Mount Pleasant
© Hema Maps

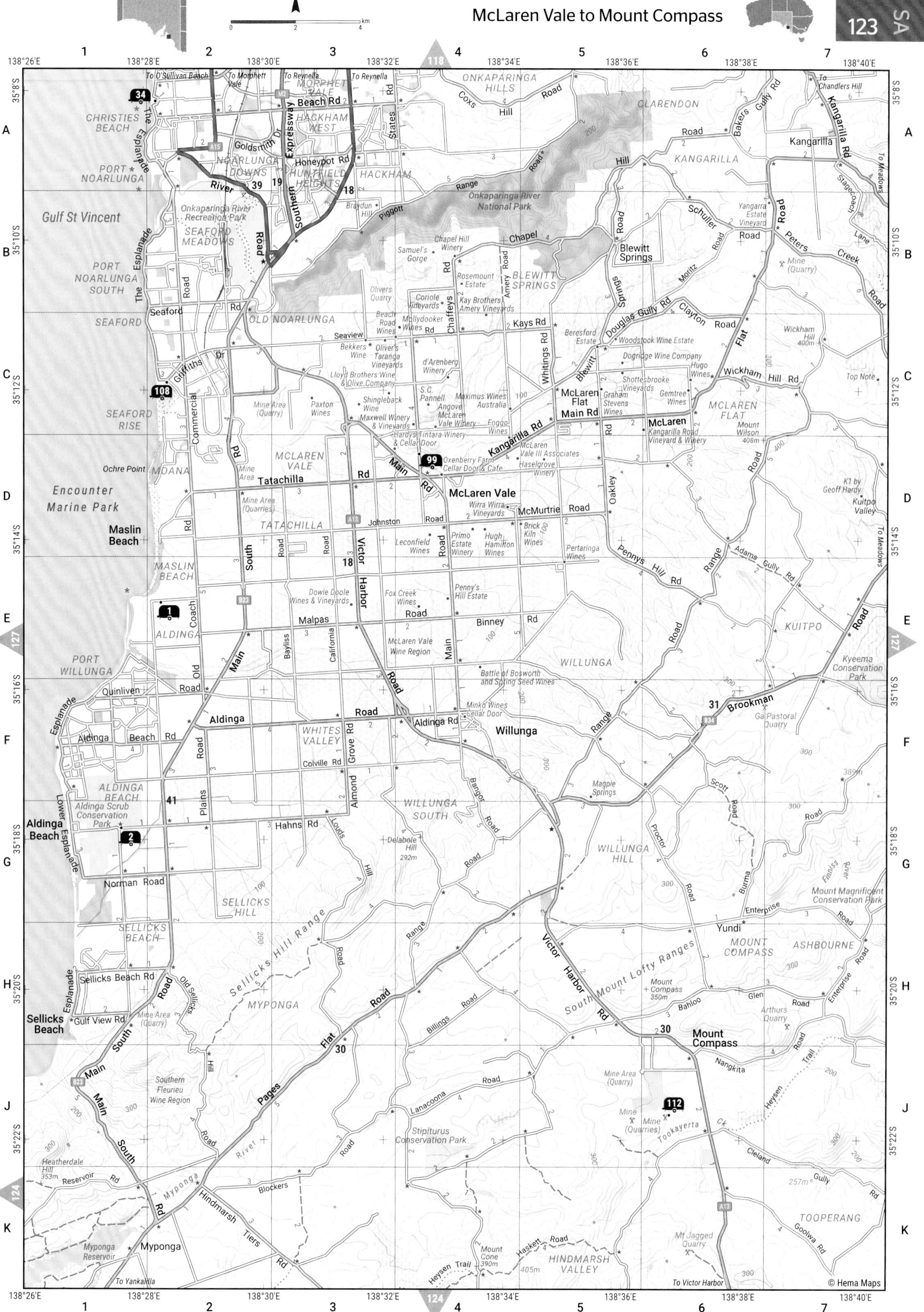

Eyre Peninsula
To Whyalla
Uteralitera Plain
Mangalo
Emu Plain
Wild Horse Plain
Watchanie
Utera 105
Utera Plain
Danger Corner
Company Corner
Mitchellville
Ferns
Ulgera Gap
'Glenville'
'Middle Camp'
Yabmana 115
Cleve
Elbow Hill
Cowell
Lucky Bay
Franklin Harbor Marine Park
Old Maratta
'Carrawa'
'The Knob'
Windmill Beach
Franklin Harbor
The Knob
Churinga'
Carpa
159
Port Gibbon
Twelve Mile Plain
Mills Beach
'Fairview'
Redbanks
Arno Bay
Cape Driver
Lincoln Highway
To Port Neill
Sea
SA
To Port Pirie
Merriton
Clements Gap
Redhill
Ingram Gap
Mundoora
Port Broughton
Hitchcock Plain
Hope Gap
Kanyaka Plain
108
Bews
Wokurna
Tickera Bay
Kadina Plain
Bruce field
Lincolnfields
123
Alford
Bute
Snowtown
Wallaroo Plain
Adams Plain
Wallaroo Bay
Wallaroo
Kadina
Hill Vista'
Nantawarra
Pat Plain
Paskeville
Cunliffe
60
Kulpara
Tiparra Bay
Moonta
Cape Elizabeth
52
Kainton
70
Agery
'The Pines'
Port Wakefield
Port Clinton
Weetulta
Arthurton
Eastern Spencer Gulf Marine Park
Spencer Gulf
Yorke Peninsula
Dowlingville
63
Middle Spit
Balgowan
Maitland
Petersville
Cunningham
Ardrossan
Sir Joseph Banks Group Marine Park
Point Pearce
Red Cliffs
Wardang Island IPA
South Kilkerran
Wardang Island
Wardang Island Aboriginal Area
Port Victoria
Urania
Sandilands
Pine Point
46
'Stonehaven'
Hardwicke Bay
Port Rickaby
37
Bluff Beach
Parsons Beach
Curramulka
Dowcer Bluff
Minlaton
'Ribo'
Port Vincent
'Andervale'
66
69
Rogers Corner
Point Souttar
Corny Point
Berry Bay
Hardwicke Bay
Peesey Swamp
Weaver
Stansbury
'Orrie Cowie'
Warooka
Yorketown
Gambier Islands Group Marine Park
White Hut
Formby Bay
'Tuckokcowie'
'Coonarie Park'
Lake Fowler
Edithburgh
'Waltham'
Wedge Island
Browns Beach
Happy Valley
'Hillsview'
'Seaweed'
Foul Bay
Sturt Bay
Waterloo Bay
West Cape
Marion Lake
Marion Bay
Stenhouse Bay
Cape Spencer
Lower Yorke Peninsula Marine Park
Gulf St Vincent
Investigator Strait
Southern Spencer Gulf Marine Park
To Gladstone
Gulnare
Spalding
To Jamestown
'Tiverville'
Yacka
Booborowie
Koolunga
'Narrioota'
'Geralka'
Leighton
'Arlie'
Rochester
'Gum Vale'
Clare Valley Wine Region
Burnsfield
Mt Surmon Wines
Jim Barry Wines
Clare
Blyth
Bumbunga Lake
Sevenhill Cellars
Paulett Wines
Farrell Flat
Penworthham
Mintaro
Martindale Hall
Everard Central
Mount Templeton
Watervale
Hoyleton
Auburn
Manoora
Stow
Wanappe
Beaufort
Goyder
Halbury
Whitwarta
Saddleworth
Bowmans
Balaklava
Riverton
Salter Springs
Tarlee
Avon
Pinery
Owen
Alma
Mary Burts Corner
Barabba
Hamley Bridge
Kangaroo Plain
Long Plains
Mallala Motor Sport Park
Mallala
Freeling
Wasleys
Korunye
Adelaide International Bird Sanctuary NP - Winaityinaityi Pangkara NP
Roseworthy
Two Wells
Gawler
See Page 127
Upper Gulf St Vincent Marine Park
Middle Beach
Virginia
Angle Vale
Torrens Island
Houghton
Lefevre Peninsula
Adelaide
Adelaide Hills Wine Region
Summertown
Uraidla
Balhannah
Hahndorf
Kangarilla
Echunga
Clarendon
Mount Bold Reservoir
Meadows
McLaren Vale
Maslin Beach
McLaren Vale Wine Region
Kuitpo Valley
Aldinga Beach
Willunga
Ashbourne
Sellicks Beach
Mt Compass
Normanville
Carrickalinga
Myponga Reservoir
Southern Fleurieu Wine Region
Yankalilla
Second Valley
Middleton
Port Elliot
Goolwa
Delamere
Inman Valley Rd
Victor Harbor
Encounter Marine Park
Morgans Beach
Cape Jervis
Lands End
Cape Jervis
Fishery Beach
Tunkalilla Beach
Waitpinga
Waitpinga Beach
Cape Cassini
Cape D'Estaing
Emu Bay
Cape Rouge
Bay of Shoals
Bay Of Shoals Wines
'Stokes Bay Station'
Cape Dutton
Kingscote
Brownlow
Cygnet River
American River
Penneshaw
Cape Forbin
Western River Wilderness Protection Area
'Snug Cove'
'Yakilo'
'Pioneer Bend'
Cape Coutts
Dudley Wines
Sunset Winery
Cape St Albans
Cape Borda
Cape Torrens
Playford
59
Parndana
48
Pelican Lagoon
Salt Lagoon
Dudley Peninsula
Cape Willoughby
Flinders Chase NP
'Brigadoon'
Andermel Marron
Two Wheeler Creek Wines
'Warrawee'
White Lagoon
Bay
Cape Hart
Cape Bedout
Kangaroo Island
Kelly Hill Caves
Murray Lagoon
'Hawks Nest'
Kangaroo Island Wine Region
Maupertuis Bay
Karatta
107
Cape du Couedic
Cape Younghusband
Cape Bouguer
Cape Kersaint
Cape Gantheaume Wilderness Protection Area
Cape Linois
Cape Gantheaume
Great Australian
Western Kangaroo Island Marine Park
Southern Kangaroo Island Marine Park
136°40'E
137°30'E
138°20'E
34°10'S
35°S
35°50'S

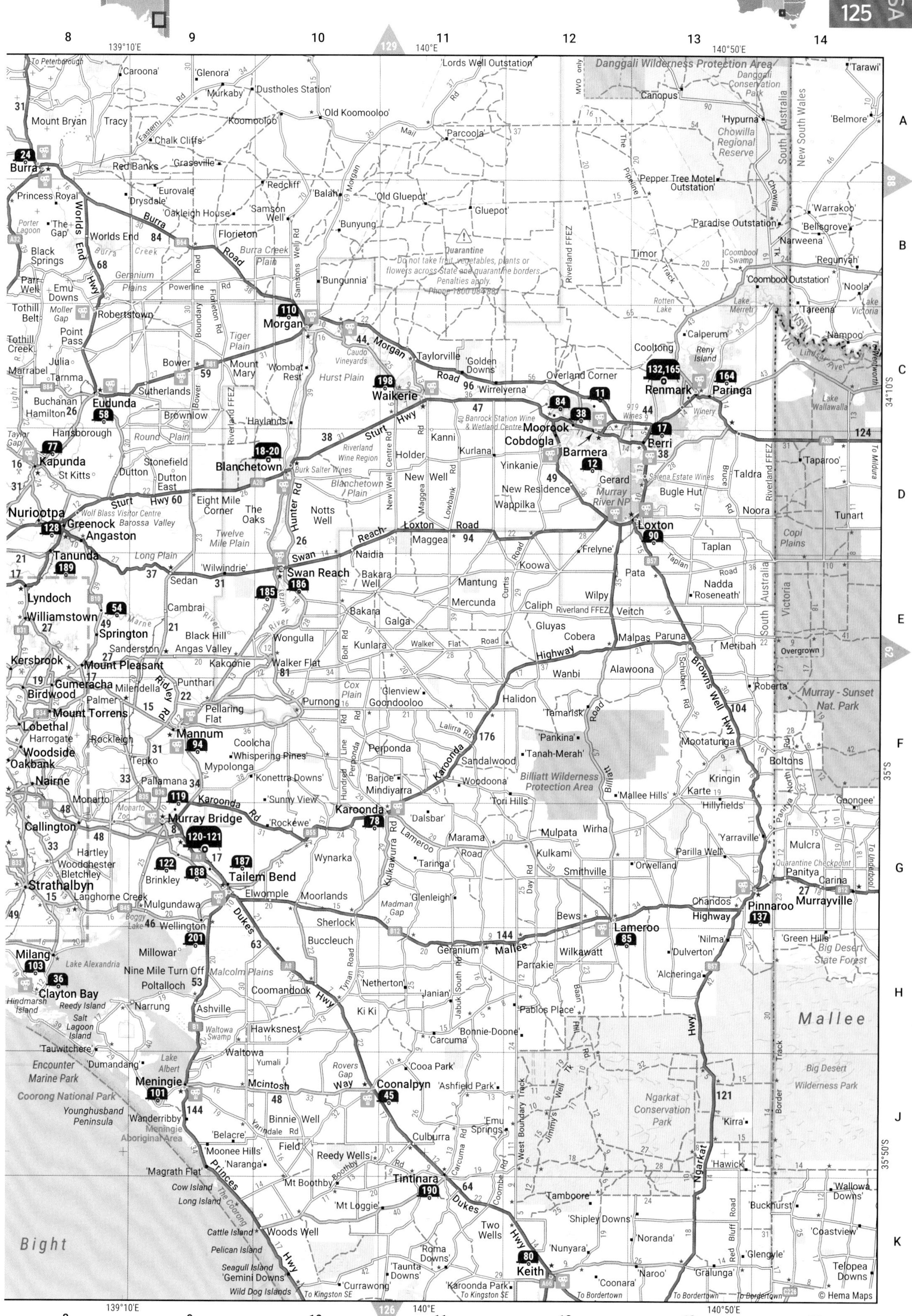

Keith to Mount Gambier

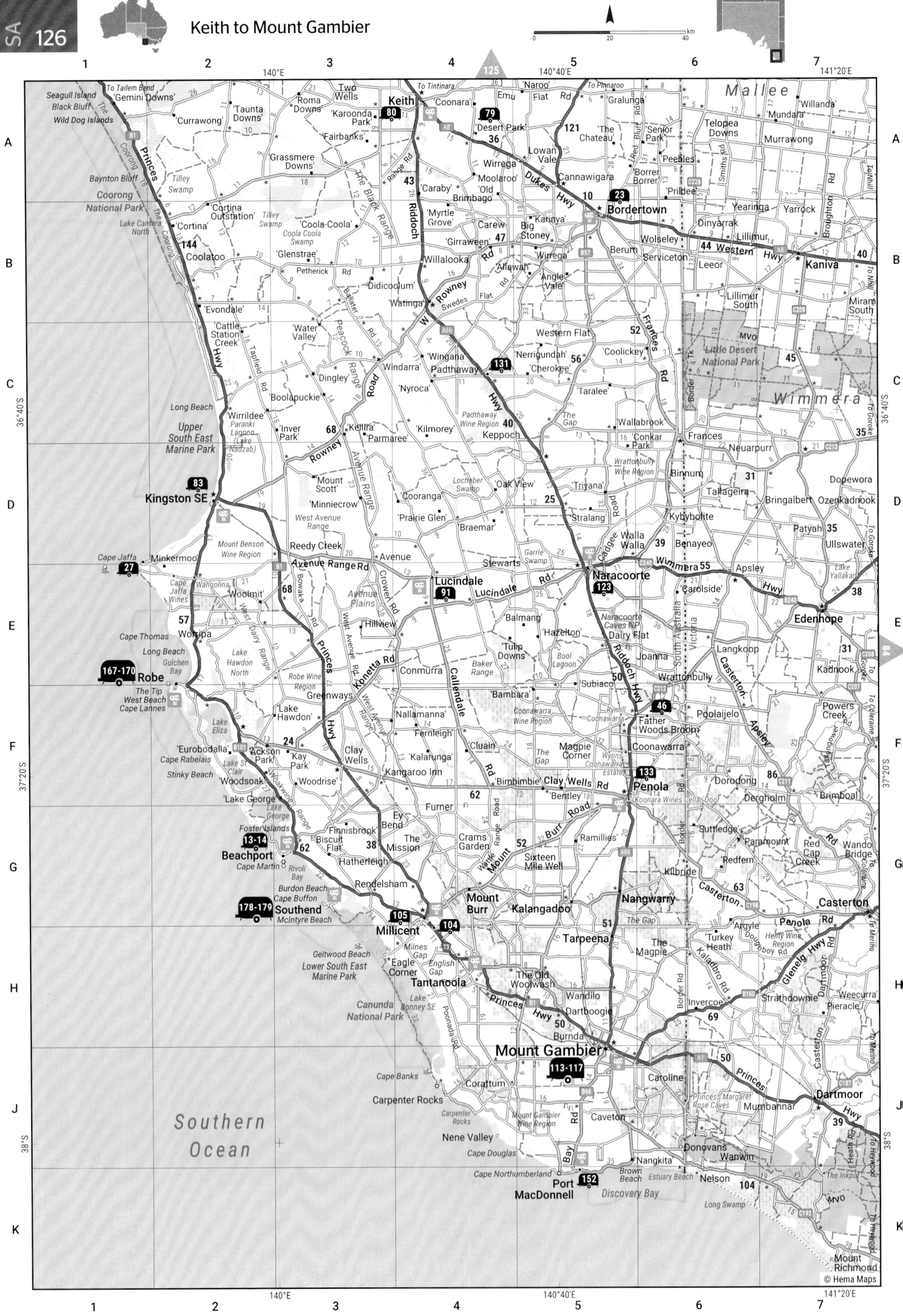

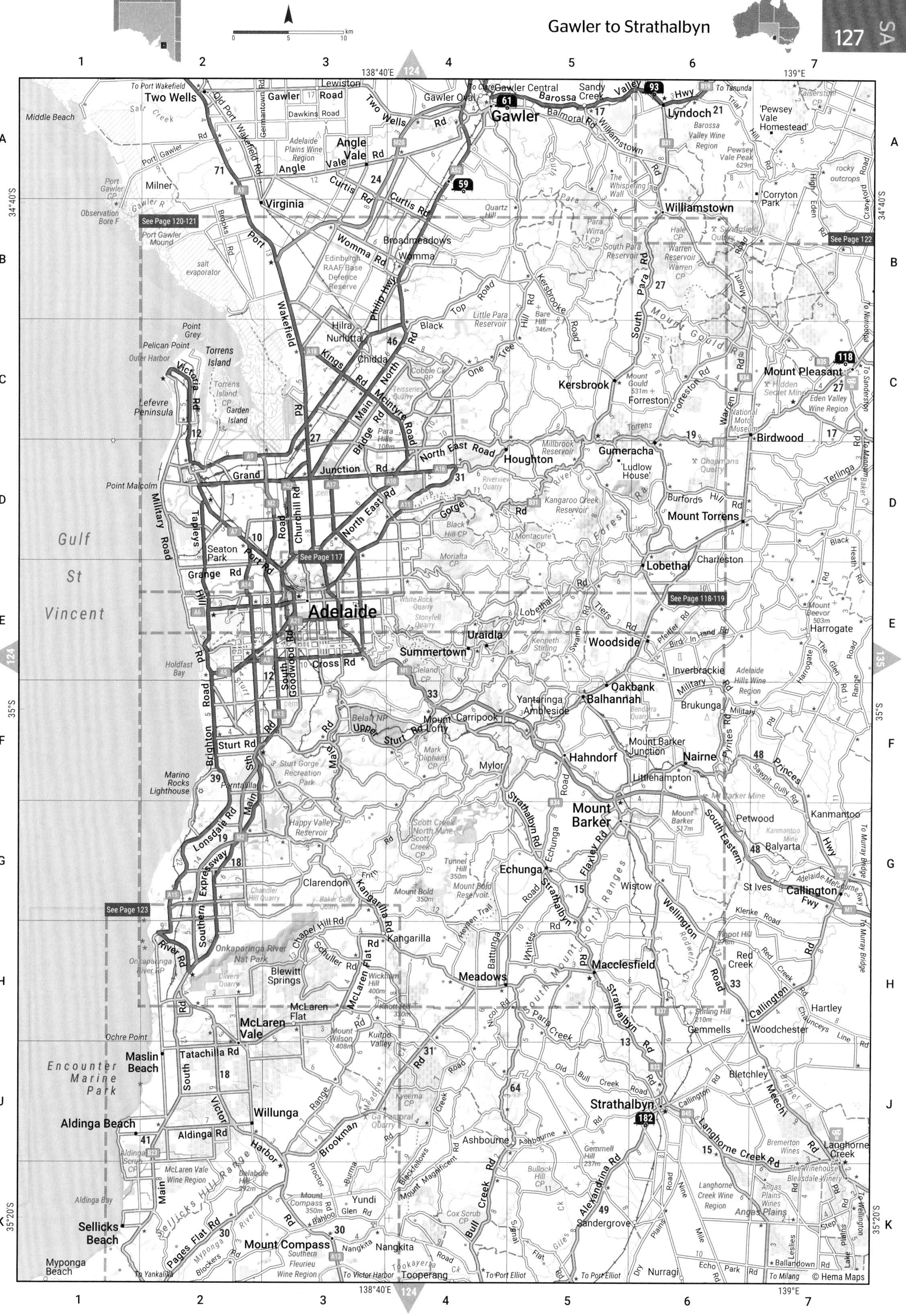

Woomera to NSW Border

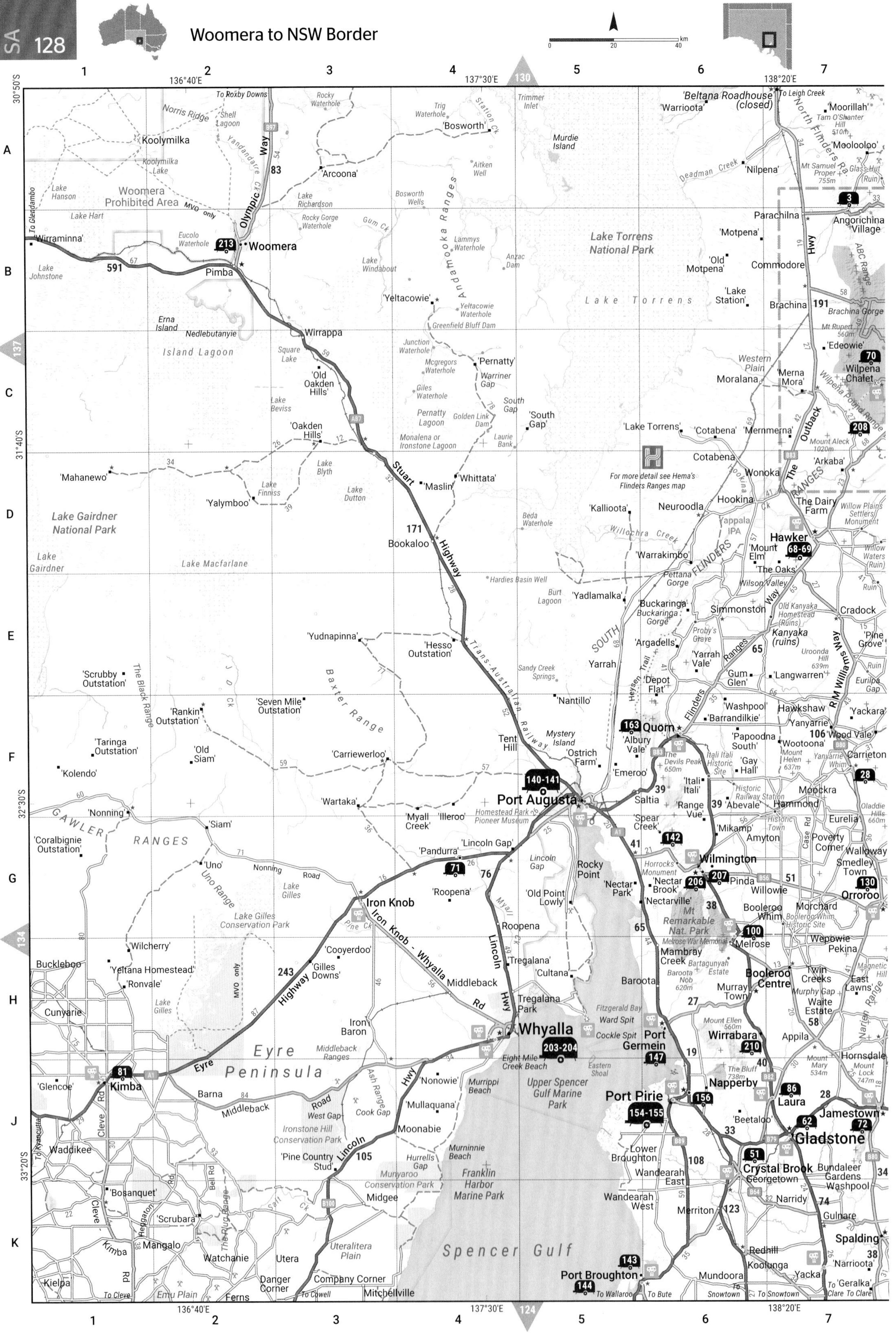

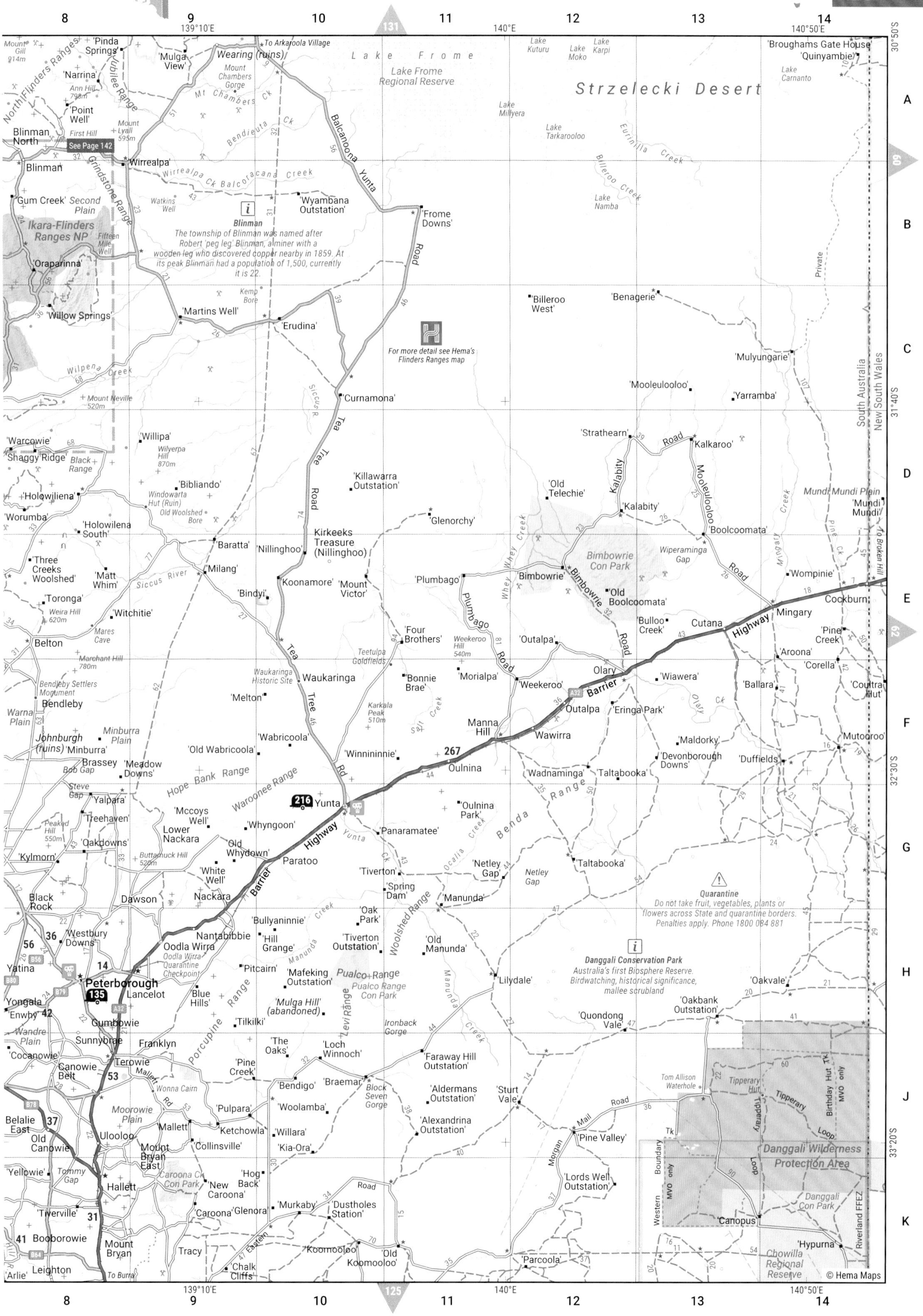

Lake Frome
Lake Frome Regional Reserve
Strzelecki Desert
Lake Kuturu
Lake Moko
Lake Karpi
Lake Millyera
Lake Tarkarooloo
Lake Namba
Lake Carnanto
'Broughams Gate House'
'Quinyambie'
To Arkaroola Village
Wearing (ruins)
'Mulga View'
Mount Chambers Gorge
Mt Chambers Ck
Bendieuta Ck
Balcanoona Yunta
'Pinda Springs'
'Narrina'
Ann Hill 798m
'Point Well'
Mount Gill 914m
North Flinders Ranges
Jubilee Range
Mount Lyall 595m
First Hill
Blinman North
See Page 142
Blinman
'Wirrealpa'
Wirrealpa Ck
Balcoracana Creek
Grindstone Range
'Gum Creek'
Second Plain
Watkins Well
'Wyambana Outstation'
'Frome Downs'
Road
Ikara-Flinders Ranges NP
Fifteen Mile Well
Blinman
The township of Blinman was named after Robert 'peg leg' Blinman, a miner with a wooden leg who discovered copper nearby in 1859. At its peak Blinman had a population of 1,500, currently it is 22.
'Oraparinna'
'Willow Springs'
Kemp Bore
'Martins Well'
'Erudina'
For more detail see Hema's Flinders Ranges map
Wilpena Creek
Mount Neville 520m
'Curnamona'
Siccus R.
Tea Tree Road
'Billeroo West'
'Benagerie'
Eurinilla Creek
Billeroo Creek
Private
'Mulyungarie'
'Mooleulooloo'
'Yarramba'
South Australia
New South Wales
'Strathearn'
Road
'Kalkaroo'
Mooleulooloo
Kalabity
'Kalabity'
'Old Telechie'
'Willipa'
Wilyerpa Hill 870m
'Warcowie'
'Shaggy Ridge'
Black Range
'Bibliando'
Windowarta Hut (Ruin)
Old Woolshed Bore
'Holowiliena'
'Worumba'
'Holowilena South'
'Killawarra Outstation'
'Glenorchy'
Whey Whey Creek
Bimbowrie Con Park
Wiperaminga Gap
'Boolcoomata'
Mundi Mundi Plain
'Mundi Mundi'
To Broken Hill
'Baratta'
'Nillinghoo'
Kirkeeks Treasure (Nillinghoo)
'Three Creeks Woolshed'
'Matt Whim'
'Milang'
Siccus River
'Koonamore'
'Mount Victor'
'Plumbago'
'Bimbowrie'
Bimbowrie Road
'Old Boolcoomata'
Road
'Wompinie'
Cockburn
'Toronga'
Weira Hill 620m
'Witchitie'
'Bindyi'
Mingary
Cutana
Highway
'Bulloo Creek'
'Pine Creek'
Mares Cave
'Four Brothers'
Weekeroo Hill 540m
Plumbago Road
'Outalpa'
'Aroona'
'Corella'
Belton
Marchant Hill 780m
Teetulpa Goldfields
'Morialpa'
Olary
'Wiawera'
Waukaringa Historic Site
Waukaringa
'Bonnie Brae'
'Weekeroo'
Barrier
'Ballara'
'Coutra Hut'
Bendleby Settlers Monument
Bendleby
'Melton'
Karkala Peak 510m
Salt Creek
Outalpa
'Eringa Park'
Olary Ck
Warna Plain
Johnburgh (ruins)
'Minburra'
Minburra Plain
'Wabricoola'
Manna Hill
Wawirra
'Maldorky'
'Mutooroo'
'Old Wabricoola'
'Winninnie'
267
Oulnina
'Devonborough Downs'
'Duffields'
Brassey
Bob Gap
'Meadow Downs'
Hope Bank Range
Waroonee Range
'Wadnaminga'
'Taltabooka'
Steve Gap
'Yalpara'
216
Yunta
'Oulnina Park'
Benda Range
'Mccoys Well'
Lower Nackara
'Whyngoon'
'Treehaven'
Peaked Hill 550m
'Oakdowns'
'Panaramatee'
Yunta Ck
Ocalla Creek
'Kylmorn'
Old Whydown'
Paratoo
Buttamuck Hill 520m
'Tiverton'
'Netley Gap'
Netley Gap
'Taltabooka'
'White Well'
Nackara
'Spring Dam'
Black Rock
Dawson
'Manunda'
Quarantine
Do not take fruit, vegetables, plants or flowers across State and quarantine borders. Penalties apply. Phone 1800 084 881
'Oak Park'
Woolshed Range
'Bullyaninnie'
Nantabibbie
'Westbury Downs'
Oodla Wirra
Oodla Wirra Quarantine Checkpoint
'Hill Grange'
'Tiverton Outstation'
'Old Manunda'
Danggali Conservation Park
Australia's first Biosphere Reserve. Birdwatching, historical significance, mallee scrubland
Yatina
Peterborough
135
Lancelot
'Pitcairn'
Manunda Creek
'Mafeking Outstation'
Pualco Range
Pualco Range Con Park
'Lilydale'
'Oakvale'
Yongala
'Enwby'
Blue Hills'
Porcupine Range
'Mulga Hill' (abandoned)
Levi Range
Ironback Gorge
'Oakbank Outstation'
'Quondong Vale'
Gumbowie
'Tilkilki'
Wandre Plain
Sunnybrae
Franklyn
'The Oaks'
'Loch Winnoch'
'Cocanowie'
Canowie Belt
Terowie
'Pine Creek'
'Faraway Hill Outstation'
Tom Allison Waterhole
Tipperary Hut
Tipperary
Birthday Hut Tk
MVO only
Mallett Rd
Wonna Cairn
'Bendigo'
'Braemar'
Block Seven Gorge
'Aldermans Outstation'
'Sturt Vale'
Mail Road
Moorowie Plain
'Pulpara'
'Woolamba'
'Alexandrina Outstation'
Belalie East
'Mallett'
Ulooloo
'Ketchowla'
'Willara'
'Pine Valley'
Tk
Loop
Danggali Wilderness Protection Area
Old Canowie
Mount Bryan East
'Collinsville'
'Kia-Ora'
'Yellowie'
Tommy Gap
Caroona Ck Con Park
Hallett
'New Caroona'
'Hog Back'
Road
Morgan
'Lords Well Outstation'
Western Boundary
MVO only
Danggali Con Park
'Tiverville'
'Caroona'
'Glenora'
'Murkaby'
'Dustholes Station'
'Canopus'
Booborowie
Mount Bryan
Tracy
Eastern
'Koomooloo'
'Old Koomooloo'
Chowilla Regional Reserve
'Hypurna'
Riverland FFEZ
'Arlie'
Leighton
To Burra
'Chalk Cliffs'
'Parcoola'
© Hema Maps
139°10'E
140°E
140°50'E
30°50'S
31°40'S
32°30'S
33°20'S

Roxby Downs to Cameron Corner

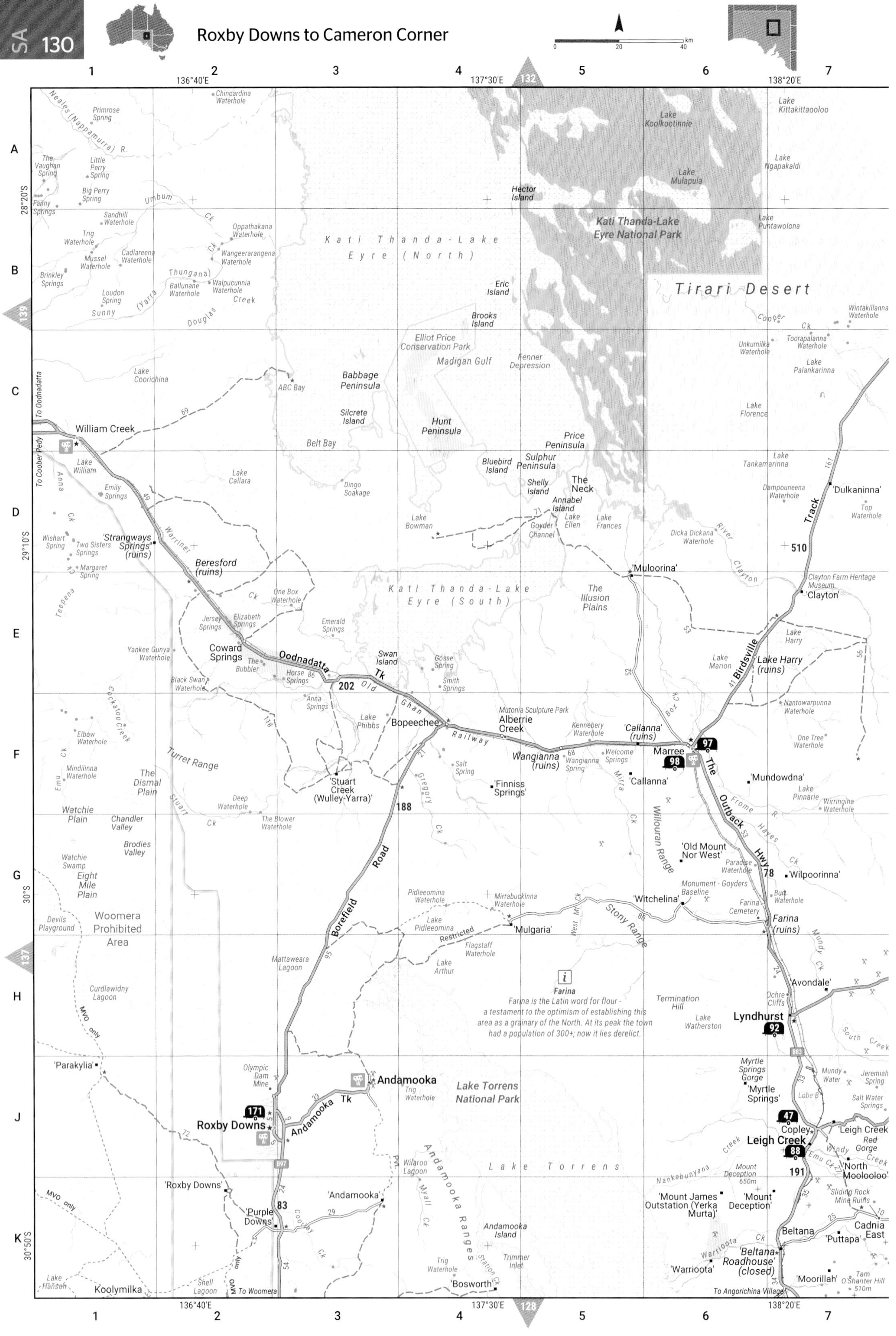

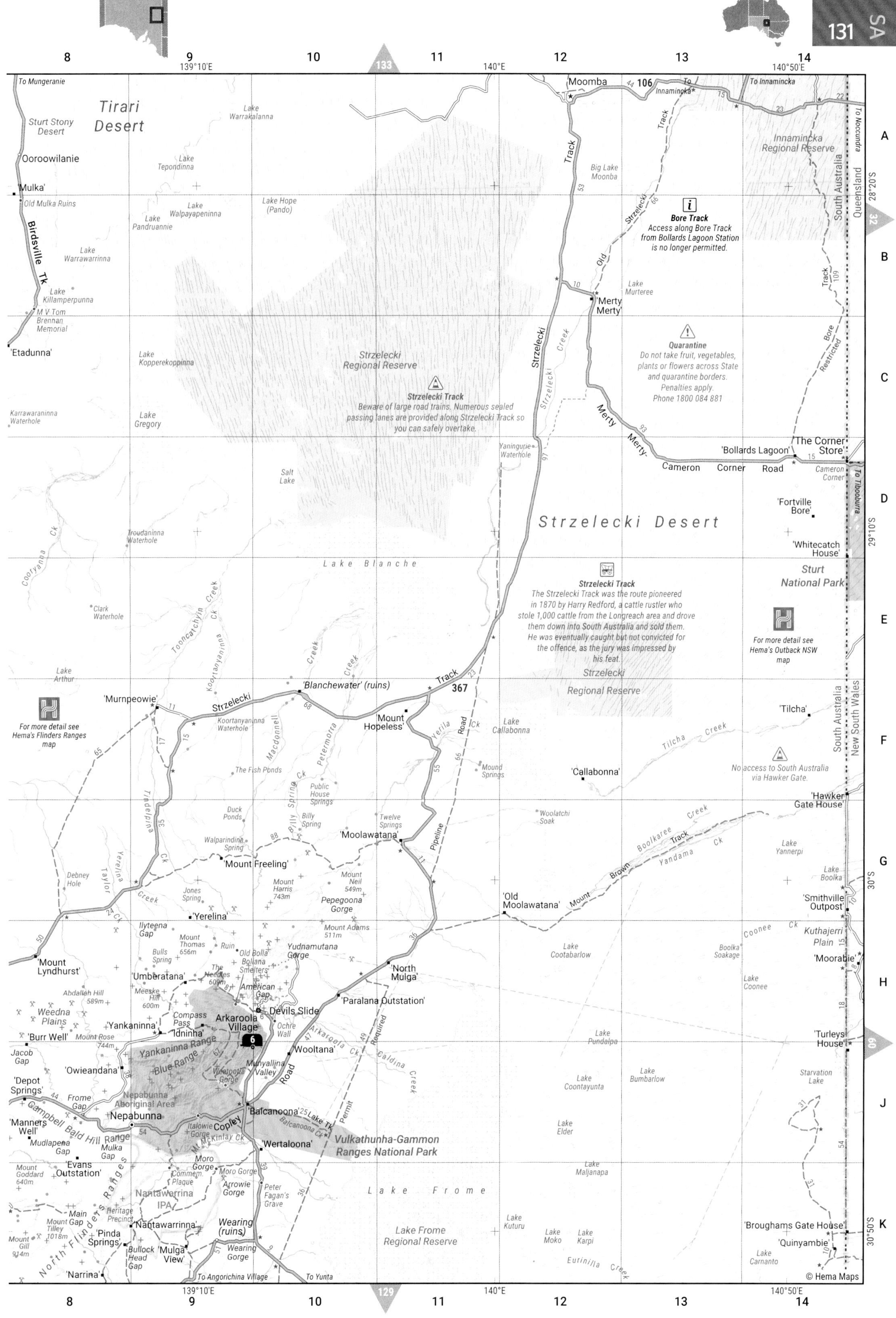

Tirari Desert
Sturt Stony Desert
Ooroowilanie
'Mulka'
Old Mulka Ruins
Birdsville Tk
Lake Warrakalanna
Lake Tepondinna
Lake Walpayapeninna
Lake Pandruannie
Lake Hope (Pando)
Lake Warrawarrinna
Lake Killamperpunna
M V Tom Brennan Memorial
'Etadunna'
Moomba
To Innamincka
Innamincka Regional Reserve
To Noccundra
South Australia
Queensland
Big Lake Moomba
Bore Track
Access along Bore Track from Bollards Lagoon Station is no longer permitted.
Lake Murteree
'Merty Merty'
Quarantine
Do not take fruit, vegetables, plants or flowers across State and quarantine borders. Penalties apply. Phone 1800 084 881
Lake Kopperekoppinna
Strzelecki Regional Reserve
Strzelecki Track
Beware of large road trains. Numerous sealed passing lanes are provided along Strzelecki Track so you can safely overtake.
Karrawaraninna Waterhole
Lake Gregory
Yaningurie Waterhole
Merty Merty-Cameron Corner Road
'Bollards Lagoon'
'The Corner Store'
Cameron Corner
To Tibooburra
Salt Lake
'Fortville Bore'
Strzelecki Desert
'Whitecatch House'
Troudaninna Waterhole
Lake Blanche
Sturt National Park
Strzelecki Track
The Strzelecki Track was the route pioneered in 1870 by Harry Redford, a cattle rustler who stole 1,000 cattle from the Longreach area and drove them down into South Australia and sold them. He was eventually caught but not convicted for the offence, as the jury was impressed by his feat.
Clark Waterhole
For more detail see Hema's Outback NSW map
Lake Arthur
'Blanchewater' (ruins)
367
Strzelecki Regional Reserve
'Murnpeowie'
For more detail see Hema's Flinders Ranges map
Koortanyaninna Waterhole
'Mount Hopeless'
Lake Callabonna
'Tilcha'
New South Wales
The Fish Ponds
Mound Springs
'Callabonna'
No access to South Australia via Hawker Gate.
Public House Springs
Duck Ponds
Billy Spring
Twelve Springs
Woolatchi Soak
'Hawker Gate House'
'Moolawatana'
Walparindina Spring
'Mount Freeling'
Lake Yannerpi
Debney Hole
Mount Neil 549m
Mount Harris 743m
Jones Spring
Pepegoona Gorge
'Old Moolawatana'
Lake Boolka
'Smithville Outpost'
'Yerelina'
Ilyteena Gap
Mount Thomas 656m
Mount Adams 511m
Kuthajerri Plain
Yudnamutana Gorge
'Mount Lyndhurst'
Bulls Spring
Old Bolla Bollana Smelters
Lake Cootabarlow
Boolka Soakage
'Moorabie'
'Umberatana'
The Needles 609m
'North Mulga'
American Gap
Abdallah Hill 589m
Meeske Hill 600m
Lake Coonee
Devils Slide
'Paralana Outstation'
Weedna Plains
'Yankaninna'
Compass Pass
Arkaroola Village
'Idninha'
Ochre Wall
'Burr Well'
Mount Rose 744m
Lake Pundalpa
'Turleys House'
Jacob Gap
Yankaninna Range
'Wooltana'
Blue Range
'Owieandana'
Weetootla Gorge
Munyallina Valley
Starvation Lake
'Depot Springs'
Lake Coontayunta
Lake Bumbarlow
Frome Gap
Nepabunna Aboriginal Area
'Balcanoona'
'Manners Well'
Nepabunna
Campbell Bald Hill Range
Copley
Italowie Gorge
Lake Elder
'Mudlapena Gap'
Mulka Gap
'Wertaloona'
Vulkathunha-Gammon Ranges National Park
Moro Gorge
Mount Goddard 640m
'Evans Outstation'
Commemorative Plaque
Lake Maljanapa
Arrowie Gorge
Peter Fagan's Grave
Lake Frome
Nantawarrina IPA
Main Gap
Heritage Precinct
Mount Tilley 1018m
Mount Gill 914m
'Pinda Springs'
'Nantawarrinna'
Wearing (ruins)
Lake Frome Regional Reserve
Lake Kuturu
Lake Moko
Lake Karpi
'Broughams Gate House'
'Quinyambie'
North Flinders Ranges
Bullock Head Gap
'Mulga View'
Wearing Gorge
Eurinilla Creek
Lake Carnanto
'Narrina'
To Angorichina Village
To Yunta
© Hema Maps

Simpson Desert to Innamincka

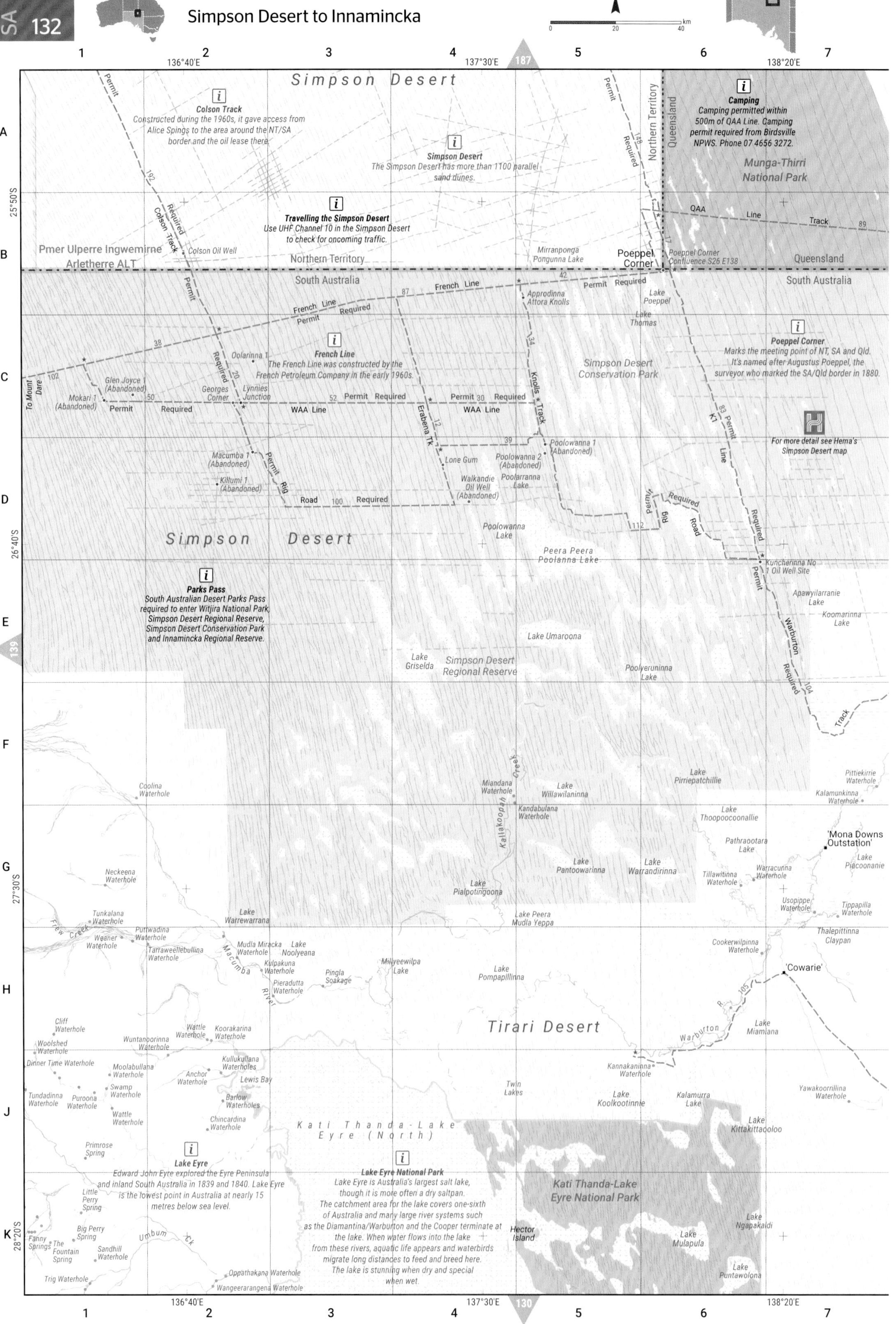

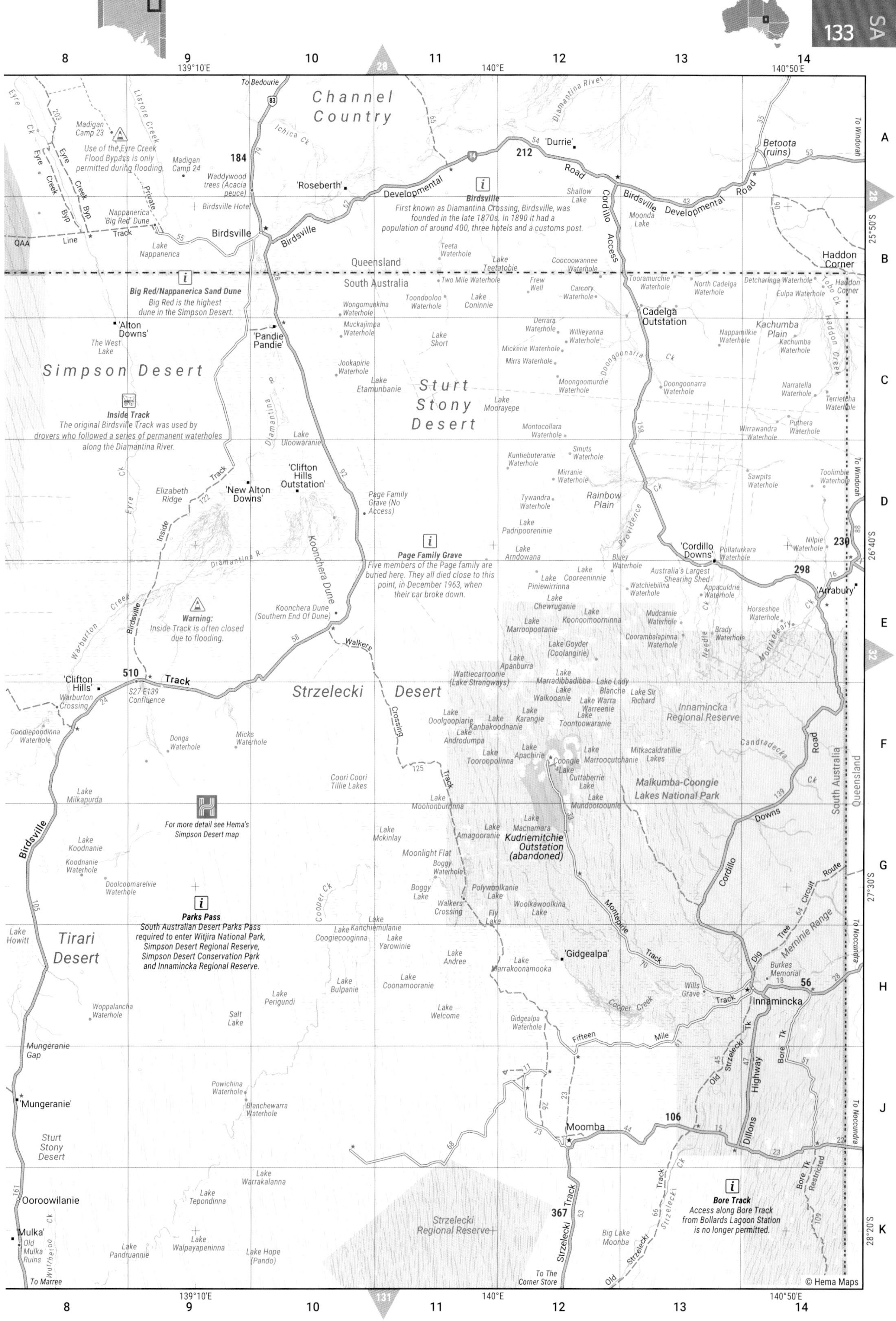

Channel Country
Simpson Desert
Sturt Stony Desert
Strzelecki Desert
Tirari Desert
Birdsville
First known as Diamantina Crossing, Birdsville, was founded in the late 1870s. In 1890 it had a population of around 400, three hotels and a customs post.
Big Red/Nappanerica Sand Dune
Big Red is the highest dune in the Simpson Desert.
Use of the Eyre Creek Flood Bypass is only permitted during flooding.
Inside Track
The original Birdsville Track was used by drovers who followed a series of permanent waterholes along the Diamantina River.
Warning:
Inside Track is often closed due to flooding.
Page Family Grave
Five members of the Page family are buried here. They all died close to this point, in December 1963, when their car broke down.
For more detail see Hema's Simpson Desert map
Parks Pass
South Australian Desert Parks Pass required to enter Witjira National Park, Simpson Desert Regional Reserve, Simpson Desert Conservation Park and Innamincka Regional Reserve.
Bore Track
Access along Bore Track from Bollards Lagoon Station is no longer permitted.
Queensland
South Australia
Birdsville Developmental Road
Birdsville Track
Cordillo Access
Cordillo Downs Road
Strzelecki Track
Old Strzelecki Track
Walkers Crossing Track
Montepirie Track
Dig Tree Circuit Route
Fifteen Mile Track
Dillons Highway
Innamincka Regional Reserve
Malkumba-Coongie Lakes National Park
Strzelecki Regional Reserve
Birdsville
Betoota (ruins)
Haddon Corner
'Durrie'
'Roseberth'
Cadelga Outstation
'Alton Downs'
'Pandie Pandie'
'New Alton Downs'
'Clifton Hills Outstation'
'Cordillo Downs'
'Arrabury'
'Clifton Hills'
Kudriemitchie Outstation (abandoned)
'Gidgealpa'
Innamincka
Moomba
'Mungeranie'
Ooroowilanie
'Mulka'
Old Mulka Ruins
To Marree
To The Corner Store
To Bedourie
To Windorah
To Noccundra
Lake Eyre
Coongie Lake
Lake Hope (Pando)
Merninie Range
Cooper Creek
Diamantina R.
Warburton Creek
Koonchera Dune
Rainbow Plain
Kachumba Plain
Burkes Memorial
Wills Grave
© Hema Maps

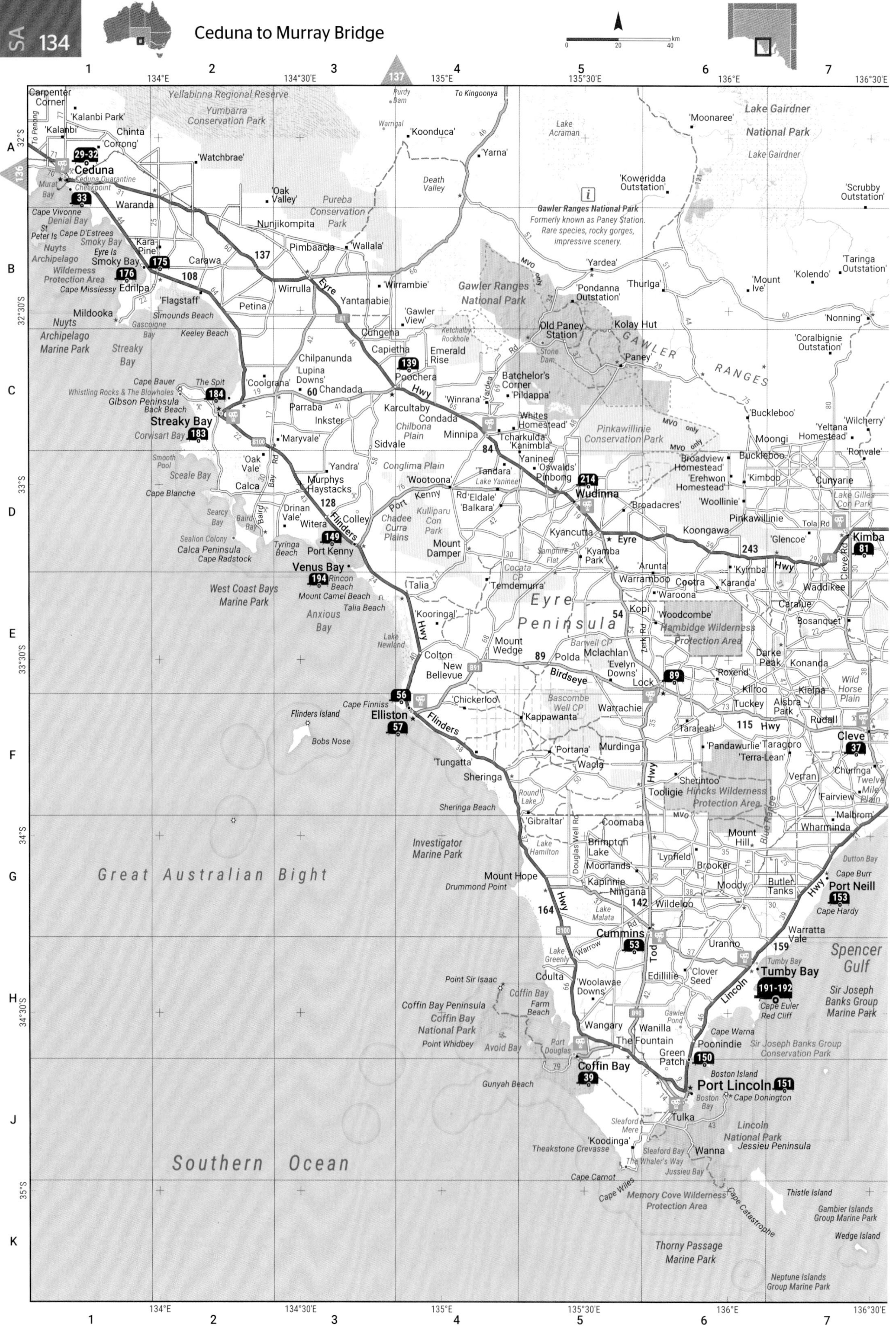

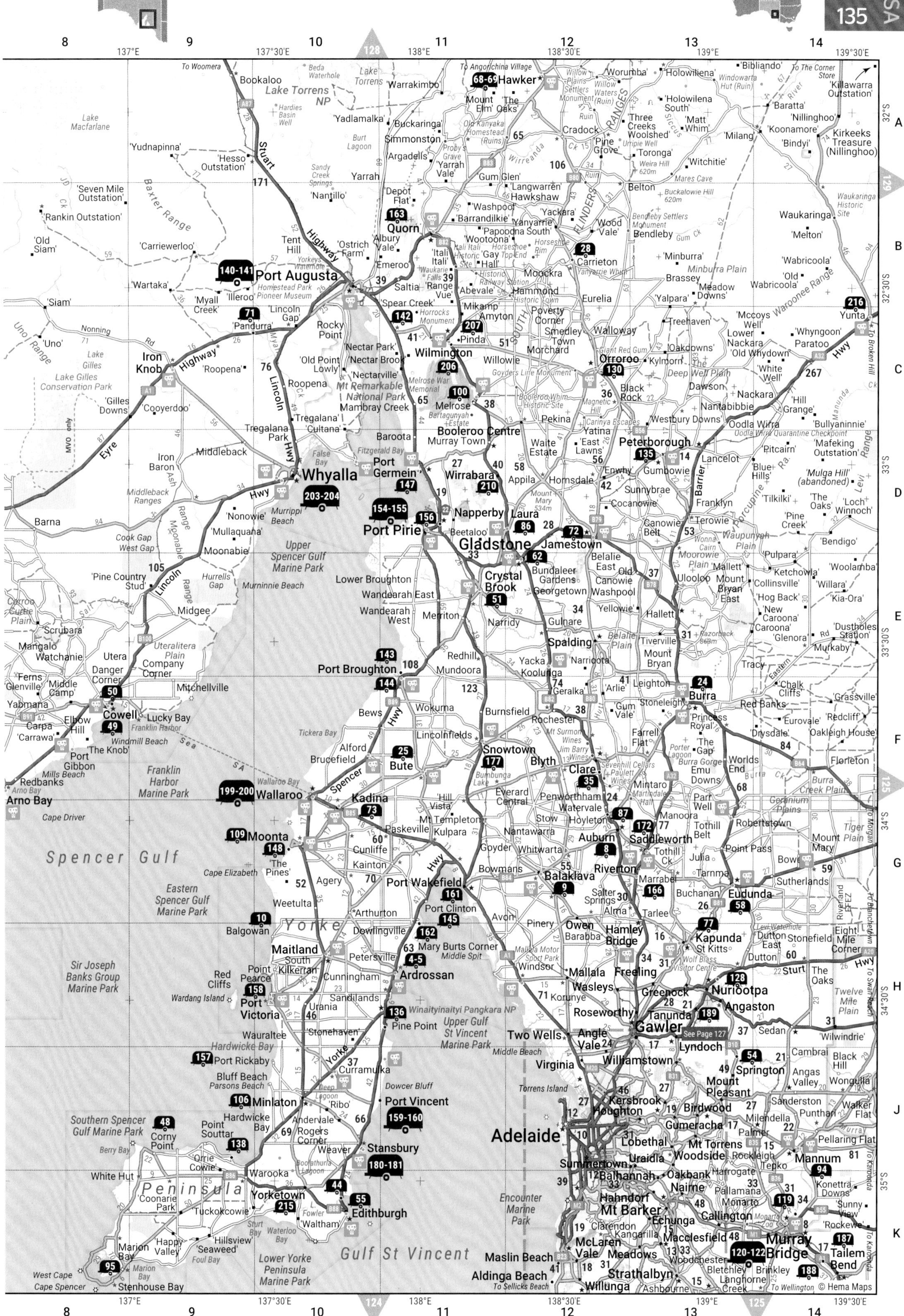

8
9
10
11
12
13
14
137°E
137°30'E
138°E
138°30'E
139°E
139°30'E
128
129
125
124
A
B
C
D
E
F
G
H
J
K
32°S
32°30'S
33°S
33°30'S
34°S
34°30'S
35°S
To Woomera
Bookaloo
Lake Torrens NP
Lake Torrens
Lake Macfarlane
'Yudnapinna'
'Hesso' Outstation'
Stuart
171
'Seven Mile Outstation'
'Rankin Outstation'
Baxter Range
'Old Siam'
'Carriewerloo'
Tent Hill
Highway
Port Augusta
140-141
'Wartaka'
'Myall Creek'
'Illeroo'
'Siam'
71
'Pandurra'
'Lincoln Gap'
Uno Range
'Uno'
Nonning
Iron Knob
Highway
'Roopena'
76
Lincoln
Lake Gilles
Lake Gilles Conservation Park
'Gilles Downs'
'Cooyerdoo'
Eyre
Middleback
Iron Baron
Tregalana Park
Hwy
Whyalla
203-204
Middleback Ranges
'Nonowie'
'Mullaquana'
Barna
Cook Gap
West Gap
Moonabie
105
'Pine Country Stud'
Lincoln
Hurrells Gap
Midgee
'Scrubara'
Mangalo
Watchanie
Utera
Uteralitera Plain
Company Corner
Danger Corner
'Ferns Glenville'
'Middle Camp'
Mitchellville
50
Yabmana
Carpa
Elbow Hill
Cowell
49
Lucky Bay
Franklin Harbor
Windmill Beach
'Carrawa'
'The Knob'
Port Gibbon
Mills Beach
Redbanks
Arno Bay
Cape Driver
Franklin Harbor Marine Park
Spencer Gulf
Cape Elizabeth
Eastern Spencer Gulf Marine Park
Sir Joseph Banks Group Marine Park
Wardang Island
Upper Spencer Gulf Marine Park
Murninnie Beach
Murrippi Beach
Yarrah
'Nantillo'
'Yadlamalka'
Hawker
68-69
'Warrakimbo'
'Buckaringa'
Simmonston
Argadells
'Mount Elm'
'The Oaks'
65
'Depot Flat'
163
Quorn
'Ostrich Farm'
'Albury Vale'
'Emeroo'
39
Saltia
'Spear Creek'
142
Rocky Point
'Nectar Park'
'Nectar Brook'
'Old Point Lowly'
'Nectarville'
Roopena
Mt Remarkable National Park
Mambray Creek
'Tregalana'
'Cultana'
Baroota
Fitzgerald Bay
False Bay
Port Germein
147
154-155
156
Port Pirie
41
Wilmington
206
65
100
Melrose
38
Booleroo Centre
Murray Town
27
Wirrabara
210
40
58
Appila
19
Napperby
Laura
86
Beetaloo
Gladstone
33
Crystal Brook
51
Lower Broughton
Wandearah East
Wandearah West
Merriton
Narridy
Redhill
Mundoora
143
Port Broughton
108
144
123
Bews
Wokurna
Lincolnfields
Alford
Brucefield
25
Bute
Wallaroo
199-200
Kadina
73
109
Moonta
148
'The Pines'
52
Agery
Cunliffe
Kainton
70
Paskeville
Port Wakefield
161
Port Clinton
145
Weetulta
Arthurton
10
Balgowan
Yorke
Dowlingville
162
Mary Burts Corner
Middle Spit
Maitland
South Kilkerran
Petersville
4-5
Ardrossan
63
Cunningham
Point Pearce
Red Cliffs
158
Port Victoria
Sandilands
Urania
46
136
Pine Point
Winaityinaityi Pangkara NP
Upper Gulf St Vincent Marine Park
'Stonehaven'
Wauraltee
Hardwicke Bay
157
Port Rickaby
Bluff Beach
Parsons Beach
37
Curramulka
Dowcer Bluff
106
Minlaton
Port Vincent
159-160
Hardwicke Bay
Southern Spencer Gulf Marine Park
48
Corny Point
Point Souttar
138
69
Rogers Corner
66
Weaver
Stansbury
180-181
Berry Bay
White Hut
Peninsula
Warooka
Yorketown
215
44
55
Edithburgh
'Coonarie Park'
Tuckokcowie
Waterloo Bay
'Waltham'
Happy Valley
'Hillsview'
'Seaweed'
Foul Bay
Marion Bay
95
West Cape
Cape Spencer
Stenhouse Bay
Lower Yorke Peninsula Marine Park
Gulf St Vincent
Maslin Beach
Aldinga Beach
To Sellicks Beach
Worumba
'Holowilena'
'Bibliando'
To The Corner Store
'Killawarra Outstation'
'Holowilena South'
'Three Creeks Woolshed'
'Matt Whim'
'Baratta'
'Nillinghoo'
'Koonamore'
Kirkeeks Treasure (Nillinghoo)
'Bindyi'
'Milang'
Cradock
Pine Grove
'Toronga'
106
'Witchitie'
'Gum Glen'
'Langwarren'
Hawkshaw
Belton
'Washpool'
'Barrandilkie'
'Yanyarrie'
'Papoodna South'
'Yackara'
Flinders Ranges
'Wood Vale'
Bendleby
Waukaringa
'Melton'
'Wootoona'
'Gay'
'Hall'
28
Carrieton
'Minburra'
Minburra Plain
'Wabricoola'
'Old Wabricoola'
Moockra
Brassey
'Abevale'
Hammond
'Meadow Downs'
'Yalpara'
Eurelia
216
Yunta
'Mikamp'
Amyton
207
Pinda
Poverty Corner
Smedley Town
Walloway
'Treehaven'
'Mccoys Well'
Lower Nackara
'Whyngoon'
Paratoo
51
Morchard
'Oakdowns'
Orroroo
130
'Kylmorn'
'Old Whydown'
'White Well'
267
Willowie
Deep Well Plain
Black Rock
36
Dawson
Nackara
Nantabibbie
'Hill Grange'
Pekina
'Westbury Downs'
Oodla Wirra
'Bullyaninnie'
Yatina
Peterborough
135
'Pitcairn'
'Mafeking Outstation'
Waite Estate
'East Lawns'
56
Gumbowie
14
Lancelot
Blue Hills'
'Mulga Hill' (abandoned)
Hornsdale
42
'Enwhy'
Sunnybrae
'Cocanowie'
Barrier
Franklyn
'Tilkilki'
'The Oaks'
'Loch Winnoch'
28
72
Jamestown
Canowie Belt
Terowie
53
'Pine Creek'
'Bendigo'
62
Bundaleer Gardens
Belalie East
Old Canowie
37
Waupunyah Plain
'Pulpara'
Georgetown
Washpool
Ulooloo
Mount Bryan East
'Mallett'
'Ketchowla'
'Woolamba'
'Collinsville'
'Willara'
'Hog Back'
'Kia-Ora'
34
Gulnare
'Yellowie'
Hallett
'New Caroona'
'Caroona'
Spalding
Belalie Plain
Tiverville
Mount Bryan
31
'Glenora'
'Dustholes Station'
'Murkaby'
Yacka
Koolunga
'Narrioota'
Tracy
74
Geralka
41
'Arlie'
Leighton
24
Burra
'Chalk Cliffs'
'Grassville'
38
'Gum Vale'
Stoneleigh
Red Banks
Burnsfield
Rochester
'Princess Royal'
'Eurovale'
'Redcliff'
Farrell Flat
'Drysdale'
'Oakleigh House'
Snowtown
177
Blyth
Clare
'The Gap'
Worlds End
84
Florieton
35
Emu Downs
Burra Gorge
68
Everard Central
Penwortham
Mintaro
24
Waterlale
87
Hoyleton
172
77
Saddleworth
Manoora
Tothill Belt
Park Well
Robertstown
'Hill Vista'
Mt Templeton
Kulpara
Nantawarra
Stow
Auburn
8
Riverton
Tothill Ck
Julia
Point Pass
Mount Mary
Goyder
Whitwarta
Bowmans
Balaklava
9
Marrabel
166
Tarnma
Sutherlands
59
Buchanan
Eudunda
58
Salter Springs
Alma
Tarlee
26
Avon
Pinery
Owen
Barabba
Hamley Bridge
16
77
Kapunda
St Kitts
Dutton East
Stonefield
Eight Mile Corner
Dutton
60
Windsor
Mallala
Freeling
34
31
Sturt
The Oaks
Wasleys
128
Nuriootpa
Greenock
15
71
Korunye
28
21
189
Angaston
Roseworthy
Tanunda
Two Wells
Gawler
See Page 127
37
Sedan
31
Angle Vale
24
17
Lyndoch
'Wilwindrie'
Middle Beach
Virginia
Williamstown
54
Springton
21
Cambrai
Black Hill
49
Angas Valley
Wongulla
Torrens Island
46
27
Mount Pleasant
27
Kersbrook
Houghton
19
Birdwood
Sanderston
Punthari
Walker Flat
Milendella
22
Palmer
Pellaring Flat
Adelaide
Gumeracha
17
31
Lobethal
Mt Torrens
15
Urairda
Woodside
Rockleigh
Tepko
Mannum
81
94
Summertown
Balhannah
Oakbank
Harrogate
Konetta Downs
39
Nairne
Pallamana
33
31
34
Hahndorf
Monarto
119
'Sunny View'
Mt Barker
48
Encounter Marine Park
Echunga
Callington
19
Clarendon
Kangarilla
Macclesfield
48
Murray Bridge
187
'Rockewe'
McLaren Vale
Meadows
13
33
120-122
Tailem Bend
17
Woodchester
Brinkley
188
18
31
Strathalbyn
Bletchley
Langhorne Creek
Willunga
Ashbourne
15
To Wellington
© Hema Maps
To Broken Hill
To Morgan
To Blanchetown
To Swan Reach
To Karoonda

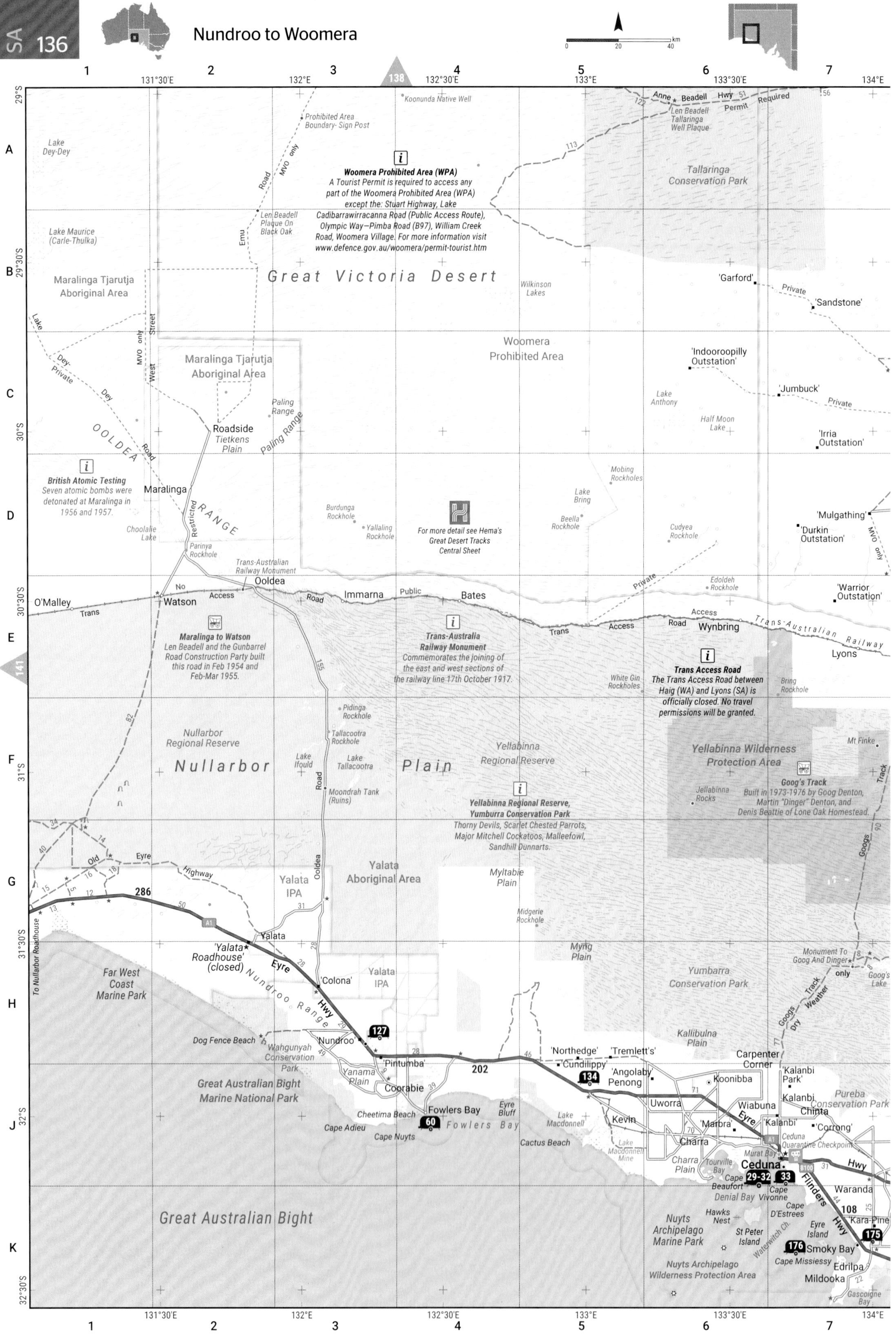
Woomera Prohibited Area (WPA)
A Tourist Permit is required to access any part of the Woomera Prohibited Area (WPA) except the: Stuart Highway, Lake Cadibarrawirracanna Road (Public Access Route), Olympic Way—Pimba Road (B97), William Creek Road, Woomera Village. For more information visit www.defence.gov.au/woomera/permit-tourist.htm
Great Victoria Desert
Maralinga Tjarutja Aboriginal Area
Tallaringa Conservation Park
Woomera Prohibited Area
British Atomic Testing
Seven atomic bombs were detonated at Maralinga in 1956 and 1957.
For more detail see Hema's Great Desert Tracks Central Sheet
Maralinga to Watson
Len Beadell and the Gunbarrel Road Construction Party built this road in Feb 1954 and Feb-Mar 1955.
Trans-Australia Railway Monument
Commemorates the joining of the east and west sections of the railway line 17th October 1917.
Trans Access Road
The Trans Access Road between Haig (WA) and Lyons (SA) is officially closed. No travel permissions will be granted.
Nullarbor Regional Reserve
Nullarbor Plain
Yellabinna Regional Reserve
Yellabinna Wilderness Protection Area
Googs Track
Built in 1973-1976 by Goog Denton, Martin "Dinger" Denton, and Denis Beattie of Lone Oak Homestead.
Yellabinna Regional Reserve, Yumburra Conservation Park
Thorny Devils, Scarlet Chested Parrots, Major Mitchell Cockatoos, Malleefowl, Sandhill Dunnarts.
Yalata Aboriginal Area
Yalata IPA
Far West Coast Marine Park
Great Australian Bight Marine National Park
Great Australian Bight
Yumbarra Conservation Park
Nuyts Archipelago Marine Park
Nuyts Archipelago Wilderness Protection Area
Pureba Conservation Park
Wahgunyah Conservation Park
Maralinga
Watson
O'Malley
Ooldea
Immarna
Bates
Wynbring
Lyons
Roadside
Yalata
'Yalata Roadhouse' (closed)
'Colona'
Nundroo
'Pintumba'
Coorabie
Fowlers Bay
Penong
Koonibba
Kalanbi
Uworra
Wiabuna
Charra
Kevin
Ceduna
Chinta
Waranda
Kara-Pine
Smoky Bay
Edrilpa
Mildooka
Eyre Hwy
Flinders Hwy
Trans-Australian Railway
Dog Fence Beach
Cheetima Beach
Cape Adieu
Cape Nuyts
Cactus Beach
To Nullarbor Roadhouse

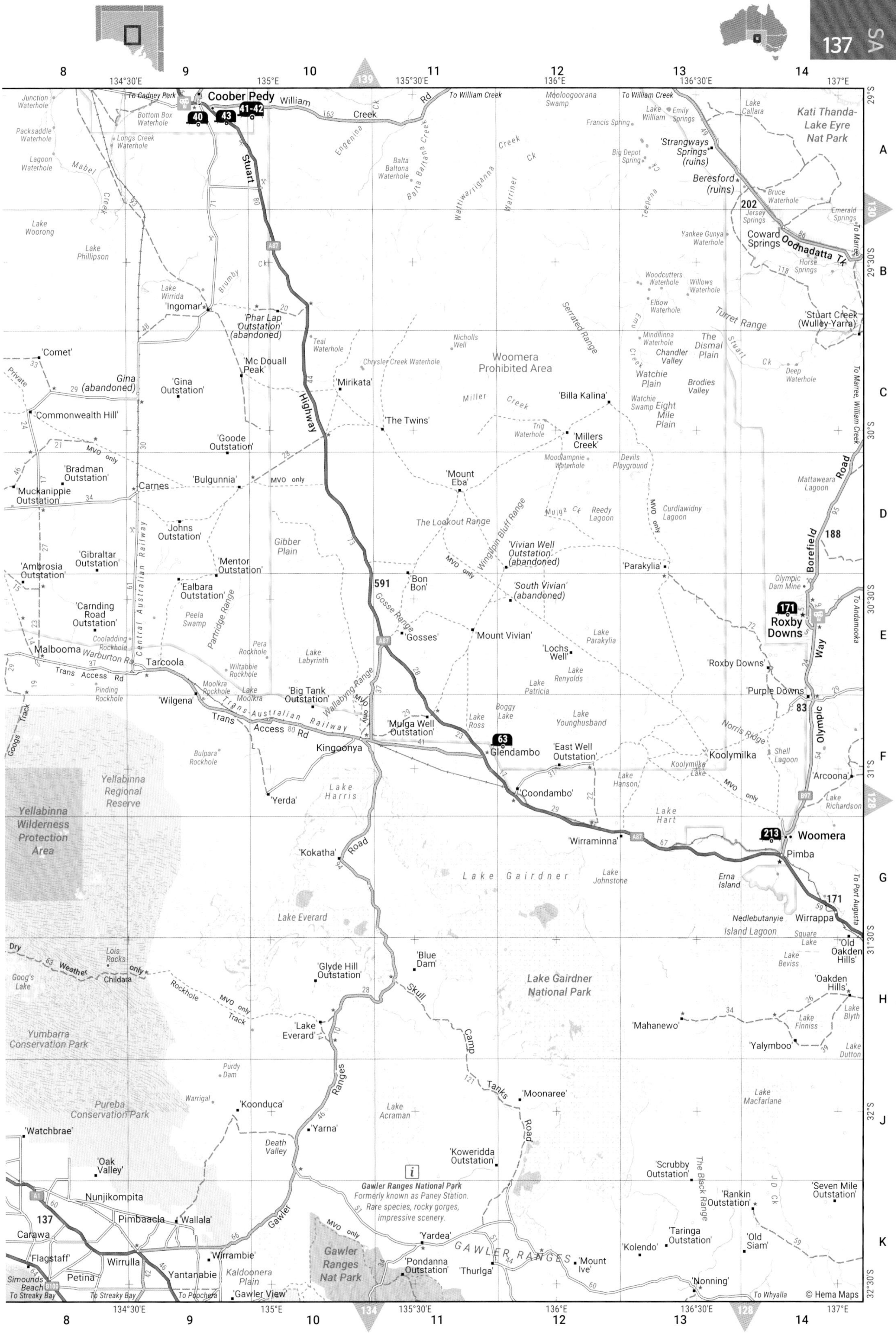

Coober Pedy
Stuart Highway
Woomera Prohibited Area
Kati Thanda-Lake Eyre Nat Park
Oodnadatta Tk
Roxby Downs
Borefield Road
Olympic Way
Woomera
Pimba
Glendambo
Kingoonya
Tarcoola
Trans Access Rd
Trans-Australian Railway
Central Australian Railway
Lake Gairdner
Lake Gairdner National Park
Lake Everard
Yellabinna Wilderness Protection Area
Yellabinna Regional Reserve
Yumbarra Conservation Park
Pureba Conservation Park
Gawler Ranges Nat Park
Gawler Ranges National Park Formerly known as Paney Station. Rare species, rocky gorges, impressive scenery.
GAWLER RANGES
Nunjikompita
Wirrulla
Yantanabie
Petina
Wirrappa
Kokatha Road
Skull Camp Tanks Road
© Hema Maps

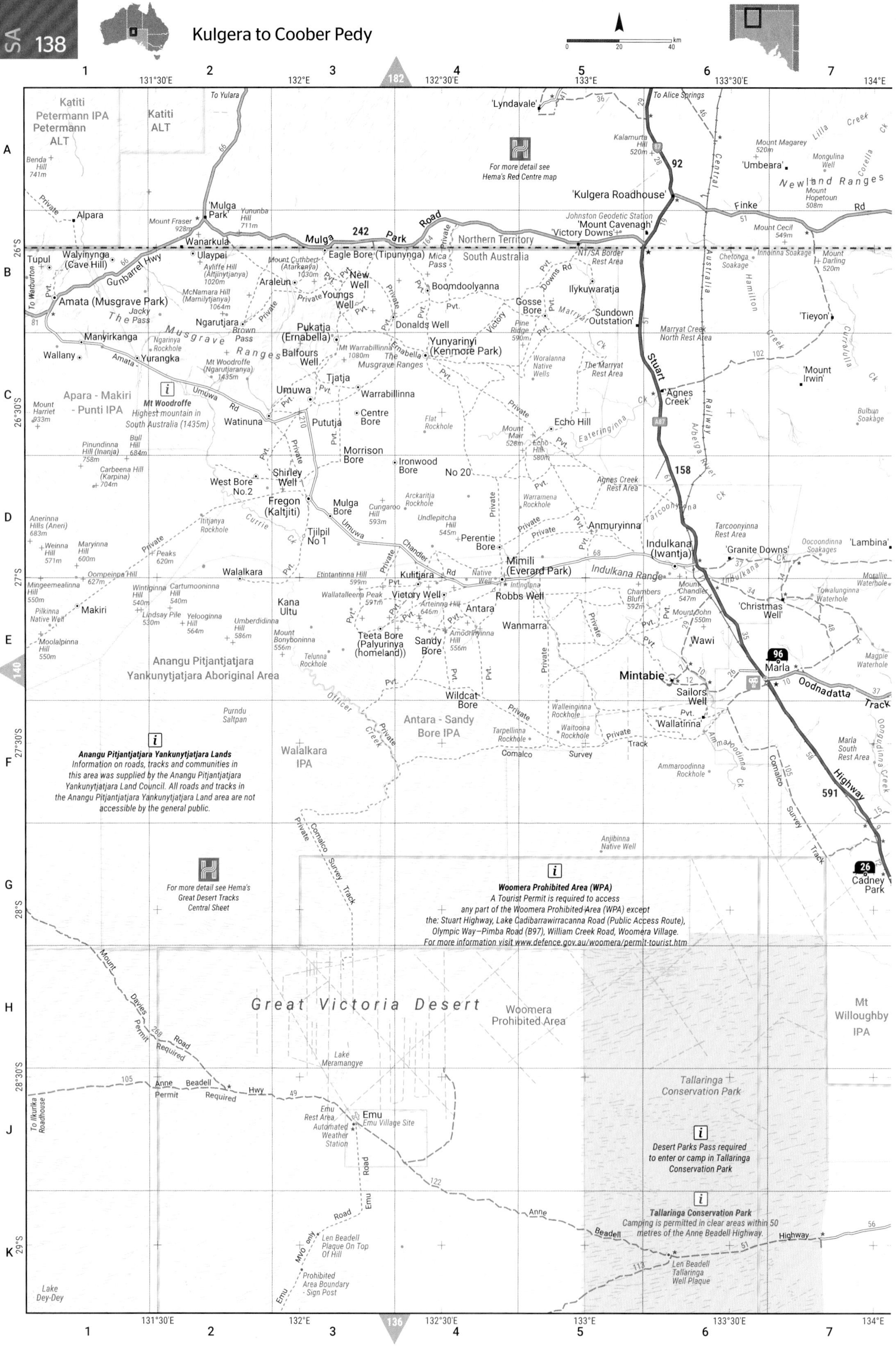

To Yulara
To Alice Springs
'Lyndavale'
For more detail see Hema's Red Centre map
Katiti Petermann IPA
Katiti Petermann ALT
Katiti ALT
Kalamurta Hill 520m
'Umbeara'
Mount Magarey 520m
Mongulina Well
Newland Ranges
Mount Hopetoun 508m
'Kulgera Roadhouse'
Finke
Rd
Central Australia Railway
Alpara
'Mulga Park'
Yununba Hill 711m
Mount Fraser 928m
Wanarkula
Mulga Park Road
Johnston Geodetic Station
'Mount Cavenagh'
'Victory Downs'
Mount Cecil 549m
Northern Territory
South Australia
NT/SA Border Rest Area
Innamincka Soakage
Mount Darling 520m
Chetonga Soakage
Tupul
Walyinynga (Cave Hill)
Ulaypei
Aylilffe Hill (Altjinytjanya) 1020m
Mount Cuthbert (Atarkanya) 1030m
Eagle Bore (Tipunyinga)
Mica Pass
Gunbarrel Hwy
Araleun
New Well
Boomdoolyanna
Ilykuwaratja
Amata (Musgrave Park)
McNamara Hill (Mamilytjanya) 1064m
Youngs Well
Gosse Bore
Marryat Ck
'Sundown Outstation'
Hamilton Creek
'Tieyon'
Jacky The Pass
Ngarutjara
Brown Pass
Pukatja (Ernabella)
Donalds Well
Pine Ridge 590m
Marryat Creek North Rest Area
Manyirkanga
Ngarinya Rockhole
Musgrave Ranges
Balfours Well
Mt Warrabillinna 1080m
Yunyarinyi (Kenmore Park)
Woralanna Native Wells
The Marryat Rest Area
Stuart Highway
Wallany
Yurangka
Mt Woodroffe (Ngarutjaranya) 1435m
The Musgrave Ranges
Ernabella
Tjatja
'Mount Irwin'
Apara - Makiri - Punti IPA
Umuwa
Warrabillinna
'Agnes Creek'
Mount Harriet 933m
Mt Woodroffe Highest mountain in South Australia (1435m)
Watinuna
Pututja
Centre Bore
Flat Rockhole
Mount Mair 528m
Echo Hill
Echo Hill 580m
Eateringinna Ck
Alberga River
Bulbun Soakage
Bull Hill 684m
Pinundinna Hill (Inanja) 758m
Morrison Bore
Carbeena Hill (Karpina) 704m
Shirley Well
Ironwood Bore
No 20
Agnes Creek Rest Area
West Bore No.2
Fregon (Kaltjiti)
Mulga Bore
Cungaroo Hill 593m
Arckaritja Rockhole
Warramena Rockhole
Tarcoonyinna Ck
Anerinna Hills (Aneri) 683m
Itjtjanya Rockhole
Currie Ck
Undlepitcha Hill 545m
Anmuryinna
Tarcoonyinna Rest Area
Ooconndinna Soakages
'Lambina'
Weinna Hill 571m
Maryinna Hill 600m
Peaks 620m
Tjilpil No 1
Umuwa Chandler Rd
Perentie Bore
Indulkana (Iwantja)
'Granite Downs'
Oompeinna Hill 627m
Walalkara
Etintantinna Hill 599m
Kulitjara
Native Well
Mimili (Everard Park)
Indulkana Range
Indulkana Ck
Mottlie Waterhole
Mingeemealinna Hill 550m
Wintiginna Hill 540m
Cartumooninna Hill 540m
Wallatalleena Peak 591m
Victory Well
Robbs Well
Chambers Bluff 592m
Mount Chandler 547m
Towalunginna Waterhole
'Christmas Well'
Makiri
Pilkinna Native Well
Lindsay Pile 530m
Yeloogginna Hill 564m
Kana Ultu
Arteinng Hill 646m
Antara
Mount Oohn 550m
Umberdidinna Hill 586m
Mount Bonyboninna 556m
Teeta Bore (Palyurinya (homeland))
Sandy Bore
Amoorinyinna Hill 556m
Wanmarra
Wawi
Moolalpinna Hill 550m
Anangu Pitjantjatjara Yankunytjatjara Aboriginal Area
Telunna Rockhole
Mintabie
Marla
Oodnadatta Track
Magpie Waterhole
Officer Creek
Wildcat Bore
Sailors Well
Purndu Saltpan
Walleinginna Rockhole
'Wallatinna'
Antara - Sandy Bore IPA
Tarpellinna Rockhole
Waitoona Rockhole
Walalkara IPA
Comalco Survey Track
Marla South Rest Area
Oongudinna Creek
Ammaroodinna Ck
Ammaroodinna Rockhole
Anangu Pitjantjatjara Yankunytjatjara Lands
Information on roads, tracks and communities in this area was supplied by the Anangu Pitjantjatjara Yankunytjatjara Council. All roads and tracks in the Anangu Pitjantjatjara Yankunytjatjara Land area are not accessible by the general public.
Anjibinna Native Well
Cadney Park
For more detail see Hema's Great Desert Tracks Central Sheet
Woomera Prohibited Area (WPA)
A Tourist Permit is required to access any part of the Woomera Prohibited Area (WPA) except the: Stuart Highway, Lake Cadibarrawirracanna Road (Public Access Route), Olympic Way–Pimba Road (B97), William Creek Road, Woomera Village.
For more information visit www.defence.gov.au/woomera/permit-tourist.htm
Great Victoria Desert
Woomera Prohibited Area
Mt Willoughby IPA
Mount Davies Road Permit Required
Lake Meramangye
Tallaringa Conservation Park
Anne Beadell Permit Required Hwy
To Ilkurlka Roadhouse
Emu Rest Area
Automated Weather Station
Emu
Emu Village Site
Emu Road
Desert Parks Pass required to enter or camp in Tallaringa Conservation Park
Tallaringa Conservation Park
Camping is permitted in clear areas within 50 metres of the Anne Beadell Highway.
Anne Beadell Highway
Len Beadell Plaque On Top Of Hill
MVO only
Len Beadell Tallaringa Well Plaque
Prohibited Area Boundary - Sign Post
Lake Dey-Dey
131°30'E
132°E
132°30'E
133°E
133°30'E
134°E
26°S
26°30'S
27°S
27°30'S
28°S
28°30'S
29°S
182
136
140

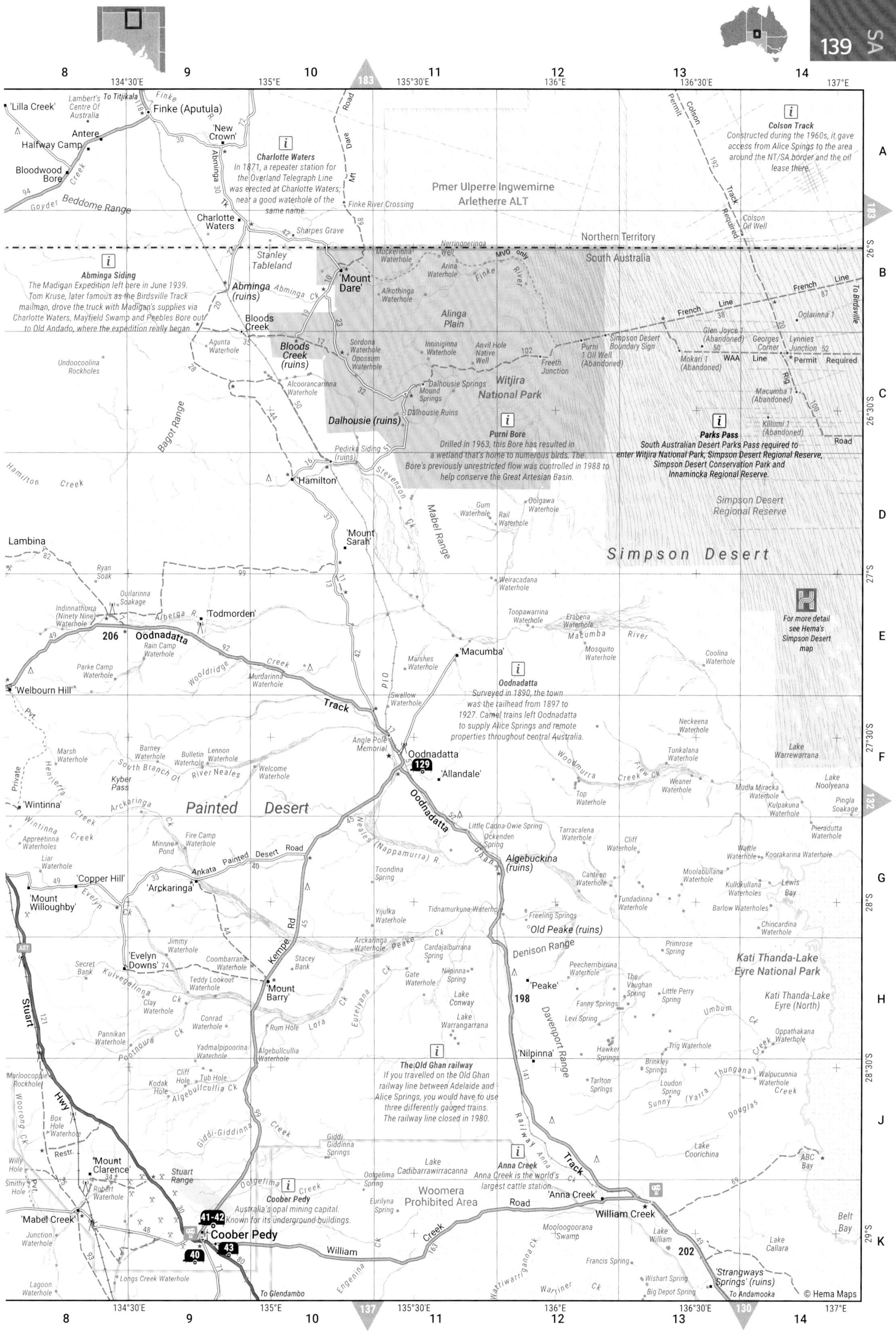

8
9
10
11
12
13
14
134°30'E
135°E
135°30'E
136°E
136°30'E
137°E
183
137
130
132
A
B
C
D
E
F
G
H
J
K
26°S
26°30'S
27°S
27°30'S
28°S
28°30'S
29°S
'Lilla Creek'
Lambert's Centre Of Australia
To Titjikala
Finke (Aputula)
'New Crown'
Antere
Halfway Camp
Bloodwood Bore
Beddome Range
Charlotte Waters
Charlotte Waters
In 1871, a repeater station for the Overland Telegraph Line was erected at Charlotte Waters, near a good waterhole of the same name.
Finke River Crossing
Pmer Ulperre Ingwemirne Arletherre ALT
Colson Track
Constructed during the 1960s, it gave access from Alice Spings to the area around the NT/SA border and the oil lease there.
Colson Oil Well
Permit Required
Sharpes Grave
Northern Territory
South Australia
Stanley Tableland
Abminga Siding
The Madigan Expedition left here in June 1939. Tom Kruse, later famous as the Birdsville Track mailman, drove the truck with Madigan's supplies via Charlotte Waters, Mayfield Swamp and Peebles Bore out to Old Andado, where the expedition really began.
Abminga (ruins)
Bloods Creek
Bloods Creek (ruins)
'Mount Dare'
Mount Dare
Alinga Plain
French Line
To Birdsville
Simpson Desert Boundary Sign
Purni 1 Oil Well (Abandoned)
Freeth Junction
Georges Corner
Lynnies Junction
WAA Line
Dalhousie Springs
Witjira National Park
Dalhousie (ruins)
Dalhousie Ruins
Purni Bore
Drilled in 1963, this Bore has resulted in a wetland that's home to numerous birds. The Bore's previously unrestricted flow was controlled in 1988 to help conserve the Great Artesian Basin.
Parks Pass
South Australian Desert Parks Pass required to enter Witjira National Park, Simpson Desert Regional Reserve, Simpson Desert Conservation Park and Innamincka Regional Reserve.
Bagot Range
Pedirka Siding (ruins)
'Hamilton'
Mabel Range
Simpson Desert Regional Reserve
Simpson Desert
Lambina
'Mount Sarah'
For more detail see Hema's Simpson Desert map
'Todmorden'
Oodnadatta
'Macumba'
Macumba River
Oodnadatta
Surveyed in 1890, the town was the railhead from 1897 to 1927. Camel trains left Oodnadatta to supply Alice Springs and remote properties throughout central Australia.
'Welbourn Hill'
Oodnadatta Track
Angle Pole Memorial
Oodnadatta
129
'Allandale'
'Wintinna'
Painted Desert
Kyber Pass
Lake Warrewarrana
Lake Noolyeana
Algebuckina (ruins)
Painted Desert Road
'Copper Hill'
'Arckaringa'
'Mount Willoughby'
Old Peake (ruins)
Denison Range
'Evelyn Downs'
Kempe Rd
'Mount Barry'
'Peake'
198
Kati Thanda-Lake Eyre National Park
Kati Thanda-Lake Eyre (North)
Davenport Range
Stuart Hwy
'Nilpinna'
The Old Ghan railway
If you travelled on the Old Ghan railway line between Adelaide and Alice Springs, you would have to use three differently gauged trains. The railway line closed in 1980.
'Mount Clarence'
Anna Creek
Anna Creek is the world's largest cattle station.
Woomera Prohibited Area
'Anna Creek'
William Creek
Coober Pedy
Australia's opal mining capital. Known for its underground buildings.
'Mabel Creek'
Coober Pedy
41-42
40
43
William Creek Road
202
'Strangways Springs' (ruins)
To Glendambo
To Andamooka
© Hema Maps

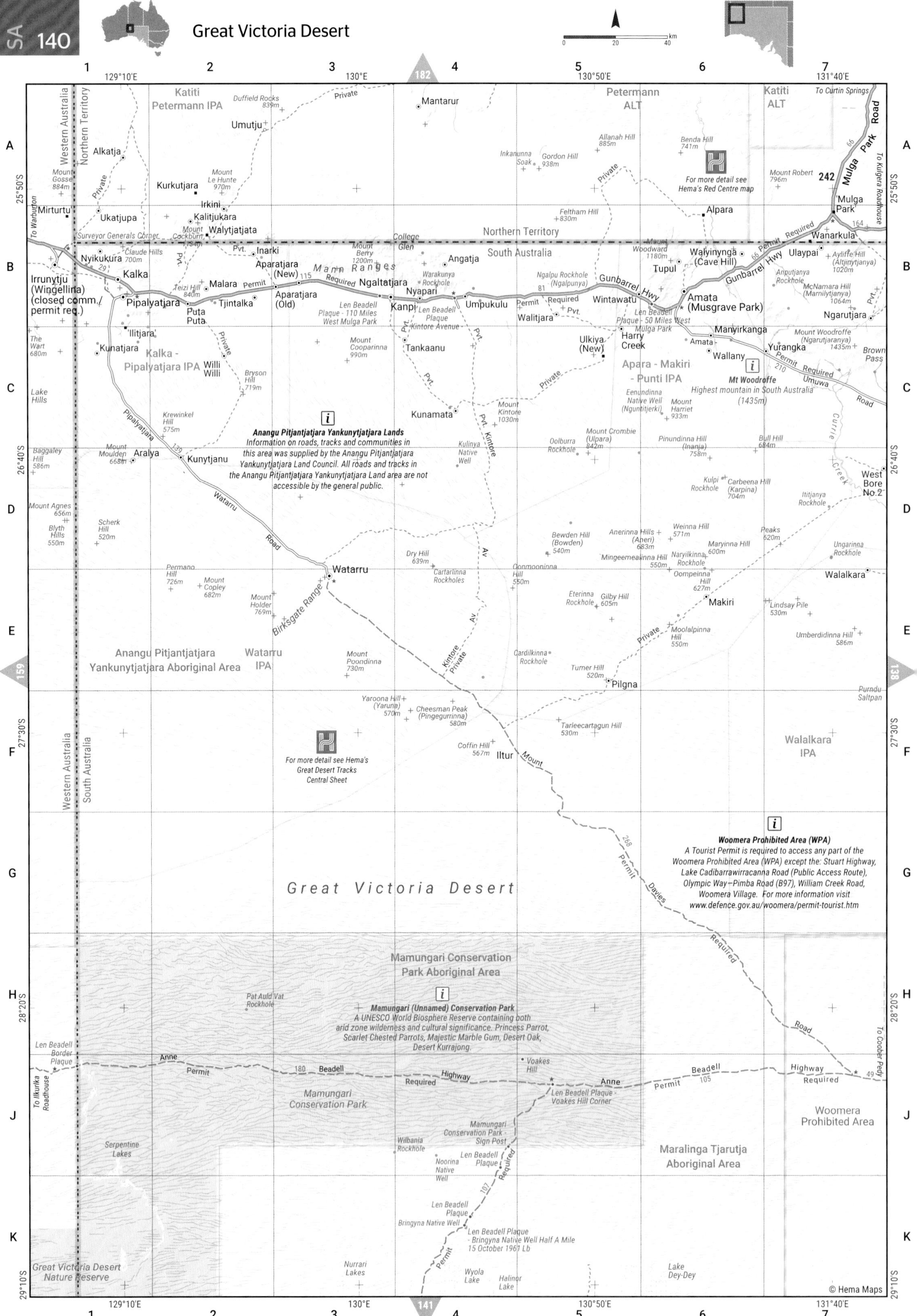

Katiti Petermann IPA
Duffield Rocks 839m
Private
Mantarur
Petermann ALT
Katiti ALT
To Curtin Springs
Mulga Park Road
Umutju
Alkatja
Western Australia
Northern Territory
Inkanunna Soak
Gordon Hill 938m
Allanah Hill 885m
Benda Hill 741m
For more detail see Hema's Red Centre map
Mount Robert 796m
242
To Kulgera Roadhouse
Mount Gosse 884m
Kurkutjara
Mount Le Hunte 970m
Irkini
'Mulga Park'
Mirturtu
To Warburton
Ukatjupa
Kalitjukara
Feltham Hill 830m
Alpara
Mount Cockburn 754m
Walytjatjata
Surveyor Generals Corner
Northern Territory
Wanarkula
College Glen
South Australia
Permit Required
Nyikukura
Claude Hills 700m
Inarki
Mount Berry 1200m
Angatja
Mount Woodward 1180m
Walyinynga (Cave Hill)
Ulaypai
Ayliffe Hill (Altjinytjanya) 1020m
Irrunytju (Wingellina) (closed comm./ permit req.)
Kalka
Aparatjara (New)
Mann Ranges
Warakunya Rockhole
Ngalpu Rockhole (Ngalpunya)
Tupul
Gunbarrel Hwy
Anputjanya Rockhole
McNamara Hill (Marnilytjanya) 1064m
Pipalyatjara
Teizi Hill 840m
Malara
Aparatjara (Old)
Ngaltatjara
Nyapari
Kanpi
Umpukulu
Wintawatu
Amata (Musgrave Park)
Ngarutjara
Puta Puta
Tjintalka
Len Beadell Plaque - 110 Miles West Mulga Park
Len Beadell Plaque Kintore Avenue
Walitjara
Len Beadell Plaque - 50 Miles West Mulga Park
'Ilitjara'
Harry Creek
Manyirkanga
The Wart 680m
Kunatjara
Kalka - Pipalyatjara IPA
Willi Willi
Mount Cooparinna 990m
Tankaanu
Ulkiya (New)
Amata
Wallany
Yurangka
Mount Woodroffe (Ngarutjaranya) 1435m
Brown Pass
Lake Hills
Bryson Hill 719m
Apara - Makiri - Punti IPA
Mt Woodroffe
Highest mountain in South Australia (1435m)
Umuwa Road
Krewinkel Hill 575m
Kunamata
Mount Kintore 1030m
Eenundinna Native Well (Nguntitjerki)
Mount Harriet 933m
Anangu Pitjantjatjara Yankunytjatjara Lands
Information on roads, tracks and communities in this area was supplied by the Anangu Pitjantjatjara Yankunytjatjara Land Council. All roads and tracks in the Anangu Pitjantjatjara Yankunytjatjara Land area are not accessible by the general public.
Pipalyatjara Road
Baggaley Hill 586m
Mount Moulden 668m
Aralya
Kunytjanu
Kulinya Native Well
Pvt. Kintore
Oolburra Rockhole
Mount Crombie (Ulpara) 842m
Pinundinna Hill (Inanja) 758m
Bull Hill 684m
Currie Creek
West Bore No.2
Kulpi Rockhole
Carbeena Hill (Karpina) 704m
Ititjanya Rockhole
Mount Agnes 656m
Wataru Road
Blyth Hills 550m
Scherk Hill 520m
Bewden Hill (Bowden) 540m
Anerinna Hills (Aneri) 683m
Weinna Hill 571m
Peaks 620m
Maryinna Hill 600m
Ungarinna Rockhole
Dry Hill 639m
Mingeemeainna Hill 550m
Naryilkinna Rockhole
Permano Hill 726m
Mount Copley 682m
Watarru
Cartarlinna Rockholes
Conmooninna Hill 550m
Oompeinna Hill 627m
Walalkara
Mount Holder 769m
Birksgate Range
Eterinna Rockhole
Gilby Hill 605m
Makiri
Lindsay Pile 530m
Moolalpinna Hill 550m
Umberdidinna Hill 586m
Anangu Pitjantjatjara Yankunytjatjara Aboriginal Area
Watarru IPA
Mount Poondinna 730m
Kintore Private
Cardilkinna Rockhole
Turner Hill 520m
Pilgna
Purndu Saltpan
Yaroona Hill (Yaruna) 570m
Cheesman Peak (Pingegurrinna) 580m
Tarleecartagun Hill 530m
South Australia
For more detail see Hema's Great Desert Tracks Central Sheet
Coffin Hill 567m
Iltur
Mount
Walalkara IPA
Woomera Prohibited Area (WPA)
A Tourist Permit is required to access any part of the Woomera Prohibited Area (WPA) except the: Stuart Highway, Lake Cadibarrawirracanna Road (Public Access Route), Olympic Way–Pimba Road (B97), William Creek Road, Woomera Village. For more information visit www.defence.gov.au/woomera/permit-tourist.htm
268 Permit Davies Required Road
Great Victoria Desert
Mamungari Conservation Park Aboriginal Area
Pat Auld Vat Rockhole
Mamungari (Unnamed) Conservation Park
A UNESCO World Biosphere Reserve containing both arid zone wilderness and cultural significance. Princess Parrot, Scarlet Chested Parrots, Majestic Marble Gum, Desert Oak, Desert Kurrajong.
Len Beadell Border Plaque
To Ilkurlka Roadhouse
Anne Beadell Highway
Permit Required
Voakes Hill
Len Beadell Plaque - Voakes Hill Corner
To Coober Pedy
Mamungari Conservation Park
Mamungari Conservation Park - Sign Post
Wilbania Rockhole
Woomera Prohibited Area
Serpentine Lakes
Noorina Native Well
Len Beadell Plaque
Maralinga Tjarutja Aboriginal Area
Len Beadell Plaque
Bringyna Native Well
Len Beadell Plaque - Bringyna Native Well Half A Mile 15 October 1961 Lb
Great Victoria Desert Nature Reserve
Nurrari Lakes
Wyola Lake
Halinor Lake
Lake Dey-Dey
© Hema Maps
129°10'E
130°E
130°50'E
131°40'E
25°50'S
26°40'S
27°30'S
28°20'S
29°10'S
182
159
138
141

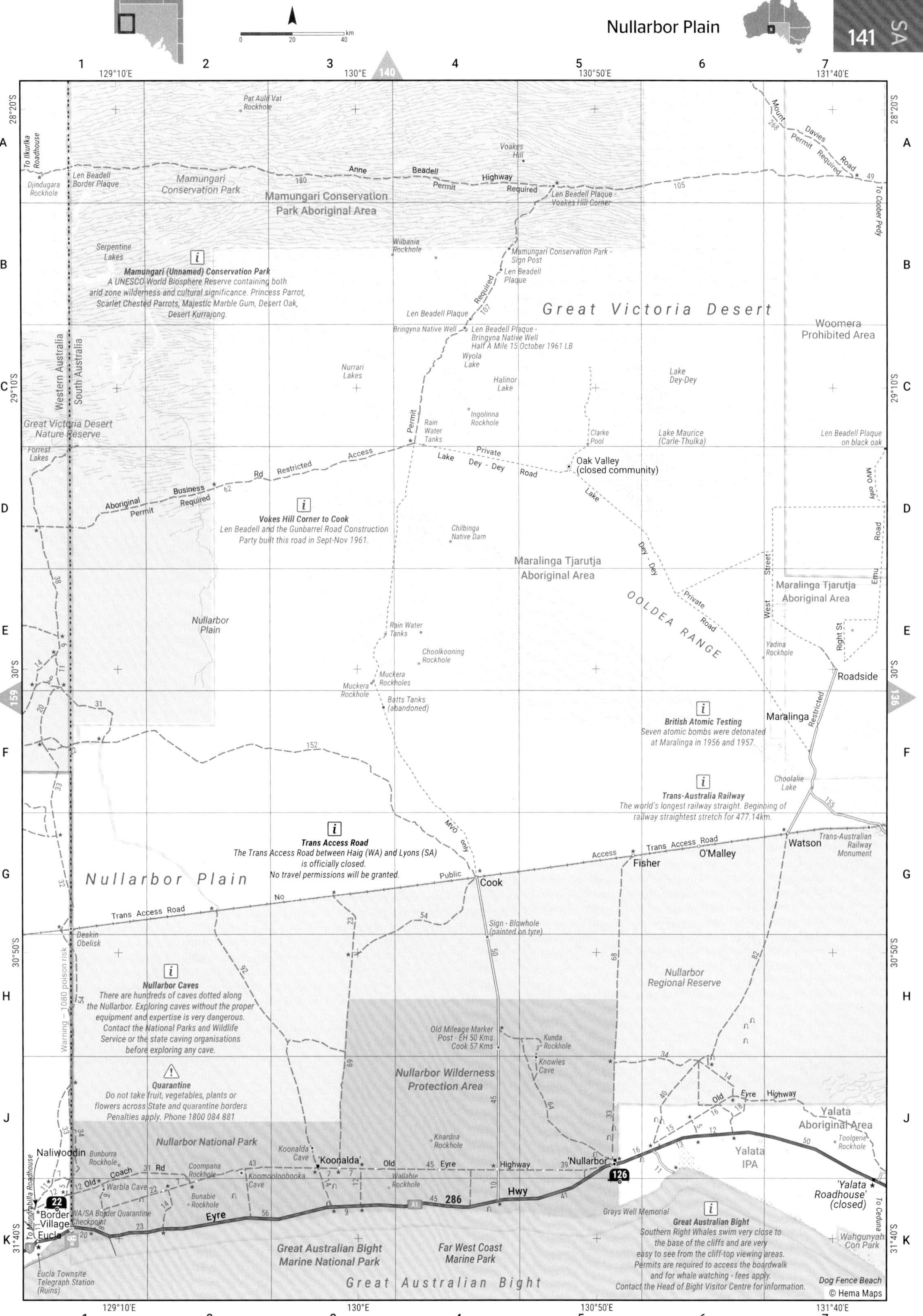
Mamungari (Unnamed) Conservation Park
A UNESCO World Biosphere Reserve containing both arid zone wilderness and cultural significance. Princess Parrot, Scarlet Chested Parrots, Majestic Marble Gum, Desert Oak, Desert Kurrajong.
Great Victoria Desert
Woomera Prohibited Area
Mamungari Conservation Park
Mamungari Conservation Park Aboriginal Area
Anne Beadell Highway Permit Required
Len Beadell Plaque Voakes Hill Corner
Vokes Hill Corner to Cook
Len Beadell and the Gunbarrel Road Construction Party built this road in Sept-Nov 1961.
Aboriginal Business Permit Required Restricted Access Rd
Oak Valley (closed community)
Maralinga Tjarutja Aboriginal Area
OOLDEA RANGE
British Atomic Testing
Seven atomic bombs were detonated at Maralinga in 1956 and 1957.
Maralinga
Roadside
Trans-Australia Railway
The world's longest railway straight. Beginning of railway straightest stretch for 477.14km.
Trans Access Road
The Trans Access Road between Haig (WA) and Lyons (SA) is officially closed. No travel permissions will be granted.
Nullarbor Plain
Cook
Fisher
O'Malley
Watson
Nullarbor Caves
There are hundreds of caves dotted along the Nullarbor. Exploring caves without the proper equipment and expertise is very dangerous. Contact the National Parks and Wildlife Service or the state caving organisations before exploring any cave.
Quarantine
Do not take fruit, vegetables, plants or flowers across State and quarantine borders Penalties apply. Phone 1800 084 881
Nullarbor Regional Reserve
Nullarbor Wilderness Protection Area
Nullarbor National Park
Naliwoodin
Border Village
Eucla
'Koonalda'
'Nullarbor'
Eyre Hwy
Yalata Aboriginal Area
Yalata IPA
'Yalata Roadhouse' (closed)
Great Australian Bight
Southern Right Whales swim very close to the base of the cliffs and are very easy to see from the cliff-top viewing areas. Permits are required to access the boardwalk and for whale watching - fees apply. Contact the Head of Bight Visitor Centre for information.
Great Australian Bight Marine National Park
Far West Coast Marine Park
Great Australian Bight
Western Australia
South Australia
© Hema Maps

Ikara - Flinders Ranges National Park

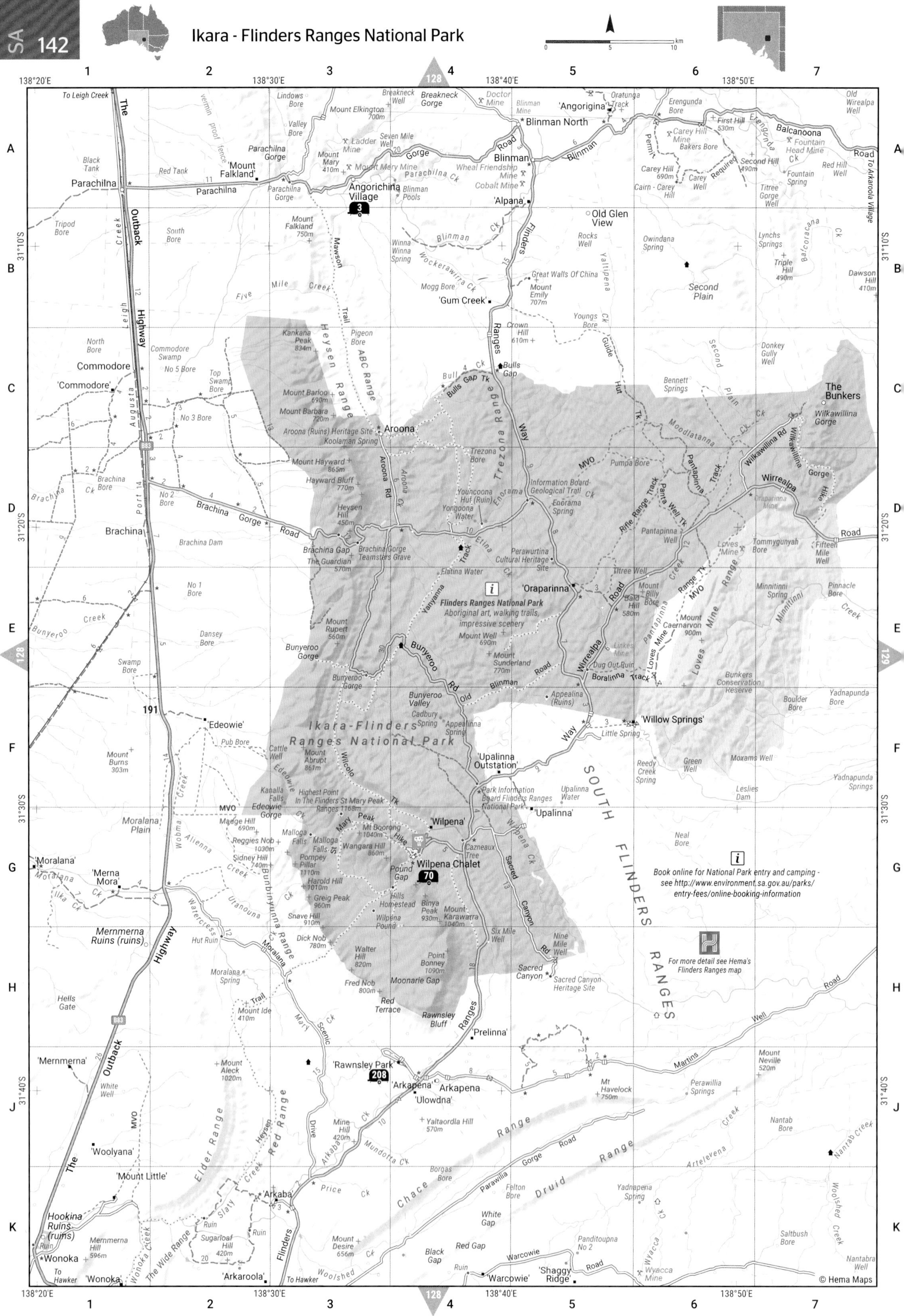

Aldinga

1 BIG4 Port Willunga Tourist Park

22 Tuit Rd. 3 km NE of PO
www.big4.com.au
08 8556 6113 HEMA 123 E2 35 14 50 S 138 28 17 E

Aldinga Beach

2 Aldinga Beach Holiday Park

Cox Rd. 4.5 km E of PO
www.aldingaholiday.com.au
08 8556 3444 HEMA 123 G1 35 17 51 S 138 27 37 E

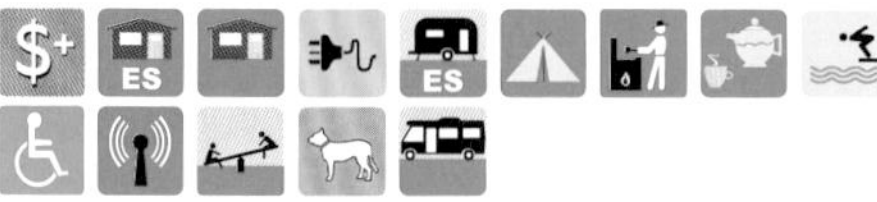

Angorichina Village

3 Angorichina Tourist Village

Parachilna Gorge
www.angorichinavillage.com.au
08 8648 4842 HEMA 142 A3 31 07 35 S 138 33 39 E

Ardrossan

4 Ardrossan Caravan Park

1 Park Tce
www.ardrossancaravanpark.com.au
08 8837 3262 HEMA 124 D5 34 25 13 S 137 55 09 E

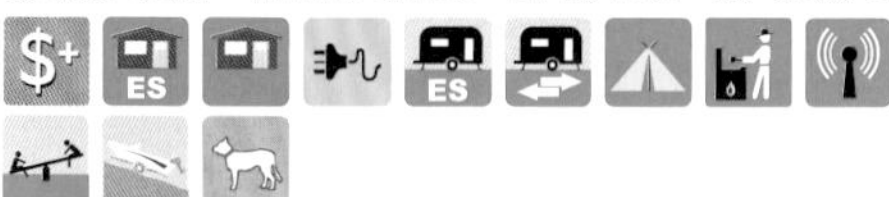

5 Highview Holiday Village

15 Highview Rd
www.highviewholiday.com
08 8837 3399 HEMA 124 D5 34 24 51 S 137 55 01 E

Arkaroola Village

6 Arkaroola Wilderness Sanctuary

Northern Flinders Ranges
www.arkaroola.com.au
08 8648 4848 HEMA 131 H10 30 18 42 S 139 20 10 E

Arno Bay

7 Arno Bay Caravan Park

Park Lane. 1 km S of PO
www.arnobaycaravanpark.com
08 8628 0157 HEMA 124 B1 33 55 03 S 136 34 24 E

Auburn

8 Auburn Community Caravan Park

Saddleworth Rd
0417 550 781 HEMA 124 C7 34 01 42 S 138 41 30 E

Balaklava

9 Balaklava Caravan Park

18 Short Tce. Next to swimming pool. Fee for showers
0400 264 075 HEMA 124 C6 34 08 57 S 138 25 08 E

Balgowan

10 Balgowan Caravan & Camping Area

Main St. All enquires to 11 Main St
08 8836 3233 HEMA 124 D4 34 19 26 S 137 29 38 E

Barmera

11 Barmera North Lake Caravan Park

525 Queen Elizabeth Dr
08 8588 7353 HEMA 125 C12 34 12 07 S 140 27 46 E

12 Discovery Holiday Parks Lake Bonney

1 Lakeside Dr
www.discoveryholidayparks.com.au
08 8588 2234 HEMA 125 C12 34 15 03 S 140 27 10 E

Beachport

13 Beachport Caravan Park

Beach Rd. 500m S of PO
www.beachportcaravanpark.com.au
08 8735 8128 HEMA 126 G3 37 28 44 S 140 00 55 E

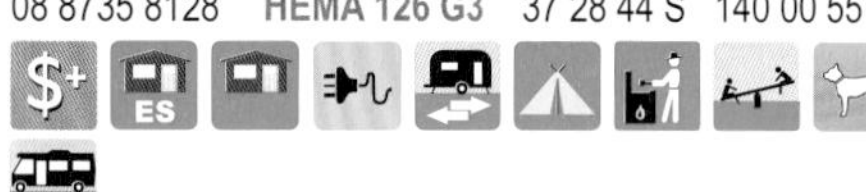

14 Southern Ocean Tourist Park

Somerville St
www.southernoceantouristpark.com.au
08 8735 8153 HEMA 126 G3 37 29 05 S 140 00 41 E

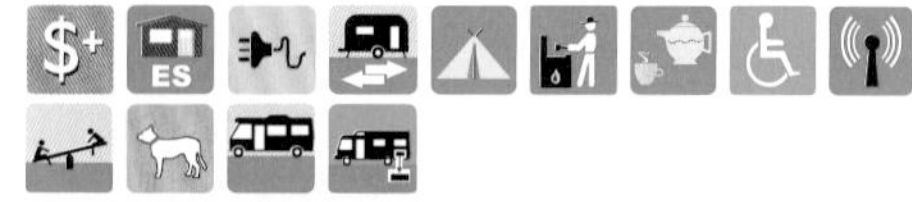

Bedford Park

15 Marion Holiday Park

323 Sturt Rd. 12 km S of PO
www.marionhp.com.au
08 8276 6695 HEMA 118 D2 35 01 02 S 138 33 40 E

Belair

16 Belair National Park Caravan Park

Upper Sturt Rd
www.belaircaravanpark.com.au
08 8278 3540 HEMA 118 D6 35 00 38 S 138 38 09 E

Berri

17 Berri Riverside Caravan Park

87 Riverview Dr
www.berricaravanpark.com.au
08 8582 3723 HEMA 125 D13 34 17 11 S 140 36 35 E

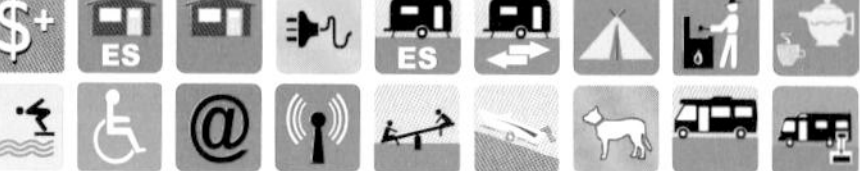

Blanchetown

18 Blanchetown Caravan Park

River Dr
www.blanchetowncaravanpark.com
08 8540 5073 HEMA 125 D10 34 20 32 S 139 37 08 E

19 River Palms Holiday Park

9109 Sturt Hwy
08 8540 5035 HEMA 125 D10 34 20 25 S 139 37 08 E

20 Riverside Holiday Park

16 Sanders St
www.blanchetownriverside.com.au
08 8540 5070 HEMA 125 D10 34 21 15 S 139 36 59 E

Bolivar

21 Highway One Caravan & Tourist Park

925 Port Wakefield Rd
www.highway1touristpark.com
08 8250 3747 HEMA 120 D4 34 45 36 S 138 35 28 E

Border Village

22 Border Village Caravan Park

Eyre Hwy
www.bordervillageroadhouse.com.au
08 9039 3474 HEMA 141 K1 31 38 18 S 129 00 12 E

Bordertown

23 Bordertown Caravan Park

41 Penny Tce
www.bordertowncaravanpark.com
08 8752 1752 HEMA 126 B5 36 18 26 S 140 46 20 E

Burra

24 Burra Caravan & Camping Park

12 Bridge Tce
08 8892 2442 HEMA 125 A8 33 40 44 S 138 56 15 E

Bute

25 Bute Caravan Park

21 Railway Tce
08 8826 2011 HEMA 124 B5 33 51 57 S 138 00 22 E

Cadney

26 Cadney Park Roadhouse

Cadney Roadhouse, Stuart Hwy
08 8670 7994 HEMA 138 G7 27 54 18 S 134 03 24 E

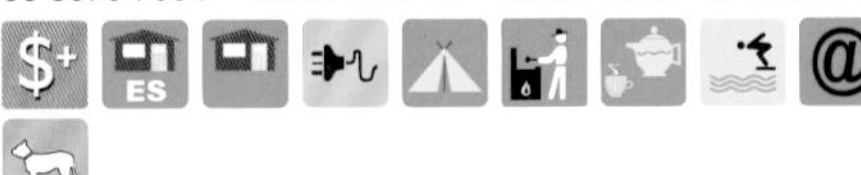

Cape Jaffa

27 Cape Jaffa Caravan Park

18 King Dr
www.capejaffacp.com.au
08 8768 5056 HEMA 126 D1 36 56 33 S 139 41 10 E

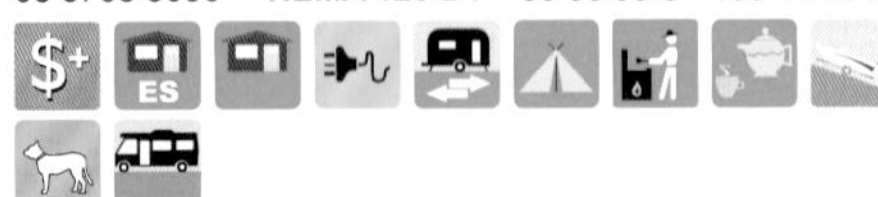

Carrieton

28 Carrieton Caravan Park

Fourth St
08 8658 9090 HEMA 128 F7 32 25 29 S 138 31 55 E

Ceduna

29 A1 Cabins & Caravan Park

41 McKenzie St
08 8625 2578 HEMA 134 A1 32 07 25 S 133 40 49 E

30 BIG4 Ceduna Tourist Park

29 McKenzie St
www.cedunatouristpark.com
08 8625 2150 HEMA 134 A1 32 07 28 S 133 40 41 E

31 Ceduna Airport Caravan Park

Eyre Hwy
www.cedunaholidayaccommodation.com.au
08 8625 2416 HEMA 134 A1 32 07 21 S 133 41 25 E

32 Ceduna Foreshore Caravan Park

25 Poynton St
www.cedunaforeshorecaravanpark.com.au
08 8625 2290 HEMA 134 A1 32 07 38 S 133 40 25 E

33 Shelly Beach Caravan Park

178 Decres Bay Rd. 3 km E of PO
www.cedunacaravanpark.com.au
08 8625 2012 HEMA 134 A1 32 08 55 S 133 41 24 E

Christies Beach

34 Christies Beach Tourist Park

39 Sydney Cres
www.christiesbeachtouristpark.com.au
08 8326 0311 HEMA 118 H1 35 08 08 S 138 28 12 E

Clare

35 Discovery Holiday Parks Clare

8511 Horrocks Hwy
www.discoveryholidayparks.com.au
08 8842 2724 HEMA 124 B7 33 51 51 S 138 37 17 E

Clayton Bay

36 Clayton Bay Riverside Holiday Park

Island View Dr
www.claytonbayrhp.com.au
08 8537 0372 HEMA 125 H8 35 29 32 S 138 55 18 E

Cleve

37 Birdseye Roadhouse Caravan Park

1 Birdseye Hwy
www.cleve.com.au
08 8628 2019 HEMA 124 B1 33 42 08 S 136 29 59 E

Cobdogla

38 Cobdogla Station Caravan Park

14 Shueard Rd. 500m W of PO
www.cobdoglacaravanpark.com.au
08 8588 7164 HEMA 125 C12 34 14 35 S 140 24 01 E

Coffin Bay

39 Coffin Bay Caravan Park

91 Esplanade. 50m NE of PO
www.coffinbaycaravanpark.com.au
08 8685 4170 HEMA 134 H5 34 37 29 S 135 28 25 E

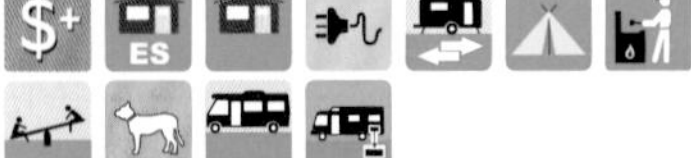

Coober Pedy

40 BIG4 Stuart Range Outback Resort

Cnr Hutchison St & Stuart Hwy
www.stuartrangeoutbackresort.com.au
08 8672 5179 HEMA 137 A9 29 01 19 S 134 45 29 E

41 Oasis Tourist Park

Hutchison St. 800m N of PO
www.familyparks.com.au
08 8672 5169 HEMA 137 A9 29 00 20 S 134 45 18 E

42 Opal Inn Caravan Park

Hutchison St. 200m S of PO
www.opalinn.com.au
08 8672 5054 HEMA 137 A9 29 00 52 S 134 45 16 E

43 Riba's Underground Camping & Tourist Park

Lot 1181 William Creek Rd
www.camp-underground.com.au
08 8672 5614 HEMA 137 A9 29 02 08 S 134 48 14 E

Coobowie

44 Coobowie Caravan Park

23 Beach Rd
www.coobowiecaravanpark.com
08 8852 8132 HEMA 124 F4 35 02 47 S 137 43 39 E

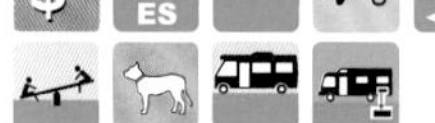

Coonalpyn

45 Coonalpyn Soldiers Memorial Caravan Park

Richards Tce. Adjacent to swimming pool
0427 399 089 HEMA 125 J10 35 41 33 S 139 51 27 E

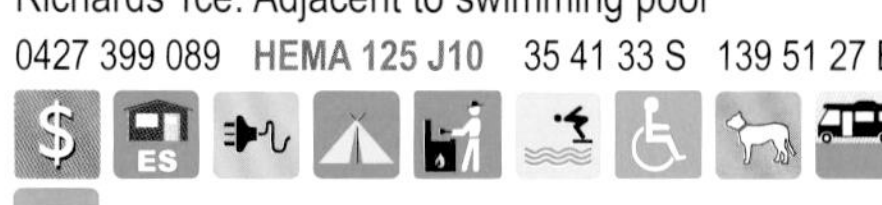

Coonawarra

46 Coonawarra Bush Holiday Park

Lot 1 Comaum School Rd
www.cbhp.com.au
0455 146 647 HEMA 126 F5 37 13 35 S 140 52 48 E

Copley

47 Copley Caravan Park

Railway Tce. 100m S of PO
www.copleycaravan.com.au
08 8675 2288 HEMA 130 J7 30 33 21 S 138 25 24 E

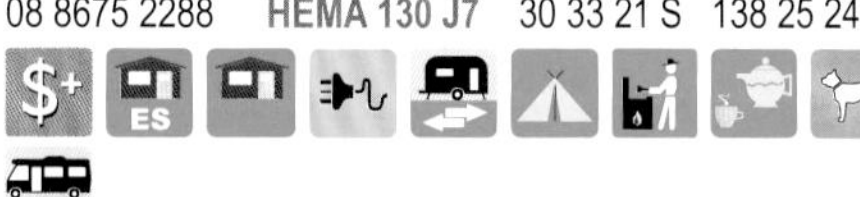

Corny Point

48 Corny Point Caravan Park

1 West Coast Rd. 2 km E of General Store
www.cornypoint.com.au
08 8855 3368 HEMA 124 F2 34 55 31 S 137 04 52 E

Cowell

49 Cowell Foreshore Caravan Park & Holiday Units

The Esplanade
08 8629 2307 HEMA 124 A2 33 41 07 S 136 55 35 E

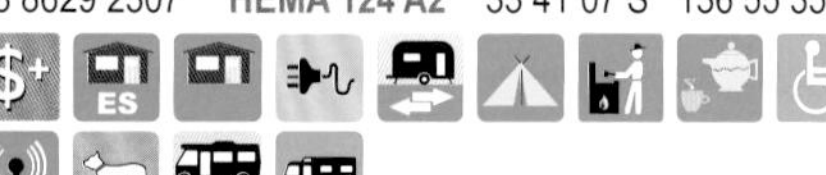

50 Harbour View Caravan Park

91 Harbourview Dr
www.harbourviewcaravanpark.com.au
08 8629 2216 HEMA 124 A2 33 40 25 S 136 56 20 E

Crystal Brook

51 Crystal Brook Caravan Park

330 Goyer Hwy
www.crystalbrookcaravanparksa.com
08 8636 2640 HEMA 128 J6 33 20 48 S 138 12 13 E

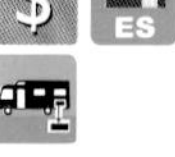

Cudlee Creek

52 Cudlee Creek Tavern Caravan Park

Gorge Rd
www.cudleecreektavern.com.au
08 8389 2319 HEMA 121 G11 34 50 23 S 138 48 58 E

Cummins

53 Cummins Community Caravan Park

25 Roe St. 2 km S of PO. Check in at Cummins Deli, Bruce Tce
08 8676 2011 HEMA 134 G6 34 16 15 S 135 43 23 E

Eden Valley

54 Eden Valley Caravan Park

1845 Eden Valley Road
08 85681934 HEMA 122 J7 34 39 15 S 139 06 07 E

Edithburgh

55 Edithburgh Caravan Park

O'Halloran Pde
www.edithburghcaravanpark.com.au
08 8852 6056 HEMA 124 G4 35 05 20 S 137 44 49 E

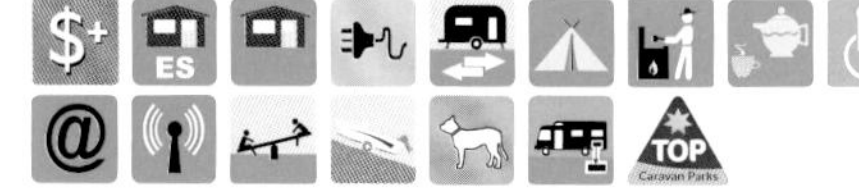

Elliston

56 Elliston Caravan Park

Flinders Hwy. 1 km NW of PO
www.ellistoncaravanpark.com.au
08 8687 9061 HEMA 134 F4 33 38 11 S 134 52 59 E

57 Waterloo Bay Tourist Park

10 Beach Tce
www.visitelliston.net
08 8687 9076 HEMA 134 F4 33 38 48 S 134 53 14 E

Eudunda

58 Eudunda Caravan Park

Oval Cres, adjacent to the swimming pool. 4 sites
www.caravanpark.eudunda.com
0414 703 345 HEMA 125 C8 34 10 44 S 139 05 19 E

Evanston South

59 Gawler Gateway Tourist Park

3134 Main North Rd
www.gawlergatewaytouristpark.com.au
08 8254 6699 HEMA 127 A4 34 39 08 S 138 42 51 E

Fowlers Bay

60 Fowlers Bay Eco Caravan Park

11 The Esplanade
www.fowlerscaravanpark.com
08 8625 6143 HEMA 136 J4 31 59 20 S 132 26 12 E

Gawler

61 Gawler Caravan Park
7 Main North Rd. 500m N of PO
www.gawlercaravanpark.com.au
08 8522 3805 **HEMA 127 A4** 34 35 33 S 138 44 48 E

Gladstone

62 Gladstone Caravan Park
6 West Tce. 1 km W of PO
08 8662 2522 **HEMA 128 J7** 33 16 08 S 138 21 05 E

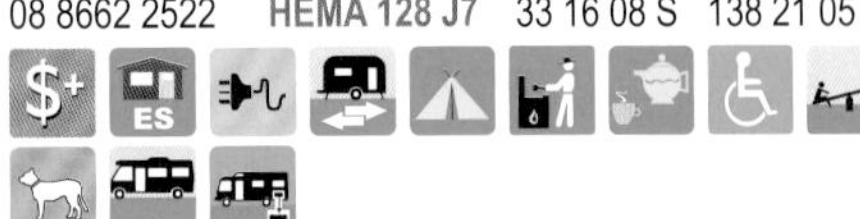

Glendambo

63 Glendambo Outback Resort
Stuart Hwy
08 8672 1030 **HEMA 137 F11** 30 58 10 S 135 45 01 E

Goolwa

64 Goolwa Camping & Tourist Park
40 Kessell Rd
www.goolwatouristpark.com.au
08 8555 2144 **HEMA 124 H7** 35 29 52 S 138 46 28 E

65 Hindmarsh Island Caravan Park
Madsen St. Hindmarsh Island
www.hicaravanpark.com.au
08 8555 2234 **HEMA 124 H7** 35 30 12 S 138 48 54 E

Hackney

66 Adelaide Caravan Park
46 Richmond St. 2km NE of PO
www.adelaidevanpark.com.au
08 8363 1566 **HEMA 117 C6** 34 54 32 S 138 36 55 E

Hahndorf

67 Hahndorf Resort Tourist Park
145A Mount Barker Road
www.hahndorfresort.com.au
08 8388 7921 **HEMA 119 D10** 35 01 14 S 138 47 59 E

Hawker

68 Hawker Caravan Park
Cnr Wilpena Rd & Chaceview Tce
www.hawkercaravanpark.com.au
08 8648 4006 **HEMA 128 D7** 31 53 15 S 138 25 34 E

69 Hawker Overflow
Carpenter Rd. Closed in summer
www.hawkercaravanpark.com.au
08 8648 4006 **HEMA 128 D7** 31 53 04 S 138 24 51 E

Ikara-Flinders Ranges NP

70 Wilpena Pound Resort
Wilpena Pound. 60 km N of Hawker
www.wilpenapound.com.au
08 8648 0048 **HEMA 142 G4** 31 31 37 S 138 36 23 E

Iron Knob

71 Nuttbush Retreat Caravan Park
Pandurra Station, Eyre Hwy. 40 km W of Port Augusta
www.nuttbush.com.au
08 8643 8941 **HEMA 128 G4** 32 37 40 S 137 25 47 E

Jamestown

72 Jamestown Country Retreat Caravan Park
Cnr Ayr St & Bute St. 200m E of Main St
08 8664 0077 **HEMA 128 J7** 33 12 19 S 138 36 01 E

Kadina

73 Kadina Caravan Park
Lindsay Tce
www.kadinacaravanpark.com.au
08 8821 2259 **HEMA 124 B4** 33 57 25 S 137 43 06 E

Kangaroo Island

74 KI Shores Caravan Park & Camping
Lot 501 Talinga Tce. Penneshaw
www.seafront.com.au/ki-shores
08 8553 1028 **HEMA 124 J5** 35 43 09 S 137 56 24 E

75 Kingscote Tourist Park & Family Units
First & Third St
www.kingscotetouristpark.com.au
08 8553 2394 **HEMA 124 J4** 35 40 16 S 137 36 47 E

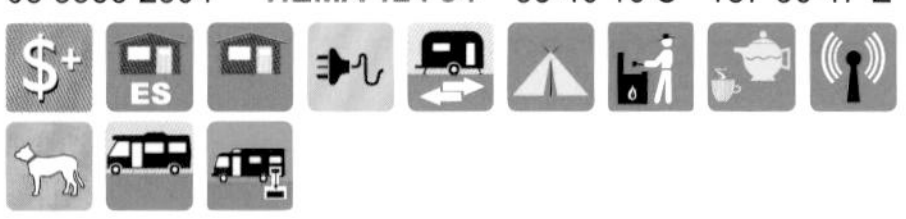

76 Western KI Caravan Park & Wildlife Reserve
South Coast Rd. 3 km E of Flinders Chase
www.westernki.com.au
08 8559 7201 **HEMA 124 K2** 35 57 39 S 136 48 28 E

Kapunda

77 Kapunda Tourist Park
51 Baker Street off Montfiore St. 1 km W of PO
www.kapundatouristpark.com
08 8566 2094 **HEMA 125 D8** 34 20 13 S 138 54 28 E

Karoonda

78 Karoonda Cabin & Caravan Park
11 Railway Tce
www.karoonda.org
08 8578 1004 **HEMA 125 G11** 35 05 47 S 139 53 23 E

Keith

79 Cockatoo Downs Farmstay
Eckerts Rd, off Dukes Hwy
www.cockatoodownsfarmstay.com.au
08 8756 7042 **HEMA 126 A4** 36 09 21 S 140 28 44 E

80 Keith Caravan Park
Naracoorte Rd
www.keithcaravanpark.com.au
0427 876 993 **HEMA 125 K12** 36 06 04 S 140 21 04 E

Kimba

81 Kimba Caravan Park, Roadhouse & Motel
15442 Eyre Hwy
08 8627 2222 **HEMA 128 J1** 33 08 45 S 136 24 54 E

Kingston Park

82 Brighton Caravan Park
4 Burnham Rd
www.brightoncaravanpark.com.au
08 8377 0833 HEMA 118 E2 35 02 18 S 138 30 57 E

Kingston SE

83 Kingston Caravan Park
34 Marine Pde. 2 km from PO
www.kingstonforeshorecaravanpark.com.au/
08 8767 2050 HEMA 126 D2 36 50 12 S 139 50 45 E

Kingston-on-Murray

84 Kingston-on-Murray Caravan Park
461 Holmes Rd
www.komcaravanpark.com.au
08 8583 0209 HEMA 125 C12 34 13 22 S 140 21 06 E

Lameroo

85 Lameroo Caravan Park
Cnr Mallee Hwy & Varden Tce. Payment & keys at Lameroo Hotel
www.lameroohotelmotel.com.au
08 8576 3006 HEMA 125 G12 35 19 41 S 140 31 17 E

Laura

86 Laura Community Caravan Park
Cnr Main North Rd & North Tce. 500m N of PO
08 8663 2296 HEMA 128 J7 33 10 54 S 138 18 02 E

Leasingham

87 Leasingham Village Cabins & Caravan Park
Lot 94 Main North Rd. 6 km N of Auburn
www.leasinghamvillagecabins.com.au
08 8843 0136 HEMA 124 C7 33 58 56 S 138 39 01 E

Leigh Creek

88 Leigh Creek Caravan Park
Acacia Rd
0429 012 445 HEMA 130 J7 30 35 17 S 138 24 29 E

Lock

89 Lock Caravan Park
South Tce
08 8689 1020 HEMA 134 E6 33 34 10 S 135 45 24 E

Loxton

90 Loxton Riverfront Holiday Park
Sophie Eddington Dr
www.lrcp.com.au
08 8584 7862 HEMA 125 D12 34 26 55 S 140 33 00 E

Lucindale

91 Lucindale Caravan Park
Oak Ave
08 8766 2038 HEMA 126 E4 36 58 08 S 140 21 59 E

Lyndhurst

92 Lyndhurst Hotel-Motel & Caravan Park
3 Short St
08 8675 7781 HEMA 130 H7 30 17 16 S 138 21 08 E

Lyndoch

93 Barossa Caravan Park
Lot 1154 Barossa Valley Hwy
08 8524 4262 HEMA 127 A6 34 35 28 S 138 52 03 E

Mannum

94 Mannum Caravan Park
Purnong Rd
www.mannumriversidecaravanpark.com.au/
08 8569 1402 HEMA 125 F9 34 54 31 S 139 19 02 E

Marion Bay

95 Marion Bay Caravan Park
17 Willyama Dr
www.marionbaycp.com.au
08 8854 4094 HEMA 124 G2 35 14 39 S 136 58 38 E

Marla

96 Marla Travellers Rest Caravan Park
Stuart Hwy
www.marla.com.au
08 8670 7001 HEMA 138 E6 27 18 15 S 133 37 20 E

Marree

97 Drovers Run Tourist Park
Cnr Birdsville Track & The Outback Hwy
www.droversrunmarree.com.au
08 8675 8248 HEMA 130 F6 29 39 11 S 138 04 25 E
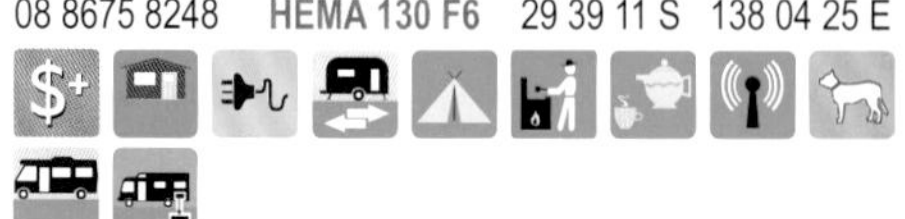

98 Oasis Caravan Park
Railway Tce South
www.marreelakeeyreflights.com.au
08 8675 8352 HEMA 130 F6 29 38 49 S 138 03 46 E

McLaren Vale

99 McLaren Vale Lakeside Caravan Park
48 Field St
www.mclarenvale.net
08 8323 9255 HEMA 123 D4 35 12 51 S 138 32 36 E

Melrose

100 Melrose Caravan Park
Joes Rd
www.melrosecaravanpark.com.au
08 8666 2060 HEMA 128 H6 32 49 30 S 138 11 11 E

Meningie

101 Lake Albert Caravan Park
25 Narrung Rd. 1 km W of PO
www.lakealbertcaravanpark.com.au
08 8575 1411 HEMA 125 J9 35 41 27 S 139 19 45 E
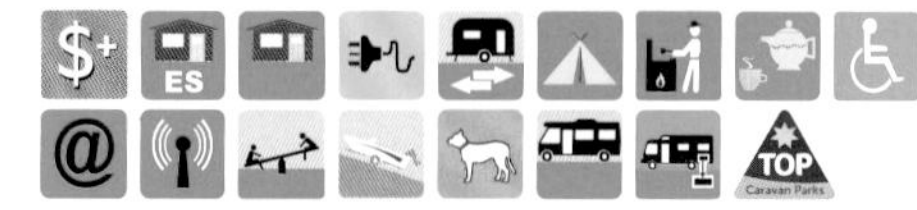

Middleton

102 Middleton Caravan Park
23 Goolwa Rd. Adjacent to General Store
www.middletoncaravanpark.com.au
08 8554 2383 HEMA 124 H7 35 30 32 S 138 42 28 E

Milang

103 Milang Lakeside Caravan Park

1 Woodrow Dr
www.kuiparks.com.au
08 8537 0282 HEMA 125 H8 35 24 27 S 138 58 24 E

Millicent

104 Hillview Caravan Park

Dalton St. 2.6 km SE of PO
www.hillviewcaravanpark.com.au
08 8733 2806 HEMA 126 H4 37 36 42 S 140 22 19 E

105 Millicent Lakeside Caravan Park

12 Park Tce. 1 km S of PO
www.millicentlakesidecarapark.com.au
08 8733 1188 HEMA 126 G4 37 35 28 S 140 20 22 E

Minlaton

106 Minlaton Caravan Park

Cnr of Bluff Rd & Minlaton Rd
www.minlatoncaravanpark.com.au
08 8853 2435 HEMA 124 E4 34 45 58 S 137 35 47 E

Mitcham

107 Brownhill Creek Tourist Park

Brownhill Creek Rd. 7 km SE of PO
www.brownhillcreekcaravanpark.com.au
08 8271 4824 HEMA 118 C5 34 59 06 S 138 37 36 E

Moana Beach

108 Moana Beach Tourist Park

44 Nashwauk Cres
www.moanabeachtouristpark.com.au
08 8327 0677 HEMA 123 C2 35 11 54 S 138 28 23 E

Moonta Bay

109 Moonta Bay Caravan Park

5 Tossell St
www.moontabaycaravanpark.com.au
08 8825 2406 HEMA 124 C4 34 03 14 S 137 33 49 E

Morgan

110 Morgan Riverside Caravan Park

Main Rd
www.morganriversidecaravanpark.com.au
08 8540 2207 HEMA 125 C10 34 02 18 S 139 40 18 E

Mount Barker

111 Mount Barker Caravan & Tourist Park

40 Cameron Rd
www.mountbarker.sa.gov.au/caravanpark
08 8391 0384 HEMA 119 F12 35 03 42 S 138 51 37 E

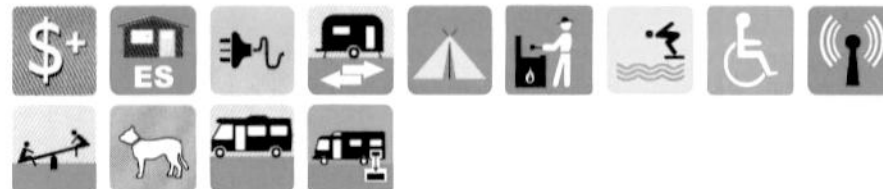

Mount Compass

112 Mount Compass Caravan Park

83 Heysen Blvd
www.mountcompasscaravanpark.com.au
08 8556 8600 HEMA 123 J6 35 21 40 S 138 36 49 E

Mount Gambier

113 Blue Lake Holiday Park

Bay Rd. 2 km SW of PO
www.bluelakeholidaypark.com.au
08 8725 9856 HEMA 126 J5 37 50 43 S 140 46 11 E

114 Kalganyi Holiday Park

Cnr Penola Rd & Bishop Rd
www.kalganyi.com.au
08 8723 0220 HEMA 126 J5 37 48 16 S 140 47 37 E

115 Limestone Coast Tourist Park

Corner of Princes Highway & Hawkins Road E. 3.5 km SE of PO
www.limestonecoasttouristpark.com.au
08 8723 2469 HEMA 126 J5 37 50 29 S 140 49 24 E

116 Mount Gambier Central Caravan Park

6 Krummel St. 900m SE of PO
www.mountgambiercentralcaravanpark.com.au
08 8725 4427 HEMA 126 J5 37 49 51 S 140 47 06 E

117 Pine Country Caravan Park

Cnr. Bay Road and Kilsby Road
www.pinecountry.com.au
08 8725 1899 HEMA 126 J5 37 51 19 S 140 45 45 E

Mount Pleasant

118 Talunga Park Caravan Park (Showgrounds)

Melrose St, at Showgrounds
08 8568 1934 HEMA 127 C7 34 46 34 S 139 02 34 E

Murray Bridge

119 Avoca Dell Caravan Park
Avoca Dell Drive via Mitchell Ave
www.avocadell.com.au
08 8532 2095 HEMA 125 G9 35 05 22 S 139 18 30 E

120 Murray Bridge Resort Caravan Park
100 Roper Rd. 3 km S of PO
www.murraybridgemarina.com.au
08 8532 6900 HEMA 125 G9 35 08 04 S 139 18 03 E

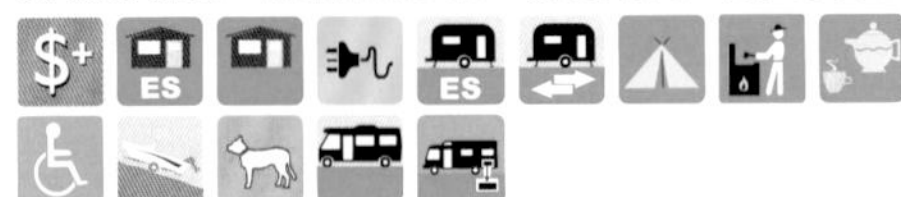

121 Murray Bridge Tourist Park
315 Adelaide Rd. 5 km W of PO
www.murraybridgetouristpark.com.au
08 8532 2860 HEMA 125 G9 35 08 08 S 139 14 03 E

122 White Sands Riverfront Caravan Park
11 White Sands Rd. Limited sites
0407 715 480 HEMA 125 G9 35 11 19 S 139 19 03 E

Naracoorte

123 Naracoorte Holiday Park
81 Park Tce
www.big4.com.au
08 8762 2128 HEMA 126 E5 36 57 06 S 140 44 37 E

Normanville

124 Beachside Holiday Park
157 Williss Drive
www.beachside.com.au
08 8558 2458 HEMA 124 H6 35 27 30 S 138 18 14 E

125 Jetty Caravan Park
34 Jetty Rd
www.jettycaravanparknormanville.com.au
08 8558 2038 HEMA 124 H6 35 26 47 S 138 18 34 E

Nullarbor

126 Nullarbor Roadhouse
Eyre Hwy
08 8625 6271 HEMA 141 J5 31 27 00 S 130 53 46 E

Nundroo

127 Nundroo Hotel Motel Caravan Park
Eyre Hwy
www.nundrooaccommodation.com
08 8625 6120 HEMA 136 H3 31 47 33 S 132 13 29 E

Nuriootpa

128 Barossa Tourist Park
Penrice Rd
www.barossatouristpark.com.au
08 8562 1404 HEMA 122 B4 34 28 08 S 139 00 06 E

Oodnadatta

129 The Pink Roadhouse Caravan Park
Ikaturka Tce
www.pinkroadhouse.com.au
08 8670 7822 HEMA 139 F11 27 32 56 S 135 26 53 E

Orroroo

130 Orroroo Caravan Park
Second St. 200m W of PO
08 8658 1444 HEMA 128 G7 32 43 57 S 138 36 36 E

Padthaway

131 Padthaway Caravan Park
75 Beeamma-Parsons Road
www.padthawaycaravanpark.com.au
08 8765 5212 HEMA 126 C4 36 35 59 S 140 30 14 E

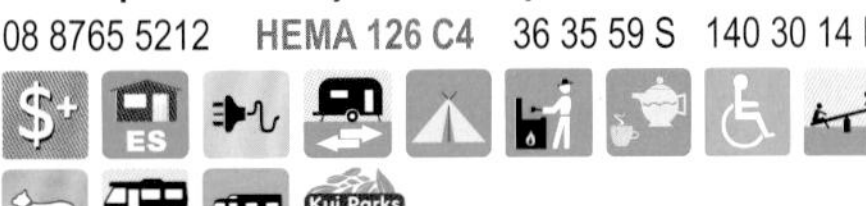

Paringa

132 Paringa Caravan Park
24 Sturt Hwy. 200m S of PO
www.paringacaravanpark.com.au
08 8595 5178 HEMA 125 C13 34 10 53 S 140 47 02 E

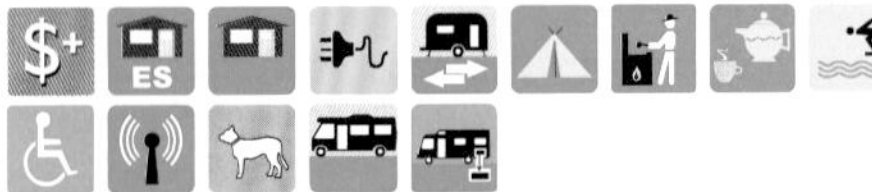

Penola

133 Penola Caravan Park
Cnr Riddoch Hwy & South Tce
www.penolacaravanpark.com.au
08 8737 2381 HEMA 126 F5 37 23 09 S 140 50 06 E

Penong

134 Penong Caravan Park
3 Stiggants Rd. 500m N of PO
08 8625 1111 HEMA 136 J5 31 55 31 S 133 00 32 E

Peterborough

135 Peterborough Caravan Park
36 Grove St. 1 km S of PO
08 8651 2545 HEMA 129 H8 32 58 52 S 138 50 01 E

Pine Point

136 Pine Point Caravan Park
Main Coast Rd
www.pinepointcpk.com.au
08 8838 2239 HEMA 124 E5 34 34 28 S 137 52 40 E

Pinnaroo

137 Pinnaroo Caravan Park
Mallee Hwy
0430 465 304 HEMA 125 G14 35 15 46 S 140 54 35 E

Point Turton

138 Point Turton Caravan Park
Bayview Rd
www.pointturtoncp.com.au
08 8854 5222 HEMA 124 F3 34 56 03 S 137 21 04 E

Poochera

139 Poochera Hotel Caravan Park
6-8 Barnes St
08 8626 3257 HEMA 134 C3 32 43 10 S 134 50 12 E

Port Augusta

140 Discovery Holiday Parks Port Augusta
Cnr Eyre Hwy & Stokes St
www.discoveryholidayparks.com.au
08 8642 2974 HEMA 128 F5 32 28 47 S 137 45 18 E

141 Shoreline Caravan Park
Gardiner Ave
www.shorelinecaravanpark.com.au/
08 8642 2965 HEMA 128 F5 32 28 29 S 137 45 44 E

SOUTH AUSTRALIA

142 Spear Creek Caravan Park
Spear Creek Sheep Station, Old Wilmington Rd.
25 km SE of Port Augusta
www.spearcreekcaravanpark.com.au
0428 822 644 HEMA 128 G6 32 34 10 S 137 59 23 E

Port Broughton

143 Broughton Bayside Caravan Park
528 John Lewis Dr
0408 352 140 HEMA 124 A5 33 35 09 S 137 56 01 E

144 Port Broughton Caravan Park
2 Barker St
www.portbroughtoncaravanpark.com.au
08 8635 2188 HEMA 124 A5 33 36 19 S 137 55 44 E

Port Clinton

145 Port Clinton Caravan Park
Cnr Duryea St & The Parade. 200m S of PO
08 8837 7003 HEMA 124 C5 34 13 32 S 138 01 12 E

Port Elliot

146 Port Elliot Holiday Park
Port Elliot Rd
www.portelliotholidaypark.com.au
08 8554 2134 HEMA 124 H7 35 31 49 S 138 41 23 E

Port Germein

147 Port Germein Caravan Park
Cnr High St & The Esplanade
www.portgermein.com.au/caravan-park
08 8634 5266 HEMA 128 H6 33 01 21 S 138 00 00 E

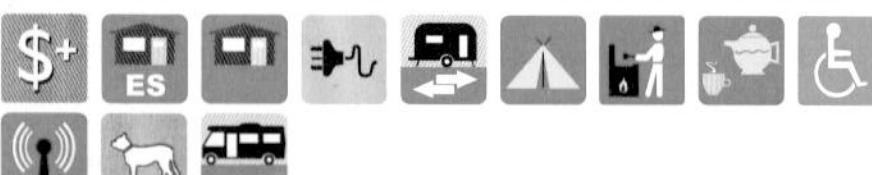

Port Hughes

148 Port Hughes Tourist Park
South Tce. 3.5 km from PO
www.porthughestouristpark.com.au
08 8825 2106 HEMA 124 C4 34 04 47 S 137 32 56 E

Port Kenny

149 Port Kenny Caravan Park
Flinders Hwy
08 8625 5076 HEMA 134 D3 33 10 12 S 134 41 32 E

Port Lincoln

150 Port Lincoln Caravan Park
1004 Lincoln Hwy, North Shields
www.plcp.com.au
08 8684 3512 HEMA 134 J6 34 37 47 S 135 51 49 E

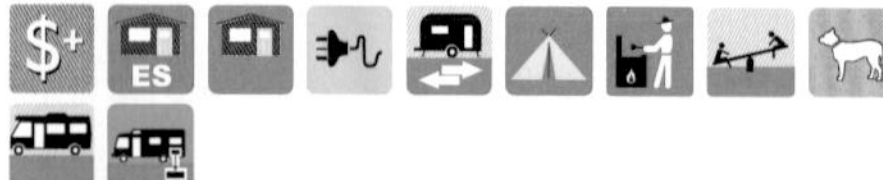

151 Port Lincoln Tourist Park
11 Hindmarsh St
www.portlincolntouristpark.com.au
08 8621 4444 HEMA 134 J6 34 43 41 S 135 53 00 E

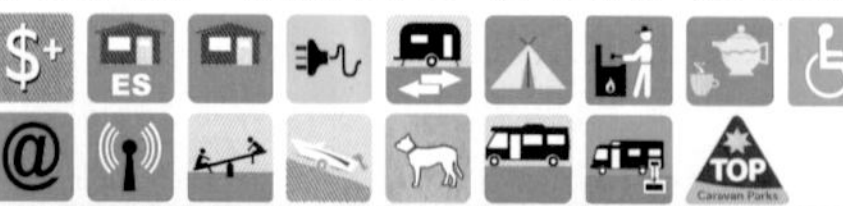

Port MacDonnell

152 Port MacDonnell Foreshore Tourist Park
12 Eight Mile Creek Rd
www.woolwash.com.au
08 8738 2095 HEMA 126 K5 38 03 00 S 140 42 58 E

Port Neill

153 Port Neill Caravan Park
1-20 Peake Tce
08 8688 9067 HEMA 134 G7 34 07 09 S 136 21 04 E

Port Pirie

154 Hillsview Cabin & Caravan Park
Port Broughton Rd
www.cabincaravanpark.com.au
08 8633 0577 HEMA 128 J6 33 13 15 S 138 00 41 E

155 Port Pirie Beach Caravan Park
Beach Rd. 1.5 km E of PO
www.portpiriebeachcaravanpark.com.au
08 8632 4275 HEMA 128 J6 33 10 57 S 138 01 22 E

156 Rangeview Caravan & Cabin Park
Highway A1. 5 km E of PO
www.rangeviewcaravanandcabinpark.com.au
08 8634 4221 HEMA 128 J6 33 10 06 S 138 04 06 E

Port Rickaby

157 Port Rickaby Caravan Park
Waimana Crt
www.portrickaby.com
08 8853 1177 HEMA 124 E4 34 40 21 S 137 29 44 E

Port Victoria

158 Gulfhaven Caravan Park
Davies Tce
www.gulfhaven.com.au
08 8834 2012 HEMA 124 D4 34 29 39 S 137 29 02 E

Port Vincent

159 Port Vincent Caravan Park & Seaside Cabins
12-17 Minlacowie Rd
www.portvincentcaravanpark.com.au
08 8853 7011 HEMA 124 E5 34 46 53 S 137 51 38 E

160 Port Vincent Foreshore Caravan Park
Marine Pde
www.portvincentfcp.com.au
08 8853 7073 HEMA 124 E5 34 46 41 S 137 51 48 E

Port Wakefield

161 Port Wakefield Caravan Park
Wakefield St
08 8867 1151 HEMA 124 C6 34 11 10 S 138 08 44 E

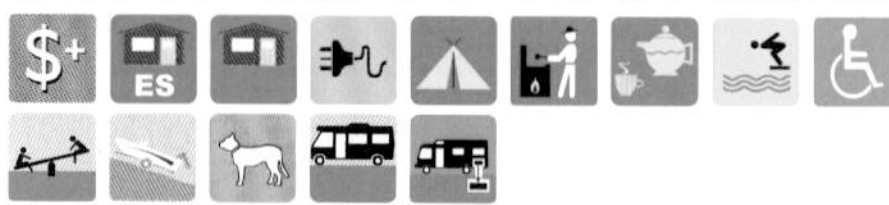

Price

162 Price Caravan Park
14 Fowler Tce
www.pricecaravanpark.com.au
08 8837 6311 HEMA 124 D5 34 17 14 S 137 59 48 E

Quorn

163 Quorn Caravan Park
8 Silo Rd
www.quorncaravanpark.com.au
08 8648 6206 HEMA 128 F6 32 20 34 S 138 02 23 E

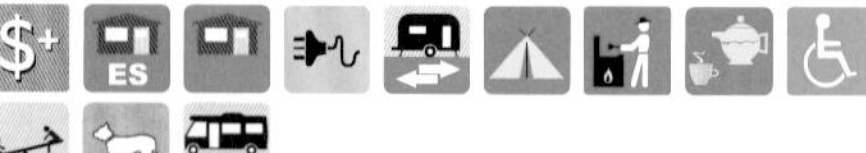

Renmark

164 BIG4 Renmark Riverfront Holiday Park
Sturt Hwy. 2 km E of PO
www.big4renmark.com.au
08 8586 8111 HEMA 125 C13 34 10 43 S 140 45 50 E

165 Riverbend Caravan Park
101 Sturt Hwy. 3 km E of PO
www.riverbendrenmark.com.au
08 8595 5131 HEMA 125 C13 34 10 45 S 140 46 31 E

Riverton

166 Riverton Caravan Park
Cnr Oxford Tce & Torrens Rd
www.rivertoncaravanpark.com.au
08 8847 2419 HEMA 124 C7 34 09 20 S 138 44 59 E

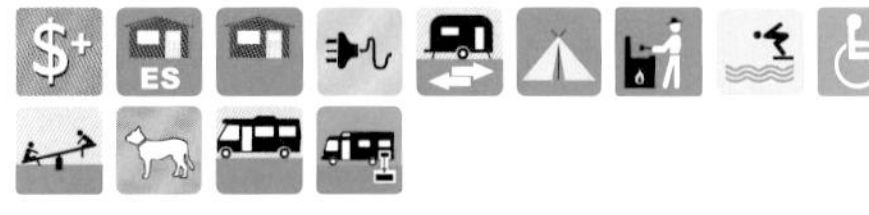

Robe

167 Discovery Holiday Parks Robe
70 The Esplanade. Call park to book with pets
www.discoveryholidayparks.com.au
08 8768 2237 HEMA 126 E2 37 09 51 S 139 47 01 E

168 Lakeside Tourist Park
24 Main Rd
www.lakesiderobe.com.au
08 8768 2193 HEMA 126 E2 37 09 58 S 139 46 15 E

169 Robe Holiday Park
Cnr Main Rd & Nora Creina Rd
www.robeholidaypark.com.au
0488 727 269 HEMA 126 F2 37 10 05 S 139 46 38 E

170 Sea-Vu Caravan Park
1 Squire Dr
www.seavucaravanpark.com.au
08 8768 2273 HEMA 126 E2 37 09 47 S 139 45 45 E

Roxby Downs

171 Discovery Holiday Parks Roxby Downs
56-94 Burgoyne St
www.discoveryholidayparks.com.au
08 8671 1991 HEMA 130 J2 30 34 03 S 136 53 35 E

Saddleworth

172 Saddleworth Oval Caravan Park
Via Belvedere Rd & Marrabel Rd
08 8847 4439 HEMA 124 C7 34 05 10 S 138 47 05 E

Second Valley

173 Second Valley Caravan Park
2 Park Ave
www.secondvalleycaravanpark.com
08 8598 4054 HEMA 124 H6 35 30 49 S 138 13 08 E

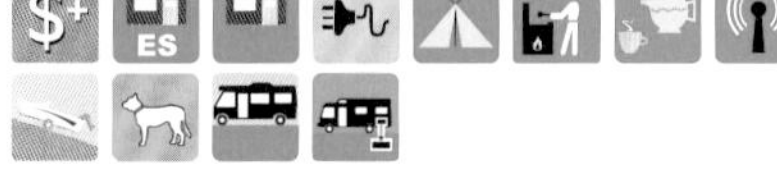

Semaphore Park

174 Discovery Holiday Parks Adelaide Beachfront
349 Military Rd. 15 km W of GPO
08 8449 7726 HEMA 120 G1 34 51 10 S 138 28 43 E

Smoky Bay

175 Baldwins Holiday Units & Van Park
117 Smoky Bay Rd
08 8625 7040 HEMA 134 B1 32 22 28 S 133 56 53 E

176 Smoky Bay Caravan Park
64 South Tce
www.smokybaycaravanpark.com.au
08 8625 7030 HEMA 134 B1 32 22 37 S 133 56 03 E

Snowtown

177 Snowtown Centenary Park Caravan Park
North Tce. See notice board for payment & keys
08 8865 2252 HEMA 124 B6 33 46 42 S 138 12 59 E

Southend

178 Southend on Sea Tourist Park
1 Eyre St
www.southendcaravanpark.com.au
08 8735 6035 HEMA 126 G3 37 34 11 S 140 07 21 E

179 Southend Sands Caravan Park
Cnr of Leake & Eliza Sts
www.southendsandscaravanpark.com.au
08 8735 6200 HEMA 126 G3 37 34 07 S 140 07 38 E

Stansbury

180 Oyster Point Drive Caravan Park
395 Oyster Point Drive. 2 km S of PO
www.stansburycaravanpark.com.au
08 8852 4171 HEMA 124 F4 34 55 00 S 137 47 46 E

181 Stansbury Foreshore Caravan Park
395 Anzac Pde
www.stansburycaravanpark.com
08 8852 4171 HEMA 124 F5 34 54 42 S 137 48 10 E

Strathalbyn

182 Strathalbyn Caravan Park
4 Ashbourne Rd
www.strathalbyncaravanpark.com.au
08 8536 3681 HEMA 127 J6 35 15 33 S 138 53 09 E

Streaky Bay

183 Discovery Holiday Parks Streaky Bay
82 Wells St. 1.5 km W of PO
www.discoveryholidayparks.com.au
08 8626 1666 HEMA 134 C2 32 47 50 S 134 11 53 E

184 The Streaky Bay Islands Caravan Park
101 Little Islands Road
www.streakybayislandscaravanpark.com.au
08 7600 0020 HEMA 134 C2 32 45 04 S 134 14 47 E

Swan Reach

185 Punyelroo Caravan Park
Punyelroo Rd
08 8570 2021 HEMA 125 E10 34 36 13 S 139 36 08 E

186 Swan Reach Caravan Park
35 Victoria St
08 8570 2010 HEMA 125 E10 34 34 05 S 139 35 46 E

Tailem Bend

187 Rivers Edge Caravan Park
216 Princes Hwy
www.riversedgecp.com
08 8572 3307 HEMA 125 G9 35 14 25 S 139 26 26 E

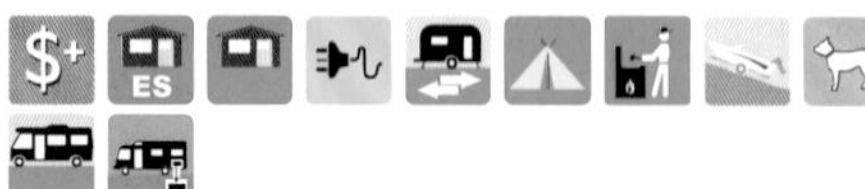

188 Westbrook Park River Resort
Jaensch Rd, off Princes Hwy
08 8572 3794 HEMA 125 G9 35 13 09 S 139 24 18 E

Tanunda

189 Discovery Holiday Parks Barossa Valley
Barossa Valley Way. 1.5 km S of PO
www.discoveryholidayparks.com.au
08 8563 2784 HEMA 122 E3 34 31 51 S 138 57 03 E

Tintinara

190 Cafe Tinti Motel & Caravan Park
19 Becker Tce
www.cafetintiandmotel.com.au
08 8757 2095 HEMA 125 J11 35 52 57 S 140 03 18 E

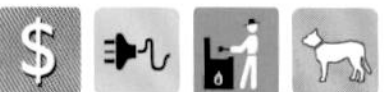

Tumby Bay

191 Tumby Bay Caravan Park
47 Tumby Tce. 1.5 km S of PO
www.tumbybaycaravanpark.com/
08 8688 2208 HEMA 134 H6 34 23 10 S 136 06 18 E

192 Tumby Bay CWA & Caravan Park
3 The Esplanade
0438 031 476 HEMA 134 H6 34 22 29 S 136 06 13 E

Vale Park

193 Levi Park Caravan Park
1A Harris Road
www.levipark.com.au
08 8344 2209 HEMA 120 H5 34 53 22 S 138 37 35 E

Venus Bay

194 Venus Bay Caravan Park
32 Matson Tce
www.venusbaycaravanparksa.com.au
08 8625 5073 HEMA 134 D3 33 13 59 S 134 40 29 E

Victor Harbor

195 Adare Caravan Park & Holiday Units
18 Wattle Dr
www.unitingvenuessa.org.au
08 8552 1657 HEMA 124 H7 35 32 30 S 138 37 39 E

196 Victor Harbor Beachfront Holiday Park
114 Victoria St. 1.5 km W of PO
www.victorbhp.com.au
08 8552 1111 HEMA 124 H7 35 33 32 S 138 36 45 E

197 Victor Harbor Holiday & Cabin Park
19 Bay Rd. 2 km W of PO
www.victorharborholiday.com.au
08 8552 1949 HEMA 124 H7 35 33 29 S 138 36 31 E

Waikerie

198 Waikerie Holiday Park
44 Peake Tce
www.waikerieholidaypark.com.au
08 8541 2651 HEMA 125 C11 34 10 33 S 139 58 49 E

Wallaroo

199 North Beach Tourist Park
1 Pamir Crt
www.wallaroonorthbeachtouristpark.com.au
08 8823 2531 HEMA 124 B4 33 55 13 S 137 37 59 E

200 Office Beach Holiday Cabins & Caravan Park
11 Jetty Rd. 500m N of PO. Entry via Heritage Dve
www.officebeachcaravanpark.com.au
08 8823 2722 HEMA 124 B4 33 55 39 S 137 37 25 E

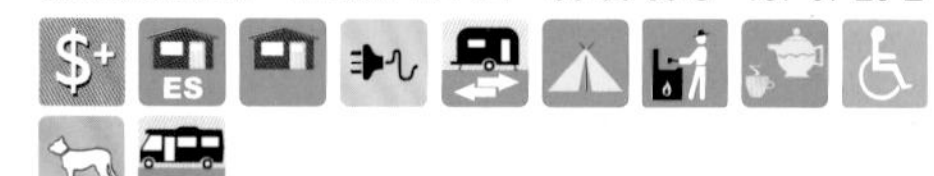

Wellington

201 Wellington Caravan Park
Main Rd
08 8572 7302 HEMA 125 G9 35 19 50 S 139 22 55 E

West Beach

202 Big 4 West Beach Parks
1 Military Rd. 3 km N of Glenelg PO
www.adelaideshores.com.au
08 8355 7320 HEMA 118 A2 34 56 53 S 138 30 19 E

BIG4

Whyalla

203 Discovery Holiday Parks Whyalla Foreshore

53 Broadbent Tce
www.discoveryholidayparks.com.au
08 8645 7474 HEMA 128 H4 33 02 33 S 137 34 39 E

204 Whyalla Caravan Park

Mullaquana Rd
www.whyallacaravanpark.com.au
08 8645 9357 HEMA 128 H4 33 02 50 S 137 32 39 E

Williamstown

205 Williamstown Queen Victoria Jubilee Park

Cnr Springton Rd & Mt Crawford Rd
www.williamstowncaravanpark.org.au
08 8524 6363 HEMA 122 K2 34 40 26 S 138 54 15 E

Wilmington

206 Beautiful Valley Caravan Park

Main North Rd. 1 km S of PO
www.beautifulvalley.com.au
08 8667 5197 HEMA 128 G6 32 39 39 S 138 06 30 E

207 Stony Creek Bush Camp Caravan Park

Stony Creek Rd
0488 156 850 HEMA 128 G6 32 38 54 S 138 08 06 E

Wilpena Pound

208 Rawnsley Park Station

Wilpena Rd. 21 km S of Wilpena
www.rawnsleypark.com.au
08 8648 0008 HEMA 142 J4 31 39 02 S 138 35 38 E

Windsor Gardens

209 Windsor Gardens Caravan Park

78 Windsor Gr
www.windsorgardenscaravanpark.com.au
08 8261 1091 HEMA 120 H6 34 52 41 S 138 38 50 E

Wirrabara

210 Wirrabara Oval Caravan Park

Via Crew Rd. 400m dirt road. N end of town.
Payment & Key at Wirrabara Craft House
08 8668 4250 HEMA 128 H6 33 01 51 S 138 15 53 E

Wirrina Cove

211 Wirrina Cove Holiday Park

199 Paradise Drive (11 km S of Normanville off Main South Rd)
www.wirrinacoveholidaypark.com.au
08 8598 3125 HEMA 124 H6 35 30 16 S 138 15 28 E

Woodcroft

212 Woodcroft Park Caravan Park

Lot 1 Bains Rd
www.woodcroftpark.com.au
08 8325 1233 HEMA 118 H2 35 06 51 S 138 33 23 E

Woomera

213 Woomera Travellers Village

Old Pimba Rd
www.woomera.com
08 8673 7800 HEMA 128 B2 31 12 02 S 136 49 05 E

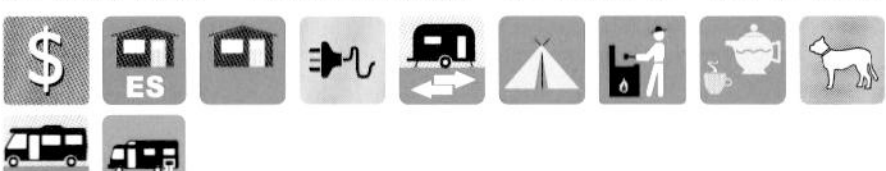

Wudinna

214 Gawler Ranges Motel & Caravan Park

Eyre Hwy. 1 km E from PO
www.gawlerrangesmotel.com.au
08 8680 2090 HEMA 134 D5 33 03 20 S 135 28 01 E

Yorketown

215 Yorketown Community Caravan Park

Memorial Dr
www.yorketowncp.com.au
0499 213 605 HEMA 124 F4 35 01 13 S 137 36 37 E

Yunta

216 Ray & Pams Roadhouse

Railway Tce
08 8650 5013 HEMA 129 G10 32 34 58 S 139 33 35 E

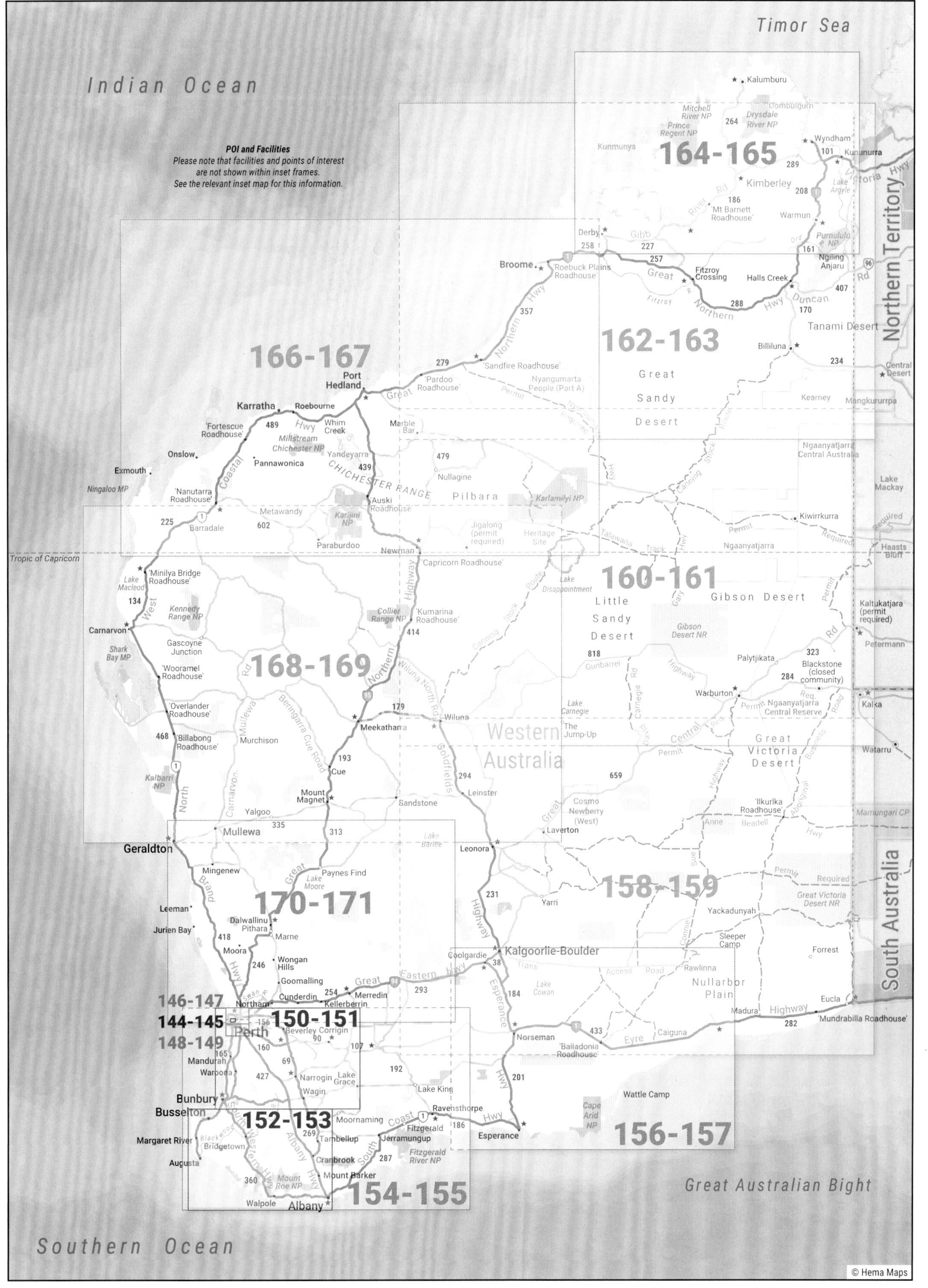
Timor Sea
Indian Ocean
POI and Facilities
Please note that facilities and points of interest are not shown within inset frames.
See the relevant inset map for this information.
164-165
162-163
166-167
160-161
168-169
158-159
170-171
146-147
144-145
150-151
148-149
152-153
156-157
154-155
Great Sandy Desert
Little Sandy Desert
Gibson Desert
Great Victoria Desert
Nullarbor Plain
Western Australia
Northern Territory
South Australia
Great Australian Bight
Southern Ocean
Tropic of Capricorn
Broome
Port Hedland
Karratha
Exmouth
Carnarvon
Geraldton
Perth
Bunbury
Albany
Esperance
Kalgoorlie-Boulder
Norseman
Eucla
Wyndham
Kununurra
Halls Creek
Fitzroy Crossing
Derby
Newman
Meekatharra
Leonora
© Hema Maps

Inner Perth

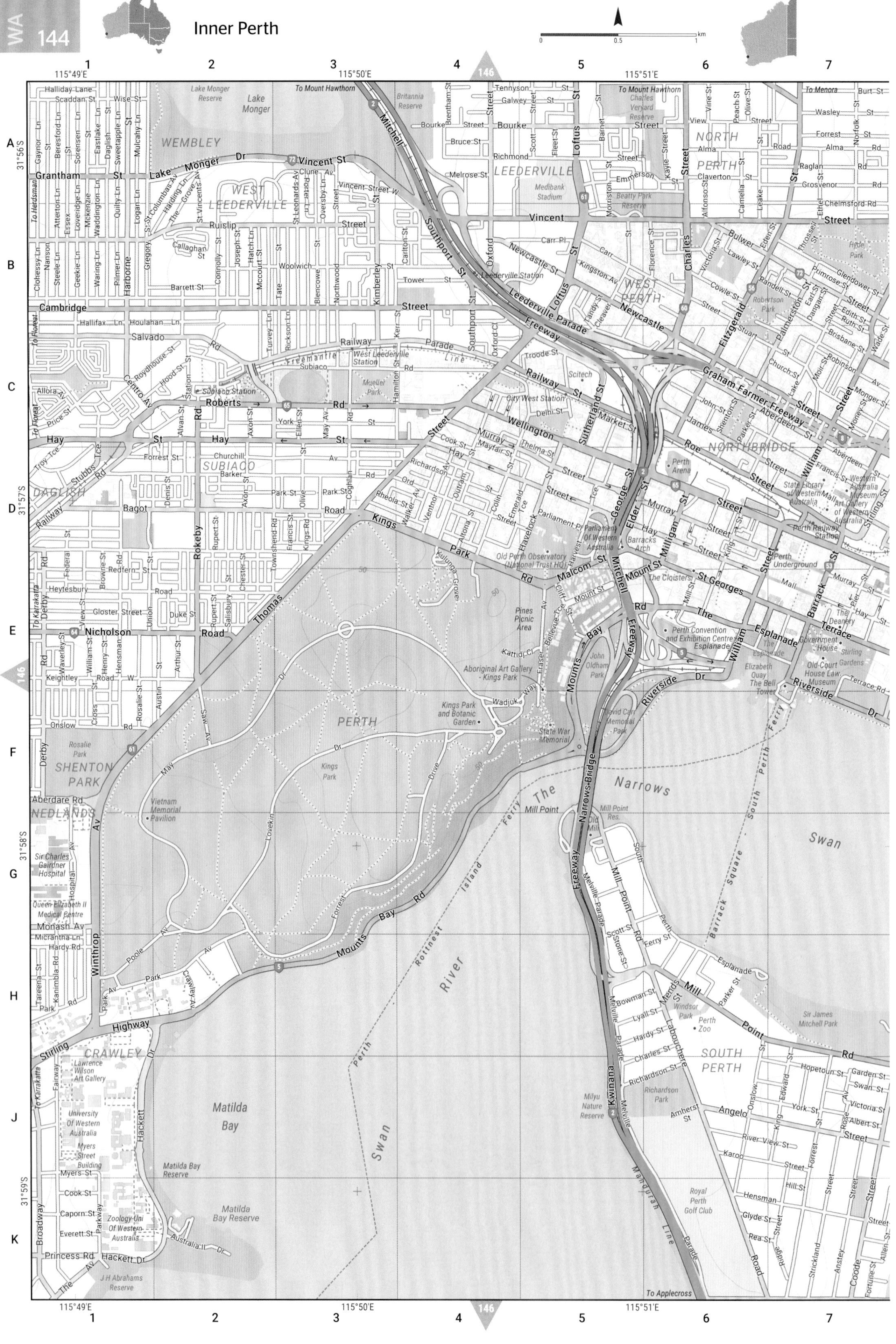

km
0
0.5
1
146
115°49'E
115°50'E
115°51'E
31°56'S
31°57'S
31°58'S
31°59'S
WEMBLEY
Lake Monger
Lake Monger Reserve
WEST LEEDERVILLE
LEEDERVILLE
NORTH PERTH
WEST PERTH
NORTHBRIDGE
SUBIACO
DAGLISH
SHENTON PARK
NEDLANDS
CRAWLEY
PERTH
SOUTH PERTH
Kings Park
Kings Park and Botanic Garden
State War Memorial
Aboriginal Art Gallery - Kings Park
Vietnam Memorial Pavilion
Pines Picnic Area
Old Perth Observatory (National Trust HQ)
Parliament of Western Australia
Barracks Arch
The Cloisters
Perth Convention and Exhibition Centre
Esplanade
Elizabeth Quay
The Bell Tower
Government House
Stirling Gardens
Old Court House Law Museum
Perth Arena
State Library of Western Australia
Western Australia Museum
Art Gallery of Western Australia
Perth Railway Station
Perth Underground
Leederville Station
City West Station
Subiaco Station
West Leederville Station
Scitech
Medibank Stadium
Beatty Park Reserve
Robertson Park
Hyde Park
Britannia Reserve
Mueller Park
John Oldham Park
David Carr Memorial Park
Mill Point
The Narrows
Narrows Bridge
Swan River
Rottnest Island Ferry
Perth Ferry
Barrack Square - South Perth Ferry
Sir James Mitchell Park
Windsor Park
Perth Zoo
Richardson Park
Milyu Nature Reserve
Royal Perth Golf Club
Matilda Bay
Matilda Bay Reserve
Lawrence Wilson Art Gallery
University Of Western Australia
Zoology-Uni Of Western Australia
J H Abrahams Reserve
Sir Charles Gairdner Hospital
Queen Elizabeth II Medical Centre
Rosalie Park
Mitchell Freeway
Kwinana Freeway
Graham Farmer Freeway
Mounts Bay Rd
Stirling Highway
Thomas Road
Kings Park Rd
Winthrop Av
Vincent Street
Cambridge Street
Roberts Rd
Hay St
Wellington Street
Murray Street
St Georges Terrace
Riverside Dr
Mill Point Rd
Mandurah Line
Fremantle Line
To Mount Hawthorn
To Menora
To Herdsman
To Floreat
To Karrakatta
To Applecross

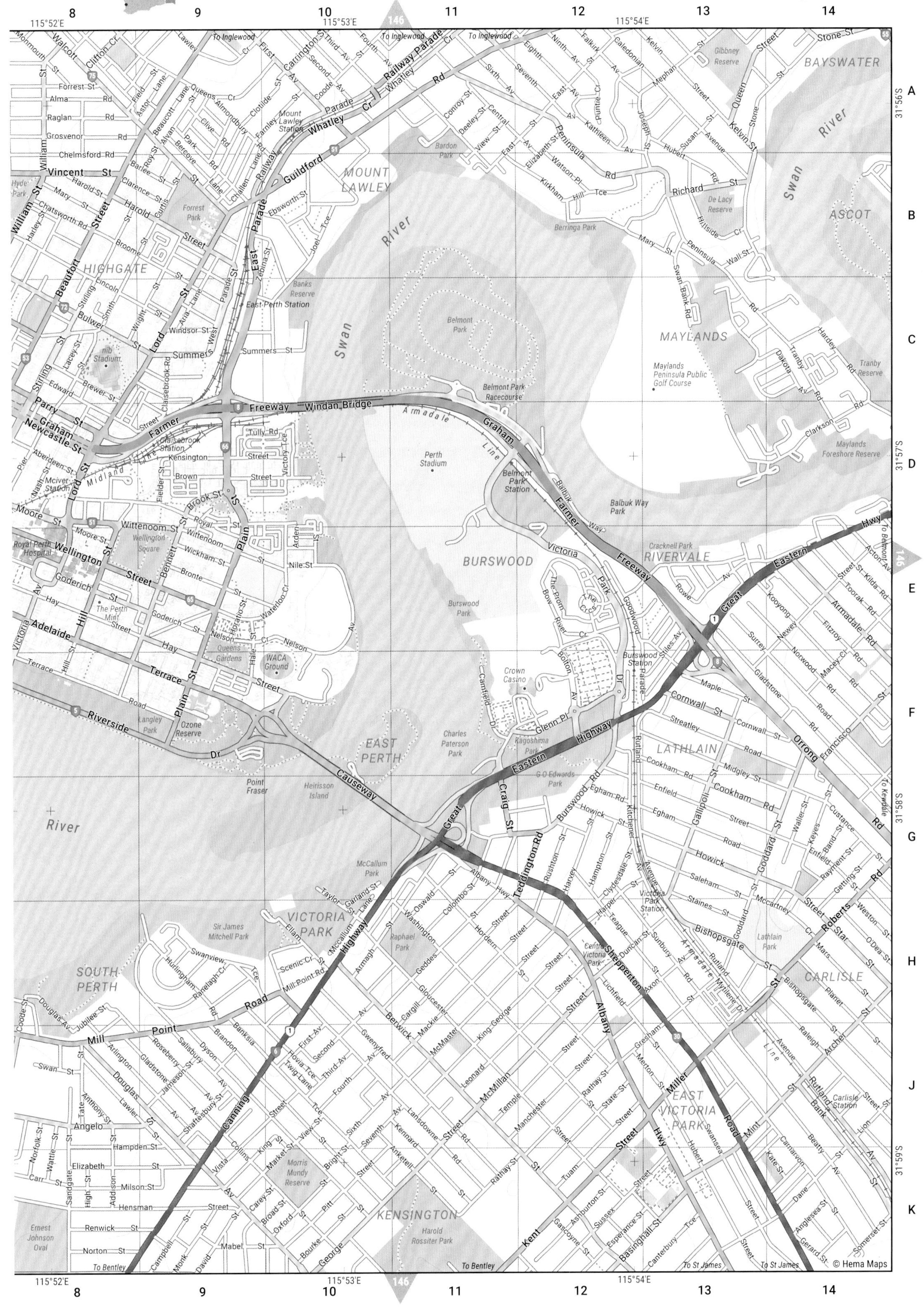
8
9
10
11
12
13
14
115°52'E
115°53'E
115°54'E
146
A
B
C
D
E
F
G
H
J
K
31°56'S
31°57'S
31°58'S
31°59'S
To Inglewood
To Inglewood
To Inglewood
BAYSWATER
MOUNT LAWLEY
HIGHGATE
ASCOT
MAYLANDS
RIVERVALE
BURSWOOD
EAST PERTH
LATHLAIN
VICTORIA PARK
SOUTH PERTH
CARLISLE
EAST VICTORIA PARK
KENSINGTON
Swan River
River
Gibbney Reserve
De Lacy Reserve
Bardon Park
Berringa Park
Forrest Park
Hyde Park
Banks Reserve
Belmont Park
Belmont Park Racecourse
Maylands Peninsula Public Golf Course
Tranby Reserve
Maylands Foreshore Reserve
Perth Stadium
Balbuk Way Park
Cracknell Park
Burswood Park
Crown Casino
Charles Paterson Park
Kagoshima Park
G O Edwards Park
Heirisson Island
Point Fraser
McCallum Park
Sir James Mitchell Park
Raphael Park
Lathlain Park
Morris Mundy Reserve
Harold Rossiter Park
Ernest Johnson Oval
Langley Park
Ozone Reserve
Queens Gardens
WACA Ground
The Perth Mint
Royal Perth Hospital
Wellington Square
nib Stadium
Mount Lawley Station
East Perth Station
Claisebrook Station
Mclver Station
Belmont Park Station
Burswood Station
Victoria Park Station
Carlisle Station
Centre Victoria Park
Windan Bridge
Graham Farmer Freeway
Great Eastern Hwy
Guildford Rd
Whatley Cr
Railway Parade
Causeway
Riverside Dr
Canning Highway
Albany Hwy
Shepperton Rd
Orrong Rd
Mill Point Road
Kent Street
Miller Street
Roberts Rd
To Belmont Av
To Kewdale
To Bentley
To Bentley
To St James
To St James
© Hema Maps

Northern Perth Suburbs to Mundaring

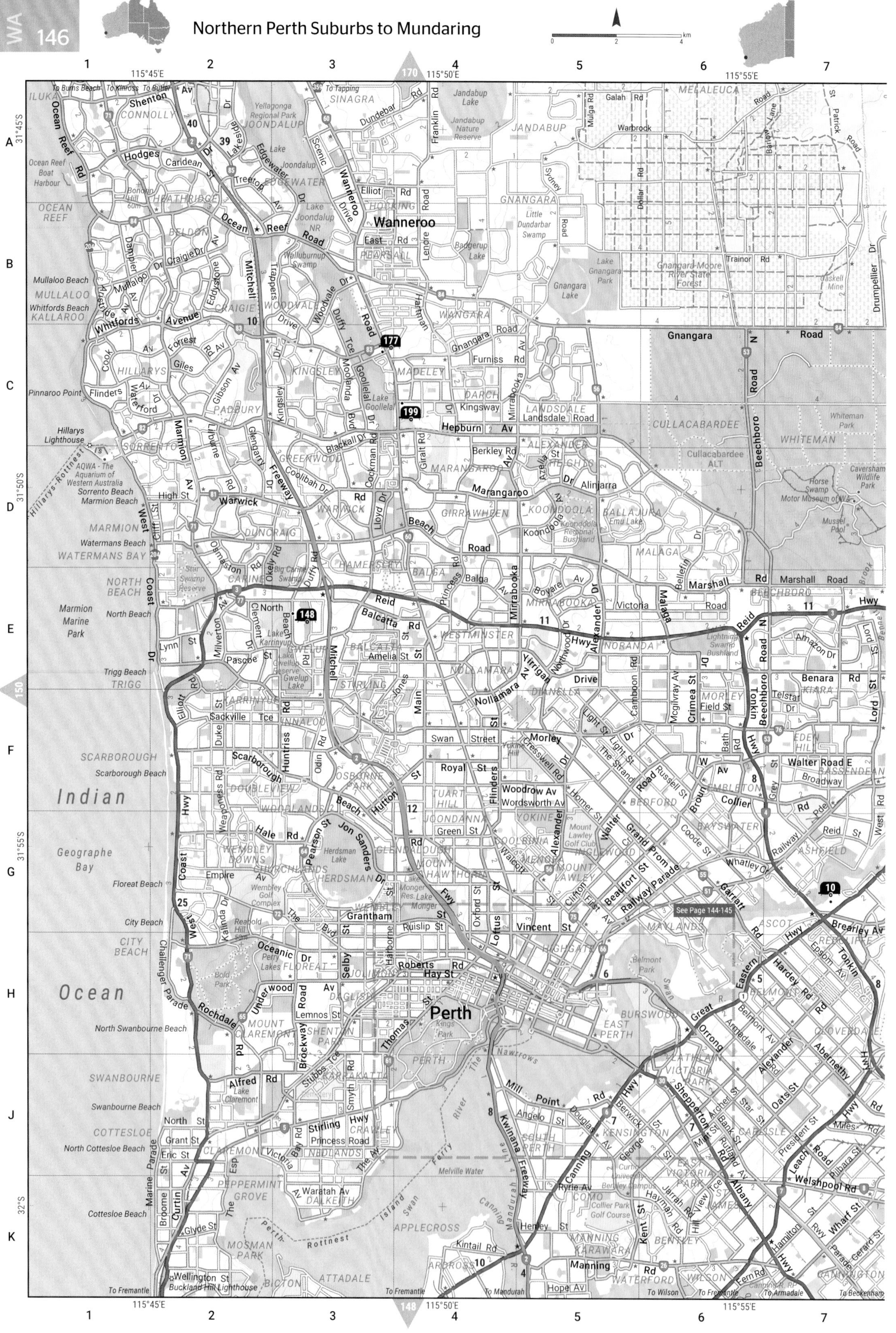

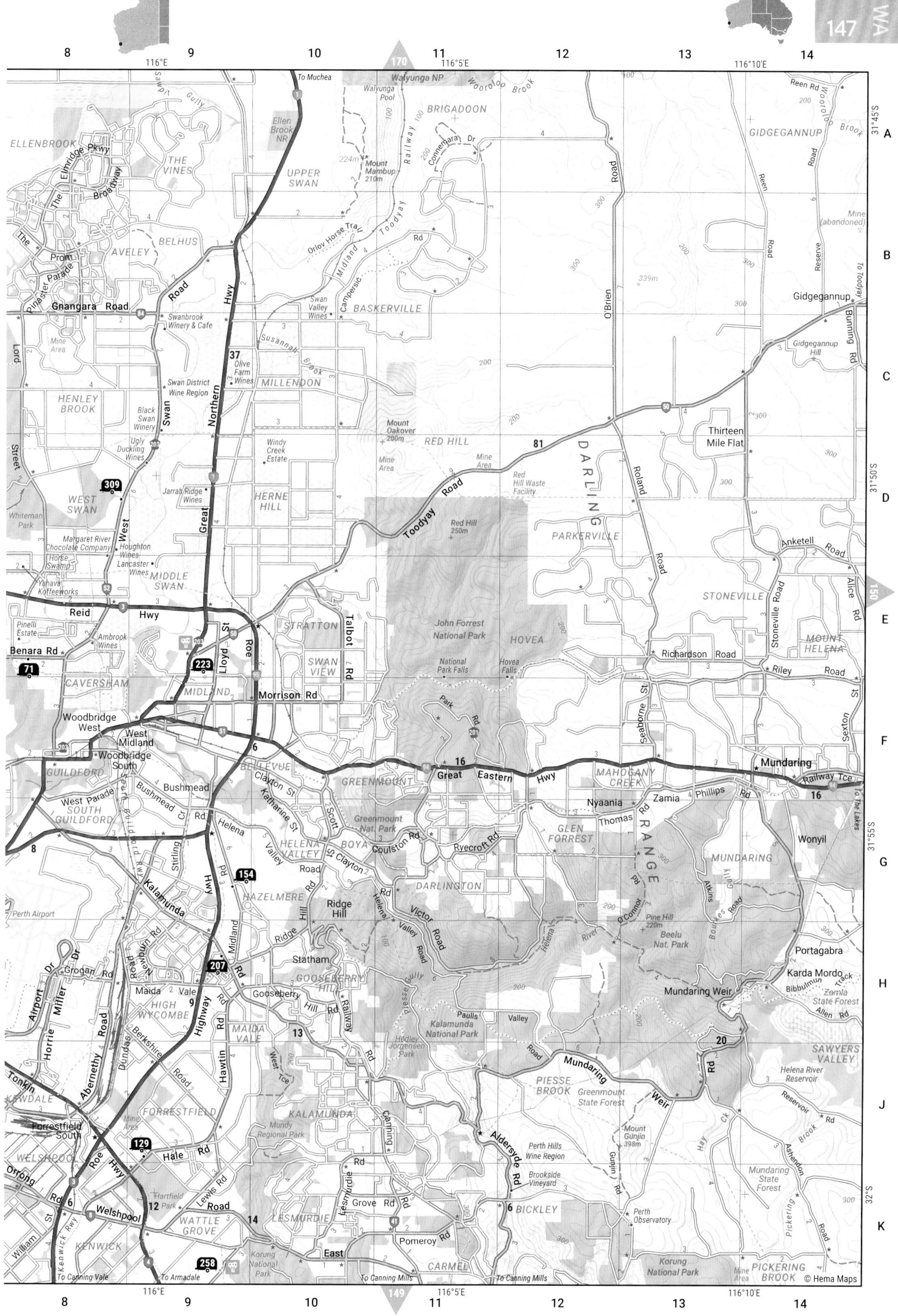
Walyunga NP
BRIGADOON
UPPER SWAN
THE VINES
ELLENBROOK
AVELEY
BELHUS
BASKERVILLE
MILLENDON
HENLEY BROOK
RED HILL
HERNE HILL
WEST SWAN
MIDDLE SWAN
STRATTON
SWAN VIEW
CAVERSHAM
MIDLAND
John Forrest National Park
HOVEA
PARKERVILLE
STONEVILLE
MOUNT HELENA
GIDGEGANNUP
Gidgegannup
Thirteen Mile Flat
DARLING RANGE
Mundaring
GREENMOUNT
BELLEVUE
GUILDFORD
SOUTH GUILDFORD
HELENA VALLEY
BOYA
DARLINGTON
GLEN FORREST
MAHOGANY CREEK
MUNDARING
HAZELMERE
Beelu Nat. Park
Mundaring Weir
SAWYERS VALLEY
HIGH WYCOMBE
MAIDA VALE
GOOSEBERRY HILL
Kalamunda National Park
PIESSE BROOK
KALAMUNDA
FORRESTFIELD
KEWDALE
WELSHPOOL
WATTLE GROVE
LESMURDIE
KENWICK
BICKLEY
CARMEL
Korung National Park
PICKERING BROOK
Perth Airport
Great Eastern Hwy
Great Northern Hwy
Toodyay Road
Reid Hwy
Roe Hwy
Tonkin Hwy
Mundaring Weir Rd
© Hema Maps

Southern Perth Suburbs to Armadale

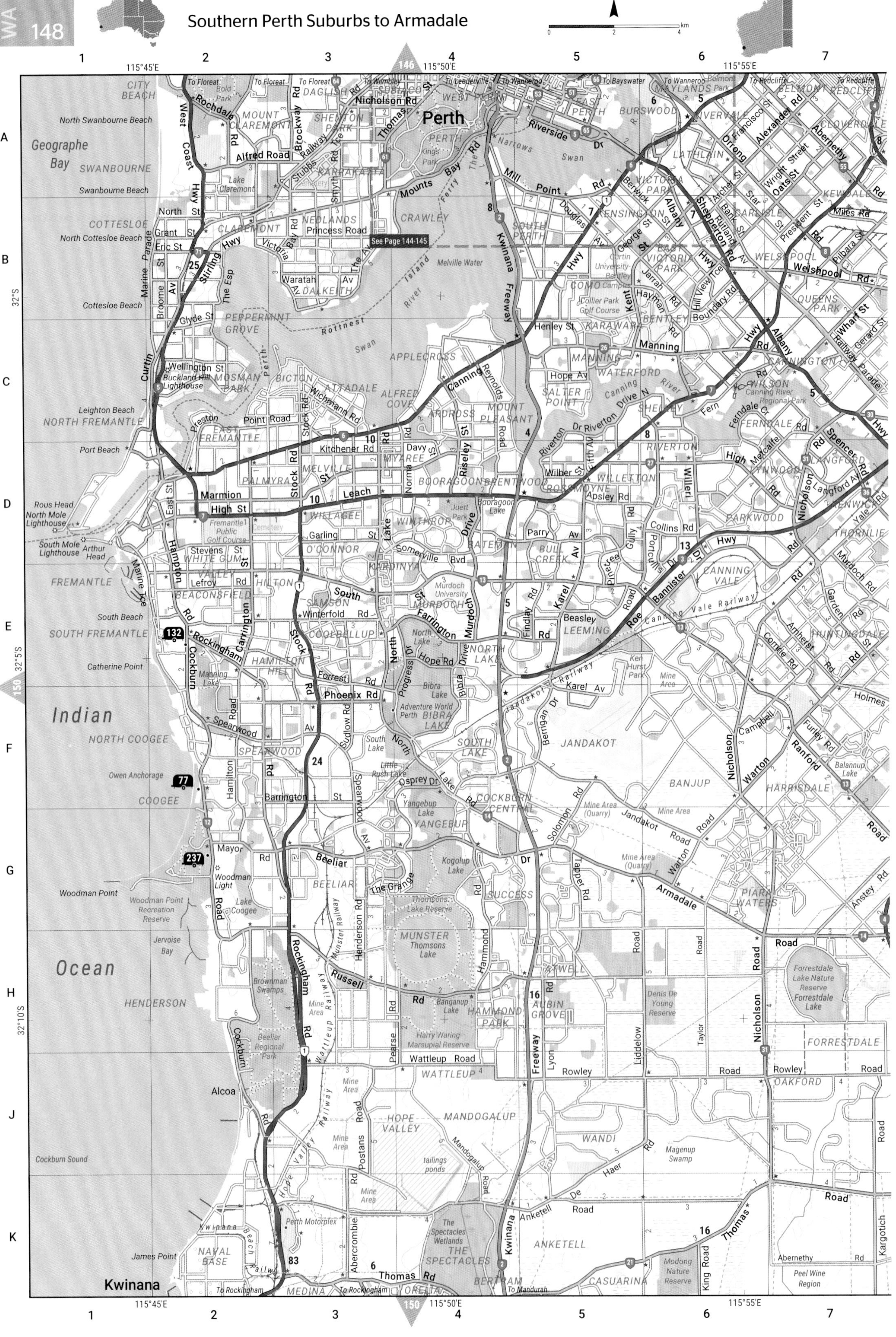

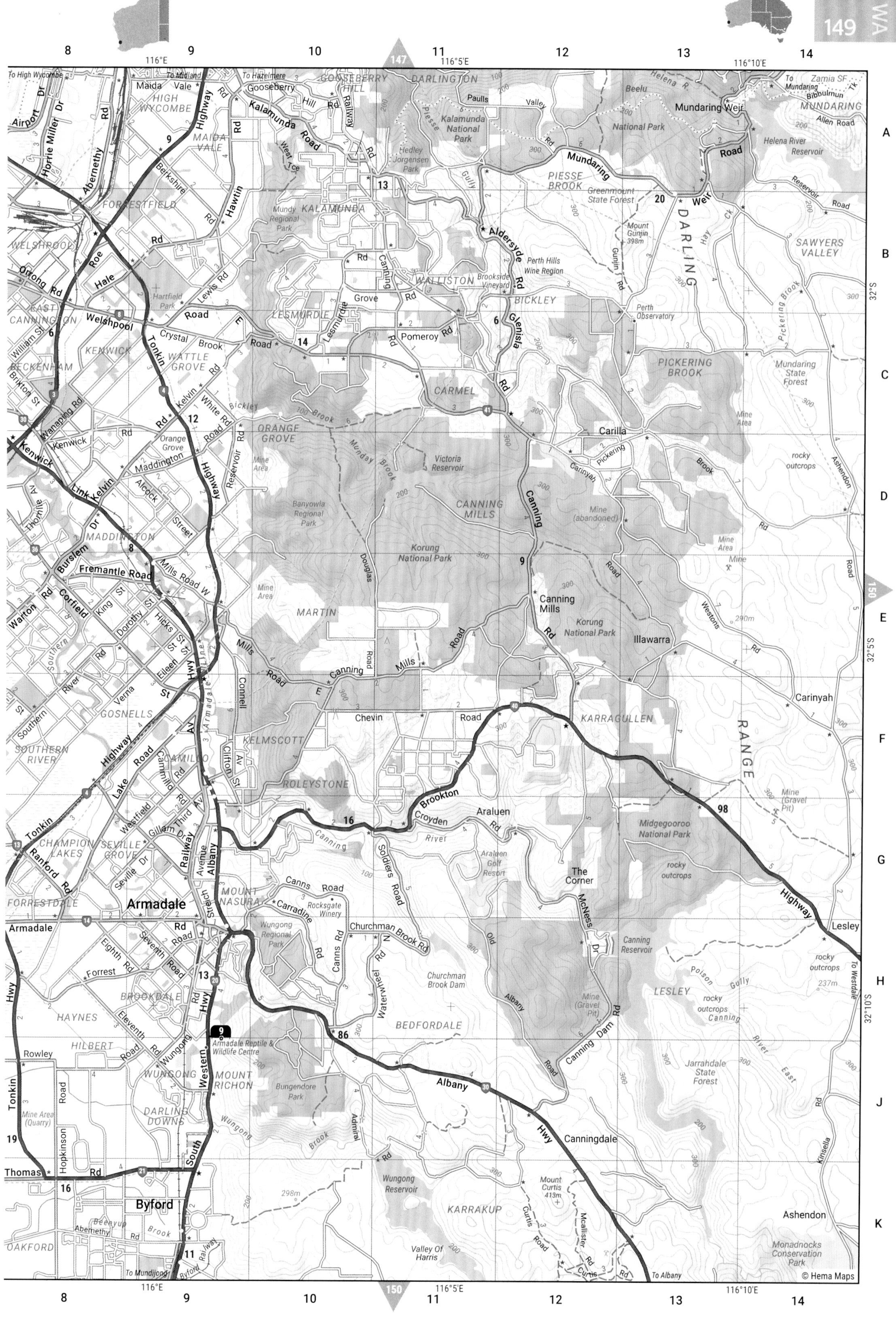

Mundaring Weir
Kalamunda National Park
Kalamunda
Darlington
Gooseberry Hill
Maida Vale
High Wycombe
Forrestfield
Welshpool
Lesmurdie
Walliston
Bickley
Carmel
Pickering Brook
Sawyers Valley
Mundaring State Forest
Perth Observatory
Piesse Brook
Darling Range
Carilla
Canning Mills
Korung National Park
Martin
Orange Grove
Kenwick
Maddington
Gosnells
Kelmscott
Roleystone
Karragullen
Illawarra
Canning Mills
Araluen
The Corner
Midgegooroo National Park
Armadale
Mount Nasura
Bedfordale
Brookdale
Haynes
Hilbert
Wungong
Mount Richon
Darling Downs
Byford
Oakford
Canningdale
Karrakup
Wungong Reservoir
Canning Reservoir
Churchman Brook Dam
Jarrahdale State Forest
Lesley
Ashendon
Monadnocks Conservation Park
Valley Of Harris
Mount Curtis 413m
Champion Lakes
Seville Grove
Forrestdale
Southern River
Camillo
Kenwick
Beckenham
Wattle Grove
Armadale Reptile & Wildlife Centre
Bungendore Park
Wungong Regional Park
Rocksgate Winery
Araluen Golf Resort
Banyowla Regional Park
Victoria Reservoir
Mundy Regional Park
Hartfield Park
Hedley Jorgensen Park
Greenmount State Forest
Helena River Reservoir
Zamia SF
Bibbulmun Trk
Albany Hwy
Brookton Hwy
Tonkin Hwy
South Western Hwy
Great Eastern Hwy
To Albany
To Westdale
To Mundijong
To Midland
To Hazelmere
To High Wycombe
To Mundaring
116°E
116°5'E
116°10'E
32°S
32°5'S
32°10'S
© Hema Maps

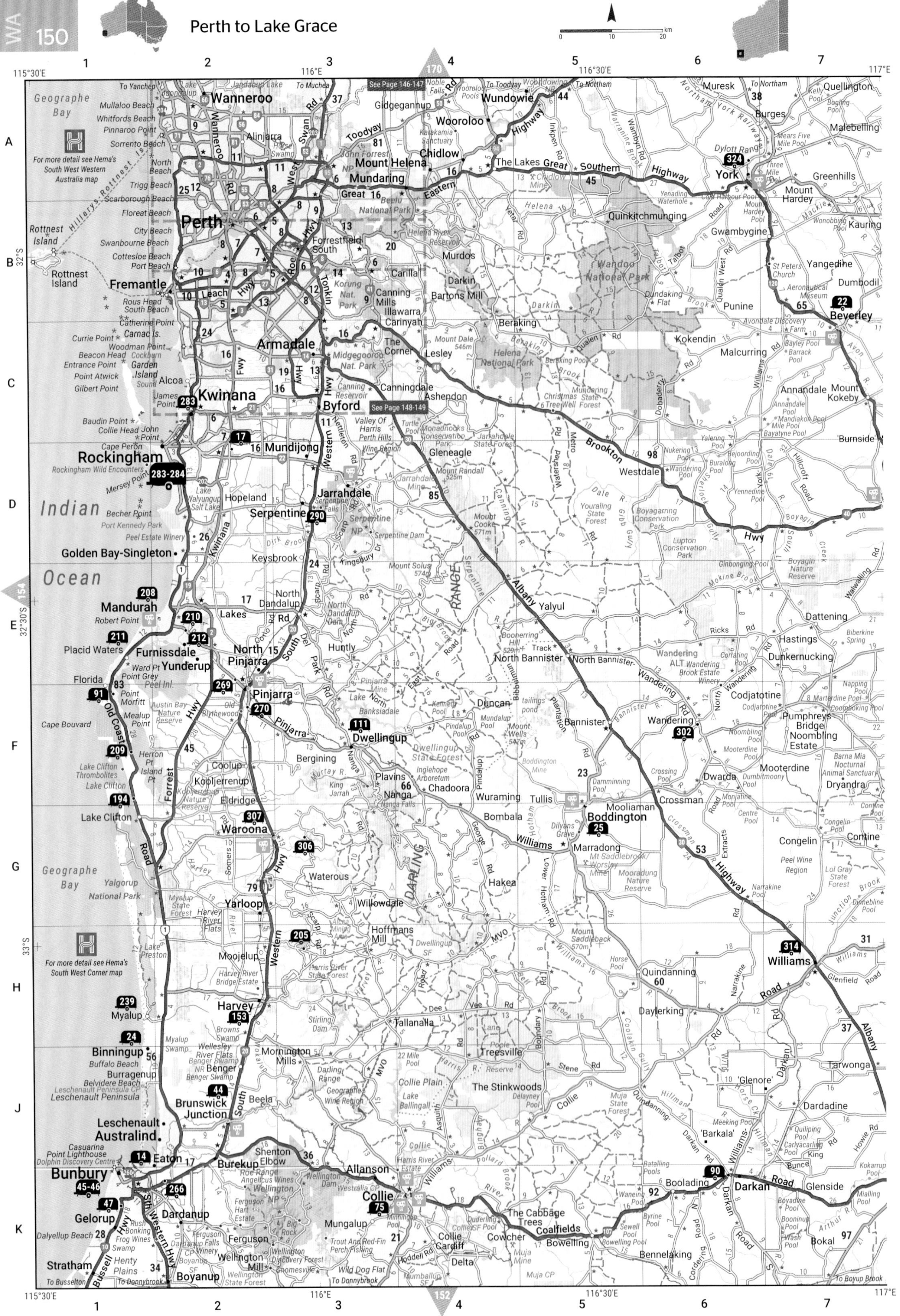

See Page 146-147
See Page 148-149
For more detail see Hema's South West Western Australia map
For more detail see Hema's South West Corner map
Geographe Bay
Indian Ocean
Wanneroo
Mullaloo Beach
Whitfords Beach
Pinnaroo Point
Sorrento Beach
North Beach
Trigg Beach
Scarborough Beach
Floreat Beach
City Beach
Swanbourne Beach
Cottesloe Beach
Port Beach
Rottnest Island
Fremantle
Rous Head
South Beach
Catherine Point
Carnac Is.
Currie Point
Woodman Point
Beacon Head
Entrance Point
Point Atwick
Gilbert Point
Garden Island
Alcoa
Kwinana
Baudin Point
Collie Head
John Point
Cape Peron
Rockingham
Rockingham Wild Encounters
Mersey Point
Becher Point
Port Kennedy Park
Peel Estate Winery
Golden Bay-Singleton
Mandurah
Robert Point
Placid Waters
Furnissdale
Yunderup
Florida
Point Morfitt
Mealup Point
Cape Bouvard
Herron Pt
Island Pt
Lake Clifton Thrombolites
Lake Clifton
Yalgorup National Park
Myalup
Binningup
Buffalo Beach
Burragenup
Belvidere Beach
Leschenault Peninsula
Leschenault
Australind
Casuarina Point Lighthouse
Dolphin Discovery Centre
Eaton
Bunbury
Gelorup
Dalyellup Beach
Stratham
To Busselton
Perth
Alinjarra
Gidgegannup
Toodyay
Mount Helena
Mundaring
Chidlow
Wooroloo
Wundowie
Forrestfield South
Carilla
Canning Mills
Illawarra
Carinyah
Armadale
Midgegooroo Nat. Park
Canningdale
Byford
Mundijong
Jarrahdale
Serpentine
Serpentine NP
Hopeland
Keysbrook
North Dandalup
Lakes
North Pinjarra
Pinjarra
Huntly
Dwellingup
Bergining
Coolup
Kooljerrenup
Eldridge
Waroona
Waterous
Yarloop
Willowdale
Hoffmans Mill
Moojelup
Harvey
Mornington Mills
Benger
Brunswick Junction
Beela
Burekup
Shenton Elbow
Allanson
Collie
Mungalup
Ferguson
Dardanup
Wellington Mill
Boyanup
Henty Plains
To Donnybrook
Noble Falls
Chidlow Mine
Beraking
Lesley
The Corner
Ashendon
Gleneagle
Murdos
Darkin
Bartons Mill
Helena National Park
Yalyul
North Bannister
Bannister
Duncan
Chadoora
Plavins
Nanga
Wuraming
Tullis
Bombala
Boddington
Mooliaman
Marradong
Hakea
Tallanalla
Treesville
The Stinkwoods
Collie Plain
Lake Ballingall
Collie Cardiff
Delta
Cowcher
Coalfields
Bowelling
The Cabbage Trees
Mount Saddleback 570m
DARLING RANGE
The Lakes
Great Southern Highway
Quinkitchmunging
Wandoo National Park
Dundaking Flat
Brookton
Westdale
Kokendin
Malcurring
Punine
Muresk
To Northam
Burges
Dylott Range
York
Gwambygine
Mount Hardey
Greenhills
Quellington
Malebelling
Kauring
Yangedine
Dumbodil
Beverley
Annandale
Mount Kokeby
'Burnside'
Ricks
Dattening
Hastings
Dunkernucking
Wandering
Codjatotine
Pumphreys Bridge
Noombling Estate
Mooterdine
Dryandra
Dwarda
Crossman
Congelin
Contine
Williams
Quindanning
Daylerking
Tarwonga
'Glenore'
Dardadine
'Barkala'
Darkan
Booladine
Glenside
Bennelaking
Bokal
To Boyup Brook
Albany Highway
Williams Rd
Crossman Rd
Kwinana Fwy
Forrest Hwy
South Western Hwy
Old Coast Road

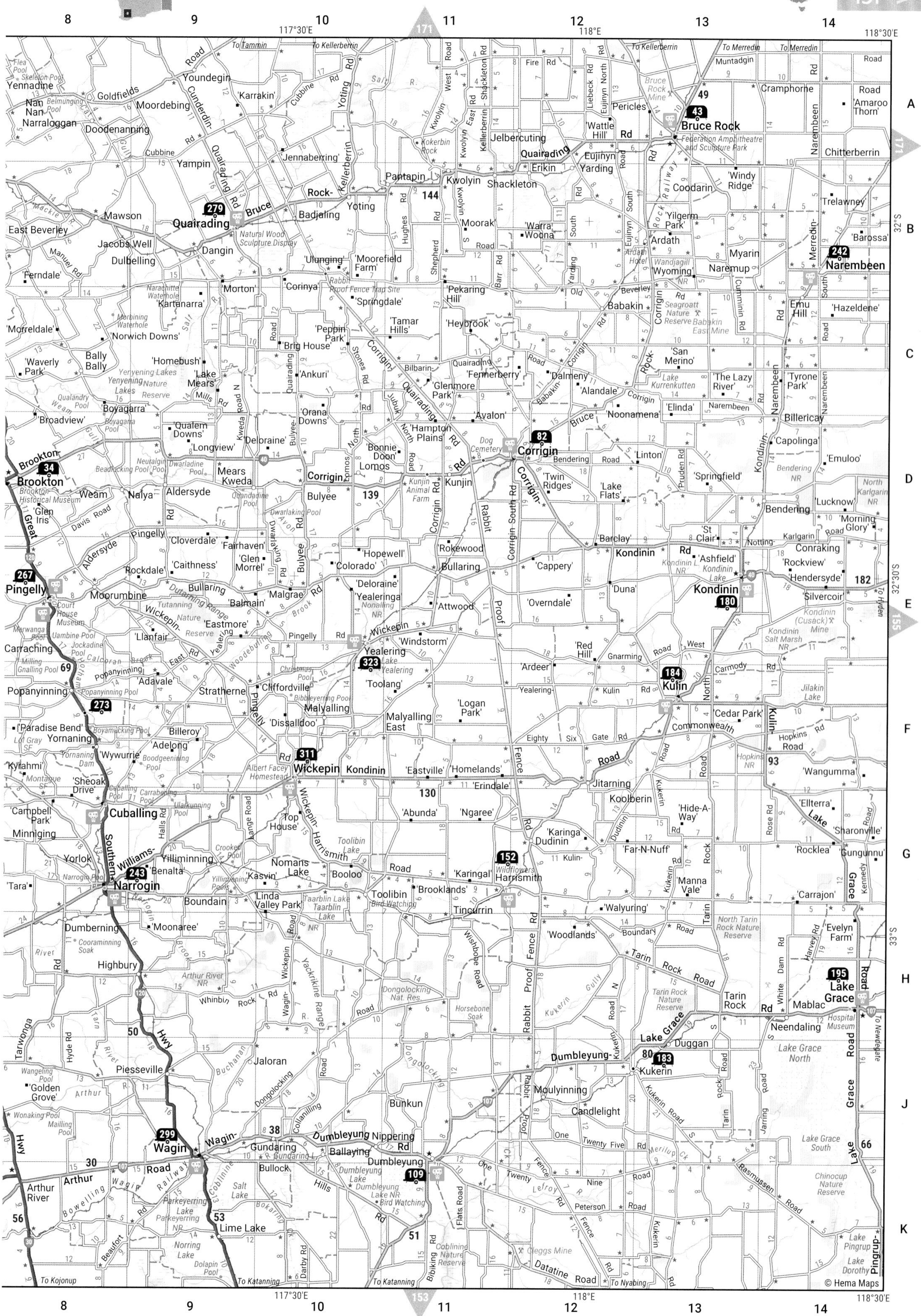

Busselton to Albany

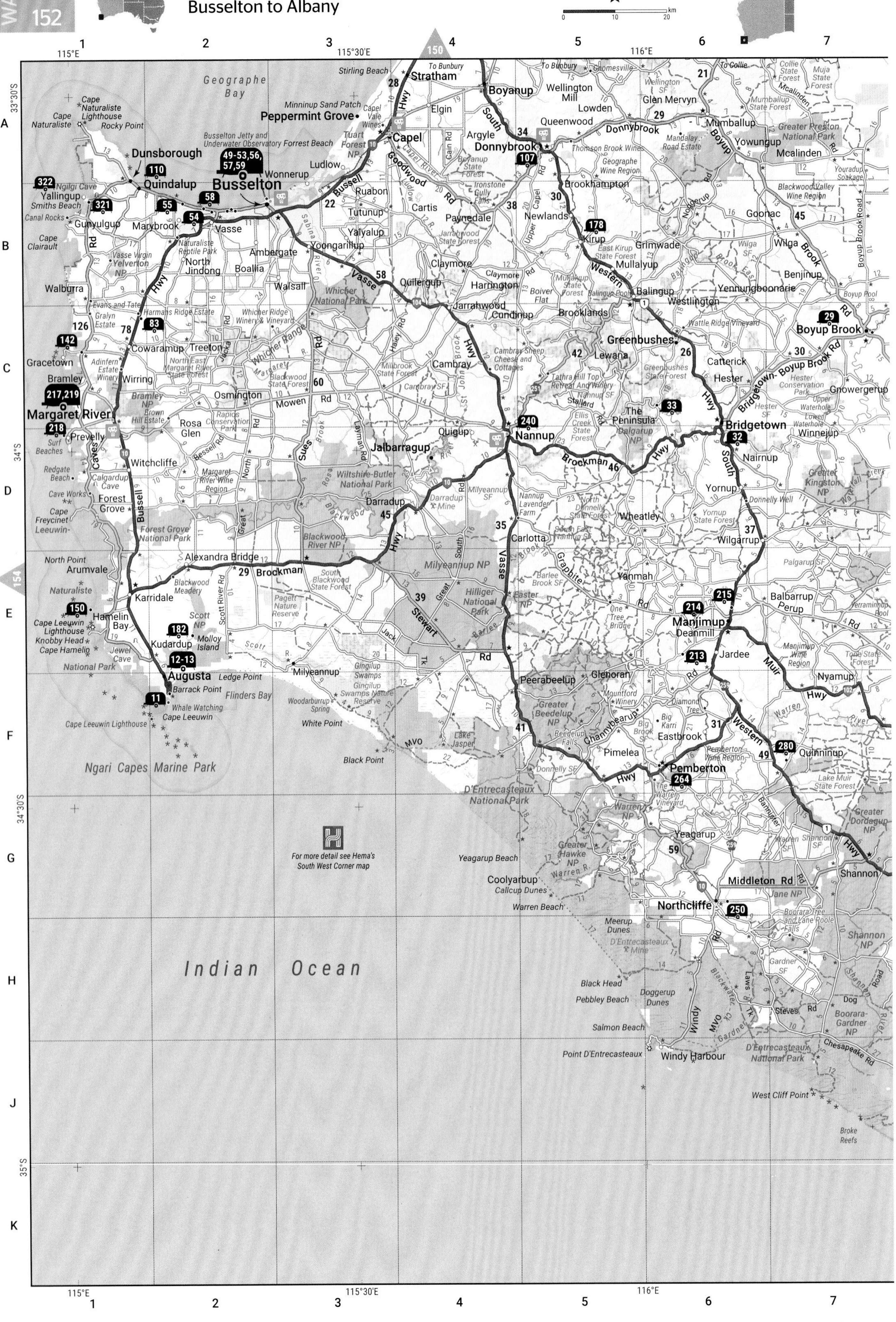

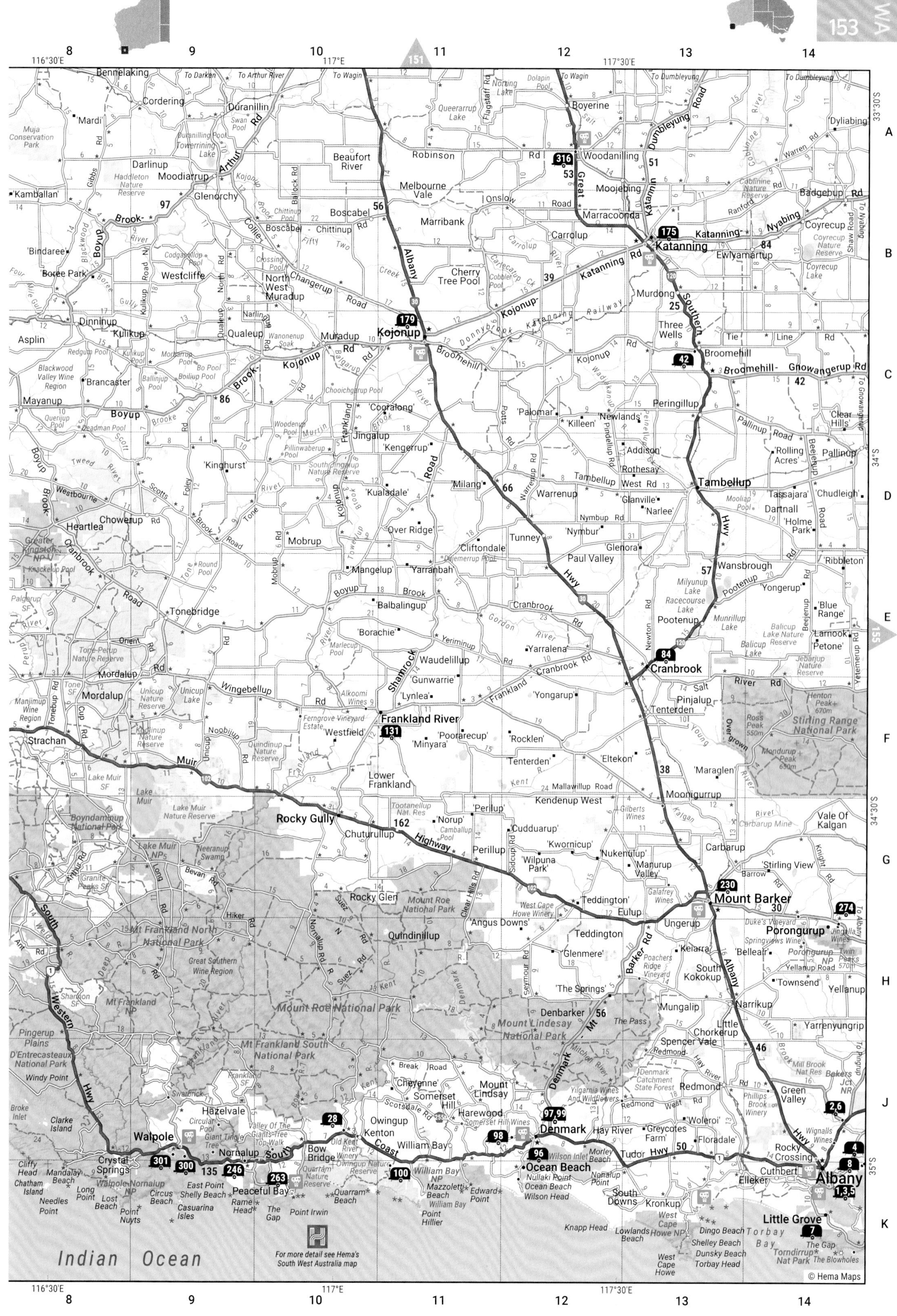

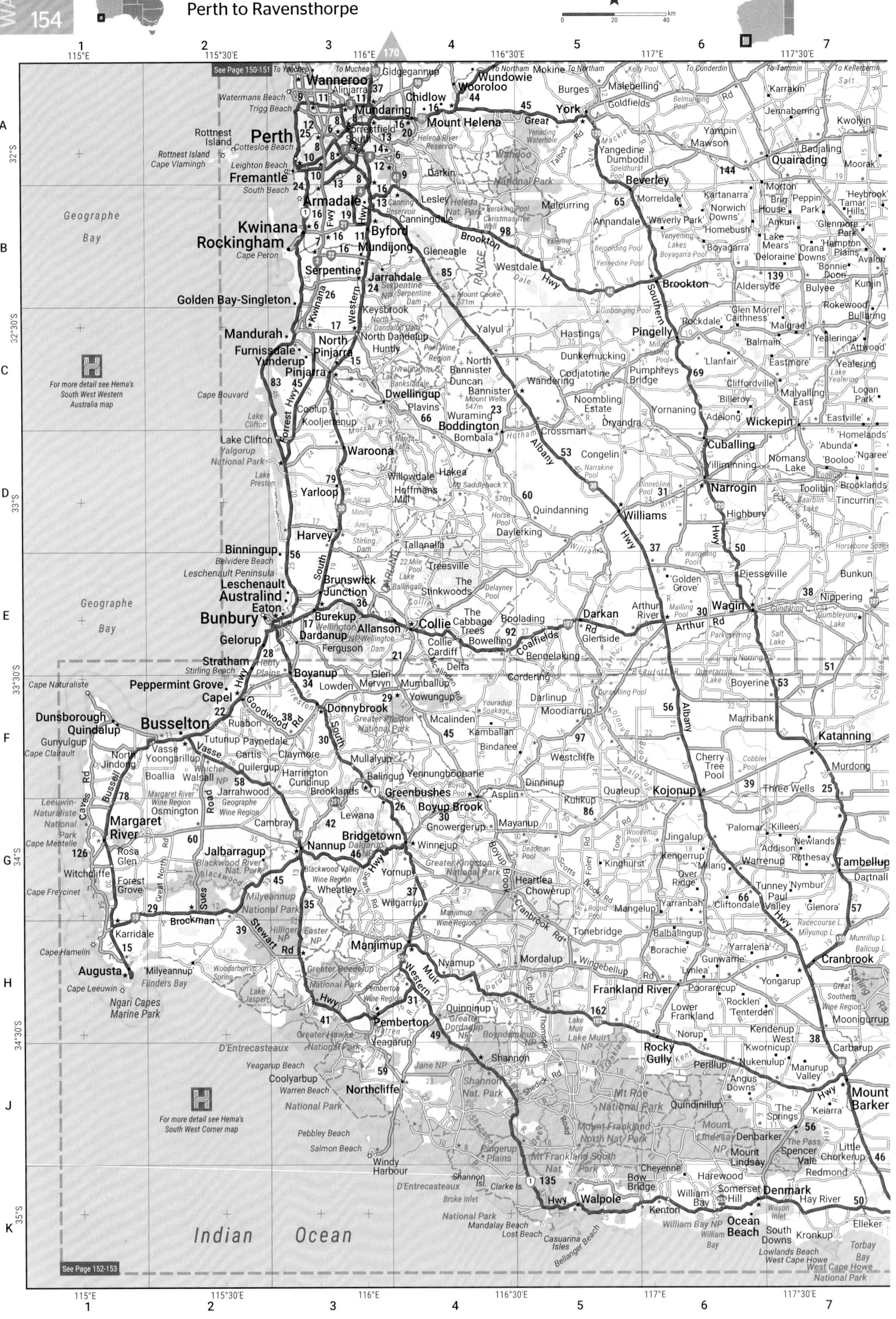
See Page 150-151
See Page 152-153
Wanneroo
Perth
Fremantle
Rottnest Island
Cottesloe Beach
Armadale
Kwinana
Rockingham
Cape Peron
Mundaring
Mount Helena
Chidlow
Wooroloo
Wundowie
York
Beverley
Brookton
Pingelly
Byford
Mundijong
Serpentine
Jarrahdale
Golden Bay-Singleton
Mandurah
Furnissdale
Yunderup
Pinjarra
North Pinjarra
Dwellingup
Boddington
Waroona
Yarloop
Harvey
Binningup
Leschenault
Australind
Eaton
Bunbury
Gelorup
Stratham
Capel
Peppermint Grove
Dunsborough
Quindalup
Busselton
Margaret River
Augusta
Cape Leeuwin
Cape Naturaliste
Geographe Bay
Nannup
Bridgetown
Donnybrook
Collie
Darkan
Williams
Narrogin
Wagin
Wickepin
Cuballing
Katanning
Kojonup
Boyup Brook
Manjimup
Pemberton
Northcliffe
Walpole
Denmark
Mount Barker
Cranbrook
Frankland River
Rocky Gully
Tambellup
Quairading
Indian Ocean
D'Entrecasteaux National Park
For more detail see Hema's South West Western Australia map
For more detail see Hema's South West Corner map

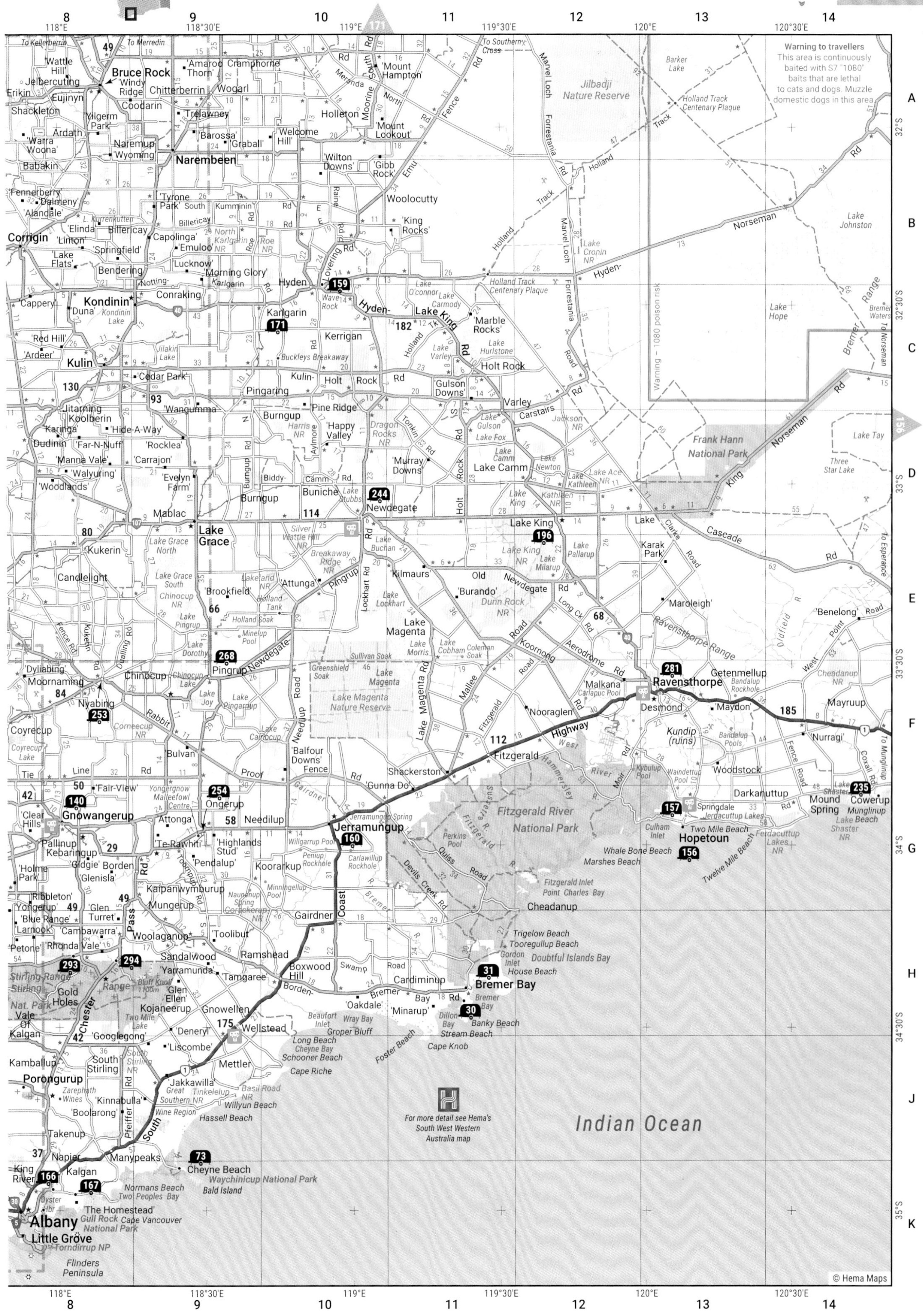

Warning to travellers
This area is continuously baited with S7 "1080" baits that are lethal to cats and dogs. Muzzle domestic dogs in this area.
Warning – 1080 poison risk
118°E
118°30'E
119°E
119°30'E
120°E
120°30'E
32°S
32°30'S
33°S
33°30'S
34°S
34°30'S
35°S
To Kellerberrin
To Merredin
To Southern Cross
To Norseman
To Esperance
To Munglinup
Bruce Rock
'Amaroo Thorn'
Cramphorne
'Mount Hampton'
Jilbadji Nature Reserve
Barker Lake
Holland Track Centenary Plaque
'Wattle Hill'
Jelbercuting
Erikin
Eujinyn
'Windy Ridge'
Chitterberrin
Wogarl
Coodarin
Shackleton
Yilgerm Park
'Trelawney'
Holleton
'Mount Lookout'
Ardath
'Warra Woona'
Naremup
'Wyoming'
'Barossa'
'Graball'
'Welcome Hill'
Babakin
Narembeen
'Wilton Downs'
'Gibb Rock'
'Fennerberry'
'Dalmeny'
'Alandale'
'Tyrone Park'
South Kumminin
Woolocutty
'Elinda'
Billericay
'King Rocks'
Lake Johnston
Corrigin
'Linton'
Capolinga'
'Springfield'
'Emuloo'
'Lake Flats'
Bendering
'Lucknow'
'Morning Glory'
Karlgarin
Hyden
Lake O'connor
Lake Carmody
Lake Cronin NR
Holland Track Centenary Plaque
'Cappery'
Kondinin
'Duna'
Conraking
Kondinin Lake
Wave Rock
Karlgarin
'Marble Rocks'
Lake Hope
Bremer Range
Kerrigan
Lake Hurlstone
Lake Varley
'Red Hill'
'Ardeer'
Kulin
Jilakin Lake
Buckleys Breakaway
Holt Rock
'Cedar Park'
Kulin-Holt Rock Rd
'Gulson Downs'
130
93
Pingaring
Varley
Jitarning
Koolberin
'Wangumma'
'Pine Ridge'
Burngup
Lake Gulson
Lake Fox
Jackson NR
Karinga'
'Hide-A-Way'
Harris NR
'Happy Valley'
Dragon Rocks NR
Frank Hann National Park
Lake Tay
Dudinin
'Far-N-Nuff'
'Rocklea'
Lake Camm
Lake Newton
'Manna Vale'
'Carrajon'
'Murray Downs'
Lake Camm
Lake Kathleen
Lake Ace NR
Three Star Lake
'Walyuring'
'Woodlands'
'Evelyn Farm'
Biddy-Camm Rd
Buniche
Lake Stubbs
Lake King
Kathleen NR
Mablac
Burngup
114
Newdegate
Lake Grace
Lake King
Lake
Cascade
80
Kukerin
Lake Grace North
Silver Wattle Hill NR
Lake Buchan
Lake King NR
Lake Pallarup
Karak Park
Breakaway Ridge NR
Lake Milarup
Candlelight
Lake Grace South
'Attunga'
Kilmaurs'
Old Newdegate Rd
'Brookfield'
Holland Tank
Lake Lockhart
'Burando'
Dunn Rock NR
'Maroleigh'
Chinocup NR
Lake Pingrup
66
Holland Soak
Lake Magenta
68
Long Ck Rd
'Benelong'
Minelup Pool
Lake Cobham
Coleman Soak
Lake Morris
Aerodrome Rd
Ravensthorpe Range
Lake Dorothy
Sullivan Soak
Koornong Road
Pingrup
Greenshield Soak
Lake Magenta
Ravensthorpe
Getenmellup
Cheadanup NR
Bandalup Rockhole
'Dyliabing'
Moornaming
Chinocup
Chinocup Lake
Lake Magenta Nature Reserve
Malkana
Carlapuc Pool
84
Nyabing
Lake Joy
Lake Pingarnup
Desmond
'Maydon'
Mayruup
185
Nooraglen
Coyrecup
Corneecup NR
Lake Carrocup
Kundip (ruins)
Bandalup Pools
'Nurragi'
Coyrecup Lake
Bulvan
'Balfour Downs'
112
Fitzgerald
Hammersley
Tie
Line
Proof Rd
Shackerston
Kybulup Pool
Waindettup Pool
'Woodstock'
42
50
'Fair-View'
Yongergnow Malleefowl Centre
Ongerup
'Gunna Do'
Darkanuttup
Lake Shaster
Cowerup
235
140
Gnowangerup
'Clear Hills'
Attonga
58
Needilup
Jerramungup
Jerramungup Spring
Fitzgerald River National Park
157
Springdale
Jerdacuttup Lakes
Mound Spring
Munglinup Beach
Shaster NR
Culham Inlet
Two Mile Beach
Hopetoun
Jerdacuttup Lakes NR
Pallinup
Kebaringup
29
'Te-Rawhiti'
'Highlands Stud'
160
Willgarrup Pool
Perkins Pool
Whale Bone Beach
Marshes Beach
156
Twelve Mile Beach
'Holme Park'
'Gidgie'
Borden
'Pendalup'
Koorarkup
Peniup Rockhole
Carlawillup Rockhole
Quiss Road
'Glenisla'
Kaipanwymburup
Fitzgerald Inlet
Point Charles Bay
'Ribbleton'
49
Mungerup
Naupenup Spring
Minningellup Pool
Cheadanup
'Yongerup'
49
'Glen Turret'
Corackerup NR
Gairdner
'Blue Range'
'Larnook'
'Cambawarra'
Woolaganup
'Toolibut'
Trigelow Beach
Tooregullup Beach
'Petone'
'Rhonda Vale'
Ramshead
Gordon Inlet
Doubtful Islands Bay
293
294
Sandalwood
Boxwood Hill
Swamp Road
31
House Beach
Stirling Range
'Yarramunda'
Tamgaree'
Cardiminup
Bremer Bay
Gold Holes
Bluff Knoll 1100m
'Glen Ellen'
Borden-Bremer Bay Rd
Bremer Bay
Nat. Park
Two Mile Lake
Kojaneerup
Gnowellen
'Oakdale'
'Minarup'
Dillon Bay
30
Banky Beach
Vale Of Kalgan
Chester Pass Rd
'Deneryl'
175
Wellstead
Beaufort Inlet
Wray Bay
Stream Beach
Groper Bluff
42
'Googlegong'
'Liscombe'
Long Beach
Cheyne Bay
Foster Beach
Cape Knob
Schooner Beach
Kamballup
South Stirling
South Stirling NR
Mettler
Cape Riche
Porongurup
Zarephath Wines
'Jakkawilla'
Great Southern NR
Tinkelelup
Basil Road NR
'Kinnabulla'
Willyun Beach
'Boolarong'
Wine Region
Hassell Beach
For more detail see Hema's South West Western Australia map
Indian Ocean
Takenup
South Coast Hwy
37
Napier
Manypeaks
73
Cheyne Beach
King River
166
Kalgan
167
Waychinicup National Park
Normans Beach
Two Peoples Bay
Bald Island
Oyster Hbr
'The Homestead'
Albany
Gull Rock National Park
Cape Vancouver
Little Grove
Torndirrup NP
Flinders Peninsula
© Hema Maps

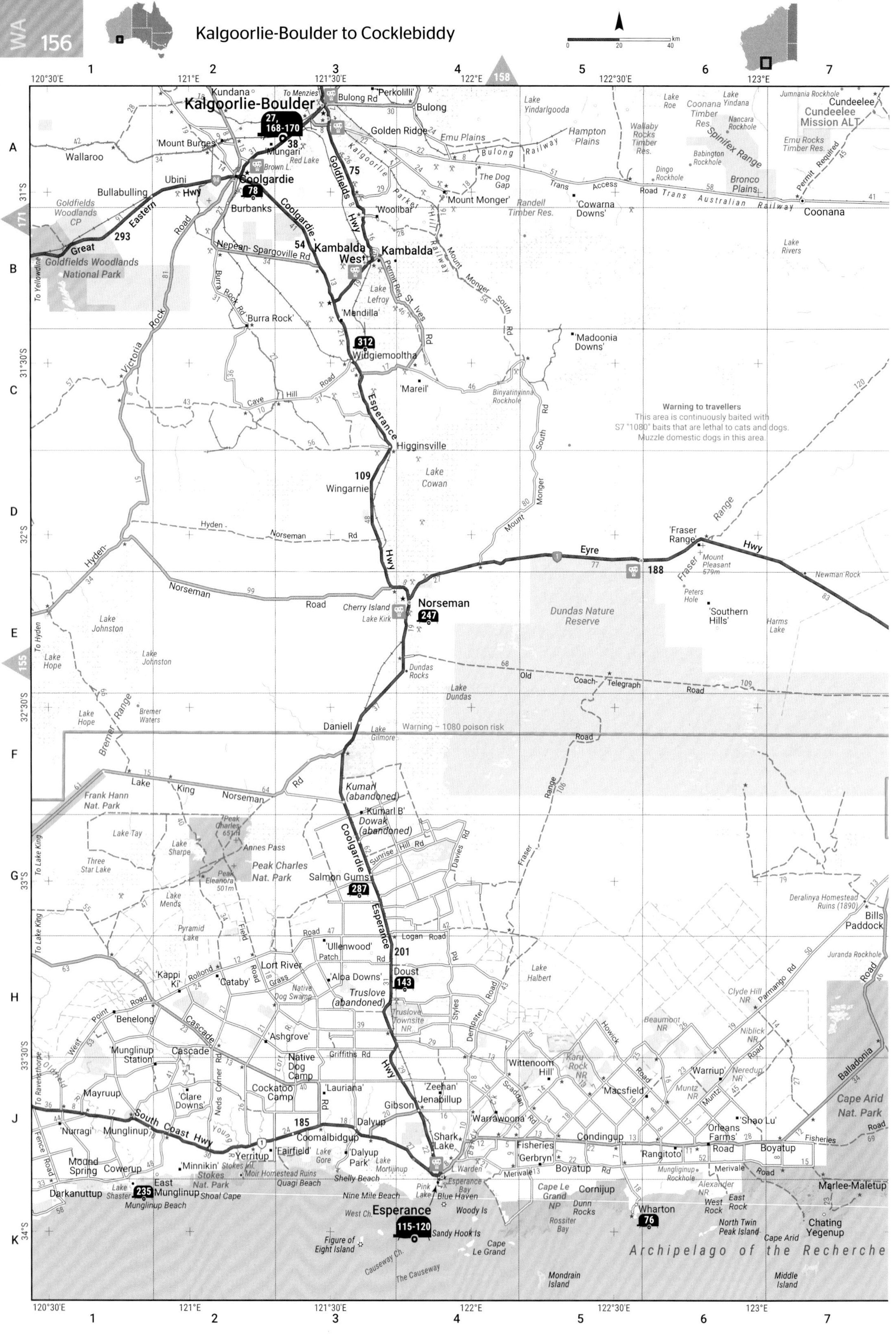
Kalgoorlie-Boulder
Kundana
Bulong
Golden Ridge
Mount Burges
Mungari
Wallaroo
Ubini
Coolgardie
Bullabulling
Burbanks
Great Eastern Hwy
Goldfields Woodlands National Park
Goldfields Woodlands CP
Kambalda West
Kambalda
Lake Lefroy
Mandilla
Burra Rock
Widgiemooltha
Mareil
Higginsville
Lake Cowan
Wingarnie
Norseman
Cherry Island
Lake Kirk
Dundas Nature Reserve
Dundas Rocks
Lake Dundas
Eyre Hwy
Fraser Range
Mount Pleasant 579m
Peters Hole
Southern Hills
Newman Rock
Harms Lake
Madoonia Downs
Randell Timber Res.
Mount Monger
The Dog Gap
Woolibar
Hampton Plains
Cowarna Downs
Trans Australian Railway
Coonana
Cundeelee
Cundeelee Mission ALT
Bronco Plains
Spinifex Range
Lake Yindarlgooda
Lake Rivers
Warning to travellers
This area is continuously baited with S7 "1080" baits that are lethal to cats and dogs. Muzzle domestic dogs in this area.
Old Coach-Telegraph Road
Lake Johnston
Lake Hope
Bremer Range
Daniell
Lake Gilmore
Warning – 1080 poison risk
Frank Hann Nat. Park
Lake King
Norseman Rd
Kumarl (abandoned)
Kumarl B
Dowak (abandoned)
Peak Charles Nat. Park
Lake Tay
Lake Sharpe
Three Star Lake
Annes Pass
Salmon Gums
Coolgardie-Esperance Hwy
Lake Mends
Pyramid Lake
Ullenwood
Lort River
Doust
Kappi Ki
Cataby
Alpa Downs
Truslove (abandoned)
Truslove Townsite NR
Benelong
Cascade
Ashgrove
Munglinup Station
Native Dog Camp
Cockatoo Camp
Clare Downs
Lauriana
Zeehan
Jenabillup
Gibson
Mayruup
Nurragi
Munglinup
South Coast Hwy
Yerritup
Fairfield
Coomalbidgup
Dalyup
Dalyup Park
Shark Lake
Lake Halbert
Beaumont NR
Wittenoom Hill
Warrawoona
Macsfield
Warriup
Muntz NR
Shao Lu
Orleans Farms
Condingup
Fisheries
Gerbryn
Boyatup
Rangitoto
Cape Arid Nat. Park
Bills Paddock
Deralinya Homestead Ruins (1890)
Juranda Rockhole
Clyde Hill NR
Balladonia Road
Mound Spring
Cowerup
Darkanuttup
East Munglinup
Stokes Nat. Park
Shoal Cape
Munglinup Beach
Quagi Beach
Shelly Beach
Nine Mile Beach
Esperance
Blue Haven
Woody Is
Sandy Hook Is
Figure of Eight Island
Cape Le Grand
Cape Le Grand NP
Cornijup
Dunn Rocks
Rossiter Bay
Wharton
Alexander
West Rock
East Rock
Marlee-Maletup
Chating Yegenup
Cape Arid
Archipelago of the Recherche
Mondrain Island
Middle Island

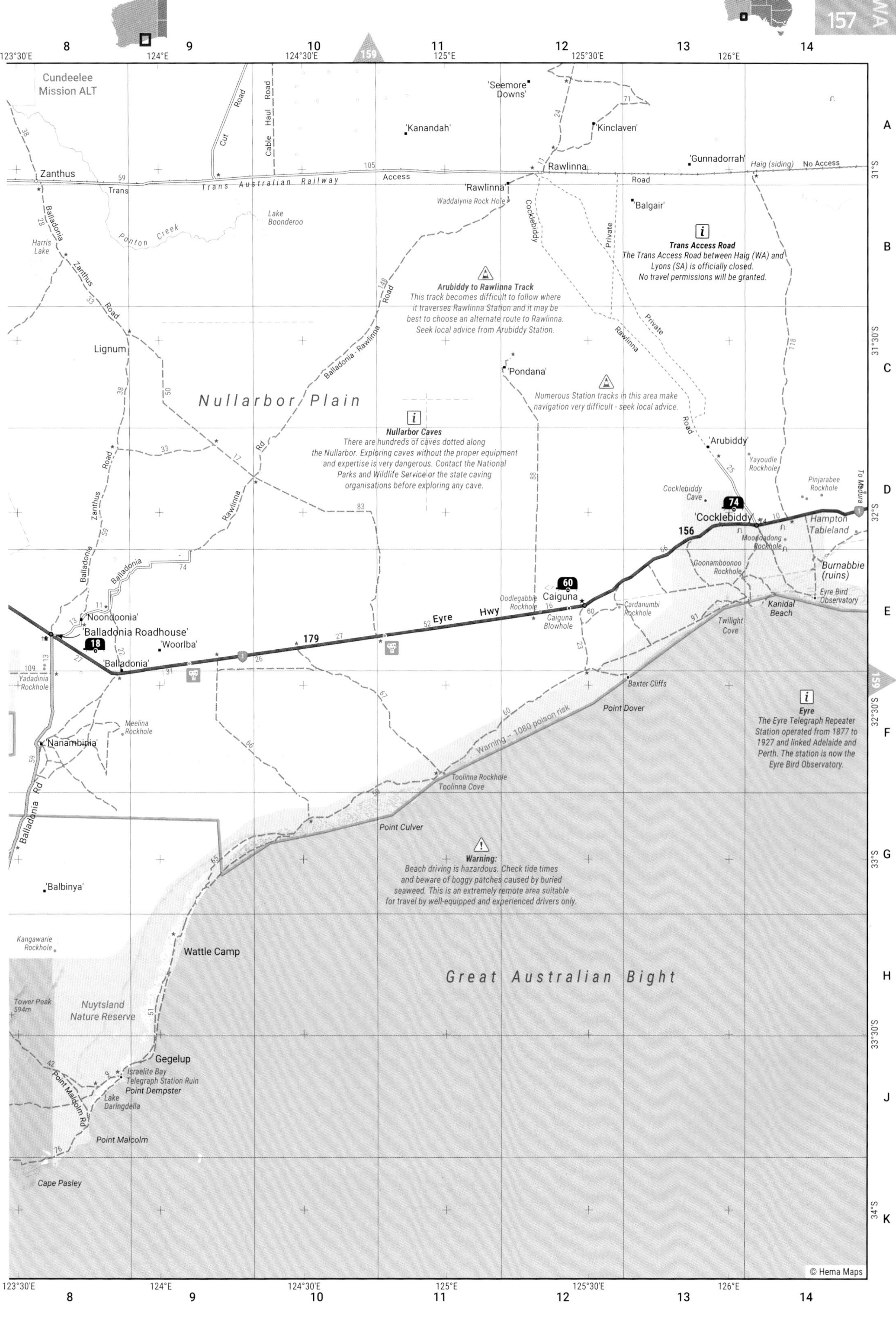

Cundeelee Mission ALT
'Seemore Downs'
'Kanandah'
'Kinclaven'
Zanthus
Trans Australian Railway
Access
Rawlinna
'Rawlinna'
'Gunnadorrah'
Haig (siding)
No Access
Road
Waddalynia Rock Hole
'Balgair'
Lake Boonderoo
Harris Lake
Ponton Creek
Trans Access Road
The Trans Access Road between Haig (WA) and Lyons (SA) is officially closed.
No travel permissions will be granted.
Arubiddy to Rawlinna Track
This track becomes difficult to follow where it traverses Rawlinna Station and it may be best to choose an alternate route to Rawlinna. Seek local advice from Arubiddy Station.
Lignum
'Pondana'
Numerous Station tracks in this area make navigation very difficult - seek local advice.
Nullarbor Plain
Nullarbor Caves
There are hundreds of caves dotted along the Nullarbor. Exploring caves without the proper equipment and expertise is very dangerous. Contact the National Parks and Wildlife Service or the state caving organisations before exploring any cave.
'Arubiddy'
Yayoudle Rockhole
Cocklebiddy Cave
'Cocklebiddy'
Pinjarabee Rockhole
To Madura
Hampton Tableland
Moonadong Rockhole
Goonamboonoo Rockhole
Burnabbie (ruins)
Eyre Bird Observatory
Kanidal Beach
Twilight Cove
Caiguna
Oodlegabbie Rockhole
Caiguna Blowhole
Cardanumbi Rockhole
Eyre Hwy
'Noondoonia'
'Balladonia Roadhouse'
'Woorlba'
'Balladonia'
Yadadinia Rockhole
Baxter Cliffs
Point Dover
Eyre
The Eyre Telegraph Repeater Station operated from 1877 to 1927 and linked Adelaide and Perth. The station is now the Eyre Bird Observatory.
Meelina Rockhole
'Nanambinia'
Warning – 1080 poison risk
Toolinna Rockhole
Toolinna Cove
Point Culver
Warning:
Beach driving is hazardous. Check tide times and beware of boggy patches caused by buried seaweed. This is an extremely remote area suitable for travel by well-equipped and experienced drivers only.
'Balbinya'
Kangawarie Rockhole
Wattle Camp
Great Australian Bight
Tower Peak 594m
Nuytsland Nature Reserve
Gegelup
Israelite Bay Telegraph Station Ruin
Point Dempster
Lake Daringdella
Point Malcolm Rd
Point Malcolm
Cape Pasley
© Hema Maps

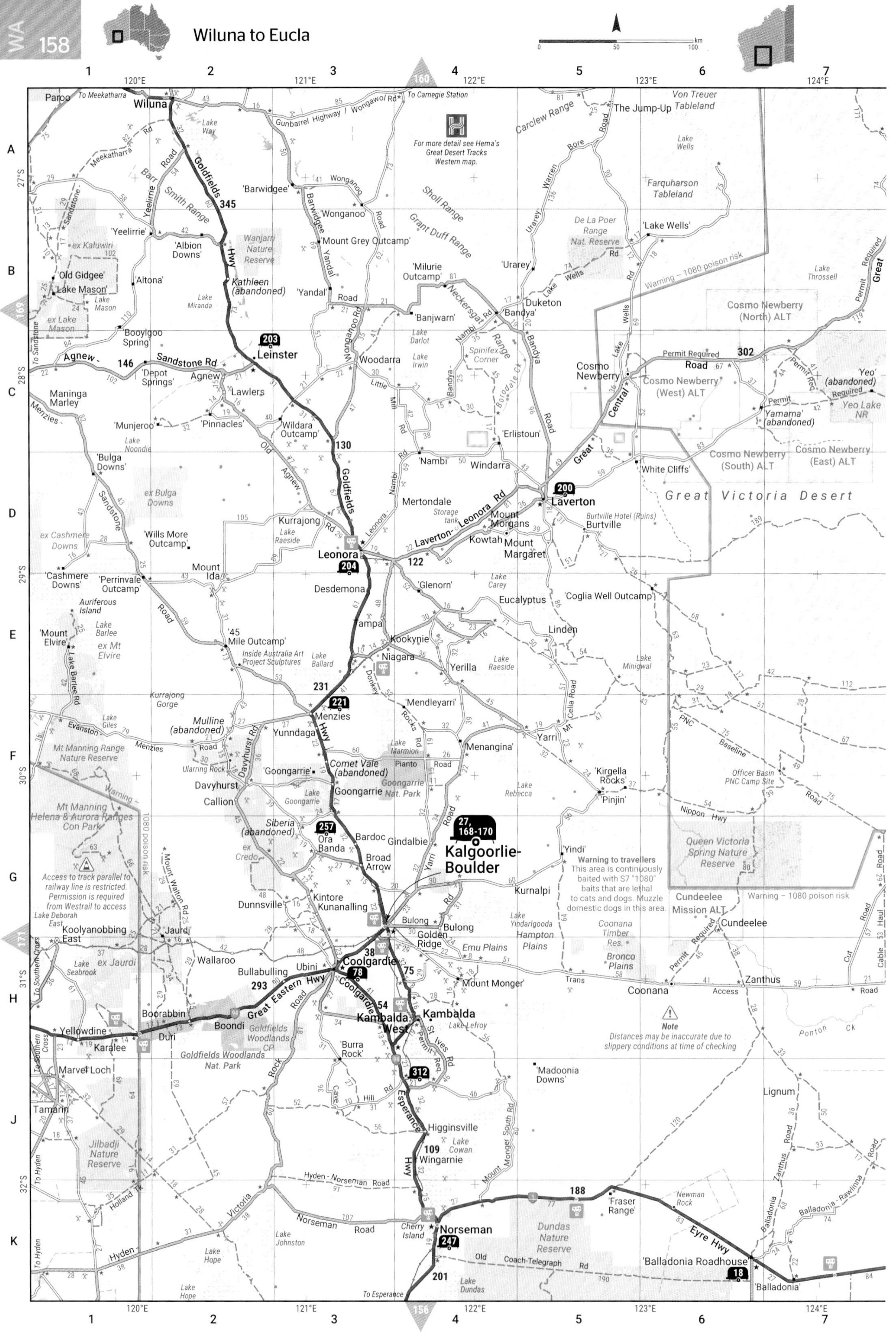
Wiluna to Eucla
For more detail see Hema's Great Desert Tracks Western map.
Warning to travellers
This area is continuously baited with S7 "1080" baits that are lethal to cats and dogs. Muzzle domestic dogs in this area.
Access to track parallel to railway line is restricted. Permission is required from Westrail to access Lake Deborah East
Note
Distances may be inaccurate due to slippery conditions at time of checking
Warning – 1080 poison risk
Wiluna
Paroo
To Meekatharra
To Carnegie Station
Gunbarrel Highway / Wongawol Rd
Goldfields Hwy
Carclew Range
The Jump-Up
Von Treuer Tableland
Lake Wells
Farquharson Tableland
'Lake Wells'
'Barwidgee'
'Wonganoo'
'Mount Grey Outcamp'
Sholl Range
Grant Duff Range
De La Poer Range Nat. Reserve
'Yeelirrie'
'Albion Downs'
Wanjarri Nature Reserve
Smith Range
'Old Gidgee'
'Lake Mason'
'Altona'
Kathleen (abandoned)
'Yandal'
'Milerie Outcamp'
'Urarey'
Duketon
'Bandya'
Lake Throssell
Cosmo Newberry (North) ALT
'Booylgoo Spring'
'Banjwarn'
Leinster
Agnew
Lawlers
'Depot Springs'
Sandstone Rd
Woodarra
Spinifex Corner
Cosmo Newberry
Cosmo Newberry (West) ALT
'Yeo' (abandoned)
Yeo Lake NR
'Yamarna' (abandoned)
Maninga Marley
'Munjeroo'
'Pinnacles'
'Wildara Outcamp'
'Erlistoun'
'Nambi'
Windarra
'White Cliffs'
Cosmo Newberry (South) ALT
Cosmo Newberry (East) ALT
'Bulga Downs'
ex Bulga Downs
Mertondale
Laverton
Great Victoria Desert
Kurrajong
Lake Raeside
'Wills More Outcamp'
Mount Morgans
Kowtah
Mount Margaret
Burtville Hotel (Ruins)
Burtville
Leonora
Laverton-Leonora Rd
'Cashmere Downs'
'Perrinvale Outcamp'
Mount Ida
Desdemona
'Glenorn'
Lake Carey
Eucalyptus
'Coglia Well Outcamp'
Auriferous Island
'Mount Elvire'
Lake Barlee
'45 Mile Outcamp'
Inside Australia Art Project Sculptures
Tampa
Kookynie
Niagara
Yerilla
Linden
Lake Minigwal
Kurrajong Gorge
Menzies
'Mendleyarri'
Mulline (abandoned)
Yunndaga
Menangina
Yarri
Mt Manning Range Nature Reserve
Comet Vale (abandoned)
Goongarrie
Goongarrie Nat. Park
'Goongarrie'
Davyhurst
Callion
Ularring Rock
'Kirgella Rocks'
'Pinjin'
Officer Basin PNC Camp Site
Nippon Hwy
PNC Baseline Road
Mt Manning Helena & Aurora Ranges Con Park
Siberia (abandoned)
Ora Banda
Bardoc
Gindalbie
Broad Arrow
Kalgoorlie-Boulder
'Yindi'
Queen Victoria Spring Nature Reserve
Kurnalpi
Cundeelee Mission ALT
Cundeelee
Dunnsville
Kintore
Kunanalling
Bulong
Golden Ridge
Emu Plains
Hampton Plains
Coonana Timber Res.
Bronco Plains
Koolyanobbing East
'Jaurdi'
Wallaroo
Bullabulling
Ubini
Coolgardie
Great Eastern Hwy
'Mount Monger'
Coonana
Zanthus
Trans Access
Boorabbin
Boondi
Goldfields Woodlands CP
Goldfields Woodlands Nat. Park
Yellowdine
Karalee
Duri
Kambalda West
Kambalda
Lake Lefroy
'Burra Rock'
Marvel Loch
'Madoonia Downs'
Ponton Ck
Lignum
Tamarin
Higginsville
Lake Cowan
Wingarnie
Jilbadji Nature Reserve
Hyden-Norseman Road
'Fraser Range'
Newman Rock
Eyre Hwy
Norseman Road
Cherry Island
Norseman
Dundas Nature Reserve
Old Coach-Telegraph Rd
'Balladonia Roadhouse'
'Balladonia'
Lake Johnston
Lake Hope
Lake Dundas
Hyden
To Hyden
To Esperance
To Southern Cross
Esperance Hwy
Mount Monger South Rd
Balladonia-Rawlinna Road
Zanthus Road
Cable Haul Road

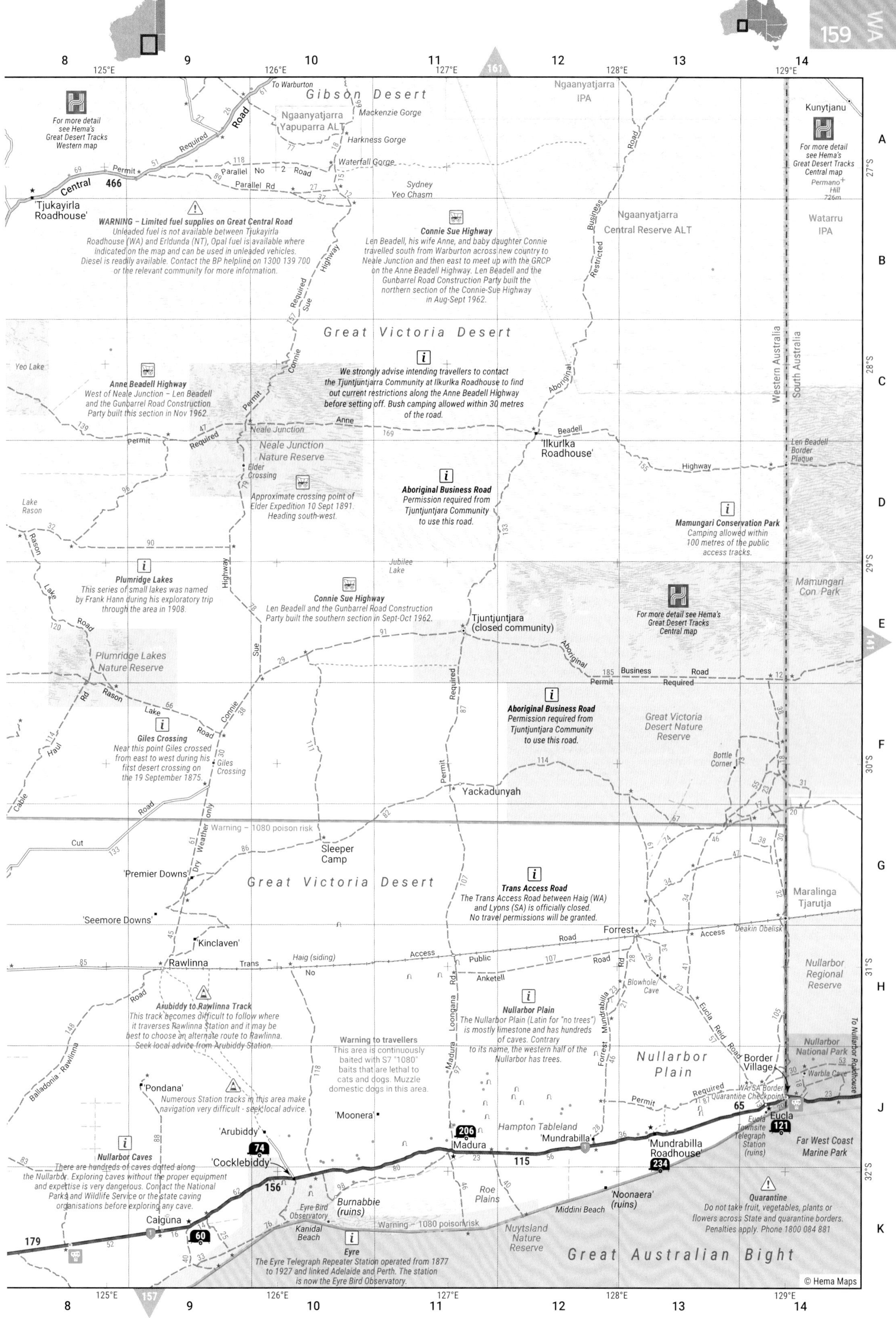
8
9
10
11
12
13
14
125°E
126°E
127°E
128°E
129°E
161
A
B
C
D
E
F
G
H
J
K
27°S
28°S
29°S
30°S
31°S
32°S
To Warburton
Gibson Desert
Ngaanyatjarra IPA
Kunytjanu
For more detail see Hema's Great Desert Tracks Western map
Ngaanyatjarra Yapuparra ALT
Mackenzie Gorge
Harkness Gorge
Waterfall Gorge
For more detail see Hema's Great Desert Tracks Central map
Permano Hill 726m
Required
Road
Permit
Parallel No 2 Road
Parallel Rd
Central
466
Sydney Yeo Chasm
'Tjukayirla Roadhouse'
WARNING – Limited fuel supplies on Great Central Road
Unleaded fuel is not available between Tjukayirla Roadhouse (WA) and Erldunda (NT), Opal fuel is available where indicated on the map and can be used in unleaded vehicles. Diesel is readily available. Contact the BP helpline on 1300 139 700 or the relevant community for more information.
Connie Sue Highway
Len Beadell, his wife Anne, and baby daughter Connie travelled south from Warburton across new country to Neale Junction and then east to meet up with the GRCP on the Anne Beadell Highway. Len Beadell and the Gunbarrel Road Construction Party built the northern section of the Connie-Sue Highway in Aug-Sept 1962.
Ngaanyatjarra Central Reserve ALT
Watarru IPA
Business
Restricted
Great Victoria Desert
Western Australia
South Australia
Yeo Lake
Anne Beadell Highway
West of Neale Junction – Len Beadell and the Gunbarrel Road Construction Party built this section in Nov 1962.
We strongly advise intending travellers to contact the Tjuntjuntjara Community at Ilkurlka Roadhouse to find out current restrictions along the Anne Beadell Highway before setting off. Bush camping allowed within 30 metres of the road.
Aboriginal
Anne
Beadell
Highway
Neale Junction
Neale Junction Nature Reserve
Elder Crossing
'Ilkurlka Roadhouse'
Len Beadell Border Plaque
Approximate crossing point of Elder Expedition 10 Sept 1891. Heading south-west.
Aboriginal Business Road
Permission required from Tjuntjuntjara Community to use this road.
Lake Rason
Mamungari Conservation Park
Camping allowed within 100 metres of the public access tracks.
Jubilee Lake
Plumridge Lakes
This series of small lakes was named by Frank Hann during his exploratory trip through the area in 1908.
Connie Sue Highway
Len Beadell and the Gunbarrel Road Construction Party built the southern section in Sept-Oct 1962.
Mamungari Con Park
For more detail see Hema's Great Desert Tracks Central map
Tjuntjuntjara (closed community)
141
Plumridge Lakes Nature Reserve
Rason Lake Road
Aboriginal Business Road Permit Required
Aboriginal Business Road
Permission required from Tjuntjuntjara Community to use this road.
Great Victoria Desert Nature Reserve
Giles Crossing
Near this point Giles crossed from east to west during his first desert crossing on the 19 September 1875.
Giles Crossing
Haul
Bottle Corner
Yackadunyah
Cable
Dry Weather only
Cut
Warning – 1080 poison risk
Sleeper Camp
'Premier Downs'
Great Victoria Desert
Trans Access Road
The Trans Access Road between Haig (WA) and Lyons (SA) is officially closed. No travel permissions will be granted.
Maralinga Tjarutja
'Seemore Downs'
Forrest
Deakin Obelisk
'Kinclaven'
Rawlinna
Trans
Haig (siding)
Access
No
Public
Anketell
Road
Nullarbor Regional Reserve
Blowhole/Cave
Arubiddy to Rawlinna Track
This track becomes difficult to follow where it traverses Rawlinna Station and it may be best to choose an alternate route to Rawlinna. Seek local advice from Arubiddy Station.
Nullarbor Plain
The Nullarbor Plain (Latin for "no trees") is mostly limestone and has hundreds of caves. Contrary to its name, the western half of the Nullarbor has trees.
Balladonia - Rawlinna
Warning to travellers
This area is continuously baited with S7 "1080" baits that are lethal to cats and dogs. Muzzle domestic dogs in this area.
Madura Loongana Rd
Forrest Mundrabilla Rd
Nullarbor Plain
Eucla Reid Road
Border Village
To Nullarbor Roadhouse
Nullarbor National Park
Warbla Cave
'Pondana'
Numerous Station tracks in this area make navigation very difficult - seek local advice.
'Moonera'
Hampton Tableland
WA/SA Border
Quarantine Checkpoint
Eucla
Eucla Townsite Telegraph Station (ruins)
'Arubiddy'
74
206
Madura
'Mundrabilla'
'Mundrabilla Roadhouse'
121
Far West Coast Marine Park
Nullarbor Caves
There are hundreds of caves dotted along the Nullarbor. Exploring caves without the proper equipment and expertise is very dangerous. Contact the National Parks and Wildlife Service or the state caving organisations before exploring any cave.
'Cocklebiddy'
115
234
156
Roe Plains
'Noonaera' (ruins)
Quarantine
Do not take fruit, vegetables, plants or flowers across State and Quarantine borders. Penalties apply. Phone 1800 084 881
Burnabbie (ruins)
Eyre Bird Observatory
Middini Beach
Caiguna
60
179
Kanidal Beach
Warning – 1080 poison risk
Nuytsland Nature Reserve
Great Australian Bight
Eyre
The Eyre Telegraph Repeater Station operated from 1877 to 1927 and linked Adelaide and Perth. The station is now the Eyre Bird Observatory.
© Hema Maps
157

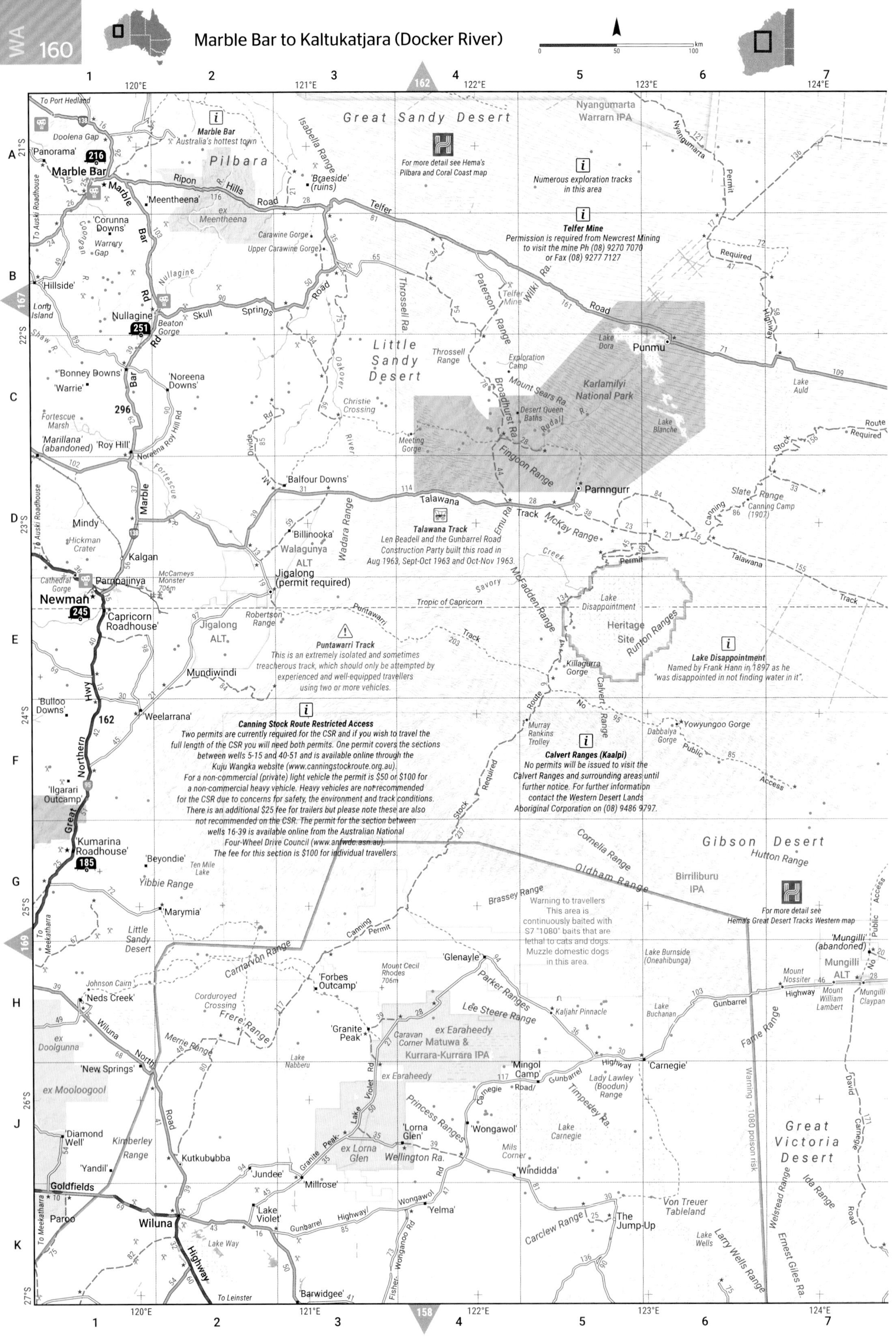
0 50 100 km
1 2 3 4 5 6 7
120°E 121°E 122°E 123°E 124°E
A B C D E F G H J K
21°S 22°S 23°S 24°S 25°S 26°S 27°S
162
167
169
158
To Port Hedland
Doolena Gap
'Panorama'
216
Marble Bar
Marble Bar
Australia's hottest town
Pilbara
Ripon Hills Road
'Meentheena'
ex Meentheena
To Auski Roadhouse
'Corunna Downs'
Warrery Gap
Coongan R.
Carawine Gorge
Upper Carawine Gorge
'Braeside' (ruins)
Isabella Range
Great Sandy Desert
For more detail see Hema's Pilbara and Coral Coast map
Nyangumarta Warrarn IPA
Nyangumarta
Numerous exploration tracks in this area
Telfer Mine
Permission is required from Newcrest Mining to visit the mine Ph (08) 9270 7070 or Fax (08) 9277 7127
Telfer Road
Permit
Required
'Hillside'
Long Island
Nullagine
Nullagine
251
Beaton Gorge
Skull Springs Road
Shaw R.
Throssell Ra.
Paterson Range
Wilki Ra.
Telfer Mine
Little Sandy Desert
Throssell Range
Exploration Camp
Lake Dora
Punmu
Karlamilyi National Park
Mount Sears Ra.
Desert Queen Baths
Rudall R.
Lake Blanche
Highway
Lake Auld
'Bonney Downs'
'Warrie'
'Noreena Downs'
296
Fortescue Marsh
'Marillana' (abandoned)
'Roy Hill'
Noreena Roy Hill Rd
Oakover
Christie Crossing
River
Meeting Gorge
Broadhurst Ra.
Fingoon Range
Route Required
Stock
Mt Divide Rd
'Balfour Downs'
Talawana Track
Parnngurr
Slate Range
Canning Camp (1907)
Canning
Fortescue
Marble Bar Rd
Mindy
Hickman Crater
Kalgan
'Billinooka'
Walagunya ALT
Wadara Range
Talawana Track
Len Beadell and the Gunbarrel Road Construction Party built this road in Aug 1963, Sept-Oct 1963 and Oct-Nov 1963.
Emu Ra.
McKay Range
Creek
Permit
Cathedral Gorge
Parnpajinya
McCameys Monster 706m
Jigalong (permit required)
Savory
McFadden Range
Lake Disappointment
Heritage Site
Runton Ranges
Track
Newman
245
Tropic of Capricorn
'Capricorn Roadhouse'
Jigalong ALT
Robertson Range
Puntawarri
Track
Puntawarri Track
This is an extremely isolated and sometimes treacherous track, which should only be attempted by experienced and well-equipped travellers using two or more vehicles.
Killagurra Gorge
Lake Disappointment
Named by Frank Hann in 1897 as he "was disappointed in not finding water in it".
Mundiwindi
'Bulloo Downs'
162
'Weelarrana'
Northern Hwy
Canning Stock Route Restricted Access
Two permits are currently required for the CSR and if you wish to travel the full length of the CSR you will need both permits. One permit covers the sections between wells 5-15 and 40-51 and is available online through the Kuju Wangka website (www.canningstockroute.org.au). For a non-commercial (private) light vehicle the permit is $50 or $100 for a non-commercial heavy vehicle. Heavy vehicles are not recommended for the CSR due to concerns for safety, the environment and track conditions. There is an additional $25 fee for trailers but please note these are also not recommended on the CSR. The permit for the section between wells 16-39 is available online from the Australian National Four-Wheel Drive Council (www.anfwdc.asn.au). The fee for this section is $100 for individual travellers.
No Route
Calvert Range
Murray Rankins Trolley
Calvert Ranges (Kaalpi)
No permits will be issued to visit the Calvert Ranges and surrounding areas until further notice. For further information contact the Western Desert Lands Aboriginal Corporation on (08) 9486 9797.
Yowyungoo Gorge
Dabbalya Gorge
Public Access
Stock Required
'Ilgarari Outcamp'
Great
'Kumarina Roadhouse'
185
'Beyondie'
Ten Mile Lake
Yibbie Range
Cornelia Range
Oldham Range
Gibson Desert
Hutton Range
Birriliburu IPA
Brassey Range
Warning to travellers This area is continuously baited with S7 "1080" baits that are lethal to cats and dogs. Muzzle domestic dogs in this area.
For more detail see Hema's Great Desert Tracks Western map
'Marymia'
To Meekatharra
Little Sandy Desert
Canning Permit
Carnarvon Range
'Glenayle'
Lake Burnside (Oneahibunga)
'Mungilli' (abandoned)
Mungilli ALT
Mount Nossiter
Johnson Cairn
'Neds Creek'
Corduroyed Crossing
Frere Range
'Forbes Outcamp'
Mount Cecil Rhodes 706m
Parker Ranges
Lee Steere Range
Kaljahr Pinnacle
Lake Buchanan
Gunbarrel Highway
Mount William Lambert
Mungilli Claypan
Fame Range
ex Doolgunna
Wiluna North
Merrie Range
'Granite Peak'
Caravan Corner
ex Earaheedy
Matuwa & Kurrara-Kurrara IPA
'Mingol Camp'
'Carnegie'
Lake Nabberu
ex Earaheedy
Gunbarrel
Highway
Lady Lawley (Boodun) Range
Warning – 1080 poison risk
David
'New Springs'
ex Mooloogool
Lake Violet Rd
Carnegie Road
Timpedey Ra.
Princess Ranges
'Diamond Well'
Kimberley Range
'Yandil'
Kutkububba
'Lorna Glen'
ex Lorna Glen
Wellington Ra.
'Wongawol'
Lake Carnegie
Mils Corner
'Windidda'
Great Victoria Desert
Carnegie
Goldfields
'Jundee'
Granite Peak
'Millrose'
Wongawol Rd
'Yelma'
Von Treuer Tableland
Welstead Range
Ida Range
Road
Paroo
Wiluna
'Lake Violet'
Gunbarrel Highway
Carclew Range
The Jump-Up
Lake Wells
Larry Wells Range
Ernest Giles Ra.
To Meekatharra
Lake Way
Highway
Fisher-Wonganoo Rd
'Barwidgee'
To Leinster

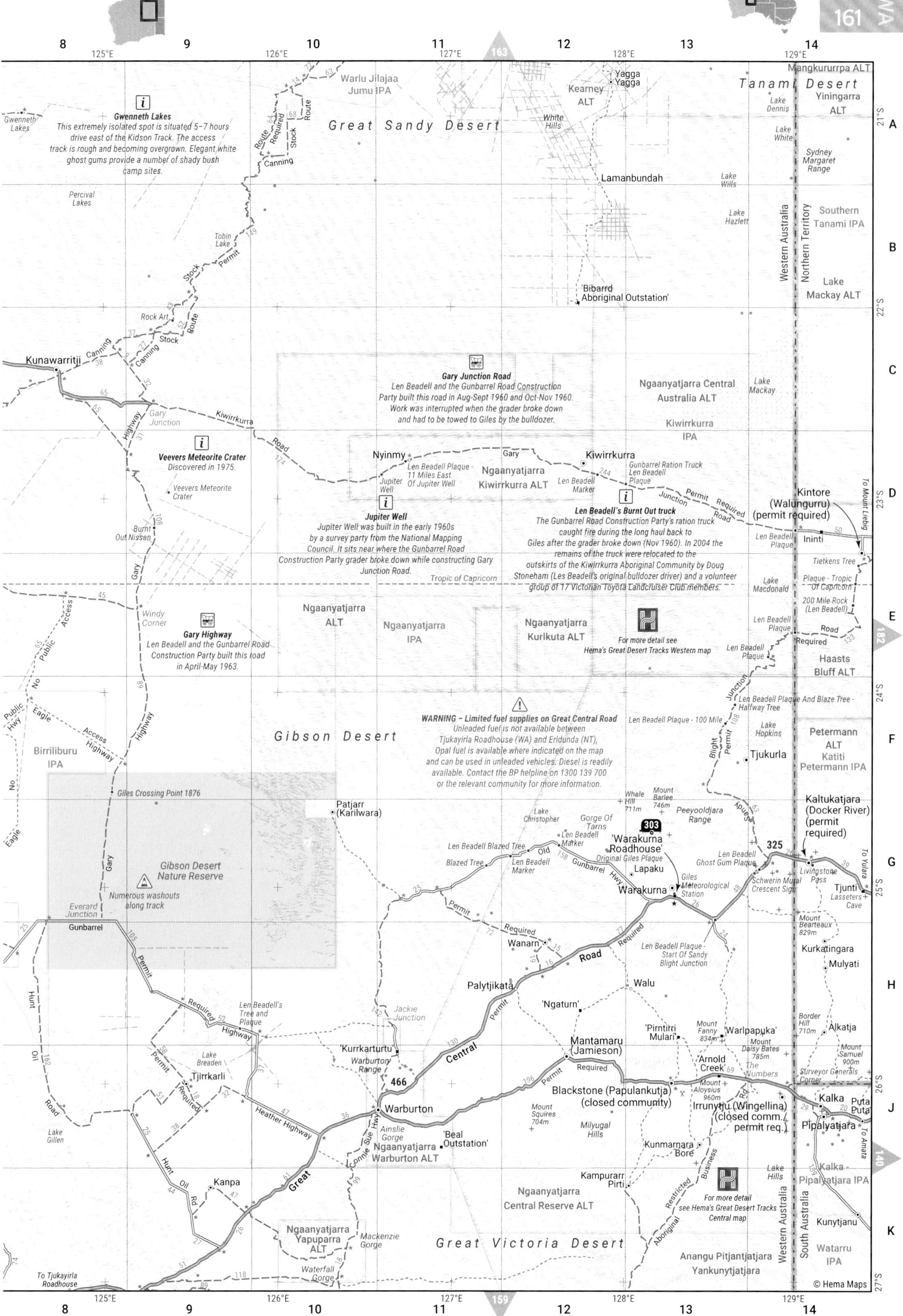

Gwenneth Lakes
This extremely isolated spot is situated 5–7 hours drive east of the Kidson Track. The access track is rough and becoming overgrown. Elegant white ghost gums provide a number of shady bush camp sites.
Great Sandy Desert
Warlu Jilajaa Jumu IPA
Kearney ALT
Yagga Yagga
Tanami Desert
Mangkururrpa ALT
Yiningarra ALT
Lamanbundah
Southern Tanami IPA
Lake Mackay ALT
'Bibarrd Aboriginal Outstation'
Western Australia
Northern Territory
Kunawarritji
Gary Junction
Gary Junction Road
Len Beadell and the Gunbarrel Road Construction Party built this road in Aug-Sept 1960 and Oct-Nov 1960. Work was interrupted when the grader broke down and had to be towed to Giles by the bulldozer.
Ngaanyatjarra Central Australia ALT
Kiwirrkurra IPA
Veevers Meteorite Crater
Discovered in 1975.
Nyinmy
Kiwirrkurra
Ngaanyatjarra Kiwirrkurra ALT
Jupiter Well
Jupiter Well was built in the early 1960s by a survey party from the National Mapping Council. It sits near where the Gunbarrel Road Construction Party grader broke down while constructing Gary Junction Road.
Len Beadell's Burnt Out truck
The Gunbarrel Road Construction Party's ration truck caught fire during the long haul back to Giles after the grader broke down (Nov 1960). In 2004 the remains of the truck were relocated to the outskirts of the Kiwirrkurra Aboriginal Community by Doug Stoneham (Les Beadell's original bulldozer driver) and a volunteer group of 17 Victorian Toyota Landcruiser Club members.
Kintore (Walungurru) (permit required)
Tropic of Capricorn
Gary Highway
Len Beadell and the Gunbarrel Road Construction Party built this road in April-May 1963.
Ngaanyatjarra ALT
Ngaanyatjarra IPA
Ngaanyatjarra Kurlkuta ALT
For more detail see Hema's Great Desert Tracks Western map
Haasts Bluff ALT
WARNING – Limited fuel supplies on Great Central Road
Unleaded fuel is not available between Tjukayirla Roadhouse (WA) and Erldunda (NT), Opal fuel is available where indicated on the map and can be used in unleaded vehicles. Diesel is readily available. Contact the BP helpline on 1300 139 700 or the relevant community for more information.
Gibson Desert
Birriliburu IPA
Petermann ALT
Katiti Petermann IPA
Tjukurla
Patjarr (Karilwara)
Gibson Desert Nature Reserve
Numerous washouts along track
Kaltukatjara (Docker River) (permit required)
'Warakurna Roadhouse'
Warakurna
Lapaku
Wanarn
Palytjikata
Walu
Mantamaru (Jamieson)
Blackstone (Papulankutja) (closed community)
Irrunytju (Wingellina) (closed comm. permit req.)
Warburton
Ngaanyatjarra Warburton ALT
'Beal Outstation'
Tjirrkarli
Kanpa
Kalka
Pipalyatjara
Kalka - Pipalyatjara IPA
Kunytjanu
Ngaanyatjarra Central Reserve ALT
For more detail see Hema's Great Desert Tracks Central map
Ngaanyatjarra Yapuparra ALT
Great Victoria Desert
Anangu Pitjantjatjara Yankunytjatjara
South Australia
Watarru IPA
To Tjukayirla Roadhouse
© Hema Maps

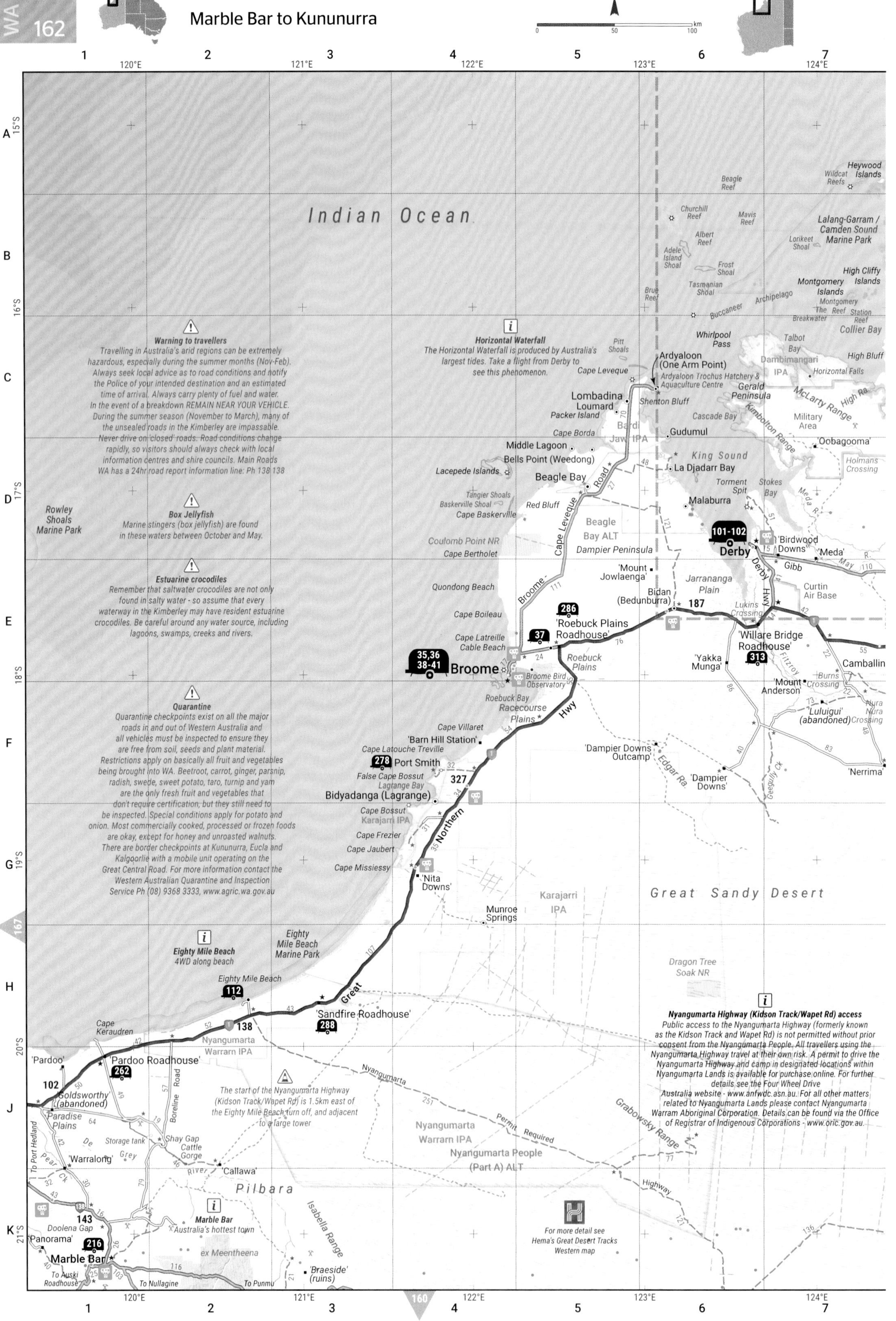
Indian Ocean
Warning to travellers
Travelling in Australia's arid regions can be extremely hazardous, especially during the summer months (Nov-Feb). Always seek local advice as to road conditions and notify the Police of your intended destination and an estimated time of arrival. Always carry plenty of fuel and water. In the event of a breakdown REMAIN NEAR YOUR VEHICLE. During the summer season (November to March), many of the unsealed roads in the Kimberley are impassable. Never drive on 'closed' roads. Road conditions change rapidly, so visitors should always check with local information centres and shire councils. Main Roads WA has a 24hr road report information line: Ph 138 138
Box Jellyfish
Marine stingers (box jellyfish) are found in these waters between October and May.
Estuarine crocodiles
Remember that saltwater crocodiles are not only found in salty water - so assume that every waterway in the Kimberley may have resident estuarine crocodiles. Be careful around any water source, including lagoons, swamps, creeks and rivers.
Quarantine
Quarantine checkpoints exist on all the major roads in and out of Western Australia and all vehicles must be inspected to ensure they are free from soil, seeds and plant material. Restrictions apply on basically all fruit and vegetables being brought into WA. Beetroot, carrot, ginger, parsnip, radish, swede, sweet potato, taro, turnip and yam are the only fresh fruit and vegetables that don't require certification, but they still need to be inspected. Special conditions apply for potato and onion. Most commercially cooked, processed or frozen foods are okay, except for honey and uncooked walnuts. There are border checkpoints at Kununurra, Eucla and Kalgoorlie with a mobile unit operating on the Great Central Road. For more information contact the Western Australian Quarantine and Inspection Service Ph (08) 9368 3333, www.agric.wa.gov.au
Horizontal Waterfall
The Horizontal Waterfall is produced by Australia's largest tides. Take a flight from Derby to see this phenomenon.
Eighty Mile Beach
4WD along beach
The start of the Nyangumarta Highway (Kidson Track/Wapet Rd) is 1.5km east of the Eighty Mile Beach turn off, and adjacent to a large tower
Marble Bar
Australia's hottest town
Nyangumarta Highway (Kidson Track/Wapet Rd) access
Public access to the Nyangumarta Highway (formerly known as the Kidson Track and Wapet Rd) is not permitted without prior consent from the Nyangumarta People. All travellers using the Nyangumarta Highway travel at their own risk. A permit to drive the Nyangumarta Highway and camp in designated locations within Nyangumarta Lands is available for purchase online. For further details see the Four Wheel Drive Australia website - www.anfwdc.asn.au. For all other matters related to Nyangumarta Lands please contact Nyangumarta Warram Aboriginal Corporation. Details can be found via the Office of Registrar of Indigenous Corporations - www.oric.gov.au.
For more detail see Hema's Great Desert Tracks Western map
Broome
Derby
Port Smith
Bidyadanga (Lagrange)
Marble Bar
'Pardoo Roadhouse'
'Sandfire Roadhouse'
'Roebuck Plains Roadhouse'
'Willare Bridge Roadhouse'
Camballin
Great Sandy Desert
Pilbara
Eighty Mile Beach Marine Park
Rowley Shoals Marine Park
Lalang-Garram / Camden Sound Marine Park
Buccaneer Archipelago
King Sound
Dampier Peninsula
Great Northern Hwy
Cape Leveque Road
Broome - Cape Leveque Road
Derby Hwy
Gibb
Nyangumarta Highway
Permit Required
To Port Hedland
To Nullagine
To Punmu
To Auski Roadhouse

167
160

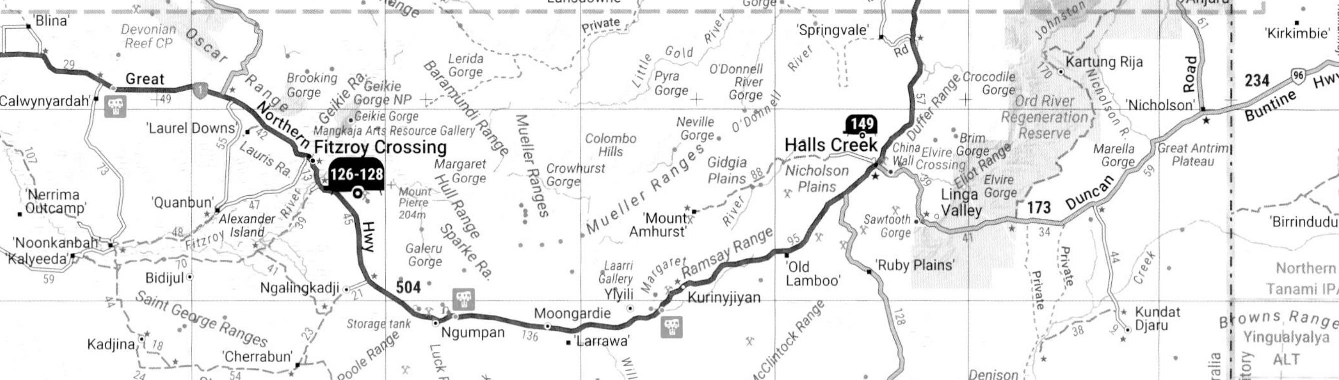

Kalumburu
Travellers wishing to visit Kalumburu are asked to leave their caravans at Drysdale River Station.

Munja Track
Permission is required from Mount Elizabeth station to use the Munja Track

For more detail see Hema's The Kimberley map

Fitzroy River
The magnificent Fitzroy River flows through rugged hills and plains for over 750km. When in flood it can reach up to 15km wide and the flood waters have carved through the limestone of the Devonian reef to form Geikie Gorge.

Wolfe Creek Meteorite Crater
At 850m wide and 50m deep, this interplanetary phenomenon is an amazing sight in its flat surroundings

Canning Stock Route Restricted Access
Two permits are currently required for the CSR and if you wish to travel the full length of the CSR you will need both permits. One permit covers the sections between wells 5-15 and 40-51 and is available online through the Kuju Wangka website (www.canningstockroute.org.au). For a non-commercial (private) light vehicle the permit is $50 or $100 for a non-commercial heavy vehicle. Heavy vehicles are not recommended for the CSR due to concerns for safety, the environment and track conditions. There is an additional $25 fee for trailers but please note these are also not recommended on the CSR. The permit for the section between wells 16-39 is available online from the Australian National Four-Wheel Drive Council (www.anfwdc.asn.au). The fee for this section is $100 for individual travellers.

Gwenneth Lakes
This extremely isolated spot is situated 5-7 hours drive east of the Kidson Track. The access track is rough and becoming overgrown. Elegant white ghost gums provide a number of shady bush camp sites.

See Page 164-165

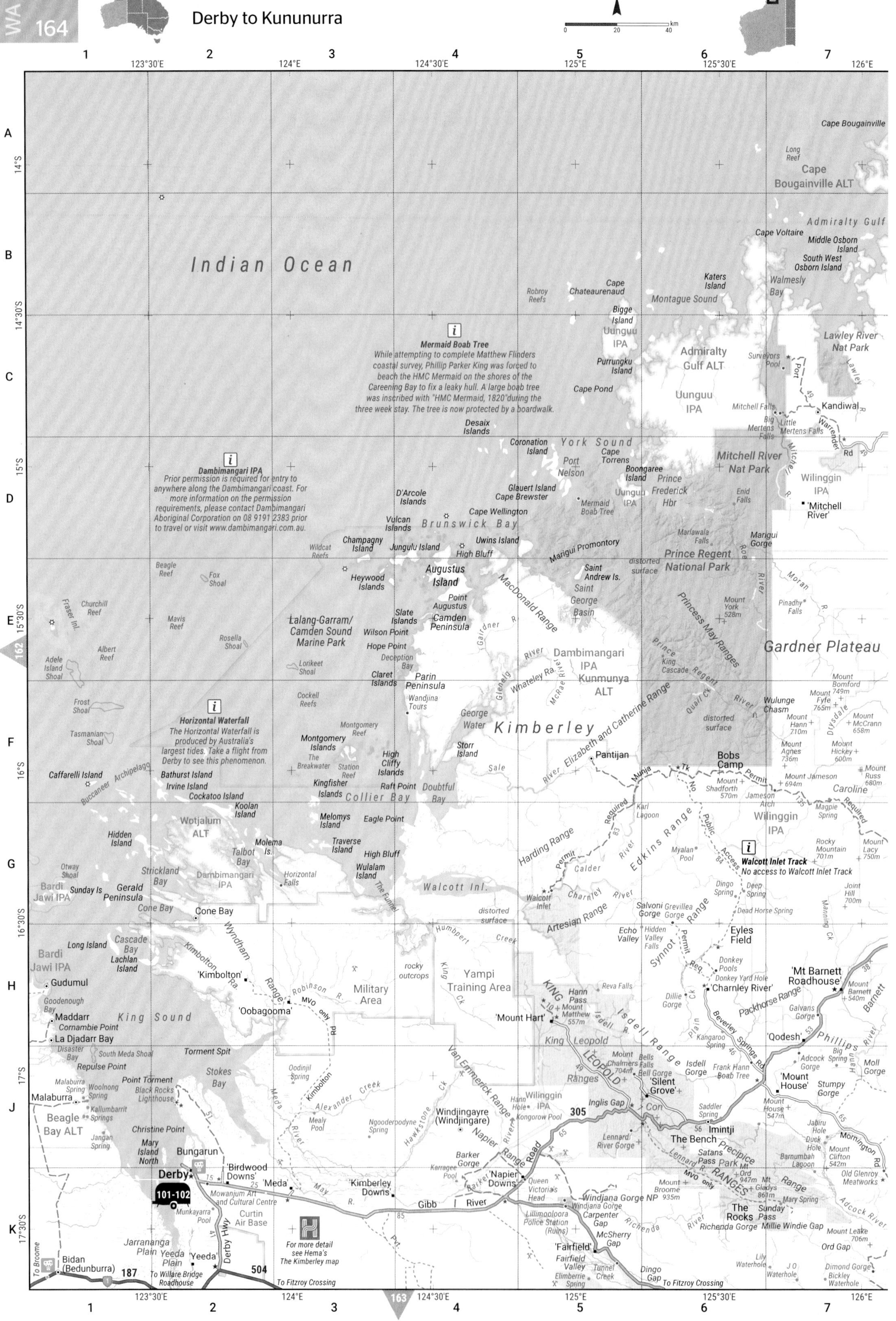

Indian Ocean
Mermaid Boab Tree
While attempting to complete Matthew Flinders coastal survey, Phillip Parker King was forced to beach the HMC Mermaid on the shores of the Careening Bay to fix a leaky hull. A large boab tree was inscribed with "HMC Mermaid, 1820" during the three week stay. The tree is now protected by a boardwalk.
Dambimangari IPA
Prior permission is required for entry to anywhere along the Dambimangari coast. For more information on the permission requirements, please contact Dambimangari Aboriginal Corporation on 08 9191 2383 prior to travel or visit www.dambimangari.com.au.
Horizontal Waterfall
The Horizontal Waterfall is produced by Australia's largest tides. Take a flight from Derby to see this phenomenon.
Walcott Inlet Track
No access to Walcott Inlet Track
Cape Bougainville
Cape Bougainville ALT
Admiralty Gulf
Cape Voltaire
Middle Osborn Island
South West Osborn Island
Walmesly Bay
Katers Island
Montague Sound
Cape Chateaurenaud
Robroy Reefs
Bigge Island
Uunguu IPA
Admiralty Gulf ALT
Purrungku Island
Cape Pond
Lawley River Nat Park
Surveyors Pool
Port
Kandiwal
Mitchell Falls
Little Mertens Falls
Big Mertens Falls
Warrender Rd
Desaix Islands
Coronation Island
York Sound
Port Nelson
Cape Torrens
Boongaree Island
Prince Frederick Hbr
Mitchell River Nat Park
Wilinggin IPA
'Mitchell River'
Enid Falls
Glauert Island
Cape Brewster
Mermaid Boab Tree
D'Arcole Islands
Vulcan Islands
Brunswick Bay
Cape Wellington
Uwins Island
High Bluff
Champagny Island
Jungulu Island
Wildcat Reefs
Marlawala Falls
Marigui Gorge
Marigui Promontory
Prince Regent National Park
distorted surface
Augustus Island
Heywood Islands
Beagle Reef
Fox Shoal
Saint Andrew Is.
Saint George Basin
MacDonald Range
Princess May Ranges
Point Augustus
Camden Peninsula
Slate Islands
Lalang-Garram/ Camden Sound Marine Park
Wilson Point
Hope Point
Deception Bay
Churchill Reef
Fraser Inl.
Mavis Reef
Rosella Shoal
Albert Reef
Adele Island Shoal
Lorikeet Shoal
Mount York 528m
Gardner Plateau
Pinadhy Falls
Moran R.
Dambimangari IPA
Kunmunya ALT
Gardner R.
Glenelg River
Whateley Ra.
McRae River
Prince Regent River
King Cascade
Claret Islands
Parin Peninsula
Wandjina Tours
George Water
Kimberley
Frost Shoal
Cockell Reefs
Elizabeth and Catherine Range
Quail Ck
distorted surface
Wulunge Chasm
Mount Bomford 749m
Mount Fyfe 765m
Mount Hann 710m
Mount McCrann 658m
Drysdale
Tasmanian Shoal
Montgomery Reef
Montgomery Islands
The Breakwater
Station Reef
High Cliffy Islands
Storr Island
Sale River
Pantijan
Bobs Camp
Mount Agnes 736m
Mount Hickey 600m
Caffarelli Island
Buccaneer Archipelago
Bathurst Island
Irvine Island
Cockatoo Island
Kingfisher Islands
Raft Point
Doubtful Bay
Collier Bay
Munja
Tk
Permit
Mount Shadforth 570m
Jameson Arch
Mount Jameson 694m
Mount Russ 680m
Caroline
Koolan Island
Wotjalum ALT
Melomys Island
Eagle Point
Karl Lagoon
Required
No Public Access
Wilinggin IPA
Magpie Spring
Hidden Island
Molema Is.
Talbot Bay
Traverse Island
High Bluff
Harding Range
Edkins Range
Myalan Pool
Rocky Mountain 701m
Mount Lacy 750m
Otway Shoal
Strickland Bay
Dambimangari IPA
Horizontal Falls
Wulalam Island
The Funnel
Walcott Inl.
Calder River
Bardi Jawi IPA
Sunday Is
Gerald Peninsula
Cone Bay
Walcott Inlet
Charnley River
Dingo Spring
Deep Spring
Joint Hill 700m
Salvoni Gorge
Grevillea Gorge
Synnot Range
Dead Horse Spring
Artesian Range
distorted surface
Humbert Creek
Echo Valley
Hidden Valley Falls
Eyles Field
Manning Ck
Long Island
Cascade Bay
Lachlan Island
Kimbolton Ra
Wyndham Range
rocky outcrops
Military Area
Yampi Training Area
Donkey Pools
Donkey Yard Hole
'Mt Barnett Roadhouse'
Mount Barnett 540m
Barnett
Gudumul
'Kimbolton'
Robinson R.
MVO only
King Ck
Reva Falls
Hann Pass
'Charnley River'
Packhorse Range
Dillie Gorge
Galvans Gorge
Goodenough Bay
Maddarr
Cornambie Point
King Sound
'Oobagooma'
Rd
'Mount Hart'
Mount Matthew 557m
Isdell R.
Isdell Range
King Leopold Ranges
Kangaroo Spring
Beverley Springs Rd
'Qodesh'
Phillips River
La Djadarr Bay
Disaster Bay
South Meda Shoal
Torment Spit
Repulse Point
Van Emmerick Range
Mount Chalmers 704m
Bells Falls
Bell Gorge
Isdell Gorge
Frank Hann Boab Tree
Adcock Gorge
Big Spring
Moll Gorge
Malaburra Spring
Woolnong Spring
Point Torment
Black Rocks Lighthouse
Stokes Bay
Oodinjil Spring
Kimbolton
Alexander Creek
Meda River
Hann Hole
Wilinggin IPA
'Silent Grove'
'Mount House'
Stumpy Gorge
Malaburra
Kallumbarrit Springs
Beagle Bay ALT
Christine Point
Mealy Pool
Ngooderbodyne Spring
Hawkstone Ck
Windjingayre (Windjingare)
Napier Range
Kongorow Pool
Inglis Gap
305
Cor
Saddler Spring
Mount House 547m
Jabiru Hole
Duck Hole
Mornington Rd
Jangan Spring
Mary Island North
Bungarun
Barker Gorge
Lennard River Gorge
56 Imintji
The Bench
Precipice Range
Barnumbah Lagoon
Mount Clifton 542m
Derby
101-102
'Birdwood Downs'
'Meda'
Karragee Pool
'Napier Downs'
Queen Victoria's Head
Satans Pass
Park
Mt Ord 947m
Mt Gladys 861m
Old Glenroy Meatworks
'Kimberley Downs'
Mowanjum Art and Cultural Centre
Gibb River Road
Munkayarra Pool
Curtin Air Base
Windjana Gorge NP
Windjana Gorge
Mount Broome 935m
Lennard R.
MVO only
Mary Spring
Adcock River
Carpenter Gap
Lillimooloora Police Station (Ruins)
Richenda River
The Rocks
Sunday Pass
Richenda Gorge
Millie Windie Gap
Mount Leake 706m
Jarrananga Plain
Yeeda Plain
'Yeeda'
Derby Hwy
For more detail see Hema's The Kimberley map
Pt.
'Fairfield'
McSherry Gap
Ord Gap
Bidan (Bedunburra)
187
To Willare Bridge Roadhouse
504
To Fitzroy Crossing
Fairfield Valley
Elimberrie Spring
Tunnel Creek
Dingo Gap
To Fitzroy Crossing
Lily Waterhole
J O Waterhole
Dimond Gorge
Bickley Waterhole
To Broome
162
163

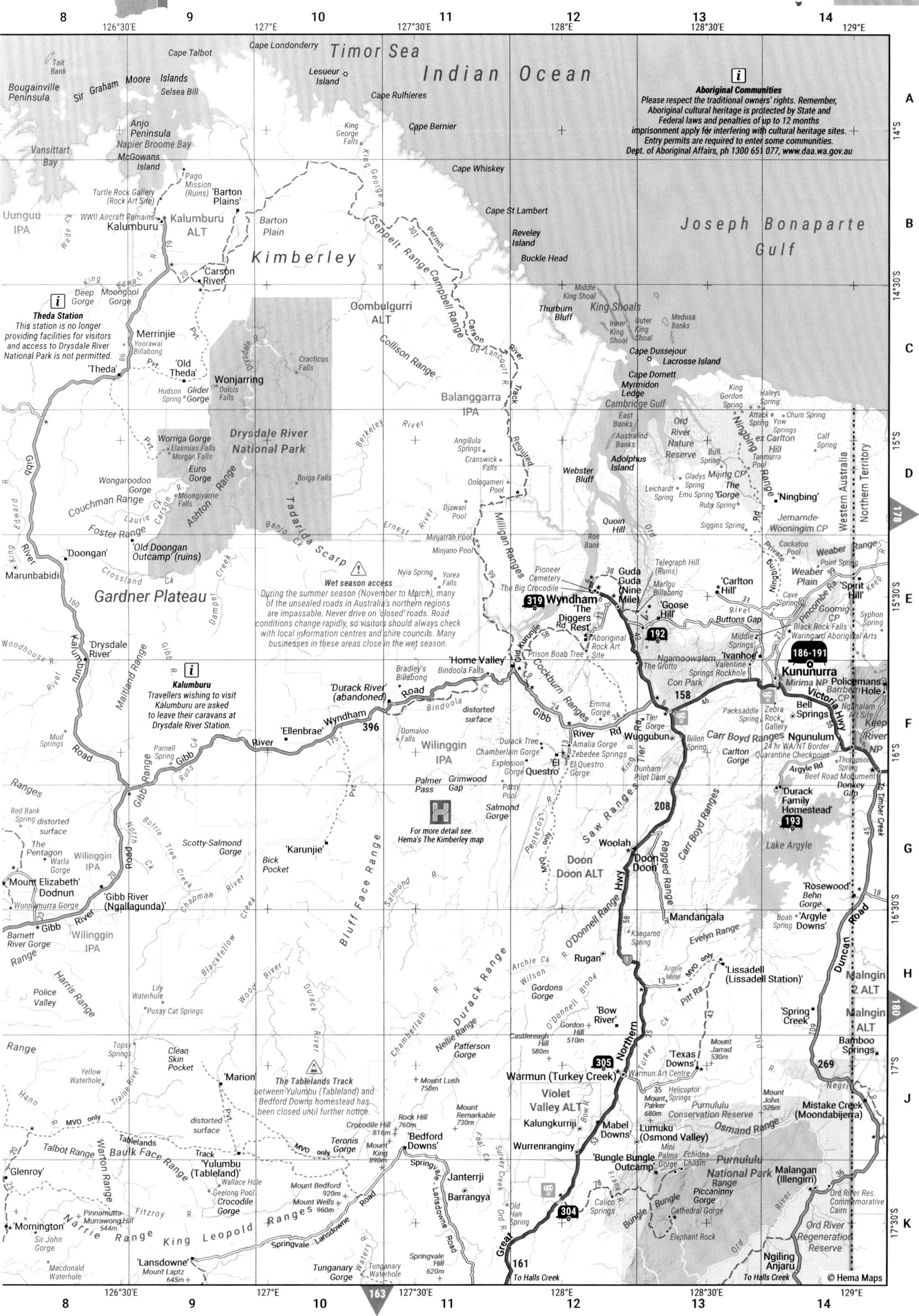
Timor Sea
Indian Ocean
Joseph Bonaparte Gulf
Kimberley
Aboriginal Communities
Please respect the traditional owners' rights. Remember, Aboriginal cultural heritage is protected by State and Federal laws and penalties of up to 12 months imprisonment apply for interfering with cultural heritage sites. Entry permits are required to enter some communities. Dept. of Aboriginal Affairs, ph 1300 651 077, www.daa.wa.gov.au
Theda Station
This station is no longer providing facilities for visitors and access to Drysdale River National Park is not permitted.
Wet season access
During the summer season (November to March), many of the unsealed roads in Australia's northern regions are impassable. Never drive on 'closed' roads. Road conditions change rapidly, so visitors should always check with local information centres and shire councils. Many businesses in these areas close in the wet season.
Kalumburu
Travellers wishing to visit Kalumburu are asked to leave their caravans at Drysdale River Station.
For more detail see Hema's The Kimberley map
The Tablelands Track
between Yulumbu (Tableland) and Bedford Downs homestead has been closed until further notice.
Cape Londonderry
Cape Talbot
Bougainville Peninsula
Sir Graham Moore Islands
Anjo Peninsula
Napier Broome Bay
Vansittart Bay
Kalumburu
Kalumburu ALT
Uunguu IPA
Drysdale River National Park
Gardner Plateau
Oombulgurri ALT
Balanggarra IPA
Cape Dussejour
Lacrosse Island
Cambridge Gulf
Ord River Nature Reserve
Wyndham
Kununurra
Gibb River Road
Victoria Hwy
Great Northern Hwy
Wilinggin IPA
'Home Valley'
'El Questro'
Lake Argyle
'Durack Family Homestead'
Warmun (Turkey Creek)
Purnululu National Park
Purnululu Conservation Reserve
Western Australia
Northern Territory
To Halls Creek
To Timber Creek
© Hema Maps

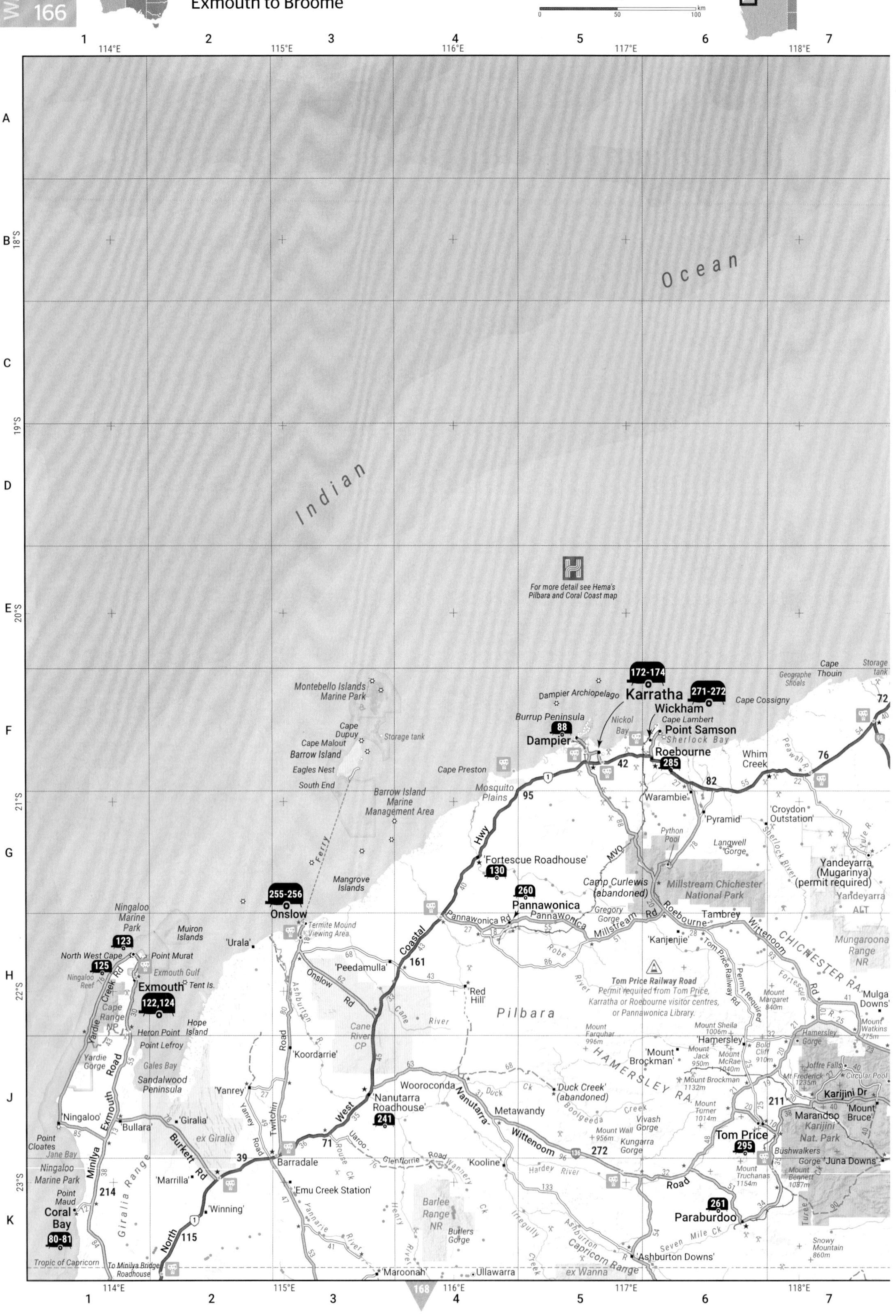
Indian
Ocean
For more detail see Hema's Pilbara and Coral Coast map
Karratha
172-174
271-272
Wickham
Point Samson
Roebourne
285
Dampier
88
Dampier Archipelago
Burrup Peninsula
Cape Lambert
Sherlock Bay
Nickol Bay
Cape Cossigny
Cape Thouin
Geographe Shoals
Storage tank
Whim Creek
Montebello Islands Marine Park
Cape Dupuy
Cape Malout
Barrow Island
Eagles Nest
South End
Storage tank
Barrow Island Marine Management Area
Cape Preston
Mosquito Plains
Mangrove Islands
Onslow
255-256
Termite Mound Viewing Area
'Urala'
Muiron Islands
Ningaloo Marine Park
123
125
North West Cape
Point Murat
Exmouth Gulf
Ningaloo Reef
Exmouth
122,124
Tent Is.
Cape Range NP
Hope Island
Heron Point
Point Lefroy
Yardie Gorge
Gales Bay
Sandalwood Peninsula
'Ningaloo'
'Bullara'
'Giralia'
ex Giralia
Point Cloates
Jane Bay
Ningaloo Marine Park
Point Maud
Coral Bay
80-81
214
Tropic of Capricorn
To Minilya Bridge Roadhouse
'Marrilla'
'Winning'
115
39
Barradale
71
'Yanrey'
'Koordarrie'
'Peedamulla'
161
'Red Hill'
Cane River CP
'Fortescue Roadhouse'
130
260
Pannawonica
Camp Curlewis (abandoned)
Gregory Gorge
Millstream Chichester National Park
Python Pool
'Pyramid'
Warambie
Langwell Gorge
'Croydon Outstation'
Yandeyarra (Mugarinya) (permit required)
Yandeyarra ALT
Tambrey
'Kanjenjie'
Mungaroona Range NR
Tom Price Railway Road
Permit required from Tom Price, Karratha or Roebourne visitor centres, or Pannawonica Library.
Pilbara
Mount Margaret 840m
'Mulga Downs'
Mount Watkins 775m
Hamersley Gorge
Mount Farquhar 996m
HAMERSLEY RA.
'Mount Brockman'
Mount Jack 950m
Mount McRae 1040m
Mount Sheila 1006m
'Hamersley'
Bold Cliff 910m
Mount Brockman 1132m
Joffre Falls
Mt Frederick 1235m
Circular Pool
Karijini Dr
'Duck Creek' (abandoned)
Wooroconda
'Nanutarra Roadhouse'
241
Metawandy
Vivash Gorge
Kungarra Gorge
Mount Wall 956m
Mount Turner 1014m
211
Marandoo
'Mount Bruce'
Karijini Nat. Park
Tom Price
295
Bushwalkers Gorge
'Juna Downs'
Mount Truchanas 1154m
Mount Bennett 1087m
272
'Kooline'
'Emu Creek Station'
Barlee Range NR
Bullers Gorge
261
Paraburdoo
'Ashburton Downs'
Capricorn Range
ex Wanna
'Maroonah'
Ullawarra
Snowy Mountain 860m
North West Coastal Hwy
Onslow Rd
Burkett Rd
Minilya Exmouth Road
Yardie Creek Rd
Nanutarra Wittenoom Road
Roebourne Wittenoom Rd
Pannawonica Rd
Millstream Rd
Tom Price Railway Rd
Permit Required
CHICHESTER RA.
Ashburton R.
Fortescue
Robe River
Hardey River
Henry River
Yannarie River
Sherlock River
Yule R.
Peawah R.
Twitchin Road
Yanrey Road
Glenflorrie Road
Uaroo
Duck Ck
Boolgeeda Creek
Seven Mile Ck
Irregully Creek
Giralia Range
Turee Ck
42
76
82
72
95
168

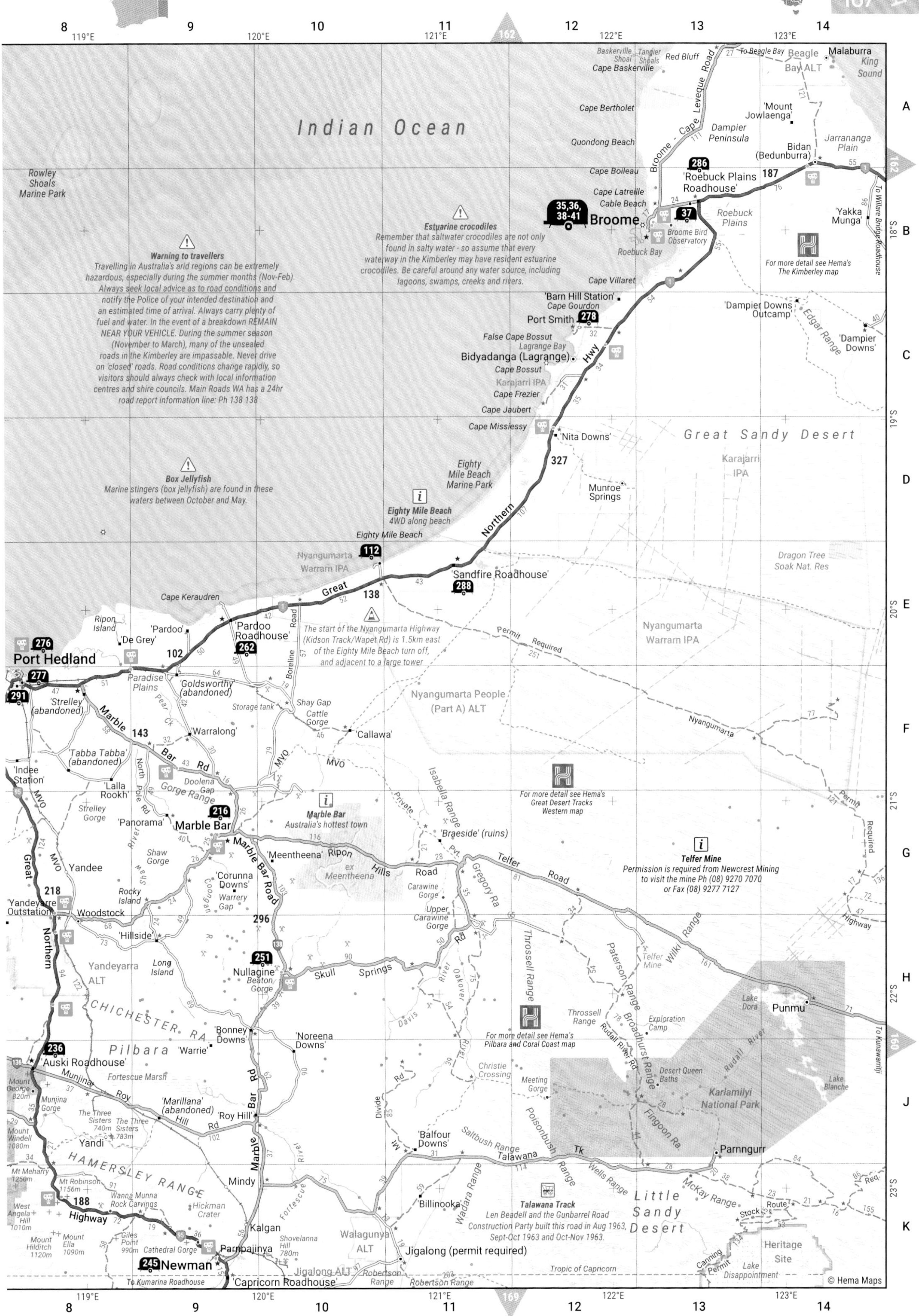

Indian Ocean
Rowley Shoals Marine Park
Warning to travellers
Travelling in Australia's arid regions can be extremely hazardous, especially during the summer months (Nov-Feb). Always seek local advice as to road conditions and notify the Police of your intended destination and an estimated time of arrival. Always carry plenty of fuel and water. In the event of a breakdown REMAIN NEAR YOUR VEHICLE. During the summer season (November to March), many of the unsealed roads in the Kimberley are impassable. Never drive on 'closed' roads. Road conditions change rapidly, so visitors should always check with local information centres and shire councils. Main Roads WA has a 24hr road report information line: Ph 138 138
Estuarine crocodiles
Remember that saltwater crocodiles are not only found in salty water - so assume that every waterway in the Kimberley may have resident estuarine crocodiles. Be careful around any water source, including lagoons, swamps, creeks and rivers.
Box Jellyfish
Marine stingers (box jellyfish) are found in these waters between October and May.
Eighty Mile Beach
4WD along beach
The start of the Nyangumarta Highway (Kidson Track/Wapet Rd) is 1.5km east of the Eighty Mile Beach turn off, and adjacent to a large tower
For more detail see Hema's The Kimberley map
For more detail see Hema's Great Desert Tracks Western map
For more detail see Hema's Pilbara and Coral Coast map
Marble Bar
Australia's hottest town
Telfer Mine
Permission is required from Newcrest Mining to visit the mine Ph (08) 9270 7070 or Fax (08) 9277 7127
Talawana Track
Len Beadell and the Gunbarrel Road Construction Party built this road in Aug 1963, Sept-Oct 1963 and Oct-Nov 1963.
Broome
Port Hedland
Marble Bar
Newman
Nullagine
Port Smith
Bidyadanga (Lagrange)
'Roebuck Plains Roadhouse'
'Sandfire Roadhouse'
'Pardoo Roadhouse'
'Auski Roadhouse'
'Capricorn Roadhouse'
Jigalong (permit required)
Punmu
Parnngurr
Great Sandy Desert
Little Sandy Desert
Karlamilyi National Park
Pilbara
CHICHESTER RA
HAMERSLEY RANGE
Great Northern Hwy
Marble Bar Rd
Telfer Road
Ripon Hills Road
Skull Springs Rd
Talawana Tk
Nyangumarta
Permit Required
Broome - Cape Leveque Road
Cape Baskerville
Cape Bertholet
Quondong Beach
Cape Boileau
Cape Latreille
Cable Beach
Roebuck Bay
Cape Villaret
'Barn Hill Station'
Cape Gourdon
False Cape Bossut
Lagrange Bay
Cape Bossut
Karajarri IPA
Cape Frezier
Cape Jaubert
Cape Missiessy
'Nita Downs'
Munroe Springs
Eighty Mile Beach Marine Park
Nyangumarta Warrarn IPA
Cape Keraudren
Ripon Island
'De Grey'
'Pardoo'
Nyangumarta People (Part A) ALT
Dragon Tree Soak Nat. Res
Beagle Bay ALT
Malaburra
King Sound
'Mount Jowlaenga'
Dampier Peninsula
Bidan (Bedunburra)
Jarrananga Plain
'Yakka Munga'
Roebuck Plains
Broome Bird Observatory
'Dampier Downs Outcamp'
Edgar Range
'Dampier Downs'
'Goldsworthy' (abandoned)
'Strelley' (abandoned)
'Tabba Tabba' (abandoned)
'Indee Station'
'Lalla Rookh'
'Warralong'
Shay Gap
Cattle Gorge
'Callawa'
Doolena Gap
Gorge Range
Strelley Gorge
'Panorama'
'Meentheena'
ex Meentheena
'Braeside' (ruins)
Isabella Range
Gregory Ra
Carawine Gorge
Upper Carawine Gorge
Yandee
'Corunna Downs'
Warrery Gap
Rocky Island
Shaw Gorge
'Yandeyarra Outstation'
Woodstock
'Hillside'
Yandeyarra ALT
Long Island
Beaton Gorge
Throssell Range
Paterson Range
Wilki Range
Telfer Mine
Throssell Range
Exploration Camp
Rudall River
Broadhurst Range
Desert Queen Baths
Fingoon Ra
Lake Dora
Lake Blanche
Christie Crossing
Meeting Gorge
Poisonbush Range
'Bonney Downs'
'Noreena Downs'
'Warrie'
Fortescue Marsh
'Marillana' (abandoned)
'Roy Hill'
Munjina Gorge
The Three Sisters 740m
Yandi
Mount Windell 1080m
Mount George 820m
Mt Meharry 1250m
Mt Robinson 1156m
Wanna Munna Rock Carvings
Hickman Crater
West Angela Hill 1010m
Mount Hilditch 1120m
Mount Ella 1090m
Giles Point 990m
Cathedral Gorge
Parnpajinya
Mindy
Kalgan
Shovelanna Hill 780m
Walagunya ALT
Jigalong ALT
Robertson Range
'Balfour Downs'
'Billinooka'
Wadara Range
Saltbush Range
Wells Range
McKay Range
Heritage Site
Lake Disappointment
Canning Stock Route
Tropic of Capricorn
To Kumarina Roadhouse
To Kunawarritji
To Willare Bridge Roadhouse
To Beagle Bay
© Hema Maps

Geraldton to Newman

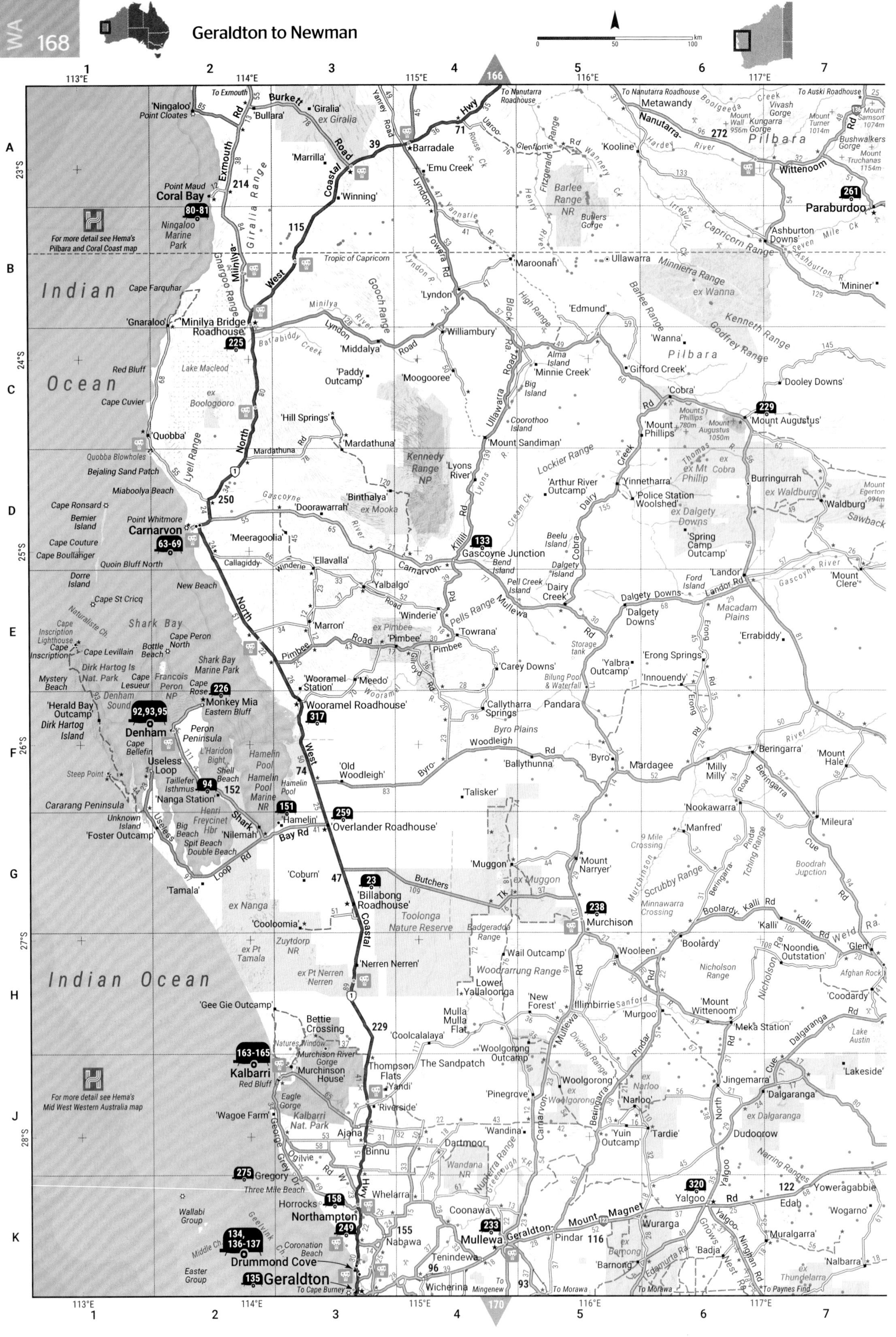

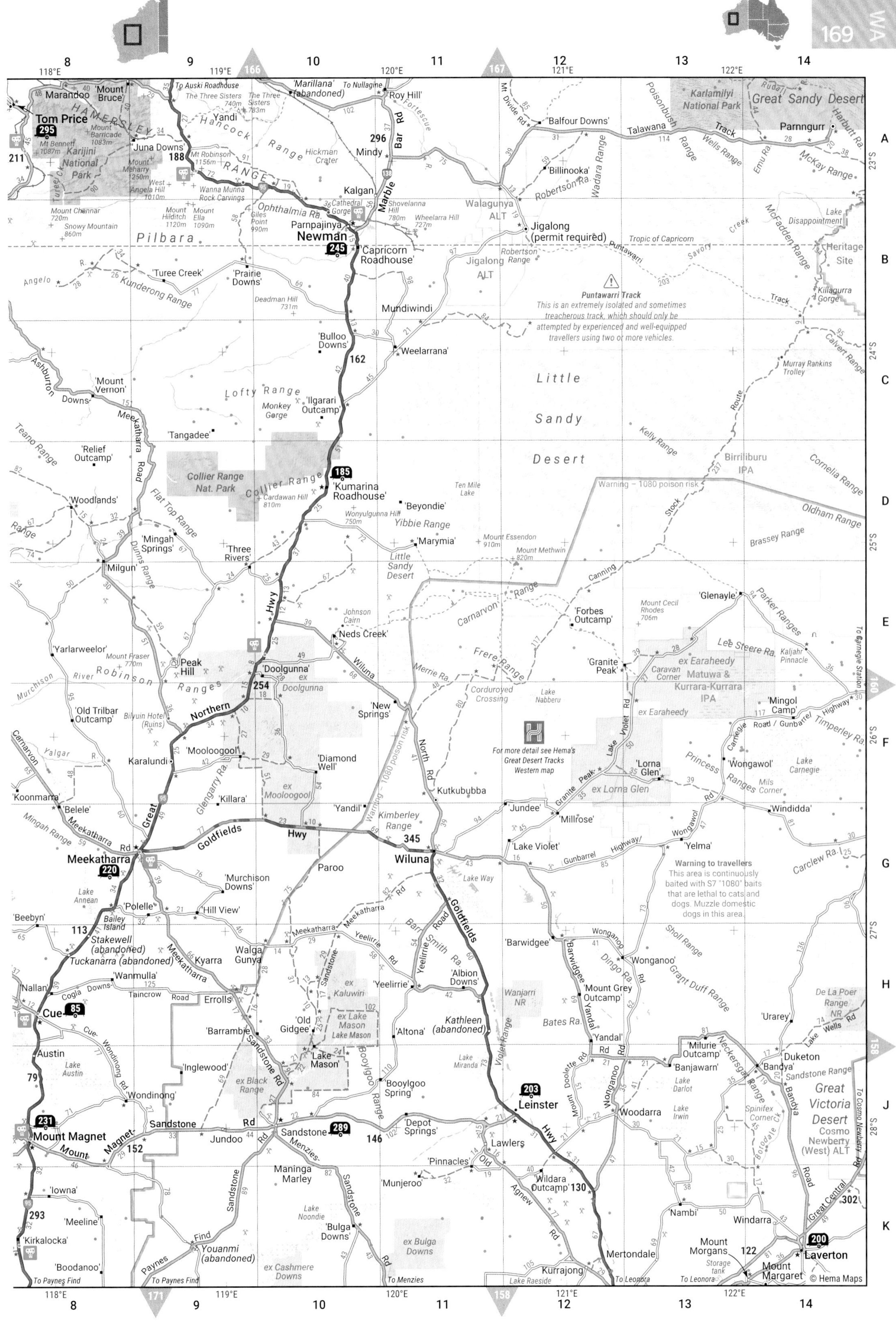

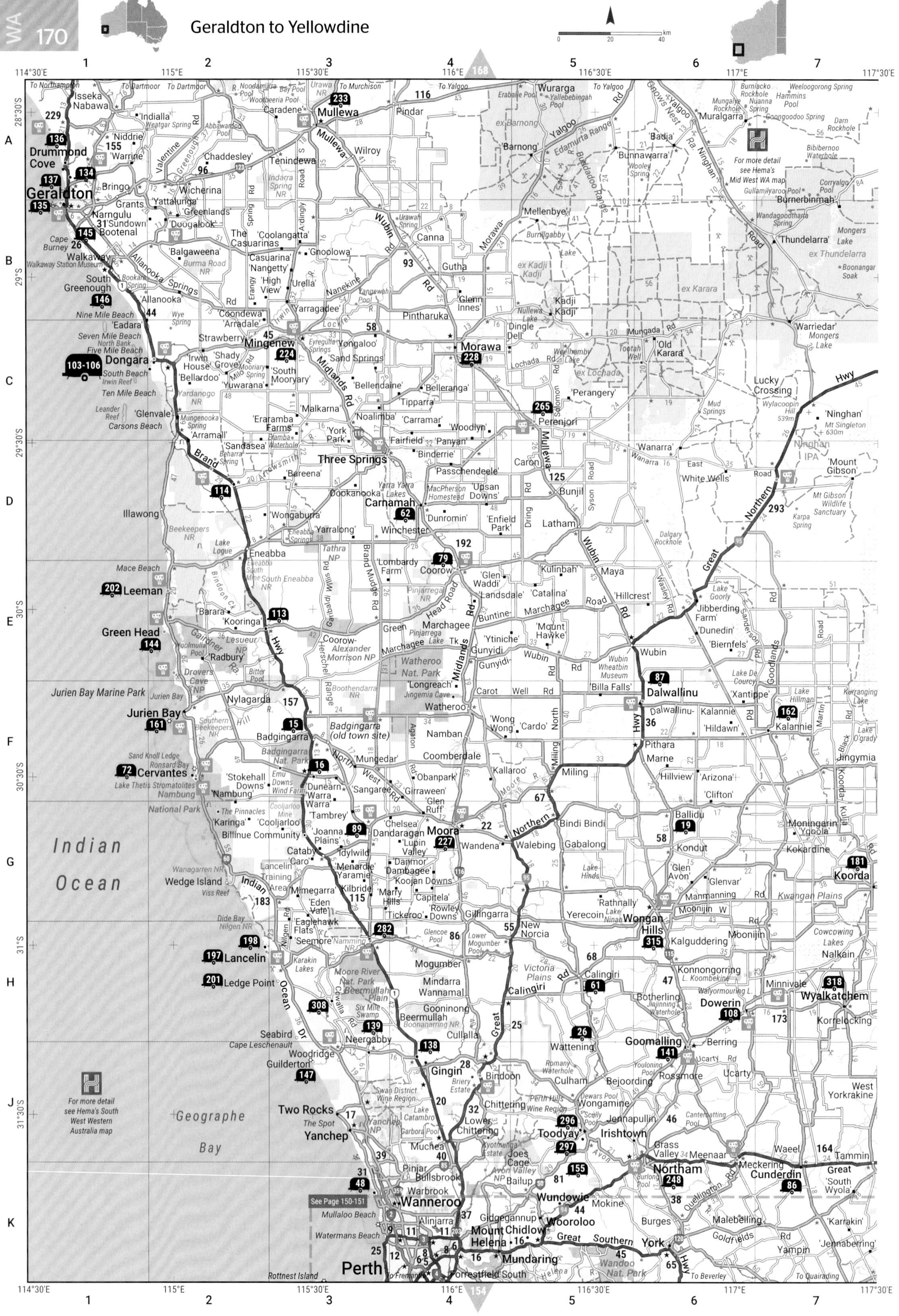
Indian Ocean
Geographe Bay
Geraldton
Mullewa
Mingenew
Dongara
Morawa
Perenjori
Three Springs
Carnamah
Coorow
Leeman
Green Head
Jurien Bay
Cervantes
Badgingarra
Moora
Dalwallinu
Wongan Hills
Lancelin
Ledge Point
Gingin
Toodyay
Northam
Cunderdin
Wyalkatchem
Koorda
Dowerin
Goomalling
Two Rocks
Yanchep
Wanneroo
Perth
Mundaring
York
For more detail see Hema's Mid West WA map
For more detail see Hema's South West Western Australia map
See Page 150-151

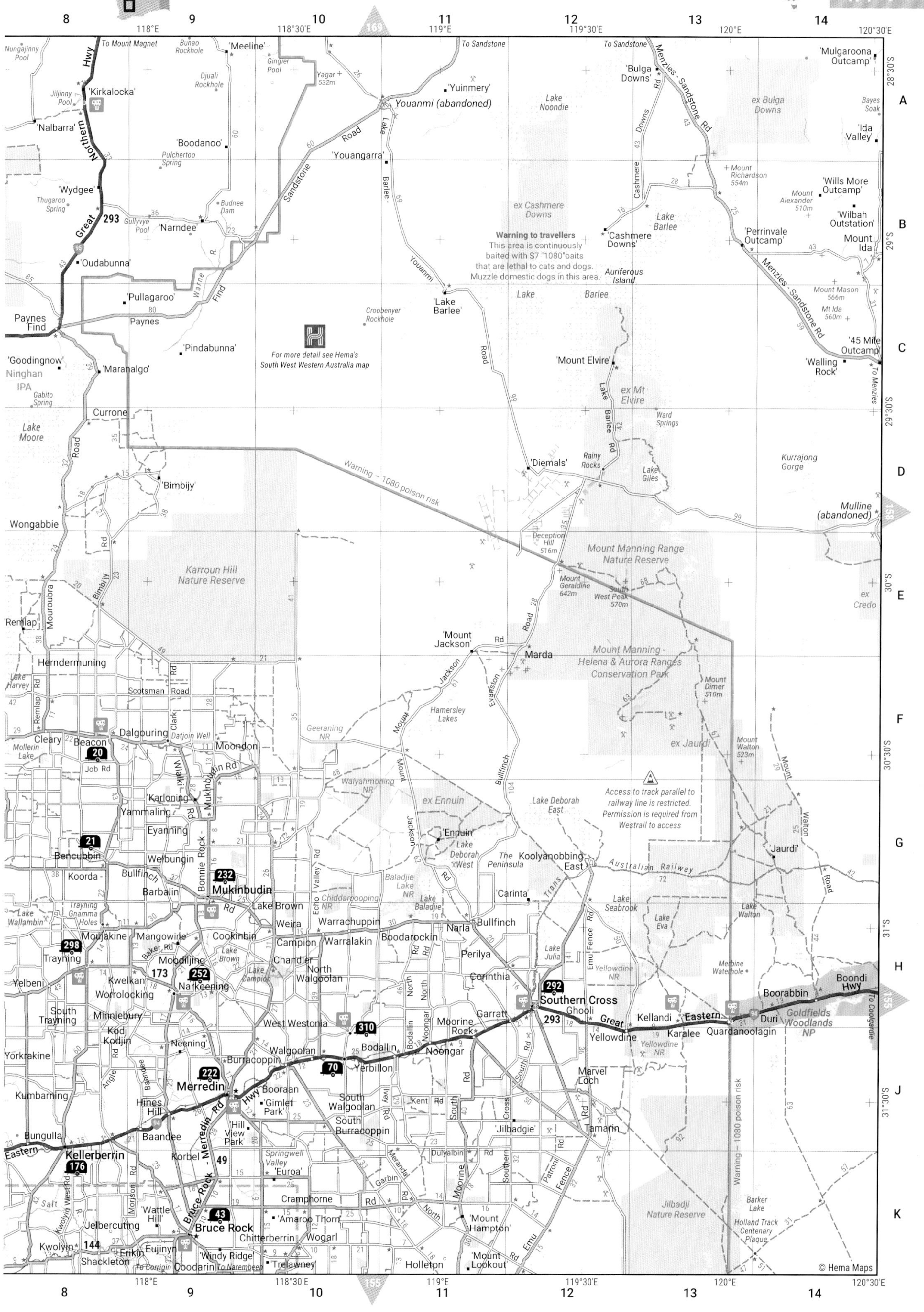

8
9
10
11
12
13
14
118°E
118°30'E
119°E
119°30'E
120°E
120°30'E
169
To Mount Magnet
To Sandstone
Nungajinny Pool
Bunao Rockhole
'Meeline'
Gingier Pool
Yagar 532m
Djuali Rockhole
'Yuinmery'
'Bulga Downs'
'Mulgaroona Outcamp'
28°30'S
A
Jiljinny Pool
'Kirkalocka'
Youanmi (abandoned)
Lake Noondie
ex Bulga Downs
Bayes Soak
'Nalbarra'
'Ida Valley'
'Boodanoo'
Pulchertoo Spring
'Youangarra'
Mount Richardson 554m
'Wydgee'
Thugaroo Spring
Budnee Dam
ex Cashmere Downs
Mount Alexander 510m
'Wills More Outcamp'
'Wilbah Outstation'
293
Gullyvye Pool
'Narndee'
Lake Barlee
B
'Cashmere Downs'
'Perrinvale Outcamp'
Mount Ida
29°S
Warning to travellers
This area is continuously baited with S7 "1080"baits that are lethal to cats and dogs. Muzzle domestic dogs in this area.
'Oudabunna'
Auriferous Island
'Pullagaroo'
Paynes
Lake
Barlee
'Lake Barlee'
Mount Mason 566m
Mt Ida 560m
Paynes Find
Croobenyer Rockhole
For more detail see Hema's South West Western Australia map
'Pindabunna'
'Goodingnow'
'Maranalgo'
'Mount Elvire'
'45 Mile Outcamp'
'Walling Rock'
C
Ninghan IPA
Gabito Spring
ex Mt Elvire
To Menzies
Currone
Lake Moore
Ward Springs
29°30'S
Rainy Rocks
'Diemals'
Kurrajong Gorge
D
'Bimbijy'
Warning – 1080 poison risk
Lake Giles
Wongabbie
Mulline (abandoned)
158
Deception Hill 516m
Mount Manning Range Nature Reserve
Karroun Hill Nature Reserve
Mount Geraldine 642m
South West Peak 570m
30°S
E
ex Credo
Remlap
'Mount Jackson'
Marda
Mount Manning - Helena & Aurora Ranges Conservation Park
Herndermuning
Lake Harvey
Scotsman Road
Mount Dimer 510m
Hamersley Lakes
F
Geeraning NR
Dalgouring
Datjoin Well
Cleary
Beacon
Mollerin Lake
20
Job Rd
Moondon
ex Jaurdi
Mount Walton 523m
30°30'S
Walyahmoning NR
Lake Deborah East
Access to track parallel to railway line is restricted. Permission is required from Westrail to access
'Karloning'
Yammaling
ex Ennuin
Eyanning
'Ennuin'
Lake Deborah West
21
Bencubbin
Welbungin
The Peninsula
Koolyanobbing East
'Jaurdi'
G
Australian Railway
Koorda
Bullfinch
Barbalin
232
Mukinbudin
Baladjie Lake NR
'Carinta'
Lake Brown
Chiddarcooping NR
Lake Baladjie
Lake Seabrook
Lake Walton
Lake Wallambin
Trayning Gnamma Holes
Weira
Warrachuppin
Narla
Bullfinch
Lake Eva
31°S
Moujakine
'Mangowine'
Cookinbin
Campion
Warralakin
Boodarockin
298
Trayning
Lake Brown
Chandler
Perilya
Lake Julia
Emu Fence Rd
173
Moodiljing
Yellowdine NR
Metbine Waterhole
Yelbeni
Kwelkan
252
Narkeening
Lake Campion
North Walgoolan
Corinthia
H
Worrolocking
Boondi
292
Southern Cross
Boorabbin
Hwy
155
South Trayning
Minniebury
West Westonia
310
Moorine Rock
Garratt
Ghooli
Great
Kellandi
Eastern
Duri
Goldfields Woodlands NP
To Coolgardie
Kodj Kodjin
'Neening'
Bodallin
293
Yellowdine
Karalee
Quardanoolagin
Yellowdine NR
Yorkrakine
Burracoppin
Walgoolan
Noongar
70
Yerbillon
Marvel Loch
222
Merredin
Booraan
Kumbarning
Hines Hill
'Gimlet Park'
South Walgoolan
Kent Rd
J
31°30'S
Warning – 1080 poison risk
Bungulla
South Burracoppin
'Jilbadgie'
Tamarin
Hill View Park'
Eastern
Kellerberrin
Baandee
Dulyalbin
Korbel
49
Springwell Valley
176
'Euroa'
Garbin
Salt
'Wattle Hill'
Cramphorne
Rd
Jilbadji Nature Reserve
Barker Lake
K
43
Jelbercuting
Bruce Rock
'Amaroo Thorn'
'Mount Hampton'
Holland Track Centenary Plaque
Kwolyin
144
Erikin
Eujinyn
Chitterberrin
Wogarl
Shackleton
To Corrigin
Coodarin
'Windy Ridge'
To Narembeen
'Trelawney'
Holleton
'Mount Lookout'
© Hema Maps
Great Northern Hwy
Sandstone Road
Lake Barlee Rd
Youanmi Road
Menzies - Sandstone Rd
Cashmere Downs Rd
Warne R.
Find
Mouroubra Road
Bimbijy Rd
Remlap Rd
Evanston Road
Mount Jackson Rd
Bullfinch Rd
Jackson Rd
Mount Walton Road
Wialki Rd
Mukinbudin Rd
Bonnie Rock Rd
Echo Valley Rd
Baker Rd
Merredin - Bruce Rock Rd
Kwolyin West Rd
Morison Rd
Baandee Rd
Angle Rd
Moorine Rd
South Rd
Southern Cross Rd
Merandal Rd
North Rd
Ivey Rd
Patroni Rd
Fence Rd
Emu Rd
Trans
Boondi Hwy

Albany

1 Albany Gardens Holiday Resort
22 Wellington St. 1 km N of PO
www.albanygardens.com.au
08 9841 4616 HEMA 153 K14 35 00 39 S 117 52 20 E

2 Albany Happy Days Caravan Park
1584 Millbrook Rd. 10 km NE of PO
www.albanycaravanpark.com
08 9844 3267 HEMA 153 J14 34 56 09 S 117 54 09 E

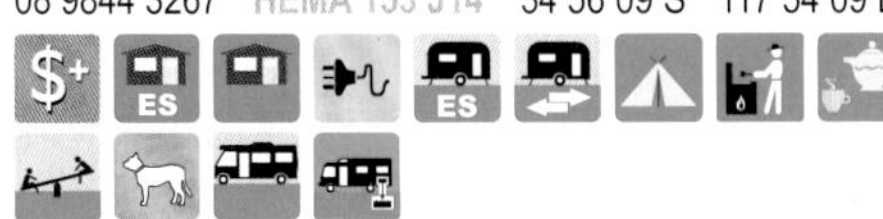

3 Albany Holiday Park
550 Albany Hwy
www.albanyholiday.com.au
08 9841 7800 HEMA 153 J14 34 59 07 S 117 51 11 E

4 BIG4 Emu Beach Holiday Park
8 Medcalf Pde
www.emubeach.com
08 9844 1147 HEMA 153 K14 35 00 00 S 117 56 16 E

5 BIG4 Middleton Beach Holiday Park
28 Flinders Pde, Middleton Beach
www.holidayalbany.com.au
08 9841 3593 HEMA 153 K14 35 01 20 S 117 54 55 E

6 King River Palms Caravan Park
795 Chester Pass Rd
08 9844 3232 HEMA 153 J14 34 56 19 S 117 54 13 E

7 Panorama Holiday Cottages & Caravan Park
71 Panorama Rd
08 9844 4031 HEMA 153 K14 35 04 43 S 117 53 09 E

8 Rose Garden Beachside Holiday Park
45 Mermaid Ave. 8 km NE of PO
www.acclaimparks.com.au
08 9844 1868 HEMA 153 K14 34 59 51 S 117 56 31 E

Armadale

9 Hillside Garden Village
270 South Western Hwy. Limited sites
08 9399 6376 HEMA 149 H9 32 10 09 S 116 00 58 E

Ascot

10 Perth Central Caravan Park
34 Central Ave
www.perthcentral.com.au
08 9277 1704 HEMA 146 G7 31 55 44 S 115 56 32 E

Augusta

11 Flinders Bay Caravan Park
Albany Tce. 4 km S of PO. Closed Jun - Aug
www.flindersbaypark.com.au
08 9758 1380 HEMA 152 F2 34 20 21 S 115 10 03 E

12 Turner Caravan Park
1 Blackwood Ave. 1 km S of PO
www.turnerpark.com.au
08 9780 5633 HEMA 152 F2 34 19 23 S 115 09 45 E

13 Westbay Retreat Caravan Park
Lot 934 Bussell Hwy. 1 km N of PO
08 9758 1572 HEMA 152 E2 34 18 05 S 115 08 56 E

Australind

14 Australind Tourist Park
65 Old Coast Rd
www.australindtouristpark.com/
08 9725 1206 HEMA 150 J1 33 18 15 S 115 42 07 E

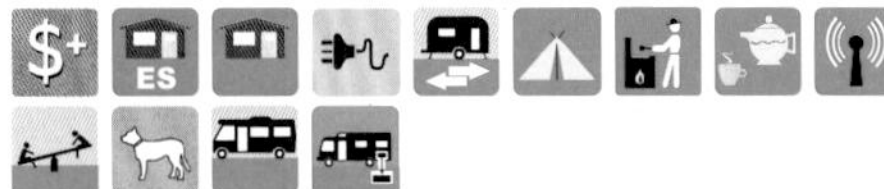

Badgingarra

15 Badgingarra Caravan Park
Reimers St
08 9652 9051 HEMA 170 F3 30 23 34 S 115 30 02 E

16 Waddi Bush Resort
Koonah Rd
www.bushresorts.com.au
08 9652 9071 HEMA 170 F3 30 29 58 S 115 30 07 E

Baldivis

17 Bonneys Water Ski Park
136 St Albans Rd
www.bonneyswaterskipark.com.au
08 9524 1401 HEMA 150 D2 32 16 55 S 115 51 12 E

Balladonia

18 Balladonia Hotel Motel Caravan Park
Eyre Hwy
www.balladoniahotelmotel.com.au
08 9039 3453 HEMA 157 E8 32 21 09 S 123 37 02 E

Ballidu

19 Ballidu Caravan Park
7 Wallis St. Payment collected, see info at site
08 9674 1114 HEMA 170 G6 30 35 44 S 116 46 22 E

Beacon

20 Beacon Caravan Park
Lucas St
0488 025 853 HEMA 171 F8 30 27 07 S 117 52 13 E

Bencubbin

21 Bencubbin Caravan Park
Kellerberrin Rd
08 9685 1202 HEMA 171 G8 30 49 07 S 117 51 44 E

Beverley

22 Beverley Caravan Park
22 Council Rd, off Main Hwy. N end of town
0457 344 434 HEMA 150 C7 32 06 28 S 116 55 25 E

Billabong

23 Billabong Homestead Hotel Motel & Caravan Park
North West Hwy
www.billabonghotelmotel.com
08 9942 5980 HEMA 168 G3 26 49 01 S 114 36 52 E

Binningup

24 Binningup Beach Caravan Park
31 Portland Dr
www.binningupbeachcaravanpark.com.au
08 9720 1057 HEMA 150 J1 33 08 47 S 115 41 26 E

Boddington

25 Boddington Caravan Park
Waruming Ave
08 9883 8018 HEMA 150 G5 32 48 00 S 116 28 22 E

Bolgart

26 Bolgart Caravan Park
George St
08 9627 5220 HEMA 170 H5 31 16 17 S 116 30 31 E

Boulder

27 Discovery Holiday Parks Boulder
201 Lane St. 800m S of PO
www.discoveryholidayparks.com.au
08 9093 1266 HEMA 156 A3 30 47 30 S 121 29 17 E

Bow Bridge

28 Ayr Sailean Chalets & Camping
1 Tindale Rd. Cnr Sth Coast Hwy
www.ayrsailean.com.au
08 9840 8098 HEMA 153 J10 34 57 09 S 117 01 08 E

Boyup Brook

29 Flax Mill Caravan Park
Jackson St. E end of the town. AH 0427 651 437
08 9765 1200 HEMA 152 C7 33 50 06 S 116 23 59 E

Bremer Bay

30 Bremer Bay Beaches Resort & Tourist Park
333 Wellstead Road. 3 km S of PO
www.bremerbaybeaches.com.au
08 9837 4290 HEMA 155 H11 34 25 37 S 119 22 21 E

31 Bremer Bay Caravan & Camping Park
Lot 130 Borden Bremer Rd
www.bremerbaycaravanpark.com.au
08 9837 4018 HEMA 155 H11 34 23 32 S 119 23 27 E

Bridgetown

32 Bridgetown Caravan Park
55 South Western Hwy
www.bridgetowncaravanpark.com.au
08 9761 1900 HEMA 152 D6 33 58 19 S 116 08 10 E

33 Maranup Ford Caravan Park
600 Maranup Ford Rd
www.maranupford.com.au
08 9761 1200 HEMA 152 C6 33 56 12 S 116 01 27 E

Brookton

34 Brookton Caravan Park & Camping Ground
Brookton Hwy. Behind recreation ground
08 9642 1106 HEMA 151 D8 32 22 07 S 117 00 08 E

Broome

35 Broome Caravan Park
14 Wattle Dr
www.broomecaravanpark.com
08 9192 1776 HEMA 162 E5 17 54 48 S 122 14 58 E

36 Broome Vacation Village
122 Port Dr. 4 km SW of PO
www.broomevillage.com.au
08 9192 1057 HEMA 162 E4 17 58 31 S 122 12 48 E

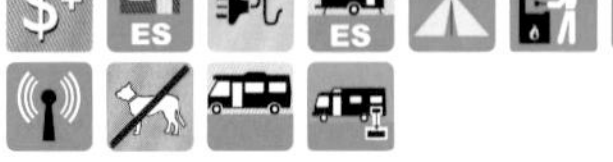

37 Broome's Gateway
3000 Broome Rd. 29 km E of Broome or 5 km W of Roebuck Plains Roadhouse
www.broomesgateway.com
0437 525 485 HEMA 162 E5 17 51 22 S 122 27 24 E

38 Cable Beach Caravan Park
8 Millington Rd. 5 km NW of PO
08 9192 2066 HEMA 162 E4 17 55 41 S 122 12 48 E

39 Discovery Parks Broome
91 Walcott St. 2 km S of PO
www.discoveryparks.com.au
08 9192 1366 HEMA 162 E4 17 58 15 S 122 14 02 E

40 Palm Grove Holiday Resort
Cnr Murray Rd & Cable Beach Rd. 5 km NW of PO
www.palmgrove.com.au
08 9192 3336 HEMA 162 E4 17 56 08 S 122 12 51 E

41 Tarangau Caravan Park
16 Millington Rd. Cable Beach
www.tarangaucaravanpark.com
08 9193 5084 HEMA 162 E4 17 55 25 S 122 13 02 E

Broomehill

42 Broomehill Caravan Park
Cnr of Morgan Rd & Journal St, book in via shire office, after hours arrivals, 0428 253 073
08 9825 3555 HEMA 153 C13 33 50 54 S 117 38 10 E

Bruce Rock

43 Bruce Rock Caravan Park
Dunstall St
08 9061 1377 HEMA 151 A13 31 52 26 S 118 09 05 E

Brunswick Junction

44 Brunswick Junction Caravan Park
South Western Hwy. 2 km N of PO
08 9726 1544 HEMA 150 J2 33 14 58 S 115 50 30 E

Bunbury

45 Bunbury Glade Caravan Park
Cnr Timperley Rd & Bussell Hwy. 4 km S of PO
www.glade.com.au
08 9721 3800 HEMA 150 K1 33 21 13 S 115 38 24 E

46 Discovery Holiday Parks Bunbury Foreshore
Koombana Dr
www.discoveryholidayparks.com.au
08 9791 3900 HEMA 150 K1 33 19 18 S 115 38 40 E

47 Discovery Holiday Parks Bunbury Village
Cnr Bussell Hwy & Washington Ave
www.discoveryholidayparks.com.au
08 9795 7100 HEMA 150 K1 33 22 29 S 115 38 44 E

Burns Beach

48 Burns Beach Sunset Village
35 Ocean Pde
www.burnsbeachsunsets.com.au
08 9305 5000 HEMA 170 K3 31 43 50 S 115 43 10 E

Busselton

49 Amblin Holiday Park
583 - 585 Bussell Hwy
www.amblin-holidaypark.com.au
08 9755 4079 HEMA 152 B2 33 39 36 S 115 16 32 E

50 BIG4 Beachlands Holiday Park
10 Earnshaw Rd. 3 km W of PO
www.beachlands.net
08 9752 2107 HEMA 152 B2 33 39 25 S 115 18 28 E

51 Busselton Holiday Village
118 Peel Tce
www.busseltonholidayvillage.com.au
08 9752 4499 HEMA 152 B3 33 39 05 S 115 21 17 E

52 Busselton Jetty Tourist Park
Cnr Marine Tce & Brown Street. 700m N of PO
08 9752 1516 HEMA 152 B2 33 38 45 S 115 20 53 E

53 Busselton Villas & Caravan Park
163 Bussell Hwy
www.busseltonvillasandcaravanpark.com.au
08 9752 1175 HEMA 152 B2 33 39 20 S 115 19 23 E

54 Busselton Youth & Family Camp
228 Caves Rd
www.busseltoncamp.adventist.org.au
08 9755 4399 HEMA 152 B2 33 39 23 S 115 14 03 E

55 Four Seasons Holiday Park
585 Caves Rd
www.fourseasonsresort.com.au
08 9755 4082 HEMA 152 B2 33 38 58 S 115 11 50 E

56 Lazy Days Holiday Park
452 Bussell Hwy
08 9752 1780 HEMA 152 B2 33 39 36 S 115 17 22 E

57 Mandalay Holiday Resort & Tourist Park
652 Geographe Bay Rd, Mandalay Entrance, Broadwater
www.mandalayresort.com.au
08 9752 1328 HEMA 152 B2 33 39 23 S 115 17 47 E

58 RAC Busselton Holiday Park
97 Caves Rd
www.parksandresorts.rac.com.au
08 9755 4241 HEMA 152 B2 33 39 40 S 115 14 54 E

59 Sandy Bay Holiday Park
2 Norman Rd, Broadwater
www.sandybayholidaypark.com.au/
08 9752 2003 HEMA 152 B2 33 39 27 S 115 16 57 E

Caiguna

60 John Eyre Motel & Caravan Park
Eyre Hwy
08 9039 3459 HEMA 157 E12 32 16 13 S 125 29 14 E

Calingiri

61 Calingiri Caravan Park
21 Cavell St
08 9628 7004 HEMA 170 H5 31 05 25 S 116 26 54 E

Carnamah

62 Carnamah Caravan Park
King St. 1 km NE of PO. Next to Niven Park, 0419 772 575
08 9951 1785 HEMA 170 D4 29 41 10 S 115 53 28 E

Carnarvon

63 BIG4 Plantation Caravan Park
589 Robinson St. 5.5 km E of PO
www.big4.com.au
08 9941 8100 HEMA 168 D2 24 51 44 S 113 42 01 E

WESTERN AUSTRALIA

64 Capricorn Holiday Park
1042 North West Coastal Hwy. 5 km E of PO
www.capricornholidaypark.com.au
08 9941 8153 HEMA 168 D2 24 51 45 S 113 42 12 E

65 Carnarvon Caravan Park
477 Robinson St. 3 km E of PO
08 9941 8101 HEMA 168 D2 24 51 57 S 113 41 20 E

66 Coral Coast Tourist Park
108 Robinson St. 700m E of PO
www.coralcoasttouristpark.com.au
08 9941 1438 HEMA 168 D2 24 52 45 S 113 39 38 E

67 Norwesta Caravan Park
24 Angelo St. 3.5 km E of PO
www.norwesta.com.au
08 9941 1277 HEMA 168 D2 24 51 55 S 113 41 03 E

68 Outback Oasis Caravan Park
49 Wise St. 3 km E of PO
www.outbackoasis-caravanpark.com
08 9941 1439 HEMA 168 D2 24 52 02 S 113 40 56 E

69 Wintersun Caravan & Tourist Park
546 Robinson St. 4 km E of PO
www.wintersuncaravanpark.com.au
08 9941 8150 HEMA 168 D2 24 51 52 S 113 41 45 E

Carrabin

70 Carrabin Roadhouse Motel & Caravan Park
Great Eastern Hwy
08 9046 7162 HEMA 171 J10 31 22 44 S 118 40 41 E

Caversham

71 Discovery Parks Swan Valley
91 Benara Rd
www.discoveryholidayparks.com.au
08 9200 4383 HEMA 147 E8 31 52 34 S 115 57 52 E

Cervantes

72 RAC Cervantes Holiday Park
35 Aragon St. 500m N of PO
www.big4.com.au
08 9652 7060 HEMA 170 F2 30 29 50 S 115 03 58 E

Cheynes Beach

73 Cheynes Beach Caravan Park
12 Bald Island Rd
www.cheynesbeachcaravanpark.com.au
08 9846 1247 HEMA 155 K9 34 53 02 S 118 24 20 E

Cocklebiddy

74 Cocklebiddy Caravan Facility
Eyre Hwy
08 9039 3462 HEMA 157 D14 32 02 15 S 126 05 49 E

Collie

75 Collie River Valley Tourist Park
1 Porter St. 2 km W of PO
www.colliecaravanpark.com.au
08 9734 5088 HEMA 150 K4 33 21 44 S 116 08 44 E

Condingup

76 Orleans Bay Caravan Park
Lot 1 Wharton Rd, via Fisheries Rd & Orleans Bay Rd, Known as "The Duke"
08 9075 0033 HEMA 156 K5 33 55 25 S 122 34 40 E

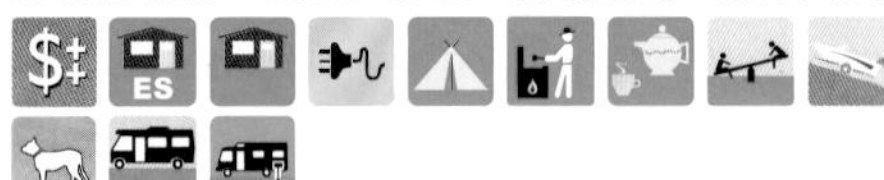

Coogee

77 Discovery Holiday Parks Coogee Beach
3 Powell Parade (off Cockburn Rd)
www.discoveryholidayparks.com.au
089418 1810 HEMA 148 F2 32 06 49 S 115 45 51 E

Coolgardie

78 Coolgardie Tourist Village
99 Bayley St
08 9026 6009 HEMA 156 A2 30 57 18 S 121 09 35 E

Coorow

79 Coorow Caravan Park
Station St. Past bulk wheat silos. Pay at council office or honesty box
08 9952 0100 HEMA 170 E4 29 52 51 S 116 01 02 E

Coral Bay

80 Ningaloo Coral Bay
Robinson St
www.ningaloocoralbay.com
08 9385 6655 HEMA 166 K1 23 08 32 S 113 46 23 E

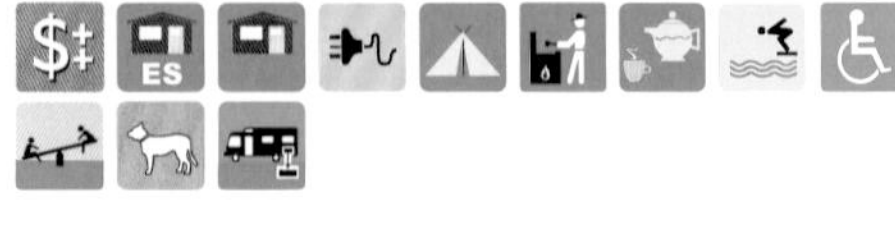

81 Peoples Park Coral Bay
Robinson St
www.peoplesparkcoralbay.com.au
08 9942 5933 HEMA 166 K1 23 08 35 S 113 46 14 E

Corrigin

82 Corrigin Caravan Park
Cnr Larke Crescent & Kirkwood St
08 9063 2515 HEMA 151 D12 32 19 52 S 117 52 41 E

Cowaramup

83 Taunton Farm Holiday Park
8113 Bussell Hwy
www.tauntonfarm.com.au
08 9755 5334 HEMA 152 C1 33 48 40 S 115 07 21 E

Cranbrook

84 Cranbrook Caravan Park
Mason St. 1 km SW of PO
0429 942 825 HEMA 153 E13 34 17 48 S 117 32 47 E

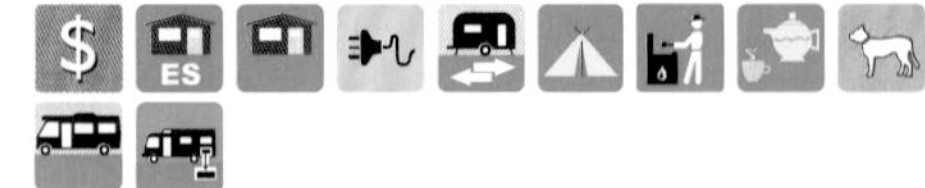

Cue

85 Cue Tourist Park
Austin St
08 9963 1107 HEMA 169 H8 27 25 18 S 117 53 57 E

Cunderdin

86 Cunderdin Caravan Park

74 Olympic Ave
08 9635 1258 HEMA 170 K7 31 38 48 S 117 14 13 E

Dalwallinu

87 Dalwallinu Caravan Park

10 Dowie St
08 9661 1253 HEMA 170 F6 30 16 27 S 116 40 08 E

Dampier

88 Dampier Transit Caravan Park

The Esplanade. 1.5 km N of PO. 3 night max
08 9183 1109 HEMA 166 F5 20 39 09 S 116 42 56 E

Dandaragan

89 Dandaragan Transit Park

Cnr Moora Rd & Caro Rd
08 9651 4071 HEMA 170 G3 30 40 13 S 115 42 12 E

Darkan

90 Darkan Caravan Park

Lot 274 Coalfields Rd
08 9736 2222 HEMA 150 K6 33 20 04 S 116 43 30 E

Dawesville

91 Dawesville Holiday Village

1149 Old Coast Rd
www.dawesvilleholiday.com.au
08 9582 1417 HEMA 150 F1 32 38 09 S 115 38 20 E

Denham

92 Blue Dolphin Caravan Park & Holiday Village

Lot 5 - 12 Hamelin Rd. 400m E of PO
www.ozpal.com/bluedolphin
08 9948 1385 HEMA 168 F2 25 55 45 S 113 32 17 E

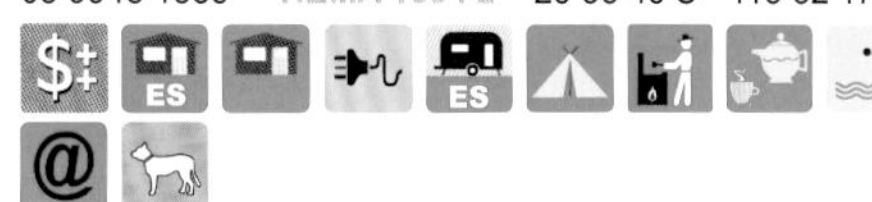

93 Denham Seaside Caravan Park

1 Stella Rowley Dr
www.sharkbay.com.au
08 9948 1242 HEMA 168 F2 25 55 31 S 113 31 48 E

94 Nanga Bay Resort

Nanga Bay. Shark Bay World Heritage Area
www.nangabayresort.com.au
08 9948 3992 HEMA 168 F2 26 15 21 S 113 48 25 E

95 Shark Bay Caravan Park

6 Spaven Way
www.sbvan.com
08 9948 1387 HEMA 168 F2 25 55 29 S 113 32 15 E

Denmark

96 Big4 Denmark Ocean Beach Holiday Park

Ocean Beach Rd
www.big4.com.au
08 9848 1105 HEMA 153 K12 35 01 15 S 117 19 30 E

97 Denmark Rivermouth Caravan Park

Inlet Rd
www.denmarkrivermouthcaravanpark.com.au
08 9848 1262 HEMA 153 J12 34 58 11 S 117 22 02 E

98 Karri Aura Caravan Park & Motel Suites

443 Mount Shadforth Rd
www.karriaura.com.au
08 9848 2200 HEMA 153 J12 34 57 43 S 117 18 48 E

99 Riverbend Caravan Park & Chalets

40 Riverbend Lane. 3 km NE of PO
www.riverbend-caravanpark.com.au
08 9848 1107 HEMA 153 J12 34 56 40 S 117 21 41 E

Denmark Area

100 Boat Harbour Chalets & Camping

26 km W of Denmark on South Coast Hwy, turn S into Boat Harbour Rd
www.boatharbourchalets.com.au
08 9840 8212 HEMA 153 K11 35 00 08 S 117 06 01 E

Derby

101 Kimberley Entrance Caravan Park

2 - 12 Rowan St
www.kimberleyentrancecaravanpark.com
08 9193 1055 HEMA 164 K2 17 18 25 S 123 37 45 E

102 Site Closed

Dongara

103 Dongara Denison Holiday Park
250 Ocean Drive Rd
www.ddbeachholidaypark.com
08 9927 1131 HEMA 170 C2 29 16 13 S 114 55 22 E

104 Dongara Denison Top Tourist Park
8 George St, Port Denison
www.dongaratouristpark.com.au
08 9927 1210 HEMA 170 C2 29 16 40 S 114 55 03 E

105 Leander Reef Holiday Park
123 Point Leander Drive, Port Denison. Limited sites
www.leanderreefholidaypark.com.au
08 9927 1840 HEMA 170 C2 29 16 06 S 114 55 31 E

106 Seaspray Beach Holiday Park
79-81 Church St. 1 km W of PO. All sites ensuite
www.seaspraybeachholidaypark.com.au
08 9927 1165 HEMA 170 C2 29 15 11 S 114 55 15 E

Donnybrook

107 Donnybrook Transit Park
Egan Park, 18 Reserve St. 3 night max
08 9731 1897 HEMA 152 A5 33 34 16 S 115 49 12 E

Dowerin

108 Dowerin Motel & Caravan Park
12 Goldfields Rd
08 9631 1135 HEMA 170 H6 31 11 43 S 117 01 55 E

Dumbleyung

109 Dumbleyung Caravan Park
Harvey St & Dawson St. AH Caretaker 0458 851 709
08 9863 4012 HEMA 151 J11 33 18 49 S 117 44 25 E

Dunsborough

110 Dunsborough Lakes Holiday Resort & Caravan Park
29 Commonage Rd
www.dunsholiday.com
08 9756 8300 HEMA 152 B1 33 37 50 S 115 07 16 E

Dwellingup

111 Dwellingup Chalets & Caravan Park
23 Del Park Rd. Next to Fire Brigade
www.dwellingupcaravanpark.com.au
08 9538 1157 HEMA 150 F3 32 42 38 S 116 03 29 E

Eighty Mile Beach

112 Eighty Mile Beach Caravan Park
Eighty Mile Beach Rd
www.eightymilebeach.com.au
08 9176 5941 HEMA 162 H2 19 45 19 S 120 40 18 E

Eneabba

113 Halfway Mill Roadhouse Caravan Facility
Brand Hwy. 30 km S of Eneabba, entry at cnr of Coorow Rd
08 9952 9054 HEMA 170 E2 30 03 27 S 115 19 50 E

Eneabba North

114 Western Flora Caravan Park
Brand Hwy
08 9955 2030 HEMA 170 D2 29 37 32 S 115 13 02 E

Esperance

115 Bathers Paradise Caravan Park
45 Westmacott St. 3 km NE of PO
www.batherscpark.com.au
08 9071 1014 HEMA 156 J4 33 50 10 S 121 54 53 E
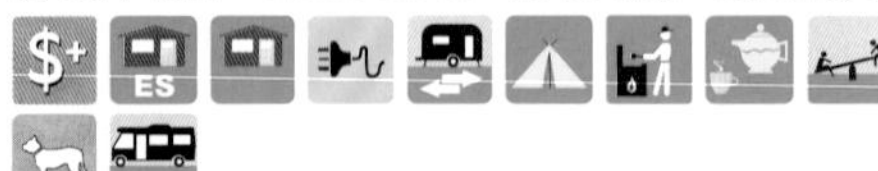

116 Bushlands Holiday Village
225 Collier Rd
08 9071 1346 HEMA 156 J4 33 50 18 S 121 51 21 E

117 Esperance Bay Holiday Park
162 Dempster St. 1 km S of PO
www.esperancebayholidaypark.com.au
08 9071 2237 HEMA 156 K4 33 52 09 S 121 53 25 E

118 Esperance Seafront Caravan Park
Cnr Goldfields Rd & Norseman Rd
www.topparks.com.au
08 9071 1251 HEMA 156 J4 33 50 44 S 121 54 07 E

119 Pine Grove Holiday Park
817 Harbour Rd. 3 km N of PO
www.acclaimparks.com.au
08 9071 4100 HEMA 156 J4 33 49 58 S 121 53 25 E
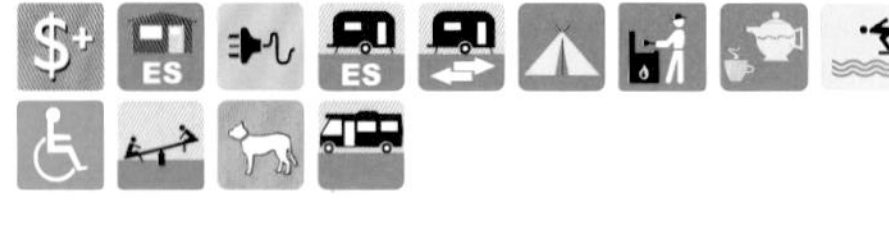

120 Pink Lake Tourist Park
113 Pink Lake Rd. 2 km W of PO
www.pinklakepark.com.au
08 9071 2424 HEMA 156 K4 33 51 29 S 121 52 10 E

Eucla

121 Eucla Roadhouse Caravan Park
Eucla-Reid Rd (No water avaliable other than for showers & toilet)
08 9039 3468 HEMA 159 J14 31 40 37 S 128 53 04 E

Exmouth

122 Ningaloo Caravan & Holiday Resort
1112 Murat Road
www.exmouthresort.com
08 9949 2377 HEMA 166 H1 21 56 05 S 114 07 42 E

123 Ningaloo Lighthouse Holiday Park
Yardie Creek Rd
www.ningaloolighthouse.com
08 9949 1478 HEMA 166 H1 21 48 29 S 114 06 51 E

124 RAC Exmouth Cape Holiday Park
3 Truscott Cres. 1.5 km S of PO
www.racexmouthcape.com.au
08 9949 1101 HEMA 166 H1 21 56 15 S 114 07 50 E

125 Yardie Homestead Caravan Park
Yardie Creek Rd
www.yardie.com.au
08 9949 1389 HEMA 166 H1 21 53 15 S 114 00 51 E

Fitzroy Crossing

126 Crossing Inn Caravan Park
Skuthorp Rd
www.crossinginn.com.au
08 9191 5080 HEMA 163 F9 18 11 08 S 125 35 00 E

127 Fitzroy River Lodge
Great Northern Hwy
www.fitzroyriverlodge.com.au
08 9191 5141 HEMA 163 F9 18 12 39 S 125 34 51 E

128 Tarunda Caravan Park
272 Forrest Rd
08 9191 5330 HEMA 163 F9 18 11 37 S 125 34 07 E

Forrestfield

129 Discovery Holiday Parks Perth Airport
186 Hale Rd
www.discoveryholidayparks.com.au
08 9453 6677 HEMA 147 J9 31 59 30 S 115 59 50 E

Fortescue Roadhouse

130 Fortescue River Roadhouse
North West Coastal Hwy
08 9184 5126 HEMA 166 G4 21 17 42 S 116 08 17 E

Frankland River

131 Frankland River Caravan Park
Moir St, off the Wingebellup Rd, behind town hall. Caretaker collects fees
0428 302 489 HEMA 153 F11 34 21 42 S 117 04 57 E

Fremantle

132 Fremantle Village
25 Cockburn Rd. 3 km S of PO
08 9430 4866 HEMA 148 E2 32 04 49 S 115 45 39 E

Gascoyne Junction

133 Junction Pub & Tourist Park
4 Viveash Way
08 9943 0868 HEMA 168 D4 25 03 13 S 115 12 25 E

Geraldton

134 Batavia Coast Caravan Park
239 Hall Rd. 10 km N of PO
www.bataviacoastcp.com.au
08 9938 1222 HEMA 170 A1 28 41 51 S 114 38 15 E

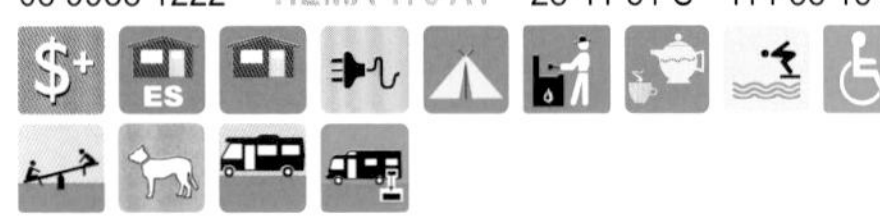

135 Belair Gardens Caravan Park
463 Marine Tce, West End
www.belairgardenscaravanpark.com.au
08 9921 1997 HEMA 170 B1 28 46 43 S 114 34 58 E

136 Drummond Cove Holiday Park
1633 North West Coastal Hwy, Drummond Cove
www.drummondcove.com
08 9938 2524 HEMA 170 A1 28 39 12 S 114 37 12 E

137 Sunset Beach Holiday Park
4 Bosley St
www.sunsetbeachpark.com.au
08 9938 1655 HEMA 170 A1 28 43 24 S 114 37 13 E

Gingin

138 Gingin Roadhouse & Caravan Park
973 Dewar Rd
08 9575 2258 HEMA 170 J4 31 19 45 S 115 52 21 E

139 Willowbrook Farm Caravan Park
1679 Gingin Brook Rd
www.willowbrookfarm.com.au
08 9575 7566 HEMA 170 J3 31 19 01 S 115 41 58 E

Gnowangerup

140 Gnowangerup Caravan Park
Richardson St. Pay at CRC or IGA. AH 0473 194 524, bond required
08 9827 1635 HEMA 155 G8 33 56 32 S 118 00 32 E

Goomalling

141 Goomalling Caravan Park
Throssell St. 1 km SE of PO
08 9629 1183 HEMA 170 J6 31 17 59 S 116 49 57 E

Gracetown

142 Gracetown Caravan Park
744 Cowaramup Bay Rd. 3 km E of PO
www.gracetowncaravanpark.com.au
08 9755 5301 HEMA 152 C1 33 51 29 S 115 01 02 E

Grass Patch

143 Grass Patch Park & Stay
Sheperd St. Limited sites. Phone on arrival. No Eftpos in town.
0488 510 701 HEMA 156 H3 33 13 44 S 121 42 52 E

Green Head

144 Green Head Caravan Park
9 Green Head Rd
www.greenheadcaravanpark.com.au
08 9953 1131 HEMA 170 E2 30 04 04 S 114 58 01 E

Greenough

145 Double Beach Holiday Village
4 Hull St, Cape Burney
www.doublebeach.com.au
08 9921 5845 HEMA 170 B1 28 51 38 S 114 38 27 E

146 S-bend Caravan Park
27 Company Rd, South Greenough
08 9926 1072 HEMA 170 B1 28 59 04 S 114 46 25 E

Guilderton

147 Guilderton Caravan Park
2 Dewar St. 500m S of PO
www.guildertoncaravanpark.com.au
08 9577 1021 HEMA 170 J3 31 21 01 S 115 30 04 E

Gwelup

148 Karrinyup Waters Resort
467 North Beach Rd. 14 km NW of PO
08 9447 6665 HEMA 146 E3 31 51 45 S 115 47 27 E

Halls Creek

149 Halls Creek Caravan Park
4 Roberta Ave
08 9168 6169 HEMA 163 F12 18 13 41 S 127 40 05 E

Hamelin Bay

150 Hamelin Bay Holiday Park
Hamelin Bay West Rd
www.hamelinbayholidaypark.com.au
08 9758 5540 HEMA 152 E1 34 13 15 S 115 01 46 E

Hamelin Pool

151 Hamelin Pool Caravan Park
5 km along Hamelin Pool Rd
www.hamelinpoolcaravanpark.com
08 9942 5905 HEMA 168 G3 26 24 02 S 114 09 55 E

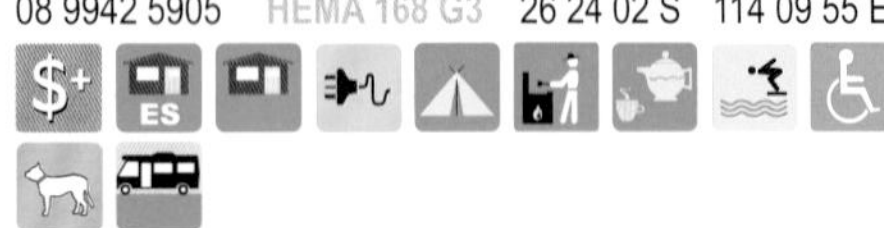

Harrismith

152 Harrismith Caravan Park
Cnr Railway Ave & Baylon St
08 9883 1010 HEMA 151 G11 32 56 10 S 117 51 44 E

Harvey

153 Harvey Rainbow Caravan Park
199 Kennedy St. 1 km NE of PO
08 9729 2239 HEMA 150 H2 33 04 46 S 115 54 09 E

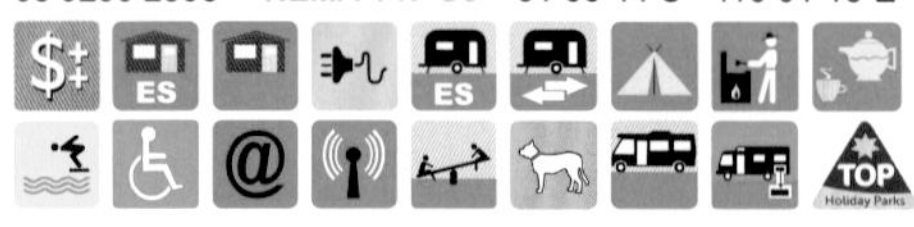

Hazelmere

154 Banksia Tourist Park
219 Midland Rd
www.banksiatourist.com.au
08 9250 2398 HEMA 147 G9 31 55 44 S 116 01 19 E

Hoddys Well

155 Hoddywell Archery Carvan Park
1027 Clackline - Toodyay Rd. Summer closure
www.hoddywellarchery.com.au
08 9574 2410 HEMA 170 J5 31 37 57 S 116 28 33 E

Hopetoun

156 Hopetoun Caravan Park
30 Esplanade. 400m W of PO
www.hopetouncaravanpark.com
08 9838 3096 HEMA 155 G13 33 57 02 S 120 07 22 E

157 Wavecrest Village Tourist Park
279 Hopetoun Ravensthorpe Rd. 3 km N of PO
www.wavecrestvillage.net.au
08 9838 3888 HEMA 155 G13 33 55 06 S 120 08 13 E

Horrocks Beach

158 Horrocks Beach Caravan Park
1 North Court. Opposite PO
www.horrocksbeachcaravanpark.com.au
08 9934 3039 HEMA 168 K3 28 22 51 S 114 25 49 E

Hyden

159 Wave Rock Caravan Park
1 Wave Rock Rd
08 9880 5022 HEMA 155 B10 32 26 30 S 118 53 52 E

Jerramungup

160 Jerramungup Caravan Park
1 Mooreshead St
www.jerramungupcaravanpark.com
08 9835 1174 HEMA 155 G10 33 56 36 S 118 55 14 E

Jurien Bay

161 Jurien Bay Tourist Park
1 Roberts St
www.jurienbaytouristpark.com.au
08 9652 1595 HEMA 170 F2 30 18 11 S 115 02 16 E

Kalannie

162 Kalannie Caravan Park
Roche St North
08 9661 0500 HEMA 170 F7 30 21 34 S 117 06 51 E

Kalbarri

163 Kalbarri Anchorage Holiday Village
Cnr Anchorage Lane & River Rd
www.kalbarrianchorage.com.au
08 9937 1181 HEMA 168 J3 27 41 59 S 114 10 12 E

164 Kalbarri Tudor Holiday Park
10 Porter Rd
www.kalbarritudor.com.au
08 9937 1077 HEMA 168 J3 27 42 43 S 114 10 09 E

165 Murchison River Caravan Park
92 Grey St
www.murcp.com
08 9937 1005 HEMA 168 J3 27 42 27 S 114 10 03 E

Kalgan

166 Kalgan River Chalets & Caravan Park
247 Nanarup Rd, Kalgan. 11 km E of PO
www.kalganrivercaravanpark.com.au
08 9844 7937 HEMA 155 K8 34 56 31 S 117 58 33 E

167 Two Peoples Caravan Park
273 Two Peoples Bay Rd
0407 431 778 HEMA 155 K8 34 57 19 S 118 03 10 E

Kalgoorlie

168 Discovery Holiday Parks Kalgoorlie
286 Burt St
www.discoveryholidayparks.com.au
08 9039 4800 HEMA 156 A3 30 46 55 S 121 28 10 E

169 Goldminer Caravan Park
Cnr Atbara St & Great Eastern Hwy. 3.5 km W of PO
www.acclaimparks.com.au
08 9021 3713 HEMA 156 A3 30 46 22 S 121 26 29 E

170 Prospector Holiday Park
Cnr Great Eastern Hwy & Ochiltree St
www.acclaimparks.com.au
08 9021 2524 HEMA 156 A3 30 45 56 S 121 27 13 E

Karlgarin

171 Tressies Museum & Caravan Park
4313 Kondinin-Hyden Rd
08 9889 5043 HEMA 155 C10 32 29 44 S 118 42 43 E

Karratha

172 Discovery Holiday Parks Balmoral
Balmoral Rd. Open May - Aug
www.discoveryholidayparks.com.au
08 9185 3628 HEMA 166 F5 20 43 50 S 116 48 34 E

173 Discovery Holiday Parks Pilbara Karratha
70 Rosemary Rd
www.discoveryholidayparks.com.au
08 9185 1855 HEMA 166 F5 20 45 11 S 116 48 53 E

174 Karratha Caravan Park
Lot 1060 Mooligunn Rd. Limited sites
08 9185 1012 HEMA 166 F5 20 45 56 S 116 51 31 E

Katanning

175 Katanning Caravan Park & BP Roadhouse
68 Cornwall St
www.katanningcaravanpark.com
08 9821 1155 HEMA 153 B13 33 42 04 S 117 33 36 E

Kellerberrin

176 Kellerberrin Caravan Park
Cnr Moore & George St
0428 138 474 HEMA 171 J8 31 37 30 S 117 43 01 E

Kingsley

177 Cherokee Village Mobile Home & Tourist Park
10 Hocking Rd. 1 km N of PO
www.cherokeevillage.com.au
08 9409 9039 HEMA 146 C3 31 48 06 S 115 48 59 E

Kirup

178 Kirup Tavern Caravan Park
47 South Western Hwy
08 9731 6311 HEMA 152 B5 33 42 28 S 115 53 34 E

Kojonup

179 Kojonup Caravan Park
75 Newstead Rd
www.kojonupcaravanpark.com.au
08 9831 1127 HEMA 153 C11 33 49 51 S 117 10 10 E

Kondinin

180 Kondinin Caravan Park
Gordon St. Key & pay at Roadhouse - Hotel
08 9889 1006 HEMA 151 E13 32 29 43 S 118 15 49 E

Koorda

181 Koorda Caravan Park
Scott St. 1 km N of PO
www.koorda.wa.gov.au
08 9684 1219 HEMA 170 G7 30 49 20 S 117 29 12 E

Kudardup

182 Molloy Caravan Park
Fisher Rd. 8 km E of Bussell Hwy
www.molloycaravanpark.com.au
08 9758 4515 HEMA 152 E2 34 15 29 S 115 12 32 E

Kukerin

183 Kukerin Caravan Park
31 Bath St. Bookings & keys Kukerin Hotel
08 9864 6338 HEMA 151 J12 33 11 09 S 118 04 59 E

Kulin

184 Kulin Caravan Park
82 Johnson St. Donation - conditions apply
0439 469 850 HEMA 151 F13 32 40 02 S 118 09 31 E

Kumarina Roadhouse

185 Kumarina Roadhouse Caravan Park
Goldfields Hwy (nonpotable water)
08 9981 2930 HEMA 160 G1 24 42 38 S 119 36 27 E
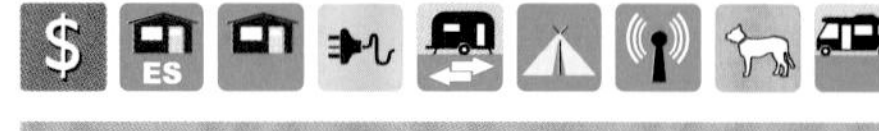

Kununurra

186 Discovery Holiday Parks Lake Kununurra
Lakeview Dr
www.discoveryholidayparks.com.au
08 9168 1031 HEMA 165 F14 15 47 29 S 128 43 14 E

187 Hidden Valley Tourist Park
Weaber Plains Rd
08 9168 1790 HEMA 165 F14 15 45 56 S 128 44 45 E

188 Ivanhoe Village Caravan Park
Cnr Coolibah Dr & Ivanhoe Rd
www.ivanhoevillageresort.com
08 9169 1995 HEMA 165 F14 15 46 15 S 128 43 54 E

189 Kimberleyland Waterfront Holiday Park
1519 Victoria Hwy
www.kimberleyland.com.au
08 9168 1280 HEMA 165 F14 15 47 06 S 128 44 11 E

WESTERN AUSTRALIA

190 Kununurra Lakeside Resort
50 Casuarina Way. 2 km SE of PO
www.lakeside.com.au
08 9169 1092 HEMA 165 F14 15 46 58 S 128 44 35 E

191 Kununurra Town Caravan Park
40 Bloodwood Dr
www.townpark.com.au
08 9168 1763 HEMA 165 F14 15 46 38 S 128 44 14 E

192 Parry Creek Farm Tourist Resort & Caravan Park
Parry Creek Rd
www.parrycreekfarm.com.au
08 9161 1139 HEMA 165 E13 15 36 03 S 128 16 37 E

Lake Argyle

193 Lake Argyle Caravan & Camping Park
Lake Argyle Rd
08 9168 7777 HEMA 165 G14 16 06 45 S 128 44 28 E

Lake Clifton

194 Lake Clifton Caravan Park
3232 Old Coast Rd
www.lccaravanpk.wix.com/caravan
08 9739 1255 HEMA 150 F1 32 47 15 S 115 40 25 E

Lake Grace

195 Lake Grace Caravan Park
Mather St
08 9865 1263 HEMA 151 H14 33 05 59 S 118 27 33 E

Lake King

196 Lake King Caravan Park
Critchley Ave. 500m N of PO. Pay at Tavern across road
www.lakekingtavernmotel.com.au
08 9874 4048 HEMA 155 D12 33 05 02 S 119 41 18 E

Lancelin

197 Experience Lancelin Holiday Park
Hopkins St
08 9655 1056 HEMA 170 H2 31 01 29 S 115 19 50 E

198 Lancelin North End Caravan Park
28 Bootoo St
08 9655 1115 HEMA 170 H2 31 00 20 S 115 19 40 E

Landsdale

199 Kingsway Tourist Park
Cnr Kingsway & Wanneroo Rd. 300m N of PO
www.acclaimparks.com.au
08 9409 9267 HEMA 146 C4 31 48 49 S 115 49 19 E

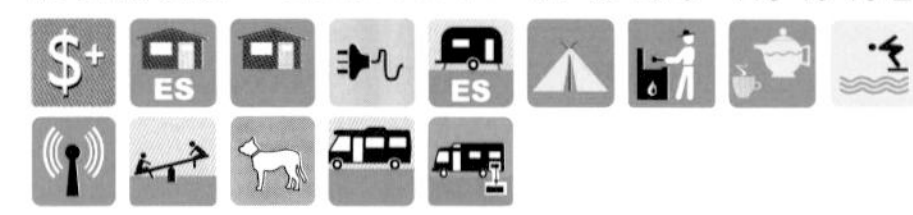

Laverton

200 Laverton Caravan Park
211 Weld Dr
08 9031 1072 HEMA 158 D5 28 37 30 S 122 24 22 E

Ledge Point

201 Ledge Point Holiday Park
742 Ledge Point Rd
www.ledgepointholidaypark.com
08 9655 2870 HEMA 170 H3 31 06 25 S 115 22 21 E

Leeman

202 Leeman Caravan Park
43 Thomas St
08 9953 1080 HEMA 170 E2 29 57 08 S 114 58 36 E

Leinster

203 Leinster Caravan Park
Mansbridge St. Payment at Supermarket
0436 661 725 HEMA 158 C2 27 55 07 S 120 41 53 E

Leonora

204 Leonora Caravan Park
42 Rochester St
www.opl.net.au
08 9037 6568 HEMA 158 D3 28 53 07 S 121 19 43 E

Logue Brook Dam

205 Lake Brockman Tourist Park
Turn E onto to Logue Brook Dam Rd off South Western Hwy. 6 km S of Yarloop
www.lakebrockman.com.au
08 9733 5402 HEMA 150 H3 33 00 20 S 115 58 27 E

Madura

206 Madura Pass Roadhouse Motel & Caravan Park
Eyre Hwy. (no water other than for showers & toilets)
08 9039 3464 HEMA 159 J11 31 53 58 S 127 01 10 E

Maida Vale

207 Advent Park Campground & Caravan Park
345 Kalamunda Rd
www.adventpark.adventist.org.au
08 9454 5341 HEMA 147 H9 31 56 42 S 116 01 08 E

Mandurah

208 Belvedere Caravan Park
153 Mandurah Tce. 1 km N of PO
www.belvederecp.com.au
08 9535 1213 HEMA 150 E2 32 31 18 S 115 43 44 E

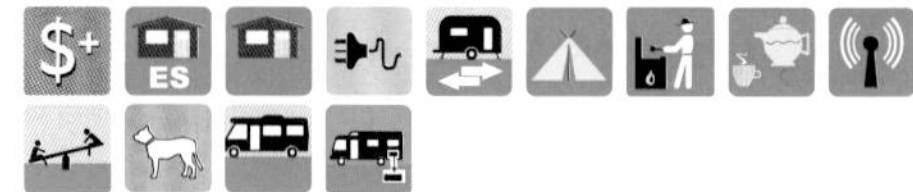

209 Estuary Hideaway Holiday Park
2151 Old Coast Rd
www.estuaryhideaway.com.au
0407 838 061 HEMA 150 F1 32 43 13 S 115 40 12 E

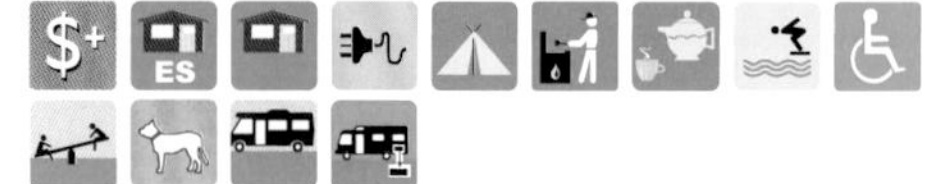

210 Mandurah Caravan & Tourist Park
522 Pinjarra Rd
www.mandurahcaravanpark.com.au
08 9535 1171 HEMA 150 E2 32 32 40 S 115 46 07 E

211 Miami Holiday Park
627 Old Coast Rd, Falcon
www.miamipark.com.au
08 9534 2127 HEMA 150 E1 32 34 53 S 115 39 46 E

212 Peel Caravan Park
598 Pinjarra Rd. Limited sites
08 9535 4343 HEMA 150 E2 32 33 03 S 115 46 37 E

Manjimup

213 Fontys Pool Chalets & Caravan Park

699 Seven Day Rd
www.fontyspool.com.au
08 9771 2105 HEMA 152 E6 34 17 14 S 116 04 02 E

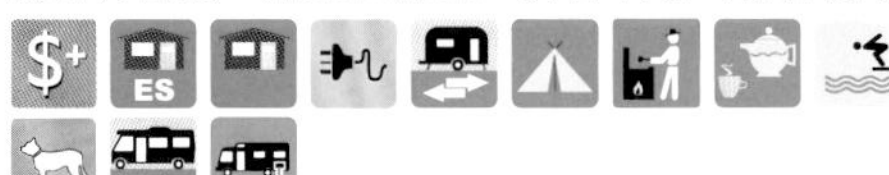

214 Manjimup Central Caravan Park

Lot 561 Mottram St
www.manjimupcentralcaravanpark.com.au
08 9777 2355 HEMA 152 E6 34 14 27 S 116 08 56 E

215 Warren Way Caravan Park

South Western Hwy
www.warrenwaycaravanpark.com.au
08 9771 1060 HEMA 152 E6 34 13 19 S 116 09 09 E

Marble Bar

216 Marble Bar Holiday Park

64 Contest Rd
08 9176 1569 HEMA 160 A1 21 10 27 S 119 44 42 E

Margaret River

217 Margaret River Tourist Park

44 Station Rd
www.mrtouristpark.com
08 9757 2180 HEMA 152 C1 33 57 32 S 115 04 09 E

218 Prevelly Caravan Park

99 Mitchell Dr
www.prevellycaravanpark.com.au
08 9757 2374 HEMA 152 D1 33 58 43 S 114 59 40 E

219 Riverview Tourist Park

8-10 Willmott Ave
www.riverviewtouristpark.com
08 9757 2270 HEMA 152 C1 33 57 06 S 115 04 59 E

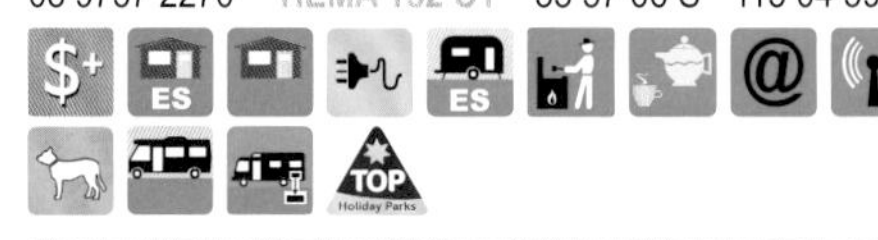

Meekatharra

220 Meekatharra Accomodation Centre

64 Main St
08 9981 1253 HEMA 169 G9 26 35 45 S 118 29 35 E

Menzies

221 Menzies Caravan Park

Shenton St, access via Brown St, AH 0448 242 041
08 9024 2702 HEMA 158 F3 29 41 40 S 121 01 44 E

Merredin

222 Merredin Tourist Park

2 Oats St
www.merredintouristpark.com.au
08 9041 1535 HEMA 171 J9 31 29 05 S 118 17 29 E

Midland

223 Midland Tourist Park

6 Toodyay Rd, Middle Swan
www.midlandtouristpark.com.au/
08 9274 3002 HEMA 147 E9 31 52 30 S 116 00 42 E

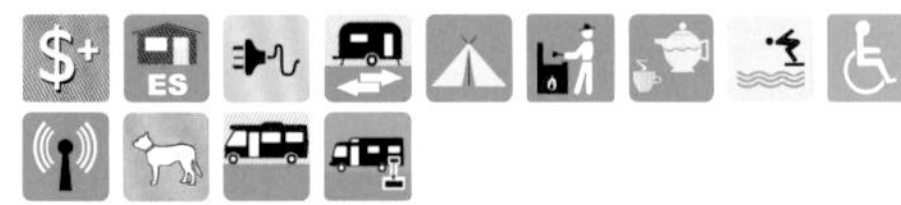

Mingenew

224 Mingenew Spring Caravan Park

Lee-Steere St. 1 km SW of PO
08 9928 1019 HEMA 170 C3 29 11 34 S 115 26 17 E

Minilya

225 Minilya Bridge Roadhouse

North West Coastal Hwy
08 9942 5922 HEMA 168 B2 23 48 53 S 114 00 33 E

Monkey Mia

226 RAC Monkey Mia Dolphin Resort

Monkey Mia Rd
www.racmonkeymia.com.au
08 9948 1320 HEMA 168 F2 25 47 39 S 113 43 07 E

Moora

227 Moora Shire Caravan Park

Dandaragan St. Behind swimming pool
08 9651 0000 HEMA 170 G4 30 38 17 S 116 00 16 E

Morawa

228 Morawa Caravan Park

26 Winfield St, Onsite Caretaker, pay shire during office hours or use honesty box, weekend check ins for chalets at Roadhouse
08 9971 1204 HEMA 170 C4 29 12 31 S 116 00 27 E

Mount Augustus

229 Mount Augustus Tourist Park

Caravan Park 280 km NE of Gascoyne Junction via Dairy Creek or 360 km NW of Meekatharra
www.mtaugustustouristpark.com
08 9943 0527 HEMA 168 C6 24 18 29 S 116 54 32 E

Mount Barker

230 Mount Barker Caravan Park

Lot 584 Albany Hwy
www.mtbarkercaravanpark.com
08 9851 1691 HEMA 153 G13 34 37 01 S 117 39 38 E

Mount Magnet

231 Mount Magnet Caravan Park

Lot 397 Hepburn St
08 9963 4198 HEMA 169 J8 28 03 42 S 117 50 58 E

Mukinbudin

232 Mukinbudin Caravan Park

Cruickshank St. 700m SW of PO
www.mukinbudin.wa.gov.au
0429 471 103 HEMA 171 G9 30 55 09 S 118 12 21 E

Mullewa

233 Mullewa Caravan Park

Lovers Lane. Mon-Fri 8.30-4.30pm, Aug-Oct caretaker
0439898762 HEMA 170 A3 28 32 19 S 115 30 14 E

Mundrabilla

234 Mundrabilla Roadhouse Caravan Park

Eyre Hwy
08 9039 3465 HEMA 159 J13 31 49 06 S 128 13 31 E

Munglinup Beach

235 Munglinup Beach Caravan Park

714 Munglinup Beach Rd
www.munglinupbeach.com.au
08 9075 1155 HEMA 155 G14 33 51 48 S 120 47 50 E

Munjina

236 Auski Tourist Village

Great Northern Hwy
www.auskitouristvillage.com.au
08 9176 6988 HEMA 167 J8 22 22 38 S 118 41 29 E

Munster

237 Discovery Holiday Parks Woodman Point

Cnr 132 Cockburn Rd & Magazine Ct. 10 km S of Fremantle
www.discoveryholidayparks.com.au
08 9434 1433 HEMA 148 G2 32 07 44 S 115 46 00 E

Murchison

238 Murchison Oasis Roadhouse & Caravan Park

Carnarvon Mullewa Rd
08 9961 3875 HEMA 168 G5 26 53 46 S 115 57 26 E

Myalup

239 Myalup Beach Caravan Park

Myalup Beach Rd
www.myalupbeachcaravanpark.com.au
08 9720 1113 HEMA 150 H1 33 06 10 S 115 41 27 E

Nannup

240 Nannup Caravan Park

4 Brockman St
www.nannupcaravanparks.com.au
08 9756 1211 HEMA 152 D4 33 58 34 S 115 45 54 E

Nanutarra

241 Nanutarra Roadhouse Caravan Park

North West Coastal Hwy
08 9943 0521 HEMA 166 J3 22 32 34 S 115 30 03 E

Narembeen

242 Narembeen Caravan Park

Currall St (Free 72 hour parking for self-contained)
08 9064 7308 HEMA 151 B14 32 03 49 S 118 23 46 E

Narrogin

243 Narrogin Caravan Park

80 Williams Rd. Caretaker 0427 478 333
08 9881 1944 HEMA 151 G8 32 56 14 S 117 09 48 E

Newdegate

244 Newdegate Motel & Caravan Park

Lot 201 Newdegate North Rd
08 9871 1685 HEMA 155 D10 33 05 30 S 119 01 45 E

Newman

245 Whaleback Village

1983 Cowra Dr, max stay 14 days, no open fires, no generators.
0407703340 HEMA 160 E1 23 21 02 S 119 44 31 E

Nornalup

246 Valley of the Giants Ecopark

6398 South Coast Hwy
www.valleyofthegiantsecopark.biz
08 9840 1313 HEMA 153 K9 34 59 45 S 116 50 41 E

Norseman

247 Gateway Caravan Park

Prinsep St
www.acclaimparks.com.au
08 9039 1500 HEMA 156 E4 32 11 25 S 121 46 42 E

Northam

248 Northam Caravan Park

150 Yilgarn Ave
www.northamcaravanpark.com
08 9622 1620 HEMA 170 K6 31 38 32 S 116 41 57 E

Northampton

249 Northampton Caravan Park

North West Coastal Hwy
www.northamptoncaravanpark.com.au
0439 979 489 HEMA 168 K3 28 21 08 S 114 37 50 E

Northcliffe

250 Aroundtu-It Eco Caravan Park

190 Muirillup Rd
www.aroundtu-it.com.au
08 9776 7276 HEMA 152 G6 34 38 03 S 116 08 35 E

Nullagine

251 Nullagine Caravan Park

Gallop St
08 9176 2090 HEMA 160 B2 21 53 17 S 120 06 25 E

Nungarin

252 Nungarin Caravan Park

Danberrin Rd, Brown Dr. Behind Recreation Centre
08 9046 5006 HEMA 171 H9 31 11 29 S 118 05 29 E

Nyabing

253 Nyabing Caravan Parking Facility

Martin St. Key at Shire Office
08 9829 1051 HEMA 155 F8 33 32 40 S 118 08 49 E

Ongerup

254 Ongerup Gardens Caravan Park

Cnr Walker St & Lamont St
0428 282 127 HEMA 155 G9 33 58 04 S 118 29 12 E

Onslow

255 Discovery Holiday Parks Onslow

557 Beadon Creek Rd
www.discoveryholidayparks.com.au
08 9184 6007 HEMA 166 H3 21 38 51 S 115 07 39 E

256 Ocean View Caravan Park

Second Ave
08 9184 6053 HEMA 166 H3 21 38 04 S 115 06 41 E

Ora Banda

257 Ora Banda Historical Inn
Gimlet St
www.orabanda.com.au
08 9024 2444 HEMA 158 G3 30 22 34 S 121 03 41 E

Orange Grove

258 Crystal Brook Caravan Park
388 Kelvin Rd
www.crystalbrookcaravanpark.com.au
08 9453 6226 HEMA 147 K9 32 01 05 S 116 01 08 E

Overlander

259 Overlander Roadhouse
North West Coastal Hwy
08 9942 5916 HEMA 168 G3 26 24 42 S 114 27 50 E

Pannawonica

260 Pannawonica Transit Park
Sports Way next to Tony Lyons Park. Limited sites, max 3 days
08 9184 1038 HEMA 166 H4 21 38 12 S 116 19 29 E

Paraburdoo

261 Paraburdoo Caravan Park
Camp Rd. Pay & key at Rocklea Palms Hotel
08 9189 5018 HEMA 166 K6 23 12 14 S 117 40 06 E

Pardoo

262 Pardoo Roadhouse Caravan Park
Great Northern Hwy
www.pardoo.com.au
08 9176 4916 HEMA 162 J1 20 03 14 S 119 49 39 E

Peaceful Bay

263 Peaceful Bay Caravan Park
Peaceful Bay Rd
www.peacefulbaywa.com.au
08 9840 8060 HEMA 153 K10 35 02 25 S 116 55 42 E

Pemberton

264 Pemberton Caravan Park
1 Pump Hill Rd. 700m W of PO
www.pembertonpark.com.au
08 9776 1300 HEMA 152 F6 34 26 36 S 116 01 30 E

Perenjori

265 Perenjori Caravan Park
137 Crossing Rd
08 9973 1193 HEMA 170 C5 29 26 09 S 116 17 17 E

Picton East

266 Waterloo Village Caravan Park
14749 South Western Hwy
www.waterloovillage.com.au
08 9725 4434 HEMA 150 K2 33 20 21 S 115 43 25 E

Pingelly

267 Pingelly Caravan Park
26 Sharrow St. Pay & key at Craft Centre
08 9887 1351 HEMA 151 E8 32 32 09 S 117 05 07 E

Pingrup

268 Pingrup Caravan Park
18 Sanderson St. Pay at CRC, AH on notice board
08 9820 1101 HEMA 155 F9 33 32 05 S 118 30 40 E

Pinjarra

269 Pinjarra Cabins & Caravan Park
1716 Pinjarra Rd
www.pinjarracaravanpark.com.au
08 9531 1374 HEMA 150 E2 32 36 59 S 115 51 23 E

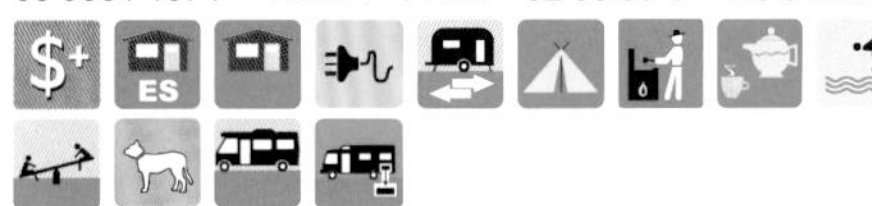

270 Pinjarra Holiday Park
326 Pinjarra Williams Rd. Blythewood. 3.5 km S of PO
08 9531 1604 HEMA 150 F2 32 39 22 S 115 52 39 E

Point Samson

271 Samson Beach Caravan Park
44 Bartley Ct
www.samsonbeach.com.au
08 9187 1414 HEMA 166 F6 20 37 50 S 117 11 46 E

272 The Cove Holiday Village
Lot 259 Macleod St
www.thecoveholidayvillage.com.au
08 9187 0199 HEMA 166 F6 20 37 56 S 117 11 48 E

Popanyinning

273 LazeAway Holiday Farm & Caravan Park
Great Southern Hwy. 4 km S of PO
08 9887 5027 HEMA 151 F8 32 41 34 S 117 08 40 E

Porongurup

274 Porongurup Range Tourist Park
7 Boxhill Rd
www.porongurupranegetouristpark.com.au
08 9853 1057 HEMA 153 H14 34 39 35 S 117 53 40 E

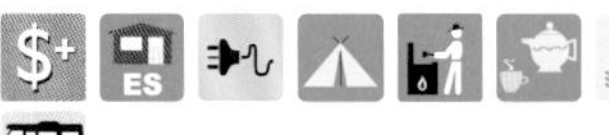

Port Gregory

275 Port Gregory Caravan Park
13 Sanford St
www.portgregorycaravanpark.com.au
08 9935 1052 HEMA 168 J3 28 11 17 S 114 15 04 E

Port Hedland

276 Discovery Holiday Parks Port Hedland
Cnr Athol St & Taylor St. 8 km E of PO
www.discoveryholidayparks.com.au
08 9173 1271 HEMA 167 F8 20 18 36 S 118 38 17 E

277 Port Tourist Park
945 Great Northern Hwy
www.porttouristpark.com.au
08 9172 4111 HEMA 167 F8 20 22 30 S 118 38 01 E

Port Smith

278 Port Smith Caravan Park
Port Smith Rd
www.portsmithcaravanpark.com.au
08 9192 4983 HEMA 162 F4 18 31 00 S 121 48 52 E

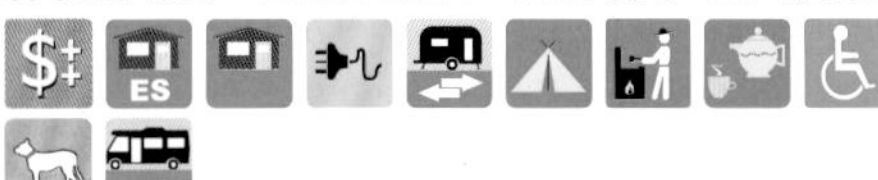

Quairading

279 Quairading Caravan Park
McLennan St
08 9645 1001 HEMA 151 B9 32 00 44 S 117 24 09 E

Quinninup

280 Quinninup Eco Tourist Park
Wheatley Coast Rd
08 9773 1329 HEMA 152 F7 34 26 11 S 116 14 44 E

Ravensthorpe

281 Green Haven Tourist Park
South Coast Hwy
www.greenhaventouristpark.com.au
0439 369 838 HEMA 155 F13 33 34 47 S 120 03 11 E

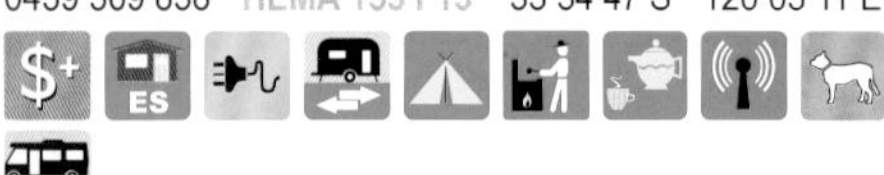

Regans Ford

282 Regans Ford Caravan Park
Harris St
08 9655 0007 HEMA 170 H3 30 58 58 S 115 42 08 E

Rockingham

283 Cee & See Caravan Park
2 Governor Rd
08 9527 1297 HEMA 150 C2 32 15 46 S 115 44 56 E

284 Rockingham Holiday Village
147 Dixon Rd
08 9527 4240 HEMA 150 D2 32 16 35 S 115 46 58 E

Roebourne

285 Harding River Caravan Park
Jiwuna Way, via De Grey St
08 9182 1063 HEMA 166 F6 20 46 35 S 117 09 01 E

Roebuck Plains

286 Roebuck Plains Roadhouse & Caravan Park
Great Northern Hwy
www.roebuckroadhouse.com
08 9192 1880 HEMA 162 E5 17 50 53 S 122 30 03 E

Salmon Gums

287 Salmon Gums Community Caravan Park
Nulsen St. Caretaker collects fees
HEMA 156 G3 32 58 55 S 121 38 53 E

Sandfire

288 Sandfire Roadhouse
Port Headland Rd
08 9176 5944 HEMA 162 H3 19 46 07 S 121 05 26 E

Sandstone

289 Alice Atkinson Caravan Park
Irvine St, no bookings required
08 9963 5859 HEMA 169 J10 27 59 23 S 119 17 50 E

Serpentine

290 Serpentine Falls Park Home & Tourist Village
2489 South Western Hwy
www.serpentinepark.com.au
08 9525 2528 HEMA 150 D3 32 22 00 S 115 59 31 E

South Hedland

291 Black Rock Tourist Park
2115 North Circular Rd
www.blackrocktouristpark.com.au
08 9172 3444 HEMA 167 F8 20 23 36 S 118 36 15 E

Southern Cross

292 Southern Cross Caravan Park & Motor Lodge
Great Eastern Hwy
08 9049 1212 HEMA 171 H12 31 13 45 S 119 20 11 E

Stirling Range

293 Mt Trio Bush Camp & Caravan Park
4850 Salt River Rd, Amelup
www.mounttrio.com.au
0419 751 801 HEMA 155 H8 34 18 14 S 118 02 49 E

294 Stirling Range Retreat
8639 Chester Pass Rd, 300m N Bluff Knoll turnoff
www.stirlingrange.com.au
08 9827 9229 HEMA 155 H8 34 18 57 S 118 11 32 E

Tom Price

295 Tom Price Tourist Park
Nameless Valley Dr
www.tompricetouristpark.com.au
08 9189 1515 HEMA 166 J6 22 41 48 S 117 45 49 E

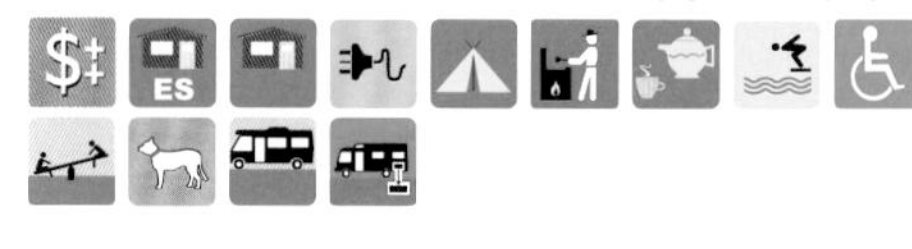

Toodyay

296 Toodyay Caravan Park
122 Railway Rd
08 9574 2612 HEMA 170 J5 31 32 43 S 116 27 07 E

297 Toodyay Holiday Park & Chalets
188 Racecourse Rd
www.toodyaycaravanparks.com.au
08 9574 2534 HEMA 170 J5 31 34 18 S 116 27 36 E

Trayning

298 Shire of Trayning Caravan Park
Bencubbin - Kellerberrin Rd. Next to sportsground
08 9683 1001 HEMA 171 H8 31 06 38 S 117 47 37 E

Wagin

299 Wagin Caravan Park
Cnr of Arthur Rd & Scadden St. 1 km W of PO. AH 0419 611 057
www.wagin.wa.gov.au
08 9861 1177 HEMA 151 J9 33 18 39 S 117 20 05 E

Walpole

300 Coalmine Beach Holiday Park
Coalmine Beach Rd
www.coalminebeach.com.au
08 9840 1026 HEMA 153 J9 34 59 22 S 116 44 24 E

301 Rest Point Holiday Village
Rest Point Rd
www.restpoint.com.au
08 9840 1032 HEMA 153 J9 34 59 13 S 116 43 11 E

Wandering

302 Wandering Caravan Park
Cheetaning St. Pay at Shire Office, AH at tavern
08 9884 1056 HEMA 150 F6 32 41 03 S 116 40 29 E

Warakurna

303 Warakurna Roadhouse
Great Central Rd
www.warakurnaroadhouse.com.au
08 8956 7344 HEMA 161 G13 25 02 34 S 128 18 12 E

Warmun

304 Bungle Bungle Caravan Park
Great Northern Hwy, at entrance to Bungle Bungle NP. Limited power. Open April - Sept.
www.bunglebunglecaravanpark.com.au
08 9168 7220 HEMA 165 K12 17 25 49 S 127 59 34 E

305 Warmun Roadhouse Caravan Park
Great Northern Hwy
www.warmunroadhouse.com
08 9168 7882 HEMA 165 J12 17 00 59 S 128 13 01 E

Waroona

306 Lake Navarino Holiday Park
147 Invarell Rd
www.navarino.com.au
08 9733 3000 HEMA 150 G3 32 50 42 S 115 58 37 E

307 Waroona Caravan Village
45 Logue St. All ensuite sites
www.waroonavillage.com.au
08 9733 1518 HEMA 150 G3 32 51 00 S 115 55 47 E

West Gingin

308 Back to Nature Caravan Park
1800 Cowalla Rd, Wanerie
www.backtonaturecaravanpark.com.au
08 9655 3025 HEMA 170 H3 31 09 55 S 115 34 04 E

West Swan

309 Swan Valley Tourist Park
6581 West Swan Rd. 6.5 km N of Guilford PO
www.acclaimparks.com.au
08 9274 2828 HEMA 147 D8 31 50 20 S 115 59 25 E

Westonia

310 Westonia Caravan Park
Cnr Kaolin & Wolfram St
08 9046 7063 HEMA 171 J10 31 18 16 S 118 41 50 E

Wickepin

311 Wickepin Caravan Park
Wogolin Rd. Behind Police Station
0428 177 952 HEMA 151 F10 32 46 52 S 117 30 12 E

Widgiemooltha

312 Widgiemooltha Roadhouse Motel & Caravan Park
Lot 124 Kingswood St
08 9020 8030 HEMA 156 C3 31 29 45 S 121 34 44 E

Willare

313 Willare Bridge Roadhouse & Caravan Park
Great Northen Hwy
08 9191 4775 HEMA 162 E6 17 43 35 S 123 39 15 E

Williams

314 Williams Motel & Shady Acre Caravan Park
Williams St
08 9885 1192 HEMA 150 H7 33 01 55 S 116 52 53 E

Wongan Hills

315 Wongan Hills Caravan Park
65 Wongan Road
www.wonganhillscaravanpark.com.au
08 9671 1009 HEMA 170 G6 30 53 21 S 116 42 53 E

Woodanilling

316 Woodanilling Caravan Park
Cnr Robinson Rd & Great Southern Hwy
08 9823 1681 HEMA 153 A12 33 33 51 S 117 25 26 E

Wooramel

317 Wooramel Roadhouse Caravan Park

North West Coastal Hwy
08 9942 5910 HEMA 168 F3 25 46 13 S 114 17 40 E

Wyalkatchem

318 Wyalkatchem Travellers Park

Lot 408 Hands Drv (Goomalling-Merredin Rd)
0475 263 099 HEMA 170 H7 31 10 59 S 117 22 46 E

Wyndham

319 Wyndham Caravan Park

9 Baker St
www.wyndhamcaravanpark.com
08 9161 1064 HEMA 165 E12 15 28 53 S 128 06 53 E

Yalgoo

320 Yalgoo Caravan Park

Gibbons St
08 9962 8472 HEMA 168 K6 28 20 40 S 116 40 54 E

Yallingup

321 Caves Caravan Park

23 Yallingup Beach Rd
www.cavescaravanpark.com.au
08 9755 2196 HEMA 152 B1 33 38 47 S 115 01 55 E

322 Yallingup Beach Holiday Park

186 Yallingup Beach Rd
www.yallingupbeach.com.au
08 9755 2164 HEMA 152 B1 33 38 25 S 115 01 32 E

Yealering

323 Lake Yealering Caravan Park

Sewell Rd
0428 787 426 HEMA 151 E10 32 35 37 S 117 37 32 E

York

324 York Caravan Park

2 Eighth Rd, off Bland Rd
08 9641 1421 HEMA 150 A6 31 51 52 S 116 46 11 E

Key Map

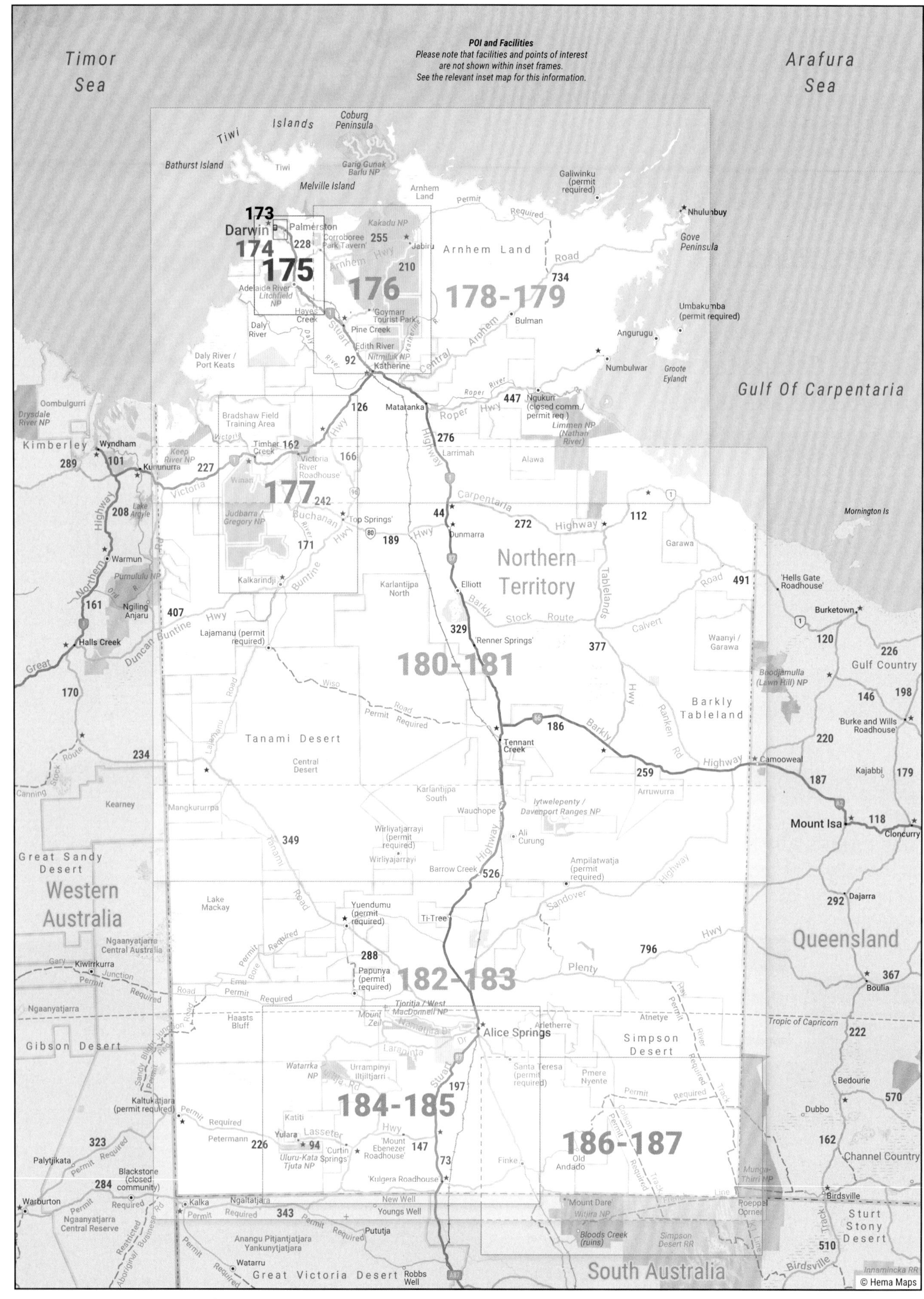
POI and Facilities
Please note that facilities and points of interest are not shown within inset frames.
See the relevant inset map for this information.
Timor Sea
Arafura Sea
Gulf Of Carpentaria
Northern Territory
Western Australia
Queensland
South Australia
173
174
175
176
177
178-179
180-181
182-183
184-185
186-187
Darwin
Palmerston
Katherine
Tennant Creek
Alice Springs
Mount Isa
© Hema Maps

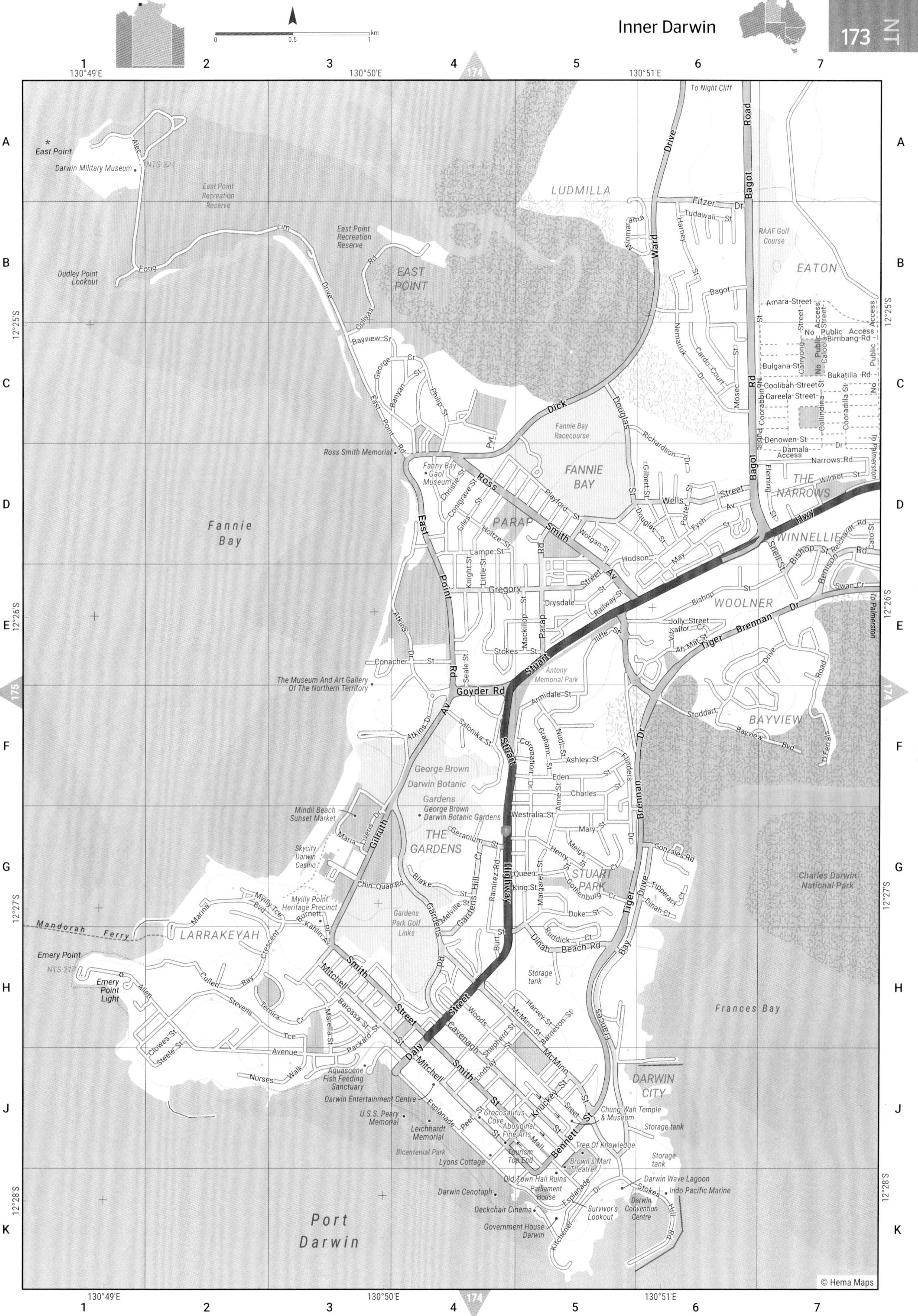
East Point
Darwin Military Museum
East Point Recreation Reserve
Dudley Point Lookout
LUDMILLA
EAST POINT
EATON
RAAF Golf Course
Ross Smith Memorial
Fannie Bay Gaol Museum
Fannie Bay Racecourse
FANNIE BAY
THE NARROWS
PARAP
WINNELLIE
Fannie Bay
WOOLNER
The Museum And Art Gallery Of The Northern Territory
Antony Memorial Park
BAYVIEW
George Brown Darwin Botanic Gardens
Mindil Beach Sunset Market
Skycity Darwin Casino
THE GARDENS
STUART PARK
Charles Darwin National Park
Myilly Point Heritage Precinct
Mandorah Ferry
LARRAKEYAH
Gardens Park Golf Links
Emery Point
Emery Point Light
Storage tank
Frances Bay
Aquascene Fish Feeding Sanctuary
DARWIN CITY
Darwin Entertainment Centre
U.S.S. Peary Memorial
Leichhardt Memorial
Crocosaurus Cove
Aboriginal Fine Arts
Chung Wah Temple & Museum
Tree Of Knowledge
Bicentenial Park
Lyons Cottage
Tourism Top End
Brown's Mart Theatre
Old Town Hall Ruins
Parliament House
Darwin Wave Lagoon
Indo Pacific Marine
Darwin Cenotaph
Deckchair Cinema
Survivor's Lookout
Darwin Convention Centre
Government House Darwin
Port Darwin
Stuart Highway
Tiger Brennan Dr
Dick Ward Drive
Bagot Road
East Point Rd
Smith Street
Mitchell St
Daly St
Cavenagh St
Knuckey St
Bennett St
Esplanade
Gilruth Av
Goyder Rd
Ross Smith Av
To Night Cliff
To Palmerston
© Hema Maps

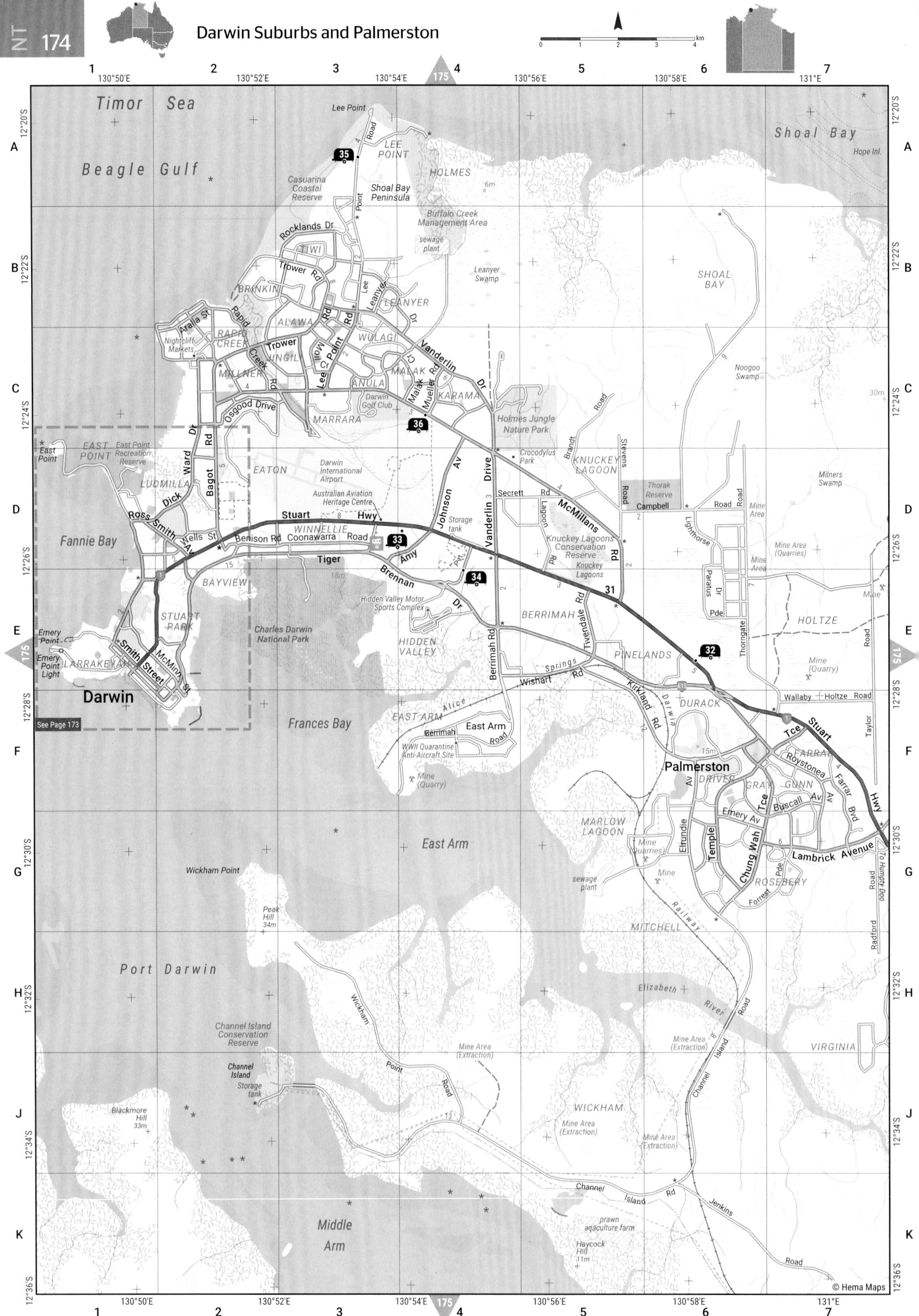
Timor Sea
Beagle Gulf
Shoal Bay
Fannie Bay
Frances Bay
East Arm
Port Darwin
Middle Arm
Darwin
Palmerston
Lee Point
Shoal Bay Peninsula
Casuarina Coastal Reserve
Buffalo Creek Management Area
Leanyer Swamp
Holmes Jungle Nature Park
Darwin International Airport
Australian Aviation Heritage Centre
Charles Darwin National Park
Hidden Valley Motor Sports Complex
Knuckey Lagoons Conservation Reserve
Thorak Reserve
WWII Quarantine Anti-Aircraft Site
Channel Island Conservation Reserve
Wickham Point
Emery Point Light
Nightcliff Markets
Darwin Golf Club
Crocodylus Park
Stuart Hwy
See Page 173
© Hema Maps

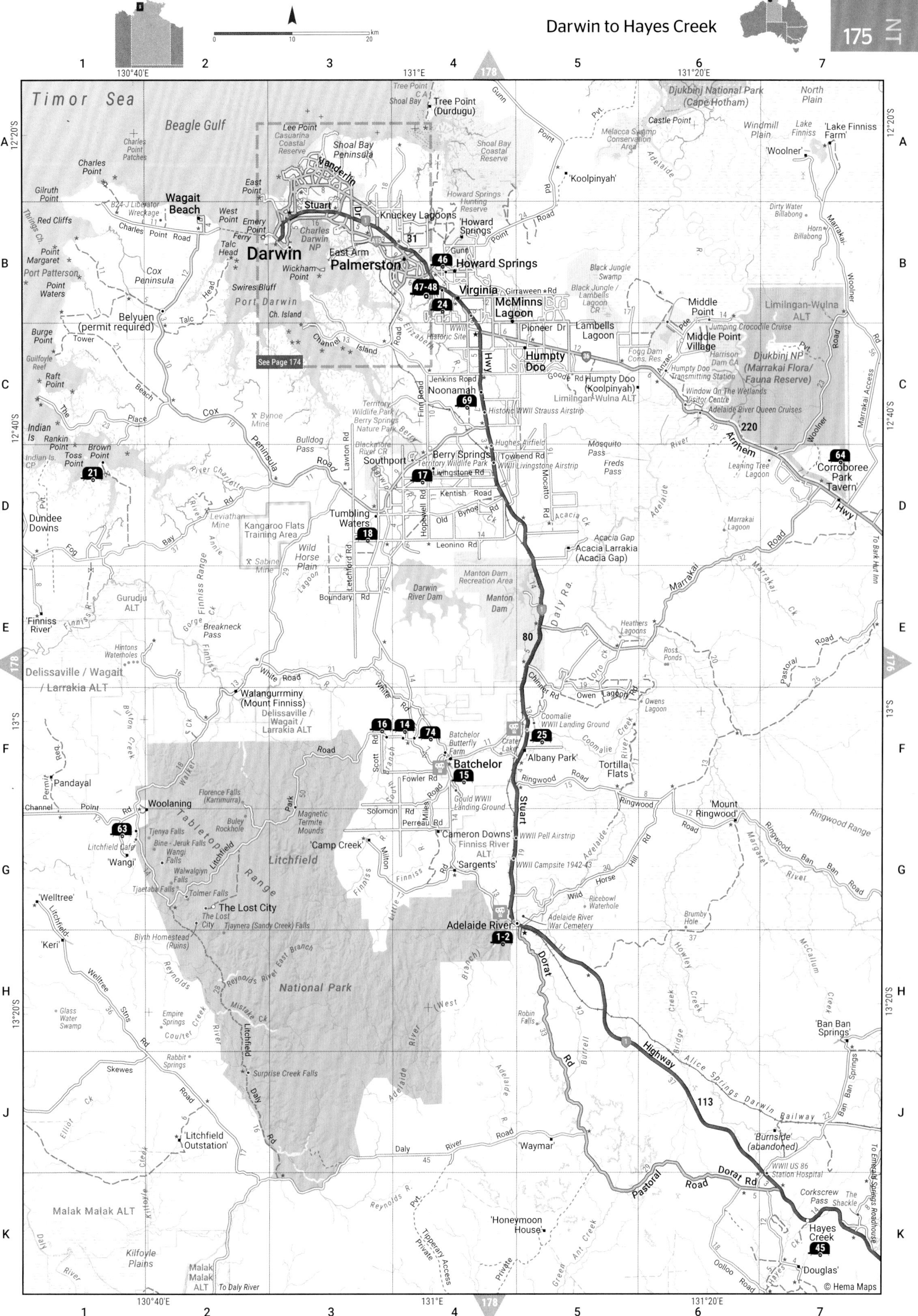
Timor Sea
Beagle Gulf
Darwin
Palmerston
Howard Springs
Virginia
McMinns Lagoon
Humpty Doo
Noonamah
Berry Springs
Tumbling Waters
Batchelor
Adelaide River
Hayes Creek
Litchfield National Park
Tabletop Range
Djukbinj NP (Marrakai Flora/Fauna Reserve)
Stuart Hwy
Arnhem Hwy
Dorat Rd
© Hema Maps

Kakadu National Park

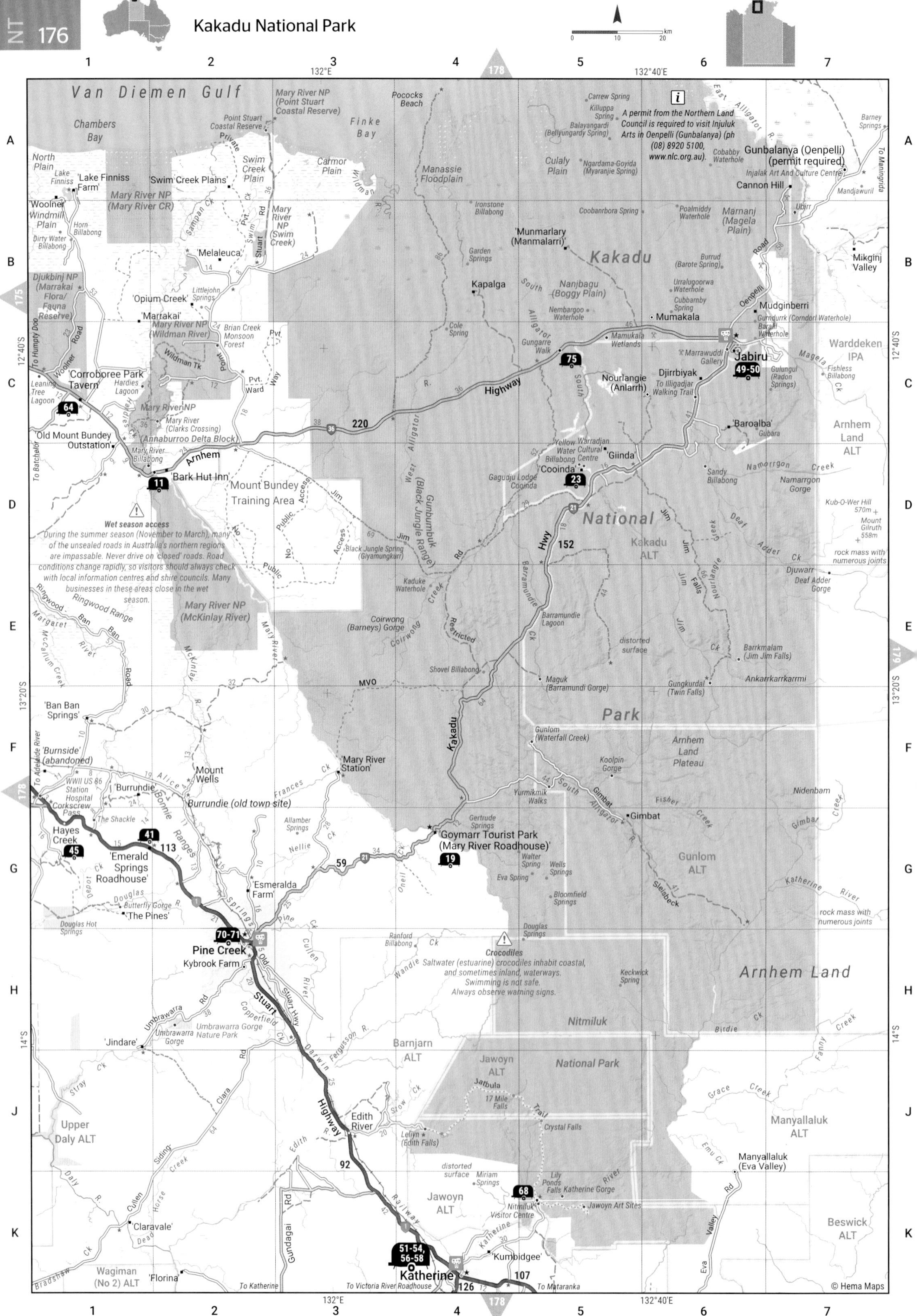

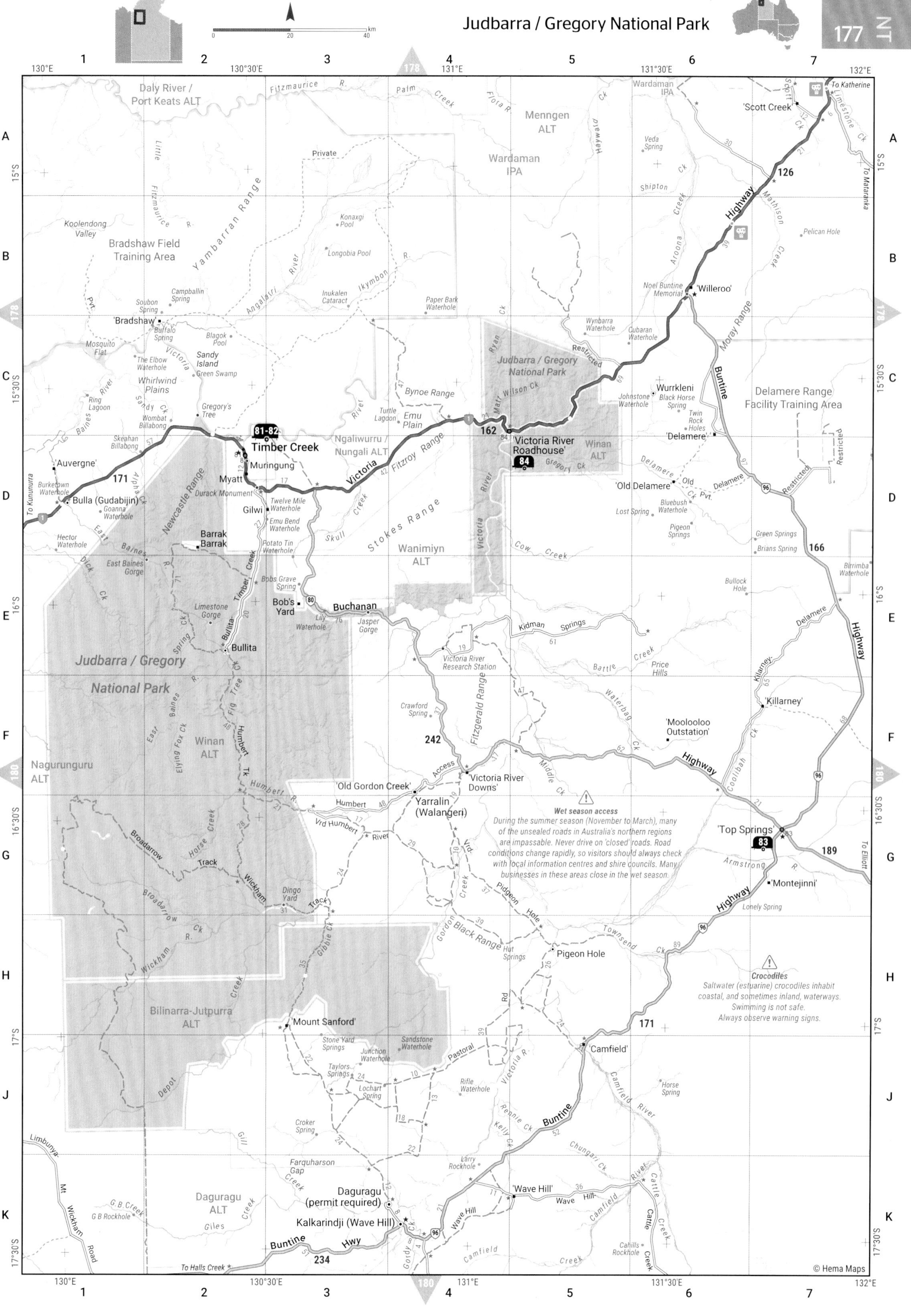
Daly River / Port Keats ALT
Menngen ALT
Wardaman IPA
Bradshaw Field Training Area
Yambarran Range
Koolendong Valley
'Bradshaw'
Judbarra / Gregory National Park
Timber Creek
Muringung
Myatt
Gilwi
Barrak Barrak
Bob's Yard
Buchanan
Bullita
Ngaliwurru / Nungali ALT
Victoria River Roadhouse
Winan ALT
Wanimiyn ALT
Stokes Range
Newcastle Range
Bulla (Gudabijin)
'Auvergne'
'Willeroo'
Delamere Range Facility Training Area
'Delamere'
'Old Delamere'
Wurrkleni
Victoria River Research Station
'Killarney'
'Mooloolooo Outstation'
Nagurunguru ALT
'Old Gordon Creek'
'Victoria River Downs'
Yarralin (Walangeri)
'Top Springs'
'Montejinni'
Pigeon Hole
Bilinarra-Jutpurra ALT
'Mount Sanford'
'Camfield'
Daguragu ALT
Daguragu (permit required)
Kalkarindji (Wave Hill)
'Wave Hill'
Buntine Hwy
To Katherine
To Kununurra
To Halls Creek
To Elliott
To Mataranka
Wet season access
During the summer season (November to March), many of the unsealed roads in Australia's northern regions are impassable. Never drive on 'closed' roads. Road conditions change rapidly, so visitors should always check with local information centres and shire councils. Many businesses in these areas close in the wet season.
Crocodiles
Saltwater (estuarine) crocodiles inhabit coastal, and sometimes inland, waterways. Swimming is not safe. Always observe warning signs.
© Hema Maps

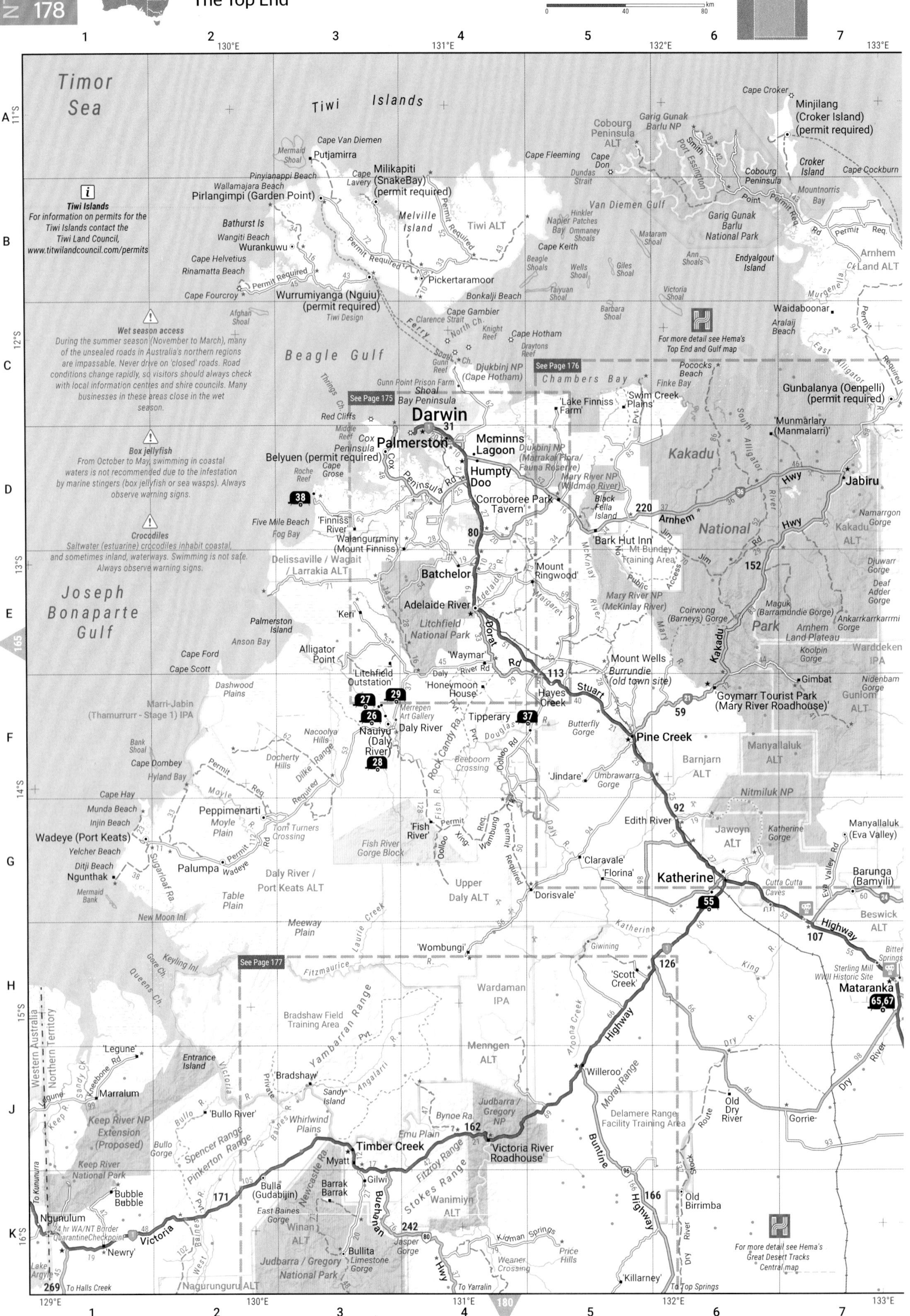
Timor Sea
Tiwi Islands
Tiwi Islands
For information on permits for the Tiwi Islands contact the Tiwi Land Council, www.titwilandcouncil.com/permits
Wet season access
During the summer season (November to March), many of the unsealed roads in Australia's northern regions are impassable. Never drive on 'closed' roads. Road conditions change rapidly, so visitors should always check with local information centres and shire councils. Many businesses in these areas close in the wet season.
Box jellyfish
From October to May, swimming in coastal waters is not recommended due to the infestation by marine stingers (box jellyfish or sea wasps). Always observe warning signs.
Crocodiles
Saltwater (estuarine) crocodiles inhabit coastal, and sometimes inland, waterways. Swimming is not safe. Always observe warning signs.
Joseph Bonaparte Gulf
Beagle Gulf
Darwin
Palmerston
Katherine
Pine Creek
Batchelor
Adelaide River
Jabiru
Kakadu National Park
Litchfield National Park
Mataranka
Timber Creek
For more detail see Hema's Top End and Gulf map
For more detail see Hema's Great Desert Tracks Central map
See Page 175
See Page 176
See Page 177

Arafura Sea
Crocodiles
Saltwater (estuarine) crocodiles inhabit coastal, and sometimes inland, waterways. Swimming is not safe. Always observe warning signs.
Visiting Aboriginal land
Permits are required to travel on most roads within Aboriginal land trust areas. Exceptions include the Roper Highway, Carpentaria Highway, Stuart Highway, Tanami Road and Tanami Mine-Lajamanu Road. In many Aboriginal communities entry permits are also required and alcohol restrictions can apply. For areas north of Tennant Creek contact the Northern Land Council, ph (08) 8920 5100, www.nlc.org.au or permits@nlc.org.au. For areas south of Tennant Creek contact the Central Land Council ph (08) 8951 6211 or www.clc.org.au. When visiting Aboriginal land please respect the traditional owners' rights. Remember, Aboriginal cultural heritage is protected by State and Federal laws and penalties apply for interfering with cultural heritage sites.
Box jellyfish
From October to May, swimming in coastal waters is not recommended due to the infestation by marine stingers (box jellyfish or sea wasps). Always observe warning signs.
Aboriginal Land
When visiting Aboriginal land please respect the traditional owners' rights. Remember, Aboriginal cultural heritage is protected by state and federal laws and penalties apply for interfering with cultural heritage sites.
For more detail see Hema's Top End and Gulf map
Central Arnhem Road
Central Arnhem Road is often closed during the wet season (Oct-Apr). Alcohol restrictions apply, and no liquor or firearms are to be carried in vehicles. No hunting or fishing is allowed. Visitors must complete the trip within 24 hours. No caravans, campervans or motorbikes are permitted.
Groote Eylandt
For information on permits for Groote Eylandt contact the Anindilyakwa Land Council, ph (08) 8987 4006 or www.anindilyakwa.com.au
Hogmanay Shoal
Cape Wessel
Marchinbar Island
South West Cape
North Crocodile Reef
Ngijipin
Warruwi (Goulburn Island)
Wunyu Beach
Junction Bay
Maningrida Arts & Culture Centre
Cape Stewart
Boucaut Bay
Elcho Island
Galiwinku (permit required)
Elcho Island Arts Centre
Cape Wilberforce
Arnhem Land
Mangardubu
Maningrida
Milingimbi (permit required)
Howard Island
Napier Peninsula
Buckingham Bay
Cape Newbald
Marthakal IPA
Nhulunbuy
Yirrkala
Oenpelli
Nabarlek
Spencer Range
Djelk IPA
Gamardi
Castlereagh Bay
Flinders Peninsula
Ulundurwi Bay
Everett Island
Arnhem Bay
Ramingining (permit required)
Gapuwiyak (Lake Evella) (permit required)
Cape Arnhem
Gove Peninsula
Dhimurru IPA
Manmoyi
Kolorbidahdah
Arafura Swamp (Muckaninnie Plains)
Gurrumuru
Laynhapuy - Stage 1 IPA
Mirrnatja
Central Arnhem Rd
Warddeken IPA
Malgawa
Caledon Bay
Bukudal
Cape Grey
Gan Gan
Arnhem Land
Barrapunta
Mitchell Ranges
Bulman Gorge
Gorpulyul
Arnhem Land ALT
Parsons Range
Cape Shield
Mount Jean
Weemol
Bulman (Gulin Gulin)
South-East Arnhem Land IPA
Coast Range
Blue Mud Bay
Cape Barrow
Bickerton Island (Amakalyuwakba)
Anindilyakwa IPA
Groote Eylandt
Andanangki
Mount Catt
Arnhem Land Plateau
Yarrawirrie Plains
Dharni
Milyakburra
Alyangula
Umbakumba (permit required)
Spit End
Endungwa Beach
Angurugu
Anindilyakwa ALT
Mainoru
Manyallaluk ALT
Miwul
Yanbakwa
Numbulwar
Urapunga ALT
Quirindi Gorge
Boomerang Lagoon
Mumpumampu
Wanmarri
Cape Beatrice
Beswick ALT
Beswick (Wugularr)
Badawarrka (Five Mile Camp)
Nummerloori
Wiyakipa Beach
Wuyagiba
Gulf of Carpentaria
Walmudga Plain
Wukointyarra Plains
Nawaparr Gorge
Rainbow Springs
'Moroak'
Ngukurr (Roper River) (closed comm./permit req.)
St Vidgeon (Ruins)
Limmen Bight Marine Park
Jilkminggan (Elsey)
Elsey NP
The Roper Savannah Way Hwy
Kewulyi (Roper Valley)
Rocky Bar Crossing
Limmen Bight
Elsey Cemetery
Mangarrayi ALT
Alawa 1 ALT
Marra ALT
Minyerri (Hodgson Downs)
Sundown Plain Paddock
Maria Lagoon
Sir Edward Pellew Group
Stuart Hwy
WWII Gorrie Air Strip
Larrimah
WWII Hospital Historic Site
Burketown Crossing
Limmen NP (Nathan River)
'Nathan River'
Yiyintyi Range
West Island
North Island
Cape Pellew
Cape Vanderlin
Vanderlin Island
Bing Bong Loading Facility
Yanyuwa (Barni - Wardimantha Awara) IPA
Alawa ALT
'Bing Bong'
'Lorella Spring'
'Maryfield'
Alexander Forrest Commemorative Cairn
'Nutwood Downs'
Minamia (Cox River)
Western Lost City
Centre Island
King Ash Bay
Pelican Spit
WW2 Daly Waters Aerodrome
Limmen NP (Billengarah)
Tawallah Range Road
Lynott's Lookout
Old Police Station Museum
Manangoora
Murrenginya Island
'Sunday Creek'
Jandanku ALT
Borroloola
Garawa
Burketown Crossing
Warby
'Jangurrie'
'Old Tanumbirini'
Daly Waters
Stuart Tree
Carpentaria Hwy
To Elliott
To Cape Crawford
Garawa ALT
Bujan (Bujana)
'Greenbank'
© Hema Maps

Timber Creek to Camooweal

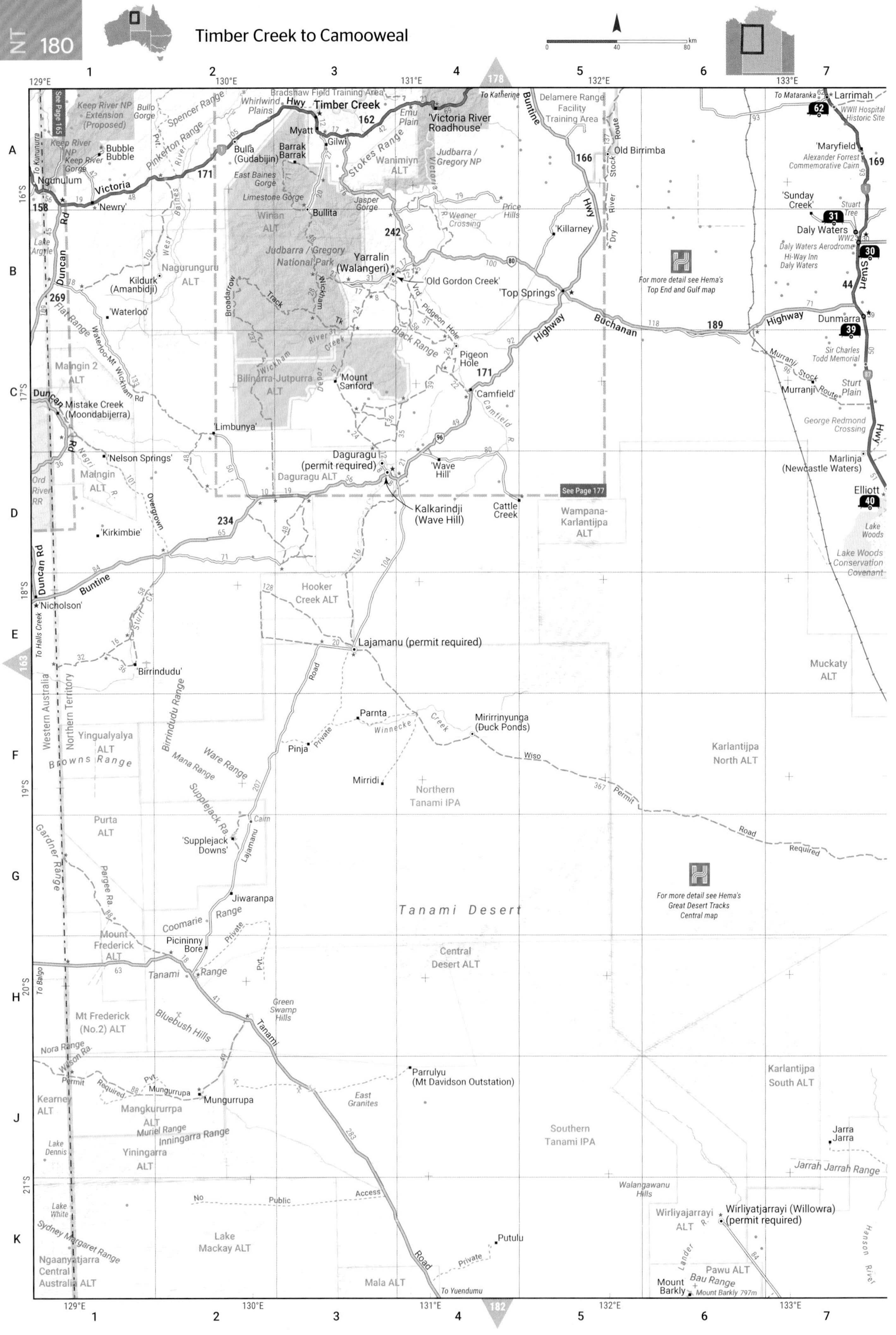

See Page 165
See Page 177

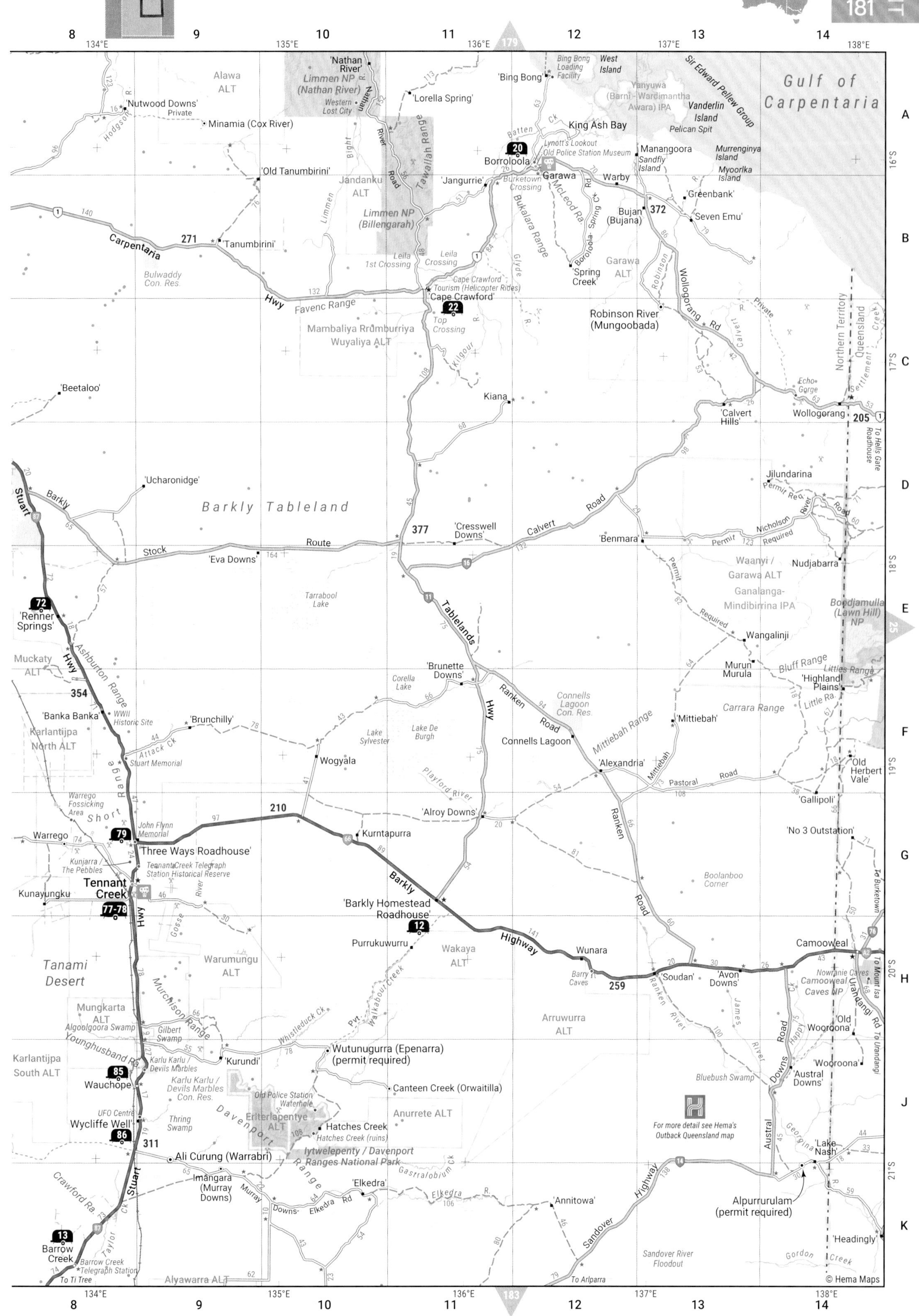

Gulf of Carpentaria
Limmen NP (Nathan River)
Limmen NP (Billengarah)
Barkly Tableland
Tanami Desert
Borroloola
King Ash Bay
Cape Crawford
Robinson River (Mungoobada)
Wollogorang
Calvert Road
Carpentaria Hwy
Stuart Hwy
Barkly Highway
Tablelands Hwy
Sandover Highway
Tennant Creek
Three Ways Roadhouse
Barkly Homestead Roadhouse
Camooweal
Wauchope
Wycliffe Well
Barrow Creek
Renner Springs
Ali Curung (Warrabri)
Wutunugurra (Epenarra) (permit required)
Canteen Creek (Orwaitilla)
Alpurrurulam (permit required)
Iytwelepenty / Davenport Ranges National Park
Boodjamulla (Lawn Hill) NP
Camooweal Caves NP
Karlu Karlu / Devils Marbles Con. Res.
For more detail see Hema's Outback Queensland map
© Hema Maps

The Red Centre

Tanami Desert

Karlantijpa North ALT

Karlantijpa South ALT

Mt Frederick (No.2) ALT

Nora Range

Bluebush Hills

Mungurrupa

Mangkururrpa ALT

Kearney ALT

Muriel Range

Inningarra Range

Yiningarra ALT

Parrulyu (Mt Davidson Outstation)

East Granites

Central Desert ALT

Jarra Jarra

Jarrah Jarrah Range

Walangawanu Hills

Southern Tanami IPA

Wirliyajarrayi ALT

Wirliyajarrayi (Willowra) (permit required)

Putulu

Lake Dennis

Lake White

Sydney Margaret Range

Murraba Ranges

No Public Access

Alcohol restrictions apply

Be aware that alcohol restrictions apply in some indigenous communities. For more information for the Northern Territory refer to their website – www.dob.nt.gov.au – and go to Liquor under Gambling and Licensing, then Liquor restricted areas under Liquor restrictions. For more information for Western Australia contact the Department of Racing, Gaming and Liquor on ph (08) 9425 1888 or their website (www.rgl.wa.gov.au). For more information for South Australia contact the Office of the Liquor and Gambling Commissioner on ph 131 882 or their website (www.olgc.sa.gov.au).

Mala ALT

Tanami Road

Bau Range

Mount Barkly 797m

Mount Barkly

Pawu ALT

Nanga Range

John McDouall Stuart Memorial

Mount Esther (abandoned)

Mt Judith 705m

Johns Range

Mount Leichhardt 1030m

Yundurbulu Range

Lander River

Ngaanyatjarra Central Australia ALT

Mount Singleton 806m

Wabudali Range

Mount Doreen 860m

Mount Hardy 810m

Yuendumu ALT

Rock Hill 880m

'Mount Denison'

Mount Treachery 720m

Giles Range

Anakeye ALT

Ti-Tree

Nturiya (permit req.)

Pmara Jutunta (Six Mile) (permit req.)

Lake Mackay

Lake Mackay ALT

Treuer Range

Djagamara Peak 814m

'Vaughan Springs'

Yuendumu (permit req.)

Wangala Hills

Yalpirakinu ALT

Yuelamu (Mount Allan) (permit req.)

Crown Hill 786m

Reynolds Range

Denison Rd

Mount Thomas 1113m

Anyungyumba (Pine Hill)

Mount Davenport 800m

Injirramurri

Permit Required

Wayililinypa

Laramba (permit req.)

Mt Caroline 751m

Mount Freeling 970m

Patty Hill 748m

Western Australia

Northern Territory

Nyirripi (Waite Creek) (permit required)

Mount Gurner 710m

Karrinyarra

'Aileron Roadhouse'

Alyuen

Campbell Range

'Newhaven'

Potato Creek Gorge

Stuart Bluff Range

The Wirmbrandt Aboriginal Art Gallery

Tilmouth Crossing

Napperby Road

Ryans Well Historic Reserve

Mount Stanley 710m

Mount Cockburn 770 m

Yunkanjini ALT

Lake Bennett

Owl Gorge

'Central Mount Wedge'

Ngalurrtju ALT

Emu Bore Required

Kiwirrkurra IPA

For more detail see Hema's Red Centre map

Lake Lewis

Injulkama

Len Beadell Plaque

Ininti

Kintore (Walungurru) (permit required)

Len Beadell Plaque

Sandy Blight Junction

Permit Required

Mount Russell 790m

Mount Liebig (permit required)

Liebig Bore Plaque

Papunya (permit required)

Mount Larrie 1070m

Junction Rd

Mount Chapple 1206m

'Amburla'

Ngutjul

Tietkens Tree

Mount Lyell Brown 872m

Ehrenberg Range

See Page 184-185

Talipata Gorge

Mangeraka Gorge

Gary Junction Rd

Mount Zeil 1531m

Redbank Hill 1090m

Mount Hay 1230m

Ceilidh Hill 922m

Adla Hill 745m

Lake Macdonald

Tropic of Capricorn

Mount Kata Kuta 750m

Winparku

Haasts Bluff (Ikuntji) (permit req.)

Mount Razorback 1274m

Tyurretye ALT

Mount Sonder 1380m

Tjoritja / West MacDonnell Nat Park

Iwupataka (Jay Creek)

Mount Udor 920m

Mount Udor (West) 849m

Mount Putardi 950m

Mount Stirling 1006m

Nguman

Pvt.

Mount Rennie 723m

Bonython Range

Len Beadell Plaque

Permit Junction

200 Mile Rock (Len Beadell)

Kungkayunti

Yateman's Bore

Mereenie Range

Mereenie Bluff 1110m

Kulpitarra

Point Helena 830m

MacDonnell Ranges

Namatjira Drive

Mount Forbes 759m

Haasts Bluff ALT

Mount Winter 800m

Lay Cocks Hill 810m

Mount Solitary 799m

That Hill 870m

Permit Required

Gosses Bluff North 830m

Larapinta Drive

Dr Owen Springs

Len Beadell Plaques

Blight

Sandy

Watson Range

Gardiner Range

Hermannsburg (Ntaria) (permit required)

Old Owen Springs (ruins)

Owen Springs Res.

Hugh

Mount Olifent 775m

Dare Plain

Mount Bowson 770m

Lake Hopkins

Carmichael Crag 906m

Walker Plain

Middle Range

Wild Eagle Plain

Mount Merrick 740m

Finke Gorge NP

Wallace Rockhole (permit required)

Petermann ALT

For more detail see Hema's Great Desert Tracks Central map

Watarrka NP

Luritja Rd

George Gill Range

Urrampinyi Iltjiltjarri ALT

Tempe Downs

James Ranges

'Orange Creek'

Tjukurla

Lake Neale

Trickett Bluff 730m

Ayers Lookout Range

Big Stone Plain

Dead Bullock Plain

Souths Range

Longs Range

Katiti Petermann IPA

Land Settlement ALT

Ukaka

Ernest Giles Road

Weather only

Ngaanyatjarra Central Reserve ALT

Bloods Range

Pinyinna Range

Rowley Range

Mt Harris

Mt Carruthers

Lake Amadeus

Angas Downs IPA

Seymour Range

Palmer River

Finke R.

Walu

McNichols Range

Liddle Hills

Luritja Rd

Stuart Hwy

Len Beadell Ghost Gum Plaque

Kaltukatjara (Docker River) (permit required)

Livingstone Pass

Ilyaralona Range

Katiti ALT

Angas Downs

Basedow Ra.

Mount Ebenezer 702m

Erldunda Range

'Mount Ebenezer Roadhouse'

Mt Sunday Ra

Schwerin Mural Crescent Sign

Petermann Ranges

Lasseters Cave

Tjunti

Tjukaruru Road (Docker River Road)

Puta Puta

Permit Required

Lasseter Highway

Yulara

Kata Tjuta / Mount Olga 1066m

Uluru-Kata Tjuta ALT

'Erldunda'

Mount Deering 853m

Mount Bearteaux 829m

Mount Fagan 870m

Pottoyu Hills

Mount Phillips 874m

Mount McCulloch 832m

Uluru / Ayers Rock 863m

Curtin Springs

Murphys Range

To Warakurna Roadhouse

Kurkatingara

Mulyati

Pilakatal

Katamala Cone 800m

Mantapayika

Mutitjulu (permit required)

Mount Conner 820m

See Page 140

Duffield Rocks 839m

Stevenson Peak 1025m

Private

Uluru -Kata Tjuta NP

See Page 138-139

'Lyndavale'

Butler Dome 1102m

Umutju

Mount Jenkins 844m

Allanah Hill 885m

Benda Hill 741m

Mount Robert 796m

Mulga Park Road

Mount Daisy Bates 785m

Alkatja

Private

Gordon Hill 938m

Von Doussa Hill 908m

'Kulgera Roadhouse'

Irrunytju (Wingellina) (closed comm./ permit req.)

'Mulga Park'

Mulga Park Road

Ayers Range

Mt Gosse 884m

To Blackstone

Mount Charles 1332m

Northern Territory

South Australia

Alpara

Hwy

Mount Mann 1169m

Walytjatjata

Mount Fraser 928m

New Well

Ilykuwaratja

Inarki

Mann Ranges

Mount Morris 1303m

Gosse Bore

Kalka

Gunbarrel

Kanpi

Umpukulu

Amata (Musgrave Park)

Youngs Well

Yunyarinyi (Kenmore Park)

Ngaanyatjarra IPA

Pipalyatjara

Puta Puta

Permit Required

Ngaltatjara

Anangu Pitjantjatjara Yankunytjatjara

Apara - Makiri - Punti IPA

Ngarutjara

Balfours Well

Mount West 858m

Kalka

Pipalyatjara IPA

Mount Hardy 1061m

Tankaanu

Yurangka

To Indulkana

WA

SA

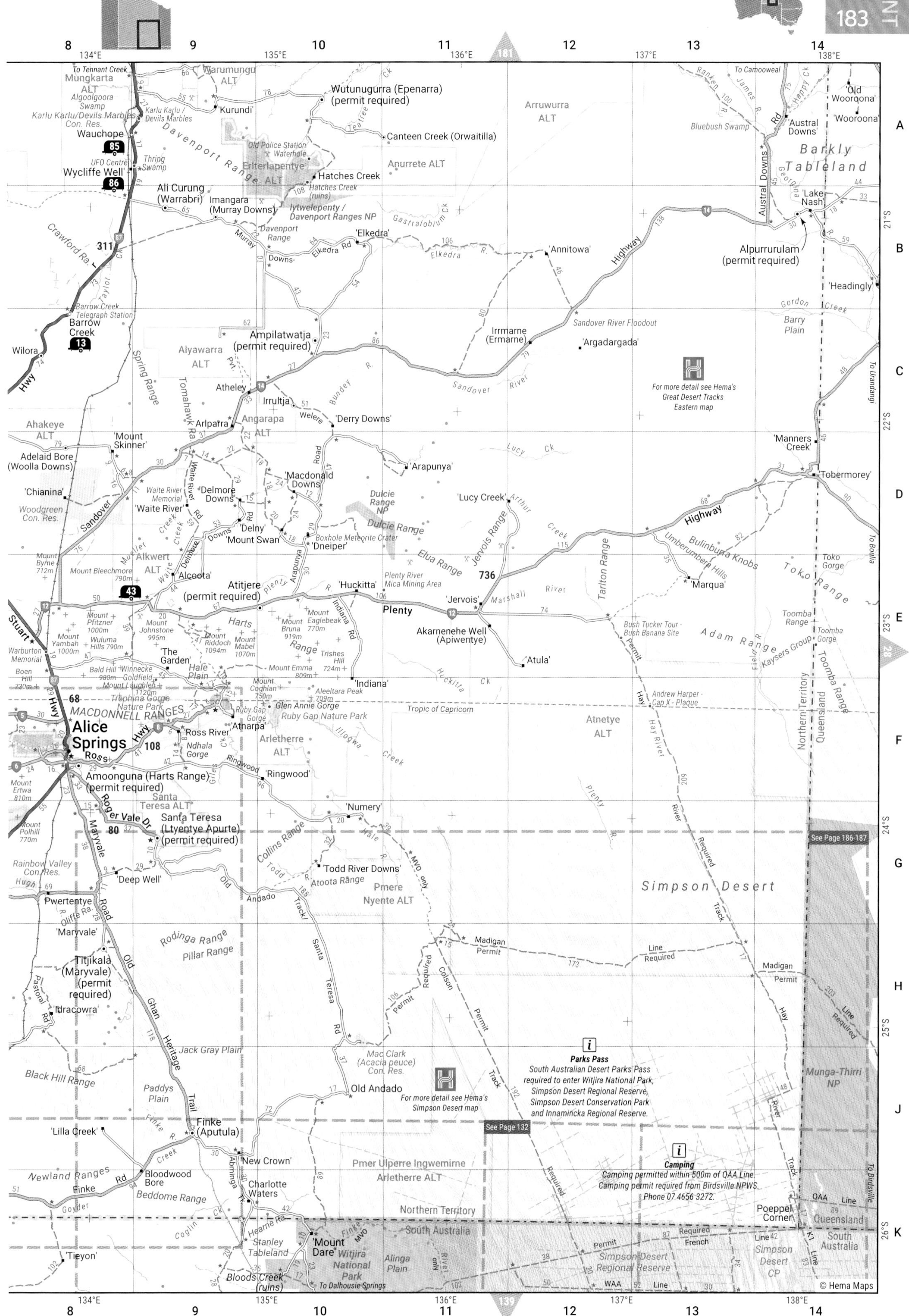

To Tennant Creek
Mungkarta ALT
Warumungu ALT
Algoolgoora Swamp
Karlu Karlu/Devils Marbles Con. Res.
'Kurundi'
Wutunugurra (Epenarra) (permit required)
Canteen Creek (Orwaitilla)
Arruwurra ALT
To Camooweal
Ranken R.
James R.
Bluebush Swamp
'Austral Downs'
'Old Wooroona'
'Wooroona'
Barkly Tableland
Wauchope
Davenport Range
Old Police Station Waterhole
Erlterlapentye ALT
Hatches Creek
Hatches Creek (ruins)
Anurrete ALT
UFO Centre
Thring Swamp
Wycliffe Well
Ali Curung (Warrabri)
Imangara (Murray Downs)
Iytwelepenty / Davenport Ranges NP
Gastralobium Ck
Austral Downs Rd
'Lake Nash'
Alpurrurulam (permit required)
Crawford Ra
Davenport Range
Murray Downs Rd
'Elkedra'
Elkedra Rd
Elkedra R.
'Annitowa'
Highway
'Headingly'
Taylor Ck
Barrow Creek Telegraph Station
Barrow Creek
Wilora
Stuart Hwy
Ampilatwatja (permit required)
Alyawarra ALT
Sandover River Floodout
Irrmarne (Ermarne)
'Argadargada'
Gordon Creek
Barry Plain
For more detail see Hema's Great Desert Tracks Eastern map
To Urandangi
Spring Range
Tomahawk Ra
Atheley
Irrultja
Welere
Bundey R.
Sandover River
'Derry Downs'
Arlparra
Angarapa ALT
Ahakeye ALT
'Mount Skinner'
Adelaide Bore (Woolla Downs)
'Arapunya'
Lucy Ck
'Manners Creek'
'Tobermorey'
'Chianina'
Woodgreen Con. Res.
Waite River Memorial
'Waite River'
'Delmore Downs'
'Macdonald Downs'
Dulcie Range NP
Dulcie Range
'Lucy Creek'
Arthur Creek
Jervois Range
Bulinbuna Knobs
Umberumberka Hills
Highway
To Boulia
Sandover
Waite Creek
Delmore Downs Rd
'Delny'
Mount Swan
'Dneiper'
Boxhole Meteorite Crater
Elua Range
Tarlton Range
'Marqua'
Toko Gorge
Toko Range
Mount Byrne 712m
Mount Bleechmore 790m
Alkwert ALT
Mueller Ck
'Alcoota'
Atitjere (permit required)
Plenty River Mica Mining Area
'Huckitta'
Indiana Rd
'Jervois'
Marshall River
Plenty
Akarnenehe Well (Apiwentye)
'Atula'
Bush Tucker Tour - Bush Banana Site
Adam Range
Kaysers Group
Toomba Range
Toomba Gorge
Mount Pfitzner 1000m
Mount Yambah 1000m
Wuluma Hills 790m
Mount Johnstone 995m
Harts Range
Mount Riddoch 1094m
Mount Mabel 1070m
Mount Bruna 919m
Mount Eaglebeak 770m
Trishes Hill 724m
Warburton Memorial
'The Garden'
Boen Hill 730m
Bald Hill 980m
Winnecke Goldfield
Mount Laughlen 1120m
Hale Plain
Mount Emma 809m
'Indiana'
Huckitta Ck
Mount Coghlan 750m
Aleeltara Peak 709m
Andrew Harper - Cap X - Plaque
Hay Permit
Trephina Gorge Nature Park
MACDONNELL RANGES
Ruby Gap Gorge
Glen Annie Gorge
Ruby Gap Nature Park
Tropic of Capricorn
Atnetye ALT
Northern Territory
Queensland
Alice Springs
Hwy
'Ross River'
'Atnarpa'
Ndhala Gorge
Arletherre ALT
Illogwa Creek
Hay River
Ross
Amoonguna (Harts Range) (permit required)
Ringwood
'Ringwood'
Plenty R.
Mount Ertwa 810m
Santa Teresa ALT
'Numery'
Roger Vale Dr
Santa Teresa (Ltyentye Apurte) (permit required)
Mount Polhill 770m
Maryvale
Collins Range
Hale R.
MVO only
River Required
See Page 186-187
Rainbow Valley Con. Res.
'Deep Well'
Todd R.
'Todd River Downs'
Atoota Range
Pmere Nyente ALT
Simpson Desert
Hugh R.
Old Andado Track
Pwertentye
Oliffe Ra.
Road
'Maryvale'
Rodinga Range
Pillar Range
Santa Teresa Rd
Madigan Permit
Line Required
Colson Permit
Titjikala (Maryvale) (permit required)
Old Ghan Heritage Trail
Madigan Permit
Pastoral Rd
'Idracowra'
Permit
Permit Required
Line Required
Hay River
Jack Gray Plain
Mac Clark (Acacia peuce) Con. Res.
Parks Pass
South Australian Desert Parks Pass required to enter Witjira National Park, Simpson Desert Regional Reserve, Simpson Desert Conservation Park and Innamincka Regional Reserve.
Black Hill Range
Paddys Plain
Old Andado
For more detail see Hema's Simpson Desert map
Munga-Thirri NP
Finke R.
Finke (Aputula)
See Page 132
'Lilla Creek'
'New Crown'
Camping
Camping permitted within 500m of QAA Line. Camping permit required from Birdsville NPWS. Phone 07 4656 3272.
Pmer Ulperre Ingwemirne Arletherre ALT
Track Required
To Birdsville
Newland Ranges
Bloodwood Bore
Finke Rd
Beddome Range
Charlotte Waters
Goyder
Northern Territory
South Australia
Poeppel Corner
QAA Line
Queensland
South Australia
Hearne Rd
Coglin Ck
Stanley Tableland
'Mount Dare'
Witjira National Park
Alinga Plain
Finke MVO only
River only
Permit
Required French
Simpson Desert Regional Reserve
Simpson Desert CP
K1 Line
'Tieyon'
Bloods Creek (ruins)
To Dalhousie Springs
WAA Line
© Hema Maps

Uluru / Ayers Rock to Alice Springs

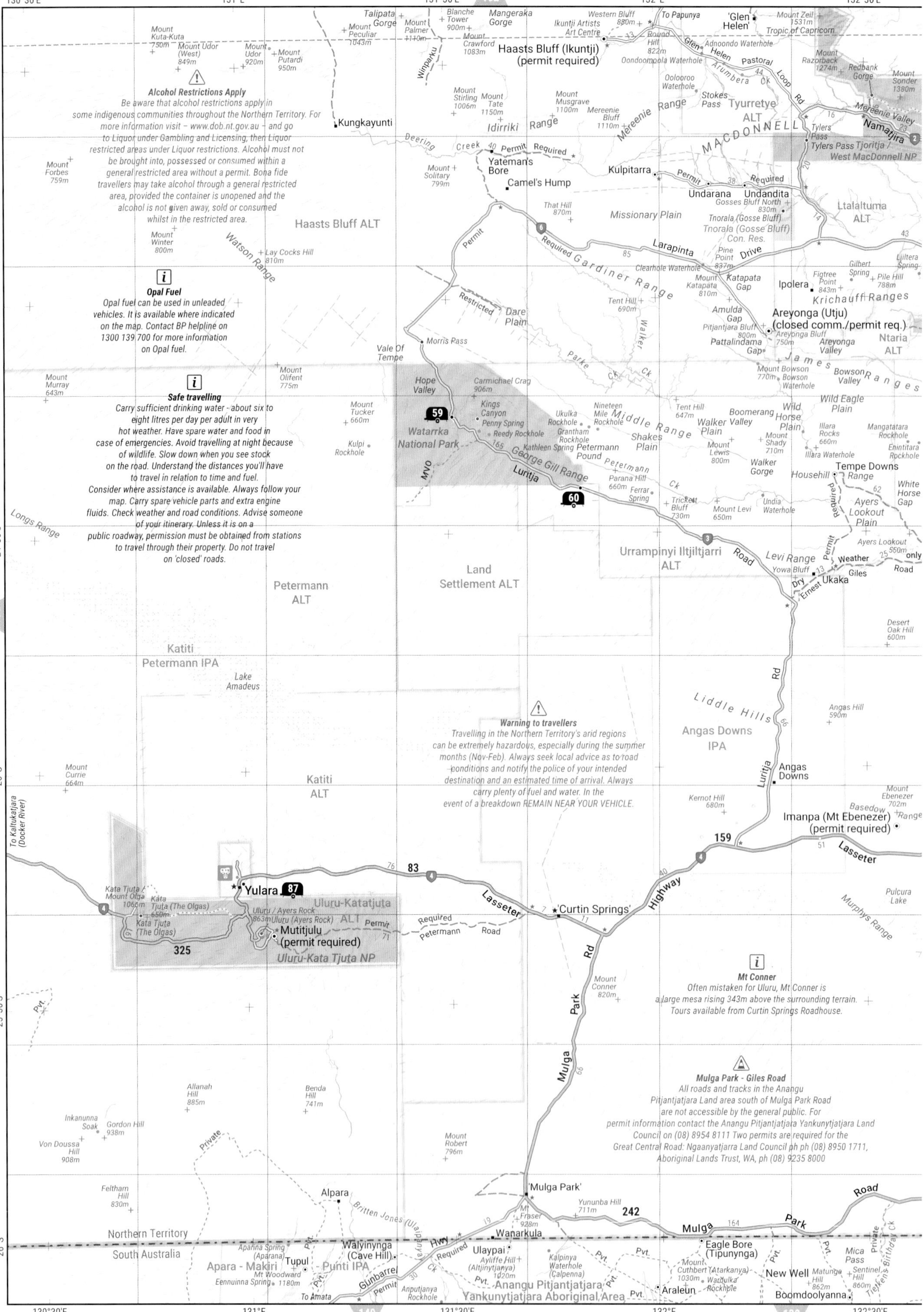

0
20
40
km
130°30'E
131°E
131°30'E
132°E
132°30'E
23°30'S
24°S
24°30'S
25°S
25°30'S
26°S
182
140
138
Alcohol Restrictions Apply
Be aware that alcohol restrictions apply in some indigenous communities throughout the Northern Territory. For more information visit – www.dob.nt.gov.au – and go to Liquor under Gambling and Licensing, then Liquor restricted areas under Liquor restrictions. Alcohol must not be brought into, possessed or consumed within a general restricted area without a permit. Bona fide travellers may take alcohol through a general restricted area, provided the container is unopened and the alcohol is not given away, sold or consumed whilst in the restricted area.
Opal Fuel
Opal fuel can be used in unleaded vehicles. It is available where indicated on the map. Contact BP helpline on 1300 139 700 for more information on Opal fuel.
Safe travelling
Carry sufficient drinking water - about six to eight litres per day per adult in very hot weather. Have spare water and food in case of emergencies. Avoid travelling at night because of wildlife. Slow down when you see stock on the road. Understand the distances you'll have to travel in relation to time and fuel. Consider where assistance is available. Always follow your map. Carry spare vehicle parts and extra engine fluids. Check weather and road conditions. Advise someone of your itinerary. Unless it is on a public roadway, permission must be obtained from stations to travel through their property. Do not travel on 'closed' roads.
Warning to travellers
Travelling in the Northern Territory's arid regions can be extremely hazardous, especially during the summer months (Nov-Feb). Always seek local advice as to road conditions and notify the police of your intended destination and an estimated time of arrival. Always carry plenty of fuel and water. In the event of a breakdown REMAIN NEAR YOUR VEHICLE.
Mt Conner
Often mistaken for Uluru, Mt Conner is a large mesa rising 343m above the surrounding terrain. Tours available from Curtin Springs Roadhouse.
Mulga Park - Giles Road
All roads and tracks in the Anangu Pitjantjatjara Land area south of Mulga Park Road are not accessible by the general public. For permit information contact the Anangu Pitjantjatjara Yankunytjatjara Land Council on (08) 8954 8111 Two permits are required for the Great Central Road: Ngaanyatjarra Land Council ph ph (08) 8950 1711, Aboriginal Lands Trust, WA, ph (08) 9235 8000
Haasts Bluff (Ikuntji) (permit required)
Kungkayunti
Haasts Bluff ALT
Yateman's Bore
Camel's Hump
Kulpitarra
Undarana
Undandita
Missionary Plain
Larapinta Drive
Gardiner Range
Watarrka National Park
Kings Canyon
Hope Valley
Morris Pass
Vale Of Tempe
Dare Plain
Areyonga (Utju) (closed comm./permit req.)
Ipolera
Krichauff Ranges
Ntaria ALT
Ltalaltuma ALT
Tyurretye ALT
MACDONNELL
Tylers Pass Tjoritja / West MacDonnell NP
Namatjira
'Glen Helen'
Tropic of Capricorn
Petermann ALT
Land Settlement ALT
Urrampinyi Iltjiltjarri ALT
Katiti Petermann IPA
Lake Amadeus
Katiti ALT
Angas Downs IPA
Angas Downs
Liddle Hills
Imanpa (Mt Ebenezer) (permit required)
Lasseter Highway
Yulara
Uluru-Katatjuta ALT
Uluru-Kata Tjuta NP
Mutitjulu (permit required)
Kata Tjuta (The Olgas)
Uluru / Ayers Rock
'Curtin Springs'
Mulga Park Rd
Luritja Rd
Ernest Giles Road
'Mulga Park'
Wanarkula
Northern Territory
South Australia
Apara - Makiri - Punti IPA
Anangu Pitjantjatjara Yankunytjatjara Aboriginal Area
Alpara
Walyinynga (Cave Hill)
Ulaypai
Eagle Bore (Tipunyanga)
New Well
Araleun
Boomdooyanna
To Amata
To Kaltukatjara (Docker River)
To Papunya
Pulcura Lake
Murphys Range
Tempe Downs
Levi Range
Wild Eagle Plain
Walker Valley
Shakes Plain
Peterman Pound
George Gill Range
Ayers Lookout Plain
James Ranges
Middle Range

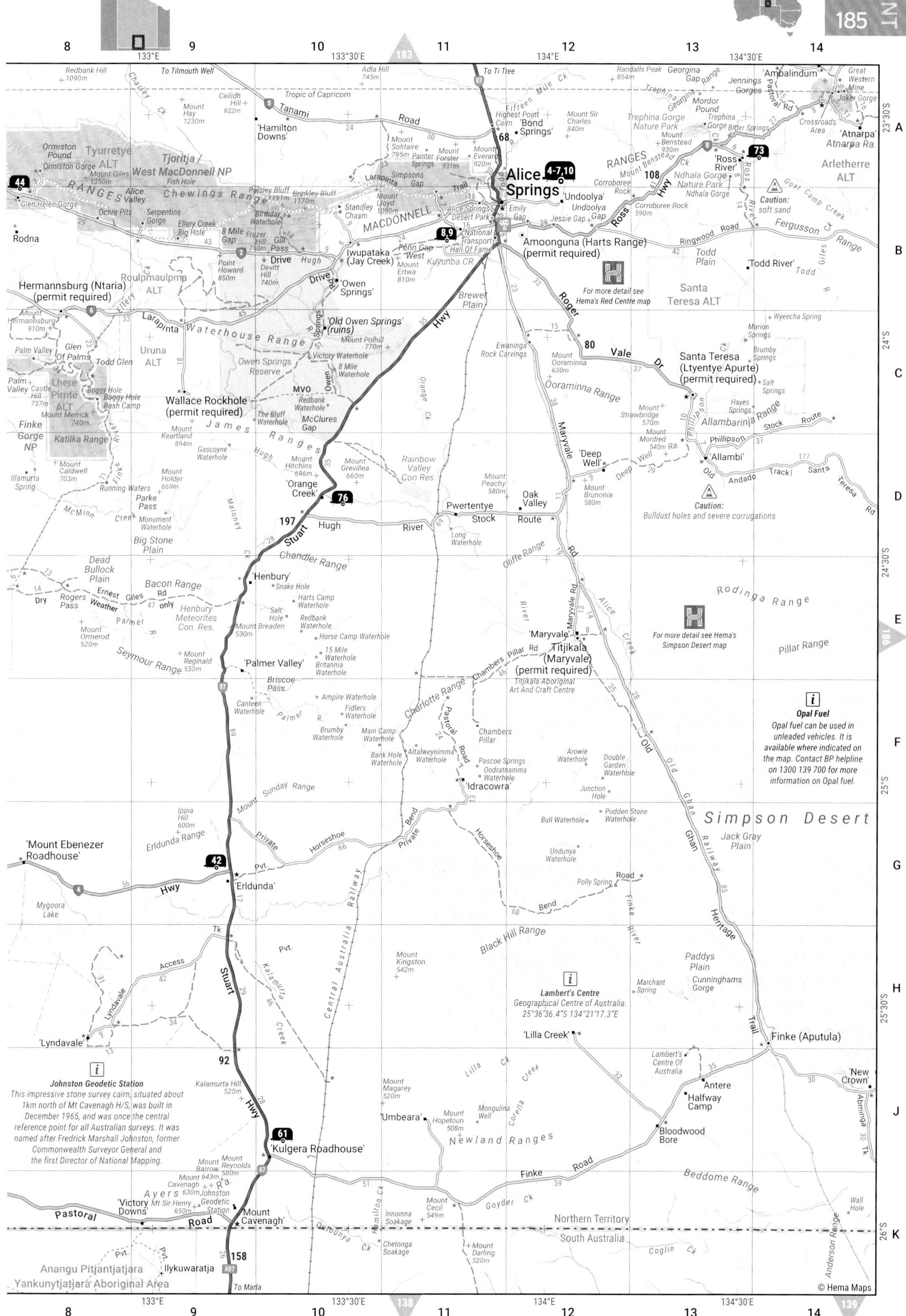
8
9
10
11
12
13
14
133°E
133°30'E
134°E
134°30'E
183
A
B
C
D
E
F
G
H
J
K
23°30'S
24°S
24°30'S
25°S
25°30'S
26°S
186
Alice Springs
4-7,10
Tropic of Capricorn
To Tilmouth Well
To Ti Tree
Tanami Road
'Hamilton Downs'
Redbank Hill 1090m
Mount Hay 1230m
Ceilidh Hill 922m
Adla Hill 745m
Ormiston Pound
Ormiston Gorge
Tyurretye ALT
Tjoritja / West MacDonnell NP
44
Glen Helen Gorge
RANGES
Chewings Range
Alice Valley
Ochre Pits
Serpentine Gorge
Ellery Creek Big Hole
8 Mile Gap
Frazer Hill 710m
Gill Pass
Birthday Waterhole
Paisley Bluff 1191m
Brinkley Bluff 1170m
Standley Chasm
MACDONNELL
Mount Lloyd 1050m
Larapinta Trail
Simpsons Gap
Mount Solitaire 795m
Painter Springs
Mount Forster 931m
Mount Everard 920m
Alice Springs Desert Park
Penn Gap
West Kuyunba CR
Mount Ertwa 810m
National Transport Hall Of Fame
8,9
Iwupataka (Jay Creek)
Rodna
Point Howard 850m
Devitt Hill 740m
Drive
Hugh
Hermannsburg (Ntaria) (permit required)
Roulpmaulpma ALT
Mount Hermannsburg 910m
'Owen Springs'
'Old Owen Springs' (ruins)
Mount Polhill 770m
Waterhouse Range
Larapinta
Owen Springs Reserve
Victory Waterhole
8 Mile Waterhole
Palm Valley
Glen Of Palms
Todd Glen
Uruna ALT
Lhere Pirnte ALT
Palm Valley
Castle Hill 737m
Boggy Hole
Boggy Hole Bush Camp
Mount Merrick 740m
Finke Gorge NP
Katilka Range
Wallace Rockhole (permit required)
MVO
Redbank Waterhole
The Bluff Waterhole
McClures Gap
James Ranges
Mount Keartland 894m
Gascoyne Waterhole
Mount Caldwell 703m
Illamurta Spring
Mount Holder 669m
Running Waters
Parke Pass
McMinn Creek
Monument Waterhole
Big Stone Plain
Mount Hitchins 696m
Mount Grevillea 660m
'Orange Creek'
76
197
Rainbow Valley Con Res.
Hugh River
Stuart Hwy
Dead Bullock Plain
Chandler Range
'Henbury'
Bacon Range
Ernest Giles Rd
Dry Weather only
Rogers Pass
Henbury Meteorites Con. Res.
Snake Hole
Harts Camp Waterhole
Salt Hole
Redbank Waterhole
Mount Breaden 530m
Horse Camp Waterhole
Mount Ormerod 520m
Seymour Range
Mount Reginald 530m
'Palmer Valley'
15 Mile Waterhole
Britannia Waterhole
Briscoe Pass
Ampire Waterhole
Canteen Waterhole
Fidlers Waterhole
Brumby Waterhole
Main Camp Waterhole
Bank Hole Waterhole
Altalweynimma Waterhole
Emily Gap
Jessie Gap
'Bond Springs'
Highest Point Cairn
68
Fifteen Mile Ck
Mount Sir Charles 840m
'Undoolya'
Undoolya Gap
Corroboree Rock
Amoonguna (Harts Range) (permit required)
For more detail see Hema's Red Centre map
Brewer Plain
Ewaninga Rock Carvings
Roger Vale Dr
80
Mount Ooraminna 630m
Ooraminna Range
Maryvale
Mount Peachy 580m
Oak Valley
Pwertentye Stock Route
Long Waterhole
Oliffe Range
Mount Brunonia 580m
'Deep Well'
Deep Well
'Maryvale'
Titjikala (Maryvale) (permit required)
Titjikala Aboriginal Art And Craft Centre
Chambers Pillar Rd
Charlotte Range
Chambers Pillar
Pascoe Springs
Oodratnamma Waterhole
'Idracowra'
Arowie Waterhole
Double Garden Waterhole
Junction Hole
Pudden Stone Waterhole
Bull Waterhole
Undunya Waterhole
Polly Spring
Randalls Peak 854m
Georgina Gap Range
Jennings Gorges
'Ambalindum'
Great Western Mine
Joker Gorge
Mordor Pound
Trephina Gorge Nature Park
Trephina Gorge
Bitter Springs
Crossroads Area
'Atnarpa'
Atnarpa Ra.
Mount Benstead 930m
RANGES
108
N'dhala Gorge Nature Park
Ndhala Gorge
Ross Hwy
'Ross River'
73
Arletherre ALT
Caution: soft sand
Goat Camp Creek
Corroboree Rock 590m
Ringwood Road
Fergusson Range
Todd Plain
'Todd River'
Santa Teresa ALT
Wyeecha Spring
Marion Springs
Brumby Springs
Santa Teresa (Ltyentye Apurte) (permit required)
Salt Springs
Hayes Springs
Mount Strawbridge 570m
Mount Mordred 540m
Allambarinja Range
Phillipson Stock Route
'Allambi'
Old Andado Track
Santa Teresa Rd
Caution: Bulldust holes and severe corrugations
Rodinga Range
For more detail see Hema's Simpson Desert map
Pillar Range
Opal Fuel
Opal fuel can be used in unleaded vehicles. It is available where indicated on the map. Contact BP helpline on 1300 139 700 for more information on Opal fuel.
Old Ghan Railway Heritage Trail
Simpson Desert
Jack Gray Plain
'Mount Ebenezer Roadhouse'
42
'Erldunda'
Erldunda Range
Ippia Hill 600m
Mount Sunday Range
Private Horseshoe Bend
Horseshoe
Bend
Mygoora Lake
Black Hill Range
Mount Kingston 542m
Central Australia Railway
Kalamurta Creek
Access
Lyndavale
'Lyndavale'
Stuart Hwy
92
Paddys Plain
Cunninghams Gorge
Marchant Spring
Lambert's Centre
Geographical Centre of Australia. 25°36'36.4"S 134°21'17.3"E
'Lilla Creek'
Lilla Ck
Finke (Aputula)
Lambert's Centre Of Australia
Antere
'Halfway Camp'
'New Crown'
Abminga Tk
Bloodwood Bore
Johnston Geodetic Station
This impressive stone survey cairn, situated about 1km north of Mt Cavenagh H/S, was built in December 1965, and was once the central reference point for all Australian surveys. It was named after Fredrick Marshall Johnston, former Commonwealth Surveyor General and the first Director of National Mapping.
Kalamurta Hill 520m
Mount Magarey 520m
'Umbeara'
Mount Hopetoun 508m
Mongulina Well
Newland Ranges
61
'Kulgera Roadhouse'
Finke Road
Beddome Range
Mount Barrow 643m
Mount Reynolds 580m
Mount Cavenagh 630m
Ayers Ra.
Johnston Geodetic Station
'Victory Downs'
Mt Sir Henry 650m
Pastoral Road
'Mount Cavenagh'
Goyder Ck
Mount Cecil 549m
Innoinna Soakage
Hamilton Ck
Chetonga Soakage
Mount Darling 520m
Wall Hole
Northern Territory
South Australia
Coglin Ck
Anderson Range
Alberga Ck
158
To Marla
Ilykuwaratja
Anangu Pitjantjatjara Yankunytjatjara Aboriginal Area
© Hema Maps
138
139

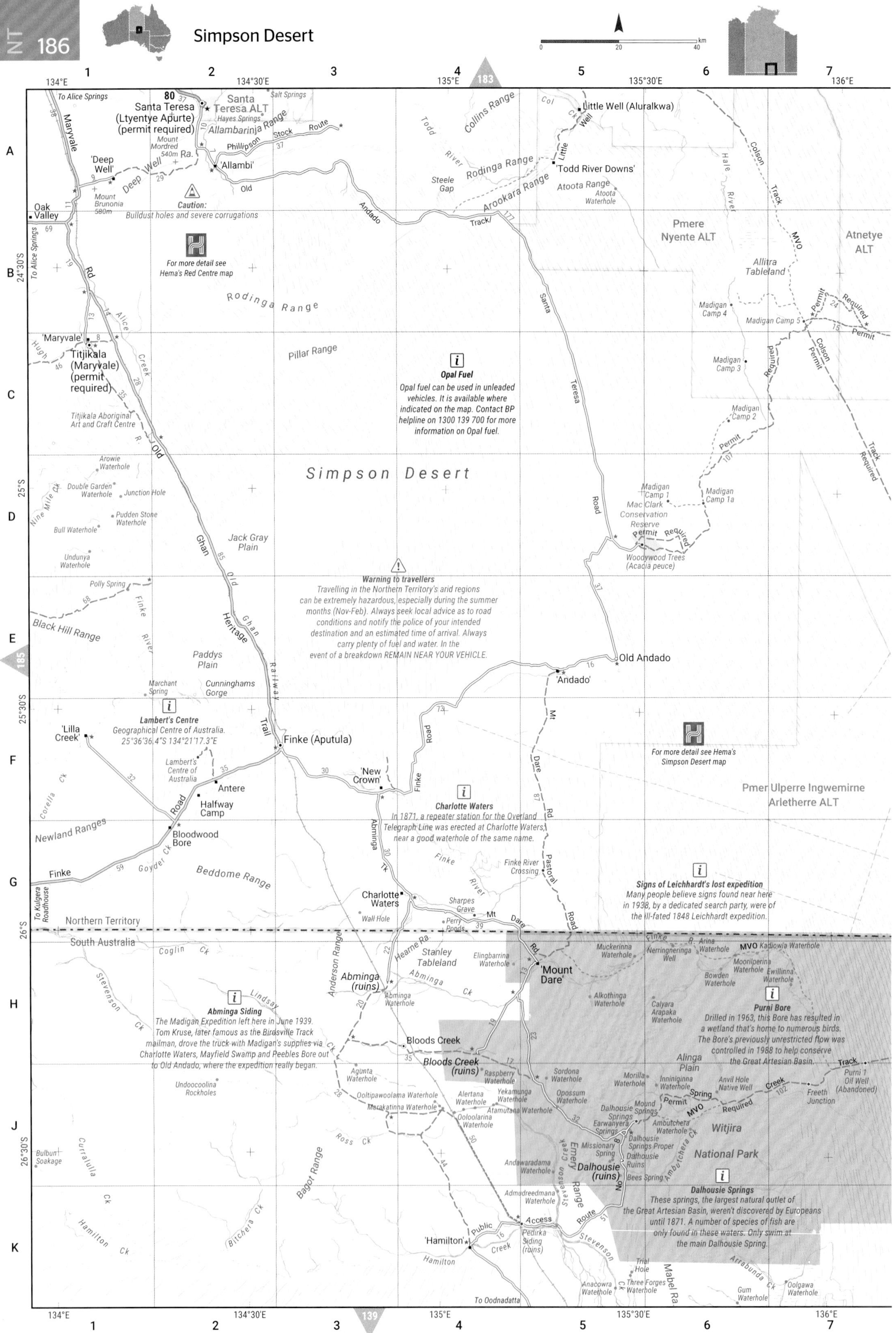
Simpson Desert
To Alice Springs
Santa Teresa (Ltyentye Apurte) (permit required)
Santa Teresa ALT
Salt Springs
Hayes Springs
Allambarinja Range
Mount Mordred 540m
Phillipson Stock Route
'Allambi'
'Deep Well'
Deep Well
Old Andado
Mount Brunonia 580m
Caution:
Bulldust holes and severe corrugations
Oak Valley
To Alice Springs
Maryvale Rd
For more detail see Hema's Red Centre map
Collins Range
Todd River
Rodinga Range
Steele Gap
Arookara Range
Track
Little Well (Aluralkwa)
Col Ck
Little Well
'Todd River Downs'
Atoota Range
Atoota Waterhole
Hale River
Colson Track
MVO
Pmere Nyente ALT
Atnetye ALT
Allitra Tableland
Madigan Camp 4
Madigan Camp 5
Permit Required
Madigan Camp 3
Colson Permit Required
Madigan Camp 2
Permit
Track Required
Madigan Camp 1
Madigan Camp 1a
Mac Clark Conservation Reserve
Permit Required
Woodywood Trees (Acacia peuce)
Santa Teresa Road
Rodinga Range
Pillar Range
'Maryvale'
Titjikala (Maryvale) (permit required)
Hugh
Alice Creek
Titjikala Aboriginal Art and Craft Centre
Opal Fuel
Opal fuel can be used in unleaded vehicles. It is available where indicated on the map. Contact BP helpline on 1300 139 700 for more information on Opal fuel.
Simpson Desert
Arowie Waterhole
Double Garden Waterhole
Junction Hole
Nine Mile Ck
Pudden Stone Waterhole
Bull Waterhole
Undunya Waterhole
Jack Gray Plain
Old Ghan Heritage Trail
Ghan Railway
Warning to travellers
Travelling in the Northern Territory's arid regions can be extremely hazardous, especially during the summer months (Nov-Feb). Always seek local advice as to road conditions and notify the police of your intended destination and an estimated time of arrival. Always carry plenty of fuel and water. In the event of a breakdown REMAIN NEAR YOUR VEHICLE.
Polly Spring
Finke River
Black Hill Range
Paddys Plain
Marchant Spring
Cunninghams Gorge
Old Andado
'Andado'
Mt Dare Rd
Lambert's Centre
Geographical Centre of Australia.
25°36'36.4"S 134°21'17.3"E
'Lilla Creek'
Finke (Aputula)
For more detail see Hema's Simpson Desert map
Lambert's Centre of Australia
Antere
Halfway Camp
'New Crown'
Finke Road
Corella Ck
Pmer Ulperre Ingwemirne Arletherre ALT
Charlotte Waters
In 1871, a repeater station for the Overland Telegraph Line was erected at Charlotte Waters, near a good waterhole of the same name.
Newland Ranges
Bloodwood Bore
Road
Abminga Tk
Finke River Crossing
Pastoral Road
Finke
Goyder Ck
Beddome Range
Signs of Leichhardt's lost expedition
Many people believe signs found near here in 1938, by a dedicated search party, were of the ill-fated 1848 Leichhardt expedition.
To Kulgera Roadhouse
Charlotte Waters
Wall Hole
Sharpes Grave
Perry Ponds
Mt Dare Rd
Northern Territory
South Australia
Coglin Ck
Hearne Ra
Stanley Tableland
Elingbarrina Waterhole
Muckerinna Waterhole
Nerringneringa Well
Arina Waterhole
MVO Kadiowla Waterhole
Moorilperina Waterhole
Ewillinna Waterhole
Bowden Waterhole
'Mount Dare'
Anderson Range
Abminga (ruins)
Abminga Ck
Abminga Waterhole
Stevenson Ck
Lindsay Ck
Alkothinga Waterhole
Calyara Arapaka Waterhole
Abminga Siding
The Madigan Expedition left here in June 1939. Tom Kruse, later famous as the Birdsville Track mailman, drove the truck with Madigan's supplies via Charlotte Waters, Mayfield Swamp and Peebles Bore out to Old Andado, where the expedition really began.
Purni Bore
Drilled in 1963, this Bore has resulted in a wetland that's home to numerous birds. The Bore's previously unrestricted flow was controlled in 1988 to help conserve the Great Artesian Basin.
Bloods Creek
Bloods Creek (ruins)
Alinga Plain
Track
Purni 1 Oil Well (Abandoned)
Agunta Waterhole
Undoocoolina Rockholes
Raspberry Waterhole
Sordona Waterhole
Morilla Waterhole
Inninginna Waterhole
Anvil Hole Native Well
Creek
Freeth Junction
Ooltipawoolama Waterhole
Alertana Waterhole
Yekamunga Waterhole
Opossum Waterhole
Spring Permit Required
MVO
Merakatinna Waterhole
Atamutana Waterhole
Dalhousie Springs
Mound Springs
Ooloolarina Waterhole
Earwanyera Springs
Ambutchera Waterhole
Witjira
Ross Ck
Missionary Spring
Dalhousie Springs Proper
Ambutchera Ck
National Park
Bulbun Soakage
Curralulla Ck
Bagot Range
Emery Range
Andawaradama Waterhole
Dalhousie (ruins)
Dalhousie Ruins
Bees Spring
Stevenson Creek
Dalhousie Springs
These springs, the largest natural outlet of the Great Artesian Basin, weren't discovered by Europeans until 1871. A number of species of fish are only found in these waters. Only swim at the main Dalhousie Spring.
Admudreedmana Waterhole
Hamilton Ck
Bitchera Ck
Access Route
Public
'Hamilton'
Creek
Pedirka Siding (ruins)
Stevenson
Hamilton
Arrabunda Ck
Trial Hole
Mabel Ra
Anacowra Waterhole
Three Forges Waterhole
Gum Waterhole
Oolgawa Waterhole
To Oodnadatta

Atnetye ALT
Madigan's Route
Dr Cecil Madigan led the first scientific-based expedition across the Simpson Desert in 1939. The GPS positions shown on this map mark his campsites. In places the shown track is indicative only as it is not always clearly visible, particularly early in the season. Permits are required for eastern and western ends of the route.
Rough track follows Hay River bed between Camp 15 and Claypan.
Simpson Desert
Geosurveys Hill 150m
Colson Track
Constructed during the 1960s, it gave access from Alice Spings to the area around the NT/SA border and the oil lease there.
Geographical Centre of The Simpson Desert
Beachcomber No.1 Oil Well (Abandoned)
Munga-Thirri National Park
French Line
The first route across the Desert, it was constructed by the French exploration company, Delhi International, in 1963. It is now the most popular and shortest route across the Desert.
Travelling the Simpson Desert
Use UHF Channel 10 in the Simpson Desert to check for oncoming traffic.
Approdinna Attora Knolls
The first European to see these two low, flat-topped hills was David Lindsay when he crossed the Desert in 1886. They were named by Ted Colson on his 1936 crossing.
Pmer Ulperre Ingwemirne Arletherre ALT
Colson Oil Well
Northern Territory
South Australia
Queensland
Poeppel Corner
Poeppel Corner Confluence S26 E138
Simpson Desert Conservation Park
Simpson Desert Regional Reserve
Poeppel Corner
Marks the meeting point of NT, SA and Qld. It's named after Augustus Poeppel, the surveyor who marked the SA/Qld border in 1880.
Lone Gum
This coolabah, and how it got here, is an oddity as these trees are generally associated with flood-out country!
Parks Pass
South Australian Desert Parks Pass required to enter Witjira National Park, Simpson Desert Regional Reserve, Simpson Desert Conservation Park and Innamincka Regional Reserve.
Poolowanna Lake
Peera Peera Poolanna Lake
Lake Griselda
Kuncherinna No 1 Oil Well Site
To Birdsville
To Jervois
© Hema Maps

Adelaide River

1 Adelaide River Inn & Resort
106 Stuart Hwy
www.adelaideriverresort.com.au/
08 8976 7047 HEMA 175 G4 13 14 19 S 131 06 23 E

2 Adelaide River Show Society Caravan Park
Dorat Rd
www.arss.org.au
08 8976 7032 HEMA 175 H5 13 14 49 S 131 06 36 E

Aileron

3 Aileron Hotel & Roadhouse
Stuart Hwy
www.aileronroadhouse.com.au
08 8956 9703 HEMA 182 D7 22 38 38 S 133 20 43 E

Alice Springs

4 Alice Springs Tourist Park
70 Larapinta Dr
www.alicespringstouristpark.com.au/
08 8952 2547 HEMA 185 B11 23 42 01 S 133 51 45 E

5 BIG4 MacDonnell Range Holiday Park
Palm Place. 4.5 km S of PO
www.macrange.com.au
08 8952 6111 HEMA 185 B11 23 44 03 S 133 52 11 E

6 G'day Mate Tourist Park
23 Palm Circuit. 4.8 km S of PO
www.gdaymatecaravanpark.com.au
08 8952 9589 HEMA 185 B11 23 44 00 S 133 52 04 E

7 Heritage Caravan Park
40 Ragonesi Rd. 5 km SE of PO
www.heritagecaravanpark.com.au
08 8953 1418 HEMA 185 B11 23 44 10 S 133 52 18 E

8 Temple Bar Caravan Park
875 Ilparpa Rd. 0418 835 859 AH number
0455 922 533 HEMA 185 B11 23 45 37 S 133 47 13 E

9 Wanngardi Caravan Park
915 Ilparpa Rd 15 km SW of PO
08 8953 3738 HEMA 185 B11 23 45 28 S 133 46 52 E

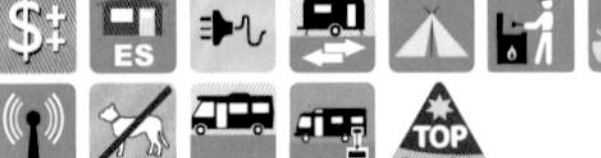

10 Wintersun Cabin & Caravan Park
North Stuart Hwy. 2 km N of PO
www.wintersun.com.au
08 8952 4080 HEMA 185 B11 23 40 55 S 133 52 27 E

Annaburroo

11 Mary River Wilderness Retreat
Mary River Crossing, Arnhem Hwy
www.maryriverretreat.com.au/
08 8978 8877 HEMA 176 D2 12 54 16 S 131 39 04 E

Barkly Homestead

12 Barkly Homestead
Junction of Barkly Hwy & Tableland Hwy
www.barklyhomestead.com.au
08 8964 4549 HEMA 181 G11 19 42 38 S 135 49 39 E

Barrow Creek

13 Barrow Creek Roadhouse & Caravan Park
Stuart Hwy
08 8956 9753 HEMA 181 K8 21 31 52 S 133 53 21 E

Batchelor

14 Banyan Tree Caravan & Tourist Park
Litchfield Park Rd
www.banyan-tree.com.au
08 8976 0330 HEMA 175 F4 13 01 34 S 130 58 29 E

15 Batchelor Holiday Park
37 Rum Jungle Rd
www.batchelorholidaypark.com.au
08 8976 0166 HEMA 175 F4 13 02 36 S 131 01 28 E

16 Litchfield Tourist Park
2916 Litchfield Park Rd
www.litchfieldtouristpark.com.au
08 8976 0070 HEMA 175 F3 13 01 29 S 130 57 18 E

Berry Springs

17 AAOK Lakes Resort & Caravan Park
170 Doris Rd, off Cox Peninsula Rd
www.lakesresortcaravanpark.com.au
08 8988 6277 HEMA 175 D4 12 43 12 S 131 00 56 E

18 Tumbling Waters Holiday Park
Cox Peninsula Rd
www.tumblingwatersholidaypark.com.au
08 8988 6255 HEMA 175 D3 12 46 24 S 130 56 46 E

Bokanj

19 Mary River Roadhouse
Kakadu Hwy. 60 km NE of Pine Creek
www.parksaustralia.gov.au
08 8975 4229 HEMA 176 G4 13 36 20 S 132 13 10 E

Borroloola

20 McArthur River Caravan Park
781 Robinson Rd
www.mcarthurcaravanpark.com.au
08 8975 8734 HEMA 179 K13 16 04 12 S 136 18 27 E

Bynoe Harbour

21 Crab Claw Island Resort
Via Fog Bay Rd
www.crabclawisland.com.au
08 8978 2313 HEMA 175 D1 12 42 25 S 130 37 20 E

Cape Crawford

22 Heartbreak Hotel Caravan Park
Cnr Carpentaria Hwy & Tableland Hwy
08 8975 9928 HEMA 181 B11 16 40 59 S 135 43 36 E

Cooinda

23 Cooinda Campground & Caravan Park
Off Kakadu Hwy. Via Jim Jim. 56 km S of Jabiru
www.kakadutourism.com
08 8979 1500 HEMA 176 D5 12 54 18 S 132 31 16 E

Coolalinga

24 Coolalinga Caravan Park
Lot 2 Stuart Hwy
www.coolalingacaravanpark.com.au
08 8983 1026 HEMA 175 B4 12 31 22 S 131 02 26 E

Coomalie

25 Coomalie Creek RV Park
6375 Stuart Hwy, Coomalie Creek
08 8976 0501 HEMA 175 F5 13 01 12 S 131 07 05 E

Daly River

26 Banyan Farm Tourist Park
Woolianna Rd. Closed during wet season
www.banyanfarm.com.au
08 8978 2461 HEMA 178 F3 13 42 47 S 130 40 22 E

27 Daly River Barra Resort
6228 Woolianna Rd
www.dalyriverbarra.com.au
08 8978 1193 HEMA 178 F3 13 39 52 S 130 39 13 E

28 Daly River Mango Farm
Off Port Keats Rd. 7 Km NW of Daly River Crossing. Closed during wet season
www.mangofarm.com.au
08 8978 2464 HEMA 178 F3 13 44 22 S 130 41 05 E

29 Woolianna on the Daly
Woolianna Rd. Closed during wet season
www.woolianna.com.au
08 8978 2478 HEMA 178 F3 13 40 14 S 130 38 28 E

Daly Waters

30 Daly Waters Hi-Way Inn
Cnr Stuart Hwy & Carpentaria Hwy
www.dalywaters-hi-wayinn.webs.com
08 8975 9925 HEMA 179 K8 16 18 28 S 133 23 06 E

31 The Daly Waters Pub
16 Stuart St. 3 km W of Hwy
www.dalywaterspub.com
08 8975 9927 HEMA 179 K8 16 15 14 S 133 22 11 E

Darwin

32 Darwin Free Spirit Resort
901 Stuart Hwy, Holtze
www.darwinfreespiritresort.com.au
08 8935 0888 HEMA 174 E6 12 27 30 S 130 58 14 E

33 Discovery Holiday Parks Darwin
11 Farrell Cres, Winnellie
www.discoveryholidayparks.com.au
08 8984 3330 HEMA 174 D4 12 25 40 S 130 54 03 E

34 Hidden Valley Holiday Park
25 Hidden Valley Rd, Berrimah
www.hiddenvalleyholidaypark.com.au
08 8984 2888 HEMA 174 E4 12 26 13 S 130 54 56 E

35 Lee Point Village Resort
Lee Point Rd, Lee Point
www.leepointvillageresort.com.au
08 8945 0535 HEMA 174 A3 12 20 32 S 130 53 30 E

36 Malak & KOA Caravan Parks
Mc Millans Rd, Malak. Pets at KOA only
www.leepointvillageresort.com.au
08 8927 3500 HEMA 174 C4 12 24 05 S 130 54 25 E

Douglas Daly

37 Douglas Daly Tourist Park
Oolloo Rd. 8 km S of Hot Springs turnoff
www.douglasdalypark.com.au
08 8978 2479 HEMA 178 F5 13 47 14 S 131 21 09 E

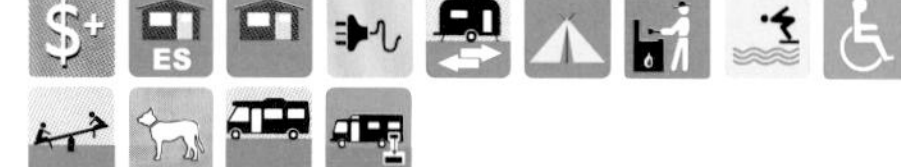

Dundee Beach

38 Dundee Beach Holiday Park
20 Dundee Place
www.dundeebeachholidaypark.com.au
08 8978 2557 HEMA 178 D3 12 43 03 S 130 21 03 E

Dunmarra

39 Dunmarra Wayside Inn
Stuart Hwy
08 8975 9922 HEMA 180 B7 16 40 47 S 133 24 45 E

NORTHERN TERRITORY

Elliott

40 Midland Caravan Park
102 Stuart Hwy. S end of town
08 8969 2037 HEMA 180 D7 17 33 21 S 133 32 52 E

Emerald Springs

41 Emerald Springs Roadhouse
Caravan Park, Stuart Hwy
www.emeraldsprings.com.au
08 8976 1169 HEMA 176 G1 13 37 53 S 131 37 47 E

Erldunda

42 Erldunda Roadhouse
Cnr Stuart Hwy & Lasseter Hwy
www.erldundaroadhouse.com
08 8956 0984 HEMA 185 G9 25 11 50 S 133 12 03 E

Gemtree

43 Gemtree Cabins & Caravan Park
Plenty Hwy. Bookings are essential
www.gemtree.com.au
08 8956 9855 HEMA 183 E9 22 58 05 S 134 14 28 E

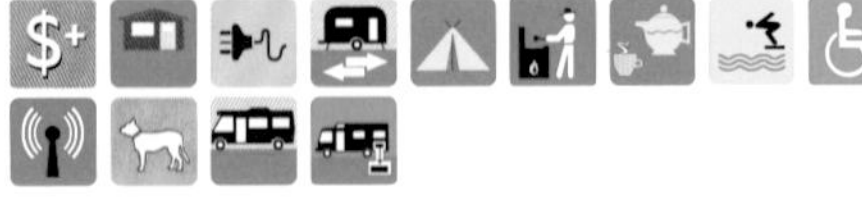

Glen Helen

44 Glen Helen Homestead Lodge
Namatjira Dr. West MacDonnell Ranges
www.glenhelenlodge.com.au
08 8956 7208 HEMA 185 B8 23 41 08 S 132 40 22 E

Hayes Creek

45 Hayes Creek Wayside Inn & Caravan Park
455 Stuart Hwy
08 8978 2430 HEMA 175 K7 13 34 56 S 131 27 30 E

Howard Springs

46 BIG4 Howard Springs Holiday Park
170 Whitewood Rd
www.big4howardsprings.com.au
08 8983 1169 HEMA 175 B4 12 29 47 S 131 02 02 E

47 Darwin Boomerang Motel & Caravan Park
30 Virginia Rd, Virginia. 6 km SW of Howard Springs PO
www.darwinboomerang.com.au
08 8983 1202 HEMA 175 B4 12 31 03 S 131 01 45 E

48 Oasis Tourist Park
17 Morgan Rd
www.oasistouristpark.com.au
08 8983 1048 HEMA 175 B4 12 30 30 S 131 01 05 E

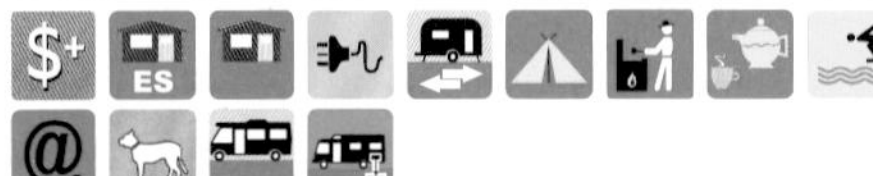

Jabiru

49 Anbinik Kakadu Resort
83 Jabiru Drive
www.kakadu.net.au/
08 8979 3144 HEMA 176 C6 12 40 01 S 132 50 14 E

50 Kakadu Lodge & Caravan Park
Jabiru Drive
www.auroraresorts.com.au
08 8979 2422 HEMA 176 C6 12 39 54 S 132 50 13 E

Katherine

51 BIG4 Katherine Holiday Park
20 Shadforth Rd. 5 km W of PO
www.katherineholidaypark.com.au
08 8972 3962 HEMA 176 K4 14 29 18 S 132 14 59 E

52 Boab Caravan Park
42 Victoria Hwy
www.boabcaravanpark.com.au
08 8971 2433 HEMA 176 K4 14 28 33 S 132 15 26 E

53 Ibis Styles Katherine Caravan Park
Cnr Cyprus St & Stuart Hwy. 3 km S of PO
08 8972 1744 HEMA 176 K4 14 28 18 S 132 17 27 E

54 Knotts Crossing Resort
Cnr Giles St & Cameron St. 2.5 km NE of PO
www.knottscrossing.com.au
08 8972 2511 HEMA 176 K4 14 26 46 S 132 16 12 E

55 Manbulloo Homestead Caravan Park
Murnburlu Rd, 9 km SW of Katherine off Victoria Hwy. 1 km dirt road
www.manbulloohomesteadcaravanpark.com.au
08 8972 1559 HEMA 178 G6 14 31 09 S 132 11 57 E

56 Site Closed

57 Riverview Tourist Village
440 Victoria Hwy
www.riverviewtouristvillage.com.au/
08 8972 1011 HEMA 176 K4 14 29 08 S 132 15 26 E

58 Shady Lane Tourist Park
257 Gorge Rd
www.shadylanetouristpark.com.au
08 8971 0491 HEMA 176 K4 14 25 52 S 132 17 43 E

Kings Canyon

59 Kings Canyon Resort
Luritja Rd, Watarrka National Park
www.kingscanyonresort.com.au
08 8956 7442 HEMA 184 D4 24 15 02 S 131 30 41 E

Kings Creek

60 Kings Creek Station
Luritja Rd
www.kingscreekstation.com.au
08 8956 7474 HEMA 184 D5 24 24 15 S 131 49 06 E

Kulgera

61 Kulgera Roadhouse & Caravan Park
Cnr Kulgera Cr & South Stuart Hwy
08 8956 0973 HEMA 185 J10 25 50 22 S 133 18 01 E

Larrimah

62 Larrimah Pink Panther Hotel
5 Mahoney St, off Stuart Hwy
08 8975 9931 HEMA 179 J8 15 34 27 S 133 12 52 E

Litchfield

63 Litchfield Safari Camp
Litchfield Park Rd. Via Batchelor
www.litchfieldsafaricamp.com.au
08 8978 2185 HEMA 175 G1 13 07 37 S 130 39 17 E

Marrakai

64 Corroboree Park Tavern
Lot 3095 Arnhem Hwy
www.corroboreeparktavern.com.au
08 8978 8920 HEMA 175 D7 12 45 42 S 131 30 02 E

Mataranka

65 Bitter Springs Cabins & Camping
255 Martins Rd, Bitter Springs
www.bitterspringscabins.com.au
08 8975 4838 HEMA 178 H7 14 54 43 S 133 05 01 E

66 Mataranka Homestead Tourist Resort
Homestead Rd. Pets by prior arrangement
www.matarankahomestead.com.au
08 8975 4544 HEMA 179 H8 14 55 20 S 133 07 55 E

67 Territory Manor Caravan Park
51 Martins Rd. 300m E of water tower
www.matarankamotel.com
08 8975 4516 HEMA 178 H7 14 55 10 S 133 04 02 E

Nitmiluk

68 Nitmiluk Tours & Accommodation
Nitmiluk National Park (Katherine Gorge), Gorge Rd
www.nitmiluktours.com.au
08 8972 1253 HEMA 176 K5 14 19 11 S 132 25 21 E

Noonamah

69 Noonamah Tourist Park
1807 Stuart Hwy, Noonamah
www.noonamahtouristpark.com.au
08 8988 4480 HEMA 175 C4 12 38 02 S 131 04 26 E

Pine Creek

70 Lazy Lizard Caravan Park
299 Millar Tce
www.lazylizardpinecreek.com.au
08 8976 1019 HEMA 176 H2 13 49 18 S 131 50 05 E

71 Pine Creek Service Station Caravan Park
Moule St
08 8976 1217 HEMA 176 H2 13 49 29 S 131 50 06 E

Renner Springs

72 Renner Springs Desert Inn
Stuart Hwy
www.rennerspringshotel.com.au
08 8964 4505 HEMA 181 E8 18 19 08 S 133 47 43 E

Ross River

73 Ross River Resort
7829 Ross Hwy
www.rossriverresort.com.au
08 8956 9711 HEMA 185 A13 23 35 34 S 134 29 35 E

Rum Jungle

74 Pandanus on Litchfield
275 Litchfield Park Rd, 9 km W of Batchelor via Rum Jungle Rd
www.pandanuslitchfield.com.au
08 8976 0242 HEMA 175 F4 13 01 35 S 130 59 17 E

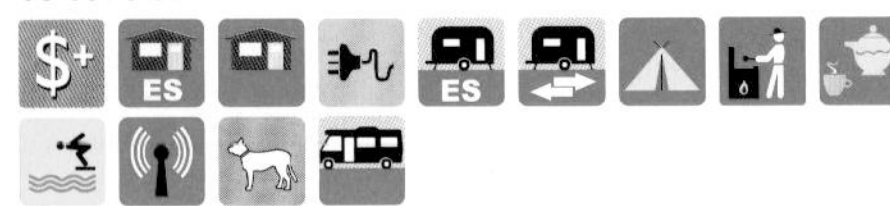

South Alligator

75 Aurora Kakadu Caravan and Camping
Arnhem Hwy, South Alligator, Kakadu National Park
www.auroraresorts.com.au
08 8979 0166 HEMA 176 C5 12 40 27 S 132 28 45 E

Stuarts Well

76 Stuarts Well Roadhouse
South Stuart Hwy
www.stuartswellroadhouse.com.au
08 8956 0808 HEMA 185 D10 24 20 26 S 133 27 31 E

Tennant Creek

77 Outback Caravan Park
71 Peko Rd
www.outbacktennantcreek.com.au
08 8962 2459 HEMA 181 G8 19 38 49 S 134 11 56 E

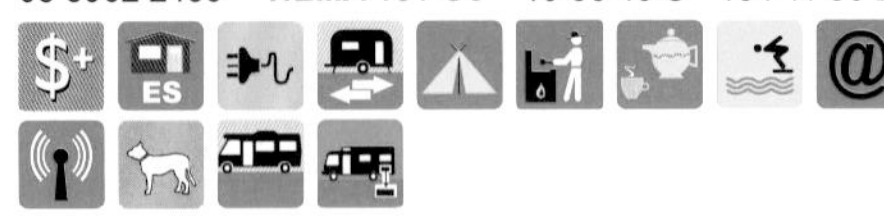

78 Tennant Creek Caravan Park
208 Paterson St
www.tennantcreekcaravanpark.com.au
08 8962 2325 HEMA 181 G8 19 38 18 S 134 11 31 E

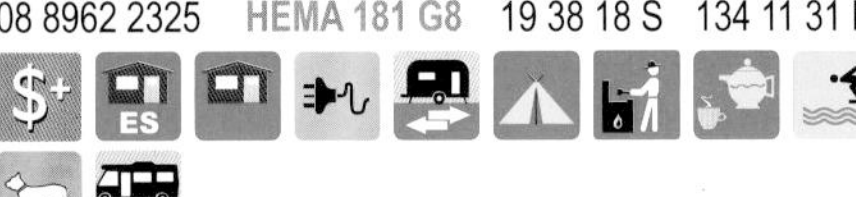

Threeways

79 Threeways Roadhouse & Tourist Park
Cnr Stuart Hwy & Barkly Hwy
www.threewaysroadhouse.com.au
08 8962 2744 HEMA 181 G8 19 26 12 S 134 12 30 E

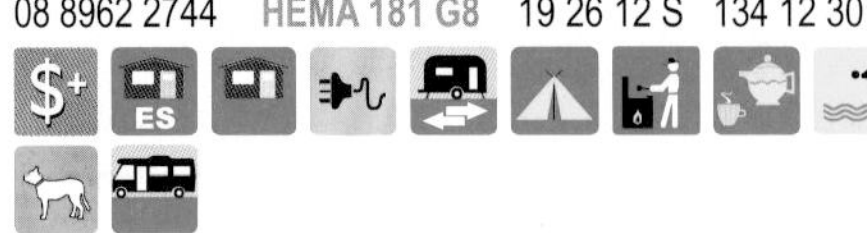

Ti Tree

80 Ti-Tree Roadhouse Caravan Park
Stuart Hwy
08 8956 9741 HEMA 182 D7 22 07 53 S 133 25 00 E

Timber Creek

81 Timber Creek Hotel & Caravan Park
Victoria Hwy
08 8975 0722 HEMA 177 D2 15 39 40 S 130 28 51 E

82 Wirib Tourism Park & Store
Lot 13 Victoria Hwy
wirib.com.au
08 8975 0602 HEMA 177 D2 15 39 46 S 130 28 52 E

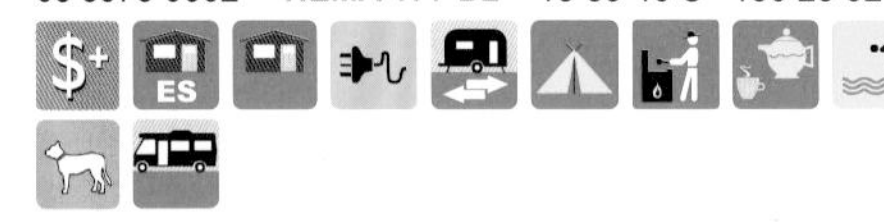

Top Springs

83 Top Springs Hotel
Cnr Buchanan Hwy & Buntine Hwy
www.topspringshotel.com.au
08 8975 0767 HEMA 177 G7 16 32 36 S 131 47 49 E

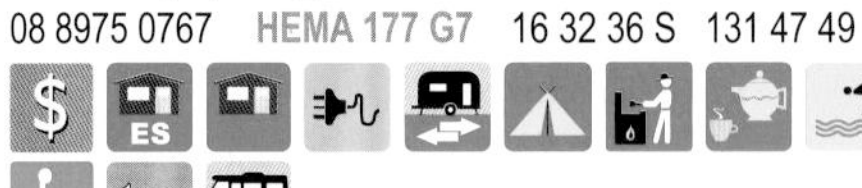

Victoria River

84 Victoria River Roadhouse Caravan Park
9405 Victoria Hwy, Gregory
08 8975 0744 HEMA 177 C4 15 36 57 S 131 07 38 E

Wauchope

85 Devils Marbles Hotel
Stuart Hwy
www.wauchopehotel.com.au
08 8964 1963 HEMA 181 J9 20 38 26 S 134 13 20 E

Wycliffe Well

86 Wycliffe Well Holiday Park
Stuart Hwy
08 8964 1966 HEMA 181 J9 20 47 45 S 134 14 12 E

Yulara

87 Ayers Rock Resort Campground
Yulara Dve, within Ayers Rock Resort
www.ayersrockresort.com.au
08 8957 7001 HEMA 184 G2 25 14 17 S 130 59 26 E

Public Dump Points

With environmental issues becoming more of a concern to travellers, the disposal of grey and black water is of major importance. A comprehensive public dump point list has been compiled to assist you in locating the facilities for responsible disposal of your waste water.

The list is alphabetical by town within each State or Territory, with location details and contact phone numbers where available. Note that public dump points are also indicated on the maps. See "Symbols used on the maps" below for an explanation of the meaning of these map symbols.

Be aware that some situations may change and the accuracy of accessibility and type of facility cannot be guaranteed.

The use of chemicals in 'black water' is of concern, so it is advisable to use those which are biodegradable and eco-friendly rather than those containing chemicals such as formaldehyde.

Most of the dump points accessible by big rigs would require the use of a waste hose, preferably 3 metres or more in length.

Please leave the facility clean and tidy, otherwise the use may be withdrawn if abused.

Where the information is available, listings show whether the dump point is suitable for cassettes or holding tanks and whether big rigs can access it.

Please respect the courtesy extended to you if you avail yourself of this service.

Explanation of a sample Public Dump Point listing

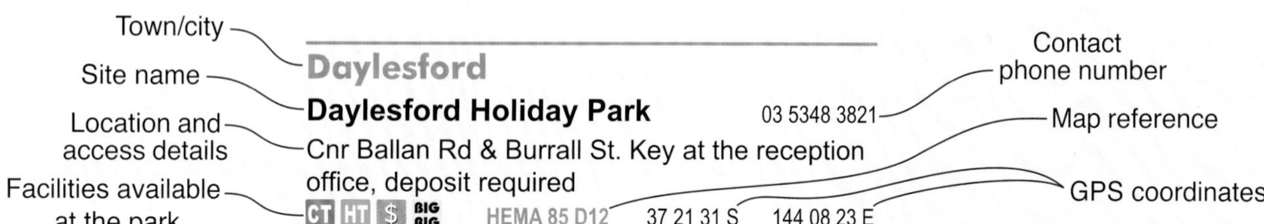

EXPLANATION OF PUBLIC DUMP POINT

SYMBOLS USED IN LISTING

CT CASSETTE TOILET USE

BIG RIG ACCESS SUITABLE FOR BIG RIGS

HT HOLDING TANK USE

$ FEES APPLICABLE

WATER AVAILABLE

SYMBOL USED ON THE MAPS

 PUBLIC DUMP POINT NOT AT A LISTED PARK

QUEENSLAND

Adels Grove

Adels Grove Dumpoint 07 4748 5502
Adels Grove Airfield, outside the Airport fence. GPS is approximate
CT HT HEMA 25 F3 18 41 29 S 138 31 53 E

Agnes Water

Council Depot
Agnes Water - 1770 Rd. 4.2 km N of Round Hill Rd intersection. Turn L at SES HQ sign
CT HT BIG RIG HEMA 16 E5 24 10 49 S 151 52 59 E

Allora

Allora Apex Park
New England Hwy, S end of town near Anglican Church, opposite Dalrymple Rd
CT HT BIG RIG HEMA 12 H1 28 02 09 S 151 59 18 E

Alpha

Alpha Dump Point
Clermont- Alpha Rd, opposite showgrounds
CT HT BIG RIG HEMA 29 F14 23 38 47 S 146 38 11 E

Aramac

Aramac Shire Caravan Park & Camping Grounds 07 4652 9999
Booker St. Public access
CT HT HEMA 29 E12 22 58 02 S 145 14 20 E

Atherton

Atherton Sewerage Works 07 4091 7937
Grove St, off Tolga Rd, over railway. N end of town
CT HT BIG RIG HEMA 22 J2 17 15 18 S 145 28 49 E

Augathella

Augathella Dump Point
Brassington Park, Bendee St - Old Charleville Augathella Rd
CT HT BIG RIG HEMA 34 A3 25 48 08 S 146 35 18 E

Ayr

Shell Burdekin Travel Centre
Cnr Bruce Hwy & Bower St
CT HT BIG RIG HEMA 18 B1 19 34 59 S 147 23 56 E

Babinda

Babinda Rotary Park 07 4067 1008
Rest Area at Babinda. Just east of town over railway. S end of Howard Kennedy Dr
CT HT BIG RIG HEMA 21 H6 17 20 54 S 145 55 35 E

Balgal Beach

Balgal Beach
At Rest Area 6 km E of Rollingstone. Turn E off Bruce Hwy 1 km S of Rollingstone. 5 km E of Hwy. N end of town near boat ramp
CT HT BIG RIG HEMA 19 F3 19 00 37 S 146 24 18 E

Baralaba

Baralaba Dump Point 07 4992 9500
Wooroonah St, near caravan park, behind the showgrounds
CT HT BIG RIG HEMA 31 G9 24 11 08 S 149 48 56 E

Barcaldine

Barcaldine Showground 07 4651 5600
Capricorn Hwy, E end of town
CT HT BIG RIG HEMA 29 F12 23 33 02 S 145 17 37 E

Lloyd Jones Weir
15 km SW of Barcaldine. Turn W off Landsborough Hwy 5 km S of Barcaldine for 9 km. 1 km dirt Rd
CT HT BIG RIG HEMA 29 F12 23 39 00 S 145 12 57 E

Beaudesert

Beaudesert Caravan & Tourist Park 07 5541 1368
Albert Street. Public access, fee applies. Must call at office first
CT HT S BIG RIG HEMA 6 G7 27 59 31 S 153 00 16 E

Bedourie

Bedourie Dump Point
Diamantina Development Rd. 500m N of Roadhouse
CT HT BIG RIG HEMA 28 G3 24 21 07 S 139 28 05 E

Bedourie Area

Cuttaburra Crossing Rest Area
Rest Area 121 km N of Birdsville or 68 km S of Bedourie
CT HT BIG RIG HEMA 28 H3 24 54 49 S 139 38 58 E

Monkira Rest Area
Rest Area on Diamantina Development Rd, 121 km E of Eyre Develpment Rd Jcn or 138 km W of Birdsville Development Rd Jcn
CT HT BIG RIG HEMA 28 H5 24 49 11 S 140 32 28 E

No 3 Bore Rest Area
Rest Area on Diamantina Development Rd. 28 km E of Eyre Development Rd Jcn
CT HT BIG RIG HEMA 28 G4 24 28 31 S 139 48 33 E

Beenleigh

Hugh Muntz Park 07 3412 3412
Reisers Rd
CT HT HEMA 4 H6 27 43 01 S 153 12 33 E

Beerwah

Beerwah Caravan Park 07 5494 0365
205 Burys Rd, Beerwah. Public access
CT HT BIG RIG HEMA 11 H12 26 52 30 S 152 58 43 E

Beerwah Sportsground 07 5494 0513
Entry off Simpson St, off roundabout
CT HT BIG RIG HEMA 11 H12 26 51 50 S 152 57 21 E

Benaraby

Boyne River Rest Area
At Rest Area 49 km SE of Mount Larcom or 49 km N of Miriam Vale. 1 km S of Benaraby
CT HT BIG RIG HEMA 16 D4 24 00 39 S 151 20 26 E

Betoota

Betoota Rest Area
At rest area
CT HT BIG RIG HEMA 28 J5 25 41 36 S 140 44 52 E

Morney Rest Area
Rest Area 108 km W of Windorah or 95 km E of Betoota on the Diamantina Development Rd
CT HT BIG RIG HEMA 28 J7 25 22 50 S 141 37 24 E

Biggenden

Biggenden Dump Point 07 4217 1177
Isis Hwy. 50m W of caravan park
CT HT BIG RIG HEMA 13 C2 25 30 52 S 152 02 20 E

Biloela

Biloela Dump Point
119 Lake Callide Drive
CT HT BIG RIG HEMA 16 F2 24 22 19 S 150 36 41 E

Rural Hinterland Visitor Information Centre 07 4992 2400
Heritage Park complex, Exhibition Avenue, NW end of town
CT HT BIG RIG HEMA 16 F1 24 24 15 S 150 30 04 E

Birdsville

Birdsville Dump Point
Adelaide St, South side of Rd past the Airstrip
CT HT BIG RIG HEMA 28 K3 25 54 14 S 139 20 41 E

Birdsville East Dump Point
E side of Birdsville. 500m E of windmill on Eyre Development Rd
CT HT BIG RIG HEMA 28 K3 25 54 28 S 139 22 39 E

Blackall

Blackall Dump Point 07 4657 4637
Corner Garden St & Blackall - Isisford Rd. Opposite Barcoo River Camp
CT HT BIG RIG HEMA 29 G13 24 25 31 S 145 27 45 E

Blackall Showgrounds
Blackall-Jericho Rd
CT HT BIG RIG HEMA 29 G13 24 25 33 S 145 28 29 E

Blackbutt

Blackbutt Showgrounds 07 4163 0633
Bowman Rd, by water tanks
CT HT BIG RIG HEMA 10 H1 26 52 52 S 152 06 08 E

Blackwater

Blackwater Dump Point
Turpentine St, near the Showgrounds
CT HT BIG RIG HEMA 30 F7 23 35 35 S 148 52 31 E

Bluewater

Bluewater Park
Rest Area at Bluewater, 80 km S of Ingham or 29 km N of Townsville
CT HT BIG RIG HEMA 19 G4 19 10 35 S 146 33 05 E

Bollon

Bollon Dump Point 07 4620 8844
William St
CT HT BIG RIG HEMA 34 G5 28 01 51 S 147 28 40 E

Boonah

Boonah Showgrounds 07 5463 4080
Entry via Melbourne St
CT HT BIG RIG HEMA 6 G3 27 59 51 S 152 41 06 E

Boulia

Boulia Dump Point
West side of Diamantina Hwy, 1 km N of Boulia
CT HT BIG RIG HEMA 28 E4 22 54 28 S 139 54 15 E

Bowen

Bowen Showground 07 4786 5353
Mt Nutt Rd, N side of town
CT HT BIG RIG HEMA 18 D4 19 59 42 S 148 13 42 E

Bowenville

Bowenville Rest Area
CT HT BIG RIG HEMA 35 E14 27 18 16 S 151 29 29 E

Bundaberg

Hinkler Lions Park
Isis Hwy, opposite airport. if locked, key at Waste Transfer Station
CT HT BIG RIG HEMA 14 B1 24 53 49 S 152 18 51 E

Burketown

Burketown Dump Point
Sloman St. Opposite caravan park
CT HT BIG RIG HEMA 25 D4 17 44 31 S 139 32 48 E

Caboolture

Caboolture Showgrounds 07 5495 2030
4 km N of Town Centre
CT HT BIG RIG HEMA 4 A4 27 03 53 S 152 56 54 E

Cairns

Cairns Wastewater Depot 07 4044 8200
8-38 Macnamara St, Manunda
CT HT BIG RIG HEMA 22 C7 16 54 46 S 145 45 00 E

QUEENSLAND

Calliope
Calliope Dump Point
Cnr Taragoola Rd & Dawson Hwy
CT HT BIG RIG HEMA 16 D3 24 00 27 S 151 12 02 E

Caloundra
Caloundra Dump Point 07 5420 6240
Behind the Information Centre, Caloundra Rd. If locked, key at Info Centre
CT HT HEMA 11 G14 26 47 53 S 153 06 51 E

Camooweal
Camooweal Dump Point
E end of town, opposite the water tower
CT HT BIG RIG HEMA 25 H2 19 55 18 S 138 07 27 E

Capalaba
John Fredericks Park 07 3829 8999
2 -14 Old Cleveland Rd
CT HT BIG RIG HEMA 4 F6 27 31 09 S 153 11 19 E

Capella
Bridgeman Park Showground
Hibernia Rd, in SW corner of grounds near horse stables
CT HT BIG RIG HEMA 30 E6 23 05 21 S 148 00 58 E

Carmila Beach
Carmila Beach 1300 472 227
6 km E of Carmila. 1 km dirt Rd. Last 300m narrow, sandy track
CT HT BIG RIG HEMA 17 D3 21 54 50 S 149 27 47 E

Carnarvon National Park
Takarakka Bush Resort 07 4984 4535
Carnarvon Gorge Rd. Fee for all users
CT $ HEMA 30 H6 25 04 13 S 148 16 17 E

Cecil Plains
Cecil Plains Rural Retreat Caravan Park 0428 913 779
Taylor St, in caravan park. Public access
CT HT BIG RIG HEMA 35 E14 27 31 59 S 151 11 45 E

Charleville
Charleville Dump Point 07 4656 8355
Qantas Drive (Airport access Rd)
CT HT BIG RIG HEMA 34 B2 26 24 59 S 146 15 07 E

Charters Towers
Columbia Mine Poppet Head 07 4761 5533
Flinders Hwy Bypass
CT HT BIG RIG HEMA 19 K3 20 04 21 S 146 16 35 E

Charters Towers Area
Fletcher Creek
Rest Area 42 km N of Charters Towers or 157 km SE of Greenvale
CT HT BIG RIG HEMA 19 J2 19 48 57 S 146 03 14 E

Childers
Childers Rest Area
Crescent St, behind Post Office
CT HT BIG RIG HEMA 13 A3 25 14 06 S 152 16 44 E

Chillagoe
Chillagoe Rodeo Grounds 07 4094 7119
From Queen St turn W onto Frew St, entrance 700m on R
CT HT BIG RIG HEMA 27 D8 17 09 29 S 144 30 58 E

Chinchilla
Chinchilla Dump Point 07 4662 7056
Park St (Chinchilla-Wondai Rd)
CT HT BIG RIG HEMA 35 C12 26 44 07 S 150 37 50 E

Clermont
Clermont Dump Point 07 4983 1133
Lime St, next to bowls club
CT HT BIG RIG HEMA 30 D5 22 49 08 S 147 38 40 E

Clermont Area
Theresa Creek Dam 07 4983 2327
22 km SW of Clermont
CT HT BIG RIG HEMA 30 E5 22 58 16 S 147 33 13 E

Cleveland
William St Marine Facility 07 3829 8999
William St, off Shore St Nth
CT HT BIG RIG HEMA 4 F7 27 30 53 S 153 17 13 E

Clifton
Clifton Recreation Grounds 131 872
N side of town in Morton St, via Clark & Devonport Sts
CT HT BIG RIG HEMA 12 H1 27 55 34 S 151 54 45 E

Cloncurry
Cloncurry Dump Point 07 4742 4100
Mary Kathleen Memorial Park, adjacent Visitor Centre, 34 Flinders Hwy
CT HT HEMA 25 J6 20 42 26 S 140 31 06 E

Terry Smith Lookout
Rest Area 103 km S of Burke & Wills Roadhouse or 78 km N of Cloncurry
CT HT BIG RIG HEMA 25 H6 20 04 49 S 140 13 39 E

Coen
Coen Dump Point 07 4060 1135
Peninsula Developmental Rd, N side of town. E side of Rd. S side of Library
CT HT BIG RIG HEMA 23 G4 13 56 43 S 143 12 06 E

Collinsville
Collinsville Showgrounds 07 4785 5795
Entry from Railway Rd next to Showgrounds
CT HT BIG RIG HEMA 18 F3 20 33 24 S 147 50 57 E

Cooktown
Cooktown Dump Point 07 4069 5444
Access from Charlotte St, opposite Sovereign Hotel
CT HT HEMA 20 A3 15 27 58 S 145 14 57 E

Cooroy
Cooroy RV Stop 07 5485 3244
7 Mary River Rd, enter at driveway between Car Club & Horse & Pony Club
CT HT BIG RIG HEMA 11 A11 26 24 49 S 152 54 25 E

Croydon
Croydon Dump Point
Alldridge St, outside the caravan park
CT HT BIG RIG HEMA 26 F5 18 12 05 S 142 14 43 E

Cunnamulla
Cunnamulla Council Dump Point
Williams St, adjacent to showground fence
CT HT BIG RIG HEMA 33 G14 28 04 05 S 145 41 49 E

Dalby
Dalby Dump Point
5 Black St
CT HT BIG RIG HEMA 35 D14 27 10 34 S 151 14 41 E

Dalveen
Jim Mitchell Park
Rest Area at Dalveen. Mountain Park Rd
CT HT BIG RIG HEMA 12 K1 28 29 21 S 151 58 14 E

Dayboro
Dayboro Showgrounds 07 3425 1156
Mt Mee Rd
CT HT BIG RIG HEMA 4 B3 27 11 25 S 152 49 25 E

Dirranbandi
Dirranbandi Dump Point 07 4620 8844
Theodore St, beside showground
CT HEMA 34 H7 28 34 33 S 148 13 52 E

Duaringa
Duaringa Rest Area
Rest Area at Duaringa. E end of town
CT HT BIG RIG HEMA 31 F8 23 43 18 S 149 40 20 E

Dululu
Dululu Rest Area
Bryant St, next to toilet block
CT HT BIG RIG HEMA 16 D1 23 50 54 S 150 15 40 E

Eidsvold
Eidsvold Dump Point 07 4166 9918
Cnr Burnett Way & Esplanade St
CT HT BIG RIG HEMA 16 J3 25 22 18 S 151 07 24 E

Einasleigh
Einasleigh Dump Point
Baroota St
CT HT BIG RIG HEMA 26 F7 18 30 55 S 144 05 36 E

Emerald
Emerald Showgrounds 0428 396 448
Capricorn Hwy
CT HT BIG RIG HEMA 30 F6 23 31 23 S 148 09 07 E

Eulo
Eulo Dump Point
Bulloo Development Rd, outside Airport adjacent to toilets
CT HT BIG RIG HEMA 33 G13 28 09 46 S 145 02 43 E

Eumundi
Eumundi RV Stop Over 0412 566 671
Parking Area at Eumundi, Cnr Albert St & Napier St
CT HT BIG RIG HEMA 11 B12 26 28 34 S 152 57 13 E

Fernvale
Fernvale Dump Point
Clive St
CT HT BIG RIG HEMA 4 E1 27 27 14 S 152 39 01 E

Forsayth
Forsayth Rest Area
Einasleigh-Forsayth Rd, next to the public toilet block
CT HEMA 26 F6 18 35 10 S 143 36 10 E

Gatton
Gatton Dump Point
23 East St
CT HT HEMA 12 F2 27 33 19 S 152 16 29 E

Gatton Showgrounds
Woodlands Rd, Behind toilet block, near grassed area at rear of grounds
CT HT BIG RIG HEMA 12 F2 27 33 31 S 152 16 51 E

Gayndah
Zonhoven Park
Burnett Hwy. E end of town
CT HT HEMA 13 C1 25 37 44 S 151 37 33 E

Georgetown
Georgetown Dump Point
Normanton St, opposite toilets in Heritage Park
CT HT BIG RIG HEMA 26 F6 18 17 30 S 143 32 53 E

QUEENSLAND

Gin Gin

Gin Gin Dump Point
Bruce Hwy, N end of town. LH side of gravel parking area opposite service stations
CT HEMA 16 H6 24 59 02 S 151 57 01 E

Glenden

Glenden Dump Point
Gilbert Ave, at Golf Club
CT HT BIG RIG HEMA 18 H3 21 21 01 S 148 07 23 E

Goomeri

Goomeri Showgrounds 0419 720 407
Cnr Burnett Hwy & Laird St. S end of town
CT HT BIG RIG HEMA 12 A2 26 11 11 S 152 04 09 E

Goondiwindi

Caltex Truck Stop 07 4671 0999
Boundary Rd, E end of town
CT HT BIG RIG HEMA 35 H11 28 31 42 S 150 18 37 E

Redmond Park
Anderson St, near the driver reviver area
CT HT BIG RIG HEMA 35 H12 28 33 01 S 150 19 12 E

Gregory Downs

Council Dump Point 07 4745 5100
Wills Development Rd, next to the toilets
CT BIG RIG HEMA 25 E4 18 38 59 S 139 15 14 E

Gympie

Archery Park
Cnr Cross St & Bruce Hwy. 4 km N of town centre
CT HT BIG RIG HEMA 12 A4 26 11 19 S 152 39 13 E

Six Mile Creek Rest Area
Bruce Hwy, 6 km S of Gympie
CT BIG RIG HEMA 12 A4 26 13 54 S 152 41 49 E

Hervey Bay

Hervey Bay RV Stop Info Centre 1800 811 728
Hervey Bay Information Centre. Cnr Urraween Rd & Hervey Bay Rd
CT HT BIG RIG HEMA 14 E4 25 17 59 S 152 48 34 E

Home Hill

Home Hill Dump Point
Sixth St. W of railway crossing
CT BIG RIG HEMA 18 C1 19 39 59 S 147 24 52 E

Hughenden

Hughenden Dump Point 07 4741 1958
Corner of McLaren St & Swanston St. Near white tower
CT HT BIG RIG HEMA 26 K7 20 51 03 S 144 11 32 E

Hughenden RV Parking Area 07 4741 2970
Parking Area at Hughenden. E end of Stansfield St on N side of road
CT HT BIG RIG HEMA 26 K7 20 50 41 S 144 12 20 E

Ilfracombe

Ilfracombe Dump Point 07 4658 2233
Murray St, opposite caravan park
CT HT BIG RIG HEMA 29 F11 23 29 27 S 144 30 37 E

Imbil

Imbil Showgrounds
Imbil Brooloo Rd
CT HT BIG RIG HEMA 11 B8 26 27 50 S 152 40 42 E

Ingham

Tyto Wetlands RV Stop 07 4776 4792
Cnr Bruce Hwy & Cooper St. S of town on W side of Hwy
CT HT BIG RIG HEMA 19 E2 18 39 18 S 146 09 11 E

Inglewood

Inglewood Rest Area
Brook St, off Cunningham Hwy. E end of town
CT HT BIG RIG HEMA 35 H13 28 24 51 S 151 05 02 E

Injune

Injune Truck Stop 07 4626 1581
Hutton St, near Roadhouse
CT HT BIG RIG HEMA 34 A7 25 50 24 S 148 34 03 E

Innisfail

Innisfail Dump Point 07 4063 2655
Haddrell Park, Bruce Hwy. Opposite Barrier Reef Motel. S side of town
CT HT BIG RIG HEMA 21 J6 17 32 01 S 146 01 47 E

Ipswich

Ipswich Showgrounds 07 3281 1577
Cnr Warwick & Salisbury Rds
CT HT BIG RIG HEMA 4 G2 27 37 38 S 152 45 33 E

Isisford

Barcoo River Weir Camping Grounds 07 4658 8900
Saint Francis St. At toilet block, SE end of town
CT HT HEMA 29 G11 24 15 28 S 144 26 36 E

Jandowae

Jandowae Dump Point
Dalby St, between High & Hickey Sts. Adjacent to Lions Park, N side of town
CT HT BIG RIG HEMA 35 C13 26 46 45 S 151 06 33 E

Jandowae Showgrounds 07 4668 5268
Warra St
CT HT BIG RIG HEMA 35 C13 26 47 13 S 151 06 38 E

Jericho

Jericho Showground 07 4651 4129
1 km NE of Jericho, at E end of town, turn N just E of railway crossing
CT HT BIG RIG HEMA 29 F14 23 35 45 S 146 07 53 E

Jondaryan

Jondaryan Woolshed 07 4692 2229
264 Jondaryan Evanslea Rd. 3 km S of Jondaryan
CT HT BIG RIG HEMA 35 E14 27 23 32 S 151 34 30 E

Julia Creek

Julia Creek Dump Point
Hickman St, near Junction of Allison St
CT HT BIG RIG HEMA 26 K4 20 39 10 S 141 44 30 E

Julia Creek Racecourse
In the Racecourse off Kynuna Road. Near the blue toilet block. GPS at entry
CT HT BIG RIG HEMA 28 A7 20 39 50 S 141 44 32 E

Jundah

Jundah Dump Point 07 4658 6133
800m N of Jundah on Thomson Developmental Rd, near turn off to outpatient entrance
CT HT BIG RIG HEMA 29 H9 24 49 11 S 143 03 52 E

Kalbar

Kalbar Showground 0499 970 119
George St. N end of town
CT BIG RIG HEMA 6 G3 27 56 15 S 152 37 32 E

Karumba

Truck Stop 07 4745 2240
Cnr Yappar St & Karumba Development Rd
CT HT BIG RIG HEMA 25 C7 17 29 29 S 140 50 07 E

Kenilworth

Kenilworth Show & Recreation Grounds 0438 849 947
Elizabeth St. S side of town
CT HT BIG RIG HEMA 11 D9 26 35 56 S 152 43 34 E

Kia Ora

Standown Caravan Park 07 5486 5144
91 Radtke Rd. Public access for fee
CT HT $ BIG RIG HEMA 13 E5 26 02 08 S 152 47 32 E

Kilkivan

Weir Oval
Wide Bay Hwy, beside the toilet block
CT HT BIG RIG HEMA 13 E3 26 05 01 S 152 14 33 E

Kingaroy

Lions Park 07 4162 6230
Baron St, off Kingaroy St
CT HEMA 12 B1 26 32 47 S 151 50 16 E

Laidley

Laidley Dump Point
John St, near swimming pool
CT HT BIG RIG HEMA 12 F3 27 37 55 S 152 23 34 E

Lawnton

Pine Rivers Showground 0459 023 346
Gympie Rd
CT HT BIG RIG HEMA 4 C4 27 17 07 S 152 59 13 E

Longreach

Longreach Dump Point
Cnr Landsborough Hwy & Kite St
CT HT BIG RIG HEMA 29 F11 23 26 24 S 144 14 57 E

Longreach Showground 07 4658 1745
Sandpiper St, off Eagle St. W end of town
CT HT BIG RIG HEMA 29 F11 23 26 20 S 144 14 56 E

Lowood

Lowood Showgrounds & Caravan Park 0455 187 201
Station St. Turn L at entry, between buildings
CT HT BIG RIG HEMA 8 H2 27 27 45 S 152 35 01 E

Mackay

Mackay Rest Area
At the Information Centre, Bruce Hwy. Access from Nthbound only. Turn in between BP & Information Centre. Dump is on the left
CT BIG RIG HEMA 17 A1 21 09 56 S 149 09 14 E

Maleny

Maleny Showgrounds 07 5494 2008
13 Maleny-Stanley River Rd
CT HT BIG RIG HEMA 11 F10 26 45 47 S 152 50 44 E

Mareeba

Eales Park Dump Point 07 4092 5674
Doyle St, opposite Davies Park. W side of town
CT HT BIG RIG HEMA 22 D1 16 59 42 S 145 24 50 E

Maroochydore

Maroochydore Dump Point
Commercial Rd
CT HT BIG RIG HEMA 11 E13 26 39 09 S 153 03 34 E

Maryborough

Airport
Access via Airport Dr off Saltwater Creek Rd. Follow signs around to right. 2 km from town on Rd to Hervey Bay
CT HT HEMA 14 G3 25 31 06 S 152 42 33 E

QUEENSLAND

Maryborough Showground & Equestrian Park 1300 794 929
Bruce Hwy. N end of town. Veer R past entry gates
CT HT BIG RIG HEMA 14 G3 25 30 22 S 152 39 46 E

McKinlay
McKinlay Dump Point
Middleton St, at the truck stop
CT HT BIG RIG HEMA 26 K3 21 16 14 S 141 17 23 E

Meandarra
Leo Gordon Apex Park
Cnr Meandarra & Dillon Sts
CT HEMA 35 E10 27 19 24 S 149 52 50 E

Miles
Miles Council Dump Point
Industry Lane, via Leichhardt Hwy (Sth), Waterworks Rd
CT HT BIG RIG HEMA 35 C11 26 39 59 S 150 11 07 E

Millmerran
Millmerran Showgrounds 0427 957 176
Millmerran-Cecil Plains Rd
CT HT BIG RIG HEMA 35 F14 27 51 37 S 151 16 40 E

Walpole Park
Charles St, between Walpole & Charlotte Sts. Dump Point opposite park
CT HT BIG RIG HEMA 35 F14 27 52 17 S 151 16 28 E

Mirani
Mirani Dump Point 1300 622 529
Victoria St, opposite Council Customer Service Centre
CT HT BIG RIG HEMA 18 G6 21 09 34 S 148 51 52 E

Miriam Vale
Granite Creek (Bernie Christensen) Rest Area
Rest Area 36 km S of Miriam Vale or 63 km N of Gin Gin
CT HEMA 16 F5 24 36 44 S 151 40 04 E

Mission Beach
Mission Beach Dump Point
Porter Promenade, outside caravan park
CT HT BIG RIG HEMA 19 B2 17 51 53 S 146 06 29 E

Mitchell
Mitchell Showgrounds 07 4623 8171
Alice St, near entrance
CT BIG RIG HEMA 34 B6 26 29 47 S 147 58 45 E

Monto
Monto Community Rest Stop
Railway Yard, Gladstone-Monto Rd
CT HT HEMA 16 G3 24 51 46 S 151 07 15 E

Monto Showground 07 4166 9918
Oxley St, W side of town
CT HT BIG RIG HEMA 16 G3 24 51 57 S 151 06 53 E

Morven
Morven Recreation Ground 07 4654 8281
S side of town via Victoria St
CT HT BIG RIG HEMA 34 B4 26 25 06 S 147 06 58 E

Mossman
Mossman Dump Point
Cnr Foxton Ave & Park St (Outside Aquatic Centre)
CT HT BIG RIG HEMA 21 A2 16 27 18 S 145 22 18 E

Mount Isa
Mount Isa Dump Point
Cnr George St & East St
CT HT BIG RIG HEMA 25 J4 20 43 16 S 139 30 10 E

Mount Molloy
Rifle Creek Rest Area
Rest Area 1 km N of Mt Molloy, 33 km S of Mossman or 41 km N of Mareeba
CT HEMA 21 C2 16 39 58 S 145 19 42 E

Mount Perry
Mount Perry Dump Point 07 4156 3850
54 Heusman Street, in front of the caravan park
CT HT BIG RIG HEMA 13 A1 25 10 29 S 151 38 24 E

Mount Surprise
Mount Surprise Dump Point 07 4062 1233
Main Rd, outside toilet block
CT HT BIG RIG HEMA 26 F7 18 08 50 S 144 19 03 E

Moura
Moura Dump Point
Moura Bindaree Rd, E end of town
CT HT BIG RIG HEMA 31 H9 24 33 54 S 149 58 27 E

Mt Isa
World War 2 Historical Site
Rest Area 50 km NW of Mt Isa or 139 km E of Camooweal. Near monument on Barkly Hwy
CT HT BIG RIG HEMA 25 J4 20 22 22 S 139 15 52 E

Mundubbera
Mundubbera Dump Point 07 4165 5700
Bauer St, near the Lyons St intersection & the tennis courts
CT HT BIG RIG HEMA 16 K4 25 35 33 S 151 18 03 E

Mungallala
Mungallala RV Stop
Camp Spot at Mungallala. Warrego Hwy
CT HT BIG RIG HEMA 34 B5 26 26 44 S 147 32 29 E

Murgon
Murgon RV Stop 07 4189 9387
3 Krebs St
CT HT BIG RIG HEMA 12 A1 26 14 32 S 151 56 17 E

Murgon Area
Bjelke Petersen Dam.
Via Haager Dr, Yallakool Park in parking area opposite tennis courts
CT BIG RIG HEMA 12 A1 26 18 12 S 151 59 44 E

Muttaburra
Muttaburra Caravan Park 07 4658 7191
Caravan Park at Muttaburra. Cnr Mary & Bridge Sts
CT HT BIG RIG HEMA 29 D11 22 35 36 S 144 33 07 E

Nambour
Nambour Dump Point
Off Bli Bli Rd. Located in the side road on the Sth side of the roundabout when taking the Western exit off Bruce Hwy. Signposted. Locked, call number on gate for combination
CT HT BIG RIG HEMA 11 D12 26 36 59 S 152 58 44 E

Nanango
Tipperary Flat Park
Rest Area at Nanango. 1.5 km S of PO. Next to BP service station
CT HT BIG RIG HEMA 12 B1 26 40 48 S 151 59 47 E

Nebo
Nebo Rest Area
Peak Downs Hwy
CT HT BIG RIG HEMA 18 J5 21 40 58 S 148 41 34 E

Nindigully
Nindigully
At the rear of new toilet block, near hotel
CT HT BIG RIG HEMA 35 G8 28 21 17 S 148 49 15 E

Normanton
Bang Bang Rest Area
Rest Area 112 km S of Normanton or 90 km N of Burke & Wills Roadhouse
CT HT BIG RIG HEMA 25 E6 18 31 36 S 140 39 11 E

Normanton Council Depot 07 4745 2200
Old Hospital Rd. Business hours only
CT HT BIG RIG HEMA 25 D7 17 40 51 S 141 04 36 E

Oakey
Oakey Dump Point
Cnr York St & Lorrimer St next to Works Depot
CT HT BIG RIG HEMA 12 F1 27 26 27 S 151 43 27 E

Petrie
Wyllie Park Rest Area
Old Bruce Hwy, beside North Pine River. Gates open 8.00am - 6.00pm
CT HT BIG RIG HEMA 4 C4 27 16 22 S 152 58 49 E

Pittsworth
Pittsworth Dump Point
Railways St, outside Showgrounds next to SES building
CT HT BIG RIG HEMA 36 F2 27 42 41 S 151 38 31 E

Pomona
Pomona Showgrounds 07 5485 1477
Exhibition St
CT HT BIG RIG HEMA 12 A4 26 21 36 S 152 51 28 E

Proserpine
Proserpine Dump Point 07 4945 1554
79 Anzac Rd. On road outside caravan park
CT HT BIG RIG HEMA 18 E5 20 24 14 S 148 34 17 E

Quilpie
Quilpie Dump Point 07 4995 8657
John Waugh Park. Quarrion St
CT HT BIG RIG HEMA 33 C11 26 36 57 S 144 15 46 E

Rainbow Beach
Rainbow Beach Sewerage Works 07 5481 0800
By sewerage pumping station. Clarkson Drive (Inskip Point Rd)
CT HT BIG RIG HEMA 14 K6 25 54 03 S 153 05 18 E

Ravenshoe
Ravenshoe Dump Point 07 4096 2244
Outside sewerage works, Ascham St
CT HT BIG RIG HEMA 21 K3 17 36 55 S 145 28 49 E

Redcliffe
Redcliffe Showgrounds 07 3283 0405
Scarborough Rd, near hospital. Daylight hours only
CT HT BIG RIG HEMA 4 C5 27 13 30 S 153 06 22 E

Richmond
Richmond RV Parking Area
At 72 hr RV parking Area. 300m off Main Rd, via Harris St & Hillier St
CT HT BIG RIG HEMA 26 K6 20 43 44 S 143 08 36 E

Rockhampton
Music Bowl Park
Nuttall Street, off bruce Hwy, N of city. Across from sports fields
CT HT BIG RIG HEMA 16 B2 23 19 08 S 150 30 51 E

QUEENSLAND

Rolleston

Beazley Park
In Rest Area, Beazley Park, Meteor St & Dawson Hwy
CT HT BIG RIG HEMA 30 G7 24 27 48 S 148 37 28 E

Rollingstone

Bushy Parker Park
Rest Area at Rollingstone. Turn E off Bruce Hwy just N of Rollingstone, across railway line
CT HT BIG RIG HEMA 19 F3 19 02 46 S 146 23 37 E

Roma

Roma Dump Point 07 4622 1266
Station St, between Lewis & Major Sts. In front of council Depot
CT HT BIG RIG HEMA 35 C8 26 34 34 S 148 47 46 E

Roma Showgrounds 0408 988 002
Northern Rd. N end of town
CT HT BIG RIG HEMA 35 C8 26 33 13 S 148 47 06 E

Sapphire

Sapphire Reserve
Rifle Range Rd, opposite general store
CT HT BIG RIG HEMA 30 F5 23 27 57 S 147 43 13 E

Sarina

Sarina Dump Point 07 4956 2251
Tourist Centre, Railway Square off the Bruce Hwy
CT HT BIG RIG HEMA 17 B2 21 25 33 S 149 13 02 E

Scarborough

Scarborough Boat Ramp
Thurecht Parade. Next to public toilets, raised off the ground
CT HEMA 4 B5 27 11 39 S 153 06 15 E

Shorncliffe

Shorncliffe Boat Ramp
In boat ramp car park, off Sinbad St. Next to toilet block. Cassettes only, raised off ground
CT HEMA 4 D5 27 20 02 S 153 04 50 E

Springsure

Springsure Dump Point 07 4984 1166
At toilet block near museum
CT HEMA 30 G6 24 07 05 S 148 05 22 E

Springsure Showgrounds 0427 841 612
Barcoo St. S side of town
CT HT BIG RIG HEMA 30 G6 24 07 19 S 148 05 02 E

St George

St George Showground 07 4620 8844
McGahan St, behind E end of showground
CT HT BIG RIG HEMA 35 G8 28 01 39 S 148 35 27 E

St Lawrence

St Lawrence Recreational Reserve 1300 472 227
1 km W of St Lawrence
CT HT BIG RIG HEMA 17 F3 22 21 04 S 149 31 11 E

Stanthorpe

Apex Park 07 4681 5500
Folkestone St, off Maryland St at toilet block
CT HT BIG RIG HEMA 36 H3 28 39 29 S 151 55 55 E

Surat

Surat Fishing & Restocking Club Park 07 4626 5058
Carnarvon Hwy, 1 km N of Surat
CT BIG RIG HEMA 35 D9 27 08 57 S 149 04 23 E

Talwood

Talwood Sports Ground 07 4671 7400
Recreation Street
CT HT BIG RIG HEMA 35 H10 28 29 12 S 149 28 08 E

Tambo

Tambo Lake
Landsborough Hwy, S end of town
CT HT BIG RIG HEMA 29 H14 24 52 55 S 146 15 35 E

Tara Lagoon

Tara Lagoon Parklands 1300 268 624
In Camp Area at Tara Lagoon
CT HT BIG RIG HEMA 35 E12 27 16 21 S 150 27 36 E

Taroom

Taroom Dump Point
Wolsey St. 700m N of Post Office, between Rose Rd & North St. Outside Council Depot
CT HT BIG RIG HEMA 31 J9 25 38 03 S 149 47 56 E

Texas

Texas Dump Point 07 4652 1444
Flemming St, outside Council Depot
CT HT BIG RIG HEMA 35 J13 28 51 12 S 151 10 25 E

Thallon

Thallon Recreation Ground 0427 259 095
Henry St
CT HT BIG RIG HEMA 35 H8 28 37 58 S 148 51 59 E

Thargomindah

Thargomindah Dump Point
Watts St off Adventure Way. N of town, Opposite council building near cooling ponds
CT HT BIG RIG HEMA 33 F10 27 59 23 S 143 49 11 E

Theodore

Theodore Dump Point 07 4992 9500
Eastern Lane, off 7th Avenue. Next to Tennis Courts
CT HT BIG RIG HEMA 31 H9 24 56 43 S 150 04 36 E

Thuringowa

Ross River Dam 07 4773 8411
At entrance to Ross River Dam Park, Upper Ross River Rd, via Kelso
CT HT BIG RIG HEMA 19 H4 19 24 27 S 146 44 00 E

Tin Can Bay

Tin Can Bay Dump Point
Snapper Creek Rd, turning point at tip
CT HT BIG RIG HEMA 14 K5 25 55 24 S 152 59 27 E

Toogoolawah

Toogoolawah Showgrounds 0459 603 666
Ivory Creek Rd
CT HT BIG RIG HEMA 12 D3 27 04 41 S 152 22 31 E

Toowoomba

Toowoomba Showground 07 4634 7400
Glenvale Rd. 8.00am-5.00pm Monday to Friday
CT HT $ BIG RIG HEMA 12 F1 27 33 36 S 151 53 04 E

Townsville

BP Bohle's Little Acre
900 Ingham Rd. 'Daylight hours only'. $10.00 Key deposit, dump point at rear of service station
CT HT BIG RIG HEMA 19 G4 19 15 43 S 146 42 53 E

Willows Shopping Centre
Kern Brothers Dr. In shopping centre car park, S side on far right
CT HT BIG RIG HEMA 19 G4 19 19 02 S 146 43 31 E

Tully

Tully Showground 07 4068 2288
Butler St, outside Showgrounds
CT HT BIG RIG HEMA 19 B2 17 56 02 S 145 55 47 E

Wallumbilla

Wallumbilla Showgrounds
Main Rd at the W end of town
CT HT BIG RIG HEMA 35 C9 26 35 14 S 149 11 01 E

Wandoan

Wandoan Dump Point
28-30 Jerrard St, near water tower
CT HT BIG RIG HEMA 35 A11 26 07 21 S 149 57 35 E

Wandoan Water Tower-Duplicate 07 4627 5148
Jerrard St, near tower
CT HT BIG RIG HEMA 35 A11 26 07 21 S 149 57 35 E

Warwick

Matilda Roadhouse 07 4661 7450
Cnr Cunningham Hwy & Ogilvie Rd. Nth end of town
CT HT BIG RIG HEMA 12 J2 28 11 41 S 152 02 39 E

Weipa

Weipa Dump Point
Kerr Point Rd, outside Weipa Camping Ground
CT HT BIG RIG HEMA 23 D1 12 38 23 S 141 51 42 E

Windorah

Windorah Dump Point
Quilpie Windorah Rd (near water tower). E side of Town
CT HT BIG RIG HEMA 29 J8 25 25 04 S 142 39 35 E

Winton

Winton Dump Point
In Riley St parking area. Cnr of Riley & Jundah Rd
CT HT BIG RIG HEMA 29 D9 22 23 30 S 143 02 23 E

Winton Recreation Ground 07 4657 1188
Vindex St, next to skate park
CT BIG RIG HEMA 29 D9 22 23 14 S 143 01 56 E

Wondai

Wondai RV Stop 07 4189 9251
Haly St, adjacent to Old Rail Station
CT HT BIG RIG HEMA 12 A1 26 19 02 S 151 52 26 E

Woodford

Woodford Showgrounds 0437 390 862
Camp Area at Woodford. Neurem Rd
CT HT BIG RIG HEMA 11 J9 26 56 51 S 152 46 12 E

Wyandra

Wyandra Dump Point
Mack St, near Cooper St
CT HT BIG RIG HEMA 34 D1 27 14 44 S 145 58 43 E

Yeppoon

Merv Anderson Park 07 4939 4888
Yeppoon Emu Park Rd, 200m E of Visitor Info Centre
CT HT BIG RIG HEMA 16 B2 23 08 16 S 150 45 00 E

Yowah Opal Field

Yowah Rest Area
Rest Area at Yowah. Gemwood St, first turn L after school.
CT HT BIG RIG HEMA 33 F12 27 58 01 S 144 37 59 E

Yungaburra

Yungaburra Dump Point
Lot 550 Mulgrave Rd. On road outside sewerage works
CT HT BIG RIG HEMA 22 J4 17 15 45 S 145 34 44 E

NEW SOUTH WALES

Aberdeen

Taylor Park
New England Hwy. N end of town. At fence on N side of park
CT HT BIG RIG HEMA 54 H6 32 09 39 S 150 53 18 E

Abermain

Abermain Bowling & Recreation Club 02 4930 4285
Entry via Goulburn St. Key at reception
CT HT BIG RIG HEMA 45 H7 32 48 26 S 151 25 36 E

Adelong

Adelong Dump Point
Travers St, off Snowy Mountain Hwy
CT HT BIG RIG HEMA 66 C5 35 18 24 S 148 03 42 E

Albury

Albury City Dump Point 1300 252 879
Railway Place. Enter at Cnr Smollett & Young St to Railway Station, turn S to dump location
CT HT BIG RIG HEMA 66 G1 36 05 07 S 146 55 26 E

Appin

Appin Park Rest Area
Appin Road
CT HT BIG RIG HEMA 51 B11 34 11 53 S 150 47 19 E

Armidale

Armidale Dump Point
Galloway St. Approx 1 km S of City off Waterfall Way. Follow signs for Arboretum
CT HEMA 55 A8 30 31 15 S 151 38 47 E

Ashford

Ashford Caravan Park 02 6725 4014
57 km N of Inverell. Bukkulla St
CT HT BIG RIG HEMA 56 F5 29 19 24 S 151 05 52 E

Balranald

Swimming Pool Car Park
Church St. In car park next to water tower
CT HT BIG RIG HEMA 62 H7 34 38 07 S 143 33 43 E

Baradine

Baradine Dump Point
Lions Park, cnr Wellington & Darling Sts
CT HT BIG RIG HEMA 58 H4 30 56 59 S 149 04 00 E

Camp Cypress 02 6843 1035
1 km W of PO at showground. Lachlan St
CT HT BIG RIG HEMA 58 H4 30 56 49 S 149 03 21 E

Barellan

Barellan Dump Point
Myall St beside Barellan Hall
CT HT BIG RIG HEMA 63 G14 34 17 06 S 146 34 16 E

Barooga

Barooga Dump Point
Nangunia St, adjacent to the Lions bus shelter
CT HT BIG RIG HEMA 69 H8 35 54 25 S 145 41 44 E

Barraba

Council Works Depot
77 Cherry St. Outside depot
CT HT BIG RIG HEMA 54 A5 30 22 49 S 150 36 46 E

Batehaven

City Park
Beach Rd, in car park opposite shops. Cassette only access may be blocked by cars
CT HEMA 67 E12 35 43 53 S 150 12 00 E

Bathurst

Bathurst Council Depot 02 6336 6011
205 Morrisset St. Access 24/7, both sides of road
CT HT BIG RIG HEMA 52 D5 33 24 10 S 149 34 26 E

Bathurst Showground 02 6331 1349
Kendell Ave
CT HT BIG RIG HEMA 52 D5 33 25 05 S 149 35 22 E

Batlow

Batlow Dump Point
Memorial Avenue, opposite Wakehurst Ave Jcn
CT HT BIG RIG HEMA 66 D5 35 31 12 S 148 09 00 E

Bega

Bega Showground
Upper St. Next to the toilets
CT HT BIG RIG HEMA 67 J11 36 40 40 S 149 50 50 E

Bellingen

Bellingen Dump Point 02 6655 2310
Black St, opposite Bellingen Showground
CT HT BIG RIG HEMA 55 A13 30 26 55 S 152 53 54 E

Bendeela

Bendeela Recreation Area
In Camp Area 7 km W of Kangaroo Valley. Dump point near toilet block in campgrounds 1 & 2. Cassette only
CT HEMA 51 J8 34 44 21 S 150 28 15 E

Berridale

Berridale Dump Point
At rear of the Southern Cross Motor Inn. Access off Middlingbank Rd
CT HT BIG RIG HEMA 66 H7 36 21 35 S 148 49 52 E

Berrigan

Berrigan Dump Point
Hayes Park, Jerilderie St
CT HT HEMA 69 G9 35 39 38 S 145 48 50 E

Berry

Berry Showground 0427 605 200
500m S of PO. Alexandra St
CT HT BIG RIG HEMA 51 J10 34 46 46 S 150 41 46 E

Bingara

Bingara Showground 02 6724 0066
Bowen St, inside 2nd entrance gate
CT BIG RIG HEMA 56 H4 29 52 00 S 150 33 20 E

Cunningham Park
Copeton Dam Rd, fee for water
CT HT BIG RIG HEMA 56 H4 29 52 15 S 150 34 08 E

Blayney

Blayney Showground 02 6368 2104
Western Hwy
CT BIG RIG HEMA 52 E4 33 31 06 S 149 15 31 E

Henry St Toilet Block 02 6368 2104
Henry St. S end, behind PO
CT HT HEMA 52 E4 33 31 58 S 149 15 23 E

Boggabri

Jubilee Park 02 6799 6760
Hull St, next to the entrance
CT HT BIG RIG HEMA 54 B3 30 42 20 S 150 02 56 E

Bomaderry

Bomaderry Country Winnebago 02 4421 0122
314 Princes Hwy. Enter at rear via Cambewarra Rd, near McDonalds. Business hours only
CT HEMA 51 K9 34 50 36 S 150 35 43 E

Bombala

Bombala Caravan Park 0488 257 928
Monaro Hwy. Public access, pay fee to office
CT HT $ HEMA 67 K9 36 54 30 S 149 14 20 E

Boorowa

Boorowa Dump Point
Park St, next to caravan park
CT HT $ BIG RIG HEMA 52 J2 34 26 01 S 148 43 12 E

Bourke

Back O Bourke Information Centre 08 6872 1321
Kidman Way
CT HT BIG RIG HEMA 61 D11 30 04 51 S 145 57 00 E

Braidwood

Braidwood Dump Point 02 4842 9231
Cnr of Kingsway & McKellar Sts, N side of town
CT HT BIG RIG HEMA 67 D11 35 26 24 S 149 48 07 E

Branxton

Branxton Oval
John Rose Ave
CT HT BIG RIG HEMA 45 A5 32 39 18 S 151 21 05 E

Brewarrina

Brewarrina Dump Point
At rear of the Information Centre on Bathurst Rd. Only accessible when info centre open. 0830-1700 weekdays
CT HT HEMA 61 D13 29 57 35 S 146 51 28 E

Broken Hill

Broken Hill Information Centre 08 8088 9700
Cnr Bromide & Blende Sts. Key at Information Centre
CT HT BIG RIG HEMA 62 A2 31 57 34 S 141 27 39 E

Broken Hill Racecourse 0437 250 286
5 km NE of Broken Hill, Racecourse Rd, off Tibooburra Rd. Fee if not staying at Racecourse
CT HT $ BIG RIG HEMA 60 H2 31 54 48 S 141 28 51 E

Bulahdelah

Bulahdelah Showgrounds 02 4997 4981
Cnr Stuart & Prince Sts. Near helipad
CT HT BIG RIG HEMA 55 J10 32 24 18 S 152 12 16 E

Bungendore

Bungendore Showground 0455 174 463
On the Bungendore - Sutton Rd. See Caretaker
CT HT BIG RIG HEMA 71 C7 35 14 30 S 149 24 37 E

Burren Junction

Burren Junction Bore Baths 02 6828 1399
Kamilaroi Hwy
CT HT BIG RIG HEMA 58 F4 30 06 52 S 148 59 44 E

Burrinjuck

Reflections Holiday Parks Burrinjuck Waters 02 6227 8114
Burrinjuck Dam, State Park, 25 km S of Bookham
CT HT HEMA 71 A1 34 58 46 S 148 37 11 E

Bylong

Bylong Community Sportsground
Bylong Valley Way, opposite store
CT HT BIG RIG HEMA 54 K3 32 24 58 S 150 06 52 E

Canowindra

Canowindra Caravan Park 0428 233 769
Tilga St. Next to swimming pool. 300m S of PO. Public access
CT HT BIG RIG HEMA 52 E2 33 34 08 S 148 39 50 E

NEW SOUTH WALES

Casino

Casino Showground 02 6660 0300
Grafton Rd, S end of town
CT HT BIG RIG HEMA 57 D12 28 53 02 S 153 02 48 E

Cessnock

Cessnock Showground 0412 235 447
Access gates beside indoor sports centre Mount View Rd. Close Feb & early Mar for show. Fee if not staying at showground
CT HT BIG RIG HEMA 45 J4 32 49 51 S 151 20 26 E

Clarence Town

Bridge Reserve 02 4984 2680
Durham St
CT HT BIG RIG HEMA 47 A14 32 34 58 S 151 46 56 E

Cobar

Cobar RSL

Cobar Visitors Centre 02 6836 2448
Barrier Highway
CT HT BIG RIG HEMA 61 G11 31 29 53 S 145 50 33 E

Cobargo

Cobargo Hotel 02 6493 6423
Princes Hwy
CT HT HEMA 67 H11 36 23 22 S 149 53 09 E

Coffs Harbour

Coffs Harbour Dump Point 02 6648 4000
Phil Hawthorne Dr, off Stadium Dr roundabout. S of town off Pacific Hwy
CT HT BIG RIG HEMA 55 A13 30 19 26 S 153 05 47 E

Coleambally

The Coly Club 02 6954 4170
Entry from Kingfisher Ave & Kidman Way
CT BIG RIG HEMA 63 J12 34 47 52 S 145 52 46 E

Collarenebri

Collarenebri Primitive Campground
Gwydir Hwy, E end of town. Next to football grounds. Beside toilet block
CT HEMA 58 D3 29 32 56 S 148 34 55 E

Conargo

Bills Park 03 5880 1200
Rest Area at Conargo. W end of town, near school
CT HT BIG RIG HEMA 63 K10 35 18 24 S 145 10 38 E

Condobolin

River View Caravan Park 02 6895 2611
Diggers Ave. S end of town. Public access
CT HT BIG RIG HEMA 64 E2 33 05 40 S 147 08 50 E

Coolongolook

Coolongolook Dump Point
King St, off Pacific Hwy. Cassette only
CT HEMA 55 J11 32 13 08 S 152 19 21 E

Cooma

Cooma Dump Point
Cnr of Geebung St & Polo Flat Rd
CT HT BIG RIG HEMA 67 G8 36 13 30 S 149 08 52 E

Coonabarabran

Neilson Park
Rest Area at Coonabarabran. Essex St, Eastern end of park
CT HT BIG RIG HEMA 58 J5 31 16 16 S 149 16 46 E

Coonamble

Coonamble Riverside Caravan Park 02 6822 1926
138 Castlereagh St. Inside caravan park, public access. Big Rigs call ahead
CT HT BIG RIG HEMA 58 H3 30 57 48 S 148 23 21 E

Cootamundra

Cootamundra Dump Point
Apex Park, Hurley St off Olympic Hwy. Near toilet block
CT HT BIG RIG HEMA 64 J4 34 38 40 S 148 01 30 E

Corowa

Corowa Dump Point
Rowers Park, Bridge Rd. Near the toilets
CT HT BIG RIG HEMA 69 J11 36 00 15 S 146 23 38 E

Cowra

Cowra Overnight Rest Area
Lachlan Valley Way
CT HT BIG RIG HEMA 52 F2 33 50 08 S 148 40 55 E

Crookwell

Crookwell Caravan Park 0408 250 652
Caravan Park at Crookwell. Laggan Rd
CT HT BIG RIG HEMA 52 J5 34 27 17 S 149 28 03 E

Cumnock

Cumnock Showgrounds 0403 054 754
Baldry Road
CT HT BIG RIG HEMA 52 B2 32 55 43 S 148 44 46 E

Dareton

Dareton Dump Point
Tiltao St, next to service station
CT HEMA 62 G3 34 05 44 S 142 02 29 E

Darlington Point

Darlington Point Lions Park 02 6968 4166
Darlington St. N side of town, 200m E of caravan park
CT BIG RIG HEMA 63 H12 34 34 00 S 146 00 29 E

Delungra

Delungra Recreation Ground 02 6724 8275
Reedy St, W end of town
CT HT BIG RIG HEMA 56 G4 29 39 04 S 150 49 33 E

Deniliquin

Deniliquin Rest Area
Cobb Hwy, N side of Town, adjacent to public toilet
CT HT BIG RIG HEMA 68 G6 35 31 31 S 144 58 41 E

Dorrigo

Dorrigo Dump Point
Waterfall Way (Armidale Rd) S of showground
CT HT BIG RIG HEMA 55 A12 30 20 29 S 152 42 02 E

Dubbo

Western Plains Zoo
At Western Plains Zoo. Turn R after entering through main gate. In caravan parking area
CT HT BIG RIG HEMA 64 C5 32 16 18 S 148 35 09 E

Dunedoo

Dunedoo Dump Point
156 Bolaro St, next to Town Hall
CT HT BIG RIG HEMA 54 H1 32 00 58 S 149 23 24 E

Dungog

Dungog Showground 02 4992 1810
Chapman St
CT HT BIG RIG HEMA 55 J9 32 24 19 S 151 45 03 E

Eugowra

Byrne's Park
Byrne's Park, Myall St, adjacent to bridge
CT HT BIG RIG HEMA 52 D1 33 25 40 S 148 22 11 E

Euston

Euston Dump Point 03 5026 4244
Nixon St, entrance between Euston Club & Motel. If locked key at club
CT HT BIG RIG HEMA 62 H5 34 34 47 S 142 44 41 E

Evans Head

Evans Head Industrial Estate 02 6682 4392
Memorial Airport Dr, near council depot, between Winjeel Dr & Sir Valston Hancock Dr
CT HT BIG RIG HEMA 57 E13 29 06 15 S 153 25 20 E

Finley

Finley RV Stop
Endeavour St, beside old railway station
CT HT BIG RIG HEMA 69 G8 35 38 41 S 145 34 37 E

Forbes

Forbes Lions Park
Rest Area at Forbes. Cnr of Lachlan & Junction Sts. 500m S of PO, beside lake
CT HT BIG RIG HEMA 64 F4 33 23 22 S 148 00 14 E

Shire Works Depot 02 6850 1300
Newell Hwy. Near BP Roadhouse, Fitzgeralds Bridge. 1.5 km S of PO. Business hours only
CT HT BIG RIG HEMA 64 F4 33 24 07 S 147 59 05 E

Glen Innes

Glen Innes Lions Park
Cnr East Ave & Ferguson St
CT HT BIG RIG HEMA 57 G8 29 44 03 S 151 44 04 E

Gloucester

Gloucester Holiday Park 02 6558 1720
Denison St. 700m W of PO. Call at reception for payment & directions
CT $ HEMA 55 H9 32 00 23 S 151 57 12 E

Goolgowi

Goolgowi Caravan Park 02 6965 1900
Combo St. 1 km NE of PO
CT HT BIG RIG HEMA 63 F12 33 58 47 S 145 42 22 E

Goolgowi Dump Point
Napier St, in the lane beside the fire station
CT HT HEMA 63 F12 33 58 47 S 145 42 28 E

Goulburn

Goulburn Recreation Area
Braidwood Rd
CT HT BIG RIG HEMA 50 J1 34 46 12 S 149 42 52 E

Marsden Weir Park
Fitzroy Street off Crookwell Rd. Limited access
CT HEMA 50 J1 34 44 08 S 149 42 25 E

Grafton

Grafton Greyhound Racing Club Campground 02 6642 3713
Cranworth St
CT BIG RIG HEMA 57 G12 29 40 27 S 152 55 32 E

Grafton Showground 0468 482 919
Prince & Dobie St
CT HT BIG RIG HEMA 57 G12 29 41 03 S 152 56 24 E

Grenfell

Grenfell Old Railway Station 02 6343 1212
West St, near old railway station. Take 2nd driveway from cnr of Camp St
CT HT BIG RIG HEMA 64 G4 33 53 43 S 148 09 21 E

NEW SOUTH WALES

Griffith

Willow Park 02 6962 4145
Kookora St toilet block
CT RIG HEMA 63 G12 34 17 16 S 146 01 55 E

Gulgong

Gulgong Dump Point 02 6374 1202
Saleyards Lane off Station St, front of shire depot
CT HT RIG HEMA 54 J1 32 21 30 S 149 32 46 E

Gulgong Showground 0499 246 434
Entrance on Cnr of Grevillia & Guntawang Rds
CT HT RIG HEMA 54 J1 32 22 15 S 149 31 41 E

Gundagai

Gundagai Dump Point
Railway Parade
CT HT RIG HEMA 66 B5 35 03 55 S 148 06 45 E

Gunnedah

Gunnedah Lions RV Park
Oxley Highway (Mullaley Rd)
CT HT RIG HEMA 54 C3 30 58 43 S 150 14 24 E

Gunnedah Showground 02 6740 2125
South St. Located just inside entrance
CT HT RIG HEMA 54 C4 30 58 48 S 150 14 53 E

Gunning

Gunning Dump Point
Cnr of Yass & Gundaroo Sts
CT HT RIG HEMA 52 K4 34 46 49 S 149 16 13 E

Guyra

Mother of Ducks Lagoon
Rest Area at Guyra. White St. S end of town, turn W off Hwy into McKie Parkway
CT HT RIG HEMA 56 J7 30 13 21 S 151 40 10 E

Harden

Harden-Murrumburrah Showgrounds 0488 509 977
Woolrych St
CT HT RIG HEMA 52 J1 34 32 45 S 148 21 27 E

Hay

Hay Showground 02 6993 1087
Dunera Way, N end of town. Outside emergency service building. 200m W of showground
CT HT RIG HEMA 63 H10 34 29 51 S 144 50 17 E

Henty

Henty Dump Point
Henty Pleasant Hills Rd, behind the library
CT HT RIG HEMA 66 D1 35 30 57 S 147 01 58 E

Hillston

Hillston Lions Park
Kidman Way, next to the caravan park
CT HT RIG HEMA 63 E11 33 28 47 S 145 32 04 E

Holbrook

Holbrook Motor Village 02 6036 3100
Bardwell St, off Hume Hwy. Public access. Must advise park office
CT HT HEMA 66 E2 35 43 46 S 147 18 30 E

Howlong

Lowe Square Recreation Reserve
Riverina Hwy, between High & Larmer Sts. Near toilet block.
CT HT RIG HEMA 69 J12 35 58 50 S 146 38 02 E

Inverell

Inverell Showground 02 6722 3435
1 km E of town, enter off Tingha Rd, in between Sporting Complex & Pioneer Village
CT HT RIG HEMA 56 G5 29 46 57 S 151 07 14 E

Jamberoo

Jamberoo Dump Point
Kevin Walsh Oval. Churchill St
CT HT HEMA 51 G11 34 38 49 S 150 46 28 E

Jerilderie

Lakeside Parking Area 03 5886 1200
Newell Hwy car park, 100m W of Civic Centre, beside church
CT HT RIG HEMA 63 K12 35 21 19 S 145 43 23 E

Jugiong

Jugiong Showground
Riverside Dr. Donation requested for use
CT HT RIG HEMA 52 K1 34 49 24 S 148 19 34 E

Junee

Laurie Daley Oval 02 6924 8100
Park Lane, 70m from entry
CT HT RIG HEMA 66 A3 34 51 34 S 147 34 24 E

Kempsey

Kempsey Showground 02 6562 5231
19 Sea St
CT HT RIG HEMA 55 D12 31 04 24 S 152 49 45 E

Kew

Kew Information & Community Centre 02 6559 4400
133 Nancy Bird Walton Dr
CT HT RIG HEMA 55 F12 31 38 05 S 152 43 18 E

Khancoban

Khancoban Dump Point 02 6948 9100
Scott St, near cnr Mitchell Ave
CT HT RIG HEMA 66 G5 36 13 03 S 148 07 24 E

Kurri Kurri

Kurri Kurri Central Oval
10 Allworth St
CT HT RIG HEMA 47 D11 32 49 24 S 151 28 51 E

Kyogle

Kyogle Showground 0459 537 601
N end of town. Fee if not staying at showground
CT HT $ RIG HEMA 57 C12 28 36 57 S 153 00 00 E

Lake Cargelligo

Lake Cargelligo Shire Dump Point 02 6895 1900
Narrandera St
CT HEMA 63 D13 33 18 17 S 146 22 23 E

Leeton

Leeton Showground 02 6953 6481
Racecourse Rd
CT HT RIG HEMA 63 H13 34 33 32 S 146 24 10 E

Lightning Ridge

Lightning Ridge Dump Point 02 6829 1670
Onyx St
CT RIG HEMA 58 D2 29 25 32 S 147 58 21 E

Lismore

Lismore Showgrounds 02 6621 5916
Camp Area at Lismore. Alexandra Parade, North Lismore. Fee if not staying
CT HT RIG HEMA 57 C13 28 47 50 S 153 16 25 E

Lithgow

Lithgow Showground 02 6353 1775
Entry off George Coates Ave. Daylight hours
CT HT RIG HEMA 48 B1 33 28 51 S 150 08 42 E

Lockhart

Lockhart Caravan Park 0458 205 303
Green St. 300m W of PO
CT HEMA 63 K14 35 13 13 S 146 42 46 E

Lyndhurst

Lyndhurst Primitive Campground 0427 201 824
Camp Area at Lyndhurst. In Recreation Ground, entrance off Harrow St
CT HT RIG HEMA 52 E3 33 40 24 S 149 02 20 E

Macksville

Gumma Crossing Reserve 02 6568 2555
Camp Area 7.5 km E of Macksville
CT HT RIG HEMA 55 B13 30 42 24 S 152 59 00 E

Maclean

Maclean Showground
At Maclean Showground, entry off Cameron St
CT HT RIG HEMA 57 F13 29 27 50 S 153 11 58 E

Maitland

Maitland Dump Point
High St, in Visitor Information car park. Limited turrning circle
CT HT HEMA 47 C11 32 44 32 S 151 34 01 E

Manildra

Manildra Showground 0428 697 685
Orange St
CT HT RIG HEMA 52 C2 33 10 38 S 148 41 16 E

Manilla

Manilla Park 02 6785 1304
Charles St
CT HT RIG HEMA 54 B5 30 44 21 S 150 42 57 E

Mathoura

Mathoura Dump Point
Laneway behind Bowling Club. Enter off Mitchell St. Drive through
CT HT RIG HEMA 68 H6 35 48 30 S 144 53 56 E

Menindee

Menindee Lakes Caravan Park 08 8091 4315
Menindee Lakes Shore Drive. Public access, pay fee at reception
CT HT $ RIG HEMA 60 K4 32 21 15 S 142 24 12 E

Merriwa

Merriwa Dump Point 02 6548 2607
Blaxland St, next to caravan park
CT HT RIG HEMA 54 H4 32 08 17 S 150 21 03 E

Milton

Milton Showground 0429 934 067
Milton Showground. Croobyar Rd
CT HT RIG HEMA 67 C13 35 19 09 S 150 25 48 E

Moama

Rich River Golf Club Resort 03 5481 3333
Twenty Four Lane, via Perricoota Rd. ID required, report to reception for key
CT HT RIG HEMA 68 J5 36 04 35 S 144 43 35 E

Moree

Moree Dump Point
Webb Ave, off Newell Hwy
CT HT RIG HEMA 58 D6 29 27 26 S 149 50 40 E

Moruya

Moruya Dump Point
Shore St. Near sewer pump station opposite tennis courts. Via Church St off Princes Hwy
CT HT RIG HEMA 67 F12 35 54 27 S 150 04 35 E

NEW SOUTH WALES

Moulamein

Moulamein Dump Point
Moulamein Rd, between Tallow St & Sainsberry St
CT HT BIG RIG HEMA 63 K8 35 05 16 S 144 01 53 E

Mudgee

Mudgee Showground 0447111329
Douro St, 200m from cnr Nicolson St. Phone first to check if dump open
CT HT BIG RIG HEMA 52 A5 32 36 10 S 149 34 53 E

Mulwala

Purtle Park
Melbourne St
CT HT BIG RIG HEMA 69 J10 35 59 08 S 146 00 34 E

Mungindi

WH Smith Park
Cnr Wirrah & Loftus Sts
CT HT BIG RIG HEMA 58 C4 28 58 53 S 148 59 30 E

Murrurundi

Wilson Memorial Park
New England Hwy. Best entrance via Mount St through back gate
CT HT BIG RIG HEMA 54 G6 31 45 51 S 150 50 11 E

Nabiac

Nabiac Dump Point
Nabiac St, by the tennis courts and public toilets
CT HT BIG RIG HEMA 55 H11 32 05 56 S 152 22 52 E

Nambucca Heads

Nambucca Heads Visitor Information Centre 02 6568 6954
Cnr Pacific Hwy & Riverside Dr. Key available between 0900- 700
CT HEMA 55 B13 30 39 09 S 152 59 25 E

Nambucca Service Centre
Pacific Hwy, within the Service Centre
CT HT BIG RIG HEMA 55 B13 30 37 38 S 152 58 18 E

Narrabri

Cameron Park
Rest Area at Narrabri. 700m S of Information Centre
CT HEMA 54 A2 30 19 37 S 149 46 43 E

Narrabri Showground 02 6792 3913
Belar St
CT HT BIG RIG HEMA 54 A2 30 20 19 S 149 45 48 E

Narrandera

Narrandera Showground 0407 105 846
Elizabeth St, E side of town. Behind hall in grounds
CT BIG RIG HEMA 63 J14 34 44 57 S 146 33 52 E

Narromine

Narromine Dump Point
Derribong Street Narromine (located on the western side of the long vehicle parking area at the Narromine Railway Station.
CT HT BIG RIG HEMA 64 C4 32 14 15 S 148 14 49 E

Newcastle Area

Australian Motorhomes, Bennetts Green Dump Point 02 4948 0433
At rear of Australian Motorhomes, enter via Groves Rd, Statham St, 2nd driveway on R. Mon - Fri 0900-1700
CT HT BIG RIG HEMA 47 F13 32 59 50 S 151 41 25 E

Norah Head

Norah Head Holiday Park 02 4396 3935
Victoria St. Fee for non guests
CT HT $ HEMA 47 J11 33 17 00 S 151 33 58 E

Nowra

Nowra Showground 1300 662 808
West St
CT HT BIG RIG HEMA 51 K9 34 52 30 S 150 35 31 E

Nyngan

Teamsters Rest Area
Teamsters Rest Area, Pangee St. Approx 300m W of Information Centre
CT HT BIG RIG HEMA 58 J1 31 33 43 S 147 11 40 E

Oberon

Jenolan Caravan Park 02 6336 0344
Cunynghame St. Public access
CT HT $ HEMA 52 E6 33 42 06 S 149 51 28 E

Orange

Total Park
Bathurst Rd, behind service station. E end of town
CT HT BIG RIG HEMA 52 D3 33 17 27 S 149 06 34 E

Parkes

Kelly Reserve
Rest Area at Parkes. N end of town
CT HEMA 64 E4 33 07 28 S 148 10 23 E

Parkes Showground 02 6862 2580
Victoria St. Not available during show August or Elvis Festival 1-14 Jan
CT HT BIG RIG HEMA 64 E4 33 07 52 S 148 09 47 E

Peak Hill

Peak Hill Dump Point
Warrah St, between Mingelo St & Bogan St. W side of Hwy
CT HT BIG RIG HEMA 64 D4 32 43 38 S 148 11 10 E

Picton

Picton Dump Point
Walton Street, next to the car park. Off Menangle St W
CT HT HEMA 51 A10 34 10 04 S 150 36 40 E

Port Macquarie

Port Macquarie Dump Point
Chestnut Rd, off Lake Rd. Adjacent to sewer pumping station
CT HEMA 55 E13 31 27 06 S 152 53 23 E

Portland

Kremer Park
Kiln St
CT HT BIG RIG HEMA 52 D6 33 21 11 S 149 58 28 E

Quirindi

Rose Lee Park
Kamilaroi Highway
CT HT BIG RIG HEMA 54 F5 31 31 04 S 150 40 34 E

Rylstone

Rylstone Caravan Park 0448 251 440
6 Carwell St. Public access. Fee applies
CT HT $ BIG RIG HEMA 52 B6 32 48 02 S 149 58 04 E

Seal Rocks

Seal Rocks Dump Point
Seal Rocks Rd, opposite entry to caravan park. Near public toilets
CT BIG RIG HEMA 55 K11 32 25 57 S 152 31 28 E

South West Rocks

Trial Bay Gaol Dump Point 02 6566 6168
Next to amenities block in day use area. $10 deposit & key collection from office at campground
CT HEMA 55 C13 30 52 37 S 153 04 19 E

Talbingo

Talbingo Dump Point 02 6941 2555
Murray Jackson Dr, between Lampe & Bridle Sts. At entrance to water depot station
CT BIG RIG HEMA 66 D5 35 34 43 S 148 17 59 E

Tamworth

South Tamworth Rest Area
Lions Park Rest Area, 470 Goonoo Goonoo Rd (New England Hwy), opposite power sub-station
CT HT BIG RIG HEMA 54 D6 31 07 57 S 150 55 22 E

Tamworth Airport Rest Area
On Hwy opposite airport
CT HT BIG RIG HEMA 54 D6 31 04 40 S 150 51 02 E

Tamworth Rest Area
3 km NE of Tamworth on New England Hwy. Limited turning circle
CT HT HEMA 54 D6 31 06 30 S 150 57 16 E

Tarcutta

Tarcutta Dump Point
Sydney St. In "Truck changeover bay". Beside toilets
CT HT BIG RIG HEMA 66 C4 35 16 33 S 147 44 17 E

Taree

Taree Rotary Park
Manning River Dr, via Victoria St. Just W of Information Centre
CT HT BIG RIG HEMA 55 G11 31 53 57 S 152 29 27 E

Tea Gardens

Tea Gardens Rest Area
Rest Area 1 km W of Tea Gardens. Cnr Myall Way & Viney Creek Rd
CT HT HEMA 53 A14 32 38 23 S 152 08 39 E

Temora

Temora Dump Point 02 6980 1100
Northern end of Airport St. Approx 200m from Hwy
CT HT BIG RIG HEMA 64 H3 34 25 40 S 147 31 09 E

Temora Showground 0427 280 339
Entry via Mimosa St
CT HT BIG RIG HEMA 64 H3 34 26 23 S 147 31 17 E

Tenterfield

Tenterfield Showground 02 6736 6000
Miles St. Entry at back gate
CT HT BIG RIG HEMA 57 D9 29 03 25 S 152 00 55 E

The Rock

The Rock Recreation Ground
Parking Area at the Rock. Wilson St, via Urana & Cornwall Sts
CT HT BIG RIG HEMA 66 C1 35 15 55 S 147 06 37 E

Tilligerry

Lemon Tree Passage Boat Ramp
Henderson Park, 54 Cook Parade, near wharf
CT HT HEMA 53 A13 32 43 47 S 152 02 22 E

Tocumwal

Town Beach 03 5874 2517
From Tocumwal - Corawa Rd turn W onto Hennessy St then S on Town Beach Rd. 700m dirt Rd
CT HT BIG RIG HEMA 69 H8 35 49 06 S 145 33 43 E

Tooleybuc

Tooleybuc Recreation Reserve
Lockhart Rd
CT HT BIG RIG HEMA 62 J6 35 01 22 S 143 20 17 E

NEW SOUTH WALES

Trundle
Trundle Showgrounds 02 6892 1260
Camp Area at Trundle Showgrounds, Austral St
CT HT BIG RIG HEMA 64 D3 32 55 33 S 147 42 06 E

Tullamore
Tullamore Showground 02 6892 5194
Camp Area at Tullamore. Cornet St
CT HT BIG RIG HEMA 61 K14 32 37 39 S 147 34 11 E

Tumbarumba
Tumbarumba Dump Point
Cnr Cape & Bridge Sts. 100m from Visitors Centre
CT HT BIG RIG HEMA 66 E4 35 46 37 S 148 00 33 E

Tumut
Tumut Dump Point 02 6941 2555
Elm Drive
CT HT HEMA 66 C5 35 18 11 S 148 13 42 E

Ungarie
Ungarie Showground
Camp Area at Ungarie, Crown Camp Rd, entrance beyond school. Behind toilets, signposted
CT HT BIG RIG HEMA 64 F2 33 38 07 S 146 58 43 E

Uralla
Uralla Dump Point
John St, at the Pioneer Cemetery
CT HT BIG RIG HEMA 55 B8 30 38 31 S 151 29 35 E

Uranquinty
Uranquinty Rest Area
Rest Area, main street
CT HT BIG RIG HEMA 66 C2 35 11 34 S 147 14 46 E

Urunga
Urunga Recreation Reserve
Morgo St, S of town centre heading to Hungry Head. 250m S of intersection with South St E
CT HT BIG RIG HEMA 55 A13 30 30 06 S 153 01 16 E

Wagga Wagga
Wagga Wagga Showgrounds 02 6925 2180
Urana St. Fee if not staying at showgrounds
CT HT $ BIG RIG HEMA 66 B2 35 07 35 S 147 21 15 E

Wilks Park
Rest Area at Wagga Wagga. Turn E off Olympic Hwy at Travers St, across bridge to Hampden Ave. N side of town, E side of Murrumbidgee River
CT HT BIG RIG HEMA 66 B2 35 05 59 S 147 22 17 E

Walcha
Walcha Dump Point
North St, in front of Council depot
CT HT BIG RIG HEMA 55 C8 30 58 40 S 151 35 18 E

Walgett
Alex Trevallion Park
Castlereagh Hwy. S end of town
CT HT BIG RIG HEMA 58 F3 30 02 04 S 148 06 55 E

Wallerawang
Lake Wallace
Barton Ave, beside lake. Turn N off Great Western Hwy 8 km W of Lithgow or 57 km E of Bathurst
CT HT BIG RIG HEMA 52 D7 33 24 56 S 150 04 24 E

Warialda
Saleyards Rest Area
Saleyards Rest Area, Gwydir Hwy. E side of town
CT HT BIG RIG HEMA 56 G4 29 32 44 S 150 34 53 E

Warragamba
Warragamba Picnic Area
Off Warradale Rd
CT HT HEMA 48 G5 33 53 37 S 150 36 06 E

Warren
Warren Dump Point
Oxley Park, Coonamble Rd. Near the water tower
CT BIG RIG HEMA 58 K2 31 41 48 S 147 50 23 E

Wauchope
Wauchope Showgrounds 0475 111 074
Camp Area at Wauchope, enter via High St
CT HT BIG RIG HEMA 55 E12 31 27 28 S 152 43 27 E

Wee Waa
Dangar Park 02 6799 6760
Cnr Cowper & George Sts, next to toilet block
CT HT BIG RIG HEMA 58 F5 30 13 25 S 149 26 39 E

Wellington
Wellington Showground
Bushrangers Creek Rd
CT HT BIG RIG HEMA 52 A3 32 33 15 S 148 56 03 E

Wentworth
Fort Courage Caravan Park 03 5027 3097
20 km W of Wentworth on Old Renmark Rd. Beside Murray River
CT HT BIG RIG HEMA 62 G2 34 05 03 S 141 43 53 E

West Wyalong
Ace Caravan Park 02 6972 3061
Cnr Newell & Mid Western Hwy's. Fee applies
CT $ HEMA 64 G2 33 55 23 S 147 11 55 E

West Wyalong Showground 0428 518 329
At the showground. Entry by Duffs Rd only off the West Wyalong bypass Rd
CT HT BIG RIG HEMA 64 G2 33 56 18 S 147 12 50 E

White Cliffs
Opal Pioneer Caravan & Camping Tourist Park 08 8091 6688
Johnstone St
CT HT BIG RIG HEMA 60 F5 30 50 58 S 143 05 23 E

Wilcannia
Wilcannia Dump Point
Myers St
CT HT BIG RIG HEMA 60 H6 31 33 23 S 143 22 29 E

Wingham
Wingham Showground 0427 570 229
Gloucester Rd
CT HT BIG RIG HEMA 55 G11 31 52 25 S 152 21 43 E

Woodburn
Woodburn Dump Point 02 6660 0267
Pacific Hwy. Beside public toilets next to Coraki turnoff
CT HEMA 57 E13 29 04 25 S 153 20 20 E

Woodenbong
Woodenbong Campground 02 6635 1300
W end of town, next to swimming pool. Deposit for key at Ampol
CT HT BIG RIG HEMA 57 B11 28 23 20 S 152 36 21 E

Wyalong
Cooinda Reserve
Copeland St, off Newell Hwy
CT HT BIG RIG HEMA 64 G2 33 55 27 S 147 14 06 E

Wyangala Dam
Relections Holiday Park Wyangala Waters 02 6345 0877
Day fee to enter park. See reception
CT $ BIG RIG HEMA 52 G3 33 57 46 S 148 57 17 E

Wyong
Caltex Service Station 02 4352 2944
Both sides of F3 Freeway. Go through truck parking to find the site
CT HEMA 47 J10 33 15 10 S 151 24 12 E

Yass
Yass Dump Point
1428 Yass Valley Way, outside council depot
CT HT BIG RIG HEMA 52 K3 34 49 18 S 148 54 21 E

Yetman
Apex Park
River St (Bruxner Hwy) next to picnic area
CT HT BIG RIG HEMA 59 C8 28 54 10 S 150 46 48 E

Young
Young Showground 02 6382 2079
In showground at Young. Entry from Whitman Ave
CT HT BIG RIG HEMA 52 H1 34 18 58 S 148 18 50 E

AUSTRALIAN CAPITAL TERRITORY

Canberra
Epic Exhibition Park
Federal Hwy, Lyneham. Adjacent to camping area. Call ahead as site often closed during Dec - Jan/ Easter
CT HT BIG RIG HEMA 72 B5 35 13 36 S 149 08 55 E

VICTORIA

Alexandra

Leckie Park
23 Station St
CT HT BIG RIG HEMA 89 G5 37 11 11 S 145 42 54 E

Ararat

Ararat Dump Point
Alexandra Ave, enter via Queen St
CT HT BIG RIG HEMA 85 C8 37 16 50 S 142 55 59 E

Avoca

Avoca Caravan Park 03 5465 3073
Liebig St. 1.2 km W of PO. Outside the caravan park
CT HT BIG RIG HEMA 85 B10 37 05 36 S 143 28 07 E

Ballarat

Eureka Stockade Caravan Park 03 5331 2281
104 Stawell Street South. Public access, must stop at reception, fee applies
CT HT $ BIG RIG HEMA 85 D11 37 33 49 S 143 53 09 E

Beechworth

Lake Sambell Caravan Park 03 5728 1421
Peach Dr. 1.5 km from PO. Must call at reception first
CT HT $ BIG RIG HEMA 92 C3 36 21 28 S 146 42 00 E

Benalla

Benalla Dump Point
Off Samaria Rd, at old Airport Terminus Building. Signposted
CT HT BIG RIG HEMA 89 D6 36 33 11 S 145 59 50 E

Bendigo

Bendigo Showgrounds
Holmes Rd. 2 km N of PO. Not available during major events
CT HT BIG RIG HEMA 85 A13 36 44 18 S 144 16 23 E

Birchip

Birchip Dump Point
At Community Leisure Centre, access from Cnr Morrison & Johnson Rds. Veer L to toilet block
CT HT BIG RIG HEMA 87 G8 35 58 46 S 142 54 41 E

Boort

Boort Park Showground 03 5494 3489
Malone St
CT HT BIG RIG HEMA 87 H11 36 06 37 S 143 43 46 E

Bridgewater

Bridgewater Recreation Reserve 03 5494 3489
Bridgewater-Maldon Rd. Key from Bridgewater Bakery, 6 Main St
CT HT BIG RIG HEMA 87 K12 36 36 23 S 143 56 41 E

Bright

BIG4 Bright 03 5755 1064
1-11 Mountbatten Ave. 500m E of PO
CT HT $ BIG RIG HEMA 96 D4 36 43 31 S 146 57 54 E

Bright Pine Valley Tourist Park 03 5755 1010
7-15 Churchill Ave
CT HT $ BIG RIG HEMA 96 D4 36 43 50 S 146 58 15 E

NRMA Bright Holiday Park 03 5755 1141
Cherry Lane
CT HT $ BIG RIG HEMA 96 D4 36 43 39 S 146 57 53 E

Bruthen

Bruthen Caravan Park 03 5157 5753
Tambo Upper Rd. 600m E of PO. Pay fee at reception
CT HT $ BIG RIG HEMA 98 G4 37 42 43 S 147 50 08 E

Cann River

Cann River Rainforest Caravan Park 03 5158 6369
7536 Princes Hwy, just W of Cann River Bridge
CT HEMA 93 H12 37 33 59 S 149 08 46 E

Casterton

Island Park Caravan Park 0457 414 187
Caravan Park at Casterton. M Carmichel Dr off Murray St, adjacent to swimming pool. Next to amenities block. Public access
CT BIG RIG HEMA 84 E3 37 34 58 S 141 24 19 E

Charlton

Travellers Rest Caravan Park 0448 276 631
43-45 High Street
CT HEMA 87 H10 36 16 02 S 143 21 05 E

Chiltern

Chiltern Dump Point
Lake Anderson Dr, adjacent to caravan park
CT HT BIG RIG HEMA 92 B3 36 09 08 S 146 36 44 E

Clunes

Clunes Dump Point
70 Bailey St. Key at bottle museum
CT HEMA 85 C11 37 17 37 S 143 46 50 E

Cobram

Cobram Dump Point
Cobram Showgrounds, entrance from Banks St into Ivy St. Follow past tennis courts to southern corner
CT HT BIG RIG HEMA 89 A5 35 55 18 S 145 39 09 E

Cohuna

Cohuna Dump Point
Cohuna Island Rd, near caravan park
CT HT BIG RIG HEMA 87 F13 35 48 17 S 144 13 33 E

Colac

Central Caravan Park 03 5231 3586
Caravan Park at Colac. Bruce St. At showground
CT HT $ BIG RIG HEMA 83 E9 38 20 09 S 143 36 12 E

Corop

Greens Lake Recreation Reserve
Camp Area 16 km W of Stanhope or 24 km E of Elmore
CT HT BIG RIG HEMA 89 D2 36 26 16 S 144 49 42 E

Corryong

Corryong Dump Point
Next to toilet block at Saleyards, Donaldson St (School Lane)
CT BIG RIG HEMA 92 B7 36 11 17 S 147 53 56 E

Cullulleraine

Bushmans Rest Caravan Park 03 5028 2252
70 Sturt Hwy
CT HT BIG RIG HEMA 88 D4 34 16 23 S 141 35 13 E

Daylesford

Daylesford Holiday Park 03 5348 3821
Cnr Ballan Rd & Burrall St. Key at the reception office, deposit required
CT HT $ BIG RIG HEMA 85 D12 37 21 31 S 144 08 23 E

Dimboola

Dimboola Dump Point 03 5391 4444
Wimmera St, near caravan park entrance
CT HEMA 86 J5 36 27 24 S 142 01 30 E

Dinner Plain

Scrubbers End Overnight Parking 1800 444 066
Parking Area at Dinner Plain Alpine Village. Enter via Big Muster Dr & Scrubbers End Lane, E side of village
CT HEMA 95 B12 37 01 28 S 147 14 36 E

Donald

Donald Apex Park
Rest Area at Donald. N end of town
CT HT BIG RIG HEMA 87 J8 36 22 03 S 142 58 39 E

Eagle Point

Eagle Point Caravan Park 03 5156 1183
Camp Park Rd. 12 km S of Bairnsdale. Opposite reception
CT HT BIG RIG HEMA 98 J3 37 53 32 S 147 40 53 E

Echuca

Echuca Rotary Park RV Stop
Rotary Park. Entry Cnr Rose & Crossen Sts
CT HT BIG RIG HEMA 89 B2 36 08 43 S 144 44 02 E

Elmore

Aysons Reserve (Campaspe River) 03 5481 2200
At Camp Area 8 km NE of Elmore. Turn N off Midland Hwy 32 km W of Stanhope or 5 km NE of Elmore along Burnewang Rd for 3 km
CT HT BIG RIG HEMA 87 J14 36 27 34 S 144 40 08 E

Euroa

Euroa Freeway Service Centre
At Service Centre, off M31
CT HT BIG RIG HEMA 89 E5 36 44 38 S 145 35 27 E

Kirkland Ave Rest Area
Kirkland Ave East. Adjacent to caravan park
CT HEMA 89 E5 36 45 15 S 145 34 34 E

Foster

Foster Dump Point
Cnr Main St & Nelson St, at service station
CT HT BIG RIG HEMA 91 G8 38 39 08 S 146 12 13 E

Girgaree

Girgarre Town Park
Corner of Winter Rd & Station St. Dump beside hall near toilets
CT HT BIG RIG HEMA 89 C2 36 23 53 S 144 58 48 E

Harcourt

Harcourt Dump Point
Cnr High & Bridge Sts
CT HT BIG RIG HEMA 85 B13 36 59 40 S 144 15 43 E

Heathcote

Heathcote Dump Point 03 5433 3121
Barrack St, outside of Queen Meadow Caravan Park
CT HT BIG RIG HEMA 85 B14 36 55 24 S 144 42 47 E

Heyfield

Heyfield RV Rest Area 0418 108 691
700m SE of Heyfield Post Office, cnr MacFarlane & Clark Sts
HT HEMA 91 C10 37 59 06 S 146 47 15 E

Heywood

Heywood RV Stop
Hunter St East
CT HT BIG RIG HEMA 84 G4 38 07 51 S 141 37 57 E

VICTORIA

Hollands Landing
Hollands Landing Dump Point 03 5142 3333
Hollands Landing Rd. Near public toilets at the jetty
CT BIG RIG HEMA 91 D13 38 03 13 S 147 27 36 E

Hopetoun
Hopetoun Rest Area
At Rest Area 1 km NE of Hopetoun, corner of Henty Hwy & Evelyn St
CT BIG RIG HEMA 86 F6 35 43 21 S 142 21 53 E

Horsham
Horsham Dump Point
Firebrace St, outside caravan park
CT HT BIG RIG HEMA 84 A6 36 43 21 S 142 11 58 E

Jeparit
Jeparit Dump Point
Dimboola - Rainbow Rd, outside the shire depot
CT HT BIG RIG HEMA 86 H5 36 08 24 S 141 59 23 E

Kaniva
Kaniva Caravan Park 0458 687 054
Caravan Park at Kaniva. Baker St. Dump is near Dungey St gates. Public access
CT BIG RIG HEMA 86 J2 36 22 54 S 141 14 25 E

Kerang
Kerang Dump Point
Markets Rd
CT HT BIG RIG HEMA 87 F12 35 44 14 S 143 55 39 E

Korumburra
Korumburra Showgrounds 03 5655 2923
Victoria St. Rear entrance gate, next to toilet block. Key from Korumburra Tourist Park, Bourke St. Deposit required
CT HT BIG RIG HEMA 81 J14 38 25 40 S 145 49 02 E

Kyabram
Kyabram Dump Point 03 5852 2883
Fauna Park Road, off Lake Rd. Next to toilet block. If locked, obtain key from Fauna Park office
CT HEMA 89 C3 36 19 16 S 145 02 52 E

Kyneton
South Kyneton Mineral Springs
Parking Area 3.5 km W of Kyneton on Burton Ave
CT HEMA 85 C13 37 14 09 S 144 25 10 E

Lake Bolac
Lake Bolac Dump Point
In service Rd, next to the Glenelg Hwy
CT HT BIG RIG HEMA 85 E8 37 42 40 S 142 50 32 E

Lakes Entrance
Lakes Entrance-Gippsland Lakes Fishing Club
Opposite Information Centre. Bullock Island Rd
CT HT BIG RIG HEMA 98 J6 37 52 58 S 147 58 18 E

Leitchville
Leitchville Dump Point
Leitchville Recreation Reserve, Cohuna - Leitchville Rd
CT HT BIG RIG HEMA 87 G13 35 54 13 S 144 17 55 E

Leongatha
Leongatha Caravan Park 03 5662 2753
14 Turner St. 800m N of PO. Fee for non guests
CT $ HEMA 90 F6 38 28 18 S 145 56 52 E

Lockington
Lockington Travellers Rest 0447 787 581
In Camp Area at Lockington, Main St
CT HT HEMA 87 J14 36 16 15 S 144 32 08 E

Lorne
Lorne Dump Point 1300 891 152
Behind Lorne Visitors Centre. Turn into Otway St, follow road towards the spit. Dump is on the RH side at 2nd toilet block
CT HEMA 83 G11 38 32 06 S 143 58 37 E

Macarthur
Macarthur Recreation Reserve
700m S of town, off Port Fairy-Hamilton Rd, entry to reserve just S of river crossing. Signposted
CT HT BIG RIG HEMA 84 G5 38 02 15 S 142 00 27 E

Maffra
Gippsland Vehicle Collection 03 5147 3223
1A Sale Rd. Access by arrangement
CT HT $ BIG RIG HEMA 91 C11 37 58 24 S 146 59 05 E

Maffra RV Park
Parking Area at Maffra. Cnr of Johnson & Moroney St's
CT HT HEMA 91 C11 37 58 11 S 146 58 50 E

Mallacoota
Mallacoota Dump Point
Buckland Drive, next to toilet block
CT HEMA 93 H14 37 33 20 S 149 45 21 E

Mallacoota Foreshore Holiday Park 03 5158 0300
Allan Drive
CT HT BIG RIG HEMA 93 H14 37 33 26 S 149 45 32 E

Mansfield
Mansfield Dump Point 1800 039 049
Stock Route off High St, N side of rail trail. 200 metres W of Info Centre
CT HT BIG RIG HEMA 94 C1 37 03 00 S 146 04 43 E

Maryborough
Maryborough dump Point
Reservoir Rd, off the Ballarat - Maryborough Rd
CT HT BIG RIG HEMA 85 B11 37 03 52 S 143 43 55 E

Meeniyan
Meeniyan Recreation Reserve
Meeniyan Recreation Reserve, Hanily Street
CT HT BIG RIG HEMA 90 G7 38 34 32 S 146 00 44 E

Mildura
Mildura Dump Point 03 5018 8450
Benetook Avenue, between 11th & 14th Sts. Front of council depot, opposite TAFE
CT HT BIG RIG HEMA 88 D6 34 12 17 S 142 10 06 E

Mirboo North
BP Service Station
Ridgway St, Mirboo North. Key from attendant, fee if no fuel purchased
CT HT $ BIG RIG HEMA 90 F7 38 24 04 S 146 09 39 E

Murrabit
Murrabit Recreation Reserve
Browning Ave, inside Rec Reserve
CT HT BIG RIG HEMA 87 E12 35 31 49 S 143 57 09 E

Murtoa
Murtoa Dump Point
Lake St, near the showground & caravan park
CT HT BIG RIG HEMA 86 A7 34 37 20 S 142 27 59 E

Nathalia
Nathalia Dump Point
Weir St, next to the toilets
CT HT BIG RIG HEMA 89 B3 36 03 20 S 145 12 03 E

Neerim South
Neerim South Recreation Reserve
Neerim East Rd
CT HT BIG RIG HEMA 90 C7 38 00 59 S 145 57 24 E

Newstead
Newstead Racecourse & Rec Reserve 03 5476 2360
Racecourse Rd
CT HT BIG RIG HEMA 85 B12 37 07 01 S 144 03 23 E

Nhill
Nhill Aerodrome RV Stop
3 km N of Nhill. Via Propodollah & Aerodrome Rds
CT HT BIG RIG HEMA 86 H4 36 18 27 S 141 38 53 E

Nicholson
Nicholson River Reserve
Toilet block at boat ramp car park. Cassette only
CT HEMA 98 H3 37 49 02 S 147 44 24 E

Numurkah
Numurkah Showgrounds
Enter via Tunnock Rd. Locked, key at Visitor Information Centre or adjacent caravan park. $20 deposit
CT HT BIG RIG HEMA 89 B4 36 05 38 S 145 26 45 E

Nyah
Nyah Recreation Reserve
River St, adjacent to Harness Club
CT BIG RIG HEMA 87 C10 35 10 18 S 143 22 53 E

Orbost
Orbost Dump Point
Forest Road behind the truck wash
CT HT HEMA 93 J9 37 42 28 S 148 27 05 E

Ouyen
Ouyen Caravan Park 03 5092 1426
10 Calder Hwy
CT HT BIG RIG HEMA 88 J7 35 04 26 S 142 19 08 E

Oxley
Oxley Recreation Reserve
Rest Area 3 km S of Oxley, via Oxley Meadowcreek Rd
CT HT BIG RIG HEMA 89 D7 36 28 14 S 146 23 06 E

Paynesville
Paynesville Progress Jetty 03 5153 9500
Toilet block on The Esplanade
CT HEMA 98 K3 37 55 09 S 147 43 10 E

Port Albert
Port Albert Parking Area
In Parking Area Wharf St, near boat ramp. Collect key from Port Albert General Store
CT HT BIG RIG HEMA 91 G10 38 40 22 S 146 41 38 E

Portland
Henty Park
Henty Park, adjacent to amenities block, near the Cable Tram depot
CT HT BIG RIG HEMA 84 H4 38 21 16 S 141 36 22 E

Pyramid Hill
Pyramid Hill Caravan Park 0438 557 012
Caravan Park at Pyramid Hill. 1 km E of PO. At the rear of the amenities block
CT HT BIG RIG HEMA 87 G12 36 03 19 S 144 07 30 E

VICTORIA

Rainbow

Rainbow Dump Point
Park St, off the Rainbow - Nhill Rd. Next to the bowling club
CT HT BIG RIG HEMA 86 G5 35 54 05 S 141 59 30 E

Rawson

Rawson Dump Point
Pinnacle Drive
CT HT BIG RIG HEMA 91 C9 37 57 22 S 146 23 49 E

Robinvale

Robinvale Dump Point
Riverside Park, Robin St
CT HT BIG RIG HEMA 87 A1 34 34 52 S 142 46 24 E

Rosebud

Capel Sound Foreshore Reserve 03 5986 4382
Port Nepean Rd, entry at section B just N of Elizabeth Ave. Near amentities block 3
CT HEMA 80 J7 38 21 49 S 144 52 24 E

Rosedale

Rosedale Bowling Club
1 Dawson St. Near Wood St
CT HEMA 91 D10 38 09 21 S 146 46 49 E

Rupanyup

Rupanyup Memorial Park 0428 193 874
Cnr of Wimmera Hwy & Minyip-Rupanyup Rds
CT HT HEMA 86 K7 36 37 35 S 142 37 45 E

Sale

Port of Sale
Canal Rd, behind Council Office. Cassettes only, access via steps behind toilet block
CT HEMA 91 D12 38 06 45 S 147 03 46 E

Sale Showground Caravan & Motorhome Park 03 5144 6432
Sale-Maffra Rd
CT HT BIG RIG HEMA 91 D12 38 05 31 S 147 03 58 E

Wellington Visitor Information Centre 1800 677 520
8 Foster Street
CT BIG RIG HEMA 91 D12 38 06 44 S 147 03 27 E

Sea Lake

Sea Lake Recreation Reserve Caravan Park 0427 701 261
71-91 Calder Hwy
CT HT BIG RIG HEMA 87 E8 35 30 11 S 142 50 57 E

Seymour

Seymour Dump Point
Cnr Wallis & High Street's
CT HT HEMA 89 F3 37 01 14 S 145 08 05 E

Shepparton

Ken Muston Automotive Dump Point 03 5821 6688
At the rear of business. Enter via Florence St or Doyles Rd into laneway, then through gates, signposted. Business hours only, donation required
CT HT $ BIG RIG HEMA 89 C4 36 23 08 S 145 25 41 E

Shepparton Dump Point 1800 808 839
Fryers St, rear of the Showgrounds, access from Archer St at Eastern end.
CT HT HEMA 89 C4 36 22 50 S 145 24 39 E

St Arnaud

St Arnaud Sports Club 03 5495 1268
Dunstan St, off Charlton St Arnaud Rd, behind sports club
CT HT BIG RIG HEMA 87 K9 36 36 32 S 143 15 34 E

Stawell

Stawell Dump Point
Scallen St, near public toilets
CT HEMA 85 B8 37 03 15 S 142 46 52 E

Strathmerton

Strathmerton Dump Point
Murray Valley Hwy, lane behind toilet block. Opposite pub
CT HT BIG RIG HEMA 89 A4 35 55 33 S 145 28 46 E

Sunshine

Sunshine 7 Eleven Service Station 03 9310 2694
Western Ring Road, Northbound. Take truck lane, past diesel pumps. Marked as Bus Effluent point
CT BIG RIG HEMA 76 G2 37 48 16 S 144 48 16 E

Sunshine 7 Eleven Service Station 03 9310 2615
Western Ring Road, Southbound. Take truck lane, past diesel pumps. Marked as Bus Effluent point
CT BIG RIG HEMA 76 G3 37 48 16 S 144 48 33 E

Swan Hill

Swan Hill Showgrounds
Entry via Stradbroke Ave. Left of the grandstand
CT HT BIG RIG HEMA 87 D10 35 20 20 S 143 22 04 E

Tallangatta

Tallangatta Showgrounds 02 6071 2621
Camp Area at Tallangatta. Weramu St. Gold coin donation for water
CT HT BIG RIG HEMA 92 B5 36 13 10 S 147 10 05 E

Tatura

Tatura Park
Hastie St, entrance opposite Davy St
CT BIG RIG HEMA 89 D3 36 26 44 S 145 13 58 E

Terang

Terang Community Caravan Park 03 5592 1687
Warrnambool Rd off Princes Hwy, outside the caravan park
CT HT BIG RIG HEMA 82 D4 38 14 31 S 142 54 34 E

Tidal River

Tidal River 131 963
At Camp Area
CT HT HEMA 91 K8 39 01 48 S 146 19 16 E

Timboon

Timboon Recreation Reserve
Curdies River Rd. DP key at Timboon Fuel
CT HT BIG RIG HEMA 82 G4 38 28 41 S 142 57 56 E

Wahgunyah

Wahgunyah
Victoria St, opposite Main St
CT HT BIG RIG HEMA 92 A2 36 00 44 S 146 24 04 E

Walwa

Walwa Dump Point
Ohalloran St, off River Rd. At the football oval
CT HT BIG RIG HEMA 92 A7 35 57 44 S 147 44 11 E

Warracknabeal

Warracknabeal Caravan Park 0400 915 125
2 Lyle St. Public access
CT HT HEMA 86 H6 36 15 11 S 142 23 15 E

Warrnambool

Surfside Holiday Park 03 5559 4700
Pertobe St. Public access. Call first, fee for non guests
CT HT $ HEMA 82 F1 38 23 31 S 142 29 02 E

Warrnambool Holiday Village 03 5562 3376
81 Henna St
CT HT $ HEMA 82 F1 38 22 41 S 142 28 43 E

Wedderburn

Wedderburn Pioneer Caravan Park 03 5494 3301
Caravan Park at Wedderburn. Hospital St. 1 km E of PO. Public access, report to office
CT HT BIG RIG HEMA 87 J11 36 24 47 S 143 36 59 E

Willaura

Willaura Recreation Grounds 0429 953 150
Delacome Way.
CT HT BIG RIG HEMA 84 D7 37 32 41 S 142 44 36 E

Winchelsea

Barwon Hotel 03 5267 2046
Palmer St. Locked, see Hotel or information on sign
CT HT HEMA 83 D11 38 14 34 S 143 59 27 E

Wulgulmerang

Wulgulmerang Recreation Reserve 03 5155 0253
Snowy River Rd
CT HT BIG RIG HEMA 93 F8 37 04 06 S 148 15 37 E

Wycheproof

Wycheproof Caravan Park 03 5493 7278
Caravan Park at Wycheproof. Calder Hwy 500m N of PO
CT HT BIG RIG HEMA 87 G9 36 04 10 S 143 13 33 E

Yarram

Yarram Recreation Reserve
Railway Ave, via Buckley St
CT HT BIG RIG HEMA 91 G10 38 33 25 S 146 40 25 E

Yarrawonga

Yarrawonga Showgrounds 03 5744 1989
Dunlop St. Next to cream brick amenities block
CT HT BIG RIG HEMA 89 B6 36 01 03 S 146 00 32 E

Yea

Yea Water Discovery Centre 03 5797 2663
2 Hood St
CT HT BIG RIG HEMA 89 G4 37 12 36 S 145 25 37 E

TASMANIA

Arthur River

Arthur River Dump Point 03 6452 4800
S side of river, turn R to Gardiner Point. Dump point is situated at the end of the road at the "Edge of the World Lookout"
CT BIG RIG HEMA 108 F1 41 03 27 S 144 39 37 E

Beaconsfield

Beaconsfield Recreation Ground 03 6383 6350
York St, off Grubb St. E side of town
CT HT BIG RIG HEMA 106 D6 41 11 57 S 146 49 19 E

Bicheno

Bicheno Dump Point 03 6375 1333
Cnr of the The Esplanade & Fraser Sts
CT HT BIG RIG HEMA 105 J14 41 52 19 S 148 18 25 E

Bothwell

Bothwell Dump Point 03 6259 5503
Market Place, rear of Council CP, behind golf museum
CT HEMA 111 H13 42 22 59 S 147 00 31 E

Burnie

Cooee Point Reserve 03 6431 1033
Cooee Point. 3 km W of Burnie, via Turrung St & Cooee Point Rd
CT HT BIG RIG HEMA 104 C1 41 02 19 S 145 52 37 E

South Burnie Dumpoint
Esplanade, Reeve St public toilets near yacht club
CT HT HEMA 104 C1 41 03 44 S 145 54 54 E

Cambridge

Cambridge Memorial Oval 03 6245 8600
Cambridge Rd
CT HT BIG RIG HEMA 101 E7 42 50 10 S 147 26 41 E

Campbell Town

King Street Oval
King St, Western end of oval
CT HT BIG RIG HEMA 102 A3 41 55 47 S 147 29 17 E

Cradle Mountain

Cradle Mountain Dump Point
Behind the Visitor Information Centre, near the bus car park
CT HT BIG RIG HEMA 104 G1 41 34 52 S 145 56 16 E

Cygnet

Burtons Reserve 03 6264 8448
Off Charlton St, S end of town. Adjacent to toilet block
CT HT BIG RIG HEMA 113 G11 43 09 48 S 147 04 55 E

Deloraine

Deloraine East Overnight Park 03 6393 5300
Racecourse Dr, near tennis courts
CT HT BIG RIG HEMA 104 G5 41 31 19 S 146 39 43 E

Devonport

Devonport South Dump Point
Miandetta-Devonport Rd, at the sewerage facility next to bridge near Horsehead Creek
CT HT BIG RIG HEMA 104 D3 41 11 59 S 146 21 19 E

Devonport East

Girdlestone Park 03 6424 4466
Car park at football ground in John St
CT HT BIG RIG HEMA 104 D4 41 11 10 S 146 22 45 E

Evandale

Morven Park
Barclay St. W end of town. Behind clubhouse
CT HT BIG RIG HEMA 105 G8 41 34 04 S 147 14 38 E

Fingal

Fingal Park
Talbot St, beside public toilets
CT BIG RIG HEMA 105 H12 41 38 17 S 147 58 06 E

Franklin

Franklin Foreshore Reserve 0428875619
Adjacent to toilet block
CT HT BIG RIG HEMA 113 F10 43 05 34 S 147 00 33 E

Geeveston

Heritage Park
Parking Area at Geeveston. Arve Rd, entry opposite roadhouse
CT HT BIG RIG HEMA 113 G10 43 09 44 S 146 55 28 E

George Town

George Town Rest Area
Main Rd. S end of town, behind information centre
CT HT BIG RIG HEMA 106 B6 41 06 33 S 146 50 18 E

Gordon

Gordon Recreation Reserve 03 6211 8200
At Reserve, Channel Hwy
CT HT BIG RIG HEMA 113 G12 43 15 42 S 147 14 33 E

Hamilton

Hamilton Camping Ground 03 6286 3202
W end of town. Beside river
CT HT $ BIG RIG HEMA 111 J12 42 33 33 S 146 49 50 E

Hobart

BP Service Station 03 6234 3549
200 Brooker Hwy
CT HEMA 100 E2 42 52 12 S 147 19 18 E

Hobart Showgrounds 03 6272 6812
Howard Rd, Glenorchy
CT HT BIG RIG HEMA 101 E3 42 50 02 S 147 17 06 E

Montrose Bay Reserve
Foreshore Rd, off Brooker Hwy
CT HT BIG RIG HEMA 101 D3 42 49 17 S 147 16 08 E

Huonville

Huonville Foreshore 03 6264 0326
Channel Hwy. Next to the toilets
CT HT BIG RIG HEMA 113 F11 43 02 06 S 147 03 02 E

Kempton

Victoria Memorial Hall 03 6259 3011
Old Hunting Ground Rd, off Main St
CT HEMA 102 E1 42 31 54 S 147 12 01 E

Kingston

Kingston Wetlands Site 03 6211 8242
At entrance to Wetlands Reserve, Channel Hwy
CT HT BIG RIG HEMA 101 K4 42 58 27 S 147 18 50 E

Latrobe

Latrobe Motorhome Stop 03 6421 4444
Rear of Wells Supermarket, access off Cotton St
CT HT BIG RIG HEMA 104 D4 41 14 14 S 146 24 37 E

Launceston

Inveresk Showgrounds (York Park Precinct) 03 6323 3383
Forster St, off Invermay Rd. In all day parking area near the Round House. Entry near South St
CT HT BIG RIG HEMA 107 K11 41 25 22 S 147 08 24 E

Low Head

East Beach Self Contained RV Park 03 63821 000
CT HT BIG RIG HEMA 106 A5 41 03 43 S 146 48 40 E

New Norfolk

New Norfolk Dump Point
Page Ave, next to caravan park
CT HT BIG RIG HEMA 113 D11 42 46 34 S 147 03 57 E

Nubeena

Nubeena Dump Point 03 6251 2400
Nubeena Rd, opposite Police Station. N end of town
CT HT BIG RIG HEMA 103 G3 43 05 44 S 147 44 36 E

Oatlands

Oatlands Dump Point
Cnr William & Wellington Sts
CT HT BIG RIG HEMA 102 C2 42 17 52 S 147 21 58 E

Penguin

Penguin Dump Point 03 6429 8979
Cnr of Main & Johnsons Beach Rds, on the beach side. If locked, key at Information Centre
CT HT BIG RIG HEMA 104 D2 41 06 36 S 146 04 10 E

Pontville

Brighton Pontville RV Stop 03 62681254
Glen Lea Rd, off the Midland Hwy
CT HT BIG RIG HEMA 102 F1 42 41 12 S 147 15 37 E

Port Albert

Bakers Point Campground (3) 03 6428 6277
In Camp Area 18 km N of B71/C740 junction. 6 km dirt road
CT HEMA 106 C1 41 09 44 S 146 34 05 E

Springlawn Campground 03 6428 6277
In Camp Area 13.5 km N of B71/C740 junction. 2 km dirt road
CT HEMA 106 C2 41 08 52 S 146 36 09 E

Port Huon

Shipwrights Point Regatta Ground 03 6264 0300
In Camp Area at Port Huon. Just N of wharf area, beside river. Signposted
CT HT BIG RIG HEMA 113 G10 43 09 31 S 146 58 47 E

Port Sorell

Port Sorell Jetty 03 6426 2693
Darling St. N end, next to caravan park
CT HT BIG RIG HEMA 106 C1 41 09 51 S 146 33 23 E

Queenstown

Queenstown Dump Point
Lyell Hwy (Batchelor St), near Mary St beside works building
CT BIG RIG HEMA 110 F6 42 04 38 S 145 33 34 E

Railton

Railton Motorhome Stop
At Camp Spot on the Esplanade. N side of Foster St opposite Hotel
CT HT BIG RIG HEMA 104 E4 41 20 39 S 146 25 23 E

Rosebery

Rosebery Dump Point
Park Rd, opposite the caravan park
CT HT BIG RIG HEMA 110 D5 41 46 38 S 145 32 06 E

Ross

Ross Caravan Park 03 6330 1463
In the Caravan Park, the Esplanade, off High St. Locked, pay fee at office
CT HT $ BIG RIG HEMA 102 A3 42 01 50 S 147 29 26 E

Scottsdale

Northeast Park
Ringarooma Rd. 1 km E of Post Office
CT HT BIG RIG HEMA 105 D10 41 09 56 S 147 31 23 E

TASMANIA

Sheffield
Sheffield Recreation Ground
Spring St, on road to Recreation Grounds
CT HT BIG RIG | HEMA 104 F3 | 41 22 58 S | 146 20 09 E

Sisters Beach
Sisters Beach Dump Point
Behind Fire Station, cnr Honeysuckle Ave & Cumming St
CT | HEMA 108 E6 | 40 55 05 S | 145 33 54 E

Smithton
Smithton Esplanade
West Esplanade, on W side of Duck River Bridge. RH side
CT HT BIG RIG | HEMA 108 D4 | 40 50 20 S | 145 07 12 E

Sorell
Sorell RV Stop 03 6269 0000
Montague St
CT BIG RIG | HEMA 102 G3 | 42 47 02 S | 147 33 24 E

St Helens
St Helens Sporting Complex 03 63767900
Tully St
CT HT BIG RIG | HEMA 105 E14 | 41 19 00 S | 148 14 08 E

St Leonards
St Leonards Park Dump Point
Station Rd, off Johnston Rd
CT HT BIG RIG | HEMA 105 F8 | 41 27 45 S | 147 11 35 E

St Marys
St Marys Sportsground & Golf Course 03 63767900
22 Harefield St
CT HT BIG RIG | HEMA 105 G13 | 41 35 05 S | 148 11 02 E

Stanley
Stanley Public Dump Point
Tatlow's Wharf Rd, beyond caravan park, next to toilet block
CT HT | HEMA 108 D5 | 40 45 50 S | 145 17 45 E

Strahan
Council Depot
96 Harvey St (Ocean Beach Rd), outside depot
CT HT BIG RIG | HEMA 110 F4 | 42 08 59 S | 145 18 48 E

Swansea
Boat Ramp Car Park 03 6257 8155
The Esplanade, near toilets & play ground
CT HT BIG RIG | HEMA 102 B6 | 42 07 51 S | 148 04 28 E

Triabunna
Triabunna Dump Point 03 6257 4772
Via Boyle St, Esplanade East. Veer L over bridge
CT HT BIG RIG | HEMA 102 E5 | 42 30 33 S | 147 55 10 E

Ulverstone
Ulverstone Dump Point 03 6425 2839
Cnr of Victoria St & Beach Rd. In car park, access can be limited if busy
CT | HEMA 104 D3 | 41 09 06 S | 146 10 27 E

Waratah
Waratah Dump Point 03 6443 8342
Annie St. Opposite Council Works Depot
CT HT BIG RIG | HEMA 108 J6 | 41 26 36 S | 145 31 51 E

Wynyard
Wynyard Solid Waste Transfer Station 03 6443 8342
Goldie St (W end). Business hours only
CT HT BIG RIG | HEMA 108 E7 | 40 59 33 S | 145 43 01 E

Zeehan
Zeehan Dump Point
Mulchahy - Packer St, off B27 300m from intersection on RHS
CT HT BIG RIG | HEMA 110 D4 | 41 53 25 S | 145 20 45 E

SOUTH AUSTRALIA

Alford
Alford Community Park
Camp Area at Alford opposite tennis courts in South Tce
CT HT BIG RIG | HEMA 124 B5 | 33 49 01 S | 137 49 18 E

Andamooka
Andamooka Caravan & Camping Ground 0456 578 604
Camp Area 1 km W of Andamooka
CT HT BIG RIG | HEMA 130 J3 | 30 27 11 S | 137 09 39 E

Ardrossan
Ardrossan RV Stop
Cnr Second St & West Tce at rear of Bowling Club & Tennis Courts, enter from West Tce
CT HT BIG RIG | HEMA 124 D5 | 34 25 28 S | 137 54 52 E

Arno Bay
The Arno Bay Hotel 08 8628 0001
Camp Area at Arno Bay. Tel El Kebir Tce, foreshore end
CT HT BIG RIG | HEMA 124 B1 | 33 54 59 S | 136 34 22 E

Balaklava
Balaklava Caravan Park 0400 264 075
Short Tce. Next to swimming pool
CT HT BIG RIG | HEMA 124 C6 | 34 08 57 S | 138 25 08 E

Barmera
Barmera RV Park (Bruce Oval)
Sims St
CT HT BIG RIG | HEMA 125 D12 | 34 15 13 S | 140 28 03 E

Beachport
Surf Beach
Millicent - Beachport Rd. In car park 500m W of Robe turnoff (Southern Ports Hwy)
CT HT BIG RIG | HEMA 126 G3 | 37 28 26 S | 140 01 52 E

Berri
Martins Bend Campground 08 8582 2423
At Camp Area 3 km E of Berri, via Riverview Rd. Follow signs. See caretaker before using
CT | HEMA 125 D13 | 34 17 24 S | 140 37 49 E

Blanchetown
Blanchetown Oval
South Terrace at Lower Blanchetown Oval
CT HT BIG RIG | HEMA 125 D10 | 34 21 19 S | 139 37 00 E

Blyth
Blyth Sportsground 0428 445 218
Parking Area at Blyth. Entry off South Tce
CT HT BIG RIG | HEMA 124 B7 | 33 50 53 S | 138 29 24 E

Bolivar
Bolivar Service Station Dump Point
Behind OTR service station. Access via Hodgson Rd off Port Wakefield Rd
CT HT BIG RIG | HEMA 120 D4 | 34 46 05 S | 138 35 33 E

Border Village
Border Village Caravan Park 08 9039 3474
Eyre Hwy. Outside entrance
CT HT BIG RIG | HEMA 141 K1 | 31 38 18 S | 129 00 12 E

Bordertown
Bordertown Recreation Lake
Off Golf Rd, at Rest Area
CT HT BIG RIG | HEMA 126 B5 | 36 18 21 S | 140 46 31 E

Bower
Bower Reserve
Camp Area at Bower. Next to tennis court, use donation box
CT HT $ BIG RIG | HEMA 125 C9 | 34 07 23 S | 139 21 11 E

Burra
Burra Caravan & Camping Park 08 8892 2442
12 Bridge Tce. Fee for use, see reception
CT HT $ BIG RIG | HEMA 125 A8 | 33 40 44 S | 138 56 15 E

Burra Showgrounds 0447 938 152
Hall Tce
CT HT $ BIG RIG | HEMA 125 A8 | 33 40 05 S | 138 55 28 E

Bute
Bute Dump Point
Railway Tce. Near toilets
CT BIG RIG | HEMA 124 B5 | 33 51 54 S | 138 00 32 E

Cadell
Cadell Recreation Ground 0497 799 284
Dalzell Rd
CT HT BIG RIG | HEMA 125 C10 | 34 02 16 S | 139 45 26 E

Callington
Callington Recreation Grounds
Callington Rd
CT HT BIG RIG | HEMA 127 G7 | 35 06 47 S | 139 02 22 E

Ceduna
BP Service Station 08 8625 3407
Eyre Hwy. W end of town at Fruit Fly Checkpoint
CT HT BIG RIG | HEMA 134 A1 | 32 06 48 S | 133 40 21 E

Clayton Bay
Clayton Bay Dump Point
Island View Dr, next to Boat Club entrance
CT HT BIG RIG | HEMA 125 H8 | 35 29 33 S | 138 55 21 E

Cleve
Cleve Dump Point
Rudall Road. 1.8 km W of PO
CT HT BIG RIG | HEMA 124 A1 | 33 41 52 S | 136 28 33 E

Coffin Bay
Coffin Bay Boat Ramp
Entry from Esplanade, near toilets
CT HT BIG RIG | HEMA 134 H5 | 34 36 58 S | 135 27 51 E

Coober Pedy
Coober Pedy Dump Point
Hutchinson St, next to Information Centre
CT HT BIG RIG | HEMA 137 A9 | 29 00 55 S | 134 45 22 E

Coonalpyn
Coonalpyn Soldiers Memorial Caravan Park 0427 399 089
Richards Tce
CT HT BIG RIG | HEMA 125 J10 | 35 41 33 S | 139 51 27 E

Cowell
Cowell
16073 Lincoln Hwy, Opp the BP service station
CT HT BIG RIG | HEMA 124 A2 | 33 40 48 S | 136 55 32 E

SOUTH AUSTRALIA

Crystal Brook

Jubilee Park
Railway Tce. Between Cunningham & Bowman Sts
CT HT BIG RIG HEMA 128 J6 33 21 13 S 138 12 23 E

Cummins

Cummins Community Caravan Park 08 8676 2011
62 Bruce Tce. 2 km S of PO
CT HT BIG RIG HEMA 134 G6 34 16 15 S 135 43 23 E

Curramulka

Curramulka Sports Complex
Mount Rat Rd
CT HT BIG RIG HEMA 124 E4 34 41 52 S 137 42 24 E

Dublin

Dublin Lions Park
In Rest Area. Old Port Wakefield Rd. Behind toilet block
CT HT BIG RIG HEMA 124 D6 34 27 07 S 138 21 05 E

Edithburgh

Edithburgh Dump Point
Blanche St, opposite caravan park
CT HT BIG RIG HEMA 124 G4 35 05 24 S 137 44 44 E

Elliston

Eliston Dump Point
Beach Tce, at Info Centre
CT HT BIG RIG HEMA 134 F4 33 38 51 S 134 53 28 E

Eudunda

Eudunda Camping Area 0417 703 345
Oval Cres via Morgan Rd
CT HT HEMA 125 C8 34 10 47 S 139 05 17 E

Gladstone

Gladstone Dump Point
Main North Rd, behind caravan park
CT HT BIG RIG HEMA 128 J7 33 16 06 S 138 20 59 E

Goolwa South

Bristow-Smith Park
Barrage Road, Goolwa

Hamley Bridge

Hamley Bridge Community & Sports Centre
Stockport Rd
CT HT BIG RIG HEMA 124 D7 34 21 14 S 138 40 53 E

Hawker

Hawker Town Park
Rest Area at Hawker. Elder Tce
CT HT BIG RIG HEMA 128 D7 31 53 15 S 138 25 16 E

Iron Knob

Knobbies Camping & Caravan Area
Dickens St
CT HT $ BIG RIG HEMA 128 G3 32 43 56 S 137 09 02 E

Jamestown

Jamestown Dump Point 08 8664 0077
130 Ayr St. Outside caravan park
CT HT BIG RIG HEMA 128 J7 33 12 19 S 138 36 03 E

Kadina

Kadina Dump Point 08 8821 1600
Doswell Tce, opposite medical centre
CT HT BIG RIG HEMA 124 B4 33 57 32 S 137 43 16 E

Kangaroo Island

American River Dump Point
Tangara Dr, in front of toilet block
CT HT BIG RIG HEMA 124 J4 35 47 15 S 137 46 15 E

Christmas Cove - Penneshaw
Christmas St, off Howard Dr. Cassette only, access is limited
CT HEMA 124 J5 35 43 09 S 137 56 02 E

Kingscote
Third St. Adjacent to Nepean Bay Tourist Park
CT HT BIG RIG HEMA 124 J4 35 40 15 S 137 36 42 E

Parndana Dump Point 08 8553 4500
Jubilee Ave, adjacent to Health Centre
CT BIG RIG HEMA 124 J3 35 47 17 S 137 15 38 E

Western KI Caravan Park & Wildlife Reserve 08 8559 7201
South Coast Rd. 3 km E of Flinders Chase. Fee for non guests, must call into reception
CT HT $ BIG RIG HEMA 124 K2 35 57 39 S 136 48 28 E

Kapunda

Kapunda Harness Racing Club 0428 956 462
Hancock Rd
CT HT BIG RIG HEMA 125 D8 34 20 26 S 138 54 08 E

Karoonda

Karoonda Cabin & Caravan Park 08 8578 1004
Entry off Karoonda Rd, follow track to behind Oval toilet block. Signposted
CT HT BIG RIG HEMA 125 G11 35 05 47 S 139 53 23 E

Keith

Keith Caravan Park 0427 876 993
Naracoorte Rd. Public access
CT HT HEMA 125 K12 36 06 04 S 140 21 04 E

Kimba

Kimba Recreation Reserve 08 8627 2026
Buckleboo Rd, extension of North Tce. Entry through archway
CT HT BIG RIG HEMA 128 J1 33 08 04 S 136 24 54 E

Kingston SE

Kingston SE Dump Point
Railway Tce, off Cape Jaffa/ Robe Hwy, at Sale Yards
CT HT BIG RIG HEMA 126 D2 36 50 03 S 139 51 45 E

Lameroo

Lake Roberts
500m E of PO, entry to day use & caravan park
CT HT BIG RIG HEMA 125 G12 35 19 41 S 140 31 17 E

Langhorne Creek

Langhorne Creek Dump Point
Meechi Rd, adjacent to public toilets. 85 m N of Bridge Rd intersection
CT HT HEMA 127 J7 35 17 44 S 139 02 11 E

Laura

Laura Dump Point
North Tce, on road outside Laura Caravan Park
CT HT BIG RIG HEMA 128 J7 33 10 54 S 138 18 03 E

Lock

Lock Caravan Park 08 8689 1020
Caravan Park at Lock. South Tce, near town centre
CT HT BIG RIG HEMA 134 E6 33 34 10 S 135 45 24 E

Loxton

Loxton Dump Point 08 8584 8071
AW Traeger Drive. Opposite Loxton Sporting Club
CT HT BIG RIG HEMA 125 D13 34 27 06 S 140 34 42 E

Loxton Lions Park Reserve 08 8584 8071
Grant Schubert Dr
CT HT BIG RIG HEMA 125 D12 34 26 53 S 140 33 01 E

Lucindale

Lucindale Dump Point
Centenary Ave, in the Sports Oval near the toilets via Western entrance before the Agriculture Field grounds
CT HT BIG RIG HEMA 126 E4 36 58 18 S 140 21 51 E

Maitland

Maitland Showground 08 8832 2171
Rogers Tce. Signposted, near shed on right
CT HT BIG RIG HEMA 124 D4 34 22 18 S 137 40 39 E

Mannum

Haythorpe Reserve 08 8569 0100
In parking area 1 km NE of Mannum, on Bowhill Rd. E side of river. N of ferry crossing
CT HEMA 125 F9 34 54 33 S 139 19 24 E

Mannum Caravan Park 08 8569 1402
Purnong Rd. Public access. Fee if not a guest, must contact office
CT HT $ BIG RIG HEMA 125 F9 34 54 31 S 139 19 02 E

Marla

Marla Dump Point
Cockatoo Crescent
CT HT BIG RIG HEMA 138 E6 27 18 08 S 133 37 22 E

Marree

Drovers Run Tourist Park 08 8675 8248
Cnr Birdsville Track & Oodnadatta Track. Inside the park
CT HT BIG RIG HEMA 130 F6 29 39 11 S 138 04 25 E

Meadows

Meadows Recreation Ground
Access from Mawson Rd. Not available during sports or events
CT HT BIG RIG HEMA 119 K9 35 10 47 S 138 45 35 E

Melrose

Melrose Showground 0428 662 140
Main North Rd. N end of town
CT HT BIG RIG HEMA 128 G6 32 48 36 S 138 11 46 E

Meningie

Meningie Dump Point
Princes Hwy, in parking bay at Southern entrance to town
CT HT BIG RIG HEMA 125 J9 35 41 40 S 139 20 12 E

Millicent

Millicent Information Centre 08 8733 0904
1 Mt Gambier St, behind Info centre
CT HT BIG RIG HEMA 126 G4 37 35 50 S 140 21 27 E

Minnipa

Minnipa Dump Point
Minnipa Oval. Mosley Tce
CT HT HEMA 134 C4 32 51 24 S 135 09 24 E

Moonta

Moonta Dump Point
Cnr of Blyth & Frances Terraces
CT HT BIG RIG HEMA 124 C4 34 03 43 S 137 35 15 E

Moorook

Moorook Riverfront Camping & Picnic Area 08 8584 7221
Kingston-Loxton Rd
CT HT HEMA 125 D12 34 17 17 S 140 22 06 E

Morgan

Morgan Dump Point
Morgan Oval, North East Tce
CT HT BIG RIG HEMA 125 C10 34 01 46 S 139 40 08 E

SOUTH AUSTRALIA

Mount Barker

Mount Barker Dump Point
Alexandrina Rd
CT HEMA 119 F12 35 04 26 S 138 51 43 E

Mount Gambier

Mount Gambier Showgrounds 0408 492 182
Pick Ave
CT HT $ BIG RIG HEMA 126 J5 37 50 16 S 140 47 51 E

Mount Pleasant

Talunga Park Caravan Park (Showgrounds) 08 8568 1934
Melrose St. At showground
CT HT BIG RIG HEMA 127 C7 34 46 34 S 139 02 34 E

Murray Bridge

Murray Bridge Dump Point
Railway Tce. 200m NE of PO
CT HT BIG RIG HEMA 125 G9 35 06 57 S 139 16 25 E

Naracoorte

Naracoorte Showgrounds 0414 453 360
Smith St
CT HT BIG RIG HEMA 126 E5 36 57 16 S 140 44 48 E

Orroroo

Orroroo Caravan Park 08 8658 1444
Second St. 200m W of PO. At back of the park. Call at reception to pay fee
CT $ BIG RIG HEMA 128 G7 32 43 57 S 138 36 36 E

Penola

McCorquindale Park
Off Cameron St, entrance between Portland St & Gordon St
CT HT BIG RIG HEMA 126 F5 37 22 29 S 140 50 27 E

Peterborough

Peterborough Dump Point
Don Ferguson Drive, entry beside Tourist Information Centre
CT HT BIG RIG HEMA 129 H8 32 58 25 S 138 50 02 E

Pinnaroo

Pinnaroo
Cnr Mallee Hwy & Homburg Tce
CT HT BIG RIG HEMA 125 G14 35 15 37 S 140 54 46 E

Point Lowly

Point Lowly 08 8645 7900
Port Bonython Rd, S side past gas plant. 500m from camp spot
CT HT BIG RIG HEMA 128 H5 32 59 34 S 137 46 51 E

Port Augusta

Port Augusta Motorhome Park
Power Station Rd
CT HT BIG RIG HEMA 128 F5 32 30 40 S 137 47 09 E

Port Broughton

Port Broughton Dump Point 08 8635 2107
Cnr Mundoora & Bute Rds, next to council depot
CT HT BIG RIG HEMA 124 A5 33 36 10 S 137 56 09 E

Port Germein

Port Germein Recreation Grounds
West Tce, adjacent to First St
CT HT BIG RIG HEMA 128 H6 33 01 09 S 137 59 39 E

Port Gibbon

Port Gibbon Foreshore 08 8629 2019
Port Gibbon Foreshore Access from B100 at Port Gibbon sign, through Igloo Rd
CT HT BIG RIG HEMA 124 B2 33 48 07 S 136 48 06 E

Port Julia

Port Julia Oval (Reichenbach Memorial Park) 08 8853 8115
Osprey St, behind toilets. Fee if not staying
CT $ HEMA 124 E5 34 39 46 S 137 52 38 E

Port Lincoln

Port Lincoln Dump Point
Windsor Ave, off Proper Bay Road. Next to Ravendale Sportsgrounds
CT HT BIG RIG HEMA 134 J6 34 44 35 S 135 51 18 E

Port MacDonnell

Port MacDonnell Recreation Reserve
Elizabeth Street
CT HT BIG RIG HEMA 126 K5 38 03 04 S 140 42 01 E

Port Pirie

Port Pirie Dump Point
Globe Oval, Geddes Rd
CT HT BIG RIG HEMA 128 J6 33 11 09 S 138 01 25 E

Port Victoria

Port Victoria Oval
Kuhn Tce
CT HT BIG RIG HEMA 124 D4 34 29 46 S 137 29 16 E

Quorn

Quorn Dump Point
Silo Rd
CT HT BIG RIG HEMA 128 F6 32 20 26 S 138 02 52 E

Renmark

Renmark Swimming Pool Car Park
Cnr Cowra & Fifteenth St. In swimming pool car park
CT HT BIG RIG HEMA 125 C13 34 10 08 S 140 44 41 E

Riverton

Riverton Caravan Park 08 8847 2419
Cnr Oxford Tce & Torrens Rd, at Town Oval. Fee if not a guest
CT HT $ HEMA 124 C7 34 09 20 S 138 44 59 E

Robe

Robe Dump Point
Corner White & Robe Sts
CT HT BIG RIG HEMA 126 F2 37 10 30 S 139 45 40 E

Robertstown

Robertstown Oval
Parking Area at Robertstown. Entry from Church St
CT HT BIG RIG HEMA 125 C8 33 59 35 S 139 04 49 E

Roxby Downs

Roxby Downs Dump Point
Near BP Service Station, Olympic Hwy. $10.00 key deposit
CT HT BIG RIG HEMA 130 J2 30 33 15 S 136 53 36 E

Saddleworth

Saddleworth Oval Caravan Park 08 8847 4439
off Main Rd via Belvedere Rd & Marrabel Rd
CT HT BIG RIG HEMA 124 C7 34 05 10 S 138 47 05 E

Snowtown

Snowtown Centenary Park Caravan Park 08 8865 2252
In Caravan Park at Snowtown. North Tce. Use Eastern entry for higher vehicles
CT HT BIG RIG HEMA 124 B6 33 46 42 S 138 12 59 E

Southend

Southend Dump Point
Bridges Dr, behind the public toilet at beach car park
CT BIG RIG HEMA 126 G3 37 34 14 S 140 07 05 E

St Kilda

St Kilda Adventure Park
Parking Area at St Kilda, via Mangrove St. Dump is W end of boat ramp car park. Key at Kiosk
CT HEMA 120 C3 34 44 31 S 138 32 00 E

Stansbury

Stansbury Dump Point
Anzac Parade, just past caravan park rear entrance
CT HT BIG RIG HEMA 124 F5 34 54 48 S 137 48 12 E

Streaky Bay

Streaky Bay Lions Park
East Tce, off Flinders Hwy
CT HT BIG RIG HEMA 134 C2 32 47 42 S 134 13 05 E

Swan Reach

Tenbury - Hunter Reserve 08 8569 0100
Take ferry N across to W side of river. 500m E of ferry crossing. Next to toilets
CT HT BIG RIG HEMA 125 E10 34 33 43 S 139 36 01 E

Tailem Bend

Tailem Bend Dump Point
Main Rd, in parking bay at S end of town
CT HT BIG RIG HEMA 125 G9 35 16 07 S 139 27 30 E

Tantanoola

Railway Reserve Tantanoola
Opposite hotel in rest area
CT HT BIG RIG HEMA 126 H4 37 41 46 S 140 27 20 E

Tumby Bay

Tumby Bay Self Contained RV Park 08 8688 2087
Northern Access Rd. N end of town
CT HT BIG RIG HEMA 134 H6 34 21 31 S 136 06 03 E

Waikerie

Waikerie Dump Point
Corner of Civic Ave & Dowling St, access off Civic Ave
CT HT BIG RIG HEMA 125 C11 34 10 56 S 139 59 14 E

Wallaroo

Wallaroo Dump Point 08 8823 2023
Owen Tce. Next to Mobil Service Station
CT HT BIG RIG HEMA 124 B4 33 56 04 S 137 37 53 E

Whyalla

Foreshore Rest Area
Lincoln Hwy. 350m S of McDouall Stuart Ave
CT HT BIG RIG HEMA 128 H4 33 02 46 S 137 31 35 E

Jubilee Park Dump Point (Whyalla Showgrounds)
Jenkins Ave. Signposted at entry. Daytime only, gates locked at night
CT HT BIG RIG HEMA 128 H4 33 02 20 S 137 30 31 E

William Creek

William Creek Camping Ground 08 8670 7880
At public toilets just outside campground
CT HEMA 130 C1 28 54 28 S 136 20 18 E

Wilmington

Wilmington Centenary Park
Melrose Tce
CT HT BIG RIG HEMA 128 G6 32 39 13 S 138 06 06 E

SOUTH AUSTRALIA

Wilpena Pound

Wilpena Pound Dump Point
At Wilpena Pound. At the back of the long term car park. GPS approximate
CT RIG HEMA 142 G4 31 31 40 S 138 36 29 E

Wudinna

Gawler Ranges Motel & Caravan Park
08 8680 2090
Eyre Hwy. 1 km E from PO. Behind the caravan park ablution block
CT HT RIG HEMA 134 D5 33 03 20 S 135 28 01 E

Yacka

Yackamoorundie Park
0408 794 891
Cnr of Main Nth Rd & North Tce
CT RIG HEMA 124 A6 33 34 06 S 138 26 43 E

Yankalilla

Yankalilla Dump Point
Arthur St
CT HT RIG HEMA 124 H6 35 27 31 S 138 21 06 E

Yunta

Yunta Centennial Park
08 8650 5009
Rest Area at Yunta. Next to Telecentre on Hwy
CT HT RIG HEMA 129 G10 32 34 54 S 139 33 46 E

WESTERN AUSTRALIA

Albany

Albany Dump Point
At Information Bay, Albany Hwy N of town. S of Drome Rd
CT HT RIG HEMA 153 J14 34 59 28 S 117 51 21 E

Brig Amity Park
08 9841 9290
Off Princess Royal Dr, Amity Quay
CT HT RIG HEMA 153 K14 35 01 44 S 117 52 45 E

Badgingarra

Badgingarra Community Recreation Centre
08 9652 0800
North West Rd
CT HT RIG HEMA 170 F3 30 23 12 S 115 29 59 E

Balladonia Area

Baxter Rest Area
At Rest Area 67 km W of Caiguna or 115 km E of Balladonia
CT HT RIG HEMA 157 E11 32 21 26 S 124 47 14 E

Woorlba Homestead Rest Area
Rest Area 132 km W of Caiguna or 50 km E of Balladonia
CT HT RIG HEMA 157 E9 32 26 12 S 124 06 17 E

Beacon

Beacon Dump Point
Lucas St, adjacent to the Information Bay, opposite the Beacon Co-op
CT HT HEMA 171 F8 30 27 04 S 117 51 49 E

Beasley River

Beasley River Rest Area
Rest Area 171 km E of Nanutarra Rdhouse or 53 km W of Paraburdoo/Wittenoom Rd junction
CT HT RIG HEMA 166 K5 22 56 56 S 116 58 40 E

Beverley

Beverley Dump Point
Council Dr. Just past & opposite the caravan park entrance
CT HT RIG HEMA 150 C7 32 06 27 S 116 55 26 E

Bindoon

Bindoon Transit Park
08 9576 1020
Next to toilets at the oval
CT HT RIG HEMA 170 J4 31 23 08 S 116 05 52 E

Boddington

Boddington RV Stop
1 Wuraming Ave
CT HT RIG HEMA 150 G5 32 47 52 S 116 28 39 E

Brookton

Brookton Caravan Park & Camping Ground
08 9642 1106
Brookton HIghway
CT HT RIG HEMA 151 D8 32 22 07 S 117 00 08 E

Broome

Broome Dump Point
08 9195 2200
Hamersley St, at the Visitor Information Centre. Locked, get key from inside
CT HT RIG HEMA 162 E4 17 57 12 S 122 14 28 E

Discovery Parks Broome
08 9192 1366
91 Walcott St. 2 km S of PO. Have to park outside, cassette only, must see reception
CT $ HEMA 162 E4 17 58 15 S 122 14 02 E

Bruce Rock

Bruce Rock Caravan Park
08 9061 1377
Dunstall St. Public access
CT HT RIG HEMA 151 A13 31 52 26 S 118 09 05 E

Brunswick Junction

Brunswick Junction Showgrounds
08 9726 1244
At Showgrounds, Ridley St. Turn R inside grounds. Key at Eziway Supermarket, business hours
CT HT RIG HEMA 150 J2 33 15 11 S 115 50 14 E

Busselton

Busselton Dump Point
08 9781 0444
Behind Churchill Park Hall, Adelaide St. Call to receive access code to unlock
CT HT RIG HEMA 152 B3 33 38 47 S 115 21 03 E

Capel

Capel Park
Buchanan Rd. Locked, Key & refundable deposit payable at Colroys Cafe
CT HT RIG HEMA 152 A3 33 33 10 S 115 33 44 E

Carnarvon

Carnarvon Dump Point
08 9941 1146
Hill St, off Robinson St
CT HT RIG HEMA 168 D2 24 52 55 S 113 39 34 E

Carnarvon Area

Blowholes (Point Quobba)
0408 942 945
At Camp Area 72 km N of Carnarvon. Turn W off North West Coastal Hwy 24 km N of Carnarvon or 115 km S of Minilya Roadhouse
CT HEMA 168 D1 24 29 16 S 113 24 44 E

Cervantes

Cervantes 24 Hour Dump Point
08 9652 0800
Cadiz St, near Visitor Centre
CT HT RIG HEMA 170 F2 30 30 07 S 115 04 03 E

Waste Transfer Station
08 9652 0806
Seville St, entry at Estella Pl. Limited opening hours
CT HT RIG HEMA 170 F2 30 29 52 S 115 04 48 E

Cleaverville Beach

Cleaverville Beach
08 9186 8555
At Camp Area. Turn N 28 km E of Karrratha Rdhouse or 14 km W of Roebourne. 13 km dirt Rd. Open May - Sep
CT HEMA 166 F5 20 39 40 S 116 59 53 E

Collie

Collie River Valley Tourist Park
08 9734 5088
Porter St. 2 km W of PO. Please call in at reception first
CT HEMA 150 K4 33 21 44 S 116 08 44 E

Collie Visitor Centre
08 9734 2051
156 Throssell St, donation for water, fee for hot showers, caravan parking
CT HT RIG HEMA 150 K4 33 21 31 S 116 08 57 E

Eddie Woods Memorial Park
Throssell St, opposite pub
CT HT RIG HEMA 150 K4 33 21 40 S 116 09 33 E

Coolgardie

Railway Museum
Woodward St, cnr of Lefroy St
CT HT RIG HEMA 156 A2 30 57 22 S 121 09 47 E

Coorow

Coorow Caravan Park
08 9952 0100
Station St. Public access
CT HT RIG HEMA 170 E4 29 52 51 S 116 01 02 E

Coronation Beach

Coronation Beach
08 9920 5011
At Camp Area. Turn W 28 km N of Geraldton or 24 km S of Northampton
CT HEMA 170 A1 28 33 12 S 114 33 52 E

Corrigin

Corrigin Dump Point
08 9063 2203
Walton St, behind toilet block
CT HEMA 151 D12 32 19 51 S 117 52 23 E

Cuballing

Cuballing RV Parking Area
08 9883 6031
Parking Area at Cuballing, Western Side of road between the Hwy & Railway line
CT HT HEMA 151 G8 32 49 15 S 117 10 48 E

Cue

Cue Dump Point
Dowley St, next to shire hall
CT HT RIG HEMA 169 H8 27 25 21 S 117 53 46 E

Dalwallinu

Dalwallinu Caravan Park
08 9661 1253
Dowie St. Public access
CT $ HEMA 170 F6 30 16 27 S 116 40 08 E

WESTERN AUSTRALIA

Dandaragan

Dandaragan Transit Park 08 9651 4071
Pioneer Park, 3550 Dandaragan Rd
CT HT BIG RIG HEMA 170 G3 30 40 13 S 115 42 12 E

De Grey River

De Grey River
At rest area 82 km NE of Port Hedland or 71 km SW of Pardoo Roadhouse
CT HEMA 167 F8 20 18 28 S 119 15 11 E

Denham

Denham Dump Point
Denham - Hamelin Rd, in info bay on approach to town
CT HT BIG RIG HEMA 168 F2 25 55 37 S 113 32 36 E

Denmark

Denmark Dump Point 08 9848 2055
17 Ocean Beach Rd, at the Information Centre
CT HT BIG RIG HEMA 153 J12 34 57 46 S 117 21 01 E

Denmark Area

Cosy Corner (East)
At Camp Area 30 km W of Albany or 38 km E of Denmark
CT HEMA 153 K13 35 03 33 S 117 38 44 E

Derby

Kimberley Entrance Caravan Park 08 9193 1055
Rowan St. See reception, donation to RFDS
CT HT BIG RIG HEMA 164 K2 17 18 25 S 123 37 45 E

Dongara

Dongara Dump Point
Waldeck St, next to the Oval
CT HT BIG RIG HEMA 170 C2 29 14 51 S 114 55 58 E

Donnybrook

Donnybrook Transit Park 08 9731 1897
Reserve St, W end of oval
CT HT BIG RIG HEMA 152 A5 33 34 16 S 115 49 12 E

Dowerin

Dowerin Dump Point
Stewart St, opposite the hotel
CT HT BIG RIG HEMA 170 H6 31 11 43 S 117 01 50 E

Dumbleyung

Stubbs Park
Bahrs Rd, in oval
CT HT BIG RIG HEMA 151 J11 33 19 04 S 117 44 36 E

Eighty Mile Beach Area

Stanley Rest Area
Rest Area 108 km NE of Sandfire Roadhouse or 181 km SW of Roebuck Plains Roadhouse. 5 km N of Nita Downs turnoff
CT HT BIG RIG HEMA 162 G4 19 02 36 S 121 39 56 E

Eneabba

Arrowsmith Rest Area
Rest Area 30 km N of Eneabba or 50 km S of Dongarra
CT HT BIG RIG HEMA 170 D2 29 34 43 S 115 08 09 E

Esperance

Esperance Dump Point
Shelden Rd, off Norseman Rd
CT HT BIG RIG HEMA 156 J4 33 50 35 S 121 53 54 E

Exmouth

Sports & Recreation Ground 08 9949 1176
Murat Rd, in recreation reserve near visitors centre. Directions available at visitors centre
CT HT BIG RIG HEMA 166 H1 21 55 56 S 114 07 47 E

Fitzroy Crossing Area

Ellendale Rest Area
Rest Area 125 km SE of Derby turnoff or 88 km W of Fitzroy Crossing
CT BIG RIG HEMA 163 E7 17 57 38 S 124 50 10 E

Ngumpan Cliff Lookout
Rest Area 96 km SE of Fitzroy Crossing or 192 km W of Halls Creek
CT HT BIG RIG HEMA 163 G10 18 44 53 S 126 06 31 E

Geraldton

Geraldton RV Park
Parking Area at Geraldton. Cnr of Francis St & Marine Tce
CT HT BIG RIG HEMA 170 B1 28 46 33 S 114 36 11 E

Geraldton Area

Fig Tree Picnic & Camping Ground 08 9920 5011
Camp Area 21 km NE of Geraldton. North West Coast Hwy, Chapman Valley Scenic Drive for 12 km
CT HEMA 170 A1 28 39 32 S 114 42 15 E

Gnoorea Point (40 Mile)

Gnoorea Point (40 Mile) 08 9186 8555
Near Camp area at Forty Mile Beach. Turn W 54 km N of Fortescue River Roadhouse or 40 km S of Karratha Roadhouse.12 km dirt Rd. Open May - Sep
CT HT BIG RIG HEMA 166 F4 20 50 26 S 116 20 51 E

Gnowangerup

Gnowangerup Caravan Park 08 9827 1635
Richardson St
CT HEMA 155 G8 33 56 32 S 118 00 32 E

Goomalling

Goomalling Caravan Park 08 9629 1183
Throssel St. 1 km SE of PO
CT HT BIG RIG HEMA 170 J6 31 17 59 S 116 49 57 E

Green Head

Green Head Dump Point
Green Head Rd. In Recreation Centre carpark
CT HT BIG RIG HEMA 170 E2 30 04 01 S 114 58 07 E

Harrismith

Harrismith Caravan Park 08 9883 1010
Caravan Park at Harrismith. Cnr Railway Ave & Baylon St
CT HT BIG RIG HEMA 151 G11 32 56 10 S 117 51 44 E

Hopetoun

Hopetoun Dump Point 08 9839 0000
Cnr Hopetoun-Ravensthorpe Rd & Senna Rd. 3 km N of Hopetoun
CT HT BIG RIG HEMA 155 G13 33 55 08 S 120 08 13 E

Jarradale

Jarrahdale Old Mill
Parking Area at Jarradale, Millars Rd off Jarradale Rd
CT HT BIG RIG HEMA 150 D3 32 20 03 S 116 04 07 E

Jurien Bay

Jurien Bay Dump Point
Bashford St (adjacent to Caltex service station)
CT HT BIG RIG HEMA 170 F2 30 18 10 S 115 02 35 E

Sandy Cape Recreational Park 08 9652 0800
2 km N of Jurien Bay or 18 km S of Green Head. 6 km dirt road
CT HT BIG RIG HEMA 170 E2 30 11 23 S 115 00 07 E

Kalbarri

Kalbarri Dump Point
Porter St, 1.7 km from turn off, in industrial area
CT HT BIG RIG HEMA 168 J3 27 42 08 S 114 10 03 E

Kalgoorlie

Boulder Dump Point
Hamilton St, between Piesse & Richardson Sts
CT HT BIG RIG HEMA 156 A3 30 47 00 S 121 29 29 E

Kalgoorlie Dump Point 08 9021 1966
Forrest St. N of railway station
CT HT BIG RIG HEMA 156 A3 30 44 38 S 121 28 12 E

Kambalda

Kambalda West RV Stop
Parking Area at Kambalda West. Behind Rec centre off Barnes Drive
CT HT BIG RIG HEMA 156 B3 31 12 23 S 121 37 17 E

Karratha

Karratha Dump Point
North Coast Hwy, near intersection of De Witt Rd
CT HT BIG RIG HEMA 166 F5 20 47 36 S 116 51 47 E

Karratha Outback Travel Dump Point 08 9143 0116
At the Outback Travel Centre, Cnr of Dampier Hwy & Exploration Dr
CT HT BIG RIG HEMA 166 F5 20 44 13 S 116 45 58 E

Katanning

All Ages Playground
Cnr Clive St & Great Southern Hwy
CT HT HEMA 153 B13 33 41 47 S 117 32 52 E

Kojonup

Kojonup Rest Area 08 9831 0500
Gordon St. S end of town
CT HT BIG RIG HEMA 153 C11 33 50 13 S 117 09 32 E

Kondinin

Kondinin Caravan Park 08 9889 1006
Gordon St
CT HT BIG RIG HEMA 151 E13 32 29 43 S 118 15 49 E

Kookynie

Niagara Dam 08 9024 2041
Downstream from dam wall
CT HT HEMA 158 E3 29 24 15 S 121 25 40 E

Kulin

Kulin Overnight Stop 08 9880 1204
Johnston St at the public toilets
CT BIG RIG HEMA 151 F13 32 40 13 S 118 09 20 E

Kununurra

Kununurra Dump Point 08 9169 1188
5 Messmate Way, BP Ord River Roadhouse, key required
CT HT $ HEMA 165 F14 15 46 42 S 128 44 25 E

Kununurra Area

Cockburn Rest Area
Rest Area at Victoria Hwy junction or 152 km N of Turkey Creek, 56 km S of Wyndham or 45 km W of Kununurra
CT HT BIG RIG HEMA 165 F13 15 52 07 S 128 22 17 E

Lake Grace

Lake Grace Dump Point
Sport Precinct, Stubbs St
CT HT BIG RIG HEMA 151 H14 33 06 03 S 118 27 22 E

WESTERN AUSTRALIA

Lake Macleod

Lake MacLeod Rest Area
Rest Area 49 km S of Minilya Roadhouse or 90 km N of Carnarvon
CT HT BIG RIG HEMA 168 C2 24 14 57 S 114 02 11 E

Lancelin

Lancelin Dump Point
Rock Way off Gingin Rd
CT HT BIG RIG HEMA 170 H2 31 01 13 S 115 19 59 E

Learmonth

Burkett Road Rest Area
16 km NE of Minilya Roadhouse or 111 km SW of Nanutarra Roadhouse. 1 km N of Exmouth turnoff
CT HT BIG RIG HEMA 166 K2 22 59 01 S 114 36 47 E

Leeman

Leeman Dump Point
Wann Park Oval, Rudduck St
CT HT BIG RIG HEMA 170 E2 29 56 42 S 114 58 52 E

Leonora

Leonora Dump Point
Goldfields Hwy, at the Information bay, S of town
CT HT BIG RIG HEMA 158 D3 28 53 37 S 121 19 47 E

Mandurah

Mandurah Dump Point
Cnr Sholl St & Hackett St. In car park
CT HT BIG RIG HEMA 150 E2 32 31 42 S 115 43 21 E

Marble Bar

Marble Bar Dump Point
At Rest Area in General St. Near the General Store & Service Station
CT HT BIG RIG HEMA 160 A1 21 10 17 S 119 44 37 E

Marble Bar Area

Des Streckfuss Rest Area
Rest Area 74 km NW of Marble Bar or 79 km SE of Hwy 1 junction.
CT HT BIG RIG HEMA 160 A1 20 49 33 S 119 30 44 E

Margaret River

Margaret River Dump Point
Gloucester Park access Rd, off Wallcliffe Rd. Behind Youth Zone Room. Locked, key available at Civic Admin Centre or Margaret River Recreation Centre
CT HT BIG RIG HEMA 152 C1 33 57 14 S 115 04 12 E

Mary River

Mary Pool (Mary River)
Rest Area 180 km E of Fitzroy Crossing or 108 km W of Halls Creek
CT HEMA 163 G11 18 43 37 S 126 52 19 E

Meckering

Meckering Memorial Park
Kelly St
CT HT BIG RIG HEMA 170 J6 31 37 58 S 117 00 26 E

Meekatharra

Meekatharra Dump Point 08 9981 1002
In lane way between Savage & Porter St's behind Shire Office
CT HT HEMA 169 G9 26 35 37 S 118 29 45 E

Meekatharra Area

Gascoyne River (South Branch)
Rest Area 148 km NW of Meekatharra, 276 km S of Newman or 108 km S of Kumarina Roadhouse
CT HT BIG RIG HEMA 169 E10 25 34 44 S 119 14 19 E

Merredin

Merredin Tourist Park 08 9041 1535
2 Oats St. Public access
CT HT HEMA 171 J9 31 29 05 S 118 17 29 E

Midland

Midland Tourist Park 08 9274 3002
6 Toodyay Rd, Middle Swan
CT HT $ BIG RIG HEMA 147 E9 31 52 30 S 116 00 42 E

Mingenew

Mingenew Dump Point
Midlands Rd, in parking bay 100m W of Palm Roadhouse
CT HT BIG RIG HEMA 170 C3 29 11 25 S 115 26 19 E

Minilya

Lyndon River
Rest Area 48 km NE of Minilya Roadhouse or 179 km SW of Nanutarra Roadhouse
CT HT BIG RIG HEMA 166 K2 23 28 58 S 114 16 32 E

Lyndon River (West)
Rest Area 32 km N of Minilya Roadhouse or 190 km S of Exmouth on Minilya-Exmouth Rd
CT HT BIG RIG HEMA 168 B2 23 32 32 S 113 57 47 E

Minilya River
Rest Area 1 km S of Minilya Roadhouse or 141 km N of Carnarvon
CT HT BIG RIG HEMA 168 B2 23 49 01 S 114 00 38 E

Minnivale

Minnivale Rest Area
Cnr of Amery Benjaberring & Berry Rd. Next to disused tennis courts
CT HT BIG RIG HEMA 170 H7 31 08 20 S 117 11 04 E

Moora

Moora RV Short Stay & Dump Point 08 9651 0000
Padbury St, Moora
BIG RIG HEMA 170 G4 30 38 32 S 116 00 30 E

Moore River

Moore River Bridge
Rest Area 33 km N of Yanchep NP turnoff or 2 km SE of Guilderton turnoff
CT HT BIG RIG HEMA 170 J3 31 18 12 S 115 33 18 E

Mount Barker

Mount Barker Visitors Centre 08 9851 1163
Albany Highway
CT HT BIG RIG HEMA 153 G13 34 37 38 S 117 39 49 E

Mount Magnet

Mount Magnet Caravan Park 08 9963 4198
Lot 397 Hepburn St
CT $ HEMA 169 J8 28 03 42 S 117 50 58 E

Mount Magnet Area

Kirkalocka Rest Area
Rest Area 64 km S of Mt Magnet or 80 km N of Paynes Find
CT HT BIG RIG HEMA 171 A8 28 35 50 S 117 46 51 E

Mukinbudin

Mukinbudin Caravan Park 0429 471 103
Cruickshank St
CT HT HEMA 171 G9 30 55 09 S 118 12 21 E

Mullewa

Mullewa Caravan Park 0439898762
Lovers Lane
CT HT BIG RIG HEMA 170 A3 28 32 19 S 115 30 14 E

Munjina (Auski)

Mulga Parking Area
Parking Area 39 km N of Auski Roadhouse or 180 km S of Hwy 1 junction
CT HT BIG RIG HEMA 167 H8 22 03 10 S 118 48 10 E

Murchison

Murchison Oasis Roadhouse & Caravan Park 08 9961 3875
Murchison Settlement
CT HT BIG RIG HEMA 168 G5 26 53 46 S 115 57 26 E

Nannup

Nannup Dump Point
Brockman St, next to the caravan park
CT HT BIG RIG HEMA 152 D4 33 58 34 S 115 45 47 E

Narembeen

Narembeen Caravan Park 08 9064 7308
Currall St
CT HT BIG RIG HEMA 151 B14 32 03 49 S 118 23 46 E

Narrogin

Narrogin Dump Point 08 9881 2064
Cnr Park & Fairway Sts, behind Dryandra Country Visitor Centre
CT HT HEMA 151 G8 32 56 14 S 117 10 46 E

Nerren Nerren

Nerren Nerren Rest Area
Rest Area 82 km N of Kalbarri turnoff or 46 km S of Billabong Roadhouse
CT HEMA 168 H3 27 12 43 S 114 36 44 E

Newdegate

Newdegate Rest Area
Maley St
CT HEMA 155 D10 33 05 34 S 119 01 27 E

Newman

Newman Visitors Centre
2 Fortescue Ave. Key required from Information centre open 8.00am - 5.00pm daily
CT HT BIG RIG HEMA 160 E1 23 21 33 S 119 43 40 E

Newman Area

Mt Robinson Rest Area
Rest Area 109 km NW of Newman or 86 km SE of Auski Roadhouse. 800m E of Hwy
CT HT BIG RIG HEMA 167 K8 23 02 34 S 118 50 57 E

Norseman

Norseman Rest Area
68 Roberts St, Key required from Tourist Information Centre. Open business hours
CT HEMA 156 E4 32 11 46 S 121 46 51 E

Norseman Area

Fraser Range Rest Area
Rest Area 109 km W of Balladonia or 83 km E of Norseman
CT HT BIG RIG HEMA 156 D5 32 04 24 S 122 35 36 E

Northam

Northam Dump Point 08 9622 2100
Peel Terrace, opposite Caltex Service Station
CT HT BIG RIG HEMA 170 K6 31 38 59 S 116 40 38 E

Northampton

Northampton Lions Park 08 9934 1488
Bateman St, access off Essex St, in the long vehicle car park, opposite IGA (Hampton Road)
CT HT HEMA 168 K3 28 20 54 S 114 37 49 E

WESTERN AUSTRALIA

Northhampton Area

Galena Bridge (Murchison River)
Rest Area 13 km N of Kalbarri turnoff or 115 km S of Billabong Roadhouse
CT HT BIG RIG HEMA 168 J3 27 49 39 S 114 41 24 E

Nullagine

Nullagine
Cnr Cooke & Walter Sts, in the Rest Stop
CT HT BIG RIG HEMA 160 B2 21 53 10 S 120 06 28 E

Nungarin

Nungarin Dump Point
Main St, opposite Heritage Machinery & Army Museum
CT HT BIG RIG HEMA 171 H9 31 11 05 S 118 06 10 E

Onslow

Onslow Dump Point 08 9184 6644
Cameron Avenue, adjacent to basketball court. S of PO
CT HT BIG RIG HEMA 166 H3 21 38 28 S 115 06 47 E

Orange Grove

Crystal Brook Caravan Park 08 9453 6226
388 Kelvin Rd
CT $ HEMA 147 K9 32 01 05 S 116 01 08 E

Paynes Find Area

Mount Gibson Rest Area
Rest Area 82 km N of Wubin or 74 km S of Payes Find
CT HT BIG RIG HEMA 170 D7 29 36 32 S 117 08 32 E

Peaceful Bay

Peaceful Bay Dump Point
Peaceful Bay Rd, near public toilets
CT HT BIG RIG HEMA 153 K10 35 02 30 S 116 55 40 E

Perenjori

Perenjori Caravan Park 08 9973 1193
Caravan Park at Perenjori. Crossing Rd
CT HT BIG RIG HEMA 170 C5 29 26 09 S 116 17 17 E

Pingelly

Pingelly Dump Point 08 9887 1066
Hall Street, behind caravan park
CT HT BIG RIG HEMA 151 E8 32 32 05 S 117 05 06 E

Pingelly Recreation Ground
Entry off Somerset St. Near swimming pool
CT HT BIG RIG HEMA 151 E8 32 31 53 S 117 05 25 E

Pinjarra

Pinjarra RV Parking Area
Williams Rd, 100m E of Premier Hotel, just before RV stop
CT HT BIG RIG HEMA 150 F2 32 37 46 S 115 52 45 E

Port Hedland

Port Hedland Racecourse 08 9173 1711
Enter via McGregor St opposite Civic Centre
CT HT BIG RIG HEMA 167 F8 20 18 31 S 118 36 45 E

Port Hedland Area

Mundabullangana
At Rest Area, cnr Great Northern Hwy & North West Coastal Hwy 40 km S of Port Hedland
CT HT BIG RIG HEMA 166 F7 20 34 27 S 118 26 18 E

Port Smith Area

Goldwire Rest Area
Rest Area 168 km NE of Sandfire Roadhouse or 121 km SW of Roebuck Plains Roadhouse
CT HT BIG RIG HEMA 162 F4 18 36 14 S 121 57 59 E

Quairading

Quairading Dump Point 08 9645 1001
Next to public toilets, stockyards on Quairading - York Rd. W side of town
CT HT BIG RIG HEMA 151 B9 32 00 43 S 117 23 42 E

Ravensthorpe

Ravensthorpe Dump Point
42 Dunn Street, next to CRC Centre
CT HT BIG RIG HEMA 155 F13 33 34 50 S 120 02 46 E

Regans Ford

Regans Ford
Rest Area 43 km N of Gingin or 32 km S of Cataby
CT HT BIG RIG HEMA 170 H3 30 59 20 S 115 42 17 E

Robe River

Robe River
Rest Area 117 km N of Nanutarra Roadhouse or 43 km S of Fortescue River Roadhouse
CT HT BIG RIG HEMA 166 H4 21 36 55 S 115 55 21 E

Roebuck Plains Area

Nillibubbica Rest Area
At rest area 71 km E of Roebuck Plains Roadhouse or 60 km W of Willare Bridge Roadhouse
CT HT BIG RIG HEMA 162 E6 17 39 21 S 123 07 57 E

Southern Cross

Southern Cross Dump Point
Corner of Achernar & Sirius Sts. Eastern end near old Shire yards
CT HT BIG RIG HEMA 171 H12 31 13 50 S 119 19 51 E

Southern Cross Area

Boorabbin Rest Area
Rest Area 114 km W of Coolgardie or 68 km E of Southern Cross
CT HT BIG RIG HEMA 171 H13 31 16 08 S 120 01 00 E

Karalee Rock & Dam 08 9049 1001
At Camp Area 137 km W of Coolgardie or 52 km E of Southern Cross. Turn N 133 km W of Coolgardie or 48 km E of Southern Cross. 5 km of dirt Rd
CT HT BIG RIG HEMA 171 H13 31 15 03 S 119 50 24 E

Three Springs

Three Springs Dump Point
Hall St, adjacent to council building
CT HT BIG RIG HEMA 170 D3 29 32 10 S 115 45 52 E

Tom Price Area

Halfway Bridge
Parking Area 36 km S of Tom Price or 44 km N of Paraburdoo
CT HEMA 166 K7 22 56 11 S 117 50 50 E

Trayning

Shire of Trayning Caravan Park 08 9683 1001
Caravan Park at Trayning. Entry off Bencubbin-Kellerberrin Rd, behind the swimming pool. Public Access
CT HT BIG RIG HEMA 171 H8 31 06 38 S 117 47 37 E

Wagin

Wagin Showgrounds RV Area 08 9861 1177
Great Southern Hwy
CT HT BIG RIG HEMA 151 J9 33 18 20 S 117 20 10 E

Walkaway

Ellendale Pool 08 9921 0500
At Camp Area 22 km NE of Walkaway, via Walkaway-Nangetty Rd & Ellendale Rd
CT HEMA 170 B2 28 51 33 S 114 58 22 E

Walpole

Walpole Visitor Information Centre
South Coast Hwy
CT HT HEMA 153 J9 34 58 32 S 116 43 55 E

Warmun (Turkey Creek) Area

Spring Creek
Rest Area 107 km NE of Halls Creek or 56 km SW of Turkey Creek
CT HT BIG RIG HEMA 165 K12 17 25 59 S 127 59 21 E

Waroona

Waroona Memorial Oval 08 9733 1506
Enter from Millar St, off South Western Hwy. Adjacent to the Walmsley Memorial Pavilion toilets
CT HT BIG RIG HEMA 150 G2 32 50 42 S 115 55 25 E

Wellstead

Wellstead Dump Point
South Coast Hwy, in truck stop
CT HT BIG RIG HEMA 155 H9 34 29 36 S 118 36 15 E

Westonia

Westonia Dump Point
Cnr Westonia - Carrabin & Boodarockin Rds
CT HT BIG RIG HEMA 171 J10 31 17 48 S 118 41 21 E

Whim Creek area

Peawah River
26 km NE of Whim Creek or 92 km SW of Port Hedland
CT HEMA 166 F7 20 50 51 S 118 04 06 E

Wickepin

Wickepin Caravan Park 0428 177 952
At caravan park at Wickepin. Wogolin Rd, behind Police Station
CT HT HEMA 151 F10 32 46 52 S 117 30 12 E

Wongan Hills

Wongan Hills Dump Point 08 9671 1973
Wongan Hills Rd. At Information Centre
CT HT BIG RIG HEMA 170 G6 30 53 35 S 116 42 59 E

Woodanilling

Woodanilling Recreation Reserve 08 9823 1506
Parking Area in Woodanilling, Yairabin St
CT HT BIG RIG HEMA 153 A12 33 33 36 S 117 25 59 E

Wooramel Area

Edaggee Rest Area
Rest Area 43 km N of Wooramel Roadhouse or 81 km S of Carnarvon
CT HT BIG RIG HEMA 168 E2 25 27 34 S 114 03 31 E

Yannarie River

Barradale Rest Area
Rest Area 156 km NE of Minilya Roadhouse or 70 km SW of Nanutarra Roadhouse
CT HT BIG RIG HEMA 166 J3 22 51 49 S 114 57 05 E

Yealering

Lake Yealering Caravan Park 0428 787 426
Sewell Rd. Public access
CT HT BIG RIG HEMA 151 E10 32 35 37 S 117 37 32 E

York

Avon Park
Lowe St at rear of public toilets
CT HT BIG RIG HEMA 150 A6 31 53 19 S 116 46 13 E

WESTERN AUSTRALIA

Yule River

Marble Bar Turn Off

Parking Area 95 km N of Auski Roadhouse or 124 km S of Hwy 1 junction

CT HT BIG RIG HEMA 167 G8 21 34 40 S 118 48 57 E

Two Camel Creek

Rest Area 83km North of Auski Roadhouse or 137km South of Hwy 1 jcn, GPS at entry - 1km to area

CT HT BIG RIG HEMA 167 H8 21 40 32 S 118 49 10 E

NORTHERN TERRITORY

Adelaide River

Adelaide River Dump Point 08 8976 0058

Hopwell St, adjacent to the fire station

CT HT HEMA 175 G4 13 14 13 S 131 06 13 E

Alice Springs

Alice Springs Dump Point 1800 645 199

Commonage Rd, S of The Gap. LHS of Rd, next to Blatherskite Park

CT HT BIG RIG HEMA 185 B11 23 43 57 S 133 51 37 E

Batchelor

Batchelor Dump Point 08 8976 0058

Nurndina St, adjacent to public toilets

CT HT BIG RIG HEMA 175 F4 13 02 49 S 131 01 43 E

Borroloola

Tamarind Park 1800 245 091

Broad St, near airport gate

CT HT HEMA 179 K13 16 04 19 S 136 18 22 E

Coomalie

Coomalie Creek RV Park 08 8976 0501

Camp Area at Coomalie Creek. 25 km N of Adelaide River or 88 km S of Darwin

CT HT BIG RIG HEMA 175 F5 13 01 12 S 131 07 05 E

Darwin

Winnellie Greyhound Club 08 8936 2499

Hook Rd, Winnellie

CT HT BIG RIG HEMA 174 D3 12 25 41 S 130 53 40 E

Jabiru

Jabiru Dump Point 08 8979 2230

Jabiru Dr, 300m past tourist information board, opposite turnoff to cemetery

CT HT BIG RIG HEMA 176 C6 12 39 52 S 132 50 19 E

Katherine

Katherine Dump Point

200m from Information Centre. 300m along Lindsay St, just beyond Second St

CT HT BIG RIG HEMA 176 K4 14 27 53 S 132 16 02 E

Katherine Area

Vince Connolly Crossing (Limestone Creek)

Rest Area 58 km SW of Katherine or 138 km NE of Victoria River

CT HT BIG RIG HEMA 177 A7 14 49 42 S 131 55 00 E

King River

King Rest Area

Rest Area 59 km N of Mataranka or 46 km S of Katherine

CT HT BIG RIG HEMA 178 G7 14 38 40 S 132 37 58 E

Larrimah Area

Warloch Rest Area

Rest Area 41 km N of Larrimah or 37 km S of Mataranka

CT HT BIG RIG HEMA 179 J8 15 14 12 S 133 06 53 E

Mataranka

Mataranka Dump Point

Cnr Stuart Hwy & Martin Rd, near white tower

CT HT BIG RIG HEMA 178 H7 14 55 17 S 133 03 56 E

Nhulunbuy

Nhulunbuy Dump Point 08 8939 2200

Bottlebrush Ave (between Hindle Oval 1 and 2), signage from Melville Bay Rd

CT HT BIG RIG HEMA 179 C14 12 11 20 S 136 47 19 E

Pine Creek

Pine Creek Dump Point 1800 245 091

Ward St, outside council depot

CT HT BIG RIG HEMA 176 H2 13 49 28 S 131 49 55 E

Tennant Creek

Tennant Creek Dump Point 08 8962 3388

Ambrose St, near showgrounds

CT HT BIG RIG HEMA 181 G8 19 38 36 S 134 11 34 E

Victoria River Area

Mathison Rest Area

Rest Area 104 km SW of Katherine or 92 km NE of Victoria River

CT HT BIG RIG HEMA 177 B6 15 08 23 S 131 41 01 E

Yulara

Yulara Dump Point 08 8956 2171

Cnr Berry Ed & Tuit Crescent, off Giles St. Behind AAT Kings depot, on the ground under metal plate

CT HT BIG RIG HEMA 184 G2 25 13 24 S 130 58 31 E

Caravan Park Index

Goondiwindi mist, image by Paula Thomas

A

B

C

AUSTRALIA WIDE

M

N

Legend in Brief

The sample below explains how each caravan park listing is laid out for easy interpretation. Most of the symbols are self-explanatory, but some have been designed to fit certain criteria.

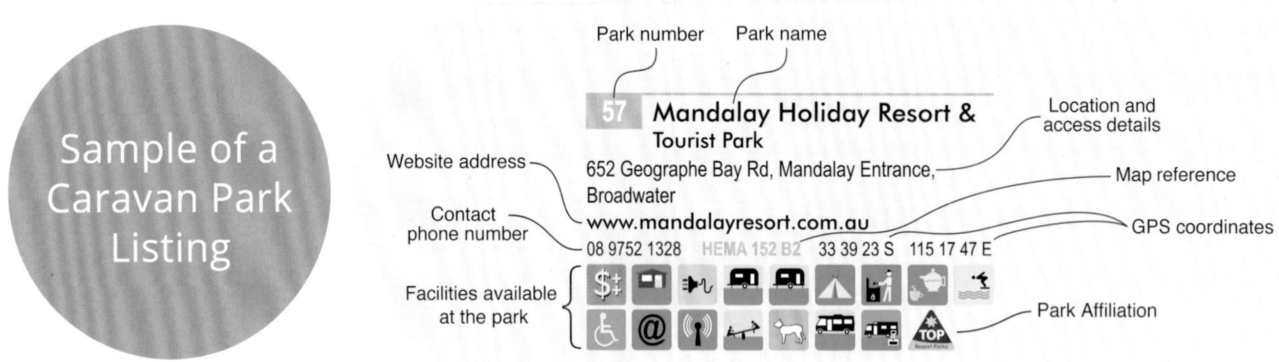

EXPLANATION OF SYMBOLS IN SITE LISTINGS (A detailed explanation is available starting at page 10)

- NIGHTLY COST $27 OR LESS
- NIGHTLY COST $28-$39
- NIGHTLY COST $40 PLUS
- ENSUITE CABINS
- CABINS
- POWERED SITE
- ENSUITE SITE
- DRIVE THROUGH SITES
- TENT SITES
- BARBEQUE
- CAMP KITCHEN
- POOL
- DISABLED FACILITIES
- INTERNET
- PETS NOT ALLOWED
- PETS ALLOWED
- SUITABLE FOR LARGE MOTORHOMES
- DUMP POINT
- BOAT RAMP AVAILABLE
- CHILDREN'S PLAYGROUND
- WI-FI FACILITIES

Explanation of a sample Public Dump Point listing

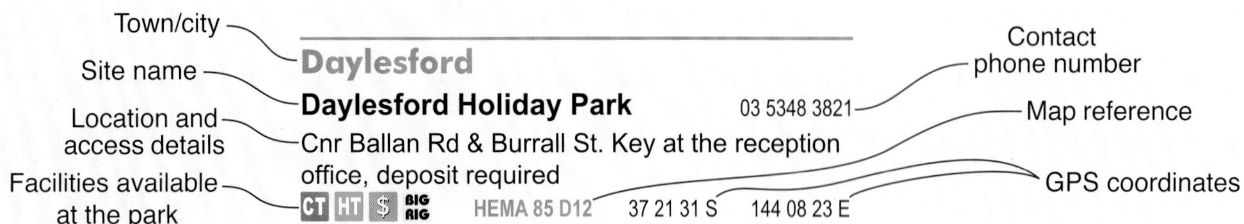

EXPLANATION OF PUBLIC DUMP POINT

SYMBOLS USED IN LISTING

- CT CASSETTE TOILET USE
- BIG RIG ACCESS SUITABLE FOR BIG RIGS
- HT HOLDING TANK USE
- $ FEES APPLICABLE
- WATER AVAILABLE

SYMBOL USED ON THE MAPS

- PUBLIC DUMP POINT NOT AT A LISTED PARK